THE ECONOMIC EFFECTS OF ADVERTISING

THE ECONOMIC
EFFECTS OF
ADVERTISING

by

NEIL H. BORDEN, M.B.A.

Professor of Advertising
Graduate School of Business Administration
George F. Baker Foundation
Harvard University

A STUDY MADE POSSIBLE BY A GENEROUS GIFT OF
MRS. ERICKSON TO THE HARVARD BUSINESS SCHOOL
AS A MEMORIAL TO HER HUSBAND,
ALFRED W. ERICKSON

1944

RICHARD D. IRWIN, INC.
CHICAGO

FIRST PRINTING, JANUARY, 1942
SECOND PRINTING, MAY, 1942
THIRD PRINTING, DECEMBER, 1943

PRINTED IN THE UNITED STATES OF AMERICA
BY W. B. CONKEY COMPANY, HAMMOND, IND.

TO

E. P. B.

PREFACE

AMONG students of marketing and advertising the need for an exhaustive factual analysis of the economic effects of advertising has long been evident. Discussions of advertising have reached large proportions, the arguments on either side have frequently been lacking in fact, and the issues involved have been of great public importance.

Recognizing the need for a factual study by an impartial organization, the officers of the Advertising Research Foundation early in 1937 proposed that the Harvard Business School undertake such a project. As a result of conversations between School and Foundation, the former consented to undertake the research, provided the Foundation would furnish the necessary funds and would agree to the usual understanding attached to any research gifts accepted by the School, namely, that it would be an entirely free agent both in the conduct of the project and in the findings, and that those findings, whatever they might be, would be published.

About this time, June, 1937, Mrs. Alfred W. Erickson of New York, as a memorial to her husband, made a gift of $30,000 to the President and Fellows of Harvard College for the use of the Business School, with the provision that it be used for such research projects as should be deemed important and likely to be fruitful. In view of the fact that Mr. Erickson had spent his lifetime in advertising work, and in view of the recent conversations on the need of a study of the economics of advertising, it was decided that such a study was the most fitting and profitable for which this money could be employed.

To Mrs. Erickson, the School, and the author in particular, are deeply indebted for the research opportunity made possible by her gift.

The task of directing the project was entrusted to the author, and to give him counsel and assistance an advisory committee was appointed consisting of Professor Howard T. Lewis, then Director of Research, as chairman, and Professors Theodore H. Brown, Edmund P. Learned, Malcolm P. McNair, and Harry R. Tosdal.

In the conduct of the project, the Committee asked for and received generous assistance, other than financial, from the Advertising Research Foundation. A mass of intimate data was needed from business concerns, if the study was to be worth while. The School had a long experience in collecting confidential information from business organizations, already had a large quantity in its files of value for the study, and anticipated no great difficulty in securing more. Nevertheless, the Foundation, with its wide support among leading advertisers and advertising agencies, was in a position to give valuable suggestions regarding sources and to provide a helpful entrée to many business concerns. Accordingly, an offer of active cooperation by the Foundation to aid in opening avenues of information was gladly accepted. The Foundation appointed Dr. L. D. H. Weld as its representative to counsel with the author and his assistants on sources and such other matters as the author might wish. The author and the School are grateful to the Foundation and Dr. Weld for this help. Not only Dr. Weld but officers and members of the Foundation freely gave their time and effort whenever called upon.

While as author, I was given the responsibility for the conduct of the study and a corresponding freedom in the direction of the investigations and the determination and statement of findings, the Advisory Committee played an important part in the project. I gladly attribute a large measure of whatever merit the study may have to my associates, each of whom gave many hours to the task. Drawing unstintedly and unselfishly upon their store of knowledge and experience, they offered suggestions which materially improved the organization and conduct of the research and the statement of findings. Under the stimulus of their keen criticism, my thinking about the economics of advertising was sharpened. Many of the ideas contained in the study I owe to them.

The Advisory Committee took a part also in laying out the original plan of the study. The members also were consulted about method during the course of the research. After the first draft of the report was written, the Committee gave suggestions regarding rearrangement in the organization of the text. Then, leading up to the final draft, each member made a detailed and painstaking criticism of the manuscript.

Although the study was greatly improved by the suggestions of my Advisory Committee, I hasten to absolve it from the weaknesses of the work. Final decisions as to methods and as to findings always rested with me. Moreover, since the collection and analysis of data and the presentation of the manuscript were my duties, the Committee was always limited in its influence over the final report by the shortcomings in my ability to direct the collection of material, to analyze the tremendous amount of data available, and to present effectively my analysis and findings. The report would be better had I been more able in my analysis, more skillful in my use of language, and more adept in the use of my associates' suggestions.

In addition to my acknowledgements to Mrs. Erickson, the Advertising Research Foundation, Dr. Weld, and my Advisory Committee, I owe thanks to a long list of individuals who have assisted and have contributed to the study in one way or another. During the course of the research, my principal assistants were Mrs. Mabel Taylor Gragg, Dr. James D. Scott, Mr. Edward K. Cratsley, and Mr. Bertram Promboin. All of these at one time or another assisted in library research and the first three were engaged in case collection and field interview work. In addition to the above tasks, Mrs. Gragg investigated merchandise testing, supervised the survey of consumer attitudes, and analyzed the data from the consumer questionnaires. Dr. Scott carried out the survey among manufacturers upon their marketing and production costs. He also analyzed cost data in the files of the Harvard Bureau of Business Research and of the Association of National Advertisers. Mr. Cratsley conducted the survey among large-scale distributors regarding their prices, pricing policies, and branding policies. Mr. Promboin compiled figures of traceable advertising expenditures for industries and individual companies.

Members of the Harvard Business School Faculty other than members of the Advisory Committee were consulted about various questions and each contributed valuable information or criticisms. These include Professors Richard S. Meriam, Nathan Isaacs, Joseph L. Snider, J. Philip Wernette, Ralph M. Hower, Charles A. Bliss, and Stanley F. Teele. Mr. Richmond F. Bingham drew various charts.

I was fortunate in having my manuscript read and criticized by a number of individuals outside the Harvard Business School Faculty. For suggestions which corrected errors and materially improved the report, I am indebted to Professor George B. Hotchkiss of New York University, Dr. John E. Dalton, Mr. Ralph Starr Butler, and Dr. Weld through whom several officers of the Advertising Research Foundation also offered their comments. I am particularly grateful to Mr. Butler, who at my request found time in a busy life to make a detailed and painstaking criticism of the manuscript. He brought to the task an academic background, a long and fruitful experience as sales and advertising executive, and a penetrating mind. His criticisms and suggestions were especially helpful.

My secretary, Mrs. Margaret C. Auerdahl, shouldered the burden of administering endless details connected with the study and saw the manuscript through the stages of galley and page proof. Miss Marian V. Sears edited the manuscript and checked reference material.

I would be remiss if I failed to mention my indebtedness to hundreds of business executives who gave the data which made this factual study possible. Often they sacrificed considerable time and incurred substantial expense to assemble confidential figures and to give information relating to their advertising and business activities.

Finally, I wish to acknowledge my debt to Dean Wallace B. Donham. When the task of analyzing data and preparing manuscript proved to be greater than had been foreseen, he relieved me of class duties for a full year, in order that I might give my full time and energies to the work. Without such assistance from him, the completion of the study would have been longer delayed.

NIEL H. BORDEN.

Boston, Massachusetts
January 1, 1942

TABLE OF CONTENTS

PART III—THE EFFECT OF ADVERTISING ON THE COSTS OF PRODUCTS AND SERVICES

PART IV—THE RELATION OF ADVERTISING TO PRICES AND PRICING PRACTICE

PART V—THE EFFECT OF ADVERTISING ON THE RANGE OF PRODUCTS, ON QUALITY, AND ON CONSUMER CHOICE

PART VI—THE EFFECT OF ADVERTISING ON INVESTMENT AND VOLUME OF INCOME

PART VII—ETHICAL ASPECTS OF ADVERTISING

PART VIII—SUMMARY

APPENDICES

THE SIGNIFICANCE OF THE STUDY

A STATEMENT BY THE ADVISORY COMMITTEE

D URING the dozen years since the end of the business boom period of the 1920's there has been increasing public consciousness of advertising as a problem. The growth of this consciousness stems from a variety of sources: Disillusion fostered by depression caused many people to turn critical eyes on numerous practices of business. Popular interest in consumption economics gained force, and the Consumer Movement attracted a substantial following. Modern economists in their theories of imperfect, or monopolistic, competition began to pay special attention to the effects of aggressive selling costs on prices. A vigorous revival of antitrust sentiment on the part of the government took as one of its targets certain advertising practices of large business concerns. At the same time, through an increasing utilization of a new medium, the radio, advertising was becoming even more omnipresent and inescapable in its clamor for attention. Simultaneously, also, the emphasis of advertising on appeals to emotion and instinct rather than to reason apparently increased. The composite net result of all these and numerous other factors has been to place a perceptible question mark on the social usefulness of present-day advertising expenditures and practices.

As the critics of advertising have waxed in numbers and strength, the defenders have not been lacking. Strong statements have come from both camps: On the one hand, "advertising is a waste and a social liability"; on the other, "advertising is a principal factor in placing goods in consumers' hands at ever lower costs." Unfortunately, neither side has been strongly fortified with facts; and so, as the public has gradually grown aware that there are important social problems with respect to advertising, because of this paucity of facts it has had little ability to judge the real merits of the controversy.

The Harvard Business School consequently welcomed the opportunity to make an initial comprehensive factual study of consumer advertising,[1] with special reference to the economic problems. Because

---

[1] Although at various points throughout Professor Borden's analysis reference in one form or another is made to industrial advertising, the predominant emphasis throughout the book is laid on consumer advertising since it is in this area that most of the controversy over the economic issues created by advertising has been waged. Limitations of
(Footnote continued on next page)

of the importance of these questions, a committee, representing several points of view among the Faculty, was appointed to exercise broad supervision over the investigation, the general conduct of which was entrusted to Professor Borden. That the confidence which the Committee had in Professor Borden was fully justified is, in its opinion, fully substantiated by the results.

Although it was essential that the study be comprehensive in scope, it was also important that the particular problems to be studied should be carefully defined. In the economic area this definition of problems focused the analysis on the place of advertising in a dynamic system of free enterprise: i.e., the assumptions of an individualistic competitive economy were taken as a setting for the study rather than any assumptions appropriate to a socialistic or totalitarian economy. In establishing this ideological framework for the investigation the author had the full approval of the Committee.

The Committee nevertheless desires to point out that, because the chief concern of this analysis was to examine the economic problems of advertising within the framework of the capitalistic system of free enterprise, it by no means follows that the findings are wholly devoid of significance for those who advocate some other form of social organization. Advertising serves certain functional purposes in any economy, whether the regime be one of private capitalism or of state socialism. In any type of social organization which is not to be wholly static, the function of providing information for consumers in regard to the sorts, qualities, quantities, uses, and special attributes of the products available, and the places where they can be obtained, is a needful one. In fact it may be an even more needful one because of the desire of the state to direct consumption along certain lines. Even if advertising were to be called propaganda and the costs borne by the state, still it would behoove the managers of advertising, and indeed the managers of the state, to understand the problems and the kind of evidence that are presented in this survey. Therefore those who believe (as the Committee and the author do not) that the day of private enterprise in the United States is fast drawing to a close should not on that account dismiss this study as merely part of the swan song of capitalistic ideology.

---

both time and funds rather than any lack of appreciation of its importance made a correspondingly careful analysis of industrial advertising impossible. It is earnestly to be hoped that such a study, comparable in scope to the present one in the consumer area, may be made possible.

THE NATURE OF THE PROBLEMS

Three Kinds of Problems Studied

The existence in the social structure of advertising or, more generally, of aggressive promotional practices, gives rise to at least three broad interrelated categories of problems: business problems, economic problems, and ethical problems. The concern of the businessman is with the profitable use of advertising as a tool of sales promotion. The concern of the economist is with the effects of advertising on the national income and on the social welfare generally. The concern of the moralist is with the relation of advertising to the prevailing social code as expressed in law or in accepted conventions of behavior and good taste.

The Business Problem

The businessman asks, "Where is the opportunity for the successful use of advertising to enhance profits? Where will advertising do a more effective job than some other tool of sales promotion? How can advertising be improved? How can its costs be lowered in relation to its results? How can its results be more accurately determined and predicted?" Chapters IV and V of this volume set forth these problems of the business use of advertising. Many business executives and serious students of business will find little or nothing that is new in these chapters and may safely omit them in reading this book. For general readers, on the other hand, especially those who do not have a thorough grasp of the problems which concern businessmen and a good understanding of the limitations on the information that is available to businessmen, these chapters should be particularly useful. That is why they are placed early in the volume. In the opinion of the Committee it is necessary to possess a sound understanding of the business problems of advertising in order to have a good background for evaluating the economic and ethical problems.

The Economic Problem

The economist inquires, "Does advertising enhance the social welfare? Does it operate to increase or decrease the national income? Does advertising make prices rigid and unresponsive to changes in economic conditions? Does it increase or restrict the freedom of consumer choice?" The nature of these problems as they grow out of economic theory is outlined in Chapter VI. The development of these issues, since this is primarily a study of the economics of advertising, constitutes the bulk of the book.

For the benefit of the lay reader, whose general acquaintance with economic doctrines is probably confined mostly to the main outlines of thought of nineteenth and twentieth century English and American economists, the fact that more recent economic thought covers a wider range needs to be emphasized. Instead of remaining within the traditional channels of the private-enterprise system, it envisages other forms of economic organization, both tried and untried. The discussion of advertising by modern economists reflects this current width of range, and some of the criticisms of advertising proceed from assumptions different from those of the nineteenth century economists. It is therefore appropriate at this point to indicate precisely how the economic issues were defined in undertaking this investigation of advertising.

Advertising is sometimes criticized on the ground that as part of the capitalistic system of free enterprise it leads consumers to buy the wrong things and spend too much for them, whereas consumers would be better off if they bought different things and spent their money in different ways. When this criticism implies, as it often does, that someone in authority might better decide what things should be bought and how consumers should spend their incomes, then the essential clash is between the rival ideologies of individualism and authoritarianism; and the basic argument is not really about advertising at all. Therefore, whenever criticisms of advertising carry the implication that some other form of social organization would be preferable to one based on freedom of consumer choice and freedom of enterprise, the debate passes beyond the scope of this study.

In the same way there are excluded from the scope of this study those criticisms of advertising which take issue with its emphasis on enhancement of material values at the expense of spiritual values. As to whether or not the satisfaction of material wants interferes with the good life, and as to whether the sum total of human happiness would be greater or smaller in a world of more asceticism and less gratification of desire, this study must be silent. These broad issues both of moral and economic ideology must be contested on other battlegrounds.

Therefore the basic economic issue which was propounded for this investigation may be phrased as follows: Within the framework of a dynamic capitalistic system of free enterprise does advertising (and sales promotional practices generally) help or hinder the successful functioning of the economy and the advance toward a greater measure of well being? By "a dynamic capitalistic system of free enterprise" is meant a system in which consumers are free to decide how they will spend their incomes, in which businessmen are free to decide the direction and scope of their activities and free to set prices for their goods and services, in which labor is free to bargain collectively or individually as it desires, in which investors are free to place their funds in whatever enterprises they see fit, in which the liberties of individuals, including the liberty to own and enjoy property, are safeguarded by the state, and in which change and innovation are accepted as the normal expectation, the whole being subject to such restraints as are imposed voluntarily by the community for the better protection of these several freedoms. Such a system is substantially that under which the whole economic and cultural development of the United States has taken place.

At this juncture the general reader, unless he is familiar with some important lines of development in economic thought during the past twenty years, may well ask, "How does the hypothesis arise that advertising may hinder the successful functioning of a capitalistic economy?" To answer this question it is necessary to outline briefly some of the recent thinking of economists with regard to the character of present-day competition.

Modern economists are more realistic than some of their predecessors. They recognize that the concepts of pure competition and pure monopoly are simply concepts and not very good descriptions of the actual world. The concept of pure competition assumes a market in which there are a large number of buyers and sellers, in which the commodity traded is essentially homogeneous and nondifferentiated, in which competition is entirely on the basis of price, and in which price is determined impersonally in the market place, since no seller or buyer is large enough to affect the calculations of any other seller or buyer. In such a market advertising to convince buyers that they ought to prefer the product of a particular seller would be neither necessary nor competitively possible, since the product is homogeneous and competition is solely on a price basis. It goes without saying, of course, that almost nowhere in the modern business world does such a market actually exist. Only in the case of certain agricultural commodities is this concept of pure competition at all closely approached.

At the opposite extreme lies the concept of pure monopoly, which envisages a single seller in control of the complete supply of a commodity and thus able, by virtue of this control of supply, to set and maintain the price at the level which he deems most likely to maximize his total profits. Again it is true that in the world of today there are very few instances of such pure monopolies (except in the case of some government monopolies). Perhaps the closest approach in the business world is the De Beers diamond syndicate, and even that has close governmental affiliations.

In establishing these concepts of competition and monopoly the eighteenth and nineteenth century economists by no means imagined that they were describing the actual world of business. On the contrary, they recognized that there were numerous imperfections in competition in the real world. However, they dismissed the imperfections as being relatively unimportant and concentrated their attention on the *tendencies* toward competition and toward monopoly. This general point of view persisted for a long time. Although some nineteenth century economists examined the curious riddle of duopoly (a situation in which two competing firms control the whole supply), it remained for economists of the twentieth century, especially in the twenty-odd years between the first and second World Wars, to recognize that in the real world actual competition is so different from the concept of pure competition that instead of dismissing the imperfections and dwelling on the abstract concepts, thoughtful students needed to focus attention on the imperfections themselves and build their theories around them.

Take cigarettes as an example of present-day competition. The individual sellers differentiate their products, hoping to gain consumer preference. Although Camels and Lucky Strikes are in competition they are not, strictly speaking, homogeneous products. They represent different blends of tobacco, different processes of curing and preparation; and each company has a monopoly of sorts; that is to say, it has a monopoly of its own brand. Cigarette competition is largely on a non-price basis, taking the form of advertising, sales promotional efforts and devices of all kinds, as well as differentiation of both product and package. Furthermore, four companies account for approximately 70% of the sales of cigarettes in the United States; and clearly none of these companies can make any competitive move without considering the probable reactions of the other large companies to that move. To be sure, price competition breaks out occasionally in flurries of price cutting; but between these price wars are long periods during which prices remain relatively constant, and in these prices are included the costs of advertising and sales promotional efforts.

Present-day economists, devoting their attention to such imperfections of the market as just illustrated, rather than to abstract concepts, have evolved the theory of monopolistic or imperfect competition, that is, a type of competition embracing aspects both of competition and of monopoly. In this volume the author has used the term "imperfect competition" as being generally synonymous with monopolistic competition.[2] It is extremely important for the general reader to recognize that except for the names there is nothing new about this kind of competition. The terms "monopolistic competition" or "imperfect competition" merely describe competition as it has existed in the world and particularly in the United States for these many years. Here it may be remarked parenthetically that the term "monopolistic competition" has acquired implications that are emotionally disturbing to some businessmen because it seems to suggest something immoral or illegal. The important question is not whether these kinds of competition exist; everyone concedes that. Monopolistic or imperfect competition is merely a label applied to the everyday realities of American business. The really important question is whether out of this species of competition there flow any consequences seriously different from the general results of the competitive system as postulated by the earlier economists. The real problems are how this competition works and what are its social consequences. Since much of the current criticism of advertising is closely related to the various theories of imperfect competition, businessmen therefore are urged to understand the concept of imperfect competition and the issues which it raises. Chapter VI, developing these issues, is written primarily for the business reader.

Criticisms of advertising grow out of theories based on the important characteristics of monopolistic or imperfect competition. These characteristics include some or all of the following:

(1) Individual sellers differentiate both the products themselves and the brands and packages in order to develop a basis for consumer preference.

(2) Competition takes a variety of forms of sales promotional effort, including advertising, display, and personal selling, rather than taking predominantly the form of price reductions.

---

[2] Among economists both terms have their supporters, but minor shades of meaning are not significant for purposes of this study.

(3) Consumers are urged to buy merchandise because of claimed improvements in quality and special features rather than because of reductions in price.

(4) There is a tendency toward a concentration of supply in certain industries in the hands of a relatively small number of large concerns.

(5) Under such conditions the individual concern has substantial control of its own price. It does not have to accept an impersonal price established in the market place on a take-it-or-leave-it basis; on the contrary, it may elect to exercise its "monopolistic" control over the preferences of some part of its customers and sell a reduced output at a higher price.

From these characteristics of imperfect competition certain serious consequences to the economic system are apprehended by many present-day economists. Among the consequences suggested by these economists the following may be noted:

(1) Consumers are confused by the large number of meaningless product differentiations and consequently do not make wise choices.

(2) Consumers do not have sufficient opportunity to buy goods at low prices. In this sense their freedom of choice is restricted.

(3) Since business firms seek to recover costs of advertising and sales promotion, and since under conditions of imperfect competition they refrain to a large extent from using the weapon of price, consumers are forced to pay too much for the goods they buy.

(4) Many aggressive marketing costs thus are wastes which retard the growth of the national income of real goods.

(5) Because of these consequences, imperfect competition is not automatically self-regulating in the social interest; that is, it does not direct investment into certain channels and away from other channels in such a way as to meet the community's real demands.

(6) The result of this improper allocation of capital investment is under-utilization of productive capacity and underemployment.

(7) Since imperfect competition is accompanied by relatively rigid prices it prevents the price mechanism from absorbing the shocks of change in the economic system, and these shocks thus fall on output and employment. Thus imperfect competition increases the severity of cyclical fluctuations in business.

It is obvious that the argument about imperfect competition is considerably broader than the argument about advertising, but it is also obvious that the criticisms of advertising are so closely intertwined with the theory of imperfect competition that businessmen cannot understand one without some grasp of the other.

With reference to the economic problems of advertising, therefore, it was the task of this investigation, taking cognizance of the theories of imperfect competition and the position of advertising in those theories, to collect and examine facts bearing on the effects of advertising in the United States on demand, on cost, on price, on the quality and variety of goods, and on the general level of national income. In examining these facts, it was deemed appropriate to take not merely a static view but also a dynamic view. In other words, it was not considered sufficient to look merely at the effects of advertising at a particular level of economic development but it was thought necessary to look also at advertising in relation to the process of economic change —to consider its effects on the flow of investment and on the mechanisms by which the qualities of goods are improved and the standard of living raised, i.e., the way in which the community moves from one level of income to a higher one. With this longer time span of judgment it is also more readily possible to observe the action of any counteracting forces which may operate to modify the results suggested by a more static type of analysis.

Just as it is important that businessmen should understand the current economic theories of imperfect competition, it is likewise important that economists, in the further development of these theories, should take into account the kinds of information which this study has sought to assemble, in order to see whether the existing doctrines of imperfect competition are adequate as a theory of economic progress.

The Ethical Problem

Somewhat apart from the economic problem, which has been discussed at some length and which constitutes the chief objective of this study, there are certain ethical problems with respect to advertising. To what standards of conduct, either as written into statutes or expressed in the conventions and codes of the business community, should advertising be expected to conform? How far does it so conform?

But first, why should these problems be treated separately? It would be foolish to suppose that with respect to advertising there are no connections between the economic problems and the ethical problems. Advertising is forced to change in order to meet changing ethical concepts, and these changes in advertising naturally have a bearing on its economic results. Nevertheless a separate treatment of the two kinds of problems is amply justified. The kinds of advertising claims which may not be inappropriate to the taste of one generation may offend the ethical sensibilities of a succeeding generation; such changing influences are readily traceable in the history of advertising in the United States. Thus the ethical standards for advertising, in common with other ethical standards, are on a pragmatic basis. They change as the views of the community change. On the other hand, the science of economics concerns itself with cause and effect in the economic realm rather than with the desirability or undesirability of particular ends and objectives; and the logic of this cause and effect, so far as it is correctly apprehended, does not change, is not in any sense pragmatic. Thus economic problems and ethical problems, although not devoid of interconnection, need to be approached with different assumptions.

Some critics take the chief ethical problem of advertising to be the question whether any influence or persuasion is properly admissible in dealings between buyers and sellers, their answers to this problem being predominantly in the negative. But again, as in the case of some of the economic criticisms of advertising, this denial of the propriety of persuasion in economic affairs resolves itself at bottom into a profound ideological cleavage. What significance can be attached to the designation of a society as "free" if there is no freedom to exercise persuasion in the relationship between buyers and sellers? Persuasion and counterpersuasion are exercised freely from pulpit, press, rostrum, classroom, and government agencies for information. If the use of persuasion were to be forbidden in economic relations, practically all semblance of free society would vanish at the same time.

The really significant ethical problem in regard to advertising, therefore, is not *whether* persuasion should be exercised but *how* it should be exercised. In other words, what are the ethics of influence in economic relationships? Not only do such ethical standards change from time to time as suggested above, but they are also pragmatic in another sense. Codes of ethics and ethical standards are by no means uniform for all professions or all occupations at the same time. They differ according to what is appropriate to the circumstances. The ethical standards which govern a judge on the bench are vastly different from those which are appropriate to the prosecutor and the attorney for the defense. For a judge to fail to be impartial would be highly unethical, but for an advocate before the bar to present only one side of the case is in no sense unethical.

The ethical problems which are appropriate for the study of advertising, therefore, are the ethics of the use of influence in competitive commercial relations. What changes are taking place in these standards of advertising conduct? How rapidly are they being written into statutory law? Is the law moving sufficiently fast to keep pace with the ethical sense of the business community? What are the effects of those standards of advertising conduct which are not yet embodied in law but have crystallized in certain conventions, in business codes, and in the activities of particular extralegal organizations, such as the Better Business Bureaus? What do consumers think about advertising? Are businessmen themselves sufficiently aware of changing standards of good taste with respect to advertising? The evidence on all these problems is examined in Part VI.

THE MAJOR FINDINGS OF THE STUDY

The material included in this study represents by far the largest body of evidence that has yet been gathered on advertising. The commodities selected for analysis so far as possible represent a sample of market conditions; yet the quality of the evidence is uneven. Some parts are much better than others, and in some important areas evidence is scanty or lacking. It is understandable that this first effort to make a comprehensive survey of the facts should reveal many areas in which satisfactory data are not as yet obtainable. For instance, evidence as to the effects of advertising on costs is disappointing in both quantity and quality. This particular defect in the evidence is part and parcel of the general truth that the businessman's knowledge of costs, and, indeed, the behavior of costs in business, by no means presents the clear-cut picture that the economist is prone to visualize. Some of the evidence that the economist looks for probably does not exist. In a broad sense most of the defects in the evidence presented in this volume must be regarded as unavoidable in any initial study having consideration for reasonableness of research outlays.

It would be a mistake to suppose that the evidence presented in this volume yields simple "yes" and "no" answers to all the major questions about advertising. Nevertheless the material on which this study is based, comprising hundreds of case histories, hundreds of interviews with business executives, thousands of pages of records examined, a substantial number of industry studies, and other special investigations—all this (in the opinion of the Committee) constitutes a factual array that cannot be ignored when advertising is discussed honestly and thoughtfully. In the future, as the facts uncovered in this survey are augmented, corrected, and refined, there can no longer be any real excuse for either the critics or the supporters of advertising to jump at quick conclusions. There is ample evidence here to show that the facts of each advertising situation have to be carefully examined before they are used as a basis for any generalizations.

In each chapter of Parts II–VI of this book, considered generalizations regarding the questions at issue are undertaken, with appropriate qualifications, to as great an extent as the evidence warrants. In order to give the general reader a preview of the findings of this investigation, some of the principal generalizations which are supported by a preponderance of the evidence are listed here. Minor qualifications of these will be found in the respective chapters.

Generalizations on the Quantitative Aspects of Advertising

  I. Since 1920, advertising expenditures in the United States have probably averaged in excess of $2,000,000,000 a year, or roughly 3% of the national income.

  II. For 1935, advertising expenditures amounted to 1.4% of the total sales volume of businesses using an appreciable quantity of advertising, but to only 0.9% of the total dollar sales transactions of all types of business.

  III. These expenditures for advertising comprised 7% of the total outlay for the distribution of goods and services.

  IV. The public gets an important indirect benefit from advertising through the contribution of advertising revenue to the gross expenses of newspapers, magazines, and radio broadcasting. Roughly one-fifth of total advertising outlays, or $400,000,000 in the year 1935, was returned to consumers in the form of lower costs for publication and radio entertainment.

  V. In the aggregate, wages of salesmen, traveling, and other costs attending personal selling efforts on the part of manufacturers, wholesalers, and retailers are several times as large as the outlays chargeable to advertising.

Generalizations on the Business Use of Advertising

  I. The businessman generally seeks to use advertising with the objective of obtaining long-run profits rather than immediate returns. The purpose of advertising is to induce continued patronage.

  II. Opportunities for the successful use of advertising vary widely. Advertising is not a business stimulator which can be turned on and off at will with the assurance that results will be commensurate with expenditures. Successful advertising depends on the right combination of numerous factors. Among factors favorable to the successful use of advertising are the following:

A. The trend of demand in the particular industry should be rising.

B. There should be an opportunity to stimulate selective demand, i.e., brand preference for the particular product. This opportunity is most likely to be present under such circumstances as the following:

    1. When there is substantial chance for differentiation of product.

    2. When consumer satisfaction depends largely on hidden qualities that cannot easily be judged at the time of purchase, for instance, toilet soap as contrasted with green vegetables.

    3. When strong emotional buying motives exist, such as protection of health or enhancement of social position.

C. The combination of potential unit sales times rate of gross margin must be high enough to permit necessary advertising expenditures in the particular market.

Where a preponderance of these conditions is present there is much greater opportunity for effective advertising than where the reverse is true. For instance, cosmetics exemplify the type of product for which most of the foregoing conditions are present, whereas sugar is a type of product for which many of these conditions are not present.

III. Advertising is not homogeneous, isolated, or unique. Instead, it is an integral part of a business plan. Where the opportunity for successful advertising exists, the business use of advertising will still not be fully successful unless the following conditions are met:

A. There must be a correct appraisal of the most suitable combination of advertising and price policy. Advertising affects the unit sales volume and thus indirectly the production cost per unit. Price likewise affects the unit sales volume and also affects the total dollar income and the total amount of gross margin. Advertising, in addition to affecting unit sales, of course increases marketing expense outlays. Gross margin less marketing and administrative expense equals net profits. Thus, with a view to maximizing profits there must be a correct appraisal of the best balance of the combination of advertising and price.

B. Advertising must be effectively coordinated with the other parts of the marketing and merchandising program, including the personal selling effort and all aspects of relations with middlemen.

C. The advertising task itself must be skillfully executed, especially with reference to the following factors:

    1. There must be a correct determination of the audience to be addressed.

    2. Selling appeals must be selected which are most likely to influence those to whom advertisements are addressed.

    3. Techniques and methods must be developed for effectively presenting the appeals.

    4. The most effective media available for reaching the audience must be judged on a basis of cost in relation to influence on the audience.

5. It is necessary to determine the best size and frequency of advertisements to produce the maximum effect with a given expenditure.

IV. Where the foregoing tasks of judgment and execution are not effectively accomplished, advertising results in waste. Businessmen are aware of this waste as it affects their own profits, and they seek to reduce it through the improvement of techniques.

    A. The dynamic character of business makes control and measurement of advertising results highly important, yet difficult, because of changing living habits and attitudes, changing fashions, changing population, changing price structure, changing competitive situation, and the increased tempo of change.

    B. Useful techniques for reducing advertising waste include the following:

        1. Market studies are increasing in number and are utilizing greater technical refinements.

        2. Improved methods are being developed for controlling marketing operations, such as the use of sales quotas and distribution cost analysis.

        3. The search continues for methods of measuring advertising results, such as keyed responses, controlled experiments, use of coupons, tests of readership and listening habits, test campaigns, and pretesting of advertisements by consumer juries.

    C. There are various obstacles to the full development of techniques for preventing advertising waste.

        1. Some businessmen have unlimited faith in the ability of advertising to operate automatically to increase profits, and others are unduly skeptical.

        2. The practice sometimes followed of having advertising agencies compete for accounts on a speculative basis leads to inadequate preliminary study.

        3. Some advertisers show unwillingness to furnish agents with adequate information on their businesses.

        4. Some businessmen and advertising agents rely too much on hunch and unchecked promotional artistry.

    D. The development of techniques for preventing waste in the field of advertising has not equaled the corresponding development of techniques for preventing waste in production and in certain aspects of marketing. Nevertheless, advertising presents a more difficult problem than these other areas, and encouraging progress has been made.

Generalizations on the Economic Results of Advertising

I. The Effects of Advertising on Demand.

    A. For many products advertising tends to speed up favorable trends of demand; that is, if underlying conditions are favorable to an increase in demand for the product, e.g., cigarettes during recent years, the use of advertising tends to enhance and accelerate the rising trend of demand.

B. In the case of a declining trend in demand, e.g., cigars, advertising is powerless to halt or reverse the trend. It can do no more than temporarily delay it.

C. Where possibilities of expanding a market do not exist, or where there is a declining trend of demand, cooperative industry advertising campaigns have not been able to succeed.

D. By aiding in the expansion of markets through accelerating a rising trend of demand, advertising also helps to increase the elasticity of demand.

   1. As greater numbers of people become acquainted with a product there is more opportunity to increase dollar sales volume through price reductions.

   2. This expansion of markets often is needed in order to make it profitable for a businessman to reduce prices.

   3. The expansion may make possible lower costs for individual firms, which can be reflected in price reductions.

E. The expansion of the market also makes it possible for new competitors to enter.

F. The building of the market by means of advertising and other promotional devices not only makes price reductions attractive or possible for large firms, it also creates an opportunity to develop private brands, which generally are offered at lower prices. Many national advertisers consider such competition as parasitic, since there is frequently present an element of trading on the reputation of established brands. The private branding concerns would have much less opportunity to operate if advertising by others did not precede their activities. In spite of the disfavor in which they may be held by national advertisers, private branders who elect to compete on a price basis serve a definitely useful economic function.

G. As a general rule, businessmen, particularly manufacturers, have not fully recognized the opportunities for increasing sales volume and profits through the exploitation of demand elasticity. In general they have been too ready to assume that demand is inelastic, and have not been sufficiently willing to experiment with price strategy.

H. Possibilities for the use of advertising by individual companies vary widely. If the right combination of conditions is present, the effect of advertising is to increase the demand for the particular company's product. There are situations, however, in which it does not pay a company to advertise, because of insufficient product differentiation, lack of strong consumer buying motives, insufficient size and frequency of sale, and so on, e.g., matches, wheat, and nails. Advertising in these cases is highly unlikely to increase the demand for a particular concern's product.

I. Where advertising does operate to increase the demand for the individual concern it tends to make the consumer demand for that product inelastic. That is, it enables the company to maintain its prices when there is a general market decline, and it enables the company to ignore, within limits, price changes on directly or indirectly competing products. This tendency is observed for commodities which are highly differentiated from others and commodities for which consumers have strong emotional buying motives.

J. In the longer run, however, competitive forces tend to weaken the condition of a company which relies on advertising to bring about an inelasticity of its individual demand and thus enable it to ignore price competition, especially during periods of depression. Either other manufacturers or private branders competing on a price basis eventually take business away from the concern which seeks to maintain high prices in the face of lower market levels.

II. The Effects of Advertising on Costs.

   A. The Effects of Advertising on Total Marketing Costs.

      1. Advertising is not in itself the cause of high distribution costs. In a society characterized by increasing complexity of goods and increasing divisions of labor, marketing costs inevitably become a major part of the final price paid by consumers. In such a society the consumers and producers are widely separated in space, time, and knowledge; and division of labor appears not only in manufacturing but also in distribution. As manufacturing costs are reduced by a larger scale of operations, marketing costs usually account for a larger share of the final price. Because consumers and producers are so widely separated and because the products of a modern economy are so varied, informational costs, whether they be incurred for advertising or for personal selling, must make up some substantial part of total marketing costs. Advertising is a part of present-day high distribution costs, but it is not a basic cause of the high proportion of these costs.

      2. It is not possible to state precisely whether the presence of advertising in the economic system has the effect of increasing or of reducing marketing costs generally.

         a. Although there is a substantial body of information available in regard to marketing costs, there are too many gaps and discontinuities in it. For instance, there is inadequate information on the marketing costs of manufacturers and of certain types of distributors.

         b. It is not possible to trace on a large statistical scale the effects of advertising by manufacturers on the expenses and margins of distributors and dealers who handle advertised products. Advertising ordinarily tends to give low selling costs among distributors for the brands advertised. In individual cases it is well established that advertising manufacturers accord smaller margins to middlemen than they normally take on unbranded or privately branded merchandise. Whether these reductions in margins are more or less than sufficient to cover the manufacturers' cost of advertising is uncertain; the evidence is both inadequate and conflicting.

c. In addition there is the further complication which comes from the shifting of promotional functions. A department store or chain store organization with numerous private brands may have a relatively high cost of doing business, but adequate information is not yet available to show how much the performance of these promotional functions by the distributor may have lowered the manufacturers' marketing costs.

d. Although it is frequently argued that advertising may tend to reduce distribution costs because it is an effective substitute for personal selling costs (which commonly run larger than advertising costs), the evidence available does not prove that this contention always holds true. In many instances advertising proves to be a more economical selling method than is personal selling. In other instances advertising is an economical and effective complement to personal selling. But frequently the use of advertising does not bring a reduction in personal selling costs or total marketing costs. Advertising and personal selling are not necessarily interchangeable.

3. There is some evidence pointing to the conclusion that among certain types of middlemen, e.g., department stores, large concerns have higher percentage costs (including advertising) than small companies. Such comparisons, however, are likely to be very misleading.

a. Frequently the variety of merchandise handled by the large firms differs greatly from that handled by the smaller firms.

b. Many large concerns embrace in their activities a considerably greater number of marketing functions than do the small concerns; that is, they reach back directly to the manufacturer instead of being approached by the manufacturer through various intermediaries.

Thus, when some large concerns spend proportionately more for advertising than do their smaller competitors, it is quite possible that they are taking the place of the manufacturer or of some other middleman with respect to such expenditures, and that the sum total cost borne by the consumer may be even less in their case than in that of some of the smaller companies.

4. What interests the consumer, of course, and society at large is the lowest possible combination of production and distribution costs. The fact that while the ratio of marketing costs has been rising final prices to consumers for many articles of merchandise have been lowered, lends credence to the presumption that in

the past higher distribution costs have been more than offset by lower production costs. But it is not possible to make the generalization that higher distribution costs today are always offset by lower production costs. There is evidence that this is true in many cases, but there is no certainty that increased costs of distribution do not, in some instances, result in higher prices to consumers.

B. The Effects of Advertising on Total Manufacturing Costs.

1. In many industries the large scale of operations made possible in part through advertising has resulted in reductions in manufacturing costs.

2. The claim that a large concern which advertises necessarily gains advantages in production costs over nonadvertising or smaller firms is not always based on fact. The evidence shows that small nonadvertising companies sometimes have as low production costs as large companies.

3. Many small firms "ride on the coat tails" of their larger competitors. They avoid information costs and let the larger concerns bear the burden of developing the demand. In some of these cases the lower advertising and general marketing costs of these small companies are offset by their higher production costs. This situation suggests that it may be a mistake to view each concern, institution, or function atomistically; that comparisons between small and large concerns or between advertising and nonadvertising concerns are necessarily imperfect; and that costs have organic aspects in society which defy traditional methods of analysis.

4. A special study of production and distribution costs of manufacturers made in connection with this investigation yielded meager and largely unsatisfactory data; but this study did indicate that economists in their reasoning have made unwarranted assumptions about the businessman's knowledge of costs.

   a. Businessmen are quite generally unable to furnish the types of cost information required by economic analysis.

   b. In general businessmen do not have the precise information about certain categories of cost which the economist's reasoning presupposes.

   c. They do not typically use this type of information in their actual operations, because they do not find practical the types of cost information assumed in theory.

   A sufficient body of fact does not now exist to warrant many of the statements about cost that have been made both by the proponents and by the opponents of advertising.

III. The Effects of Advertising on Price.

A. The long-run effect of advertising and aggressive selling costs on price is closely related to the concept of innovation and growth costs. Since the burden of developing demand is a substantial and costly one, pioneers in any business fairly often must make large outlays before they begin to get any return on their investment. After they have developed a demand, the path is easier for the imitators who follow them, since the latter do not have to incur the same developmental expenses but at the same time are able to take some of the market. Fearing this situation, the pioneer, of course, seeks to get back his growth costs and assure himself of a long-run profit by utilizing various devices such as patents and trade-marks to obtain something like a temporary monopoly for his product. Brands, product differentiation, and advertising are some of the means which he uses to try to protect his position. The extent to which the pioneer's hope is attained and the extent to which his growth costs actually enter into the equilibrium price depends on the strategy and timing of activities by the imitators. If some of them elect, as they frequently do, to use price competition (which they can readily do since they have lower marketing costs), the pioneer may have difficulty in recovering his growth costs; and these then do not enter into long-run price equilibrium.

To the extent that such growth costs do enter into equilibrium price and are borne by society, they may be regarded as part of the price of economic progress. For without some protection for these costs pioneers would be fewer and the opportunities for investment would be more scarce. When all the imitators follow the leaders' policies, however, and do not elect to use price competition, then the cost paid by society for progress may be too high.

B. The evidence of the study indicates that advertising has the effect of slowing up the development of price competition but that it rarely succeeds in preventing price competition over longer periods.

   1. Price competition commonly reasserts itself in periods of depression, though it is clear that many businessmen delay too long in reducing prices at such a time.

   2. Competing firms carry on a continual contest for advantage, and this rivalry takes many forms which are in lieu of price competition (e.g., special concessions, favors, rebates, and so on), but which ultimately break out in the form of price competition.

   3. In many industries the large scale of operations made possible in part through advertising has resulted in reductions in costs, which frequently have been passed on in considerable part to consumers.

C. Advertising in general operates in the direction of increasing price stability and, to some extent, lessens the flexibility of the price system.

D. In some industries advertising has contributed to concentration of demand and hence has been a factor in bringing about concentration of supply in the hands of a few dominant firms, a situation which, according to the doctrine of imperfect competition, tends to keep prices at unduly high levels. The preponderance of evidence, however, indicates that advertising is not a basic cause for the concentration of supply in the hands of a few concerns.

IV. The Effects of Advertising on Quality and Range of Merchandise.

    A. Advertising tends to improve the quality and range of merchandise offered to consumers.

        1. Advertising and aggressive selling have led to a more rapid adoption of new major inventions than would otherwise have been possible.

        2. Advertising has played an indirect but nevertheless real and important part in stimulating product improvement, because it has brought about competition in product improvement for the sake of developing selling arguments. Although some people believe that in the short run this type of competition results in product differentiations that are trivial or foolish, it is through numerous small developments over a period of time that major product improvements ultimately take place; and in a free society it is only through trial and error in the market that the seller can know whether a differentiation is significantly important to the consumer.

        3. In addition to stimulating product improvement, advertising has had a desirable effect on product quality through the stimulus which it offers to the maintenance of quality of products sold under advertised brand names.

    B. Because nonprice competition has had these important effects on the improvement in quality and range of merchandise, it cannot be dismissed as a socially undesirable form of competition.

V. The Effect of Advertising on Consumer Choice.

    A. Advertising and aggressive selling have had their most direct and important influence on consumer choice in widening the range of merchandise available to consumers, particularly through product differentiation. It is sometimes objected that these product differentiations are not significant ones for consumers; but in economics the worth-whileness of product differentiations must be determined in the end by consumers' behavior.

    B. Significant product differentiations for the consumer are those things which give him satisfaction. He expresses his judgment of them by buying or refusing to buy. Evidence of the study indicates clearly that consumers accept some differentiations and not others. Over a long period, competition in product differentiation leads to significant improvements in products.

    C. The main task of advertising for business concerns is to make sales mutually satisfactory to buyers and sellers at low cost, but there is evidence that advertising, as now practiced, is not giving consumers sufficient product information to serve as a wholly effective guide to consumer choice.

D. Nevertheless advertising has been the principal source of information available to consumers, and thus, in spite of inadequacies, has been essential to the functioning of the economy.

E. The inadequacy of information furnished by advertising has justified the development of the Consumer Movement in so far as the aims of that movement are to provide greater information and educate consumers to be better buyers.

F. The evidence suggests that in some situations consumers do not have enough opportunity to buy goods at low prices; and that where such options are available consumers either are not sufficiently aware of them, perhaps because of lack of advertising, or else, being aware, they do not choose to avail themselves of these options.

VI. The Effect of Advertising on Investment and the Level of National Income.

A. Advertising and aggressive selling have been significant forces in advancing the technology of production and increasing the investment in productive facilities—two developments which largely explain the four-fold increase of real national income per capita during the past one hundred years.

1. From a long-range point of view, advertising and aggressive selling have played a very large though not precisely measurable part in the formation of mental attitudes necessary to a high level of consumption, especially such attitudes as expectation of change and the notion of progress. In other words, advertising has helped to develop a mobile as opposed to a static society.

2. Advertising has stimulated new wants with the result that the luxuries of one generation have become the necessities of the succeeding generation.

3. The possibility of using advertising and aggressive selling to bring businesses more quickly into the profit-making zone has facilitated the performance of the entrepreneurial function.

4. Advertising and aggressive selling have speeded up technological change.

5. Advertising and aggressive selling have had their greatest influence on investment in new industries, though they have also helped to increase the demand for the products of established industries.

B. The gains from new investment in plants to produce new products and from investment in labor- or capital-saving machines are not all net gains to the consumer group, since the new plant causes obsolescence of the old. But such losses from obsolescence should not be overemphasized. In spite of losses and dislocations that have occurred in the process of change and growth, the balance in terms of real consumer income and rising standards of living appears to rest in favor of change.

VII. The Effect of Advertising on Business Cycles.
  A. Advertising may slightly accentuate the swings of cyclical fluctuation in business.
    1. The evidence indicates that the volume of advertising expands during a boom and contracts during a depression.
    2. Businessmen make relatively little attempt to use advertising to offset cyclical movements.
  B. Far-sighted business management might be able to employ advertising effectively in launching new products to combat cyclical downswings. Some managements have done so.
  C. There is no convincing evidence that advertising and aggressive selling constitute a cause of cyclical fluctuations.
    1. It is true that advertising is probably one of the contributory causes to lack of flexibility in price structure. This inflexibility is found in both upward and downward price movements.
    2. But the argument which makes such lack of flexibility in the price structure a significant cause of cyclical fluctuations is not well supported.
  D. The "bullish" point of view typical of the entrepreneur who makes substantial use of advertising and other aggressive selling devices is essential to the revival of private investment needed for business recovery in any period of depression.

VIII. Principal Dangers in the Contemporary Use of Advertising.
  A. There is a tendency among businessmen to assume too readily that demand is inelastic and consequently to refrain from sufficient use of price as a competitive weapon.
  B. Consumers sometimes do not have sufficient freedom of choice to buy nonadvertised or privately branded goods on a price basis.
  C. In some instances, owing to the dominating position of large advertisers there may be insufficient freedom of entry of new enterprises into established industries.
  D. The advance in distribution costs may be reaching the point where greater than corresponding declines in production costs are no longer forthcoming, and where the conveniences and services associated with present-day distribution may be proving too expensive a luxury for some pocketbooks.
  E. Present-day advertising does not give consumers sufficient information to enable them to buy with full economic effectiveness.

IX. Important Counterbalancing Forces.
  A. A substantial number of firms elect to compete on a price basis.
    1. Many small manufacturers cater to the demands of private branding distributors and therefore sell at low prices.

2. A considerable number of large companies also make up merchandise for sale under private brands.

3. There has been a substantial growth of strong distributive enterprises, such as chain stores, which sell private brands to a considerable extent on a price basis and which pit their strong buying power (and sometimes their own manufacturing facilities) against the monopolistic tendencies of some manufacturers. This development has done much to keep the situation in balance.

4. New types of enterprise in the distributive field usually elect to compete on a price basis, e.g., supermarkets.

B. The growing influence of the Consumer Movement through its emphasis on price as related to objective product qualities tends to offset in part the practice of some advertisers to lay heavy stress on appeals to emotion and instinct.

C. Efforts of businessmen to reduce wastes in advertising and selling through the use of improved techniques of market study, budgeting, and measurement of advertising results operate in the direction of lightening the burden of cost carried by consumers

X. Final Conclusions on the Economic Problem.

On balance, the general conclusion to be drawn from the evidence is that the functional objectives of advertising in a dynamic economy are socially desirable and that advertising as it is now conducted, though certainly not free from criticism, is an economic asset and not a liability.

Generalizations on the Ethical Problems of Advertising

I. The use of influence in commercial relations is one of the attributes of a free economy. Therefore the ethics of advertising is the ethics of influence in the buyer and seller relationship.

II. In a competitive system where numerous sellers compete for the patronage of buyers the appropriate ethics for the seller are the ethics of the advocate. In other words, the seller's biased point of view is not inherently unethical.

III. As advertising and aggressive selling have developed, ethical standards governing their use have evolved on a pragmatic basis.

A. In this pragmatic evolution of ethical standards for advertising, certain advertising practices have come to be regarded as sufficiently serious abuses to be condemned by law, e.g., the so-called model advertising statutes which have been enacted in 25 states with the support of the advertising profession.

1. It is to be expected that crystallization of the views of the community into rigid statutes should lag somewhat behind the evolution of these community opinions.

2. Occasionally the law lags too far behind the sentiment of the community; such a situation probably existed for several years

prior to 1935. But since that date the lag has been very substantially narrowed by the enactment of such measures as the Copeland amendments to the Pure Food and Drug Act, the Wheeler-Lea amendments to the Federal Trade Commission Act, and the Wool Labeling Act. It will take time to make these laws fully workable and overcome the administrative problems; and for that reason further major crystallizations into law of the ethical sense of the community with respect to advertising do not appear desirable for the time being.

     a. The evidence from reports both of the Federal Trade Commission and of the Better Business Bureaus points to the conclusion that a relatively small percentage of present-day advertising material is of such a character as to be misleading or false under the definitions used by those organizations.

B. Going beyond the crystallizations in the form of law are the tentative formulations of the ethical sense of the business community represented by codes of professional conduct of various organizations, such as the code promulgated by the National Association of Better Business Bureaus.

C. But present-day advertising practice of some concerns falls short of these standards, since the latter represent tentative formulations which the public opinion of the community is not yet strong enough to enforce.

IV. In addition to observing ethical standards codified into law or sanctioned by the business community, advertisers should also give close heed to the sentiments of the consuming public, since these sentiments are likely to be significant indicators of newly developing crystallizations of community ethics. In this connection a survey of consumer opinions of advertising undertaken as part of this general study yielded the following significant results:

A. These consumers generally expected advertising to be biased.

B. But they had little tolerance for anything regarded as untrue, though they were somewhat lenient in their interpretation of what was true and what was false.

C. They possessed a fairly strong belief that advertising should be strictly true and purely informative.

D. They criticized a considerable body of advertising on the score of exaggerated claims, bad taste, use of fear, and use of questionable testimonials.

E. On the whole they apparently had somewhat better opinions of advertised products than of the advertising of the sponsors of those products.

F. A majority of them apparently believed that advertising increases prices.

In conjunction with other studies of consumer views on advertising, this survey suggests that with respect to certain advertising practices at least part of the business group may be lagging dangerously behind the sentiments of the consuming public.

V. On the other hand, business cannot raise standards much more rapidly than the general community will accept them; and the public, in spite of the opinions which it makes known in surveys, still accepts, and by its acceptance makes profitable, business practices which many businessmen would prefer not to employ but whose use by a minority forces the majority to fall in line.

SUGGESTIONS

Apart from the present emergency of national defense the problem of both business and government is how to keep the economic machine functioning, and from a practical standpoint that means functioning within the general structure of the private enterprise system. Very few people in business, in government, or in the community at large desire to see drastic social changes. But if such changes are to be avoided and if the economic machine is to be made to function effectively, it is necessary that businessmen, instead of being blindly antagonistic to all criticism, should become more acutely aware of the social consequences of their business acts and should seek to understand such criticisms of existing business practices as those which are dealt with in this study of advertising.

This study shows that advertising properly carried out contributes to the maintenance of a dynamic economy and helps to raise the level of real income. The functioning of advertising along these lines, however, can be substantially improved if businessmen will study their problems more carefully and make better use of price strategy. The existing economic machine can also be made to run more smoothly if businessmen will behave more boldly and fearlessly in pushing pioneering ventures and in keeping the door open to new types of enterprise. Efforts to choke off the entry of new enterprises, whether by means of patents, tying agreements, enormous advertising expenditures, or restrictive price control measures, such as price maintenance laws and not-selling-below-cost laws, will lead to the eventual disruption of the private enterprise system.

Businessmen can help consumers by providing more product information. It is short-sighted of businessmen to oppose the development of a strong Consumer Movement. Under a free-enterprise system consumers have fully as much right to organize as does labor. Furthermore, the Consumer Movement is one of the corrective forces which keeps the economic machine in proper balance.

·Advertisers are in some danger of not paying sufficient attention to public sentiment. The practitioners of advertising have developed some interesting research techniques to find out what people like in advertisements and to find out what they like about products. It might be wise to use such types of opinion survey to keep in closer touch with evolving ethical standards by finding out what the public really thinks about many contemporary practices in advertising. There is a need to get at the facts instead of replying to criticisms by means of emotional statements based on half truths, because such replies serve only to encourage further emotional statements based on partial truths by the other side.

The same admonition may be addressed to the critics of advertising. They are urged to examine the facts collected in this study, because an effort has been made impartially to appraise advertising and aggressive selling practices. The economists are urged to understand the organic functions of advertising in a dynamic economy. If this view of the function of advertising in a system of private enterprise is sound, advertising has a permanent place in modern life; and both the critics and the practitioners must work together to make advertising and aggressive selling serve even more effectively than in the past in the interests of the whole of society.

Signed:

> THEODORE H. BROWN,
> EDMUND P. LEARNED,
> HOWARD T. LEWIS,
> MALCOLM P. MCNAIR,
> HARRY R. TOSDAL,
> *Advisory Committee*

Soldiers Field,
Boston, Massachusetts,
January, 1942.

PART I

The Development and Use of Advertising by Businessmen—Economic Background

CHAPTER I

THE SETTING OF THE PROBLEM

ADVERTISING is under fire. Its adverse critics come from many camps and their complaints tend to become increasingly vehement. Certain economists complain that its extensive use involves undue costs and is a bar to free competition, with a resultant adverse effect on the operation of the free price system. Home economics teachers charge it with being a poor guide to consumption. Students of ethics accuse it of showing frequent display of poor taste and misrepresentation. Businessmen themselves have not infrequently doubted its effectiveness for business purposes.

Proponents of advertising claim that it represents an economical means of effecting exchange; that it helps to lower costs because it makes possible large-scale operations in industries operating under decreasing costs; that it is an essential source of product information in an advanced economy; that it encourages product development and technological improvement by inducing consumers to want the new and improved things offered; in short, that it contributes to a high standard of living.

The discussions on both sides have often been characterized by sweeping generalization, by paucity of fact, and by lack of closely-knit, logical reasoning. There has been much wishful thinking and rationalization, because the issues involved have frequently turned upon questions of basic philosophies toward life that have a high emotional content, or because advertising has been a calling and a source of livelihood to those who have spoken out.

The adverse criticism has reached such proportions that neither businessmen nor the public can dismiss it as they have so often done in the past. Neither will unsupported counterclaim suffice. Either these criticisms are sound or they are not sound. Either they can be supported by evidence or they cannot be so supported. If advertising performs a useful economic function, it should be possible to demonstrate that fact. If, as opponents aver, costs are vastly out of proportion to benefits realized, that conclusion should be demonstrable.

3

The Need for Factual Studies

What is needed is evidence bearing upon the issues, for there has been little attempt to get at sources of information and certain types of information have not been available. A mere restatement of printed materials or resort to *a priori* reasoning will not serve to resolve the complex issues involved in such discussions of advertising.

The lack of factual material upon which to base conclusions cannot be blamed on those who have taken part in the dispute. Businessmen who are advocates of advertising as a rule have had neither the training nor the time to undertake large-scale analysis of such an economic problem. In turn, the critics of advertising, generally high-minded, serious individuals, have lacked resources for obtaining the needed evidence. The type of information called for is largely facts and figures of business concerns, which for competitive reasons have ordinarily been closely guarded. Collection of such material is a difficult, laborious task requiring time and assistance on a scale not ordinarily available to the individual student. Time-consuming, difficult, and expensive also are the collation and analysis of facts from government documents, from advertising measuring services, and from industrial and economic monographs. Finally, special skills are needed in collection and use of the needed materials. Data from such widely-scattered sources are at best likely to be fragmentary, particularly since voluntary submittal of confidential data from business firms is involved; consequently the analyst should have a broad familiarity with advertising and business practice if he is to arrive at a correct and complete picture of business and advertising practice upon which economic analysis may depend. In brief, hope for solution of the problem rests, on the one hand, on a willingness of businessmen to provide needed evidence and, on the other hand, on adequate financial support to enable properly equipped investigators to collect and analyze the evidence.

The Attempt to Amass Factual Evidence

The study presented in this volume is an attempt to collect evidence that will furnish at least tentative or partial answers to the issues raised by the opponents and proponents of advertising. A generous gift made possible assistance in gathering and collating information relating to these issues on a scale never before attempted. Businessmen evinced interest in such a factual study, and as a rule were highly cooperative in providing desired information. In order that the reader may not have a mistaken idea as to the size of the project, however, it should be pointed out that the effort was small relative to the job that might have been done. For comparison, less money was spent for this research than is often spent by individual business concerns for a single market investigation. Although the study required investigation in many fields, the expenditure for collection of data was but a small fraction of that spent by the Federal Government through the Temporary National Economic Committee to investigate the working of the national economy. Clearly, the study can be deemed only a start which may throw some light where there has been much confusion. If it does no more than point the way to further factual study, it will have justified itself.

That such studies are worth making is beyond doubt. Advertising is an extensive activity in our economic structure, involving the energies of thousands of individuals and the expenditure by consumers of hundreds of millions of dollars. Not only is the activity important, but the economic implications are so controversial that it is desirable in the interests both of the public and of business to attempt to substitute facts for unstudied opinions.

If the facts reveal abuses or errors, business should make corrections. If the facts reveal injustice of criticisms, critics should recognize their misconceptions. Eventually a better understanding of advertising in the economic order should be the outcome.

Complexity of the Problem—
Definition of Underlying Postulates

At best the problem is complex. Much of its apparent complexity, however, and the confusion which has attended its discussion have been the result of controversy relating to basic philosophies of life which are not amenable to scientific proof or disproof. These basic ideologies of people are determined primarily by their sentiments, not by a logical analysis of evidence. The fact that the criticisms have their origin largely in the emotions, which are the mainspring of human belief and action, has led to much wishful thinking and rationalization about advertising. In some cases the underlying ideologies have guided the assembling of facts which justify the answers desired.

If a study is to avoid this confusion, it must clearly define the underlying postulates. Then within the framework of these postulates, the issues should be drawn and the pertinent facts submitted to logical analysis. Such a procedure cannot supply the ultimate answers regarding the relative merits of the fundamental philosophies, but it provides the only available basis for scientific treatment of such data regarding advertising and its economic effects.

To illustrate, in attacking advertising and aggressive selling, critics often are attacking not advertising as such, but the capitalistic system. Obviously, if one's underlying economic philosophy favors distribution of goods and services by governmental allotment to consumers, then advertising and selling directed by men actuated by profit appear unnecessary and even undesirable.

Again, advertising has been attacked because it has been a force to stimulate the manufacture of countless products and has been used to make people want these many things. To these critics the everpresent advertisement, with its frequent emotional appeals, represents a powerful agency leading away from the non-egoistic, simple life, which they favor, toward what they consider a magnification of personal vanities and desires and an objectionable emphasis upon material things. Manifestly, advertising which is employed to make people desire material things is objectionable to those whose underlying philosophy rejects either the view that human happiness and welfare depend in appreciable measure on the satisfaction of material wants or the view that the stimulus of wants is desirable or, at least, not counter to human welfare and happiness.

Differences in viewpoint arising from such differences in basic ideology clearly cannot be resolved in the study here undertaken. There is no logical, scientific way of proving that one ideology is preferable to another. Adequate evidence regarding results attained under various ideologies, such as those of Russia and of Germany, probably does not exist. Furthermore, even if such evidence were available, it would be beyond the scope of this study to gather it, because the task undertaken here has been a rigorous analysis of the facts within the framework of a free, capitalistic society.

The most important basic postulate made here is that advertising is to be studied in the framework of a free, capitalistic society, such as has existed in the United States.

That the full implications of this postulate may be realized, certain further subordinate postulates of such a society must be laid down. These are stated simply, without elaboration or extensive qualification. In their simple form they are subject to qualifications which will be evident as the chapter proceeds. These are the postulates:

(1) A free, capitalistic society is one in which the members are free to follow such economic endeavor as they see fit.

(2) Private initiative and private enterprise are relied upon to supply desired goods and services to be consumed.

(3) The direction of economic endeavor depends essentially upon a free exchange of goods and services among the members of the society, not upon socialized control and allotment.

(4) Accordingly, members are free to manufacture such products as they think other members will desire, so long as they observe the legal or social controls that have been imposed to prevent abuses. In turn, men are free to sell their products and services at such values as they may wish to put upon them. Correspondingly, members are free to buy merchandise at such values as they care to offer.

(5) The use of influence by individuals in dealing with other individuals is permitted in economic affairs just as it is permitted in religion, in politics, in education, and in other human affairs.[1] Since influence and persuasion involve ethical considerations, however, they must be carried on according to the controls established by the social group to prevent abuses.

In keeping with the postulate that influence is permitted, the values placed by members of society on merchandise or services are determined as a result of opportunity for free interchange of information, opinion, and persuasion. Since individuals differ in needs, in likes and dislikes, in attitudes, and in wealth, it is not to be expected that all buyers and all sellers will agree in their valuations of merchandise. Buyers can indicate their valuations by their willingness to buy what is offered and can show the attainment of satisfactions with goods and services by continuing to buy.

The second basic postulate upon which the study rests is closely related to the first; namely, in a free society the primary objective of economic activity as well as of other human endeavor is assumed to be the happiness and welfare of the individual, not the enhancement of the state or the performance of duty as set up by totalitarian philosophies. The state is presumed to exist to serve the individual, not the

---

[1] A substantial body of critics of advertising apparently reject this postulate so far as advertising is concerned or, in fact, so far as economic exchange is concerned. They would deny to businessmen the right to use influence or persuasion in exchange transactions, reducing selling and advertising efforts solely to providing factual data of merchandise and sources.

See Max Radin, *The Lawful Pursuit of Gain* (Boston, Houghton Mifflin Company, 1931). A. S. J. Baster, *Advertising Reconsidered* (London, P. S. King & Son, Ltd., 1935).

individual to serve the state. In the necessary guiding and control of human relationships and institutions, it is accepted that the democratic ideal will hold. The combined opinions of individuals will govern, and the guiding objective in that governing will be the happiness and welfare of the individual.

It is assumed further that what contributes to the welfare and happiness of any man will be determined by the man himself within the controls always needed to assure amiable and just relationships among members of the society. It will not be dictated by authority. Since self-determination will guide him in the pursuit of happiness, it is to be expected that the views of one person may not accord with those of all others.

In keeping with this assumption is the further premise which to all appearances has guided the American economy, namely, that an individual's happiness and welfare depend in appreciable measure upon the degree to which his wants are satisfied. Further, the stimulation of his wants is not considered counter to his welfare and happiness. Those with an ascetic view of life, who eschew things material, are free to follow that view. But, in turn, those who aspire to a high material standard of life may seek that end. Accordingly, it is assumed that the achievement of the ends of economic activity may be measured by a high standard of material welfare. The test for such material welfare is assumed to rest in the attainment of satisfaction of a large number of wants by the great body of consumers.

Acceptance of the above postulates and criteria removes many controversial points regarding advertising discussion. But such limitation is necessary in order to avoid confusion and sterile argument over issues for which answers cannot be derived by the logical, scientific method of adducing facts which are subject to verification.

The basic problem undertaken in the study may be phrased thus: Does advertising contribute to or does it interfere with the successful functioning of a dynamic, free, capitalistic economy, the aim of which is a high material welfare for the whole social group? The issues involved in this broad problem are so many that a full chapter is devoted to their statement and to an explanation of how they arise through economic analysis. Some of the more important of these issues are the following: whether advertising is a necessary function in modern economy; to what extent it has served as a desirable guide to consumers; whether it has led to correct or incorrect valuations;

what effect it has had on production and marketing costs of business concerns; whether it has interfered with free price competition; whether it has contributed to the development of monopolies; whether it has interfered with the entry of new firms into industry; whether it has aided or hindered the attainment of a higher standard of living; and whether it has intensified or helped to overcome cyclical fluctuations of business.

Acceptance of the postulates of a free, capitalistic society and of the criteria by which the social worth of advertising is to be judged does not require that the failures of that society in certain respects need be overlooked, nor does it mean that the criticisms based upon different ideologies are not understood or appreciated.

Now that underlying assumptions are defined, it is possible to classify the issues which are involved in the study.

Business, Economic, and Ethical Issues

The use of advertising in a free society involves business issues, economic issues, and ethical or moral issues. These issues are interrelated. Yet, to make the many-faceted undertaking manageable, it will be necessary to draw clear distinctions among these three groups of issues.

The business issues relating to advertising revolve around questions of its sound usage by administrators under various operating conditions to help accomplish successful management of the business enterprise. The criterion which the businessman applies to the use of advertising is that of profit, generally long-range profit.

In contrast, on the economic issues the social point of view is taken. The economist studies any business activity from the standpoint of its effect upon the entire economic organization. He is interested in knowing how advertising may bring profit to the business enterprise, but he is concerned only as profit and the activities employed in making it affect the production and consumption of goods. In short, the economist's attention is devoted to the functioning of the economic system as a whole. The economist is interested in advertising not only as it contributes to consumption, but also as it may affect freedom of exchange and the distribution of wealth.

The ethical and moral issues deal with the perplexing questions of what shall be deemed fair, honest, and desirable practice in the use of influence in exchange. Individuals in a free economy, actuated by self-interest, may act in a way to injure others. They may offer harmful goods. They may misrepresent, lie, and cheat. They may employ bad taste and thus offend public sentiment. Since advertising can be and has been used in all these ways, it has been a prolific source of moral and ethical problems. A question here is whether the fault rests with the individuals who use advertising unethically, rather than with advertising itself.

In order that the broad problem may be made manageable and the analysis made clear, the economic effects of advertising are studied without reference to the moral and ethical effects. For example, in the study of the effects of advertising in shaping the demands of consumers, no attempt is made to differentiate between merchandise which is good and that which is not good for mankind. If consumers are stimulated to want products such as spirituous liquors, tobacco, patent medicines, and cosmetics, it is assumed that the products give them satisfaction. The consumer in a free society, generally speaking, is free to determine what is good for him, what gives him satisfaction. Likewise he is recognized as the final determiner of what services or merchandise are worth to him. In brief, for purposes of analysis and study a clear division is drawn between economics and ethics or morals. In a practical world, however, no such precise division can be drawn.

The Interrelationship of Economic and Ethical Issues

Ethical and moral views impinge upon and even govern business and economic activity. The functioning of a free, capitalistic economy is fashioned in large degree by constantly changing ethical and moral views and rules. In short, although the term "free society" is used, no such thing exists in reality. *Laissez faire* is a concept, not an actuality.

The individual must always conduct himself with reference to those about him and temper his desires and wishes so as to have congenial and just relationships with his fellow citizens. He must act in accord with dictates laid down by the social group to protect the individual who cannot adequately protect his own interests. He must avoid offending the religious and moral sentiments of those about him.

In economic affairs, sellers have not been entirely free to sell whatever might be profitable in whatever way they have seen fit. Nor has the individual consumer been free always to buy every product or service he desired. The action of both sellers and buyers has been restricted in numerous ways to comply with established customs and ideas as to what is good for the individual and for society. Examples are numerous. Certain products, such as contraceptives, which transgress religious or moral sentiments, have been sold under legal restraints; gambling devices or services have been interdicted; alcoholic beverages have been subjected to a greater or lesser degree of regulation, or even to prohibition; minors have not been allowed to buy tobacco.

As the variety of merchandise and services made available by an expanding, dynamic economy has become wider and wider, the social group has found an increasing need for regulating the activities of producers and sellers in order to protect individuals or groups. Unrestricted sale of harmful, habit-forming drugs has been banned for many years. Rules to govern purity and cleanliness of foods and drugs have been instituted. And so the list of examples might be extended.

Just as the products which may be sold have been subject to social control, so also the use of influence in selling products from early times has been subject to social control. For many generations the seller has not been permitted to say all the things he might wish to say in order to persuade the buyer to accept his valuations of the merchandise he has to sell. He has not been permitted under law to commit fraud, which essentially is resort to misrepresentation that leads the buyer to set his valuations upon expected satisfactions which he will not realize.

As will be developed in a later chapter, what has been deemed proper use of influence in effecting exchange of merchandise and services has been subject to constant change. Ethical viewpoints which lead to legal controls and provide the voluntary rules of the game governing individuals in their intercourse change with changing economic institutions. In turn, they play an important part in shaping those institutions. In addition to the influences arising from economic institutions themselves, religious and political institutions and ideas have always played an important part in determining the ethical viewpoints ruling economic conduct and practice, just as economic institutions and practice in turn have influenced religion and politics.

The Economic Implications of Ethical Problems

The effect of changing ethical attitudes and changing social institutions upon relations between buyers and sellers can be traced through the centuries: in Roman society, in the guild economy of the Middle Ages, and in our later economy. After the breakdown of the guild system and the slow evolution of what we have come to term a free economy, the use of influence and persuasion between buyer and seller went through a slowly changing process. The first rules governing exchange were crude. Buyer and seller stood at arm's length and were permitted freely to swap lies. With the growth of the factory system, as the number of products has increased, as the importance of exchange has grown, and as the business structure has become more complex, the buyer has been afforded an increasing degree of protection. The law of fraud has changed. Ideas as to what is proper in persuasion have changed; they are changing now.

Since ethical attitudes are subject to a constant evolution, and since they govern the way in which business is to be conducted, it is highly essential that businessmen be alert to changes in ethical viewpoints. Blindness to them can result only in legal compulsion.

Although this is a study of the economic effects of advertising, it is fitting to give attention also to these moral and ethical viewpoints, difficult and complex as they are, for they largely govern advertising practice and, accordingly, its economic effects. Failure to give such attentions would nullify any practical effects from such a study.

The Search for Positive Conclusions

In this study an attempt has been made to come as near to positive conclusions as the nature of the available information permits. In turn, effort has been made to get as complete information as possible, without reference to whether it might be deemed favorable or unfavorable to past and current advertising and business practice.

In many instances the determination of fact has been most difficult. Study of the effects of advertising calls for detailed analyses of specific industries and businesses. The collection of needed data from widely scattered business concerns was made difficult because the books of record of such concerns generally are not set up specifically to provide the type of information needed for this study. Again, many of the important considerations behind decisions relating to advertising are not available because frequently the conferences of business executives at which problems are discussed and decisions are reached, as well as the individual actions of executives, have not been recorded. Consequently it is often difficult to get such information after the event. In many instances the study has had to rely on the unverified statements of business executives regarding the facts as given in case reports.[2] Often it has been necessary to fill in desired information by analogy from known facts. Moreover, much of the needed data were looked upon as confidential, in that they involved the intimate details of business operations in highly competitive fields. It is easily understandable why some firms refused to give such information and why others supplied it only on the condition that it be treated in confidence. In such instances the facts were furnished for the study, but it was requested that they should not be published in such form as to disclose the source. In short, the study has had to deal with faulty and incomplete material; yet an attempt has been made to recognize the weaknesses of the data and to temper the conclusions accordingly.

It has, of course, been impossible to put into this volume all the actual data amassed. Hundreds of case histories have been reviewed and analyzed in the course of the investigation. Many folders of confidential figures submitted for study have been analyzed. It would not be wise to reproduce all this information even if it were possible. Yet it has provided a sounder basis for conclusions than was furnished by the limited data which it has been possible to reproduce in the study.

Inevitably in complex social phenomena, positive conclusions to some problems evade grasp because of their very complexity, or because of the investigator's inability to secure adequate and dependable data, or because of the conflicting nature both of data secured and of bases for judgment. It should be pointed out, however, that failure to reach a conclusion upon the basis of earnest effort to secure pertinent data is in itself a conclusion. It indicates that positive, scientifically derived statements cannot be made on the matter in hand. The study has indicated that some of the highly laudatory statements made by the proponents of advertising as well as some of the disparaging conclusions drawn by opponents are equally unjustified if criteria involving scientific proof are applied to them.

The Plan of the Study

The plan of this book is a simple one. The first step is to define advertising and to develop a factual picture of advertising and its importance in the national economy.

---

[2] A detailed discussion of the character of the case reports employed and of their worth as evidence will be found on p. 72 ff.

Since advertising is a business activity undertaken by businessmen in the free enterprise system, it was logical to have economic analysis preceded by a study of how and why advertising has been used in business and commerce. This part of the study involves a brief historical review of the development of business under brands and of the relationship of advertising to brands. To measure more precisely the economic importance of advertising, an attempt has been made to measure the volume of advertising and to relate it to other forms of economic activity. An appraisal of the effectiveness or ineffectiveness of advertising from the business point of view and a comparison of advertising with alternative procedures complete the general background against which studies of economic and social effects of advertising can proceed.

Part of the confusion and disagreement arising in discussions of the economics of advertising is the result of lack of clear understanding by businessmen of technical economic terminology. Consequently, it has been deemed wise to preface the chapters of factual analysis by a chapter which presents in nontechnical language the economic problems arising from the use of advertising as they are indicated to the economist by his economic theory. The theories of pure competition and of monopoly are reviewed and compared with the theory of so-called "monopolistic competition," or "imperfect competition," with which branding and advertising are associated. The place of advertising and selling in value theory is thus examined because a study of theory discloses questions regarding the economic or social effects of advertising, the answers to which must be sought in an examination of the facts. While theory may thus be valuable in crystallizing important questions, the economist recognizes that he cannot soundly recommend reform or legal control on the basis of theoretical analysis alone. He realizes the need of seeking out facts not only to test and refine his theories but also to find the practical answers to the questions which his theories raise. It is the task of the chapters following to marshal the facts bearing on the issues raised in this theoretical discussion.

The series of chapters dealing with the effects of advertising on the demand for goods and services, on their supply and costs, on prices, and on investment and growth in production constitute the principal portion of the study. In these chapters particularly are to be found the materials with which attempt has been made to differentiate this study from the *a priori* and abstract discussions which have so often been accepted uncritically by the layman.

Since business practice is subject to ethical controls and since some of the criticisms directed against advertising are ethical in nature, a chapter has been included which briefly traces the changing ethical attitudes of society that have determined codes of business conduct and legal control of advertising. This chapter is supported by a review of certain surveys of consumers' opinions and attitudes towards advertising.

Finally, the conclusions and recommendations which have come from the study are summarized in the last chapter.

CHAPTER II

THE DEVELOPMENT AND GROWTH OF ADVERTISING IN THE AMERICAN ECONOMY

THE purpose of this chapter is to define *advertising* as the word is used in this study, to trace the growth and development of advertising in the American economy, and to interpret from these historical facts its place in the business structure. Space does not permit giving a detailed history of advertising, and it is not necessary, for the task has been done adequately by others;[1] but some essential historical facts are included and interpreted because they provide needed background for the economic issues to be treated in later chapters.

Advertising Defined

The word *advertising* is used in many different ways with many varied connotations. It is desirable, therefore, to define rather carefully the concept which is used throughout this study.

[1] Among the numerous books relating to the history of advertising and of business that have appeared, the following have been consulted in preparation of this chapter:

E. W. Gilboy, "Demand as a Factor in the Industrial Revolution," an essay in *Facts and Factors in Economic History*, Articles by Former Students of Edwin F. Gay, (Cambridge, Harvard University Press, 1932).

N. S. B. Gras, *An Introduction to Economic History* (New York, Harper & Brothers, 1922).

W. C. Hazlitt, *The Livery Companies of the City of London* (London, S. Sonnenschein & Co., 1892).

G. B. Hotchkiss, *Milestones of Marketing* (New York, The Macmillan Company, 1938).

Ralph Hower, *The History of an Advertising Agency* (Cambridge, Harvard University Press, 1939).

J. M. Lambert, *Two Thousand Years of Gild Life* (Hull, A. Brown & Sons, 1891).

F. B. Millett, *Craft-Guilds of the Thirteenth Century in Paris* (Kingston, The Jackson Press, 1915).

Frank Presbrey, *The History and Development of Advertising* (New York, Doubleday, Doran & Company, Inc., 1929).

G. P. Rowell, *Forty Years an Advertising Agent, 1865–1905* (New York, Franklin Publishing Company, 1926).

Henry Sampson, *A History of Advertising from the Earliest Times* (London, Chatto & Windus, 1875).

F. I. Schechter, *The Historical Foundation of the Law Relating to Trade-Marks* (New York, Columbia University Press, 1925).

Toulmin Smith, *English Gilds* (Published for the Early English Text Society by N. Trubner & Co., 1870).

George Unwin, *The Gilds and Companies of London* (2d ed., London, Methuen & Co., Ltd., 1925).

A. P. Usher, *An Introduction to the Industrial History of England* (Boston, Houghton Mifflin Company, 1920).

Advertising includes those activities by which visual or oral messages are addressed to the public for the purposes of informing them and influencing them either to buy merchandise or services or to act or be inclined favorably toward ideas, institutions, or persons featured. As contrasted with publicity and other forms of propaganda, advertising messages are identified with the advertiser either by signature or by oral statement. In further contrast to publicity, advertising is a commercial transaction involving pay to publishers or broadcasters and others whose media are employed.

Activities Included in Advertising

Just what activities of business firms shall be labeled advertising is often a question of debate. Certain things are almost universally accepted as advertising, while arbitrary decision determines the inclusion or exclusion of other things. Clearly, advertising includes the following forms of messages: the messages carried in newspapers and magazines, on outdoor boards, on street car cards and posters, in radio broadcasts, and in circulars of all kinds, whether distributed by mail, by person, through tradesmen, or by inserts in packages; dealer help materials; window display and counter display materials and efforts; store signs; house organs when directed to dealers and consumers; motion pictures used for advertising; and novelties bearing advertising messages or signature of the advertiser.

Labels, tags, and other literature accompanying merchandise are deemed advertising in this study because they reasonably may be said to fall within the definition of advertising given above. Writers with a different purpose in mind sometimes exclude these items.

Activities Excluded from Advertising

Activities sometimes termed advertising but which in this study are placed under other classifications of sales promotional effort include the offering of premiums to stimulate the sale of products; the use of exhibitions and demonstrations at fairs, shows, and conventions; the use of samples; and the so-called publicity activities involved in sending out news releases. Likewise arbitrarily excluded from the category of advertising are the activities of personal selling forces, both regular and missionary salesmen; the offering of free goods; the payment of advertising allowances which are not used for advertising; the entertainment of customers; the conducting of demonstration stores; and the giving of the bonuses or PM's[2] to salesmen of the trade.

Often these excluded activities are embraced in advertising budgets and are directed by those in charge of advertising. On many there is room for close argument as to whether they should be called advertising or be otherwise classified. They have been excluded here for one reason or another. For example, the use of premium merchandise to gain sales is deemed more in the nature of a price inducement than an advertising message. Exhibitions and demonstrations at fairs and shows are thought to be more closely related to personal selling than to advertising. Publicity does not deal with messages identified with source. A long discussion of the pros and cons regarding inclusion or exclusion of each individual item is not necessary. One might study all aspects of aggressive selling comprehended in the activities mentioned above which are in practice divided under the heads of *advertising, sales promotion,* and *personal selling.* They all have the same economic objective of stimulating sales and bringing about exchange. In the present study, however, it has been decided to center attention only upon the activities which relate to presenting visual or oral messages to groups of people.

Advertising as a Part of the Selling Process

Advertising, even most broadly defined, must be viewed in perspective as constituting only a part of the selling process. Because it is pervasively and persistently conspicuous, there is danger that the student of advertising economics will receive a distorted impression of the position of advertising in our economy. The growth of large-scale specialized units producing a tremendous variety of merchandise and the growing lack of self-sufficiency of consuming units have necessarily been accompanied by an increase in the effort required to bring consumers and producers together. Satisfaction of consumers' needs and wants by specialized producers requires exchange, whether that exchange be effected by the volition of buyers and sellers in a competitive economy or by allotment processes in a controlled economy. In the competitive economy with which this study is concerned, it becomes obvious that either the buyer must come to the seller or the seller must go to the buyer, or they must share the burden of coming together in a

---

[2] PM stands for premium merchandise, for the sale of which special commissions are given to salesmen in retail stores in order to stimulate special selling efforts.

market, although the cost of this coming together is borne ultimately by the buyer. Otherwise, the seller cannot sell that which he must sell if he is to secure a return for his labor and materials and for the outlays which he has made for the labor and material furnished by others. Nor will the consumer be satisfied.

In the United States, the initiative in exchange is largely taken by the seller. In the selling process, the problem presented to business executives is that of choosing and putting into execution the means of effecting exchanges. Theoretically, it might be said that every selling executive works toward a selling program embodying ideal proportions of personal salesmanship, advertising, and other available means of performing selling functions so that he can effect distribution at minimum cost and maximum long-run profit for the sellers. That such an optimum proportion exists is only conjectural, but, as will be shown later, there is much evidence to support the point of view that in given situations some proportions are better than others. For example, there are many instances of improved accomplishment from the standpoint of the seller which have been effected through increase of the amount of advertising in the selling program. Nevertheless, it must be kept in mind that advertising is only a part of that selling program. For certain types of companies and certain types of selling tasks, advertising seems to have been used more commonly and more successfully than for others. The discussion proceeds, therefore, to a more detailed examination both of the types of advertising classified by institutions conducting that advertising and to the relationships of advertising to branded goods in the selling of which advertising has been relatively most widely used.

Classification of Types of Advertising

Just as definitions of advertising are somewhat arbitrary, so classifications of types of advertising are established in accordance with the purposes of writers. There are many bases on which advertising may be classified: according to media, type of product, institution, type of appeal, character of action sought, and so on. From the standpoint of this study of economics, a useful division is indicated in the following outline:

I. Manufacturers' advertising
   A. Consumers' goods advertising
      1. Advertising directed to consumers

      a. Advertising to influence direct purchase
      b. Advertising to influence purchase through tradesmen
         (1) Advertising relating to branded merchandise
         (2) Advertising relating to the maker or institution
    2. Advertising directed to dealers
  B. Industrial goods[3] advertising

II. Dealers' advertising[4]
  A. Advertising for immediate sale of merchandise
  B. Advertising for promotion of brands
  C. Advertising for promotion of institution or departments

This outline is not an all-inclusive classification, nor are the categories set up mutually exclusive. It is employed simply to delimit the area against which has been directed a large share of the adverse criticism based on economic grounds. Attention is called to the divisions made; distinction is drawn between manufacturers' and dealers' advertising. Manufacturers' advertising falls into two broad classes, that of consumers' goods and services and that of industrial goods and services. Consumers' goods advertising breaks down into that which is directed to consumers and that which is directed to tradesmen. A relatively small part of consumers' goods advertising is designed to induce purchase direct from the producer. The greater part is employed to influence the purchase of the advertisers' brands from tradesmen. It is largely indirect in action, in that its aim often is not so much to induce immediate sale as to build up the reputation of brands and to enhance their wantability, through ideas relating either to the merchandise itself or to the characteristics of the maker which might influence sale. Dealers' advertising for the most part is a direct offering of merchandise to consumers at a price. An appreciable part, however, is devoted to the building of brand and institutional reputation.

No one of the categories of the outline has been free from adverse criticism on either ethical or economic grounds. To cite a few common complaints, each has been charged at times with having employed excessive claims, with having stimulated questionable valuations of merchandise, with having provided inadequate information, or with having exhibited bad taste. While no classification has been free from disapprobation, criticism has tended to center upon advertising of

---

[3] Industrial goods include equipment, materials, and supplies that are used for industrial purposes.
[4] Dealers' advertising applies to both consumers' goods and industrial goods.

manufacturers' brands of consumers' goods. Censure of this type has developed in part because advertising expenditures for manufacturers' brands have made up a large part of the total and because copy has relatively often been deemed objectionable. Basically, however, most criticisms have related to the way in which the trade-mark or branding system has come to be used in the economy.

The criticisms are directed primarily at the practices of differentiating merchandise under brands and of devoting large amounts of selling effort to secure consumer preferences. To make their products wantable, sellers have sought to make them different in some way or other. Many of these differentiations are said by the critics to be inconsequential. Advertising and aggressive selling have been used to make them appear important and thus to build strong consumer brand preferences. As a result, manufacturers' brand advertising has been indicated as being the chief builder of brand monopolies, although this criticism also may be levelled in smaller degree against other classes of advertising devoted to brands, such as industrial goods advertising or dealer advertising. The complaint is that these brand monopolies hinder the free competition on price that would result were merchandise unbranded and standardized. To an excessive degree, it is stated, competition on these branded articles has been in advertising or in other non-price forms, with adverse price results so far as consumers are concerned. Again, the multiplicity of brands is charged with causing confusion among buyers and a costly duplication of inventory among tradesmen. Some of the proposals to put competition to a greater extent on a price basis, to reduce what are termed excessive costs of advertising and aggressive selling, and to simplify consumer buying look toward changes which would minimize the importance of brands.

In order to provide the necessary background for appraisal of such criticisms and the proposed remedies, the place of brands in the economic system and the ways in which they have come to be used in modern business should be understood. In tracing and interpreting the development of trade-mark usage, one may also trace and interpret the growth of selling methods of which trade-mark advertising is a part.

ADVERTISING AND THE TRADE-MARK SYSTEM

The historical development of the trade-mark need not be traced except in its broad outlines, for it is the modern use of trade-marks that is in question. It is worthy of note, however, that the modern trade-mark and the trade-mark law of English-speaking countries represent an evolution reaching back to the Middle Ages, while the placing of the producer's mark on pottery and other merchandise reaches back to prehistoric times.[5]

In medieval days two types of marks were employed by sellers: the merchant's mark, indicating merchant ownership, and the craftsman's mark, or regulatory mark, indicating manufacturing source or origin. Until the fifteenth century the craftsman and merchant were likely to be the same person. The merchants' marks were employed to provide evidence of proprietary rights of merchants in commerce. These marks identified goods in storage and transit. In addition, they' were particularly valuable in helping the owners to retrieve goods that were stolen by the pirates, who were a constant danger to the shipping of those times. It is not necessary to dwell upon merchants' marks, because the modern trade-mark represents a development from the craftsman's mark.

Use of the Early Craftsman's Mark for Policing Quality

The craftsman's mark under the guild system was compulsory, its purpose being not to provide buyers a symbol by which they might recognize desirable merchandise, but to furnish a "police" mark for the guilds. With these marks they could trace and punish those who did not live up to the standards of workmanship which were deemed essential under the guilds' monopoly grants. Thus the craftsman's mark was likely to be a liability to its owner instead of an asset, as is usually the case with a modern mark. The craftsman's mark, moreover, was compulsory, whereas the modern mark is voluntary. The craftsman's marks helped to keep interlopers from selling in the monopoly area of the guild. Attaching asset value to a mark was discouraged, for any effort of individual craftsmen to attract trade at the expense of other guild members was frowned upon. Goodwill was for the guild, not for individual craftsmen. Practically every guild in the exercise of its right of search or supervision affixed its seal or mark to the products of its members. To prevent individual exploitation,

---

[5] For a detailed account of trade-marks and trade-mark law, see F. I. Schechter, *op. cit.*

Among the many references consulted regarding the use of marks under the guild system, the work of Schechter was found most significant and revealing from the standpoint of this study. In tracing the law relating to trade-marks, he necessarily explored their use for business purposes. In the pages ahead, his work has been drawn upon more heavily than any other.

the craftsman's mark was generally not permitted under guild regulations to be more prominent than the guild mark.

In view of the fact that buyers in medieval times were restricted for the most part to purchasing the few products produced in their locality, they had no great need for reliance upon the trade-mark, or symbol of the craftsman, as a guarantee of the excellence of material or workmanship. Buyers were in direct contact with the craftsmen, and in the villages and small towns of the time had excellent opportunity to know their skill and their integrity.

Development of Marks as Assets in Trade

In certain industries products were transported and sold in appreciable amounts outside the local market in which a guild operated. In those cases in which the maker and the buyer were not in close contact, the marks gradually came to have an asset value in trade, inasmuch as they represented known quality of workmanship and materials. This shift from liability to asset value of marks was particularly evident in the cloth trade and the cutlery trade during the fifteenth, sixteenth, and seventeenth centuries.

In the cloth trade the marks which become important and were afforded protection were not those of the individual clothiers, but the collective marks of various cloth centers. In England the woolen trade became so important to the nation that the affixing of marks and their protection against counterfeiting was regulated by the Crown. The value of the marks in trade came to be increasingly recognized and the cloth centers strove to maintain the quality of the merchandise under their marks. Schechter cites the findings of the Privy Council in 1632 in the case of one Thomas Jupp, who was found guilty of attaching counterfeit Colchester seals to baize cloth which was manufactured at Bocking. Jupp recognized that Colchester baize was dearer than Bocking baize and assumed that it sold better "beyond the seas". The following findings of the council gave recognition to the asset value of the mark of Colchester:

That the people of this Towne of Colchester and of the parts adioyning, receive a great part of their sustenance by the making of Bayes: That for many yeeres past, by occasion of the carefull Search there made, they have beene truely and not deceitfully made, and of a knowne goodnesse: That such of them as are fully wrought are sealed with a Seale attesting their goodnesse: If upon Search any proove not so good, they are marked for such; so as the buyers both within the Realme and abroad, may bee ascertaind of the goodnesse of the Merchandize by view of the Seale, wherein (the Law requiring it) such great care hath beene had from time to time, that upon the credit of the Seale alone they were plentifully and readily vented in all places.[6]

In the case of the cutlery trade, the transition from the individual craftsman's regulatory and liability mark of the Middle Ages to the asset mark of modern times is more easily followed than in the cloth trade.[7] In the middle of the fifteenth century the Mayor and Aldermen of London recognized the asset value of the craftsman's mark by restoring to a widow still in the bladesmith business and to her new husband the Double Crescent mark of her former husband. In the following two centuries the value of the marks to their individual owners as the basis for attracting and holding patronage became increasingly appreciated, as is indicated by numerous recorded cases of trade-mark infringement in London and Sheffield. Schechter cites a certain Ephraim How of London as probably one of the first to advertise in order to repress piracy of his mark. In the *London Gazette* of May 24–27, 1703, he advertised as follows:

> Whereas several Cutlers, in the disuse of their own Marks, do imitate the mark of Ephraim HOW, of Saffron-hill, which is the Heart and Crown, by stamping a playing Spade and a Crown, and also in Imitation of his Sirname they stamp NOW: Many having been deceived by this undermining Invention, all Persons who would buy Knives of his making, are desired to observe his Name and Mark narrowly, that they may not be imposed upon; for there is no Cutler whose name is NOW.[8]

Need of Trade-Marks as Buyers and Sellers Lost Contact

A point of great significance lies in the fact that so long as the producer and consumer were in close contact, as was the case with small-town and village craftsmen, trade-marks did not develop as valuable marks for the guidance of buyers and hence as symbols of goodwill with asset value to their owners. But even in the Middle Ages, when goods were put into commerce outside the producer's area and the contact between buyer and maker was lost, the marks became guides of quality to buyers and hence valuable to the owner producers. Apparently, also, as towns grew larger and contacts of the citizens grew less intimate, the

---

[6] *Ibid.*, pp. 92–93.
[7] *Ibid.*, Chapter II.
[8] *Ibid.*, p. 119.

marks of particular craftsmen became helpful to consumers within a city as guides to good merchandise.

Today the close contact of buyer and maker that characterized the village economy has largely disappeared. The actual contact of the producer with the consuming buyer is relatively infrequent. Practically all business in consumers' goods in our present economy is through trade intermediaries. Probably less than 5% of total consumers' purchases are made direct from manufacturer to consumer at the factory, by mail order, or by house-to-house canvassers, or from the manufacturer's own retail stores. But although these sales are said to come from direct contact, it is not the sort of relationship of the small town or village, in which the consumer could learn well the skills of various craftsmen. Dealing with a distant manufacturer's local retail establishment or with his canvassing salesmen is little different from dealing with the usual tradesman. Under either method the consumer must learn from use, or from advertising, or from salesmen the probable worth of the merchandise he is to buy. To a large degree he has come to rely on brands to identify the merchandise.

In contrast to consumers' goods, direct sale of industrial goods is far more common. But again the contact between buyer and seller is not of the type that characterized the village economy. The customer generally deals with salesmen from a distant firm. While such a separation between buyer and seller indicates a need for brands, as a matter of fact, brands as guides to purchase of industrial goods do not hold so important a place relatively as in the consumers' goods field. The reasons for this anomaly are found primarily in the differences in technical skills of large, industrial goods buyers, on the one hand, and consumer buyers, on the other, in selecting and testing merchandise. The volume of total purchases by a business organization permits the employment of trained purchasing officers. For certain types of purchases, when the amount of money involved is substantial or when there are specialized needs, skilled purchasing officers can depend on their own knowledge of merchandise and that to be found in the organization, and do not need to rely on brand as an evidence of quality. They can develop their own specifications and test their products to fit their own needs. Good examples are found in primary materials, fabricating parts, and major installation equipment. In such instances the reputations of suppliers for skill and integrity are usually known, in part through advertising, and play an important part in guiding patronage. For numerous products, however, when the amount of purchases does not justify engaging in an elaborate process of developing specifications and testing products, buyers rely to a large extent on brands.[9] Many supplies and accessories fall in this class and sometimes installation equipment, accessory equipment, and fabricating parts and materials.

Historically the widening of the gap between producer and consumer was attended by a growth in aggressive selling. In fact, the growth in the use of brands is but a subordinate phase of this increase in aggressive selling, in that brands merely provided the mark of identification for merchandise as sellers extended their selling efforts. Possible reasons for this growth of aggressive selling and its economic significance are discussed at some length in a later chapter.[10] At this point it is sufficient merely to note certain changes which took place between the Middle Ages and modern times and which help to explain the growth in aggressive selling and hence in brand selling and advertising.

Two of the most significant economic developments since medieval times are found in a growing lack of self-sufficiency on the part of consumers and an increase in large-scale, specialized manufacturing units. It is to be expected that such developments would be accompanied by a growth of exchange. When the consumers were nearly self-sufficient, they did not buy an appreciable amount of merchandise; whereas when men began to specialize in their production and to rely upon others for needed products, their lack of self-sufficiency made it necessary for them to purchase products to fill their needs. Moreover, as factories came into being, those who ran them had to sell their output if the enterprise was to continue. Exchange was required, and this exchange had to be brought about either through effort on the part of buyers to seek out sellers, or of sellers to seek out buyers, or through a combination of efforts of the two. Historically, sellers tended to take greater initiative in effecting exchange during the passage from the days of the guilds to modern times.

---

[9] For a discussion of differences between industrial buying and consumer buying and the differences in brands, see:

M. T. Gragg, in collaboration with N. H. Borden, *Merchandise Testing as a Guide to Consumer Buying* (Harvard Business School, Division of Research, Business Research Studies, No. 22, 1938).

H. T. Lewis, *Industrial Purchasing, Principles and Practice* (Chicago, Richard D. Irwin, Inc., 1940).

[10] Chapter XXIV.

In medieval times the initiative for exchange within a nation's borders rested very largely upon buyers. Guild limitations discouraged craftsmen from seeking out buyers or from influencing their purchases. Buyers had to seek out sellers. The tradition thus built up against active selling was effective to some extent in Europe as late as the eighteenth century. But the burdensome restriction did not endure. Merchants who were men of enterprise and capital came into being. They were interested in gaining profit by selling beyond the limits of the local market. They developed the practice of having craftsmen outside of the guilds produce merchandise for them. Thus the so-called domestic, or putting-out, system evolved. Under this system the custom of sellers seeking out buyers grew. The merchants sold their goods in foreign markets and in distant cities and towns within their nation's borders. Moreover, the evidence indicates that with the passage of time enterprising craftsmen increasingly made known within their own towns and cities the merits of the merchandise sold under their marks.

With the introduction of machinery and power and the emergence of the factory during the Industrial Revolution, the pressure for producers to seek out buyers became even greater. Enterprise led to the building of factories, but their building and operation depended upon the entrepreneurs' seeing an opportunity to dispose of their outputs. A sales volume larger than could be disposed of in the environs of a factory was needed if the factory was to be kept busy, operate efficiently, and be profitable. In certain industries the task of getting a needed demand was shifted to selling agents; in others, the producers undertook the selling functions themselves. In England, foreign commerce expanded. Moreover, the practice of sending salesmen who rode by horse or by stage to buyers in distant towns had become common there by the middle of the eighteenth century.[11] Gradually the sellers began to use catalogues and other forms of advertising to supplement their personal selling. As the practice of large-scale production in advance of sales grew, selling effort of this kind became firmly established.[11]

Under the factory system it was natural that the practice of affixing trade-marks, which had been firmly established in medieval times, should continue. Merchants and manufacturers who had seen the opportunities of an ever-widening market were quick to sense the oppor-

[11] See footnotes, Chapter XXIV.

tunity of building and holding patronage and identifying their wares with brands.

Growth of Practice of Product Differentiation

Historical researches relating to growth in the practice of differentiating products under brands have not been made. The facts relating to growth of the asset value of brands in themselves, however, are evidence that the importance of product differentiation was early recognized. For most product lines consumers have always found that the merchandise of different producers is not identical, that it varies in quality characteristics of one kind or another. They therefore have found reason to distinguish between the merchandise of producers or sellers. In turn, sellers have found it worth while to maintain the particular qualities which have made their brands wanted. Thus the baize of Colchester was desired by consumers "for its knowne goodnesse", which the craftsmen of Colchester were careful to maintain. Likewise, linen bearing the mark of the town of Osnabrück, the center of the Westphalian linen industry, was held in great respect and esteem abroad. In England in the middle of the fifteenth century, Osnabrück linen commanded a price 20% higher than that of other Westphalian linens.[12] And so on down to present times, brands have been used to indicate merchandise of certain quality characteristics, to be distinguished from other merchandise of the same general kind.

The opportunity for individual sellers to undertake differentiation of their products and to benefit therefrom undoubtedly was not great until after the power of the guilds to control quality of merchandise and to restrict aggressive selling had waned. As noted previously, quality of products under the guilds was carefully controlled; craftsmen generally were required to meet specifications laid down; craftsmen's marks were required so as to facilitate search for deviations from required quality. These restrictions, largely set up to help the guilds maintain their monopoly grants and to prevent competition among members of the craft, eventually contributed to the loss of control by the guilds. The enterprising merchants who sought the demand of distant markets found it necessary to go to craftsmen outside the guilds to get merchandise of qualities or prices which were readily acceptable in those markets. Guild restrictions kept members from producing these desired qualities. Thus the rigidity of

---

[12] F. I. Schechter, *op. cit.*, p. 79.

quality restrictions and the failure to meet the needs of developing markets probably were factors contributing to the wane of the guilds.

With the disappearance of guild restrictions, freedom of individual producers or sellers to govern quality became firmly established. Such freedom existed while the factory system got under way and grew. Thus the enterprising producer for several centuries has been free to strive for product quality characteristics which would attract and hold patronage for his brand.

While the maintenance of quality characteristics to differentiate one brand from others has long been customary, the practices of differentiation which have been made the butt of criticism in recent years undoubtedly are relatively modern manifestations. The reference here is to the current behavior of sellers trying consciously to differentiate their merchandise from that of competitors, apparently, in many instances, largely for the purpose of providing appeals for advertising and other aggressive selling efforts. The great number of duplicative brands of merchandise to be found in markets, often differentiated in various ways that seem of minor importance to critics, has been a phenomenon of the mature economy of recent decades since the number of sellers competing in markets has become large and competition through aggressive selling has become common. The economic significance of current practices of differentiation is to be one of the main topics of this study.

Growth in Variety of Merchandise Produced and Number of Brands

The practice of product differentiation has been an important force in widening the variety of merchandise available to consumers. But variety has been increased also by invention and swift strides in technology. A host of entirely new products to meet new needs have been placed on the market by an enterprising, technologically advancing people, and there are a fabulous number of brands. Nobody knows how many there are, but there probably have been in excess of a million brands simultaneously in the United States during recent decades.[13] Some of the problems to be dealt with in this study have their origin in this tremendous number of products and brands. For example, questions have been raised as to whether it leads to complexities in consumer buying and to heavy, competitive advertising costs.

---

[13] See Chapter XXII.

The Meaning of the Trade-Mark in Modern Business

Whereas the trade-mark originally was evidence of manufacturing origin, it has now become largely a symbol of qualities which the consumer associates with the product through recommendation, through use, or through advertisement. So far as consumers are concerned, manufacturing source has lost its significance in many instances. In the case of distributors' brands the consumer has not even been informed of the manufacturing source and apparently has not cared. Moreover, manufacturers in their advertisements and labels during recent years frequently have given little or no display to the firm name but have given large display to distinctive trade-marks, on the theory that the mark, not the firm name, establishes the essential basis for attracting and holding patronage. The trade-mark has been a device to aid consumer memory, to make recall easy. Often, studied effort has been made by sellers to find easily remembered, easily pronounceable names of favorable connotation that would be the symbols around which to center their aggressive selling.

Consumer Protection Stressed in Legal Theory

Through the centuries in English-speaking countries a great body of common law has been built up about trade-marks. This law, as it has evolved, has given more and more stress to consumers' interest in trade-marks as means of identifying merchandise of known quality. The law regarding trade-marks has grown primarily from cases brought to prevent infringement or unfair trading. From these cases recognition of the property value of trade-marks in law has become firmly established. But in dealing with infringement or unfair trading, the courts have not relied solely or even primarily on the principle that the rights and property of a trade-mark owner must be protected against diversion of his business to another who has later adopted a similar, and hence a confusing, mark. In some cases the courts have followed the principle that it is their duty to promote honesty and fair dealing and to stamp out deception and fraud. Significantly, however, protection of the consumer has been the principle given greatest weight by the courts. They have held that consumers should be guarded from purchasing, because of confusion of trade-mark or name, goods other than those which consumers have come to know under a particular mark or name. Nims says: "It is now recognized that the important consideration for the court is not competition, but possible deception of the public." [14] In short, while the present system of brands and trade-marks has developed because of their value to owners, the importance of brands to consumers as guides to purchasing has evolved as the dominant consideration." [15]

Varying Importance of Brands for Different Merchandise

Even though brands are important as guides to consumer buying, it will be recognized immediately that their value for this purpose varies with different types of products. For some merchandise the consumer is largely indifferent as to whether he buys the product of one producer or vendor or that of another. For other types of products he lays great stress on getting a particular brand or one of several brands which he may consider acceptable.

Often his brand preferences are determined by objective differences in products which he can know from inspection, or the preferences may depend upon performance which can be observed and appraised. Thus, Ivory soap may be preferred by some because it floats, or because it is a mild cleanser. Association of such product characteristics or performance facts with a brand provides a basis for brand preference, irrespective of whether aggressive advertising and selling are devoted

---

[14] *The Law of Unfair Competition and Trade-Marks* (3d ed., New York, Baker, Voorhis and Company, 1929), p. iii. Also see: N. H. Borden, *Determination of Confusion in Trade-Mark Conflict Cases* (Harvard Business School, Division of Research, Business Research Studies, No. 16, 1936).

[15] Certain critics of the present branding system have suggested the adoption of mandatory specifications or government grades for merchandise to take the place of brands. While this complex issue will not be fully investigated in this study, the question may be raised whether such plans would eliminate the need for brands. The history of branding under the guilds and the difficulties of making merchandise identical even under a system of specifications and grading suggest that trade-marks probably would be of value both to consumers and to sellers under such a system. The guilds, which attempted to control product quality, required the craftsmen's mark to check against the inefficient or dishonest workman. Yet when goods were put into commerce, individual marks enjoyed buyers' preference as evidence of good quality. Moreover, within the environs of a town the output of particular local craftsmen came to be known as superior or inferior, even though guilds sought to insure a minimum of quality. A study of manufacturing indicates that in modern times control of quality would result in similar distinctions. Even were manufacturers required to use the same specifications or to conform to grades, products of different producers would still vary in many instances. Within any grades established there might be room for a range of tastes. Moreover, specifications for manufacture generally cannot be drawn so finely as to insure identical merchandise from different producers. The skill and integrity of managements and workmen are often more important in determining a satisfactory product than the specifications governing manufacture. Accordingly, even were the economic system to be altered so as to bring about adoption of governmental control of quality, history indicates the probable need for producers' trade-marks to guide consumer buying in many instances, even though the goods were supposedly identical. Correspondingly, brands might be assets to their owners because of consumer preferences. For pertinent material relating to this issue, see M. T. Gragg, *op. cit.*

to the brand. Advertising and selling, however, may be used to heighten the significance of these ideas in the minds of consumers. To wit, the advertising of Ivory soap over many years has been employed to enhance the desirability of floating and mildness as characteristics of soap and to associate these ideas with Ivory. In some instances the ideas which underlie consumers' brand preference may be almost entirely implanted by advertising and selling. Such is true, for example, of some proprietary remedies whose constituents are unknown to the purchaser and whose efficacy depends largely on a mental state. In short, consumers' brand discriminations depend upon their subjective valuations, as determined by objective product characteristics, observable performance, or implanted ideas.

Sellers have been alert to these facts; detailed analyses of their efforts to establish brand preference through objective product differentiation and advertising will be made in later chapters. At this point it suffices merely to give some examples of wide variation in the importance of brands in different product fields.

Where product differentiations are deemed of no great consequence by consumers or are readily appraisable from inspection, brand means little. Much of the merchandise displayed on open counters in hardware stores and variety stores is of this character—screws, bolts, nails, cheap electrical fixtures, small tools not submitted to any difficult strain, kitchen spoons and gadgets, clothes pins, ribbons, string, shoe laces, inexpensive toys, games, needles, pins, and many other notions. Sometimes trade-marks are affixed to such articles; in other instances they are not.

Certain products, such as granulated sugar and inexpensive sheeting, whose total demand is sufficient to warrant the sellers' desire for brand discrimination, nevertheless do not enjoy strong brand preference, because consumers do not deem product differentiations of enough consequence to lead them to pay much attention to brand or retail source of the product.

Other products to whose brands the buyer tends to be relatively indifferent are those for which design or style is the important determinant of the consumer's purchase. In such instances a consumer can observe the designs and determine whether products are to his liking. A clear-cut example is found in greeting cards. The consumer looks at illustration, verse, and paper, and decides whether a particular card is one he wants. He may be very fussy about the card he selects, but he has no interest in any trade-mark that may be placed upon such cards by seller or distributor.[16] Brand does not stand for qualities of consequence to him which he cannot appraise by sight.

The selection of merchandise on the basis of observable design, which is so clearly illustrated in the case of greeting cards, applies with greater or lesser degree to a wide range of merchandise, such as textiles, fashion clothing, neckties, and furniture. In many of these products, however, hidden quality characteristics are of some consequence in guiding consumer selection. For example, durability and color fastness of textiles are fixed characteristics which may be associated with brand. Hence, on many of these products, effort is made by sellers to have brands known to consumers as guides to these hidden characteristics. In some instances expert designers may try to make a brand stand for fashion rightness. But they do not often succeed because no designer can invariably be fashion right. The consumer is always the judge as to the acceptability of a style.

In contrast to the cases cited, brands tend to be important for any class of product for which vendors offer varying qualities and forms which purchasers ordinarily are not able to appraise adequately at time of purchase. In such cases they rely upon marks to assure themselves of getting products they know through use or reputation. Clear examples are drugs and medicines, for which brand may be important as an assurance of expected efficacy in the cure or alleviation of ills, or of purity and care in compounding. In cosmetics, brands may be important because of their promised ability to give personal beauty or charm. In foods, they may be important to assure a particular flavor or form that has been found satisfying. In mechanical goods, particularly those involving large expenditure, such as automobiles, electrical appliances, and watches, brand is relied upon for assurance of satisfactory operation.

The varying importance of brands for different types of merchandise and for different articles within any class has resulted in a wide variation in the importance of brands to sellers as a means of attracting and holding patronage. But for almost all products, brands have had enough goodwill value and have offered sufficient advantages in influencing consumer selection to lead those engaged in commerce to desire ownership or control over them. Not only have manufacturers

---

[16] See N. H. Borden, *Problems in Advertising* (3d ed., New York, McGraw-Hill Book Company, Inc., 1937), case of Colton Card Company, p. 160.

wished to sell their products under their own brands, but tradesmen also have desired either to own or to exercise control over the brands they sell. The resulting struggle for brand control and thus for control over trade, has tended to be heightened as the country's industry has expanded.

The Struggle for Brand Control

While some manufacturers in the United States placed their own brands on their merchandise before 1880, the practice of aggressive promotion of these brands to consumers as a means of controlling trade had not attained great momentum up to that time. Often they were content to sell their merchandise to tradesmen unbranded or under the latter's mark; or if they placed their own brands on their output, they usually directed their selling effort solely to wholesalers or retailers. As a rule, the latter group controlled the offering and the promotion of products to consumers. After 1880, however, manufacturers increasingly sought to make their brands well known to consumers, thereby hoping to gain control over ultimate demand and to decrease their dependence on merchants.

In his analysis of the clients of N. W. Ayer & Son, advertising agency, Hower found that, "In the 'seventies and 'eighties those who advertised through the Ayer firm were largely retailers and others who sold directly to the public. By 1890 most of these had ceased to use the Ayer agency, and its principal work was the advertising of manufacturers who sold through dealers and retailers but preferred to get control over their ultimate market." [17]

A survey of newspapers and magazines made by the author for the period 1840 to 1900 bore out Hower's observations regarding the growth of manufacturers' advertising after the 'eighties. The important advertisers, except for retailers and wholesalers, were until the 'eighties proprietary remedy manufacturers, book and periodical publishers, amusement companies, and transportation companies. Manufacturers' brands were frequently mentioned in retailers' advertisements, but the number of advertisements placed by manufacturers, excepting those producing books and medicines, were relatively few. After the 'eighties the number of manufacturers who carried their messages to consumers increased rapidly. At the same time, retailers also made increased use of advertising.

---

[17] Ralph Hower, *op. cit.*, p. 211.

Presbrey states that during the 'eighties some four to five hundred manufacturers advertised nationally each year, but for the most part in a desultory way. Only four products, except medicines, employed consistent magazine and newspaper schedules with dominant space: Sapolio, Royal Baking Powder, Pear's Soap, and Ivory Soap. Some sixty other manufacturers were listed as national advertisers employing "more or less system". After 1890, however, the growth of manufacturers' advertising was very marked. This growth was evidence of the effort of manufacturers to gain control over consumer demand.[18]

The drive on the part of manufacturers for brand dominance, which gained momentum before the turn of the century, has continued unabated up to the present time. But as manufacturers have sought to gain control of ultimate demand, wholesalers and retailers have not been passive. They have resisted full passage of brand control into the hands of manufacturers, because experience has shown them that the handling of well-known manufacturers' brands has often led to keen price competition upon these brands within the trade, with resultant reduction of trade margins. To improve their profit outlook, distributors have taken measures either to establish their own brands or to get some control over manufacturers' brands which would permit them to secure desired margins from their selling operations. Consequently there has been a continuous struggle for control of brand demand, not merely between competing manufacturers but also between distributors and manufacturers. This struggle for brand control not only has entailed heavy selling costs but has also played an important part in shaping the forms of competition governing costs and prices of merchandise.

While the competitive struggle often centers about brands and is frequently referred to as the "battle of the brands", it should be realized that the conflict goes beyond mere questions of brands to questions of control over demand and of control over the marketing process. In cases of competing manufacturers, the battle is for control over demand, with each manufacturer using such tools as product quality, price, service, aggressive advertising and promotion, and personal efforts to secure public acceptance and dealer selling support. When manufacturers and distributors compete, however, the competition essentially is to gain control over the merchandising and promotional functions of marketing. It is a question of whether the

---

[18] Frank Presbrey, *op. cit.*, p. 338 ff.

manufacturer not only will control the merchandising function, i.e., the function of determining product form, but will also reach forward and take over the promotional function, i.e., the function of stimulating and fashioning consumers' desire for his products; or whether the retailer, because of his strategic position for influencing consumers, not only will guide consumers' buying, i.e., assume the promotional function, but also may even go so far as to reach back and control the merchandising function. In the latter case he furnishes specifications to the manufacturer or has him manufacture in accordance with a sample product.

An understanding of the character of the competition growing out of this struggle for control between manufacturers and distributors is essential to an understanding of the place of advertising in the economic system. It is advisable, therefore, to inquire further why manufacturers and distributors have sought control over brands. The generalizations which follow regarding their attitudes and practices will, it is believed, be generally acceptable to businessmen. Many of them are axiomatic. They have been drawn not merely from observation of business and from conversations with businessmen but also from an analysis of hundreds of marketing cases [19] collected by the Harvard Business School over the past 20 years.

Reasons Why Manufacturers Seek Brand Control

The outstanding reason why manufacturers wish to put their marks on merchandise has already been stated, namely, the desire to secure the benefit of any consumer goodwill that may attach to the products they manufacture. When merchandise goes through the channels of trade unmarked or with the mark of a distributor upon it, any consumer preferences for or satisfaction with it does not redound to the benefit of the manufacturer but rests with the distributors who sell the merchandise. When the manufacturer is successful in establishing a consumer preference for his brand, he may have a more stable business than would hold were he to depend upon trade patronage alone. The shifting of patronage of a few large wholesalers or retailers might mean loss of a large volume of business. Consumer demand often promises greater stability, because the loss of individual customers does not materially affect total sales.

Manufacturers also wish to sell under their own brands because they

---

[19] For a description and discussion of case material, see Chapter IV, p. 72 ff.

desire better to direct and control aggressive selling efforts upon individualized merchandise. Greatest enthusiasm and interest for new types of merchandise or for new developments in established merchandise are generally found among those who have invented and fostered the new developments. They are often more inclined to take the risks involved in advertising and promoting such a new or different product to consumers than are retailers or wholesalers, who may want the assurance of established demand before stocking and selling the merchandise. Often a manufacturer has an intense interest in his single article or line of merchandise; retailers or wholesalers with their hundreds or thousands of items do not take particular interest in any one item. The manufacturer, therefore, is often forced to take the risk of convincing consumers of the desirability of his new or differentiated merchandise, and when he must take on this risk he naturally wishes to attach his own mark to the merchandise in order to profit from its promotion. In fact, it is generally essential that he attach his mark so that consumers when informed will know what to ask for. Once the manufacturer's mark is established on merchandise, his self-interest leads him to try to keep the demand active.

Again, manufacturers generally want to sell under their own brands because of their desire to influence the prices which they may receive, as a means to the end of maximizing net profits. They recognize that advertising and promotion of their brands may affect the valuations consumers place on their products. Although advertising and selling efforts may possibly, though not necessarily, increase unit costs, yet to the businessman these costs may appear justified if the advertising promises to yield a larger net income (volume times price less cost) for a differentiated product than he would obtain under alternative plans of selling unbranded goods or distributor branded merchandise.

In brief, the manufacturer who sells through distributors would like to be in a position to have consumers' preference which would make it at least desirable, if not essential, for retailers and wholesalers to stock and sell his brands, taking them irrespective of the prices he sets. In so far as advertising helps him to attain this objective, he is inclined to employ it.

The extent to which the ideal of complete control by the manufacturer can be attained varies, however, because the opportunities of influencing consumers' brand choices also vary widely. For some products a manufacturer can build a "pull" which makes it essential for retailers to handle his brand, especially when he can differentiate his product in some way that is particularly appealing to a considerable segment of consumers. For other products, however, the maker can exert so little pull that the dealer may be relatively free to select his merchandise. In between the extremes are many degrees of consumer acceptance or preference to which tradesmen may give greater or lesser heed. Hence manufacturers' opportunities to influence the merchandise which tradesmen carry will be found to vary widely and their marketing programs to vary accordingly.

Reasons Why Some Manufacturers Do Not Seek to Establish Brands

While emphasis is given above to the desire of manufacturers to establish their own brands, it is equally important to recognize that manufacturers do not always strive to sell under their own brands. Many gladly produce merchandise for sale either under distributors' brands or unbranded. They are in business to make a profit and are willing to work for profit where they see it. Since many distributors want to buy products under their own brands or unbranded, there are manufacturers willing to sell them in those forms. Of these manufacturers some produce largely for sale under the brands of others; others merely accept such business as an adjunct to sales under their own brands. In the latter cases, private brand contracts generally are taken on in order to employ plant capacity that is not taken up by sales of the manufacturer's own brands.[20] Thus the willingness of manufacturers to cater to tradesmen permits competition which includes dealers' brands as well as manufacturers' brands.

Varying Degrees of Use of Advertising by Manufacturers

In this discussion of the desire of manufacturers to gain consumer preference for their own brands, it should be recognized also that the efforts which competing manufacturers in any product field expend in attempting to build consumer preference for their brands vary markedly. Some elect to use aggressive advertising and selling; others exert little effort of this kind, though they still seek to sell merchandise bearing their own brands. The advertising costs of brands new to the

---

[20] Clear examples of such a situation are found in the cases of the Reber Silk Hosiery Company and the George Host Company in the case files of the Harvard Graduate School of Business Administration.

market differ from the costs of established brands. In a later chapter it will be shown that advertising costs incurred by manufacturers vary widely not only between product fields but within any product field. For example, the ratio of advertising expenditure among manufacturers of nationally advertised drugs and toilet goods was shown in one cost study to vary from 8% to 60% of sales; among food and grocery product manufacturers the range was from 0.25% to 47% (see Chapter XVII). Thus, not only must the competition between manufacturers' and distributors' brands be kept in mind, but equally as important, the competition among manufacturers' brands with widely varying advertising effort behind them.

From the above recitation of reasons why manufacturers have sought to get brand control the inquiry is directed to the reasons why distributors have wished similar brand control, or at least freedom from manufacturers' domination.

Reasons Why Many Distributors Have Sought Brand Control

A distributor resembles a manufacturer in his desire to gain consumer goodwill and patronage. One means the distributor has of gaining a hold on consumers is by becoming recognized as the source of satisfactory merchandise carrying his own marks, or to a lesser extent as a source of good values in unbranded merchandise for which he stands responsible for selection. He can also secure the desired result of being a sole source of merchandise among his customers by becoming an exclusive representative in his trading area for manufacturers' brands. This method, however, may involve uncertainty and risk regarding the tenure of his agency for these brands.

The distributor is actuated also by a desire to be free from the direct price comparisons upon merchandise that consumers know to be identical. The prices charged to the trade on well-established manufacturers' brands ordinarily are based on retail list prices which, if used by retailers, provide adequate recompense to distributors for their services; but for marked products which require dense distribution[21] and hence stocking by directly competing distributors, the fierce price competition which is likely to occur in both wholesale and retail channels brings a shading of list prices and a consequent narrowing

---

[21] Dense distribution applies to so-called "convenience" goods, articles of low price which the consumer has come to expect in readily accessible stores. Manufacturers of such articles seek to get stocks and display of their brands in as many stores as possible in the markets in which they sell.

of trade margins. For this reason, distributors, particularly large-scale distributors such as wholesalers, chains, and department stores, may attempt to build business about their own marks or on unbranded merchandise in order that they may be free in their buying and selling, their hope being to get suitable gross margins while building their own reputations as sources of satisfactory merchandise. One of the strongest incentives to the establishment of private brands is the hope of receiving a wider gross margin and a larger net profit than is had from the sale of manufacturers' brands.

A further reason which sometimes leads distributors to establish their own brands may be mentioned, namely, their desire to offer merchandise values that compare favorably with or excel those offered by competing merchants under their own brands or by manufacturers. While a retailer at times may eschew competing with other retailers on identical manufacturers' brands, he frequently desires to have merchandise that he can offer to his clientele as giving value as good as or better than that offered by competitors. That he may have freedom in his selection of merchandise and in its pricing to meet competitors' offerings, he may turn to selling under his own brand.

Reasons Why Some Distributors Do Not Seek Brand Control

Although the generalization that distributors desire to own or control the brands of merchandise which they sell appears justifiable from a study of business behavior, it is, of course, evident to students of marketing that not all retailers and wholesalers seek to establish their own marks. In fact in many instances little such effort is made. The distributors often not only are willing to handle manufacturers' brands, but may even prefer to do so. The reasons for such conduct are many and varied. Here only a few of the more important considerations are brought out since the purpose of this chapter is merely to give a general picture of business development which will contribute to an understanding of advertising usage and the forms of competition with which it is associated.

Distributors are in business for profit, and so long as profitable business can be secured from sale of manufacturers' brands, many distributors are glad to sell these brands. Both the urge on their part to establish their own brands as a means of avoiding harsh price competition and the opportunities for establishing their own brands vary widely among different product fields. In some instances it has been relatively easy for them to establish brands; in others, difficult. Often the costs of selling under their own brands is greater than costs of selling manufacturers' advertised brands. Moreover, the ability of distributors to sell under their own brands has been governed to considerable extent by the size of their businesses.

Effect of Size of Operations on Branding by Distributors

The development of distributors' brands has been associated primarily with large-scale retail or wholesale operations. The small independent retailer, even though he might like his own brands, usually has not been in a position by himself to contract with a manufacturer for enough merchandise under his own brand to make it worth while for the manufacturer. The costs of special labeling and packaging for the small volume he would take have precluded private branding. In addition, the small retailer has not been in a position either to check adequately the uniformity of quality in the merchandise bought, or to investigate the manufacturing sources available to him. Moreover, his reputation as a merchant often has not been such that his sponsorship would induce ready acceptance of his brands.

For certain types of products a distributor must have a particularly large scale of operations in order to get manufacturers to produce merchandise under his label. Such has been the case, for example, with high-price mechanical products: washing machines, refrigerators, radios, stoves, farm machinery, and the like. In order to get a favorable purchasing contract from a manufacturer on such merchandise, a distributor often must make a volume commitment which is beyond the reach of any except the largest of individual dealers. Even for them such a commitment may involve considerable risk, in view of the danger of obsolescence that attaches to such machines, which are subject to constant change and technological development. Accordingly, in such fields, distributors' brands have not been common.

During the latter part of the nineteenth century and the early part of the present century, wholesalers frequently established their own brands on merchandise to compete with the manufacturers' brands, which were being increasingly advertised to consumers. Wholesalers operated on a scale large enough to permit them to enter into suitable contracts with manufacturers for private labels on various types of canned products in the grocery field; on textiles, hosiery, underwear, and other articles in the dry goods field; and on drugs, hardware, and numerous other articles. Wholesalers who went in heavily for private branding tended to become specialists, devoting their attention primarily to those articles which they were branding and to sell these over a wide territory.[22] In time many became closely associated with their manufacturing sources or actually integrated with them. Whether they integrated or not, however, they were virtually in the same position as manufacturers in their attempts to induce retailers to sell their brands. Retailers had little more reason for interest in wholesalers' brands than in manufacturers' brands.

The large-scale operations of department stores and of women's specialty stores have permitted them to become private branders of many types of articles, such as hosiery, men's and women's clothing, shoes, sheets, cosmetics, and house furnishings. By and large, department stores have become conscious of their strong position in their communities to influence consumers' selection of merchandise, particularly fashion merchandise and household furnishings. Many of these organizations adhere to the policy of building goodwill for their stores by selling merchandise either bearing their own marks or unbranded rather than of acting as distributors primarily of manufacturers' brands, particularly when these brands are available through other retailers in the community.

In recent years as corporate chain stores have assumed an increasingly important place in the business structure, they have sought to build sales under their own brands for many types of merchandise. This has been true of chains in the grocery, drug, dry goods, and automotive fields, and to a lesser extent of the variety chains. The greater share of the merchandise sold under their brands has been products for which manufacturers' brands were not dominant, but the chains have ventured to some extent into those fields in which the brand leadership of manufacturers was firmly established.

The large mail-order houses from their inception have sold merchandise to a large extent under their own brands or unbranded, serving as their own guarantors of quality. The tremendous business of firms such as Sears, Roebuck and Company, and Montgomery Ward & Co., Incorporated, covers a wide range of consumer merchandise, including not only articles to the brands of which the consumer ordinarily gives little thought, but also high-price mechanical articles for

---

[22] See T. N. Beckman and N. H. Engle, *Wholesaling, Principles and Practice* (New York, The Ronald Press Company, 1937).

which the consumer is particularly desirous of having assurance of a dependable source. On such products as radios, mechanical refrigerators, vacuum cleaners, and farm machinery, to cite a few examples, they have been able to establish their brands firmly among consumers and to build large volumes of business. Their operations are conducted on such a scale as to command the interest of many manufacturing sources. Since their advent into chain store distribution, their volume of sales and the acceptance of their brands by consumers have increased.

In recent years the small retailer has entered more actively into the distributor's brand picture through the development of so-called voluntary and cooperative chains.[23] The difficulties met in getting satisfactory margins on manufacturers' brands have often borne heavily on independent retailers. In addition, the managements of these chains have realized the value of building goodwill about their own brands. Most of the voluntary groups started with the idea of promoting the brands of the sponsoring wholesaler or the brands of the voluntary organization to which the wholesaler allied himself. Upon such brands a retailer usually enjoys limited territorial selling rights and thus has a special interest in them. The managements of the voluntary chains have centered promotional activities conducted through the member retailers largely on their own brands.

Similarly the retailer cooperative chains either have developed their own brands or have entered into contracts with manufacturers to feature and promote exclusively these manufacturers' brands. As the cooperative chains have become stronger in recent years they have tended more in the direction of developing their own brands.[24]

Amount Spent on Advertising and Promotion of Distributors' Brands

In a later chapter the amount of advertising and aggressive selling accorded distributors' brands is compared with that given manufacturers' brands, so far as data permit. At this juncture only the conclusion is stated; namely, that in many cases a smaller outlay has been devoted to promotion of distributors' brands than has been given to competing manufacturers' brands.

As a rule, retailers selling under their own brands or under the

---

[23] For a full description of the development of these chains and the character of their operations and of their private branding policies, see G. C. Corbaley, *Group Selling by 100,000 Retailers* (New York, American Institute of Food Distribution, Inc., 1936).

[24] *Ibid.*, Chapter XII.

brands of voluntary chains have relied upon their close contact with the consumer to bring about purchase of their brands. Point-of-purchase display, the suggestions of salesmen, and the periodic listing of their products in direct-action advertisements have been the means most used to bring trial of their merchandise, with the hope that consequent consumer satisfaction would bring continued patronage.

Just as there has been wide variation in the extent to which different manufacturers have used advertising and promotion to establish their brands, there has been corresponding variation in retailers' use of advertising. There have been variations between retail trades and within particular trades. For example, grocery stores ordinarily spend only from 0.25% to 0.75% of sales income for advertising, whereas furniture stores on an average spend about 7%, and large department stores about 5% for advertising and publicity. Considerable deviation from these latter figures is to be found, however. Moreover, differences in methods of conducting businesses by competing tradesmen and the amount of service given lead to considerable variation in their total operating costs. In many instances low operating costs have been associated with the offering of private brands and thus may have played a part in widening the range of price choices offered consumers in the competitive market.

Variation in Balance of Brand Control in Different Product Fields

While size of operations has played an important part in governing the establishment of brands by distributors, even large aggressive chains, department stores, and wholesalers, bent on gaining control over the merchandise they sell, have had widely varying success in different product fields in building demand for their brands in competition with manufacturers' brands. Hence marked contrasts are to be found in the proportions in which consumer demand is shared between manufacturers' and distributors' brands. In some product fields competition has been largely limited to brands of manufacturers. In others the balance of control has gone heavily to retailers. In still others it has been divided in diverse proportions between manufacturers and distributors. A few examples will suffice to show the multifarious conditions met.

Distributors have been particularly desirous of establishing their own brands for many so-called convenience products, i.e., products of low price which the consumer buys on a convenience basis, because price competition in the trade on well-known manufacturers' brands of convenience goods has tended to be especially keen and hence distasteful both to wholesalers and retailers. On such goods, of which many of the articles sold by grocers and druggists are typical, manufacturers selling under their own brands generally desire dense distribution because sale of such merchandise is likely to be enhanced by wide exposure. When dense distribution is obtained on a manufacturer's brand, however, every wholesaler or retailer handling the brand is subject to direct price comparisons. The practice of distributors' using such brands as price leaders to attract patronage has often brought profitless business on those brands to distributors; hence they have had a special urge to divert demand to their own brands to avoid such competition.

Efforts of distributors to build business on their own brands have met with varying success. On certain specialties both in the drug and in the grocery fields a relatively small number of manufacturers have been so successful in building preferences for their brands that they secure the great bulk of demand. On such products distributors' brands are often few, and even when numerous, receive a relatively small ratio of total demand. Such has been the case with cigarettes, soap, canned soups, dentifrices, and many ready-to-serve breakfast foods. For other drug and grocery products, however, manufacturers have not been able to establish such dominant leadership, and retailers and wholesalers have been able to gain for their brands appreciable shares of total demand, the proportions varying for different products. In the drug field, such has been the case with cod liver oil, rubbing alcohol, and mineral oil; and in the grocery field with canned vegetables, canned fruits, canned milk, spices, and flour. Still other food products, such as fresh vegetables and meats, have passed in considerable degree through the channels of trade without brand designation. Demand for these has been guided largely by the tradesmen's selection. But the growing practice of packaging and branding foods which in former times were sold in bulk has been extended even to these products in some degree. Thus unmarked merchandise has competed with producers' brands of citrus fruits, nuts, smoked meats, and even vegetables and fresh meats, whose merits have been made known to the public.

The division of control in other fields has already been indicated. For certain high-price mechanical items, consumers have given preference to manufacturers' brands, and distributors' brands have not been important factors in demand. In the case of automobiles, for example, there are no distributors' brands. For other articles, however, such as mechanical refrigerators, radios, oil burners, and washing machines, some headway has been made by certain large-scale distributors in establishing their brands.

In many branches of the clothing field, particularly in women's clothing, where fashion is a dominant factor, control over consumer demand has come to rest primarily with retailers. Such is true also of furniture and many house furnishings. Yet in all these fields many examples are to be found of manufacturers battling to establish preferences for their brands among consumers.

Lack of Similarity in Economic Effects of Advertising in Various Product Fields

In the pages preceding, attention has been directed to several sets of facts which have brought about very dissimilar patterns of competition in individual product fields. The facts noted are the following:

(1) The opportunity to make brands significant to consumers has varied widely with different products.

(2) The amount spent on advertising and selling by manufacturers has varied markedly not only between product fields but within product fields. These differences are associated with diverse marketing methods employed.

(3) The degree to which retailers and wholesalers, on the one hand, and manufacturers, on the other, have been successful in gaining control over the choices of ultimate users has not been uniform among products.

(4) The methods of promotion, the services given, and the total costs of distributors have been dissimilar. In turn, these variations in costs have become associated with specific brands and have led to a range of price choices offered consumers.

To the above facts may be added another important consideration, which so far has merely been alluded to, namely, that the degree to which demand is concentrated within a market in a few brands or in many is subject to wide variation. Because of the widely varying patterns of competition which are met, any factual study of the economics of advertising should be directed, in part at least, to intensive study of particular product fields. Only thus can conclusions regarding the effect of advertising upon demand, supply, and prices be drawn with any certainty. From the conclusions regarding specific products, broader generalizations as to advertising's economic effects may then be built.

Thus far in this chapter the development and growth of aggressive selling and advertising of brands have been traced and their place in the business structure has been interpreted. There remains the task of indicating by actual data the extent to which advertising has been used in the American economy.

THE GROWTH OF ADVERTISING IN THE UNITED STATES

Modern advertising in the United States is a growth of the past 75 years, the period in which the developments discussed in the preceding pages occurred. An idea of its striking development since the Civil War is given by data for advertising income of newspaper and magazine publishers, as shown in Table 1, page 48. These figures for periodical advertising provide a rough index of total advertising.

During recent years, advertising in newspapers and magazines has constituted approximately 40% of the total advertising expenditure of the country; the percentage in earlier years is not known. In the very early years, outdoor advertising may have been relatively more important than during later years, although this is not certain. In the last decade radio is known to have reduced somewhat the percentages not only of magazines and newspapers but of other media as well. Nevertheless, magazines and newspapers combined have contributed an important share of the advertising during the whole period covered in the table, and probably provide a fair index of the growth of advertising.

The increase in use of advertising becomes clear when expenditures are reduced to a per capita basis. In the Civil War period newspapers and periodicals apparently received an income equivalent to nearly 25 cents for each member of the population. By 1880 this figure had tripled, and then it increased steadily to a high of $9.22 in 1929, an amount approximately 36 times that of the Civil War years and 12 times that of 1880. Evident from this table also is the marked increase which followed the first World War. In 1914 the per capita expenditure for advertising in newspapers and periodicals was $2.61, while in 1921 it was $6.26. Also notable is the effect of the 1930

TABLE 1

VOLUME OF NEWSPAPER AND PERIODICAL ADVERTISING REVENUE, PER CAPITA EXPEN-
DITURES IN THESE MEDIA, AND RATIO OF EXPENDITURES TO NATIONAL
INCOME, SELECTED YEARS, 1865–1937

YEAR	ADVERTISING REVENUE OF NEWSPAPERS	ADVERTISING REVENUE OF OTHER PERIODICALS	TOTAL	POPULATION (000 omitted)	PER CAPITA EXPENDITURE FOR NEWSPAPER AND PERIODICAL ADVERTISING	RATIO OF MAGAZINE AND NEWSPAPER ADVERTISING EXPENDITURE TO NATIONAL INCOME
						%
1865*	....	....	$ 7,584,340	35,060	$ .22	....
1866*	....	....	9,686,844	35,772	.27	....
1867*	....	....	9,600,327	36,483	.26	....
1880	....	....	39,136,306	50,262	.78	.52
1890	....	....	71,243,361	63,056	1.13	.59
1900	....	....	95,861,127	76,129	1.26	.53
1904	....	....	145,517,591	82,601	1.76	....
1909	$148,554,392	$ 53,978,853	202,533,245	90,691	2.23	.69
1914	184,047,106	71,585,505	255,632,611	97,928	2.61	.75
1919	373,501,890	154,797,488	528,299,378	105,003	5.03	.78
1921	521,685,483	155,301,227	676,986,710	108,208	6.26	.83
1923	580,937,741	212,955,728	793,893,469	111,537	7.12	1.17
1925	661,513,242	261,759,431	923,272,673	114,867	8.04	1.27
1927	724,837,083	305,383,936	1,030,221,019	118,197	8.72	1.40
1929	797,338,231	322,900,164	1,120,238,395	121,526	9.22	1.38
1931	624,953,969	243,556,044	868,510,013	124,113	7.00	1.61
1933	428,672,688	141,001,525	569,674,213	125,770	4.53	1.35
1935	500,022,708	186,097,701	686,120,409	127,521	5.38	1.24
1937	574,180,206	235,874,088	810,054,294	129,257	6.26	1.16

* For year ending June 30.

NOTE: Allowance should be made for possible inaccuracies of the figures for the Civil
War period, as derived from government tax reports, and of those for the period covered
by early reports of the Census of Manufactures.

Sources:
Population: U. S. Bureau of the Census, *Statistical Abstract of the United States, 1937*,
(Washington, U. S. Government Printing Office, 1938), p. 10.
Advertising revenue: 1880–1937 inclusive, *U. S. Census of Manufactures;* 1865–1867,
based upon reports of tax income from advertising (3% of receipts) as contained in
annual reports of the U. S. Commissioner of Internal Revenue for the years 1865,
1866, and 1867.
National income estimates: Temporary National Economic Committee, *Verbatim Record
of the Proceedings of the Temporary National Economic Committee*, Vol. 1 (Washington, The Bureau of National Affairs, Inc., 1939), Reference Data Section III, p. 41.

depression upon advertising activity, with per capita expenditure in
newspapers and periodicals in 1933 just about half that of 1929.

When the newspaper and magazine advertising expenditures are
related to the net value of the goods and services produced for the
respective years, as contained in estimates of national income, the
increase does not appear so striking as when related to population.
In the period since the first World War, expenditures for periodical
advertising have represented from less than 1% to 1.6% of the
national income, whereas in 1880 they represent only 5%. A three-

fold increase is large, but is far less striking than the per capita increase. The explanation, of course, lies in the growth in per capita production from $147 in 1880 to a postwar average in excess of $500.

The Reasons for Growth of Advertising

The reasons for such a marked growth in the volume of advertising in the short span of 75 years are found in the economic changes which accompanied the growth of the nation. At the beginning of the period, the economy was predominantly agricultural, characterized in the main by small communities;[25] by an industrial organization which, outside of a few product lines, had not advanced far beyond the household stage; and by consumption limited to a small variety of products. Now, at the end of the period, the country has a highly advanced industrial economy in which large-scale producers of an amazing variety of products sell on a nation-wide basis and in which retailers operate in markets encompassing wider areas and far larger numbers of people than previously. Some of the important developments during this period, in which are found the explanation for the increased use of advertising, have been covered in the preceding pages. They are briefly summarized here and several additional reasons are discussed.

(1) The gap between producers and consumers widened.

(2) A rapidly increasing variety of new types of merchandise came upon the market.

(3) The quest for product differentiation became intensified as the industrial system became more mature and as manufacturers had capacity to produce far beyond existing demand.

(4) During the period the competitive battle for control of demand developed.

(5) Retail markets widened as the means of transportation steadily improved, particularly after the advent of the automobile. Retailers have had little need for advertising when close and frequent contact with a well-defined group of consumers has been possible. Just as at the present time the local independent grocer spends relatively little for advertising because he is in close contact with the customers who visit his store almost daily, so in early days in small towns and villages consumers knew well the merchandise of the general stores; there was

---

[25] In 1860 there were only 141 cities in the United States with population exceeding 8,000, and these accounted for only 16.1% of the population. In 1930 there were 1,208 such cities accounting for 49.1% of the population. *Statistical Abstract of the United States, 1937*, p. 6.

little reason for the storekeeper to try to entice customers to his place of business. Today, however, the area of the retail market for many types of merchandise is far wider than previously, and competing merchants resort to advertising to attract consumers to their establishments. The development of the chain store companies has brought increased newspaper advertising for products which were formerly little advertised by retailers.

(6) The effect of the foregoing factors was to intensify competition, among both manufacturers and retailers, with businessmen placing increasing reliance on advertising as a form of competitive selling.

(7) As an aspect of increasing intensity in competition, advertisements tended to become larger and more expensive as time went by. This increase in size can be attributed in part to the increase in number of firms with operations large enough to justify use of large space, and in part to the theory that has been held by many advertisers during the period, that large-size space is proportionally more profitable than smaller space. To a considerable degree, however, the increase in size of advertisements can be attributed to the competition for consumers' attention, which grew keener as the number of advertisers became larger. Starch's studies show that in the 'sixties and 'seventies the average advertisement in the *Boston Evening Transcript* and the *New York Tribune* was about four column-inches, whereas by 1918 the average advertisement was four times this size. In magazines, half-page spaces were used about two and one-half times as often as full-page spaces in 1880; in 1890 less than two times as often; and in 1920 only one-third as often. Until 1890 only one-fifth of total advertising space in magazines consisted of full-page space, but by 1920 the ratio was approximately three to four.[26]

(8) Advertising became increasingly recognized among businessmen, when effectively planned and used, as a profitable method of building demand.

(9) Part of the remarkable growth of advertising may be ascribed to the promotion of advertising itself by the various media and by advertising agencies, which have held forth its value as an aid to profitable business operations. Manufacturers have not had to learn for themselves of the profit possibilities of advertising. They have been subjected to aggressive promotion carried on through salesmen

---

[26] Daniel Starch, *Principles of Advertising* (Chicago, A. W. Shaw Company, 1923), pp. 539–541.

and through advertisements. They have been taught of advertising possibilities by a trade press. Advertisers have organized themselves into clubs and associations to study advertising's use and to defend it against those who question its economic and social benefits. Few, if any, other forms of business activity have been the subject of such proselytizing.

In the next chapter a detailed study of the present volume of advertising is presented in order that its importance in the economy may be better appreciated.

CHAPTER III

THE ECONOMIC IMPORTANCE OF ADVERTISING AS MEASURED BY EXPENDITURES

WHATEVER combination of forces may have been responsible for the remarkable growth of advertising in the past 75 years, there can be no question of its importance in the present economy. Aside from its effect on the functioning of the economic system, which is the central theme of this study, advertising must be recognized as an important economic activity in itself, involving all or part of the working time of several millions of people and the utilization of large quantities of materials.

Practically every one of the 3,000,000 [1] business establishments of the country uses advertising to some extent. For some concerns it may be only a sign to tell the world their place of business; for other organizations advertising is one of the large items in the expense budget, amounting to thousands or even millions of dollars. The administration of advertising within business organizations, involving specialized departments whenever advertising expenditures are appreciable, has probably represented an average annual expenditure of almost $200,000,000 in the postwar period. With relatively few exceptions, advertising is an essential source of revenue to the 13,000 magazines and newspapers of the country. It has supplied some 60% to 70% of the revenue of these publications, a revenue which has exceeded a billion dollars annually in recent years, and has provided employment for 120,000 people. Some of these employees devote their attention largely to the selling of advertising space and to the production of advertising. The rest owe their employment in part to advertising, for without advertising revenue, publication of elaborate modern newspapers and magazines could not be profitably carried on. Advertising practically alone supports radio broadcasting in the United States, with its 560-odd commercial stations and some 14,500 employees, not counting the broadcasting talent employed by advertisers. Direct advertising of one type or another accounts for over 50% of the revenue which keeps a three-quarter billion dollar commercial

---

[1] This rough figure does not count the professions or agricultural ventures.

printing and lithographing industry occupied, with its 100,000 employees. The printing and publishing businesses in turn have a vital bearing on the allied printing trades—engraving, photo-engraving, and stereotyping—and are the chief customers of the huge paper industry. Advertising is the sole support of a $35,000,000 annual outdoor advertising industry, a $12,000,000 annual car-card industry, and a $75,000,-000 annual industry devoted to the production of advertising signs and advertising novelties.

In addition to all the above businesses are the numerous firms which specialize in the planning, production, and selling of advertising. Some 1,300 general advertising agencies employ over 14,000 people in their work of planning, producing, and placing advertising with media for their clients. A large but unknown number of establishments not to be classed as general agents are engaged in writing advertising copy and in doing commercial art work. Another smaller group acts as specialized counsel on advertising matters. Still another devotes itself to the planning and executing of mail campaigns and to preparing mailing lists. Another carries on advertising research in the form of market surveys or the gathering of evidence regarding advertising's effectiveness among consumers. Another is made up of special representatives for selling space in advertising media. Still another group specializes in placing window displays.

In order that the economic importance of advertising might be more accurately known, one of the projects of this study was a detailed effort to determine the national expenditure for advertising. The year 1935 was chosen as a base because it was the most recent year for which complete census data were available. Since no authoritative statement as to the quantity of advertising in total for any year has been made by a governmental or private body, the estimates of this chapter are intended to fill that gap.

The Annual Expenditure for Advertising

Expenditures for advertising in the United States for 1935 are estimated to have been in the neighborhood of $1,700,000,000 as shown in Table 2, page 54. For those who are interested, a detailed account of the surveys conducted, of sources used, and of computations made and some indication of the error involved in the estimates are supplied at length in Appendix I.

In spite of attempts to arrive at accurate estimates in the several classifications listed, many of the figures must be accepted as only rough approximations. For some, such as newspapers, periodicals other than newspapers, and radio time, there is a relatively high degree of accuracy, because federal census figures for these items are available. For others, including radio talent, sign advertising, posters, car cards, and motion pictures, there is probably a relatively small degree of error on the whole, although the percentage of error in any one of the classifications may be appreciable. For another group, including direct advertising; art work, plates, and other mechanical costs; and departmental administration costs, the error may be large, because data to permit accuracy of measurement were lacking.

TABLE 2

ESTIMATED ADVERTISING EXPENDITURES FOR THE UNITED STATES, 1935 *

		AMOUNT	% OF TOTAL
A.	Newspapers	$ 519,000,000	30.5
B.	Periodicals Other than Newspapers	200,000,000	11.8
	General Magazines	$120,811,000	
	National Farm Magazines	5,565,000	
	Trade and Business Publications	43,241,000	
	Other Periodicals	30,383,000	
C.	Radio	105,000,000	6.2
	Time	79,618,000	
	Talent	25,600,000	
D.	Signs and Advertising Novelties	74,000,000	4.4
E.	Outdoor Advertising—Space and Printing	38,000,000	2.2
	Poster Panels, Painted and Electric Display Space	35,000,000	
	Printing and Lithographing	3,000,000	
F.	Car Cards—Space and Printing	13,500,000	0.8
	Space	12,000,000	
	Printing and Lithographing	1,500,000	
G.	Direct Advertising	500,000,000	29.4
	Postage for Direct Mail	87,000,000	
	Duplicating, Addressing, Mailing, and Mailing List Service	9,000,000	
	Printing and Lithographing for Direct Mail	247,000,000	
	Consumer and Dealer Literature, Labels, Display Material, and Other Direct Advertising	157,500,000	
H.	Motion Pictures	5,000,000	0.3
I.	Art Work, Plates, and Other Mechanical	75,000,000	4.4
	Costs Billed through General Agencies.	32,000,000	
	Other, Not Billed through Agencies	43,000,000	
J.	Agency Commissions (included in figures for space costs)		
K.	Advertising Department Administration.	170,000,000	10.0
	Approximate Total	$1,700,000,000	100.0

* Since many of the estimates may involve considerable error, the figures are rounded off and only the approximate totals of the items are given.

The relative importance of the several media and of the other expense items as a part of the whole is evident in the table, but certain relationships and certain additional facts are noted as follows:

Expenditures in newspapers, which accounted for a little over 30% of the total sum, were judged to be distributed approximately as follows between advertising placed by national advertisers and that placed by all types of local advertisers.

Placed by national advertisers............$158,000,000   30%
Placed by local advertisers............... 361,000,000   70%

The census figures, used as a base for the estimates, were inflated slightly to make allowance for the fact that some publishers did not include agency commissions or discounts in their reports to the U. S. Bureau of the Census, whereas others did so.

Direct advertising, an omnibus item covering not only the usual direct-mail but also catalogues, house organs, dealer help material, and many other forms of sales literature, was the second most important category of advertising cost, accounting for almost 30% of the total. This figure was the most difficult to derive, and unfortunately because of its size may contribute considerable error to the total sum.

Magazines, accounting for about 12% of expenditures, stood third. The census figures for magazines were inflated slightly, as they were for newspapers, to allow for agency discounts not reported to the Census Bureau.

Radio, the newest form of advertising, had by 1935 risen in a few years to fourth place among media. While radio time expenditures were readily obtainable, the figures for talent costs had to be estimated, and estimates necessarily were uncertain because of the wide variation in costs of programs and lack of adequate sample-data regarding such expenditures. Estimates of talent costs for network, local, and spot broadcasts were compiled separately, the resulting total showing talent costs to be 32% as large as expenditures for time.

Outdoor advertising, although very conspicuous on the American landscape, accounted for only slightly over 2% of total expenditures, including an estimated lithography cost of $3,000,000. Space costs were judged to be divided as follows:

24-sheet posters $28,000,000
Painted display and spectaculars.................... 6,000,000
3-sheet posters 1,000,000

Agency commissions, which were known from census figures to be in excess of $70,000,000 in 1935, were not included as a separate item because the estimates for media and for art work and production included agency commissions. Certain promotional activities often considered advertising costs, such as premium merchandise, sampling, and merchandise shows and conventions, were not included in the estimates in view of the definition of advertising previously given.

Estimated Annual Volume of Advertising for the Period 1914–1938

Estimates of the annual total volume of advertising for a period of years are more difficult to derive than the figures for the year 1935. Nevertheless, estimates for the years 1914–1938 are presented in Table 3. These figures were obtained by application of the *Printers' Ink* General Index of Advertising Activity, developed by Dr. L. D. H. Weld, to the estimate for 1935. The *Printers' Ink* general index is based on volume of advertising in newspapers, general magazines, farm magazines, radio, and the outdoor media, with allowance for other media than the five named, which are covered in specialized *Printers' Ink* indexes. The estimates for individual years, given in Table 3, may be in error, not only because of the uncertainty of the 1935 advertising estimate, but also because of some uncertainty as to how accurately the *Printers' Ink* general index reflects advertising expenditures outside of those made in the major media. The estimates derived, however, appear reasonable in the light of estimates of sales volume and of national income for the period.

It will be noted that in the postwar period, advertising volume, according to the estimates made, varied directly with business activity, reaching a high of $2,600,000,000 in 1929, and a low of $1,400,-000,000 in 1933. The annual average for the whole postwar period is $2,100,000,000. Since 1930 the level of advertising expenditure has been appreciably below that reached in the 1920's.

Although the above figures for advertising volume in themselves appear large, their significance becomes clear only when they are compared with economic activities with which they are associated. Various comparisons may be made to illustrate their importance. For instance, advertising expenditures may be compared with the national income to show what part of national income arises from advertising activity. Again, advertising costs may be compared with the total volume of sales transactions of business enterprise, a type of comparison frequently made by businessmen. Advertising expenditures may further be compared with total costs of distribution, of which advertising is a part, and with other specific costs of distribution, particularly with personal selling.

The Relation of Advertising Expenditure to National Income

The figure for national income for any year represents the net value of all goods and services produced in the United States expressed in terms of market value. It is a measure of the national productive effort for the year. Some of the productive effort is devoted to advertising, partly in the form of direct labor producing advertisements, and partly indirectly in the demand for numerous goods and services, such as paper, ink, transportation, and power, consumed by the advertising industry. Accordingly, if a ratio is struck between advertising

TABLE 3

ESTIMATES OF ADVERTISING VOLUME, 1914–1938, INCLUSIVE

YEAR	"PRINTERS' INK" GENERAL INDEX (Monthly Average 1928–1932 = 100)	CONVERTED INDEX (1935 = 100)	ESTIMATED VOLUME (Billions)
1914	60.4	76.2	$1.3
1915	59.6	75.2	1.3
1916	67.4	85.0	1.4
1917	69.6	87.8	1.5
1918	65.9	83.0	1.4
1919	92.1	116.1	2.0
1920	106.8	134.7	2.3
1921	91.3	115.1	2.0
1922	97.2	122.6	2.1
1923	106.9	134.8	2.3
1924	107.0	134.9	2.3
1925	112.0	141.2	2.4
1926	118.0	148.8	2.5
1927	115.8	146.0	2.5
1928	114.7	144.6	2.5
1929	120.7	152.2	2.6
1930	104.9	132.3	2.4
1931	91.9	115.9	2.0
1932	71.8	90.5	1.5
1933	65.0	82.0	1.4
1934	74.7	94.2	1.6
1935	79.3	100.0	1.7
1936	89.1	112.4	1.9
1937	94.0	118.5	2.0
1938	81.4	102.6	1.7

Source: Derived from application of *Printers' Ink* General Index of Advertising Activity to the volume estimates for 1935.

expenditures and national income for any year, the result is the percentage of all goods and services produced in that year which was spent directly or indirectly on advertising. Or, expressed differently, such a ratio shows what part of the value of all goods and services produced in a given year was directly attributable to advertising activity.[2]

Strictly speaking, to determine the part of the national productive effort employed for advertising purposes, it would be necessary to have a net figure of advertising expenditure, because the national income figure is a net figure. The estimate of advertising for 1935 is a gross figure containing some duplication, because materials and services employed by advertisers, such as paper and ink, media, and agencies, were themselves advertised. Hence some advertising was counted twice, once directly and once indirectly in the prices of these services and materials which made up part of the estimate of total expenditures. Such duplication is relatively so small that its elimination would not materially affect the resulting ratio between national income and advertising expenditure. This ratio is derived from the gross advertising expenditure figure for 1935 of $1,700,000,000 and the national income figure for that year of $55,794,000,000.[3] Accordingly it may be said that approximately 3% of the national income for that year is traceable to advertising activities. As noted above, the part of the national income thus attributable to advertising arose both directly in the form of services to produce advertisements and indirectly in the demand for a multitude of goods and services used by the advertising industry. The statement that 3% of the national income is traceable to advertising does not, of course, take into consideration possible effects which advertising as a form of sales stimulus may have had on the economy as a whole.

The Relationship of Advertising Expenditure to Volume of Sales Transactions

Since businessmen are accustomed to relate advertising and other expenditures to volume of sales, it adds perspective to compare total advertising to total sales transactions in business and to the volume of sales transactions for those types of businesses in which it is employed in appreciable amounts. The percentage of sales income devoted

[2] The effects of advertising in stimulating economic activity through its stimulus of sales are not comprehended in this ratio.

[3] R. R. Nathan, "National Income in 1938 at 64 Billion Dollars," U. S. Bureau of Foreign and Domestic Commerce, *Survey of Current Business*, June, 1939, Table 1, p. 11.

to advertising by business firms varies from practically nil for some to over 60% for others. What was the average percentage of expenditure for 1935?

TABLE 4

DETERMINABLE SALES OR COMMISSIONS FROM SALES OR RELATED FIGURES FOR TYPES OF BUSINESS IN WHICH ADVERTISING WAS EMPLOYED IN APPRECIABLE AMOUNTS—1935

TYPE OF BUSINESS	CHARACTER OF DATA	VOLUME (000 omitted)
Group I. Sales of Tangible Products—Total.	....	$ 96,087,000
1. Manufacturers	Sales	38,821,280
2. Wholesalers	Sales	20,124,702
3. Retailers	Sales	33,161,276
4. Construction Industry	Sales—work done	1,622,862
5. Real Estate Sales through Agencies	Fees received multiplied by 20 (117,844 x 20)	2,356,880
Group II. Sales of Various Services—Total.		4,285,924
6. Service Establishments	Sales	2,029,302
7. Power Laundries and Cleaning	Sales	369,452
8. Hotels	Sales	720,145
9. Tourist Camps	Sales	24,300
10. Places of Amusement	Sales	699,051
11. Motion Picture Producers	Production Cost	188,470
12. Radio Broadcasting	Sales, Broadcasting Stations.	86,493
13. Advertising Agencies	Commissions received	70,840
14. Public Warehousing	Sales	97,871
Group III. Sales of Transportation—Total.		5,711,340
15. Motor Bus Transportation	Sales	167,933
16. Motor Trucking for Hire	Sales	530,860
17. Railways, Freight	Freight Revenue	2,831,139
18. Railways, Passenger	Passenger Revenue	358,423
19. Street Railways (Electric, Motor Bus)	Operating Revenue	666,633
20. Civil Aeronautics	Estimated Passenger and Express Revenue	16,450
21. Pullman	Total Operating Revenue	48,428
22. Express Companies	Total Operating Revenue	91,474
23. Water Transportation	Estimated Operating Revenue	1,000,000
Group IV. Financial Services—Total.		11,256,292
24. Banks	Estimated Gross Earnings	1,600,000
25. Security Dealers	Sales of New Securities	3,782,143
26. Financial Institutions Other than Banks and Security Dealers	Payroll x 2	324,520
27. Insurance, Life	Premiums	3,692,128
28. Insurance, Fire and Marine	Premiums	871,414
29. Insurance, Casualty	Premiums	953,380
30. Insurance, Mutual, Accident, and Sick Benefit	Premiums	32,707
Group V. Communication, Light, Heat, and Power Services—Total.		3,530,836
31. Electric Light and Power	Revenues from Sales of Current	1,975,304
32. Natural Gas*	Revenue from Consumers	374,546
33. Telephone	Operating Revenues	1,049,815
34. Telegraph and Radio Telegraph	Operating Revenues	131,171
Total		$120,871,392

* Manufactured gas included in the Census of Manufactures Item 1.

Two tables of sales transactions were computed, one for those businesses which employed advertising in appreciable amounts, and one for businesses whose sales transactions involved very little advertising. The first group of businesses, totaling some $120,000,000,000 in sales, are shown in Table 4; the second, totaling $72,000,000,000 in sales, are shown in Table 5. When advertising expenditures in 1935 of $1,700,000,000 are measured against the total sales transactions of $120,000,000,000 for businesses using an appreciable amount of advertising, the average advertising expenditure appears to be 1.4% of sales. When, however, the total advertising expenditure is compared

TABLE 5

VOLUME OF SALES TRANSACTIONS FOR SELECTED PRODUCTS AND SERVICES NOT
EMPLOYING APPRECIABLE ADVERTISING, 1935

A. Estimated Cash Income from Farm Marketings	$ 6,507,000,000
B. Total Fisheries, United States and Alaska	80,121,000
C. Total Mineral Products	3,650,000,000
D. Nonprofit Organizations	404,312,000
E. Sales of Various Products and Securities on Organized Exchanges (Estimated)	38,800,000,000
F. Sales by Individuals, by Small Businesses, and Miscellaneous Sales Unreported in Any Census or Reporting Service	Indeterminate
G. Pipe Lines, Operating Revenue	211,789,000
H. Sales of Professional Services, Probably over	2,000,000,000
I. Over-the-counter Security Sales, Probably over	20,000,000,000
Approximate Total	$72,000,000,000

with the total sales transactions of $192,000,000,000 of all types of business, the average advertising cost as a percentage of sales was 0.9% of total sales. The bases for the estimates of sales transactions are given in Appendix II.

The above figures for the volume of sales transactions do not, of course, represent the net market value of goods and services produced or consumed in the year, for many products are sold a number of times in their passage from producer to consumer. The net value of goods and services is contained in the figure of national income discussed in the preceding section.

Relation of Advertising Expenditure to Total Distribution Cost

Another comparison showing the relation of advertising expenditure to the economic structure is indicated by the percentage relationship of the total expenditures for all advertising to the total expenditures incurred in marketing merchandise and services in 1935.

One of the few efforts made thus far to determine the total cost of distribution of commodities is that of Paul W. Stewart and J. Frederic Dewhurst for the Twentieth Century Fund, showing for 1929 a total distribution cost for commodities of $38,500,000,000.[4] As recognized by the authors, such a figure involved estimates in which there may be a considerable degree of error. With due allowance for these reservations, their estimate can be accepted for the present purpose.

Since the Twentieth Century Fund estimate relates only to the distribution costs for commodities and is for the year 1929, it was necessary to make adjustments to derive a figure of total distribution costs for both goods and services for the year 1935 to correspond with the total advertising expenditure figure for that year. It was estimated that the cost of distributing commodities in 1935 was $23,500,000,000.[5] To this figure was added $1,750,000,000,[6] a rough estimate of marketing costs for services, giving an estimate of total distribution costs for commodities and services of $25,250,000,000. Advertising in 1935, therefore, accounted for approximately 7% of total distribution costs $\frac{\$1.7 \text{ billion}}{\$25.3 \text{ billion}}$. This percentage figure indicates that advertising, though it may be large in the aggregate, is a relatively small part of the total costs involved in effecting distribution of goods and services to consumers.

THE RELATION OF ADVERTISING COSTS TO PERSONAL SELLING COSTS

To add further perspective as to the place of advertising in the economic structure, it is enlightening to compare advertising costs with

[4] P. W. Stewart and J. F. Dewhurst, *Does Distribution Cost Too Much?* (New York, The Twentieth Century Fund, 1939), p. 118.

[5] Adjustment of the Twentieth Century Fund's estimate of distribution costs was made as follows: Sales by manufacturers, wholesalers, and retailers in 1935 were 61% of those for 1929. Accordingly, this ratio was applied to the distribution costs for 1929 to derive an estimate for 1935 of $23,500,000,000. This method of estimating is not fully satisfactory, but to build up a figure of costs from 1935 census data and from other available data would not have altered the result sufficiently to have justified the expenditure of effort. The method used is deemed to be sufficiently accurate for the purpose of determining approximately what part of total distribution costs were advertising costs.

[6] Satisfactory data for estimating marketing costs of services are not available. The estimate made was little more than an appraisal based upon inadequate knowledge of the marketing costs for services of many kinds. Difficulty was met also in determination of what part of various services was utilized by retailers, wholesalers, and the marketing departments of manufacturers which make up a part of the operating costs of those institutions and which was, therefore, included in the estimate of cost of distributing commodities. The estimate of $1,750,000,000 can be termed little more than an intelligent guess.

those of the other leading form of activity employed for stimulating sales and bringing about exchange, namely, personal selling.

The costs of personal selling are several times as great in the aggregate as are the costs of advertising. Because of the lack of adequate data, no attempt has been made to build a total personal selling cost figure against which to compare the advertising bill; but the relationship of personal selling costs to advertising costs is roughly determinable from cost studies of a wide variety of businesses.

Ratio of Personal Selling Costs to Advertising Costs— Retail Stores

In the case of retail stores, the ratio between personal selling costs and advertising costs varies widely, not only among individual stores in any one field but also among different fields, as measured in the common figures or averages. Table 6, on page 63, shows ratios for the retail trades for which data deemed representative or nearly representative of advertising and personal selling costs were available. It must be realized, however, that the designation of costs as personal selling or advertising in such studies is not clear-cut and certain; accordingly the relationships pointed out must be accepted with reservations. In the trades for which comparisons are given, only furniture retailers had advertising costs as great as personal selling costs.[7] In 1935 the advertising costs for the furniture stores included in the study quoted were slightly greater than personal selling costs. Next in the degree of reliance on advertising among the stores listed are women's specialty stores, for which selling costs were indicated, in the studies quoted, to be approximately one and one-half times as great as advertising costs. Department stores, which contribute a far greater volume of retail advertising than any other type of store, showed personal selling costs about double their advertising costs. For the shoe retailers and the men's clothing stores included in the studies quoted, the personal selling figure is two and one-half to three times the advertising figure. Hardware retailers and grocers rely primarily upon personal selling. For hardware retailers the personal selling costs reported were some ten times the advertising costs. For grocers, personal selling costs ranged

---

[7] The study quoted in the table shows a higher ratio for advertising than is shown in other furniture cost surveys, but all cost studies of furniture retailers show them to have relatively high advertising costs. See M. P. McNair, S. F. Teele, and F. G. Mulhearn, *Distribution Costs—An International Digest* (Boston, Harvard Graduate School of Business Administration, 1941).

TABLE 6
TYPICAL FIGURES FOR SELECTED RETAIL TRADES SHOWING ADVERTISING EXPENSES,
PERSONAL SELLING EXPENSES, AND THE RATIOS OF PERSONAL SELLING
EXPENSES TO ADVERTISING EXPENSES

TYPE OF FIRM	YEAR	PERCENTAGE OF SALES REPRESENTED BY		RATIO OF PERSONAL SELLING TO ADVERTISING EXPENSE	SOURCE
		Advertising and Display	Personal Selling		
Department Stores	1935				a
$ 150,000-$ 300,000		3.40	9.40	2.76	
300,000- 500,000		3.90	10.00	2.56	
500,000- 750,000		4.30	9.45	2.19	
750,000- 1,000,000		4.60	9.00	1.95	
1,000,000- 2,000,000		4.80	9.00	1.87	
2,000,000- 4,000,000		5.10	8.85	1.73	
4,000,000- 10,000,000		5.60	9.10	1.62	
10,000,000- 20,000,000		5.05	9.45	1.87	
20,000,000 or more		4.65	9.30	2.00	
Specialty Stores	1935				a
$ 300,000-$ 500,000		4.25	....	....	
500,000- 1,000,000		5.55	8.30	1.50	
1,000,000- 2,000,000		6.25	8.25	1.32	
2,000,000- 4,000,000		6.35	8.30	1.30	
4,000,000 or more		5.20	8.85	1.70	
Shoe Stores	1936				b
Chain		3.20*	8.7†	2.71	
Multiple		3.40*	11.3†	3.32	
Single		3.10*	8.0†	2.58	
Men's Clothing Stores	1935				c
Under $100,000		2.41	7.16†	2.97	
Over $100,000		3.74	8.00†	....	
Furniture and Home Furnishings	1935	7.30	6.80	.93	d
Hardware Stores	1935	0.92	9.31†	10.11	e
Independent Grocery Stores	1924	....	(10.9)‡	....	f
	1927	0.30§	4.58#	....	g
	1927	0.25	6.42†	25.68	h
	1929	0.45	7.30†	16.22	i
Chain Grocery Stores	1929	0.75	(10.3)‡	....	j
Independent Drug Stores	1932	1.10	(17.9)‡	....	k
Drug Chain	1929	1.55	(17.6)‡	....	l
Limited Price Variety Chains	1939	0.29	(16.51)‡	....	m

* No salaries or wages included.
† Wages of salesforce only.
‡ Total salaries and wages; it is estimated that approximately 70% of this represents
selling salaries.
§ No salaries or wages included.
# Hired sales help only.

Sources:
  a. Harvard Business School, Bureau of Business Research, Bulletin No. 100, *Operating
     Results of Department and Specialty Stores in 1935*, by C. N. Schmalz, pp. 13, 18,
     24, 25.

(Continued on bottom of p. 64).

from ten to twenty times advertising costs. Among druggists they were roughly eight to ten times as great.

What the average ratio of personal selling costs to advertising costs is for all retailers can be but an uncertain estimate based on judgment of probable personal selling costs and advertising costs in various fields, weighted in accordance with the annual sales of the respective fields as shown in the United States Census of Business. From such an appraisal it seems safe to conclude that personal selling costs for retailers as a whole are some three to four times their advertising costs.

Ratio of Personal Selling Costs to Advertising Costs— Wholesale Trades

The wholesale business is essentially a personal selling business. Advertising plays a relatively small part, as shown in Table 7. As with retailers, there is considerable variation in the ratios of personal selling costs to advertising costs among individual firms and among the common figures for different types of wholesale businesses. Again, the figures must be accepted with reservations as to their accuracy in giving a clear-cut division between personal selling and advertising costs. Table 7 indicates that on the average (median of the ratios) the wholesale businesses included in the study quoted had personal selling expenses probably fifteen times as large as their advertising expenditures.

---

b. National Shoe Retailers Association, *Retail Shoe Stores and Leased Shoe Departments, Analysis of Operating and Merchandising Experience for 1936*, p. 20. Compiled by Research and Statistical Division, Dun & Bradstreet, Inc. Copyright by Dun & Bradstreet, Inc.
c. *National Clothier*, April, 1937, p. 17.
d. Controllers' Division of the National Retail Furniture Association, *1936 Operating Report*, p. 3.
e. *Hardware Retailer*, "Hardware Store Survey," June, 1936.
f. Harvard Business School, Bureau of Business Research, Bulletin No. 52, *Operating Expenses in Retail Grocery Stores in 1924*, p. 23.
g. State University of Iowa, College of Commerce, Bureau of Business Research, Iowa Studies in Business, No. VI, *Operating Costs of Grocery Stores in Iowa for the Year 1927*, by W. F. Bristol, p. 12.
h. University of Nebraska, College of Business Administration, Nebraska Studies in Business, No. 22, *Operating Expenses of Retail Grocery Stores in Nebraska, 1927*, p. 12.
i. University of Nebraska, College of Business Administration, Nebraska Studies in Business, No. 27, *Operating Expenses of Retail Grocery Stores in Nebraska, 1929*, p. 25.
j. Harvard Business School, Bureau of Business Research, Bulletin No. 84, *Expenses and Profits in the Chain Grocery Business in 1929*, by M. P. McNair, p. 24.
k. U. S. Bureau of Foreign and Domestic Commerce, Domestic Commerce Series, 90, *Costs, Sales, and Profits in the Retail Drug Store* (Washington, U. S. Government Printing Office, 1934), by Wroe Alderson and N. A. Miller, p. 23.
l. Harvard Business School, Bureau of Business Research, Bulletin No. 87, *Operating Results of Drug Chains in 1929*, by C. N. Schmalz, p. 29.
m. Harvard Business School, Bureau of Business Research, Bulletin No. 112, *Expenses and Profits of Limited Price Variety Chains in 1939*, by E. A. Burnham, p. 15.

Ratio of Personal Selling Costs to Advertising Costs— Manufacturers

Common figures of expense for particular manufacturing industries are of uncertain significance, for methods of operation employed by different firms vary widely. The range of the various expense ratios

TABLE 7

TYPICAL FIGURES FOR WHOLESALE TRADE SHOWING ADVERTISING EXPENSES, PERSONAL SELLING EXPENSES, AND THE RATIOS OF PERSONAL SELLING EXPENSES TO ADVERTISING EXPENSES, 1934

	PROFITABLE FIRMS			UNPROFITABLE FIRMS		
	Percentage of Sales Represented by		Ratio of Personal Selling to Advertising Expense	Percentage of Sales Represented by		Ratio of Personal Selling to Advertising Expense
TYPE OF FIRM	Salaries, Commissions and Other Personal Selling Expense	Advertising		Salaries, Commissions and Other Personal Selling Expense	Advertising	
Automobile Parts and Accessories...........	11.14	0.75	14.85	16.05	0.76	21.11
Bakers' and Confectioners' Supplies..............	6 29	0.27	23.29	4.87	0.30	16.23
Bakery.................	18.74	1.06	17.67	24.30	0.43	56.51
Beverage..............	9.01	2.04	4.42	8.93	2.56	3.49
Boot and Shoe.........	6.58	0.60	10.96	4.45	0.10	44.50
Building Supply........	6.83	0.46	14.84	7.22	0.28	25.78
Cigar, Cigarette and Tobacco..............	2.48	0.13	19.07	2.99	0.25	11.96
Coffee and Tea.........	8.89	1.39	6.40	11.28	2.50	4.51
Confectionery..........	7.01	0.20	35.05	7.10	0.43	16.51
Dairy Products.........	3.96	0.26	15.23	6.73	0.20	33.65
Drug..................	4.09	0.17	24.05	5.13	0.65	7.89
Dry Goods.............	6.50	0.62	10.48	8.76	0.20	43.80
Electrical Household Appliances...........	6.65	1.04	6.39	10.45	0.43	24.30
Feed, Grain and Hay....	4.69	0.13	36.07	3.89	0.90	4.32
Fish and Shellfish.......	7.80	0.60	13.00	8.25	0.26	31.73
Fruits and Vegetables....	6.67	0.27	24.70	4.69	0.87	5.39
General Merchandise....	6.16	0.50	12.32	6.50	0.60	10.83
Grocery...............	3.10	0.31	10.00	3.69	0.49	7.53
Hardware..............	6.67	0.40	16.67	6.65	0.40	16.62
Hosiery and Underwear..	6.18	1.00	6.18	6.85	0.17	40.29
Jewelry................	7.86	0.31	25.35	9.43	1.27	7.42
Leather and Shoe Findings	7.23	0.90	8.03	6.23	0.40	15.57
Lumber................	6.31	0.49	12.88	6.34	0.48	13.20
Meat and Poultry.......	6.42	0.67	9.58	8.28	0.15	55.20
Paper.................	8.20	0.16	51.25	7.18	0.20	35.90
Paper and Paper Products	7.96	0.39	20.41	10.23	0.55	18.60
Petroleum..............	7.29	0.61	11.95	19.11	0.80	23.88
Plumbing Supplies.......	6.99	0.30	23.30	10.34	0.23	44.95
Seed, Bulb and Plant....	3.93	0.60	6.55	9.95	4.70	2.12
Steel and Iron Products..	5.56	0.44	12.63	11.90	0.45	26.44
Tires and Tubes.........	7.31	1.10	6.64	12.60	2.50	5.04
Wines and Liquors......	6.10	0.72	8.47	5.24	0.36	14.56

Source: Dun & Bradstreet, Inc., Research and Statistical Division, *Wholesale Survey, 1934* (New York, Dun & Bradstreet, Inc).

among the firms in a single manufacturing industry is far greater than is the range for the firms in a wholesale or a retail trade, where the methods of operation are more nearly uniform. Averages, or common figures, of expenses are of doubtful significance when expense ratios have such wide range; yet common figures for an industry may serve to show in a rough way the relative reliance in the industry upon personal selling as contrasted with advertising selling.

Tables 8 and 9 show average, or common, figures for personal selling and for advertising costs for samples of manufacturers in different industries as reported in two cost studies. Apart from the questionable significance of common figures in these tables, there is also uncertainty as to the meaning and accuracy of the figures. This uncertainty arises from several causes: from the limited samples included in the studies; from doubt as to the appropriate classification of businesses among product groups; from difficulties met by cooperating firms in adjusting their figures to the accounting forms submitted by the research agencies, in view of the fact that accounting procedures of firms vary greatly; and from the varying definitions of expense items used in different cost studies. The studies do not give a uniform division between personal selling expense and advertising expense. The Association of National Advertisers' cost study gives a division between "advertising and sales promotion," on the one hand, and "direct selling costs," on the other. The Harvard Bureau of Business Research study of grocery manufacturers makes a division between "salesforce and brokerage," on the one hand, and "sales promotion and advertising," on the other.

With recognition of the uncertain meaning of the figures in the tables and of the weakness of common figures in such cost studies, it still is clear that, among manufacturers, personal selling expense on the whole is considerably greater than advertising expenditure. Among manufacturers in some product groups, however, an average of advertising and sales promotion expense exceeds the average of personal selling expense. Such a relationship holds for manufacturers of drug and toilet articles and of tobacco products, Table 8, and for manufacturers of soaps, cleansers, polishes, and disinfectants, Table 9. These few instances, however, are exceptions to the rule. Inspection of Tables 8 and 9 indicates that among manufacturers of consumers' products, other than those mentioned, common figures of personal selling costs are from one to six and one-half times as great as com-

TABLE 8

TYPICAL FIGURES FOR SELECTED MANUFACTURING INDUSTRIES, SHOWING ADVERTISING
AND DIRECT SELLING EXPENSE AS PERCENTAGES OF SALES AND THE RATIO
OF DIRECT SELLING EXPENSE TO ADVERTISING EXPENSE, 1931

TYPE OF FIRM	EXPENSES AS PERCENTAGES OF NET SALES		RATIO DIRECT SELLING COSTS TO ADVERTISING AND SALES PROMOTION EXPENSE
	Advertising and Sales Promotion	Total Direct Selling Costs	
Consumers' Goods	%	%	%
Agricultural Equipment and Supplies..	1.58	8.24	5.22
Automotive.....................	3.99	12.85	3.22
Clothing......................	3.67	11.15	3.04
Confections and Bottled Beverages....	6.68	11.47	1.72
Drugs and Toilet Articles...........	18.36	11.31	.62
Furniture......................	6.11	14.83	2.43
Grocery Products.................	6.21	11.08	1.78
Hardware......................	2.16	9.07	4.20
Heating Equipment...............	7.90	15.78	2.00
Home Furnishings................	2.94	12.35	4.20
Household Appliances.............	6.83	12.75	1.87
Jewelry and Silverware............	6.29	11.54	1.83
Office Equipment and Supplies........	3.23	21.26	6.58
Paints and Varnishes..............	7.52	17.11	2.27
Petroleum Products...............	5.98	10.89	1.82
Radio Equipment and Supplies.......	5.33	5.38	1.00
Shoes.........................	3.67	8.72	2.38
Sporting Goods..................	3.64	8.37	2.30
Tobacco Products................	8.23	3.23	.39
Industrial Goods			
Building Materials and Supplies......	2.95	11.77	3.99
Chemicals and Allied Products.......	1.22	10.56	8.66
Electrical Equipment and Supplies....	3.04	11.99	3.94
Iron and Steel and Their Products.....	1.89	8.97	4.75
Machinery and Machine Tools.......	4.38	14.61	3.34
Nonferrous Metals................	1.07	10.20	9.53
Paper and Paper Products...........	2.52	9.42	3.74
Stove, Clay and Glass Products.......	3.05	10.04	3.29
Textiles.......................	1.26	5.10	4.05
Transportation Equipment..........	1.67	8.76	5.25

Source: Association of National Advertisers, Inc., *An Analysis of the Distribution Costs of 312 Manufacturers* (New York, The Association, 1931), p. 22 ff.

TABLE 9

TYPICAL FIGURES FOR SELECTED MANUFACTURING INDUSTRIES SHOWING MARKETING
EXPENSES AS PERCENTAGES OF SALES AND THE RATIOS OF SALESFORCE AND BROKERAGE
EXPENSES TO SALES PROMOTION AND ADVERTISING EXPENSES, 1927

TYPE OF FIRM	COMMON FIGURES AS PERCENTAGES OF NET SALES		RATIO SALESFORCE AND BROKERAGE TO SALES PROMOTION AND ADVERTISING
	Sales Promotion and Advertising (Except Administration)	Salesforce and Brokerage	
Flour Manufacturers......................	0.4	2.5	6.25
Meat Packers............................	0.1	2.5	25.00
Canned and Bottled Foods.................	2.3	5.5	2.39
Coffee, Tea, Chocolate, Extracts and Spices....	3.2	7.5	2.14
Cereals, Crackers, Macaroni, Salt and Preserves.	6.5	8.5	1.31
Soaps, Cleansers, Polishes and Disinfectants...	13.0	9.0	.69

Source: Harvard Business School, Bureau of Business Research, Bulletin No. 77, *Marketing Expenses of Grocery Manufacturers for 1927*, p. 18.

mon figures of advertising costs. Among various groups of industrial goods manufacturers, common figures of personal selling costs are from three to nine and one-half times as great as advertising costs. Data of similar cost studies of a large number of industries, made by Dun & Bradstreet, showed ratios of personal selling costs to advertising costs even greater than those for the tables above.

While the costs of personal selling by manufacturing firms were shown by these studies to be appreciably larger than advertising costs, it was deemed unwise to hazard a guess as to an average ratio of personal selling expense to advertising expense for all manufacturers because of the lack of an adequate sample and the uncertainty of such data as were available.

All in all, inspection of the cost data of retailers, wholesalers, and manufacturers indicates that costs attending personal selling efforts in the aggregate are probably several times as large as those chargeable to advertising. Hence, although this study is devoted to the phase of aggressive selling most evident to the casual observer, its costs to the consumer are not so great as those of the less obtrusive form, personal selling.

CONTRIBUTON OF ADVERTISING EXPENDITURES TO PUBLISHING AND BROADCASTING

In compilation of the facts regarding advertising expenditures it is important to include a statement about their direct effect upon the publication of newspapers and magazines and the broadcasting of radio entertainment. The newspapers of today, with their instant and widespread news coverage and their many features, are made possible at the low price of two or three cents a copy only as a result of receiving advertising revenue. Likewise many modern magazines, with their high-price feature articles, serials, short stories, and special departments, are available to consumers at the low prices charged only because of advertising income. An increasing number of business magazines, particularly trade papers, are furnished to their readers without charge, the publishers having gone so far as to rely upon advertising income wholly to support publication.[8] In the case of radio, broadcasting service in the United States is almost wholly supported by advertising revenue.

---

[8] These publishers employ so-called "controlled circulation" methods.

There has been criticism both of an advertising-supported press and of the American broadcasting plan. Some critics hold the view that reliance upon advertising revenues has made the press subject to undue influence from business. To what extent this allegation is true and whether undesirable social consequences have attended the present publishing system were not subjects of investigation in this study, because of lack of time and resources. Likewise, the relative merits of the American plan of broadcasting and of other possible plans were not studied. An effort was made, however, to determine for 1935 the part of publishing and of broadcast advertising revenues which could be termed a "net contribution" to publishing and to broadcasting.

Net contribution in the case of publishers refers to that part of the total advertising revenues left after the costs of obtaining, handling, and printing advertising are deducted. It is the amount which advertising contributes to printing the news, features, stories, and all other elements in which people are interested, other than advertising, when they subscribe to a periodical. This viewpoint makes the assumption that readers are not interested in paying for advertising messages; yet it is known that they are attracted to certain media because of the advertising they carry. In brief, the net contribution from periodical advertising equals total advertising revenue minus all costs ascribable to advertising. Similarly for radio broadcasting, the net contribution from advertising is that part of total expenditures made for radio broadcasts by advertisers which remains after the costs attending the selling and handling of advertising and profits are deducted.

In order to get the data needed in determination of the net contribution of advertising to publishing, a sample survey was conducted among publishers. In the case of radio, data from government publications were adequate as basis for an estimate of the net contribution of advertising to broadcasting. A report of the periodical survey and the analysis of data on broadcasting companies are contained in Appendix III.

The net contribution of advertising to publishing and broadcasting is an important one. In the case of newspapers, in 1935 the total revenue of publishers was some $760,000,000, of which $500,000,000 came from advertisers and $260,000,000 from subscriptions. The survey among newspapers indicates that costs ascribable to advertising were probably about half of advertising revenue. Thus the net contribution of advertising was roundly $250,000,000, or approximately half of the costs involved in publishing all parts of newspapers other than the advertising. Had the publishers attempted to issue papers with the same scale of news reporting and features as they maintained without the aid of advertising, they would probably have had to extract from subscribers a sum equal to at least one-half the advertising revenue of their papers and probably in excess of this amount. This conclusion means roughly that circulation revenue would have had to be doubled.

In the case of magazines, the total revenue of publishers in 1935 was roundly $330,000,000, of which $144,000,000 was from subscriptions and $186,000,000 from advertising. The data regarding magazines did not permit other than a rough and uncertain estimate of the net contribution from advertising to publishing, but it was judged to be at least $50,000,000. This amount is over one-third of the total subscription revenue of all magazines for that year. While for magazines as a whole, lack of advertising revenue might have necessitated increase in subscription revenue of at least one-third, such an increase would not have been adequate for many of the leading consumer publications which carry large amounts of advertising and sell for low subscription prices. Were publications of this kind to be issued in their current form without advertising revenue, their subscription prices would have to be increased substantially, probably as much as two to three times, in order to yield an amount equivalent to the net contribution which they enjoy from their advertising.

For radio broadcasting, total advertising expenditures in 1935 in round figures were $105,000,000, of which $80,000,000 was paid to broadcasting stations and networks for broadcasting time, and $25,-600,000 was paid for talent. From this total of $105,000,000 the amounts deductible for obtaining, handling, and broadcasting the advertising, for brokerage on talent, and for the profit of broadcasting stations and networks were estimated to be $28,000,000. Accordingly it would appear that advertising contributed some $77,000,000 to provide broadcasting facilities for a wide variety of free radio entertainment to the public.

To summarize, for the three media the net contribution from advertising expenditures in 1935 was roughly as follows:

Newspapers	$250,000,000
Magazines	50,000,000
Radio	77,000,000
Total	$377,000,000

Thus, almost half of the total advertising expenditure of some $824,-000,000 in these media was, in effect, returned to consumers in the form of low-cost periodicals and free radio entertainment. In that way it may be deemed to be a deduction or offset against the total advertising costs of $1,700,000,000 in all media.

CHAPTER IV

THE UTILIZATION OF ADVERTISING BY BUSINESS

WHILE the principal reason for this study is the examination of the theory and practice of advertising from the economic and social points of view, that examination cannot logically be undertaken without an understanding of the place of advertising in the distribution of commodities under a system of private enterprise. Advertising is an activity which businessmen undertake to attain profits, but the attainment of profit is not assured simply by the use of advertising. To be profitable it must be in the right form and quantity, and it must be related properly to the other means employed to effect sales. Businessmen face difficult decisions in choosing among the various alternatives open to them in their use of advertising. The risk in making these decisions is important because wrong decisions may be disastrous to the welfare of the business firm. The risk unfortunately has been large because there has been a general lack of specific knowledge as to the results that might be expected from specific selling and advertising programs. In this and the following chapter the problems met by businessmen in making choices in their use of advertising and in reducing the attendant risks are discussed.

Chapters IV and V are included in the volume primarily for those who are not fully familiar with advertising and business practice and, accordingly, are not acquainted with the forces which determine advertising usage. Businessmen and others familiar with business and advertising methods may find it preferable either to omit these chapters or quickly to scan them. The knowledge of advertising usage and its determinants held by these persons will enable them to proceed at once to the economic analysis which is taken up in Chapter VI.

Character of Evidence Used

The study of the utilization of advertising by businessmen contained in these two chapters is based primarily upon case histories collected for the Harvard Business School from business executives over a period of some 20 years. These cases are reports of problems or issues met by managements in the operation of a wide variety of business enterprises. They ordinarily, though not uniformly, contain a crystallization of specific issues as seen by the executives; statements regarding alternative policies or procedures considered for adoption; a record of facts and reasons bearing upon the issues; a record of the actions taken or of the policies adopted and the reasons therefor; and evidence regarding the success or lack of success of methods or policies employed. Over 500 cases relating specifically to advertising are in the files of the School. Supplementing these are almost 3,500 cases dealing with the subjects of marketing, sales management, and retail store management. All these pertain to problems of marketing, and many of them directly or indirectly have to do with questions of utilization of advertising. In addition to these written case studies, opportunity for intensive study of the methods and policies of business firms has been possible through many interviews and discussions with business executives, not only during the collection of some of these cases, but also on many other occasions. In other words, it has been possible to draw upon hundreds of unrecorded cases. Furthermore, periodicals in the fields of advertising and marketing generally, as well as books written by students of marketing, have been drawn upon.

These case histories and statements obtained from executives have real shortcomings as evidence upon which to base conclusions regarding the profitable utilization of advertising. Ideally, cases should include statistical data regarding advertising expenditure, sales, profits, and other measurable activities. In addition they should include such nonmeasurable materials as a faithful description of the advertising and selling methods employed and information as to the energy and skill exhibited by staffs in carrying out the advertising and selling activities, for the success of a program or policy may depend as much upon skill and energy in execution as upon proper decision regarding method and policy. The cases as collected usually have evidence both of a statistical and a nonstatistical character, but not always so complete or so certain as might be desired. Frequently much information of a statistical character is taken from company books of record, but very frequently desired statistical measurements have not been kept by the business firms. Occasionally in place of detailed sales, cost, and profit facts, generalized statements by executives regarding these facts have had to be accepted.

On decisions regarding methods or policies adopted or rejected, statements of executives have had to be relied upon without verification. Sometimes these statements are unquestionably rationalizations after the event rather than completely accurate accounts of the reasons that governed decisions at the time. The well-trained field investigator is sometimes able to keep such rationalizations out of his statement of the case, but even the best-trained man cannot be sure of obtaining all the numerous emotional and nonlogical factors which have entered into decisions. One of the greatest difficulties is that numerous business decisions are carried through with no record kept as to the reasons therefor. Active businessmen making decisions day in and day out, without record of the reasons therefor, and often without having fully crystallized their reasons, simply cannot recall after the event all that guided their decisions. For a business to keep such records would entail an undue burden. Furthermore, advertising decisions are often interwoven with other marketing and business decisions, and the full significance of the variables is not clear either to those who made the decisions or to subsequent analysts. It must be recognized also that even in those instances when the most complete records have been kept and intelligent cooperation has been given by business managements to the case reporter, the sales and profit results from the advertising decisions have not been fully determinable. In other words, standards for measuring the success of advertising and selling programs are frequently uncertain.

In spite of their shortcomings, such case histories have been highly valuable as a basis for generalization regarding the conditions governing the choices of businessmen in their utilization of advertising. Although exact standards have not been present for measuring the success of advertising methods and policies, ordinarily sales and profit results and other data are sufficient to permit advertising's contribution to be judged at least roughly. Of special significance is the fact that the evidence has been cumulative. As the number of cases has grown, comparison and contrast between cases have made possible the determination of uniformities of practice and ascertainment of reasons for variation in advertising policy and method under varying sets of conditions. Since the experiences of many concerns can be checked one against the other, the shortcomings of individual cases are overcome. Accordingly, the generalizations regarding business utilization of advertising which are contained in this and the following chapter are presented with full confidence as to their soundness.

It has been deemed inadvisable even to try to recite all the case histories and interview evidence that lie back of the statements made. The method followed is to give an exposition regarding the utilization of advertising, with representative illustrations drawn from case histories. The points made in these chapters will receive supporting evidence in later chapters, when demand and cost data of particular industries are presented in more detail.

Effect of Long-Range Profit Considerations on the Use of Advertising by Business

While decisions by business firms on whether to use advertising, how to use it, and to what extent are guided almost solely by profit considerations, a clear-cut distinction should be made between a short-range and a long-range profit viewpoint. By and large, business firms are guided in their operations by a long-range profit viewpoint, which puts emphasis upon continued patronage as contrasted with one-time sales. The importance of repeat sales is evident in the case of cigarettes or bread, which consumers purchase each day. But repeat purchases are likewise important for products whose purchase is less frequent, as in the cases of shoes or automobiles.

Advertising may, of course, be employed to help bring a quick return on sales transactions at a sacrifice of future patronage. It may be used to induce the consumer to buy goods from which he will not get satisfaction. Clearly a quick turnover profit, a drawing in of one-time buyers, is the method of fly-by-night concerns or of so-called "borax" establishments, whose objective is to make a cleanup and to move on before the district attorney moves in. Some business firms are of this type and are an irritant not only to defrauded consumers but to the business community. Such businesses, however, are not the concern of this chapter.[1] Attention is devoted rather to the great majority of business enterprises which are conducted in the hope of continuity of patronage. The hundreds of case studies which have been drawn upon for this chapter have dealt with business conducted with such a viewpoint.

Firms actuated by a long-range profit viewpoint vary markedly in their ability to manage their affairs so as to attract and to hold customers. That they occasionally yield to the pressure to show a profit for the current accounting period or a profit upon particular transac-

---

[1] In Chapter XXVII further consideration is given to the subject of business ethics.

tions is evident to any student of business. Often they may exercise mistaken judgment as to the effect of immediate acts upon continued patronage of those with whom they deal. They may be mistaken, for example, in the setting of either quality standards or prices, or in a combination of the two, with consequent harm to customer relations.

No way appears feasible to measure statistically the extent to which businesses, through choice, through mistaken judgment, or through inefficiency and ignorance, follow practices which threaten future patronage of their customers. Only opinions and impressions can be given. Innumerable individual instances of such practices are to be found. But such instances appear inevitable when businesses, like all lines of endeavor, must be run by men who are inefficient, lacking in foresight, or occasionally wanting in integrity. That they do not occur more frequently can be attributed largely to the long-range profit viewpoint which appears to permeate business.

It has become a generally accepted principle of business policy that immediate profit should be sacrificed whenever the practice which immediate profit dictates threatens to bring loss of future patronage or otherwise to harm future profitableness of an enterprise. An aphorism frequently reiterated by business managers is that one-time sales are not ordinarily profitable. The low cost of making sales to constant patrons and the stability which continued patronage gives to a going concern are the best guarantees of a maximized profit over a period of time. Even when repeat sales do not occur or are very infrequent, still the policies followed by well-managed firms ordinarily stress customer satisfaction in the hope that the reputation thus gained will help them in gaining new customers.

The long-range profit viewpoint of business management accounts for the importance attached to maintenance of quality of branded merchandise, of congenial selling contacts, of acceptable pricing, and of efficient service of one kind or another. It has a distinct bearing on advertising practices, particularly as advertising may be designed to build up ideas or attitudes regarding products or the selling institution that are conducive to continued patronage. On the negative side, it is a deterrent to adoption of advertising practices which, though possibly immediately effective, might reduce future patronage.

Customer satisfaction, upon which continued patronage depends, is not necessarily determined by a business firm's meeting the lowest prices in the market or offering merchandise deemed good values by *all* potential buyers. Continued patronage generally depends rather upon the degree to which a firm can meet the desires of some segment of the market. Different buyers have different tastes and are induced to purchase by varying sets of buying motives, of which price is only one. The offering of individualized product qualities; the provision for prompt delivery, easy credit, convenience in buying, or good repair service; a reputation for fashion, dependability, generous adjustment, or courteous salespeople—all these and numerous other considerations may be relied upon by a firm to give buyers the satisfaction that will lead them to purchase again. This multiplicity of buying and patronage motives which appeal to various segments of the market plays a fundamental part in the development of numerous competitive patterns of business with varying utilization of advertising among them.

Effects of Advertising on a Manufacturer's Operating Statement

In order that the possible contribution of advertising to a business firm's profit or deficit may be clearly before the reader, its effects upon a firm's operating statement are examined. From an accounting standpoint profit is merely the residuum of sales income after all the expenses incident to the conduct of the business have been deducted. Since the use of advertising by manufacturers is in large part different from its use by distributors, the possible effects of advertising upon the items of the operating statement of a manufacturer are studied first.

Below is a simple form of operating statement containing the essential items representative of the operations of a manufacturer:

a.	Sales income (number of units sold x price per unit)......................	xxxxx
b.	Total manufacturing costs..	xxxxx
c.	Gross margin available for marketing, for general administration, and for profits (a—b)	xxxxx
	d. Salesforce expense	xxx
	e. Sales promotion and advertising expense.........................	xxx
	f. Shipping, transportation, warehouse, and delivery expense.........	xxx
	g. Credit and collection expense..................................	xxx
	h. Marketing administration costs................................	xxx
i.	Total marketing expenses (sum of d to h inclusive).....................	xxxxx
j.	Balance remaining for general administration and for profit (c—i)..........	xxxxx
	k. General administrative costs...................................	xxx
l.	Balance for profit (j—k)...	xxxxx

A business management seeks to conduct its operations so that a profit is shown in the final item (1). What profit occurs is the result of the interplay among the items above it. It is evident that greater or lesser use of advertising may affect both the income item and the various expense items listed

The possible effects of advertising on the various operating items in different marketing situations are many. For clarity, only the broad effects are noted. When a management considers use of advertising, the questions posed are as follows:

(1) What will be the effect of an advertising program upon sales income (item a)?

Sales income is the result of the number of units sold multiplied by price per unit. Advertising is employed to increase people's desire for a product. If it accomplishes this end, it will have effect on either the number of units purchased by new and old customers, or the price they pay, or both. A management must ask: To what extent does advertising promise to affect sales income (a) through effect on units sold? (b) through effect on price obtainable?

While a management through use of advertising often can increase the desire of consumers for its products and thereby may find it possible to increase the prices which it receives per unit, it also often can materially affect the quantities of its products sold, and accordingly its sales income, by the prices it sets upon its products. It is essential, therefore, that a management properly appraise the effect of price upon the quantities of products which it may sell, if it is to get a maximum sales income. Provided a product has an elastic demand, that is, a demand in which quantities sold increase rapidly as prices are decreased, a management may increase sales income by decreasing prices. As will be indicated in later chapters, advertising for some products may have the effect of increasing the elasticity of demand to a point where it is good strategy for a management to decrease prices because sales income thereby may be increased. In short, if a management is to maximize its sales income, it must carefully appraise the effects both of price and of selling effort upon sales response.

(2) What will be the effect of advertising upon the manufacturer's production costs?

Any advertising costs undertaken may be offset in part or in whole by reduction in unit production costs. If unit production costs are to be affected by advertising, that result must come through advertising's effect upon volume of manufacture. Provided advertising helps give a sufficient volume to make lower unit costs possible, the wider gross margin per unit and the larger number of units sold give an aggregate gross margin (item c), offsetting the promotional expenditure undertaken. Accordingly, an efficient management knows the effect of volume upon manufacturing costs and, consequently, the aggregate margin which will result.

Reduced production costs per unit may come from either (a) effective utilization of existing plant, which means the spreading of fixed costs over a large number of units, or (b) employment of increased capital in order to permit a more efficient plant and scale of operations with lower unit costs.

(3) What will be the effect of advertising on the manufacturer's marketing costs?

Advertising itself (item e) is a cost that must be met. If the advertising outlay cannot be recouped through wider margins resulting from higher price or lowered production costs, or through a greater aggregate sum available from selling more units at a relatively constant margin, then possibly it may be justified from a profit standpoint, provided it represents a more economical means of securing sales volume than personal selling (item d) or other promotional methods. Or it may find its justification in making personal efforts more productive of sales volume than they otherwise would be, for advertising frequently has this effect.

This brief discussion of the interrelation between advertising expenditures and the various parts of the operating statement is, of course, oversimplified. Considerable ingenuity is required by operating executives to think out in advance the effects which advertising may produce on business operations; and often it is difficult to measure advertising effects after the event, because a decision to use advertising probably entails other changes to be made at the same time, the effects and implications of which may be widespread. Consequently it is difficult to assign any simple cause and effect relationship. Results come from the interplay of a large number of variables. Furthermore the advertiser does not judge the success of his operations from the operating statement of a single year, provided his financial resources permit him to take a longer view.

This schematic illustration is helpful to an understanding of the effects of advertising in various operating patterns or formulae which are presented in the pages ahead.

Dependence of Profitable Use of Advertising Upon
Proper Combination with Other Operating Procedures

The use of advertising as a selling tool does not automatically provide a profit to an organization. Its improper use may contribute to loss just as much as its correct use may contribute to profits. The businessman can lose money about as rapidly from making wrong decisions regarding what policies and methods of advertising to employ as he can from adoption of ineffective methods in any other branch of business endeavor.

Good use of advertising from a business standpoint depends upon finding answers to the questions cited above regarding advertising's effect upon units to be sold, prices received, production costs, and marketing costs, all of which combine to give a net profit result; but the answers to such questions often vary widely with different products and different operating conditions. The answer for one type of product and for one company may not fit another product and another company. Moreover, frequently for individual companies there are several answers as to the kind and amount of advertising to combine with other operating variables to produce a profitable result. Generally there is not just one way to produce and market a product or line of products. Any management may consider numerous alternatives for conducting its operations, alternative methods as to merchandising, pricing, channels of distribution, and selling methods. Some particular combination of methods may be most promising in a specific product field and the firms which follow these methods may thereby become dominant in the market. But other methods can be employed and can produce a profit. The outlooks of different managements may vary widely because of differences in product lines, markets sought, size of enterprise, capital, selling channels available, and their skills of merchandising, manufacturing, promotion, and general administration. The result is a wide variety of management operating patterns or formulae employed by manufacturers.

Whether advertising can be profitably used depends upon how well it is fitted into a particular operating formula as a whole. Below some of the more important considerations which govern differences in utilization of advertising in manufacturers' operating programs are discussed.

Advertising Utilization as Affected by Brand Policy

One of the main decisions of a manufacturer which govern his utilization of advertising is whether or not to affix a brand which he will promote to ultimate users. Even in fields where most manufacturers trade-mark their output and spend a considerable percentage of sales income on advertising, other manufacturers of the same product carry on without advertising because they have elected to sell to private brand distributors, to those desiring unbranded merchandise, or to those who desire a controlled manufacturer's brand.[2] An adequate volume of sales to give economical production costs may be obtained with little or no advertising when such basic operating policies have been adopted. If margins above manufacturing costs are low under such procedures, this fact is offset by low marketing costs, because promotional costs to ultimate buyers are assumed by the distributors. To cite an example, the great bulk of the dentifrice business is carried on under heavily advertised manufacturers' brands. One manufacturer visited, however, had a profitable business supplying dentifrices and other toilet articles to variety chain stores under their brands. He did no consumer advertising and had very low selling expenses to the trade. In another case, after an unsuccessful attempt to sell vacuum cleaners under his own brand, a manufacturer whose chief interest was in industrial products made a contract to sell his vacuum cleaners to a sewing machine manufacturer under the latter's brand. The sewing machine manufacturer had a chain of stores and a group of retail agencies devoting efforts primarily to his sewing machines, and desired additional items to swell the sales of his retail outlets.[3] Such instances of manufacturing for private brand or under controlled manufacturers' brands are common. While such business may be profitable in many cases, the methods of operation do not appeal to many aggressive managements.

Advertising Utilization as Affected by Choice of Selling Methods

The extent to which advertising is employed by a manufacturer selling under his own brand is determined in large degree by his choice among alternative methods for influencing sales. In some product fields,

---

[2] The term "controlled" is applied to those brands which are sold exclusively to one buyer, usually with some understanding that he will continue to have exclusive selling rights.

[3] N. H. Borden, *Problems in Advertising* (3d ed., New York, McGraw-Hill Book Company, Inc., 1937), case of Rand Company, p. 134.

such as certain toilet goods or proprietary remedies, the decision to rely heavily upon advertising may be readily made because experience has shown it to be a more effective and economical means for influencing sales of such products than is large use of personal selling. Data collected showed these industries typically to have heavier advertising costs than personal selling costs. Many such manufacturers have no salesmen, relying upon advertising to create a consumer pull which leads distributors to carry their products. But for other products it is very often difficult to forecast just what the relative effectiveness of various combinations of advertising and personal selling may be. Consequently differences of opinion develop as to the correct combinations to use, and varying operating procedures are chosen by different companies. For example, several large refiners of cane sugar [4] have elected to advertise their packaged sugar to consumers. They have done so on the hypothesis that advertising, even though not highly effective in influencing consumer demand for sugar, would build enough brand recognition among consumers to induce retailers to prefer their brands to competing brands. Each has reasoned that under this policy he might secure not higher prices than competitors, but a larger and more stable volume of business over a period of time than he would obtain without advertising. In order to attain this end, they have aimed to sell an increasing proportion of their sugar in packages rather than in bulk and have adopted the policy of offering a full line of packaged sugars—powdered sugar, cube sugar, brown sugar, and so on. Each has expected to recoup rather modest advertising costs, that is, small in proportion to sales volume, primarily from production economies to be had from full and constant utilization of manufacturing capacity, for fixed costs of sugar refineries are large.

In contrast to the methods adopted by these refiners, others have elected not to use consumer advertising. Some of these nonadvertising refiners have small capacity and low costs. They have seen in their nearby markets opportunity to dispose of their entire potential production without entering the package business. Selling their output largely in bulk, they have had no need for consumer advertising. Other nonadvertisers [5] have elected to strive for package business, but in lieu of consumer advertising they have relied primarily upon good delivery

---

[4] Cases of American Sugar Refining Company and National Sugar Refining Company, files of the Harvard Business School.

[5] N. H. Borden, *Problems in Advertising* (3d ed.), case of Sucrosa Sugar Refining Company, p. 80.

and other services to the trade as a basis for getting patronage. Thus do directly competing manufacturers follow divergent policies.

In the shoe business some manufacturers elect to carry their message to the consumer, with a modest amount of general advertising over their names and larger advertising efforts directed to consumers through retailers. A considerable volume of shoe business carried on under manufacturers' brands, however, is sought almost solely through personal selling and advertising directed to the trade. In such instances there is no advertising to consumers through general media, and sometimes little or no advertising directed through retailers.[6] Such promotion as is conducted is left largely to the retailer to carry out. Still other manufacturers follow a policy of selling unbranded merchandise to retailers, while others sell all or a substantial volume under dealers' labels.

Widely divergent selling methods and policies are found in the candy business. A certain manufacturer[7] of chocolate candy selling at $1 and $1.50 a pound has been a heavy user of magazine advertising. Advertising featuring this candy as a gift sure to be recognized and appreciated has been accepted by the management as a profitable tool to help bring volume at these prices. Other manufacturers[8] of equally high-grade chocolates have offered their products at the same prices, but have adopted the alternative practice of devoting their promotion efforts primarily to missionary work with retail dealers. They have depended upon fine packaging, skillful display, and quality recognizable through use as sound bases for building a profitable volume of sales. Certain other candy manufacturers have relied upon controlled chains of retail stores to dispose of their products, some making considerable use of advertising, others employing it sparingly.

In the drug field companies frequently face the alternatives of promoting their medicines to consumers or of selling them on a so-called ethical basis, i.e., promoting their sale through doctors or dentists.[9] The two types of business are distinctly different and make use of different operating patterns. Whenever a company chooses to promote

[6] *Ibid.*, case of Weyenberg Shoe Manufacturing Company, p. 201.

[7] See: Eldridge Peterson, "Whitman's is Unique," *Printers' Ink,* March 23, 1939, p. 11.

[8] N. H. Borden, *Problems in Advertising* (2d ed., 1932), case of Chocolate Candy Company, p. 487.

[9] The files of the Harvard Business School contain a large quantity of case material illustrative of the so-called ethical approach as against the consumer advertising approach in the promotion of drug products. Typical of these is the case of the Sargent Dental Company, in *Problems in Advertising,* by N. H. Borden (3d ed.), p. 103.

its product to consumers, it uses a heavy program of advertising in general media and generally little personal selling effort to the trade. When the decision is made, however, to promote a product to doctors, advertising expenditures are smaller and are employed chiefly for professional magazines and for direct mail. This advertising in turn is often accompanied by relatively heavy expenditures for so-called detail work, i.e., promotional work by missionary or specialty salesmen among physicians, dentists, or other professional groups to build the reputation of the products and to lead these professional men to use or specify the products among patients. In addition, considerable missionary selling among druggists is carried on. In either of the above instances, the total promotional costs are relatively heavy, but the utilization of advertising is widely different in the two approaches.

Advertising Utilization as Affected by Channels of Distribution Chosen

The channels of distribution chosen by a manufacturer generally have a marked effect on his utilization of advertising. While specific products tend to go to consumers through the same channels, individual manufacturers may see opportunity profitably to employ different channels, and this divergence of method leads to differing use of advertising. For example, in the silk hosiery industry, manufacturers marketing under their own brands [10] generally have sold through selected retail distributors. As a rule, their advertising has been directed to consumers primarily through these retailers; there has been relatively little general advertising in magazines and newspapers over the manufacturers' names.

General advertising has been deemed a relatively inefficient and unprofitable form of promotion for the hosiery manufacturers distributing through a limited number of selected retailers, because in the keen competition with private brands and unbranded merchandise, advertising does not have sufficient influence to draw consumers to the relatively few selected retail outlets employed. The limited funds available for advertising accordingly have been largely directed to cooperative advertising over the retailers' names.

One manufacturer of silk hosiery, however, has continued to adver-

---

[10] It has been estimated that approximately 75% of the silk hosiery business of recent years has been carried on under the labels of retailers or on unbranded lines sold by them; only 25% has been sold under manufacturers' brands. Case of Reber Silk Hosiery Company, files of Harvard Business School.

tise extensively in general media, such as magazines and radio. Such advertising has been deemed wise in the marketing formula of this company because its distribution has been conducted not through selected retailers, but through house-to-house canvassers. It has used advertising primarily to pave the way for these salesmen and to increase the productivity of their efforts.

Another example of the effect of channels upon the utilization of advertising is found in the vacuum cleaner industry. Certain companies selling through regular retail channels employ considerable programs of consumer advertising. Other companies selling direct to housewives through canvassers employ relatively little consumer advertising and place almost the full burden on personal selling. Still another vacuum cleaner manufacturer was found who eliminated personal selling and relied entirely upon mail-order selling.

Advertising Utilization as Affected by Merchandising Policies

Basic merchandising policies usually determine whether a management can or cannot use advertising profitably. These merchandising policies govern matters of product form, quality, packaging, pricing, and related details that affect the segment of the market to which appeal may be made. A management must decide what market it wishes to reach, the sort of product needed to satisfy this market, and the kind of promotional policy that is essential to establish the product in that market. Different decisions involve different uses of advertising. For example, a New England textile manufacturer operating under conditions of relatively high manufacturing costs concluded that he could not profitably produce low-grade and medium-grade sheeting at the competitive prices that held for those grades. Accordingly he elected to use a skilled labor group and an experienced organization to produce a fine, high-count percale sheeting. He consciously set out to differentiate his product and to make it superior to the sheetings generally produced. In order to get a profitable volume of business, the management deemed it essential to make its brand widely known among consumers as a fine product, made for those wanting fine things. Prices were set high enough to allow margins needed for the building of this reputation. In this instance, profitable conduct of the enterprise depended upon the use of advertising.[11]

---

[11] Based on recorded interview with executives.

In contrast, many low-cost mills have found an opportunity to make a profit by going after business in the low-count sheeting field. To obtain a suitable volume of sales, consumer advertising has not been deemed an essential part of an operating program. The effect on volume of business to be obtained or on prices to be secured for low-count sheeting has not been great enough to justify an expenditure for such advertising. Rather, promotion to retailers by personal selling and trade advertising has been the selling method followed.

Again, a manufacturer of fountain pens faces a similar basic merchandising policy decision. He may choose to sell pens without benefit of reputation and without individualizing features at retail prices ranging from 20 cents to $3, depending upon quality. A number of fountain pen manufacturers, however, have striven to develop products of fine quality with individualizing features for which consumers have been willing to pay from $3 to $10. The marketing of pens within this price range, however, involves an operating formula entirely different from that used for the low-price pens. The high-price pen must bear a name recognized by consumers as standing for those characteristics found in high-grade pens. Manufacturers generally take the view that the attainment of such a reputation depends not only upon manufacturing a good product, but also upon spending considerable sums for advertising to establish the reputation. In a few instances, manufacturers of high-price pens have decided to make their bid for business with relatively little consumer advertising, relying instead on selected dealers, impelled by liberal margins, to persuade consumers to purchase their brands.

Considerations Governing Choices among Alternative Advertising Policies and Methods

In all the above illustrative situations it should be recognized that advertising is not an operating method to be considered as something apart, as something whose profit value to the enterprise is to be judged alone. An able management does not ask, "Shall we use or not use advertising?" without consideration of the product and of other management procedures to be employed. Rather the question is always one of finding a management formula giving advertising its due place in the combination of manufacturing methods, product form, pricing, promotion and selling methods, and distribution methods. As pointed out, different formulae, i.e., different combinations of methods, may be profitably employed by competing manufacturers.

The broad generalizations as to whether advertising will or will not be a profitable tool for a manufacturing enterprise become self-evident. They may be stated as follows:

(1) There must be a correct appraisal of what advertising is likely to accomplish in a particular operating formula. Alternative methods must be appraised.

(2) Effective use depends upon skillful building of advertisements correctly placed. Even a potentially profitable use of advertising can become unprofitable if the advertising space or radio time purchased is not skillfully and effectively employed to accomplish desired objectives. Effective execution requires a search for:

(a) Selling appeals most likely to influence those to whom advertisements are addressed.

(b) Techniques for effectively presenting the appeals to create the desired impression or to induce the desired action.

(c) The combination of size and frequency of advertisements that will produce the maximum effect from an expenditure.

(d) The most efficient media available, as judged on a basis of cost in relation to influence upon those addressed.

(3) Profitable use of advertising depends upon its proper coordination with the other marketing and merchandising elements of a program. If it is assumed that a profit-promising plan has been adopted and that skillful advertising in right amounts has been included therein, there is still need for seeing that all parts of the basic plan are well executed. Poor execution of any part of the program or failure to coordinate the parts may bring lack of success of the whole program. If advertising is to influence not only consumers but sales organizations and distributors as well, then the sales managers must make sure that the sales organizations and distributors are duly informed regarding the advertising and are led to time their selling and promotional efforts so as to maximize the selling effect of the program as a whole.

This outline of the broad conditions governing profitable use of advertising provides the topics for further discussion in this and the following chapter.

Need of Proper Appraisal of What Advertising Can Accomplish in Specific Situations

In applying the foregoing generalizations about profitable utilization of advertising, the manufacturer of a specific product begins with careful appraisal of ultimate demand for his product and of his chances of influencing that demand within required cost limitations. In studying this problem, he must consider the effect of advertising not only on consumers but also on those engaged personally in influencing and guiding consumer buying, namely, the company's own sales organization and its dealer organization. The appraisal calls for estimates of the possible effect of advertising upon the prices he can ask and the number of units he might sell at alternative prices. It involves a realistic study of the conditions governing demand, the competition met, the buying habits and attitudes of consumers and of the trade, and the chances of influencing those attitudes.

A study of the opportunity to influence consumer demand may be broken down into two parts: (a) that of stimulating primary demand, i.e., demand for the type of product, and (b) that of stimulating selective demand, i.e., demand for the product of the particular seller. This topic of demand, which involves analysis of the extent to which advertising can affect the price and sales volume of particular products and the reasons therefor, is one of the main topics dealt with in this study, and it is discussed at length in subsequent chapters. Accordingly, a detailed study of demand factors is reserved for those chapters; in this chapter are presented only a few examples of good and poor decisions by manufacturers in appraising what advertising might do profitably to stimulate the demand for their products. But the possible combinations of operating method involving advertising and the types of programs and conditions governing demand for different products which have to be appraised are so numerous that the few illustrations which can be given do not begin to span the wide range of issues met. They will serve, however, to bring out some of the more important guiding considerations which manufacturers must observe when judging whether advertising can profitably be used to influence demand; likewise, they will show the importance to them of right decisions. Attention is directed first to instances in which the problem of manufacturers is essentially one of appraising opportunity to stimulate primary demand, and then to cases where the task is that of appraising opportunity to stimulate selective demand.

Profitable Advertising Utilization as Related to Correct Appraisal of Opportunity to Stimulate Primary Demand

Clear examples of attempts to use advertising and other promotion to stimulate primary demand, i.e., demand for a type of product, occur when competing producers or sellers combine to advertise cooperatively. While such advertising has not played a relatively large part in the advertising picture, numerous cooperative campaigns have been undertaken in the last 20 years. A study of such campaigns has led to the conclusion that many have been of questionable value to the contributors.[12] The short duration of many of them is evidence of the lack of confidence which contributors have had in their effectiveness. In some instances, the lack of success undoubtedly should be attributed to poor execution of advertising and sales plans, to poor coordination between the selling and merchandising efforts of those involved, and to poor financing. The task of securing proper planning and coordination in cooperative campaigns is difficult as compared with that met in the campaigns of individual enterprises.

But ineffective planning and execution have not been the only reasons for ineffective expenditure. Equally if not more important in many instances has been the failure of those undertaking the programs to appraise properly the opportunity to stimulate the demand for the product through advertising. Advertising often has been assigned a task that it could not profitably perform. Accordingly, expenditures have outstripped any returns which might yield a profit. For example, the shoe industry in 1928 launched an ambitious program to increase the per capita consumption of men's shoes.[13] The program was abandoned after advertising had been carried on for about half the time planned. Comments made to the author by contributors to the campaign have provided further evidence of its lack of success. While numerous difficulties undoubtedly contributed to the failure of the campaign, a basic one was the failure to appraise the extent to which the proposed advertising could be expected to change men's attitudes regarding shoe usage and to induce them to spend a larger part of their income on shoes. Strong trends in living habits had operated to reduce shoe consumption, and the ideas to be conveyed through advertising were of questionable effectiveness in overcoming these influences.

---

[12] N. H. Borden, *Cooperative Advertising,* Harvard Business Reports, Vol. 11, (New York, McGraw-Hill Book Company, Inc., 1932).

[13] *Ibid.,* p. 105.

Other examples of promotional programs which, in the opinion of the author, presented questionable opportunity for expanding demand through cooperative advertising are those of the sterling silverware manufacturers during 1926–27 and the furniture industry, whose campaign ran in magazines over the name of "National Home Furnishings Program" during 1930 and 1931.

In contrast, there are numerous examples of programs undertaken by trade associations or by cooperative marketing associations which have been considered by contributors as successful in inducing profitable sales results. Among these are the campaigns carried on by the California Fruit Growers Exchange for citrus fruits [14] and those of the Portland Cement Association.[15]

Appraisal of Opportunity to Stimulate Primary Demand by Individual Manufacturers

Among individual manufacturers the extent to which advertising designed to expand primary demand succeeds is often very difficult to determine, because it is often accompanied by selective or competitive advertising and selling efforts. Not infrequently, however, when manufacturers attempt to increase sales by inducing consumers to accept their products for uses to which they are not ordinarily put, they clearly have had to appraise the chance to influence primary demand. Such has been the case, for example, when new product uses have been featured in efforts to overcome seasonality of sales, as when lemons have been advertised as a preventive of colds and as a beauty aid. In such situations failure to appraise properly the consumer's acceptance of and satisfaction with the product for any new use leads to unprofitable advertising and promotional expenditure.[16]

A clear example of an unprofitable advertising expenditure undertaken to stimulate primary demand was afforded some years ago by a manufacturer of Stillson wrenches, who attempted through an advertising campaign to increase the demand for his wrench among householders. He advertised it as "The handy tool about the home." Appreciable expenditures in general magazines, coupled with selling efforts through the trade, failed to bring a volume of business among home owners commensurate with the advertising cost. Promotional

---

[14] See Chapter VII.
[15] N. H. Borden, *Cooperative Advertising*, p. 150 ff.
[16] See Chapter XIX.

margin on units sold in the consumer market did not nearly equal advertising expenditures. The need for pipe wrenches among house-holders was not great enough to induce wide purchase. Moreover, since a wrench was a one-time purchase and did not involve a repetitive buying habit, the promotional plan was particularly ill-conceived in view of the weak appeals that could be made.[17] The type of case illustrates the common-sense conclusion that any effort to promote products of known worth to groups which have little need for such products is bound to be unprofitable and wasteful.

Another clear-cut example of unprofitable expenditure is found in the experience of a textile manufacturer who in the 1920's developed a new type of cotton webbing with strands of exposed rubber woven through it, for use in men's trousers as the curtain, the strip of fabric which forms the inside waistband of the trousers. The exposed rubber strands provided a sort of nonskid device to overcome what the adver-tisements referred to as "the sad problem of the bulgy shirt," that is, to keep the shirt down and the trousers up. Since the new fabric did not meet with ready acceptance by manufacturing tailors, the company undertook a program of advertising to consumers to induce them to buy the material to sew into trousers, and to lead them to accept and possibly specify that the trousers of new suits be equipped with the material. It was hoped that with such consumer acceptance manu-facturing tailors in time would widely adopt the new material. The company, however, failed to appraise properly the opportunity to stim-ulate a demand for the product. Consumers were not greatly troubled by bulging shirts or drooping trousers. Neither consumers nor the trade were influenced to buy. In a few months over $100,000 was spent in advertising; no appreciable volume of sales resulted.

Again, manufacturers face the problem of appraising their chances of stimulating primary demand when they launch products of an entirely new type upon the market. Consumers must be influenced to fill a new want or to meet an established want in a noncustomary way. New habits must be established; prejudices against the new and unknown must be broken down.[18] Aggressive selling is often essential if the expansion of demand is to be speeded up, but care must be exercised to keep the amount of advertising for these new products or

---

[17] N. H. Borden, *Problems in Advertising* (3d ed.), case of the Holmes Manufac-turing Company, p. 54.
[18] See discussion of introduction of mechanical refrigerators, Chapter XIV.

uses geared to the actual volume of sales which may be expected, if operating losses are to be avoided. For example, in recent years under conditions of lowered buying power, the difficulties met by manufacturers of air-conditioning equipment in inducing large sales of their product for homes represent a situation in which advertising expenditures have had to be carefully controlled and directed to avoid loss. For this new product expansion of demand would be aided by aggressive presentation of the merits of air conditioning, but it has been difficult to arouse desire for such a high-price item to the point where appreciable numbers of home owners would place its purchase ahead of the many other wants pressing in upon them. Here, as is often the case with introduction of new products, in order to avoid operating losses, manufacturers have had to keep promotional costs within the limits dictated by the small number of sales that they could induce.

A long list of examples might be cited of new products which have failed to gain a place in the market, even though appreciable amounts have been expended in advertising to bring consumer adoption. In some such instances it might be argued that more skillful management or more skillfully designed advertising might have brought the business ventures to profitable fruition. Still, many are the cases which failed from improper appraisal of the underlying need for the products and the want or desire that might be aroused for them among users. When improper appraisal is made of the opportunity to influence consumers, advertising and other selling expenditures are doomed to failure from a profit standpoint.

Profitable Advertising Utilization as Affected by Correct Appraisal of Opportunity to Establish a Selective Demand

While manufacturers always must keep in mind the primary demand for their product, ordinarily when appraising the opportunity to use advertising, they think in terms of selective demand. The great bulk of manufacturers' advertising is selective and is designed to secure or hold for the manufacturer his desired share of the existing market for the type of product advertised. But whether a manufacturer is using advertising to stimulate primary demand or selective demand, the question posed for him is the same: "Will the advertising help me to maintain or to increase sales volume at a profit?"

When appraising the effectiveness of advertising to build brand preference, the manufacturer usually must first be sure of two basic requirements: (1) there must be present in the product some differentiation which serves as a basis for consumer brand preference over similar products on the market; and (2) there must be present in appreciable degree opportunity to affect consumer valuations for the product through advertising and selling appeals. In other words, there must be action-compelling ideas which can be built into or associated with a brand, making it wanted above other brands lacking the association of such ideas.

Examples of manufacturers who have been successful in correctly appraising their opportunities to use advertising to stimulate a selective demand might be taken almost at random from the long lists of well-known advertised brands that have good profit records. Numerous instances are cited in later chapters. Since the purpose at this point is to center attention upon certain of the more important considerations involved in correct appraisal by manufacturers of their opportunities to stimulate a selective demand and to devise profitable operating programs, two cases are discussed in some detail, one dealing with a product which was successful in the market and the other with a product which was unsuccessful.

The soap powder Rinso is an example of a product for which a manufacturer judged correctly the chance to build a profitable demand with the aid of advertising. In this instance advertising was so important a part of the marketing program that it clearly can be credited with a large part of the sales success attained for the product. Detailed data regarding advertising costs and sales volume for several years after this product was put on the market are given in a later chapter.[19] It will suffice here merely to give an outline of important considerations involved in the appraisal. When Lever Brothers launched this product there were numerous laundry soaps and soap powders on the market. The soap market was a large one, however, since every family was a consumer. Since repeat purchases of housewives were relatively frequent, a brand which met with favor could be expected to enjoy a continuing demand. Moreover, the relatively new type of blown soap powder gave promise of being preferred by consumers for certain laundry uses. Clothes soaked in water containing the powder were effectively cleansed with less labor than was required with certain other types of laundry soap. Accordingly there was reason to believe that soap of this kind, whose virtues were effectively pre-

---

[19] See Chap. XVII.

sented to the public, might be expected to achieve a large volume of
sales. Before launching the product, however, the management had
to feel absolutely certain that the new soap compared favorably with
similar products on the market. Unless it gave satisfaction in use equal
to or greater than that given by competing products, there was little
reason to believe that repeat sales and a long-range profit could be
attained. Success depended upon continued patronage. The management believed the appeals to be strong enough to induce consumer
trial of the product, particularly in view of the fact that the cost of
a package was so low as to entail small price sacrifice on the part
of consumers.

Since certainty as to the quality of the product was vital to success,
the management undertook extensive preliminary tests to determine
whether consumers liked it, before embarking upon an extensive marketing effort. The management conducted tests also to be sure that
it had a selling and advertising program that would induce stocking
of the product by the trade and purchase by consumers. After the
preliminary product and selling tests had been made, the company
proceeded on a bold scale, risking large expenditures on the chance
that the product once known and used would attain and hold a volume
of sales that would be profitable. It chose to follow a type of operating
program employed for many leading soaps, namely, to place a heavy
selling burden upon advertising and to support this advertising with
an aggressive personal selling program. Advertising expenditures the
first year were over $500,000 and after the first year were in excess of
$1,000,000 a year.

Among the pricing alternatives open to the management, it chose
to price its product in line with directly competing brands. Such a
price gave a margin wide enough to support the heavy selling program,
provided consumers responded in sufficient number to its selling efforts,
and provided a substantial percentage of these purchasers continued
to buy.

Data given in Chapter XVII show [20] that the advertising and
other promotion were successful in inducing consumers to try the
product. Moreover, the fact that the product enjoyed a large volume of
repeat sales is evidenced by the growing sales volume, which rose from
less than 9,000,000 pounds in 1920 to 108,000,000 pounds in 1930.
Advertising costs were so heavy as related to sales during the first few

---

[20] See Chapter XVII, Table 111.

years that a profit showing was not possible, but rising volume thereafter brought the ratio of costs down to a point permitting profit. From
a long-range profit viewpoint the advertising expenditures had been
correctly appraised in the light of volume of sales and margins to be
attained with the help of the aggressive selling program.

In contrast to the above example of a correct appraisal of the
opportunity to stimulate a selective demand may be cited the case of
another soap product, which was unsuccessful. A New England manufacturer had an idea for a differentiated type of cleanser for household
use; it involved enclosing a cleaning powder in a sponge rubber
holder.[21] When wet, the powder was converted into a paste, which
oozed out the porous surface of the holder. In the opinion of the
inventor and of those who saw and used the product, it was an
effective, handy, and quick cleanser for mirrors, windows, bathtubs,
porcelain, and tile surfaces. Here was a new and individualized type
of product which, it was believed, would appeal to some users more
than other types of cleansers used for glass and porcelain surfaces.
The manufacturing cost was estimated to be five cents a unit.

The marketing situation faced by the management was as follows:
Numerous well-established soaps and cleansers suitable for washing
windows and mirrors were on the market, and most of them were
advertised. While the company's product was deemed by the management superior to competing products, it had the handicap of requiring
a noncustomary method of cleansing. In order to meet the established
competition and to overcome any consumer hesitance toward use of the
new methods, the management rightly decided that advertising and
promotion to consumers were essential. An approach to the trade alone
could not be taken. Unless the company induced at least a small
and persistent consumer demand for the product when exposed to
sale, the trade was not likely to handle it. Since expenditures for such
purposes had to be covered in the prices asked, any decision regarding
the use of advertising was accordingly inextricably bound up with the
decision regarding the price to ask for the product. It seemed clear
that a price giving a fairly wide margin was essential to give the
promotional margin needed. But price could not be increased at
will without affecting the number of units that could be sold. Just
what price could best be combined with the advertising costs in order

21 N. H. Borden, *Problems in Advertising* (3d ed.), case of The Expello Corporation, p. 75.

to maximize profits was hard to judge. Consumer behavior towards prices for such an article ordinarily reflects a complex of influences— the influence of customary price, of prices of competing soap products, and of opinions or attitudes as to the cost of the new product.

The company set a retail price of 15 cents on its rubber sponge cleaner and launched a marketing campaign in the New England area which included a program of aggressive personal selling among retailers and a $7,000 newspaper advertising campaign for consumers. A total promotional and advertising expenditure of some $10,000 was incurred in a six months' period. Sales for the period amounted to only $5,000. Distributors failed to reorder, stating that initial sales were slow and repeat sales few. The evidence of lack of repeat purchases by housewives at the price asked convinced the company that advertising would be ineffectual in inducing consumers to purchase the cleanser. The program was dropped. Another type of promotion, the use of store demonstrators, was tried, and although it proved to be more effective in inducing purchase, it was rejected as being too costly to promise a profitable result.

The failure of this venture in the grocery field may be attributed to a number of causes. The case illustrates clearly the importance of proper appraisal of the effectiveness of the combination of specific elements used in a marketing program, of which advertising is one. Since numerous variables were involved, numerous questions may be asked regarding the failure. For example, did the company get the maximum selling effectiveness from its expenditure of $7,000 for advertising space? Some advertising practitioners might have deemed the copy and space schedule which were used to be poorly designed.

In the next place, did the company expect too much from the advertising in view of the price asked? Was a 15-cent price high in view of the price of soap powders and other cleansers available? Would a reduction of price, even though it gave less margin for promotion and hence less for advertising to influence consumers, have brought a larger sales response than a price of 15 cents with the schedule of advertising employed?

Next, was the product itself satisfactory? It was different from other window cleansers, but did its differentiating features really satisfy customers? The fact that the product involved a new use habit probably made first sales difficult. The lack of substantial repeat sales, after initial sales were made, indicates, however, that the management probably overestimated the extent to which the product would satisfy consumers as compared with competing cleansers, particularly at a 15-cent price. Of course, unless such repurchase did occur, the heavy promotional costs of inducing initial sales could not possibly be recouped.

Again, was an adequate expenditure made to establish the product in the market? It was entering into a field where competition was keen and where well-intrenched products were supported by considerable advertising and promotional expenditure. Here was a situation in which the product not only had to be satisfactory and pleasing to users when compared with other products, but probably had to have a considerable amount of publicity to make it appear worthy of consideration. The management relied on small-space advertisements (70 lines) appearing approximately twice a week for six months. While case reports indicate successful launching of grocery and drug products on a small scale with schedules no larger than this, it must be recognized that no great impression on public consciousness is likely to be made with such a schedule. Another company, which subsequently successfully launched a different type of window cleanser, employed in its introductory program some 10,000 lines of newspaper advertising as compared with the 3,000 lines used by the company described above.[22] The successful company's advertisements ranged in size from 600 lines down to 112 lines, as compared with the small 70-line advertisements used for the sponge rubber cleaner. An expenditure of larger size involved a considerable risk, of course. It meant that every market opened would show an operating loss which could be recouped only after sales had been gradually built up to a point where promotional costs were covered by aggregate margins. In the light of this second window cleanser case it may be argued that the marketing failure of the sponge rubber cleaner might possibly be attributed, in part at least, to the company's failure to risk more on its initial advertising program. There is little doubt, however, that the lack of suitability of the product to consumers was the decisive factor in the lack of success. The lack of repeat purchases was the main reason for giving up the effort. No matter how much the company might have spent, there is little reason to believe that the venture would have been profitable.

The case illustrates that a management in its appraisal of marketing opportunity must study carefully the wants of people, the ability

[22] *Ibid.*, case of Athena Corporation, p. 262.

of its product to give satisfaction as compared with competing products, the strength of the appeals that it can employ, the price that it can charge, the probable influence of advertising in gaining and holding sales for the product, the probable effectiveness of specific advertisements and schedules, and the amount of promotional costs which it can risk.

While the above cases indicate some of the fundamental issues with which manufacturers must deal when appraising their opportunities to influence selective demand, they do not cover the wide range of problems met in such appraisals. For example, these cases deal with an appraisal of advertising utilization for single, differentiated products. Often manufacturers face the issue of whether it might be desirable to promote a considerable number of items under a "family" trade-mark. This method of promotion is likely to be used when all or a considerable share of the items produced lack differentiating elements which might be promising as the basis for individual promotional programs for each, or where promised volume of sales from single items evidently would not support a separate program. The question then posed is whether the advertising and promotional expenditure to build a reputation for the group of items will be conducive to a profitable result. Again, the two cases do not show the problems met by an organization in appraising the value of so-called "institutional" advertising, which is designed to build attitudes toward the advertiser's organization and the services he offers which will attract patronage for all his products.[23]

---

[23] In institutional advertising the advertiser seeks not to build mental associations about the products he sells but to establish in the minds of consumers attitudes toward the advertiser's organization, or institution. Such advertising is sometimes undertaken to help a company solve a public relations problem by conveying ideas regarding its contribution to economic and social welfare. It may be undertaken sometimes to improve morale among the employees of an organization. Interest in such advertising in this study, however, relates primarily to its use to induce patronage, for the ideas presented ordinarily are appeals to patronage motives.

A patronage motive is the reason or incentive impelling a buyer to trade with a particular firm in preference to patronizing other firms which offer similar commodities. Developed in institutional advertisements are ideas relating to the extensive research conducted by a company which connotes dependability of product; the consumer research undertaken which promises wantable merchandise; the long life and reputation for integrity which leads one to expect honesty in product and fair dealing; the variety of merchandise offered for selection; and the ability of the advertiser to give prompt delivery, to provide dependable repair service, to offer courteous, friendly employees, and so on.

The specialized institutional campaign is used most frequently by large organizations rather than small; by service organizations such as railroads, public utilities, and hotels, to a greater extent than by product manufacturing organizations; and among product manufacturing organizations largely by those whose products require technical skill and extensive research to keep in the van in a fast moving technological world. Among the

The two cases cited, furthermore, do not show the wide range of effectiveness of advertising for stimulating selective demand for various products. That the opportunities to influence brand preferences vary widely has already been mentioned. Since such differences will be made the subject of intensive study in the chapters on demand, further cases are not discussed at this point. These variations apply to products ranging from proprietary remedies and certain cosmetics, on the one hand, to staple groceries and certain industrial products, on the other hand. In the former cases, those who aggressively market under their own brands to consumers are likely to conclude that a heavy expenditure for advertising is essential if they are to develop a considerable volume of sales for their products. In the latter cases, even when advertising is used, the amount which can be expended is a relatively small percentage of sales, because advertising is not effective in influencing consumer purchases. Such variations in advertising effectiveness must be correctly judged by the advertiser.

The cases discussed above are sufficient to show the need of realistic appraisal of alternative programs if a manufacturer is to stimulate selective demand at a profit. Attention may be turned now to the bearing of skills in advertising technique upon profitable utilization of advertising.

Profitable Utilization as Affected by Skill in Advertising Techniques

Skill in techniques, such as is involved in building advertisements, in selecting media, and in planning size and frequency of insertion, has already been named as an essential to effective and profitable utilization of advertising. In the case of the window cleanser cited above, it was recognized that possible reasons for failure may have been the ineffectiveness of the advertising messages used and inadequacy of the space schedule employed. Dollars buy space in media, but the message in the space is what influences consumers' behavior.

The wide variation in effectiveness of advertising copy is generally

---

more extensive institutional campaigns of manufacturers have been those of General Motors Corporation, General Electric Company, Westinghouse Electric & Manufacturing Company, Parke, Davis & Company, and E. R. Squibb & Sons. Among service organizations, institutional advertisers have included railroads, hotels, insurance companies, and public utilities.

Whereas specialized institutional campaigns are relatively infrequent among product manufacturers, such advertisers often weave patronage appeals into their product advertising. Thus institutional attitudes akin to those arising from specialized campaigns may be established over a period of time.

recognized among advertisers and accounts for the recent intensification of almost 40 years of effort to develop copy testing techniques which would enable the advertiser to get greater return for his advertising dollars. Only mail-order advertisers have an accurate basis for measurement of the actual sales return from advertising effort. Most measurements of advertising effectiveness must rest on evidence short of actual sales or profit value from the expenditure. A few examples will serve, however, to illustrate the wide variation in the sales effectiveness of advertisements or at least in attention given to them.

Rudolph, in the preface of his study of inquiries from magazine advertising, gives the following generalization: "When measured in terms of keyed response or actual, traceable sales, it is not uncommon for different advertisements to vary as much as 300 per cent in effectiveness." [24] Starch, in various writings, has pointed out the widely varying difference in effectiveness of advertisements, as in the following statement:

Few business concerns fully realize the literally enormous differences in the effectiveness of the various advertisements in any given series or campaign. They are not aware of it because the great majority of businesses have no direct way of ascertaining the actual effectiveness or lack of effectiveness of any given advertisement or even of a series of advertisements.

To illustrate this point, let us note the following actual cases:

Of a series of fifteen advertisements for a player piano, the best one brought 258 replies, while the poorest one brought one reply. The other thirteen advertisements brought returns scattered all the way between these two extremes . . .

Of a series of five lathe advertisements, the best one brought 40 times as many inquiries as the poorest one.

Of a series of eight advertisements of a book sold entirely by mail, the best advertisement sold three times as many copies as the poorest one, differences in seasons and mediums being considered.[25]

In their tests of the consumer opinion method of testing advertisements, Borden and Lovekin[26] secured 16 series of advertisements from advertisers, for which response in sales or in inquiries closely related to sales response gave clear statistical evidence of variation in effectiveness traceable to copy alone; in numerous instances certain advertisements in a series produced over three times as many returns as others.

[24] H. J. Rudolph, *Four Million Inquiries from Magazine Advertising* (New York, Columbia University Press, 1936), p. 7.

[25] Daniel Starch, *op. cit.,* p. 306.

[26] N. H. Borden and O. S. Lovekin, *A Test of the Consumer Jury Method of Ranking Advertisements* (Harvard Business School, Division of Research, Business Research Studies, No. 11, 1935).

Among published data relating to specific advertisers, the inquiry costs of the California Walnut Growers Association [27] indicate the wide variation in advertisements in attracting readers and in inducing inquiry for the offer made. During the period 1927–1935, when the recipe booklet offered in advertisements was much the same, the cost per inquiry varied from $70 down to 33 cents. In the 1929–1930 season alone there was a variation from $26 to 46 cents. While these inquiry costs do not provide conclusive evidence of sales effectiveness of the advertisements run, yet the extreme variation in inquiries undoubtedly reflects a wide variation in the ability of advertisements to attract consumer interest and reading. This variation was the result largely of differences in copy, in media, and in season of advertising, although other variables affecting inquiry also were involved.

Further evidence as to the variation in the interest of readers in advertisements is available in reader survey reports. In the case of the California Walnut Growers Association, the percentage of observation and reading of advertisements was obtained from a magazine reader survey service. This service extended the ratios of observation and reading obtained from its sample surveys to total magazine circulations and then computed for individual advertisements figures of costs per time each advertisement had been "seen" "read some," and "read most." For the year 1933–1934, the costs per time "seen" for California walnut advertisements ranged from .27 cents to .91 cents, while the costs per time "read most" for these advertisements varied during the same season from 1.21 cents to 8.04 cents.

To cite an example from another research study, in which ratings were based merely on a percentage of observers and readers found in the samples surveyed, an advertiser found that a certain type of copy had been observed by 24% of the magazine readers surveyed. By changing his copy approach, he secured an observation from 58% of the magazine readers.[28] A tooth paste manufacturer whose copy in one type of advertisement was found to be read by only 1% of the readers of a magazine, raised the percentage of reading by changing to comic-strip type of copy, getting a 75% reading of the comic strip and a 12% reading of the body copy.[28]

---

[27] H. C. Hensley and N. H. Borden, *Marketing Policies of the California Walnut Growers Association* (Washington, Farm Credit Administration, Cooperative Division, 1937), Bulletin No. 10.

[28] *The Clark Magazine Advertisement Service—Its Purpose and Use* (New York L. M. Clark, Inc.).

Such evidence regarding the variation in the effectiveness of adver-tisements might be multiplied many times over. As stated previously, except for the mail-order field, where sales results are traceable to advertisements, the evidence regarding sales or profit effectiveness of advertisements is not final; yet the variations in reader interest shown by inquiry returns and reader surveys are often so wide as to give a clear presumption of variation in sales effectiveness.

The more important a part advertising plays in affecting consumer valuations and in inducing buying action in any marketing venture, the more important it is from the standpoint of success of the venture that the advertising be effective. For concerns selling products such as soap, breakfast foods, dentifrices, and numerous proprietary rem-edies, sales volume depends so much upon advertising that effective and able presentations of advertising may to a considerable degree determine the profitability of the enterprise. In contrast, ineffective advertising of sugar, while undesirable, would not be nearly so hurtful to the business venture because it plays relatively so small a part in the whole operating picture.

Importance of Media Selection to Profitable Utilization of Advertising

An important part of advertising and marketing technique is the careful definition of markets for a product and the selection of media which will reach these markets economically and effectively. That improper selection of media may lead to unprofitable advertising expen-diture is axiomatic among advertising practitioners. Fundamental from a profit standpoint is the selection of media which will reach pros-pects who can readily be induced to buy, because advertising addressed to poor prospects entails high costs. But even when competing peri-odicals ostensibly reach the right people for a particular advertiser, there still may be a marked difference in their advertising effectiveness, because of differences in the extent to which subscribers read the period-icals and the varying interest aroused for different products by the editorial contents and by the physical setting which advertisements are given.[29] Involved also is the difficult problem of appraising the relative effectiveness of different types of media for different products.[30]

[29] For a general discussion of problems involved in media selection, see H. E. Agnew and W. B. Dygert, *Advertising Media* (New York, McGraw-Hill Book Company, Inc., 1938). See also:
McCall Corporation, *A Qualitative Study of Magazines—Who Reads Them and Why* (a continuing study inaugurated in October, 1939).

Examples of possible waste involved in selection of media could be multiplied. They are brought into clearest focus in mail-order advertising or in advertising designed to get sales leads, for here the variation in cost of getting sales can be traced to particular media. As examples, the following cases may be cited:

A company selling vacuum cleaners on a mail-order basis found that it could secure sales through advertising in newspapers in cities near its factory at a much lower cost than in magazines. In turn it discovered, however, that sales through newspapers in cities distant from its factory could be made only at high cost.[31]

The Parker-Kalon Company, which sold self-tapping screws and bolts, found one year that the average cost per inquiry for trade and industrial journal advertising was $30; for carefully directed mail, approximately $7; and for a campaign in a weekly magazine of general circulation, $100 for desirable inquiries.[32]

The Dennison Manufacturing Company conducted an extensive survey among women who had written in for booklets on paper craft offered in the company's advertising in order to learn, as far as possible, the amount of sales induced by these booklets. An analysis of inquiry data and of the sales information obtained from the survey, while not conclusive, indicated not only that costs of traceable inquiries varied widely between media, but also that there was a large variation in the quality of inquirers as purchasers of Dennison products. For example, not only did publications whose circulation was primarily in small towns and rural areas produce inquiries at a relatively high cost, but those who wrote for the booklets subsequently bought a relatively small amount of Dennison products.[33]

Among direct-mail advertisers the importance of building a mailing list of responsive prospects is regarded as fundamental. Efficient mail-order companies using direct mail as one of their media ordinarily carry on extensive mailings only after preliminary sampling tests of

Life's Continuing Study of Magazine Audiences (Time Incorporated), Report No. 1, December 1, 1938; No. 2, May 1, 1939; No. 3, January 1, 1940; No. 4, September 1, 1940.

P. B. West, *Circulation Analysis*. Bulletin of the Association of National Advertisers, 1931. Advertising Research Foundation, *The Continuing Study of Newspaper Reading* (New York, Inaugurated—June, 1939).

[30] For a case showing the analysis of one large advertiser in attempting to appraise the effectiveness of different types of media, see N. H. Borden, *Problems in Advertising* (3d ed.), case of California Fruit Growers Exchange, p. 581.

[31] *Ibid.*, case of Rand Company, p. 134.

[32] *Ibid.*, case of Parker-Kalon Company, p. 645.

[33] *Ibid.*, case of Dennison Manufacturing Company, p. 458.

their lists give assurance of profitable returns.[34] Illustrative of the importance of proper compilation of lists is the case of the Harvard Economic Service in selling its *Review of Economic Statistics*. Analysis of its mailing results indicated that it could sell profitably on the average only to companies with an estimated net worth in excess of $300,000. Mail campaigns addressed to lists of companies of lower net worth induced sales at costs of two to three times the maximum amount deemed allowable by the management.[35]

While such variation in the effectiveness of different media can be measured by companies which can trace sales or sales-producing inquiries to particular advertisements, as in the examples above, it follows, however, that variation in media effectiveness applies as well to advertisers employing indirect action advertising, particularly when their markets are selective or thin. Even direct-action advertisers vary widely in the care and skill with which they analyze their inquiries and delimit their markets. The far greater difficulty met by indirect-action advertisers of measuring effectiveness of media undoubtedly leads many to employ media of questionable effectiveness for them.

Discussion of further problems involving advertising techniques is not necessary to indicate their importance for effective utilization of advertising. It matters not whether the differences in effectiveness are attributable to copy, to the media in which advertisements are placed, to the season of placement, to size of advertisement, to the frequency of repetition, to use of color as against black and white, or to other variables under control of the advertiser. The variation shows the importance of employing proper techniques in order to secure effective and consequently profitable use of advertising.

Profitable Utilization of Advertising as Affected by Skill in Coordinating the Elements of a Selling Campaign

Profitable utilization of advertising requires not only a marketing plan offering profit possibilities and effective advertisements well placed, but also skillful coordination among the various elements in the execution of the marketing plan. The reason for coordination is

[34] J. K. Crippen, *Successful Direct-Mail Methods* (New York, McGraw-Hill Book Company, Inc., 1936), ch. 8–9.

C. R. Greer, *Advertising and Its Mechanical Production* (New York, Thomas Y. Crowell Company, 1931).

E. B. Pope, "At Last! A Formula for Determining Size of Mailing List Tests," *Printers' Ink*, October 20, 1939, p. 17.

[35] N. H. Borden, *Problems in Advertising* (3d ed.), case of Harvard Economic Service, p. 65.

evident; each kind of advertising used is but one element in an entire program designed to bring about sales. Full effectiveness of the selling program is attained only when the various parts are properly meshed. The task of coordination involves, first of all, the proper timing and execution of whatever kinds of advertising may be needed in a program, such as advertising directed to consumers through consumer media, advertising directed to the trade, dealer cooperative advertising, and point-of-purchase display. It includes also establishment of a correct relationship between advertising and other types of promotional effort and between advertising and personal selling efforts not only of the company's salesforce but also of distributors and of their salespeople.

The need of coordination of advertising with other selling methods is heightened by the fact that in most manufacturers' selling programs advertising is largely indirect in its action. The general consumer advertising of manufacturers through periodicals, posters, or radio in a high percentage of instances is not designed to consummate sales immediately, as is true, for example, of mail-order advertising. Whereas the mail-order advertisement is a selling document, complete enough in itself to induce immediate action by the consumer either in the form of placing an order or that of seeking additional information before placing an order, the usual manufacturer's advertisement is indirect. An indirect action advertisement is one designed not to induce immediate response of some kind on the part of the reader, but to build mental associations or beliefs regarding the product, with the hope that some later stimulus will lead to desired buying action.[36]

Manufacturers' Need for Direct Stimuli in Their Selling Programs

Since their advertising is generally indirect in action, manufacturers strive to provide in their selling campaigns the stimulus needed

---

[36] Manufacturers' brand advertisements often involve a strategy designed to get some immediate consumer response to an advertisement or an action quicker than ordinarily might be had from a purely indirect action advertisement. Examples of such strategy are the coupon, the premium, and the contest. These direct-action methods in themselves present interesting questions as to their long-range selling effectiveness. They also usually must be carefully coordinated with other selling efforts. Although the use of such techniques by manufacturers has increased in recent years, by and large space advertising may be characterized as predominantly indirect in character.

See also:

E. T. Gundlach, *Facts and Fetishes in Advertising* (Chicago, Consolidated Book Publishers, Inc., 1931), ch. 14, 15, 16.

E. T. Gundlach, "Coupons in Advertising," *Printers' Ink,* December 17, 1936, p. 96.

N. H. Borden, "Problems for Premium Users," *Printers' Ink Monthly,* August, 1936.

H. L. Hansen, "Premium Merchandising," *Harvard Business Review,* Winter, 1941, p. 185.

to bring consummation of sales. This stimulus ordinarily becomes effective when the consumer actually is in the market place to buy. The impression made by advertising sometimes is strong enough to lead to recall when the consumer is making up a shopping list or when he is in a store to buy a product for which he has a need. Often, however, the subsequent urge may come from some further stimulus supplied by the advertiser or the storekeeper. Of such direct-action stimuli there are several, some of which are to be classed as personal selling; some of which are advertising. They include (1) direct action advertising by retailers in newspapers, mail, or other media; (2) display of product at or near the point of purchase; (3) display of poster or dealer help materials at or near the point of purchase; (4) salesmen's suggestions in the retail store; (5) demonstration within the retail store; (6) actual sales solicitation of customers in their homes.

For most products the need for one or more of these stimuli as part of a complete promotional campaign means that manufacturers must rely upon and try to secure cooperation from retailers. Some products are so nearly unique and the advertising appeals employed for them are so strong that they can be pulled through the retailer with little or no active cooperation on his part. Such is the case with proprietary remedies; soaps; highly individualized grocery specialties, such as breakfast foods and coffee substitutes; and cosmetics. But even those brands enjoying the strongest of pulls through consumer requests for specific brands can have their sales greatly curtailed through lack of dealer support at the point of purchase. Whenever display is denied a product and active efforts are made by retailers to effect substitution,[37] sales of a product can be materially reduced, even though the dealer carries it in stock. Accordingly, most manufacturers, even when they have a strong pull resulting from space advertising, strive at the same time to get active dealer support in the stocking and display of products, in the use of counter and window displays, in the offering of selling suggestions by sales clerks, and in the mention of products in the retailer's direct-action advertising.

The need for dealer cooperation in stocking a product and in point-

---

[37] For examples of the ability of retailers to affect the sales of proprietary remedies and cosmetics, see *Price Control under Fair Trade Legislation,* by E. T. Grether (New York, Oxford University Press, 1939), ch. IV. Dealer alienation resulting from price cutting of well-known brands has been an important factor in leading certain manufacturers to support price maintenance legislation.

of-purchase effort accounts in large part for the increased amount of missionary work and direct selling to retailers that has developed among advertising manufacturers in the past two decades. The large number of products carried by wholesalers has led to a passive attitude in selling manufacturers' brands to retailers. Accordingly manufacturers have sent their own salesmen to retailers to take orders for wholesalers' accounts. The chief task of these missionary men, however, is to keep alive retailer interest in the product, generally to get him to install or permit installation of a product display, and sometimes to secure his cooperation in special promotional efforts, such as may be involved in a premium offer or a special sales plan.

Different products call for different combinations of the various types of advertising and selling efforts to induce final sale. The sale of some products, so-called "impulse" items, is especially subject to increase through good display and through use of point-of-purchase signs. For example, display is particularly effective with a product such as candy,[38] the more sight of which is likely to excite the salivary glands, with resultant impulse to buy. Neckties, inexpensive jewelry, and perfumes are other products for which display is advantageous. Manufacturers of such products selling under their own brands will strive to get dealer cooperation in display efforts, and a considerable part of their promotional expenditure will be directed to this end. So-called missionary or specialty salesmen loom large in their marketing budgets. In sharp contrast, the manufacturer of a proprietary remedy[39] will devote most of his effort to space advertising in various media wherein he can present at length consumer health problems to which his product will offer a solution, relying upon the strength of the appeal to lead to actual request for the product when the consumer goes to market. But even for him, display is to be desired. Between the extremes of candy, on the one hand, and proprietary remedies, on the other hand, different products have different combinations of the various types of selling effort devoted to them in order to secure completion of sale.

For products in the high-price ranges, the manufacturer selling under his own brand is especially dependent upon the personal selling and advertising efforts of his retail representatives. While advertising

---

[38] See N. H. Borden, *Problems in Advertising* (3d ed.), case of Carmen Chocolate Company, p. 140.
[39] *Ibid.*, case of Lydia E. Pinkham Medicine Company, p. 103.

may arouse consumers' desire for the type of product and may help to build a brand reputation, personal salesmanship plays a relatively important part in the consummation of sales. Accordingly for those products of high price for which selected distribution is used, the manufacturer seeks as far as possible to make the retailer essentially his sales representative to consumers. For such products the manufacturer's selling is ordinarily either direct to the retailer or through exclusive wholesale distributors, selling methods which permit development of close cooperation in promotional efforts. He often goes to considerable lengths in offering to his retailers advertising, selling, and display procedures which he has found from comparative study to be effective. It is highly desirable to him that retailers cooperate in carrying out his plan.

Problems Met by Manufacturers in Securing Desired Coordination for Products Requiring Dense Distribution

Although coordination between advertising and the other parts of the selling program is essential to attainment of best sales results, it is often hard to secure, especially full coordination between personal selling and advertising. Since the coordination problems met in cases of products requiring dense retail distribution are quite different from those of products for which selected distribution is employed, the two are discussed separately in the order named.

For branded products of low price for which consumers desire and expect convenience in their buying, practically complete distribution among stores handling the type of product is a much-desired objective. It is essential if full potential sales are to be attained. Moreover, only with wide distribution can general indirect action advertising (i.e., product reputation advertising) be fully effective. Without good distribution, possible brand sales are lost; advertising influence is lost.

For only a relatively few products is the pull of advertising upon consumers strong enough to force retailers to handle them. Generally manufacturers must carry on personal selling and promotional work among retailers, so far as their gross margins permit. The marketing plan adopted by a management should recognize the sales value of dealer work; the execution of a plan should aim to accomplish the objective of obtaining stocking and display so far as this is feasible. Yet frequently the personal selling force may be charged with failure to do well its allotted part in gaining distribution and the needed point-of-purchase selling effort, without which advertising expenditure is rendered ineffective.

To cite a clear example, which involved the launching of a new household product, the plan adopted called for the usual missionary work in various city markets in advance of the launching of advertising and promotional efforts. The missionary selling force employed to carry out the project in certain cities was inadequate, however, and at the time the advertising started, less than one-third of the independent retailers and no chain stores had been canvassed to stock the product, although chain stores accounted for over 50% of grocery sales. It should be recognized that the small volume of sales secured by a large percentage of grocers would make it advisable for a manufacturer to limit his coverage of retailers to those whose probable sales would warrant the expense of a call. Yet release of advertising to consumers with such incomplete distribution as was attained resulted in wasted advertising effort.

Other case material studied, as well as discussions with sales executives in the field, has indicated that similar lapses in sales management may be charged with reducing the effectiveness of sales plans and hence with rendering advertising partially ineffective, not only for new products but for products long upon the market.

Closely allied to the question of inducing stocking of a product is the problem of securing the needed point-of-purchase display to accompany general advertising. Almost invariably manufacturers who sell convenience products under their own brands furnish window and counter display material. Among advertisers, however, it is recognized that such material often involves ineffective expenditure. This ineffectiveness may arise first from the lack of immediate selling power of the display itself; secondly, from the loss of sales which a manufacturer suffers when he fails to get needed point-of-purchase advertising used at the proper time; thirdly, from non-use of printed material supplied to retailers. A considerable literature has developed relating not only to the designing of purchase display material, but to the problems involved in bringing about its effective use.[40]

A further cause of ineffectiveness in the marketing of convenience

[40] For example, see:

Michael Gross, *Dealer Display Advertising* (New York, The Ronald Press Company, 1936).

W. H. Leahy, *Window Display for Profit* (New York, Harper & Brothers, 1931).

Metropolitan Life Insurance Company, Policyholders' Service Bureau, *Reducing Waste of Dealer-Helps* (New York, 1932).

type products arises from poor administration of advertising allowances. For example, a marketing cooperative selling a fruit product with distribution through brokers and thence through regular grocery channels relied for its brand promotion on a thin schedule of magazine advertising, with a great share of its advertising appropriation allotted to retailers in the form of allowance for advertising and promotional effort to be carried on by them. Full effectiveness of the plan required that the management check and control the advertising conducted by the retailers given allowances. In this case, however, as has been found to be true in many other instances where such allowances have been made, effective use of and proper accounting for allowances was not secured. Investigation indicated that the management got small promotional effort from many of the allowances given. Special studies of considerable magnitude which have been made of advertising allowance practice indicate that the wastes attending their use have often been large.[41]

Problems of Securing Coordination for Products Given Selective Distribution

From these comments regarding coordination problems attending the selling of convenience type products, attention is directed to difficulties in coordination met by manufacturers whose products are given selected distribution, i.e., sale through only one or a few chosen stores in each locality. Selected distribution applies particularly to high-price specialty products sold under manufacturers' brands.

When distribution is limited to selected outlets, it is particularly important for manufacturers to secure active promotional and selling effort from the selected dealers. Lack of wide exposure of a manufacturer's brand to sale must be compensated for by zeal on the part of the selected retailers to attract patronage for the brand to their establishments. In such cases the manufacturer, if he is to attain maximum sales for his brand, cannot afford to be passive regarding his dealer selling and promotional efforts. He must make certain that his selected dealers are known in the community and that they employ aggressive direct selling effort, both advertising and personal. The manufacturer is likely to divide his advertising appropriation, using

---

[41] For further discussion of advertising allowances, see:

L. C. Lockley, *Vertical Cooperative Advertising* (New York, McGraw-Hill Book Company, Inc., 1931).

L. S. Lyon, *Advertising Allowances* (Washington, The Brookings Institution, 1932).

part of it in indirect action advertising over his own name, to build brand reputation, and part of it for advertising over the dealer's name, largely for the purpose of making the local sources of supply known and to attract immediate purchasers to these local sources.

Three types of perplexing and difficult problems having to do with coordination are met by manufacturers using selected distribution: first, to devise a marketing plan which provides an optimum division between advertising and personal selling expenditures; secondly, to apportion advertising expenditures most productively between general reputation advertising and advertising directed through retailers; and third to secure fully effective execution of the plan by salesforce, wholesale distributors, and retailers. Involved also is the problem of how best to arouse their interest, enthusiasm, and cooperation in the selling plan.

Among many cases of selected distribution studied, wide variations in marketing plans were found, even among manufacturers of similar products with similar distribution and brand policies. For example, some manufacturers apportioned a relatively small part of their marketing appropriation to advertising, devoting their efforts mostly to personal selling, while other manufacturers followed the opposite policy. In the division of the advertising appropriation, some manufacturers devoted a large part to brand reputation advertising placed in general media over their own names with little or no allowance for advertising over dealers' names. Others reversed this procedure and directed the major share of their appropriation through their dealers. In some instances dealers contributed heavily to advertising of the manufacturers' brands; in other instances they spent little. Analysis of the cases and discussion of the varying practices with the managements employing them frequently revealed uncertainty on their part regarding the relative value of alternative plans open to them. There are reasonable operating hypotheses to justify many of the variations found among the programs of these manufacturers. Difference in plans such as mentioned above may stem from differences in the strength of product appeals, the number of selected dealers employed in localities, the gross margins granted dealers, the size of operations, and the length of the lines sold.

A detailed analysis of these cases, however, to determine possible principles governing selection among alternative marketing plans is

not a purpose of this study.[42] The point of interest here is the conclusion that there was a wide variation in the effectiveness of the sales
plans adopted and in the skill with which they were executed. For
example, the relatively large share of appropriations devoted to general reputation advertising over the manufacturers' names by certain
manufacturers of women's hosiery and of paint appeared questionable,
in view of the limited advertising appropriations at the disposal of
the managements. In these instances the pull that could be exerted by
general advertising did not appear to have been great enough to attract
consumers to the stores of the selected dealers. The large share of the
appropriation given to general advertising, moreover, left little to be
expended upon advertising through dealers. Accordingly, proper provision was not made for them to become known as sources of the
manufacturers' brands in their communities or to carry through direct
action advertising and promotion over their names. This lack of provision for proper coordination in the plans resulted in lack of sales
productiveness.

In another case the management of a tire comany had taken a
passive attitude toward the promotional and advertising effort carried
on through dealers. In its advertising, emphasis was directed largely
to the building of reputation through general advertising. Although
the company offered to supply advertising helps to its dealers and to
contribute to local advertising over the dealers' names, the management did not actively seek such cooperation and, consequently, the
selling force did not secure adequate cooperation from many of its
exclusive agency dealers in carrying out such efforts. As a result,
relatively few consumers in many communities knew where to buy the
product. Moreover, in such communities the tire was not so well
known as in communities where effective cooperation with retailers had
been secured by the selling force. The facts to support this conclusion
were developed in an investigation conducted in some 270 cities and
towns among approximately 25,000 people.

Further examples are not needed to illustrate the difficulties met
by manufacturers using selected distribution in setting up properly
coordinated marketing plans and in securing care in their execution.
Those cited show the importance of proper coordination to profitable
utilization of advertising.

[42] Critical analysis of a group of 17 cases dealing with this issue will be found in
the doctoral thesis of Mr. James D. Scott, in the files of the Harvard Business School
Library.

Problems of Securing Needed Coordination in Cooperative Campaigns

Comment has already been made upon the fact that many advertising campaigns carried on cooperatively among competitors are reduced in effectiveness because the advertising is not carefully coordinated with the selling efforts of the individual manufacturers engaged in the campaign. Frequently in such campaigns the individual managements are not cognizant of the need of making their own advertising and selling efforts fit closely with the selling effort of the cooperative advertising if maximum results are to be attained.

In a case study of cooperative advertising campaigns by competitors made by the author, the common occurrence of faulty coordination led him to make the following comment in the introduction of the volume in which the cases were presented:

One of the greatest causes of ineffectiveness of cooperative promotional and advertising programs lies in the difficulty of securing effective coordination between the selling and advertising activities of the individual companies and the association activities. It is unnecessary here more than to mention the importance of planning and carrying through a fully coordinated program of advertising and selling efforts. In several of the commentaries I have dealt with the topic at considerable length. If, when an association launches an advertising program of merely an educational sort, cooperating firms sit back and expect wonders from it, they are doomed to disappointment. When an individual company undertakes advertising, it expects the advertising to be merely a part of a complete program of selling and promotional strategy. Not advertising alone, but a coordinated program of selling efforts, produces results. If each part of a selling campaign is not carefully thought out in relation to other parts, ineffectiveness is likely to be the outcome. Too frequently, cooperative programs have not been carefully enough devised with the ultimate objective of sales in mind. And often even a well-constructed plan has fallen through because of the failure of the cooperating firms properly to do their part. Such effectiveness as some association campaigns have attained, as in the case of the American Paint and Varnish Manufacturers Association, seems to have come not so much from the advertising by the association as from the stimulation of more aggressive selling by all factors in the industry. The maintenance of active interest and cooperation is essential.[43]

THE UTILIZATION OF ADVERTISING BY RETAILERS

The discussion thus far in this chapter has been devoted to the considerations governing utilization of advertising by manufacturers. The

---

[43] N. H. Borden, *Cooperative Advertising, op. cit.*, p. 25.

difficulties of appraising consumer and distributor response to alternative methods of promoting and marketing products have been outlined. In turn the importance from a profit standpoint of skill in the use of advertising techniques and in the execution and coordination of programs has been indicated. Attention is now directed to the utilization of advertising by retailers, the objectives and methods of which, on the whole, are in contrast to those of manufacturers' brand advertising.[44]

The main purpose of most retail advertising is to attract customers to a store and to create traffic within the store, the hypothesis being that such traffic leads to sales and that sales well made bring continued patronage. Consequently the space advertising of retailers is predominantly direct action in character, in contrast to the indirect action methods typical of the space advertising of manufacturers. Generally the retailer's advertisement says, "Here is certain merchandise at a price; come and get it." For example, probably 80% to 90% of department store advertisements are designed primarily to attract people to the store at the time the advertisement appears. This fact accounts for the common practices among such stores of advertising special promotions and of using comparative prices in their advertisements as a most effective direct action stimulant.

Since the aim of retail advertising is to develop store traffic, it is deemed good retail advertising practice to offer merchandise that people want, items in current fashion, or of known demand; on the other hand, it is deemed bad practice to advertise merchandise "mistakes," that is, goods that have been found not readily saleable. To advertise the latter is likely neither to attract immediate buyers nor to add to the store's reputation for selling wanted merchandise.

Experience has shown that the most effective means of attracting immediate buyers is to offer recognizably good values. This conclusion explains the practice among retailers, particularly chain grocers and chain druggists, of featuring manufacturers' brands at reduced prices. In addition to listing known brands, they also offer standard unbranded merchandise whose values are currently known in the market, such as fresh butter, fresh eggs, sugar, potatoes, and so on. The constant featuring of recognizably low prices not only attracts

---

[44] In Appendix I, the volume of local advertising, which is largely retail advertising, has been roughly estimated for 1935 at $600,000,000. This figure includes classified advertising. It covers the advertising of local advertisers in all media.

customers, but is counted upon to help build the retailer's reputation for good values.

Individual Items Receive Varying Advertising Emphasis

Different types of products receive varying emphasis in the space advertising of retailers, just as different classes of merchandise receive varying amounts of advertising and promotion among manufacturers. Since the usual purpose of the direct-action advertising of a retailer is to attract patrons, those items which are most promising in attracting patronage will be more frequently presented than items that will not draw people to the store. Small items purchased only sporadically by consumers as needed will not generally be listed. On the other hand, products for which there is a constant and recurring demand, with resultant presence in the market of a large number of users, will be presented often. In a grocery store, for example, items such as spices, extracts, anchovies, and paraffin are not often advertised, whereas the staple commodities of everyday use, such as butter, cheese, sugar, and coffee, are frequently offered, as are the well-known brands of grocery specialties, such as cereals, gelatin and powdered desserts, canned meats, soups, and the like.

In the case of department stores, some departments will get more advertising than other departments, partly because the merchandise in those departments has greater drawing power, partly because it is a policy of the store to build up the reputation of particular departments. The expenditures for space advertising and total publicity for selected departments of large department stores are shown in Table 10, measured in percentage of sales. As will be noted, there is considerable variation between departments in the total costs of publicity, which covers all types of advertising and display effort. For example, coats and suits; blouses and sportswear; knit apparel; furs; home furnishings; men's clothing; and juniors', misses', and women's dresses represent departments with publicity expense in excess of 7% of sales. In contrast, ribbons; laces, trimmings, and embroideries; and restaurants are departments with expense of less than 3%, and a considerable number of departments have a publicity expense under 4%. Even more marked is the variation in the use of newspaper space. Departments handling patterns, laces, trimmings, and ribbons use less than 1% of sales income for newspaper advertising, while departments selling women's suits and radios spend in excess of 6% of sales for newspaper space.

TABLE 10

TYPICAL NEWSPAPER ADVERTISING AND TOTAL PUBLICITY COSTS, IN PERCENTAGE OF
SALES, FOR SELECTED DEPARTMENTS OF DEPARTMENT STORES WITH
SALES VOLUME OF $10,000,000 AND OVER, 1937

DEPARTMENT	NEWSPAPER SPACE COSTS (% OF SALES)	TOTAL PUBLICITY (% OF SALES)
Restaurant, Luncheonette, and Fountain	0.3	1.1
Patterns	0.4	6.1
Laces, Trimmings, and Embroideries	0.7	2.3
Ribbons	0.9	2.4
Umbrellas and Canes	1.9	3.1
Wash Goods and Linings	2.4	3.9
Children's Hosiery	2.4	3.8
Woolen Dress Goods	2.6	3.9
Art Needlework and Art Goods	2.8	4.0
Books and Stationery	2.9	4.4
Books and Magazines	2.9	4.9
Stationery	2.9	3.9
Infants' Wear	3.1	4.5
Silk and Muslin Underwear and Slips	3.6	5.2
Men's Furnishings	4.0	5.5
Hosiery, etc.	4.1	5.0
Women's and Misses' Dresses	4.2	7.0
Piece Goods, Domestics, Blankets, etc.	4.6	6.0
Blouses and Skirts	4.7	7.0
Major Household Appliances	4.9	7.0
Coats and Suits	5.0	7.0
Silverware	5.1	6.0
Women's and Misses' Coats and Suits	5.2	7.3
Men's Clothing	5.3	7.4
Home Furnishings	5.4	7.2
Men's and Boys' Wear	5.5	6.7
Blouses, Sportswear	5.5	7.7
Juniors', Misses', and Women's Dresses	5.7	7.3
Furs	5.8	8.4
Sportswear, Knit Apparel, etc.	5.8	8.1
Aprons, House Dresses, and Uniforms	5.9	7.3
Juniors', Misses', and Women's Suits	6.0	7.8
Radios, Talking Machines, and Records	6.2	7.4
Total Basement	5.2	6.2
Total Store	4.0	5.8

Source: *1937 Departmental Merchandising and Operating Results of Department
Stores and Specialty Stores* (New York, Controllers' Congress, National Retail Dry Goods
Association, June, 1938), p. 61.

Within departments, moreover, there is the same distinction drawn
between advertisable and nonadvertisable items as pointed out above
for grocery stores. For example, in the white goods department, sheets,
an item of universal and constant usage with need of replacement, are
advertised frequently, whereas cheesecloth receives little space advertising because it lacks "drawing" power. Packaged cheesecloth, however, may be given prominent point-of-purchase display because display of a low-price package may lead to impulse purchase. Likewise,

candy will not be advertised often by a grocer; yet he may give it prominent display to attract impulse purchase.

Retailers Use Advertising Also to Build Reputation

While retail advertising is employed primarily to attract immediate patronage, it is used also to build favorable mental associations, that is, to enhance the store's reputation. Often a minor part of a retailer's advertising appropriation is devoted to featuring merchandise in ways that will build up the reputation of particular departments or of the institution for those things which induce continuous patronage. Without featuring action-impelling price inducements, a department or specialty store may advertise fashion merchandise with copy devoted mostly to discussion of current fashions and the success of the store or department in being fashion correct. Or the wide variety of selection in particular departments may be stressed in an advertisement by presentation of numerous items and emphasis in the copy on the wide variety that is available. Again, a small part of a store's promotional appropriation may be devoted to purely institutional advertisements to build its reputation for easy credit, good delivery service, low prices, liberal returns and adjustments, and other practices by which the store seeks to build continuous patronage. Or these same institutional appeals may be woven into regular day-to-day direct-action selling advertisements. Moreover, the illustrations, type, and copy of all its advertisements may be given tonal qualities that will produce a desired store reputation, say, of the bargain mart or of the exclusive shop.

The retailer is generally aware of the importance of product display, of sales suggestions, and of point-of-purchase advertising materials of one type or another in the consummation of sales. Good advertising practice requires careful coordination of his point-of-purchase efforts with his space advertising.

Whenever a retailer serves as the selected distributor for a manufacturer in a community, the point-of-purchase display material and frequently his space advertising are designed for him by the manufacturer. It is important to him as well as to the manufacturer that he be known in the community as the sole or one of a few sources where the particular brand of product may be secured. The retailer's space advertisements for these selected agency products do not so frequently employ the immediate action stimuli of low price as do the run-of-mine advertisements of department, grocery, and drug stores. The advertisements often reflect the manufacturer's indirect-action advertising, with the retailer's signature given as local source for the product. Since such advertising is not likely to induce the immediate action desired by retailers, however, such retailers sometimes seek in their newspaper advertising to devise immediate action strategies to bring buyers into their establishments, such as trade-in allowances, premiums, contests, and so on.

Generalizations Regarding Profitable Utilization of Advertising by Retailers

The above outline of common practices of retail advertising indicates some of the important requirements for its effective utilization by individual retailers. These may be summarized thus:

(1) The amount of advertising used must be adjusted to fit the scale of operations and the needs of the particular store. Obviously the amount spent upon advertising must accord with gross margin and with other expenses if a profit is to result. As part of this task the retailer must determine the place of advertising in his specific program, inasmuch as different retail operating programs call for different burdens to be placed upon advertising. For example, grocery stores which serve a neighborhood are in such close and constant touch with neighborhood buyers that they need little advertising other than point-of-purchase display. In contrast, stores which draw customers from a wide radius, such as department stores and furniture stores, generally find space advertising an economical and effective means of attracting business. But, even among retailers within a trade, differences in operating methods frequently call for different utilization of advertising. For example, in shopping centers many stores, particularly small stores, find it desirable to rely primarily upon their windows and heavy traffic past their stores to attract patronage. Even so large and successful an institution as S. Klein's wearing apparel store in New York has not employed space advertising to attract customers. Variety chains, generally speaking, have not used advertising.

(2) The advertising should be carefully planned and its objectives clearly defined. Otherwise advertising efforts are likely to be haphazard, particularly in large retail institutions such as department stores, whose success as a whole depends upon the skill with which individual departments are operated. To attain best results, advertising should be made an integral part of the store's operation. Effec-

tive planning requires that the various types of merchandise or the various departments of the business get proper advertising support. The advertising plan accordingly must fit into the merchandising plans of these departments. Promotions should be properly timed, and the merchandise selected for advertising of these promotions should be effective not only in creating immediate sales for the departments but in building for them reputations conducive to continued patronage. Moreover, the advertising plan should comprehend the need of development of institutional reputation, if a long-range profit viewpoint is held.

(3) Skill in advertising techniques should be sought. The wide variation in advertising effectiveness arising from varying skills in techniques, which was discussed in connection with manufacturers' advertising, applies to retail advertising as well. Accordingly, effective utilization of advertising by retailers requires that they attempt to build effective advertisements and to place them in the right media.

CHAPTER V

THE UTILIZATION OF ADVERTISING BY
BUSINESS—Continued

THE difficulties met by business executives in securing effective utilization of advertising, as described in the preceding chapter, have been only partly overcome by the development of management techniques. Consequently, even with the best of intentions, some ineffectiveness and waste is unavoidable in the use of advertising as in all lines of endeavor. For the great run of businesses whose products are clearly socially desirable, advertising expenditure that does not effectively accomplish the purposes for which it was planned involves waste and is not in the public interest, just as waste in any form of economic activity is undesirable. Because of their desire to have their enterprises succeed, businessmen have exerted effort to reduce the risks involved in the use of advertising and hence to reduce its wastes. In this chapter these efforts are analyzed and appraised.

Lack of Adequate Techniques for Control and Measurement of Advertising

It is evident from what has been said previously that the designing of profitable management programs embodying advertising, the building of effective advertisements, and the satisfactory execution of selling campaigns are far from exact sciences. The margin of error in the prediction of human behavior in response to selling programs is large. Accordingly, waste in advertising may be attributed in some degree to the inability of managements to predict sales and profit results from its use. Psychological research has not yet provided business managements with good tools for measurement or prediction of response, nor does psychology give much promise of developing methods for accurate measurement. Since accurate prediction depends to a substantial degree upon the availability of data by which to guide judgments, ineffectiveness in advertising utilization may be ascribed chiefly to the lack of precise techniques for accounting for and measuring the effects of advertising and other selling efforts, and to the failure of many businesses fully to use the techniques that are available. The number of companies that have had competent managements and resources sufficient to conduct economically the research needed to reduce errors in their selling activities has represented a relatively small part of business as a whole. That wisdom and competence in use of advertising are not more general is but a reflection of the varying capacities of men to be found in all lines of endeavor and of the complexity of the problems faced in advertising management. The waste in advertising due to human incompetence is probably no greater than in other phases of business administration.

Variables Affecting Results of Sales Promotion Programs

The measurement of advertising effectiveness is complicated by the fact that advertising is only a part of a total sales plan. It is but one variable among many that affect the sales results of an advertiser. Human response to the plan may be measured in terms of sales, but just how each of the many variables contributed to the sales result cannot be exactly determined. Accordingly, in most instances the contribution of advertising can only be guessed at. That this statement is true may readily be seen from an hypothetical example which in outline conforms to facts frequently encountered in business.

Let it be assumed that a manufacturer late in 1932 decided to advertise an item in his line which he had not previously advertised but for which he had fairly extensive distribution and annual sales of $250,000. The decision to advertise came as a result of an improvement which the company had made in its product. As a part of the decision to advertise, the package was redesigned, the sales organization was expanded, and efforts were made to arouse among new and old salesmen an enthusiasm for the new product, in the hope that this enthusiasm would be transmitted to dealers and their salespeople. By 1937, sales had reached $350,000 a year. In the meantime, prices on this and competing products had increased somewhat. Throughout the period the company, as well as competing sellers, from time to time employed free deals and combination offers to the trade and to consumers in an effort to stimulate sales. Moreover, largely because of the increased sales activity of this manufacturer, competitors countered with product changes, new packages, and increased selling effort. Several instituted premium and sampling programs from time to time. By 1937 the increase in aggregate gross margin on this product a little more than offset the increase in expenses which had been incurred from advertising and selling.

Just what did advertising contribute to the sales and profit results of this company? What did it contribute from period to period during these years? Were copy and media changes effectively made from time to time? These questions cannot be answered precisely, for it is readily seen that a large number of variables had a bearing upon the volume of sales which the company attained. The sales increases were not attributable to advertising alone but were merely concomitant with changes in a large number of forces. The following list contains only the most evident of these variables.

(1) *Changing buying power.* Between 1932 and 1937, expanding buying power of consumers in itself should have accounted for some increase in sales.

(2) *Changing product formulae.* Not only did the change in the company's product have an effect on its subsequent sales, but the changes later made by competitors likewise had an effect.

(3) *Changing price structure.* During the period not only changes in price by this manufacturer but also those made by direct and indirect competitors, and changes in the price structure as a whole had a bearing on the sales attained by each. Not only listed price changes but the equivalent of price changes occurring from free deals and combination offers had an effect on the distribution of sales among the various sellers.

(4) *Changing personal selling effort.* The increase in personal selling effort by this company affected its sales, but during the period competitors also altered their salesforces. This change in personal selling probably took various forms, such as change in number of salesmen, in frequency of sales calls, and in the character of sales presentations,—just to name a few.

(5) *Changing promotional methods.* The employment of premiums and sampling by certain competitors probably affected not only their own sales but those of all concerns in the industry. Use of other forms of promotional effort, such as store demonstrators and display counters and racks for retailers, also may have been varied.

(6) *Changing advertising.* The company's inauguration of advertising was designed to increase its sales. During the period, however, competitors countered with changing advertising efforts; and all these changes had an effect on distribution of sales among those in the industry.

(7) *Changing packages.* Since packages influence sales, the new

package designs used by the company and by its competitors represented a variable to appraise in any analysis of sales results.

To the above list of variables clearly applicable to the hypothetical case, which has been set up from a composite of actual cases, may be added others whose presence must necessarily be weighed in any effort to appraise advertising's effects upon sales of a product. Some of the more important additional changes which in particular marketing situations might have considerable effect on sales are the following:

(8) *Changing number of competitors by entrance or departure.* Changes in a company's sales may be affected materially by new, direct competitors entering the field; likewise they may be affected by new indirect competition. For example, the development and widespread offering of tomato juice and of pineapple juice affected the sales of oranges and other fruit juices for breakfast use.

(9) *Changing fashion.* For many products fashion is the most important element in determination of sales fluctuation for a product, far outweighing any promotional effort in its effect on sales. Change in fashion generally calls for change in product design; accordingly this variable may be closely related to variable (2) above.

(10) *Changing distribution methods and policies.* The constant flux in the selling operations of distributors may affect the sales of producers' brands. Wholesale and retail distribution methods and policies employed by competing manufacturers are subject to changes which may affect the sales of all in the industry. In some instances they may be of minor importance, as when dealers here or there shift between brands with consequent effects upon the sales of brands in those market areas. Again, alteration in the margins or in the services given to distributors by a manufacturer may have material effect upon trade attitudes toward competing brands and hence may affect the distribution of sales among brands.

(11) *Changing living habits and attitudes.* The demands for all products and hence the sales of individual business firms are subject in greater or less degree to the effect of changing living habits and attitudes. These changes underlie so-called basic trends, to which businesses must adjust themselves, and which must be weighed in an appraisal of changing sales results. They will be discussed at some length in the chapter on demand.

From the above discussion of variables associated with changing sales, it is evident that changes in sales very frequently cannot be ascribed definitely to any one of the variables, such as advertising. The contribution of advertising must be judged in the light of all the other variables. How educated a management's judgment is depends upon the evidence it has gathered regarding the variables and upon its skill in weighing these data. Because of the constant changes in the market, the seller needs sensitive guides to inform him from time to time regarding his absolute and relative sales position in an industry. He needs to have evidence also regarding changes in all the variables that may account for these changes in sales position. In addition, he desires methods for measuring the effect upon consumer behavior of his various selling efforts, of which advertising is only one. With such information he may try to judge the changes needed in his operating plans from time to time in order to maintain a profit.

The Increasing Tempo of Change in Business Operations

Rapid change in sales outlook makes for difficulty in advertising and sales measurement and hence in management. That the last 20 years have witnessed a marked increase in the tempo of change in business operations is the common opinion of students of business. This conclusion appeared in many of the individual reports of economists who contributed to the study of *Recent Economic Changes,* made by the National Bureau of Economic Research, in 1929. The situation was summarized thus by Copeland in that study:

A characteristic of many American industries during the nineteenth century and the early twentieth century was mass production of more or less standardized articles, a system which reached its zenith in the Ford plant. That method of operation permitted the economical utilization of labor and resulted in great economies in production. Since 1920, however, a different set of conditions has been apparent, as indicated by the new tempo of demand, the rapidity of style changes, and the receptivity of consumers to new varieties and types of products. Whether these new conditions are permanent or not, they must be faced. Some conditions, such as the change in rural markets and the rise in standards of living, are working for a continuance of frequently changing demand. There is some evidence of a reaction against widespread standardization of products, at least in the case of display merchandise. This tendency toward greater variety may be regretted, but it is a fact that cannot be disregarded by alert business executives. These conditions have placed a premium on keen foresight in product planning, that is, on constructive merchandising.[1]

[1] National Bureau of Economic Research, *Recent Economic Changes* (New York, McGraw-Hill Book Company, Inc., 1929), Vol. I, ch. 5, p. 329, "Marketing," by M. T. Copeland.

Lough, in his study *High-Level Consumption,* reached similar conclusions:

One plain characteristic of high-level, in contrast with low-level, consumption is its fickleness. Offerings to consumers, if they are to hold their markets, must be continually remodelled—always with a risk that the supposed improvements will fail to "click." Popular demands are apt to shift suddenly, undermining whole industries.[2]

It is in this world of change that the modern businessman has to operate. The predicting of sales returns has been difficult; the measuring of advertising effectiveness has been correspondingly difficult.

Development of Techniques for Reducing Risk in Selling Programs

Until the passing of the so-called seller's market which existed roughly up to 1921, the need for refining selling techniques, and hence for developing methods of measuring their effectiveness, was not pressing upon American manufacturers. In comparison the postwar period has been one of marked advance in such effort. Particularly has the past decade seen a growth in employment and study of market research, of sales planning, and of marketing control procedures.

Efforts to measure and increase advertising effectiveness have followed three lines. One of these has been in market studies of diverse types. There have been analyses of consumer demand for various products; audits to verify the volume and character of circulation of advertising media of different types; reports of advertising experience in the form of case studies; investigation of marketing procedures and policies employed by marketing institutions; and so on at length. A great deal of market research, however, has been designed to get evidence which would be of value to specific sellers for predicting probable trade or consumer response to proposed marketing programs involving issues regarding product form, or price, or methods of selling and advertising. In such instances direct evidence from consumers or distributors has been sought in the field to supplement evidence gained from past experience.

A second approach has been that of perfecting records of sales and expenses and of gathering evidence regarding the variables affecting sales, such as have been listed in the preceding pages. For a

---

[2] W. H. Lough, *High-Level Consumption* (New York, McGraw-Hill Book Company, Inc., 1935), p. 2.

marketing program composed of many types of promotional effort and subject to the constantly changing variables noted, exact measurement of the profit contribution of various elements of the program to final sales volume and profit is impossible. Management has been forced to measure the final results of its selling efforts, as shown in sales and profits, and of appraising as best it can the part played by each type of effort. The management ideal of measuring the exact profit contribution of each element of a marketing program is unattainable, but good records provide needed data for the exercise of judgment.

A third type of effort for increasing advertising efficiency has been to devise techniques of measuring past advertising operations in a narrow sense, the aim being to secure maximum efficiency in selecting for future use the strongest appeals, in devising effective advertisements employing those appeals, in getting the most productive combinations in size and frequency of advertisements, and in selecting the most efficient media available.

It is not within the scope of this study to analyze in detail the various research techniques that have been developed. On the other hand, it is desirable to indicate the character of and the promise and limitations of the efforts made by businessmen to reduce the risks of advertising. Impelled by the desire to increase profits businessmen have experimented widely. From these efforts to reduce waste the economy as a whole has undoubtedly benefitted. In the following pages the increasing use of market studies of diverse types is outlined. Various organizations taking part in such research are indicated. The objectives of the data sought and the difficulties in obtaining information are pointed out and the present state of the art of market research of various types is appraised. Next, the efforts to perfect records of sales and expense for individual companies by which they may guide marketing programs are presented. Finally, efforts to measure copy effectiveness and other advertising elements are discussed.

Growth in the Use of Market Studies

Market research of all kinds is relatively recent. Hower[3] describes what was probably the first crude market research undertaken by an advertising agency for a client, a study made by N. W. Ayer & Son in

---

[3] R. M. Hower, *The History of an Advertising Agency* (Cambridge, Harvard University Press, 1939), pp. 88–94.

1879 for Nichols-Shepard Company, manufacturer of threshing machines, to show the geographical distribution of markets for threshers, as indicated by crop data, and to provide a suitable list of media to reach these markets. Work of this kind did not at once become a part of regular agency service, however. It was given only occasionally when some special need arose. But gradually this agency, like others, extended this service to advertisers and began to take over the function of studying actual and possible markets for commodities and of devising advertising plans to capture the markets. By 1900 the preparation of plans had become a part of the regular service which it offered; but market surveys ordinarily were very limited and crude. Not until 1908 did this agency have a fully developed Plans Department.

Regarding agencies generally, Presbrey reports: "Around 1910 began the formation of research departments to obtain a variety of country-wide data and equip the agency with detailed information on which to base the advertising plan. . . ." [4]

Types of Organization Engaged in Market Research

After World War I, the larger advertising agencies generally, though not universally, established research departments to make market studies for their clients. Small agencies as a rule did not offer organized research service, however, nor did small clients employ field investigation organizations on any considerable scale. But even for small advertisers employing agencies, the hit-or-miss use of advertising of early days disappeared. In recent years some attempt to delimit markets, to lay out schedules and copy approach, and to select proper media to reach markets has become an established part of advertising agency work even for the small advertiser, while the studies made for large advertisers are often elaborate.

Numerous advertising media, following the lead of the Curtis Publishing Company whose Commercial Research Division was begun in 1911,[5] have established research departments. The aim of these departments has been to gather facts regarding their advertising linage, the successes of their advertisers, the character of their audiences, the possible demands of these audiences as purchasers, and the intensity of readership by subscribers. Such research undoubtedly has been help-

---

[4] Frank Presbrey, *The History and Development of Advertising* (New York, Doubleday, Doran & Company, Inc., 1929), p. 527 ff.

[5] J. C. Oswald, editor, *The Advertising Year Book for 1924* (New York, Doubleday Page & Company, Inc., 1925), p. 358.

ful to agencies and advertisers in many cases, but frequently it has suffered from the bias of being a special pleader.

With the advent of the 1930 depression, specialized market research organizations, which had begun to appear a few years previously, increased in number and have come into wider use in recent years. A number of these, headed by capable research executives and employing trained field investigators, are leaders in the development of research techniques.

While business enterprises to a large degree have relied on outside organizations of one type or another for aid in formal market research of any magnitude, a limited number of large business organizations have established their own market research departments, some of which employ a considerable personnel.[6] Some idea of the extent of organized research among manufacturers in recent years was afforded by a survey relating to the year 1937, made by the Market Data Section of the U. S. Department of Commerce.[7] Questionnaires were mailed to 869 manufacturers of whom two-thirds made some reply. Ninety-four of the manufacturers responding to the inquiry, reported that they themselves conducted marketing research for which they spent about $2,000,000 annually. In terms of the average company, approximately $21,000 annually was spent for research by its own organization. Forty-two companies reported that they spent $8,000 for outside research. Three full-time employees devoted all their time to research and four others gave part time to the activity. The most common subjects of investigation were: (1) study of potential markets, (2) study of competitive products, (3) analysis of markets by sales territories, and (4) study of sales and profit possibilities of new products. While this study indicates that business concerns often do not have formal research organizations, there are probably few which do not employ market analysis to some extent.

A large amount of research that has been valuable in reducing ineffective advertising expenditure has been carried on under the sponsorship of cooperative groups of concerns engaged in advertising. Noteworthy among such efforts was the formation of the Audit

---

[6] Among advertisers with well-developed market research departments may be mentioned: Procter & Gamble Company, Lever Brothers Company, General Foods Corporation, General Motors Corporation, General Electric Company, and American Telephone & Telegraph Company.

[7] U. S. Bureau of Foreign and Domestic Commerce, Market Research Series No. 21, *Marketing Research Activities of Manufacturers*, by E. S. Moulton, (Washington, The Bureau, 1939), pp. 5, 8, 10.

Bureau of Circulations in 1914, designed to provide dependable data regarding the volume and distribution of the circulation of newspapers and magazines and the methods by which circulation was obtained. Thus advertisers were assured of dependable information upon which to base judgments regarding the worth of the media space to them. With the objective of providing dependable data regarding the circulation methods of controlled circulation publications,[8] the Controlled Circulation Audit, Inc., was established in 1931. To insure reliable data regarding the circulation and coverage of outdoor advertising, the Traffic Audit Bureau, Inc., was established in 1931. Evidence regarding radio listening habits was ushered in by the formation of the Cooperative Analysis of Broadcasting in 1930. Of similar significance have been studies of the several advertising trade associations and of the Advertising Research Foundation.

The Extent of Published Market Research Work in Recent Years

In addition to the above market research efforts, studies have been carried on by the Federal Government, state governments, colleges, universities, foundations, trade associations, and chambers of commerce. The magnitude of such work is indicated by the fact that the 1938 (seventh) edition of *Market Research Sources,* Domestic Commerce Series No. 55, published by the U. S. Bureau of Foreign and Domestic Commerce, required 240 pages for listing some 1,040 research organizations and their published studies for the years 1933–1937 inclusive. This document included only known researches of which published copies or records were available to the public. Accordingly the large quantity of confidential market research conducted by thousands of business firms, by approximately 1,500 advertising agencies, and by the smaller number of specialized research organizations, which was of direct significance in the planning of specific programs, was omitted from this source list, as was much of the confidential research data of trade associations and of the cooperative groups mentioned above.

Varying Quality of Market Research

That the quality and worth of published studies vary widely is known to all students of marketing. Many of these published re-

---

[8] Controlled circulation periodicals are those sent without charge to selected lists of persons or organizations determined by the publisher.

searches, as well as the specific market researches conducted by or for business firms to guide them in the formulation of market plans, may be said to suffer from the immaturity of social research generally.[9] Those engaged in market research are fully cognizant of the crudity of their techniques. For example, only in recent years has studious attention been given to the difficult problem of proper sampling among consumers. Although progress has been made, the problems of sampling procedure in market study are far from solved, and the sampling methods employed often involve considerable error.[10]

Progress in the techniques of interviewing consumers in field investigation work likewise leaves much to be desired. Techniques of interviewing designed to obtain simple facts of consumer or trade behavior have been developed, but relatively little is known about interviewing procedures suitable for determining with certainty the attitudes or opinions of consumers or distributors. Nor have good methods been devised to measure the intensity or significance of these opinions as they may bear upon behavior.

All in all, the past 20 years have seen a remarkable growth in the effort of business organizations, service organizations, schools and governmental agencies to gather data and to conduct studies which might reduce the margin of error in selling programs. If the general run of such studies is judged by rigorous scientific standards or if the criterion of their success in elimination of waste is applied, it must be concluded that there is still much to be desired. Such a generalization, however, fails to give adequate recognition to the promising

---

[9] For an analysis and estimate of the literature relating to consumer demand and of the research techniques employed, see the essay by H. R. Tosdal, "The Study of Consumer Demand in Relation to Capitalistic Society," *Business and Modern Society* (Cambridge, Harvard University Press, 1938). Also see:
W. E. Spahr and R. J. Swenson, *Methods and Status of Scientific Research* (New York, Harper & Brothers, 1930).

[10] Discussion of current techniques of market research is given in *The Technique of Marketing Research*, prepared by the American Marketing Society (New York, McGraw-Hill Book Company, Inc., 1937). Also see:
L. O. Brown, *Market Research and Analysis* (New York, The Ronald Press Company, 1937).
T. H. Brown, *The Use of Statistical Techniques in Certain Problems of Market Research* (Harvard Business School, Division of Research, Business Research Studies, No. 12, 1935).
E. D. Smith, "Market Sampling," *Journal of Marketing,* July, 1939, p. 45.
E. L. Lloyd, "Sampling Problems in Current Trade Statistics," *Journal of Marketing,* April. 1939, p. 373.
R. A. Fisher, *Statistical Methods for Research Workers* (4th ed., London, Oliver and Boyd, 1932).
R. A. Fisher, *The Design of Experiments* (London, Oliver and Boyd, 1935).
G. U. Yule and M. G. Kendall, *An Introduction to the Theory of Statistics* (London, C. Griffin & Company, Ltd., 1937).

progress that has been made to meet problems that have become increasingly complex under the accelerated demand changes of the recent period. The important thing to note is that the effort to reduce risk and waste in marketing operations is widespread.

Development of Accounting and Statistical Techniques for Controlling Marketing Operations

Consideration is turned now from market studies of diverse types to efforts to develop control techniques which will aid management in its accounting for advertising expenditures and in directing expenditures effectively. With the increase in scale and complexity of marketing operations and the sharpening of competition since 1920, increased attention has been given to budgetary control of marketing operations and of cost accounting analysis for selling work.

In order to assure profitable operation, management has found it increasingly necessary to know which item or groups of items and which customers or types of customers are profitable, and how effort should be related to the needs of the different items and markets. Good management has found it unwise merely to appropriate funds for advertising and selling to be spent over broad territories with a check only on final profit results, for the final profit result, even though favorable, may represent a combination of losses in some markets and profits in others. Moreover, good management recognizes that selling effort should be fitted to the needs of particular markets of a size whose operations can be readily appraised and directed.[11] Success in business depends to a large degree on seeing that a multitude of small things are done well.

Thus in addition to efforts to know profitability of lines of merchandise and of customers, there has grown an increasing practice of breaking the total market into trading or marketing areas to which sales can be traced and to which expenses can be allocated. Under such a plan not only can sales and expense for an area be determined with more or less precision, but operating executives for the area may note the behavior of the variable elements affecting sales. Thus advertising expenditures as well as other selling efforts may be adjusted to the selling tasks faced in particular areas.

In order to make certain that the attainments in market areas may

11 For a discussion of the determination of market areas, see: N. H. Seubert, "How Big Is a Market Area," and V. D. Reed, "Statistical Possibilities of Defining Market Areas," *Journal of Marketing*, July, 1938, pp. 34 and 39.

be in accordance with their potentialities, efforts have been made to improve the techniques of setting standards in the form of quotas or buying power indexes against which to measure attainment. Thus for any area management desires not only the record of sales and of the costs of getting those sales, but a figure which reflects potential sales that good management might attain. Such a standard or potential index may serve as a beacon or flag to indicate to management the need for careful analysis and possible adjustment of its operations.

While hopeful progress can be reported in the development of techniques for distribution control, as yet high attainment cannot be claimed. Cost accounting as applied to marketing operations presents difficult problems and results thus far attained are much less accurate than those secured in factory costing. Large parts of total marketing costs must be allocated, because efforts to set up systems of direct charges for specific operations generally encounter difficulty, whether accounting for commodity costs, customer costs, or market area costs. Moreover, in many instances the determination of sales for particular market areas is inexact, because of the difficulty met by a manufacturer of tracing the sales of wholesalers or chains. Consequently, the cost figures for individual commodities or customers or markets are usually rough, not precise, measurements.

Likewise, in the setting of standards in the form of quotas or indices of sales possibilities, it can be said with assurance that the art is still in an immature stage. The standards worked out by some sales organizations have provided helpful indicators for managements, but the degree of accuracy needed, if a standard is to be of great value to management, has probably been attained by relatively few companies.[12]

It should be recognized also that the quality of the distribution accounting and statistical control techniques employed varies widely among business managements. Accordingly, the amount of waste which comes from failure to employ improved methods varies widely among business organizations.

Development of Current Statistics of Competition

The establishment of market research to enable sellers to have a record not only of their own sales at retail but those of competing

---

[12] L. D. H. Weld, "Scientific Determination of Regional Sales Potentials," *Seventh International Management Congress, Distribution Papers* (New York, The National Management Council of the U. S. A., 1938), p. 15.

brands, together with evidence of the main promotional efforts of these competitors, and possibly of their resale prices, is a recent development. This evidence may come through field surveys among a sample of retail stores[13]; or it may be provided in part through a continuing survey among an adequate sample of consumers regarding their purchases and usage of products by brands.[14] Such data are valuable not only because they reflect sales trends of competing brands, but because they may reflect more accurately what is occurring on the actual sales front of consumer buying than do a manufacturer's own sales figures, which merely show the flow of merchandise into trade channels. Between the manufacturer's sales to the trade and consumers' buying is a lag, which unfortunately is not constant.

With such records a management can watch the trend of sales of all competing brands and match against these trends the marketing efforts of the various sellers. Changes in asked prices, special dealer promotions, changes in volume of advertising, changes in advertising appeal, employment of premium offers and contests, and so on may be noted in relation to sales response. By such means does management seek to secure a refinement of data on which to base judgments which might reduce error in marketing operations.

Market research of this type, however, when well done is costly, and unless well done it is worthless. Thus far only a relatively small number of advertisers have made use of it, and these have been large organizations whose scale of operations would support such costly research. The expenditures for research and accounting control must not exceed the possible savings they may contribute.

The Search for Methods of Measuring the Profit Contribution of Advertising

While the techniques of accounting for sales and promotional effort and for securing records of competitors' efforts described above are valuable for guiding marketing activity, they do not enable a management to know the specific profit contribution of advertising. The uncertainty comes from the difficulty that has been noted, namely, that of ascertaining the extent to which sales results may be ascribed to specific variables associated with those results.

---

[13] For a discussion of this type of market research, see F. K. Leisch, *Profits from Marketing Research,* Consumer and Industrial Marketing Series C. M. 24 (New York, American Management Association, 1937).

[14] For a discussion of such research, see H. C. Link and Irving Lorge, "The Psychological Sales Barometer," *Harvard Business Review,* January, 1935, p. 193.

In the mail order business or in businesses employing advertising for the sole purpose of getting leads to prospective buyers the *profit contribution of advertising* to the business is readily determinable. For every advertisement, and hence for the whole advertising program, accurate sales results are traceable as a result of keyed responses.[15] Accordingly the cost of advertising can be compared with the profit that comes from sales. Under such a scheme, advertising is employed only as long as the sales obtained provide a margin that will more than absorb advertising expense. A quick and accurate check on the results predicted for an advertisement can be obtained. The situation is ideal for controlling advertising and for experimenting to find ways of improving returns or of keeping the cost of returns within the prescribed limits.

Difficulties in Measuring Advertising's Profit Contribution in Sales Programs as a Whole

For other types of sales programs, the relation between advertising and sales is not so directly evident. In businesses in which the selling burden is placed very largely on advertising and in which other selling efforts are negligible in importance as compared with advertising, sensitive sales and advertising records permit managements roughly to judge advertising's sales contribution, although the contribution of individual advertisements cannot be determined. As advertising becomes relatively less important in the sales picture, the difficulty of appraising its sales contribution increases. In any case, the advertiser may endeavor to ascertain the profit contribution of the advertising part of his program by sales tests, that is, experiments in which advertising efforts are varied while other factors affecting sales are held constant, so far as is possible, or are allowed for. The experiments may be carried on in either of two ways: (1) by changing the amount or type of advertising in any given area over a period of time; (2) by varying the amount or type of advertising in different areas for which sales results and expense figures are available.

---

[15] For discussion of methods of such businesses, see:

N. H. Borden, *Problems in Advertising* (3d ed., New York, McGraw-Hill Book Company, Inc., 1937), cases of Rand Company, p. 134, and Harvard Economic Service, p. 65.

John Caples, *Tested Advertising Methods* (New York, Harper & Brothers, 1933).

A. T. Falk, "Analyzing Advertising Results," *Harvard Business Review,* January and April, 1929, pp. 185 and 312.

E. T. Gundlach, *Facts and Fetishes in Advertising* (Chicago, Consolidated Book Publishers, Inc., 1931).

C. C. Hopkins, *My Life in Advertising* (New York, Harper & Brothers, 1927).

W. A. Shryer, *Analytical Advertising* (Detroit, Business Service Corporation, 1912).

The results obtainable from such experimentation are not as a rule highly satisfactory. The chief difficulty is that the variables affecting sales, other than mere volume of advertising, cannot be held constant. Accordingly, a management does not know how much allowance is to be given to changing factors other than advertising, and the troublesome question persists as to whether all variables have even been considered.[16] Rough approximations may be drawn, but precision in measurement is lacking.

Another troublesome difficulty in such experiments is the time necessary for advertising or the lack of advertising to display its full effect on sales and profit. This difficulty accounts in part for the fact that advertisers proceed for long periods of time with no more than *a priori* reasoning to guide them in the use of certain types of advertisements, such as institutional advertisements, which are very indirect and slow in action.

Whenever the burden placed upon advertising in the sales program is relatively small, or whenever the number of sales that might be expected in a given period is restricted because of a limited number of prospects or infrequency of purchase, the chances of learning much about the sales contribution of advertising from a differential experiment of the type mentioned above are small. A variation in advertising effort in such cases does not produce enough effect on sales to permit confidence to be felt in the experimental data, in view of the difficulties met in controlling variables which have a much heavier influence on sales than does advertising.

In those marketing programs in which advertising has a relatively large and a relatively quick effect upon sales, however, the attempt to get light regarding advertising's profit contribution through differential experiments is not so hopeless, even though the measurement of contribution is not exact. For example, in the cases of certain grocery and drug specialties and cigarettes, for which advertising plays an important part in consumer response, the differences in the volume of sales in different periods or in different areas under different volumes and programs of advertising provide clear evidence of advertising's contribution to sales, although it cannot be said that even here management has a refined tool for measurement.

---

[16] An analysis which shows the difficulty of tracing the sales effect of varied volume of advertising will be found in *Marketing Policies of the California Walnut Growers Association,* by H. C. Hensley and N. H. Borden, Bulletin No. 10, Farm Credit Administration, Washington, D. C.

Techniques for Measuring Consumer Response to Advertisements—Criteria Employed

Attention is now turned to the techniques that have been evolved to control the various phases of strictly advertising operations in order that each may be done well and that management may get the most from its expenditure, even though it may not be certain what the profit contribution of the expenditure is.[17] Methods of measuring appeal and the techniques of presentation are considered first.

Inasmuch as all consumer advertising is designed ultimately to lead to consumer action, the ideal evidence with regard to the effectiveness of advertisements would be found in consumer behavior, the behavior of purchase. To what extent is this evidence ascertainable? To what extent must the advertiser accept less satisfactory evidence?

Techniques for Measuring Response to Direct-Action Advertisements

For advertising of the mail-order type, in which the relationship between consumer response to advertisements and sales, and accordingly profits, is definitely ascertainable, management can attain the ideal of varying the appeal and character of presentation in accordance with sales effectiveness. Traceable responses provide the basis for measurement of effect of the important variables. All that is necessary when evidence of the effect of any variable is being sought is care either in keeping other variables constant or in making proper allowance for them. It becomes possible under such conditions for management to construct advertisements with a relatively high degree of predictability of responses and profit contribution. The management can know by a change in traceable response when changing conditions or long usage of a certain approach entail waning effectiveness. Thus it can be led to new experimentation to find an advertising approach which will induce profitable consumer response. In such operations the hypotheses guiding advertising practice are subject to constant check.

---

[17] For a general discussion of the details of advertising testing methods and an appraisal of these, see:
L. E. Firth, *Testing Advertisements* (New York, McGraw-Hill Book Company, Inc., 1934).
Advertising Research Foundation, *Copy Testing* (New York, The Ronald Press Company, 1939).
G. B. Hotchkiss, *An Outline of Advertising* (rev. ed., New York, The Macmillan Company, 1940), ch. XXVI.
C. H. Sandage, *Advertising Theory and Practice* (rev. ed., Chicago, Richard D. Irwin, Inc., 1939), ch. XXIII–XXVII.

Another category of advertisements employed by manufacturers seeks direct inquiries from readers for information. These inquiries are then used to induce purchases from the trade.[18] Responses in these cases can be traced to specific advertisements, but the sales value of such responses is not evident. But even though the sales value of the inquiries is not known, it is evident that, so long as such marketing strategy is employed, it is highly desirable for the management to try to increase the number of responses received for each dollar of advertising expense. In attaining this objective the keyed responses are valuable.

The Use of Coupons in Advertisements
Whose Main Objective Is Indirect

Partly to get evidence as to consumer interest in their advertising, and partly to provide a means for placing samples or sales literature in the hands of purchasing prospects, manufacturers in recent years have turned more and more to the strategy of making an offer calling for direct action in what are essentially indirect action advertisements. This practice raises the issue of the value of such responses as an indication of the effectiveness of such advertisements.[19] The management expects no immediate purchases of its products to be made by the persons who read or hear its advertisements, and the direct action offer carried in them ordinarily is not given much prominence. The advertisements are designed primarily to build around a brand mental associations which will be conducive to buying. Subsequent stimulus of some kind must be relied upon to bring buying action, although the mental associations built up may contribute materially to the ultimate buying response.

The inquiries received from advertisements of this kind are not records of sales. The total effect of the advertisements is not limited to their effect upon those who write in. The question raised is whether the number of inquiries received from different advertisements provides an index of their relative sales effectiveness.

As yet no one has given clear evidence that the number of inquiries received is such an index. Yet, whenever in a series of advertisements

---

[18] For a discussion of such a case, see *Problems in Advertising* (3d ed.), by N. H. Borden, case of Dennison Manufacturing Company, p. 458 ff.

[19] For a discussion of the use of inquiries of this type, see:

H. J. Rudolph, *Four Million Inquiries from Magazine Advertisements* (New York, Columbia University Press, 1936).

H. C. Hensley and N. H. Borden, *op. cit.*

the offer is hidden or is not given undue prominence, the number of inquiries appears to provide evidence of the relative degrees to which the various advertisements had been seen and had induced reading. Often the differences in the number of responses to the same offer in different advertisements are amazing.

Even though it is not definitely established that variation in number of inquiries is certain evidence of the relative sales effectiveness of what are essentially indirect-action advertisements, yet many advertisers are using inquiries to guide their selection of appeals and their copy presentation, in the belief that it is better to proceed with this evidence of consumer reading of advertisements than to proceed with no evidence at all. And this belief is deemed to have substance, so long as the inquiry-producing offers are not given an emphasis which detracts from the main objective of the advertisements in building mental associations, and so long as the prominence of the offer is uniform in all advertisements.

The Use of Consumer Readership Surveys

Another type of evidence regarding consumer response to indirect action advertisements is available in reports of the degrees to which consumers remember having noticed and read advertisements and of the degrees of their recall when name-identifying marks have been removed from the advertisements. Under this scheme consumers are asked to indicate which advertisements they have read in a specific periodical and the extent of their reading.[20] Such reader reports are now continuously available for leading magazines from certain research organizations; and if desired, recognition or recall tests can be made readily for advertisements in widely circulated periodicals.

As with the inquiry data just discussed, recognition and recall tests are not definitely established as measures of sales effectiveness or profit contribution of advertisements. Yet many advertisers use such evidence on the ground that to build advertisements on the basis of appeals and techniques which are known to attract the attention and interest of readers is better than to proceed with an hypothesis of building advertising against which there is no check. The reading of advertisements is to be desired if people are to be influenced; accordingly it is helpful to know to what extent advertisements are read.

---

20 For a discussion of this type of testing, see:
L. E. Firth, *op. cit.*
C. H. Sandage, *op. cit.*

A related type of measurement which has proved valuable in guiding radio advertising is the survey of listening habits of consumers. Periodic checks of listening are not measurements of sales effectiveness, but they permit the broadcaster to estimate the size of his audience, to know how his program stands in relation to other programs, and to know whether trend of listening is up or down.[21] They can guide him in building a program and enable him to check how well he has built.

Copy Testing through Test Campaigns

Still another technique for measuring roughly the effectiveness of different copy approaches and appeals, and one of some value for products for which advertising plays an important part in sales and enjoys a quick response, is found in sales tests in which the main differentiation in marketing procedures between areas or in time periods is made in the advertising copy. The records for such sales tests are generally secured from a check of retailers' sales, as mentioned earlier.

The shortcomings of tests of this kind already have been given. The proper control of the variables or allowance for them is most difficult. Unless the advertising is very quick in inducing response and the differences in sales results are considerable and appear clearly to be attributable to the varying copy approaches, then the test cannot mean much as a measure of copy effectiveness. Thus far such sales tests have been of greater value in testing the likelihood of success of whole marketing plans, particularly in the launching of new products, than in measuring the effectiveness of copy approaches.

Other Techniques

In addition to these techniques, which are those most widely applied, are certain others, to some of which only reference can be made.

The method of pretesting by a consumer jury, that is by getting opinions from a sample of potential buyers, still lacks adequate proof of its validity for predicting relative sales effectiveness of advertisements.[22] The reliability of the consumer jury method as

21 For a discussion of such checks, see:

J. J. Karol, "Measuring Radio Audiences," *Printers' Ink*, November 19, 1936.

L. D. H. Weld, "Radio Checking Methods Are Here Evaluated and Analyzed," *Printers' Ink*, August 18, 1939.

C. E. Hooper, "Radio's System of Checking Buying Habits May Suggest Idea to Other Media," *Printers' Ink*, March 22, 1940.

22 For a discussion of such tests, see *A Test of the Consumer Jury Method of Ranking Advertisements,* by N. H. Borden and O. S. Lovekin (Harvard Business School, Division of Research, Business Research Studies, No. 11, 1935).

applied to indirect action advertisements has been tested by comparison of rankings based on inquiries, or reader recognition tests with rankings obtained from consumer juries. But such experiments have not indicated the method's value for measuring relative sales effectiveness, for neither inquiry rankings nor the consumer reader report rankings are known to be rankings of sales effectiveness. Even though ratings by the consumer jury test method may have correlated highly with the known sales effectiveness of advertisements, i.e., mail-order advertisements, there still remains the question of whether the ability of a consumer jury to rank mail-order advertisements is proof of its ability to rank indirect-action advertisements. Moreover, there remains a question as to whether the method is reliable for detecting other than wide differences in effectiveness. In spite of these uncertainties, many advertisers are using consumer jury tests in conjunction with other measuring methods in their search for guides by which to improve their advertising.

To a limited extent advertisers have experimented to measure the strength of mental associations that may have been established among products, brands, and ideas by advertising and selling programs. As has been brought out previously, manufacturers' advertising is designed in large part to build strong associations with brands, the hypothesis being that reiteration of selling ideas in connection with brand names may eventually lead to sales. Recall tests are designed, therefore, to show to what extent brand names are known and to what extent rememberable ideas have been employed in association with them. Such tests fail to relate advertising effort specifically to sales or profit contribution; yet they represent a type of information which management might well desire in view of the advertising hypothesis which they follow. Accordingly, recall tests are being experimented with by market researchers, but thus far they have not been perfected or widely used.

Reference may be made also to the experimentation of the past few years with specially devised cameras to record the eye movement of readers in their perusal of advertisements. Such cameras may be used to check specific advertisements before publication. Moreover, from data gathered are sought principles to guide planning of layout and typography, use of illustration, and selection of ideas, which may permit the advertiser to increase the drawing power of his advertisements. Such research is still in an early stage of development.[23]

Attention is called also to the widespread efforts made to build "check lists," or lists of points by which to appraise or judge advertisements before publication, in order to be assured of their effectiveness in attracting interest and attention. Ever since students of advertising started to dissect advertisements to determine what made them effective, formulae to guide construction of advertisements have been sought. The efforts to build check lists have been aided in recent years by the fact that evidence regarding the extent to which advertisements are being seen and read, and evidence of response through inquiries has increased. More examples of effective and ineffective advertisements from which to crystallize guiding principles have been available. Such lists can be helpful as guides to the balanced appraisal which must be employed in building individual advertisements. They do not, however, provide an automatic formula of an advertisement's sales contribution.

Measurements of Variables Other Than Copy

In the preceding pages attention has been directed to techniques of measuring the effectiveness of copy. As indicated previously, associated with any study of the effectiveness of copy are the collateral problems of the relative effectiveness of varying sizes of advertisements, frequency of insertion, and media used.

When it comes to measuring the sales effectiveness of the size and frequency of advertisements, the situation is not a happy one. Generalizations have been advanced with some supporting evidence regarding the effect of size in gaining the attention of consumers, the conclusion reached by many research workers being that, excepting very small advertisements, attention-gaining value varies roughly in accordance with the square root of the area. In building advertising schedules, however, advertisers have not generally followed this hypothesis. Other considerations, such as competitive practice and desire for prestige, have overbalanced trust in an hypothesis that is not backed by evidence relating to known sales return.

---

[23] For a discussion of such experimentation see:
"Look's Camera," *Tide*, October 15, 1939, pp. 12–13; November 1, 1939, pp. 20–21; December 1, 1939, pp. 12–13; January 1, 1940, pp. 22–23; February 1, 1940, pp. 20–21; April 1, 1940, pp. 30, 32; May 1, 1940, pp. 16–17.
"Eye Tracings of the Scanacord in Newspapers and Magazines," *Advertising & Selling*, March, 1940.

Regarding the effect of frequency of insertion of advertisements, little of a definitive character is known. Most decisions regarding size and frequency are based on *a priori* reasoning regarding the amount of space needed to make a desired impression or to meet a competitive schedule, or on the dictates of a limited appropriation. The evidence to support or disprove such hypotheses as are followed would rest in sales records, but the difficulty of isolating the effect of the variable makes generalizations uncertain. This difficulty, of course, does not apply with so much force to the mail-order type of advertising, where the effect of changes in size and frequency can be determined, within limits, by tests. In the case of indirect action advertisements analysis of inquiries and tests of reader recognition and recall may possibly give some evidence, though usually inconclusive, regarding the effect of size and frequency.

As to measuring with precision the part that particular media play in sales results, the advertiser faces all the difficulties that have been enumerated above. When advertisements providing traceable responses are used, an idea of relative effectiveness of different media can be gained. Otherwise the advertiser must rely upon some type of experiment and analysis in which he seeks to control or to make allowance for variables other than media, with all the uncertainties that come in trying to exercise such control or to make correct allowances. It should be remembered, however, that advertisers have made much progress in providing information for use in determining to what extent various media reach those whom they wish to address and the extent to which consumers see and read those media. Hence the data upon which to base selection of media are far better now than they were in previous years.

From this appraisal of the techniques of market studies, of budgetary control methods, and of advertising testing methods, it is seen that considerable strides have been made in the effort to reduce the uncertainty and risk that attend the use of advertising. Nevertheless a large amount of uncertainty and consequently ineffective expenditure remains. The wastes arise largely from the complexity of the problems met, from the immaturity of the management techniques for dealing with them, and from the varying capacities of management to employ the methods available. Because advertising and selling are employed to influence human behavior and because their control depends on measurement and prediction of human behavior, these forces cannot be expected to be reduced to an exact scientific or engineering type of control. Relatively little progress has been made in developing techniques by which to measure and predict complex human behavior, and it does not appear likely that rapid strides in this direction are in the offing. Accordingly, considerable uncertainty in the measurement of advertising and selling efforts and in the prediction of results from their use may be expected to continue. Nevertheless there has been and still is much room for improving the techniques of control of these business efforts. Fortunately, those working in this area have been impressed by the intensive drive in recent years to develop improved methods for reducing ineffective expenditure.

Practice and Attitudes Operating against Adoption of Improved Measurement Techniques

In spite of the encouraging increase in use of improved management techniques, much ineffective advertising persists because of the peculiar attitudes of some business executives and advertising practitioners towards advertising. Some executives have fallen into the error of placing unfounded faith in the ability of advertising to influence people and somehow to contribute to profits. To those who have opportunity to follow advertising closely and intimately there is little doubt that a large volume of advertising even in recent years has been based on such unfounded faith, without adequate effort by management or advertising counsel either to secure needed evidence by which to judge its sales and profit possibilities or to apply hard thinking regarding these possibilities from such facts as are readily at hand. While facts on which to base judgments are desirable and much needed, a bit of common sense ordinarily will go a long way in preventing some of the wastes that occur. Case material, discussion with businessmen, and observation lie back of this opinion as to the lack of "tough-mindedness" in regard to advertising expenditure. Further evidence is to be found in certain practices in the advertising field which have not been uncommon.

One such piece of evidence is found in the methods often applied in the selection and use of advertising counsel. That advertising agents vary in abilities for handling specific accounts may be accepted. Instead of selecting agents on the basis of careful investigation of their suitability for an account, however, many advertisers have been guilty of encouraging agents to compete for their accounts on a speculative basis.[24] In such solicitation, agents have been given neither adequate time nor adequate pay for making the careful industry studies generally needed to devise an advertising program, nor have they been given complete company data essential for building advertising into a good management program. Yet they have been asked to produce ideas or plans or to give examples of brilliant and dynamic copy which might effect a flow of sales. The worth of the plans or ideas presented in such solicitations is often judged by advertisers without the careful study needed for building or appraising sales plans. Again, advertisers and agency men, according to reports obtained, have been guilty not infrequently of making poor selection of advertising counsel because of friendship or politics.[25] Moreover, after advertising counsel have been selected, whether on a sound or an unsound basis, many advertisers have not made effective use of them. Unfortunately, under the advertising agency system as established, advertisers often have been unwilling to give to their agents the intimate sales and operating data necessary for effectively devising and executing a program. Because of the relatively frequent turnover of advertising agency accounts, they have feared that intimate records of sales operations might later be used to their disadvantage. The fact that such a view exists probably operates against fully effective advertising practice.

While advertising agency executives have done much to improve advertising practice, the agency system has not always been conducive to improvement. Some advertising agents have not appeared greatly interested in applying the control and measurement techniques that

---

[24] Numerous articles have appeared in the trade press regarding the so-called "speculative solicitation of accounts." Although no statistical evidence regarding the extent of the practice is available, the fact that it is fairly common is indicated in trade articles published, e.g.:
B. A. Grimes, "The Pros and Cons of Agency Speculative Plans," *Printers' Ink Monthly*, November, 1932; "Advertising Solicitation Error," *Printers' Ink*, November 1, 1934; "Agency Solicitation as Seen from the Agency Side," *Printers' Ink*, December 6, 1934; "Agency Solicitation, How Much and When," *Printer's Ink*, December 13, 1934.
Lee Bristol, "On Selecting and Paying an Advertising Agency," *Printers' Ink*, September 13, 1934.
T. G. McGowan, "Advertising Agency Selection" and "Advertising Agency Solicitations," *Advertising & Selling*, January 30, 1936, and February 13, 1936.
"Advertising Solicitation Methods Draw Fire of Many Advertisers," *Printers' Ink*, May 3, 1940.

[25] Not only were examples found of questionable agency selection based on friendship, but it was stated that media selection often has been directed more by friendship than by rigorous analysis of media needs. For the published observations of an advertising agent of long experience regarding what he considered unsound advertising practice induced in part by the peculiar relationship of advertisers and agency and media representatives, see: E. T. Gundlach, *op. cit.*

have been developed or in furthering their improvement. They have sometimes given the impression that they prefer to proceed as the "experts" or "authorities," without careful check against the sales and profit contributions of the advertisements they produce. Some excuse for such an attitude may be found in the fact that control and measurement techniques have been so crude that they have carried the threat of giving erroneous ideas as to the worth of the advertising among executives not aware of the limitations of the testing methods. The above statement regarding attitudes of some agents should not be taken, however, to mean that all advertising agents have been indifferent or hostile to the development of techniques to reduce advertising risk. As a matter of fact, advertising agency men have played a leading part not only in improving advertising techniques but also in developing the improved methods of control and measurement which have been discussed. Moreover, many of them have regretted the frequent lack of opportunity to work closely with clients. In the conduct of this advertising study research workers were told confidentially of some cases in which advertising agencies resigned from accounts because managements insisted on operating without the careful planning and testing which the agents deemed essential.

That many large advertisers have not been sympathetic with attempts to apply controls and measurement techniques to advertising is indicated from conversations with business executives and from case material. Discussions with certain executives controlling very large advertising expenditures indicated a belief on their part that advertising success depended not so much upon careful planning and checking as upon brilliance of ideas and upon a superselling sense which enabled some individuals to formulate or pick ideas that would click, as against those which would fail. One such executive stated that he released very large advertising campaigns primarily on his judgment as to their probable success, with little or no testing. This man expressed his viewpoint thus: "Advertising is in reality an art rather than a science, and its effectiveness depends upon the real merchandising ability of the individual who is responsible for that advertising and the expenditure of monies. Poor or mediocre advertising is undoubtedly wasteful. I believe that 90% of advertising expenditure would fall under this heading, but the other 10% spent by merchants, artists in their line, is so valuable that it carries the 90% of waste and makes the whole method a benefit."

This company has been profitable and undoubtedly a considerable part of its success may be attributed to its use of advertising, because advertising plays an important part in its selling program. The executive admitted, however, that a number of his hunches had proved disappointing and confessed his inability to predict with certainty that a piece of copy or a copy theme would be successful.

While the executive risked large sums on untested copy themes, his advertising was conducted carefully in other respects. Media were carefully checked; expenditures were budgeted in accordance with the needs of territories; sales results were followed carefully, and campaigns which were not pulling were not carried for an undue amount of time. Further inquiry showed that his advertising department was experimenting with copy testing techniques.

This example is believed indicative of a trend. The number of executives and agencies in business who rely upon hunch and unchecked promotional artistry have been many, and there are still many who profess adherence to this viewpoint. The importance of creative ability in advertising is not to be questioned; ability to develop promotional ideas and plans that will induce buying will always be at a premium so long as selling influence is permitted. Yet the need of submitting ideas and promotional plans to the various checking procedures outlined above has become increasingly recognized. As with the executive quoted, although numerous advertisers may vehemently argue that advertising is an art instead of a science, nevertheless, in actual practice they have adopted many of the management techniques developed to test and check advertising.

While some businessmen have made wasteful expenditure because of an unfounded faith in advertising, others have gone to the other extreme of unwisely rejecting advertising as a helpful sales and profit tool because they have insisted on concrete proof of its contribution to sales and profit. This attitude has been held particularly by some executives with a mathematical type of mind, who, lacking concrete evidence of the part which advertising might play in influencing sales, have turned instead to selling methods, such as personal selling, with which the chances of tracing results to particular efforts are more feasible. Consequently they have failed to give adequate consideration to the full possibilities of advertising as a complementary selling force for increasing sales and profit.

Probably the answer to the most profitable use of advertising lies between the two extremes of use by those who have an unfounded faith in advertising and are willing to proceed without seeking facts to check its contribution, and of use by those who insist on mathematical proof of advertising results. Failure to seek and use facts to guide judgments of advertising's contribution inevitably leads to waste. On the other hand, the large number of variables and the lack of precise techniques for accounting for and measuring advertising and selling efforts makes foolish the demand of executives for mathematical precision in measurement. Advertising's worth in a selling program must be determined by a balanced judgment from data regarding the many variables which affect demand, data generally incomplete and unsatisfactory, yet increasingly to be sought after in order to decrease management error.

Development of Control and Measuring Techniques for Retail Advertising

Behind the varying usage of advertising by retailers mentioned in the last chapter are business judgments regarding the part which advertising may play for particular stores in selling merchandise and in attracting patronage. As with manufacturers, retailers' decisions relating to advertising expenditure have not been based on exact knowledge of sales and profit contribution of particular advertisements or groups of advertisements, because the precise contribution of advertising to retail profit has not been readily demonstrable. Advertising is only one among many factors contributing to the sales volume enjoyed by a store on any day or week. Others are skill in the selection and pricing of merchandise; the skill of its selling force; location of the store; and the strength of the patronage motives which it has established among consumers through its reputation for integrity, fairness in adjusting complaints, the quality and variety of its merchandise, its good values, and its credit and delivery service.

Difficulties met by the retailer in tracing the sales contribution of particular advertisements are comparable to those met by manufacturers in tracing their advertising results. Even though a considerable percentage of the retailers' advertisements are designed to lead to immediate action of consumers in buying the merchandise featured, yet it is hard to determine to what extent sales can be attributed to specific advertisements. On any day the average retailer enjoys the major share of his sales from normal patronage without reference to any advertising done. Few retail institutions, however, have been able to devise formulae for determining the normal patronage for articles or departments on any day; hence they cannot know advertising's contribution to sales with any precision. In addition, numerous variables affecting sales enter to complicate advertising measurement: the fickleness of the weather, the advertising of competitors, and the imponderable involved in the salability of particular merchandise offered in an advertisement, particularly when fashion is involved.

Most department and specialty stores employ records showing the sales of advertised merchandise and total sales of the corresponding departments. These provide a basis for rough rule-of-thumb grading of advertisements as to sales effectiveness. These rough ratings of advertisements serve as one guide to judgments regarding the effectiveness of different advertising techniques and the appeal of types of merchandise in attracting consumers.

Among a large number of retailers interviewed in the course of this study, three were found to have developed methods which they believed measured with rough accuracy the sales contribution of specific advertisements. Their methods at least promised to help them find better solutions than previously regarding advertising questions as to selection of merchandise to offer, price lines to feature, appeals to make, media to employ, day of week or season to advertise, size of advertisement to use, and so on.[26]

The studies made by these stores have been restricted to the special promotion or sales type of advertisements. Since such advertisements are designed to induce immediate response, their effectiveness can be measured by immediate returns. For the advertisements whose purpose is largely to build reputation for departments or for a store, the measurement of effectiveness is more difficult, because response is delayed and consequently cannot be determined. The measurement of such advertisements has not been attempted, so far as is known.

That retail advertisements vary in effectiveness, just as do the advertisements of manufacturers, is to be expected. After one of the stores mentioned, Macy's in New York, had devised a formula for determin-

---

[26] For a short statement regarding one of these researches, carried on by R. H. Macy & Co., see Paul Hollister, "A Trend in Retail Advertising," *Eleventh Boston Conference on Distribution, 1939* (Boston, Retail Trade Board and Boston Chamber of Commerce, 1939). Similar analysis of advertisements has been carried out by the associated store, L. Bamberger & Co., Newark. An unusual test of advertising measurement by a retail cleansing establishment will be found in the case of Cary Cleansers, Inc., (B), *Problems in Advertising* (3d ed.), by N. H. Borden, p. 436.

ing the normal sales return for an advertisement, it was able to rate its quick-action advertisements on the basis of their contribution to volume above normal. They found a wide variation in the effectiveness of the advertisements they had employed.[27] Thus able to classify advertisements according to sales effectiveness, the management was able to study the probable causes of variation. It sought to increase the response of these advertisements, reportedly with the successful result of reducing the ratio of advertising cost to sales above normal expectancy from 19% in the spring of 1936 to 13% in the fall of 1938.[28]

Macy's, however, represents one of the most progressive of retail advertisers, advanced in its efforts to increase advertising effectiveness. The extent to which Macy's professes to have improved direct-action advertising is indicative of a similar improvement that might be made in perhaps even greater degree among numberless retail advertisers, were advertising effectiveness known to them. The lack of techniques for measuring retail advertising contribution has tended to perpetuate a considerable degree of ineffective expenditure, even though progress has been made in decreasing haphazard and unprofitable retail advertising through improved planning and budgeting methods.[29]

In this chapter the efforts of businessmen to develop management techniques to reduce the risks attending the use of advertising have been discussed. Both for retail advertising and manufacturers' advertising the problems of measurement and of control which must be solved are difficult, and as yet only a start towards their solution has been made. Moreover, many managements have not taken advantage of such methods as are available. Consequently there can be little doubt that the wastes arising from use of advertising are considerable. Nevertheless, it is encouraging that both manufacturers and retailers have shown so much interest and have been willing to experiment to such a marked degree in recent years to improve the tools which will reduce this waste.

---

[27] The other stores which had made studies testified likewise regarding wide variation in effectiveness of advertisements.

[28] Paul Hollister, *op. cit.*

[29] Considerable progress has been made in recent years in the adoption of improved methods of planning and budgeting retail advertising, particularly by large retailers. Some progress has been made also in developing market research and internal store statistics helpful in guiding advertising decisions regarding what to promote, how to promote it, and to whom to promote it. For a discussion of these topics, see C. M. Edwards, Jr., and W. H. Howard, *Retail Advertising and Sales Promotion* (New York, Prentice-Hall, Inc., 1936), ch. IV, V, XX, XXI.

CHAPTER VI

THE ECONOMIC EFFECTS OF ADVERTISING
AS INDICATED BY VALUE THEORY

IN THE preceding chapters an effort has been made to give a realistic analysis of the use of advertising by businessmen. Its development as a tool of business to secure sales needed for profitable operation of large-scale enterprise; the struggle of manufacturers and distributors to maintain stable, profitable volume of sales by building consumer preferences for their brands; and the difficulties met by them in the competitive struggle to devise profitable operating programs in a dynamic world and to reduce the risks attending the use of advertising in those programs have been discussed. All these considerations serve as needed background for the economic study to which attention is now turned.

A discussion of factual findings relating to the economics of advertising should be preceded by a clear understanding of the questions or issues which the science of economics raises regarding advertising. The main question posed by the businessman regarding advertising, namely, whether it will help assure a profit, is only one of many questions to be dealt with in an economic investigation. Economists are interested in advertising as it affects the functioning of the economic system as a whole. They wish to determine how advertising and various other economic forces bear upon one another in contributing to the social effectiveness of the system. One can view social effectiveness from many angles, but certainly one of the important considerations is the sum total of satisfactions derived by people from the consumption of goods and services. Other considerations obviously include effects on investment and employment. The part of economics which deals with these problems is value theory, and it is from certain developments in value theory that some of the principal criticisms of advertising arise.[1]

---

[1] Those interested in a detailed and technical discussion of value theory are referred to the following authorities who, in addition to their own contributions on theory, cite extensive further references:
Edward Chamberlin, *The Theory of Monopolistic Competition* (2d ed., Cambridge, Harvard University Press, 1936).

Unfortunately laymen have not fully comprehended the technical terms used by economists or the full significance of the economic issues or questions which have been raised in value theory.[2] This misunderstanding has arisen in part from the method of theoretical analysis, which is to apply logic to certain sets of assumptions in an effort better to understand economic behavior. Since economic forces are many and their workings complex, theorists commonly find it advisable to resort to simplifications in their analyses. By employing a certain set of assumptions regarding demand and supply they have been able to reason regarding prices under conditions approximating the assumptions. They then may move to a new set of assumptions to see what conclusions are indicated with a new set of forces in operation. In the history of theory, economists continually have attempted to refine their theory and from time to time have given recognition in their analyses to new sets of conditions which inductive study of the economic world has shown to be applicable.

Although theorists over a long period have analyzed various sets of assumptions, not until recent years have they paid much attention to the place of aggressive selling and advertising in their theory of value. Among the theoretical analyses made, those which have been most widely studied in texts relate to so-called "pure competition" and "pure monopoly." In neither of these theories is allowance made for aggressive selling. In recent years, however, certain economists who have been dissatisfied with these older theories of value because they failed to take full account of actual facts in the world of reality have sought to bring into their analyses the facts of aggressive selling and

---

Alfred Marshall, *Principles of Economics* (8th ed., London, Macmillan & Co., Ltd., 1920).
Joan Robinson, *The Economics of Imperfect Competition* (London, Macmillan & Co., Ltd., 1933).
Robert Triffin, *Monopolistic Competition and General Equilibrium Theory* (Cambridge, Harvard University Press, 1940).

[2] While value theory is employed in this study to indicate the questions regarding the economic effects of advertising to be investigated in the factual study, laymen should recognize that economists' conclusions are not guided solely by value theory. Value theory is one specialized field of economics and does not include all that economists have to say about various economic subjects. They have many theories. They also investigate the practical workings of business. In these various segments of endeavor different aspects of the same phenomenon may be examined. For example, in value theory they set up assumptions to help them understand prices under conditions of monopoly. On the other hand, they have made many other studies regarding monopoly and its effects. Accordingly, in the field of monopoly, as in many other areas, the conclusions or statements based on theoretical analysis should not be taken to indicate the final conclusions or all that economists may have to say about the subject.

certain other business methods.[3] From these efforts has grown a theory of so-called imperfect, or monopolistic, competition.[4] It is through this latter theory that economic issues regarding advertising are brought into focus. These issues are likely to be better understood, however, if the more familiar theories of pure competition and pure monopoly are outlined and compared with the theory of imperfect competition. Accordingly in this chapter the three theories are reviewed in non-technical language, and the questions or issues which flow from them as to the possible effects of advertising in a free economy are pointed out. The discussion is not a full, detailed statement of the theory of value and is not meant for economists whose interest lies in refinements of economic theory. It is intended rather to provide an interpretation for the layman in order that he may understand the assumptions underlying the theories of pure competition and of pure monopoly and appreciate how the introduction of facts regarding aggressive selling has clarified the economic questions regarding advertising and aggressive selling which have been the subject of the factual investigation discussed in later chapters.

---

[3] There is plenty of evidence in economic theory to show that the older economists were fully aware of the actual facts of the business world, but simply did not make them a part of their value analysis. In turn, although a large part of the original impetus to develop the more recent theory consisted of an exploration of the facts of the real world, these theories once started have been amplified and developed by a considerable group of economists who appear to be more interested in refinements of theoretical methodology than in following the real world and determining whether their theoretical conclusions stand the test of inductive method.

[4] It was suggested to the author that he employ the phrase *non-price competition* to refer to the concepts ordinarily referred to by economists under either the term *monopolistic competition* or that of *imperfect competition*. The layman fails to comprehend the latter phrases because he is unfamiliar with the technical and restricted economic definitions of competition and monopoly, as given in the pages above. To the layman the phrase monopolistic competition appears made up of mutually contradictory words and is generally meaningless. Moreover the word monopoly carries connotations of undesirability. Imperfect competition does not mean much more to him because he is unaware that the word competition in the phrase refers essentially to price competition as assumed in the theory of pure competition. The suggested term, non-price competition, of course, signifies the fact that much of the competition of business is carried on not in price but in non-price forms. On the other hand, this descriptive phrase fails to comprehend fully the concepts covered under the theory of monopolistic or imperfect competition. For example, imperfect competition assumes that generally some degree of price competition as well as non-price competition is present. Again, one part of the theory is that, when there are a limited number of sellers, they may behave as monopolists and may not compete either in price or in non-price forms, because to do so might lead to retaliatory action by competing sellers. Moreover, the large amount of discussion devoted in recent years to monopolistic or imperfect competition has made both these phrases familiar and firmly accepted among students of economics. Because the suggested term does not fully describe the concept, and because the terms monopolistic competition and imperfect competition have become firmly established among economists, the author has elected to employ the accepted economic terminology in this volume. Of the two terms, that of imperfect competition has been employed generally. Frequent reference has been made to non-price forms of competition.

Before comparing the various value theories, however, it is needful to make a brief statement about the methodological tools of the economist.

Methodological Tools of Economists

Economists have made a number of assumptions in connection with their reasoning about value. They have postulated man as a rational animal who, impelled by self-interest and seeking the lowest prices in all his purchases of any class of product, apportions the expenditure of his limited income in accordance with the subjective satisfactions to be had from the various products and services available to him. The valuations set by manufacturers or sellers in parting with their merchandise, on the other hand, are based not so much on the satisfactions in use which they themselves would derive from their merchandise as upon the valuations necessary to cover their costs and to give a profit; in short, the valuations necessary to provide the incentive to continue in business. In the long run, consumer valuations guide production. Resources are allocated to producing various products[5] in so far as the valuations or demands of consumers meet the necessary costs of production.

As methodological devices, economists make use of demand and supply schedules. A demand schedule represents the quantities of products which are demanded in a market at various prices; a supply schedule represents the quantities which are offered at various prices. The concept of these schedules may be used within short-run or long-run analyses. When a supply schedule is long run, it is a cost schedule; that is, it portrays the costs which must be covered if producers are to continue in business to supply the various quantities over the long run. Also, both these schedules may be constructed to apply to an individual firm or to an industry. The schedules commonly are plotted graphically and the price resulting from the interaction of the forces of demand and supply is portrayed at the intersection of the two curves. In short, the two curves depict an interaction of forces causing prices or, as the textbooks commonly say, they act much in the way that the two blades of a pair of scissors both function in cutting a piece of paper.

---

[5] For simplification, the single term *products* frequently has been used in this discussion. It should be understood that economic goods cover not only products but services of all types.

The Demand Schedule

The demand for any product arises from the utility [6] of that product to individuals in the market. Each consumer has numerous wants which he desires to gratify. His separate demand for each of many different products is determined by the character of his many wants and by his income. In purchasing to fill all these wants, the individuals within a market create a combined demand which we may term the aggregate demand, as contrasted with the demand of any individual.

Since the purchasing power of most consumers is limited, each ordinarily has to exercise choice in deciding the wants which he will satisfy or the extent to which he will satisfy his various wants. At any time the individual consumer, driven by the necessity of apportioning his income among purchases to satisfy his various wants, has for each type of product a demand curve. Theoretically he has a schedule of the amounts of each which he will purchase at market prices. His demand curve for a product is affected by the utility of successive units of the product to him. It is subject, on the one hand, to the law of diminishing utility, which is a recognition of the fact that the additional benefits which he derives from a given purchase of a commodity diminish with every increase in the stock already in his possession. It is governed, on the other hand, by the strength of his desire for other products, because purchase of one thing may well mean foregoing another thing.

Demand for the economist is a considerably more precise concept than it is for the marketer, as is indicated in the following quotation:

To measure demand, the economists take money as the standard measure and refer to price. Money is a satisfactory measure when its own value does not fluctuate, i.e., when the general price level does not change. It is important to remember that demand helps to explain prices only when the general price level is assumed and that *demand and supply really explain relative prices, not the general level of prices.*

Assuming the general level of prices, we measure demand by the prices the buyers are ready to pay for different quantities. *Demand refers to both quantities and prices, not to either of them alone.* A given demand may be expressed either in tabular or in diagrammatic form. A demand schedule states the demand situation as follows:

---

[6] The utility of a product is its ability to fill a want or desire of consumers.

Price	Quantity
$9	1
8	2
7	3
6	4
5	5
4	6
3	7
2	8
1	9
0	10

This means that if the price is $9 one unit will be taken, and if the price is $7 three units will be taken; and conversely, that if only one is put on the market the price will be $9, whereas if eight are put on the market the price will be $2. If eight are sold rather than one, it does not mean an increased demand; it means that, with an unchanged buyers' attitude toward the commodity, the price is lower for the larger quantity.

The same demand situation is presented in diagrammatic form in the following Figure as a demand curve DD'.

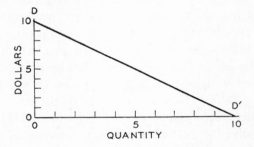

The entire situation, i.e., the whole statement of quantities and prices, is referred to as the demand. It is a convention among economists to represent physical quantity on the horizontal axis and price on the vertical axis.

The demand schedule and the demand curve both illustrate the general law of demand: *other things being equal, the larger the quantity put on the market, the lower the price; or the lower the price, the larger the quantity sold.*

An increase or decrease in demand must be represented by a new curve. *An increase in demand means that, at the same series of prices as before, increased quantities can be sold.* An increased demand is represented by a new curve, lying to the right of the original curve. A special case of an increased demand is one brought about by the seller through advertising or other sales promotion; this is called, in marketing, the expansibility of demand.

To be distinguished from an increase in demand is the elasticity of demand. Although the general law of demand states that larger quantities bring lower prices, it does not say how much lower. An elastic demand exists when the larger quantity brings a relatively small decline in price; an inelastic demand exists when the larger quantity brings a relatively large decline. In more precise language, *demand is elastic when, with a larger quantity offered, the necessary reduction in price is so small that the total receipts (the net price times the number of units sold) are greater for a large quantity than for a lesser one; and demand is inelastic when, with a larger quantity offered, the necessary reduction in price is sufficiently substantial to make the total receipts smaller. Conversely, of course, elastic demand means that when a smaller quantity is placed on the market the consequent advance in price is not sufficient to increase the total receipts, whereas inelasticity means that with a smaller quantity placed on the market the consequent advance in price is sufficiently great to increase the total receipts. The boundary case is that where the elasticity is one, where the total receipts are the same whatever the number of units sold.* There is no reason why the elasticity of demand for a particular commodity should be the same throughout; the same commodity might have an elastic demand for one range of prices and quantities and an inelastic demand for another.[7]

The Supply Schedule

A supply schedule is a representation of the quantities that will be put on the market at various prices. In the very short run, where goods already exist in manufacturers' or merchants' inventories, the quantities which will appear on the market at the several prices on the supply schedule bear little relation to the cost of production. In a longer period, when the goods have to be produced by existing facilities, the quantities offered will be in relation to prime or variable costs, and prices may or may not cover fixed costs. In the considerably longer run, when either replacement or expansion of existing productive facilities is involved, so-called fixed costs become of importance as determinants of supply since prices then must cover all outlays necessary to maintain or augment supply. Under these conditions some return to capital also may be considered as a cost since in the absence of such a return, or the prospect of it, investment does not take place.

The Theories of Pure Monopoly and of Pure Competition

The theory of monopoly explains price in those instances in which a single producer in a market has complete control over the supply of the product. Control over supply makes it possible for the monopolist to set price as he desires. The price set is that which maximizes profit or net return. In theory the monopolist determines the cost of producing various amounts of his product; he appraises so far as possible the quantities that can be sold at different prices; and he then estab-

---

[7] M. P. McNair and R. S. Meriam, *Problems in Business Economics* (New York, McGraw-Hill Book Co., Inc., 1941), pp. 82–84.

lishes his output at a point which maximizes his net return. Economic analysis indicates that usually this point is above the point at which the demand schedule and supply schedule would equate, provided no control of supply were exercised. The theory of monopoly assumes the demand curve of consumers to be known.

At the other extreme from pure monopoly is the concept of pure competition. Actually in real life cases of pure competition are almost as difficult to find as cases of pure monopoly, but both concepts are very useful for analytical purposes. In the theory of pure competition the products or services of any particular category are assumed to be identical or standardized. The market is assumed to contain a large number of sellers and a large number of buyers, the action of any one of whom has no appreciable effect in the final price determination. In the theory, a given demand schedule may be assumed, and the effect thereof on equilibrium value worked out. Then new assumptions regarding demand may be made, and the effect thereof studied; for instance, an increase in the demand at each of several prices might be assumed and its effects noted. When studying pure competition and pure monopoly, theorists thus have recognized the effects of demand changes upon equilibrium value. But in the building of the theories they gave little attention to reasons why demand changed. Sometimes they referred to new discoveries, new inventions, or shifts in consumers' desires; but practically never did they refer to aggressive selling as a cause of change in demand. For that reason aggressive selling costs, i.e., educational costs and persuasion costs on the part of sellers, are not included in the theory of pure competition. As a matter of fact, the concept provides no reason for the seller to spend money for aggressive selling, for the basic assumptions preclude such expenditure. Consumers are assumed to have given wants and perfect knowledge of the market. For example, for such a product as soap, they are assumed to be indifferent to what producer's soap they take, because all soap is assumed to be identical, and they are aware of all the satisfactions which soap might give them. Further it is assumed that producers can sell all they can produce at the market price and accordingly that no producer can add to the supply at the given moment at the existing price. Under such conditions there would be no gain to the producer from aggressive selling efforts. Under such conditions of pure competition, the curves of demand and supply for a product define the point at which demand and supply are equated

in a market. This point is the price at which the opposing economic
forces of demand and supply tend to balance.

Simplifications Involved in Theories of Pure Monopoly and Pure Competition

Economists have realized that the conditions assumed in the theories
both of value under pure monopoly and of value under pure competition are fictions. They are simplifications which give first approximations in the effort to understand and measure price in a complex,
dynamic economy. The theories have helped students to understand
value in a system containing few, if any, examples of pure competition and perfect monopoly, a system rather that is characterized by
imperfect competition. Even though specific products do not have
conditions of demand and supply which are in accord with the conditions assumed in these theories, yet the theories can be of help in
guiding judgments regarding price behavior, in so far as the conditions for a specific product accord more with those assumed in the
theory of pure monopoly, on the one hand, or more with those of
pure competition, on the other hand.

As a matter of fact, there are no such things as pure monopoly and
pure competition. There is no monopoly, because every product is to
some extent in competition with all other products for the consumer's
dollar; and nearly every product has some substitutes which the consumer may accept to fill his needs. For example, even the most complete monopolies known, such as an exclusive electric plant, are not
without competition. If electric rates are too high, many people will
forego using much electricity and will direct their expenditures to
products filling entirely different needs, or they may elect to substitute
other products or services which would fill the needs or desires which
electricity might fill, e.g., gas for cooking or light. The closest
approach to pure competition is found in only a few raw material
markets, such as grain, fiber, and major metals. In such markets are
large numbers of buyers and sellers who are anonymous, and ordinarily
no one has an appreciable effect upon price.

Conditions Incorporated in the Theory of Imperfect Competition

The earlier economists were well aware that the theories of competition and monopoly did not describe all the facts. They saw the

imperfections in the market, which were not covered by their theories, but they did not try to incorporate these "imperfections" in their theories. This point of view marks the difference between the older economists of the 19th century and some of those of more recent years, since the later group definitely have undertaken to build their theories around the "imperfections" of the market. This new body of systematic theory is variously described as monopolistic, or imperfect, competition. The theory of imperfect competition gives recognition to the following important conditions met in the world of reality which are not covered in the assumptions of the more simplified theories:

(1) Goods in competition ordinarily are not identical, but differentiated.

(2) Instead of consumers with perfect knowledge and definitely known demand, the market generally is made up of consumers whose knowledge is imperfect and whose demands are subject to influence. These facts lead to two important conditions affecting value:

   (a) Aggressive selling affects the demand schedule for products.

   (b) Aggressive selling costs enter as elements of greater or less importance into the costs of supply.[8]

(3) Competition, instead of taking place solely in terms of price, is carried on in part in advertising, sales promotion, product quality, service guarantees, and other non-price forms.

(4) Instead of markets with a large number of sellers, none of whom has appreciable effect on price, many markets are dominated by a small number of concerns, each of which is big enough to affect prices. As to whether they will attempt to influence price, two assumptions are generally made:

   (a) That the tendency of entrepreneurs is to maximize profits; hence that, so far as possible, they generally will adopt pricing practices which promise maximization of profits.

   (b) That most producers of manufactured products operating with appreciable overhead costs, and well aware of the disastrous possibilities of price cutting, tend to appraise carefully competitors' reactions to any change in

---

[8] It is only a fair statement that the newer theories have placed special emphasis on the cost aspects of aggressive selling. Though recognizing that aggressive selling affects demand schedules, these theorists actually have done little inductive exploration of these effects.

policy, with the result that prices tend to remain well above variable costs.

(5) Sellers in their pricing frequently do not operate with perfect knowledge of their costs, of the conditions governing demand for their products, or of the price activities of competitors. The assumption of this condition of sellers' ignorance has not received so much recognition in the theoretical analysis of students of imperfect competition as have the conditions listed above. It will be noted that this assumption goes somewhat counter to the assumption contained in item (4a) above, i.e., that entrepreneurs seek to maximize profits; for, even if the desire to maximize profits is assumed in analysis, it must be recognized by students of pricing that sellers' ignorance of costs, demand, and competitors' reactions acts as a hindrance to a rational setting of prices so as to maximize profits.

All these sets of conditions, which have an important bearing upon the extent to which products are demanded by consumers and supplied by producers, may be closely associated with and even depend upon the use of advertising. In so far as they involve advertising use, numerous questions or issues correspondingly arise regarding the effect of advertising upon the functioning of the economic system. Accordingly, the significance of each of the points listed above upon the functioning of the economy is discussed briefly in the order of listing, the possible relations to advertising are indicated, and the economic issues to be investigated in the factual chapters are enumerated.

EFFECTS OF PRODUCT DIFFERENTIATION UPON VALUE

The fact of differentiation, which has been described in preceding chapters, can be accepted; the question is one regarding its effects upon value as indicated by economic analysis. From the standpoint of theory, differentiation represents an element of monopoly through which the seller gets a limited control over price. Competition based solely on price, with buyers indifferent as to the product bought, as assumed in the theory of pure competition, no longer is held to obtain. Consumers prefer some brands over others and will pay more for preferred brands. When there is any degree of differentiation, each seller has a monopoly over his own individualized product or brand; he is subject not to direct competition on that brand, but only to the competition of substitute products or brands. As differentiation becomes more important, the element of monopoly theoretically becomes greater; the brand owner tends to be further removed from direct competition because of increasing strength of consumer preferences. In any case, however, whenever there is differentiation, prices tend to be adjusted somewhat in accordance with the principles of monopoly rather than those of pure competition.

Questions Regarding Economic Effects of Advertising Arising from Differentiation

What is the relation of this fact of product differentiation to advertising, and consequently, what are the issues which should be investigated in this study of the economic effects of advertising? The specific questions raised for investigation are as follows:

(1) In what ways, if any, does advertising contribute to the practice of product differentiation?

(2) To what extent does product differentiation for various products contribute to a monopoly position which permits substantial control over price?

   (a) Is the control over price obtained through differentiation practically important in the whole economic picture, or is it relatively unimportant?

(3) Does the practice of product differentiation contribute in any way to economic progress and thereby enhance the general social well-being?

(4) Or, conversely, are the differentiations employed by sellers in their attempts to get away from direct price competition inconsequential and therefore undesirable from the standpoint of consumer satisfactions to be derived from them?

   (a) Does this differentiation lead to undesirable complexity in consumer buying which might be avoided?

   (b) Does it increase costs because of the resulting large number of brands, with but minor differences among them, which distributors must carry?

   (c) Does making so many brands known lead to undue advertising costs?

EFFECTS OF IMPERFECT KNOWLEDGE UPON VALUE THEORY

The assumption of perfect knowledge and of known demands on the part of consumers, which is part of both the theory of pure monopoly and that of pure competition, is far from reality. Instead of knowing the full utility of all products to them, consumers are relatively ignorant of the satisfactions they may expect from the wide range of merchandise at their command, particularly since each brand is differentiated in some respect from other brands. Moreover, instead of having known and easily predictable demands, their demands are in constant flux in this dynamic world. Part of the fluctuation in demand comes from the use of influence by sellers. That these are the facts is not open to question.

The analysis of these facts shows that imperfect knowledge and unpredictable demands of consumers have an important bearing upon value because these facts affect both the demand curves and the cost curves for a product. Demand curves are affected because advertising and selling are employed both to move the curves to the right, i.e., increase the demand, and also to change their shape, i.e., affect elasticity. The cost curves are affected because advertising, personal selling, and other non-price efforts employed by businessmen to influence sales involve costs which must be included in the cost curves. Consequently, two groups of questions regarding the economic effects of advertising are brought to the fore: (1) those relating to advertising's effects upon the demand for products and (2) those relating to its effects upon the costs of products.

The Effect of Advertising upon Demand

Advertising and aggressive selling represent forces exercised by sellers chiefly to shift the demand curve, although they also may be used to change the shape of the demand curve for a product.[9] Adver-

---

[9] Advertisers probably do not think in terms of changing the shape of the demand curves of their products through the use of advertising, but their pricing practice sometimes indicates that they act in the hope that brand reputation built by advertising may have made the demand for their brands inelastic. This would appear true, for example, in cases in which heavily advertised brands during periods of falling prices have sometimes been held to their old prices or have been reduced but little, apparently in the hope that the preferences built for the products would lead consumers to continue buying them even though little or no reduction in price was made. Since the holding of prices in a falling price market is the equivalent of a price rise, sellers following this practice act as though they hoped brand reputation had made the demand for their products inelastic. It is not apparent that advertising necessarily has this effect, for as is indicated in later chapters, advertisers have sometimes suffered as the result of following a policy of having "sticky" prices. See Chapter XXI.

tisers wish to move the demand curve to the right, that is, to bring greater sales at a particular price or to get a higher price for a particular quantity than they would have without such selling effort. To do this they appeal to consumers' buying motives, with the aim of changing the marginal utility[10] of individual consumers for the class of product featured and accordingly to change its aggregate demand. For them advertising performs the economic function of leading consumers to arrive at evaluations which influence the price and volume received in such manner as may enable the enterprise to succeed.

The advertising appeals employed to change the utility of products to consumers may be classified as primary or selective. When appeal is made to primary buying motives, the objective is to increase primary demand, i.e., to induce people to buy products of the class in which the advertised article falls. It is offered as a solution to a want, or desire, of the consumer. For example, the featuring of the leisure that the housewife may experience from having labor-saving household devices, such as washing machines or vacuum cleaners, is designed to lead to the purchase of such articles. In the case of cosmetics, say skin creams, the featuring in advertisements of the romance that comes from having a fine skin is designed to lead to the use of beautifying creams which may bring romance.

In contrast, appeals to selective motives are designed to bring out some superiority of a brand to other brands, i.e., to affect selective demand, or demand for brands within a product class. Want or desire for the class of product is assumed by the seller. For example, a washing machine may be advertised as having a particularly effective mechanism for loosening dirt, a vegetable shortening as being particularly effective in the making of pies and cakes, a sheet as offering durability. Such appeals are designed to establish mental associations between brand and product, i.e., ideas regarding product quality or performance which will induce ready acceptance or even preference for the brand.

Whenever a product is so highly individualized that consumers are inclined to think not in terms of product classifications but rather in terms of brand names, the advertiser can make effective use of pri-

---

[10] The term marginal purchase has been used by economists to describe the unit of a commodity which the buyer "is only just induced to purchase because he is on the margin of doubt whether it is worth his while to incur the outlay necessary to obtain it. The utility of his marginal purchase may be called the marginal utility of the thing to him." Alfred Marshall, *op. cit.*, p. 93.

mary appeals for securing a selective result. Accordingly when the face cream manufacturer features a woman winning romance because of her beautiful skin, the solution offered to satisfy this desire is not face cream in general but a specific brand. With proprietary remedies, alleviation or cure of a particular ailment is a primary appeal; but the solution offered to the consumer problem is a specific remedy. Thus for a substantial number of products for which differentiation exists or can be established in part by ideas conveyed in the advertising, advertisers use primary appeals as a basis of building a selective demand for their particular brands.

In turn it may be pointed out that advertising by competing sellers, even when they employ selective appeals, under certain conditions has a primary effect. It may increase total demand for any class of product, provided this demand is *expansible,* as explained in the next section.

The Concept of Expansibility of Demand

A study of demand shows that different products vary widely in the susceptibility of their primary demand to increase as a result of advertising and aggressive selling. For example, the demand for oranges has increased under aggressive selling; the demand for shoes has not so responded. The term frequently employed to express this susceptibility of demand for products to increase is "expansibility of demand." [11]

Expansibility of demand should be distinguished from elasticity of demand. Elasticity of demand is a concept relating to the shape of the demand curve, i.e., to the quantities that will be taken at various prices, other things being equal, and the position of the demand curve itself being unchanged; if, as prices fall the product of price times quantity increases, then the demand is elastic. [12] The concept

---

[11] This term is believed to have been used first by Professor M. T. Copeland in his marketing classes about 1925. The term was not employed in his *Principles of Merchandising* (Chicago, A. W. Shaw Company, 1924), although the enlarging of demand was commented upon (p. 8). The term was used in classes shortly thereafter. The concept of expansibility of demand relates to change of demand, which can come about from a number of causes. For example, changes in the level of income occurring from cyclical fluctuation have the effect of shifting demand curves. In periods of depression, when buying power is low, they are shifted to the left, while in periods of high income they are shifted to the right.

[12] Some economists have attempted to explain the responsiveness of various classes of products to advertising and selling effort in terms of elasticity of demand. A study of products will show that generally, though not always, products possessing an elastic demand are responsive to advertising and selling effort, but an explanation of responsiveness to advertising in terms of elasticity is not fully satisfactory. Any given demand schedule

of expansibility of demand is a part of change in demand, i.e., change in the attitude of the market towards a product, change in the position of the demand curve. Such changes may come about for reasons in no way connected with the activities of businessmen, for example, rise of interest in winter sports, decline in popularity of miniature golf; but if a business concern, or group of business concerns, by various methods of sales promotion induces the market to absorb a greater quantity of a product at the same price, or even at a higher price, then the demand may be termed "expansible." A product with an expansible demand is one for which a business can increase demand readily, price being constant, through appeal to consumers' buying motives. Conversely, a product has an inexpansible demand when its sales cannot be readily increased by appeals to buying motives.

The increase in sales of a product may come (1) from individual consumers being induced to use more of it for the purposes to which they were already putting it, (2) from present users being induced to buy more of the product for new uses featured in selling appeals, (3) from former nonusers having their desire for the product raised to the point where they become buyers. The seller attempts to change the marginal utility of the product among individuals in the market. One of the important problems faced by sellers when considering the possible profitability of advertising to expand demand is that of forecasting its expansibility, or its responsiveness to appeals.[13]

Advertising and Selective Demand

Observation and case study indicate that a preponderant share of advertising, whether employing primary or selective appeals, is used not so much with the thought of expanding demand for the class of product as with that of securing for each seller's brand a larger share of the consumer's expenditure upon that class of product than would be his without such advertising; i.e., the aim is to affect selective demand. In striving for this end the seller seeks to establish his brand

---

of the economist depicts a static situation. It shows the quantities of products which may be taken in a particular period of indefinite length at the prices named and assumes that forces other than price affecting demand are static.

Demand schedules are not static, however; they are subject to constant change. The quantities that will be taken in a period at particular prices are not in accordance with the quantities that will be taken in another period at these prices. In the preceding chapter it was noted that the demand for particular products is subject to constant change; change brought about by shifts in buying power, by alteration of living habits, by shifts in buying attitudes developed by aggressive selling, and so on.

[13] See Chapter V, p. 120 ff.; also, N. H. Borden, *Cooperative Advertising, op. cit.*, pp. 3–26.

as an individualized commodity. Through advertising and aggressive selling he hopes to establish a demand curve for his own brand to the right[14] of where it would be if he did not employ advertising; that is, he hopes that at any price more units will be demanded than would be the case without advertising.

While distinction has been drawn between primary and selective advertising appeals and between primary demand and selective demand, it is well to note that in the world of reality consumers generally set values not upon classes of products, e.g., shoes, but upon brands or sources of products, such as "Keds" or shoes of the Jones Shoe Store. The merchandise of different sellers in any product group is not identical. Accordingly, in place of visualizing a single demand schedule for a product class, it is more in keeping with actuality in most product fields to think of each seller at any time as having a demand curve for his brand, the quantities demanded at various prices being determined in large part by the valuations set by consumers for his brand in comparison with those set for competing brands, although, of course, indirect substitutes are also a factor. The above statement gives recognition to the fact that each seller, through differentiation and reputation, attempts to gain for his brand a limited monopoly position. It is limited because substitution is easy.

While there may be separate demand schedules for each differentiated product and therefore it may be difficult to visualize a single demand schedule for all producers making a given class of products, nevertheless the student of demand can arbitrarily use product classes and through industry statistics can study the trend of demand of each class in units and dollars, relating thereto the advertising and selling efforts exerted by the industry. Such a procedure will be followed in the factual studies.

Competitive Nature of Both Primary and Selective Advertising

In passing it may be well to consider from an economic theory standpoint the view taken by some commentators, both economists and businessmen, that primary advertising is preferable to selective

---

[14] The statement regarding shifting a demand curve to the right refers to the graphic presentation of demand schedules. Provided advertising were successful in stimulating consumer desire for a product, more units would be sold at any price than would be sold without advertising. Accordingly, in a graphic presentation of demand schedules, the schedule of increased quantities demanded under advertising usage would be to the right of the schedule of quantities demanded without advertising usage.

advertising. While the supporting arguments for this view are often hard to ascertain, the main points advanced appear to be three: first, that primary advertising, through stressing the utility of specific types of products, gives a more desirable sort of information to consumers than does selective advertising, which plays up points of product differentiation; secondly, that primary advertising is to be preferred because it is designed to strengthen an industry, and hence all firms within an industry, while selective advertising represents a battle among competitors with each seeking a larger slice of the total business of the industry; third, that primary demand advertising serves to expand total consumption, whereas selective advertising does not contribute to expansion of total demand.

To conclude on the basis of these reasons that primary demand advertising in all instances should be deemed economically preferable to selective advertising is questionable from a theoretical viewpoint. From the standpoint of the economy as a whole, all advertising is competitive, whether it uses primary or selective appeals. All producers are in competition for a share of consumers' expenditures and in this they employ both primary and selective advertising to affect consumer valuations. In this competition a shift in demand from firms in one industry to firms in another industry may or may not contribute any more to consumers' satisfactions than a shift in demand among firms within an industry. The question posed is what final distribution of consumer expenditure gives greatest satisfaction. From the standpoint of guidance in buying the consumer may benefit as much through being advised of the good features of a brand, when the differentiation of that brand can be of significance to him, as through being told in primary advertising of the benefits to him of a whole class of products. Primary and selective appeals are equally subject to misrepresentation and abuse. Moreover, the effects upon the volumes of individual producers and upon their costs and prices need not necessarily be favorable for one type of advertising and unfavorable for the other.

The question of how advertising theoretically may affect total consumption is considered later in this chapter. It will suffice here merely to state that advertising can have an effect in expanding total consumption only as it may influence investment and thus increase the capacity of the economy to produce, and as it may aid in securing fuller utilization of existing capacity. While primary advertising may lead consumers to desire new types of products and thus may encourage investment, the selective advertising by individual companies upon their differentiated brands may also lead to a demand requiring new investment. Moreover, primary demand advertising is not employed solely for new products for which expansion of production is expected, but often is used to try to save moribund or declining industries. The effect of such advertising is not to add to total consumption, but to protect the position of existing institutions. In short, it cannot be concluded that primary demand advertising is necessarily preferable from a social standpoint to selective advertising. Individual situations of advertising use must be studied separately whenever one seeks to appraise their economic effects.

Issues to Be Investigated Relating to Advertising's Effect upon Demand

Now that the effects of advertising upon demand have been outlined in theory, the issues to be investigated in the factual chapters may be listed. These issues relate to the extent to which demand for specific products has been changed by advertising and whether the satisfactions derived from consumption have been favorably or unfavorably affected. The questions may be stated as follows:

(1) To what extent has advertising affected the primary demand for various specific products?

(a) How does its effect upon primary demand vary for different products?

(2) To what extent has advertising affected the selective demand for various specific products?

(a) How does its effect upon selective demand vary for different products?

(3) Are advertising and aggressive selling necessary functions in a modern free economy?

(4) To what extent has advertising, as conducted, served as a desirable guide to consumers?

(a) Has it led to correct valuations?

(b) Has it led to incorrect valuations?

(c) What is the basis for determining what are correct and what are incorrect valuations?

(5) To what extent are there effective substitutes for advertising to provide information and education?

With this statement of issues relating to demand, attention may be directed to the topic of the effects of advertising upon the costs of products.

Advertising Costs in Economic Theory

In order that the issues for factual study relating to costs may be better understood, it is desirable to outline in some detail the character and behavior of costs as viewed in economic theory. The theories of pure competition and pure monopoly include no cognizance of costs of aggressive selling.[15] The exclusion of aggressive selling costs does not mean, however, that all marketing or distribution costs are excluded from these theories and only manufacturing costs included. Those marketing costs involving place and time utility are included, i.e., costs needed to get merchandise to the place desired by consumers at the time wanted, such as costs of transportation and stocking of merchandise. Although not generally mentioned by theorists, "information" costs also would be admitted, ". . . making and maintaining effective contact between buyers and sellers—in other words of finding out about markets and customers, and telling customers about the kinds, the quantities, the qualities and the prices of the goods which are being offered for sale."[16] Such costs would be recognized as essential in a complex society in which contact between producer and consumer is lacking, whereas they would not be incurred in a simple village economy, where buyers and producers are in close contact with each other. Under conditions of pure competition, however, such information would be the very minimum necessary to provide sellers with knowledge of the market's demands, and buyers with knowledge of the quality and price of merchandise available. While the function of providing information is covered by the activities of a market research department, salesforce, advertising department, and display men, the efforts of these departments devoted to persuading the consumer to buy more of any seller's merchandise than he would buy if left to himself, would not be considered a part of information. Information here means only what is needed for the "perfect" knowledge of price and source essential to buying standardized merchandise at the lowest price by consumers who realize product qualities and

---

[15] See Chapter VI, p. 157.
[16] Dorothea Braithwaite and S. P. Dobbs, *The Distribution of Consumable Goods* (London, George Routledge & Sons, Ltd., 1932), p. 14.

their own needs. It will be noted that such a distinction between information and aggressive selling, or "advertising persuasion," is more clearly perceived in abstract and logical thinking than in actual practice. Elements of information, as above defined, and elements of persuasion could not be easily separated one from the other among the operations of a salesforce, of an advertising department, or of a market research department.

While the older theories of value do not make provision for aggressive selling costs, it is evident that any analysis of product values in the world of reality must make provision for them, as has been done in the theory of imperfect competition, because in the aggregate they represent a vast expenditure. For any particular seller, marketing expenditures represent outlays which, like other costs, he must recoup in the long run if he is to continue in business. They represent to the consumer in each purchase an amount ranging from a very small percentage to a very appreciable percentage of the product price.

Effect of Aggressive Selling Costs on Unit Costs and Prices

While it is true that producers and sellers in the long run seek to make consumers pay for aggressive selling costs incurred, it does not necessarily follow that final product costs and consequently prices to consumers are increased as the result of aggressive selling efforts. Such efforts may give lower unit costs, although not always. The effect of advertising and selling upon unit costs of individual producers depends upon how the various selling forces influence the total number of units produced and sold in relation to the effect upon total costs. That advertising and aggressive selling may perform for business the economic function of developing uniformities of demand needed for large-scale production has been indicated in preceding chapters. Whether the conditions are those of perfect competition, imperfect competition, or monopoly, economic theory recognizes that an increased scale of operations may produce varying effects upon unit production costs and marketing costs of producers. The effect of advertising upon the unit costs of products under these varying cost conditions is obviously part of the information needed for a factual study.

Theory of the Effect of Advertising upon Costs under Conditions of Increasing or Constant Costs

In so far as advertising might succeed in increasing demand in an industry in which the combination of processing and nonaggressive marketing costs increase with increasing volume of operations, the result would be an increase in unit costs and hence in prices to consumers. To the increased processing and nonaggressive marketing costs per unit brought about by increased volume, there would have to be added the aggressive selling costs as well. Such conditions of increasing costs are relatively rare, if they exist at all, in manufacturing industries, and, accordingly, are not considered further.

In those instances where the combination of unit processing and nonaggressive marketing costs is constant as volume increases, final unit costs must be increased at least by the amount per unit devoted to aggressive selling. In the long run, therefore, the price to the consumer is increased under those conditions. He must pay what the product would cost without aggressive selling, plus the cost of being told about the product and of being induced to buy it. In this case, as in the preceding, the increased volume induced by aggressive selling does not permit him to save anything on production or nonaggressive marketing costs.

From a theory standpoint, is the consumer justified in paying more than he would have paid without advertising? Theoretically it is possible to distinguish between instances in which demand has shifted among sellers within a product classification and those in which the shift is between product classifications. But the result from the standpoint of effect upon consumer satisfactions is the same. Clearly, if the consumer in shifting his purchases has been misled in his expectations about the product aggressively sold, he is economically harmed by the aggressive selling efforts. Provided the advertising and selling give him ideas about the product which increase his satisfaction from use, he gains. But even when he gets satisfaction from his new valuations, there still remains the question of whether with the shift of demand he, as an individual, or society is better off from the redistribution of productive resources, part of which are devoted to aggressive selling efforts. This question is purely speculative, involving issues as to the correctness of valuations induced by advertising which have already been listed for possible factual investigation under the discussion of demand.

Theory of the Effect of Advertising upon Cost and Prices under Conditions of Decreasing Costs

Decreasing unit costs of products occur when increasing size of operations makes possible increased efficiency in organization and in operating methods, and hence lower costs. Theoretically for any industry there is an optimum size of plant and organization, i.e., a size which gives greatest efficiency and hence lowest costs. Costs decrease until such size is attained, after which they may increase with further expansion.[17]

In those instances where decreasing costs apply, the increased sales volume which the seller gets from advertising and aggressive selling may bring economies in production and marketing costs which may either partially offset, just offset, or more than offset his aggressive selling costs. When the savings in other costs do not offset aggressive selling costs, final unit costs and hence price to the consumer in the long run must be sufficient to cover the net addition in costs. When savings in other costs and aggressive selling costs balance, final unit costs, and hence price, may be unaffected. When savings in other costs overbalance aggressive selling costs, final unit costs, and hence the price which the consumer may well pay, will thus be less than they would be were no aggressive selling efforts undertaken.[18]

In those instances in which lower costs and prices result from the volume induced by aggressive selling, from a theoretical viewpoint consumers clearly benefit in so far as they get the same volume of merchandise at a lower total expenditure than previously or in so far as they get a larger amount of merchandise for the same outlay. Whenever the total expenditure of consumers upon the product is increased as the result of aggressive selling, however, and demand is

---

[17] The phenomenon of low costs from attainment of a more efficient size is to be distinguished from that of low costs secured from full utilization of an existing plant, which permits spreading of fixed costs over a large output. The question of advertising's relation to overhead is discussed in Chapter XIX.

[18] There is much argument among economists as to whether conditions of decreasing costs occur except under conditions of monopoly or of monopolistic competition. If decreasing costs were continuous, it would seem logical for the large concern to get larger and larger. With the advantage of lower costs coming from increasing size, the growing concerns would ultimately drive other suppliers from the market. Even when it is recognized that costs do not decrease continuously, but that there are optimum sizes, it would appear that the market would probably gravitate to a limited number of firms, each approaching this optimum size. Consequently the conditions would not be those assumed in pure competition. Accordingly, in the statement above it must be recognized that prices under conditions of decreasing costs probably are not the prices indicated by the theory of pure competition.

thus diverted from other products to the aggressively sold product, question can be raised as to whether consumers are better off than, or as well off as, they would be were demand not shifted. The question plunges one into a purely speculative realm as to whether the persuasive efforts of sellers have led to better or worse valuations than would have held without aggressive selling. In instances where total consumer expenditures for a product increase, even though aggressive selling may bring lower prices for the product, it may be argued in any specific case by those who disagree with the new consumer valuation that it would be better not to have resorted to persuasive selling, for consumers would be better off with income devoted to the old distribution of goods rather than the new.[19] Here again, from a theoretical consideration of costs the same questions regarding the correctness of valuations induced by advertising are brought to the fore as were raised from the theoretical consideration of demand several pages back.

Advertising Costs Versus Alternative Selling Costs

Theory indicates that the costs of individual firms play an important part in the ultimate prices paid by consumers, because under conditions of free competition the lower the costs of marginal producers, the lower are the prices paid by consumers. Competition is assumed to lead to an effort on the part of individual concerns to find efficient methods of operation in order that they may keep below the costs of marginal producers. Although theory does not delve into the matter of the practical efficiency of specific operating methods, it recognizes the importance of finding efficient operating formulae. Accordingly, in a study of the relation of advertising to the costs of products, the costs of alternative methods of marketing employed by different firms should be considered.

---

[19] The reasoning underlying such a conclusion is stated thus by Braithwaite and Dobbs, *op. cit.,* p. 99: "If we consider that the new set of valuations resulting from advertisement are less likely to be correct than the old, the consumer may or may not benefit from this transfer. He will benefit from it so long as the excess of the total price paid for the amount produced with advertisement over the total price paid for the amount produced without advertisement is no more than the total utility of the additional units. In other words, since with the new demand curve some units are produced at a price exceeding their utility as shown by the old demand curve, the consumer will gain so long as the total amount of the excess is less than the saving on the original units together with the consumer's surplus on those additional units whose price is less than their utility."

Issues To Be Investigated Relating to Advertising's Effect upon the Costs of Products and Services

From the above discussion of costs the following issues dealing with advertising's relation to the costs of merchandise and services are indicated as requiring inclusion in the factual study:[20]

(1) What effect has advertising had on the production costs of various concerns as a result of its contribution to increased scale of operations?

(2) What effect has advertising had on the marketing costs of various concerns as a result of its contribution to the scale of operations?

(3) What are the actual costs of advertising for various products? Are they substantial or relatively small?

(4) To what extent does advertising provide a lower cost of selling than do alternative methods of selling?

(5) What are the costs of alternative operating formulae?

EFFECTS OF THE PRACTICE OF COMPETITION IN ADVERTISING UPON VALUE OF PRODUCTS

Now that the questions relating to the effect of advertising upon demand and cost have been noted, attention is directed to the effects upon value of a third condition, which was not included in the older value theories, but which has been incorporated in the theory of imperfect competition, namely, that in the world of reality competition between sellers takes place not solely in terms of price but in part in advertising, sales promotion, product quality, service guarantees, and other non-price forms. What does the theory of imperfect competition have to say with regard to the effects of such non-price competition upon the production and consumption of goods that should be investigated in the factual study of advertising?

Dependence of Competition in Advertising upon Price Influence

In the preceding discussion of the effect of decreased costs upon the prices of products, it was assumed that the setting of prices by

---

[20] Omitted in this list are the questions as to whether advertising leads to correct valuations for consumers, inasmuch as they were included in the list of questions relating to advertising's effect upon demand.

a manufacturer was determined on the competitive principle and accordingly that any operating economies enjoyed by marginal producers as a result of their aggressive selling efforts were passed on to consumers. But it has already been noted that for most merchandise, competition is imperfect. Sellers through product differentiation and through the building of product and firm reputation by means of advertising and selling seek to avoid the conditions assumed in the theory of pure competition and to attain some of the freedom in pricing that is enjoyed by the monopolist. It is possible that consumer preference for a seller's product and firm may be strong enough to give the latter considerable freedom in his pricing. Thus he may, in so far as he can operate in accordance with monopoly theory, set his price so as to maximize his profits rather than to maximize consumer satisfactions by naming a lower price and undertaking a larger output.

Or it may happen that, although he sets a price high relative to his production and nonaggressive marketing costs, he may expend a large part of the net which remains between these costs and price for aggressive selling efforts of one type or another. In such a case, according to the terms of theory, a limited monopoly price would be set, but the profits would not be those presumed to follow in the statement of pure monopoly theory with its assumption of a fixed demand and no persuasion costs. Instead, the presumed profit margin would be devoted in greater or lesser part to aggressive selling costs.

So long as demand schedules are subject to changes because of advertising's effects upon consumers' valuations, it is readily perceived that the tendency toward efficiency and low costs visualized in that theory does not necessarily hold. Under that theory it is indicated that the producer or seller, if he is to continue in business, must adopt efficient methods and keep his costs down in order to meet the market price. His hope of attaining good profits rests in his ability to conduct his production and marketing operations so skillfully that his costs will be below those of marginal producers. Such reasoning does not hold, however, when in theoretical analysis the fact is recognized that sellers by aggressive selling methods can escape a competitive price. Sellers can increase expenditures so long as they can command prices covering such expenditures. They need not strive to keep costs low.

The danger that aggressive selling costs may become large must be recognized. Theoretically, if all sellers in a field were to embark upon aggressive selling programs, they could do so only at the expense of their own profits or by generally raising prices to cover such costs, except in so far as economies from large volume might offset selling expenditures and thus permit low prices. If offsetting economies did not develop, however, there might arise a situation in which the general level of prices among sellers in an industry would be set at a relatively high point to cover these selling costs. In such an instance competition for the industry would be on the basis of advertising and aggressive selling rather than on price. Conceivably if there were no check upon the tendency to raise prices to cover ever-increasing selling outlay, a larger and larger part of the national dividend might be devoted to aggressive selling efforts.

While such a contingency is conceivable, it will be recognized at once that there are checks against a continuous increase in aggressive selling costs. Competitors need not fight aggressive selling with aggressive selling. A firm may compete with the aggressive seller through prices lower than aggressive-selling competitors can charge because of their high selling costs. Accordingly, consumers may have an option. They may buy at one price products with differentiating features of one kind or another behind which there may be a considerable advertising and selling expenditure, or they may buy at a lower price products supported by what may be considered a normal or even a small aggressive selling expenditure. Moreover, another possible check upon runaway promotional expense is found in the fact that aggressive selling expenditures may bring decreasing returns. Additional expenditures may fail to bring the necessary sales volume at desired prices to make the expenditure worth while. Such a condition may hold because consumers' subjective valuations cannot be influenced beyond a certain point. Direct substitutes and indirect substitutes theoretically would prevent unlimited manipulation of demand. Consumers would soon cease to deem differentiation and product reputation worth the price asked for them. In theory, the check to keep advertising and other aggressive selling expenditures from getting unduly out of line would appear to rest, therefore, in the alternative types of selling procedure available to sellers and in the alternative choices available to consumers.

Advertising as a Growth Cost

In the preceding section and in this section advertising costs have been treated as normal costs which enter into the long-time balance or equilibrium of supply and demand. There is a sound basis in theory, however, for considering some part of advertising costs as growth costs which are not involved in long-run economic equilibrium. The treatment of advertising costs as normal costs has been common in the theory of imperfect competition, and this view accounts for the objection to advertising by some economists on the ground that competitive use of advertising and promotion by all sellers leads to higher prices. Some advertising costs, however, are undertaken by concerns to develop a business. Like research expenditures incurred in developing a new product they contribute to the growth of an industry. To regard such costs as normal costs entering into equilibrium price leads to a static concept and fails to explain how the economy gets from one level to another.

Certain theoretical aspects of growth costs have been explained by Professor R. S. Meriam as follows:

> Growth costs, sometimes called development costs or innovation costs, have a theoretical position very different from other costs. No growth costs are involved in a position of economic equilibrium, where consumption, price, cost, production, and production facilities are nicely balanced. In a condition of equilibrium, the so-called normal costs include the outlays necessary to maintain the equilibrium but not the outlays which have been necessary to reach the equilibrium. Many marketing costs are growth costs.
>
> Growth costs are closely connected with business enterprise, especially new business ventures, and therefore with business profits. Through such devices as patents, growth costs of originators receive protection against the full impact of the competition of imitators. Growth costs are thus connected with the theory of monopolies. If the nature of growth costs is clearly understood, the paradoxical proposition that a certain amount of monopoly is a necessary condition of economic progress is seen to be no nonsense. Yet the protection of growth costs may account for some of the difficulties of keeping the economic system in perfect balance.[21]

Issues for Factual Investigation Resulting from the Condition of Competition in Advertising

The issues to be studied in the factual chapter relating to the effects of competition in advertising are readily evident from the above discussion. They may be stated as follows:

---

[21] M. P. McNair and R. S. Meriam, *op. cit.*, p. 235.

(1) To what extent is competition carried out through advertising and other non-price forms in specific product fields?

(2) To what extent do competing sellers employ alternative selling methods with varying costs?

(3) Is there effective competition from sellers with lower operating costs which serves to check the heavy use of advertising and other forms of aggressive selling?

   (a) Are consumers given the option of buying unadvertised or little-advertised products at prices reflecting their low selling costs?

   (b) To what extent do consumers exercise the option of low price extended to them?

(4) To what extent does consumer education promise to check heavy competition in advertising?

(5) What evidence is there that some advertising costs may be looked upon as growth costs?

EFFECT OF CONCENTRATION OF SUPPLY UPON VALUE

With this listing of issues regarding the effects of competition in advertising and other non-price forms upon the value of products, there remains for consideration one further set of facts or conditions which has been given prominent place in the theory of imperfect competition, namely, that for many products a small number of concerns hold dominant positions in their industries and consequently are able materially to influence the prices of these products in the market.[22] It will be recognized at once that this statement merely avers that for these products the conditions assumed in the theory of pure competition do not hold; that is, no buyer or seller has an appreciable effect upon price, because buyers and sellers are so many. With many buyers and sellers, price is assumed in economic analysis to depend upon free play between them. Conversely, it is assumed that with few sellers, prices will be set somewhat in accordance with monopoly theory, because the behavior of sellers accords with that assumed in monopoly theory.

---

[22] The theory of imperfect competition recognizes also that buyers may be in a position to influence prices. Buyers may be so large that they can bring strong pressure upon suppliers to reduce their prices. They may stay out of the market for a time; they may play one supplier against another; they may work upon a supplier who is known to be in a weak position in order to get goods at a low price. In this study no effort was made to make a factual study of the problems raised by buyer influence.

It is presumed that sellers will try to maximize profits and in so doing will attempt to influence price rather than to adjust their supply to the prices which free play in the market would produce. They will consider the effect of their actions upon the behavior of other sellers and act accordingly. For example, they may avoid cutting prices as a means of increasing sales volume because they realize that such moves may lead to quick reductions by competitors, with no material benefit to the one who initiated the reduction. Small competitors, moreover, may follow the lead of dominant firms in setting prices instead of setting them in accordance with their own supply schedules based on their costs plus the profits which would lead them to continue in business. All these actions might occur without any collusion between sellers and for a variety of reasons.

The discussions of imperfect competition by various economists suggest that another factor may be important as an element in leading important sellers to influence prices rather than to permit free play of the market to determine them, namely, the effect on their pricing views arising from large fixed costs. Because of their high fixed costs these producers in the long run have a wide spread between their prices and their variable costs. Consequently in times of depression they may hesitate to initiate price changes because possibly prices might be driven eventually almost as low as variable costs.[23] It is assumed that producers, in order to avoid such a contingency, feel that it is wise to maintain their prices on the supposition that other producers also will do so; and even though the volume of sales may fall, the effect upon the operating statement will be better from a policy of maintaining prices than from one of materially reducing them. In contrast, in certain industries, such as the agricultural industries, such maintenance of price schedules by sellers does not develop even though their fixed costs are relatively very high; the reason for the sensitivity of their prices rests in the fact that the prices are set through a free play of a large number of buyers and sellers. The possible significance of insensitivity of prices upon cyclical fluctuations will be explained later.

What, if any, is the possible relationship of advertising to the development of a small number of dominant firms? To begin with, adver-

---

[23] In a free price market producers find it to their advantage, if market conditions make it necessary, to produce and sell products at any prices which more than cover variable costs. Anything above variable costs represents a contribution to fixed costs.

tising possibly may be an important element in building the dominant positions of many firms. Of course, advertising alone is not responsible for a concern's leadership, because it is associated with other operating policies and methods which may contribute to dominance. In the second place, brand leadership built through advertising possibly might become so strong that free entry of new competitors is hampered, particularly the entry of small competitors. Thus, advertising possibly may be used to perpetuate concentration of supply.

Issues Regarding the Economic Effects of Advertising Arising from Concentration of Supply

The special issues for factual investigation arising from the concentration of supply are indicated from the above discussion to be as follows:

(1) To what extent in specific industries does domination of leading concerns depend upon advertising?

(2) To what extent is entry into these industries made difficult because of the advertising of the leading concerns?

    (a) What is the evidence regarding entry of new concerns?

(3) To what extent have leading concerns whose dominance has been built through advertising been able to influence prices as a result of their advertising?

    (a) Does this control over prices involve relatively large price differences, or are the differences small?

    (b) Are prices of leading concerns in the industry evidently set with reference to the prices of competitors?

(4) To what extent have smaller firms set prices with reference to those of leading concerns?

(5) For products which have been widely advertised, what is the price history over a period of time?

    (a) To what extent have any economies from large-scale production and from technological development been passed on in lower prices?

    (b) To what extent have they been retained, or spent for aggressive selling?

    (c) To what extent have manufacturers of advertised products reduced their prices and their gross margins as their relatively new, differentiated products (specialties) have tended to lose their individuality and to become closely similar to competing merchandise?

(6) In specific industries, what evidence is found of large profits which are apparently attributable to dominant advertising?

(7) To what extent are the prices of advertised products less sensitive than prices of nonadvertised products?

(8) To what extent does advertising lead to stability of operation for particular concerns and particular industries?

EFFECT OF IMPERFECT KNOWLEDGE OF SELLERS UPON VALUE

As a rule analysts of value under conditions of imperfect competition have included in their reasoning not only the assumption that sellers control their pricing activities so as to maximize profits, but also the assumption that sellers have a knowledge which permits them to set prices so as to attain maximum profits. In other words, it is assumed that sellers have knowledge of their costs, of the character of the demand curve, and of the behavior of other sellers. Some theorists have recognized, however, that these assumptions cannot be used to explain all prices under imperfect competition.[24] The assumptions may or may not be true in specific market situations. Inductive study indicates that sellers do not always act so as to maximize profits. Moreover, far from having a perfect knowledge to guide prices so as to attain maximum profits, they set their prices with great ignorance as to the effects upon costs and demand. Recognition of those facts indicates the need of basing analysis on the conditions met in any particular situation, if valid conclusions regarding value for that situation are to be had.

When the assumption is made that sellers control their pricing actions with regard to the behavior of other sellers and consequently with regard to the total influence of all sellers upon price, the tendency will be toward monopoly price, as was indicated in the discussion of the preceding section. But if sellers in the market ignore the possible price behavior of competitors and adjust their prices in accordance with their individual estimates of the strength of demand and their individual desires to get business, the tendency, even with a few sellers,

---

[24] The need of making value analyses conform with the facts found in specific fields is indicated particularly by Triffin, *op. cit.* Also see Edward Chamberlin, *op. cit.*, Section II, "The Effect of Uncertainty," p. 51.

will be for price to approach the level indicated in the theory of pure competition.

In instances where there is ignorance or imperfect knowledge among sellers regarding their own costs, the demand curves for their products, and competitors' pricing activities, an analysis based on the assumption of perfect knowledge with price set to maximize profit will probably be invalid. Likewise, in instances where there is friction among sellers, with a consequent tendency to price wars or at least to a setting of prices guided by personal animus, an analysis based on the assumption that prices are guided by a desire to maximize profits is invalid. In all instances where ignorance, uncertainty, and friction exist, prices may tend to behave in accordance neither with the theory of pure competition nor with the theory of monopoly. Instead, the theorist cannot predict the level at which prices will be established in the market.

From what has been stated above it should be recognized that conclusions of imperfect competition theory regarding value must be considered as tentative, subject to refinement or change as inductive method may show need of refinement of the assumptions to be included in the analysis. Accordingly in conducting the factual study of advertising it was recognized that no single set of assumptions employed in theoretical analysis would be suitable for all the product situations studied.

QUESTIONS RELATING TO POSSIBLE EFFECTS OF ADVERTISING UPON THE LEVEL OF THE NATIONAL INCOME

The issues for factual study listed so far in this chapter relate for the most part to the effect of advertising upon the balance between demand and supply of specific products. While these questions are important, it is fully as important to determine whether advertising has any effect upon total demand and supply of goods and services, that is, upon the size of the national dividend, which determines the standard of living enjoyed by the community.

The size of the national income at any time is determined, first, by the productive capacity of the economic machine, and secondly, by the extent to which the productive capacity is used. Since the advent of the factory system, the growth of productive capacity on a per capita basis has been tremendous. The increase has come primarily from four sources: (1) increasing investment in factories and productive machines, (2) technological development, (3) improved organization and management techniques, and (4) discovery and use of new resources.

Accompanying such growth of supply, there must have been a corresponding growth in consumers' purchasing power. Investment in productive resources by entrepreneurs has depended upon the outlook for a profitable demand. An important question for historical investigation to be dealt with in the factual chapters is raised, therefore, as to whether or not advertising and aggressive selling have contributed to the growth in demand that has called forth investment.

Although the capacity of the productive machine has greatly increased with the passage of time, unfortunately business has been subject periodically to severe cyclical maladjustments with consequent fluctuation in employment, income, and consumption. Theoretically, advertising may have a direct effect upon cyclical fluctuation in accordance with the variation in its use by businessmen. As a form of business activity using men and materials, advertising in itself may either accentuate or alleviate cyclical employment, according to the extent to which it is used in good times and in bad times. Moreover, as a force to influence the demand for products, it may either reduce or increase fluctuations in sales, and thus in business activity, according to whether the amount used is in inverse or direct relationship to cyclical swings.

Apart from this direct effect, advertising in theory may have a possible indirect effect upon cyclical maladjustments, as it may contribute to the imperfect competition which is accompanied by rigid prices. Among other things, the maladjustments of cyclical fluctuation involve price relationships. Theoretically, if competition were free and labor and capital were mobile, adjustments in price relationships would automatically take place. New equilibria between the demand and supply of various products would be established so as to utilize productive resources. But labor and capital are not highly mobile, nor are prices quickly adjustable.

The rigidity of prices of many manufactured products already mentioned has been held by some economists to have interfered with the self-adjusting character of the economic system. They allege that price rigidity has accentuated cyclical maladjustments and has tended to prolong cyclical depression. Advertising alone is not held to be the cause of price rigidities, but merely a part of the imperfect competition of which rigidity is one of the symptoms.

From the above theoretical considerations come several questions for factual investigation:

(1) Has advertising contributed in any way to the growth in demand that has called forth investment?

(2) What has been the relationship between fluctuations in advertising expenditures and fluctuations in business activity as a whole?

(3) As a source of employment has advertising increased or decreased the extent of cyclical fluctuation?

(4) From the standpoint of its effect upon demand, has advertising had any effect upon cyclical fluctuation?

(5) Has advertising had any effect in producing price rigidities, which, in turn, have accentuated cyclical maladjustments?

THE NEED FOR FACTUAL STUDIES

This chapter has outlined the major economic questions about advertising with which this study is concerned. It was the aim of the investigation, so far as possible, to obtain facts bearing on these questions. Only in this way can real understanding of the economics of advertising be established. But it is perhaps not inappropriate to suggest that factual studies, for which it is hoped that this one will furnish at least initial pattern, are likewise important to economists whose chief interest lies in the further development of the theories of imperfect competition. These theories in their present form unquestionably represent an advance in economic thinking towards greater reality; nevertheless the author ventures to suggest that in several respects the current doctrine of imperfect competition would benefit from further inductive study, for instance the following:

(1) The effects of aggressive selling on demand have not been sufficiently explored, since the students of imperfect competition have been more particularly concerned with the effects of aggresive selling on costs. Much more work needs to be done on the effects on change in demand, on elasticity or inelasticity of demand, and on total demand in the aggregate, especially in its relation to investment.

(2) In giving attention to the effects of aggressive selling on costs, modern economists have lacked the facts on which to base sound assumptions as to what information on costs business-

men actually have. Furthermore, these economists have reasoned about the effects of aggressive selling on costs within a framework of relatively static assumptions about costs which do not take into account some other important aspects of costs such as the "growth" or "innovation" costs that characterize a dynamic economy.

In short, there is a basic question as to whether the doctrine of imperfect competition in its present stage of development is adequate as a theory of economic progress.

THE RELATION OF ADVERTISING TO THE THEORY OF EQUILIBRIUM BELOW FULL EMPLOYMENT

Thus far in this chapter the discussion of the theoretical effects of advertising, as indicated by economic analysis, has followed the traditional pattern of assuming, as part of the analysis, full employment of workers and full utilization of other productive resources of the economy. This assumption of full employment has an important bearing upon the conclusions of economic analysts on many issues. For example, it influences the conclusions of those who, apparently believing that only a minimum of advertising for informational purposes is necessary, reason that heavy competition in advertising is unfortunate economically because it may result in much of the national dividend being devoted merely to the building of product reputation. These people conclude that it would be desirable to divert men engaged in persuasive advertising into manufacturing work or into services which they deem desirable from a consumption standpoint. They point out that with such diversion to manufacturing, the amount of goods and services available for consumption, other than persuasive advertising services, would be increased, because, according to the assumption of full employment, men and resources not employed for advertising would be employed in other endeavor.

In recent years, under the leadership of J. M. Keynes, a new body of economic thought has been presented, which includes in its analysis the assumption that the equilibrium or balance between total demand and total supply in a modern, mature economy does not involve full employment of workers or other resources. Instead, there is an equilibrium reached with large segments of the working population unemployed and with factories and machines idle. The theory seeks to explain the chronic unemployment of recent years. In the analysis many conclusions regarding the interaction of economic forces reached in older theory, under the assumption of full employment, have been materially revised.

No effort is made in this study to outline fully the complex economic reasoning and the conclusions embodied in this theory of equilibrium below full employment, because it is not here used as a guide to factual investigation nor are its conclusions widely enough accepted to serve as a base for final judgment of advertising's contribution. For those who desire a more complete statement, not only are the works of Mr. Keynes[25] available, but also there is a lucid, nontechnical explanation by Mrs. Joan Robinson.[26] Here only enough of the theory is presented to indicate that under it advertising finds a theoretical justification not afforded under a theory assuming full employment.

The new theory attributes unemployment and the lack of use of resources to the fact that free enterprise in a mature society results in a *deficiency of demand.* In simple terms the reasoning is thus: The amount of employment in a free economy is determined by the decisions of individual employers. Their decisions as to the number of people they employ, the amount of products they produce, and the investment they make in new plant are guided largely by the outlook for profits, which depend upon the opportunity to sell goods profitably, i.e., upon demand. Demand, however, depends upon money expenditure by individuals. The ability of people or corporations to expend money for goods, in turn, depends upon the expenditures of other people or corporations. One man's expenditure is another man's income. While it is desirable to keep expenditures and income operating in constant unison, at full tilt, such a condition is not attained, for men desire to save; they do not spend their full incomes. Their savings unfortunately do not go into investment at once, i.e., into real capital, such as factories or machines, which would flow out at once as income. Investment rests upon the decisions of business executives, as determined by their outlook for profit. The very act of saving, however, reduces the outlook for profit because it reduces demand for goods. In short, the decision of individuals to save reduces demand for consumers' goods without increasing the demand for capital goods. The

[25] J. M. Keynes, *The General Theory of Employment, Interest and Money* (New York, Harcourt, Brace and Company, 1936).

[26] Joan Robinson, *Introduction to the Theory of Employment* (London, Macmillan & Co., Ltd., 1938).

result is unemployment. There cannot be full employment of resources, according to the theory, if the amount that businessmen are willing to invest is less than the amount that all individuals combined would want to save out of incomes which full employment of resources would entail.

The full analysis deals with the effect upon employment of resources arising from changes in investment rate, changes in thriftiness, changes in prices, and changes in the rate of interest. The reasoning regarding the interaction of these forces provides an hypothesis regarding the upward and downward cyclical spirals of business activity. A highly significant part of the theory, however, is the conclusion that in a mature economy full employment is never attained. It is held that when employment of resources falls to a very low point in a depression and is followed by the usual rise in money wages that is a part of recovery, the demand for money increases and the rate of interest thereupon is driven up. This rise adversely affects the desire of entrepreneurs to invest, because the rate of interest affects the profit outlook. Consequently, full employment of resources is not attained.

Several tenets under this theory appear to have an important bearing regarding the effects of advertising under such conditions. First of all, because of the effect of saving on the employment of resources, the theory lays stress upon the propensity of people to consume. It holds that a desire to save beyond what businessmen require for investment has an adverse effect upon demand and hence upon employment. Accordingly, an increase in the propensity of people to consume or a reduction in the rate of their thriftiness would lead to fuller employment of resources. If this reasoning is accepted, it appears that aggressive selling effort designed to make people want products and to increase their expenditures will have a tendency to induce fuller employment and higher income than would hold with greater saving. In other words, advertising and selling would tend to cut down the deficiency of demand.

In the next place, under the theory of equilibrium below full employment, advertising appears to be a means of helping to reduce chronic unemployment in so far as it adds to consumers' desires for new inventions. If, with the help of advertising, demand for new inventions develops, the rate of investment increases, employment increases, income increases, and the well-being of the community follows. Thus advertising theoretically may play a part in overcoming unemployment in a mature society if by leading to a demand for new products it calls forth investment.

One further point. Those accepting the theory of equilibrium below full employment take the view that unemployed resources should be put to some use, even though their contribution is not deemed to be of great consequence to society. Unemployed workers represent resources that are unused and, therefore, lost. They should be put to work. Those who accept the theory even go so far as to say that useless employment, under such conditions, is not to be considered undesirable economically. The employment of persons who otherwise would be idle may involve expenditure, but it also brings income to the community. The national dividend is not less because they are working rather than idle. Society would have to support these people anyway. Accordingly their employment merely provides a means of dividing the national dividend among the total group. Proceeding from this point, they hold that if those employed make any contribution at all to wealth, there is a real gain socially. The national dividend will be larger if they work than it will be if they are left unemployed. This reasoning accounts for the advocacy of government unemployment projects by those who subscribe to the theory.

The above discussion of the theoretical effects of advertising under an assumption of equilibrium below full employment is, of course, incomplete and does not touch upon all issues regarding advertising, many of which would be the same under this theory as under the theories assuming full employment. Only as much has been presented as has been deemed essential to indicate how, theoretically, advertising appears to promise a contribution to the economy, if it is assumed that the economy in the years ahead is to operate under continued unemployment.

If this reasoning is applied to advertising and selling work, the objections against advertising effort by those who judge persuasive selling efforts to be a relatively unproductive type of service lose much force. The theory tends to break down many of the distinctions between what is waste and what is economy that held under the older theories. Because of the importance attached to a high propensity to consume and to new inventions as a stimulus to investment, those who hold to the theory of equilibrium below full employment probably would conclude that advertising makes at least some social contribution and, therefore, has economic justification.[27] Under the theory it would add to social well being because it would provide occupation for many who otherwise would be unemployed and at the same time would provide some contribution to the national dividend. If a factual investigation were to be dictated by this theoretical analysis, the task here suggested would be that of determining whether, on the whole, advertising appeared to provide some net addition to socially desirable services and products.

Even though the work of Mr. Keynes and his followers represents a challenging and stimulating contribution to economic analysis, and appears to provide a basis for clearer theoretical justification of advertising than older theory, the author has nevertheless elected in this factual study to examine the economic problems of advertising in the light of the more conventional economic tenets, which do not permit so convenient a solution.

---

[27] It is recognized, of course, that there is the possibility that some might take an extreme view that advertising is a disservice. For these people the reasoning above would not be valid.

PART II

The Effect of Advertising on the Demand for Products and Services

Chapter VII

PROBLEMS INVOLVED IN DEMAND MEASUREMENT

THIS chapter and the nine that follow give factual evidence regarding the effects of advertising on demand, the issues regarding which have been listed in the preceding chapter (page 168). An effort is made quantitatively to measure the effects of advertising on the primary and selective demand of specific products. These products were so chosen as to afford a wide range of examples in accordance with the extent to which advertising has been employed in their marketing. While previous studies relating to the economics of advertising have devoted attention to the effect of advertising on demand, in general they have given little objective data to indicate the extent to which demand for types of products and for brands has been influenced by advertising. Consequently the literature contains vague and conflicting statements regarding advertising's ability to influence demand. In some instances advertising is credited with having a marked effect in shaping demand, while in other instances it is assumed to have little effect. From the analysis of demand included in these chapters it will be seen that the effect of advertising varies widely with different products.

Difficulties of Measurement—Need of Knowledge of Factors Influencing Demand

The reader is warned in advance that the answers regarding the quantitative effects of advertising upon demand are not precise. In many instances they are very uncertain, not more than considered opinions. The reasons for such uncertainty were pointed out in Chapter V, where the difficulties met by the individual businessman in appraising advertising results were outlined. The number of variables concomitant with demand is large, it is often difficult even to determine just what variables are present, and frequently it is impossible to get data by which to measure those that are known. Under such circumstances the careful investigator must avoid the error so frequently made of assuming a simple cause and effect relationship between advertising and change in consumption of a brand or product.

Appraisal of the reasons for demand changes requires an understanding of human behavior and of the effect of sociological forces upon behavior. Consumption patterns flow out of people's ways of living and out of attitudes that are developed by the whole complex of forces that shape society and its mode of living. Advertising is but one force involved in molding consumption attitudes and in guiding consumer expenditure. Advertising enthusiasts would be naive to claim too great credit for this force in shaping people's consumption habits. Successful users of advertising do not make this mistake, for they have learned that when they seek to mold people's viewpoints they must be careful to shape their own merchandising and promotional efforts to meet clearly defined consumer wants and preferences.

As will be shown in examples to come, advertising can be profitably used only when it holds forth something that consumers need or can easily be made to desire. Advertising creates needs only in the sense that it makes consumers aware that a product offers a satisfactory solution to a need. Often, particularly in the case of new products, consumers are unaware that the products will fill certain needs or desires; advertising serves to let them know what the product will do for them, but the latent desires or needs must be present. A great proportion of new inventions are doomed to oblivion. Their failures generally can be attributed to the fact that they do not offer an improved solution to consumer problems or wants; on the other hand, inventions that satisfactorily meet needs generally can support only small advertising programs until their desirability is demonstrated by a growing demand. Thus, as demand increases, the amount that can be employed upon advertising increases. In such instances, advertising alone is not to be credited with creating demand. Such new products would generally succeed in securing some demand without advertising, because they satisfactorily fill consumer wants and desires. Advertising serves merely as a force to speed up their consumption.

The inability of advertising alone to shape demand is shown, likewise, in the case of products whose demand is decreasing. Businessmen in mature industries often find themselves competing for part of an ever-decreasing total of business. Changing consumption patterns coming from a dynamic world are stronger than their efforts to mold and shape consumers' habits. Their advertising may serve to allay a more rapid shift from the product, but it cannot prevent it.

Effect of Changing Living Habits—Basic Trends

In any quantitative study of demand it is essential to have a clear understanding of consumer living habits and attitudes that relate to the consumption of the specific product. Any changes in the rate of consumption of the product must be interpreted in the light of possible operation of basic demand trends, which are attributable to changing living habits and attitudes. It is beyond the compass of this study to trace or appraise all the underlying causes for such demand trends. To attempt to do so in particular cases leads only to speculation, for these demand changes have their roots in the intricate play of forces that form the character of our free society, a mobile society little hampered by traditions of class or caste. The products whose trends of usage are investigated in themselves represent one force affecting society's form and people's behavior. For example, the growth in automobile usage helped bring improved roads, but improved roads in turn have been a factor in increased automobile usage. What have been termed the "causes" of changes in demand more properly in many cases should be looked upon merely as phenomena accompanying such product trends. The various changes are related, but it is impossible to disentangle cause and effect.

In order that the meaning of such trends and their bearing upon the problem of measuring advertising effects may be better understood, a few examples are cited.

Examples of Basic Trends—Foods

In the food field, distinct trends in the consumption of various types of products have been noted for many years.[1] Leo Wolman, in a study

---

[1] For advertising cases which contain a discussion of trends in product consumption, see the following, found in *Problems in Advertising,* by Neil H. Borden (3d ed., New York, McGraw-Hill Book Company, Inc., 1937):
National Live Stock and Meat Board, p. 10.
Associated Salmon Packers, p. 3.
Bureau of Milk Publicity—State of New York, p. 44.
See also H. C. Hensley and N. H. Borden, *Marketing Policies of the California Walnut Growers Association* (Farm Credit Administration, Washington, D. C., March, 1937, Bulletin No. 10).
The following is only a partial list of treatises which discuss changes in food consumption and possible reasons therefor:
Edith Hawley, *Economics of Food Consumption* (New York, McGraw-Hill Book Company, Inc., 1932).
P. H. Nystrom, *Economic Principles of Consumption* (New York, Ronald Press Company, Inc., 1929).
Raymond Pearl, *The Nation's Food* (Philadelphia, W. B. Saunders Company, 1920).
Washington Platt, "A Study of Bread Consumption," *The Northwestern Miller and American Baker,* January 1, 1936, p. 37.
(Footnote continued on bottom of next page.)

of "Consumption and the Standard of Living,"[2] in 1929 arrived at the following conclusions:

(1) For many years there has been a significant and practically continuous trend toward smaller food requirements per capita, in the physiological sense.

(2) Consumption of cereals, notably wheat and corn, has declined.

(3) Consumption of dairy products, sugar, and miscellaneous vegetables has increased.

Federal government studies reported in the 1939 *Yearbook of Agriculture*[3] substantiate this appraisal of the marked change of diet of this country during two generations. It states that the proportion of calories derived from milk, cheese, fruits, and succulent vegetables has doubled in 50 years; that greater emphasis has been given to sugars and fats; and that the proportion of grains and meats has declined. The changes are summarized in Table 11. Advertisers and aggressive sellers have had to adapt themselves to these trends.

What is the explanation of such changes? Analysis indicates that the changes in the foods demanded are largely in accord with changes in the consumer group. There has been a change in the age distribution of population; a larger proportion is found in the older age groups. Food requirements of older people differ from those of younger people.[4] Furthermore, population has become more and more

---

U. S. Department of Agriculture, "Food and Life," *Yearbook of Agriculture, 1939* (Washington, U. S. Government Printing Office, 1939).

W. C. Waite and Ralph Cassady, Jr., *The Consumer and the Economic Order* (New York, McGraw-Hill Book Company, Inc., 1939).

Holbrook Working, "The Decline in Per Capita Consumption of Flour in the United States," *Wheat Studies of Food Research Institute* (Stanford University, July, 1926).

[2] National Bureau of Economic Research, *Recent Economic Changes* (New York, McGraw-Hill Book Company, Inc., 1929), Vol. 1, Ch. 1.

[3] U. S. Department of Agriculture, *op. cit.*

[4] Many manufacturers in recent years have given serious thought to the probable effects upon their businesses of the changing distribution of population by age groups as the population of the United States approaches stability. The decline in the American birth rate began before the Civil War, but for many years was obscured by immigration. With the Immigration Quota Act of 1924, immigration as an important factor in populating the United States ended. This act corresponded closely with the peak in number of births. It also marked a point when the decline in the birth rate was accelerated. Thus this date marks the approximate crest of population increase in this country. Since that date one age classification after another in the children's group has reached its numerical peak and an absolute decline has set in. In the years ahead, unless there is an unexpected alteration in population trends, the peak numerical market in various age groups will have been reached, to be followed by a subsequent decline and then a gradual leveling off as stability is reached. That such changes will materially affect the demand for products is evident. Already those who sell school supplies, children's clothes, and toys have felt the force of this population change.

For a more complete discussion, see:

R. E. Chaddock, "Age and Sex in Population Analysis," *The Annals of the American Academy of Political and Social Science*, November, 1936, p. 185 ff.

W. S. Thompson, *Population Problems* (New York, McGraw-Hill Book Company, Inc., 1930), p. 237 ff.

W. C. Bober, "Population Still Short of Its Prime," *Barron's*, January 9, 1939.

TABLE 11

CITY AND VILLAGE FAMILY FOOD: TRENDS IN AVERAGE PER CAPITA CONSUMPTION
PER YEAR OF SPECIFIED FOODS BY LEVEL OF FOOD EXPENDITURE, 1885-1937*

LEVEL OF FOOD EXPENDITURE AND PERIOD†	GRAIN PRODUCTS, Pounds	MEAT, FISH, POULTRY, Pounds	MILK, OR ITS EQUIVALENT, Quarts	EGGS, Dozen	LEAFY, GREEN, AND YELLOW VEGETABLES, Pounds‡	TOMATOES, CITRUS FRUITS, Pounds
$1.25-$1.87 a person a week:						
1885-1904	294	123	41	12	24	10
1905-1914	240	124	90	12	31	15
1915-1924	174	84	101	15	35	38
1925-1934	152	85	112	12	43	37
1935-1937	155	85	118	16	53	45
$1.88-$2.49 a person a week:						
1885-1904	222	169	90	24	29	22
1905-1914	239	157	90	14	39	46
1915-1924	176	87	186	18	62	57
1925-1934	172	104	135	15	70	39
1935-1937	160	106	150	23	76	75
$2.50-$3.12 a person a week:						
1885-1914	218	204	84	20	48	59
1915-1924	204	115	180	26	67	73
1925-1934	163	129	144	24	83	68
1935-1937	174	139	191	27	95	98

* Based on averages from many scattered family dietary studies, published and unpublished, compiled by the Bureau of Home Economics.
† Adjusted to 1935 levels by use of U. S. Bureau of Labor Statistics Index of Retail Food Costs.
‡ Does not include sweet potatoes.

Source: U. S. Department of Agriculture, "Food and Life," *Yearbook of Agriculture, 1939* (Washington, U. S. Government Printing Office, 1939), p. 313.

urban. Along with this development important changes have been made in the conditions of labor. There has been a steady trend toward more sheltered occupations. White-collar workers have become a larger part of the social group. Increased mechanization has reduced physical exertion of those still performing physical labor. The hours of labor have become less with every passing decade. The wider use of the automobile probably has affected the amount of physical exertion commonly expended. Better housing, wider use of central heating, and a consequent smaller exposure to cold may have had an effect on the need for heat- and energy-producing foods.

Research and education in dietetics have gone on apace. The virtues of vitamins and of mineral constituents in diet have been widely broadcast and popularized. Foods probably have been subject to fashion influence; consumers tend to copy the food styles of those who are looked upon as accepted leaders of their social groups.[5]

[5] See H. K. Stiebeling, "Food Habits, Old and New," an essay in *Yearbook of Agriculture, 1939*, p. 130.

The availability of certain foods has undergone a distinct change. Development of cheap and quick transportation and improved methods of refrigeration have been followed by geographic specialization in vegetable and fruit raising. As a consequence many fresh fruits and vegetables, once to be had only during short seasons, now are available throughout the year. Food preservation processes also have been perfected. Canning and drying processes have been improved and now freezing processes are coming into larger use.

Food has been made available in many new and attractive forms. Many specialties, products of individualized character, such as breakfast foods, desserts, and beverages, have been continuously developed and marketed.

Changes in amount of purchasing power and changes in the distribution of purchasing power are intimately related to the changes in food consumption as they are to changing consumption of many other products.[6] Recent studies by the Department of Agriculture have brought into clear focus the differences in food consumption at different income levels.[7] There is still a marked challenge in the fact that underconsumption and poorly balanced diets persist among the lower income groups of this country. Yet a rise in family income over a long period, even in the lower strata in the United States, has made possible a wider and better selection of foods.

Since the caloric intake of Americans on the average has probably tended to decrease or at least remain constant,[8] increase in consumption of one type of food has meant decrease in another. Thus, a favorable trend for one class of product may be a reason for an unfavorable trend for another.

While the above list of variables is only a partial outline of developments affecting people's living habits, which in turn are related to changes in food consumption, yet it serves to indicate the complexity of the forces which shape demand and bring the continuous change to which food producers must adjust their selling programs.

[6] See U. S. National Resources Committee, *Consumer Expenditures in the United States* (Washington, U. S. Government Printing Office, 1939).
U. S. National Resources Committee, *The Structure of the American Economy*, Part I, ch. II (Washington, U. S. Government Printing Office, 1939).
U. S. Bureau of Foreign and Domestic Commerce, Market Research Series No. 5, *Consumer Use of Selected Goods and Services by Income Classes* (Washington, The Bureau, 1935).
[7] See, for instance, an address by Milo Perkins on "The Challenge of Underconsumption," before the Fourth Annual Farm Institute, Des Moines, Iowa, February 24, 1940; also, H. K. Stiebeling and C. M. Coons, "Present-Day Diets in The United States," an essay in *Yearbook of Agriculture, 1939*, p. 296 ff.
[8] See Raymond Pearl, *op. cit.*; Leo Wolman, *op. cit.*, p. 13.

Basic Trends—Shoes

The per capita consumption of men's shoes[9] has shown a decline since 1910, from approximately three pairs to approximately two pairs. Such a decline occurred in spite of an increase in per capita income, which held until the period of the depression, and in spite of a considerable amount of aggressive selling of men's shoes. Women's and misses' shoes, on the other hand, subjected apparently to a somewhat different set of forces, have shown no such consumption decline, but a slight increase from approximately 2.5 pairs in 1914 to approximately 3.3 pairs in 1935 (see Table 12).

TABLE 12

APPROXIMATE PER CAPITA CONSUMPTION OF LEATHER SHOES BY MEN AND WOMEN, SELECTED YEARS, 1899–1935

YEAR	APPROXIMATE PER CAPITA CONSUMPTION	
	Men's	Women's
1899	2.7 pairs	3.0 pairs
1904	3.0 "	2.6 "
1914	2.9 "	2.5 "
1923	2.6 "	2.9 "
1927	2.2 "	3.0 "
1935	2.1 "	3.3 "

Source: Based on Table 91.

Why have men consumed fewer shoes? Again it is necessary to speculate. The automobile has brought less walking; urban living and less rigorous occupations may have contributed to the decline; the improved quality of shoes may have entailed less replacement; a fashion change which brought general use of low shoes throughout the year, and hence fewer shoes in the wardrobe, may have brought decreased fashion obsolescence.

In contrast, women's shoes have been subject to the fashion force in a different way. Highly styled, inexpensive shoes have been in demand since the early 1920's. The quick swing of fashion changes has apparently entailed an obsolescence offsetting any adverse effects on consumption arising from changed living habits.

Basic Trends—Other Examples

In the tobacco field[10] the trend of demand for different types of products has been marked. Cigars reached a peak of consumption per

[9] See N. H. Borden, *Problems in Advertising* (3d ed.), case of National Shoe Retailers' Association, p. 33.
[10] See Tables 25 and 26, pp. 213, 214.

capita of 86.4 cigars in 1907 and had declined by 1937 to 42. Chewing tobacco had a per capita usage of 2.8 pounds in 1890, but by 1930 this had shrunk to .8 pound. Per capita consumption of smoking tobacco was 2.4 pounds in 1916, but only 1.8 pounds in 1937. Snuff had a steady consumption of approximately .3 pound from 1905 to 1930. In contrast to the above, cigarettes had a hundredfold increase in demand, from 10.6 per capita in 1880 to 1,005 in 1930, a trend which has continued since that time, the figure for 1938 being in excess of 1,300. Here again, advertising, which has been used for all forms of tobacco, has had to be employed in accordance with these trends; it has affected them but has not caused them.

Changing conditions of work may have accounted for some of the changes in tobacco usage, particularly in the chewing of tobacco. The increase of factory and office work did not favor chewing. Moreover, both fashion and the weakening of moral taboos against tobacco, phenomena which have their genesis in basic living habits and attitudes, have had an important bearing not only upon tobacco consumption as a whole, but also upon the forms of tobacco used, as will be developed at greater length in later chapters.

Hosiery is another product whose demand has been subject to market trends. In 1926 the United States Tariff Commission in a study of cotton hosiery reported that "Hosiery, at one time almost as staple a product as sugar, is now subject to the vagaries of fashion. The most pronounced effect of style influence in the years since the war has been the change from lisle to silk hosiery."[11] In 1914 over 80% of the hosiery produced was cotton, but by 1923 cotton's share was only 59%. The downward trend has continued since, particularly in the case of women's hosiery. Since 1927 the Census of Manufactures has segregated data of production of women's hosiery from other hosiery. In 1927, 24% of the women's hosiery produced was all-cotton, while silk and silk with cotton tops, toes, and heels accounted for 47% of production. By 1937 only 7% of women's hosiery was all-cotton, while all-silk hosiery accounted for 57% of production, and silk with cotton tops, toes, and heels for another 26%. Again, these trends have not been attributable to aggressive selling efforts. Sellers, instead, have had to adapt their selling efforts to the trends.

The big element in the alteration of hosiery demand has undoubt-

---

[11] U. S. Tariff Commission, *Cotton Hosiery* (Washington, U. S. Government Printing Office, 1929), p. 9.

TABLE 13

PRODUCTION OF WOMEN'S HOSIERY, BY KIND, IN THE UNITED STATES, 1927 AND 1937

	1927		1937	
	Dozens of Pairs (000 omitted)	Percentage	Dozens of Pairs (000 omitted)	Percentage
All cotton........................	10,828	24.2	3,866	7.2
All silk...........................	3,376	7.5	30,736	57.2
Silk with cotton tops, toes, and heels..	17,611	39.4	14,155	26.4
Other mixtures.....................	12,902	28.9	4,959	9.2
	44,717	100.0	53,717	100.0

Source: Derived from *U. S. Census of Manufactures*, 1927, 1937.

edly been fashion. The fashion for sheer silk came into full play, however, only with decreased costs of silk and with technological improvements in hosiery manufacture.

A somewhat different type of trend is found in the case of Portland cement. Portland cement manufacturers enjoyed a very favorable trend for their product in the field of road building during the period of 1910–1930, a trend that was arrested by the depression. These facts are shown in Table 14.

TABLE 14

SQUARE YARDS OF CONCRETE PAVEMENT CONTRACTS AWARDED IN UNITED STATES

YEAR	ROADS	STREETS	ALLEYS	TOTAL	TOTAL BUILT
1910	151,148	682,637	107,874	941,659	....
1915	12,050,909	5,933,879	612,921	18,597,709	....
1920	29,326,689	8,814,782	907,184	39,048,635	....
1925	63,895,104	35,664,427	4,509,810	104,069,341	101,428,272
1930	108,008,062	35,212,793	2,600,800	145,821,655	150,588,913
1935	30,971,959	12,470,290	207,031	43,649,280	37,613,224

Source: Portland Cement Association, *Cement and Concrete Reference Book*, 1937, p. 24.

Contracts for less than 1,000,000 square yards of concrete pavement were awarded in 1910. In 1915 over 18,000,000 square yards were awarded, and the upward trend continued rapidly until a peak in excess of 140,000,000 square yards was reached by 1930.[12] Advertising was used to help stimulate this demand, but the extent to which consumption would have increased without advertising is unknown.

The trend of demand for Portland cement for pavements rests, of course, in the effect of the automobile and the truck. The demand for

[12] For a discussion of the use of advertising in stimulating use of concrete for highways and streets, see the case of the Portland Cement Association in *Cooperative Advertising*, by N. H. Borden, *op. cit.*, p. 140.

concrete pavement may be looked upon as complementary to the demand for the automobile. Full satisfaction from automobile usage has required improved highways. The heavy pounding of cars and trucks has favored a strong, rigid pavement.

Other examples of such basic product trends could be multiplied at great length.[13] Horse-drawn buggies have practically disappeared, but in the span of one generation automobiles have progressed from an inventor's dream until there are four passenger cars for every five families in the land. The demand for kerosene for lighting purposes grew and waned; gas lighting then had its day, only to lose out to electricity. The demand for sterling silverware failed to keep pace with the growth of population and of wealth in the United States. Ready-made clothing has become more and more widely purchased; correspondingly has come a decline in sales of textile piece goods to consumers. The amount of cloth in garments has changed widely over periods of time. After the advent of radio, piano sales declined markedly. The increased expenditures for services of many types represent one of the most striking trends of post-war consumption, services such as those provided by public utilities, laundries, and cleaning establishments; hairdressers; auto repair shops; and professional groups, such as doctors and dentists. On the other hand, there has been a marked trend downward in domestic service.

The National Resources Committee in a study of *Patterns of Resource Use* has constructed a chart which reflects the trend of change in the purchases of particular items, corrected for the variable of of change in income.[14] This is reproduced as Chart I, pages 204–205. It shows graphically the average annual rate of increase or decrease that has been operating for various classes of consumer goods. Some 20 classes of goods show positive trends; 11 show negative trends; and 3 show no up or down tendency. Back of all such trends lie basic changes in the character of the population and its way of living: changes in urban distribution, in occupation, in age distribution, in sex distribution, in family size, in housing, in education, and in modes of transportation and communication. Such sociological changes are slow and hence bring slow but persistent change in demand.

---

[13] For an interesting estimate of consumer spending by product classes for the period 1909–1931, see W. H. Lough, *High-Level Consumption* (New York, McGraw-Hill Book Company, Inc., 1935), p. 236 ff.

[14] U. S. National Resources Committee, *The Structure of the American Economy* (Washington, U. S. Government Printing Office, 1930), Part I "Basic Characteristics," p. 20.

When the inquiry into demand changes is extended, two forces come to the fore in example after example as the molders of change in living habits and in consumption attitudes, namely, invention, or technological development, and fashion. The effect of these upon the business of a manufacturer may be direct and relatively quick, as is illustrated in the case of clothing, where fashion swings bring shifts in demand for particular textiles; or as in the case of the safety razor, where in a relatively few years there was a considerable shift from the old, straight-edge razor to the safety type. Or the effect may be slow and indirect, but nevertheless powerful, through the influence on people's living habits and wants, and consequently the distribution of their spending power among various classes of merchandise. An example of a long-time, slow fashion swing is the case of tobacco products. The outstanding example of a long-time, indirect competitive effect from invention is the automobile, which has been charged with being responsible for the ills of many industries. Rightly has it been credited with bringing a revolution in consumption. Its effect upon people's living habits and hence upon product consumption was cited in the case of men's shoes and concrete pavement. Numerous similar examples might be cited. Certain sterling silverware manufacturers have taken the view that the coming of the automobile greatly reduced the desire for sterling as a mark of social distinction.[15] One of the most notable effects of the automobile in shifting consumer habits is its replacement of railroads for travel. Its possible indirect effect upon the demand for numerous products is readily seen from the figures of per capita expenditures of Americans for local transportation in the form of automobiles, bicycles, and horse-drawn equipment, and for local fares. Based on Lough's [16] estimates, these total per capita expenditures rose from approximately $12 in 1909 to $70 in 1929, with a subsequent decrease in the depression year of 1931 to $45. In terms of family expenditure this increase meant a rise from approximately $50 in 1909 to a 1929 peak of over $280, and a 1931 figure of $180. This overall increase in the transportation item is attributable almost solely to the automobile, its operation, and its maintenance. The National Resources Committee's estimates of automobile expenditures alone, based on a study of some 60,000 family budgets, gives an aver-

[15] See N. H. Borden, *Problems in Advertising* (3d ed.), case of Silverware Association, p. 26.
[16] W. H. Lough, *op. cit.*, p. 236.

CHART I

Trends of Change in Consumer Wants
Average Annual Rate of Change*

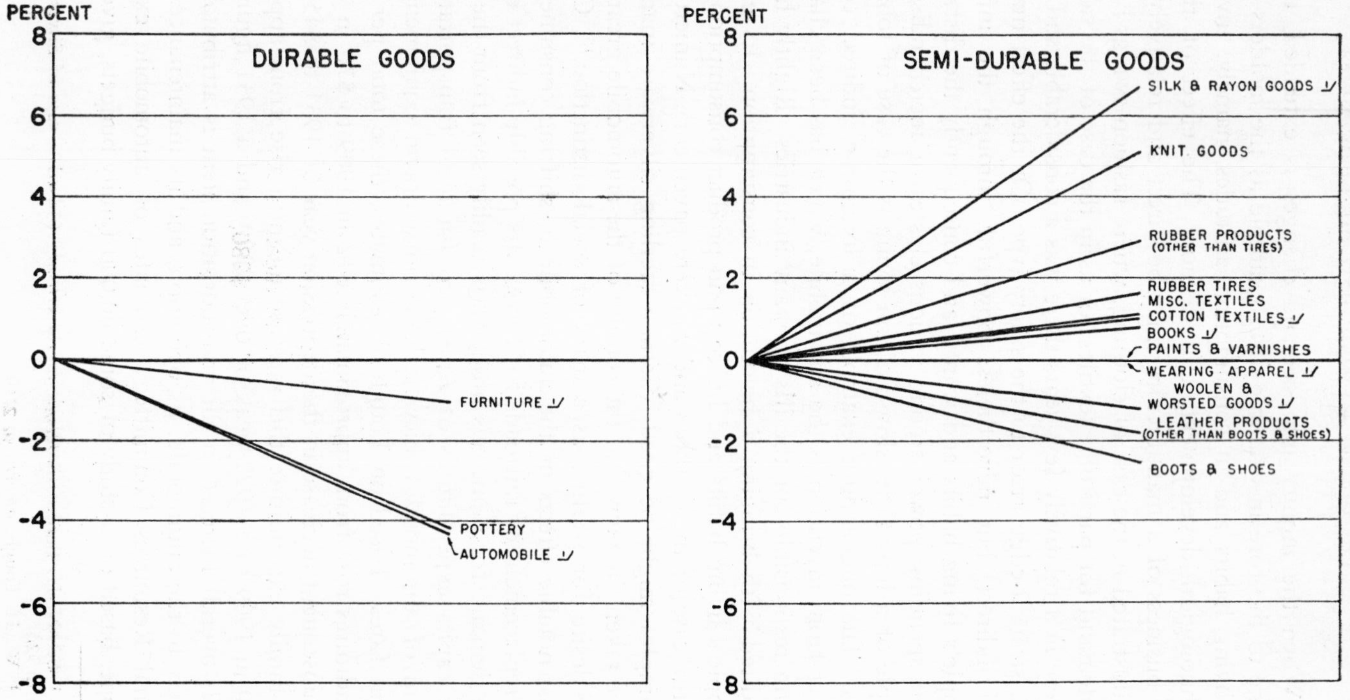
PERCENT
8
6
4
2
0
-2
-4
-6
-8
DURABLE GOODS
FURNITURE 1/
POTTERY
AUTOMOBILE 1/
PERCENT
SEMI-DURABLE GOODS
SILK & RAYON GOODS 1/
KNIT GOODS
RUBBER PRODUCTS
(OTHER THAN TIRES)
RUBBER TIRES
MISC. TEXTILES
COTTON TEXTILES 1/
BOOKS 1/
PAINTS & VARNISHES
WEARING APPAREL 1/
WOOLEN &
WORSTED GOODS 1/
LEATHER PRODUCTS
(OTHER THAN BOOTS & SHOES)
BOOTS & SHOES

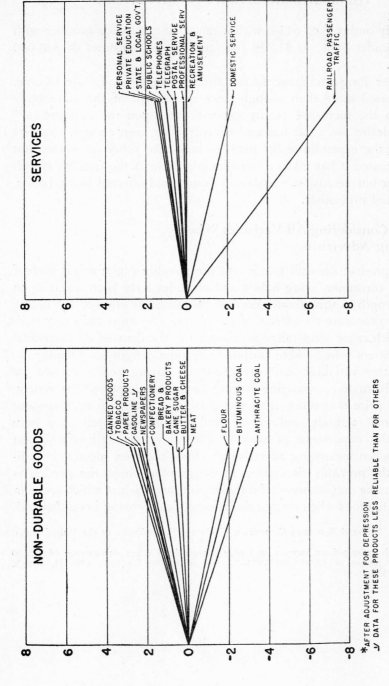

NON-DURABLE GOODS

CANNED GOODS
TOBACCO
PAPER PRODUCTS
GASOLINE ⟋
NEWSPAPERS
CONFECTIONERY
BREAD &
BAKERY PRODUCTS
CANE SUGAR
BUTTER & CHEESE
MEAT
FLOUR
BITUMINOUS COAL
ANTHRACITE COAL

SERVICES

PERSONAL SERVICE
PRIVATE EDUCATION
STATE & LOCAL GOV'T.
PUBLIC SCHOOLS
TELEPHONES
TELEGRAPH
POSTAL SERVICE
PROFESSIONAL SERV
RECREATION &
AMUSEMENT
DOMESTIC SERVICE
RAILROAD PASSENGER
TRAFFIC

*AFTER ADJUSTMENT FOR DEPRESSION
⟋ DATA FOR THESE PRODUCTS LESS RELIABLE THAN FOR OTHERS

Source: United States National Resources Committee, *The Structure of the American Economy* Part I, "Basic Characteristics" (Washington, U. S. Government Printing Office, 1939), p. 20. Based on the formulas shown in the respective summaries of the report, *Patterns of Resource Use*, National Resources Committee. The rate of change is computed from the net relationship with time shown in each formula when the other factors are held constant.

age family outlay [17] of $114, with a range from $15 for families with incomes under $500, to $1,759 for families with incomes of $20,000 and over.

Another long-time basic factor affecting demand, family income, has increased more than enough since the advent of the automobile to absorb the increased family expenditures upon the automobile.[18] Yet the desire for a car has undoubtedly been keen enough to affect markedly the expenditure for items in numerous other categories, not merely because it has taken a considerable share of the family's spending power but because it has shifted desires and affected living habits, as indicated previously.

Need of Considering All Variables When Measuring Advertising

Basic product demand trends and the possible explanations thereof found in consumer living habits and attitudes have been dwelt upon at such length in this chapter because they must be allowed for in any attempt to measure the effects of advertising. So must the many variables which cause short-range fluctuations in the demand of individual manufacturers which were outlined at some length in Chapter V. These latter variables, such as changing buying power caused by cyclical fluctuation, changing buying formulae employed by sellers, changing price structures, changing personal selling efforts, changing promotional methods, and so on, need not be elaborated upon here because the importance of making allowance for their effect upon demand when measuring advertising's effect has been adequately indicated in the previous discussion. In the chapters ahead the attempt is made to make due allowance for the important variables which apply in specific situations when tracing the effects of advertising upon demand.

---

[17] U. S. National Resources Committee, *Consumer Expenditures in the United States*, p. 23.

[18] Lough estimated an increase in family income from a pre-war average of $1,600 to post-war figures of $2,900 for 1923–27, and of $2,100 for 1931 (W. H. Lough, *op. cit.*, p. 53).

CHAPTER VIII

THE EFFECT OF ADVERTISING ON THE DEMAND FOR TOBACCO PRODUCTS—CIGARETTES

TOBACCO was included as one of the products to be studied for several reasons: first, tobacco has been heavily advertised over a long period of time; second, the economic effects of this advertising have been the subject of sharp controversy;[1] and, third, the data regarding consumption, prices, costs, advertising expenditures, and competitive practices, though far from complete and satisfactory, are sufficient to give a basis for analysis.

Heavy Advertising of Tobacco Products

Tobacco products have been one of the most heavily advertised of products during the past 75 years. Shortly after the Civil War, Bull Durham smoking tobacco was widely publicized and the trade-mark became one of the best-known marks in the business.[2] J. B. Duke is reported to have spent what were deemed huge sums on advertising in the '80's and '90's upon cigarettes and smoking tobacco, as much as $750,000 or $800,000 a year upon individual brands.[2] The old American Tobacco Company was reportedly formed in the nineties in part to do away with heavy advertising costs, and apparently accomplished this aim in some degree. Nevertheless, considerable sums were expended in all branches of the business throughout the period of its existence.[3] The study made by the U. S. Commissioner of Corporations gives excellent data regarding advertising costs of the Tobacco Combination for the period from 1893 until its dissolution in

---

[1] For varying appraisals, see:
L. D. H. Weld, "Advertising and Tobacco," *Printers' Ink*, October 7, 1937, and October 21, 1937.
U. S. Bureau of Corporations, *Report of the Commissioner of Corporations on the Tobacco Industry*, Part III, "Prices, Costs, and Profits" (Washington, U. S. Government Printing Office, 1915), p. xxxii.
J. J. Gottsegen, *Tobacco* (New York, Pitman Publishing Corporation, 1940), ch. VII.
Reavis Cox, *Competition in the American Tobacco Industry* (New York, Columbia University Press, 1933), ch. IX.
[2] J. W. Jenkins, *James B. Duke, the Master Builder* (New York, George H. Doran Company, 1927), ch. 4 and 5.
Also see: Frank Presbrey, *op. cit.*, p. 501. "Camels of Winston-Salem," *Fortune*, January, 1931.
[3] U. S. Bureau of Corporations, *op. cit.*, pp. 4, 5, 165.

1911. The average cost figures for the various products are shown in Tables 15 to 21 inclusive. For its numerous varieties of plug tobacco the average expenditure for individual years varied from 5% to 12% of the net price received. The corresponding range for smoking tobacco was from 4% to 16%; for fine cut chewing tobacco, from 1% to 23%; for cigarettes, from about 1% to 20%; for snuff, from 2% to 11%. The range in different years for cigars was from 5% to 50% of net price, the latter percentage during a period when the Combination was endeavoring to strengthen its position in the cigar branch of the industry. For 1910 the Commissioner reported advertising expenditures of a large part of the tobacco industry to be somewhat in excess of $13,000,000, as shown in Table 22. In 1913, after the dissolution, they had jumped to $25,000,000.

The very large advertising expenditures typical of recent years are shown in Table 23, in which an estimate based on traceable expenditures is made for cigarettes, cigars, and smoking tobacco for 1939. The total for that year is estimated to be from $55,000,000 to $60,000,- 000; a corresponding figure for the peak advertising year of 1931 was

TABLE 15

ENTIRE CIGARETTE BUSINESS OF THE COMBINATION*: PRICES, COSTS, AND PROFIT
IN DOLLARS PER THOUSAND AND RELATION OF ITEMS OF COST AND PROFIT
TO NET PRICE LESS TAX, 1893–1910 †

YEAR	NET PRICE	TAX	NET PRICE LESS TAX	MANUFACTUR-ING COST		SELLING COST		ADVERTISING		FREIGHT		PROFIT	
1893..	$3.52	$0.50	$3.02	$1.28†	42.4%†	$0.09	3.0%	$0.37	12.2%	$....	...%	$1.28	42.4%
1894..	3.49	0.50	2.99	1.17†	39.1 †	0.13	4.4	0.33	11.0	.....	.....	1.36	45.5
1895..	3.27	0.50	2.77	1.02	36.8	0.17	6.1	0.33	11.9	0.04	1.5	1.21	43.7
1896..	2.96	0.50	2.46	0.90	36.6	0.15	6.1	0.31	12.6	0.04	1.6	1.06	43.1
1897..	2.94	0.67	2.27	0.89	39.2	0.12	5.3	0.22	9.7	0.04	1.7	1.00	44.1
1898..	3.27	1.25	2.02	0.79	39.1	0.12	5.9	0.03	1.5	0.03	1.5	1.05	52.0
1899..	3.51	1.50	2.01	0.73	36.3	0.12	6.0	0.01	0.5	0.03	1.5	1.12	55.7
1900..	3.66	1.50	2.16	0.78	36.1	0.11	5.1	0.08	3.7	0.03	1.4	1.16	53.7
1901..	3.61	1.27	2.34	0.85	36.3	0.13	5.6	0.31	13.2	0.02	0.9	1.03	44.0
1902..	3.86	1.01	2.85	1.29	45.3	0.14	4.9	0.58	20.3	0.03	1.1	0.81	28.4
1903..	4.05	1.01	3.04	1.50	49.3	0.12	4.0	0.36	11.8	0.03	1.0	1.03	33.9
1904..	4.00	1.00	3.00	1.45	48.3	0.13	4.3	0.43	14.4	0.03	1.0	0.96	32.0
1905..	4.09	1.00	3.09	1.56	50.5	0.12	3.9	0.31	10.0	0.03	1.0	1.07	34.6
1906..	4.26	1.01	3.25	1.70	52.3	0.12	3.7	0.32	9.9	0.05	1.5	1.06	32.6
1907..	4.24	1.02	3.22	1.77	55.0	0.12	3.7	0.36	11.2	0.05	1.5	0.92	28.6
1908..	4.42	1.02	3.40	1.80	52.9	0.13	3.8	0.38	11.2	0.04	1.2	1.05	30.9
1909..	4.49	1.02	3.47	1.74	50.1	0.14	4.0	0.46	13.3	0.03	0.9	1.10	31.7
1910..	4.66	1.15	3.51	1.70	48.4	0.17	4.9	0.60	17.1	0.04	1.1	1.00	28.5

* Exclusive of exports and foreign manufacturing business.
† Includes freight.

Source: U. S. Bureau of Corporations, *Report of the Commissioner of Corporations on the Tobacco Industry* (Washington, D. C., Government Printing Office, 1915), Part III, pp. 155, 157, 158.

TABLE 16

ENTIRE SMOKING TOBACCO BUSINESS OF THE COMBINATION: PRICES, COSTS, AND PROFIT IN CENTS PER POUND AND RELATION OF ITEMS OF COST AND PROFIT TO NET PRICE LESS TAX, 1893–1910

Year	Net Price	Tax	Net Price Less Tax	Manufacturing Cost		Selling Cost		Advertising		Freight		Profit	
1893...	29.8¢	6.0¢	23.8¢	15.4¢*	64.7%*	1.2¢	5.0%	3.3¢	13.9%	....¢	....%	3.9¢	16.4%
1894...	29.3	6.0	23.3	14.1*	60.5*	1.3	5.6	2.8	12.0	.....	......	5.1	21.9
1895...	31.0	6.0	25.0	14.6	58.4	2.2	8.8	3.9	15.6	1.3	5.2	3.0	12.0
1896...	30.7	6.0	24.7	14.7	59.5	1.9	7.7	2.4	9.7	1.3	5.3	4.4	17.8
1897...	29.7	6.0	23.7	13.1	55.3	1.8	7.6	2.8	11.8	1.4	5.9	4.6	19.4
1898...	32.1	8.5	23.6	13.7	58.1	2.1	8.9	3.4	14.4	1.3	5.5	3.1	13.1
1899...	33.1	12.0	21.1	13.2	62.6	1.9	9.0	2.1	9.9	1.3	6.2	2.6	12.3
1900...	34.8	12.0	22.8	13.6	59.6	1.5	6.6	2.2	9.6	1.2	5.3	4.3	18.9
1901...	34.3	11.0	23.3	13.6	58.4	1.1	4.7	2.6	11.2	1.1	4.7	4.9	21.0
1902...	33.8	8.0	25.8	13.8	53.5	1.0	3.9	3.6	13.9	1.1	4.3	6.3	24.4
1903...	33.2	6.0	27.2	14.1	51.8	1.3	4.8	4.2	15.5	1.2	4.4	6.4	23.5
1904...	34.6	6.0	28.6	15.2	53.1	1.4	4.9	4.0	14.0	1.2	4.2	6.8	23.8
1905...	33.7	6.0	27.7	15.1	54.5	1.4	5.1	2.6	9.4	1.2	4.3	7.4	26.7
1906...	34.3	6.0	28.3	15.8	55.8	1.6	5.7	2.4	8.5	1.3	4.6	7.2	25.4
1907...	34.6	6.0	28.6	17.2	60.1	1.6	5.6	1.5	5.2	1.3	4.6	7.0	24.5
1908...	35.2	6.0	29.2	17.3	59.2	1.3	4.5	1.4	4.8	1.4	4.8	7.8	26.7
1909...	35.4	6.0	29.4	18.2	61.9	1.5	5.1	1.3	4.4	1.4	4.8	7.0	23.8
1910...	36.4	6.9	29.5	18.1	61.4	1.6	5.4	1.9	6.4	1.4	4.8	6.5	22.0

* Includes freight.

Source: U. S. Bureau of Corporations, *op. cit.*, pp. 87, 89, 90, 91.

TABLE 17

DOMESTIC CIGAR BUSINESS OF THE COMBINATION: PRICES, COSTS, AND PROFIT IN DOLLARS PER THOUSAND AND RELATION OF ITEMS OF COST AND PROFIT TO NET PRICE LESS TAX, 1901–1910 *

Year	Net Price	Tax	Net Price Less Tax	Manufacturing Cost		Selling Cost		Advertising		Freight		Profit	
1901	$31.13	$3.30	$27.83	$23.44‡	84.2%‡	$0.87	3.1%	$3.69	13.3%	$.....	...%	$0.17†	0.6%†
1902	27.98	3.00	24.98	20.31‡	81.3‡	0.93	3.7	9.35	37.5	.....	.....	5.61†	22.5†
1903	28.08	3.00	25.08	14.61‡	58.2‡	0.77	3.1	12.52	49.9	.....	.....	2.82†	11.2†
1904	26.58	3.00	23.58	16.23	68.8	1.27	5.4	6.80	28.8	0.32	1.4	1.04†	4.4†
1905	26.96	3.00	23.96	18.21	76.0	1.12	4.7	2.85	11.9	0.34	1.4	1.44	6.0
1906	27.69	3.00	24.69	19.07	77.2	0.90	3.7	1.78	7.2	0.30	1.2	2.64	10.7
1907	26.74	3.00	23.74	19.08	80.4	0.79	3.3	1.19	5.0	0.30	1.3	2.38	10.0
1908	26.82	3.00	23.82	20.25	85.0	1.27	5.3	1.09	4.6	0.29	1.2	0.92	3.9
1909	27.06	3.00	24.06	19.16	79.6	1.20	5.0	1.32	5.5	0.31	1.3	2.07	8.6
1910	27.50	3.00	24.50	20.32	82.9	1.25	5.1	1.17	4.8	0.33	1.4	1.43	5.8

* Excludes stogies, cheroots, and package cigars.
† Loss.
‡ Includes freight.

Source: U. S. Bureau of Corporations, *op. cit.*, pp. 197, 198, 199.

TABLE 18

HAVANA CIGAR BUSINESS OF THE COMBINATION: PRICES, COSTS, AND PROFIT IN DOLLARS PER THOUSAND AND RELATION OF ITEMS OF COST AND PROFIT TO NET PRICE LESS TAX, 1902–1910 *

Year	Net Price	Tax	Net Price Less Tax	Manufacturing Cost		Selling Cost		Advertising		Freight		Profit	
1902	$57.72	$3.00	$54.72	$47.10	86.1%	$2.17	4.0%	$3.52	6.4%	$0.45	0.8%	$1.48	2.7%
1903	52.39	3.00	49.39	42.68	86.4	2.51	5.1	2.50	5.1	0.42	0.8	1.28	2.6
1904	54.99	3.00	51.99	45.40	87.3	2.58	5.0	1.42	2.7	0.44	0.9	2.15	4.1
1905	56.08	3.00	53.08	43.10	81.2	2.52	4.7	1.71	3.2	0.45	0.9	5.30	10.0
1906	56.83	3.00	53.83	43.07	80.0	2.12	4.0	2.16	4.0	0.48	0.9	6.00	11.1
1907	56.02	3.00	53.02	44.08	83.1	1.93	3.6	1.73	3.3	0.46	0.9	4.82	9.1
1908	54.13	3.00	51.13	50.21	98.2	2.45	4.8	2.40	4.7	0.44	0.8	4.37†	8.5†
1909	53.91	3.00	50.91	49.87	98.0	2.40	4.7	2.10	4.1	0.45	0.9	3.91†	7.7†
1910	53.16	3.00	50.16	43.11	86.0	2.45	4.9	1.56	3.1	0.46	0.9	2.58	5.1

* Excludes Havana cigars not manufactured in the United States.
† Loss.
Source: U. S. Bureau of Corporations, *op. cit.,* pp. 201, 202, 203.

TABLE 19

ENTIRE PLUG BUSINESS OF THE COMBINATION: PRICES, COSTS, AND PROFIT IN CENTS PER POUND AND RELATION OF ITEMS OF COST AND PROFIT TO NET PRICE LESS TAX, 1893–1910

Year	Net Price	Tax	Net Price Less Tax	Manufacturing Cost		Selling Cost		Advertising		Freight		Profit	
1893	34.0¢	6.0¢	28.0¢	....¢	..%	....¢	....%	....¢	....%	..¢	...%	2.6¢*	9.3%*
1894	35.1	6.0	29.1									1.2	4.1
1895	21.5	6.0	15.5									4.5*	29.0*
1896	18.9	6.0	12.9	12.9	100.0	2.3	17.8	1.4	10.9	0.7	5.4	4.4*	34.1*
1897	18.2	6.0	12.2	11.5	94.3	1.6	13.1	0.7	5.7	0.8	6.6	2.4*	19.7*
1898	25.2	8.5	16.7	15.0	89.8	2.1	12.6	1.9	11.4	0.6	3.6	2.9*	17.4*
1899	33.0	12.0	21.0	15.5	73.8	1.5	7.1	1.0	4.8	0.8	3.8	2.2	10.5
1900	34.8	12.0	22.8	14.9	65.3	1.3	5.7	2.0	8.8	0.8	3.5	3.8	16.7
1901	36.0	10.9	25.1	14.4	57.4	0.8	3.2	2.6	10.3	0.8	3.2	6.5	25.9
1902	35.5	7.8	27.7	14.7	53.1	0.6	2.2	3.2	11.5	0.8	2.9	8.4	30.3
1903	35.4	6.0	29.4	15.2	51.7	0.9	3.1	2.6	8.8	0.9	3.1	9.8	33.3
1904	35.9	6.0	29.9	16.5	55.2	1.4	4.7	3.3	11.0	0.9	3.0	7.8	26.1
1905	36.2	6.0	30.2	16.3	34.0	1.6	5.3	3.5	11.6	1.0	3.3	7.8	25.8
1906	36.0	6.0	30.0	15.8	52.7	1.6	5.3	2.7	9.0	1.0	3.3	8.9	29.7
1907	36.2	6.0	30.2	16.6	55.0	1.7	5.6	2.5	8.3	1.0	3.3	8.4	27.8
1908	36.3	6.0	30.3	17.8	58.8	1.4	4.6	2.0	6.6	1.1	3.6	8.0	26.4
1909	35.7	6.0	29.7	20.0	67.3	1.7	5.7	1.8	6.1	1.1	3.7	5.1	17.2
1910	36.0	6.9	29.1	19.5	67.0	1.9	6.5	1.9	6.5	1.1	3.8	4.7	16.2

* Loss.
Source: U. S. Bureau of Corporations, *op. cit.,* pp. 51, 55, 56.

TABLE 20

ENTIRE FINE-CUT CHEWING TOBACCO BUSINESS OF THE COMBINATION: PRICES, COSTS, AND PROFIT IN CENTS PER POUND AND RELATION OF ITEMS OF COST AND PROFIT TO NET PRICE LESS TAX, 1893–1910

Year	Net Price	Tax	Net Price Less Tax	Manufacturing Cost		Selling Cost		Advertising		Freight		Profit	
1893...	31.5¢	6.0¢	25.5¢	18.6¢*	72.9%*	2.9¢	11.4%	2.0¢	7.9%	...¢	...%	2.0¢	7.8%
1894...	31.6	6.0	25.6	18.9*	73.8*	2.1	8.2	0.5	2.0	...	...	4.1	16.0
1895...	33.0	6.0	27.0	19.3	71.5	2.5	9.2	0.2	0.7	0.8	3.0	4.2	15.6
1896...	33.2	6.0	27.2	19.9	73.2	2.5	9.2	0.4	1.5	0.8	2.9	3.6	13.2
1897...	32.6	6.0	26.6	18.1	68.1	2.0	7.5	0.3	1.1	0.7	2.6	5.5	20.7
1898...	34.4	8.5	25.9	18.1	69.9	2.3	8.9	5.9	22.8	0.6	2.3	1.0†	3.9†
1899...	36.4	12.0	24.4	18.1	74.2	1.8	7.4	1.8	7.4	0.7	2.8	2.0	8.2
1900...	34.9	12.0	22.9	18.7	81.7	1.4	6.1	2.1	11.3	0.8	3.5	0.6†	2.6†
1901...	37.2	10.9	26.3	21.3	81.0	1.1	4.2	5.4	20.5	0.8	3.0	2.3†	8.7†
1902...	41.2	7.8	33.4	22.1	66.1	1.1	3.3	3.4	10.2	0.5	1.5	6.3	18.9
1903...	35.4	6.0	29.4	18.2	61.9	1.4	4.8	2.3	7.8	0.8	2.4	6.8	23.1
1904...	36.8	6.0	30.8	19.4	63.0	1.4	4.5	2.1	6.8	0.8	2.6	7.1	23.1
1905...	36.6	6.0	30.6	19.0	62.1	1.3	4.3	1.8	5.9	0.9	2.9	7.6	24.8
1906...	35.9	6.0	29.9	18.4	61.5	1.3	4.4	1.9	6.4	1.0	3.3	7.3	24.4
1907...	36.0	6.0	30.0	20.2	67.4	1.3	4.3	1.1	3.7	1.0	3.3	6.4	21.3
1908...	36.4	6.0	30.4	20.1	66.1	1.1	3.6	0.8	2.7	1.1	3.6	7.3	24.0
1909...	36.2	6.0	30.2	22.0	72.8	1.5	5.0	0.6	2.0	1.1	3.6	5.0	16.8
1910...	37.5	7.0	30.5	22.9	75.1	1.6	5.2	0.9	3.0	1.2	3.9	3.9	12.8

* Includes freight.
† Loss.
Source: U. S. Bureau of Corporations, *op. cit.,* pp. 129, 131, 133.

TABLE 21

ENTIRE SNUFF BUSINESS OF THE COMBINATION: PRICES, COSTS, AND PROFIT IN CENTS PER POUND AND RELATION OF ITEMS OF COST AND PROFIT TO NET PRICE LESS TAX, 1900–1910

Year	Net Price	Tax	Net Price Less Tax	Manufacturing Cost		Selling Cost		Advertising		Freight		Profit	
1900...	41.7¢	12.0¢	29.7¢	15.5¢	52.2%	3.5¢	11.8%	3.2¢	10.8%	2.1¢	7.0%	5.4¢	18.2%
1901...	41.4	11.0	30.4	15.8	52.0	2.6	8.5	1.7	5.6	2.3	7.6	8.0	26.3
1902...	40.3	8.0	32.3	15.3	47.4	2.3	7.1	1.5	4.7	2.3	7.1	10.9	33.7
1903...	40.2	6.0	34.2	15.0	43.9	2.3	6.7	2.0	5.9	2.2	6.4	12.7	37.1
1904...	42.6	6.0	36.6	15.2	41.5	2.2	6.0	1.7	4.7	2.3	6.3	15.2	41.5
1905...	43.8	6.0	37.8	16.3	43.1	2.1	5.6	1.3	3.4	2.3	6.1	15.8	41.8
1906...	43.5	6.0	37.5	14.9	39.7	1.9	5.1	1.3	3.4	2.2	5.9	17.2	45.9
1907...	43.5	6.0	37.5	15.4	41.1	2.0	5.3	1.4	3.7	2.2	5.9	16.5	44.0
1908...	44.2	6.0	38.2	16.8	44.0	1.9	5.0	0.7	1.8	2.1	5.5	16.7	43.7
1909...	44.1	6.0	38.1	16.5	43.3	1.6	4.2	1.1	2.9	2.2	5.8	16.7	43.8
1910...	44.8	6.9	37.9	16.2	42.7	1.3	3.4	1.5	4.0	1.9	5.0	17.0	44.9

Source: U. S. Bureau of Corporations, *op. cit.,* pp. 139, 141, 142.

TABLE 22

TOTAL SELLING AND ADVERTISING COSTS IN THE TOBACCO INDUSTRY, 1910–1913

	1910			1913		
	Selling Costs	Advertising Expenditures	Total	Selling Costs	Advertising Expenditures	Total
Cigarettes.............	$ 1,669,303	$ 4,305,560	$ 5,974,863	$ 3,264,844	$13,764,072	$17,028,916
Cigars, Total.........	1,587,452	1,549,206	3,136,658	....	....	....
Cigars..............	$ 1,476,832	$ 1,339,318	....	....	....	....
Little Cigars........	110,620	209,888		191,546	426,509	618,055
Chewing and Smoking Tobacco and Snuff, Total............	7,478,968	7,364,687	14,843,655	8,926,658	10,890,213	19,816,871
Plug................	$ 3,389,424	$ 3,001,698		$ 3,433,264	$ 3,409,969	
Fine Cut............	156,809	88,577		193,708	70,671	
Smoking Tobacco....	3,049,500	3,690,082		4,079,381	6,393,623	
Mixed Products.....	492,634	156,747		626,474	170,857	
Snuff...............	390,601	427,583		593,831	845,093	
Total................	$10,735,723	$13,219,453	$23,955,176	$12,383,048	$25,080,794	$37,463,842

NOTE: The following data indicate the extent to which the figures presented cover the industry:

Plug: In 1913 there were 50 concerns, other than successor companies, producing plug and twist tobaccos. Data were secured from 16 of the companies, including all the larger ones, representing, in 1913, 65% of the total production of all companies other than successor companies.

Smoking tobacco: The companies covered produced 78% of the total smoking tobacco produced by all companies other than the successor companies in 1913.

Cigarettes: In domestic Virginia cigarettes no material is given: first, no important independent manufacturer operated throughout the entire period 1893–1910; second, nearly all were either too insignificant or operated only a short period of time. Data cover all larger independent Turkish cigarette manufacturers; companies covered produced over 50% of total output of all companies other than successor companies.

Cigars: There were 20,485 manufacturers in 1912; of this number there were only a comparatively few large concerns. Data cover 14 of the larger companies.

Sources:

(a) Figures covering the combination and successor companies from table on pp. 17 and and 18, U. S. Bureau of Corporations, *op. cit.*

(b) Data on "other companies" computed by multiplying the number of pounds sold of the various types of products times the advertising cost per pound for each corresponding type of product. See pages 393, 395, 401, 403, 410, 412, 417, 418, 423, 424, 429, 431, 436, 438, 442, 444, U. S. Bureau of Corporations, *op cit.*

probably about $75,000,000. Since chewing tobacco and snuff advertising is not large [4] at the present time, the estimates given for cigars, cigarettes, and smoking tobacco are close to the total for the industry.

Further evidence of size of advertising expenditures in recent years is indicated in figures of percentage of sales expended for tobacco products. The average advertising expenditures of four tobacco product

---

[4] The magazine, newspaper, and radio space and time expenditures for these items are so small that they do not appear in the reports of companies which measure and record advertising.

TABLE 23

ESTIMATE OF ADVERTISING EXPENDITURE FOR CIGARETTES, CIGARS, AND
SMOKING TOBACCO, 1939

	CIGARETTES	CIGARS	SMOKING TOBACCO	TOTAL
Traceable Expenditure in Magazines, Farm Journals, Newspapers, and Chain Radio	$24,956,000	$3,197,000	$5,082,000	$33,235,000
Estimated Total (Traceable Expenditures as 60% of Total).......................	41,600,000	5,300,000	8,470,000	55,400,000
Estimated Total (Traceable Expenditures as 55% of Total).......................	45,375,000	5,812,000	9,240,000	60,427,000

NOTE: Association of National Advertisers' estimates of National Advertising Budgets, 1932-1933 and 1934-1935 show that the space and time items accounted for approximately 55% to 60% of total advertising budgets of drug and toilet article manufacturers and about 50% of the budgets of grocery product manufacturers. The budgets of these manufacturers are believed to correspond most closely to budgets of tobacco companies. Accordingly, it was thought that time and space expenditures would represent 55% to 60% of total expenditures for the above tobacco products. Association of National Advertisers, Inc., *An Analysis of 285 National Advertising Budgets, 1932–1933* (New York, 1933), and *A Survey of 299 National Advertising Budgets, 1934–1935* (New York, 1936).

Source: American Newspaper Publishers' Association, Bureau of Advertising, *Expenditures of National Advertisers in Newspapers, Magazines, Farm Journals and Chain Radio in 1939* (Media Records measurements), p. 14 ff.

manufacturers in 1931, as reported in the Association of National Advertisers' study of costs of distribution, were 8.23%.[5] Confidential information received by the author on advertising expense of individual tobacco companies for recent years indicates a range from approximately 6% to about 30%.

Comment upon the industry's heavy use of advertising has been common ever since the days of the Tobacco Combination, when the tobacco industry became the subject of recurrent investigation by governmental bodies and economics students. Probably no specific industry provides a wider array of conflicting statements regarding the economic effects of its advertising. Critics who have held advertising to be counter to social welfare have been answered by others who have contended that the economic effects have been favorable. In the course of this study the various issues that have been drawn will be discussed. In this chapter attention is directed to an appraisal of the effect of advertising upon the demand for tobacco products as a whole and for cigarettes. The following chapter deals with the demand for other tobacco products. While an understanding of demand issues requires

[5] Association of National Advertisers, *An Analysis of the Distribution Costs of 312 Manufacturers* (New York, 1933), p. 15.

separate study of each type of tobacco product, a survey of total tobacco consumption is made first because it reveals several interesting relationships between the component parts.

EFFECTS OF ADVERTISING UPON TOBACCO CONSUMPTION AS A WHOLE

The facts regarding consumption since 1870 are shown in Tables 24, 25, 26. For the 1870–1895 period (Table 25), total per capita consumption on a poundage basis had to be built in part from estimates of the weight of cigars and cigarettes then consumed. As a result of this estimating process the data for total consumption in pounds in Table 25 are not so accurate as they are for the period after 1900 (Table 26), but they are believed to be fairly accurate.[6]

The tables show a steady increase in annual per capita consumption after 1870 from slightly less than 3 pounds to over 5 pounds in 1900 and on to a war peak in 1917 of nearly 7¾ pounds. Since 1917 consumption has been relatively stable, around 7 pounds except for the 1933 depression period, when under the impact of decreased buying power it dropped temporarily to 6 pounds.

The causes of this consumption increase will be discussed in conjunction with each of the several types of tobacco, but certain considerations relating to total consumption are worthy of note here.

The growth in tobacco usage subsequent to the Civil War was probably influenced by an increase in the production and consumption of mild tobaccos. Bright leaf tobacco with its fine flavor and texture

---

[6] G. K. Holmes, *Tobacco Crop of the United States, 1612–1911* (U. S. Department of Agriculture, Bureau of Statistics, Circular 33, Washington, 1912) gives estimates of consumption for this period based on a formula of production plus net imports minus domestic exports. His figures are as follows:

YEAR	POUNDS	YEAR	POUNDS
1839	5.65	1871–75	1.78
1847 ⎫		1876–80	3.65
1849 ⎬ weighted average	3.03	1881–85	5.43
1853 ⎭		1886–90	5.12
1859	8.27	1891–95	5.14
1866–70	3.07		

Since his formula does not give figures which represent consumption for any certain year, and since the figures for subsequent periods vary markedly and thereby do not accord with the consumption statistics as reflected in the reports of the Commissioner of Internal Revenue, they are not believed to represent consumption as accurately as do the data of Table 26.

TABLE 24

CONSUMPTION OF TOBACCO PRODUCTS AT FIVE-YEAR INTERVALS, 1870–1935

Fiscal Year Ending June 30	No. Large Cigars	No. Small Cigars	No. All Cigars	No. Large Cigarettes
1870	1,139,470,774		1,139,470,774	
1875	1,926,661,780		1,926,661,780	
1880	2,367,803,250		2,367,803,250	
1885	3,358,972,633		3,358,972,633	
1890	4,087,889,983		4,087,889,983	
1895	4,163,972,440		4,163,972,440	1,073,397
1900	5,316,273,561	646,896,820	5,963,170,381	4,448,392
1905	6,860,414,577	728,422,630	7,589,337,207	8,420,933
1910	7,140,229,837	1,073,126,667	8,213,426,504	21,532,707
1915	7,058,122,323	992,263,280	8,050,385,603	15,703,061
1920	7,732,629,000	684,409,000	8,417,038,000	32,258,000
1925	6,530,915,000	487,235,000	7,018,150,000	15,200,000
1930	6,328,646,000	402,015,000	6,730,661,000	9,042,000
1935	4,660,366,000	191,652,000	4,852,018,000	2,407,000

Fiscal Year Ending June 30	No. Small Cigarettes	No. All Cigarettes	Pounds Snuff	Pounds Chewing and Smoking Tobacco
1870	13,881,417	13,881,417	1,168,077	89,120,006
1875	167,175,329	167,175,329	3,334,478	116,101,396
1880	408,708,365	408,708,365	3,966,308	132,309,527
1885	1,058,749,238	1,058,749,238	6,361,794	174,415,619
1895	2,233,254,680	2,233,254,680	9,221,641	229,068,517
1890	3,327,403,780	3,328,477,177	10,831,474	248,269,638
1900	2,635,451,393	2,639,899,785	14,917,418	278,977,035
1905	3,368,212,740	3,376,633,673	21,131,861	334,489,110
1910	7,863,215,808	7,884,748,513	31,969,111	436,608,898
1915	16,740,776,912	16,756,479,973	29,839,074	402,474,275
1920	50,412,535,000	50,444,793,000	38,410,000	415,004,000
1925	75,009,865,000	75,025,065,000	37,520,000	371,788,000
1930	119,935,433,000	119,944,475,000	40,646,000	335,101,000
1935	128,482,392,000	128,484,799,000	36,176,000	302,046,000

Sources: Annual Reports of U. S. Commissioner of Internal Revenue.

* From 1920 on, *First Annual Report on Tobacco Statistics,* U. S. Department of Agriculture (Washington, D. C., U. S. Government Printing Office, May, 1937).

TABLE 25

PER CAPITA CONSUMPTION OF TOBACCO PRODUCTS IN THE UNITED STATES AT FIVE-YEAR INTERVALS, 1870–1895

Year Ending June 30	Cigars, Number*	Cigarettes, Number*	Cigars, Pounds†	Cigarettes, Pounds‡	Manufactured Tobacco, Pounds*	Snuff, Pounds*	Total, Pounds
1870	29.48	.36	.56	.001	2.306	.030	2.90
1875	43.34	.93	.82	.004	2.612	.075	3.51
1880	47.11	8.13	.89	.031	2.632	.079	3.63
1885	59.29	18.69	1.12	.071	3.078	.112	4.38
1890	64.83	35.42	1.22	.134	3.633	.146	5.13
1895	59.84	47.84	1.13	.181	3.579	.145	5.04

* Total quantities consumed taken from Annual Reports of the Commissioner of Internal Revenue for the years 1870, 1875, 1880, 1885, 1890, and 1895. These figures were then divided by population figures taken from the "Annual Midyear Estimates for Continental United States and Certain Outlying Territories and Possessions," *Statistical Abstract of the U. S., 1937,* p. 10.

† Derived by dividing per capita consumption of cigars by 53. The average conversion rate for the years 1900–1909 was 51.5 but was falling, therefore a more conservative figure was adopted.

‡ Derived by dividing per capita consumption of cigarettes by 264, the average conversion rate in the 10-year period 1900–1909.

TABLE 26

PER CAPITA CONSUMPTION OF TOBACCO PRODUCTS IN THE UNITED STATES, 1900–1937

YEAR*	LARGE CIGARS, NUMBER	SMALL CIGARETTES, NUMBER	CIGARS, POUNDS†	CIGARETTES POUNDS,	CHEWING TOBACCO, POUNDS	SMOKING TOBACCO, POUNDS	SNUFF, POUNDS	TOTAL, POUNDS
1900	70.5	34.9	1.33	0.14	2.39	1.31	0.20	5.37
1901	75.0	29.5	1.42	.12	2.38	1.44	.22	5.58
1902	77.7	33.6	1.47	.13	2.28	1.51	.23	5.62
1903	84.6	37.8	1.62	.14	2.29	1.58	.24	5.87
1904	82.0	39.4	1.57	.15	2.22	1.80	.25	5.99
1905	82.3	40.4	1.59	.15	2.09	1.92	.25	6.00
1906	84.4	44.5	1.65	.16	2.16	2.01	.27	6.25
1907	86.4	59.5	1.75	.21	2.16	2.10	.27	6.49
1908	78.2	61.0	1.57	.22	2.06	2.07	.25	6.17
1909	75.1	67.7	1.54	.24	2.15	2.17	.30	6.40
1910	76.7	93.7	1.59	.34	2.17	2.30	.34	6.74
1911	77.8	107.8	1.65	.40	1.98	2.23	.31	6.57
1912	77.6	139.0	1.65	.49	1.96	2.28	.33	6.71
1913	80.1	163.7	1.72	.60	1.96	2.27	.34	6.89
1914	75.3	168.5	1.67	.62	1.84	2.28	.31	6.72
1915	71.4	180.6	1.58	.67	1.77	2.36	.33	6.71
1916	76.1	250.4	1.71	.93	1.90	2.37	.34	7.25
1917	80.1	340.7	1.79	1.29	1.98	2.34	.34	7.74
1918	72.0	366.0	1.65	1.39	1.76	2.25	.36	7.41
1919	69.0	426.4	1.61	1.59	1.53	2.17	.34	7.24
1920	79.8	418.8	1.87	1.56	1.43	1.98	.34	7.18
1921	64.3	470.1	1.50	1.72	1.19	2.05	.33	6.79
1922	65.7	487.5	1.48	1.48	1.26	2.21	.35	6.78
1923	66.2	577.9	1.52	1.74	1.24	2.10	.35	6.95
1924	61.9	627.3	1.44	1.88	1.13	2.17	.34	6.96
1925	60.3	696.1	1.39	2.07	1.10	2.14	.33	7.03
1926	59.7	767.6	1.40	2.23	1.08	2.11	.33	7.15
1927	58.3	822.2	1.36	2.40	.99	2.00	.34	7.09
1928	56.6	883.7	1.34	2.52	.95	1.92	.34	7.07
1929	56.4	979.6	1.32	2.77	.90	1.88	.33	7.20
1930	50.1	972.0	1.17	2.73	.80	1.87	.33	6.90
1931	45.3	914.2	1.08	2.58	.69	1.95	.32	6.62
1932	37.5	828.9	.89	2.32	.57	1.93	.29	6.00
1933	36.5	888.7	.89	2.53	.55	1.87	.29	6.13
1934	38.4	992.0	.94	2.87	.56	1.87	.29	6.53
1935	39.5	1,055.6	.96	3.01	.55	1.83	.28	6.63
1936	42.0	1,192.7	1.03	3.40	.55	1.86	.29	7.13
1937‡	42.8	1,258.2	1.05	3.59	.53	1.80	.28	7.25

* Available data 1900–09 do not include tax-paid products from the Philippine Islands and Puerto Rico and are for the fiscal year beginning July; 1910–35 data include tax-paid products from the Philippine Islands and Puerto Rico and are for the calendar year. In the former group, January population was used, while in the latter group July population was used, to determine the per capita consumption.

† Pounds of cigars and cigarettes represent unstemmed equivalent of tobacco used in the manufacture of these products, as reported in the annual reports of the Commissioner of Internal Revenue. Both large and small cigars and large and small cigarettes are included.

‡ Preliminary.

Sources: U. S. Department of Agriculture, Statistical Bulletin No. 58, *First Annual Report on Tobacco Statistics, 1937* (Washington, The Department, May, 1937), p. 100; Statistical Bulletin No. 67, *Annual Report on Tobacco Statistics, 1938*, p. 79.

was developed in 1852,[7] received wide local adoption, and became well known during the Civil War to soldiers both of the North and

[7] W. W. Young, *The Story of the Cigarette* (New York, D. Appleton and Company, 1916), p. 82.

TABLE 27

AVERAGE PRICES RECEIVED BY THE TOBACCO COMBINATION FOR TOBACCO PRODUCTS,
1893–1910, AND OF SUCCESSOR COMPANIES, 1912–1913

Year	Plug Business Average per Pound	Smoking Tobacco Business Average per Pound	Cigarette Business Average per Thousand	Domestic Cigar Business Average per Thousand	Snuff Business Average per Pound
1893	$0.340	$0.298	$3.52	$......	$......
1894	0.351	0.293	3.49	....	....
1895	0.215	0.310	3.27	....	....
1896	0.189	0.307	2.96	....	....
1897	0.182	0.297	2.94	....	....
1898	0.252	0.321	3.27	....	....
1899	0.330	0.331	3.51	....	....
1900	0.348	0.348	3.66	....	41.7
1901	0.360	0.343	3.61	31.13	41.4
1902	0.355	0.338	3.86	27.98	40.3
1903	0.354	0.332	4.05	28.08	40.2
1904	0.359	0.346	4.00	26.58	42.6
1905	0.362	0.337	4.09	26.96	43.8
1906	0.360	0.343	4.26	27.69	43.5
1907	0.362	0.346	4.24	26.74	43.5
1908	0.363	0.352	4.42	26.82	44.2
1909	0.357	0.354	4.49	27.06	44.1
1910	0.360	0.364	4.66	27.50	44.8
1912	0.372	0.396	4.73	....	45.3
1913	0.371	0.404	4.62	....	45.1

Source: U. S. Bureau of Corporations, *op. cit.*, pp. 51, 87, 139, 155, 197, 224, 252, 309, 324.

of the South.[8] About 1869 its suitability for cigarettes was learned. Matthewson records that mild white burley tobacco made its appearance in 1864;[9] it met with unusual success. The mild tobaccos with their better flavor probably encouraged a consumption that might not have occurred had the harsher tobaccos of the pre-Civil War period prevailed.[10]

Increased consumption of tobacco products as a whole over this period was not encouraged by decreasing prices; in fact, prices of tobacco tended upward somewhat, as indicated in the discrete price series presented in Tables 27 and 28.[11] The increase was not marked

[8] J. W. Jenkins, *op. cit.*, ch. 4.
[9] E. H. Matthewson, *Export and Manufacturing Tobaccos of the United States with Brief Reference to Cigar Types,* Bulletin 244 (Washington, U. S. Department of Agriculture, Bureau of Plant Industry, 1912).
[10] See J. J. Gottsegen, *op. cit.*, pp. 6, 41.
[11] No retail price series covering the period, and no fully satisfactory wholesale price data were found. Accordingly the discrete series contained in Tables 27 and 28 have been used. For the purposes of this study they are adequate to show price trends.

but was about in line with prices generally (see Table 28). Thus, it is to be noted that the demand for tobacco expanded in this period. Increasing consumption took place without decrease in prices.

Since the first World War, however, the picture has changed. In this period, per capita consumption has been practically stationary. Both the wholesale and retail prices of tobacco have tended downward, as indicated in Tables 28 and 29; but the extent of the downward price trend of tobacco products, excepting smoking tobacco, has not been so great as has been the drop in the wholesale price index for all commodities. A level of tobacco prices somewhat higher than

TABLE 28

ANNUAL AVERAGE WHOLESALE PRICES OF TOBACCO PRODUCTS AND INDEX OF PRICES—1926=100, COMPARED WITH U. S. BUREAU OF LABOR STATISTICS COMBINED INDEX OF WHOLESALE PRICES, 1913–1938

YEAR	PLUG TOBACCO, 15-oz. Plug	INDEX OF PRICE 1926=100	SMOKING TOBACCO, Gross 1-oz. Bags	INDEX OF PRICE 1926=100	CIGARETTES, per Thousand	INDEX OF PRICE 1926=100	CIGARS, per Thousand	INDEX OF PRICE 1926=100	SNUFF, ½ Gross of 1½ oz. Average Container	INDEX OF PRICE 1926=100	B.L.S. Combined INDEX OF WHOLESALE PRICES 1926=100
1913	$0.470	55.9	$5.640	67.8	$......	......	$......	......	$......	......	69.8
1914	0.470	55.9	5.680	68.3	......	......	......	......	......	......	68.1
1915	0.490	58.2	5.760	69.2	......	......	......	......	......	......	69.5
1916	0.490	58.2	5.760	69.2	......	......	......	......	......	......	85.5
1917	0.585	69.5	5.760	69.2	......	......	......	......	......	......	117.5
1918	0.747	88.7	8.080	97.1	......	......	......	......	......	......	131.3
1919	0.909	107.9	9.176	110.3	......	......	......	......	......	......	138.6
1920	0.778	111.7	9.920	119.2	......	......	......	......	......	......	154.4
1921	0.714	102.5	9.920	119.2	......	......	......	......	......	......	97.6
1922	0.701	100.7	9.920	119.2	......	......	......	......	......	......	96.7
1923	0.701	100.7	9.920	119.2	......	......	......	......	......	......	100.6
1924	0.696	100.0	8.453	101.6	......	......	......	......	......	......	98.0
1925	0.696	100.0	8.320	100.0	......	......	......	......	......	......	103.5
1926	0.696	100.0	8.320	100.0	5.660	100.0	52.808	100.0	5.292	100.0	100.0
1927	0.696	100.0	8.320	100.0	5.660	100.0	52.845	100.7	5.292	100.0	95.4
1928	0.696	100.0	8.320	100.0	5.422	95.8	52.714	99.8	5.292	100.0	96.7
1929	0.696	100.0	8.320	100.0	5.398	95.4	52.427	99.3	5.292	100.0	95.3
1930	0.696	100.0	8.320	100.0	5.645	99.7	51.044	96.7	5.292	100.0	86.4
1931	0.696	100.0	7.017	84.3	5.851	103.4	49.767	94.2	5.292	100.0	73.0
1932	0.696	100.0	5.120	61.5	6.042	106.7	49.053	92.9	5.292	100.0	64.8
1933	0.597	85.8	5.120	61.5	4.902	86.6	46.420	87.9	5.292	100.0	65.9
1934	0.642	92.2	5.120	61.5	5.370	94.9	46.875	88.8	5.292	100.0	74.9
1935	0.642	92.2	5.120	61.5	5.380	95.0	46.199	87.5	5.292	100.0	80.0
1936	0.642	92.2	5.120	61.5	5.380	95.0	45.996	87.1	5.292	100.0	80.8
1937	0.642	92.2	5.120	61.5	5.057	89.3	46.044	87.2	4.887	92.3	86.3
1938	0.642	92.2	5.120	61.5	5.513	97.4	46.056	87.2	4.502	85.1	78.6

Sources:
B. L. S. Index, Years 1913–1927: U. S. Bureau of Labor Statistics, Bulletin No. 493, *Wholesale Prices*, August, 1929, p. 237. Years 1928–1938: *Statistical Abstract of the United States*, 1940.
Tobacco prices: U. S. Department of Agriculture, Statistical Bulletin No. 67, *Annual Report on Tobacco Statistics*, 1938, op. cit., pp. 37 and 38.

general prices may have tended to slow down the consumption increase since 1918, but it is believed that not very much weight should be given to the price factor as an explanation of the halt in growing per capita consumption. A slowing down in the rate of consumption increase had set in some years before the first World War, when tobacco prices were below the general level of prices, as shown by wholesale price indices. Moreover, the tenacity of tobacco usage, once established, gives the product a relatively inelastic demand and hence a tendency to be little affected by moderate price change.[12] It would appear, rather, that in the more mature market of recent years consumers' habits and attitudes have not changed in such a way as to bring the expansion of the preceding period, nor have heavy promotional expenditures been a force adequate to expand consumption.

The picture within the industry is one of conflicting demand trends. Cigarettes have had a remarkable growth, over a thousandfold, since 1870, from practically nothing to a total per capita consumption of 1,258 in 1937. Per capita consumption of cigars had an upward trend which reached its peak in 1917 with a steady decline since that time.

TABLE 29

RETAIL PRICES OF TOBACCO PRODUCTS, AVERAGE IN 32 CITIES, DECEMBER, 1920–21 AND 1926–37 *

YEAR	CIGARETTES, PER PACK OF 20	CIGARS, EACH	CIGARETTE TOBACCO, PER OZ.	PIPE TOBACCO, PER OZ.	PLUG TOBACCO, PER OZ.
1920	19.8¢	11.0¢	8.8¢	8.9¢	7.8¢
1921	18.7	10.2	8.8	8.6	7.5
1926	14.6	8.4	8.6	7.2	7.3
1927	14.4	8.1	8.4	7.2	7.2
1928	13.7	8.1	8.4	7.2	7.3
1929	13.4	7.6	8.4	7.1	7.1
1930	13.3	6.0	8.5	6.8	6.8
1931	14.2	5.2	6.3	6.6	6.8
1932	14.2	4.7	5.9	7.0	6.5
1933	12.2	4.7	5.7	6.8	6.5
1934†	13.1	5.2	5.8	6.6	6.6
1935‡	13.3	4.6	5.7	6.4	6.4
1936	13.3	4.6	5.6	6.6	6.3
1937§	13.8	4.6	5.6	6.6	6.3

* Prices were obtained from approximately 4 dealers in each of 32 large cities as of the 15th of the month, for the brand and/or package size most in demand in their stores, and have been weighted by population of the metropolitan areas and of adjacent areas, where the retail prices were obtained. Sales taxes are included wherever applicable.
† November.
‡ October.
§ September.

Source: U. S. Department of Agriculture, Statistical Bulletin No. 67, *Annual Report on Tobacco Statistics, 1938*, p. 39.

---

12 See Reavis Cox, *op. cit.*, p. 144.

Chewing tobacco has shown a steady downward trend for the greater part of the period. Smoking tobacco reached its peak during the first World War and has since lost ground. The consumption of snuff moved upward until 1910, with a slight decline after the depression. In short, for the period of relatively stable consumption since 1917 the increase in the use of cigarettes has about offset the decreased consumption in other categories.

TABLE 30

CHANGES IN ANNUAL PER CAPITA CONSUMPTION OF CIGARETTES, 1911–1937

YEAR	INCREASE OR DECREASE OVER PRECEDING YEAR, NUMBER OF CIGARETTES	YEAR	INCREASE OR DECREASE OVER PRECEDING YEAR, NUMBER OF CIGARETTES
1911	+14	1925	+69
1912	+31	1926	+72
1913	+25	1927	+55
1914	+5	1928	+62
1915	+12	1929	+96
1916	+70	1930	−8
1917	+90	1931	−58
1918	+25	1932	−85
1919	+60	1933	+60
1920	−8	1934	+103
1921	+51	1935	+64
1922	+17	1936	+137
1923	+90	1937	+66
1924	+49		

Source: Based on Table 26.

The data regarding advertising expenditures which have been presented are complete enough to indicate the important part advertising has played in the marketing of tobacco products throughout most of the period. For all types a considerable percentage of sales income has been devoted to advertising. Because consumption has been large, the total sums available for advertising have therefore been large. The result has been a heavy barrage of selling persuasion during the entire period. That such advertising must have had some influence in increasing per capita consumption from less than three pounds in 1870 to the seven pounds attained by 1916 appears a reasonable conclusion; but judgment is withheld until the numerous factors influencing the demand for individual tobacco products have been examined.

EFFECT OF ADVERTISING UPON CIGARETTE DEMAND

The Primary Demand

Perusal of Tables 24 and 26 shows a remarkable expansion in cigarette consumption, an expansion still in progress. Following the beginnings of cigarette manufacture in the Civil War period, consumption was very small until the 1880's. At that time a spurt traceable to several factors occurred. The Bonsack cigarette-making machine, introduced about 1875 and perfected in 1883 by Duke,[13] reduced costs. A reduction in the internal revenue tax on cigarettes from $1.75 to 50 cents a thousand also came in 1883. Thereupon Duke cut the price of cigarettes from 10 cents to 5 cents a package, and launched heavy advertising to secure a demand for the output of his machine-equipped factory. The market expanded rapidly. Advertising in this case appeared to be an important factor for this manufacturer in making low production costs possible through the stimulation of his sales volume.

Remarkable Growth in Demand

Although the percentage increase was rapid throughout the following period, excepting a slight setback between the years 1896 and 1901, per capita consumption had not yet reached 100 cigarettes a year by 1910. This amount is less than one-tenth of the consumption figure for years subsequent to 1935. When it is recognized that the 1935 figure was attained with cigarette usage among only 50% of the adult male population and less than 20% of the female, it becomes apparent that consumption in 1910 was limited to a relatively small percentage of men and to a very small fraction of women. The annual percentage of increase for more recent years has not only been large, excepting in depression years, but the aggregate expansion, as shown in annual per capita consumption, has been many times greater than for the earlier period. As shown in Table 26, in five instances the annual per capita consumption increased by an amount approximating or even exceeding the total per capita consumption of 1910, which was 94 cigarettes; and that figure represented the growth of over 40 years. The annual increases of considerable size date from the period of the first World War and continue to the present, with losses or lack of material increases limited only to years of marked business recession.

---

[13] J. W. Jenkins, *op. cit.*, ch. 5.
U. S. Bureau of Corporations, *op. cit.*, p. 149.

What is the explanation for this remarkable expansion of demand?

Consumption of the various forms of tobacco has been subject to a rise and decline in extent of usage, which gives to each the semblance of a long-time fashion curve. By definition, fashion is merely common acceptance of a style or mode of use.[14]. Knowledge of fashion causes is hazy. As defined, fashion, or common acceptance of a style, is not merely a matter of emulation of the accepted social leaders of a group, or of imitation, or of the tendency to conform to accepted social practice, although these are potent motivating forces in bringing about consumption change of the kind involved in fashion cycles. Working with emulation, imitation, and desire for approval are consumer attitudes or sentiments flowing out of social environment, which help determine prevailing forms of usage. Accordingly, changes in consumption must be studied in the light of a changing social background.[15]

Possible Reasons for the Growth of Cigarette Consumption

The following are held to be the more important reasons for growth in cigarette consumption since 1870:

(1) Breakdown of prejudices and taboos.
   (a) Social, moral prejudices.
   (b) Prejudice against women's usage.
(2) War influence.
   (a) Smoking as a nervous release.
   (b) Widened social contacts.
(3) Changing living habits.
   (a) The quickened tempo of modern life conducive to use of a short smoke.
(4) Low cost of cigarettes.
(5) Increased income of the population.
(6) Advertising and aggressive selling.

It is impossible to set up any clear cause and effect relationship among so many variables of uncertain validity. In enlarging upon a few of them it is recognized that there is room for disagreement regarding advertising's part in demand increase.

---

[14] P. H. Nystrom, *Economics of Fashion* (New York, The Ronald Press Company, 1928), ch. 1.

[15] A detailed and scholarly effort to trace the causes of tobacco fashion will be found in the study by Dr. J. J. Gottsegen, *op. cit.*, ch. IV and V.

The Role of Advertising in Helping to Break Down Prejudices against Tobacco Usage

Undoubtedly the weakening of taboos and prejudices against ciga-rettes has been one of the most important factors in the widening con-sumption among both men and women. Probably the increased per capita consumption has come more from increasing the number of users than from stimulating larger use per smoker. Once adopted, usage tends to be habitual and persistent.

Ever since its introduction, tobacco has suffered from a social prej-udice which at times has brought organized proselyting against its use and widespread laws curbing its sale or use. Among tobacco products, the cigarette, particularly, has been subject to attack. The author recalls that during his childhood there was ardent solicitation among school children to join the Anti-Cigarette League, with its pledge to abstain from using "coffin nails." He recalls also that the women in his small university town vehemently criticized the new university presi-dent for smoking cigarettes and thus setting a bad example for youth. Not infrequently businessmen refused to hire cigarette smokers. The best evidence of the extent and intensity of prejudice is the fact that 14 states passed statutes between 1896 and 1921 prohibiting the sale of cigarettes. The last of these laws was not repealed until 1927. All states except Texas have laws prohibiting the sale of tobacco to minors.[16]

Such prejudices against tobacco usage have their basis in beliefs and sentiments coming from medicine, religion, and morality. The disap-pearance of these prejudices rests in part in changes occurring in medicine, religion, and moral attitude. The campaigns of testimonials featuring well-known personages and the picturing of the "right" kind of people smoking have undoubtedly had an influence in breaking down such prejudices. But the full explanation undoubtedly lies much deeper in a variety of forces operating in the social group.

Effect of the First World War on Primary Demand

The large annual increases in per capita consumption of cigarettes date from the period of the first World War. War generally has tended to break down social restrictions upon personal behavior. In addition, war has served to bring young men of the nation together

---

[16] J. J. Gottsegen, *op. cit.*, p. 152.

under conditions favoring the use of tobacco. Various writers have commented upon the spread of the tobacco habit during the Civil War. Certainly it grew among the young men of this nation during the first World War, particularly the use of cigarettes. The cigarette was easy to use and easily carried; it fitted into army routine because it was a short smoke. The public was encouraged to send tobacco, largely cigarettes, to the soldiers. The distribution of cigarettes by the Army and Navy helped popularize the habit. The low price of cigarettes made them favored among the men in the service. A few years tended to bring widespread acceptance of this form of smoking among the young men of the nation. Cigar and pipe smoking, which had been the dominant forms of smoking in poundage of consumption, lost ground consistently thereafter as cigarettes forged ahead.

The Effect of Changing Living Habits on Primary Demand

Nervous tension, which may have had a part in the increased usage in time of war, is but a characteristic of the increased tempo of modern life. Present conditions of living tend to favor the short smoke rather than the leisurely smoke of former times. The rules of factory and office, the use of trolleys and busses, all favor the short smoke. Cigarette usage is more prevalent in large cities than in small towns and rural areas.[17] Thus, changing habits of living may have played a part in the developing fashion of cigarette usage.

Advertising's Part in Expanding the Market among Women

Advertising has been credited with expanding the demand for cigarettes in recent years through its stimulation of the practice of smoking among women. This appears to be a reasonable conclusion, but again it must be recognized that advertising's part has probably been one of merely accelerating a usage which had considerable acceptance before cigarettes were advertised to women.

Cigarette manufacturers apparently hesitated for some time before making direct appeals to women or before picturing women smokers in their advertisements; probably they feared social disapprobation.[18]

---

[17] See page 226.
[18] Mr. George Washington Hill in court testimony in 1938 referred to the fear of the tobacco companies of advertising directly to women: "We never dared to talk about women smoking cigarettes, until what is known in the trade as the Lucky Strike campaign. We had a series of testimonials of opera singers, and among others was Madame Schumann-Heink. She was the first woman that ever publicly came out and testified that she smoked cigarettes, and she had rather an unpleasant experience. She was in the West

In the early 1920's they suggested that women might be interested in smoking, but desisted from direct appeals or illustration of women smoking.[19] The taboo against smoking by women had been one of long standing. Although there had been considerable smoking by women in Colonial times, it became socially unacceptable by the nineteenth century; the remains of this taboo extend up to the present time in the form of well-established prejudices.[20] Statistical support of this observation is furnished by a survey made among 250 women by the Market Research Corporation in 1937. Eighty-one per cent of the women interviewed, including smokers and nonsmokers, looked with disfavor upon women's smoking in the street; 94% of nonsmokers condemned the practice. Among 250 men interviewed, 72% looked with disfavor upon women's smoking in the street.[21] It is interesting to learn from this study that the drinking of alcoholic beverages by women was not only more common than smoking, but their drinking at bars was disapproved by a smaller percentage of both men and women than disapproved of their smoking upon the street.

The first advertising campaign directed to women and featuring women as smokers was launched by the American Tobacco Company for its Lucky Strike cigarettes in 1927. It was quickly followed by campaigns of other manufacturers. By this time, however, smoking among women had reached considerable proportions. The more daring spirits undoubtedly had taken up smoking in spite of prejudices, in order to gain the same satisfactions which men had enjoyed therefrom. In an article in *Printers' Ink*, January 31, 1925, by Curtis A. Wessel, Managing Editor of the *United States Tobacco Journal,* is recorded the guess of an experienced cigarette executive that female consumption at that time was probably 3,000,000,000 cigarettes a year, out of a total consumption of approximately 60,000,000,000 cigarettes. Moody's *Investors' Service* in 1929 made a not too certain estimate of the volume of cigarettes consumed by women, of 14,000,000,000

---

and she had some dates with some girls' colleges to sing out there, and as soon as she published this she began to get cancellations on some of those dates, and she quit. But that was the start of the breaking down of the prejudice, and from that time on, of course, all cigarette manufacturers have developed all the romance they could use, using women's testimonials and women in romantic situations." H. L. Stephen, "How Hill Advertises Is at Last Revealed," *Printers' Ink*, November 17, 1938, p. 93.

[19] "Women and Cigarettes," *Printers' Ink*, February 18, 1932.

One such advertisement pictured an attractive girl saying to her escort, "Blow some my way."

[20] J. J. Gottsegen, *op. cit.*

[21] *Sales Management*, September 1, 1937, p. 30; September 15, 1937, p. 36.

cigarettes, or 12% of consumption for that year.[22] The Moody study indicated that use of cigarettes by women had been growing for several years and associated it with the greater freedom of behavior following the first World War. It stated: "Among the visible results of these tendencies [for greater freedom] were the gradual concessions made by public opinion with regard to smoking by women, particularly in public places. While in Europe this change in public opinion had taken place much earlier, it seemed that it was not before 1923 and 1924 that widespread smoking among women in this country began."

There is no basis for measuring the amount of increase in consumption among women since the advent of advertising addressed to them in comparison with the years before. Personal observation leads to the belief that it has been rapid. The *Fortune* report on the American Tobacco Company avers that public cigarette smoking among women was greatly increased after the Lucky Strike campaign.[23]

The best evidence available of women's usage is contained in a survey made by *Fortune* in the spring of 1935. Among what was probably an adequate sample, *Fortune* found that 26.2% of women under 40, and 9.3% of women over 40, were smokers, or about 18% of the total group. Considerable variation was found in the extent of smoking in cities and in small towns and rural areas. In cities over 100,000, from 30% to 40% of the women were smokers; in small cities of 25,000 to 100,000, only 21% were smokers; while in small towns and rural areas only about 9% of the women were smokers.[24] A survey of the Market Research Corporation [25] among 250 urban women in the spring of 1937 reported 26% as regular smokers and an additional 23% as occasional smokers.

That the extent of cigarette smoking among women is still below that of men is indicated by the fact that the *Fortune* survey showed 66% of men under 40 years old as cigarette smokers, and 44% of those over 40, or 53% of the total sample. A study made by the Psychological Corporation in 1935 indicated that approximately 63% of men were cigarette smokers and an additional 17% were cigar or pipe smokers.[26] From the above data it is concluded that the large

[22] *Printers' Ink*, February 18, 1932.
[23] "Lucky Strike—The American Tobacco Company," *Fortune*, December, 1936.
[24] "The Fortune Survey," *Fortune*, July, 1935, p. 111.
[25] *Sales Management*, September 15, 1937, p. 36.
[26] H. C. Link, "Significance of Change in Cigarette Preference," *Advertising & Selling*, June 6, 1935, p. 44.

increases in annual per capita consumption since the first World War and particularly those which have occurred since 1927 have undoubtedly been brought about in considerable degree by a growing use by women. Advertising undoubtedly has played a part in speeding up social acceptance of women's smoking and thus in hastening a trend which had already been under way for some years preceding any appeals directly to women.

The Effect of Emulation and Imitation on Primary Demand

Smoking is a social habit. The form of smoking adopted by an individual is undoubtedly influenced largely by emulation. The prevailing usage, as indicated above, may be influenced by attitudes governed by many social forces. But as accepted social leaders adopt a usage, emulation provides a basis for its spread.

Cigarette advertising has made much use of this motive of emulation. Well-known personages have been pictured using cigarettes; their testimonials have been presented. Advertising illustrations have pictured people worthy of emulation. Thus has advertising provided a force tending to speed up a usage that undoubtedly would have reached considerable magnitude without advertising.

The Effect of Advertising on Primary Demand

The above analysis leads to the conclusion that advertising has been an important factor in speeding up a favorable trend of demand for cigarettes, a trend which has its roots in the changing habits of life and social attitudes arising from the whole complex of forces that is called social environment. It is evident that the remarkable increase in consumption should not be attributed solely to the force of advertising. In fact, the large sums devoted to cigarette advertising in recent years may possibly be deemed as much an effect as a cause of increased consumption. Tobacco manufacturers have centered their expenditures on this product, because business management knows that advertising and aggressive selling are more profitable for a product enjoying a favorable trend than for one operating with an adverse trend. In 1936, *Fortune,* in its report on the advertising and selling activities of The American Tobacco Company, pointed out that the company concentrated its advertising largely on Lucky Strike cigarettes, although it produced approximately 500 items in lines covering all tobacco products except snuff. Lucky Strikes were said to account for 75%

of company sales and 65% of net profits. Certain items were reported to give greater margins than cigarettes, but in view of the fact that they were being sold to a shrinking market, they were not heavily advertised, because, says the report: "President Hill never bucks a trend." [27] Under such promotional practice, the increase in cigarette consumption, determined in large part by sociological forces, has provided ever larger aggregate sums to be devoted to advertising by manufacturers desiring a share of an increasing market. In turn, however, this advertising has been a force to speed up the favorable trend. Without advertising, cigarette use would probably have grown; with advertising, the increase has been amazing.

THE EFFECT OF ADVERTISING UPON SELECTIVE DEMAND

What have been the effects of advertising upon selective demand, i.e., the distribution of demand among suppliers? Without doubt advertising has been an essential business tool to cigarette manufacturers desirous of building profitable volume. In this industry competition has been carried out largely through advertising. As will be developed in a later chapter there has not been the close price competition characteristic of fields where products are more nearly identical and brands are of small consequence in guiding consumer purchase. Instead, cigarettes have been so priced that margins have been available for advertising and promotion to stimulate brand preference. Consumers have responded to advertising efforts. Operating in a constantly expanding field of large volume, manufacturers, especially since the first World War, have had available large promotional funds. These have been devoted in greater proportion to advertising than to personal selling.

Heavy Reliance upon Advertising in Cigarette Marketing

The evidence regarding the important part of advertising in shaping selective demand is unmistakable. The extent to which managements have employed advertising and the corresponding volumes of sales are indicated in Tables 31, 32, and 33. As will be noted in Table 31, traceable expenditures for space and time in newspapers, magazines, farm publications, and chain radio have varied from approximately

---

[27] *Fortune*, December, 1936, p. 98.

TABLE 31

CIGARETTE CONSUMPTION BY BRAND AND TRACEABLE ADVERTISING EXPENDITURE IN NEWSPAPERS, MAGAZINES, FARM PUBLICATIONS, AND CHAIN RADIO, 1929–1939

YEAR	CAMEL		CHESTERFIELD		LUCKY STRIKE		TEN-CENT BRANDS		ALL OTHER		GRAND TOTAL	
	Consumption, Billions of Cigarettes	Traceable Advertising Expenditure, Thousands of Dollars	Consumption, Billions of Cigarettes	Traceable Advertising Expenditure, Thousands of Dollars	Consumption, Billions of Cigarettes	Traceable Advertising Expenditure, Thousands of Dollars	Consumption, Billions of Cigarettes	Traceable Advertising Expenditure, Thousands of Dollars	Consumption, Billions of Cigarettes	Traceable Advertising Expenditure, Thousands of Dollars	Consumption, Billions of Cigarettes	Traceable Advertising Expenditure, Thousands of Dollars
1929	40.0	$ 1,942	26.0	$ 5,254	36.4	$ 6,589	......	$	16.6	$ 7,022	119.0	$20,806
1930	38.0	4,813	25.0	5,968	42.6	10,095	......	......	14.0	5,142	119.6	26,018
1931	33.0	10,006	24.6	9,130	44.6	13,649	......	......	11.2	5,210	113.4	37,996
1932	24.6	2,389	21.0	11,138	37.0	10,850	12.0	26	9.0	4,058	103.6	28,461
1933	26.5	10,248	29.0	7,590	37.5	7,192	8.5	100	10.3	2,340	111.8	27,471
1934	32.0	10,382	33.5	9,575	33.5	8,120	13.0	143	13.6	3,441	125.6	31,661
1935	37.0	9,265	36.0	9,443	32.5	5,588	13.1	68	16.0	4,852	134.6	29,216
1936	43.0	9,042	38.0	8,909	37.0	6,846	16.0	827	19.2	6,848	153.2	32,472
1937	45.0	8,529	38.0	8,948	38.5	5,617	19.0	470	22.1	7,191	162.6	30,755
1938	41.0	8,362	37.4	9,279	38.3	4,095	24.0	483	23.0	4,866	163.7	27,085
1939	40.0	7,367	36.5	7,776	39.5	4,214	30.0	1,157	26.4	4,442	172.4	24,956
Average..	36.4	7,486	31.4	8,455	37.9	7,532	17.0	409	16.5	5,037	134.5	28,809

Sources:
(1) Volume of sales: *Standard Trade and Securities*, "Basic Survey—Tobacco," June 7, 1940, Vol. 96, No. 20, Section 3, p. T0–13.
(2) Volume of traceable advertising expenditures: For the three brands, Camel, Chesterfield, and Lucky Strike, and for the grand total for the years 1929–1937 inclusive, Media Records, "Nine-Year History of Cigarettes, 1929–1937." In view of the fact that Media Records' study grouped all brands other than Camel, Chesterfield, and Lucky Strike under a heading "All Other Brands," a special compilation was necessary to separate the 10-cent brands from the "All Other Brands." Compilations were made for radio, magazines, and farm journals from annual reports of the Publishers' Information Bureau, and for newspapers from the linage figures of Media Records. Newspaper figures were then multiplied by a rate of approximately 40 cents per line, in order to convert them to a dollar basis. The basis for conversion is explained in Appendix IV. The totals of all media for the 10-cent brands and "other brands" were then altered slightly in order to make their sum correspond to the total figure for the "all other" group provided in the Media Records study, *op. cit.*
Expenditures for 1938: American Newspaper Publishers' Association, Bureau of Advertising. *Expenditures of National Advertisers in Newspapers, 1938, op. cit.*
Magazines, farm journals, and chain radio expenditures were obtained from the Publishers' Information Bureau.
Expenditures for 1939 were based upon the American Newspaper Publishers' Association study, *Expenditures of National Advertisers in Newspapers, Magazines, Farm Journals, and Chain Radio, 1939, op. cit.*

TABLE 32

TRACEABLE EXPENDITURES ON CIGARETTE ADVERTISING, 1938

	GENERAL MAGAZINES	FARM JOURNALS	RADIO	NEWSPAPERS	TOTAL
Avalon*................	$........	$.......	$ 144,898	$ 2,368	$ 147,266
Camel.................	2,258,275	219,813	500,092	5,383,573	8,361,753
Chesterfield...........	2,169,198	247,248	1,218,638	5,544,202	9,279,286
Craven "A"...........	1,550	....	....	....	1,550
Deities...............	2,975	....	....	8,480	11,455
Domino*..............	2,482	....	....	58,107	60,589
Fatima................	....	....	....	101,770	101,770
Herbert Tareyton......	....	....	....	98,318	98,318
Kool..................	321,580	....	285,829	95,230	702,639
Lucky Strike..........	163,493	191,878	2,224,757	1,514,468	4,094,596
Marlboro..............	49,239	....	....	6,858	56,097
Marvels*..............	....	....	....	208,838	208,838
Old Gold..............	688,709	....	644,905	344,885	1,678,499
Pall Mall.............	5,700	....	257,335	19,233	282,268
Philip Morris..........	221,730	....	1,068,354	55,649	1,345,733
Raleigh...............	....	....	285,829	560	286,389
Sensation*............	....	....	....	53,589	53,589
Spud..................	92,309	....	....	140,166	232,425
Twenty Grand*........	....	....	....	147	147
Viceroy...............	2,815	....	....	....	2,815
Virginia Rounds.......	13,880	....	....	55,464	69,344
Wings*................	....	....	....	10,086	10,086
All Cigarettes........	$5,993,935	$658,939	$6,730,637	$13,701,941	$27,085,452

* So-called 10-cent brands.

Sources:

Newspapers: American Newspaper Publishers' Association, Bureau of Advertising, *Expenditures of National Advertisers in Newspapers, 1938, op. cit.*, p. 7 ff.

Magazines, Farm Journals, Radio: Publishers Information Bureau.

$20,000,000 in 1929 to a high of $38,000,000 in 1931.[28] Total advertising expenditures were probably almost double the amount of these traceable expenditures. While not all cigarette brands employ sufficient space or time advertising to appear in the measuring services from which Tables 31, 32, and 33 are constructed, the sales of companies not listed are small. Advertising has been employed by all companies enjoying substantial sales volume.

Use of Advertising by the "Big Three"

The three leading brands built their domination largely through the use of advertising. The R. J. Reynolds Company, with its Camel brand, started the practice of concentrating expenditures on a single brand[29] that has held in the recent period. At the dissolution of the

[28] These estimates of traceable advertising expenditure are rough approximations, not exact measurements of space and time expenditures. See Appendix IV.

[29] Mr. George Washington Hill testified in 1938 regarding the policy of concentra-

TABLE 33
TRACEABLE EXPENDITURES ON CIGARETTE ADVERTISING, 1939

	GENERAL MAGAZINES	FARM JOURNALS	RADIO	NEWSPAPERS	TOTAL
Avalon*................	$ 11,612	$	$ 520,940	$ 63,982	$ 596,534
Camel.................	1,661,520	160,475	1,132,116	4,462,964	7,417,075
Chesterfield............	1,402,196	206,201	1,601,549	4,902,363	8,112,309
Deities.................	....	....	....	4,840	4,840
Domino*...............	2,191	....	....	81,158	83,349
Dunhill................	....	....	37,180	32,202	69,382
Fatima.................	....	....	....	21,964	21,964
Herbert Tareyton........	....	....	....	17,035	17,035
Kool...................	202,110	....	185,559	128,503	516,172
Lucky Strike............	1,506,154	209,593	1,837,833	660,408	4,213,988
Marlboro...............	7,480	....	....	12,203	19,683
Marvels*...............	....	....	30,495	145,827	176,322
Old Gold...............	257,454	....	482,451	412,153	1,152,058
Pall Mall...............	1,950	....	257,593	100,271	359,814
Philip Morris............	242,406	....	1,159,846	103,524	1,505,776
Raleigh................	2,406	....	461,454	23,414	487,364
Sensation*..............	....	....	177,982	3,788	181,770
Spud...................	160,060	....	....	50,081	210,141
Twenty Grand*..........	....	....	48,470	55	48,525
Virginia Rounds.........	20,194	....	....	57,144	77,338
Wings*................	....	....	64,050	6,471	70,521
Total..............	$5,477,733	$576,269	$7,977,608	$11,290,350	$25,341,960

* So-called 10-cent brands.

Source: American Newspaper Publishers Association, Bureau of Advertising, *Expenditures of National Advertisers in Newspapers, Magazines, Farm Journals, and Chain Radio in 1939*, p. 18 ff.

tion followed by his company. He said: "The success of The American Tobacco Company has been largely due to a policy of concentration. You see, Mr. Duke had developed the tobacco business to a point where he had approximately 92 per cent of the cigarette business, 80-odd per cent of the smoking tobacco business, and 80-odd per cent of the plug business. Mr. Duke had accomplished that result through great merchandising ability and through the purchase of other companies. . . Mr. Duke's problem was a little different from the problem that confronts us in merchandising today. With such a large proportion of the total volume of consumption in the United States Mr. Duke had to be sure that the salesmen that he had that went around were courteous to the dealers and did not impose with the great authority that they had by reason of the huge control of the business that he had.

"The result was that Mr. Duke's policy, particularly in latter years, and my father's policy in latter years was decentralization rather than concentration. . . .

. . . For a while we continued by force of habit in Mr. Duke's policy of operating our company on the basis of departments, but we soon found that we had plenty of competition from the outside without creating more from the inside internally. So we changed our policy, and before my father's death I had convinced my father that that was a proper change and a practical change from a merchandising view to make, and on my father's passing the first thing that I did in the development of the companies was to insist on this policy of concentration which has gone through the operation of The American Tobacco Company's business since that time and has been often a subject of comment and criticism among other merchants.

. . . With the growth in cigarettes it became clear to me that the policy of concentration on cigarettes was the right policy for my company, and we did concentrate on cigarettes and we concentrated on the exploitation of the one type of cigarette, the Lucky Strike." H. L. Stephen, *op. cit.*, pp. 13, 14.

Tobacco Combination, the R. J. Reynolds Company was allotted no cigarette business. Among other brands launched by this company to get a share of the cigarette market, Camel, a blend based on bright leaf tobacco, immediately caught popular fancy.[30] On this brand the company centered all its promotional and advertising effort.[31] From having only .2% of total cigarette sales in 1913,[32] Reynolds had captured 40% of the total by 1917, and 45% by 1925.[31] The success attending the Reynolds Company's blend and its promotional policy led the Liggett & Myers Tobacco Company to change its Chesterfield brand, which had been launched in 1912, from a straight domestic [33] to a domestic blend, and the American Tobacco Company to launch its Lucky Strike brand in 1917.[34] Since that date all three companies have used heavy advertising for their leading brands, as indicated by the average of annual traceable time and space costs for the 11-year period, 1929–1939, which were approximately $7,500,000 for Camel and Lucky Strike, and nearly $8,500,000 for Chesterfield (Table 31). The total advertising expenditures were probably almost double these figures.

Advertising Usage by Lorillard and Philip Morris

Other brands for which a foothold in the domestic blended field has been sought have made headway only with the use of advertising. The P. Lorillard Company in 1926 decided to enter this field with its Old Gold brand. While its various cigarette brands had accounted in 1913 for 24% of total business,[35] it had lost ground with the shift of demand to domestic blends. Recognizing the need for adequate funds to finance not only manufacturing facilities and the large leaf inventories required for the new brand, but also the heavy advertising required to obtain a place in the market, it floated a debenture bond issue of $15,000,000 in 1927.[36] In spite of large advertising expenditures, as indicated in Tables 32 and 33, Old Gold has not had appreciable success in getting near the leading three.

---

[30] For a description of this blend, see pp. 239-240.
[31] For a case history of Camel cigarettes, see "Camels of Winston-Salem," *op. cit.* Considerable reference to Camel is also found in "Lucky Strikes—American Tobacco Company," *op. cit.*
[32] U. S. Bureau of Corporations, *op. cit.*, p. 12.
[33] A straight domestic blend contains only domestic tobaccos; a domestic blend contains mostly domestic tobaccos, but has some Turkish added.
[34] "Lucky Strike—The American Tobacco Company," *op. cit.*
[35] U. S. Bureau of Corporations, *op. cit.*, p. 12.
[36] Brokers' circular, Guaranty Trust Company of New York, June, 1927.

Philip Morris, now firmly entrenched in fourth place in the competitive race, launched its new blend of 15-cent cigarettes in January, 1933. Unlike the Lorillard Company, it did not fortify itself with fresh capital to break into the market, but relied upon earnings to finance the new venture. Since the start it has made advertising one of the chief elements in its successful program of building demand for its brand.[37] The new blend was introduced first on an experimental basis in large metropolitan cities. The success there led the president to write his stockholders to this effect:

> We think that the public likes the quality of this product and we have therefore entered into an advertising program on this account that is more pretentious than anything ever undertaken by us heretofore. We feel that we are justified in spending, if necessary, considerable money in the promotion of Philip Morris English Blends, and that if it continues to respond in the same measure that it has during the past three months, we will greatly benefit thereby . . . If this program is carried out, it will unquestionably mean a temporary reduction in the net earnings of the company, and I want this fact to be made perfectly plain to you. We feel that now is the time when our advertising dollar can be spent most advantageously as, on account of cheapening of price in competitors' brands, both cigarette dealers and smokers are prone to give us more support than would ordinarily be the case.

With increased advertising financed out of earnings, traceable expenditures of Philip Morris by 1939 exceeded $1,500,000.

Philip Morris was launched on the market at a firm 15-cent retail price when leading brands were selling at 12½ cents a package. Shortly thereafter, leading brands reduced wholesale cigarette prices and sold at 10 cents and 11 cents in chain stores,[38] but Philip Morris retail prices were generally held at 15 cents. Philip Morris has encouraged the trade to maintain its suggested price. At this 15-cent price, advertising clearly appears to have been an essential to Philip Morris to break into the market. Its advertising is believed by its executives and by many advertising men to have been an important factor in its success in gaining volume. It should be stated, however, that the brand was greatly benefitted by being able to trade down [39]

---

[37] Case of Philip Morris Company, files of the Harvard Business School.
[38] *The Tobacco Leaf*, January 7, 1933, February 18, 1933, January 13, 1934.
[39] The term "trading down" refers to the practice of attaching a trade-mark, which has become associated in consumers' minds with a certain quality or grade, to a lower grade, sold at a lower price. As a rule the lower grade profits as a result of the reputation enjoyed by the higher grade.

on the prestige attached to the name Philip Morris, which had been used as a brand for Turkish blend cigarettes long sold for 35 cents a package. Moreover, the company's ability to induce retailers and wholesalers to maintain its suggested prices brought trade margins greater than were enjoyed on leading brands and thus gained valuable trade support that undoubtedly had much to do with its success. In addition, as later pointed out, it had struck an acceptable blend and may have benefitted from a new hygroscopic (moisture retaining) agent which it employed.[40]

Entry of the 10-cent Cigarettes

In contrast to Philip Morris, the 10-cent brands were launched without substantial advertising support. Before 1931 there were a few such brands, but they had insignificant sales volume, limited distribution, and were not real factors in cigarette competition. At that time there were only two brands of consequence, Coupon, sold by Liggett & Myers, and Paul Jones, which had been introduced by the Continental Tobacco Company in 1928.[41]

Following an increase in price in the leading brands in June, 1931, from $6.40 to $6.85 a thousand, the sales of 10-cent cigarettes jumped. Other companies entered the field: in September, Larus & Brothers, Inc.; in March, 1932, Brown & Williamson Tobacco Company reduced the price on its Wings [42] to put it in the 10-cent class; in May, 1932, Sunshines, manufactured by the Pinkerton Tobacco Company, were put in the 10-cent class; in June, 1932, Axton-Fisher entered its new brand, Twenty Grand; during the same month, Scott & Dill came into the scramble; and in September, Stephano Brothers brought out Marvels. The rise in sales of the 10-cent brands during the depression was phenomenal. Starting almost from nothing in 1931 they accounted for over 20% of the domestic cigarette market for a few months during the fall of 1932, as shown in Table 34.

A substantial retail price differential made possible in large part by use of cheaper tobaccos, offered at a time when consumer buying

---

[40] Case of Philip Morris Company, files of the Harvard Business School.

[41] U. S. Federal Trade Commission, *Report of the Federal Trade Commission on Agricultural Income Inquiry*, Part I, "Principal Farm Products" (Washington, U. S. Government Printing Office, 1938), p. 460.

[42] Wings, one of the leading 10-cent brands, was launched experimentally with advertising in June, 1930, at a retail price of 15 cents. Its price was dropped in 1932 to 10 cents, and therewith "circus" advertising and fancy packaging previously employed were dropped. *Printers' Ink*, April 6, 1933, p. 74.

power was greatly curtailed explains the amazing increase in demand for these cigarettes with little advertising support. The leading tobacco companies had followed the mistaken policy of raising the wholesale prices of cigarettes subsequent to the advent of the depression from $6 a thousand, first to $6.40 (October, 1929), and then to $6.85 (June, 1931). These prices resulted in a retail price for these brands of 14 cents to 15 cents. The 10-cent brands offered the consumer a 4-cent to 5-cent saving per package. Not until January 3, 1933, after the 10-cent cigarettes and the roll-your-own practice, abetted by the depression, had made substantial inroads upon their sales, was the wholesale price of the leading brands reduced, first to $6 a thousand,

TABLE 34

PERCENTAGE OF TOTAL CIGARETTE SALES SECURED BY THE 10-CENT BRANDS BY MONTHS FROM JANUARY, 1931, TO FEBRUARY, 1936, INCLUSIVE

MONTH	1931	1932	1933	1934	1935	1936
January	0.26%	2.33%	16.76%	10.00%	10.85%	10.59%
February	.27	3.30	11.60	9.96	11.71	10.51
March	.28	3.26	7.07	10.43	11.25	.....
April	.27	6.13	8.55	11.11	11.70	.....
May	.23	6.59	6.43	10.37	11.72	.....
June	.28	9.12	7.03	10.01	11.36	.....
July	.57	12.46	9.58	12.09	11.87	.....
August	1.82	17.76	8.67	12.38	13.72	.....
September	2.00	19.57	9.78	11.62	13.53	.....
October	2.41	19.00	9.54	12.46	11.01	.....
November	2.39	22.78	11.21	13.13	12.15	.....
December	2.88	21.31	9.26	12.28	12.54	.....

Source: U. S. Federal Trade Commission, *op. cit.,* p. 462.

then, in February, 1933, to $5.50.[43] Retail prices of the leading brands, which had been 14 cents and 15 cents, fell to 12½ cents, and then to 10 and 11 cents.[44] The heavy inroads of the 10-cent cigarettes on the leading brands were checked. The sales of 10-cent cigarettes fell from 21.3% of total cigarette sales in December, 1932, to 6.4% of the total in May, 1933. Smokers returned to the standard brands after the price differential had been removed or reduced to a matter of 1 cent or 2 cents.

---

[43] "Tobacco and Tobacco Products, Basic Survey," *Standard Trade and Securities,* Vol. 88, No. 22, June 15, 1938, p. To-83.

[44] *The Tobacco Leaf,* January 7, 1933; February 18, 1933; January 13, 1934; also see Table 29. We have also drawn upon case material from producers of 10-cent cigarettes for the above discussion. The retail prices given above do not apply to states wherein state cigarette taxes were levied. In such states the spread in cents between the lower- and higher-price cigarettes is the same as in states not levying a tax.

In January, 1934, the price of leading brands was increased to $6.10 a thousand, and in January, 1936, to $6.25, bringing retail prices to 12½ cents or 13½ cents a package. Again the 10-cent brands offered the consumer a price differential of some magnitude, but far less than in 1932. There was no sudden jump in the percentage of the market held by 10-cent brands, but in the months that followed they held fairly constantly from 10% to 12% of the market (Table 34); later this percentage increased until in 1939 it was over 17%.

In recent years, particularly since 1936, most managements pro-

TABLE

ESTIMATED DOMESTIC CONSUMPTION OF LEADING CIGARETTE BRANDS IN BILLIONS

YEAR	CAMEL		CHESTERFIELD		LUCKY STRIKE		OLD GOLD	
	Cigarettes, Billions	% of Total	Cigarettes, Billions	% of Total	Cigarettes, Billions	% of Total	Cigarettes, Billions	% of Total
1929	40.0	33.6	26.0	21.8	36.4	30.6	8.0	6.7
1930	38.0	31.8	25.0	20.9	42.6	35.6	8.0	6.7
1931	33.0	29.1	24.6	21.7	44.6	39.3	7.6	6.7
1932	24.6	23.7	21.0	20.7	37.0	35.7	5.7	5.5
1933	26.5	23.7	29.0	25.9	37.5	33.1	5.5	4.9
1934	32.0	25.5	33.5	26.7	33.5	26.7	5.0	4.0
1935	37.0	27.4	36.0	26.7	32.5	24.1	5.3	3.9
1936	43.0	28.1	38.0	24.8	37.0	24.2	6.8	4.4
1937	45.0	27.7	38.0	23.4	38.5	23.7	7.9	5.0
1938	41.0	25.0	37.4	22.8	38.3	23.4	6.3	3.8
1939	40.0	23.2	36.5	21.2	39.5	22.9	5.3	3.1

ducing 10-cent cigarettes have employed advertising to help gain volume. Although the margins available for advertising and promotion at the 10-cent price have not permitted the heavy advertising available to higher-priced brands, the managements of these companies have concluded that in order to build desired volume for these brands,[45] a limited amount of advertising is needed in addition to the retail price differential which they offer the consumer.

The relation of sales growth of 10-cent cigarettes to the promotional effort expended upon them is interesting. Traceable advertising expenditures in newspapers, magazines, farm publications, and chain radio, for the various cigarette brands are shown in Tables 32 and 33. The 10-cent brands are marked with an asterisk. Since several of the 10-cent brands have used spot radio advertising extensively, the table may not indicate fully the amount of the space and time advertising of the 10-cent brands. The expenditure per unit of sale, however, is undoubtedly much less than that used for the leading brands. The

[45] Based on case material gathered in 1938, files of Harvard Business School.

average expenditure for traceable time and space per billion of cigarettes is shown in Table 35 to have been only about one-fifth or even less of that employed for the leading brands. Discussions with executives of cigarette companies likewise indicated that the advertising expenditure of 10-cent brands is probably one-fifth as much per unit as for leading brands. With the support of advertising and the price differential enjoyed it is interesting to note from Table 35 that the 10-cent cigarettes have been making steady progress, their estimated volume in 1939 comprising 17.4% of consumption, a rise from less

35
OF CIGARETTES, AND PERCENTAGE OF TOTAL CONSUMPTION BY BRANDS, 1929–1939

PHILIP MORRIS		MENTHOLATED BRANDS		COMBINED TEN-CENT BRANDS		ALL OTHER BRANDS		TOTAL BILLIONS	% OF TOTAL REPRESENTED BY THREE LEADING BRANDS
Cigarettes, Billions	% of Total	Cigarettes, Billions	% of Total	Cigarettes, Billions	% of Total	Cigarettes, Billions	% of Total		
....	....	....	....	....	....	8.6	7.2	119.0	86.0
....	....	....	....	....	....	6.0	5.0	119.6	88.3
....	....	*	....	*	....	3.6	3.2	113.4	90.1
*	....	*	....	12.0	11.6	3.3	3.2	103.6	80.1
*	....	*	....	8.5	7.6	4.8	4.3	111.8	82.7
2.8	2.2	3.3	2.6	13.0	10.4	2.5	2.0	125.6	78.9
3.8	2.8	4.1	3.0	13.1	9.7	2.8	2.1	134.6	78.2
5.0	3.3	3.7	2.4	16.0	10.4	3.7	2.4	153.2	77.1
7.5	4.9	2.6	1.6	19.0	11.7	4.1	2.5	162.6	74.8
9.2	5.6	1.9	1.2	24.0	14.7	5.6	3.4	163.7	71.2
11.0	6.4	2.0	1.2	30.0	17.4	8.1	4.7	172.4	67.3

* Included in "All Other Brands."
Source: *Standard Trade and Securities*, "Basic Survey—Tobacco," June 7, 1940, Vol. 96, No. 20, Section 3, p. To–13.

than 6% in 1933. Further comment upon the effect of advertising as an offset to price on cigarettes will be made later. It must be remembered in connection with the above discussion, however, that the 10-cent cigarettes are not identical with the other cigarettes. They are made of lower-price and lower-quality leaf. Thus a quality variation is mingled with price and advertising variation.[46]

---

[46] Mr. George Washington Hill, in court testimony referred to in previous footnotes, testified as follows regarding the decision of his company not to go into the manufacture of 10-cent cigarettes: "It [the 10-cent cigarette] had been suggested as far back as 1930 and there had been constant urgings that The American Tobacco Company put out a 10-cent cigarette. The 10-cent cigarette is not practical—not today practical. You can't sell a 10-cent cigarette and pay the farmer the proper price for his tobacco—a living wage. When you buy tobacco and put it into a 10-cent cigarette you make such an inferior product that the consumer does not like it and the history of the 10-cent cigarette shows that to be so every time a new brand of 10-cent cigarette comes out and everybody runs to the new brand and tries it regardless of what the brand is, showing that they like the price of 10 cents but they don't like the quality of 10-cent cigarettes or any of them that have been put out. They are not what the trade wants, not standard brands. Based on that policy of ours of concentration I was resisting the suggestion on anybody's part that my company put out a 10-cent cigarette." H. L. Stephen, *op. cit.*, p. 90.

Psychological Evidence Regarding Effect of Advertising on Valuation

Evidence that consumer valuations or preferences for cigarette brands are subjective values built by advertising is deduced from the fact that cigarette users in blindfold tests are not able to distinguish their customary brand by taste and smell from competing brands with similar blends. Moreover, over 90% of total cigarette volume is of blended tobaccos. Guided by these considerations, some investigators have reached the conclusion that consumer cigarette values are primarily determined by advertising.[47]

Husband and Godfrey[48] carried on an experiment among 51 subjects, all of whom smoked regularly and generally stuck to one brand. Each subject was tested with four cigarettes, three leading brands and one other. Each was told that his own brand would be among the four, which were presented in random order. Adequate time was allowed between smokes to compensate for taste confusion and fatigue. Only 31% of the smokers guessed their own brand. Chance alone would have given a 25% identification. The identification of the

TABLE 36

IDENTIFICATION OF DIFFERENT CIGARETTE BRANDS IN BLINDFOLD TEST—51 SUBJECTS

BRAND	PER CENT OF SUBJECTS IDENTIFYING BRAND IN COLUMN 1 AS:					
	Camel	Lucky Strike	Chester-field	Twenty Grand	Spud	Miscel-laneous
Camel..................	31%	14%	38%	6%	2%	10%
Lucky Strike............	19	41	21	4	0	14
Chesterfield............	27	23	33	2	0	15
Twenty Grand..........	38	26	3	17	0	15
Spud..................	0	6	6	0	76	11

Source: R. W. Husband and Jane Godfrey, "An Experimental Study of Cigarette Identification," *Journal of Applied Psychology,* Vol. XVIII, No. 2, April, 1934, p. 222.

individual brands is shown in Table 36. From the table it will be seen that, except for the mentholated cigarette, Spuds, no brand had a high degree of identification. The high percentage of identification of Lucky Strike is in accord with trade belief that this cigarette is most easily recognized among the popular brands.[49]

Such a study as that of Husband and Godfrey substantiates the

---

[47] See J. J. Gottsegen, *op. cit.,* p. 193.
[48] R. W. Husband and Jane Godfrey, "An Experimental Study of Cigarette Identification," *Journal of Applied Psychology,* Vol. XVIII, No. 2, April, 1934, p. 222.
[49] "Camels of Winston-Salem," *op. cit.,* p. 55.

conclusion reached on the basis of advertising and sales data, that advertising is an important element in building consumer brand preference for cigarettes. One must not jump to the conclusion, however, that advertising is so important an element in determining consumer valuation that a cigarette brand can be carried to a strong market position merely through dominance in advertising expenditure. To do so would go counter to the history of the cigarette business.

The Importance of Blending and Flavor

That consumers have definite likes and dislikes of flavor or taste in cigarettes is indicated by the shifts in cigarette preference which have occurred over a long period of time. According to Young[50] the first cigarettes in this country were made by hand from Turkish leaf. About 1869 it was discovered that bright leaf tobacco gave a superior quality of cigarette and the demand shifted almost entirely to cigarettes made of this tobacco. During the '80's and '90's cigarettes were made almost exclusively from bright leaf. In the period 1895–1900, however, a decided change took place in the nature of demand for cigarettes. Those manufactured from the bright leaf of Virginia and North Carolina lost their demand to some extent, while the demand for those made from Turkish leaf increased rapidly.[51] After 1900 the old domestic brands were supplanted not only by brands of Turkish but by brands made of so-called Turkish blend, a mixture approximately 60% domestic and 40% Turkish leaf, as well as by new brands of all-domestic leaf. Between 1900 and 1910 the demand for Turkish and Turkish blend cigarettes showed rapid increase; domestic leaf brands showed decided loss in popularity. At the time of the dissolution of the tobacco trust, public preference was centered on Turkish and Turkish blend cigarettes, particularly the latter.[52]

The next shift in popular favor has been referred to previously, namely, the shift to the so-called domestic blend adopted by the Reynolds Tobacco Company for its Camel brand, which proved so decidedly popular that the other large tobacco companies shortly thereafter developed similar blends.[53] Camels quickly rose to top place,

---

[50] W. W. Young, *op. cit.*

[51] U. S. Bureau of Corporations, *op. cit.*, p. 149.

[52] Interview with executives of leading cigarette companies; also U. S. Bureau of Corporations, *op. cit.*

[53] Since the composition of blends used in the various brands is carefully guarded, varying reports have been made as to the approximate composition of blends of popular
(Footnote continued on next page.)

displacing the Fatima brand, the blended cigarette of the Liggett & Myers Tobacco Company, which was leader at the dissolution of the combination.

Further evidence of the importance of blending and flavor to commercial success of a cigarette brand was given in the opinions of executives in the tobacco business who were interviewed. It was the consensus among executives of five companies from whom case histories were obtained that the success of any cigarette is determined to a considerable extent by the success of the manufacturer not only in finding an acceptable flavor or blend but also in maintaining its standard of quality. All these companies had added new brands to their lines in recent years and they had a uniform story of the painstaking and extensive efforts made to develop an acceptable blend. For example, in the case of the Philip Morris English Blend cigarette, a large number of blends were worked out. From this group the blenders chose what they considered the 20 best blends and sent them to the company executives for final selection. The executives through a process of elimination chose the blend which was used in the Philip Morris English Blend cigarettes and which has met with popular favor.[54]

Failure to develop an acceptable blend, according to executives, may play a large part in the lack of success of a cigarette. This fact is borne out specifically in a confidential report upon one brand of cigarette which failed to meet with success, although it was launched with a large program of advertising. During the first three months the new cigarette was on the market it attained large sales, reportedly one of the most successful introductions enjoyed by any new cigarette. But shortly thereafter it became evident to company executives that it was not winning consumer favor. An investigation indicated that although advertising induced smokers to try the cigarette, a large percentage of them did not repurchase. Executives concluded that the product had failed in large part because consumers did not like the

---

cigarettes. Many different leaves are used in most of them. For example, *Standard Trade and Securities*, "Tobacco, Basic Survey," Part I, May 31, 1939, p. TO-12, gives the following approximate proportions of leaf in the average blending:

Flue-cured [bright leaf]	53%
Burley	32%
Maryland [fast-burning]	5%
Imported Tobaccos	10%

Also see "Camels of Winston-Salem," *op. cit.*, p. 55.

[54] Case of Philip Morris, Inc., files of Harvard Business School.

blend of tobacco used, even though the management had thought that it approximated the leading brands.[55]

Further evidence of the importance of blend is found in the case of Pall Mall cigarettes, introduced in 1937 and featured in advertising as containing no flavoring. The blend was similar to that of cigarettes manufactured for English consumers, who preferred straight tobacco without flavoring. After its introduction, the company reached the decision, however, that the blend of tobacco used for Pall Mall cigarettes with flavor omitted was not so acceptable to the taste of the American consumer as it had hoped. Accordingly, in August, 1939, in an effort to increase the demand for Pall Malls, the management considered further means which it might adopt to increase demand. It decided to increase the size of Pall Malls, making them 85 millimeters instead of 70 millimeters long. This increased the tobacco content approximately 20%, but still kept the product within the limits of three pounds per 1,000 cigarettes, the limit for classification for tax purposes as a small cigarette. To quote from the case obtained from The American Tobacco Company:

> On August 1, Mr. George Washington Hill decided to manufacture such a cigarette for the Pall Mall brand. Since he was making this change it seemed to him an appropriate time to change the blend. Consequently a new blend, which included flavoring, was developed. The wording on the package was rephrased, and the words "King Size" were added. By August 23 the new cigarettes were distributed to the trade.[56]

Newspaper advertising of the new cigarette appeared in October. Subsequent trade reports indicated that the brand enjoyed appreciable sales increases.

That maintenance of quality is important is borne out by a confidential case history relating to a 10-cent cigarette which compromised with quality in order to keep costs down in a period of rising leaf prices. According to the management, the executives were of the opinion that deterioration of quality reacted against the sale of the cigarette, and it was not until pains were taken to restore and maintain quality that sales volume was regained. It should be added here, however, that advertising was also used in the effort to build up sales.

In recent years various companies have experimented with the blending and flavoring of tobaccos in the hope of finding a combination

---

[55] Confidential case report, files of Harvard Business School.
[56] Case of American Tobacco Company, files of Harvard Business School.

that would be distinctive and still meet popular favor. These have been tried for new brands and in the rehabilitation of old brands. As noted above, when Pall Mall, formerly a Turkish blend cigarette, was brought to new life as a domestic blend by the American Tobacco Company in 1936, the company featured the fact that no sweetening or flavor was added to the tobacco. Spuds and Kools have been mentholated; other brands have been given distinctive flavors or aromas. The mentholated cigarettes have found a substantial group of followers although they have failed to hold the volume attained in 1935–1936 (Table 35). By and large, manufacturers desirous of securing volume demand have deemed it essential to approximate the taste found in the leading brands, whose large sales indicate popular preference in a wide range of choice. Yet they exercise great care in trying to find an acceptable flavor in a domestic blend, indicating thereby a belief which goes contrary to any conclusion that quality or taste is of little consequence and that advertising is the chief determinant of preference.

In recent years some experimenting in product formulae has related to the hygroscopic agent employed. The older brands have used glycerin. Philip Morris has employed a new hygroscopic agent which it claims is less irritating to the membranes. This new agent has also been adopted by other recently launched brands.[57] Since these new products have met with apparent success in their marketing, it is concluded, though not with certainty, that the change in formula may be an element which meets with popular favor.[58]

Relation of Advertising Expenditure to Volume of Demand

The charge has been made by some critics that mere weight of expenditure by the so-called Big Three has given them virtual control of the market, and that other manufacturers have been forestalled

---

[57] *Fortune,* December, 1936, and confidential case reports.

[58] *Tide,* December 15, 1940, p. 14, reported the launching of a new cigarette, Pinehurst, which eliminated glycerine as the hygroscopic agent and substituted therefor an extract of the root of ginseng, *panax quinquefolium.* The patent application for the new process stated:

> "On contact with the saliva when smoking, . . . [the ginseng extract forms] a mucilage strongly demulcent which acts to coat the mucous membranes and results in a mild sweet smoke without irritation and with a pleasant aroma and taste."

Whether the new cigarette would be successful was a topic of interest among those in the industry. Said *Tide,* "Others in the industry aren't especially optimistic about Pinehurst's chances. The reason, of course, is the high mortality rate of new brands and small companies. To these observations, Pinehurst's backers reply with the success of Philip Morris."

from getting a substantial volume of business because they could not match these expenditures. This view implies that the securing of sales volume in the cigarette business is merely a matter of size of advertising expenditure. An analysis of industry data for recent years and of case material does not substantiate this viewpoint.

In the decade 1930–1939, expenditures of each of the three leaders generally have either approximated or greatly exceeded the expenditures of all other brands combined; yet the three leaders have not held their relative positions in the industry. Moreover, a study of advertising expenditure data as related to the sales of brands indicates that the gaining of sales is not a mere function of the number of dollars spent.

As will be noted in Table 35, the Big Three in 1930–1931 accounted for 90% of total consumption. By 1939 their share had fallen away to 67.3%. While they have lost in relative position, two other types of cigarettes have forged ahead: (1) the 10-cent brands and (2) the other advertised brands, for the most part domestic blend brands. The gain of the 10-cent brands from less than 8% of the market in 1933 to over 17% in 1939 has already been commented upon. The other advertised brands have progressed from a low point of 8.6% of total consumption in 1932 to 15.3% in 1939 (Table 35).

Table 37, presented graphically as Chart II, contains interesting

TABLE 37

BILLIONS OF CIGARETTES SOLD AND TRACEABLE ADVERTISING EXPENDITURE IN NEWS-PAPERS, MAGAZINES, FARM JOURNALS, AND CHAIN RADIO, OF CIGARETTE BRANDS, IN THOUSANDS OF DOLLARS, FOR EACH BILLION OF CIGARETTES SOLD, 1929–1939

YEAR	CAMEL		CHESTERFIELD		LUCKY STRIKE		TEN-CENT BRANDS		ALL OTHERS	
	Advertising, Thousands of Dollars per Billion Cigarettes	Billions of Cigarettes Sold	Advertising, Thousands of Dollars per Billion Cigarettes	Billions of Cigarettes Sold	Advertising, Thousands of Dollars per Billion Cigarettes	Billions of Cigarettes Sold	Advertising, Thousands of Dollars per Billion Cigarettes	Billions of Cigarettes Sold	Advertising, Thousands of Dollars per Billion Cigarettes	Billions of Cigarettes Sold
1929......	48.5	40.0	202.1	26.0	180.2	36.4	....	....	413.0	16.6
1930......	126.7	38.0	238.7	25.0	237.0	42.6	....	....	367.3	14.0
1931......	303.2	33.0	371.1	24.6	306.0	44.6	....	....	473.7	11.2
1932......	97.1	24.6	530.4	21.0	293.3	37.0	2.4	12.0	450.9	9.0
1933......	386.7	26.5	261.7	29.0	191.8	37.5	11.8	8.5	227.2	10.3
1934......	324.4	32.0	285.8	33.5	242.4	33.5	11.0	13.0	253.0	13.6
1935......	250.4	37.0	262.3	36.0	171.9	32.5	5.2	13.1	303.3	16.0
1936......	210.3	43.0	234.4	38.0	185.0	37.0	51.6	16.0	230.3	19.2
1937......	189.5	45.0	235.5	38.0	145.9	38.5	24.7	19.0	309.8	22.1
1938......	203.9	41.0	248.1	37.4	106.9	38.3	20.1	24.0	211.6	23.0
1939......	184.2	40.0	213.1	36.5	106.7	39.5	38.6	30.0	168.3	26.4
Average..	211.4	36.4	280.3	31.4	199.0	37.9	20.7	17.0	309.8	16.5

Source: Based on Table 31.

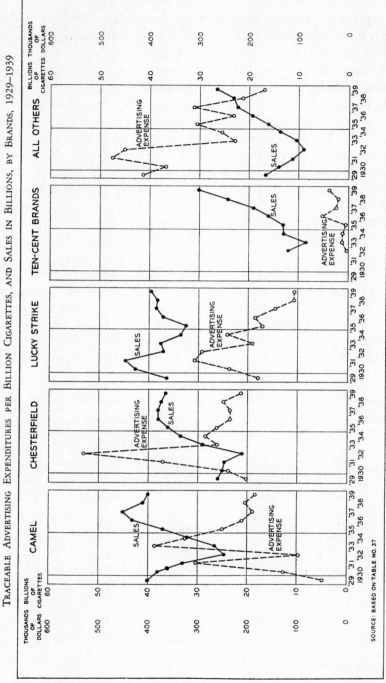

CHART II

TRACEABLE ADVERTISING EXPENDITURES PER BILLION CIGARETTES, AND SALES IN BILLIONS, BY BRANDS, 1929–1939

SOURCE: BASED ON TABLE NO. 37

data relating to the part that advertising has played in building sales volume for different brands. Over the period 1929–1939, the average annual traceable expenditures of the Big Three brands were not far apart, although there were wide variations in years. Those of Camel and Lucky Strike were approximately $7,500,000 each; that of Chesterfield $8,500,000 (Table 31). The sales return for dollar of expenditure has not been the same, however, as measured by the figures of traceable advertising cost per billion of cigarettes sold, as shown in Table 37. Over the 10-year period Chesterfield is shown as having spent an average of $280,000 for time and space for every billion cigarettes sold, whereas Camel spent only $211,000 and Lucky Strike only $199,000. It must be recognized that these figures of advertising expenditure may be subject to considerable error because not all advertising media employed are included and because they are based on space measurements whose price is not exactly determinable. Yet they represent an approximation of expenditures in the major media for all three brands. Although there may be varying errors from year to year, it is believed that over the 11-year period the figures probably are significant as indicators of relative expenditures.

When trends of costs for each billion of cigarettes sold are examined, as shown in Chart II, it is seen that since 1932 Lucky Strike has consistently spent less for time and space than have its two large competitors. While it lost volume as against competitors' gains in the period 1932–1935, it bettered its position relative to its competitors in the period 1935–1939, and by 1940 was again making its bid for first place; and this gain was secured by an average traceable space and radio time expenditure over these years of $143,000 per billion cigarettes as contrasted with $238,000 for Chesterfield and $219,000 for Camel.

The remarkable gains made by the 10-cent cigarettes with relatively low advertising expenditure have been commented upon. As will be noted in Table 37, their advertising space and time expenditure per billion of cigarettes averages less than $30,000,[59] as against the $100,000 to $300,000 or more for the more heavily advertised brands. Given the price differential which they have enjoyed since 1933 and this relatively modest advertising expenditure, in a few short years they have gained for themselves a substantial percentage of the

---

[59] Based upon the years 1938–39, for which the data are more dependable than for other years.

cigarette business. Although they are made of less expensive tobaccos, they are acceptable to a large portion of the market at the price differential which they afford.

Among the less advertised brands, the average expenditure for time and space has been considerably heavier for each billion of cigarettes sold than has held for the Big Three. Of individual brands for which estimates of both volume and advertising expenditure are available, Old Gold has failed to hold its ground, but others, notably Philip Morris, have made good progress; consequently, as a whole they have made substantial gains. Old Gold has lost ground in spite of the fact that its expenditures, as related to its sales volume, have been relatively large. Based on 1938–1939 figures of sales and traceable advertising expenditures, approximately $277,000 for time and space has been spent for every billion of cigarettes sold. In contrast, Philip Morris, which has made a steady sales increase, spent on an average for these two years only $142,000 for time and space per billion cigarettes sold, much less than Camel and Chesterfield spent.

That it is not possible to make sales response a simple function of price or of price and advertising expenditure is indicated in the case of Philip Morris. As noted previously, this brand has made headway with a relatively low rate of advertising expenditure, although selling much of the time at a price around two cents higher per package than that of the leading advertised brands. In this case the trade margin made possible by the firm retail price has apparently brought valuable dealer cooperation in selling.

From what has been said above, it is concluded that the sales trends of the various brands have not been determined solely by the amount of advertising. The full explanation of the changes that have taken place in the relative standing of the different brands can be merely hypothetical. The more important influences on the shifting volume of the brands are believed to be the following:

(1) Variation in effectiveness of advertising campaigns.
(2) Variation in volume of advertising.
(3) Variation in trade support of brands.
(4) Variation in effectiveness of personal selling forces of manufacturers.
(5) Variation in price differentials between brands.
(6) Variation in consumer response to product flavor and quality of competing brands.

There is no way of measuring statistically the effect of these variables upon the demand for the different brands.

Effect of Advertising upon the Stability of Demand for Cigarettes

One of the claims made for advertising is that it may gain for a manufacturer a stability of demand which will permit economical use of production facilities and of marketing and production organization. What is the record so far as the cigarette is concerned?

It is impossible to determine whether greater stability has been attained under the system of heavily advertised brands than would hold were cigarettes sold unbranded. The question is purely hypothetical because cigarettes are not identical merchandise. Under a scheme of identical merchandise, stability of demand of a manufacturer would depend primarily on always giving as favorable a price as he could and secondarily upon giving service. Failure to meet competitive prices would mean loss of demand.

The shifting of demand between sellers for the most part has not been the result of price differentials between the brands. Instead, prices have been relatively stable for any brand. Price changes ordinarily have been met by competing brands of similar type, although Philip Morris and Pall Mall, among other domestic blends, have sold at higher prices than those of their chief competitors. Demand shifts are accounted for by consumer likes for product characteristics and by aggressive selling activities.

It is clear from a study of the shifting position of brands that the use of advertising by managements has not given assurance of stability of demand. The various managements are matching wits to capture through merchandising and promotional effort a larger share of cigarette business. Their weapons are primarily product quality and aggressive selling effort, with the 10-centers using a price differential as their chief weapon. Among the advertisers no one management has been consistently the winner in the competitive race. No one has been able through advertising to hold even a constant volume.

Yet the business of the well-established companies has been relatively stable, as contrasted with many industries. The stability, however, should be attributed not to the use of advertising but to the character of consumer demand for this product. Cigarettes, a product of habitual use, are not likely to be discarded even in times of reduced income; accordingly they have a relatively steady demand. This steadiness of consumption has been supplemented by a favorable demand trend. Accordingly companies within the business have had reason to hope for relatively stable volume.

Such evidence of consumer habits as is available indicates that cigarette smokers do not shift brands frequently; [60] yet there is some shifting and new smokers are coming continually into the market. Each manufacturer relies upon advertising to help hold its present users against competitive advertising onslaughts and to gain as large a share as possible of new users. Hence advertising is at one and the same time a weapon employed to secure stability and a weapon in the hands of others to cause instability. Accordingly any charge that advertising is a cause exclusively either of stability or of instability in the cigarette business would not appear to be well-founded.[61]

Summary of Conclusions Regarding Selective Demand

To summarize the discussion of the preceding pages, the following conclusions are listed regarding the effect of advertising upon selective demand: (1) In the marketing of cigarettes, advertising is one of the more important determinants of consumer valuation, and thus of selective demand. (2) Sales volume of any brand is not a direct reflection merely of weight of advertising expenditure; rather advertising campaigns have varied in sales effectiveness. Other variables affecting sales must also be recognized. (3) Advertising reputation to be effective must be built upon an acceptable product flavor and quality; in other words, advertising has not been the sole determinant of preference. (4) For many smokers brand preference is measurable in terms of relatively small price differences. Up to a certain price differential these consumers apparently will pay more for well-known brands, but when the price of heavily advertised brands exceeds these limits the volume tends to shift to the brands of lower price which are less

---

[60] The 1935 *Fortune* Survey gives the following response to the question, "How many years have you been smoking this brand?":

1 year	12.6%
2 years	12.9%
3 years	10.0%
4 years	5.9%
5 years	10.1%
Over 5 years	44.3%
Don't know	4.2%

"The Fortune Survey," *op. cit.*, p. 114.

[61] See J. J. Gottsegen, *op. cit.*, p. 212.

heavily advertised. (5) In the case of the 10-cent cigarettes the value of reputation to be attained through advertising has been recognized by the managements selling them; in the drive for sales a number of them have employed such advertising as they have been able to squeeze from a narrow margin in order to supplement the effects of the price differential. (6) Advertising cannot be considered as a cause exclusively of either stability or instability of selective demand.

CHAPTER IX

THE EFFECT OF ADVERTISING ON THE DEMAND FOR
CIGARS AND SMOKING TOBACCO

EFFECT OF ADVERTISING ON THE PRIMARY
DEMAND FOR CIGARS

THE more important facts regarding the demand for cigars have already been noted in the preceding discussion relating to the consumption of all tobacco products and of cigarettes. In brief, the per capita consumption of cigars increased steadily during the period 1870 to 1907, and has had a downward trend since the latter date. This decrease has occurred in spite of a substantial amount of advertising and in spite of a falling price trend. These facts lead to the conclusion that social changes and the growth of cigarette usage have in recent years combined to make cigars less fashionable than they were in a former period, a change which advertising did not forestall.

The facts regarding per capita consumption contained in Tables 25 and 26 are recalled briefly. By 1870 per capita consumption was approximately 29.5 cigars. By 1907 this figure had risen to 86.4 cigars, although the peak consumption in pounds was not reached until 1920 because there was a decreasing proportion of small cigars in the total. Since 1907 per capita consumption has dropped steadily, the low of 36.5 having been reached in the depression year of 1933. Since then there has been a recovery so that consumption in recent years has been somewhat above 40, which is still well below that reached in the late 1920's.

Decreasing Prices of Cigars

The fall in demand has occurred in the face of decreasing prices of cigars and a shift towards low-price cigars. The facts regarding cigar prices were indicated in Tables 17, 27, 28, and 29. Although the price data for the early period are inadequate, such evidence as is available in Table 17 indicates that the trend of the average return per thousand to the Tobacco Combination for the years 1901–1910 was slightly downward, from \$31.13 a thousand in 1901 to \$27.50 a thousand in 1910. For the period since 1926, Bureau of Labor Statistics price data (Table 28) indicate that wholesale cigar prices have fallen from \$52.80 a thousand to \$46.06 a thousand. This decrease, however, has not been so rapid as the fall of wholesale prices in general. These price figures, however, fail to reflect what has occurred in the cigar business, namely, the transfer of demand from the higher-price to lower-price cigars. These facts are reflected more clearly in Table 29, which shows the retail price of tobacco products in 32 cities. Whereas in 1920 the average price paid in 32 cities for the fastest selling brands of cigars was 11 cents, by 1935 the average amount paid was only 4.6 cents a cigar. That the trend since 1920 has been definitely toward the cigar selling for 5 cents or less is shown in Table 38, which gives figures of tax withdrawals by price classes. In 1920, Class A cigars, those selling for 5 cents or less, accounted for only 24% of demand. By 1935 they accounted for 88% of demand.

In short, since 1920 aggressive selling has been devoted more and

TABLE 38

CONSUMPTION OF LARGE CIGARS BY PRICE CLASSES, 1920–1937

YEAR	CLASS A	CLASS B	CLASS C	CLASSES D AND E
1920	24.0%	30.8%	42.8%	2.4%
1921	30.8	27.3	39.2	2.7
1922	39.8	22.4	35.7	2.1
1923	38.8	22.1	36.9	2.2
1924	41.4	19.7	36.5	2.4
1925	43.7	16.5	37.1	2.7
1926	45.1	13.7	37.5	2.7
1927	50.2	11.0	36.2	2.6
1928	53.2	9.6	34.7	2.5
1929	56.4	8.5	32.6	2.5
1930	62.1	6.4	29.2	2.3
1931	71.0	3.1	24.2	1.7
1932	79.6	1.1	18.0	1.3
1933	85.7	0.7	12.5	1.1
1934	86.1	1.2	11.7	1.0
1935	88.1	1.3	9.7	0.9
1936	88.0	1.0	10.1	0.9
1937	87.9	1.0	10.2	0.9

Class A—not over 5 cents each.
Class B—more than 5 cents each; not over 8 cents.
Class C—more than 8 cents each; not over 15 cents.
Class D—more than 15 cents each; not over 20 cents.
Class E—more than 20 cents each.
Source: Based on volume of tax withdrawals *Annual Reports of Commissioner of Internal Revenue*, U. S. Office of Internal Revenue, (Washington, U. S. Government Printing Office, respective years).

more to lower-price cigars. These lower prices may be attributed to a number of conditions, among the more important of which are lower costs within the industry after the advent of machine-manufacturing methods in 1917, and low tobacco leaf costs during the period. In addition to these lower costs there was intense direct competition within the cigar industry and keen indirect competition with cigarettes.

Extent of Advertisement of Cigars

The facts with regard to the amount of advertising over the period are far from complete. It would not appear, however, that advertising and aggressive selling were any less intense during the last 20 years of falling consumption than in the preceding period of rising consumption.

The only evidence available of advertising during the early period was gained from the report of the U. S. Commissioner of Corporations in his study of the Tobacco Combination which is presented in Table 17. From 1901–1904, inclusive, when the Tobacco Combination was trying to build a dominating place in the cigar business, it spent heavily for advertising without greatly improving its position in the industry. For example, in 1903 it spent approximately 50% of its net income upon cigar advertising. In 1902 it spent 37½%; in 1904, 29%. These heavy expenditures were largely responsible for losses which its cigar business showed during this period. After 1905 it reduced its advertising expenditures to an average figure of about 5% of net selling price, an amount at which it was able to show a profit, although a much smaller profit than it made in the other branches of its business. Competing cigar companies outside the combination spent from 3% to 4% of net sales for advertising.

Data regarding the aggregate volume of advertising of cigars in 1910–1913, though far from complete, show a substantial amount of advertising. The industry consisted of over 20,000 companies, only a few of which were of considerable size, and the study of the U. S. Commissioner covered but 14 of the large operators; yet in 1910 a total of over $1,500,000 of advertising for cigars was shown by this small number of leading firms.

For the period 1914–1929 there is evidence of only a part of the advertising expenditure of cigar companies, namely, that carried on in leading magazines, as given in Table 39. This table shows substantial amounts of magazine advertising subsequent to 1916, when the

TABLE 39

ADVERTISING EXPENDITURES FOR CIGARS IN LEADING MAGAZINES, 1914–1929

1914	$ 62,444
1915	35,283
1916	178,737
1917	175,862
1918	355,357
1919	357,242
1920	399,415
1921	392,929
1922	266,840
1923	211,527
1924	230,750
1925	225,517
1926	120,138
1927	141,436
1928	142,963
1929	292,792

Source: Curtis Publishing Company, Advertising Department, *Leading Advertisers* (Philadelphia, respective years).

General Cigar Company started national advertising.[1] But it represents only a small part of the whole advertising effort and it is doubtful whether it is even indicative of the trend of volume for the industry, in view of the fact that the predominant medium for advertising cigars has been newspapers. Newspaper advertising was particularly important before 1920, because a large part of the cigar business was then centered on local brands which had to utilize media reaching their restricted markets.[1]

The extent of advertising from 1929 to 1939 reflected in Table 40, which shows that the volume of traceable advertising in newspapers, magazines, farm journals, and chain radio in 1929, was well over $6,000,000. During the depression this dropped away to somewhat less than $2,500,000 and came back in 1939 to over $3,000,000. Total advertising expenditures for advertisers included in these tables for these years probably were almost twice these amounts. Such figures, however are probably well below the total for the industry, because of the large number of small operators whose advertising does not show up in the media measured. Even so, advertising expenditures for the industry as a whole have been small as compared with those for cigarettes. The traceable advertising expenditures for cigars for the 11-year period, 1929–1939, which averaged approximately $3,900,000 a year, are only about one-seventh as large as those for cigarettes.

[1] Case of General Cigar Company, Inc., files of Harvard Business School.

TABLE 40

TRACEABLE NEWSPAPER, MAGAZINE AND FARM JOURNAL SPACE EXPENDITURES AND CHAIN RADIO TIME FOR CIGARS SOLD NATIONALLY, 1929–1939

YEAR	NEWSPAPERS (Value Estimated)*	GENERAL MAGAZINES	FARM JOURNALS	RADIO	TOTAL
1929	$5,939,678	$184,161†	$ 3,674‡a	$ 481,704‡c	$6,609,217
1930	5,545,745	315,323§	10,773‡b	767,392‡	6,639,233
1931	3,602,039	187,436§	....	2,246,529‡	6,036,004
1932	2,213,290	26,800§	....	1,381,911‡	3,622,001
1933	1,757,551	25,200§	672‡	642,571‡b	2,424,994
1934	2,325,165	34,170§	643#	227,932#	2,587,910
1935	1,986,168	20,461§	....	362,965‡	2,369,594
1936	2,777,759	36,101#	1,242‡c	83,934‡d	2,899,036
1937	2,779,784	43,707#	1,846#	83,468#	2,908,805
1938	2,199,294	99,514#	....	410,776#	2,709,584
1939	2,059,992	219,621#	....	781,860#	3,061,473

a Extended from 10 months.
b Extended from 11 months.
c Extended from 9 months.
d Extended from 8 months.

Sources:

* 1929–1939 lineage taken from Media Records, Inc., *Newspapers and Newspaper Advertisers*; 1938–1939 dollar figures from American Newspaper Publishers' Association, *Expenditures of National Advertisers*. Conversion ratio calculated from data for 1938 and 1939—38 cents per line—applied to other years. See Appendix IV regarding conversion rate.
† Crowell Publishing Company, Advertising Department, *National Markets and National Advertising* (New York, 1929).
‡ National Advertising Records, Inc., *National Advertising Records, 1929–1936*.
§ Curtis Publishing Company, *Leading Advertisers, 1930–1935*.
# Publishers' Information Bureau, Inc., *National Advertising Records*.

When the demand figures for cigars are viewed in the light of such price and advertising data as are available, it is impossible to say with certainty just what the effect of advertising on primary demand has been. It is clear, however, that the aggressive selling efforts of the industry have not been able to forestall a declining trend since 1907. This adverse trend cannot be attributed to failure of the industry to continue its advertising. During the 1920's, when demand had a persistent down trend, advertising was apparently still following the pattern employed in the years before 1907 when cigar sales moved ahead persistently. Volume of sales was still large enough to permit substantial promotional expenditures. It is true, of course, that cigars have lost ground to cigarettes during a time when cigarettes have had increasing amounts of advertising devoted to them. But it must be remembered that the increasing volume of cigarette advertising has been possible largely because favoring fashion trends have brought increasing cigarette consumption. Conversely, cigar advertising has been arrested because the fashion trend operating against cigars has reduced sales revenues. Manufacturers have not been able profitably to spend increasing sums.

In the case of cigarettes it was concluded that advertising has been an important element, but one whose relative importance cannot be weighed mathematically, in speeding up a favorable demand trend made possible by underlying social change; in the case of cigars it is concluded that advertising may have been a force to check an adverse trend arising from the same social change, but not strong enough to reverse it. Cigarettes have gained new users. Cigarette smokers are typically young people. Cigar smokers, however, are reportedly predominantly older men.[2] This fact suggests that cigar manufacturers apparently have held many habitual users, but have not been so successful as cigarette manufacturers in gaining new users.

EFFECT OF ADVERTISING UPON SELECTIVE DEMAND FOR CIGARS

Cigar manufacturers have continued to spend considerable sums upon advertising despite the downward trend of demand in recent decades, because there has been a large volume of business for individual producers to strive for and advertising has been considered helpful for securing sales. Further examination discloses, however, that certain conditions which have seemed to favor large programs of selective advertising by cigarette manufacturers in recent decades have not prevailed for cigar manufacturers. Conditions in the cigarette industry have led to a competition by large producers carried out largely through advertising. The cigar industry, however, has been a demoralized, unstable industry, composed of a large number of small producers, among whom competition has tended to center upon price to a considerable degree, rather than upon brand advertising. Only in recent years has there been a tendency toward concentration of demand upon individual brands which has permitted really large scale advertising.

Large Number of Small Producers in Cigar Industry

In contrast to the cigarette industry, which ever since 1875 has used machines that have favored large-scale operations, the cigar industry until the past two decades has largely relied upon hand manufacture

2 "The Problem of Cigar Promotion," *The Tobacco Leaf*. May 6, 1933, pp. 3 and 14.

and has been characterized by small-scale factories. The cigar-making machine,[3] which in recent years has been revolutionizing the industry, was not perfected until 1917. Until the advent of the machine, a condition of decreasing manufacturing costs did not operate to favor large-scale operations. The lack of need for large investment made possible thousands of small factories. The machine, however, gave important savings to its users, as much as $5.50 to $6.00 a thousand cigars, even after royalty and machine overhead were allowed.[4] Its adoption has led to larger factories and has tended toward elimination of small operators. The Commissioner of Internal Revenue in 1912 reported 20,485 manufacturers of large cigars in the United States, only a few of whom were large concerns.[5] In 1921 there were 14,578 factories, of which only 11 companies had an annual production of over 40,000,000 cigars and accounted for 15.7% of total production. By 1938 the number of factories had been reduced to 4,430, of which 28 had an annual production of over 40,000,000 cigars and accounted for 61.3% of total output (Table 41). From these data it can be seen that only in the last decade has the move toward concentration of the industry gone far. But even now there remains a large number of relatively small-scale operators.

The large number of small producers operating even in recent years is reflected in the number of brands. Instead of a small number of dominating brands, as in the cigarette business during the past 25 years, there have been many cigar brands, fewer than formerly, yet thousands in all. Of these a large percentage have had only local distribution. Private brands and wholesalers' brands have been common.[6] The number of brands to be found in a single market is shown in the figures issued by *The Milwaukee Journal,* which for 1938 reported 235 brands of cigars being used in the Milwaukee market.[7] In contrast, only 30 brands of cigarettes were reported.

In passing it may be pointed out that the charge sometimes made that advertising tends to multiply brands does not hold true in the

---

[3] Case of General Cigar Company, Harvard Business School files. See also: U. S. Bureau of Labor Statistics, "Technological Changes in the Cigar Industry and Their Effects on Labor," *Monthly Labor Review,* December, 1931, p. 11.

[4] Case of General Cigar Company, Harvard Business School files. U. S. Bureau of Labor Statistics, *op. cit.*

[5] U. S. Bureau of Corporations, *op. cit.,* p. 451.

[6] Cases of General Cigar Company, Inc., and Multan Cigar Company, Harvard Business School files.

[7] *The Milwaukee Journal,* "1938 Consumer Analysis of the Greater Milwaukee Market," p. 74.

TABLE 41

NUMBER OF CIGAR MANUFACTURERS, CLASSIFIED AS TO OUTPUT AND PERCENTAGE OF
PRODUCTION IN EACH CLASS—CALENDAR YEARS, 1921, 1926, 1934, 1938

OUTPUT OF CIGARS	1921		1926		1934		1938	
	No. of Factories	% of Total Production	No. of Factories	% of Total Production	No. of Factories	% of Total Production	No. of Factories	% of Total Production
Under 500,000......	13,149	13.7	9,281	8.0	5,708	5.9	4,087	3.3
500,000 to 40,000,000	1,418	70.6	943	67.0	424	39.8	315	35.4
Over 40,000,000.....	11	15.7	23	25.0	28	54.3	28	61.3

Source: *Annual Reports of the Commissioner of Internal Revenue*, 1922 Annual Report, p. 120; 1927 Annual Report, p. 100; 1935 Annual Report, p. 117; 1939 Annual Report, p. 119.

cigar industry. Here, as is usually true, multiplicity of brands arises from the fact that unidentical merchandise is offered by a large number of sellers under their marks. Advertising when successful is a force tending to bring diminution in number of brands, because it aims to attract a large number of users to the advertised brands. As will be brought out in a later chapter, however, forces other than advertising primarily determine the number of brands in any field.[8]

Tendency to Keen Price Competition

A market containing so large a number of small producers would in itself lead one to expect keen price competition rather than competition carried out largely through advertising and promotion with relatively stable prices, such as has been characteristic of the cigarette industry. The additional fact that this large number of small cigar producers has been operating under conditions of a declining demand has accentuated the price competition. The demoralized conditions of the industry were emphasized in a report of the National Recovery Administration[9] in 1936 and are evident also from case material collected in this study.

The keen price competition of the industry is not reflected in usual price data but is determinable from detailed knowledge of the industry. Since the early days of the cigar business there has been a strong tendency for cigars to be sold in certain retail price classes, such as two for 5 cents, 5 cents each, three for 10 cents, two for 15 cents, 10 cents each, three for 20 cents, and so on. The federal tax schedule has

[8] See Chapter XXII for a further discussion of the forces affecting the number of brands.
[9] U. S. National Recovery Administration, Division of Review, Industry Studies Section, *The Tobacco Study, Tobacco Unit* (March, 1936), pp. 191–192.

probably been a factor in the continuation of these traditional prices. Although at times producers have found it advisable to price their cigars so that resulting retail prices have departed from customary prices, odd prices have not been popular with consumers, and in general manufacturers have fixed their prices to the trade so as to avoid noncustomary prices.[10] Competition has taken the form of the offering of cigars whose quality and size would win favor in a particular price class. Consequently, to influence sales volume manufacturers have sometimes changed quality. In other instances, they have shifted a brand from one price class to a lower price class, with quality retained, as when cigars selling at two for 15 cents have been reduced to three for 20 cents, then to 5 cents each. In still other instances, price competition has taken the form of sellers offering larger discounts to the trade without suggesting change of retail price. Price competition in the industry has been in part responsible for the marked shift of demand from Class B and Class C cigars to Class A cigars, a change previously noted.

Extent of Use of Advertising by Cigar Manufacturers

The margins which have been available and the scale of operations of cigar producers have not permitted advertising and aggressive selling on so large a scale as has held in the cigarette industry. Whereas cigarette manufacturers who have relied heavily upon advertising have devoted to advertising from about 6% to 9% of selling price, including taxes, or from 15% to 20% of net sales less taxes, cigar manufacturers have spent a smaller percentage. Such data as were obtainable indicate that cigar manufacturers have spent for advertising in recent years from 2% to 9% of sales value, less taxes.[11] Confidential expense figures from manufacturers show advertising expenditures ranging from 2% to 8% of sales. Correspondence with manufacturers of leading brands indicated that the expenditures on 5-cent cigars have ranged from one-tenth to two-tenths of a cent per cigar, which is equivalent to 3% to 6% of the manufacturers' selling

---

[10] See U. S. Federal Trade Commission, *Report of the Federal Trade Commission on Agricultural Income Inquiry*, Part I, "Principal Farm Products," 1937, p. 453.

[11] For cigars the percentages of advertising expense figured before tax deduction are not greatly different from those based on sales less taxes, because cigar taxes represent less than 10% of manufacturers' selling prices. Thus a manufacturer's price of approximately $33 a thousand for 5-cent cigars has included only $2 taxes. An advertising cost percentage based on $31, the sales return less taxes, is not greatly different from one based on $33.

prices less taxes. One manufacturer stated, however, that advertising expenditures for leading national brands of 5-cent cigars ran in the neighborhood of three-tenths of a cent per cigar, which is equivalent to approximately 9% of the manufacturers' selling prices less taxes. Undoubtedly there is a considerable range in the percentages of advertising expenditure of various manufacturers, but even the highest figures are below those common in the cigarette business.

While there apparently are many minor cigar brands given relatively little advertising support, generally cigar producers have used advertising and promotion to influence sales volume in so far as margins have permitted. This fact was indicated from numerous interviews with executives in the industry and from study of case histories. Many of the local and regional brands of small operators have not been accorded appreciable space advertising, but they have often been given considerable promotion to and through the trade.[12] The extent to which some 38 brands, distributed nationally, have used newspaper, magazine, and radio advertising during the years 1938 and 1939 is shown in Table 42. Of these 38 brands, 8 had expenditures in these media in excess of $100,000 in 1939, while the two leading brands had really substantial expenditures, the amount spent for Bayuk's Phillies being almost $1,000,000, and that for White Owl approximately $663,000.

Increasing Concentration in the Industry

These large advertising appropriations for individual brands during recent years are related directly to the gradual concentration of production that has been taking place since the advent of the cigar-making machine. During the past 20 years the leading cigar companies have adopted machine manufacture and concurrently have followed the policies of decreasing the number of brands offered, of concentrating advertising and promotion on brands in the low-price field, and of developing their markets nationally. An illustration of such policies is found in the case of the General Cigar Company; this case illustrates also the reliance which a leading company has placed upon advertising to build sales volume for its brands.

The General Cigar Company, Inc., launched a policy of brand concentration and of seeking a widened area of demand in 1913. At

---

[12] An example is found in the case of the Mello Cigar Company, Harvard Business School files.

TABLE 42
Traceable Space and Time Advertising Expenditure for Cigar Brands Sold Nationally, 1938–1939

BRAND	VOLUME OF ADVERTISING IN DOLLARS	
	1938	1939
Adlon	$ 630	$ 483
Admiration	62,036	54,747
Alfred Dunhill	760	.....
American Tobacco Company	.....	17
Blackstone	33,865	.....
Charles Denby	29,856	34,279
Cinco	6,672	19
Deisel-Wemmer-Gilbert	.....	62
Dutch Masters	90,980	86,747
El Producto	216,362	202,131
El Roi Tan	88,620	168,108
El Sidelo	.....	8,098
El Verso	.....	5,807
Emerson	.....	14,075
Garcia Y Vega	175	.....
Girard	11,176	.....
Harvester	117,492	41,986
Havana	6,159	.....
Havana Ribbon	4,965	.....
Henrietta	7,819	16,540
La Azora	10,114	48,207
La Fendrich (and Charles Denby)	29,856	33,826
La Palina	187,962	187,221
P. Lorillard	99,948	.....
Lovera	48,440	38,054
Mozart	2,374	.....
Muriel	.....	166,445
Phillies	839,300	975,477
R. G. Dun	.....	12,217
Robert Burns	186,363	136,579
San Felice	.....	9,496
Tom Moore	11,353	.....
Van Dyck	119,418	193,542
Webster	79,787	73,065
White Owl	533,628	663,465
Yankee	.....	25,738
"44"	5,196	540
7-20-4	516	.....
	$2,831,822	$3,196,971

Sources:
1938 newspaper: American Newspaper Publishers' Association, *Expenditures of National Advertisers in Newspapers in 1938.*
1938 magazine, farm journal, radio: Publishers' Information Bureau, *National Advertising Records,* 1938.
1939 figures: American Newspaper Publishers' Association, *Expenditures of National Advertisers in Newspapers, Magazines, Farm Journals and Chain Radio in 1939.*

that time the executives were of the opinion that advertising alone could not bring an insistence for its brands strong enough to obtain the dense retail distribution which the management desired. Accordingly, the company placed considerable reliance upon personal selling to retailers, and between 1916 and 1935 distributed approximately 75% of its output direct to retailers through its own wholesale branches. Although it resumed sale to retailers through tobacco wholesalers in 1935, it continued to rely upon personal promotion to retailers to help consummate sales.

The company advertised nationally after 1916, concentrating first on the Robert Burns 10-cent cigar. In 1922 the national advertising was extended to include White Owl, then an 8-cent cigar, which was reduced to 7 cents in 1926, then to 6 cents, and to 5 cents in 1931. These latter reductions in price and a substantial campaign of advertising were instituted at a time when the American Tobacco Company was making a strong bid to establish itself as a leader in the cigar market with heavy advertising of its 5-cent Cremo cigar, reportedly being advertised at the rate of $2,000,000 annually.[13] The countering moves of reduced price and of advertising by the General Cigar Company and by other companies was apparently an important factor in leading the American Tobacco Company to drop its heavy advertising of Cremo cigars in the summer of 1931. White Owl not only had the advantage of trading on its reputation as a higher-price cigar, but was a larger cigar than Cremo. It is evident from this instance that although this leading company used advertising in its competitive battle, it also used price.

In keeping with its policy of concentration, the company, after 1931, devoted most of its advertising and promotion for 5-cent cigars upon White Owl, instead of upon the William Penn brand, which had been the advertised brand in this class.

The General Cigar Company, Inc., adopted machine manufacturing for its low- and medium-price cigars after 1923. This change brought an increasing pressure on management to secure a large sales volume in order to secure the lower costs afforded by machine operation. In turn, as the economies of machine operation were available, this company, like other large operators, apparently had somewhat wider margins available for advertising and promotional work than had small companies. Thus, advertising has probably been an element along with lower production costs in bringing concentration in the industry. Concentration as yet has not gone far, however. In 1935, the General Cigar Company, Inc., was reported to sell about one-seventh of

---

[13] "Lucky Strike—The American Tobacco Company," *Fortune*, December, 1936, p. 156. Also see Chapter XX.

the country's total output of cigars as compared with approximately one-fourteenth in 1920.[14] General Cigar Company, Inc., and Bayuk Cigars, Inc., the two largest producers in recent years, are reported to have accounted for less than one-fourth of total cigar production.[15]

From the above discussion it appears evident that advertising has been an effective tool for the managements of cigar companies in helping to guide selective demand. As is always true, its effect cannot be measured mathematically; yet its universal use and the success which has come to well advertised brands in recent years leaves little doubt of its value as a sales aid to cigar concerns. Advertising has not, however, influenced selective demand for cigars to so large an extent as it has that for cigarettes.

EFFECT OF ADVERTISING UPON THE PRIMARY DEMAND FOR SMOKING TOBACCO

The general pattern of demand for smoking tobacco has been previously noted. Like cigars, it enjoyed for a long period of time a steadily increasing consumption, its peak demand coming in 1917, 10 years later than that of cigars. But since World War I the demand trend has been downward. As with cigars, this decrease has occurred in spite of a substantial amount of advertising and in spite of a falling price trend. Pipe smoking has become less fashionable in the last 25 years than it was formerly. The same social attitudes previously outlined that have made cigarettes the popular form of tobacco use have apparently operated against pipe smoking, just as they have against cigars.

The Trend of Demand

In 1870 annual per capita consumption of smoking tobacco was about .6 pounds. By 1900 this had risen to 1.3 pounds, and continued its climb to a high of approximately 2.4 pounds in 1916. From that time on there has been a steady decline until in 1937 per capita consumption was only 1.8 pounds. (Table 26.)

The decline was temporarily stemmed in the depression years of 1932–1933. This interruption is accounted for, so far as can be judged, not by an increase in pipe smoking during those years but by

---

[14] Standard Statistics Company, Inc., *Standard Corporation Records*, Individual Reports Section, Bulletin G-16, February 25, 1935.
[15] Case of General Cigar Company, Inc., Harvard Business School files.

the practice of many cigarette smokers of rolling their own cigarettes. In short, the persistent upward trend in cigarette smoking was not stemmed even by the 1930 depression, as the consumption figures for manufactured cigarettes seem to indicate. Cigarette smoking continued unabated; the consumption merely switched to a cheaper form of cigarette. During the depth of the depression a number of smoking tobacco companies made heavy appeals on a "roll your own" theme, particularly Bull Durham.[16] That hand rolling was widely adopted is indicated in the reports of the Commissioner of Internal Revenue, which show over a five-fold increase in the withdrawal of packages of cigarette papers during the depression years following 1930. The large number of packages of cigarette papers withdrawn, even after manufactured cigarettes resumed their upward surge in 1933 indicates that the practice of smokers of rolling their own cigarettes must have continued in considerable degree; but the decline in per capita consumption of smoking tobacco set in again after 1932.

The decrease in consumption has occurred in spite of a general decrease in prices of smoking tobacco since the first World War. As compared with the Bureau of Labor Statistics combined index of wholesale prices, the price of tobacco during the first World War had not risen so high as had commodities in general. (Table 28.) Based on 1926 as 100, the index for the price of smoking tobacco was only 119 in 1920; the Bureau of Labor Statistics combined index was 154. Prices were not reduced until 1924, however, and they then remained constant until 1931. With a second drop in 1932, the price of tobacco products was placed at a lower level than prices of commodities generally, as indicated by the Bureau of Labor Statistics index, and have remained at this low point. It will be noted that stability of prices for long periods has been characteristic of the product.

Extent of Advertising

Smoking tobacco over a long period of years has been given strong advertising support. The heavy advertising of Bull Durham and Duke's Mixture has been referred to previously; that of smoking tobacco in general during the period of the Tobacco Combination is indicated in Table 16, which shows the average expenditure over the period 1893–1910 to have been in excess of 10% of net sales (less

---

[16] "Lucky Strike—American Tobacco Company," *op. cit.* The appeal was, "Roll your own and save your roll" (p. 101).

taxes). During the later years of the Combination, however, when it controlled 75% of smoking tobacco production, the percentage expended was only half this amount. In 1910 the United States Commissioner of Corporations in his study of the tobacco trust reported that approximately $3,700,000 was spent in the advertising of smoking tobacco. After the dissolution of the trust, when the successor companies greatly increased the extent of their aggressive selling, the advertising expenditure also was greatly increased, with the result that in 1913 the total was approximately $6,400,000 (Table 22). The Commissioner's report indicated that in 1912 and 1913 the successor companies were again spending approximately 10% of net receipts upon advertising.[17] Companies which had not been in the combination, however, were spending only about 3% on advertising.[17]

For the period 1913–1929 the available record of advertising relates solely to magazine advertising, as shown in Table 43. During this period a substantial percentage of the space advertising expenditure for smoking tobacco is believed to have been devoted to magazines; yet the practice of marked variations in media employed from year to year probably render the table a poor indicator of trend of expenditure. It will be noted, however, that the magazine expenditures in all years represented an appreciable sum, and in the later 1920's averaged over $1,000,000 a year.

TABLE 43

ADVERTISING EXPENDITURES FOR SMOKING TOBACCO IN LEADING MAGAZINES, 1914–1929

YEAR	ADVERTISING EXPENDITURES
1914	$ 605,207
1915	673,696
1916	611,413
1917	683,831
1918	342,046
1919	689,387
1920	378,945
1921	496,566
1922	540,159
1923	424,465
1924	478,789
1925	529,062
1926	1,077,318
1927	1,366,400
1928	1,018,639
1929	811,051

Source: Curtis Publishing Company, *op. cit.*, respective years.

[17] U. S. Bureau of Corporations, *op. cit.*, pp. 255, 415.

Since 1929 a more complete estimate of space and radio time expenditures (Table 44) gives a better picture of the substantial volume of advertising devoted to smoking tobacco, ranging from the space expenditures of approximately $1,500,000 in the depression year of 1933 to approximately $3,500,000 for the years 1936 and following. Total advertising expenditures probably are in the neighborhood of twice these amounts. If an estimate of total advertising expenditure of approximately $7,000,000 for 1937 is related to the value of smoking tobacco as reported in the 1937 Census of Manufactures, $117,700,000, it is seen that the advertising expenditure was apparently approximately 6% of the value of the manufactured product. This result would indicate that advertising expenditures probably have ranged in the neighborhood of 5% to 10%, a figure in line with the practices recorded in the report of the U. S. Commissioner of Corporations for the early period, 1893–1913. It is in accord likewise with confidential figures obtained from a few companies from which cases relating to this product were collected. One relatively small company, using little space advertising but relying largely on dealer work and deals for promotion of the product, spent

TABLE 44

TRACEABLE ADVERTISING EXPENDITURES IN MAGAZINES, NEWSPAPERS, FARM JOURNALS, AND CHAIN RADIO FOR SMOKING TOBACCO, 1929–1939

YEAR	NEWSPAPERS*	GENERAL MAGAZINES	FARM JOURNALS	RADIO	TOTAL
1929	$ 268,590	$ 811,051†	$110,804‡a	$	$1,190,445
1930	370,490	1,209,648†	148,316b	88,211‡a	1,816,665
1931	1,322,004	845,267†	151,000‡	657,709‡	2,975,980
1932	1,756,172	546,830†	36,139‡	164,233‡	2,503,374
1933	802,032	317,960†	56,826‡	302,446‡b	1,479,264
1934	1,390,487	336,753†	92,165§	321,527§	2,140,932
1935	509,432	280,954†	109,613§	597,135‡	1,497,134
1936	1,391,856	1,057,753§	279,448‡c	939,369‡c	3,668,426
1937	1,169,819	1,360,611§	388,490§	725,831§	3,644,751
1938	1,069,832	1,195,621§	447,730§	708,586§	3,421,769
1939	585,260	1,043,006§	396,563§	1,588,336§	3,613,165

a Extended from 10 months.
b Extended from 11 months.
c Extended from 9 months.

Sources:
* 1929–1939 linage taken from Media Records, Inc., *Newspapers and Newspaper Advertisers*; 1938–1939 dollar figures from American Newspaper Publishers' Association, *Expenditures of National Advertisers*. Conversion ratio calculated from data for 1938 and 1939 (48¢) applied to other years. For an explanation of conversion rate see Appendix IV.
† Curtis Publishing Company, *Leading Advertisers*, respective years.
‡ National Advertising Records, Inc., *National Advertising Records*, respective years.
§ Publishers' Information Bureau, Inc., *National Advertising Records*, respective years.

only a little over 1% of sales on advertising. Three larger companies using space advertising reported spending approximately 6%, 7%, and 9%, respectively, for advertising in a recent year.

An appraisal of the above data relating to consumption, prices, and advertising does not permit one to state with certainty the extent to which advertising has affected the primary demand of smoking tobacco over this long period, just as was the case with cigars and cigarettes. For the period before the first World War it is reasonable to suppose that the large amount of advertising tended to accelerate the fashion of pipe smoking. In turn, however, the equally large or larger sums devoted to advertising since the first World War have failed to forestall a swing away from this form of tobacco. They may have retarded a declining trend; but as with cigars the social attitudes arising from social change presented forces that advertising and aggressive selling could not overcome.

THE EFFECT OF ADVERTISING UPON SELECTIVE DEMAND FOR SMOKING TOBACCO

The ratios of advertising expenditures to sales of smoking tobacco of individual manufacturers have been indicated above, ranging according to our small sample from 1% to approximately 10% of net sales. It should not be concluded from these figures, however, that all smoking tobacco brands of the manufacturers are accorded these amounts of promotion. As in the cigar field, producers of smoking tobacco have many brands to which they do not accord space advertising. Some of the brands are even withheld from the market for considerable periods of time; some are given a limited amount of promotion to and through dealers. Only a small number are heavily advertised. The policy of concentrating advertising on particular brands has apparently been followed more widely in the last 25 years than in the period preceding. The practice that was successful with cigarettes has been carried over to other tobacco products.

Varying Use of Advertising for Smoking Tobacco

With manufactured tobacco as with cigars and even with cigarettes to a lesser degree, certain brands are kept in distribution with little promotion because there exists a consumer demand persistent enough to make them profitable. For example, one manufacturer of tobacco products, chiefly smoking tobacco, reported having 51 active brands, representing various mixtures and cuts. Only two were promoted with a substantial volume of advertising; the others were given varying amounts of promotion through special deals and point of purchase display. Executives of the company reported that these brands, many of long standing, had a persistent following. They stated that many pipe smokers apparently continue to use a brand for many years; although there is some switching of brands among users, it is more the custom of new pipe smokers.

The American Tobacco Company is an example of a big tobacco company having a large number of brands with advertising concentrated on a limited number. *Fortune's* report on this company contains the following statement:

> The American Tobacco Co. makes and sells every nicotinic product except snuff. There are nearly 500 items in the line, ranging from Boot Jack and Gold Rope and Old Honesty plugs to Roi Tan and Chancellor cigars to Egyptian Prettiest and Royal Nestor and Svoboda cigarettes. The formulas and processes by which all these brands differ from each other are in the safe-keeping of Charles F. Neiley, Vice President of Manufacturing, one of Mr. Hill's three over-$100,-000-a-year men. On the accuracy of his control depends the continued profit from such items as Nigger Hair, a smoking tobacco that will have sold some 425,000 pounds in the Milwaukee district this year with no promotion at all, simply because people there seem to like it.[18]

Evidence of Selective Effect of Advertising

Partial evidence of the effectiveness of advertising in guiding demand appears in the fact that the great bulk of demand in the country as a whole is concentrated on the 27 leading brands included as national advertisers in Table 45. Distribution of demand among brands in one market is illustrated in the annual analyses of the Greater Milwaukee Market by the *Milwaukee Journal*. The distribution for 1940 is shown in Table 46. The *Milwaukee Journal* found that 112 brands of smoking tobacco were in use in that market in 1940. In its sample, only 21 brands were used by 1% or more of pipe or "roll-your-own" cigarette smokers, accounting for 90% of such tobacco users. The other 91 brands were smoked by the remaining 10%. It will be noted in the table that 15 of the 21 brands listed in the survey are among the national advertisers included in Table 45. These

---
[18] "Lucky Strike—The American Tobacco Company," *op. cit.*, p. 98.

TABLE 45

TRACEABLE ADVERTISING EXPENDITURES FOR SMOKING TOBACCO IN NEWSPAPERS,
MAGAZINES, FARM JOURNALS, AND CHAIN RADIO, 1938–1939

BRAND	1938	1939
Big Ben	$ 77,715	$ ....
Blue Boar	3,942	....
Bond Street	8,900	23,704
Briggs	65,925	82,270
Bugler	79,713	456,243
Craven	2,713	....
Crosby Square	6,997	....
Dill's Best	217,560	250,106
Edgeworth	96,724	53,749
Eton	700	....
Granger	370,732	336,103
Half and Half	249,830	243,094
Heine's	6,236	....
Kentucky Club	107,417	293,747
London Dock	4,524	....
P. Lorillard Tobaccos	....	69
Middleton's	154	....
Model	217,560	255,224
Peper's	1,841	....
Pipe Major	....	8,884
Prince Albert	2,133,584	1,809,826
Revelation	....	19,140
Sir Walter Raleigh	115,360	422,680
Union Leader	115,301	135,111
Velvet	440,177	455,534
Walnut	7,316	....
Yule Blend	175	....
Total	$4,331,096	$4,845,484

Sources:

1938: General magazine, farm journal and radio, Publishers' Information Bureau, *National Advertising Records*, 1938.
Newspaper, American Newspaper Publishers' Association, *Expenditures of National Advertisers in Newspapers in 1938*.
1939: American Newspaper Publishers' Association, *Expenditures of National Advertisers in Newspapers, Magazines, Farm Journals, and Chain Radio in 1939*.

nationally advertised brands account for approximately three-fourths of all users. Eight Brothers, an old brand of the Penn Tobacco Company, which stands fourth in the survey list but is not listed as a national advertiser in Table 45, had distribution only in a restricted geographical area which included Milwaukee; it had been given considerable advertising in that area for several years previous to 1939. It will be noted that the non-advertised Nigger Hair, referred to in the quotation above, was used by 1.5% of the smokers interviewed. Most brands with little advertising were in the miscellaneous group being used by less than 1% of those interviewed.

Cases from manufacturers of smoking tobacco were obtained on a confidential basis; accordingly detailed information regarding the

TABLE 46

DISTRIBUTION OF CONSUMER PREFERENCES AMONG 112 BRANDS OF SMOKING TOBACCO
USED IN GREATER MILWAUKEE MARKET, 1940

BRAND	% OF ALL MEN BUYING SMOKING TOBACCO WHO USED EACH BRAND
Half and Half	16.1
Prince Albert	10.0
Union Leader	8.4
Eight Brothers	8.3
Sir Walter Raleigh	6.4
Kentucky Club	6.3
Model	4.8
Velvet	4.2
Friends	4.2
Granger	3.4
Big Ben	3.2
Briggs	2.8
Edgeworth	2.4
Plow Boy	2.1
Bond Street	1.9
Crosby Square	1.6
Nigger Hair	1.5
Peerless	1.4
Revelation	1.3
Dills Best	1.0
Tuxedo	1.0
Miscellaneous*	9.9

* Included all brands (91) used by less than 1% of the total men who smoke pipes.
Source: *The Milwaukee Journal,* "1940 Consumer Analysis of the Greater Milwaukee Market," p. 73.

effect of advertising in building demand for these companies has to be presented in disguised form. In several instances the evidence from these cases is unmistakable regarding the positive contribution of advertising in building selective demand.

In one case the manufacturer decided to advertise a brand of long-cut tobacco[19] which had not previously been given much promotional help. The trend of sales for long-cut tobacco of which the company had several brands had been downward for some years and the declines in the years 1932, 1933, and 1934 had been serious, approximating about 12% each year. By 1935 it had become apparent to the company that the business revival which was gaining momentum at the time would not cause enough improvement to bring sales of long-cut tobacco back to 1929 levels. It decided, therefore, to concentrate advertising and promotion on what it considered its best brand of

[19] In order to keep the tobacco user of 50 years ago from having to carry both a plug of chewing tobacco and a package of smoking tobacco, James B. Duke developed long-cut tobacco, which was suitable for either smoking or chewing. Such tobacco has had a marked downward trend in demand in recent decades.

that type of tobacco. As the result of a survey in the trade it changed the size and wrapping of its packages and altered prices somewhat to put them in line with those of competing brands. Thereupon, early in 1936, the company launched a selling program, in which radio advertising played the most important role. Personal selling efforts to the trade were not increased. The expenditure for advertising over the next five years was approximately 5% of sales. Sales of the brand immediately turned upward. Sales for 1936 were 12% above those for 1935; those for 1937 were 23% above those for 1936; and those for 1938 were 3% above those for 1937. Although sales turned downward in 1939, with a change of advertising program in January, 1941, the upward trend was resumed. The increase in sales of this tobacco is the more impressive because there has been a decided down trend in the use of long-cut tobaccos in the past two decades. Company executives estimated that the number of pounds of long-cut tobacco sold by the industry in 1939 was only 44% of those sold in 1917.

In another case a new brand of straight pipe tobacco, which will here be called Bluegrass tobacco, was launched by the Morro Tobacco Company[20] with the help of advertising at prices the same as those of leading competitive brands. Much study was given by the management to the development of a blend which would find favor. The company followed the plan of developing sectional markets. In 1937, four years after the product was launched, sales exceeded 5,000,000 pounds. The management was convinced that it could not have made this record in such a highly competitive field without advertising.

This same management conducted an interesting experiment to check the effect of its advertising. Late in 1934, a question was raised as to whether the smoking public would have accepted its new Bluegrass brand of tobacco without advertising. In order to answer this question objectively, it was decided to conduct an experiment with its Guardsman brand of smoking tobacco. The company proposed gradually to change the blend of tobacco of the Guardsman brand, month by month, until it was exactly the same as the Bluegrass blend. No advertising was to be used. Company officials reasoned that a close check on sales results, month by month, would show whether or not the change in the blend of the Guardsman brand without advertising would stimulate the sales of the product.

Table 47, which shows the yearly percentage changes in the sales

---

[20] Fictitious name.

TABLE 47

MORRO TOBACCO COMPANY

PERCENTAGE CHANGE IN SALES OF GUARDSMAN BRAND OF SMOKING TOBACCO,
1928 TO 1934 (IN POUNDS)

YEAR	% CHANGE FROM PREVIOUS YEAR
1928	— 2
1929	— 3
1930	— 3
1931	+ 6
1932	+190
1933	— 46
1934	— 56

Source: Company records.

of Guardsman brand tobacco from 1928 through 1934, gives a sales history of the blend prior to the proposal of the experiment.

As Table 47 shows, the sales of this brand had declined by small amounts during 1928, 1929, and 1930.

In 1931 and 1932 the company had undertaken an aggressive sales promotional campaign to extend the distribution of this product and to stimulate its sales. Company salesmen called upon retailers to get window and counter display; free deals were offered to the retailers; pipe deals were featured; and special sales were run. As a result of this aggressive program, the sales of Guardsman brand were increased 6% in 1931 and 190% in 1932. The extra pressure exerted merely served to overstock the jobbers and the retailers with this brand, however, and sales exhibited a serious decline during 1933 and 1934. In 1933 and thereafter the company had relied entirely upon the jobbers' salesmen to sell to the retailers; no special dealer promotional efforts were undertaken and no advertising was used.

In January, 1935, the company started its proposed experiment by changing the blend of the Guardsman brand pipe tobacco. The blend was modified gradually, so that it would not be noticeable. By July, 1935, the change had been completed, and the Bluegrass blend was being sold under the Guardsman name. No changes were made in the sales program during the period of the test.

The results of the experiment are shown in Table 48.

A comparison of the monthly sales for 1935 and 1936 with corresponding months in previous years indicates clearly that the downward trend in sales volume continued uninterrupted throughout the period of the experiment. Also, the total sales for 1935 declined

TABLE 48

MORRO TOBACCO COMPANY

MONTHLY SALES OF GUARDSMAN BRAND SMOKING MIXTURE, 1934–1936 (POUNDS)

MONTH	1934	1935	1936
January	2,745	1,444	1,103
February	2,169	1,143	832
March	2,612	1,254	1,004
April	2,485	1,367	868
May	2,122	1,228	1,071
June	2,007	971	1,028
July	1,988	1,389	944
August	1,878	1,250	693
September	1,709	1,107	871
October	1,726	951	889
November	1,045	1,058	690
December	1,440	801	704
	23,926	13,963	10,697

Source: Company records.

42% from the 1934 level; 1936 sales were 23% lower than sales for 1935; similarly, the brand continued to decline for four years following.

The change in blend may have alienated some habitual users, who had become accustomed to the old blend; yet the flavor, which had been so widely accepted and successful in the brand which the company advertised, did not win over old Gaurdsman users and bring additional users. The executives concluded from this experiment that a good blend was not enough in itself to attract demand for its smoking tobaccos, but that aggressive advertising was essential in addition.

From the preceding discussion it is concluded that the persistent use of a brand by individuals has permitted many brands of smoking tobacco to be sold with little advertising and promotional support. However, the predominant position of advertised brands in the market as well as the case material cited attest the part which advertising plays in influencing selective demand.

THE DEMAND FOR CHEWING TOBACCO AND SNUFF

In this study no effort was made to get case material on chewing tobacco and snuff. Hence only the incidental evidence gained during the investigation of other tobacco products is presented.

Chewing tobacco shows the characteristic rise and decline in consumption that has held for cigars and smoking tobacco. With chewing tobacco, however, the peak in consumption came about 1890, when per capita consumption was 2.8 pounds. Chewing tobacco may have been the fashion for the robust, outdoor worker of the nineteenth century, but it has lost its place with the urban population of recent decades. It was pointed out by one tobacco company executive that formerly chewing tobacco was not only commonly used in rural areas but, to a larger extent than now, among factory workers who were not permitted to smoke on the job. With the steady and persistent change in population from rural to urban, and with the increasing number of white collar workers, the habit of chewing tobacco has decreased, until now annual per capita consumption is approximately .5 pounds as compared with the 2.8 pounds of 1890.

Although Tables 19 and 20, pages 210 and 211, show substantial percentages of sales devoted to advertising between 1893–1910 by the Tobacco Combination, 10% or more in some years, there is little evidence regarding advertising expenditures in recent years. Nor does case material add much. References in case material collected from companies manufacturing chewing tobacco in addition to other tobacco products indicate that such advertising as has been done in recent years has taken the form largely of dealer work and point-of-purchase display. The records of space measuring organizations have not shown space expenditures for chewing tobacco.

The evidence regarding snuff is even less than that for chewing tobacco, largely because advertising has played a smaller part in its distribution than in that of other products. Table 21, page 211, shows that the expenditures of the Tobacco Combination on snuff advertising typically varied between 2% and 4% of sales, less than for most other products. After the dissolution of the Tobacco Combination the successor companies increased their advertising expenditures to 5% and 7% in 1912 and 1913.[21] In recent years the advertising measuring services have not shown advertising expenditures of snuff in magazines, newspapers, or radio. Brief discussion with tobacco executives indicated that advertising is limited largely to point-of-purchase display. References by other investigators indicate that brand habits in snuff are relatively well fixed and early established.[22] In view of these facts and the limited consumption of the product, it is

---

[21] U. S. Bureau of Corporations, *op. cit.*, p. 312.
[22] J. J. Gottsegen, *op. cit.*, p. 195; also *Standard Trade and Securities*, "Basic Survey Tobacco," June 7, 1940, p. To–18.

evident that space advertising probably would not be effective in influencing demand.

Without the aid of space advertising per capita consumption of snuff has been relatively constant for a long period of time, as indicated in Tables 25 and 26, pages 215 and 216, having increased from .03 pound in 1870 to .3 pound in 1910, with little subsequent variation from that figure. While snuff was fashionable in the eighteenth century,[23] it has not in the period since the Civil War followed the normal fashion movement which has characterized other forms of tobacco. Its use now is apparently confined largely to laboring classes in the South, particularly negroes, and to certain midwestern areas, particularly among the Scandinavians of Wisconsin and Minnesota.[24]

Both chewing tobacco and snuff illustrate products for which advertising does not promise profitable return and consequently is not used.

---

[23] J. J. Gottsegen, *op. cit.*, p. 120 ff.
[24] U. S. Department of Agriculture, Circular 249, *American Tobacco Types, Uses and Markets*, by C. E. Gage (Washington, The Department, January, 1933), p. 56.

CHAPTER X

THE EFFECT OF ADVERTISING ON THE
DEMAND FOR SUGAR

SUGAR was included as a product to be studied because it probably comes as close to standardization as any consumer product on the market. It was deemed advisable to inquire to what extent manufacturers have employed advertising and aggressive selling for a product so nearly standardized, and to determine to what extent such promotion has affected demand.

Standardization of Sugar

All the sugar produced by various refiners is not identical. First of all there is a clear differentiation in the trade and among consumers between cane and beet sugar. In spite of the fact that the beet sugar producers as a group have carried on a limited amount of advertising and publicity to establish the merits of beet sugar, this product has always sold in American markets at a differential under cane sugar. When reference is made to standardization of sugar, standardization either among cane sugars or among beet sugars is meant. In view of the fact that between 75% and 80% of the sugar consumed in this country in the last decade was cane sugar,[1] attention will be directed primarily to that product.

In recent years, roughly 6,300,000 tons of refined sugar have been consumed in the United States annually, of which approximately 70% has been cane sugar refined by continental refiners; approximately 10% cane sugar refined in the tropics, i.e., in Cuba and in American insular possessions; and some 20% beet sugar.

Among cane sugars, there are numerous types in the market. There are various types and sizes of cube sugar and a lack of uniformity among refiners as to the types each offers. There are brown sugars as contrasted with white sugars. There are likewise various degrees of fineness of sugars; some large refiners put out specialties such as extra-fine powdered sugar for use on fruits and cereals, specially

---

[1] Myer Lynsky, *Sugar Economics, Statistics, and Documents* (New York, U. S. Cane Sugar Refiners' Association, 1938; Supplement, 1939), p. 32.

shaped tablets for party purposes, sugar and cinnamon mixtures, and so on. For such specialties, differentiation has provided a basis for brand recognition and preference by consumers.

Even among granulated sugars there is some lack of standardization. For example, some refiners produce a thermophilic sugar, that is, sugar which is treated to reduce danger of spoilage by bacteria, thereby making it especially suitable for canning purposes. Moreover, certain refiners produce special types of sugars which make them particularly suitable for certain industrial purposes. It has been possible for these refiners to get recognition and preference among industrial users for these specialized products.

While these various specialties are differentiated, the product which accounts for about 95% of sugar sold to householders,[2] common, granulated sugar, approaches standardization. The word *approaches* is used advisedly because the executives of refineries who were interviewed, as well as sugar brokers, all agreed that there was not complete standardization between the output of one refinery and that of another. For example, a number of those interviewed expressed the view that one refiner had been particularly successful in maintaining a high standard of quality, having apparently paid particular attention to establishing controls which assure high quality of its product. Those interviewed likewise offered the opinion that greater uniformity of quality was found in the output of the leading domestic refiners than in the output of certain small domestic refiners and of so-called "offshore" sugar refiners.[3]

Although these differences in granulated sugar were recognized by those in the trade, they generally agreed that, so far as consumers ordinarily were concerned, the product of one refiner could not be distinguished from the similar product of other leading refiners. To all intents and purposes, sugar is sugar. The opportunity for differentiation in this product of universal demand has been very small indeed.

In spite of this standardization, the refiners have packaged their sugar, have adopted carefully designed, individualized labels bear-

---

[2] This estimate is based on confidential data of sales by types of sugars received from several refiners.

[3] So-called "off shore" refined sugar, that refined in the tropics, is almost always sold in bulk. There are no specialties made in the tropics, such as brown sugar or powdered sugar. Likewise, beet sugar refiners do not sell a full line. This is partly due to technical reasons, since it is impossible to make a brown or yellow beet sugar; and partly due to economic reasons, since the output of a beet refinery is so small that it cannot afford to enter extensively into the production of specialties.

ing their trade-marks, and have devoted a limited amount of advertising to their packaged product, seeking thereby to gain a degree of consumer and trade preference.[4]

The Effect of Advertising upon Primary Demand

Although sugar has been advertised, advertising has played no appreciable part in the remarkable growth in sugar consumption during the past century.

Advertising of sugar is a relatively recent phenomenon in the long history of the product, and the quantity of advertising has been small. Sugar was not packaged and branded for consumers until 1901. Only small amounts of consumer advertising occurred before 1915, when Mr. Earl D. Babst, an exponent of packaged sugar, joined the American Sugar Refining Company. Thereafter this company increased its advertising appropriations, but for a company so large, they have always been modest. In the early years the American Sugar Refining Company advertised in magazines in amounts ranging from a high of $63,000 in 1917 to $14,000 in 1918. Excepting 1917, the amounts were always under $50,000, and generally under $40,000.[5] Not until 1927 did the National Sugar Refining Company launch consumer advertising, to be followed by certain other refiners. But even at the peak of advertising expenditure in the industry, the total was small, as indicated in Table 49, which gives a record of traceable advertising in leading media.

There is no satisfactory continuing record of consumer space advertising previous to 1929. Since that date the traceable expenditures in newspapers, magazines, farm journals, and chain radio reached a high of approximately $1,000,000 a year in 1929 and 1930, followed by a downward trend until the total in 1939 was only about $218,000. Previous to 1927 the totals were small, as compared with those for the period shown in the table, for, so far as was ascertainable, no

---

[4] A packaged item in the sugar refining industry is any item not sold in a barrel or in a 100-pound bag. A 25-pound sack of sugar is a package. All the sugar sold to food manufacturing industries is sold in barrels or 100-pound bags. Most of that sold to institutions, such as hotels, restaurants, hospitals, and so on, is sold in 100-pound bags. No figures are available for the industry as a whole as to the percentages of total sales made in bulk and in packages. It is estimated that in recent years approximately three-fourths of the sugar sold in packages to household consumers has been in 5, 10, and 25-pound bags; the other fourth has been sold in cardboard cartons and containers of smaller size. Since 1936 there has been a substantial trend away from the use of cotton bags to paper bags.

[5] Curtis Publishing Company, Advertising Department, *Leading Advertisers* (Philadelphia), annual editions.

TABLE 49

Estimated Value of Traceable Space and Time in Newspapers, Magazines, Farm
Journals, and Chain Radio Placed by the Sugar Industry, 1929–1939

Year	General Magazines	Newspapers	Farm Journals	Radio	Total
1929		$989,331		$ 60,515*	$1,049,846‡
1930		984,926		93,378	1,078,714‡
1931		809,467		187,350	996,817‡
1932		497,179		87,108	584,287‡
1933		379,378		122,164†	501,542‡
1934		473,271		60,300	533,571
1935		262,765			262,765
1936	$ 88,960	274,612			363,572§
1937	194,342	297,531	$5,612		497,485§
1938	38,000	288,065	2,575		328,640§
1939	12,682	202,085	3,587		218,354§

 * Extended from 8 months' data.
 † Extended from 11 months' data.
 ‡ Includes advertising by the Sugar Institute (Association of Sugar Refiners) as follows:
         1929—$469,944   1932—$9,045
         1930— 403,407   1933— 3,514
         1931— 220,408
 § Includes considerable expenditures by associations for public relations purposes. See Table 56.

Sources:
Magazines and farm journals: Publishers' Information Bureau, Inc., *National Advertising Records*, 1936–1939.
Radio: 1929 to 1933, inclusive, National Advertising Records, Inc., *National Advertising Records*; 1934, Publishers' Information Bureau, Inc., *National Advertising Records.*
Newspapers: Dollar figures for 1938 and 1939 from American Newspaper Publishers' Association, *Expenditures of National Advertisers.* Lineage, 1929 to 1939, from Media Records, Inc., *Newspapers and Newspaper Advertisers.* Conversion rate calculated from 1938 and 1939 data (32 cents per line) applied to other years. See Appendix IV regarding conversion rate.

company other than the American Sugar Refining Company then employed consumer space advertising.

The relatively large expenditures in the period 1929–1931 were accounted for by a cooperative advertising effort carried on under the auspices of the Sugar Institute, designed to offset attitudes then in vogue which were thought to be adverse to sugar consumption. There was current the fashion of the slim figure. Dieting had been given considerable attention in magazine articles. The American Tobacco Company had launched its program featuring the slogan, "Reach for a Lucky instead of a sweet." Numerous foods had advertised their nonfattening characteristics. Drug products also had featured appeals tying in with the vogue of the slim figure. Fearing the effect of such attitudes, the sugar refiners publicized offsetting appeals, as stated in *Printers' Ink* when the program was launched:

The Sugar Institute advertising copy will include not only the facts about the proper place of sugar in the diet but will also point out the harmful effects which frequently follow self-starvation by women and girls, and will emphasize the fact that properly balanced meals are essential for health and stamina . . . All the advertising will be submitted to the American Medical Association and other public health authorities before publication.[6]

The program was laid out to run for a five-year period, but substantial expenditures were made for only three years, 1929, 1930, and 1931. The advent of the depression and decreasing emphasis upon dieting and the slim figure led to the decision to reduce the program and finally to discontinue it after 1933.

In the years 1936 to 1939 inclusive, three separate groups in the sugar industry, the U. S. Cane Sugar Refiners, the U. S. Beet Sugar Refiners' Association, and the Hawaiian Sugar Planters' Association carried on magazine campaigns, the combined space expenditures of which were approximately $336,000. Of this amount almost $200,000 was spent in 1937.[7] The campaigns were not designed to increase sugar consumption, but were essentially public relations programs, undertaken to further the political interests of the respective groups. Accordingly, they had no appreciable effect upon demand and therefore are not given further consideration in this study.

All in all the amount of advertising of sugar has been very small when related to the size of the industry. For example, at the heyday of advertising in 1929, when traceable space expenditures amounted to over $1,000,000 and total advertising expenditures probably were near $2,000,000, the advertising probably represented about one-third of one per cent of the combined value of cane and beet sugar, which was reported as $602,000,000 for that year.[8] The exact percentages of sales devoted to advertising in 1939 for seven of the principal cane sugar refiners and five of the leading beet sugar refiners are available from reports of the Federal Trade Commission.[9] The average for the cane refiners was 0.21% and for the beet refiners was 0.09%. These figures indicate that the average for the whole sugar industry was probably well under 0.2% of sales in 1939. In terms of consumer purchases this expenditure represents less than one-hundreth of a cent for each pound of sugar consumed in the country.

The growth in consumption of sugar occurred in large part before

6 "Sugar Institute Starts National Advertising Campaign," *Printers' Ink*, February 21, 1929, pp. 57 and 58.

7 For detailed expenditures see Table 49, p. 278.

8 *Statistical Abstract of the United States, 1937*, p. 677.

9 U. S. Federal Trade Commission, Industrial Corporation Reports, *Cane Sugar Refining Corporations*, December 31, 1940, and *Beet Sugar Refining Corporations*, December 10, 1940.

the modest amount of consumer advertising above described was undertaken. As shown in Tables 50 and 51, there was a tenfold growth in sugar consumption in the century from 1830 to 1930. In 1830, per capita consumption amounted to only 12 pounds; by 1850 it had risen to 23 pounds; by 1900, which marked the earliest advent of any consumer promotion, to 70 pounds; and by 1920 to 100 pounds.

In short, until 1900 there was practically no advertising, and since that date, the amount of advertising devoted to sugar has been too

TABLE 50

SUGAR CONSUMPTION, SELECTED YEARS, 1830–1929 (IN TERMS OF RAW SUGAR)

YEAR	AVAILABLE FOR CONSUMPTION, TONS	PER CAPITA CONSUMPTION OF SUGAR, POUNDS	YEAR	AVAILABLE FOR CONSUMPTION, TONS	PER CAPITA CONSUMPTION OF SUGAR, POUNDS
1830	83,653	12.2	1880-84	1,243,449	46.5
1835	113,244	.....	1885-89	1,524,389	50.9
1840	128,612	14.1	1890-94	2,131,644	64.3
1845	201,586	.....	1895-99	2,264,380	62.2
1850	287,291	23.0	1900-04	2,875,638	71.7
1855	437,340	29.9	1905-09	3,483,547	78.9
1860	514,542	30.7	1910-14	4,101,356	85.6
1865	399,833	21.4	1915-19	4,280,668	83.2
1870-74	844,924	40.7	1920-24	5,782,790	104.5
1875-79	902,999	38.1	1925-29	6,658,207	111.8

Sources:
1830–1865—Willett & Gray, Inc., *Weekly Statistical Sugar Trade Journal* (New York), respective years. Long tons of Willett & Gray converted to short tons.
1870–1929—*Statistical Abstract of the United States, 1938*, p. 674.

TABLE 51

UNITED STATES CONSUMPTION OF FINISHED SUGAR AND PER CAPITA CONSUMPTION, 1925–1938

YEAR	U. S. CONSUMPTION, SHORT TONS (Refined Value) (Thousands)	POPULATION (Thousands)	PER CAPITA CONSUMPTION, POUNDS (Refined Value)
1925	6,140	114,867	106.91
1926	6,307	116,532	108.24
1927	6,018	118,197	101.83
1928	6,269	119,862	104.60
1929	6,318	121,526	103.98
1930	6,452	123,091	104.83
1931	6,231	124,113	100.41
1932	5,992	124,974	95.89
1933	5,999	125,770	95.40
1934	5,963	126,626	94.18
1935	6,248	127,521	97.99
1936	6,317	128,429	98.37
1937	6,278	129,257	97.34
1938	6,275	130,000 (est.)	96.54

Source: Myer Lynsky, *op. cit.*, (1938 edition), Table 1, p. 3.

small to have had any appreciable effect upon consumption. Beyond
these considerations, until the Sugar Institute campaign, the appeals
employed were chiefly selective, not primary. They were designed
to get consumer preference for the refiners' brands.

While the advertising undertaken by the Sugar Institute, which was
supported by other industries making large use of sugar, may have
had some effect in counteracting attitudes adverse to consumption,
there is no way of measuring to what extent this result occurred. As
a matter of fact, a perceptible downward trend in sugar consumption
(Table 51) occurring after 1926 was not noticeably affected by the
campaign. It must be recognized, however, that a heavy depression
set in just after the campaign got under way.

The reasons for the long-time increase in sugar consumption can
only be surmised. That a rising standard of living in this country
would bring a marked increase in consumption from the low levels
of the early nineteenth century seems apparent. Sugar directly satisfies
one of the elementary taste sensations. Accordingly, as technological
developments brought lower sugar costs and increased productivity
brought higher consumer incomes, it was to be expected that consumers would increase their consumption of sugar without exhorta-
tion from sellers. At the same time, part of the increased demand
was complementary to the increased consumption of other products.

TABLE 52

NET IMPORTS OF CERTAIN BEVERAGES IMPORTANT TO SUGAR CONSUMPTION, SELECTED
YEARS, 1830–1935 (POUNDS PER CAPITA)

YEAR	COFFEE	TEA	CHOCOLATE AND COCOA
1830...................	2.99	0.54	....
1840...................	5.04	0.99	....
1850...................	5.58	1.21	....
1851-1860..............	6.78	0.76	....
1861-1870..............	4.66	0.91	....
1871-1880..............	7.19	1.32	0.104
1881-1890..............	8.52	1.34	0.238
1891-1895..............	8.61	1.34	....
1896-1900..............	10.07	1.17	0.42
1901-1905..............	11.65	1.18	0.786
1906-1910..............	10.29	1.05	1.15
1911-1915..............	9.65	0.99	1.675
1916-1920..............	11.20*	1.03*	3.34
1921-1925..............	11.73	0.83	3.30
1926-1930..............	12.30	0.74	3.59
1931-1935..............	12.79	0.69	3.87

* Average, July 1, 1915–December 31, 1920.

Source: *Statistical Abstract of the United States, 1938*, pp. 679 and 680. Per capita
figures for chocolate and cocoa derived from quantity figures given.

For example, a marked increase in the consumption of coffee and chocolate (Table 52) entailed an increased use of sugar. Moreover, the development of a number of industries with increased consumption of their products brought a substantial industrial use of sugar. Particularly large has been the use of sugar in the confectionery, beverage, canning and preserving, and bakery products industries, as shown in Table 53. In recent years industrial use has accounted for approximately 30% of total cane and beet sugar consumption, as shown in Table 54.

TABLE 53

INDUSTRIAL CONSUMPTION OF BEET AND CANE SUGAR, 1929 AND 1937

INDUSTRY	1929			
	BEET AND CANE		BEET SUGAR	
	Quantities Tons Refined (Thousands)	Share of Usage, %	Quantities Tons Refined (Thousands)	Value (Thousands)
Beverages	102	5.8	6	$ 618
Bread and Bakery Products	489	27.6	145	14,453
Canning and Preserving	336	18.9	84	8,087
Chewing Gum	30	1.7	10	982
Chocolate and Cocoa Products	86	4.8	25	2,356
Confectionery	357	20.0	95	9,187
Dairy Products	117	6.6	20	1,992
Flavoring Extracts and Syrups	112	6.3	6	613
Food Products Not Elsewhere Classified	67	3.7	6	558
Tobacco Industries			1	98
Other Industries	79	4.6	2	19
Totals	1,775	100.0	399	$38,963

INDUSTRY	1937				
	CANE SUGAR		BEET AND CANE COMBINED		
	Quantities Tons Refined (Thousands)	Value (Thousands)	Quantities Tons Refined (Thousands)	Share of Usage, %	Value (Thousands)
Beverages	158	$ 15,512	164	8.6	$ 16,130
Bread and Bakery Products	390	38,439	536	28.0	52,892
Canning and Preserving	239	21,352	314	16.4	29,439
Chewing Gum	20	1,842	30	1.6	2,824
Chocolate and Cocoa Products	101	9,280	126	6.6	11,636
Confectionery	291	27,459	386	20.2	36,646
Dairy Products	50	4,930	71	3.7	6,922
Flavoring Extracts and Syrups	161	15,950	167	8.7	16,563
Food Products Not Elsewhere Classified	91	8,559	97	5.1	9,117
Tobacco Industries	19	1,552	20	1.0	1,650
Other Industries	1	136	2	.1	155
Totals	1,512	$145,012	1,913	100.0	$183,975

Source: Myer Lynsky, *op. cit.*, 1939 Supplement, Table 7b, p. 311.

TABLE 54

HOUSEHOLD DOMESTIC AND INDUSTRIAL CONSUMPTION OF SUGAR, 1929 AND 1937

CONSUMPTION	1929		1937	
	QUANTITY, TONS	%	QUANTITY, TONS	%
Industrial......................	1,775,000	28.1	1,913,000	30.4
Household Domestic..............	4,543,000	71.9	4,378,000	69.6
Total United States...........	6,318,000	100.0	6,291,000	100.0

Source: Myer Lynsky, *op. cit.*, compiled from 1938 edition, Table 1, p. 3, and 1939 Supplement, Table 7b, p. 311.

The increasing consumption of sugar was favored by a lowering of cost, brought in large part by technological developments. In 1742 sugar was priced at $2.75 a pound in England.[10] Early methods of sugar production were crude, but time has wrought many and important refinements in methods. In 1830 the spread in price between raw and refined sugar was 10 cents a pound; by 1876 this spread had been reduced to 3 cents a pound; since 1895 it has been in the neighborhood of 1 cent a pound. The full wholesale price of refined sugar in recent years has been less than one-half the amount of the spread between the prices of raw and refined sugar as of 1830. Low prices have favored heavy consumption. Prices since 1895 are shown in Table 55.

From the above survey of demand growth, the small use of advertising, and price data, it is concluded that advertising has not been an appreciable factor in the expansion of sugar consumption.

THE EFFECT OF ADVERTISING UPON SELECTIVE DEMAND

To what extent has advertising been effective in influencing selective demand among the various refiners for granulated cane sugar, a product so nearly standardized? As a result of study of case histories secured from five refining organizations and from discussions with sugar brokers, it is concluded that advertising has had a relatively small effect in guiding selective demand. It has produced no brand preference strong enough to bring a differential in price to the

---

[10] L. A. Wills, "The Sugar Industry," Ch. XIV in *The Development of American Industries*, J. G. Glover and W. B. Cornell, Editors (New York, Prentice-Hall, Inc., 1932), pp. 269 and 270.

TABLE 55

YEARLY AVERAGE QUOTATIONS SUGAR PRICES, SELECTED YEARS 1895–1939
(IN CENTS PER POUND)

YEAR	RAW—96 DEGREE CENTRIFUGAL DUTY PAID—NEW YORK	REFINED—GRANULATED NET CASH	SPREAD
1895	3.270	4.152	0.882
1900	4.566	5.320	0.754
1904	3.974	4.772	0.798
1909	4.007	4.765	0.758
1914	3.814	4.683	0.869
1919	7.724	9.003	1.279
1921	4.763	6.207	1.444
1923	7.020	8.441	1.421
1925	4.334	5.483	1.149
1927	4.730	5.828	1.098
1929	3.769	5.025	1.256
1931	3.329	4.425	1.096
1933	3.208	4.308	1.100
1935	3.217	4.302	1.085
1936	3.595	4.660	1.065
1937	3.449	4.567	1.118
1938	2.940	3.948	1.008
1939	2.989	4.032	1.043

Source: Willett & Gray, Inc., *Weekly Statistical Sugar Trade Journal,* respective years.

advertised brands, as has been true of the other products selected for study. There is some evidence, however, that consumers have more readily accepted known brands of sugar than those unknown. There is further evidence that advertising has been of some help in influencing the trade to stock advertised brands. At least, some refiners have deemed a relatively small appropriation worth while as a means of trying to gain these ends. They have believed that the sale of packaged, branded sugar is likely to be somewhat more stable than the sale of bulk sugar and that a limited appropriation to increase their sales of packaged, branded items is worth while. Other refiners, however, have reached other conclusions and have rejected advertising as a management tool to influence sales.

The Extent of Advertising of Brands

The amount expended for advertising by the various refineries, so far as it can be traced and estimated for the period 1929–1939 is contained in Table 56. The table cannot be deemed a full and accurate record of space advertising, for it is believed that small expenditures by certain refiners, particularly beet sugar refiners, do not appear. Yet the record is complete enough to indicate the small and sporadic character of space advertising activity. Since 1915, the American Sugar

Refining Company has been a consistent advertiser of both its Domino brand and its Franklin brand. The National Sugar Refining Company launched its program of consumer space advertising in 1927 and for the period covered by the table has been the largest space advertiser. So far as the records show, no other refiners have been consistent advertisers to consumers. Some, as shown in the table, have advertised sporadically, others not included in the table have employed no consumer space advertising. Since the sales operations of all refiners are regional, space advertising has been conducted mostly in newspapers. The small percentages of sales devoted to advertising by refiners have already been cited.

Effect of Brand Advertising

First of all, brand advertising and promotion have enabled no brand to obtain a price differential. Such was the testimony of every sugar man interviewed. Traditionally, competition in the sugar industry has been centered upon price. The base price, that for a 100-pound bag of standard granulated sugar, has been subject to frequent change. Roughly it follows the fluctuations in the price of raw sugar. The chance to make a trading profit on price fluctuations has led the trade to make purchases largely on days of price moves. A price initiated by any refiner ordinarily is met by other refiners within 24 hours. No refiner, according to the testimony obtained, has attempted to get a differential above competitors, either for his bulk sugar or for his branded sugar. The price of packaged granulated sugar has been quoted in terms of a differential above the base price. The size of the differential has approximated package costs, and different refiners always have met competitive prices on package items.

It was testified further that sugar buyers take advantage of any opportunity to buy at a price advantage, even if it means trade with sources other than those usually patronized. A broker cited the instance of a refinery which reentered a certain market, after having dropped out for some months, with a price 5 cents below that of other refiners. It immediately secured a substantial volume of orders in spite of the fact that it had done no advertising and had not made substantial efforts to establish strong personal relations with wholesalers and retailers. All executives interviewed stated that price in the sugar industry has been and is the most important determinant in the flow of trade. So long as prices are met, however, then competition turns upon per-

TABLE 56

ESTIMATED VALUE OF TRACEABLE SPACE AND TIME ADVERTISING IN NEWSPAPERS, MAGAZINES, FARM JOURNALS, AND CHAIN RADIO PLACED BY SUGAR REFINERS AND ASSOCIATIONS OF REFINERS 1929–1939

Company or Brand	1929	1930	1931	1932	1933	1934	1935	1936	1937	1938	1939
American Sugar—Domino	$152,828	$129,818	$144,984	$64,627	$52,442	$94,786	$78,751	$75,678	$34,731	$170,685	$70,583
American Sugar—Franklin	24,360	23,668	11,867	16,515	11,199	27,188	19,909	15,263	22,910	33,081	14,405
California and Hawaiian			110,351	74,124			5,144				
Dixie Crystals			12,415		10,744	14,221	16,836		3,463		
Godchaux Sugar		35,818	14,966								
Hawaiian Sugar Planters' Assoc.	39,254	59,346	32,583		3,246	23,620	4,933	20,685	83,842	42,700	10,212
Imperial Sugar								18,148	27,721	2,575	2,194
National Sugar, Jack Frost	323,277	421,589	380,292	382,306	403,609	286,906	113,195	128,775	150,192	122,299	85,888
Quaker Sugar								12,855	34,433		
Sea Isle			67,304	36,167							
Snow Flake	3,222										
Spreckel's	8,166	10,664									
Sunny Cane						22,805	23,997	23,893	21,600		
Utah and Idaho Sugar									5,993		1,393
Sugar Institute	498,739	397,811	222,055	8,977	3,514						
Farmers and Mfr's Beet Sugar Association						39,025					
Cane Sugar Industry					16,788	25,020					33,959
U. S. Beet Sugar Association				1,571				68,275	64,500		
U. S. Cane Sugar Refiners									46,000		
Total	$1,049,846	$1,078,714	$996,817	$584,287	$501,542	$533,571	$262,765	$363,572	$497,485	$328,640	$218,354

Sources:

Magazine and farm journals: Publishers' Information Bureau, Inc., *National Advertising Records.*

Radio: 1929 to 1933, inclusive, National Advertising Records, Inc., *National Advertising Records;* 1934, Publishers' Information Bureau, Inc., *National Advertising Records.*

Newspapers: Dollar figures for 1938 and 1939 from American Newspaper Publishers' Association, *Expenditures of National Advertisers.* Line-age, 1929 to 1939 from Media Records, Inc., *Newspapers and Newspaper Advertisers.* Conversion rate calculated from 1938 and 1939 data (32 cents per line) applied to other years. See Appendix IV.

sonal friendship, upon the ability of a seller to give service, and last of all upon the strength of brand acceptance in the market.

The importance of price in the wholesale market has been carried into the retail market and has there operated against strong brand influence. Sugar has been one of the favorite sales leaders among retailers with the customary featuring of price. One refiner estimated that sugar has accounted for 6% of the average retailer's sales and for some 12% of wholesalers' sales; yet he stated that the keen price competition within the trade has reduced margins to a point where net profit has been eliminated.

No evidence from consumer surveys as to strength of consumer preferences for brands of sugar was made available, although one advertising refiner stated that surveys made by his advertising agency indicated that preferences were weak.

An advertising test made by another advertiser was also inconclusive, but the sales results seemed to be more dependent upon personalities in the market than upon the advertising that was done. The test was carried on in two areas, one of which had been less productive of sales than the other. During the course of the year, 35 advertisements were run in the weak area. In the strong area, only 26 advertisements of similar size were run.[11] At the end of the year, sales revealed a 19% increase in the weak area and a 6% decrease in the strong area. While these results on their face would indicate that the more intense advertising schedule had had greater effect upon sales than the lighter schedule, an analysis of the two areas made by the sales department indicated that other more powerful factors were at work. In the area where sales had increased it was found that a certain broker, for reasons not connected with the advertising program, had switched from a competing company to the advertised brand, and as a result certain important wholesalers who were friendly to the broker had also switched to the advertised brand. In the area where sales decreased, a popular salesman had died, and one of the refiner's well-known broker representatives had gone out of business.

Almost invariably those interviewed testified that distributors were far more important in determining the brands of sugar sold in a com-

---

[11] The test was likely to be inconclusive, even had variables other than advertising held relatively constant, because the difference in use of advertising in the two areas was probably not large enough to have appeared in current sales figures.

munity than were consumers. The fact that the trade might change the brands of sugar handled without any apparent reaction from consumers was indicated by the case of one refiner who temporarily adopted in a large city market a certain sales policy which alienated dealers. As a result, a substantial number of wholesalers and retailers in that area switched to a competing brand and had since stayed with competing brands to a large degree. Consumer preferences were not strong enough to stop the switch. It was the opinion of those interviewed, however, that the company which had lost sales would not be precluded from regaining its former place in this market because consumers had bought other brands in the meantime; they would accept the company's brand if retailers offered it.

Further evidence of the unimportance of brand to consumers was the small number of brands which retailers find it advisable to carry. For example, in 1935 in Greater Milwaukee there were nine brands of packaged sugar being consumed. Only 1½% of the retailers sampled were found to handle as many as three brands. Sixteen per cent handled only two brands, while 65% handled only one brand; 18% at the time of the survey were not handling packaged sugar.[12]

From what has been said above it should not be inferred that brand is meaningless in the selling of granulated sugar. Invariably those interviewed stated that in certain markets there was some evidence of brand preference. The instance most frequently cited was that of Arbuckle sugar, sold in certain portions of West Virginia, Ohio, and Kentucky. One informant, a broker, stated that when Arbuckle sugar was out of that market for a short time a few years ago, dealers offered as much as 10 cents a hundred pounds over the regular market price in their effort to get Arbuckle packaged sugar to satisfy their consumers' preference. The strength of this brand was attributed to early development of packaged sugar sales in the areas by Arbuckle salesmen, who had previously built up substantial sales of Arbuckle coffee. Their favorable relationships with the trade enabled them to secure excellent distribution for Arbuckle sugar. The distinctive Arbuckle package, carrying a picture of Brooklyn Bridge, then became so well-known in that market that an unusual consumer preference for the brand developed. Among the sugar men interviewed, several mentioned the fact that certain consumers recognized and evidently

---

[12] *The Milwaukee Journal,* "Consumer Analysis of the Greater Milwaukee Market," 1935.

preferred packages which were known to them. In addition to this incident, it was reported that in certain areas consumers asked for sugar in the yellow package, referring to the Domino brand.

Further evidence that brand names on granulated sugar mean something was found in the testimony of one refiner who was opening new markets. He stated that in his experience chain stores ordinarily had given preference to brands which were generally accepted and known by consumers. Thus he found it difficult to sell his packaged sugar to chain stores until after he had attained distribution through independent outlets and the brand had become known in the community. In some instances the company used space advertising when opening up new markets.

Evidence of the possible value of brand promotion was found in the fact that the refineries which have been consistent advertisers of branded sugar have been successful in attaining the objective of getting a substantial percentage of their total sales of sugar to householders in branded packages rather than in bulk. Evidence as to their objective and their success in attaining this objective is contained in the following excerpts from Annual Reports of the American Sugar Refining Company:

1913: Believing that the demand for sugar in packages was a growing one, the company has in recent years appropriati d considerable sums for the purpose of advertising such sugars under the Crystal Domino and other brands, as well as a new brand of table syrup. As a result, the package business of the company is showing very satisfactory growth. (p. 7.)

1921: During the last three years [1919–1921] our package products have constituted about half of the production of the company which goes to the households of the country. (p. 12.)

1923: In 1923 we sold nearly 600,000,000 pounds of package sugar. (p. 16.)

1924: Our package business has shown a healthy growth during 1924 in which year these sales amounted to over 625,000,000 pounds. (p. 8.)

1927: About one-half of the sugar refined by the company which reached the household in 1927 was in package form under the trade names Domino and Franklin. It amounted to almost 750,000,000 pounds. (p. 16.)

1929: We delivered over 800,000,000 pounds of Domino and Franklin package sugars, a record for all time, but about an equal quantity of our sugar still goes in bulk form to the households. (p. 9.)

1931: Our Domino and Franklin package sugars continue to make steady increases in volume. (p. 14.)

1932: Our Domino and Franklin package sugars have held their volume notwithstanding the decline in our meltings. (p. 17.)

It is believed that the American Sugar Refining Company has prob-ably succeeded in getting a larger percentage of its sales in package form than have other refiners.

Refiners' Desire for Trade Support

In view of the slight pull that can be obtained from brands on packaged sugar, the question may be raised as to why certain refiners have followed the policy of advertising. The answer lies in the belief of the managements that even a relatively small expenditure has been of value in helping to obtain support from brokers, wholesalers, and retailers, that otherwise would be lacking.

As noted above, all those interviewed in the sugar trade agreed that the determination of selective demand rested largely with the trade. This influence over selective demand rests in part with brokers, in large part with wholesalers, and in part with retailers. Since these distributors have had so much influence over selective demand, the promotional efforts of refiners have been directed primarily to them.

Most sugar has been sold through two types of brokers: the gen-eral sugar broker and the exclusive brokerage representative. The general broker has sold the sugar of all refiners in a market. Accord-ingly wholesalers, chains, or large retailers buying through a general broker have specified the brand desired. The exclusive broker has represented one sugar refiner only, although he usually has also rep-resented producers of other food items. Since he has sold only one brand of sugar he has been in a position through his personal follow-ing in the market to have considerable influence in guiding sales to the brand.

Since wholesalers and retailers have been in a position to deter-mine the brands they carried, practically all refiners were found to direct the greater part of their promotion to them. Each had a mis-sionary salesforce whose duty it was to call upon wholesalers and retailers to develop friendly relations, thereby trying to induce them to specify the refiner's brand when buying through a general broker or to buy through the refiner's exclusive brokerage representative. When calling upon retailers, the missionary men in many instances solicited orders to be placed through a wholesaler. For those retailers who were already handling their brand they arranged displays and gave other services that might be helpful. It was found, however, that the refiner's representatives usually were careful to get a wholesaler's permission to seek orders for their brands for his account. According to some refiners, failure to do this might lead to difficulties because many times wholesalers refused to accept orders for a brand of sugar not currently carried in stock.

Advertising of a brand in any market has provided a sales argument for the personal selling representatives discussed above. Apparently both wholesalers and retailers have been aware of the relative unimportance of sugar brands and have appreciated their freedom to carry such brands as they desired. On the other hand, distributors have been brand conscious and generally have been responsive to the argument that advertising and promotional help was given by manufacturers. Some managements have evidently felt that an expenditure upon consumer advertising was worth while, particularly in view of the fact that the outlay represented a very small percentage of sales value. It necessarily has had to be small because the margins available for promotion have been narrow.

It was generally agreed that such brand consciousness as has been established applied only to packaged items; it has not carried over to bulk sugar sold to householders. On the other hand, the acceptance of a brand in any market on packaged items has offered at least a small degree of stability in demand which otherwise probably would have been lacking. To the extent that a wholesaler or retailer has been inclined to favor a brand acceptable in the market, he has been likely also to place his purchases of bulk sugar with the same refinery.

On the basis of confidential case histories from a number of refineries, both advertisers and nonadvertisers, it was concluded that advertising was more likely to be used by large refiners than by small. Sugar refining has involved large overhead costs. Consequently it has been highly desirable from a standpoint of attaining profit for a refinery to operate as near to capacity as possible. Large refiners, in order to get full utilization of the large plants which they have built, have found it advisable not only to reach wider markets than have small refiners, but also to develop their markets intensively. As one means of getting business they have offered a full line of sugars. Some of the large refiners have produced as many as 150 items, distributed among some 50 types of sugars. Besides the items in most common demand they have produced various specialties not offered by small refineries because the latter have not been able to produce economically the small quantities of such items as they could sell in their restricted markets. Accordingly the large refiners have given to wholesale and retail customers the advantage of placing orders for a full line of merchandise in one place.

A full line also has provided an advantage for advertising. Since a family brand can be used to cover a wide variety of items, volume has been large enough to make the unit advertising cost small.

In contrast, some of the small refiners have offset the advantages described above with other advantages designed to gain patronage. Often, as local enterprises, they have had local prestige and strong personal contacts not enjoyed by distant refiners. Moreover, they often have held out excellent service of one kind or another as a bid for patronage. Being in a position by these means to gain the volume needed for low cost operation, they have not felt the need of offering full lines of packaged merchandise or of publicizing their brands.

There was lack of agreement among those consulted as to whether the packaged items offered any greater margin above manufacturing costs than did bulk sugar. The price of packaged items has been quoted in terms of a differential above the base price of standard granulated sugar in 100-pound bags. These price differentials have been determined in large part by the production and packaging costs involved. The price differentials have not been constant but have varied from time to time. For example, the differential received on granulated sugar packaged in 2-pound and 5-pound cartons increased from 50 cents per 100 pounds to 60 cents per 100 pounds between the years 1914 and 1924, an increase attributable to increased costs of packaging and overhead. By January, 1928, this price differential had been reduced to 50 cents per 100 pounds, and by January, 1929, to 35 cents. Between the last named date and January, 1939, there were occasional fluctuations above and below the 35-cent figure. In times of severe depression consumers were less inclined to pay the necessary differential to get packaged sugar. In order to keep their volume of packaged sugar, certain refiners shaded the differential and this price shading was immediately met by other refiners. At other times, the differential widened somewhat above the usual figure. There was lack of agreement as to whether the differential obtained more than covered the costs involved. Some maintained that packaged sugar afforded no more profit than the bulk; others expressed the view that in the long run it gave a slightly greater margin.

To summarize, it is concluded that sugar affords an excellent example of a product for which advertising has been used in only a small degree by producers because competing brands have not given to the consumer enough differentiation to lead him to pay a price differential for any of them. Yet the influence of brand has been large enough to lead all refiners to put their brand name on the product for what it may be worth, and for some to expend a very small fraction of the sales value upon advertising for the influence it might have on consumers and upon the trade. Advertising has probably had some influence in shifting the demand of household consumers from bulk to package sugar.

Chapter XI

THE EFFECT OF ADVERTISING ON THE
DEMAND FOR DENTIFRICES

THERE are several reasons why dentifrices are included in this study. They represent a product for which advertising is an important element in determination of consumer values. There are many brands on the market, but probably as much as 90% of the demand goes to a dozen brands which are heavily advertised, even though they sell at prices above many unadvertised brands. The total dentifrice advertising bill in recent years has varied apparently from $10,000,000 to $15,000,000, while retail sales were from $40,-000,000 to $55,000,000.[1] Thus, it will be seen that advertising is a large element in product price cost. In terms of manufacturers' selling price, advertising and promotional expenditure for advertised brands is believed to average about 40% of their net sales, or about 25% of retail selling price. Even though personal selling costs are low, the spread between the manufacturing cost and the retail selling price is wide.

In view of this marketing set-up there have been conflicting opinions with regard to the part played by advertising. On the one hand, advertising has been praised as a means of inculcating and keeping alive among a large segment of the population the desirable practice of care of the teeth. On the other hand, advertising has been attacked because of the heavy cost it involves and the type of persuasive appeals used. Critics maintain that consumers have been led to pay too great a price for reputation and persuasion. These conflicting views regarding the effects of the heavy advertising of dentifrices led to its choice for study.

EFFECT OF ADVERTISING ON PRIMARY DEMAND

Just how extensive the teeth-cleaning habit is in the United States is not exactly known. One view widely accepted assumes a large part of the population to be nonusers. For example, in 1936 an article

---

[1] For the bases of these estimates see Chapter XI, p. 300.

in *Fortune* relating to one of the large dentifrice producers stated, "The soap trade ruefully admits that only 50% of the people in the United States use either tooth paste or tooth powder. And only 5% more brush their teeth with toilet soap or baking soda. The rest, around 45% of the population, do without tooth brushes altogether."[2] Again, a dentist writing in *Physical Culture,* August, 1938, stated: "Less than 25% of our fellow citizens ever use a tooth brush."

Such estimates of tooth brushing are probably far from the actual situation in recent years. A leading market researcher, who has conducted surveys for a dentifrice manufacturer, gave the author the following statement: "I have checked with many others who have surveyed among consumers, from the top to pretty low down, if not absolute bottom. We all agree that somewhere around 90% use dentifrices of some kind."

This estimate from consumer surveys made by dentifrice manufacturers is in agreement with surveys made by newspapers and magazines. For example, the Scripps-Howard survey among some 53,000 housewives in 16 cities, found that 89.4% of the families interviewed had either tooth paste, tooth powder, or both on hand. Curiously, only 69% of the homes were reported as having tooth brushes.[3]

Likewise, surveys over a number of years by *The Milwaukee Journal* among families in greater Milwaukee, have indicated a use of tooth paste or tooth powder among more than 90% of the families supplying information, as shown in Table 57. The amount of duplication among homes using more than one type of dentifrice is not shown in the *Journal* surveys, but it will be noted that for surveys through 1934 over 90% of the families reported use of tooth paste. Accordingly it is assumed that in 1938–1940, following a shift in form of dentifrice used, either tooth paste, tooth powder, or liquid dentifrice was used in over 90% of the homes. Surveys in the years 1937, 1938, and 1939 showed that 99.5% of the families had tooth brushes.

Time[4] in 1932 conducted a bathroom inventory survey covering one family in every six in Appleton, Wisconsin, with interviews distributed among all income groups determined by sworn income tax returns of heads of families. The survey showed 1,778 tubes of tooth paste on hand among every 1,000 families with incomes under $5,000, and 2,461

[2] "Colgate-Palmolive-Peet," *Fortune,* April, 1936, p. 144.

[3] Scripps-Howard Newspapers, *Market Records,* "Buying Habits and Brand Preferences of Consumers in Sixteen Cities," 1938, Vol. I, p. 206 ff.

[4] "Markets by Incomes" (*Time,* Inc., New York, 1932), Vol. I, pp. 70, 71.

tubes in every 1,000 households with incomes over $5,000. Corresponding figures for tooth powder were 359 cans in every 1,000 homes with incomes under $5,000, and 764 cans in every 1,000 homes with incomes over $5,000. Each 1,000 families with incomes under $5,000 were found to have 3,750 tooth brushes, while a like number with incomes of $5,000 or more had 4,478 brushes. As the data are reported it is impossible to determine the number of nonusing families.

These surveys do not provide fully satisfactory data regarding usage; they are urban only. In addition they relate to families and not to individuals. Moreover, it is not certain that they were based on a true cross section of the city markets from which they came, particularly among homes in the lowest income brackets; yet they

TABLE 57

SURVEYS OF CONSUMER PURCHASES OF DENTIFRICES AND TOOTH BRUSHES
BY "THE MILWAUKEE JOURNAL" AMONG FAMILIES IN GREATER
MILWAUKEE MARKET, 1924, 1929, 1934, 1938, 1940

	1924	1929	1934	1938	1940
Tooth Paste, Total Number Brands in Use...........	95	70	102	83	83
% of Families Reporting Use.....................	94.7	95.3	91.8	65.0	59.2
Tooth Powders, Total Number Brands in Use........	41	36	47	76	66
% of Families Reporting Use.....................	9.2	7.0	17.5	57.3	52.4
Liquid Dentifrices, Total Brands in Use.............					9
% of Families Reporting Use......................					22.9
Tooth Brushes, Total Number Brands in Use........				184	
% of Families Reporting Use......................				99.5	

Source: *The Milwaukee Journal,* "Consumer Analysis, Greater Milwaukee Market," annual editions.

were presented as having reached all classes and they were large enough in number to be at least indicative of the extent of use of dentifrices by families in urban markets. Again, they do not show the frequency of use of dentifrices. Nevertheless, from these studies and the testimony of the market researcher referred to above, it seems clear that a very large majority of the population are now users of dentifrices in some form.

While survey data show use of dentifrices by a high percentage of families, the per capita consumption, as computed from the reports of the *U. S. Census of Manufactures,* indicates that many of the families having dentifrices on hand either use substitute products in considerable degree or that many individuals in the family do not wash their teeth frequently. Many consumers may use some form of mouth wash instead, for *The Milwaukee Journal* surveys in recent years have shown about 60% of homes as users of mouth wash. Others use substitutes, such as salt, baking soda, soap, or just plain water. As shown in Table 58, per capita consumption over a 13-year period has ranged from 21 cents to 28 cents at manufacturers' wholesale prices, sums representing retail expenditures from 32 cents to 43 cents. The usual retail prices of leading brands in recent years have been in the neighborhood of 40 cents for tubes of paste varying in weight from 2 ounces to 4 ounces and for cans of powder weighing in the neighborhood of 5 ounces. Accordingly, the annual per capita consumption has been about one tube of tooth paste or one can of powder, amounts far below what would be consumed by a steady user of either form of dentifrice.[5] When the census figures of dentifrice production are divided by the number of persons between the

TABLE 58

DENTIFRICE PRODUCTION AND INDICATED PER CAPITA CONSUMPTION, BIENNIALLY, 1925–1937

YEAR	MANUFACTURERS' WHOLESALE VALUE OF PRODUCT	INDICATED PER CAPITA CONSUMPTION	
		Wholesale Value	Retail Value, Estimated
1925	$25,736,068	$0.22	$0.34
1927	30,692,834	0.26	0.40
1929	32,463,698	0.27	0.42
1931	35,699,132	0.28	0.43
1933	25,956,856	0.21	0.32
1935	29,722,047	0.23	0.35
1937	35,559,134	0.27	0.42

Sources:

Value of product: 1927, 1933, 1935, 1937, U. S. Biennial Census of Manufactures.

Per capita consumption: Manufacturers' value divided by annual midyear estimates of population of U. S. Bureau of the Census.

Retail value: Manufacturers' wholesale value taken as 65% to derive retail value. Percentage determined from survey of selling prices of leading brands as related to manufacturers' selling prices.

ages of 5 and 65 years who more nearly represent potential dentifrice users, the resulting figures of per capita consumption do not change the conclusion materially.[6] For 1937 the per capita consumption of

[5] It is estimated that a steady user of tooth paste consumes about six regular-size tubes a year. The quantity of powder or of liquid dentifrice consumed in any period is less than that of paste.

[6] Approximately 85% of the population falls in the age classification of 5 years to 65 years.

this group of potential users would have been 50 cents at retail, representing roughly 1¼ tubes of tooth paste or 1¼ cans of powder. Thus it is apparent that although the use of tooth brushes and of dentifrice has become widespread, the amount of commercial dentifrice consumed does not represent heavy individual use on the average.

Although dentifrices have been advertised since the Civil War, consumption on the scale indicated in the preceding paragraph is of recent development. In the *Census of Manufactures* reports, dentifrices have for many years been a part of the classification "perfumes, cosmetics, and other toilet preparations." Not until 1925 was the value of dentifrice production given separately, in which year it was $25,700,000. Since 1925, dentifrices have represented from 17% to 27% of the value of "perfumes, cosmetics, and toilet preparations," reported in the various censuses. Inasmuch as the value of this entire classification was only $16,900,000 in 1914, and dentifrice value probably, though not certainly, was not more than a fourth of the total, it is clear that dentifrice production was relatively small in that year as compared with 1925. The high point in production for which figures are available came in 1931, when the manufactured value was approximately $35,700,000. Consequently it appears that the heavy development of the dentifrice market occurred in the period between 1914 and 1931.

The Advertising of Dentifrices

This period of increased consumption corresponded with the period of heavy increase in the use of advertising for dentifrices. Hence, it seems fair to assume that advertising was an important factor in stimulating the practice of brushing teeth. In the last decade, however, advertising has had no appreciable effect on per capita consumption, nor did it stem the marked decrease in consumption during the years of heavy depression. Supporting data for this conclusion follow.

Dentifrice advertising apparently began about the time of the Civil War. Presbrey, in *The History and Development of Advertising,* gives this account of early dentifrice advertising.

To the people of the 1870's and '80's Sozodont, manufactured by Hall & Ruckel of Brooklyn, N. Y., was in a measure what Kolynos, Forhan's, Ipana, Pepsodent, Mu-Sol-Dent and other latter-day dentifrices are to the people of 1928. Beginning in Civil War days and continuing through the '70's, the name Sozodont appeared everywhere on the landscape. A sample of its enterprise was the lettering of "Sozodont" on Maiden's Rock, near Redwing, Minn., in a size which made the name visible to Mississippi River steamboat passengers when they were three miles away. There was just the name—nothing more. Magazine advertising began in 1880, and the smiling Sozodont Girl in 56-line space was one of the surest items to be found in the religious weeklies and in the Century, Harper's and Scribner's in that decade. The personal attractiveness which white teeth gave was the copy appeal. Zonweiss Tooth Cream used full pages in the monthly magazines in competition with Sozodont's quarter pages, but was not so systematic in schedule. In the late '80's Rubifoam, "deliciously flavored," joined with quarter pages in suggesting the desirability of a clean mouth and good teeth, and a little later Dr. Lyon's Tooth Powder, an advertiser in small space since the '60's, began to appear regularly in quarter-pages in the standard magazines. The attitude of the masses of the people toward dentifrices as late as the '90's was expressed by a reporter for *Printers' Ink* in 1897 when he interviewed the advertising manager of Sozodont and referred to the product as "an article of luxury."

Development of truly large-scale advertising by dentifrices was slower than in some other lines. As late as 1916 expenditures of six dentifrice manufacturers in general magazines amounted to only $236,000. A few years later it came with a rush, however. Toothbrush manufacturers lagged behind the dentifrice makers both in start and volume.[7]

That there was a marked increase in dentifrice advertising after World War I is shown in Table 59, which gives a record of advertising expenditures for dentifrices in leading magazines. In 1914, three advertisers spent $132,000 in magazines; in 1919 there were six advertisers, with an expenditure of some $840,000; but during the '20's there was a rapid growth, with some ten magazine advertisers spending in 1926, 1927, and 1928 well in excess of $3,000,000 annually.

TABLE 59

ADVERTISING EXPENDITURES FOR DENTIFRICES IN LEADING MAGAZINES, 1914–1928

YEAR	NUMBER OF ADVERTISERS REPRESENTED	EXPENDITURES	YEAR	NUMBER OF ADVERTISERS REPRESENTED	EXPENDITURES
1914.........	3	$ 132,278	1922.........	9	$1,516,567
1915.........	4	142,301	1923.........	8	1,756,549
1916.........	4	136,474	1924.........	7	1,993,460
1917.........	7	381,178	1925.........	9	2,643,087
1918.........	5	552,526	1926.........	10	3,419,332
1919.........	6	843,238	1927.........	9	3,382,078
1920.........	10	1,461,162	1928.........	9	3,298,062
1921.........	10	1,430,131	....	....	....

Source: Curtis Publishing Company, Advertising Department, *Leading Advertisers* (Philadelphia), 1914–1928.

[7] Frank Presbrey, *The History and Development of Advertising* (New York, Doubleday, Doran & Company, Inc., 1929), pp. 402–403.

TABLE 60

ESTIMATED VALUE OF TRACEABLE SPACE AND TIME ADVERTISING EXPENDITURES
FOR DENTIFRICES IN NEWSPAPERS, MAGAZINES, FARM JOURNALS AND
CHAIN RADIO, 1929–1939

YEAR	GENERAL MAGAZINES	NEWSPAPERS	FARM JOURNALS	CHAIN RADIO	TOTAL
1929	$4,801,312	$2,558,473	$30,593*	$ 447,574†	$7,837,952
1930	4,848,314	1,433,757	21,740‡	1,566,164	7,869,975
1931	4,503,944	1,461,528	23,500	1,252,646	7,241,618
1932	3,539,584	1,140,941	20,790	1,363,997	6,065,312
1933	3,131,962	1,020,042	54,423	1,884,159‡	6,090,586
1934	2,662,522	1,102,567	90,746	2,344,568	6,200,403
1935	2,089,800	1,641,575	28,595	2,398,224	6,158,194
1936	2,356,375	2,039,024	97,353§	2,308,497†	6,801,249
1937	3,672,846	2,204,777	58,469	2,862,938	9,099,030
1938	2,830,639	1,881,599	40,115	2,285,308	7,037,661
1939	2,916,775	1,545,320	25,624	3,545,257	8,032,976

* Extended from 10 months.
† Extended from 8 months.
‡ Extended from 11 months.
§ Extended from 9 months.

Sources:

1929 Magazines: Crowell Publishing Company, *National Markets and National Advertising.*

1929–1933, 1935–1936 Radio and Farm Journals: National Advertising Records, Inc., *National Advertising Records.*

1930–1936 Magazines: Curtis Publishing Company, *Leading Advertisers.*

1934 Radio and Farm Journals: Publishers' Information Bureau, Inc., *National Advertising Records.*

1937, 1938 Magazines, Radio, and Farm Journals: Publishers' Information Bureau, Inc., *National Advertising Records.*

1938–1939 Newspapers: Dollar figures from American Newspaper Publishers' Association, *Expenditures of National Advertisers.*

1929–1939 linage from Media Records, Inc. *Newspapers and Newspaper Advertisers'* conversion rate of 43 cents per line, calculated from 1938–1939 data, was applied to other years. See Appendix IV regarding conversion rate.

1939: American Newspaper Publishers' Association, *Expenditures of National Advertisers.*

A more complete picture of advertising expenditures in leading media is shown in Table 60, in which are given estimated values of traceable time and space expenditures for newspapers, magazines, farm journals, and chain radio. Figures during this period range from $6,000,000 in the depression year of 1933 to $9,000,000 in 1937.

A study of individual advertising budgets of dentifrices and other toiletries leads to the belief that such space costs probably represent about 60% of the total advertising expenditure. Accordingly the estimated total advertising expenditure during the period varied from about $10,000,000 in 1933 to approximately $15,000,000 in 1937. The estimated advertising cost thus determined in census years represents 38% of the manufactured value of the product, or almost 25% of the retail price.[8]

---

[8] Retail sales in 1937 are estimated to have been in the neighborhood of $55,000,000. This estimate was based on the assumption that the manufacturer's price was 65% of retail price, an assumption based on study of a confidential report of trade margins and retail prices covering a large number of brands.

Relationship of Advertising to Primary Demand Growth

As with all the other products studied, it is impossible to say with certainty how much the marked increase in consumption of dentifrices evident in census data of 1914 and 1931 was the result of the heavy programs of advertising that were initiated after World War I. Advertising was not the only generator of favorable consumer attitudes towards tooth care during this period. As is true in most instances of increasing volumes, dentifrice manufacturers rode with a demand tide in part generated by themselves but impelled also by widespread education coming from a number of sources.

The belief that the teeth are an important adjunct to personal beauty has existed immemorially.[9] Explorers have found some of the most primitive people using rude forms of toothbrush or otherwise caring for the teeth, not so much apparently for preserving them as for improving individual appearance.

To the basic desire for attractive teeth has been added in recent times knowledge regarding the relationship of the teeth to health and the importance of care of the teeth in preventing oral ills. Throughout the nineteenth century and particularly during the twentieth century, the dissemination of such knowledge among the populace by dental societies, dental colleges, public health authorities, and public schools has grown apace. In 1801 appeared the first book on dentistry in this country, *On the Human Teeth*, by R. I. Skinner. In 1834 the first society of dental surgeons was founded in New York City, and association among dental practitioners has spread from that time. These dental societies have been focal points for disseminating knowledge regarding the care of teeth. In 1840 came the first dental school, the Baltimore College of Dental Surgery, to be followed by the establishment of dental colleges by an increasing number of schools of higher learning. Here has been another source for edu-

[9] A history of the development of dentistry and dental care may be found in the following books:

C. A. Brackett, *The Care of the Teeth* (Cambridge, Harvard University Press, 1915).

Woods Hutchinson, *Civilization and Health* (Boston, Houghton Mifflin Company, 1914).

J. J. Rosenau, *Preventive Medicine and Hygiene* (New York, D. Appleton & Company, 1927).

Thomas Ryan, *Teeth and Health* (New York, G. P. Putnam's Sons, 1921).

Clair Turner, *Personal and Community Health* (St. Louis, The C. V. Mosby Company, 1926).

F. C. Waite, *High Points in the History of Dentistry.* Reprinted from *Bulletin of the Cleveland Dental Society,* October, November, 1931; January–May, 1932.

S. S. White Company, *82 Years of Loyal Service to Dentistry* (Philadelphia, S. S. White Company, 1926).

cating the public. In 1910 came the introduction of oral hygiene instruction into the public schools, a movement which grew slowly at first, then much more rapidly in the period after World War I. The report of Dr. A. C. Fones, covering a five-year study of diseases and their prevalence among children in the Bridgewater, Massachusetts, schools, showed not only the need of education in personal hygiene, but also the value of public health work in improving the health of school children. Dr. Fones' figures showed that 30% of the children coming under his care brushed their teeth only occasionally, and 60% did not brush their teeth at all. Such figures proved an impetus to the further teaching of hygiene in the public schools.

The dental profession has cooperated in this movement by volunteering its services at minimum fees and stressing the importance of the work in its societies and practice.[10] State and city governments have cooperated by providing nurses and by printing informational literature. The bulk of such work has been done since World War I, the recent development coinciding with the extensive promotional activity of dentifrice manufacturers.

To such educational activities as are noted above should be added the educational work carried on by magazines and newspapers.

The advertising of dentifrices to a very marked degree has utilized primary appeals. The objective of the manufacturers has, of course, been chiefly selective, to secure for their brands a substantial part of existing dentifrice demand. The strong appeals, however, have been primary appeals—personal beauty, romance, and preservation of health. The products have been highly individualized; hence the association of a brand name with some individualizing copy idea has been effective in guiding selective demand. That much of the advertising throughout this period made effective appeal for the care of the teeth is undeniable. In fact, a common complaint is that much of the advertising has been too appealing, the claims and promises for both health and beauty having been overstated and in poor taste. Dental authorities seem agreed that the therapeutic value of any dentifrice is practically nil; it is merely a cleanser. Critics within and without the advertising industry agree that dentifrice advertising has been one of the sore spots in business practice.[11]

---

[10] For a study of such work see Mary Ross, *Medical Advertising* (Chicago, Julius Rosenwald Fund, 1932).

[11] See John Benson, "Pseudo-Scientific Arguments in Advertising," *Advertising & Selling*, February 23, 1927. Also see B. B. Palmer, *Paying Through the Teeth* (New York,

Be that as it may, a 30-fold increase in the volume of persuasive advertising which came about during the period 1914–1931 quite clearly must have been an important factor in bringing about the marked growth in primary demand for dentifrices. But the manufacturers were helped by other forces which gave a favorable trend and, because of these other variables affecting demand, it would be a mistake to ascribe the growth in use solely to advertising effort.

As noted previously, the per capita consumption of dentifrices apparently reached its peak in 1931. The continuing heavy programs of advertising subsequent to that date failed to stem a marked decrease in per capita consumption during the depression.

Once established, the practice of brushing teeth presumably is habitual. In view of the fact that the outlay for dentifrices is not a large item in the budget, it appears reasonable to conclude that the demand for dentifrices, at least among habitual users, should be relatively inelastic; i.e., neither an increase nor a decrease in price would have marked effect upon the quantities demanded.[12] Or, among habitual users, if prices remained constant, decreased consumer buying power during a depression would not appear likely to bring much decrease in quantities demanded. Apparently dentifrice manufacturers proceeded on the theory that dentifrice users generally were habitual users and that the demand for the whole market, therefore, was inelastic. As a matter of fact, however, during the 1933 depression there was a material decrease in the quantities of commercial dentifrices sold, as shown from the reports of the *Biennial Census of Manufactures*. Whereas 1931 showed product value of $35,700,000, the 1933 value was less than $26,000,000, a decrease of about 25%. During the depression the prices of dentifrices generally were "sticky." Accordingly, the number of units produced in the two years are believed to be in proportion to the dollar figures. Hence, it is seen the product showed itself sensitive to decreased buying power of consumers.

The Vanguard Press). In commenting upon this book, Mr. C. B. Larrabee, in an article "Dentists and Advertising," *Printers' Ink*, July 25, 1935, p. 65 ff., said: "No doubt this book will be vigorously denounced by many of the manufacturers in the field and by their friends. Like any muck-raking book—although by no means to such a large extent—it makes statements that are refutable. No amount of refutation, however, will eliminate the fact that an uncomfortably large proportion of dentifrice and mouth wash advertising has sunk to a pretty low ethical standard . . . There can be no question that Dr. Palmer represents, perhaps a little extremely, the view of a large number of well-informed dentists."

[12] This discussion waives for the moment the question of the effect of price as a means of affecting demand between brands. This question is treated in the next section.

One cannot be sure of the causes of the decrease in quantities bought, but that the market showed itself responsive to price is clear. While there may have been less brushing of teeth, it seems more likely that many consumers were not habitual users and were influenced by price to turn to substitute products. The experience indicates that executives in the industry may not have given sufficient weight to the effect of price as a stimulant of demand and, instead, have relied too much upon advertising and promotion to increase demand. It seems likely that a combination of advertising and lower prices would have produced a larger volume of sales and possibly of profits than has been attained by the industry, although these results cannot be stated with certainty.

By 1937, demand had practically reached its former high level. Since the prices of products generally in that year and in subsequent years were below predepression levels, the unchanged prices of dentifrices were relatively higher in those years than they were before 1929. Hence it may be concluded that advertising and aggressive selling had a more difficult job in inducing purchase in this past depression period than they had in the years previous to the depression.

THE EFFECT OF ADVERTISING UPON SELECTIVE DEMAND

Dentifrices provide one of the best examples available of the influence of advertising on consumer valuations of brands. Each brand has been highly individualized; there is and has been no such thing as identical merchandise. Each brand differs from others in ingredients, in taste, and in consumers' ideas regarding its efficacy. People do not buy simply tooth paste or tooth powder; they buy brands of either product.

Advertising has been so effective in building the reputation of brands as beautifiers, as protectors of oral and general health, or as aids to attainment of romance that consumers have been led to choose widely advertised brands in preference to little known brands or to substitute products, even when price differentials have been appreciable. Consumers have bought dentifrices in large quantities in spite of considerable publicity to the effect that simple, inexpensive substitutes, such as salt or baking soda, will cleanse the teeth.[13] More-

---

[13] Many consumers undoubtedly prefer to use well-known dentifrices not only because they like their taste but also because they believe they have therapeutic value. Since consumers cannot judge therapeutic value they have had to rely largely on the reputation for this quality as established through advertising. The claims for therapeutic value have been criticized by the dental profession.

over, given the choice between widely advertised brands or unadvertised brands, particularly private brands of distributors, at markedly lower prices, consumers have turned almost wholly to the most advertised brands. As noted in a later chapter, a 5½-ounce tube of unadvertised tooth paste, eligible to receive the American Dental Association emblem, could be bought at retail for 20 cents in 1940, whereas leading advertised brands, ranging in size from about two ounces to four ounces, sold in the neighborhood of 40 cents. The concentration of demand among brands is shown in Tables 61 and 62, which are based on surveys in some 17 city markets in 1938. In the neighborhood of 90% of dentifrices purchased were distributed among a dozen well-advertised brands. Concentration on a relatively few advertised brands applies alike to powders a⁢ ! pastes, which are, of course, in competition with each other. At the same time it will be noted that the range of choice of brands is wide. In Milwaukee in 1935 there were some 99 tooth paste brands in use, but 86 of these brands accounted for only 6% of the tooth pastes being used by those

TABLE 61

USAGE OF TOOTH PASTE BRANDS IN CITY MARKETS, 1938

BRAND	SCRIPPS-HOWARD INVENTORY IN 16 CITIES, PERCENTAGE OF TOOTH PASTE USERS USING BRAND	"THE MILWAUKEE JOURNAL" SURVEY, PERCENTAGE OF TOOTH PASTE USERS USING BRAND
Ipana	19.3	16.6
Colgate	19.2	18.8
Pepsodent	18.4	17.9
Listerine	6.1	8.5
Kolynos	4.1	5.8
Squibb	3.9	3.2
Phillips	3.0	3.2
Iodent	2.9	3.9
Pebeco	2.4	3.6
Dr. West	2.2	8.7
Forhan	1.8	1.4
Watkins	1.2	2.5
Avon	1.1	...
Dr. Lyon's	...	2.3
Craig-Martin	...	1.0
Others (less than 1%)	14.4	6.2 (69 brands)
Percentage of surveyed homes using tooth paste	64.6 (of 53,124 homes inventoried)	65.0 (of 6,800 homes surveyed)

Sources: Scripps-Howard Newspapers, *Market Records—Buying Habits and Brand Preference of Consumers in Sixteen Cities* (New York, 1938), pp. 206–207; *The Milwaukee Journal, op. cit.*, p. 83.

TABLE 62

USAGE OF TOOTH POWDER BRANDS IN CITY MARKETS, 1938

BRAND	SCRIPPS-HOWARD INVENTORY IN 16 CITIES, PERCENTAGE OF TOOTH POWDER USERS USING BRAND	"THE MILWAUKEE JOURNAL" SURVEY, PERCENTAGE OF TOOTH POWDER USERS USING BRAND
Dr. Lyon's	35.9	59.6
Pepsodent	19.8	8.0
Calox	10.2	3.9
Colgate	4.2	3.1
Revelation	3.3	5.0
Vince	2.0	...
Squibb	1.3	...
Pebeco	...	4.1
J. R. Watkins	...	3.5
Dr. West	...	2.6
Listerine	...	1.8
Zincora	...	1.3
Fuller	...	1.2
Others (less than 1%)	23.3	7.2 (55 brands)
Percentage of surveyed homes using powder	46.1 (of 53,124 homes inventoried)	57.3 (of 6,800 homes surveyed)

Sources: Scripps-Howard Newspapers, *op. cit.*; *The Milwaukee Journal, op. cit.*, p. 82.

TABLE 63

ESTIMATED VALUE OF TRACEABLE ADVERTISING EXPENDITURES OF DENTIFRICES

BRAND	1929	1930	1931	1932	1933
Bost				$ 16,099	$ 700
Calox Tooth Powder			$ 7,057		
Colgate Dental Cream	$1,015,760	$1,160,320	1,105,245	462,701	644,933
Colgate Tooth Powder					
Forhan Tooth Paste	963,116	789,341	197,977	147,261	86,099
Forhan Tooth Powder					
Iodent Tooth Paste	168,308	179,572	161,370	178,660	19,902
Ipana Tooth Paste	1,129,678	1,076,768	1,205,064	1,193,818	925,866
Kolynos Tooth Paste	213,560	352,543	471,381	332,573	511,439
Listerine Tooth Paste	1,021,174	1,089,478	1,006,385	1,108,553	947,428
Listerine Tooth Powder					
Dr. Lyon's Tooth Powder	138,620	195,643	202,355	211,578	401,717
Pebeco Tooth Paste	527,014	366,455	376,722	33,915	189,768
Pebeco Tooth Powder					
Pepsodent Tooth Paste	1,352,972	1,869,344	1,553,539	1,432,272	1,520,309
Pepsodent Tooth Powder					
Phillips Tooth Paste			87,777	175,863	316,643
Squibb Dental Cream	610,283	559,160	623,516	484,193	341,091
Squibb Tooth Powder					
Teel					
Dr. West Tooth Paste	438,243	180,823	126,097	190,144	161,948
Others	259,224	50,528	117,133	97,682	22,843
Total	$7,837,952	$7,869,975	$7,241,618	$6,065,312	$6,090,586

* Average for period of years determined by first appearance of advertising.
Source: See sources listed for Table 60.

interviewed; there were 63 brands of tooth powder, but 55 of the brands accounted for only 9% of usage.[14]

The tables referred to in the preceding paragraph represent findings of home surveys in various city markets. They are not an accurate representation of distribution of total sales among the various leading brands in 1938. This statement is based on study of a confidential report of the distribution of sales among brands made by a commercial research organization. The figures contained in Tables 61 and 62, however, serve to indicate the character of the dentifrice market, in which competition was carried on largely through advertising among some 15 brands of paste and powder with no brand enjoying as much as 20% of total demand.

Estimated value of the traceable advertising expenditures in newspapers, magazines, farm journals, and chain radio during the period 1929–1939 for the advertised brands is contained in Table 63. These estimates of space and time expenditures, as measured by various commercial services, cannot be looked upon as accurate. They probably are somewhat greater than actual expenditures in view of the fact that they represent measurements multiplied by unit rates and, ac-

IN NEWSPAPERS, MAGAZINES, FARM JOURNALS, AND CHAIN RADIO, 1929–1939

1934	1935	1936	1937	1938	1939	Annual Average*
....	$ 11,640	$ 2,732	....	$ 7,400	....	$ 4,821
$ 97,344	158,231	161,739	$ 281,776	145,555	$ 176,347	114,228
832,282	922,026	861,785	1,145,665	1,086,932	1,261,977	954,511
			159,828	37,896	359,175	185,633
85,550	111,069	106,664	120,818	81,272	85,384	252,232
15,500	83,899	....				16,566
....	47,031	11,621	46,816	96,864	79,244	89,944
1,160,373	1,227,703	1,395,659	1,699,294	1,601,822	1,424,953	1,276,455
635,706	529,560	436,035	337,198	396,050	370,303	416,937
882,930	670,700	834,470	812,617	643,292	516,943	862,179
			48,000	....		16,000
548,488	628,089	1,069,722	1,330,572	841,794	1,273,088	621,059
48,538	178,040	188,282	250,305	97,270	39,132	208,676
					24,438	24,438
1,094,232	1,109,237	415,003	1,051,977	378,670	219,863	1,090,674
		462,026	691,329	629,440	604,846	596,910
434,164	277,963	214,808	148,703	....	188,655	204,953
236,599	88,850	402,964	261,049	819,495	230,722	423,447
		106,123	252,049	520	203,728	140,605
			....	22,927	809,245	416,086
83,015	76,659	63,936	62,884	4,290	11,098	127,176
45,682	37,497	17,680	398,150	146,172	153,635	....
$6,200,403	$6,158,194	$6,801,249	$9,099,030	$7,037,661	$8,032,976	

[14] *The Milwaukee Journal*, "Consumer Analysis of the Greater Milwaukee Market, 1938."

cordingly, do not allow for quantity discounts given to large advertisers. Yet over the period they probably are not far wrong and serve to show the approximate range of expenditure.

Relation of Quantity of Advertising and Sales Volume

The annual rankings of different dentifrice brands by volume of advertising expenditure are shown in Table 64. A comparison of this table with Table 61, which is indicative of the relative standing of

TABLE 64

ANNUAL RANKING OF VOLUME OF ADVERTISING EXPENDITURES OF DENTIFRICE BRANDS, 1929–1939

BRAND	1929	1930	1931	1932	1933	1934	1935	1936	1937	1938	1939
Pepsodent Paste & Powder..	1	1	1	1	1	2	2	3	1	3	4
Ipana Paste...............	2	4	2	2	3	1	1	1	2	1	2
Colgate Paste & Powder....	4	2	3	5	4	4	3	4	4	2	1
Listerine.................	3	3	4	3	2	3	4	5	5	6	6
Dr. Lyon's Powder........	11	9	8	7	6	6	5	2	3	4	3
Squibb Paste & Powder....	6	6	5	4	7	8	11	6	6	5	7
Kolynos..................	9	8	6	6	5	5	6	7	7	7	8
Forhan...................	5	5	9	11	11	10	8	11	11	11	11
Pebeco Paste & Powder.....	7	7	7	12	9	....	9	9	9	9	13
Dr. West.................	8	10	11	8	10	11	12	12	12	12	14
Iodent...................	10	11	10	9	12	.....	13	13	13	10	12
Phillips..................	.....	.....	13	10	8	7	7	8	10	.....	9
Calox....................	.....	.....	14	.....	.....	9	10	10	8	8	10
Teel.....................	.....	.....	.....	.....	.....	.....	.....	.....	.....	.....	5

Source: Based on Table 63.

brand sales in various city markets, shows that brand sales in general conformed with the advertising expenditures. Those brands which were most heavily advertised were, in general, the brands in greatest demand. Pepsodent, Ipana, Colgate, Dr. Lyon's, Listerine, Squibb, and Kolynos were the leaders in usage and also were the leaders in advertising expenditures.

As with most products, varying marketing methods are followed by different manufacturers to gain business, but brands which have not been advertised to consumers have not had large sales volume. For example, a case history from one manufacturer showed a small but profitable business built with very little advertising to consumers. His promotion was limited mostly to dentists, asking their recommendation of the dentifrice among patients.[15] Another case was from a manufacturer employing no advertising other than package inserts,

[15] See N. H. Borden, *Problems in Advertising* (3d ed.), case of Sargent Dental Company, p. 103.

who sold under his own brand in variety chains, offering a large tube of tooth paste at a price far below that of advertised brands. Elimination of advertising expense and of personal selling expense permitted such sale with profit to the manufacturer. Other manufacturers sold under private brands. While manufacturers may thus sell profitably without appreciable advertising, yet the history of the dentifrice business shows that he who desires to attain any substantial volume of business must employ advertising and set his price to provide margins permitting a program of advertising sufficient to lead to consumer acceptance and use.

Relation of Advertising to Trade Distribution

The importance of advertising in stimulating a selective demand is further indicated by the fact that the advertised brands have a demand strong enough to gain dense distribution, whereas unadvertised brands have spotty distribution. A confidential trade survey (1938), made available to the author, showed that leading brands usually had almost complete distribution among drug stores, several having distribution in 80% to 99% of such stores. Some of the advertised brands with smaller sales volume had distribution in only 60% to 80% of the stores; yet even this distribution represents a substantial consumer acceptance. In contrast unadvertised or little advertised brands had spotty distribution. For example, private brands were found only in the stores controlling these brands.

The extent to which stores find it desirable to carry a number of brands of dentifrice is indicated in Table 65, which shows the number of brands carried by dealers in the Milwaukee market in January, 1935. In that year the *Journal* survey showed that out of 99 brands of tooth paste used in the market, only 13 brands were used by as many as 1% of the families interviewed. As indicated in the table, 18% of the stores limited themselves to 14 brands or less, probably the brands most frequently called for. An additional 19% carried from 15 to 19 brands, while over 50% carried 20 or more brands. In the same year, only eight brands of tooth powder out of 63 used in the market were found to be used in at least 1% of the homes surveyed. Eleven per cent of the stores carried as few as four brands; 62% carried as few as eight brands or less; 38% carried more than eight brands. From these data it becomes apparent that many brands of dentifrice had limited retail distribution.

TABLE 65

NUMBER OF DENTIFRICE BRANDS CARRIED BY RETAILERS IN GREATER MILWAUKEE
MARKET, 1935

	99 TOOTH PASTE BRANDS IN MARKET Number of Brands Carried by Dealers					
Range	0–9	10–14	15–19	20–24	25–30	Over 30
Percentage of Dealers..........	3%	15%	29%	36%	11%	6%
	63 TOOTH POWDER BRANDS IN MARKET Number of Brands Carried by Dealers					
Range	0–2	3–4	5–6	7–8	9–10	Over 10
Percentage of Dealers..........	0	11%	20%	31%	11%	27%

Source: *The Milwaukee Journal, op. cit.*, 1935.

Advertising and Shifts in Brand Demand

Further evidence of the importance of advertising in the marketing of dentifrices is found in the shifting of sales among brands. For example, Sozodont, referred to previously as the leading brand of dentifrice before 1900, is now unknown to most people. This brand was advertised in magazines as late as 1917. In 1916 over $21,000 was spent for magazine space for the brand; it was the third largest magazine advertiser among dentifrice manufacturers in that year. As other brands came forward with increasing appropriations, however, Sozodont, for reasons unknown, ceased to advertise widely. Though still upon the market in recent years, its name fails to appear in the lists of brands which enjoyed usage by as much as 1% of consumers using dentifrice, either in the Scripps-Howard or the Milwaukee market surveys.

The shifting of ranking of various brands in the Milwaukee market in selected years over a 15-year interval provides partial evidence of the relation of advertising to demand. Tables 66 and 67 show standing of brands in selected years. Comparison of these tables with Table 63, page 306, which gives the expenditure for various brands over a substantial part of this period, makes evident that the heavy, consistent advertisers have forged ahead, while those who have failed to advertise have lost position. This result is illustrated particularly in the case of tooth powders. Starting in 1934 there developed a shift towards greater use of tooth powder (see Table 57, page 296). Whereas in 1934 in Milwaukee 92% of the families reported use of tooth paste and only 17% use of tooth powder, in 1938, 65% of the families were users of tooth paste and 57% of tooth powder.[16] These

---

[16] Some families used both types; hence the percentages total over 100%.

TABLE 66

CONSUMER BRAND PREFERENCES AMONG TOOTH PASTES IN THE GREATER MILWAUKEE MARKET SELECTED YEARS, 1924–1940

TOOTH PASTE BRAND	1924		1929		1934		1938		1940	
	Rank*	%†	Rank*	%†	Rank*	%†	Rank*	%†	Rank*	%†
Colgate	1	29.9	1	19.8	2	13.0	1	18.8	1	25.6
Pepsodent	2	24.0	3	14.4	1	28.7	2	17.9	2	19.0
Ipana	7	1.4	6	8.0	5	8.4	3	16.6	3	14.7
Dr. West					3	12.2	4	8.7	6	4.6
Listerine	6	5.4	2	15.3	4	11.1	5	8.5	4	6.5
Forhan	5	8.0	4	10.5	8	2.1	8	1.4	8	1.5
Pebeco	3	11.6	5	9.2	7	3.8	7	3.6	7	4.0
Kolynos	4	8.9	7	6.4	6	5.8	6	5.8	5	4.7
Total brands mentioned	95		70		102		83		83	

USERS OF TOOTH PASTE—PERCENTAGE

Yes	No	Yes	No	Yes	No	Yes	No	Yes	No
94.7	5.3	95.3	4.6	91.8	8.2	65.0	35.0	59.2	41.8

* Rank is judged by percentage of all families buying this type of product who use each brand.
† Percentage of tooth paste users who use this brand.

Source: *The Milwaukee Journal, op cit.,* annual editions.

TABLE 67

CONSUMER BRAND PREFERENCES AMONG TOOTH POWDERS IN THE GREATER MILWAUKEE MARKET SELECTED YEARS, 1924–1940

TOOTH POWDER BRAND	1924		1929		1934		1938		1940	
	Rank*	%†	Rank*	%†	Rank*	%†	Rank*	%†	Rank*	%†
Dr. Lyon's	3	13.5	2	16.3	1	55.2	1	59.6	1	59.5
Pepsodent							2	8.0	3	7.2
Revelation	2	13.8	1	33.7	2	26.4	3	5.0	6	3.8
Pebeco							4	4.1	5	3.8
Calox			7	2.1			5	3.9	4	4.2
Vince					3	1.8				
Dr. Graves	1	23.7	3	12.7	4	1.6				
Zincora					5	1.3	10	1.3	10	1.0
Wernet			4	6.8						
Colgate	5	10.6	5	5.3	6	1.0	7	3.1	2	8.1
Pyorrhocide	4	12.0	6	2.7						
Total brands mentioned	41		36		47		76		66	

USERS OF TOOTH POWDER—PERCENTAGE

Yes	No	Yes	No	Yes	No	Yes	No
9.2	90.8	7.0	93.0	17.5	82.5	57.3	42.7

* Rank is judged by percentage of all families buying this type of product who use each brand.
† Percentage of tooth powder users who use this brand.

Source: *The Milwaukee Journal, op. cit.,* annual editions.

figures for Milwaukee indicate a greater shift in sales than actually occurred in the country as a whole; yet the trend throughout was marked. Dr. Lyon's tooth powder benefited particularly from this trend; in fact, this brand undoubtedly was in part responsible for the shift, having greatly increased its program of advertising in 1933, featuring the appeal, "Do as your dentist does; use powder," which apparently was effective. Many other dentifrice manufacturers, noting the trend, offered powders. Those who advertised forged to the head: Dr. Lyon's, Colgate, Pepsodent, Calox. On the other hand, as shown in Table 67, other brands, such as Dr. Graves, Revelation, and Pyorrho-cide, that had stood high in sales in Milwaukee in 1924 and 1929, but which had failed to hold a place in the advertising parade, dropped toward the bottom of the lists of 1938 and 1940.[17]

Advertising and Stability of Demand among Dentifrices

As was the case with cigarettes, advertising has not in itself assured stability of demand for dentifrices. That there has been a shifting of sales among advertised brands is shown in Tables 66 and 67. Evidence of a better type was had from the confidential report of a continuing survey among retailers of brand sales covering a four-year period, which showed a high degree of stability in the proportion of total dentifrice sales attained by some brands, while others had marked fluctuations in their sales and in their relative positions in the industry. As with other products, it is concluded that advertising itself does not determine stability; but skillful use of advertising in conjunction with sound merchandising and pricing policies does enable a management to attain relative stability of demand.

As with cigarettes, price has not been the chief determinant in the shifting of demand between dentifrice brands. While many of the leading brands have sold at approximately the same price per tube, the quantity in the tube has varied among the brands.[18] Moreover, a few well-advertised brands, such as Listerine, have sold at a lower price than that of others for the large size tube. Yet such variations in quantity for a price have not determined the flow of demand. Among the advertised brands, so far as could be learned variation from established prices as a means of getting business has not been much used, although free promotional deals to the trade have been

---

[17] Further evidence regarding the effects of advertising on brand leadership of denti-frices is contained in G. B. Hotchkiss and R. B. Franken, *The Measurement of Advertising Effects* (New York, Harper & Brothers, 1927), ch. 9, p. 110 ff. The authors carried out association tests to determine the strength of brand associations in 1921 and again in 1925. Their data led to the conclusion that general publicity advertising was a powerful influence in building the prestige of dentifrice trade-marks among consumers.

[18] For specific data regarding price, see Chapter XX.

employed at times. Even allowing for such free deals, dentifrice prices may be characterized as having been stable. Quite clearly the distribution of demand among brands has been determined very largely by the advertising.

The various managements have matched wits in their advertising appeals, with first one type of approach and then another; these programs have varied in their effectiveness. Acccordingly, advertising cannot be said to have been in itself a stabilizer of demand among the brands. Price has been stabilized, but the demand has shifted as first one management and then another has hit upon a stimulating advertising approach.

In recent years brands have been subject to shifts in demand, because to the variable of advertising programs has been added the variable of product form. Dentifrice manufacturers rightly look upon all sorts of dentifrices, no matter whether paste, powder, or liquid, as direct competitors. The constant effort and success of manufacturers to find new product forms which might be preferred to existing types has led in recent years to marked shifts in demand for various types of dentifrice products. Reference has been made to the trend which occurred after 1933 away from tooth paste to tooth powder. More recently, liquid dentifrices, led by Teel, a product of the Procter & Gamble Company, have brought about a further shift. During 1939–1940, liquid dentifrices made great strides. As shown in Table 57, page 296, practically 23% of the homes in the Milwaukee market were shown in the sample survey to have taken up the use of liquid dentifrices, whereas two years previously demand for such a product was practically nonexistent.[19] The Procter & Gamble Company made heavy use of advertising when ushering in its Teel. Other companies followed suit.

From the above discussion it seems evident that in order to enjoy stability of demand, managements must find advertising and promotional approaches as effective as those of competitors; and they must keep up with the trends of consumer preference so far as forms of dentifrice are concerned. In order to get quick and continuous data regarding the sales results of not only their own advertising and merchandise moves but those of competitors, some managements subscribe to the continuing surveys of sales by brands among retailers,

---

[19] Several of the older brands of dentifrice on the market were liquids, but the demand for them was small.

which have been referred to previously. Skillful use of advertising, guided by knowledge of what is occurring in the market, may thus help a manufacturer to get stability of sales. Failure to know the facts, however, and to devise skillful advertising may lead to instability of demand. Thus it is concluded, as in the case of cigarettes and other products, that advertising itself should not be termed a stabilizer of demand; instead, skillful management of advertising is needed.

Summary

Advertising has played a dominant role in guiding the selective demand for dentifrice. Among the products studied dentifrices are among those most heavily advertised when measured in percentage of sales devoted to advertising. Consumer values are much influenced by this advertising. Advertised brands often sell at prices well above those of unadvertised brands of acceptable quality. The heavily advertised brands dominate the market although there are many brands. Consumer preference for advertised brands is so strong as to force dense distribution. Competition in the industry has taken place primarily through advertising, and brands which have not been consistently advertised have lost their standing. In order to have a stability of demand, a manufacturer in this field finds it necessary to manage his advertising skillfully.

CHAPTER XII

THE EFFECT OF ADVERTISING ON THE
DEMAND FOR DOMESTIC SHEETING

AMONG several marketing and advertising executives of companies producing domestic sheeting from whom cases were
gathered in this study there was general agreement that
advertising probably had little if any effect on the total consumption
of sheets and pillowcases. Its effects rather have been to influence
distribution of demand among brands.

EFFECT OF ADVERTISING ON PRIMARY DEMAND

Satisfactory data regarding consumption of sheeting for domestic
purposes were not available to the author. Not until 1935 did the
Biennial Census of Manufactures give a separate figure for wide
sheeting production for domestic use. Table 68, which gives the
Census figures of production for the years 1935 and 1937, indicates
a per capita production for domestic use of 2.4 square yards in 1935
and 4.3 square yards in 1937. Not until 1937 were figures on the
production of manufactured sheets and pillowcases made available.
As shown in Table 69, the production per capita was .42 sheets and
.44 pillowcases.

Starting in 1927, the *Census of Manufactures* has given figures of
production for all sheeting over 40 inches wide, but these data have
covered wide sheeting intended for both domestic and industrial use,
as shown in Table 70. Unfortunately it is not possible to segregate
the production for domestic use from that for industrial use for this

TABLE 68

SHEETINGS FOR DOMESTIC USE (WIDER THAN 40 INCHES), 1935, 1937

YEAR	POUNDS	SQUARE YARDS	VALUE	INDICATED PRODUCTION PER CAPITA
1935.............	85,507,783	304,274,040	$33,093,392	2.4 square yards
1937.............	154,281,005	557,956,634	57,959,412	4.3 square yards

Source: U. S. *Biennial Census of Manufactures.*

315

TABLE 69

PRODUCTION OF FINISHED SHEETS AND PILLOWCASES, 1937

	MADE FROM OWN MATERIALS, INCLUDING PRODUCTS MADE ON COMMISSION		MADE FROM MATERIAL OWNED BY OTHERS, DOZEN	INDICATED PRODUCTION PER CAPITA, DOZEN
	QUANTITY, DOZEN	VALUE		
Sheets...........	3,518,019	$29,745,461	905,111	0.42
Pillowcases......	3,762,771	8,392,414	1,016,218	0.44

Source: U. S. *Biennial Census of Manufactures, 1937.*

period, in view of the fact that the division of demand between the two uses has not been constant.

Another difficulty lies in the fact that production figures for any year do not represent the sheeting that has gone into consumption. As will be noted from Tables 68 and 70, there have been wide fluctuations in the annual production of sheeting. While these fluctuations have been wider for sheeting for industrial use than for that for domestic use, still there has been a tendency for the trade and for manufacturers to build up inventories during periods of rising cotton prices, and conversely for inventories to become short in periods of inactivity in the textile industry. Production in any year is not a close measure of goods moving into consumption.

Thus, industry statistics do not provide a basis for determining whether there has been an increase or a decrease in per capita consumption of sheeting and pillowcases; yet there was agreement among executives interviewed that some increase occurred after 1928.

Such increase as may have occurred was not, however, attributed to the advertising carried on. The use of sheets is an old, well-established custom not likely to be readily affected by advertising appeal. Yet some room for expansion has existed, for one mill executive

TABLE 70

PRODUCTION OF ALL SHEETING OVER 40 INCHES WIDE
(FOR DOMESTIC AND INDUSTRIAL USE)

YEAR	POUNDS	SQUARE YARDS	VALUE
1927........................	157,325,425	648,054,001	$73,939,456
1929........................	124,673,996	517,859,634	53,916,903
1931........................	101,099,775	443,636,689	31,400,125
1933........................	150,001,000	603,728,000	43,086,000
1935........................	136,128,829	572,967,210	50,226,844
1937........................	202,866,103	926,936,240	78,014,280

Source: U. S. *Biennial Census of Manufactures.*

stated that consumer surveys showed either little or infrequent use of sheets in certain low-income groups. He did not know the size of such groups, but their low buying power made them poor prospects. Opportunity for increased consumption has existed also in increasing the size of sheet used.[1] Some manufacturers have encouraged the trade to sell the larger sizes, but to what extent this has been effective is not known. In an effort to increase consumption, one manufacturer conducted a short campaign which suggested the use of an extra sheet as a desirable covering in the summertime. No evidence of the effect of the campaign is available.

Extent of Advertising

The advertising directed by the various mills to housewives has been almost uniformly selective in its appeal, and the amount of advertising has been relatively small. As noted in Tables 71 and 72, total space expenditures in no year have been much in excess of $500,000, and in most years well below this amount. Although the total promotional expenditure of the advertising companies probably was from two and one-half to three times the space expenditures

TABLE 71

ADVERTISING SPACE EXPENDITURE FOR BRANDS OF DOMESTIC SHEETS AND PILLOWCASES IN LEADING MAGAZINES, 1914–1928

YEAR	PEQUOT	PEPPERELL	WAMSUTTA	UTICA STEAM & MOHAWK VALLEY COTTON MILLS	DWIGHT ANCHOR	CANNON	TOTAL
1914	$ 7,971						$ 7,971
1915	5,788						5,788
1916	10,941						10,941
1917	9,035						9,035
1918	9,119						9,119
1919	15,400						15,400
1920	19,365	$ 789					20,154
1921	19,973	11,805	$ 41,000				72,778
1922	21,516		66,000				87,516
1923	21,332		66,000				87,332
1924	21,557	30,368	55,850	$21,902			129,677
1925	30,660	64,428	44,810	59,761			199,659
1926	49,688	54,073	77,360	65,652	$24,479		271,252
1927	81,434	45,588	75,715	78,281	80,942		361,960
1928	128,395	59,578	91,673	69,528	86,004	$8,217	443,395

Source: Curtis Publishing Company, Advertising Department, *Leading Advertisers,* (Philadelphia), 1914–1928.

[1] For example, in commenting upon current sheet advertising, *Tide,* January 1, 1940, p. 32, reported with regard to the advertising of Utica sheets: "Each advertisement also plugs the long (108″) sheet for sleeping comfort, a successful innovation Utica introduced in 1931 to boost dollar volume."

TABLE 72

TRACEABLE SPACE AND TIME EXPENDITURES FOR BRANDS OF DOMESTIC SHEETS AND
PILLOWCASES IN NEWSPAPERS, GENERAL MAGAZINES, FARM JOURNALS,
AND CHAIN RADIO, 1929–1939

YEAR	PEQUOT	PEPPERELL*	WAMSUTTA	UTICA STEAM & MOHAWK VALLEY COTTON MILLS	DWIGHT ANCHOR	CANNON	TOTAL
1929.....	$153,210	$ 72,581	$119,311	$92,489	$57,492	$ 31,874	$580,087
1930.....	144,418	63,599	77,426	54,640	....	....	345,858
1931.....	111,609	20,274	63,755	56,412	....	....	252,040
1932.....	76,275	19,150	47,855	32,991	....	....	196,271
1933.....	90,513	43,550	28,715	36,525	10,149	....	209,452
1934.....	122,933	53,080	40,185	54,787	10,200	8,800	289,985
1935.....	107,177	34,890	26,965	38,592	5,625	109,365	322,614
1936.....	96,551	37,075	47,850	37,678	11,595	123,116	372,980
1937.....	126,600	106,849	64,880	58,776	13,438	135,073	544,676
1938.....	150,210	54,729	61,630	44,718	....	137,270	481,569
1939.....	143,007	75,560	64,750	46,495	....	144,460	474,412

* After 1930 Pepperell spent substantial parts of its appropriation in institutional advertising of the Pepperell family mark and of other Pepperell fabrics. Only the sheet advertising is included here.

NOTE:
Expenditures of other companies:

1929	J. C. Penney Co.	$53,130
1930	Sears, Roebuck and Co.	5,775
1936	Chatham	19,115
1937	Chatham	12,660
	Indian Head	26,400
1938	Bates	2,512
	Indian Head	30,500

Sources:
Magazines:
 1939—American Newspaper Publishers' Association, *Expenditures of National Advertisers.*
 1936 to 1938—Publishers' Information Bureau, Inc., *National Advertising Records.*
 1930 to 1935—Curtis Publishing Company, *Leading Advertisers.*
 1929—Crowell Publishing Company, *National Markets and National Advertising.*
Newspapers:
 1939—Dollar figures from American Newspaper Publishers' Association, *Expenditures of National Advertisers.*
 Linage, 1929–1939 from Media Records, Inc., *Newspapers and Newspaper Advertisers.*
 Conversion rate of 37 cents per line derived from linage and dollar figures for 1938 and 1939 for five commodities, applied to linage of other years. See Appendix IV regarding basis of conversion.
Farm Journals:
 1939—American Newspaper Publishers' Association, *Expenditures of National Advertisers.*
 1937–1938—Publishers' Information Bureau, Inc., *National Advertising Records.*
 1935–1936—National Advertising Records, Inc., *National Advertising Records.*
Radio:
 1937–1938—Publishers' Information Bureau, Inc., *National Advertising Records.*

listed, still the amounts have been relatively modest when compared with the advertising of many products. Accordingly, the view of the advertisers themselves is accepted, namely, that the effect of advertising has been chiefly to influence the distribution of demand among manufacturers of sheeting.

This use of advertising, however, has entailed two correlated changes in the character of sheeting demand which are worthy of note. First there has been a change in the buying habits of consumers, a change from buying piece goods to buying finished sheets and pillowcases. Until the turn of the century, sheeting mills sold their products only as piece goods. While manufacture of sheets and pillowcases was done by and for the trade, the major part of consumer buying was of piece goods. The Pequot Mills, one of the first manufacturers of sheeting to undertake the complete finishing of its sheets and pillowcases, sold all its output as piece goods until 1902.[2] In 1927 these mills reported that sales of finished sheets and pillowcases constituted over two-thirds of their sales of Pequot sheeting.[2] Executives of sheeting mills from whom case material was gathered in 1938 gave varying estimates of the percentage of domestic sheeting sold in the form of piece goods, ranging from 2% to 12% of the total. While advertising cannot be said to be "the cause" of this almost complete shift, the directing of advertising and aggressive selling to finished sheets and pillowcases has been a factor in influencing the change.

The second change in the character of domestic sheeting demand has been a diversion of demand to finer grades of sheeting which has been concurrent with advertising. Although there were well-known mill brands of sheeting in the nineteenth century, such as Pepperell and Pequot, no manufacturer of sheeting had employed consumer space advertising to establish his brand until the Pequot Mills undertook such advertising at the time it entered upon the manufacture of finished sheets and pillowcases. The Pequot brand was of finer construction than the muslin sheeting generally in demand at that time. The thread count of muslin sheeting in widest demand was 64 x 64, whereas Pequot construction was 68 x 72.[3]

As other manufacturers undertook consumer advertising of their brands of sheets and pillowcases subsequent to 1920, the products advertised practically without exception were of the 68 x 72 count or of finer construction. One result of their aggressive advertising and personal selling has been to shift a larger share of total sheeting demand to these finer counts. Figures are not available to the author

---

[2] N. H. Borden, *Problems in Advertising* (3d ed.), *op. cit.*, case of Naumkeag Mills, p. 179 ff.

[3] See footnote 4 on page 321 regarding thread counts and the grading of sheets.

to indicate the proportion of various constructions at various periods, but for 1938 the following division is a composite of estimates given by several executives in the field:

COUNT	PERCENTAGE OF TOTAL PRODUCTION
64 x 64 or coarser	50
68 x 72	40
Finer than 68 x 72	10

Invariably, executives consulted were agreed that these ratios represented a considerable change from the distribution before the aggressive selling of leading mills was turned to finer count sheeting.

Summary Regarding Primary Demand

The data regarding consumption of sheeting do not permit definite conclusions regarding the trend of demand. The relatively recent and relatively small amount of advertising devoted to a product long on the market, as well as the selective character of the appeals employed, lead to the conclusion that advertising probably has had no material effect on primary demand. It has been an influence, however, in bringing about a shift of demand for piece goods to a demand for finished sheets and pillowcases. It has also been a force to increase the proportion of high count sheets sold.

THE EFFECT OF ADVERTISING UPON SELECTIVE DEMAND

It is difficult to determine with certainty the extent to which advertising has affected the selective demand for sheeting. Difficulty comes in part from a paucity of specific data regarding sales within the industry; in part from the fact that there have been so many variables, other than advertising, affecting the flow of demand, and these are hard to appraise.

The selective influence of advertising is not so clear-cut as it is for products such as tobacco and dentifrices, or even for walnuts. On the other hand, advertising has had more effect on the selective demand for sheeting than on that for sugar. In the case of sugar, advertising and aggressive selling have not permitted the advertised brands to secure any price differential over unadvertised brands. In the case of sheeting, however, advertising has helped certain manufacturers to build a large and relatively stable volume of demand for their brands at prices somewhat above those received for little-known brands of similar grade. On the other hand, the evidence indicates that this price differential cannot widen much without demand turning to the lower-price, less-advertised brands.

There is confidence in this conclusion in spite of the lack of complete data and the necessity of relying on the opinion of those in the industry. Care was taken to check opinions. The views of competing manufacturers were checked against each other. These views in turn were checked against those of selling houses and of distributors. Within the trade both department store and chain store executives were interviewed. The evidence which supports the opinion is discussed below.

Grades of Sheets

The fact that advertising does not play a more important part in guiding the selective demand of sheeting is traceable in large part to the fact that the product tends to fall into clearly defined grades and the variations among sheets of leading mills within these grades are of no great practical significance. The differences among the various grades of sheeting are well defined.[4] Among sheetings of a particular grade or thread count, however, there are variations in quality. A number of manufacturers expressed the belief that their particular brands were superior to competing brands of similar count. Other manufacturers, however, stated that the differences among leading brands of a particular grade, including not only the leading advertised brands but also some mill brands not so well advertised and certain private brands, were slight, from a practical standpoint. Retailers gave a similar opinion. A department store executive, for example, stated: "Comparably priced brands of sheets have no sig-

---

[4] The grading of sheets is determined by a number of product characteristics: (1) the thread count; (2) the weight of the fabric in ounces per square yard; (3) the tensile strength; (4) the amount of sizing used; (5) the character of the yarn used; (6) the character of the hems,—size and number of stitches per inch. In the trade there have been certain rough classifications, as follows:

Light muslin sheets: These are cheap sheets having a thread count of less than 64 threads to the inch.

Medium muslin sheets: Low-price sheets of 64 x 64 construction, in large demand. This grade includes such brands as Salem and Pepperell.

Heavy muslin sheets: These are of 68 x 72 construction and comprise the majority of well-known brands, such as Pequot, Lady Pepperell, Utica, Dwight Anchor, Cannon, Cast Iron, and Pacific.

Fine count sheets: Above the 68 x 72 construction are a number of sheets of varying construction. At one time the word *percale* was applied to these sheets, but it has been greatly abused, so that its meaning as a generic term is uncertain. The Wamsutta Mills, which have expressed their aim as that of making their brand of sheets the finest on the market, have dropped the term percale and employed the registered trade name Supercale for Wamsutta sheets. Only long staple, fine grades of cotton are used, and a high count construction is employed, 96 x 108.

nificant quality differences, although there are differences in appearances and feel that make it possible for me to tell them apart." Another department store executive stated, "If the . . . . . . and the . . . . . . company exchanged products [leading brands] but continued their same advertising, sales, and other policies, their sales would not be affected." All operating executives attested to the need of careful control of production to maintain quality, indicated the dangers of lapses in quality standards, and pointed out the value of brand as an indicator of quality sponsorship. The fact that the products of certain mills are not so good as those of other mills gives basis for consumer discrimination among brands. They apparently were agreed, however, that the quality of leading brands was generally maintained.

The Urge for Differentiation

In spite of the tendency for sheeting to become standardized by grades, the cases collected from sheeting mills provide evidence of the urge of business managements to lift their products out of the rut of standardization, to differentiate and individualize them in a way to make them preferred by consumers as a means of avoiding an inexorable and unprofitable price competition that may occur on a standardized product.[5] The goal of the mills employing advertising has been profits, but more particularly the stabilizing of profits through control of demand. They have desired to have enough preference for their brands to permit them to have a constant volume of sales through trade channels. The urge for such stabilization has been great because, for a good part of the period, particularly subsequent to 1920, there has been overcapacity in the industry, which has brought lack of stabilization.

The adoption and use of advertising for sheeting should be studied in the light of this severe competitive situation, which has been thus appraised by students of the industry.

No one engaged in the cotton textile industry witnessed with regret the passing of the 1921–1931 decade. During that period, most mills were unable to make satisfactory profits, and many mills, after having experienced repeated losses, were obliged to liquidate. Indeed, the faith in the cotton textile industry fell so low that many mill shares were sold for from one-half to one-fourth of the net current asset value they represented. This condition was the consequence of several factors.

---

[5] The methods employed by manufacturers in trying to differentiate their sheets will be considered in Chapter XXII.

In spite of the increased consumption of cotton goods during that decade, mill owners were unable to obtain a reasonable price for their products because production had a constant tendency to outrun consumption. In order to operate at capacity and thus decrease their production costs, most mills have been willing to manufacture for stock. This practice quickly results in the accumulation of burdensome stocks of cotton goods, which decrease the margin of profit. Furthermore, the poor merchandising methods of the industry make it particularly susceptible to unsettling influences. Most producers make staple materials (grey goods) which have to be converted before they can be sold to the consumer. With the exception of those for the products of a few companies, no valuable brands have been established which might stabilize the sales of individual manufacturers. Because of that, competition is mainly on a price basis, and therefore keen and easily destructive, since price-cutting is a means of competition available to anyone in the industry.[6]

While the quotation relates to cotton textiles as a whole, it reflects well the difficulties met in the sheeting business, as is indicated by the following excerpts from annual statements of the manufacturer of Pequot sheets. In 1928:

The wide sheeting industry is handicapped by intense competition caused by an overcapacity to produce. Fortunately for us, however, the nation-wide popularity of our Pequot brand, which has by far the widest distribution of any sheet in the country, places this company in a much better situation than others. . . . .[7]

In 1931:

Successive reductions in the selling price of our goods, which were made necessary by unrestrained competition, with no comparable reduction in our costs, resulted in operating loss during the second half year.[8]

Similar statements regarding the severity of competition from overcapacity were made in other years as well. Advertising has been employed by a number of mills along with product development and changed selling methods to try to make profit in a demoralized industry.

Extent of Advertising

The statistical story of advertising is contained in Tables 71 and 72. Table 71 gives space advertising in leading magazines only, but it reflects rather accurately the trend of total consumer space expenditures of manufacturers, because their consumer advertising of this

---

[6] C. E. Fraser and G. F. Doriot, *Analyzing Our Industries* (New York, McGraw-Hill Book Company, Inc., 1932), ch. VI, p. 114.

[7] 1928 Annual Report, Naumkeag Steam Cotton Company.

[8] 1931 Annual Report, Naumkeag Steam Cotton Company.

product has been predominantly placed in magazines.[9] As this table shows, through 1928 every mill during this period spent less than $100,000 for magazine advertising, with only a single exception. After 1929 space expenditures were somewhat higher.

Based on a study of advertising budgets of a few companies, it is estimated that for recent years the traceable consumer space advertising represents only from one-third to two-fifths of the total advertising and promotional expenditure. A considerable portion of the advertising and promotional budget has gone into point-of-purchase advertising and into advertising and promotion to the trade.

History of Sheeting Advertising

Pequot was the first manufacturer of sheeting to undertake a consistent program of consumer advertising, starting shortly after it undertook the manufacture of finished sheets and pillowcases in 1902. Until 1920 there was no other general advertiser of the product. The Pequot Mills were the first to adopt the 68 x 72 construction, a cloth chosen after experiment and testing by the management.[10] It believed that this texture possessed advantages of moderate weight, long wear, easy laundering, and smoothness. Thus, when it undertook its advertising, Pequot sheeting provided for consumers several points of product differentiation: first, a construction which the mills had developed and for whose quality it accepted responsibility; and second, the offering of finished sheets and pillowcases as well as piece goods under the brand. In view of the fact that there never had been any standardization upon sheet construction within the industry, or any control on quality except that exercised by individual manufacturers or by the distributors, the company had a basis for inviting consumer discrimination in favor of its brand of sheets and pillowcases. It had reason to expect consumer reliance on brand, for few housewives have been or are expert judges of the quality of sheeting.

The Pequot case illustrates clearly the advantages accruing to an early advertiser of a product, especially when free from competitive advertising. With relatively small advertising expenditure, the reputation of Pequot became firmly established. It became and has re-

---

[9] For the period 1929–1939 for which newspaper, chain radio, and farm journal space data are available, these media accounted for only 5% of traceable consumer space advertising placed by manufacturers; magazines for 95%. Retailers, of course, placed their sheet advertising largely in newspapers.

[10] N. H. Borden, *Problems in Advertising* (3d ed.), case of Naumkeag Mills, p. 179 ff.

mained the leading brand of sheeting, although in recent years its share of the industry's sales has not been so great as at one time. It will be noted from Table 72 that during the period 1914–1920 the expenditure for magazine space never was as much as $20,000. The dominance which it gained from this relatively small advertising space expenditure and from its merchandising program was given by a Boston department store executive in 1938, who said: "Up to 10 to 20 years ago, Pequot had a solid hold on its grade of the sheeting business; every store sold the Pequot brand and liked it." Pequot's position was indicated by a statement contained in a letter from the treasurer of the company to stockholders, dated January 18, 1928:

> We estimate that sheets and pillowcases sold under the Pequot ticket constituted over 40% of all the sheets and pillowcases produced in the country and coming in this price group and almost 20% of the country's entire production of sheets and pillowcases of every description.

Increased Competition in Advertising after 1920

Starting in 1920 the competitive picture in the industry changed, as indicated in Table 71. In the years subsequent to 1920 several mills placed their marks on their sheeting and began to push their brands aggressively through advertising.

No longer did Pequot have the field of consumer brand advertising to itself, nor was it allowed to dominate the 68 x 72 construction[11] to such an extent as formerly. The mills sought to avoid the difficulties of keen price competition in the popular 64 x 64 grade and lower grades. Moreover, the opportunity to individualize their brands was greater in the better quality sheets. Accordingly, the advertisers devoted their promotion to finer count sheets. Under Pequot leadership, the trend of demand had been directed toward such sheets. With the exception of Wamsutta, which laid out as its goal the development of the relatively small, high-price percale market, the advertised brands during the '20's were manufactured to sell at about the same price as Pequot and were of similar texture.

To an increasing degree mills turned to advertising and the total expenditures for the industry mounted. Under a new and aggressive management, the Pepperell Manufacturing Company launched a program featuring its Lady Pepperell sheet, its chief point of individualization being a 68 x 76 construction. Whereas Pequot had been

---

[11] Regarding the textures of sheeting see page 321.

spending about $20,000 in magazine advertising, Pepperell in 1924 spent $30,000, and followed it up in the two subsequent years with expenditures of $64,000 and $54,000, respectively. The Utica Steam & Mohawk Valley Cotton Mills also started advertising its Utica steets in 1924, and for three years had space expenditures greater than those of Pequot. The Dwight Manufacturing Company began advertising its Dwight Anchor sheet in 1926; Cannon Mills, Inc., entered in 1928 to become a leading advertiser of its Cannon sheets. In 1927, apparently to protect its position, Pequot increased its expenditures. As a result of this activity, the industry, which had used only $20,000 of space in 1920, by 1929 purchased nearly $600,000 worth.

With the advent of the depression and a greatly decreased value of sheeting sales, however, the space expenditures fell below $200,000 in 1932; and thereafter during the period covered by the table, they reached a total above $500,000 only in 1937, which was a year of large textile production.

Confidential information obtained from several mills advertising sheets indicated that expenditures for advertising for recent years ranged from 1% to 3% of net sales. For a sheet selling at retail in the neighborhood of $1.50, this percentage represents an advertising expenditure by the manufacturer ranging from somewhat under 1 cent to 2½ cents. Discussions with mill executives indicated that they did not believe a larger expenditure on this highly competitive item could be made profitably. Thus, competition in price has evidently checked increasing promotional expenditures.

Character of Competition after 1920

The competitive situation which developed during the 1920's, when the advertising expenditures were growing, may be summarized as follows:[12] A large number of mills, approximately 100, manufactured sheeting. As much as 75% of the business, however, was reported to be furnished by 10 companies, of which 6 were the advertisers listed in the tables above. During this period, in the neighborhood of 50% to 60% of sales was still in the 64 x 64 construction, or coarser. Since price competition among the lower grade textures was very keen and tended to be unprofitable, the advertising mills

---

[12] Based upon information gathered from operating executives in the collection of case histories, and not supported by statistical data; consequently it must be accepted as only approximate.

as well as certain other mills which did not advertise were desirous of shifting their sales to the higher count textures which promised more profit. The promotional drive of mills and of the trade to sell better grade sheets undoubtedly has accounted for the persistent trend toward consumption of finer grades of sheets.

While there were numerous mill brands and distributors' brands of 64 x 64 texture and coarser, advertising and promotion was devoted almost entirely to the better grades of sheeting, chiefly to the 68 x 72 grade, as indicated in Table 71, page 317. The five mills which had taken up advertising in the twenties were among the leading producers in 1930.

In the field of fine percale sheeting, Wamsutta Mills carried on a consistent program of advertising and promotion after a new management had taken over the plant in 1920. The Wamsutta brand became and has remained the dominant one in its field, although in more recent years a number of mills, such as Pepperell and Cannon, have entered into competition for this business. Some department stores, mail-order houses, and chains also have established private brands of percale sheets.

Unadvertised Mill Brands

There were a number of mills of considerable capacity which employed no appreciable space advertising directed to consumers. Some of these had old brands, well known in the trade and among consumers, such as Fruit of the Loom and Indian Head. Pacific Mills, another leading textile producer, in 1922 erected a modern mill at Lyman, South Carolina, with an annual production capacity of about 15,000 cases of sheets, both in the 64 x 64 texture and in the 68 x 72 texture. In building sales of its sheets to absorb the capacity of this plant, Pacific Mills did not advertise to consumers. It sold under a number of its existing mill brands and under the private brands of wholesalers and retailers, securing volume by offering attractive wholesale prices. Later it sought to obtain wholesale prices at or near those of advertised brands and offered its retailers exclusive or selected dealerships, appealing merchandising aids, and dealer advertising aids to make its line attractive to them.[13] In very recent years, Pacific Mills has undertaken a limited amount of space advertising to help build demand for its Pacific brand.

---

[13] Case of Pacific Mills, files of the Harvard Business School.

Private Brands

Many mills, including some that advertised, sold sheeting in the piece to wholesalers, chain store companies, and mail-order houses, which made finished sheets to be sold under their own brand names, while other mills made finished sheets to be sold under the brands of distributors.[14]

While several of the leading mills were employing advertising and aggressive promotion to help establish their brands, the private brands of distributors, particularly those of large department stores and chains, were being promoted by their owners. It will be noted, for example, in Table 72 that in 1929 the J. C. Penney Company spent $53,000 on sheet advertising in magazines, and in 1930 Sears, Roebuck and Company spent approximately $6,000. This table, however, does not reflect the substantial amount of newspaper advertising or the other store promotion put behind their private brands of sheets and pillowcases by large department stores and by the chains. Reports of the Controllers' Congress of the National Retail Dry Goods Association show that approximately 5% of sales is spent in publicity of sheeting departments.[15] Much of this expenditure is devoted to private brands.

Changes in Selling Methods Accompanying Advertising

An appraisal of the effect of advertising upon the demand for various brands of sheeting is made difficult by the fact that important changes in selling methods have been adopted by a number of the mills which have employed advertising. One important marketing development relates to methods of trade distribution. The leading advertised brand, Pequot, from early days followed a policy of using selected wholesale distribution, and intensive or dense retail distribution. Because of the strength of its brand, Pequot by 1920 had unusually dense distribution for a dry goods item. This very domination, however, provided an opening for the mills then seeking to expand their brand sales, because Pequot sheets were used frequently as a price leader by dry goods and department stores, and were generally subject to keen price competition in the retail

---

[14] Case of the Carpenter Company, files of the Harvard Business School.
[15] For example, see: *1939 Departmental Merchandising and Operating Results of Department and Specialty Stores*, Controllers' Congress, National Retail Dry Goods Association (New York, June, 1940).

trade. Consequently the retail margins attained upon Pequot were not so large as desired by many retailers. For example, an executive of a leading department store in Boston stated that in the period before the advent of other advertised brands, when Pequot was the leader, the gross margin on sheets in his store was in the neighborhood of 15% of sales. Subsequently, as an exclusive representative of another advertised brand, the store obtained a gross margin in the neighborhood of 30% in its sheeting department.

Not only was this situation conducive to development of private brands by large stores, but it permitted any of the mills entering on an advertising program subsequent to 1920 to seek purchases from important retail outlets on the inducement of their being made an exclusive selected retail representative in their respective cities. A number of advertised brands, such as Pepperell and Dwight Anchor, as well as unadvertised brands, such as Pacific, adopted some such plan of selected retail distribution.

Another important marketing change accompanying advertising was adopted by a number of the leading companies, namely, the shift from selling agents to the establishment of sales organizations by the mills.[16] This procedure was accompanied in some cases by a policy of making a larger percentage of sales direct to retailers than had been the practice previously.

In a number of instances the selling programs were subjected to still other significant changes which make an appraisal of advertising effects difficult. For example, when new management undertook in 1925 to launch Lady Pepperell sheets as the leading item in its advertising and promotional program, it not only established its own sales department and undertook a large amount of direct selling to retailers, but also launched upon a program of product diversification. Whereas sheets were the principal product manufactured when the new management took over in 1924, by 1927 they represented only about one-fifth of the company's production. Moreover, the diversification program entailed a plan to advertise and firmly establish a "house mark," or family brand, which would be of benefit not only to Pepperell products but possibly to products manufactured by other manufacturers from Pepperell fabrics. Since 1930 a substantial part of the company's advertising has been devoted to this

---

[16] For example, Pepperell formed its own sales department in 1925; Pacific Mills did so in 1927; Pequot in 1936.

family brand and to other Pepperell fabrics. While Lady Pepperell sheets have been the leading item and have received a substantial volume of advertising, they probably have benefited also from the advertising of the family mark. In addition, it should be recognized that the efforts of the selling organization have been given not only to sheets but to other items as well. Hence any effort to appraise the effect of Pepperell sheet advertising would necessarily have to weigh these sales policies.

From the above discussion it is evident that numerous forces in addition to advertising have affected the flow of demand among producers. The sales attained by advertising mills must be attributed in part to changes in their selling methods which have been con-current with the use of advertising. In turn their sales have had to be gained in competition with other mills which have not advertised and with distributors who have sold aggressively under their private brands.

Evidence Regarding Mill Prices

Since detailed data regarding prices and quantities of sheet sales by individual mills are not attainable, it has been necessary to sup-plement information obtained from case material with opinions from executives in the industry and in the dry goods trade regarding quantities sold and prices received by advertisers and nonadvertisers. A study of price data is complicated by the fact that not only wholesale prices but retail prices must be considered in the efforts to trace advertising's effect.

As a rule the mill prices for the leading advertised brands in the 68 x 72 construction have been equal or nearly equal over a period of years. A possible exception is Dwight Anchor,[17] which reportedly has been sold very largely to the institutional trade and has not had such extensive retail distribution as some of the other brands. It was said by several informants to have been sold to the retail trade at somewhat less than the other advertised brands. As a rule the price changes of important competitors were said to have been quickly met.

In the 64 x 64 construction, Cannon and Pepperell Red Label, the

---

[17] In October, 1932, the Nashua Manufacturing Company purchased the sheeting busi-ness of the Dwight Manufacturing Company and since that date has manufactured and sold Dwight Anchor sheets.

leading advertised mill brands, were reported to have received an advantage in mill selling prices from 2½% to 5% over nonadvertised mill brands.

In the high-count field, Wamsutta, as a result of its advertising and merchandising policies, held an outstanding leadership in sales volume. In contrast to the situation among competing brands in other textures, Wamsutta's prices were reported to have been consistently above all competing brands. Not only did the Wamsutta management make its product desired through its advertising, but it followed the avowed policy of trying to make Wamsutta the finest cotton sheeting in the market. By concentrating its efforts it clearly was successful in building an enviable reputation among consumers. This reputation, along with a policy of encouraging price maintenance, evidently brought a large degree of retail support.

Unadvertised mill brands have been sold to the trade at a differential under the leading advertised brands. While estimates of the amount of differential varied among our informants, the figures most commonly named were 5% to 7½%, although two executives with long experience in the field stated that the differential was 10% to 15%. Apparently the amount of difference permitted between the leading brands and unadvertised mill brands has depended upon the strength of the market, sometimes having amounted to more than 15%.

Sheeting of 68 x 72 construction put out under private brands of retailers and wholesalers was sold by the mills at a differential under the advertised brands. The amount of difference apparently varied in accordance with the strength of the market and the desire of mills for orders. Such a differential is, of course, to be expected in view of the fact that for private brand merchandise, the distributors assumed the full burden of promoting sales. The differential given here was said by six informants to be approximately the same as that between the advertised and unadvertised mill brands, while the others stated that it was somewhat more; one said it was about 10%, another said 10% to 15%, while still another said it was from 10% to 30%. Most mills were reported to have accepted orders for private brands. Some mills sold the same products to the trade under private brands that they sold under their own well-known mill labels.

Advertising and Demand at Retail

The price differentials established at the mills, as outlined above, were not in all cases reflected in the retail prices asked for advertised brands and unadvertised brands.

Some retailers, particularly chains, such as J. C. Penney Company, Sears, Roebuck and Company, and Montgomery Ward & Co., Incorporated, were found to sell their private brands at a substantial differential below the prices asked for comparable advertised mill brands offered by competing stores. The differential at retail was greater than that at the mill. For example, in 1938 one chain was selling its private brand sheets at 20 cents to 30 cents under leading advertised brands of comparable quality.

In contrast to the chains, not all leading department stores sold their private brands below advertised mill brands of comparable quality. A substantial number were reported by the mill executives consulted as selling at the regular retail prices of the leading advertised brands, but some stores which featured low prices asked a price somewhat below the usual prices of leading brands. These opinions, obtained from sheet manufacturers, were in agreement with price data obtained from a limited check among leading Boston and New York stores. The fact that department store private brands were sold at relatively firm prices led some trade informants to the opinion that many such brands on the whole may even have sold at retail somewhat above the leading advertised brands, in view of the fact that the latter were more frequently used as sales leaders by retailers.

That the advertising of mills did not present undue difficulties to the sale of private brands was indicated by the fact that merchandise executives of several large department stores and chains from whom case material was obtained invariably expressed their interest in developing their private brands of sheeting. Moreover, all stated that they had been able to build a consumer acceptance of their brands in their localities. They readily admitted, however, the greater pulling power of leading advertised brands. For example, one chain store manager cited the case of holding a nine-day mark-down sale in 1938 on a leading advertised brand of sheet, size 81 x 99, for $1, this price permitting a mark-up of 18%. At the time of the sale the regular price in competing stores was $1.49.

Approximately 3,500 sheets were sold. The buyer stated that, on the basis of his experience, the same amount of newspaper advertising upon a similar mark-down of its own private brand sheet of the same grade would have produced sales of only 1,000 to 1,500 units. This difference in pull explained the store's interest in using the well-known brand as a leader.

To sum up, the limited evidence of retail demand for sheets indicates that the well-known, advertised brands evidently have been preferred by many consumers to the unadvertised mill brands or private brands. This conclusion is supported by the large volume of sales made at prices above those at which certain leading private brands have been obtainable. It is shown also by the greater pulling power of the advertised brands when sold at reduced prices.

Yet the pull of the advertising by the mills has been limited. Leading department stores have found it possible to gain sales for their private brands and for unadvertised mill brands for which they have been selected dealers, with little or no concession in price below regular prices of advertised brands. Moreover, when private brands have been sold by important chains at a differential appreciably below advertised brands, they reportedly have made substantial increases in sales.

Volumes of Sales of Mills

Opinions obtained regarding the quantities of sheeting sold by different mills, though lacking in concreteness, on the whole tended to support the evidence from retailers as to the effect of the advertising upon demand. That advertising had been helpful to the mills using it was shown by the fact that in general the brands which held a leading place in 1940 were those which had been advertised. Their leading positions had been obtained at firmer prices at the mill than those which had been secured for unadvertised mill brands and private brands. In addition, some of the brands in the 68 x 72 construction, particularly Lady Pepperell,[18] had built their demand largely after advertising was initiated in the early 1920's.

On the other hand, there appeared reason to believe that the price differential at retail between certain private brands and advertised mill brands and the desire of retailers to promote their own brands

---

[18] Although Lady Pepperell sheets have had a 68 x 76 thread count, they have been considered as directly competitive with sheets of 68 x 72 construction.

were forces strong enough to offset the consumer advertising of mill brands. Several of the private brands of leading chains were reported to have made rapid increases in sales in the last decade. Moreover, opinions received show that on the whole unadvertised mill brands and private brands in recent years, at least, have not lost ground to the advertised mill brands. Some informants insisted that although mills with advertised brands had held their share of yardage, a larger percentage of their sales than formerly was of private brand merchandise or was sold to institutions, such as hotels, hospitals, and government agencies, at practically the levels of price received for privately branded merchandise. All in all, the evidence indicates that advertising is only a moderately effective force in guiding demand so long as the differential in prices at retail is not too wide.

One final piece of evidence of the pull of advertising is found in the fact that Pequot, the brand most subject to price cutting among retailers, has been able to maintain extensive retail distribution. While many mill brands, according to inquiries in 1938, followed in general a policy of selected retail distribution, Pequot still adhered to its policy of unselected retail distribution. Accordingly, Pequot was then, as it had been for many years, subjected to frequent use as a sale leader. Inquiry among several large retailers indicated that they preferred to devote their advertising and selling efforts to a private brand or to a mill brand for which they had selected agency rights, because the need of meeting competitive prices on Pequot sheets gave them a lower margin on such sales. Yet the reputation of Pequot was so great among consumers that a majority of these stores found it advisable to carry a stock of Pequot sheets. Inquiry among Boston department stores and women's specialty stores in August, 1940, showed the following results: Out of ten leading department and women's specialty stores, eight sold sheets, two did not. Of the eight, five carried Pequot sheets, three did not. At the time of the investigation, all five stores which carried Pequot gave display space either to private brands or to other mill brands; only one store displayed Pequot sheets.

In view of the policy of unselected retail distribution employed by Pequot, it is believed that use of advertising was clearly an essential in its selling program. Without a strong consumer demand based not merely on high intrinsic quality of the product, but made effective through consistent advertising, many large stores which handled the product would not have done so. Large retailers generally seek to avoid the handling of brands which competitors sell unless there is an evident consumer call for them. A sheeting brand unsupported by advertising has not enough individuality to lead to such demand.

Since the Pequot mills have been engaged in the manufacture of only sheeting, the sales figures for which have been published in annual reports, the record of sales volume attained under its advertising and selling policies is available over a considerable period, together with its profit record. These are shown in Table 73. As indicated in the previous discussion, its sales volume must be interpreted in the light of the changing competitive situation which has been outlined.

TABLE 73

PEQUOT MILLS
OPERATING STATISTICS, 1855 AND 1911–1939

YEAR	PRODUCTION		SALES		NET PROFITS AFTER DEPRECIATION
	Pounds (000 Omitted)	Linear Yards (000 Omitted)	Linear Yards (000 Omitted)	Dollars	
1855	1,473	5,455			$ 96,280
1911		16,988	16,296	$ 2,705,634	
1912		17,322	19,153	3,182,097	
1913		17,844	18,221	3,252,545	
1914		11,575	13,067	2,188,288	
1915		6,975	7,446	1,447,942	
1916		17,397	16,139	3,298,174	
1917		19,327	19,285	4,835,015	
1918		19,453	19,363	7,057,470	
1919		15,955	17,315	6,503,226	
1920		18,252	18,379	9,360,384	
1921		20,535	20,718	7,091,476	
1922		21,461	22,566	8,282,612	
1923		21,705	22,474	9,112,872	
1924		22,115	21,660	8,725,837	
1925	13,792	22,373	22,650	9,056,447	
1926	14,552	23,644	24,678	9,072,675	423,806*
1927	19,888	32,328†	30,766	10,583,100	1,598,541
1928	13,017	20,945	20,397	7,273,535	439,898
1929	12,908	20,836	21,058	7,887,607	614,053
1930	12,692	20,086	20,335	7,162,267	535,097§
1931	12,248	19,601	19,460	5,895,003	50,733§
1932	11,382	18,240	18,466	4,184,756	127,983§‡
1933	10,221	16,363†	16,744	3,811,826	19,066
1934	12,378	21,614		4,386,188	151,909
1935	8,683	15,367†		5,717,285	1,136,322§
1936	16,791	26,925		6,722,508	434,853
1937	18,089	29,150		8,514,796	341,868
1938	17,482	26,553		6,215,972	125,424
1939	12,789	20,196		5,592,995	63,195

* After inventory markdown of $391,646.
† Company operated night shift through 1927; 1933, strike May 8 to July 19; 1935, 10-week strike.
‡ After deduction of depreciation adjustment of $36,635.
§ Deficit.

Source: Company's annual reports.

The value of the advertising in helping this mill to gain leadership in volume in the period before 1920 has already been discussed. The effect of advertising since that date is not so clear. Production in the decade 1930–1939 was about 4½% less than that of the decade 1920–1929. Moreover, in the latter decade was included an unknown percentage of private brand business. In addition, part of the production was of textures other than the 68 x 72 count of the Pequot brand.

It is impossible to draw from these data any final conclusions regarding advertising effect. Sales of this brand have been influenced so much by a mixture of competition in price and advertising and by a changing competition for retail outlets, which cannot be mathematically appraised, that any effort to measure advertising results in the sales data is futile. Also lacking is evidence of total sheeting sales for the United States with which to compare Pequot performance. Yet the continued consumer demand for Pequot sheets, which has induced widespread retail stocking of the brand, and the sale of substantial quantities in spite of an apparent lack of active selling support in retail channels provide reason to believe that the consumer advertising has influenced demand.

The lack of certainty as to the exact effect of advertising in the Pequot case applies to the industry as a whole. Such difficulty in measurement of advertising effects usually occurs when advertising is of relatively minor weight among the forces influencing demand. Clearly it has not had a strong effect on either primary or selective demand for sheeting. Yet that it has helped bring a change in the grades of sheeting consumed seems certain, while its moderate effect in guiding selective demand is borne out by such evidence as is available.

CHAPTER XIII

THE EFFECT OF ADVERTISING ON THE DEMAND FOR ORANGES, WALNUTS, AND LETTUCE

THE EFFECT OF ADVERTISING ON THE PRIMARY DEMAND FOR ORANGES

PROBABLY oranges have been cited more than any other product as an example of demand expansion through advertising. For over 30 years the California Fruit Growers Exchange has carried on a persistent, able program of advertising and promotion. During that time per capita consumption has increased 2½ fold. This increase may be attributed in part to a favoring dietary trend, which was discussed in Chapter VII, and in part to a downward trend in the price of oranges. Under these conditions a considerable consumption increase would probably have taken place had there been no advertising. But much credit for the increase should be given to advertising and promotion, for the management has been alert to speed up wide acceptance of health and dietary ideas favoring its products.

The Need for Expanding Demand

From the standpoint of citrus producers, the need of expanding the market has been a pressing one for many years, a need arising from an ever-increasing productive capacity of orchards planted by thousands of farmers.[1] Production of bearing orchards cannot be controlled as can that of manufactured products. The problem is clearly stated in the 1939 *Annual Report of the General Manager* of the California Fruit Growers Exchange:

> The season 1938–1939 was another disappointing year. While returns varied widely according to individual production, many citrus growers did not make the cost of production. This general statement applies to all of the citrus producing states.
>
> . . . . . .
>
> The reason for this general situation is not hard to find but it is most difficult to correct. The law of supply and demand will not be denied.

---

[1] One of the serious problems in the citrus field, as in numerous agricultural fields, has been a tendency for farmers to produce greater quantities than the market will take at prices which are profitable to them.

The simple fact is that the citrus industry has substantially increased its production year by year until it has reached a point where the public is unwilling or unable in present conditions to buy the volume marketed at a price which provides a living return to the average grower.

The most encouraging thing in the situation is the strong consumer demand so amply demonstrated in the operation of this season. Sales from all sources in many weeks exceeded 2,500,000 boxes, and for the year, over 200,000 carloads (90,000,000 boxes) were consumed as fresh fruit. This establishes a new record, exceeding the previous record sales of 1938 by about 19,000 carloads.

The figures on total citrus production are even more challenging than figures on shipment. The combined crop harvested in the various producing states in 1938–1939 of 135,000,000 boxes, compares with 115,000,000 boxes harvested in 1937–1938, and a five-year annual average of 55,000,000 boxes for the period 1925–1929 inclusive, which is considered the period of maximum buying power in this country in all history. Had the crop of 1938–1939 been no larger than in those prosperous days, the marketing problem would have been a simple one indeed.[2]

Oranges, to which attention is directed in this study, in recent years have accounted for 60% to 70% of the citrus production referred to in the preceding paragraph. Since 1909 orange production has increased roughly at the rate of 2,000,000 boxes a year and has reached a total in recent years of almost 80,000,000 boxes. Faced by such increases, the desirability of expanding demand for citrus fruits is evident. Failure to do so must result in losses to growers, which in time would serve to check production. The growers naturally have desired to prevent such losses.

The Increase in Consumption

Table 74 shows the steady growth over a long period of years in per capita orange consumption, based on production data. Since these data relate to oranges produced and not to oranges which have gone into commercial channels, they are probably somewhat high, but the error, as reflected in per capita figures, is small and does not disturb the trend picture. Whereas for the five-year period, 1915–1920, the average per capita consumption was approximately 14½ pounds, for 1933–1937, inclusive, it was in excess of 32 pounds, over twice as much. The increase is described in different terms in the 1937 annual report of the California Fruit Growers Exchange, which marked the completion of 30 years of Exchange advertising:

---

[2] California Fruit Growers Exchange, *Annual Report of the General Manager for the Year Ended October 31, 1939*, p. 5.

The year before Exchange advertising began, per capita orange consumption stood at 31. In 10 years it had risen to 43; in 20 years, to 52; while in the last year of full production (1935–1936), Americans bought an average of 79 oranges.[3]

TABLE 74

UNITED STATES PRODUCTION OF ORANGES, PER CAPITA CONSUMPTION, AND ADVERTISING EXPENDITURES BY CALIFORNIA FRUIT GROWERS EXCHANGE AND FLORIDA CITRUS COMMISSION, 1900, 1909, AND 1915–1937, INCLUSIVE

YEAR	TOTAL U.S. PRODUCTION PLUS IMPORTS LESS EXPORTS (NET), THOUSANDS OF BOXES	PER CAPITA CONSUMPTION		CALIFORNIA FRUIT GROWERS ADVERTISING EXPENDITURE	TRACEABLE FLORIDA EXPENDITURES
		Pounds	Index 1915-1919=100		
1900.........	6,067	6.1	....	....	....
1909.........	21,663	18.3	....	$ 50,000	....
1915.........	19,625	15.3	105	193,000	....
1916.........	22,583	16.8	116	240,000	....
1917.........	9,636	6.9	48	288,800	....
1918.........	22,423	16.8	116	129,000	....
1919.........	23,528	16.8	116	278,000	....
1920.........	30,206	21.4	147	303,600	....
1921.........	21,534	15.3	105	531,500*	....
1922.........	31,165	21.4	147	278,300	....
1923.........	36,068	24.5	169	585,800	....
1924.........	28,658	19.1	132	660,000	....
1925.........	32,455	21.4	147	538,600	....
1926.........	36,771	24.5	169	696,800	....
1927.........	30,729	19.9	137	801,700	....
1928.........	49,585	31.3	216	761,977	....
1929.........	30,683	19.1	132	1,207,345	....
1930.........	50,439	31.3	216	726,068	....
1931.........	47,019	29.0	200	1,568,324	....
1932.........	48,052	29.0	200	947,948	....
1933.........	44,118	26.7	184	826,045	....
1934.........	58,609	35.1	242	1,015,052	....
1935.........	47,916	29.0	200	1,451,514	$ 12,529
1936.........	52,475	31.3	216	866,582	97,145
1937.........	66,905	39.7	273	1,345,021	159,790
1938.........	....	....	....	1,728,378	92,084
1939.........	....	....	....	962,677	111,269

* 14 months.

Sources:

Production and exports: U. S. Department of Agriculture, *Agricultural Statistics,* 1936 and 1939.

Per capita consumption: Production for U. S. consumption in boxes was converted to pounds by multiplying the number of boxes by 76.4, a weighted average for the twelve-year period, 1927–1938, of California oranges at 70 lbs. a box and Florida oranges at 90 lbs. a box. The total poundage figure was then divided by midyear estimates of population of *Statistical Abstract of the United States,* 1938.

Advertising expenditures: For California, *Annual Reports of the General Manager* of the California Fruit Growers Exchange for years ending October 31. For Florida, 1939 figures and 1938 newspaper figure from American Newspaper Publishers' Association, *Expenditures of National Advertisers.*

1935–1939 newspaper linage: Media Records, Inc., *Newspapers and Newspaper Advertisers.* A line rate of 35 cents was calculated from the linage of 1938 and 1939 and the dollar expenditures in newspapers for the same years and applied to the other years. For conversion rate, see Appendix IV.

1937, 1938 magazines, and 1937 radio: Publishers' Information Bureau, *National Advertising Records.*

[3] California Fruit Growers Exchange, *Annual Report of the General Manager for the Year Ended October 31, 1937,* p. 24.

Price Data

There are no satisfactory price data for the entire period showing what consumers have paid for the increased quantities of oranges which have been consumed. A continuous series of the average New York auction prices for the various classes of oranges is available for the period 1924–1938, as shown in Table 75. While the variations arising from crop size give considerable irregularity to the series, the general trend has been downward. An index of prices, based on 1926 as 100, shows the price of oranges for most years below the Bureau of Labor Statistics All Commodities Index. Prices have tended to be especially low in recent years under the pressure of large production increase and lowered national income.

Accordingly, it must be recognized that the advertising and promotional efforts have not moved the ever-increasing volume of oranges without price concessions. On the other hand, the large crops probably could never have been moved, even with the price concessions made, had not consumers' desire for oranges increased over the period.

TABLE 75

PRICES OF ORANGES PER BOX—AVERAGE FOR SEASON AT NEW YORK AUCTION
AND INDEX OF PRICES, 1926=100, 1924–1938 *

YEAR	CALIFORNIA VALENCIA		CALIFORNIA NAVEL		FLORIDA		B.L.S. ALL COMMODITY Index 1926 = 100
	Price per Box†	Index 1926 = 100	Price per Box†	Index 1926 = 100	Price per Box†	Index 1926 = 100	
1924........	....	....	$5.11	108	$6.02	146	98.1
1925........	$7.15	135	4.80	101	5.10	124	103.5
1926........	5.28	100	4.74	100	4.11	100	100.0
1927........	6.00	114	5.61	118	6.24	152	95.4
1928........	7.45	141	4.10	86	3.40	83	96.7
1929........	4.63	88	5.64	119	4.94	120	95.3
1930........	7.59	144	3.54	75	3.54	86	86.4
1931........	3.97	75	3.14	66	3.43	83	73.0
1932........	3.41	65	2.73	58	2.43	59	64.8
1933........	3.12	59	2.88	61	2.78	68	65.9
1934........	4.25	80	2.93	62	2.61	64	74.9
1935........	3.45	65	3.17	67	3.04	74	80.0
1936........	4.21	80	3.84	81	3.25	79	80.8
1937........	5.13	97	2.72	57	2.26	55	86.3
1938........	3.02	57	2.86	56	2.10	48	78.6
Average per box.......	4.90		3.84		3.68		
Average per lb.........	0.07		0.055		0.041		

* Season varies from 6 to 12 months.
† Size of box: California, 70 pounds; Florida, 90 pounds.
Sources:
Prices: U. S. Department of Agriculture, *Yearbook,* 1926; U. S. Depatrment of Agriculture, *Agricultural Statistics,* 1936 and 1940.
B. L. S. Index: *Statistical Abstract of the United States,* 1939, p. 316.

Amount of Advertising of Oranges

One of the ablest agricultural marketing cooperatives in the country, the California Fruit Growers Exchange, has done an outstanding job in its efforts to secure a profitable return to its producer members. It has done this in part through establishment of a program of orderly marketing, which has involved the shipment of carefully graded fruit to individual markets in accordance with the capacity and current needs of those markets, and in part through its program of consumer advertising and dealer promotion work.

Its first advertising expenditure was in 1907, when it appropriated $10,000 for advertising with the understanding that the Southern Pacific Railroad Company would spend an equivalent amount.[4] The management was encouraged by the fact that a total of $7,000 spent on advertising Exchange oranges in the state of Iowa in that year resulted in sales 50% greater than in the preceding year in the state. The following year a total of $25,000 for advertising was authorized, and the Sunkist brand was adopted. Thus was inaugurated a program of advertising which has since been carried on consistently until, by the end of the 1939 season, the Exchange had spent on the advertising and promotion of citrus fruits a total of $28,302,000, of which probably $20,000,000 was devoted to oranges.[5] Since 1930 the average annual expenditure on oranges alone has been well in excess of a million dollars. The expenditures by years are shown in Table 74.

In the early years the promotional and advertising expenditure amounted to only about 1 cent a box for oranges; in recent years it has been 5 cents a box for normal or light crop seasons and 7 cents for certain heavy crop seasons. In terms of consumer buying, these latter amounts represent an expenditure of approximately four-tenths to five-tenths of a cent a dozen. The expenditure has represented to the Exchange over a period of time approximately 1½% of the sales price of the fruit.

In recent years, to the advertising and promotional expenditures of the California Fruit Growers Exchange there have been added substantial expenditures by the Florida citrus industry. In 1935 the Florida Citrus Commission's program was inaugurated by an act of the state legislature. This commission came into being at the behest

[4] R. M. McCurdy, *The History of the California Fruit Growers Exchange* (Los Angeles, 1925), p. 59.
[5] Estimate for whole period based on the division of total expenditures among various products during 1930–1939 decade.

of leading growers and shippers, who saw in the prospects of large increases of the Florida citrus crop a need for a program which would regulate product standards and provide for promotion of Florida fruit. Its total expenditures upon advertising and dealer promotion for the first three years of its existence were reported to have been approximately $2,000,000 for all citrus fruits, representing an assessment of 1 cent a box on oranges, 3 cents on grapefruit, and 5 cents on tangerines.[6] Table 74 shows traceable space expenditures, for oranges only, as shown by advertising measurement services.

Further promotional efforts have been devoted to oranges and other citrus fruits by the Florida Citrus Exchange, a cooperative, which since 1910 has carried on promotional work for its members. In 1939 it was reported that members of this cooperative contributed 2½ cents a box for promotional work, with a total expenditure for such effort of approximately $200,000.[7]

Character of Advertising Appeals

The advertising of the California Fruit Growers Exchange as a whole has stressed primary appeals. Only in recent years, when Florida competition has become keen, have directly competitive appeals come to the fore, and then mostly in connection with the advertising of navel oranges,[8] which are marketed in the same season as Florida oranges. The 1937 Annual Report, p. 25, expressed a note of regret that the management had felt it necessary "to interrupt the Exchange's long-standing educational program in favor of the competitive campaign."

Some selective appeals have been used in other years; yet the management has put chief emphasis on efforts to expand the orange market.

The management's viewpoint was well expressed in the 1933 report (pp. 24 and 25):

Exchange advertising, while continually changing in its application to conform with marketing and economic conditions, has three primary objectives:

---

[6] In view of the fact that the advertising of Florida oranges did not reach sizeable proportions until 1935, by which time the larger part of growth in consumption had occurred, attention in the study has been directed primarily to consideration of the advertising of the California Fruit Growers Exchange.

[7] L. W. Marvin, "Each Dollar Invested in Advertising Brings Sales Increase of $17," *Printers' Ink*, July 7, 1939, p. 11.

[8] Two important varieties of oranges are marketed by the California Fruit Growers Exchange: Navels, which ripen from November to May, and Valencias, which ripen from April to November.

(1) through educational advertising, to cause non-users to consume oranges and lemons for their healthful and refreshing qualities; (2) to cause limited users to consume more; and (3) to encourage habitual users to continue citrus fruit as a part of the daily diet in preference to other products for which are claimed the same health properties.

The present universal acceptance of citrus fruit by scientists and the general public alike, brought about by long years of scientific cultural practices, efficient handling, zealously guarded grade standards, intelligent distribution and consistent educational consumer advertising, can be perpetuated only by a continuance of the same diligent and constructive efforts.

Down through the years of Exchange advertising and marketing, the aim has been to convince the housewife to spend more of her food budget for citrus fruits. The increasing consumer expenditures for these fruits have, in many instances, come out of other foods. Today, citrus fruits encounter competition from products whose producers hope to garner for themselves a part of the food budget now expended for oranges, lemons and grapefruit.

. . . . .

The canners of tomato juice and pineapple juice are endeavoring by intensive advertising to build demand for their products. In their advertising they are making the same nutritional and health claims responsible in such a large degree for the phenomenal increase in citrus fruit consumption. Already these products, by reason of economy and convenience more than comparable food value, have found their way into American homes and institutions. The citrus fruit market thus faces a future that demands concerted advertising action as well as concerted marketing.

Other reports in recent years have recognized the importance of advertising to meet competition of substitute products.

The primary appeals used have fallen into two general categories: (1) the taste appeal, and (2) the health appeal. As part of its program of showing the deliciousness of oranges, the advertisements over a long period have featured the use of orange juice. In order further to encourage consumption of juice, the Exchange launched in 1921 an aggressive program, which has continued ever since, of selling juice extractors both for the fountain market and for home use. From 1921 through 1939 the Exchange had sold in excess of 75,000 fountain extractors, more than 100,000 electric extractors for home use, and approximately 2,600,000 reamers for home use.

To fortify itself with reasons for increasing citrus consumption, the Exchange has aided and encouraged medical and dietary research, and in turn through its advertising has carried the story of this research not only to consumers but to schools and professional groups.

In the 1936 Annual Report, p. 27, was the following statement:

Scientific nutritional and product research is the third foundation stone of an Exchange advertising program. Studying the constituents of Sunkist products and searching out their superior qualities over competitive citrus from other sections, as well as over other fruits and vegetables, gives sales ammunition to protect the leadership of the Exchange in the perishable field. And nutritional research incorporating clinical feeding studies, coupled with an analysis of the healthful qualities of citrus fruits, gives consumers new reasons for a wider consumption of these products. This third form of research helps build demand for the current season, but its greatest value is in the development of advertising news stories that build consumption to meet the constantly increasing production of the future.

The Exchange invested $22,579 in this type of research the past year, supporting twelve individual studies through college grants and fellowships at the leading educational institutions in this country.

The 1934 Annual Report contained the story of a three and one-half year research project at Mooseheart, Illinois, carried on through the cooperation of the Exchange with the University of Chicago, indicating the value of orange and lemon juice as preventives of dental caries and aids in building bone and tooth structure, particularly for children. This research provided the campaign theme for valencia oranges for the 1934–1935 season and was further employed subsequently.

The 1939 report, pp. 23–24, gives indication of the extensive effort of the Exchange's Home Economics and Educational Division:

The home economics division of the advertising department continued valuable contacts with food and nutrition editors of newspapers and magazines and teachers in this field, to whom new health facts, recipes and photographs were distributed regularly. Sunkist exhibits were made at conventions and hotel and restaurant shows. Recipes were developed for use of other food advertisers in cooperative advertising of their products with Sunkist oranges and lemons. A two-reel kodachrome color recipe film, "Citrus on Parade," was produced and shown to food classes and housewives numbering over 1,125,000, and 1,500,000 copies of a leaflet containing the recipes shown in the film were distributed at the showings.

In sixteen years in the educational field, the California Fruit Growers Exchange has distributed over 61 million pieces of educational material to schools. For the school year of 1938–39, more than 5,600,000 such pieces were placed through individual contacts with some 48,000 educators. In many cases, this educational material is used as actual teaching texts. Such unqualified acceptance of an advertiser's publications by teachers is the result of the care with which all educational numbers are edited.

A one-reel film, "The Golden Journey," was made and shown during the year to an audience of more than 2,300,000 students. Through animated maps and historical scenes, the picture shows the journey of citrus fruits from their original home in the Orient to California, and depicts grove and packing house operations. A new feature in both of the Sunkist educational films has been the provision of sound prints for schools with sound equipment.

The substantial volume of advertising by the Florida orange growers since 1935 has been an additional force to stimulate orange consumption. This advertising has contained primary appeals as well as selective.

Effect of Advertising on Consumption

To what extent this program of primary appeals increased consumption can be but a matter of conjecture. The part played by advertising in building consumer attitudes is suggested in evidence from consumer surveys made by the Exchange and recounted in the 1936 and 1937 annual reports. A survey made in 1936 showed that among orange-using families 90% used juice in the summertime and 84% in the wintertime.[9] On the basis of number of users and frequency of use it was estimated by the management that the drinking of orange juice, so assiduously encouraged by the Exchange, was by this time accounting for two-thirds of the crop.[10] The reasons given by consumers in the survey for the use of oranges reflected the ideas carried in Exchange advertising, ideas which came from the nutritional research sponsored by the Exchange. Among the leading reasons given for use of oranges were their contribution to general health, their contribution of calcium and vitamins, their laxative effect, their alkaline effect, and their value to the teeth. In all, 81% of United States families were shown as users of oranges.

The General Manager, in his 1938 annual report, p. 26, suggested as further evidence of the possible efficacy of Exchange advertising in stimulating demand for oranges and other citrus fruits, a comparison of citrus consumption and that of certain other fruits which have not had such consistent promotion. In commenting upon changes in American food habits, the report pointed out that not only citrus fruits but other fruits as well might have expected benefit from the marked dietary changes favorable thereto. Yet, whereas oranges and other citrus fruits had made marked increases in per capita consumption, certain other fruits, particularly apples, peaches, and bananas, had experienced decreases in per capita consumption. Such evidence

---

9 1936 *Annual Report,* p. 26.
10 1937 *Annual Report,* p. 24.

is strongly suggestive of advertising effect, but not conclusive because of the many variables involved which are unaccounted for.

Effect of Advertising upon Selective Demand

While the promotion of oranges of the California Fruit Growers Exchange has in large measure used primary appeals, the management has also been alert to the competitive battle with oranges grown in other states and has taken numerous measures to try to build preference for its brands. The 1938 Annual Report, p. 11, called attention to the greatly increased shipments from Florida, and stated:

> The marketing problem did not hinge so much on the size of the navel crop as on the extremely heavy production of Florida oranges which moved to the markets without regulation, coupled with low buying power throughout the country and the enormous apple crop selling at low prices. Florida's interstate shipments during the southern navel season were 10,201 cars greater than the 5-year average—an increase of 44%. Not only so, but estimates of Florida's crop were so far below actual outturn that it made it impracticable to correlate navel shipments with the unregulated national orange supply. As late as March, the estimate was 5,625 cars lower than the season's production proved to be.
>
> . . . . .
>
> Barring climatic disasters, competition from Florida promises to be even more severe in the immediate future. It must be kept in mind that her cultural and transportation costs are lower than California's; consequently, citrus fruit from that state can sell at considerably lower prices and still return a fair profit to the grower. California navels must, therefore, sell on a preference basis. It will require the united efforts of the California citrus industry in advertising and merchandising, in shipping programs, and in the maintenance of a superior product to successfully market the navel crop of the future.

From early days the Association has recognized the importance of carefully guarding and protecting the quality of the fruit sold under the Exchange's Sunkist and Red Ball brands, in order to build preference for them. Its chief brand, Sunkist, was adopted in 1908, the year after advertising was initiated. The 1909 Annual Report, p. 3, pointed out:

> But your [advertising] success will not be as great as it might be if you had some general supervision as to what *character of fruit* is put under that brand. In other words, *with* supervision you might get the 100% benefit possible from advertising, whereas you only get 50% or thereabouts *without* it.

In accordance with the stricture laid down in this statement, the Exchange has carefully guarded the quality of fruit sold under its brands. To insure shipment of only fruit acceptable to the consumer both in juice content and in appearance, the Exchange early set up a field department to try to improve and protect quality. Each year the problems met by this department and the efforts taken to solve them are recorded in the annual report. For example, in 1934 particular difficulty was met in assuring the quality of its valencia crop, which in that year was below standard. In order to protect the advertised trade-marks of the Exchange under the difficulties met, it was found necessary to establish new grade regulations and to strengthen the inspection force. The year 1937 presented extreme difficulties because of the severe freeze in January of that year, while 40% of the fruit was still on the trees. In order to segregate good from bad fruit, a new X-ray sorting machine was put into use, which by fluoroscopic methods reveals interior quality without cutting the fruit. The 1939 report records a refrigeration project which had as its goal the determination of the best conditions for pre-cooling packed fruit to assure desired quality on arrival in eastern markets.

Another important part of the effort to build preference, particularly trade preference, for Exchange products has rested in its extensive force of promotional men calling on retailers. For example, 28 dealer service representatives made over 65,000 retail calls in 911 different markets in 1939, and the regular salesforce made almost 15,000 calls upon retailers to carry out the promotional and merchandising activities of the organization.

In addition to the above steps, the management has placed much reliance upon its advertising to bring a competitive brand preference. While the advertising has been devoted largely to primary appeals, all advertisements have carried one of the Exchange's brand names, Red Ball or Sunkist, more frequently the latter, until it has undoubtedly become one of the most familiar of food marks.

The increased competition in recent years has led to more competitive appeals being woven into the copy, particularly in connection with the advertising of navel oranges. The 1937 campaign was particularly aggressive in its competition with Florida oranges. Florida in its opening campaign had featured the theme of "one-fourth more juice." The Exchange in turn featured "more vitamin content" for its Sunkist oranges.[11] In 1938 a typical advertisement pointed out that navel

---

[11] *Sales Management,* February 15, 1937, p. 300.

oranges are seedless, have the richest juice and finest flavor, and are easier to peel, slice, and separate.

In many years, particularly when there have been large crops, the advertisements have employed more of direct-action type of appeal. Low price and immediate action have been stressed. This was true, for example, of the valencia campaigns in 1935 and 1938. Such direct action copy has a selective effect.

That the California Fruit Growers Exchange has benefited from its program from the standpoint of selective demand appears evident after a survey of such data as are available. The management strongly holds this opinion. For example, on page 26 of its report to its members in 1932 is the following statement:

> Dependable fruit, sound sales policies, and many years of continuous Sunkist advertising have built a public and trade preference for not only Sunkist but for all Exchange fruit that no other fruit even approaches. Consumers willingly pay a premium for it because of their confidence in its widely known quality. Dealers are willing to pay this premium because Sunkist is easier to sell.

That there has existed a preference for the California orange is indicated in the price data. For example, in Table 75 it will be noted that the average New York auction price per box for California navels was either as high as or higher than that for Florida oranges, in all except three years of the 17-year period covered in the price series, in spite of the fact that the Florida box is considerably larger than the California box, 90 pounds as against 70 pounds. The average prices per pound based on these quotations for the California navels and Floridas, the types which are directly competitive, were as follows: navels $5\frac{1}{2}$ cents, and Floridas, $4\frac{1}{10}$ cents. In the Chicago market the average auction price per box for California oranges was higher in every year of the period than that received for Florida oranges.

Several variables might account for varying ratios of prices received for the two types of oranges at particular times, such as the relative quantity of each available, the sizes available, and the quality of the respective fruits for that year. Moreover, the oranges from the two areas differ in flavor, color, presence of seeds, and other respects. Further, the California Fruit Growers Exchange has been far more skillful in regulating the supply of its oranges in various markets than have the Florida growers. From trade reports it is concluded, also, that it has been more careful in maintaining quality under its brands over a long period of years. Accordingly a number of factors might account in part for the premium paid for California oranges. But it appears safe to conclude, in addition, that the consistent advertising of the Exchange has been a factor of considerable importance in establishing consumer preference.

Since 1935 the Florida citrus growers, under the Florida Citrus Commission previously mentioned, have adopted a sizeable program of advertising and promotion to gain for themselves such benefits as may come from aggressive selling. The total advertising and promotion expenditure for 1938–1939 was reported as $850,000. This expenditure involved use not only of space but also of sales promotion men at key points east of the Mississippi River.[12] Data have not been gathered in this study by which to determine the extent to which the efforts of this group have proved profitable, or to what extent they have succeeded in building for Florida oranges a reputation offsetting that built for California oranges.

---

[12] Ben Hibbs, "State Advertising of Farm Products," *Advertising & Selling*, January, 1940, p. 19.

EFFECT OF ADVERTISING ON THE DEMAND
FOR WALNUTS

Walnuts were included in the study as a further example of an agricultural product for which advertising has been extensively used. In this instance relatively complete data by which to measure advertising effects were available from the California Walnut Growers Association, which for many years has controlled the marketing of over 80% of the walnut crop of the United States. Since 1918 the Association has conducted a consistent program of advertising, the expenditure varying with the size of the annual crop. Each year the management has had to determine the prices at which to offer its walnuts, its aim being to move the crop and to avoid a carryover, which might be a depressant to prices the following year. Advertising has been employed to help stimulate consumption at prices as favorable as possible to the growers. The management has had the task always of appraising not only the effect of price changes upon quantities to be taken, but also the effect of advertising in expanding demand.

In 1934 the management of the California Walnut Growers Association expressed an interest in having the U. S. Farm Credit Administration make a study of the effectiveness of its marketing methods, with special reference to its advertising. All operating data possessed by the management were made available. Drawn in as a consultant, the author had opportunity, in association with Mr. Harry C. Hensley, Senior Agricultural Economist of the Cooperative Division of the Farm Credit Administration, to attempt to trace the effect of advertising not only upon the demand for walnuts as a commodity but on the demand for the association's Diamond brand.

The report of that study, which was published by the Farm Credit Administration,[13] is drawn upon to trace, so far as is possible, the effects of advertising upon the demand for walnuts. It should be recognized that this walnut study was undertaken by the Farm Credit Administration to help the association determine whether advertising had been a helpful tool to the management in increasing the returns to walnut growers. The task presented was to appraise the effect of advertising upon primary and selective demand and to judge

---

[13] H. C. Hensley and N. H. Borden, *Marketing Policies of the California Walnut Growers Association* (Washington, Farm Credit Administration, Cooperative Division), Bulletin No. 10, March 1937.

whether sales returns to the association attributable to advertising were greater than the advertising expenditures. Because of this objective, the study is presented from the viewpoint of the business management. The appraisal of advertising's effect upon demand is the same, however, as would result from an approach from the social point of view. The study is quoted at length, below.

The study illustrates well the difficulties usually met in efforts to measure the effects of advertising upon demand, even when data are relatively complete.

Appraisal of Advertising Value from Analysis of Sales and Consumption Data

The test of whether the advertising expenditures of the association have been justified is the effect they may have had upon returns to the walnut growers. Was the net income of walnut growers greater as a result of an average annual expenditure of approximately $237,000 over the last 17 years? A clear-cut answer was not obtainable.

The consistent program of consumer advertising carried on since 1918 (see Table 78, column 6) has, for the most part, been primary in character, that is, designed to stimulate a demand for walnuts, not merely to get preference for the Diamond brand. Such a sustained and fairly heavy program of primary advertising may have an effect in several directions: (1) It may increase the volume of products sold at a stated price; (2) it may increase consumers' desire for the product to a point where higher prices may be had than would be obtainable without such consumer stimulation; or (3) it may offset forces which have an adverse effect either on volume of sales or on prices.

The association's expenditures for advertising for the years 1926–1934 have not represented a large percentage of the credited value, as may be seen from Table 76. Each year, with the exception of 1932, approximately three-fourths of a cent per pound of merchantable walnuts sold was spent on advertising. Before the economic depression this expenditure represented less than 4 per cent of the credited value of the nuts sold, but as a result of lower prices during the depression, this ratio for later years was somewhat more than 4 per cent. Only in the 1932 season did the expenditure per pound and consequently the percentage of credited value become excessive. The disorganized economic conditions of that season so affected selling conditions that sales were far short of the quota upon which the advertising expenditure had been based, and for the first time the association had a large carry-over of walnuts.

An examination of advertising expenditures back to 1918 showed that the ratio of advertising expenditures to sales had been greater for the period after 1926 than for the period before. Advertising expenditures for the period 1918–1925 averaged somewhat less than one-half cent a pound for unshelled walnuts sold and only 1.8 percent of sales value.

TABLE 76

QUANTITY, PRICE, AND VALUE OF DOMESTIC SALES OF MERCHANTABLE UNSHELLED
WALNUTS, AND ASSOCIATION EXPENDITURES FOR ADVERTISING,
1926–27 TO 1934–35

CROP YEAR	(1) DOMESTIC SALES OF UNSHELLED WALNUTS, POUNDS†	(2) WEIGHTED AVERAGE PRICE PER POUND AS CREDITED TO LOCALS, CENTS	(3) APPROXIMATE VALUE CREDITED TO LOCALS, DOLLARS‡	ADVERTISING EXPENDITURES		
				(4) TOTAL, DOLLARS	(5) PER POUND OF UNSHELLED WALNUTS SOLD, CENTS §	(6) PERCENTAGE OF CREDITED VALUE PERCENT ‖
1926–27.....	18,910,900	27.5	5,200,498	114,218	0.0060	2.2
1927–28.....	69,126,800	19.7	13,617,980	525,817	.0076	3.9
1928–29.....	33,504,500	24.3	8,141,594	211,563	.0063	2.6
1929–30.....	53,050,000	19.7	10,450,850	315,341	.0059	3.0
1930–31.....	39,529,700	21.9	8,657,004	313,164	.0079	3.6
1931–32.....	33,069,900	16.0	5,291,184	247,852	.0075	4.7
1932–33*....	37,085,900	13.1	4,858,253	550,280	.0148	11.3
1933–34*....	35,800,300	15.7	5,620,647	250,589	.0070	4.5
1934–35*....	40,138,000	14.9	5,980,562	244,500	.0061	4.1

* From July 1 to June 30; other years are from October 1 to September 30.
† From the association's order files.
‡ Column 1 times column 2.
§ Column 4 divided by column 1.
‖ Column 4 divided by column 3.

Though it was stated above that expenditures do not appear to have been unduly large, except in 1932, it should be recognized that any expenditure is excessive when it does not accomplish profitable results. Thus the advertising costs must be judged only in the light of volume of sales and prices received.

Accordingly, the consumption of walnuts before and after advertising was employed was first studied. Attention was directed to unshelled walnuts because they, rather than shelled walnuts, have been the subject of advertising and represented the chief interest of the association. In order to make allowance for material increases in population over a period of time, consumption figures were reduced to a per capita basis. Because of wide annual fluctuation in consumption resulting largely from crop variations, a 3-year moving average was applied to these per capita data to provide a clearer picture of the changes in consumption that have occurred. Chart III shows the consumption of unshelled walnuts in the United States for the seasons 1910–11 to 1934–35, inclusive.

Consumption rose appreciably above former levels for some 12 years after advertising was begun. During the period 1910–11 to 1917–18, before advertising was undertaken on a considerable scale, no marked trend in consumption is apparent from the data, although average annual consumption of walnuts for this period was heavier than for the preceding 10 years. During the post-war period, 1918–19 to 1928–29, the average consumption of unshelled walnuts per capita was appreciably above that of the pre-war and war periods; average per capita consumption for 1910–11 to 1917–18 was 0.46 pound, and that for the period 1918–19 to 1928–29 was 0.61 pound. While the average consumption for this latter period was high, it will be noted that the highest level of consumption was attained in 1919–20 and that the trend was somewhat downward from then on. In the depression period a discouraging fall in per capita consumption occurred; the average for the period 1929–30 to 1934–35 was .043 pound.

In view of the fact that the association's advertising may have had an effect upon the consumption of shelled as well as unshelled walnuts, the trends in consumption of all walnuts for the period 1910–1934 were examined. These trends were not materially different from those for unshelled nuts alone.

To summarize to this point, when forces other than advertising, which might affect consumption, were temporarily disregarded, advertising would appear to have helped in the attainment of the high per capita consumption in the period 1918–19 to 1928–29. The advertising, however, was not potent in withstanding the forces adverse to walnut consumption during the depression period 1929–30 to 1934–35.

CHART III

PER CAPITA CONSUMPTION OF MERCHANTABLE UNSHELLED WALNUTS,
1910–11 to 1934–35

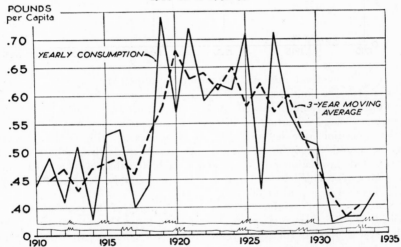

Consumption figures could not be considered alone, however, as the numerous factors affecting demand had to be weighed. Attention was next given to the prices received for walnuts during the period studied.

Effect of Advertising on Prices

No fully satisfactory series of prices for all unshelled walnuts consumed in the United States for the period was found to exist. However, a series of weighted average opening prices of the California Walnut Growers Association since 1921 reflects more or less accurately the prices received by the association for its entire crops. In many years no changes were made from opening prices, and in other instances relatively small changes were made and these only after a major part of the crop had been moved.

CHART IV

ANNUAL PER CAPITA EXPENDITURES FOR UNSHELLED WALNUTS, 1910–1934

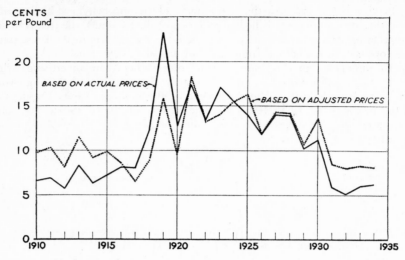

Available evidence indicates that ordinarily imported unshelled walnuts and other domestic walnuts have been sold at prices somewhat below the prices of the California Walnut Growers Association. Since the association's walnuts represent so large a portion of domestic consumption, however, the prices set by the association have determined largely the prices at which competing walnuts have been sold. Accordingly, the assumption was made that, although a series of weighted Association prices was somewhat higher than average prices for all the walnuts consumed in the United States, it might be accepted for study of variations in walnut prices from year to year.

Since a series of weighted average opening prices of the association was not available for the years previous to 1921, the opening price of No. 1 Soft-Shell walnuts was applied for these years. Since, for a large part of this period, No. 1 Soft Shells constituted a major portion of the total merchantable walnuts handled by the association, the price of these nuts apparently represented closely an average weighted price. Accordingly, the price series used is a spliced series. It is employed as the best index available of unit values for walnuts consumed.

Since the actual prices received over the period reflect in part changes in the purchasing power, or value in exchange, of the dollar, it was deemed advisable to adjust these prices in terms of the average for the period 1924–1928. The conversion was made by dividing the actual prices by an index of wholesale prices of the United States Bureau of Labor Statistics (October-December averages for 1924–1928 = 100). The fall period was used as a base, since most of the walnuts move to market during these months.

Although there were material changes from year to year in both the actual prices of walnuts and the adjusted prices, caused largely by variations in the size of crops, the adjusted walnut prices were fairly stable throughout the period of the advertising program. The adjusted price of walnuts was higher, on the whole, after advertising was started on a considerable scale, in 1918, than in the period 1910–1917. The average of adjusted prices received for the seasons 1910–11 to 1917–18 was 20.1 cents per pound; that for the entire advertising period 1918–19 to 1934–35 was 22.4 cents. When this latter period was broken up into the predepression and depression years the averages were for the seasons 1918–19 to 1928–29, 22.7 cents, and for 1929–30 to 1934–35, 21.9 cents.

Provided the opening price series employed is a satisfactory index of prices for entire seasons, the higher per capita consumption which followed after advertising had been instituted in 1918 did not occur because of lower prices of walnuts, but occurred when prices were somewhat higher than during the period previous to advertising.

Actual and Adjusted Value of Walnuts Consumed

Even though the price data were not all that might be desired, it was possible to estimate the actual value of the unshelled walnuts consumed and the adjusted value to packers and importers of walnuts for each year by multiplying the consumption in pounds by the actual price per pound and by the adjusted price per pound. These estimates are shown in Table 77.

The income to packers and importers was appreciably higher during the advertising period than in the period before advertising was undertaken. An average of the estimated annual value for the period 1910–11 to 1917–18 was slightly in excess of $7,000,000; for the period 1918–19 to 1928–29 it was $16,846,000; and for the period 1929–30 to 1934–35, $9,275,000. The estimated annual average adjusted value of the consumption for these years was as follows: 1910–11 to 1917–18, $9,000,000; 1918–19 to 1928–29, $15,567,000; and 1929–30 to 1934–35, $11,858,000.

The above estimates of total expenditures for walnuts are affected in part by the rise in consumption because of increasing population. In Table 78 are shown estimates of annual per capita expenditures, actual and adjusted, for unshelled walnuts for the period 1910–11 to 1934–35. The per capita expenditure for unshelled walnuts was considerably greater in the period after advertising was begun than in the period previous to advertising, whether figured on an actual or an adjusted basis, as shown in Chart IV. The actual average per capita expenditure for unshelled walnuts for the seasons 1910–11 to 1917–18, inclusive, was 7.2 cents; and for the advertising period 1918–19 to 1934–35, it was 12.4 cents. If we break the advertising period into the predepression and depression periods, the averages were: 1918–19 to 1928–29, inclusive, 15.0 cents; and 1929–30 to 1934–35, 7.4 cents. The estimated adjusted expenditures per capita were, for the preadvertising period, 9.2 cents, and for the entire advertising period, 12.3 cents.

From the estimated value of unshelled walnuts consumed, then, it may be concluded that the primary demand advertising of the California Walnut Growers Association may have had an effect in bringing about an appreciable increase in per capita expenditures for unshelled walnuts and accordingly in total national expenditures for them.

TABLE 77

APPARENT ANNUAL CONSUMPTION, PRICE, AND ESTIMATED VALUE OF MERCHANTABLE
UNSHELLED WALNUTS, 1910–11 TO 1934–35

CROP YEAR*	(1) APPARENT CONSUMPTION, 1,000 POUNDS	(2) PRICE PER POUND, CENTS	(3) ESTIMATED VALUE, 1,000 DOLLARS	(4) ADJUSTED PRICE PER POUND, CENTS	(5) ESTIMATED ADJUSTED VALUE, 1,000 DOLLARS
1910-11	40,881	15.0	6,132	22.2	9,076
1911-12	46,027	14.0	6,444	21.1	9,712
1912-13	39,204	14.0	5,489	19.7	7,723
1913-14	49,244	16.0	7,879	22.6	11,129
1914-15	37,436	16.5	6,177	24.1	9,022
1915-16	52,925	13.6	7,198	18.7	9,897
1916-17	54,589	13.5	8,461	16.0	8,734
1917-18	41,426	20.1	8,327	16.2	6,711
Average 1910-11 to 1917-18	45,217	15.5	7,013	20.1	9,000
1918-19	45,274	28.0	12,677	20.3	9,191
1919-20	78,175	31.5	24,625	21.4	16,729
1920-21	61,280	22.5	13,788	16.8	10,295
1921-22	78,435	24.1	18,903	25.4	19,922
1922-23	66,030	22.7	14,989	22.4	14,791
1923-24	69,743	22.5	15,692	22.6	13,762
1924-25	69,643	25.4	17,689	25.2	17,550
1925-26	81,876	24.1	19,732	23.0	18,831
1926-27	50,390▶	27.5	13,857	27.6	13,908
1927-28	84,434	19.7	16,633	20.2	17,056
1928-29	68,794	24.3	16,717	25.0	17,199
Average 1918-19 to 1928-29	68,552	24.6	16,846	22.7	15,567
1929-30	63,615	19.7	12,532	20.7	13,168
1930-31	63,558	21.9	13,919	26.6	16,906
1931-32	45,809	16.0	7,329	22.7	10,399
1932-33	48,081	13.1	6,299	20.4	9,809
1933-34	47,956	15.7	7,529	21.9	10,502
1934-35	53,997	14.9	8,043	19.2	10,364
Average 1929-30 to 1934-35	53,833	17.2	9,275	21.9	11,858

* October 1 to September 30.

Sources: [References to tables in original document.]
Column 1—Table 32, column 11.
Column 2—Opening prices, No. 1 Soft Shell, 1910–11 to 1913–14, obtained from:
    Erdman, H. E. and Fuhriman, W. U., *Walnut Supply and Price Situation.* Calif. Expt.
    Sta. Bull. 475, 60 pp. 1929. See p. 46.
    Opening prices, No. 1 Soft Shell, 1914–15 to 1920–21, obtained from California Wal-
    nut Growers Association.
    Weighted opening prices, all grades and sizes, 1921–22 to 1934–35, obtained from
    California Walnut Growers Association.
Column 3—Column 1 times column 2.
Column 4—Column 2 divided by the index of wholesale prices of all commodities of
    the U. S. Bureau of Labor Statistics, October–December average, 1924–1928=100.
Column 5—Column 1 times column 4.

An attempt was made to determine whether consumption of other leading
nuts had shown the material increase in consumption and value in the post-war
period that walnuts had enjoyed. If so, forces other than advertising would be
indicated as the important causes for increased value and consumption of wal-

TABLE 78

APPARENT ANNUAL PER CAPITA CONSUMPTION OF AND EXPENDITURE FOR
MERCHANTABLE UNSHELLED WALNUTS, AND ASSOCIATION EXPENDITURES FOR
ADVERTISING, 1910–11 TO 1934–35

CROP YEAR*	(1) PER CAPITA CONSUMPTION, POUNDS	(2) PRICE PER POUND, CENTS	(3) PER CAPITA EXPENDITURE, CENTS	(4) ADJUSTED PRICE, CENTS	(5) ADJUSTED EXPENDITURE PER CAPITA, CENTS	(6) ADVERTISING EXPENDITURES, 1,000 DOLLARS
1910-11	0.44	15.0	6.6	22.2	9.8	....
1911-12	.49	14.0	6.9	21.1	10.3	....
1912-13	.41	14.0	5.7	19.7	8.1	....
1913-14	.51	16.0	8.2	22.6	11.5	....
1914-15	.38	16.5	6.3	24.1	9.2	....
1915-16	.53	13.6	7.2	18.7	9.9	....
1916-17	.54	15.5	8.4	16.0	8.6	....
1917-18	.40	20.1	8.0	16.2	6.5	....
Average 1910-11 to 1917-18	.46	15.5	7.2	20.1	9.2	
1918-19	.44	28.0	12.3	20.3	8.9	61
1919-20	.74	31.5	23.3	21.4	15.8	120
1920-21	.57	22.5	12.8	16.8	9.6	251
1921-22	.72	24.1	17.4	25.4	18.3	164
1922-23	.59	22.7	13.4	22.4	13.2	202
1923-24	.62	22.5	14.0	22.6	14.0	128
1924-25	.61	25.4	15.5	25.2	15.4	166
1925-26	.71	24.1	17.1	23.0	16.3	160
1926-27	.43	27.5	11.8	27.6	11.9	114
1927-28	.71	19.7	14.0	20.2	14.3	526
1928-29	.57	24.3	13.9	25.0	14.2	212
Average 1918-19 to 1928-29	.61	24.6	15.0	22.7	13.8	....
1929-30	.52	19.7	10.2	20.7	10.8	315
1930-31	.51	21.9	11.2	26.6	13.6	313
1931-32	.37	16.0	5.9	22.7	8.4	248
1932-33	.38	13.1	5.0	20.4	7.8	550
1933-34	.38	15.7	6.0	21.9	8.3	251
1934-35	.42	14.9	6.3	19.2	8.1	245
Average 1929-30 to 1934-35	.43	17.2	7.4	21.9	9.5	

* October 1 to September 30.

Sources: [References to tables in original document.]
Column 1—Appendix table 33, column 9.
Column 2—See source reference for table 2, column 2.
Column 3—Column 1 times column 2.

Column 4—Column 2 divided by the index of wholesale prices of all commodities, of the U. S. Bureau of Labor Statistics, October–December average, 1924–28 equals 100.
Column 5—Column 1 times column 4.

nuts, in view of the fact that these other nuts had not been advertised. Unfortunately, records of consumption and values of the leading competing nuts prior to 1922 were not available. During the period subsequent to 1922 the leading competing nuts, as a group, had a fairly stable consumption which fell off approximately one-third during the depression, as did walnut consumption.

The average prices received by the United States producers for these competing nuts, however, tended downward during the depression period to a greater extent than did the prices of walnuts.

Up to this point it has been noted that, after the advent of advertising on a considerable scale by the California Walnut Growers Association, the United States consumption of walnuts, particularly of unshelled nuts, increased materially. It was noted further that this increase in consumption was not accompanied on the average by a decrease in prices, particularly when prices were adjusted in accordance with the change in purchasing power of the dollar. Accordingly, the value of the average annual quantity of nuts consumed was materially larger during the period of advertising than during the period prior to advertising, although the average of this value fell off materially from its peak in the depression period.

It should be kept in mind that this larger value of the product consumed was not accompanied by a heavy advertising expenditure per unit of product. On the whole, the California Walnut Growers Association was spending between one-half and three-fourths of a cent per pound of its merchantable nuts to bring about an effect upon demand. The average prices received after the institution of advertising exceeded those of the preadvertising period by a much larger margin than the amount involved in the advertising.

There is no sound basis to assert positively that the increased consumption and the increased prices were caused by advertising. Too many forces have had a bearing upon the consumption of this product even to say with certainty that advertising was a leading cause in large consumption at firm prices. But at least such an increase did occur and advertising may have had some effect. The other forces bearing upon consumption will be considered later. In the meantime evidence of the effect of advertising may be found, not in the results produced over a number of years, but in immediate effects upon annual sales of the association coming from variations in advertising expenditures.

Effect upon Demand of Variations in Advertising Appropriations

Sometimes it is possible to get an indication of the effect of advertising on sales when marked differences in expenditures have been made at different times. The wide variations in advertising expenditures from year to year, in pounds of unshelled walnuts sold, and in the average weighted prices received by the association, are shown in Table 76. No conclusions concerning any causal relationship between advertising and sales can be drawn from these figures, however. Whenever the volume of advertising was changed, other variables changed, notably the price set by the association to move the crop. Among other conditions which fluctuated from year to year were the supplies and prices of competing nuts, size of trade carry-overs, business activity, supplies and prices of imported walnuts, the sales efforts of brokers and wholesalers, the general level of prices, and the time taken to move the crop. Hence no definite conclusion concerning the effect of the advertising expenditures can be drawn merely from a comparison of variations in advertising expenditures and sales from year to year.[14]

An effort was made to get evidence of the effect of advertising by noting the sales results from varying expenditures in different territories in the light of the potentialities of those territories. The detailed analysis is omitted. The results are indicated in the further quotation.

Up to this point we have noted that after the advent of advertising, average annual sales of walnuts increased appreciably, with adjusted prices (Table 78), on the average almost 2 cents above those obtained in the years previous to advertising. On the other hand, a comparison of advertising expenditures and sales returns between territories does not provide a clear indication of the sales-producing results of advertising . . . Variables other than advertising have had a greater effect on sales than has advertising. Quite clearly any sales response to the advertising effort for the product is not immediately and readily discernible from the data.

Certain unmeasurable factors affecting demand that must be weighed in determining what advantages advertising as a marketing tool may have for the association will be considered next.

APPRAISAL OF ADVERTISING VALUE FROM OTHER STANDPOINTS

Advertising as an Aid in Getting Premium Prices

A communication from officers of the association early in the study stated that "it is the universal custom of the competition to offer unshelled walnuts equivalent to the association's grades at 1 or 2 cents under Association quotations." An independent survey among brokers and wholesalers in 10 widely separated cities substantiated this statement.

The ability to obtain better prices than those of competing sellers of walnuts indicates an effect of advertising from the competitive or selective standpoint, rather than the primary effect of increasing the sale of walnuts generally. While advertising cannot be given all or perhaps even a major part of the credit for the better prices received for the association's pack, yet it seems fair to assume that it should be given some of the credit. The outstanding work of the association in establishing and maintaining high grading standards and the recognized character of its sales management have undoubtedly been large factors in bringing about such favor by the trade. Yet the advertising of its brands to consumers and to the trade is judged to have played a considerable part in enhancing the reputation of the association's product, with a consequent disposition on the part of the trade to pay more for brands with recognized standards and with an established brand acceptance among consumers.

As previously stated, in most years advertising has cost the association from

[14] *Ibid.*, p. 25 ff.

one-half to three-fourths of a cent per pound. In so far, then, as advertising has helped move the association's pack at higher prices than those paid for competing walnuts, to that extent the expenditure has been justified.

Stimulation of Broker Activity through Advertising

While the effect of advertising upon the sales organization and upon the trade in securing effective selling efforts is immeasurable and intangible, and accordingly should not be weighed too heavily, nevertheless it is real. The evidence given by the association's officers and by brokers and tradesmen who were interviewed indicated that the association's advertising has been of value in this direction. In its advertising and selling work the association and the agency have followed a sound policy in so-called merchandising of its advertising to the trade. The consumer advertising has been employed as a talking point to secure more active and enthusiastic support by brokers and tradesmen in selling Association walnuts.

Effect of Advertising in Offsetting Influences Adverse to Walnuts

The fact that the per capita consumption of unshelled walnuts has not increased in recent years as a result of the extensive advertising of the association may be accounted for in part by the presence of two noticeable dietary trends adverse to the consumption of walnuts; namely, (1) less baking in the home, and (2) the tendency of people, particularly women, to eat less of fattening foods.

The tendency of American consumers to rely more on bakery products and less on home cookery is indicated by the following quotation:

"Even if we ignore the questionable data before 1880, the per capita product of the baking industry has shown the striking increase from $1.28 in 1879–80 to $5.33 in 1919, and to over $6.50 (in 1913 dollars) in 1921 and 1923. This reflects a huge transfer of baking from the household to the commercial bakery during this period. The expansion was most rapid between 1880 and 1890, and very much less rapid between 1890 and 1900, the decade including the severe industrial depression. In the war period the rate of expansion was greatly reduced, but the trend has been resumed since 1919. It will be noted, however, that the rate of increase is declining."*

The home demand for unshelled walnuts has been affected to the extent that less baking has been done in the home.

The large amount of publicity and advertising given to the slim figure may well have had some effect upon the consumption of a food so high in fat content as nuts. There is no statistical evidence, however, to indicate the extent and importance of this effect.

On the other hand, it is well to recognize that there may have been some

---

* H. Kyrk and J. S. Davis, *The American Baking Industry, 1849–1923, as Shown in the Census Reports.* 108 pp. illus., Stanford University, California, 1925 (Stanford University Food Research Institute, Misc. Pub. No. 2), see p. 13.

trends favoring consumption of unshelled walnuts which might have been exploited. There have been indications of various changes in dietary habits of the American people. Since the World War the per capita consumption of potatoes and wheat for food has decreased. The consumption of vegetable oils, sugar, vegetables, and fruits has increased. The consumption of salads has certainly increased since lettuce production increased almost 50 percent between 1924 and 1930,† and the number of carloads of lettuce shipped was only 8,000 in 1918 and over 55,700 in 1930. These facts would indicate the need of studying dietary trends so as to feature uses of walnuts in connection with dishes that are assuming a more important part in the diet. In the consumer investigation, salads stood second only to cakes and cookies as the favorite dish making use of walnuts.

Advertising as an Aid in Meeting Direct Competition

Walnuts have faced an increasingly difficult direct competition from other nuts, particularly pecans. . . . .

While the trend of pecan production has been upward, the price trend has been downward, particularly during the depression period . . . The adjusted price received by growers for improved pecans was fairly constant through 1930, ranging from approximately 30 to 44 cents per pound. From that point on, however, the adjusted prices dropped to around 15 to 21 cents per pound. Fluctuation has been even more marked in prices of seedling pecans. As shown above, in Table 78, the adjusted prices of unshelled walnuts remained quite constant, even throughout the period of depression; the widest range was between the price of 27.6 cents per pound in 1926 and 19.2 cents per pound in 1934.

The downward trend of pecan prices has brought difficult competition for walnuts. Whereas improved pecans were once much more expensive than walnuts, in recent years they have been sold at prices very close to those of walnuts. The consumer survey showed that about one-fourth of all housewives interviewed preferred pecans to other nuts, both for eating out of hand and for cooking purposes.

The constant advertising on the part of the association and the work which it has done with domestic science teachers have helped to offset this direct competition. Walnuts have gained the advantage of being generally specified in printed recipes. The millions of Association advertisements illustrating and specifying walnuts have undoubtedly had an influence in keeping the product in the foreground as the standard nut for cooking purposes.

Advertising as an Aid in Meeting Indirect Competition

The period during which the association has been a consistent and fairly heavy advertiser has been one of increased competition among food manufacturers and food growers for a large share of the family food budget. Just as walnuts must face direct competition with other nuts, so they must face indirect

† U. S. Department of Agriculture, *Yearbook of Agriculture*, 1924–1930.

competition from other foods. As indicated by the studies of Pearl ‡ and others, the caloric intake of the American has remained constant over a long period of years. Increased consumption of one food is likely to mean decreased consumption of another.

TABLE 79

EXPENDITURES FOR MAGAZINE ADVERTISING OF FOODS IN THE UNITED STATES, 1918–1934

YEAR	TOTAL EXPENDITURES DOLLARS	YEAR	TOTAL EXPENDITURES DOLLARS
1918	7,468,778	1927	22,840,735
1919	11,557,211	1928	23,862,264
1920	14,310,315	1929	23,864,010
1921	11,319,967	1930	26,352,050
1922	10,479,438	1931	26,391,636
1923	12,156,716	1932	19,442,439
1924	14,522,188	1933	17,888,525
1925	16,531,771	1934	18,577,638
1926	19,913,989		

Source: Curtis Publishing Company, *Leading Advertisers*, 1918–1934.

The large sums of money spent in magazine advertising of foods, as shown in Table 79, indicate the extent to which business organizations have sought more aggresively to induce consumers to buy their products in the post-war period. It must be recognized that these expenditures for advertising have been accompanied by an aggressive campaign to secure cooperation of the trade in the sale of the product advertised. While there is a corrective against excessive advertising and sales promotion in that nonadvertisers may be able to undersell and thus overcome any advantage given by the advertising, yet the advertiser with a product suited to advertising, who keeps his expenditures in line and is skillful in presentation of copy, may secure an appreciable advantage for his product in the battle for demand.

Reference has been made to the use of advertising for products which are suited for advertising. Walnuts are believed to fit in this category. They may be listed as a semiluxury or nonessential food. The greatest hope for increasing their consumption rests primarily in inducing housewives to use them more freely in cooking. They add flavor to many foods and give body and flavor to salads. Accordingly they lend themselves well to a primary type of advertising, that which suggests a wider and more frequent use. Menu suggestions in advertisements and cookbooks placed in the hands of housewives would seem to promise a positive effect upon consumption. In addition, walnuts are a seasonal product. Their advent on the market is accompanied by the traditional holiday use for eating out of hand. With the arrival of the crop, display advertising near the point of purchase is sound strategy to stimulate display and selling by retailers and to suggest use by consumers.

‡ R. Pearl, *The Nation's Food*, 274 pp. illus., Philadelphia, 1920.

Summary of Evidence Regarding the Value of Advertising

In the attempted estimate of the place of advertising in the marketing program of the California Walnut Growers Association, the investigators experienced the difficulty met in most indirect-action advertising of obtaining any clear indication of the effect on sales. It seems impossible to isolate and weigh each of the innumerable factors affecting the volume consumed and the prices received. It was noted, however, that over the period studied the volume of walnuts consumed, and possibly, the prices received for them were greater after the institution of advertising than they had been before. In the breakdown of sales by territories no clear evidence was found of a quick and strong pull from advertising.

At the end of the analysis it was impossible to assert with certainty that the growers had received greater net returns over the 17-year period because of the expenditure of over $4,000,000 for advertising by the association. Yet when the results attained by the association are weighed (a greater per capita consumption at higher adjusted prices than those received before the advent of advertising, in the face of adverse living trends and an increasingly intense direct and indirect competition) one is led to the conclusion that the advertising expenditures have been justified. It is doubtful whether the same volume of nuts would have been sold at the same average prices without the stimulus of this advertising. It is also doubtful whether the differential of 1 to 2 cents over competing walnuts would have been obtained had not the association enhanced the reputation of its product and stimulated aggressive selling of its broker and dealer organization through advertising. The total expenditures have averaged less than three-fourths of a cent per pound of merchantable nuts produced by the association. It is probable that the advertising has been worth more than three-fourths of a cent per pound in returns to the growers, not solely from suggesting more frequent use by consumers, but through providing an aggressive management with a helpful weapon in its dealer work.[15]

---

[15] *Ibid.*, p. 40 ff.

ADVERTISING AND THE DEMAND FOR LETTUCE

Lettuce has been included in this study as an example of a product which has experienced a relatively large increase in demand over a period of years without the benefit of advertising by is producers. It illustrates a point which has been reiterated in different places in this study, namely, that the demand for products rests in the wants and desires of people as developed by the complex of social forces; and when the forces are favorable they may bring a great expansion of demand for a product without any effort on the part of producers to shape consumer attitudes.

TABLE 80

TOTAL HARVESTED PRODUCTION AND PER CAPITA CONSUMPTION OF LETTUCE (COMMERCIAL CROP) AND AVERAGE PRICE PER CRATE RECEIVED BY FARMERS, 1918–1938

YEAR	HARVESTED U. S. PRODUCTION 1,000 CRATES	INDICATED PER CAPITA CONSUMPTION, POUNDS	AVERAGE PRICE PER CRATE TO FARMERS	INDEX OF PRICE 1926 = 100	B.L.S. INDEX OF WHOLESALE PRICES OF ALL COMMODITIES 1926 = 100
1918	3,787	2.6	$1.63	98	131.3
1919	4,330	2.9	1.91	118	138.6
1920	7,703	5.1	1.53	92	154.4
1921	7,214	4.7	1.89	114	97.6
1922	9,292	5.9	1.88	113	96.7
1923	10,369	6.5	1.60	96	100.6
1924	12,422	7.7	1.60	96	98.1
1925	13,704*	8.3	1.45	87	103.5
1926	16,100*	9.7	1.66	100	100.0
1927	16,984*	10.1	1.35	81	95.4
1928	18,647	10.9	1.70	102	96.7
1929	19,968	11.5	1.81	109	95.3
1930	19,770	11.4	1.71	103	86.4
1931	19,609	11.1	1.48	89	73.0
1932	17,310*	9.7	1.26	76	64.8
1933	17,279*	9.6	1.27	76	65.9
1934	18,937*	10.5	1.36	82	74.9
1935	19,412	10.7	1.44	87	80.0
1936	20,898*	11.4	1.45	87	80.8
1937	20,915*	11.3	1.57	95	86.3
1938	19,150*	10.3	1.50	90	78.6

* Quantities not harvested have been deducted from the total production figures for the years indicated.

Sources:

Production: Average price received by farmers: U. S. Department of Agriculture, *Agricultural Statistics, 1939*, p. 207, and *1940*, p. 233.

Per capita consumption for each year was derived by converting the number of crates to lbs. at 70 lbs. per crate and dividing by the estimated population of the United States.

Population: *Statistical Abstract of the United States, 1938*, p. 10.

B. L. S. Index: *Statistical Abstract of the United States, 1939*, p. 316.

The Extent of Demand

The remarkable increase in the consumption of lettuce since 1918 is indicated in Table 80. The commercial crop of 1918 amounted to less than 4,000,000 crates,[16] but increased to over 20,000,000 crates by 1936. On a pound basis, the indicated per capita consumption went from 2.6 pounds in 1918 to an average of 10.8 pounds for the decade, 1929–38. There was no overall increase in per capita consumption during this latter period; the marked increase having occurred in the previous ten years.

Decreased price has not been an appreciable factor in accounting for the growth in consumption. No satisfactory price series for the product exists, but an indicator of price is found in the average price received by farmers, which varied from as low as $1.26 a crate to $1.91. As will be noted from the table, the series shows no marked decrease in price, particularly when compared with prices in general.

Probable Reasons for Expansion of Demand

As with the other products studied, any explanation of the change in consumption of lettuce is purely speculative. In this instance, however, advertising by lettuce producers and sellers as a cause of increase is ruled out.

During the past two decades, Americans clearly have become salad eaters. This practice is but one manifestation of the basic dietary change which was discussed in Chapter VII. Lettuce has benefited from widespread advocacy of a substantial amount of leafy vegetables in the diet. Medical and dietetic research relating to the virtues of vitamins, iron, and calcium has gone on apace in the past 20 years. These virtues have been widely broadcast through newspapers and magazines, through the schools, and through the advertising of a host of other food producers.

Lettuce producers have been fortunate also because lettuce demand is complementary to that of many other products which have been heavily advertised. The producers of these advertised foods wisely have ridden with the trend toward salad use in their promotion. Their advertisements and their recipe booklets, which have been distributed by the million, have carried illustrations of appetizing salads and direc-

---

16 A crate of lettuce contains approximately 70 pounds, the number of heads varying from 4 to 6 dozen.

tions on how to make them. The growers of nuts, oranges, prunes, and avocados have played up salads, of which lettuce is ordinarily a part. The salmon packers, the tuna fish packers, the cheese manufacturers, the gelatin manufacturers, the canned goods manufacturers, and the meat packers also have done their share. And salads have been a primary interest of the salad dressing manufacturers, who have been substantial advertisers.

In response to the growing demand came geographic specialization in lettuce-raising, particularly in California and Arizona, and this development has in turn helped increase demand. While lettuce once had been largely grown commercially in truck gardens adjacent to cities, and hence subject to seasonal use, for many years now it has been available at a low price in city markets the year round.

As noted above, the upward trend in per capita consumption of lettuce was checked subsequent to 1929. Undoubtedly this was in part the result of the depression. In the meantime, as is true of many of our agricultural crops, production had tended to outstrip consumption. Lettuce growing for many years has not been profitable to many growers. The following statement was carried in the *Federal-State Market News Service* in 1940: "For the past several years it has become more and more evident that with normal growing conditions more lettuce is produced almost the year round than can be marketed under present methods."[17] The ploughing under of crops under government prorating plans has been undertaken in recent years.

The only known effort of growers to influence consumption of lettuce was carried out in 1937–1938 under the stress of this overproduction situation. The Western Growers' Protective Association, an organization of lettuce and melon growers of California and Arizona, put on a campaign involving an expenditure of approximately $175,000 during the year March, 1937, to March, 1938. Newspapers in important city markets were used. The copy approach emphasized the art of "tossing lettuce" in bowls of green salads, the assumption being that such salads made large use of lettuce and overcame the tendency of many other recipes to emphasize other ingredients. The promotional plan involved widespread distribution of recipe booklets and offered a wooden salad bowl at a low price.

The program was not continued for more than one year. The large

[17] *Federal-State Market News Service*, January 6, 1940. "Brief Review of the Arizona 1939 Fall Lettuce Season."

number of small producers and the wide separation of growing areas throughout the United States presented hurdles to the undertaking of any cooperative advertising program to influence the demand for lettuce, aside from the question of the uncertainty of profitably stimulating consumption. Whether lettuce consumption has reached a saturation point only time will tell.

CHAPTER XIV

THE EFFECT OF ADVERTISING ON THE
DEMAND FOR SHOES

SHOES have been included in this study of demand because of the contrasts afforded with the other items studied. They are a product for which varying reliance upon advertising by manufacturers is found. Many shoe manufacturers do little consumer advertising; others spend substantial amounts. Among manufacturers who do advertise to consumers, the greater part of their efforts is usually carried on through retailers, who occupy a key position in the selling plan. The shoe retailers themselves place more advertising than do manufacturers. In the study an attempt was made to determine why such widely varying advertising policies exist side by side in the market and why the retailer is the center of activities designed to influence demand.

The Amount of General Advertising by Manufacturers

The amount of advertising devoted to manufacturers' brands of shoes is small in relation to their value. The great majority of shoe manufacturers do little or no general consumer advertising for their brands over their own names. For example, in 1939 only 40 brands of shoes produced by 17 companies were listed as being nationally advertised in newspapers, magazines, farm journals, or radio in the report of the American Newspaper Publishers' Association (Table 81). Only companies spending $25,000 in the four media measured were included in the A.N.P.A. lists. One hundred thirteen shoe brands were reported as being advertised in magazines in the 1939 report of the Publishers' Information Bureau. It will be seen, in fact, that many of the expenditures for individual brands included in the table are very small in the light of modern advertising expenditures for certain other products. The figures of 17 companies and 40 brands, or even the larger figure of 113 brands, are in striking contrast to the 1,080 shoe manufacturing establishments reported in the *Biennial Census of Manufactures* of 1937. Mr. Arthur D. Anderson, editor of *Boot & Shoe Recorder,* in a letter to the author, stated that in 1940

TABLE 81
Traceable National Advertising by Leather Shoe Manufacturers in Magazines, Newspapers, Farm Journals, and Chain Radio, 1939

Company and Brand	Newspapers	Magazines	Farm Journals	Chain Radio	Total
Brown Shoe Co.					
Air Step		$ 79,583			$ 79,583
Buster Brown		30,167			30,167
Naturalizer		11,900			11,900
Odette		2,072			2,072
Roblee		123,450			123,450
Total		$247,172			$247,172
Commonwealth Shoe & Leather Co.					
Bostonian		$ 52,802			$ 52,802
Footsaver		4,950			4,950
Mansfield		10,039			10,039
Total		$ 67,791			$ 67,791
Dunn & McCarthy, Inc.					
Enna Jettick	$ 1,667	$ 83,980		$70,728	$156,375
Florsheim Shoe Co.					
Florsheim	$ 5,205	$162,585			$167,790
General Shoe Corp.					
Jarman	$13,521	$ 92,250			$105,771
Daniel Green Co.					
Daniel Green		$ 94,394			$ 94,394
House of Crosby Square					
Crosby Square		$ 29,327			$ 29,327
International Shoe Co.					
City Club		$ 4,502			$ 4,502
Conformal Personalized	$10,451				10,451
Dundeers Sport		1,424			1,424
Heel Latch		8,423			8,423
Peters		2,210			2,210
Poll Parrott		7,037			7,037
Queen Quality	14,072	9,210			23,282
Sundial Work			$1,116		1,116
Uptown Freemold		9,038			9,038
Vitality	357	69,069			69,426
Weather-bird		2,421			2,421
Winthrop		4,502			4,502
Shoes	55				55
Total	$24,935	$117,836	$1,116		$143,887
Johnson, Stephens & Shinkle Shoe Co.					
Fashion Plate		$ 2,100			$ 2,100
Rhythm Step	$12,485	34,480			46,965
Products	905				905
Total	$13,390	$ 36,580			$ 49,970
Julian & Kokenge Co.					
Foot Saver		$ 47,588			$ 47,588
Geo. E. Keith & Co.					
Walk-Over	$12,435	$ 64,805			$ 77,240
Nunn-Bush Shoe Co.					
Nunn-Bush	$ 25	$ 29,000			$ 29,025
E. P. Reed & Co.					
Matrix	$17,225	$ 21,870			$ 39,095
Tyless		4,600			4,600
Total	$17,225	$ 26,470			$ 43,695

(Continued on following page.)

TABLE 81—(Continued)

Company and Brand	Newspapers	Magazines	Farm Journals	Chain Radio	Total
Selby Shoe Co.					
Physical Culture	$ 1,034	....	....	....	$ 1,034
Selby	44,219	$ 24,050	....	....	68,239
Total	$45,253	$ 24,050	....	....	$ 69,303
U. S. Shoe Corp.					
Red Cross	$71,188	$120,506	....	....	$191,694
Wohl Shoe Co.					
Connie	....	$ 31,435	....	....	$ 31,435
Jacqueline	....	14,110	....	....	14,110
Natural Poise	....	25,709	....	....	25,709
Paris Fashion	....	29,525	....	....	29,525
Total	....	$100,779	....	....	$100,779
Wolverine Shoe & Tanning Co.					
Wolverine	....	....	$59,290	....	$ 59,290

Total number of companies advertising 17
Total number of brands advertised.......................... 40

Source: American Newspaper Publishers' Association, Bureau of Advertising, *Expenditures of National Advertisers in Newspapers, Magazines, Farm Journals, and Chain Radio in 1939*, p. 25 ff.

TABLE 82

ADVERTISING EXPENDITURES IN NATIONAL MAGAZINES
FOR SHOES OTHER THAN RUBBER, 1914–29*

Year	Amount
1914	$ 307,417
1915	311,234
1916	520,234
1917	1,136,966
1918	1,297,276
1919	1,733,819
1920	1,337,566
1921	1,028,943
1922	1,178,781
1923	1,498,782
1924	1,718,224
1925	1,609,605
1926	1,915,001
1927	1,877,302
1928	2,153,079
1929	2,103,328

* Prior to 1920 includes expenditures for rubber footwear and sundries.
Source: Curtis Publishing Company, Advertising Department, *Leading Advertisers* (Philadelphia), 1914–1929.

his publication "started collecting names used in men's, women's, and children's shoes, and when it ran over 6,000 we quit." Clearly, the great majority of shoe brands move into consumption with little or no support of advertising placed by manufacturers in general media.

Unfortunately data showing the total dollar volume of shoe advertising of manufacturers over a long period of time are not available. Table 82 shows the volume of advertising in national magazines from 1914 to 1929, expanding from $307,000 in 1914 to $2,150,000 in 1928 and declining slightly in 1929. These figures represent probably 75% or more of the shoe advertising carried in general media over manufacturers' names in those years. Estimates of traceable expenditures in newspapers, magazines, farm journals, and radio for the period subsequent to 1928 are given in Table 83. These estimates vary in amount from a high of $3,092,000 in 1929 to a low of $937,-000 in the depression year, 1933.

The total of this traceable manufacturers' advertising is small when compared with the annual value of shoe production, which has averaged during the period covered by the table in the neighborhood of

TABLE 83

ESTIMATED VALUE OF ADVERTISING OF LEATHER SHOES BY SHOE MANUFACTURERS IN MAGAZINES, NEWSPAPERS, FARM JOURNALS, AND CHAIN RADIO, 1929–1939

YEAR	GENERAL MAGAZINES	NEWSPAPERS	FARM JOURNALS	CHAIN RADIO	TOTAL
1929	$1,823,976	$861,857	$55,526*	$ 350,898§	$3,092,257
1930	628,758	627,965	50,478†	616,599	1,923,800
1931	1,092,366	233,495	....	1,148,905	2,474,766
1932	769,743	263,897	....	192,827	1,226,467
1933	778,633	124,096	27,784	7,356†	937,869
1934	1,035,864	230,579	61,943	39,660	1,368,046
1935	1,319,986	96,498	41,450	73,229	1,531,063
1936	1,387,625	69,569	43,744‡	49,058§	1,549,996
1937	1,973,389	72,939	66,975	29,910	2,143,213
1938	1,429,385	82,643	58,365	69,835	1,640,228
1939	1,345,113	204,844	60,406	70,728	1,681,091

* Extended from 10 months' data.
† Extended from 11 months' data.
‡ Extended from 9 months' data.
§ Extended from 8 months' data.

Sources:
Magazines, 1939: American Newspaper Publishers' Association, *Expenditures of National Advertisers*.
    1936–1938: Publishers' Information Bureau, Inc., *National Advertising Records*.
    1930–1935: Curtis Publishing Company, *Leading Advertisers*.
    1929: Crowell Publishing Company, *National Markets and National Advertising*.
Newspapers, 1938–1939: Dollar figures from American Newspaper Publishers' Association, *Expenditures of National Advertisers*.
    1929–1939: Lineage from Media Records, Inc., *Newspapers and Newspaper Advertisers*.
    Conversion rate, 66 cents per line, calculated from 1938 and 1939 data, applied to other years. See Appendix IV regarding conversion rate.
Radio and Farm Journals, 1939: American Newspaper Publishers' Association, *Expenditures of National Advertisers*.
    1934, 1937–1938: Publishers' Information Bureau, Inc., *National Advertising Records*.
    1929–1933, 1935–1936: National Advertising Records, Inc., *National Advertising Records*.

TABLE 84

RELATION OF TRACEABLE SHOE ADVERTISING BY MANUFACTURERS TO SHOE
PRODUCTION CENSUS YEARS, 1929–1939

YEAR	ADVERTISING PER THOUSAND PAIRS	ADVERTISING AS % OF VALUE OF PRODUCTION
1929	$9.38	.342%
1931	9.01	.406
1933	3.03	.182
1935	4.69	.262
1937	6.24	.319
1939	3.96	....

Source: Compiled from figures for product value and unit production—*Biennial Census of Manufactures*, respective years. Advertising expenditures based on Table 83.

$550,000,000 a year.[1] As shown in Table 84 this traceable advertising has been only about 0.3% of the value of shoe production during the decade 1929–1939.

This small percentage of expenditure for general advertising by manufacturers in magazines, newspapers, farm journals, and chain radio, for several reasons is not a fair representation, however, of the total advertising expenditure for shoes. First, the general advertisers put only a part of their total advertising into the general media covered by the table. Secondly, many of the companies which did not carry on advertising in general media spent in the aggregate substantial sums on trade paper advertising and upon dealer help material. Finally, a large amount of advertising of shoes was conducted by retailers.

Character of Advertising Expenditures by Manufacturers

That the reader may have a clearer picture of the extent and character of shoe advertising, the detailed data to support the generalizations made in the preceding paragraph are presented. Attention is directed first to the extent and character of expenditures of shoe manufacturers. The percentages of sales devoted to total advertising by certain shoe manufacturers are given in Table 85, which is based on reports to the Association of National Advertisers in its study of national advertising budgets. It will be seen that the average expenditure was in the neighborhood of 4% of sales, with a range reported for the year 1934 of 2% to 6.5%. These data from the Association of National Advertisers' study agree with figures obtained from case histories collected. For example, a manufacturer of men's high-price

---

[1] Based on *Biennial Census of Manufactures* figures.

orthopedic shoes during the years 1930–1938 spent from 4% to 5% of total sales of all lines annually, or approximately 40 cents a pair for the line of shoes advertised. A manufacturer of women's medium-price shoes spent in 1937, typical of recent years, 2% of sales, or 7.7 cents a pair. A manufacturer of women's high-price style shoes spent approximately 4% on advertising, or just about 33 cents a pair. A manufacturer of men's high-price shoes had an average advertising expenditure of about 3.3% of sales, approximately 25 cents for each pair of shoes sold.

A somewhat more extensive survey of expenses of shoe manufacturers, one which covered small manufacturers as well as large and consequently, by inference, included firms which were not general advertisers, was made by Dun & Bradstreet for 1934.[2] This study shows an average expenditure of 1.38% of net sales for 17 profitable concerns, and 2.18% for 10 concerns reporting a net loss for the year. These ratios are below those of the A. N. A. study and those obtained from case histories of companies known to be national advertisers. Unfortunately advertising expense ratios for a substantial number of companies known to employ no general consumer advertising are not available. One company, selling under its own brand and directing all its advertising at and through retailers, in 1928 spent less than 1% for advertising.[3] This company is believed to be representative of a substantial number of companies. Their individual appropriations have been small; yet in the aggregate they have amounted to a considerable sum. Their advertising, as noted above, has been directed largely to

TABLE 85

ADVERTISING AND SALES PROMOTIONAL BUDGET OF SHOE MANUFACTURERS, 1933–1934–1935 *

	1933	1934	1935
Number of companies reporting..............	6	8	9
Average advertising expenditures (% of sales).	4.00%	4.25%	3.97%
Range of advertising expenditures..... {High..		6.50	
{Low...		2.00	

* Included some canvas and rubber footwear manufacturers.

Source: Association of National Advertisers, *A Survey of 299 National Advertising Budgets, 1934–1935* (New York).

[2] Dun & Bradstreet, Inc., *Manufacturing Survey,* 1934.
[3] Cf. case of Weyenberg Shoe Manufacturing Company, *Problems in Advertising,* by N. H. Borden (3d ed., New York, McGraw-Hill Book Company, Inc., 1937, p. 201). In years subsequent to the date of collection of this case, the Weyenberg Shoe Company has undertaken magazine advertising.

the trade through trade papers and mail; in addition they often have provided retailers with dealer helps. For shoes sold unbranded, of which there has been a substantial volume particularly among women's style shoes, manufacturers have undertaken advertising only to make themselves known to the trade as sources for shoes. No statistics are available regarding the percentage of shoes sold unbranded, but Mr. Arthur D. Anderson, who has had a long and intimate contact with the industry, estimated in 1940 that probably 20% of men's shoes, 35% of women's shoes, and 55% of children's shoes were sold unbranded.[4]

Many companies which have advertised their brands to the public in periodicals or radio have devoted less than half of their total expenditure to such general advertising. This statement is based on data contained in case material obtained in 1937 and 1938, and upon the 1934–1935 advertising budget study of the Association of National Advertisers. An analysis of the division of budgets by various classes of expenditures among 17 shoe companies interviewed in 1937–1938 in the course of this study is contained in Table 86. Twelve spent 40% or less of their total expenditures on general advertising, the balance going to advertising directed at or through the dealers, i.e., dealer cooperative advertising, dealer helps, or trade advertising. Only among advertisers of women's shoes was half or more of the expenditure devoted to advertising in general media. The Association of National Advertisers' budget study of 1934–1935 shows that in 1934 the eight manufacturers reporting spent on the average approximately 42% of their total expenditure for magazines, newspapers, radio, and farm journals, the rest being devoted to other categories. From these data it is deduced that the traceable expenditures for general advertisers probably would have to be multiplied by three to approximate their total advertising expenditures.

The above division of advertising expenditures suggests that in the selling of shoes, whether under manufacturers' brands, unbranded, or private brands, the retailer is in a key position to guide consumer demand. Either on his own or through the support of the manufacturer, he carries out a large share of such consumer advertising as is done. Invariably in the case material collected, the retailer held a highly important place in the selling plans of shoe manufacturers, even among manufacturers of women's shoes who were devoting the larger share of their advertising appropriation to general advertising. All

---

[4] Statement contained in a letter to the author.

TABLE 86

DIVISION OF ADVERTISING EXPENDITURES OF 17 SHOE MANUFACTURERS
BY CLASSES OF EXPENDITURE, 1937–38

TYPE OF SHOE	YEAR	CONSUMER ADVERTISING IN GENERAL MEDIA, %	DEALER COOPERATION, %	DEALER HELPS, %	DEALER HELP PLUS DEALER COOPERATION, %	ADVERTISING TO TRADE, %
Women's.......	1938	60	20	20*	20–40	20*
Women's.......	1937	55	40†	5	45	0
Women's.......	1938	50	20	15	35	5
Women's.......	1937	49	9	25	34	1
Women's.......	1937	48	30	15	45	7
Men's, Women's and Children's	1938	40	30	20	50	3
Men's..........	1938	38	9	36	45	10
Men's..........	1937	34	20	37	57	2
Women's.......	1938	33	33	20	53	10
Women's.......	1937	30	33	33	66	3
Women's and Children's....	1937	30	22	19	41	2
Men's..........	1937	25	0	75‡		
Men's..........	1938	20	60	10	70	1
Men's..........	1938	18	15	44	59	16
Men's..........	1937	10	35	43	78	0
Men's, Women's and Children's	1937	4	1	47	48	38
Men's, Women's and Children's	1938	0	0	20	20	40

* Covers both dealer helps and trade papers.
† Company did not grant cooperative advertising allowances. Instead, company placed and paid for advertising over retailers' names (18%) and placed Sunday newspaper advertising listing dealers' names (22%).
‡ Includes dealer helps, trade paper, and other advertising.
Source: Doctoral thesis of Dr. J. D. Scott, *Types of Advertising Programs Used to Promote Products with Selected Distribution* (on file in Baker Library, Harvard Business School, 1940).

endeavored to get their dealers' active support in the selling and advertising of their various brands.

Further evidence of the retailers' importance in the advertising of shoes is contained in records of advertising linage for shoes in newspapers and in studies of their costs of doing business. That shoe advertising is, to a large degree, carried out over the dealer's signature is shown in Table 87, which gives the linage in newspapers of leading cities devoted to shoe advertising by boot and shoe stores and by department stores in contrast to the so-called national advertising placed by shoe manufacturers over their own signatures. In 1929 national advertising was only 4.2% of the total shoe advertising carried in city newspapers. In 1935 and in 1937 it was less than 1%, and in 1939, when there was apparently a resurgence of manufacturer's advertising in newspapers, it amounted to only 7.5%. Of the large volume of retail advertising carried out by department stores and by shoe stores,

TABLE 87

NATIONAL AND LOCAL NEWSPAPER ADVERTISING OF BOOTS AND SHOES
IN LEADING CITIES, SELECTED YEARS, 1929–1939

YEAR	LOCAL ADVERTISING				NATIONAL		TOTAL LINES
	Department Stores		Boot & Shoe Stores		Lines	%	
	Lines	%	Lines	%			
1929...	15,201,000	29.9	33,533,000	65.9	2,143,000	4.2	50,877,000
1935...	16,558,000	43.4	21,431,000	56.1	198,000	0.5	38,187,000
1937...	19,407,000	43.1	25,495,000	56.6	153,000	0.3	45,055,000
1939...	19,174,000	44.8	20,249,000	47.8	3,407,000	7.5	42,830,000

Source: Media Records, Inc., *Newspaper and Newspaper Advertisers,* respective years.

a substantial part was paid for by the manufacturers on a cooperative arrangement whereby the manufacturer ordinarily matched the expenditures of his selected dealers in their featuring of his brand. The part of the advertising budget devoted by 17 manufacturers to cooperative advertising is shown in Table 86, varying from 0% to 60% of the total. It will be noted further that most manufacturers devoted substantial proportions of their appropriations to dealer help material.

Shoe retailers' expenditures on advertising are given in various cost studies. These are shown for the most recent years available in Tables 88, 89, 90. Independent shoe retailers and shoe chains, on the average, apparently have spent in the neighborhood of 3% upon advertising in recent years. Department and specialty stores spent somewhat more, their common figure for newspaper costs alone being in excess of 3%, while their total publicity costs—newspaper advertising and point-of-purchase display—were in excess of 5% of net sales.

Case histories obtained from three manufacturers operating their own chains showed considerable variation in advertising expenditure. One manufacturer's chain handling women's high-price, style shoes appropriated 6.5% of its stores' sales for advertising by the stores. A

TABLE 88

RATIO OF ADVERTISING EXPENSES TO NET SALES
OF RETAIL SHOE STORES AND LEASED SHOE DEPARTMENTS, 1936 AND 1937

	1936	1937
Single Stores	3.1%	2.5%
Multiple Stores*	3.4	3.1
Leased Departments	1.8	2.7

* Each reporting concern operated 2, 3, or 4 stores.

Source: National Shoe Retailers Association, New York (Compiled by Dun & Bradstreet), *Retail Shoe Stores and Leased Shoe Departments.*

TABLE 89

1939 AVERAGE ADVERTISING AND PUBLICITY COSTS OF SHOE DEPARTMENTS
IN DEPARTMENT AND SPECIALTY STORES WITH ANNUAL SALES VOLUME OVER $500,000

	NEWSPAPER COSTS, % OF TOTAL SALES	TOTAL PUBLICITY COSTS, % OF TOTAL SALES
Shoe Departments	3.3	5.3
Children's Shoe Departments......	3.1	4.7
Women's Shoe Departments	3.5	5.3

Source: Controllers' Congress, National Retail Dry Goods Association, *1939 Departmental Merchandising and Operating Results of Department and Specialty Stores* (New York, 1940).

TABLE 90

AVERAGE ADVERTISING COSTS OF SHOE CHAINS, 1929 AND 1932

	1929	1932
Number of Chains Reporting	53	23
Number of Stores Reporting..................	1,361	661
Advertising and Display (% of Total Sales)	3.2%	2.98%

Sources:
C. N. Schmalz, *Operating Results of Shoe Chains in 1929* (Harvard Business School, Bureau of Business Research, Bulletin No. 86), p. 33.
M. P. McNair, *Chain Store Expenses and Profits,* an Interim Report for 1932 (Harvard Business School, Bureau of Business Research, Bulletin No. 94), p. 13.

large chain selling men's medium-price shoes had an expenditure for recent years ranging from 6% to 7%. In contrast, a large chain selling men's low-price shoes used advertising more sparingly, spending only 0.4%.

When all the above data are considered, an estimate of the total amount of money spent in the advertising of shoes in recent years can be little more than a guess. The variation in advertising practices of manufacturers and, to a lesser extent, of retailers makes averages derived from the available data entirely undependable. It would appear that about 3% of the retail value was spent on retail advertising. An appreciable part of this expense was donated on a cooperative basis by manufacturers. When deduction is made for the cooperative expenditures of manufacturers, and allowance is given for the small percentage of advertising expenditure by the great majority of manufacturers, their outlay, as a whole, probably did not represent more than 1% of their combined sales. At retail the value of shoe sales has been in the neighborhood of $1,000,000,000;[5] retail expenditures accordingly have been in the vicinity of $25,000,000 to $30,000,000,

---

[5] This estimate assumes a retail markup of 35% to 40%.

partly paid for by manufacturers. The expenditure by manufacturers for dealer helps, for trade advertising, and for the other items in the advertising budget probably represented some $5,000,000 to $6,000,000 more, giving a total of some $30,000,000 to $35,000,000. Thus retail advertising appears to have been five or six times as great as advertising issued by manufacturers.[6]

TABLE 91

ANNUAL PER CAPITA PRODUCTION OF LEATHER SHOES, SELECTED YEARS 1899–1937, AND ESTIMATED ANNUAL PER CAPITA CONSUMPTION, SELECTED YEARS 1921–1937

YEAR	PER CAPITA PRODUCTION, PAIRS		ESTIMATED PER CAPITA CONSUMPTION, PAIRS	
	Men's	Women's	Men's	Women's
1899	2.7	3.0		
1904	3.0	2.6		
1914	2.9	2.5		
1919	2.6	3.0		
1921	1.9	2.8	1.71	3.02
1923	2.6	2.9	2.48	3.04
1925	2.1	2.6	2.15	2.86
1927	2.2	3.0	2.16	2.91
1929	2.3	3.2	2.12	3.21
1931	1.8	2.6	1.74	2.79
1933	2.0	3.0	1.81	2.99
1935	2.1	3.3	2.08	3.28
1937	2.3	3.4	2.22	3.77

Sources:
Per capita production: Determined from figures of *Census of Manufactures* divided by annual mid-year estimates of population of the Bureau of the Census, with age and sex distribution determined in accordance with nearest decennial census.
Per capita consumption: Estimates of *Boot and Shoe Recorder*, December 25, 1937, p. 117.

EFFECT OF ADVERTISING ON PRIMARY DEMAND

In order to study the effect of advertising on the primary demand for shoes it is necessary to consider men's and women's shoes separately. Per capita consumption data since 1921 are given in Table 91. For the earlier years, per capita consumption estimates are not available, but production figures are satisfactory because shoe production has been geared relatively closely to consumption.

---

[6] The amount spent by wholesalers represented so small an item that it would not change the total greatly. According to the 1935 Census of Business, *Distribution of Manufacturers' Sales* (p. 124) only 16.4% of shoe sales were distributed through wholesalers. A study by Dun & Bradstreet, Inc., of operating costs of profitable wholesalers indicated an average expenditure in 1934 of 0.6% for advertising. (*Wholesale Survey*, 1934.)

Effect of Advertising on Consumption of Men's Shoes

In the case of men's shoes, consumption was downward from nearly three pairs a year, at the turn of the century, until in the 20's it was only slightly above two pairs a year, a figure around which it has stayed for the last decade. The lower figures for 1931 and 1933 were the temporary results of the marked decrease in buying power for those years.

The reasons for this downward trend in men's shoe consumption have already been discussed.[7] Changing conditions of work, changing living habits, and the increasing use of the automobile as possible causes have been mentioned. A limited amount of advertising by manufacturers in general media and a substantial retail expenditure did not check these factors that were operating against shoe consumption.

The continued down trend led the National Shoe Retailers' Association with the support of manufacturers to undertake a cooperative campaign in 1925–26.[8] This campaign was designed to induce men to include a larger number of shoes in their wardrobes and to lead to increased obsolescence with a consequent stimulation of consumption. The questionable ability of the advertising materially to affect shoe consumption, together with the difficulties of raising funds and of administering a campaign to be supported by thousands of possible participants, led to discontinuance of the campaign.

The relative stability of consumption since the late 20's indicates that the causes which were operating against decreasing consumption have become stabilized. Such advertising as has been carried on probably has been, for the most part, selective in result, rather than primary.

Effect of Advertising on Consumption of Women's Shoes

In the case of women's shoes there has been some increase in consumption since the turn of the century. Whatever decrease occurred between 1900 and 1920 has been followed by an increase, which in the last decade has carried consumption to new heights. Annual per capita consumption in recent years has been more than a pair greater than for men.

The probable reason for the growing consumption of women's shoes rests in the fact that fashion has played a more important part for

---

[7] See p. 199, Chapter VII.
[8] This campaign was discussed on p. 89 ff.

women's footwear than for men's. Style became an increasingly important element in shoe merchandising just subsequent to World War I and has been an important consideration ever since.[9] Women's shoes, in contrast to men's, have tended to be bought more to meet the dictates of fashion and consequently less to meet demands of utility. Accordingly, obsolescence has been greater and has brought greater per capita consumption. One manufacturer,[10] whose business was devoted to women's highly styled shoes, stated in an interview in 1938 that a survey conducted by his company among customers buying from its own chain stores showed regular customers typically bought five pairs of its highly styled shoes each year. Thus did fashion-conscious women with ability to buy purchase more shoes than the average woman. The survey showed, moreover, that the buyers were interested primarily in suitable style, and secondarily in comfort, while wearing qualities of the shoes were a minor consideration.

Advertising probably cannot be held to have been the leading cause of increased consumption in the case of women's shoes; yet undoubtedly it has been an important vehicle to carry fashion news to women and to stimulate their purchases of new shoe styles. What the behavior of consumers would have been without advertising is not clear, but it seems safe to say that the large body of retail advertising, as well as the more limited amount of manufacturers' general advertising devoted to new footwear in the current mode must have had an appreciable effect in directing larger expenditures to footwear than would have occurred without such stimulation. Women's shoes furnish an example of advertising serving as a vehicle to stimulate consumption through appeal to consumers to keep up with the fashion parade. It should be noted, however, that, in contrast to other products studied in the chapters on demand, the stimulus to consumption came not so much from persuasive advertising of brands by manufacturers as from the aggressive selling efforts of retailers.

EFFECT OF ADVERTISING ON SELECTIVE DEMAND

While the featuring of new styles of shoes to women in advertising has probably had an appreciable effect in increasing primary demand,

[9] See *Proceedings of the Nineteenth Annual Convention of the National Boot and Shoe Manufacturers' Association of the United States, Inc.*, January, 1923.
[10] Case of the Roycroft Shoe Company, files of the Harvard Business School.

yet a chief objective and effect of such advertising for both men's and women's shoes has been to guide selection among brands. In contrast to advertising's place in guiding selective demand for some of the products studied, however, such as dentifrices and tobacco, shoe advertising, relatively, has not been an important factor in guiding selective demand. As was noted above, few manufacturers have made appreciable use of reputation-building, persuasive advertising. Those who have employed it have used it in relatively small amounts. While retailers' advertising has been devoted in part to building the reputation of brands, its chief use has been to guide immediate buyers to stores to purchase featured merchandise and to inform buyers that stores are sources for certain kinds and brands of shoes.

Personal selling effort is judged to have been a far more important factor in guiding the selective demand for shoes than advertising has been. This view applies alike to manufacturers who have advertised their brands to consumers and to manufacturers who have limited their selling efforts to the trade. The latter have relied far more on personal selling to secure sales from distributors than upon selling through advertisements.

Reasons for Relative Weakness of Brand Advertising

An understanding of the reason for the relatively minor place of brand advertising in the marketing of shoes may come from a study of consumer attitudes and buying habits and of trade attitudes and buying habits. In the first place, although shoes are not standardized—far less so, for example, than are sugar and sheeting—yet the opportunity for manufacturers to individualize their products and to employ appeals which will greatly influence consumer selection is not great. The lack of opportunity for sellers to make their brands stand for important individualizing characteristics not available in other brands and the consequent lack of strong selective appeals have meant that heavy advertising could not profitably be employed by manufacturers on their brands for the general run of shoes.

The relative weakness of advertising in influencing selective demand for shoes is not attributable to standardization of the product, as was the case with sugar and sheeting, but to the factor of style. As a matter of fact, the element of style prevents standardization of shoes but style in itself does not provide a basis for brand advertising except as the seller may try to make his brand known as a style leader and, hence, deserving of consumer consideration. This practice applies particularly to the women's shoe field, in which it has been adopted by some manufacturers, such as I. Miller. Brand, however, cannot stand for specific style, for style is a changing thing; and the consumer can look at merchandise and determine whether it meets his desires. An advertiser who fails to provide desired styles will lose out no matter how much he may advertise. This generalization, which applies to all fashion merchandise, has been demonstrated many times in the case of shoes. Although it applies particularly to women's shoes, it holds true also for men's shoes. For example, the W. L. Douglas Shoe Company, which had been a consistent, though not heavy, advertiser of men's shoes over a long period of time, suffered a considerable decline in sales after 1920 largely because it failed to give adequate attention to the style factor. It adhered rather to its old policy of producing conservatively styled shoes of good quality. In 1934, with a change of styling policy, it frankly stated in its newspaper and magazine advertising that, although in the past it had established a reputation for producing fine quality, it had not given proper emphasis to the style element.[11] Thus it sought more deeply to impress the fact that it was then offering attractive styles. Another manufacturer of men's high grade shoes stated that in 1930 it had found it necessary to offer new and attractive styles as a result of learning in a survey that it was not getting a desired proportion of sales to young men who were more conscious of fashion than older men.[12] Still another manufacturer devoted considerable effort to developing a means of making his orthopedic shoe amenable to current styling without sacrifice of comfort, thereby hoping to widen his market.[13]

In the women's shoe field the importance of fashion merchandising has been even more important and more difficult. The difficulties met and the importance of styling were stressed in all case histories obtained from manufacturers of women's shoes, proper styling being given as probably the most important element in successful merchandising.[14] Fashion has made it possible for many manufacturers to secure sales without benefit of brand reputation, for retailers have bought a large part of their women's shoes unbranded or under their own labels.[15]

---

[11] Case of W. L. Douglas Shoe Company, files of Harvard Business School.
[12] Case of the Ruxton Shoe Company, files of Harvard Business School.
[13] Case of Burwind Shoe Company, files of Harvard Business School.
[14] Cases of Holburn Shoe Company and of Roycroft Shoe Company, files of Harvard Business School.
[15] See discussion in succeeding pages, based on retail case histories.

In the orthopedic field there has been real opportunity for individualizing a shoe brand around which appeals of considerable strength might be built. Such shoes have specialized construction and for them strong appeals can be made for health and comfort. Some of the most consistent advertisers have been these manufacturers. Such shoes, however, appeal to a limited market. And here, too, the strong influence of fashion has made it essential for manufacturers to try to offer their corrective and comfort shoes in current styles so far as possible.

To the consumer a shoe brand ordinarily stands for integrity in manufacture—durability at a particular price level. There have been a large number of good brands available in the market at the various price levels. Evidently, in so far as the consumer could judge the wearing qualities of these shoes at any level, he has apparently deemed them nearly equal. Brand preferences have existed, but brand loyalties apparently have not been particularly strong, especially for fashion merchandise. Moreover, the shoe retailer has been present as a dependable selector of merchandise for the consumer. Since he has been a specialist in shoes and since he has acted as the authority upon the fit of the shoe, an important consideration, consumers undoubtedly in many cases have put as much reliance upon the retailer as a source of footwear as upon the manufacturer's brand; often more.[16] Hence, the retailer has been a dominating influence in guiding consumer selection.

The Importance of Retailers in Guiding Selective Demand

A study of case material in the Business School files shows that the shoe retailer has been fully aware of his position in the distributing set-up.[17] He could be independent in his merchandising, and he has often tended to be. Even in instances where a retailer may have preferred to handle a certain manufacturer's brand of merchandise, he has known that his success did not depend upon handling that or any other particular brand. Moreover, among advertised brands he ordi-

---

[16] Some shoe manufacturers stress fit and comfort. In making this appeal effective they must depend upon their dealers or clerks in their own chains to do a good job of fitting.

[17] Retailer attitudes and viewpoints presented in these paragraphs were based in large degree upon study of case material obtained from retailers in the files of the Harvard Business School: Webster Company, Hawkins & Stott, Hallock Company, John Garland Company (A), John Garland Company (B), Murchase Company, Evers & Chance, Rickerton Company, Fargo & Lewis, Manford & Ross, Howes Company, Laristan Company, Minor Company, Nogworth Company, Winfield Company, Christopher Hall, Inc., Ayleward Company, Costigan Shoe Company.

narily has been able to secure the agency for some one of a number of good brands, if he is a good retailer, for in most cities available brands have been more numerous than retailers. In addition, he has known that he could guide consumer choice to a very marked degree even though he handled a little known manufacturer's brand, unbranded merchandise or his private brand. Suitable sources for unbranded or private brand merchandise have been available to him. Moreover, the fact that the consumer's choice has been guided in large part by style has tended to increase the retailer's desire for freedom in his selection of merchandise among manufacturers, particularly in his selection of women's shoes. Large independent shoe retailers, chain stores, and department stores were found to have shopped among numerous manufacturers for their women's shoes, changing sources in accordance with the judgment of buyers regarding suitability of the merchandise available. Such merchandise often has been sold unbranded or under the retailer's brand. The cases indicated also that such large retailers at times took an active part in designing the shoes which they handled.

When the retailer has sold a manufacturer's brand, almost always he has insisted upon being the only seller of that particular brand in his immediate market. Thus, shoe manufacturers selling under their own brands invariably have found it necessary to employ a program of selective distribution. Among the cases collected, a manufacturer's shoe brand typically was sold in only one store in small and medium-size cities; in larger cities a larger number were used; but always the number was a relatively small percentage of the number of stores selling shoes in the community.

Advertising has not been a force strong enough to lead retailers to handle many brands. As a matter of fact, the heavy inventory involved in a full line of shoes is such that it is not feasible or desirable for a retailer generally to handle more than one brand in a particular price line. Accordingly, when one manufacturer's brand is handled, other directly competing manufacturers are shut out. When shoes are sold unbranded or under private brands, of course, a price line can be made up from several manufacturing sources as is sometimes done, particularly by large stores.

Effect of Selective Retail Distribution on Advertising

This restricted distribution for manufacturers' brands and the re-tailers' function of guiding consumers' purchases have largely been responsible for the advertising practices in the shoe field described above. Since any brand of shoes has had a relatively small number of retail distributors, its sales have consequently been limited, and advertising appropriations have been limited in accordance with these sales. The manufacturers' problem has been one of obtaining good retailers. Since the manufacturer's brand advertising has not been strong enough to enable him to obtain directly competitive retail rep-resentatives in a community, his success has depended to a great extent upon working with his retailers to help them increase their local patron-age and to make them more aggressive sellers of his line of shoes. Moreover, the limited amount of his advertising appropriation often has not been adequate for extensive general advertising after dealer helps and dealer advertising have been provided for. The consequences of this situation become apparent; such promotional expenditures as have been made for brands have been directed largely through the re-tailer in the belief that expenditures of this type would be most effec-tive. A limited number of manufacturers' brands have been given more general advertising, primarily to help induce good retailers to act as agents for the advertised brand. Other manufacturers, however, have foregone use of advertising in this manner.

In order to overcome the difficulties met in getting desirable and adequate retail representation for their own brands, manufacturers have adopted various methods. One plan used by some has been to establish their own chains of retail stores and of leased shoe depart-ments. By such integration they have been assured of having desirable and aggressive retail outlets. Another means adopted by other manu-facturers has been the establishment of several brands for the same quality and price line of shoes, which they then might offer to dif-ferent retailers in a community. Such a policy, however, has entailed promotion of the several brands, with limited funds for the promotion of each.

Evidences of Advertising Effect from Case Histories

While manufacturers who were employing programs of general advertising to consumers as well as substantial sales aids to be utilized by the retailers had no mathematical proof of advertising contribution, generally they looked upon their consumer advertising program as an essential for the particular selling strategy which they were employing. That the viewpoint of these advertisers towards advertising as an aid in guiding selective demand may be better appreciated, digests of several cases are presented.

First of all, in order to show the importance of retail shoe advertising as an aid to securing sales of a particular brand of shoe as well as to suggest that even retail advertising is not indispensable, the case of the Thursby Shoe Company is presented.

Case of the Thursby Shoe Company.—The Thursby Shoe Company[18] was a chain selling men's shoes under its own brand. In 1938 it had over 400 stores located in 224 cities distributed among 40 states. Its close contractual relationship with one large shoe manufacturer, most of whose output it took, virtually made it a manufacturer's chain.

Between 1922 and 1929 this chain had had an exceptional growth and a good profit record. During this time it used practically no advertising other than point-of-purchase display. Advertisements announcing the opening of new stores were the only space advertising that it had employed. To attract patronage the company relied upon its merchandising policy of offering a shoe of good quality, style, and fit at a low price, varying at different dates between $3 and $4 a pair. By 1929 it had over 300 stores and was selling over 4,000,000 pairs of shoes a year.

Stores were located in the principal shopping districts of smaller industrial cities, while in large cities neighborhood shopping districts were selected in addition to central locations.

In 1929, newspaper advertising was undertaken in New York City. Sales of Thursby shoes for that year increased. It was not possible, however, to determine to what extent the increase was the result of advertising, because new executive personnel in the area, changing business conditions, and changing competition were additional elements influencing sales. However, the campaign was considered to have been helpful and accordingly was continued in subsequent years.

The fact that the company had been so successful with the use of only point-of-purchase advertising led executives to believe that other advertising was not an essential to successful operation of the enterprise. The stores were well located. The merchandise was attractive. Satisfied customers returned and brought others to the store.

---

18 Case of the Thursby Shoe Company, files of the Harvard Business School.

From the standpoint of the management the only reason for advertising would rest upon expectation of making more profit than they would have without advertising.

In 1934 a proposal was made that the company experiment with newspaper advertising outside the New York area. Several reasons were advanced for making the experiment. It had been observed that Thursby stores exhibited substantial increases in sales during the first 4 or 5 years of operation, while thereafter sales increased only slightly. The following explanation was offered for this situation. The executives believed that many people had developed fixed habits with respect to the streets that they frequented. Consequently, the window display advertising after a period of time failed to reach new potential customers. It was questioned also whether people of higher income who had not bought Thursby shoes might be induced to do so were they informed of the good quality obtainable at the price asked.

The widespread operations of the company permitted a means of checking advertising results, provided an experimental campaign was employed. Sales trends in an area where advertising was used could be compared with those of other areas where advertising was not employed. Accordingly, in the spring of 1934 the first tests were conducted in Baltimore to determine the sales effects of 16 weeks of advertising. For the 2 months prior to advertising, sales in Baltimore had increased 6% over the corresponding period of the year preceding. Sales in other parts of the Keystone district, of which Baltimore was a part, had shown an increase of 25% over the corresponding period of 1933. During the 16 weeks of the advertising campaign, Baltimore sales increased 45% over the corresponding period of 1933, while other parts of the Keystone district showed only a 21% increase. In short, sales in that district outside of Baltimore showed a somewhat slackening increase during the period of advertising, while the sales in Baltimore increased materially. The increase in Baltimore attributable to advertising was deemed large enough to make the expenditure profitable.

To check the Baltimore results, a second test was carried out in Philadelphia in which the sales increase there was compared with the sales trend of Thursby shoes for the country as a whole. With advertising, Philadelphia sales stepped ahead appreciably compared with the trend in the country as a whole.

As a result of these experiments the executives decided to extend local advertising to other cities. In 1935 they placed advertising in 17 cities besides New York. In 1936 the list was increased to 29 cities, and in 1937, to 77 cities. At the time the case was collected, July, 1938, advertising was being carried on in those markets where on the average advertising costs for the type of advertising schedule found successful in relation to existing volume were not over 5 cents a pair. Since the program had been in operation only a little over 3 years, executives considered the use of advertising still in the experimental stage. At that time, however, the sales trends in cities where advertising had been conducted showed gains over nonadvertising cities in 31 out of 40 instances, a result which led the publicity director to conclude that the advertising had been effective and profitable.

In summary, it should be noted in this case that although a profitable selling method had existed without the use of retail space advertising, yet advertising increased the volume of sales. The increase was definitely attributable to advertising in view of the evidence from control territories. It should be noted further that this advertising was conducted with no change in the price at which shoes were sold. From a profit standpoint, advertising had to find justification solely from the effect of increased volume upon the operating statement.

Case of the Holburn Company.[19]—The Holburn Company, a manufacturer of women's shoes, provides an interesting case because the same management employed different methods in the sale of two lines of shoes. One line of women's low-price shoes was unbranded; hence its only promotion was to the trade. To this operation it added the manufacture and marketing of a woman's medium-price shoe under its own brand for which advertising to consumers was employed as an essential element of the marketing program. Up to the time of the collection of the case history, this latter program had been highly successful, although the exact contribution of advertising was not determinable separately.

The management of the Holburn Company had been successful in building up sales for its women's low-price shoes to a volume of approximately 2,000 pairs a day. The management wished to expand but could see no opportunity materially to increase this volume and therefore was looking for an opportunity to acquire an already advertised brand of shoe. In accordance with this desire, it purchased in 1931 the factory and the trade-mark rights of the Diana shoe, which

---

19 Case of the Holburn Company, files of the Harvard Business School.

had been advertised extensively in women's magazines since 1905. The executives believed that they could produce the $10 Diana shoe on a large scale at a cost which would make possible cutting the retail price to $6 without any change in quality. They thought that such a radical decrease in price of a well-known, advertised brand would increase sales enough to provide the desired volume. They reasoned that the $10 price restricted the potential market of the Diana to women in upper-income groups, who represented only 5% of the total female population, whereas the same shoe at $6 would bring its potential market in the range of approximately 20% of the female population.

In accordance with this reasoning the first action of the new management was to reduce the suggested retail price from $10 to $6. The gross margin of 40% to retailers, which had been given previously, was retained.

Great care was taken to maintain the wearing and fitting qualities of the shoe. In addition, effort was made to improve the style of the line, which had been promoted primarily as an orthopedic shoe. By 1937 the line had been modified so that the orthopedic type represented approximately 40%, sport shoes 25%, and style shoes 35% of the total production. For the creation of new styles the company maintained a style department including a stylist, two assistant stylists, and three experienced factory men. In addition the consulting services of three stylists located in New York City and one living in London were obtained.

Prior to 1932 the Diana shoes were distributed through 450 retail outlets, which were granted exclusive franchises. After the new management secured control and an aggressive advertising and selling campaign had been undertaken, the number of retailers handling the Diana shoe had been increased, until it reached 1,200 by 1934. By 1938 it equalled 1,500. The very substantial increase in sales volume of Diana shoes subsequent to 1932 led 120 retail stores to handle the Diana line exclusively.

Advertising was made an integral part of the whole program. In the first year, when sales of the Diana shoe were in the neighborhood of 880,000 pairs with a value of $3,000,000, $46,000 was expended in advertising, most of which was placed in newspapers of key cities and in dealer helps. As sales increased the advertising was increased until the expenditure in 1937 was in the neighborhood of $240,000, $44,000 of which was spent in newspapers advertising over retailers' names,

$54,000 of which was used for advertisements in rotogravure sections of Sunday newspapers, $132,000 in magazines, and $10,000 for dealer helps.

In addition to the above advertising, great effort was made by the selling force to secure the active cooperation of retailers in the promotion and advertising of Diana shoes. At the beginning of each season, Holburn salesmen called upon each dealer and in conference with his sales promotion officers drew up detailed promotion plans to be supported by retailer advertising of Diana shoes. Dealers were encouraged to spend approximately 5% of their sales on local advertising. The president estimated that Diana dealers spent approximately 4 times as much on local newspaper advertising as the company spent on its key city newspaper campaign.

The sales increase for Diana shoes up to 1938, when the case was collected, was phenomenal. Within a very short time sales increased from the December, 1931, level of 500 pairs a day to 2,500 pairs a day. Prior to December, 1931, the maximum number of Diana shoes sold by the old management of the Holburn Shoe Company in any one year was only 320,000 pairs. In 1932 under the new management 880,000 pairs were sold, and by 1937 this figure had increased to approximately 3,000,000 pairs, representing sales of almost $12,000,000.

It was impossible to isolate the effect of advertising in this entire selling campaign; yet from the standpoint of the management, advertising was an essential ingredient in the program. Undoubtedly the price reduction, which was made in December, 1931, with no change in the quality of Diana shoes, was the primary factor in stimulating the large increase in sales value. The new management judged well the importance of price as a sales stimulant. The sale at $6 of a shoe known to consumers to have been priced at $10 evidently provided dramatic evidence of value both to the trade and to consumers. Advertising, however, was an important means for carrying the story of this marked reduction to consumers. Moreover, the advertising prior to 1931 had played a part in building the reputation of the Diana shoe from which the new management benefited. The advertising employed by the new management not only publicized the new value offered but also gave assurance of maintained quality and improved style. In conjunction with the pricing and styling policies it helped the company to increase its retailers over threefold and to secure their active selling support.

The president deemed it significant that the new management, so long as it had confined its efforts to the promotion of women's un-branded shoes, had been unable to increase sales volume beyond the level of 2,000 pairs a day. Practically the same group of executives, however, in a few years built a sales volume of over 12,000 pairs a day with a shoe supported by a program of national advertising.

Case of the Burwind Company.[20]—This case illustrates the use of consumer advertising to build sales volume for a man's comfort and orthopedic shoe selling in the price range of $10 to $13. The case is of interest in view of the fact that orthopedic shoes usually have been promoted under manufacturers' brands. It indicates that substantial sales apparently have been obtainable for such shoes only when the manufacturer has undertaken advertising to make known to consumers the comfort and health value of his specially constructed footwear.

Previous to 1922 the sales of the Burwind Company had been obtained almost entirely from a men's style line retailing at from $8 to $9.50; the remainder from a shoe of special construction, which it deemed superior to other orthopedic shoes on the market, and for which it had had manufacturing rights since 1914. Without advertising, this specialized comfort shoe had had no appreciable sales success. The management found that retailers were readily interested in the special construction and a number were induced to stock the line. But the retailers had difficulty in selling the shoes after placing them on their shelves. This situation reacted against the company as well as the orthopedic brand. Sales continued to be small; in 1920 only 6% of the company's total sales were of this special feature shoe.

In order to build consumer demand for the Burwind comfort shoe, the company decided in 1923 to undertake a national advertising campaign. The advertising program in the years that followed consisted of a limited amount of national advertising in magazines, a substantial amount of newspaper advertising carried on cooperatively over retailers' names, and point-of-purchase helps for retailers. The executives deemed the advertising necessary not only to build a favorable reputation for its special shoe among consumers, but to help gain retailers' cooperation and direct action on their part in the sale of the shoes.

Under the new program active interest of a substantial number

---

[20] Case of the Burwind Company, files of the Harvard Business School.

of retailers was obtained. In January, 1938, the customer lists showed approximately 1,400 active retailer accounts and approximately 700 occasional retail buyers. The restricted market for a high-price shoe of this type limited solicitation of outlets for the most part to cities of 50,000 or more. According to the executives, the company had been more successful in attaining an active and cooperative dealer organization than was ordinarily attained for shoes in its price class.

While the executives considered advertising an essential element in their marketing program, they looked upon the aggressiveness with which the dealers supported the line as the major factor in determining its success. Compared with the selling effort of dealers, consumer preference generated through the advertising was deemed of minor importance. To get this aggressive support of dealers, the company had had to grant them exclusive agencies. The advertising was deemed an important element in getting them interested in an agency and in keeping them active.

Under the aggressive plan of brand promotion undertaken after 1922, sales of the orthopedic line were built from approximately 80,000 pairs to a high of over 700,000 pairs in 1929. The company gradually shifted its production from its regular style line of shoes to the comfort line. Whereas in 1920 only 6% of total sales were of the comfort type of shoe, by 1929 almost 75% were of this type.

Following 1929 the company suffered a substantial decrease in sales volume of this line to a low of 338,000 pairs in 1932. Sales had recovered to a figure of some 475,000 pairs in 1937. Such a marked decrease in sales, however, was general among men's high-price shoes, according to executives. They felt that the company had fared relatively well as compared with competitors. Moreover, during these years the company had been subjected to increasing competition, in view of the fact that other manufacturers of high-price shoes had turned to the orthopedic field in an effort to reverse the shrinking sales volume.

In this case as in the other situations where shoes have been advertised aggressively to the consumer by manufacturers and by their retailers, partly as a result of the company's stimulation, it was impossible to say with certainty just how much advertising contributed to the demand result. The company's comfort shoes apparently afforded a larger margin of profit than did the company's line of regular shoes. A satisfactory volume on this line of shoes, however, was not attained until the program of consumer advertising was undertaken. From 1914 until 1922 without the use of advertising sales had shown little increase. Once undertaken, advertising became an integral part of the company's selling scheme to retain retailers and to induce them to carry on aggressive selling efforts. The reputation established was not great enough, however, to prevent a substantial shift of demand to lower-price shoes when a depression came upon the country. Part of the difficulty at this time probably rested in the fact that prices of Burwind feature shoes were not reduced so quickly or so radically as shoe prices in general after 1929. Prices were held at 1929 levels until the fall of 1932, when a drastic cut was made. After the reduction of prices there came an improvement in sales volume. According to executives, however, the reputation of the shoe helped it to retain a greater proportion of its previous sales volume than had been true among many other shoe brands in the same price class.

Other evidences that advertising had been helpful were the following: The retail prices established for the shoe were above those of competing comfort type shoes. The value of any such comparison, however, was recognized as open to question in view of the fact that it is very difficult to appraise the relative quality of different lines of such shoes, which often are made with different constructions.

Another indication of advertising's effect, cited by executives, lay in the large number of letters from retailers commenting upon the constant and considerable repeat demand for the shoes. Here again, however, it was recognized that it was impossible to tell to what extent this demand came from customers satisfied from use of the brand and how much from reputation established through advertising.

Company officials agreed that to eliminate their consumer advertising would probably have involved losing some of the confidence which the dealers had in their shoe line. They believed that dealers would begin to wonder whether the consumer preference for the Burwind shoes was being maintained, and they feared that the retailers would be inclined to slow up in their selling work and to cut down on the amount of money expended for local advertising and sales promotion of the brand. In addition, officials feared that the company would not get its share of the new consumer demand for corrective and comfort shoes that was constantly coming into the market. How much of a decline in sales would result, there was no way of determining, however.

Summary

While the above cases may not be said to be typical, they serve to illustrate the viewpoint of shoe manufacturing managements toward the use of advertising for shoes under their own brands and the lack of clear evidence by which to measure the effect of advertising upon the selective demand for shoes. In all, some 18 case histories from 9 shoe manufacturers were obtained, and in addition a large number of cases from shoe retailers. In none of these cases was it possible to isolate and measure the effect of advertising. In no case was advertising the major element in the sales program. Accordingly its effect on volume of sales could not be readily distinguished from those of other causal elements affecting sales volume. It was necessary always to study the effects of entire market programs or plans of selling strategy. Advertising was employed generally as much for its influence in helping to secure retailers and in providing a focal point upon which to center retailers' promotional effort as for its influence upon consumers.

It was almost impossible to judge to what extent aggressive brand selling had affected prices obtained, as compared with prices obtained for unadvertised brands. The lack of standardization in shoes and the difficult problem of setting a valuation for varying product characteristics, such as style, niceties of manufacture, comfort qualities, and so on, made it impossible to know the values of competing sellers. The cases illustrate, however, that not only manufacturers of high-price shoes used advertising to help attain desired marketing objectives, but manufacturers in the medium- and low-price ranges did likewise. While some attempted to influence prices through advertising, others did not.

While those manufacturers employing consumer advertising looked upon it as an aid in building sales volume for their brands, it is clear from these case histories as well as from other material presented in this report that advertising does not play so important a part in guiding selective demand for shoes as it does for numerous other products. Manufacturers employing consumer advertising hope thereby to secure greater sales stability than they would have if they sold shoes unbranded or under retailers' brands. But these alternatives have offered enough profit opportunity to lead many manufacturers to elect to direct their selling efforts largely to the trade rather than to consumers. As contrasted with dentifrices, cigarettes, and electric refrigerators, which are to be discussed in the next chapter, consumer advertising has not been a "must" item in the program of shoe manufacturers desirous of attaining a considerable volume of sales, even though it has been valuable to managements which have used it skillfully.

Because of the importance of the retailer in guiding the selective demand for shoes, advertising by manufacturers has been directed largely through retailers. In turn, retailers have done considerable advertising on their own account. Thus, retail advertising to large degree has taken the place of consumer advertising placed by manufacturers over their own trade-marks, and such advertising has probably played an appreciable part in directing consumer demand to retail sources. In so far as this retail advertising relates to manufacturers' brands it serves, of course, to influence the brand sales of manufacturers.

CHAPTER XV

THE EFFECT OF ADVERTISING ON THE DEMAND
FOR MECHANICAL REFRIGERATORS

THE mechanical refrigerator was selected for study as representative of many new, dynamic products which have played an important part in American life in recent years. Like most of these products, the mechanical refrigerator has generally been looked upon as giving a worth-while contribution to the comfort of living. To stimulate its purchase, manufacturers and retailers have employed aggressive selling and advertising techniques. Its rate of adoption by consumers, slow at first and then markedly accelerated, has been typical of the sales behavior of many American inventions.

The place of such products in the American scheme of life is deserving of careful attention in any economic study. They enjoy a decreasing cost of production. Accordingly, growth of demand usually entails decreasing prices to the consumer. To what extent has advertising been a factor in building an increased demand for refrigerators? Has increased demand been followed by lowered prices which have made possible wide adoption of the products? At a later point inquiry will be made as to whether advertising applied to such products may help to increase investment and to influence full utilization of resources in our advanced industrial economy.

THE GROWTH OF DEMAND

Adoption of mechanical refrigerators by householders was relatively slow for some years after their introduction. Although domestic refrigerating units were advertised in magazines as early as 1916, up to 1920 only 10,000 refrigerators or refrigerating units had been bought by householders, as shown in Table 92. Each year thereafter the number purchased increased, but consumers did not rush in to buy. Price made it a luxury for the rich. The average retail price up to 1920 was $600, and although appreciable decreases came each year, only the high income groups could afford the product. Moreover, even consumers with power to buy had to be convinced of the merits of the new method

TABLE 92

ESTIMATED SALES AND RETAIL VALUE OF DOMESTIC ELECTRIC REFRIGERATORS
IN THE UNITED STATES, 1920–1940

YEAR	TOTAL UNITS	RETAIL VALUE	AVERAGE RETAIL PRICE PER UNIT	
			Dollars	Index, 1926=100
Up to 1920.	10,000	$ 6,000,000	600	154
1921.	5,000	2,750,000	550	141
1922.	12,000	6,300,000	525	135
1923.	18,000	8,550,000	475	122
1924.	30,000	13,500,000	450	115
1925.	75,000	31,875,000	425	109
1926.	205,000	79,950,000	390	100
1927.	375,000	131,250,000	350	90
1928.	535,000	178,690,000	334	86
1929.	778,000	227,176,000	292	75
1930.	791,000	217,525,000	275	71
1931.	906,000	233,748,000	258	66
1932.	798,000	155,610,000	195	50
1933.	1,016,000	172,720,000	170	44
1934.	1,283,000	220,676,000	172	44
1935.	1,568,000	253,648,000	162	42
1936.	1,996,000	327,344,000	164	42
1937.	2,310,000	395,010,000	171	44
1938.	1,240,000	213,280,000	172	44
1939.	1,840,000	309,120,000	168	43
1940.	2,600,000	395,200,000	152	39

Sources:
1920–1925 inclusive, *Air Conditioning and Refrigeration News,* January 11, 1939. Figures not corrected for export; amount deemed inconsequential.
1926–1929 inclusive, Annual Statistical Number, *Electrical Merchandising,* January, 1936. (Based on data from *Air Conditioning and Refrigeration News.*)
1930–1940 inclusive, Annual Statistical Number, *Electrical Merchandising,* January, 1940. (Based on data from *Air Conditioning and Refrigeration News.*)

of refrigeration. Although the new invention had the possibilities of offering great satisfaction to those who could afford the relatively high outlay, sales were attained only as a result of persistent and aggressive seeking out of possible buyers, not merely through advertising but through personal solicitation.

Increase in Demand

Sales were slow, but each year the increment of new buyers was larger than the year before. In 1921, 5,000 new units were sold; in 1922, sales jumped to 12,000; in 1923, to 18,000, a continually accelerating growth as the worth of the new product became recognized and the force of emulation and imitation set in. In 1926 came a marked spurt, when annual sales jumped from 75,000 to over 200,000 units. Thereafter usage went forward rapidly: over 500,000 in 1928;

over 900,000 in 1931; just a slight setback in the depth of the depression in 1932; and then a constantly increasing number until over 2,300,000 units were sold in 1937, the high point of the 1930 decade. In 1938, a maturing market and severe business recession teamed together to bring the first material decline in mechanical refrigerator sales, but by 1940, with further price decreases, total units reached a new high.

The growth in usage of electrical refrigerators, which probably have accounted for slightly over 90% of the mechanical refrigerators sold,[1] is reflected in the ratios of number of users to the total number of homes equipped with electricity, shown in Table 93. By 1925 only 1% of wired homes had electrical refrigerators. By 1930 this percentage had increased to over 9%, by 1935 to nearly 30%; and by 1940 it was 56%. In 1940, manufacturers had to expect that the percentage of usage would be increased at a much slower rate than previously, in view of the probable low incomes of the great bulk of nonusers and the difficulties met by such a group not merely in making the initial purchase of such a high-price article, but in trying to support the luxury of re-

TABLE 93

ESTIMATED NUMBER OF ELECTRIC REFRIGERATORS IN USE, AND DEGREE OF PUBLIC ACCEPTANCE OF ELECTRICAL REFRIGERATION, AS SHOWN BY RATIO OF USERS TO NUMBER OF WIRED HOMES, AS OF JANUARY 1, 1925, AND 1928–1941, INCLUSIVE

YEAR	ESTIMATED NUMBER OF DOMESTIC ELECTRIC REFRIGERATORS IN USE AS OF JANUARY 1	PERCENTAGE OF WIRED HOMES WITH ELECTRIC REFRIGERATORS
1925	150,000	1.1
1928	755,000	4.3
1929	1,223,000	6.4
1930	1,850,000	9.4
1931	2,610,000	12.8
1932	3,498,750	17.1
1933	4,300,000	21.6
1934	4,900,000	24.6
1935	6,020,000	29.3
1936	7,250,000	34.2
1937	9,000,000	41.1
1938	11,271,000	50.6
1939	12,101,000	51.7
1940	13,701,000	56.0
1941	16,100,000	63.0

Source: Excepting 1925 and 1931, taken from January annual issues of *Electrical Merchandising;* missing years computed by author.

[1] See Arthur Hirose and Don Parsons, "Electric Refrigerators, the 'Joe Louis' Industry," *Printers' Ink Monthly,* April, 1939, p. 6.

frigeration from incomes that probably provided little more than the bare necessities of life.[2]

By 1941 a large majority of those with adequate income had purchased mechanical refrigerators, and there was little prospect of greatly expanding the market unless in the future very substantial reduction in price and operating costs occurred. This conclusion is indicated by a study of income distribution as related to refrigerators in use. If it is assumed that the mechanical refrigerators in use were distributed one to a family down through the income groups in accordance with the size of their incomes, then the 16,000,000 mechanical refrigerators in use in 1941 were to be found in part among homes with incomes from $1,000 to $1,250. This computation is based on the distribution of incomes as reported by the National Resources Committee in 1938.[3] It is true, of course, that not all homes above the $1,250 level had mechanical refrigeration and that many homes in the $1,000–$1,250 group or even lower had been sold, facts indicating that an unsold market of some size still existed in 1941. Yet it would appear that sales to new prospects after that date would be obtained with increasing difficulty, unless material reductions in price and in operating costs developed.

Increasing replacement sales were also an indicator that the market approached saturation. Surveys among retailers and consumers indicated that in 1936 replacement purchases by consumers were about 7% of total sales, but by 1939 they were in the neighborhood of 20% of the total.[4] Distributors forecast that replacements would represent at least one-fourth of 1940 sales. Since sales to new users were becoming more difficult, the industry by 1940 had to look more and more to replacements as the source of business.

Decreasing Prices of Refrigerators

The remarkable growth in the use of mechanical refrigeration was not attained without material reductions in the prices at which refrigerators were available (Table 92). New strata of buyers were reached as the unit prices were reduced. Up to 1920 the average retail price

---

[2] *Ibid.*, p. 5 ff.

[3] U. S. National Resources Committee, *Consumer Incomes in the United States* (Washington, U. S. Government Printing Office, 1938).

[4] *Electrical Merchandising*, "Review and Forecast," January, 1938, p. 12; January, 1939, p. 8; January, 1940, p. 16.

Arthur Hirose and Don Parsons, *op. cit.*, p. 76.

had been $600; by 1925 the price had fallen to $425; by 1929 it had fallen to $292. With the advent of the depression, which brought not only decreased material and labor costs but a spur to producers to get their prices down in order to keep their factories operating, prices fell rapidly. By 1932 the average price was down to $195, by 1933 to $170, and from that date through 1939 it hovered between $162 and $172. In 1940 it fell to $152.

According to data obtained from one manufacturer, the prices of comparable models in 1939 were only 55% of what they had been in 1929, although in operation, life expectancy, shelf capacity, and appointments, the 1939 machine was far superior to the 1929 machine. Equally significant is the fact that the lowest-price models had been brought down until, in 1938, a number of manufacturers offered mechanically satisfactory refrigerators in the neighborhood of $100, a price within reach of relatively low income groups, particularly since installment buying was offered.

Thus in a span of 20 years the mechanical refrigerator, with its many contributions to comfortable living, grew from small beginnings until it was to be found in a large percentage of American homes capable of buying and operating such a machine.

THE USE OF ADVERTISING

The evidence regarding the volume of advertising is fragmentary but adequate for a description of the general sweep.

TABLE 94

ADVERTISING OF HOUSEHOLD MECHANICAL REFRIGERATION IN LEADING MAGAZINES, 1916–1928

YEAR	EXPENDITURE
1916	$ 676
1917	6,341
1918	......
1919	38,080
1920	64,625
1921	......
1922	......
1923	44,642
1924	114,249
1925	406,848
1926	1,111,333
1927	1,545,336
1928	2,075,680

Source: Curtis Publishing Company, *Leading Advertisers* (Philadelphia), 1916–1928.

Advertising Previous to 1929

For the period previous to 1929, published records cover only the advertising in leading magazines, as shown in Table 94. The first magazine advertising in the field in 1916 was not of a refrigerator but of a domestic refrigerating unit, Isko, to be installed in an ice box. The advertising of this unit was continued until 1920, after which it disappeared from the scene. In 1920 the Toledo Coldmaker Company advertised, but its name does not appear thereafter in advertising records. During 1921 and 1922 there was no magazine advertising of mechanical refrigerators. Throughout this period, however, a large number of companies[5] were carrying on developmental work, and some were selling machines. Their scale of operations did not justify magazine advertising, but several thousand units were sold each year, as indicated in Table 92. Not until 1923 were magazine programs launched by brands that have since become familiar names. In 1923, Kelvinator placed some $38,000 of advertising in leading magazines, while Frigidaire started with a modest $6,366. In 1924 these two were again the only brands advertised in magazines; Kelvinator spent approximately $72,000 for space, while Frigidaire spent $42,000. After 1924 the mechanical refrigerator business was well launched. New brand names appeared in the advertising lists: Seeger and Servel in 1925; Copeland, Absopure, Hart, and Zerozone in 1926; General Electric and Electrolux in 1927; Westinghouse and Norge in 1928. In step with the growing volume of sales, the volume of magazine advertising increased rapidly as follows: $400,000 in 1925, $1,111,000 in 1926, over $1,500,000 in 1927, and over $2,000,000 in 1928.

A record of expenditures in magazines fails, however, to reflect the whole extent of the aggressive selling effort devoted to mechanical refrigerators during these years. As indicated in later discussions, the traceable expenditures in leading magazines probably have not been more than one-fifth or one-sixth of the total advertising and promotional expenditures made by manufacturers. Moreover, case material indicates that in the early stages of a brand's development, before

---

[5] In his volume, *Household Refrigeration* (4th ed., Chicago, Nickerson & Collins Company, 1933), H. B. Hull states that there were "several hundred concerns producing or developing household refrigerating equipment" during the twenties.

After 1915 the electrical trade journals from time to time announced new refrigerating units put upon the market. See: *Electrical Review*, vol. 70, p. 294; *Electrical World*, May 8, 1915, p. 1202; December 4, 1915, p. 1277; December 23, 1916, p. 1259; June 23 1917, p. 1236; August 31, 1918, p. 426.

sales were large, manufacturers tended to direct their limited advertising expenditures to local markets and through retailers to a greater extent than at a later stage when volume of sales permitted not only the necessary retailer advertising and promotional support but magazine programs as well. Hence, magazine expenditures probably do not provide a good index of total advertising for the early years.[6]

Case histories develop the further fact that in the early years a relatively heavier reliance was placed upon personal selling than in later years, when refrigerators had gained public acceptance. This change was described by one manufacturer as follows:

> During the period of growth of the company's refrigerator sales there was a gradual change in the buying habits of refrigerator purchasers. When the company originally entered the refrigeration field, the sales problem was almost entirely one of aggressively searching out customers, but with each passing year the market report showed an increasing tendency on the part of customers to go to the dealers and purchase refrigerators without the stimulus of a direct canvass.[7]

This manufacturer, like others throughout the 1920's and even into the 1930's, attempted to have his retail representatives make a systematic, home canvass of potential buyers. While this practice had not disappeared in 1940, it did not occupy the place in the marketing programs that it did in the early years before public acceptance of mechanical refrigeration had been obtained.

The public utilities played an important part, particularly in the early years, in stimulating purchase of automatic refrigerators. This was true of both electric companies and gas companies. To them installation of refrigerators meant an increase in their pay loads. Many were the selling schemes which they developed: elaborate displays of merchandise, reduced price sales, crews of canvassers, sales and advertising aids for appliance retailers, surveys of household appliances in use by which to guide sales efforts, sales and advertising work with architects and builders, commissions and bonuses given to employees for providing names of active prospects, rental of appliances, trial installation of appliances, long-time instalment selling, provision for collection of instalments for retailers, and heavy programs of adver-

---

[6] Case of Durbin Corporation, files of Harvard Business School.

[7] Case of Randolph Eaton, files of the Harvard Business School. Also see "Electric Servants," *Printers' Ink Monthly*, August, 1937, p. 7 ff. Here are described sales solicitation methods employed in 1937 for various electrical appliances.

tising.[8] At times they had great difficulty in pursuing their intensive selling efforts without antagonizing the regular retailers of household appliances, whose selling efforts they desired in order to increase use of appliances.

To summarize, the advertising of refrigerators by manufacturers before 1924 was carried on largely in local markets, to a considerable extent through retailers of electrical appliances. The aggressive personal selling that has been applied to most major household appliances was devoted to refrigerators. This aggressive personal selling continued after 1924. To supplement it an increasing amount of advertising was employed, some in magazines, a larger amount in newspapers over manufacturers' names, and an even larger amount over the names of retailers.

Advertising since 1929

An estimate of the expenditures for manufacturers' advertising in newspapers, general magazines, farm journals, and chain radio for the period 1929–1939 is shown in Table 95, the amounts of these traceable expenditures ranging from a high of over $7,000,000 in 1931 to a low of $2,700,000 in 1938, the year when refrigerator sales received their first major setback. It is significant that advertising continued on a large scale after the depression of 1929 set in. The continuance of consumer advertising on a scale as large as or larger than that of 1928–1929 is in marked contrast to the advertising of many durable merchandise items whose appropriations were severely cut with the advent of depression.

An indication of the size of the expenditures for individual brands in the four media is given in the records of 1938 and 1939, Table 96.

---

[8] The following cases contain a description of selling efforts devoted to appliances by public utilities:
Philip Cabot and D. W. Malott, *Problems in Public Utility Management* (New York, McGraw-Hill Book Company, Inc., 1930):
    Westover Electric Company (B), p. 249.
    New England Gas Association, p. 470.
C. O. Ruggles, *Problems in Public Utility Economics and Management* (New York, McGraw-Hill Book Company, Inc., 1938):
    Central Hudson Gas & Electric Corporation, p. 478.
    Niagara Hudson Power Corporation (B), p. 482.
    Hartford Electric Light Company (B), p. 485.
    The Hartford Gas Company, p. 492.
    Luckey, Platt & Co. *v.* Central Hudson Gas and Electric Corporation, p. 499.
Files of the Harvard Business School:
    New York Power & Light Corporation.
    San Joaquin Light & Power Corporation.
    Brooklyn Gas Corporation.

TABLE 95

ESTIMATED VALUE OF SPACE ADVERTISING FOR MECHANICAL REFRIGERATORS, PLACED
BY MANUFACTURERS IN NEWSPAPERS, GENERAL MAGAZINES, FARM JOURNALS,
AND CHAIN RADIO, 1929–1939

YEAR	NEWSPAPERS*	GENERAL MAGAZINES	FARM JOURNALS	CHAIN RADIO	TOTAL
1929.......	$3,628,766	$2,373,020 †	$10,754 [a] ‖	....	$6,012,540
1930.......	3,661,485	2,361,170 ‡	....	....	6,022,655
1931.......	4,121,992	3,104,621 ‡	....	$141,572 [a] ‖	7,368,185
1932.......	2,637,747	2,284,778 ‡	....	....	4,922,525
1933.......	1,941,958	1,126,446 ‡	....	66,527 [a] ‖	3,134,931
1934.......	2,040,674	1,813,553 ‡	12,060 §	192,608 §	4,058,895
1935.......	2,140,063	2,165,182 ‡	46,509 §	179,351 §	4,531,105
1936.......	2,106,146	2,120,740 §	118,117 [b] ‖	133,806 [c] ‖	4,478,809
1937.......	2,501,517	2,421,843 §	135,872 §	317,705 §	5,376,937
1938.......	1,266,838	1,270,611 §	94,911 §	86,532 §	2,718,892
1939.......	1,684,714 ¶	1,612,233 ¶	87,584 ¶	....	3,384,531

[a] Extended from 11 months.
[b] Extended from 9 months.
[c] Extended from 8 months.

Sources:

* 1929–1939 linage taken from Media Records, Inc., *Newspapers and Newspaper Advertisers;* 1938–1939 dollar figures from American Newspaper Publishers' Association, *Expenditures of National Advertisers.* Conversion ratio calculated from data for 1938 and 1939—37.8 cents—applied to other years. See Appendix IV regarding conversion rate.
† Crowell Publishing Company, *National Markets and National Advertising.*
‡ Curtis Publishing Company, *Leading Advertisers.*
§ Publishers' Information Bureau, *National Advertising Records.*
‖ National Advertising Records, Inc., *National Advertising Records.*
¶ American Newspaper Publishers' Association, *Expenditures of National Advertisers in Newspapers, Magazines, Farm Journals and Chain Radio in 1939.*

As will be seen, the campaigns of the leaders were large, even though the expenditures in these two years were considerably less than those for the years preceding.

While these figures of traceable advertising in four media give a better idea of the scale of advertising operations than do the magazine figures previous to the year 1929, they fail to reflect the full extent of advertising and promotional expenditures devoted to refrigerators. Figures of total advertising and promotional expenditures over a period of years submitted by several manufacturers show that the total for such expenditures were two and one-half to three times the value of the traceable expenditures shown in Table 96. The wide discrepancy between total advertising expenditures of these companies and the traceable space expenditures shown in the table arises from the fact that a major part of their advertising cost was of other types: namely, dealer cooperative advertising, dealer helps, advertising to the trade, and charges for production and administration. The division of adver-

TABLE 96

Estimated Value of Space Advertising Placed by Individual Manufacturers of
Mechanical Refrigerators in Newspapers, General Magazines,
Farm Journals, and Chain Radio, 1938 and 1939

Brand	1938	1939
Crosley	$ 95,075	$ 62,475
Fairbanks-Morse	. . . .	708
Frigidaire	525,758	940,896
General Electric	403,963	667,500
Gibson	. . . .	23,792
Hot Point	246,801	145,179
Kelvinator	225,449	247,119
Leonard	27,890	3,777
Norge	257,156	186,478
Philco	. . . .	120,239
Servel-Electrolux	517,301	500,992
Stewart-Warner	22,952	71,671
Superfex	20,642	17,274
Westinghouse	375,905	396,431
	$2,718,892	$3,384,531

NOTE: In instances where several products were covered by a campaign, a prorating
was made for refrigeration advertising.

Sources:

1938: Newspapers—American Newspaper Publishers' Association, *Expenditures of National
Advertisers in Newspapers, 1938.*
Magazines, Farm Journals, Radio: Publishers' Information Bureau, *National Advertising Records.*
1939: American Newspaper Publishers' Association, *Expenditures of National Advertisers
in Newspapers, Magazines, Farm Journals, and Chain Radio in 1939.*

tising expenditures in 1938 among the classifications of "general
advertising," "dealer cooperative advertising," "dealer help material,"
and "advertising to the trade,' as submitted by five refrigerator manufacturers, is shown in Table 97. As will be noted, there was
considerable variation in practice, but four of the five gave emphasis
to promotion through their dealers either in the form of dealer
cooperative advertising or dealer helps. Only one company spent as
much as half of its appropriation for general advertising in magazines,
newspapers, and other consumer media.

If the evidence of relation of traceable expenditures to known total
expenditures of the several manufacturers who made known their
expenditures, admittedly an inadequate sample, are accepted as applicable to all manufacturers, then total advertising expenditures incurred
by manufacturers of mechanical refrigerators may be deemed to have
been as much as $20,000,000 in the year of peak expenditures, 1931;
and as much as $8,000,000 in the low year of 1938.

From the limited data made available it is estimated that during the

TABLE 97

PERCENTAGE OF ADVERTISING EXPENDITURES DEVOTED TO VARIOUS TYPES OF ADVERTISING BY FIVE MECHANICAL REFRIGERATOR MANUFACTURERS, 1938

COMPANY	GENERAL ADVERTISING OVER COMPANY NAME, % OF TOTAL	DEALER COOPERATIVE ADVERTISING, % OF TOTAL	DEALER HELPS, % OF TOTAL	ADVERTISING TO TRADE, % OF TOTAL
1................	51	21	11	3
2................	44	39	12	3
3................	33	26	21	2
4................	25	20	40	10
5................	20	59	9	12

1930's refrigerator manufacturers devoted between 5% and 10% of sales income to advertising and sales promotion. In terms of the average refrigerator value, these percentages represent an expenditure in the neighborhood of $5 to $10 a unit.

Advertising by Retailers

In addition to the advertising placed by the manufacturers, a substantial amount of advertising of appliances was carried on by retailers. As indicated above, this advertising was paid for in part by the manufacturers. It was common practice for the manufacturer to match the advertising of the retailer. Generally the manufacturer did not remain passive with regard to retailer advertising, but he exerted considerable pressure upon the retailer to carry out what he had deemed an adequate amount of retail advertising. For example, one manufacturer followed the policy of urging retailers to spend 3% of their sales on local advertising. This amount was to be matched by an equal contribution paid two-thirds by the manufacturer and one-third by the wholesale distributor.[9] Another company stated that it set aside 5% of the amount billed to the distributors for the refrigerators which they purchased to build up what was called a "territorial" advertising fund. This fund was used to help the local retailers in a number of ways. Some was used to defray a portion of the newspaper and outdoor campaigns which the company conducted in the territories. It was used also to pay part of the cost of dealer helps, such as demonstrating kits, sales books, window display, and direct mail pieces, sold to dealers at reduced prices. The remainder of the fund was used to match dollar for dollar the expenditures made by dealers in local advertising campaigns.[10]

[9] Case of Durbin Corporation, files of the Harvard Business School.
[10] Case of Randolph Eaton Company, files of the Harvard Business School.

The amount of linage devoted to retail advertising of mechanical refrigerators was considerably larger than the linage placed in newspapers by the manufacturers directly. For example, in 1939 *Media Records* showed for 112 cities a total of 7,404,000 lines of electric refrigerator advertising by department stores alone, whereas the number of lines placed by manufacturers was only 4,547,000 lines.[11] In addition to the department store advertising, some 10,643,000 lines of advertising were devoted to electrical apparatus and supplies by retailers other than department stores. It is estimated that as much as 40% of this may have been devoted to refrigerators.[12] Thus retailers placed upward of 11,500,000 lines of advertising of refrigerators in 1939 as compared with the 4,500,000 placed directly by manufacturers in the 112 leading cities.

Typical percentages of sales devoted to advertising of refrigerators by retailers are given in Tables 98 and 99. In 1939, department stores

TABLE 98

TYPICAL FIGURES OF MERCHANDISING AND OPERATING RESULTS FOR MECHANICAL REFRIGERATOR DEPARTMENTS OF DEPARTMENT STORES, 1939

ITEM	PERCENTAGE OF SALES
Gross Margin	28.2
Newspaper Expense	3.6
Total Publicity Expense	5.2
Other Expense	30.6
Total Expense	36.8
Loss	8.6
Average Sale	$124

Source: National Retail Dry Goods Association, Controllers' Congress, 1939, *op. cit.*, pp. 64–65.

TABLE 99

OPERATING AVERAGES OF ELECTRIC AND GAS HOUSEHOLD APPLIANCE STORES, 1935 AND 1936

ITEM	1935	1936	PROFITABLE CONCERNS 1936
Number of Concerns Reporting	311	415	277
Typical Net Sales	$19,900	$25,000	$26,500
Cost of Goods Sold	63%	64.3%	62.8%
Gross Margin	37%	35.7%	37.2%
Total Expense	32.9%	31.0%	29.7%
Advertising Expense	1.5%	1.4%	1.3%
Profit	4.1%	4.7%	7.5%

Source: Dun & Bradstreet, Inc., *Retail Survey*, 1937.

[11] Media Records, Inc., *Newspapers and Newspaper Advertisers, 1939.*
[12] Department store advertising of mechanical refrigerators was 41% of total advertising of electric appliances and supplies, including refrigerators.

typically spent 3.6% of refrigerator sales for newspaper advertising, and 5.2% for total publicity. Typically, small retailers specializing in electrical and gas household appliances spent a smaller percentage upon advertising than did department stores, in the neighborhood of 1.5%, as shown in Table 99.

The evidence regarding the advertising of mechanical refrigerators during the 20-year period in which the market was developed may be summarized as follows:

Advertising and promotional efforts were small during the first few years while the product was being perfected. These expenditures grew rapidly after 1925, as sales grew. The advertising of manufacturers reached a high of probably as much as $20,000,000 for the year 1931. The expenditures continued to be large throughout the period of extreme business depression subsequent to 1929. During this period, except for a slight setback in 1932, sales kept mounting. Manufacturers' expenditures probably represented between 5% and 10% of sales, over half of which was devoted to advertising directed through the retailers in the form of cooperative advertising and dealer helps. Aided by manufacturers, retailers placed over their names a larger linage of retail advertising in newspapers than was placed direct by the manufacturers over their names. Throughout the period, but particularly during the early developmental years, aggressive personal selling methods were employed. For some years canvassing of consumers in their homes was a common practice. To the efforts of the usual retailers was added the intensive selling efforts of public utilities, both gas and electric, which saw in the refrigerator an opportunity to build their loads for electricity and gas.

Mechanical refrigerators provide an excellent example of a new, successful invention which was aggressively promoted and became successful because it filled a real want of consumers. In 20 years a machine requiring an outlay of from $100 to over $600 was sold to almost one-half of all American homes, probably a major share of those possessing means to purchase and operate the device.

THE EFFECT OF ADVERTISING ON PRIMARY DEMAND

No more than a considered judgment as to the part which advertising played in the remarkable growth of demand for mechanical refrigerators outlined above can be given. It may be argued that electric, gas, and kerosene refrigerators offered consumers such an advance in domestic refrigeration that a rapidly growing demand was inevitable in a country with the buying power of the United States. When a careful study is made of the character of demand growth, however, this conclusion seems improbable. It must be remembered that it took over 10 years to sell the first million machines and that almost 10,000,000 were sold in the next decade. Moreover, this latter phenomenal increase in sales occurred after the advent of the most serious depression in the history of the country. Without aggressive personal selling such as was employed, it does not seem likely that so many units of this high-price machine would have been sold during this period. Nor does it seem likely that the sale of the important first million machines by 1929 would have come without the use of persuasion.

Attention is directed to the variables which may have had a bearing upon the growth in demand. In the discussion a basic assumption, which admittedly is debatable,[13] is made, namely, that automatic refrigeration offered a material advance to consumers over old methods of preserving foods, and accordingly represented new merchandise that consumers would purchase, provided they were aware of its utility and had the buying power to convert their desires into effective demand.

The Potential Market as Affected by Income

First, the ability of people to buy, as reflected in consumer income and the changing prices of refrigerators, is examined. Refrigerators have represented a major purchase, one calling for a large sacrifice for most consumers. In order to be induced to make such an outlay they have had to be convinced of the worth of the product. Although the 1920 price had been cut by 1929, the average price of $300 still meant a heavy sacrifice for most families.

During the 1920's, however, national income and consequently the income of consumers was at a high level as compared with the period that followed. National income for the five-year period 1925–1929 averaged some $76,000,000,000 a year; for the next decade it averaged only $57,000,000,000. Even though the prices of refrigerators during this period were still relatively high as compared with prices after

---

[13] It is recognized that under the impetus of competition from automatic refrigeration great improvements were made in ice refrigerators.

1931, the sacrifice on the part of consumers was probably no greater than in the depression years. In other words, the prices of refrigerators were not so high as to have forestalled purchases by a considerable segment of American families, in view of the existing high income level. Moreover, by this time the mechanical refrigerator had been developed to a relatively high point of efficiency, even though its efficiency was far below that of a decade later. In addition, a large amount of advertising, publicity, and personal selling effort had been given to the product. Enough machines had been in use for some years to permit word-of-mouth evidence regarding the advantages of mechanical refrigeration to become known. Yet by 1929 only a small part of the total market had been tapped; probably not a third of families with incomes over $2,500 [14] had been sold. Only 1,250,000 families, representing less than 10% of the homes electrically wired at that time, had purchased electric refrigerators, while the gas refrigerator was just getting under way.

Slowness of Adoption by the Market

These facts are indicative of the slowness with which new products may find buyers even in a country such as the United States, which has had little class restriction or tradition to stand in the way of new usage, which has been amenable to change, and which has enjoyed relatively a high buying power, essential to change. For products other than those ruled by fashion, shifts in consumer usage ordinarily have not occurred quickly, even under the aggressive persuasion of sellers. This has been true particularly of merchandise of high value. Ability to buy has not meant that new, desirable products would be purchased at once by large groups of consumers. Although the growth in demand of refrigerators has been termed phenomenal, yet a phenomenal increase meant that less than 10% of potential users had been induced to buy even after a decade of intensive selling effort.

It is impossible to determine to what extent the increase in sales should be attributed to persuasive selling methods, but it is concluded that the adoption of mechanical refrigeration by consumers would have been much slower had passive selling efforts been employed.

---

[14] The National Resources Committee estimated that there were 3,645,000 in 1935 with incomes over $2,525 a year. The number was probably greater in 1929 (U. S. National Resources Committee, *op. cit.*, p. 96, Table 7B).

Just as it is impossible to say with certainty how many sales should be credited to the aggressive selling methods employed in the early days of mechanical refrigeration, so it is impossible to divide credit for those first sales between personal selling and advertising. Up to 1929 personal selling of an extremely aggressive type was employed, including canvassing, demonstration, trial usage, easy terms. Working hand in hand with this personal selling was a substantial volume of advertising by manufacturers and retailers. While competition among sellers was keen during this period, a great part of the selling effort was carried on with primary appeals. The advantages of refrigeration, particularly mechanical refrigeration, were stressed alike through advertising and by salesmen. The two forms of selling worked together to induce consumers to adopt the new form of refrigeration.

Factors in Rapid Growth after 1929

The rapid growth in demand after 1929, in the face of the extreme depression that extended through much of the period, can be attributed to a number of factors.

First of all, the pioneering efforts of the first decade of refrigerator selling undoubtedly had built a public acceptance for mechanical refrigeration which paved the way for its subsequent rapid spread. Its advantages to the housewife had been made known through advertising and personal selling. Moreover, the motives of emulation and imitation became operative on a wider scale. Each new installation provided not only a source of word-of-mouth advertising regarding the advantages of the new form of refrigeration, but each installation represented also an additional center for the working of emulation. To the aid of aggressive selling came the heightening of desire generated by an ever-widening group of users.

In the next place, this widening desire for mechanical refrigeration had an opportunity to become effective because the prices of refrigerators were quickly lowered at a time when buying power was decreased. The average price fell to $275 in 1930, to $258 in 1931, to $195 in 1932, and to $170 in 1933, the figure about which it hovered up to 1940.

Another factor which operated to make demand effective was a decreasing cost of operating the refrigerators. Decreased costs of operation came in part through improvement of the machines and in part through lower costs of electricity and gas, as shown in Table

100. In cities of 50,000 population or more, the average bill for 100 kw.-hr. of electric energy, an amount adequate for light, small appliances, and refrigerators, was $6.18 in October, 1924, but by January, 1939, it had dropped to $3.96, only 63% of the previous figure.

TABLE 100

AVERAGE TYPICAL BILLS FOR 100 KILOWATT-HOURS OF ELECTRIC ENERGY IN CITIES
OF 50,000 POPULATION OR MORE
(COVERS USAGE FOR LIGHTING, SMALL APPLIANCES, AND REFRIGERATION), 1924–1939

DATE	AVERAGE BILL FOR 100 Kw.-Hr.	INDEX OF AVERAGE BILL OCT. 1, 1924=100	AVERAGE BILL IN CENTS PER KW.-HR.
October 1, 1924*.............	$6.18	100.0	6.2
October 1, 1925*.............	6.00	97.1	6.0
October 1, 1926*.............	5.85	94.7	5.9
October 1, 1927*.............	5.58	90.3	5.6
October 1, 1928*.............	5.34	86.4	5.3
October 1, 1929*.............	5.13	83.0	5.1
October 1, 1930*.............	4.98	80.6	5.0
October 1, 1931*.............	4.72	76.4	4.7
October 1, 1932*.............	4.65	75.2	4.7
October 1, 1933*.............	4.58	74.1	4.6
October 1, 1934*.............	4.47	72.3	4.5
January 1, 1935*.............	4.45	72.0	4.5
January 1, 1935†.............	4.47	....	4.5
January 1, 1936†.............	4.21	67.8	4.2
January 1, 1937†.............	4.10	66.0	4.1
January 1, 1938†.............	4.03	64.9	4.0
January 1, 1939†.............	3.96	63.8	4.0

* Average bills are for a selected group of 150 cities.
† Average bills are for all cities of 50,000 population or more.
NOTE: Index numbers are adjusted to be comparable with earlier years.
Source: *Statistical Abstract of the United States, 1939,* p. 385.

Lower cost of operation was attained also from more efficient machines; according to the data submitted by an executive associated with one of the leading brands, the average kilowatt consumption per month of his company's refrigerator was only 40% as great after 1937 as it was previous to 1930. An executive of another electric refrigerator company made the following statement:

In 1925 the average retail price of a refrigerator was $435; in 1927 that price had been reduced to approximately $350, and this refrigerator used on an average 822 kw.-hr. annually, according to figures made available by *Electric Merchandising,* which also furnished much of the statistics and data. We have labored diligently during the last few years with the result that the average retail price of a refrigerator in 1936 was $160, and we had increased the efficiency to a point where the average consumption of kw.-hr. per unit for 1935 was 480, with the annual average of kw.-hr. consumption still falling. In other words, we have reduced the unit cost almost two-thirds, and the cost of operation approximately one-half in the last 10 years, and we are still making progress. We are giving the public more for its money, and it is responding by buying more of our products.[15]

The Part Played by Advertising

While lowered prices, lowered costs of operation, and increased number of adoptions favored expansion of demand after 1929, aggressive selling continued to play a large part in speeding up adoption. The reliance placed upon personal selling tended to be less with each passing year; more and more manufacturers counted upon advertising to bring consumers to retail establishments to buy. The program of advertising was more intense than that of the preceding period, and with each passing year it became more and more selective in its aim. The desirability of mechanical refrigeration was taken more for granted and the individualizing characteristics of each brand were emphasized. Yet many of the selective appeals, such as the convenience of box design, the beauty of appearance, the economy of operation, the liberal ice cube capacity, and the efficiency in food preservation were primary as well as selective appeals to consumers who did not have mechanical refrigerators. It will be recalled that the great bulk of sales, even in 1940, were to buyers who had not previously used mechanical refrigerators.

In short, during the 1930 decade advertising continued to play an important part in bringing expansion of demand, although its contribution cannot be measured mathematically.

EFFECT OF ADVERTISING ON SELECTIVE DEMAND

Advertising undoubtedly has played an important part in guiding selective demand among the various brands of mechanical refrigerators. That such should be the case has been determined by the part brand reputation plays in the purchase of such a mechanical product.

Consumer Reliance on Brands

To the consumer a refrigerator has represented a major expenditure calling for careful consideration of the merchandise available. Moreover, the average consumer has been unable scientifically to test or appraise the many nonstandardized machines on the market. He has had to reach a conclusion based on his judgment of the advertising

[15] "Electric Servants," *op. cit.,* pp. 8–9.

material which he has seen, the statements of friends, possibly the ratings of testing organizations, and the statements of retailers. Consequently the manufacturer generally has deemed it wise to develop for his brand a reputation which would at least lead the consumer to give it consideration when in the market.

One large manufacturer made a survey in 1936 and 1937 among purchasers of his refrigerator to determine their reasons for choosing his box. The reasons given with the percentages of buyers mentioning each are shown in Table 101.

TABLE 101

REASONS INFLUENCING CHOICE OF DURBIN REFRIGERATOR
BY PURCHASERS, 1936 AND 1937

REASON	PERCENTAGE OF BUYERS MENTIONING	
	1936	1937
Excellence of Refrigerating Mechanism.........	63.2	69.7
Economy of Operation......................	60.7	69.5
Beauty of Refrigerator.....................	51.9	56.2
Convenience Features	53.8	51.1
Opportunity for Easy Financing..............	47.4	44.8
Warranty Given	30.9	48.8
Manufacturer's Standing	41.2	43.6
Dealer's Standing	39.5	41.3
Vital Differences in Machine from Competitors..	25.4	26.7
Other Reasons	10.0	13.3

Source: Case of Durbin Corporation, files of Harvard Business School.

The advertising and selling plans of the company were drawn to build the reputation of the refrigerator about these reasons. Other manufacturers in turn have sought to build similar associations about their brand names, stressing the individualizing features deemed most significant.[16]

Leadership of Manufacturers' Brands

Competition for the most part has been between the brands of manufacturers. Through 1939 not many retailers operated on a large enough scale to undertake private branding. This was true not only of stores specializing in household appliances and of furniture stores

---

[16] A description of the advertising campaigns of refrigerator manufacturers will be found in the following articles and cases:
"Electric Servants," *op. cit.*, p. 78 ff.
Arthur Hirose and Don Parsons, *op. cit.*, p. 77 ff.
F. R. Pierce, "Product Advertising, Steadily Done, Lifts Selling Out of Competitive Class," (discussion of Frigidaire selling methods), *Printers' Ink,* June 29, 1939, p. 11 ff.
Cases of Durbin Corporation, Norge Corporation, and Randolph Eaton Company, files of the Harvard Business School.

but also of department stores, which were often larger operators. The purchase commitments required by manufacturers for private brands were greater than most department stores could dispose of. Moreover, the danger of obsolescence in a product as dynamic as the mechanical refrigerator involved heavy risk. In addition, department stores did not have established reputations for providing dependable mechanical merchandise under their own brands which would help them in selling their private brands of refrigerators. Their reputation turned more on their skill in providing correct fashion merchandise.

There were exceptions to the above rule of retailer branding, notably in the cases of the large mail-order houses and chains, Sears, Roebuck and Company and Montgomery Ward & Co., Incorporated. Their large-scale operations permitted them to make favorable contracts with manufacturers. Moreover, different from department stores, their long and successful experience in selling mechanical products under their own brands had helped to build for them patronage motives leading to acceptance by consumers of their brands of machines.

Retailers generally have sold manufacturers' brands. They have relied on the reputations of the brands handled and upon their own advertising efforts as local sources of these brands, to attract patrons to their stores. To some extent they have gone out to consumers' homes to drum up trade.

Tasks Assigned Advertising

In contrast to the situation with shoes, manufacturers of refrigerators have counted upon brand reputation to exert a strong pull in leading consumers to their selected retailers to inspect their machines. Reputation has been determined to a large extent by performance, of course, but advertising also has been an important element in building brand reputation. The fact that manufacturers have made constant improvements in their refrigerators, bringing forth new models yearly upon which to center their selling efforts, has meant that advertising has played a particularly important part in gaining consideration of consumers coming into the market. Consumers have not been able to determine current purchases by performance and design of past models. Always they have had to consider new product developments and the news regarding these has been carried to them through advertising.

According to case data, manufacturers have recognized that product reputation built through advertising was not in itself enough to consummate sales. The limited information which could be given through advertisements, and recognition of the bias of advertisements, apparently has meant that consumers ordinarily have given consideration to several machines and have turned to dealers for additional information and for demonstration which would help them determine their selection. Accordingly, most manufacturers have relied on advertising to gain consideration for their brands from a substantial number of those in the market. To make their selling programs complete, they have recognized the importance of working closely with their dealers, of inducing them to advertise in their localities, and in training them to present effectively the advantages of their particular brands. An appraisal of advertising's place was stated thus by the sales manager of one of the leading brands.

> Advertising has been a very important factor in helping to sell our refrigerators. Its function has been to create a desire in the minds of consumers and to get prospective buyers to visit a ―― dealer. A sale has not been completed, however, when a prospective buyer has come into a retail store handling ―― refrigerators. It has been necessary for the retail salesman to prove to the prospective buyer through demonstration of the product's features and through persuasive selling tactics that the ―― refrigerator has been the best one to buy.[17]

The same viewpoint was expressed by Mr. Frank R. Pierce, Manager of the Household Division of Frigidaire Division of General Motors Sales Corporation:

> "If every salesman," we said [at a sales convention], "told the Frigidaire story as the advertising tells it, he would sell more refrigerators."
> And this is true, although we do not look upon our advertising as a substitute for sales effort. Our advertising is expected to tell the sales story but not to make sales. The product itself must do that with the aid of the dealer organization. We know very well that very few, if any, people will read one of our advertisements, rush out in search of a dealer and place an order, just as salesmen seldom get an order on the first call. In behalf of the salesmen, our advertising calls again and again on prospects everywhere, those on whom dealers are already working and on many more that the dealer doesn't even know are prospects or who aren't prospects today but will be tomorrow.
> When a family does decide to buy an electric refrigerator the advertising we have been doing for years will pay dividends. It has created an acceptance, an acceptance for the Frigidaire name and for at least part of our sales story. For

---

[17] Case of Durbin Corporation, files of Harvard Business School.

example, for several years we have featured our Meter Miser. We don't know, of course, how many people who see our advertisements have read them carefully enough to know exactly what a Meter Miser is and what it does. But everyone who has seen or heard our advertisements is familiar with that name. We think the name itself has an appeal and when a salesman mentions the term "Meter Miser" to the prospect it is something with which he is already familiar. "Oh, yes," he says, or thinks, "I've heard about that and would like to know what it is."

The Meter Miser was put over with advertising. The dealer organization by itself could not have done the job. Consider how few prospects, relatively, a salesman actually sees. If we were to depend entirely upon our dealer organization for familiarizing the public with terms like "Meter Miser" and, this year, "Cold-Wall Refrigerator," it would take us years, and even then we wouldn't reach half the prospects who should know about them. This is vitally important with products that are being improved constantly. A new feature must be capitalized quickly while it is news and before still another improvement comes along.[18]

As the market became more and more developed during the 1930's, and electric refrigeration was more and more accepted by consumers, house-to-house canvassing methods became less effective. To a larger extent than formerly, manufacturers' general advertising and retail advertising were relied upon to bring consumers to retail establishments.

It is not possible to separate the effects of advertising, personal selling, variations in price, and product reputation arising from usage, as determinants of selective demand. These following points merely supplement the above analysis of the important part played by advertising in guiding demand.

Volume of Sales among Brands

Most manufacturers have relied upon advertising as an essential element in their sales programs and such data as are available show that demand has gone primarily to those brands which have been most widely advertised. This fact is shown in the brands found in homes as determined by the survey of Scripps-Howard papers among 53,124 homes in 16 cities in 1938. These brands, representing at least 1% of the 31,796 mechanical refrigerators found, are listed in Table 102.

---

[18] F. R. Pierce, *op. cit.*, p. 13 ff.

TABLE 102

BRAND OWNERSHIP OF MECHANICAL REFRIGERATORS AS REPORTED BY 31,796
HOMES AMONG 53,124 HOMES INVENTORIED IN 16 CITIES IN 1938
BY SCRIPPS-HOWARD NEWSPAPERS

BRAND	NUMBER OF REFRIGERATORS FOUND	PERCENTAGE OF TOTAL
Frigidaire	7,121	22.4
General Electric	5,930	18.6
Norge	2,738	8.6
Servel Electrolux	2,598	8.2
Kelvinator	2,543	7.9
Westinghouse	2,500	7.9
Coldspot	2,344	7.4
Crosley	949	3.0
Grunow	823	2.6
Leonard	713	2.2
Stewart-Warner	314	1.0
Others (less than 1% each)	3,223	10.2

Source: Scripps-Howard Newspapers, *Market Records—Buying Habits and Brand Preferences of Consumers in Sixteen Cities* (New York, 1938), Vol. I, p. 224.

Of the brands named, every one except Coldspot was the advertised brand of a manufacturer. The heavily advertised brands led in volume of sales. Moreover, many of the brands included in "Others," those appearing in less than 1% of the homes with mechanical refrigerators, were the advertised brands of manufacturers, such as Copeland, Apex, Hotpoint, Universal, and Gibson. Coldspot, the brand of Sears, Roebuck and Company, which was found in 7.4% of homes with mechanical refrigerators, has not been widely advertised through magazines, but it has been given a large amount of retail advertising by the various Sears, Roebuck stores, and a large volume of mail-order advertising by that company. The same is true of the refrigerator of Montgomery Ward & Co., Incorporated, which was included among Others.

Similar evidence for the Milwaukee market for various years is given in Table 103. The listed brands were those appearing in at least 1% of homes having electric refrigeration, which were 40% of the homes surveyed in 1938. Every brand named was an advertised, manufacturers' brand, with the exception of Coldspot. These listed brands accounted for almost 92% of the total machines reported, while the remaining 8% were distributed among some 47 less publicized brands.

The evidence in these two tables and in Table 96 does not tell to what extent advertising was responsible in bringing volume to the brands listed. It does indicate, however, that those manufacturers who accounted for most of mechanical refrigerator sales, looked upon advertising as an essential element in their marketing programs. As has already been indicated, they devoted a considerable amount of money to advertising, an amount probably varying between 5% and 10% of their sales. In addition, it is known that the private brands also were given a substantial amount of advertising support.

In the course of the investigation, case material and data secured from manufacturers of four of the leading brands gave direct evidence of the confidence they placed in advertising as an aid to securing sales, but no mathematical measurement of its contribution was possible.

It is impossible, furthermore, to state to what extent advertising may have aided manufacturers in securing prices for their brands greater than they would have secured without such advertising. All

TABLE 103

OWNER PREFERENCE OF LEADING MAKES OF ELECTRIC REFRIGERATORS IN GREATER MILWAUKEE, SELECTED YEARS 1934–1938

BRAND	PERCENTAGE DISTRIBUTION OF BRANDS AMONG FAMILIES WITH MECHANICAL REFRIGERATORS			
	1938	1937	1936	1934
Frigidaire	18.5	17.7	20.6	24.0
Norge	14.1	16.5	16.6	17.5
General Electric	13.4	11.8	13.4	13.0
Coldspot	11.9	9.0	5.9	1.5
Kelvinator	9.9	12.1	13.3	13.3
Westinghouse	7.0	4.9	5.0	5.0
Grunow	4.3	4.6	4.8	2.3
Crosley	3.4	3.4	2.3	....
Leonard	2.1	2.9	2.7	1.8
Stewart-Warner*	1.8	1.1	....	....
Fairbanks-Morse*	1.5	....	....	....
Apex*	1.1	1.0	....	....
Copeland	1.0	2.3	2.6	4.4
Hotpoint*	1.0	....	....	....
Gibson	1.0	1.0	1.0	....
Miscellaneous†	8.3	11.7	11.8	17.2
Percentage of Families with Electric Refrigerators	40.5	30.7	26.0	17.7

* Used by less than 1% in previous years and therefore included under "Miscellaneous" in those years.

† Represented:

YEAR	NO. OF BRANDS	YEAR	NO. OF BRANDS
1938	47	1936	33
1937	35	1934	37

Source: *The Milwaukee Journal*, "Consumer Analysis, Greater Milwaukee Market, 1938," p. 89.

have employed advertising to build brand reputation. Moreover, the lack of standardization among the various brands does not permit of ready price comparison. The private brands of Sears, Roebuck and Company, and Montgomery Ward & Co., Incorporated, probably have had less advertising expenditure per unit than have most manufacturers' brands, although this conclusion is but a speculation based on the fact that manufacturers' machines have had both general advertising and retail advertising devoted to them. These private brands have been offered to consumers at prices considerably below those of most manufacturers' brands. For example, in 1940 the leading manufacturers' brands in Boston varied in price, but ranged from approximately $115 upward, with large-size boxes in one line running as high as $535. Not all companies started their lines at the same level, nor were the prices of competing models of approximate size the same. Price varied in accordance with the various features included in any model. In contrast, prices of Sears, Roebuck and Company's Coldspot refrigerators in its Boston stores ranged from $88.50 to $169.50.[19]

To summarize: the study of refrigerators has indicated that advertising has had an appreciable effect upon both the primary and the selective demand of the product. Refrigerators represent the successful invention, one that has proved wantable to a large part of our population. But large demand for such a product did not follow immediately its launching upon the market. Even though the United States had many families of high income, the number of units sold for the first decade or more was but a small part of the potential market. Moreover, the first million machines were sold only as a result of a most aggressive type of advertising and personal selling.

Subsequent sales followed rapidly, in spite of reduced consumer income. The first million units sold were a large factor in stimulating subsequent sales, for they helped generate desire among unsold consumers. They provided a wide basis for emulation to work. Lowered prices and smaller costs of operation aided sales growth. Making the most of lowered prices and lower operating costs, manufacturers and retailers employed heavy programs of advertising and personal selling to speed up adoption. The result was a remarkable volume of sales in a decade characterized by business depression. Without advertising,

---

[19] Detailed price data are given in Chapter XX.

demand for mechanical refrigerators would have grown; with advertising, its adoption was greatly speeded up.

Since the refrigerator has been a highly individualized, rapidly changing product, brand discrimination among consumers has been high. Brand reputation has been an important element in helping to attract consumers. Advertising has played an important part in the building of such reputation, and hence in the guiding of selective demand.

CHAPTER XVI

SUMMARY OF THE EFFECTS OF ADVERTISING ON PRIMARY AND SELECTIVE DEMAND

T HE chapter on refrigerators concludes the detailed analyses of the effects of advertising upon primary and selective demand, although in the course of this investigation into the economics of advertising, industry statistics and advertising expenditure figures were assembled in greater or less detail for the following product groups: automobiles, gasoline, breakfast foods, electric clocks, electric shavers, women's hosiery, and radio receiving sets. Moreover, case histories relating to the above products and to a wide variety of additional products were gathered and studied. Detailed analyses of the effects of advertising upon the primary and selective demand for these products are not presented here. While their presentation would contribute interesting illustrations of variation in the forces affecting demand, the products discussed in the preceding pages serve adequately to show the wide differences in the place of advertising as a stimulator of primary and selective demands under the varying forces which govern demand.

In the range of industries studied, advertising has been used in widely differing amounts with varying effect upon primary and selective demands. Some industries which have used little advertising have had an expanding demand; other industries with large volume of advertising have had a contracting demand. In certain industries selective advertising expenditures of many producers have been so large that they have represented a substantial part of the final sales price, while in other industries expenditures have been a very small percentage of price. What helpful generalizations may be drawn from this selection of examples?

Theoretical Ways in Which Advertising May Affect Demand

The chapter on value theory has indicated that advertising theoretically is a force which may either shift demand curves or change their shapes. It may affect either the demand curves for classes of products as a whole (primary demand) or the demand curves of individual companies (selective demand).

Advertising may shift the demand for a class of product when the demand for that product is expansible, i.e., subject to increase through appeals to consumers' buying motives. Appeals may be made either to previous users or to nonusers. The appeals may emphasize the desirability either of old, accustomed uses or of new uses. Provided the desire for the product in the market is thereby enhanced, the demand curve is shifted to the right. When the demand can thus be increased easily, price being constant, through appeal to consumers' buying motives, a product is said to have an expansible demand; conversely a product has an inexpansible demand when its sales cannot readily be thus increased.

In influencing the shape of the demand curve for any type or class of products, advertising theoretically may make the demand either more or less elastic, i.e., responsive to price changes. Conceivably the demand for some products might be made less elastic, provided the advertising rendered the desire for the product so intense that consumers' demand would not be readily affected by price changes. More generally, however, it would be expected that demand would become more elastic as the desirability of a product became known to a wide audience and the variety of its uses became generally recognized.

Since the great bulk of advertising is carried on by individual companies to increase their sales, it is to be expected that advertising effects relate largely to the demand curves of individual companies, i.e., to selective demand. Here, advertising theoretically may not only expand the demand of the individual company which advertises, but it also may change the shape of the company's demand curve. The shifting of a concern's demand curve as a result of advertising occurs when the appeals make a branded product appear more desirable to consumers than would be the case without such selling effort. In so far as a company is able to shift its demand curve with advertising, it attains a larger share of the industry's total than before, unless primary demand expands in equal ratio. When a concern finds it possible through advertising readily to shift the demand schedule of a branded product, that product may be said to be advertisable or to offer a good advertising opportunity. Conversely, when advertising does not readily bring a change in a concern's demand schedule, the product may be described as one not presenting a good advertising opportunity. Aside from the question of shifting a demand curve, advertising theoretically may change the shape of a company's demand curve in various ways, either making it more or less responsive to price at various parts of the curve.

Conditions Governing Advertising Opportunity

The evidence has shown that no general answer can be given concerning the effects of advertising upon the demand for products. Numerous conditions bear upon the effectiveness of advertising and it is necessary for each concern carefully to appraise its opportunity for using advertising for each of its products in the light of the conditions under which it operates. It must consider both conditions affecting primary demand and those affecting selective demand. The individual concern in appraising its advertising is interested in expanding its own demand, whether the expansion comes from attracting new users to the product field or from weaning customers from competitors. The advertising of individual concerns, accordingly, may affect both primary and selective demand schedules. Aside from the relatively infrequent instances in which competitors band together to carry on co-operative campaigns in order to shift the demand of an industry, advertising's effect upon industry or primary demand comes from the aggregate effect of individual company campaigns.

In the preceding chapters the conditions favorable and unfavorable to the use of advertising by business concerns have come to light. The individual company has found it advisable to use advertising to increase sales only when advertising has served to stimulate a volume of sales at prices which have covered all costs, including the advertising outlay. The studies have shown numerous conditions which affect the opportunity to employ advertising profitably to shift the demand curves of products, but among the conditions found five stand out:

First, advertising is likely to be more effective if a company is operating with a favorable primary demand trend than if it is operating with an adverse trend. When an industry's sales are expanding, each concern can strive for part of an increasing whole. Thus in the tobacco industry some companies in recent decades have put much of their advertising and promotional effort on cigarettes, because the demand for cigarettes has been expanding and promotional effort given to them has been particularly promising of bringing increased volume of sales. In contrast, in advertising smoking tobacco and chewing tobacco, tobacco companies have operated with adverse trends and each company has been seeking to get a share of a contracting total demand.

The second condition governing a concern's opportunity to influence its demand is the presence of large chance for product differentiation. When products can be significantly differentiated, advertising is likely to be effective. Conversely, advertising is of smaller help when there is a marked tendency for the products of various producers to become closely similar. In product differentiation rests the opportunity for influencing consumers to prefer one brand to another. Advertising can be used to show consumers the significance of differentiating qualities. Moreover, differentiations have an important bearing on the gross margins which the seller can obtain. When differentiations of significance are present, gross margins can be widened. When significant differentiations are absent, margins tend to be narrow. The width of the margins in turn determines the availability of funds with which to support advertising and selling. Among the products studied, smoking tobacco, cosmetics, dentifrices, soaps, electric refrigerators, and automobiles have had product differentiations of significance to consumers and the individualizing points of different producers have been stressed in their advertising. Conversely, sugar, salt, canned fruits, and sheeting are illustrative of products which have tended to be closely similar and as a result advertising has not been a very effective means to increase the demand of individual companies.

A third condition bearing upon the advertising opportunity for any product is the relative importance to the consumer of hidden qualities of the product as contrasted with external qualities which can be seen and appreciated. When these hidden qualities are present, consumers tend to rely upon the brand, and advertising can be used to associate the presence of the qualities with the brand. Conversely, when the characteristics of a product which are significant to a consumer can be judged at time of purchase, brand tends to lose some of its significance and advertising is not needful in building mental associations regarding these characteristics. To illustrate, consumers attach importance to the hidden qualities of mechanical products such as automobiles, watches, washing machines, for satisfactory operation of a machine depends upon its hidden qualities. Manufacturers of such products use advertising to build mental associations regarding the dependability of their brands. Likewise, consumers are apt to give greater weight to the purity, potency, and other hidden qualities of such products as drugs and cosmetics. On the other hand, one reason why advertising has not been valuable to producers of green vegetables is the fact that the buyer can inspect the articles and judge their worth at the time of purchase. The seller's trade-mark can stand for no hidden qualities of great significance to the buyer, particularly in view of the perishable nature of the product. Similarly, in the case of fashion merchandise, the consumer can judge the elements of style, such as color and design, and tell whether the product suits his fancy. In such merchandise these external characteristics are more important to the buyer than hidden product qualities, such as fastness of color and durability, which may be associated with a seller's trade-mark. This fact accounts in considerable part for the relatively small use of advertising to influence the demand for the branded merchandise of producers of fashion goods.

A fourth condition having a highly important bearing upon the opportunity for use of advertising to increase the demands of individual concerns is the presence of powerful emotional buying motives which can be employed in advertising appeals to consumers. Conversely, if such strong appeals cannot be used effectively, then the advertising opportunity is not so great. In the case of oranges, effective appeals to maintenance of health have helped to build demand for the products of the California Fruit Growers Exchange, for appeals to health and personal well-being are potent. Similarly, manufacturers of cosmetics, drugs, and food specialties have found in their products bases for appeal to strong consumer buying motives. Food and drug products give promise of health, which those who are ailing or who think they are ailing, urgently desire. Cosmetics give promise of personal beauty and romance. Generally such emotional appeals, when relevant to a product, have material effect on consumers' valuations, a fact clearly illustrated in the prices obtained for advertised drug and cosmetic products. In contrast to the above, walnut growers, sugar manufacturers, sheeting manufacturers, and numerous other sellers have found their products less adapted to the use of strong emotional appeals.

A fifth condition of importance in determining the employment of advertising to increase the demand of the individual concern is whether the concern's operations provide substantial sums with which to advertise and promote its products in the markets it seeks to reach. Advertising must be carried on on a scale large enough to make an effective impression upon its market. Consequently the size of the advertising fund is an important consideration in an appraisal of advertising's opportunity. The matter of an advertising fund for any period depends upon the number of units of the product which can be sold in the period and upon the margin available for advertising. The size of the margin depends very largely upon the effectiveness of advertising in influencing consumer valuations for a product. This influence of advertising in turn is dependent upon the extent and significance of product differentiation and upon the strength of appeals which may be employed to present the differentiated qualities. The amount of margin available for aggressive selling work depends also upon conditions of competition within an industry, i.e., whether competition is carried on in price or in non-price forms. Cigarettes and dentifrices are illustrative of products which are purchased by large numbers of consumers at relatively frequent intervals and on which the margins available for advertising have been substantial proportions of selling prices. As a result of the combination of the large number of units sold and the relatively wide promotional margins, many sellers in these fields have been able to make large advertising appropriations, in spite of the fact that the unit sale is small. In contrast, although sugar has had large sales volume, its price has provided very narrow margins which might be devoted to advertising. Again, the number of units of electric refrigerators sold is not large as compared with the above products, but the size of unit sale has been large enough to provide a relatively large margin per unit for advertising, and consequently large total advertising appropriations for individual companies. On the other hand, manufacturers of products of high price which have a thin demand, such as expensive clocks and pipe organs for the home, have been small advertisers because they have not sold enough units to support extensive advertising programs.

In addition to the above important conditions, other conditions which affect the use of advertising in individual cases might be cited. For example, the percentage of gross margin which a concern is able to secure for its product and the consequent margin available for promotion often appear to be affected by the importance of the item in the consumer's budget. If an article is of relatively low price and purchase is infrequent, consumers apparently do not weigh price differences so carefully as they do where usage is frequent or price is high, and the expenditure consequently assumes a more important place in the budget. When buyers behave in this way an advertiser may be able to continue to secure a substantial volume of sales at a good margin and consequently he can continue to advertise. To illustrate, certain companies which have advertised free-running salt have been able to secure as much as 10 cents a package, whereas brands not so well known have been priced at 5 cents to 8 cents. The two-cent to five-cent difference evidently has not appeared of sufficient importance to many housewives to lead them to choose the low price brands even though the various competitive products have been much alike in quality. So too in the case of certain medicines and cosmetics, the willingness of consumers to pay a relatively high price for well-advertised brands has evidently been brought about not merely through the effectiveness with which the advertisers have associated powerful buying motives with their brands, but also through the facts that the products are used in relatively small quantities and purchases are infrequent. Even though the differential in price may be appreciable, still the fact that this price difference is spread over a considerable period of time evidently bears on consumers' selection of the brands they prefer. In short, the sacrifice in price seems small as compared with the satisfactions attached to the desired brands. Again, manufacturers of certain brands of confections and soft drinks sold at 5 cents have continued to secure over long periods of time wide percentage gross margins, which support substantial advertising programs, because for such products the price appeal of competing products is not particularly effective with many consumers. Five cents gives these consumers a satisfying amount of a drink or a candy or a gum and they continue to buy a brand which they know and like even though other brands might give them a larger quantity for 5 cents or equal quantity for less money.

The Importance of Appraising the Combination of Conditions Affecting Advertising Opportunity

Other conditions which may bear upon the opportunity of individual concerns to make effective use of advertising in influencing the demand for their brands need not be enumerated, for the five conditions mentioned above are most universal and are of first importance. It should be stressed, however, that the opportunity to use advertising effectively generally depends not so much on the presence of one of these conditions as upon the combination of conditions which exists.

The possible combinations in which these conditions are present in greater or lesser degree are almost innumerable, and each demand situation as it relates to advertising use must be considered unique although there may be similarities in some respects with other demand situations. It is this wide variation in the demand conditions of individual concerns and the uncertainty regarding advertising's influence upon sales under the conditions met which entails much of the risk involved in advertising expenditure. On the other hand, the presence or absence of some one condition or of a favorable combination of conditions serves to explain the varying extent to which advertising has been used to influence the demand of individual concerns in different industries. A few instances taken from material presented in previous chapters will serve to show the wide range of combinations met and the varying opportunities for advertising usage in different industries.

In the case of green vegetables, of which lettuce is illustrative, favorable primary demand trends have been operating, but other conditions have been adverse to use of advertising by individual producers to influence demand. The total volume of sales of any single producer has been too small to favor consumer advertising in distant markets, even if promotional margins were wide instead of narrow. Furthermore, in these cases the characteristics of the product have not been favorable for the influencing of selective demand. The highly perishable character of the products has prevented producers from effectively guaranteeing a quality under a brand. Moreover, the consumer has been able to judge by inspection whether quality has been satisfactory. Hence the chance to individualize a product under a brand and to get better prices to support aggressive selling efforts has been absent. In keeping with these conditions, competition has turned largely on price so that margins available for aggressive selling have been narrow.

In the case of sugar the presence of many of the conditions favorable to advertising use have meant little in view of the tendency of competing brands to standardize. It has made small difference that a favorable primary demand has existed and that refiners have had large volume as a result of the fact that every family uses sugar and buys frequently. Product standardization has prevented an appreciable part of the sales income received from being used for advertising, because there has been no chance for getting increased margins from product differentiations to support advertising. Nor has there been promise that ideas implanted by advertising would make consumers pay more for one brand than another.

The presence of certain favorable conditions explains why advertising has been used in industries which have had adverse trends of demand. In all such cases a substantial volume of business has been available in spite of adverse trends. Differentiation has been present. Appeals for brand preference have been effective. Prices of many producers contained appreciable margins for promotional effort. Such was the case with smoking tobacco and several other products falling in this category whose demand has been analyzed.

A still different type of demand situation is found in the case of oranges, for which demand trends on the whole have been favorable but conditions governing selective demand have been apparently unfavorable, because the products have tended to be standardized and consumers have been able to judge quality to some extent at time of purchase. A study of these situations, which are in some respects similar to those met in the marketing of avocados and prunes, will indicate why advertising was used for these products and not for perishable vegetables. Of greatest importance is the fact that growers representing a large percentage of the industry were banded together in effective marketing cooperatives. They could carry on a unified marketing program which could not be done in agricultural industries less well-organized. Because of their unified front, these cooperatives have been able to tie in their advertising and promotion with favorable trends. In the case of oranges particularly, the primary appeals available have been strong enough to speed up the trends favoring citrus consumption. Moreover, these cooperatives were in a position, by careful grading, to offer consumers a uniform quality under a brand which could be relied upon. Brand has meant something to consumers because they are not fully able to judge quality at time of purchase. Accordingly, the marketing and promotional approach has had some favorable results on selective demand as well as on primary demand.

In passing it may be pointed out that the conditions which have brought favorable results in the case of the unified industry approach for the agricultural marketing cooperatives have not been present in many industry cooperative campaigns of manufacturers. Many of these latter programs have been undertaken only after an industry has been operating against adverse trends. The advertising, accordingly, has been devoted to primary appeals too weak to overcome the adverse underlying conditions governing primary demand. Often, too, the cooperators have not been well organized nor have they had good financing for promotional work. Moreover, they have generally not been set up to carry on with a single unified marketing program as in the cases of the agricultural cooperatives. Instead, every producer carried out a separate selling program. Accordingly there has not been effective coordination of selling efforts to gain good selling results.

Conditions Most Favorable to Advertising Usage

Large expenditures for advertising and strong reliance upon advertising in the marketing of products occur when most of the conditions favorable to the stimulation of demand by individual concerns are present or when the factor of significant differentiation can be combined with strong appeals to affect valuations. Because these extremely favorable combinations were found in the cigarette and dentifrice industries the conditions present are summarized. Manufacturers in these fields have operated with favoring demand trends. The number of users has been large and the frequency of purchase has been high, particularly that of cigarettes. The amount which might be devoted to advertising has been substantial because the margins for promotion have been a considerable part of the selling price. Yet in absolute amount they have not been large enough to be a material hindrance to consumer buying. These promotional margins have been possible because the advertised brands of manufacturers have been deemed by consumers to be highly individualized, and strong appeals regarding the effectivenesses of brands have been applicable to heighten the importance of individualizing features. Accordingly, consumers have been willing to pay more per package for advertised brands than for unadvertised brands. Because of the strength of advertising in influencing valuations, competition has turned largely upon advertising, although the opportunity for consumers to buy lower-price products has been present.

Numerous other products have experienced selective demand conditions that have been similar in many respects to those enumerated, although the variations in conditions are countless. Included are such products as cosmetics, toilet articles, grocery specialties, and proprietary remedies. They are the most "advertisable" products. In the case of proprietaries, the number of units sold is often small and the total business income is not very large, but the margin for advertising is very wide. Hence advertising funds of producers are substantial. Here individualization is extreme. Each brand is practically in a class by itself. Advertising provides the chief basis not only for inducing purchase, but also for giving ideas that provide satisfaction in use. Grocery specialties, in contrast to these proprietaries, are likely to have small advertising expenditure per unit sold, but the frequency of purchase and the number of buyers serve to build the promotional fund.

Further Examples of Combinations of Conditions Affecting Advertising Opportunity

A different set of conditions has tended to make advertising important as a tool for influencing the demand of many major mechanical appliances such as automobiles, washing machines, radios, oil burners, mechanical refrigerators and so on. In the early stages of marketing, demand has not been large. Purchases have been few, but sizable promotional funds have been expended because sellers have found it necessary to provide wide margins in price to furnish the selling persuasion necessary to induce purchase of a new and unusual product of high unit value. These products for considerable periods have generally had favoring trends; the primary appeals used for them have been potent in speeding up acceptance. As volume has grown, increasing size of manufacturing plant and technological development has brought large decreases in price which have combined with advertising and aggressive personal selling greatly to stimulate demand. The consumers' attitudes toward such products have favored the use of advertising to stimulate selective demand. The prices of these articles have represented relatively large outlays. As with most mechanical contrivances, the consumer is unable to judge their qualities. He has needed guidance in purchase and has wanted assurance of dependability. The products have not been standard but individualized. Hence selective appeals carried in advertising have done a considerable part of the selling task for manufacturers. For most of these products advertising has been an important selling tool for most manufacturers and advertising expenditures have been large.

A different pattern of advertising usage is to be found for merchandise of various kinds, such as garments, furniture, shoes, and neckties, which are subject in greater or less degree to fashion dictates. Style is a highly important element in guiding consumer choice here.

But style is something that can be judged at time of purchase. Although there may be fixed characteristics of consequence to the consumer in such products, for which brand may be a symbol, the importance of variable style tends to reduce the importance of brand as a guide for consumer purchasing. Producers' brands for these products do not dominate. Retailers come to the fore as the selectors of merchandise from manufacturers, and consumers look largely to them as the source of such merchandise. Moreover, retailers generally play the leading role in advertising and promotion.

Summary Generalization Regarding Advertising's Effect on Selective Demand

The statements in the pages above regarding the combinations of conditions which govern the opportunity of individual concerns to employ advertising to stimulate their demands provide in themselves helpful generalizations as to the effect of advertising upon selective demand. These statements can be summarized in a broad generalization as follows: Advertising can and does increase the demand for the products of many individual companies, but the extent to which it does so varies widely and depends upon the circumstances under which the enterprises operate. The extent to which individual concerns in certain industries have been able with the help of advertising to build brand leadership and thus establish a concentration of selective demand has been noted in the various industry studies, but the question of the part which advertising may play as compared with other forces in bringing a concentration of demand and, in turn, a concentration in supply is examined in later chapters.

Generalizations Regarding the Effect of Advertising on Primary Demand

Attention is turned now to generalizations regarding advertising's effect upon industry or primary demand, which comes largely from the aggregate advertising effort of individual concerns. From the many cases analyzed and from the industry studies one clear and important generalization can be made, namely, that basic trends of demand for products, which are determined by underlying social and environmental conditions, are more significant in determining the expansion or contraction of primary demand than is the use or lack of use of advertising. This generalization explains why changes in primary demand of industries have occurred without relation to the amount of advertising used; why the demand for lettuce, sugar, green vegetables, and many professional services grew though little advertising was used, while that for cigars and smoking tobacco, men's shoes, wheat flour, and furniture[1] fell away in spite of considerable expenditures for advertising and promotion. Advertising has been effective in expanding demand when underlying conditions favored expansion In other instances expansion has gone ahead irrespective of whether advertising has been used. Conversely, strong advertising has not overcome contraction of demand when underlying conditions have operated to bring contraction.

When advertising has been used, its chief effect on primary demand has been either to speed up the expansion of a demand that naturally would have come without advertising, or to check or retard an adverse trend. Consumers' wants for products have been determined by the character of consumers and by their existing environment. Advertising has not changed people's basic characteristics, nor has it appreciably changed environment. It has merely played upon consumers' buying motives to intensify desire or to build favorable attitudes toward product consumption. In helping to usher in inventions and in speeding up demand for some products and slowing down contracting demand for others, advertising has had an effect in altering consumers' living habits and attitudes and thus has had an effect upon environment. But it is believed that it would be an error to magnify its direct influence in guiding and shaping living habits and thus in modifying environment.

In connection with this summary of the effect of advertising upon primary and selective demand, an observation may be made regarding appeals used to stimulate demand. In their use of advertising businessmen use primary or selective appeals in accordance with their appraisal of whether the one or the other type will be effective in helping them to gain desired patronage. For many products advertisers use primary appeals to large extent even though their objective is to affect selective demand, as in the cosmetic, drug and cigarette industries. The appeals here are often to health, romance and other primary motives. They can thus use primary appeals because their products are so individualized that consumers accept their brands as the ones offering solution to the primary need featured. Again, in the early

---

[1] Furniture advertising and promotion has been carried on chiefly by retailers.

stages of development of products entirely new to consumers, primary appeals are largely relied upon because the chief task then is the stimulation of acceptance for the type of product. As acceptance increases, however, selective appeals come into greater use. But whether appeals used are primary or selective, advertising probably has some effect upon the distribution of demand among industries. Even with selective appeals the publicity given to specific goods and the urging of consumers to buy them have helped to influence the volume of sales for those types of products in their competition with other types of products. In so far as primary appeals have been employed, they have tended to build attitudes favoring increased consumption for the industry.

The extent to which advertising programs made up in large part of selective appeals may have an influence on primary demand is evidently in accord with the generalization expressed above, namely, that advertising is likely to be effective according to whether underlying social conditions and environment favor demand expansion or not. That increased programs of advertising, largely selective, may not simply take business from competitors, but expand industry sales has been shown not only in the industries cited, but also in the case of vegetable shortening. When the vegetable shortening, Spry, was introduced by Lever Brothers with the support of heavy selective advertising, total consumption of vegetable shortening was increased without adversely affecting the sales of competing brands already on the market. In contrast, new brands of soap introduced with heavy advertising programs from time to time in recent years have had little effect upon soap consumption.[2]

---

[2] During the course of the study investigators secured from executives of several companies an interesting generalization regarding the effect of the total volume of advertising upon the total demand for special types of grocery and drug products relatively new to the market, sometimes referred to as "specialties" by the trade. These new types of products may be contrasted with articles long on the market, having firmly established, stable demands. This generalization, reportedly based on data compiled by the A. C. Nielsen Company of Chicago, was to the effect that when the total advertising and promotional efforts for any such new type of product fall or increase relative to advertising activity generally in allied fields, i.e., food or drugs, the total demand for that type of product tends to fall or increase relatively. In other words, the total demand for such products was said to be especially sensitive to the withdrawal or addition of advertising and promotional effort. It was stated that this sensitiveness applies to new types of products but not to products for which demand has become stable. Since the Nielsen figures are confidential, it was not possible personally to examine the records, although correspondence with an executive of that organization confirmed the generalization. The behavior is in keeping with what might be expected from our study of the effects of advertising upon primary and selective demand. The new types of merchandise referred to generally are operating under conditions favorable to expansion of demand. Accordingly, increase or decrease in programs of competitive advertising might well have an effect on industry demand.

The Effect of Advertising upon the Elasticity of Primary Demand

Now that the effect of advertising in shifting demand curves has been dealt with, the bearing of the evidence regarding advertising's effect upon elasticity of demand is summarized. The evidence on this point is not comprehensive and complete and conclusions must be drawn largely by inference from comparisons and contrasts of the demand behavior of different products studied. First is the question of advertising's effect upon the elasticity of primary demand for various classes of products.

It appears likely that for products whose demand is inherently inelastic, i.e., whose consumption by individuals is limited by the character of the products, advertising does not materially affect the elasticity of demand. For example, although salt has been advertised to consumers, it seems unlikely that advertising has materially shifted or changed the shape of the demand curve for salt. Its demand is and has been inelastic. Again, although advertising has helped in greatly expanding the demand for cigarettes, i.e., in shifting the demand curve, advertising does not appear to have greatly changed the shape of the curve. The sales for cigarettes fell somewhat in the 1930 depression, when leading companies generally held cigarette prices firm, an action which was equivalent to a normal price rise. But the decrease was relatively slight as compared with the decrease for many other products. This behavior of cigarette demand is in keeping with what would be expected from the fact that cigarette use is habitual with most buyers and their purchases are not appreciably affected by price change. In short, while advertising has helped induce some persons to acquire the use habit and thus has influenced total cigarette demand, advertising has not affected the shape of the demand curve, that is, the responsiveness of demand to price change.

In contrast to the above examples, for certain products advertising not only has had the effect of increasing their demand, i.e., of shifting the demand curves, but has apparently altered the shape of the curves. For example, many new products give evidence, in their early stages of marketing, of having small and relatively inelastic demand. Consumers are usually skeptical of a new product. They are not responsive to a price appeal at such times because of this skepticism and lack of an aroused desire for the product. Moreover, limited use of a product prevents the important selling forces of emulation and imitation from coming into play. As advertising and aggressive selling are employed, however, to build public acceptance for a new product and widening use brings the force of emulation into play, the shape of the product's demand curve evidently is altered. Large numbers of people come to desire the product. In short, in such cases the advertising and promotion have the effect of making demand more elastic. When public acceptance is once established, lowering of price generally serves to bring a large number of buyers into the market. Mechanical refrigerators are an example of a product whose elasticity of demand was increased by advertising and aggressive selling. Demand was built up slowly at first by aggressive selling. After the introductory period, as prices dropped, large numbers of buyers were brought into the market. Other new mechanical products which have been heavily promoted are also believed to have had their demand curves thereby rendered more elastic, products such as automobiles, radios, oil burners, and a long list of electrical appliances. Likewise, in other fields, it is believed that advertising has had the effect of increasing the elasticity of primary demand. For example, in the food field advertising and promotion have probably increased the elasticity of demand for such products as prepared breakfast foods, prepared desserts, and numerous other food innovations which have enjoyed substantial expansions of demand following their introduction to the market.

While conceivably there are products whose total demand becomes less responsive to price rise as the result of the building of strong consumers' preference for the products through advertising, no examples of this kind were found during this study, and they are believed to be few, if any. Dentifrice is a product which from *a priori* reasoning was expected to behave in this way. It was thought that the strong health and beauty appeals employed for dentifrices would have built such a strong desire for the product that an increase in price would not materially affect consumption. This reasoning was not borne out in the 1930 depression, however. When the price structure for dentifrices generally was held quite rigid in the depression, an action equivalent to a price rise in that period of declining prices, per capita sales for dentifrices fell some 25%. The contraction of dentifrice demand on this equivalent of a price rise suggests that demand for the product might be stimulated in turn by a general reduction of price. That this would actually happen is not supported by evidence. Strangely enough, price appeal has not been highly effective to individual companies in attracting selective demand.

The Effect of Advertising upon the Elasticity of Demands of Individual Concerns

The summary of the evidence relating to demand is turned now to the question of the effect of advertising upon the elasticity of demand for the products of individual concerns. Does it make the demand for brands more or less responsive to price change?

Some of the evidence given in the industry studies indicates that the advertising of brands tends, in some instances at least, to make their demands relatively inelastic for varying lengths of time. Evidence to support this conclusion is found, for example, in the relatively rigid prices which have held for advertised brands in the dentifrice and cigarette fields. That brand advertising might have this effect is not surprising, for brand advertisers seek to build strong brand preferences. Accordingly, if brand loyalty is established among consumers, some of them may be expected to stick by a brand even though its price relationships with competing brands are disturbed. Many advertisers have apparently accepted this view in their operations.

Final generalizations regarding the effect of advertising upon the elasticity of demands for individual concerns will not be presented, however, until the further data regarding the effects of advertising upon prices are presented and analyzed in later chapters. These price data relating to a wide variety of products provide needed evidence upon which to base conclusions regarding elasticity.

PART III

The Effect of Advertising on the Costs of Products and Services

CHAPTER XVII

THE EFFECT OF ADVERTISING ON THE COSTS OF MARKETING MERCHANDISE

THE effect of advertising upon the costs of merchandise, as viewed in value theory, and the issues indicated by theory as the subjects for factual investigation were presented at length in Chapter VI and need not be repeated here.[1] In this and the following chapter the effect of advertising upon the costs of marketing merchandise will be discussed, and these will be followed by a chapter in which its effects upon production costs will be traced so far as is possible.

THE SIZE OF ADVERTISING COSTS

Much evidence has already been presented regarding the absolute and relative size of advertising expenditures for different products and for different types of business. In this section certain of this evidence will be recalled, and such new data presented as will serve to bring out the characteristics of advertising costs.

Variation in Advertising Costs of Manufacturers

In preceding chapters one of the most striking things about the advertising costs of manufacturers has been reiterated, namely, the wide variation to be found in these costs, not only between industries, but also between individual companies within an industry. These facts are clearly illustrated in Table 104, which shows the advertising expenditures of various classes of manufacturers of consumer goods as reported in a study of the Association of National Advertisers. The average percentage of expenditure for these classifications varied from 34% for proprietary medicines down to less than 2% for textiles and for automobile trucks. Such average percentages are not highly significant because of the wide range of expenditures within product classifications, but even so they serve to reflect roughly the relative

---

[1] Chapter VI, pp. 169–174 inclusive.

TABLE 104

TOTAL ADVERTISING EXPENDITURES IN RELATION TO NET SALES VOLUME
FOR VARIOUS MANUFACTURING GROUPS—CONSUMER PRODUCTS, 1935

PRODUCT GROUP	NUMBER OF COMPANIES REPORTING	AVERAGE PERCENTAGE*	RANGE IN PERCENTAGES
Proprietary Medicines	7	33.78%	31.00—61.00%
Drugs and Toilet Articles	14	27.65	8.00—60.00
Soft and Carbonated Beverages	3	15.23	Within 0.3% of average
Silverware, Clocks, etc.	5	9.31	7.00—10.00
Paints, Varnishes, and Removers	7	7.40	3.25—22.00
Drug Sundries	4	6.00	4.20—10.00
Auto Accessories	4	5.90	†
Heating, Air Conditioning, Refrigerating Equipment	8	5.73	3.00— 8.00
Petroleum Products	5	5.68	Oil: 5.00—20.00
			Gas: Under 2.00
Sporting Goods	5	5.67	3.00—10.00
Confections, Ice Cream	4	5.35	2.50—16.00
Food and Grocery Products	26	5.07	0.25—47.00
Service Organizations	2	5.00	1.00— 5.00‡
Beer	3	4.67	Small deviation
Clothing and Accessories	8	4.50	1.50— 5.50
House Furnishings	8	4.50	2.00—10.00
Household Electrical Equipment	6	4.47	0.84— 8.10
Knit Goods, Hosiery	7	4.20	2.50— 9.64
Travel and Transportation	9	4.05	0.22—10.00
Footwear	9	3.97	2.00— 6.50
Agricultural Equipment	6	3.78	1.00—20.00
Hardware	3	2.67	0.50— 5.00
Office Equipment	6	2.60	Small deviation
Textiles	5	1.82	0.30— 5.00
Auto Trucks	3	1.27	0.0015–2.82

* Interquartile average.
† Not given.
‡ Range for 1934, for which average was 3.17%.

Source: Association of National Advertisers, Inc., *A Survey of 299 National Advertising Budgets, 1934–1935*, pp. 15 and 29 ff.

degree to which advertising has been an effective tool for stimulating demand for various product classes.

Within the product group the variation in percentage of sales devoted to advertising by manufacturers is often wider than that found between the common figures of groups. For example, the range in the proprietary medicine group is shown in the table to be from 31% to 61%; among food and grocery product manufacturers, from 0.25% to 47%; for agricultural equipment, from 1% to 20%; and so on. These wide variations were found in a study in which only advertising concerns reported. Similar variations between individual grocery manufacturers in several product groups are shown in greater detail in a study made by the Harvard Bureau of Business Research in 1927–1928, which is summarized in Table 105. On cer-

TABLE 105

ADVERTISING AND SALES PROMOTIONAL EXPENSE PERCENTAGES REPORTED BY CERTAIN GROCERY MANUFACTURERS IN 1928 CLASSIFIED BY PRODUCT GROUPS—PERCENTAGE OF NET SALES DEVOTED TO ADVERTISING AND SALES PROMOTION

32 Manufacturers of Coffee, Tea, Extracts, and Spices		17 Manufacturers of Canned and Bottled Foods	9 Manufacturers of Soaps and Cleansers	8 Packers of Meat	8 Manufacturers of Pickles and Preserves	7 Manufacturers of Flour	6 Manufacturers of Macaroni	4 Manufacturers of Cereals
0.00%	1.84%	0.00%	1.04%	0.02%	0.18%	0.07%	0.00%	9.01%
0.07	2.73	0.00	7.74	0.15	0.21	0.13	0.41	12.37
0.26	2.74	0.03	9.38	0.15	0.46	0.36	1.57	14.31
0.30	2.94	0.11	14.32	0.18	0.97	0.53	1.99	15.96
0.53	4.14	0.20	19.12	0.30	1.06	0.83	5.04	....
0.70	4.57	0.49	20.01	0.43	1.85	1.41	10.39	....
0.86	4.59	0.51	25.61	0.44	2.76	2.55	....	....
0.95	7.08	0.54	30.07	0.47	4.47	....	....	....
1.02	7.17	0.64	36.85	....	....			
1.15	7.84	1.43						
1.15	8.59	1.55						
1.21	10.97	1.69						
1.47	13.09	3.83						
1.54	13.34	4.07						
1.56	17.05	4.14						
1.75	21.60	4.15						
....	....	7.59						

Source: Harvard Business School, Bureau of Business Research, Bulletin No. 79, *Marketing Expenses of Grocery Manufacturers for 1927 and 1928*, p. 7 ff.

tain product groups typically much more was spent than on others. For example, soap and cleanser manufacturers typically had higher ratio of advertising cost than meat packers or flour manufacturers. Within most product groups wide variations were found. Among 32 manufacturers of coffee, tea, extracts, and spices, there was a range in advertising cost from 0.0% to 21.6% of sales; among 9 manufacturers of soaps and cleansers, a range from 1% to 37%; among 6 manufacturers of macaroni, a range from 0.0% to 10%. Only among the meat packers and flour manufacturers was there a narrow range of expenditure.[2]

To the above data may be added fresh evidence regarding the varying advertising costs and marketing costs of individual manufacturers which were obtained during the course of this advertising study.[3] The advertising and promotional costs of 32 manufacturers of consumers' goods as a percentage of 1937 sales are shown in Table 106, Column 7. They vary from 1.4% of sales value for building specialty manufac-

[2] Further tables reflecting advertising costs of manufacturers are found in Tables 7, 8, and 9, pages 65 and 67, Chapter III.

[3] A description of this cost research will be found on page 503 ff.

turer No. 10, to 55.4% of sales value for proprietary remedy manufacturer No. 31.

Reasons for Variations in Advertising Costs

The reasons for such variations in the advertising costs of manufacturers have been discussed and need little elaboration. They merely
reflect differing product and selling policies adopted by manufacturers
in their quest for profitable operating formulae under differing sets of
conditions. In order to crystallize the sort of variations in operation
that are found, some of those brought out in the chapters on demand
are summarized here. In the case of cigarettes, leading companies have
carried out competition largely on the advertising front, spending therefor from 15% to 20% of net sales, less taxes, that is, an amount in
the neighborhood of $0.006 to $0.009 per package. In contrast, the
10-cent brands, which sought patronage through lower price, have
spent less than one-fifth as much per package. In the case of sugar,
no manufacturer has spent over a fraction of 1% of sales for advertising; the average for certain leading cane sugar refiners being only
0.25% in 1939, and for leading beet refiners only 0.1%. Numerous
refiners spent even less. In contrast to sugar manufacturers, leading
dentifrice manufacturers carried on competition largely through advertising, with prices of their differentiated merchandise set so as to give
an adequate margin for advertising costs running as high as 40% of
sales. On the other hand, certain dentifrice manufacturers selling
private brands showed little or no advertising expense. Again, in the
case of sheeting, different managements employed different selling
formulae with varying advertising costs; there was no common pattern.
Certain leading mills spent from 1% to 3% of net sales on advertising,
but other mills selling under their own brands spent less, while a large
volume of sheeting went to private branders with practically no promotional or advertising expenditure made by manufacturers. Once
again, among shoe manufacturers a wide variety of selling practices
were followed, with similarly wide variation in advertising costs. Such
costs ranged from practically nothing by those selling under private
brands to as much as 7% by others who were aggressively promoting
their own brands. Finally, most refrigerator manufacturers followed
the policy of aggressive advertising to consumers, with advertising costs
reported in the neighborhood of 5% to 7% of sales; but even in this
field certain manufacturers in recent years have produced machines to

% OF SALES)		(11) PRODUCTION COSTS AS % OF SALES a	(12) ESTIMATED MFRS'. ADVERTISING EXPENDITURE PER AVER. UNIT	RATIO OF		ESTIMATED TRADE MARKUP ‖	
(9) Other Marketing	(10) Total Marketing			(13) Total Advertising to Salesforce	(14) Total Advertising to Total Marketing	(15) Wholesale	(16) Retail
2.6	7.7	74.2	....	1.96	.66	direct	40–50%
8.1	9.9	53.9	.0025	.22	.18	10–15%	30
5.0	10.3	78.0	4.45	1.06	.51	15–20	35–40
†	†	†	.54	†	†	15–20	35–40
4.6	10.2	88.6	.012	.40	.16	direct	35–40
†	†	59.2	.36	†	†	own retail chain	35–40
0.5	10.8	61.1	5.80	2.03	.64	15–20	35–40
0.9	11.5	64.2	.01	4.04	.74	10–15	30
3.9	12.1	82.8	.012	.36	.18	direct	35–40
‡	12.5	62.2	8.44	1.66	.62	20	35–40
9.4	13.4	†	....	.54	.10	†	†
4.8	19.2	78.9	.24	2.43	.53	15–20	35–40
10.2	20.1	75.8	....	.41	.14	direct	30–40
4.2	21.3	50.9	.008	2.35	.56	10–12	20
20.0	23.2	51.1	....	.16	.14	direct	25
9.0	23.8	57.1	.10	1.18	.34	direct	40–50
13.7	24.4	35.6	.04	.78	.44	30–35	30–40
19.1	26.0	58.4	.004	.36	.27	10–12	20
16.7	28.3	72.0	.05	.47	.13	20	30–40
1.9	28.3	26.6	.005	1.67	.58	20	25
25.5	29.3	†	.003	8.50	.12	direct	25
17.3	31.2	62.9	....	.22	.08	20–25	30–35
22.0	33.8	59.1	....	1.51	.21	25	35–40
‡	36.1	49.4	.08	3.75	.79	15–20	30–35
11.1	37.0	50.4	.48	1.59	.43	25	30–40
7.6	38.9	30.4	.033	3.28	.61	10–12	20
15.7	41.9	60.2	.35	1.05	.32	direct	40
3.9	44.4	16.6	.16	4.87	.76	10–15	30
4.9	46.0	36.1	.03	2.00	.60	15–20	30–35
6.7	50.2	22.6	.07	....	.87	10–15	30
§	55.4	12.8	.165	....	....	10–15	30
11.3	56.3	37.7	.09	4.69	.66	15–20	30–35

AL PRODUCTS

†	†	†	....	†	†	†	†
†	†	†	....	.29	†	†	†
1.1	9.5	83.6	....	.27	.19	†	†
†	†	†	....	†	†	†	†

wholesalers and direct to retailers.

¶ Size of Company (Millions of Dollars of Sales)
A—Under 1   D—10 to 20
B—1 to 3   E—20 to 50
C—3 to 10   F—Over 50

ADVERTISING AND MARKETING COSTS, AS A PERCENTAGE OF NET SALES, OF SELECTE

(1) MANU- FACTUR- ERS' No.	(2) PRODUCT MANUFACTURED	(3) APPROXI- MATE RETAIL PRICE PER UNIT	(4) SIZE OF COM- PANY¶	MANUFACTURERS' MARKETING COSTS			
				Advertising & Sales Promotion			(8) Sales- force
				(5) Space	(6) Other	(7) Total	
1	Watches	$20 and up	C	2.1	3.0	5.1	*
2	Hardware Specialty ...	$ .25	C	†	†	1.8	*
3	Electrical Appliance ..	$125 and up	C	3.3	2.0	5.3	*
4	Household Appliance .	$40–$75	B	1.4	1.3	2.7	†
5	Hosiery (Silk)	$ .60–$1.50	B	0.7	0.9	1.6	4.0
6	Men's Shoes	$6	C	4.1	2.1	6.2	†
7	Electrical Appliance ..	$125 and up	E	4.3	2.6	6.9	3.4
8	Drug Sundry	$ .20	D	†	†	8.5	2.1
9	Hosiery (Silk)	$ .60–$1.50	C	0.2	1.9	2.2	6.1
10	Electrical Appliance ..	$125 and up	E	5.1	2.7	7.8	4.7
11	Building Specialty ...	†	C	0.7	0.7	1.4	2.6
12	Household Appliance .	$5–$25	B	3.3	6.9	10.2	4.2
13	Tires	$8 and up	D	†	†	2.9	7.0
14	Grocery Specialty	$ .10	D	†	†	12.0	5.1
15	Oil & Gasoline	$ .15–$ .30	F	1.9	1.3	3.2	*
16	Jewelry Product	$1–$150	A	4.3	3.7	8.0	6.8
17	Auto Accessories	$ .75	†	†	†	10.7	*
18	Grocery Specialty	$ .10	B	4.1	2.8	6.9	*
19	Rubber Shoes	$1–$5	C	2.4	1.3	3.7	7.8
20	Confection	$ .05	C	8.6	7.9	16.5	9.9
21	Gasoline	$ .15	E	3.1	0.3	3.4	0.4
22	Paper Products	$ .05–$1	D	1.3	1.2	2.5	11.4
23	Radio Receivers	$20 and up	C	†	†	7.1	4.7
24	Cosmetic	$ .10–$1	B	25.6	2.9	28.5	7.6
25	Fountain Pens	$3 and up	C	13.1	2.8	15.9	10.0
26	Grocery Specialty	$ .20	B	23.2	0.7	23.9	7.3
27	Clothing Item	$2–$10	B	9.3	4.2	13.5	12.8
28	Proprietary Remedy ..	$ .50–$1	C	31.8	1.8	33.6	6.9
29	Cosmetics	$–.10–$1	C	18.8	8.6	27.4	13.7
30	Toilet Articles	$ .10–$ .50	C	25.3	18.2	43.5	0.0
31	Proprietary Remedy ..	$ .25–$1.25	A	†	†	55.4	0.0
32	Cosmetics	$ .10–$ .50	B	35.4	1.7	37.1	7.9
							INDUS
33	Machinery	$1000 and up	F	†	†	2.0	†
34	Electrical Products ...	†	D	1.3	0.7	2.0	7.0
35	Machinery	$1000 and up	D	0.5	1.3	1.8	6.7
36	Leather	†	B	1.5	0.5	2.0	†

* Included with "Other Marketing."
† Not available.
‡ Included with "Salesforce."

§ Included with "Advertising & Sales Promotion Total."
‖ Most of the companies selling convenience products sold both t
ª Does not include general administration costs or income taxes.

be sold under the trade-marks of retailers, and on these sales have incurred no advertising expense. Accordingly, wide variations in advertising costs were to be found.

The presence of certain combinations of conditions within specific industries tends to explain the variation of common figures of advertising expense among industries. Each industry must be studied separately to see what combination of conditions may explain relatively high or relatively low costs of advertising common to the industry. For example, in relatively new industries in which various producers are attempting to build demand and in which the tendency towards similarity of competing products has not progressed far, advertising costs often are relatively high. Such is the case, for example, in the various electrical household appliance fields and in grocery specialty fields. In contrast, in many established industries in which competing products have tended to become relatively standardized and demand has become fully established, costs tend to be relatively low. Such is the case, for example, with the sugar industry, canned fruits and vegetables, gasoline, and a host of other commodities. In certain industries, relatively high advertising costs have continued over long periods because the sales effectiveness of advertising, as contrasted with the effectiveness of price in stimulating demand, has led to continuation of competition in advertising and other non-price forms rather than to competition in price. Such has been true of dentifrice and numerous other toilet goods, cosmetics, proprietary remedies, and cigarettes. And so on, other industries might be cited to indicate that various combinations of conditions explain the relative reliance of those industries upon advertising as a sales tool.

It is to be expected that wide variations in the burden placed upon advertising by manufacturers under differing methods and conditions of marketing will produce corresponding differences in the use of salesforce, in margins applicable to marketing and profit, and in numerous other respects. This fact is brought out clearly in Table 106, page 444. The consumer goods companies included in this table are arranged in ascending order of marketing costs (Column 10), ranging from watch company No. 1, which used only 7.7% of sales income to market its product, to cosmetic manufacturer No. 32, who spent 56.3%. A listing in ascending order of marketing costs, however, does not give an ascending arrangement for advertising and promotional costs (Column 7). The wide differences in expenditure on salesforce, for example, are shown in Column 8, ranging from no expenditure for certain companies which rely wholly on advertising to bring about sales, to over 10% by several companies. Again, the wide differences in margins between manufacturing costs and selling costs with which to cover marketing costs, general administration, and net profit, are reflected in Column 11, which shows the percentage of sales which is accounted for by production costs. These costs ranged all the way from about 13% for proprietary remedy manufacturer No. 31, to almost 89% for hosiery manufacturer No. 5.

The Advertising Costs for Industrial Goods

The variations in the advertising costs among classes of industrial products and among companies within industrial product fields are similar to but smaller than those found in the consumer goods field. Such variations are shown in Tables 107 and 108. According to the Association of National Advertisers' study, Table 107, the average percentage of sales devoted to advertising varied from 4% for paper and paper products to 0.5% for chemicals. Employing a different classification, the National Industrial Advertisers' Association studies (Table 108) show a variation from less than 1% for primary materials to over 3% for accessory equipment and operating supplies. As in all cost and budget studies relating to manufacturers, the figures can be taken only as indicative, because in both studies the samples in certain classifications were very small. The Association of National Advertisers' study shows variation in use of advertising among individual companies in certain product groups to be fairly wide. For example,

TABLE 107

TOTAL ADVERTISING EXPENDITURES IN RELATION TO NET SALES VOLUMES FOR VARIOUS INDUSTRIAL GOODS MANUFACTURERS, 1935

PRODUCT GROUP	NUMBER OF COMPANIES REPORTING	AVERAGE PERCENTAGE*	RANGE IN PERCENTAGES
Paper and Paper Products............	6	4.00	0.25–6.00
Automotive Equipment	7	3.90	0.88–8.62
Building and Construction Materials...	9	2.44	1.50–5.00
Electrical Equipment	4	2.25	0.50–5.00
Machinery and Supplies	13	2.01	0.50–4.50
Steel and Other Metals	9	1.33	0.001–5.80
Miscellaneous	2	.75	0.11–1.00
Chemicals	2	.50	0.30–0.64

* Interquartile average.

Source: Association of National Advertisers, *A Survey of 299 National Advertising Budgets, 1934–1935, op. cit.,* pp. 89 and 100 ff.

TABLE 108

ADVERTISING EXPENDITURES IN RELATION TO GROSS SALES VOLUMES FOR
MANUFACTURERS OF VARIOUS CLASSES OF INDUSTRIAL GOODS, 1938–1939

CLASS OF PRODUCT	5-YEAR AVERAGE OF PERCENTAGES OF GROSS SALES SPENT ON ADVERTISING OF COMPANIES REPORTING IN THE	
	1939 Study	1938 Study
Major Equipment	2.4	2.45
Accessory Equipment ...:.............	3.14	3.36
Operating Supplies	2.28	4.04
Fabricating Parts	1.84	2.24
Fabricating Materials	1.37	1.58
Containers	2.22	1.01
Process Materials	2.86	.99
Primary Materials	.72	....
Building Materials	2.91	2.03
No Classification	1.86	1.73

Source: National Industrial Advertisers Association, Inc., *A National Survey of Industrial Advertising Budgets,* 1938 and 1939. (Chicago, The Association), pp. 3 and 7.

among paper and paper product manufacturers there was a range from 0.25% of sales to 6% of sales; for automotive equipment from 0.88% to 8.62%.

Comparison of the percentages of sales devoted to advertising by manufacturers of industrial products and manufacturers of consumers' products immediately brings to light two facts: (1) On the average, advertising does not account for so large a percentage of the manufacturer's selling price for various classes of industrial products as it does for consumer products. In the study of advertising budgets made by the Association of National Advertisers (Table 104), 19 out of 25 classifications of consumer products showed an average expenditure above 4%, with only 6 classes below that figure. Among the industrial goods manufacturers, however, Table 107, only one group had an average expenditure as high as 4%. Expense studies made in other years by the Association of National Advertisers and studies of the National Industrial Advertisers' Association give similar low percentages of advertising cost. (2) The highest advertising percentages found among individual companies in the industrial goods field are far below those found in the consumers' goods field, and consequently, the range of expenditure is lower than for consumer goods. The highest advertising expenditure indicated for any industrial goods covered by the Association of National Advertisers' study was 8.62% of sales for one company in the automotive equipment field. Among other product groups the highest percentage reported was 6%. Study of numerous cases gathered by the Harvard Business School did not disclose advertising cost ratios for industrial products as high as the 8% indicated in the study of the Association of National Advertisers.

In contrast to the above extremes for industrial goods manufacturers, it is not unusual to find individual companies in some consumer product classifications spending from 10% to 50% of sales, and occasionally even more, for advertising, as indicated in Table 104 and as corroborated by other budget studies and by case reports.

Reasons for Low Advertising Costs of Industrial Goods

Lack of resources did not permit an extensive study of the advertising for industrial goods as a part of this research study. Accordingly, full reasons for the low advertising costs cannot be presented with assurance. Differences in costs are attributable in large part to the well defined character of industrial markets and to the attitudes and buying habits of industrial buyers. Of prime importance is the fact that the industrial goods buyer is relatively a rational buyer. His purchases are for business reasons. His aim ordinarily is to buy in such a way as to make a profit. Consequently his valuations have not been subject to influence to such a degree as consumer valuations, particularly those determined by nonrational motives.

Further, the well-defined character of the market ordinarily makes possible the direction of advertising messages to known buyers with a minimum of waste circulation; whereas in consumer advertising the less clearly defined markets and the absence of specialized media frequently result in use of media reaching many consumers who are not good sales prospects.

Again, the portion of the selling burden placed upon advertising by a large proportion of industrial goods manufacturers is governed in large part by the fact that the bulk of their sales are made directly to users in well-defined market groups without the interposition of intermediary distributors.

The extent to which sale is direct to users is indicated in Table 109, which shows the methods of sale reported by 308 industrial goods manufacturers to the National Industrial Advertisers Association. For this entire group selling all types of industrial products, 41% sold solely on a direct basis to users, while 36% sold directly in part and in part through distributors.

TABLE 109

METHOD OF DISTRIBUTION EMPLOYED BY INDUSTRIAL GOODS MANUFACTURERS IN
VARIOUS CLASSIFICATIONS—308 REPORTING COMPANIES, 1939

TYPE OF PRODUCT	COMPANIES REPORTING	METHOD OF DISTRIBUTION (NUMBER REPORTING)		
		Direct Sale	Through Distributors	Both Methods
Major Equipment............	112	46	21	45
Accessory Equipment.........	73	27	21	25
Operating Supplies...........	15	6	3	6
Fabricating Parts.............	28	14	3	11
Fabricating Materials.........	21	13	3	5
Containers..................	8	5	2	1
Process Materials............	16	8	2	6
Primary Materials........ ...	3	....	1	2
Building Materials...........	15	2	9	4
Unclassified.................	17	5	5	7
	308	126	70	112
Percentage of Total..........	100	41	23	36

Source: National Industrial Advertisers Association, Inc., *A National Survey of Industrial Advertising Budgets for 1939*, p. 6.

Industrial marketing case material which describes channels of distribution indicates that manufacturers in certain product categories in Table 109, particularly those selling major equipment, accessory equipment, and fabricating parts and materials, probably reported functional middlemen, such as manufacturers' agents, as distributors. In fact such sellers are not true distributors in the sense that they buy and sell merchandise for their own account. Rather, they sell for the manufacturer's account and merely serve as a substitute for a salesforce under his direct supervision. Accordingly an even larger percentage of the companies than indicated in the table should be classed as direct sellers.

Where sale is direct to user, advertising is merely an auxiliary aid to a salesforce closely controlled by the producer. The selling burden is placed primarily upon the personal selling force. In contrast to consumers' goods the advertising of industrial goods is used not so much to pull a product through the channels of trade or to induce stocking and display of a product by dealers, as it is to pave the way for salesmen, to secure inquiries for follow-up by salesmen, and to provide information regarding product buying sources which may be placed in the industrial purchaser's files for use between salesmen's calls. For many types of industrial products the messages carried in space advertising in industrial and business magazines and direct-mail pieces can do little more than establish a general idea of the adequacy of a manufacturer's product to meet the industrial buyer's problems. This publicity must often be followed by skilled technical advice in order to bring about the consummation of a sale. Accordingly, personal selling looms large in relation to advertising selling.

Study of case material indicates further that where intermediary merchants are employed in distribution of industrial products, particularly for accessory equipment such as small motors, small tools, typewriters, calculating machines, and office furniture, the merchants often are made exclusive representatives for their territories. In such cases the exclusive or selected agents are urged to be aggressive sellers of the manufacturers' products; personal sales effort again looms large as contrasted with advertising effort.

For those types of industrial products, such as operating supplies, for which distributors play an important part in distribution, the advertising methods may be similar in many respects to those met in the distribution of consumers' goods. Where products of a manufacturer are differentiated in significant ways from competing products, advertising may be used to a considerable degree to help build a product reputation that will induce distributors to handle the product. In other instances, lack of significant product differentiation may lead a manufacturer to forego advertising of his product to users. Instead, selling effort is directed solely to the distributors as the real determiners of merchandise selection for their clientele.

The Size of Retailers' and Wholesalers' Advertising Costs

Attention is turned from the advertising costs of manufacturers to those of distributors. A description of the use of advertising by retailers and certain figures regarding the percentage of sales devoted to both retail and wholesale advertising are given in Chapters III and IV.[4] Apart from those instances in which wholesalers have undertaken consumer advertising of their own brands of merchandise, their advertising expenditures have been relatively small, in most trades less than 1% of their sales (Table 7, Chapter III, page 65). These expenditures have not involved imposition of a heavy charge in the ultimate price.

In the case of retailers the cost of advertising has varied by type of store and by type of merchandise sold. Hardware, drug, and

---

[4] Chapter III, pages 62 to 64, inclusive, Chapter IV, p. 113 ff.

grocery stores have had small advertising expenditures on the average, chains expending somewhat more than independents, probably because their multiple outlets have made advertising an effective expenditure. Limited-price variety chains, however, have been small advertisers, since they depend on consumer traffic and good values to bring consumers to their stores. On the other hand, department stores, women's specialty stores, shoe stores, and furniture stores have spent appreciable amounts upon advertising. This practice has come about in part because such stores attract patronage from over a wide territory. Equally important, however, is the fact that much of the merchandise handled by these stores is sold without substantial advertising or promotional costs on the part of manufacturers. These retailers sell a considerable amount of unbranded or private branded merchandise, for which they seek to establish their own reputation as a source; or, if they handle manufacturers' brands as selected outlets, they place a large share of the persuasive advertising of the manufacturers, as was indicated in the earlier study of shoes and of refrigerators. Thus a considerable part of the amounts they spent may be considered as the cost of not merely informational advertising relating to merchandise and source, but also persuasive, reputation-making advertising.

Retailers in any one field have not had uniform advertising costs, although the variation from a common figure is not nearly so great as in the case of manufacturers. Differences in location, in size of store, in size of city, and in merchandising policies have led retailers to vary the amounts of advertising employed. Thus among department stores reporting to the Harvard Bureau of Business Research in 1939 the range of percentages of advertising costs to net sales was from 0.28% to 7.24%, as shown in Table 110. Among limited price variety chains, which in some classifications of merchandise compete with department stores, the interquartile range of companies reporting to the Harvard Bureau of Business Research was from 0.19% to 0.60%.[5]

Summary Regarding Varying Rates of Advertising Expenditure

All the above evidence regarding the varying parts of sales income devoted to advertising by manufacturers and distributors is in accord

---

[5] Harvard Business School, Bureau of Business Research, Bulletin No. 112, *Expenses and Profits of Limited Price Variety Chains in 1939,* by Elizabeth A. Burnham, p. 15.

TABLE 110

TOTAL ADVERTISING EXPENSE OF DEPARTMENT STORES REPORTING TO THE HARVARD BUREAU OF BUSINESS RESEARCH, 1939 (PERCENTAGE OF NET SALES)

DEPARTMENT STORES WITH SALES OF	COMMON FIGURES	EXTREME RANGE OF REPORTING STORES	INTERQUARTILE RANGE OF REPORTING STORES
$150,000	1.90%	0.28%—4.26%	1.27%—2.48%
150,000—300,000	2.60	1.17 —5.81	2.02 —3.19
300,000—500,000	2.65	0.39 —6.78	2.05 —3.11
500,000—750,000	2.90	0.75 —7.24	2.36 —3.33
750,000—1,000,000	3.10	1.18 —4.99	2.49 —3.74
1,000,000—2,000,000	3.45	1.05 —6.93	2.82 —4.00
2,000,000—4,000,000	3.60	1.64 —6.91	2.90 —4.01
4,000,000—10,000,000	3.95	1.92 —6.75	3.28 —4.46
10,000,000—20,000,000	3.90	1.64 —6.31	3.17 —4.67
20,000,000 or more	3.40	2.38 —5.57	2.64 —3.90

Source: Based on figures submitted to the Harvard Bureau of Business Research.

with the generalizations indicated by *a priori* reasoning of theory concerning the variations to be expected when competition is imperfect, that is, when it does not conform to the economic concept of pure competition.[6] The advertising of individual producers varies widely, largely because many operating alternatives are chosen by them. Within most lines merchandise is not identical. While competition is based in part on price, patronage also is obtainable on the basis of numerous non-price competitive forms. Consequently, within any industry competition may be carried out on the basis of numerous combinations of product quality and functional services of one kind or another, to meet either a common market price or a series of prices set by competing sellers. The costs of different sellers accordingly will contain varying amounts for different functional elements, such as personal selling, advertising, delivery service, credit, product manufacture, and so on. While one seller may stress certain individualizing product qualities or certain functional services to attract patronage, another may stress different qualities or other services or price. So far as advertising is concerned, widely varying amounts are used by competing sellers; consequently, varying charges for information and persuasion are included in the prices asked. Among different types of products the extent to which consumers' patronage can be affected by advertising and aggressive selling varies widely; accordingly, the advertising expenditures which profitably can be made by sellers vary widely.

---

[6] See Chapter VI.

THE EFFECT OF VOLUME OF SALES UPON ADVERTISING AND MARKETING COSTS OF MANUFACTURERS

Now that the facts regarding the varying size of advertising expenditures have been presented, attention is directed to the effect of size of operations upon advertising and marketing costs. Advertising and aggressive selling ordinarily are undertaken to increase, or at least to maintain, sales volume. Advertising sometimes is credited with bringing lower marketing costs through its contribution to larger scale of operations. To what extent is such a generalization sound?

Just as *a priori* reasoning indicates that in the manufacture of any product there is an optimum size of operation which will bring greatest production efficiency, likewise it indicates that there may be an optimum size of operation from the standpoint of marketing costs. Actual evidence bearing on optimum size is meager, however, and the subject is one about which little is known. Studies made by the Harvard Bureau of Business Research have shown that in the department store field large size does not bring low expenses. Small department stores characteristically have lower total ratios of expense than do large stores.[7] Clearly, in any kind of business the simple assumption cannot be made that decreasing costs always apply and that increased size of operations by a concern will entail economies in marketing. For any given marketing expenditure, of course, the larger the number of units sold the smaller will be unit marketing costs, but this statement is a far different thing from saying that increasing size of operation will bring lower unit marketing costs. Under some conditions increased volume may be followed by lower unit marketing costs; under other conditions it may be accompanied by increased costs.

Effect of Increasing Volume under Uniform Expenditures

Attempts to measure the effects of size of operation upon marketing costs through study of the trends of marketing costs of individual companies are likely to contribute little, because variables other than size far outshadow size in determining marketing costs. Moreover, the effect of size as a factor in costs cannot be isolated. For example, changes made by a management in its promotion policies and in its

---

[7] Evidence bearing on this point may be found in the following publications: Harvard Business School, Bureau of Business Research, Bulletin No. 111, *Operating Results of Department and Specialty Stores in 1939*, by M. P. McNair, p. 16; Bulletin No. 113, *Operating Results of Department and Specialty Stores in 1940*, by M. P. McNair, p. 11.

profit policy, and fluctuations in prices of the elements entering into marketing costs, may be far more important in determining a company's marketing costs than is the change in volume which develops. A few examples will suffice to indicate the complexity of the problem.

Whenever a management concludes that an advertising expenditure of a particular size is adequate to make its product known in the market it wishes to reach, and keeps its appropriation more or less constant at that size, advertising costs per unit will, of course, vary in accordance with the fluctuation of sales volume. This type of situation is not infrequently met. It is illustrated very clearly by figures disclosed in the course of litigation which show the advertising costs incurred by Lever Brothers in marketing Rinso soap powder.[8]

In launching this product, Lever Brothers followed the bold policy, frequently adopted by large and experienced advertisers, of spending substantial sums to impress housewives with the virtues of its new product. The company quickly developed regional markets one after another, and then carried on nation-wide advertising. As shown in Table 111, the advertising for the eight-year period, 1921–1928, averaged $1,200,000 annually, and, excepting the year 1925, varied little from this figure.

As a result of its aggressive selling, sales increased rapidly, as shown in Column 2. Whereas in 1920 sales were only 8,853,000 pounds, in 1927 they were five times as large, 44,753,000 pounds.

Since advertising expenditures, as shown in Column 4, were held nearly constant from 1921 through 1928 (excepting 1925), the large increase in volume brought a marked decrease in advertising expenditure per unit. The high point in unit advertising cost occurred in 1921, when advertising cost per pound was $0.0918, or 56.6% of sales value. By 1928 it had dropped to $0.0238, or 19.7% of sales value.

Although complete data concerning production costs, other marketing costs, and general administrative costs are not available, it is evident that Lever Brothers followed a practice often adopted by those who develop a national market for such a specialty; that is, it incurred substantial losses during the years of establishing a demand for Rinso, in the belief that the product's quality and a reputation sustained by advertising would afford a profitable demand thereafter. A large sales volume having been built by 1928, there appears to

---

[8] *Advertising Age*, November 10, 1934, p. 1.

TABLE 111

SALES OF RINSO, ADVERTISING EXPENDITURE, AND ADVERTISING COSTS
PER UNIT, 1920–1930

YEAR	(1) POUNDS SOLD	(2) VALUE OF SALES	(3) EQUIVALENT IN SMALL RINSO PACKAGES	(4) ADVERTISING EXPENDITURES	(5) ADVERTISING COST PER POUND	(6) ADVERTISING COST PER PACKAGE	(7) ADVERTISING COST AS PERCENTAGE OF SALES VALUE
1920...	8,853,000	$ 1,497,000	25,988,000	$ 562,000	$.0635	$.0216	37.5%
1921...	12,063,000	1,955,000	35,582,000	1,107,000	.0918	.0311	56.6
1922...	17,850,000	2,545,000	52,132,000	1,189,000	.0666	.0228	46.7
1923...	22,318,000	3,173,000	64,893,000	1,256,000	.0563	.0194	39.6
1924...	23,305,000	2,213,000	68,248,000	1,207,000	.0518	.0177	54.5
1925...	24,164,000	3,173,000	66,273,000	739,000	.0306	.0112	23.3
1926...	34,189,000	4,266,000	91,170,000	1,126,000	.0329	.0124	26.4
1927...	44,753,000	5,563,000	84,222,000	1,251,000	.0280	.0149	22.5
1928...	55,416,000	6,687,000	99,549,000	1,318,000	.0238	.0132	19.7
1929...	80,118,000	9,739,000	143,348,000	1,697,000	.0212	.0118	17.4
1930...	108,205,000	13,451,000	203,680,000	2,463,000	.0228	.0121	18.3

Source, Columns 1–4: *Advertising Age*, November 10, 1934, p. 1.

have been a shift in the policy of determining advertising appropriations during the years following; namely, they were shifted in accordance with sales. The cost per unit varied but little for the period 1928–1930.

The case of a grocery manufacturer provides another striking example of decreasing advertising and total marketing costs per unit resulting from increased sales volume while advertising and selling costs were kept at relatively constant amounts. In this case the management, in order to maintain market leadership for its low price, convenience type of product, cut selling prices and its own profit margins per unit markedly. Thus price was added to advertising as a stimulant to sales volume. An effective advertising program, the expenditure for which was held constant, accompanied by the lowered prices, brought a two-fold increase in physical volume of sales. Consequently, the marketing and advertising costs per unit were practically cut in two.

In both the instances cited above, the effect of volume on marketing costs under the policies followed by the managements is easily seen. That marketing and advertising costs fell was attributable to two conditions: relatively constant expenditures, and increasing sales volume. But such conditions do not always hold.

Examples of Increasing Unit Advertising and Marketing Costs

That the marketing costs of individual manufacturers may increase markedly as sales volume increases is indicated by figures of sales volume and of operating costs over a period of years obtained in a special cost research project undertaken under the direction of the author. A description of this research project, which was undertaken to get evidence regarding the effect of advertising upon manufacturers' production and marketing costs, is given in Chapter XIX.[9] It will suffice here to state that sales and operating figures for periods covering from three to twelve years were obtained from 37 concerns. The range of companies covered, the character of their products and of their advertising costs are indicated in Table 106, page 444, which has already been commented upon.

In the case of proprietary remedy manufacturer No. 28,[10] marketing costs increased materially when sales volume increased with the aid of advertising. In a seven-year period, the unit sales of this company increased 430% while selling price was held constant. In this instance the manufacturer embarked upon a greatly increased program of advertising of his highly individualized product. Advertising cost per case of medicine rose from approximately $1.25 to $2.10; total marketing expense per case rose from $2.00 to $2.57. The resultant increase in marketing costs was offset only in part by a decreased production cost. Accordingly the margin per unit left for profit was less than in previous years, but the greatly increased volume of units sold gave a larger aggregate profit.

A similar situation was found in the case of a manufacturer of cosmetics, No. 24. Over a 10-year period, sales volume increased over 250%, primarily as the result of an enlarged program of advertising. Since advertising costs per unit in this period increased from about 5 cents to 8 cents, the profit margin per unit was reduced, but owing to the large increase in sales the aggregate profit was enlarged.

Examples of Decreasing Unit Advertising and Marketing Costs

In the case of four manufacturers selling products for which total demand was expanding during the period covered by the data sub-

---

[9] Chapter XIX, p. 503.
[10] See Table 106, p. 444.

mitted, marketing costs per unit decreased as sales volume increased. The sample is too small and the number of variables too many to justify any generalizations regarding the behavior of marketing costs for products thus subject to an expanding demand. The facts regarding these four cases are given below:

In the case of drug sundry manufacturer, No. 8, a 600% increase in sales volume over a 12-year period was accompanied by a material decrease in both advertising and total marketing costs. In this instance unit costs are not available, but the manufacturer's advertising costs for the first year of the data were 22% of net sales; for the last year, only 8.5%. Total marketing costs during the same period dropped from 28.5% to 11.5%. During this time selling prices were reduced over 50%. Accordingly the advertising and marketing costs on a unit basis were greatly reduced. In this case sales acceptance for the product, which was a type of merchandise never marketed before, was built slowly during the first few years. Gradually, however, the product gained wide acceptance. Since the product was of a type which competitors could easily copy and place upon the market, competition and the threat of competition evidently led the management to avoid any policy of maintaining high prices. Even with marked reductions in the aggregate amount spent upon advertising and upon salesforce, sales in units increased rapidly over the period. Hence there occurred a marked decrease in advertising and selling costs per unit as volume mounted.

Electrical appliance manufacturer, No. 10, had approximately a 10-fold sales growth for the appliance considered over an 11-year period covered by data. During this period of expanding demand, the salesforce expenditure per unit decreased from almost $20 during the first year covered by the data to an average of about $5 for the latter part of the period. Unit advertising costs did not undergo such a decrease, variation being between $5.70 and $11.00, with the expenditure in most years ranging from $7 to $9. Under this operating policy, total marketing costs decreased from a high of $28 per unit for the first year covered by the data to around $13 for the latter part of the period.

Electrical appliance manufacturer, No. 7, enjoyed an increase in physical volume of over 20-fold for the item studied during the period covered by the data. Marketing costs for the first year during which distribution was being gained were inordinate, over $100 a unit.

In the second year, however, they had dropped to about $27 a unit, and in the latter part of the period covered by the data they averaged only $12. In this case the same marked decrease in salesforce cost occurred that applied to company No. 10, discussed in the preceding paragraph. In the first year, salesforce costs per unit were almost $70. In the second year, they had dropped to $13, whereas in the last part of the period they averaged only $4 a unit. Advertising costs per unit did not show a declining trend, although there were marked variations in the amount of expenditure from year to year, the range being from $5.80 to $10.45.

In the case of household appliance manufacturer, No. 12, total marketing expenses over a seven-year period decreased from $2.40 per unit to $0.43 per unit. During this period salesforce expenditures were reduced from $0.42 per unit to $0.10, and advertising costs from $1.72 to $0.22. The reasons for such a marked decrease in advertising and marketing costs are not evident from the data and supporting information was not obtained from the manufacturer. It is believed, however, from evidence from another source, that the entrance of numerous competitors into the market and a generally falling price structure made necessary a marked curtailment of marketing costs concurrent with a reduction in the selling price of the article. Although advertising and personal selling expenditures were greatly reduced, the demand for the product increased rapidly. The consequence was a greatly decreased advertising and marketing cost per unit.

Summary Regarding the Effect of Size upon Manufacturers' Marketing Costs

From the instances cited above the danger of any simple generalizations regarding the relation of advertising and marketing costs to volume of sales is evident. Manufacturers' marketing costs are determined largely by the marketing formulae which they follow.[11] Their costs are affected also by their operating efficiency and by the responsiveness of markets at different periods. Consequently, an increase in sales volume gained with the aid of advertising does not necessarily entail lower unit advertising and marketing costs. In some instances lower costs occur because volume increases at a faster rate than expen-

---

[11] As indicated in Chapter IV, the prices received for merchandise by competing manufacturers operating under different formulae vary. For example, a manufacturer producing private brand merchandise sells at a low price as compared with the manufacturer who performs promotional functions himself.

ditures. In other instances, however, the opposite occurs; expenditures increase at a faster rate than sales volume, and unit costs increase. From the standpoint of the manufacturer, higher unit costs may, from a profit standpoint, be justifiable, because aggregate net profit may increase in spite of lower unit net profit, provided volume increases enough. Moreover, higher unit costs in some instances may be accompanied by higher unit price. While high unit costs may not be objectionable from the profit standpoint of the manufacturer, they cannot be looked upon as desirable from a social standpoint. The existence of checks to prevent high costs will be considered in a later chapter.

THE COSTS OF ADVERTISING VERSUS THE COSTS OF ALTERNATIVE SELLING METHODS

Since advertising may be employed by the manufacturer not for the purpose of getting the lowest distribution costs possible but rather to induce people to buy his product at the prices asked, does it provide him with an economical substitute for other forms of sales effort? Although this query has been answered in Chapters IV and V, in which the use of advertising by businessmen was discussed, it is raised again here in order to give supporting evidence and to indicate the social implications. As shown in those chapters, the manufacturer is constantly striving to attain particular objectives at as low a cost as possible; that is one of the important paths to profit. But it must be kept in mind that the objective of a manufacturer may not be the attaining of lowest possible marketing costs. His aim is rather to attain a desired volume of business at prices which more than cover the costs incurred. To attain the desired volume of sales at these prices he will, of course, try to make as economical an expenditure as possible. The fact that manufacturers have used advertising in certain amounts in specific programs indicates that they have deemed it an effective and economical means of performing particular tasks. The choice between the proportions of advertising and alternative selling and promotional methods to employ varies in different programs, because the effectiveness of the several kinds of advertising as compared with the alternative methods varies widely in different situations. A few examples will be cited, even though they cover ground previously gone over.

Examples of Choice of Alternative Selling Methods

Toilet goods manufacturer No. 30 (Table 106) employed no sales-force but relied on advertising alone. He sold a type of product which consumers bought largely on a brand basis. In order to obtain distribution in the trade and to make substantial sales it was necessary for him to lead consumers to ask for his brand or to select it from dealers' displays. Experience led him to believe that the most effective and most economical way to obtain consumer acceptance was through relatively intensive advertising. He believed that personal selling to the trade, even on a large scale, would not have accomplished the same results for his product. Personal selling direct to consumers might conceivably have brought an equal sales volume, but the cost of such selling would, of course, have been prohibitive.

While consumer advertising was the most economical means for the attainment of this manufacturer's objective, it was not the cheapest method of distributing the product that he might have followed. A competing manufacturer followed a less costly selling procedure. He did no advertising except through package inserts and sold on long contracts, with small selling expense, to variety chains that displayed his merchandise. But this competitor failed to gain the sales volume and the profit attained by manufacturer No. 30.

In striking contrast to the toilet goods manufacturer in reliance on advertising were industrial goods manufacturers No. 34 and No. 35, who for their products believed it more effective to expend three times as much for personal selling force as for advertising (Columns 7 and 8). For industrial products generally, sellers usually place most of the selling burden upon personal selling, although advertising often is an effective aid to personal selling.

Experimentation to Find Economical Selling Methods

Numerous examples are to be found of experimentation by executives to determine whether for certain objectives advertising would provide a more effective and economical selling method than personal selling. Their conclusion often is that advertising is not a substitute for personal selling but an effective aid or supplement to it.

A clear illustration of the selection of advertising in preference to personal solicitation because executives believed it promised a more economical method of building demand occurred in the case of the

Corning Glass Works [12] in the early years of marketing Pyrex industrial glass. This new glass had distinctive physical characteristics, such
as chemical stability, dielectric strength, hardness, transparency, and
high resistance to heat and to temperature change. These characteristics fitted it for a wide variety of products and industrial processes,
many of which were unknown to the company. To learn of these
possible uses the company might have employed a staff of investigating
engineers to canvass industrial firms in various industries. Instead, the
company elected to advertise the characteristics of the glass to engineers and manufacturing executives and thus to lead this group to
consider applications in their businesses. Inquiries were followed up
by Corning engineers. The management felt that only in special
instances did it have sufficient data available to permit the location
of possible markets with enough precision to make the use of a
direct investigating staff as economical as was the use of advertising
in conjunction with a smaller staff.

Another illustration in which an increase in advertising to consumers
permitted a reduction in expenditures for salesmen calling on the
trade was found in the case of a company manufacturing 10-cent cigarettes. The management established its product in the market during
1932–1933 without use of space advertising. In doing so, however,
it had placed much reliance on salesmen to the trade as a means of
getting the trade to stock and push its cigarette. Several years later
the management decided to use advertising to help build consumer
demand for its product. As part of its decision to use advertising the
management decided to reduce the number of salesmen, and in the
course of the next year cut its salesforce from approximately 200 men
to 100. The funds thus saved paid for one-fourth of the advertising
expenditure for the year. Under the new marketing program, which
placed reliance upon the pull from consumer advertising, sales volume
increased.

Another example of the use of advertising as an economical means
of reducing personal selling and total marketing expense was found
in the case of a shoe company which kept the number of its salesmen's
calls down without loss of volume by relying upon mail directed to
its dealers between calls to bring fill-in orders and to secure sales on
new styles introduced between salesmen's calls.

---

[12] N. H. Borden, *Problems in Advertising* (3d ed., New York, McGraw-Hill Book
Company, Inc., 1937), case of Corning Glass Works, p. 61.

Household appliance manufacturer No. 4 (Table 106) changed his selling policy during the period covered by the sales and cost data submitted. For the first few years a considerable part of the company's sales were made through wholesale channels. During this time advertising expenditures amounted to 10% of sales, or over $2.50 a unit. A change in emphasis in the selling plan to direct personal selling to consumers led to a reduction of advertising expenditure to less than 3% of sales, or only $0.75 a unit, while personal sales expense rose. Later the management again sold through wholesale channels and again incurred a higher advertising expenditure per unit in order to secure demand effectively through these channels. As advertising costs rose, personal selling costs again fell. In this instance changes in the amounts of personal selling and advertising were determined by decisions regarding the channels of distribution to be employed.

Changing Effectiveness of Alternative Selling Methods

The relative effectiveness and economy of advertising as compared with alternative selling methods may change as a product progresses from a stage of nonacceptance to one of acceptance. As was recounted in the discussion of electric refrigerator demand the proportions of advertising and personal selling found effective in consummating sales tended to change as mechanical refrigerators became more commonly used by consumers. In the early years, although substantial consumer advertising was employed, the companies induced distributors to carry out personal solicitation and demonstration in the homes of potential buyers, a costly though effective selling method for high-price products in the early stages of demand development. Later, advertising alone was relied upon to lead buyers to the retailers' stores. In the total program advertising, as compared with personal selling, tended to assume a larger burden. Such a shifting of sales burden to advertising with the growth of consumer use has characterized the history of numerous products. It illustrates an evolution in the character of selling costs as a result of the experimentation of sellers to find means of selling their products profitably. Prices at the various stages have had to be adjusted to cover the selling cost incurred.

Summary Regarding the Costs of Advertising as an Alternative Selling Method

Enough examples have been cited to establish the generalization that the use of advertising by businessmen in place of alternative selling methods is guided by their opinions as to its effectiveness in gaining particular marketing objectives. In some instances it is considered an effective and economical substitute to gain particular ends, in other instances other selling methods are employed. When it is employed the manufacturer is not necessarily trying to attain the lowest cost method of distribution which he might adopt; instead, he is trying to build sales volume at prices to yield a profit. In the framework of the marketing program adopted, he ordinarily attempts to get maximum effectiveness from his expenditures. As a result of the varying effectiveness of advertising in different marketing situations the wide variety of combinations of advertising and of other selling forms as elements of marketing programs are found. Such a wide variety is shown in Table 106. For example, excepting the toilet article and proprietary remedy companies which use no personal salesforce, the ratios of advertising cost to personal selling cost range from approximately 8.5:1 in the case of oil and gasoline manufacturer No. 21, to 1:5 for paper products manufacturer No. 22 and hardware specialty manufacturer No. 2.

Because businessmen cannot be certain that they have established the most effective combination of advertising promotion and personal selling methods, it is not certain that the combinations recounted in the examples which have been noted above, or those shown for the several other manufacturers in Table 106 were the most economical which could have been adopted for attaining their sales objectives, even under the brand and pricing policies pursued. Yet these combinations represent the striving of the managements for economical and effective means of gaining their ends.

Since the objective of profit may mean that sellers have not adopted methods to attain the lowest costs of marketing or to sell at the lowest prices, it is desirable from a social standpoint to carry the investigation further to see what competitive forces operate to bring low costs which may be reflected in low prices. Evidence on advertising and marketing costs has shown that among manufacturers of any particular product, wide differences exist in advertising costs and in total marketing costs. The widest differences in these costs are found between manufacturers who rely chiefly upon advertising to sell their own brands and those who use no advertising in selling merchandise to distributors under the latter's brand. Extreme examples of this kind are found in the case of toilet goods, dentifrices, and proprietary remedies, for which advertising expenditures of over 40% of selling price and total marketing costs of over 50% are not uncommon among manufacturers heavily advertising their brands. In contrast, there are manufacturers whose advertising costs are practically nil because they sell either under distributors' brands or under their own unadvertised brands to chains. Among distributors there is a variation in costs similar to, though smaller than, that found among manufacturers. Since final prices must reflect the costs not only of manufacturers but of distributors, it is desirable to have some idea regarding the combined costs of competing methods of distribution. Attention is turned to this topic in the next chapter. In the next chapter and Chapter XXV, analysis is made, also, regarding variations in services to the consumer or in contributions to the social group which may attend variations in the costs of different selling methods.

CHAPTER XVIII

THE EFFECT OF ADVERTISING ON COSTS OF MARKETING MERCHANDISE—Continued

SINCE an economical method of distributing goods from manufacturer to point of purchase is desirable from the consumer's standpoint, the relative overall advertising and selling costs incurred under competing methods of marketing are pertinent to this economic study. It was not feasible to investigate the variations in costs among all possible methods of marketing, but effort was made to determine differences between two methods which offer wide contrasts in selling procedures and opportunity for considerable variation in costs, namely, distribution under manufacturers' brands and under large-scale retailers' brands. How do the advertising and selling costs and the final marketing costs of manufacturers and distributors combined compare in instances in which the manufacturer conducts advertising and promotion for his brand, as contrasted with those in which advertising and promotional work are carried out by distributors?

In this chapter attention is devoted primarily to analysis of the costs of distribution under distributors' private brands as compared with costs of distribution under manufacturers' advertised brands. The full social significance of the differences in the costs of the two methods is analyzed in later chapters. Until that analysis is presented, however, the reader should keep in mind when comparing costs of the two methods that the private brander does not assume the burdens of developing new types of products or of promoting their demand. He puts his brands on products for which demand has been established, generally through the aggressive promotional efforts of manufacturers.[1] From a social standpoint not only the significance of the lower costs which private branders may attain, but also the significance of the development and introduction of new products by manufacturers must be weighed. These matters are discussed in subsequent chapters.

---

[1] See Chapter XXI, p. 605, and Chapter XXIV, p. 710.

Possible Economies from Integration of Marketing Functions

The practice of large-scale retailers selling under their own brands is one aspect of marketing methods involving the integration of marketing functions, which, in some instances at least, has brought economies in overall marketing costs. Under this plan of integration the retailer reaches backward and takes over from the manufacturer, among other functions, those of advertising and promotion which, under the usual manufacturer-wholesaler-retailer plan of distribution, are conducted in large part by the manufacturers. In some instances distributors undertake the manufacturing function. For example, the Great Atlantic and Pacific Tea Company has its own facilities for manufacturing its coffees, gelatin desserts, canned milk, canned salmon, and numerous other items; likewise many other chains, mail-order houses, and some large department stores manufacture some of the items which they sell under their own brands. This form of integration may be termed integration backward, in contrast to integration forward, which occurs when the manufacturer takes over the distributive function and sets up his own retail stores. Both forms of integration represent efforts by managements to gain control over the marketing process through ownership of brands and direction of retail sale. They also strive to effect economies in the performance of various marketing functions.[2] For example, in the backward type of integration the amount of advertising employed between the stages of manufacture and consumption in many instances has been reduced. Concurrently, the costs of certain other functions have sometimes been reduced either through finding a more efficient way to perform these functions or through their simplification or possible elimination. For instance, some large-scale distributors have been able to reduce the

---

[2] Evidence from case material and from expense studies points to the tentative conclusion that integration backward from retailers has certain advantages over integration forward from manufacturers. Limited evidence from the shoe industry indicates that integration backward on the whole has been more successful than forward integration. For example, many shoe chains established and conducted by some manufacturers, i.e., integrated forward, have not been highly successful either in obtaining a low rate of expense in their stores or in showing profit results in their store operations. The difficulty has appeared to rest in part upon the failure of these manufacturers to put adequate emphasis upon store operation as essential to the success of the whole enterprise. Instead of putting emphasis on a single profit realized in the final sale at the stores, they have often operated on the assumption that they should show a profit at the factory as well as at the time of final sale. The emphasis upon a factory profit in turn has led them to neglect the retail viewpoint of low operating expense, quick stock-turn, merchandising directed from close contact with consumer, and prices which attract. Consequently their store operations sometimes have not compared favorably with chains operated by retailers who have been interested in only one profit, that secured on final sale, and have devoted every effort to conduct successful store operations.

costs of warehousing and transportation between factory and stores. Again, they have simplified the function and reduced the costs of the promotional effort directed to individual store managers. Some of them have eliminated various expensive customer services, such as delivery, credit, and merchandise returns.

Examples which support the conclusion that economies sometimes are effected through the method of backward integration of marketing functions have been provided in Federal Trade Commission hearings of which the case of Bird & Son is illustrative. A complaint was made against Bird & Son [3] under the Robinson-Patman Act for selling its floor coverings at a lower price to Montgomery Ward & Co., Incorporated, than to its independent retail customers. To show that its lower prices to the mail-order house were justified by lower costs, Bird & Son filed with the Commission an analysis of marketing costs made by the public accounting firm of Price, Waterhouse & Company, showing the costs of selling to various classes of customers for the ten months ending October 31, 1936. Although any cost accounting allocations are more or less arbitrary and cannot be accepted as definitive, this study indicated that costs of selling to Montgomery Ward & Co., Incorporated, were 9% of net sales, less than the costs of selling to jobbers, and 28.5% of net sales, less than the costs of selling to independent retailers, as shown in Table 112. Large economies for the manufacturer were effected in advertising and salesforce expenses. Other economies were obtained in warehouse and freight accounts. The Commission held that the lower selling prices to Montgomery Ward & Co., Incorporated, were justified by lower costs. The selling costs of the company, as compared with those of retailers and retailers and wholesalers combined are not available, but the fact that the complaint was raised in part because the company undersold independent retailers is indicative that this concern's costs were not such as to wipe out the advantage gained in its buying.

Again, in the Federal Trade Commission action against Goodyear Tire & Rubber Company,[4] the respondent sought to justify its lower price to Sears, Roebuck and Company on the basis of lower costs of selling than were involved in selling through its regular channels. A large part of the manufacturer's saving, of course, came from the

---

[3] The selling costs of this case and others mentioned in the pages ahead are taken from a study by J. F. Thomas, "Varying Functions in Distribution, Their Costs and Influence on Retail Prices," *The Journal of Marketing*, July, 1938, p. 47.

[4] 101 F. 2nd, 620, February 16, 1939.

TABLE 112

PERCENTAGES OF EXPENSE OF BIRD AND SON, INC., FOR SELLING FLOOR COVERING TO
VARIOUS TYPES OF DISTRIBUTORS; COLUMNAR STATEMENT OF SALES AND SELLING,
DISTRIBUTING, ADMINISTRATIVE AND GENERAL EXPENSES, ETC., FOR THE TEN
MONTHS ENDING OCTOBER 31, 1936—ALLOCATED TO RESPECTIVE CLASSES
OF CUSTOMERS

	EXPENSES AS A PERCENTAGE OF SALES INCOME				
	All Types of Distributors	Mail Order Houses	Jobbers	Retailers	Others
Net sales.........................	100%	100%	100%	100%	100%
Selling, distributing, administrative and general expenses, etc.:					
Sales commissions, salaries and traveling expenses (outside).....	6.3%	5.0	6.6	6.0	....
Salaries and traveling expenses (inside).......................	1.6	1.5	1.6	1.5	2.8
Advertising expense.............	4.4	.5	4.5	4.0	7.3
Miscellaneous selling expenses.....	2.8	2.8	2.8	2.5	4.1
Warehousing expenses...........	.5	.4	.1	15.0	....
Freight paid on sales.............	9.5	4.8	9.7	10.0	7.8
General and administrative expenses	2.0	2.9	1.9	7.5	2.0
State excise taxes................	.3	.4	.3	.2	.5
Social security taxes.............	.1	.1	.1	.1	.2
Total.....................	27.7%	18.6%	27.6%	47.1%	24.9%

Source: J. F. Thomas, "Varying Functions in Distribution, Their Costs and Influence
on Retail Prices," *The Journal of Marketing*, July, 1938, p. 51.

elimination of advertising and selling, such as was devoted to its
own brands. But there were also economies in its warehousing,
shipping, and other expenses when it sold to Sears, Roebuck and
Company. Sears, Roebuck and Company furthermore undertook the
advertising and promotional functions for its own brand of tires and
spent less on these functions than did Goodyear Tire & Rubber Company for its own brands. A comparison of distribution costs in 1930
under the two methods of selling for a 450 x 20 tire is given in
Table 113, which is based on evidence submitted to the Federal Trade
Commission. The distribution cost for a Goodyear Allweather tire of
this size was $3.44, or 41% of the retail price of $8.40; the distribution
cost for a Sears, Roebuck Allstate tire through its retail stores was
$2.07, or 30.2% of its retail selling price of $6.47. The marketing
cost for the latter brand through the mail-order division was $1.16,
or 18% of a selling price of $6.17.

An example of the varying spreads between retail price and manufacturers' costs for electric refrigerators sold under different methods
of distribution has been cited in the study by Mr. Thomas.[5] The facts
as given by him are contained in the following statement:

[5] *Op. cit.*, p. 55.

TABLE 113

COMPARISON OF DISTRIBUTION COSTS, GOODYEAR AND SEARS AUTO TIRES
SIZE 450 x 20ss, 1930

	RETAIL PRICES	COST DISTRIBUTION	PERCENTAGE OF DISTRIBUTION COST TO SELLING PRICE
RETAIL STORES			
Goodyear Allweather.................	$8.40	$3.44	41.0%
Sears Allstate Retail Store............	6.47	2.07	30.2
Difference.........................	$1.93 or 23%	$1.37 or 40%	....
MAIL ORDER			
Goodyear Allweather.................	$8.40	$3.44	41.0
Sears Allstate Mail Order.............	6.17	1.16	18.0
Difference.........................	$2.23 or 26.5%	$2.28 or 63%	....

Source: J. F. Thomas, *op. cit.*, p. 53. Author cites Federal Trade Commission Docket No. 2116 as the original source.

A certain standard brand electric refrigerator has a production cost of $93.34 and is retailed for $207.50—with most of the expense between manufacturer and consumer going for sales promotion and advertising, or the marketing functions.

A large direct buyer with multiple outlets, on the other hand, contracts with a manufacturer for a comparable product at a cost of $100.00 and retails it for $158.00—performing all of its own marketing and distribution functions.

In one case selling and distribution costs amount to $114.16, or 55% of retail price,[6] and in the other, $58.00, or 36.7%. The difference of $49.50 in selling prices is due largely to the difference in selling methods used. In the indirect method, the distribution organization consists of a sales manager with zone, district, and block managers who work with retail dealers. Salesmen are used by the dealer for outside solicitation on a commission basis ranging from 10% to 15%. This effort is supplemented with national advertising by the manufacturer, and all sorts of dealer assistance amounting to approximately 10% of retail price.

The mass distributor of a private brand item of comparable quality, on the other hand, has only a sales manager to direct selling and advertising methods used by retail store managers. Store salesmen divide their time between inside and outside selling effort, working only on specific prospects furnished by the store, and are paid a commission of 4% to 6%. Advertising expense does not exceed 3%, in that part of consumer acceptance comes from good-will and gen-

[6] According to reports of the National Electrical Manufacturers' Association, over a period of years, the spread between factory price and retail price for electric refrigerators has been approximately 50%, somewhat less than the 55% cited in the example given by Mr. Thomas.
A summary of distributive margins on electric refrigerators, as estimated by the National Electrical Manufacturers' Association, is contained in U. S. Temporary National Economic Committee, Investigation of Concentration of Economic Power, Monograph No. 1, *Price Behavior and Business Policy* (Washington. U. S. Government Printing Office, 1940), p. 144.

eral advertising of the mass distributor, the cost of which is charged to many thousands of items.

Unfortunately, more extensive studies which show the full distributive costs under the two methods of distribution are not available. The individual instances cited above indicate, however, that through integration of marketing functions by large-scale retailers, economies may be effected and that these economies come in part from lower total costs of selling, promotion, and advertising.

Supplementary Information Sought Regarding Marketing Costs

In order to supplement the information given above regarding the total costs for marketing specific products under the method of private branding by distributors and under manufacturers' brands, an effort was made to determine the relative costs of large-scale retailers in selling manufacturers' advertised brands and in selling their own brands or unbranded merchandise. The statement is frequently met that the advertising and promotion of a manufacturer makes the selling effort of the distributor easy and that when the distributor sells his own brand or unbranded merchandise, instead of manufacturers' advertised brands, his costs of operation are increased. The investigation has sought to appraise the correctness of this statement. The question raised is whether the retailer's costs of handling and selling his own brands have been apparently increased by an amount as great as or greater than that made by manufacturers in advertising and promoting their own brands. It will be recalled that when the distributor sells under his own brand or sells unbranded merchandise, the manufacturer is practically relieved of consumer advertising and promotional expense, whereas the distributor assumes the full function of promotion to the consumer.

Additional evidence which throws some light upon the integrated costs under the two methods of marketing will also be presented in a later chapter in which the prices of merchandise under the two plans are compared. These two sets of prices will not in themselves show the exact differences in costs under the two methods because prices contain net profit or loss as well as costs, but substantial differences in price may be taken to imply differences in costs. Thus the evidence in the price chapter may be taken as supplementary to the evidence produced in this chapter.

Lack of Detailed Data Regarding Retailers' Costs for Individual Items

Knowledge regarding retailers' or wholesalers' costs for selling particular items of merchandise is very scanty. To obtain such information involves difficult and inexact cost accounting. Relatively few such studies have been made, and of these the results have seldom been made available outside the organizations compiling them. It was impossible in this research to make an independent study of this difficult and involved problem. Conclusions given here are based on knowledge of retailers' methods and opinions given by retailers concerning their costs. Consequently, although the conclusions must be tentative, they will perhaps clear away certain misconceptions which have been found not only among laymen but also among businessmen and economists.

Clearly, any suggestion that advertising costs incurred by manufacturers necessarily are followed by exactly offsetting decreases in the marketing costs of distributors is not justified. Yet it is a truism that in most product fields a well-known manufacturer's brand is easier to sell than a relatively unknown manufacturer's or distributor's brand or an unbranded item. The extent to which a distributor's costs will differ when handling manufacturers' advertised brands, unadvertised brands, and his own brands will vary, because the behavior of the retailer's costs is not alike under different sets of conditions.

The Bearing of Consumer Acceptance on Distributors' Selling Costs

To begin with, some products need not be advertised to enjoy a relatively low selling cost by distributors. Whether a product has been advertised by manufacturers or not, the distributors' selling costs, aside from the costs of physical handling and such services as delivery and credit, will be low when the following conditions hold: (a) when there is a ready acceptance or demand for the product among his customers, so that he need not persuade them to purchase; (b) when the relation between sales and stocks permits a sufficiently rapid turnover of stock.

That marketing costs of products tend to be low under these conditions is so evident as to need little supporting evidence. The statement applies to a large number of popular, advertised brands of manufacturers, but it applies likewise to numerous staple, unadvertised products in ready demand, for which brand is of no great consequence to consumers. Sugar, relatively speaking, is an unadvertised product as compared with soap; yet the retailers' or wholesalers' costs for selling sugar are probably no greater than those for selling well-advertised manufacturers' brands of soap. Neither calls for any appreciable promotional or selling urge on the part of the retailer. The distributor will use both as leaders to attract trade, because of the established demand for them among a large part of his patrons. On both it is possible for him to obtain a rapid stock-turn. Such conditions as these hold for other staples to which relatively small advertising and promotional costs are devoted by producers, e.g., potatoes, eggs, and flour. The retailer sells these items without appreciable selling or promotional effort, irrespective of the fact that they have received little promotion by producers.

Similarly a retailer may have low marketing costs for his private brands or for unbranded merchandise even in product categories which have strongly demanded manufacturers' brands after he has once established acceptance among his patrons for his own brands or for unbranded merchandise which he carries. For example, interviews with several executives of limited-price variety chains revealed their belief that their costs of handling numerous private or unadvertised brands of merchandise were only a little greater, if any, than the costs incurred in selling competing manufacturers' brands which were extensively advertised. Although the opinion of these executives was not supported by cost studies, it appears sound from an analysis of the cost factors for these variety chain stores. Their method of selling, which was to rely almost solely on merchandise display to induce purchase, was such that they exerted neither advertising nor personal selling effort for any of the merchandise carried. In so far as volume of sales from a well-known brand obtainable from a certain amount of counter space was greater than that for the unknown brand, the amount of sales per square foot was larger and gave for certain fixed expenses a slightly lower cost per unit for the fast-moving item than for the slow-moving item; but the difference was of very small moment in the many instances in which the store's own brands or unbranded items were accepted in appreciable amount by the buying public. The worth of the unadvertised articles was evident to consumers from display, and consumers' reliance on the store to offer dependable merchandise often brought acceptance of unadvertised brands or unbranded items. For example, several variety chain executives expressed the belief that the costs of selling their own brands of razor blades were little if any greater than their costs of selling well-advertised manufacturers' brands.

When the conditions outlined above do not hold, and the retailer finds it essential to exert considerable selling and promotional effort in order to dispose of his own brand, or when his stock-turn on merchandise of his own brand is very low, then his costs tend to become larger for his unadvertised brand than for manufacturers' advertised brands having an established demand.

EVIDENCE FROM TRADE SURVEY REGARDING MARKETING COSTS

Some evidence regarding retailers' costs of selling their own brands of merchandise, as compared with their costs of selling manufacturers' advertised brands, was obtained in an extensive survey among large-scale retailers made early in 1939 under the author's direction. The study brought to light the different relationships between the costs of selling the two groups of merchandise under different operating conditions.

The survey was conducted among a large enough group of organizations to be significant. (See Table 114.) In all, information was secured from 66 organizations, selling through approximately 73,000 retail outlets, varying in size from department stores with sales of many millions, down to small independent grocers in voluntary cooper-

TABLE 114

NUMBER AND TYPE OF DISTRIBUTORS FROM WHOM QUESTIONNAIRES WERE RECEIVED REGARDING COSTS AND PRICES FOR SELLING BRANDED MERCHANDISE

TYPE OF DISTRIBUTOR	DATA SECURED BY		APPROXIMATE NUMBER OF RETAIL STORES REPRESENTED
	PERSONAL INTERVIEW	MAIL	
Corporate chain, food distributors......	10	10	31,456
Corporate chain, drug distributors......	7	6	1,165
Voluntary food chains, headquarters....	6	1	35,997
Voluntary food chains, wholesale branches	3	8	
Dry goods and department store chains...	5	0	2,786
Limited price variety chains..........	5	0	2,042
Department stores...................	4	0	4
Large independent grocer.............	1	0	4
Total...........................	41	25	73,454

ative chains. Of the 66 sets of data and questionnaires received, 41 sets were obtained through personal interviews; 25 sets were obtained by mail as a result of an inquiry addressed to 31 corporate food chains, 21 corporate drug chains, and 40 voluntary cooperative food chains, a reply by 27% of those addressed. The questionnaire form used is reproduced in Appendix V. In the case of the voluntary food chains, data were received from operating wholesale members as well as from the group headquarters. In three instances wholesaler members reported the actual operating practices of the retailers they supplied, whereas the headquarters of the same voluntary group gave the policies and opinions of the central group. In view of the fact that reported practices and policies of wholesaler members and headquarters did not always agree, each questionnaire was treated as an entity. The replies of headquarters and of wholesaler members are segregated in tabulations, however.

Statements Regarding Costs of Selling Manufacturers' versus Private Brands

The various organizations were asked: "Have you made any studies regarding costs of handling and selling your own brands vs. handling and selling manufacturers' brands of merchandise?" Nine organizations stated that they had made such studies: three corporate food chains, two corporate drug chains, one corporate limited-price variety chain, and three voluntary food chain wholesaler members.

These organizations were also asked what their studies indicated. Their replies to the question, as stated, were as follows:

Expenses for handling and selling private brands of merchandise as compared with manufacturers' brands are—

Type of Organization	Slightly Higher	About the Same	Slightly Lower	Vary Widely with Merchandise
3 Corporate food chains	2	1		
2 Corporate drug chains			1	1
1 Variety chain				1
3 Voluntary food chain wholesaler members	2			1
Total replies	4	1	1	3

The studies supporting the findings were not made available for review, and accordingly cannot be vouched for. In general the replies indicate a somewhat higher cost for selling distributors' brands than for selling manufacturers' advertised brands, although replies from three organizations indicate variation among types of merchandise.

Those organizations which had not made such cost studies were then asked several questions as to their opinions or beliefs regarding the costs of selling their own brands as compared with the costs of selling competing manufacturers' brands. It should be recognized that the replies to these questions are largely opinion only, that those who answered did not have statistical evidence of costs for individual items and that their interest in the welfare of their own brands may have colored their answers. In spite of the shortcomings of these replies as evidence, they are given because, as a whole, particularly in conjunction with other evidence, they throw some light on the question of costs of selling under private brands and under manufacturers' brands.

The first question asked those who had not made cost studies and the replies given are indicated below:[7]

If your answer to the above question is "no," do you think that in general the costs of handling and selling private brands of merchandise, as compared with manufacturers' brands, are—

Type of Organization	Appreciably Higher	Slightly Higher	About the Same	Slightly Lower	Appreciably Lower	Vary Widely with Different Merchandise
14 Corporate food chains.	5	4	5	....	....	....
11 Corporate drug chains.	3	4	2	....	....	2
7 Voluntary food chains, wholesaler members...	1	4	2	....	....	
4 Voluntary food chains, headquarters.........	....	2	2	....	....	
2 Variety chains.......	....	....	2	....	....	
3 Dry goods chains.....	....	1	2	....	....	
2 Department stores....	....	1	1	....	....	
Total replies........	9	16	16	0	0	2

These opinions of the executives interviewed, recognizably not fully satisfactory as evidence, indicate again a higher cost for selling distributors' brands, as a rule, than for selling advertised brands, although over a third of those interviewed stated that the costs were about the same for the two. That the costs for advertising and promoting certain items under private brands were greater than for others was indicated not only in the replies listed above, but also in comments given orally and in the questionnaire. These showed clearly that the

[7] Not all gave a reply to this question.

strong standing of manufacturers' brands in certain product categories made entrance of distributors' brands costly; to establish consumer acceptance of private brands in these instances required unusual selling effort.[8] For example, relatively few of those interviewed sold their own brands of soap; likewise, few sold their own brands of canned soup or corn flakes. In all three of these fields manufacturers' brands are dominant. Moreover, they are fields in which manufacturers have established highly individualized products, usually referred to in the grocery trade as "specialties." In contrast, almost all the chains interviewed had found it not too costly to establish and to make sales of their brands on types of products for which demand had long been established and for which new product individualizations were not highly significant, such as coffee, salad dressing, and all-purpose flour.

Statements Regarding Turnover of Merchandise

A question bearing on turnover of stock and, hence, on costs was asked. The replies given were as follows:

Aside from the question of cost of handling and selling, how does rate of turnover of your own brands compare with that of nationally advertised brands?

Type of Organization	Appreciably Higher	Slightly Higher	About the Same	Slightly Lower	Appreciably Lower	Varies Widely with Different Merchandise
16 Corporate food chains	3	3	4	....	1	5
12 Corporate drug chains	....	....	1	3	3	5
11 Voluntary food chains, wholesaler members	2	1	3	3	....	2
7 Voluntary food chains, headquarters	1	....	1	2	1	2
2 Variety chains	....	....	1	....	....	1
1 Department store	....	1	....	....	....	....
Total replies	6	5	10	8	5	15

These replies indicate a wide divergence of opinion regarding the relative rate of turnover of distributors' brands as compared with manufacturers' brands. Probably the large number who indicated that the turnover experience varied with different classes of merchandise gave a sound generalization, while those giving other answers apparently attempted to give an average experience for the kinds of merchandise they handled.

---

[8] Further evidence relating to this point is given in Chapter XXI, p. 593 ff.

That turnover and the costs incident to turnover varied widely with different types of merchandise was made evident by comments of those interviewed. Seasonal products, such as canned fruits and vegetables, which had to be bought in large lots when packed under the distributors' labels, necessarily brought slower turnover than was incurred when manufacturers' advertised brands were sold. Again, for mechanical items, such as refrigerators, the turnover on private brands was not only low for some organizations, because of large contractual requirements, but low turnover entailed considerable risk because of the rapid introduction of innovations in such merchandise. Once again, one small drug chain stated that it had not tried to establish its own brand of tooth paste because to do so would have necessitated a contract for 10,000 tubes of paste, an amount which it could not hope to sell in its few outlets in a reasonable period of time. For large chains, however, purchase of many items for private brands did not appreciably affect the rate of turnover because their scale of operations was great enough to meet manufacturers' contractual requirements without resulting in large stocks in individual warehouses or stores.

Further comments regarding turnover and costs attending the handling of their own brands were mentioned by certain distributors. Two executives stated that their total inventories of particular types of merchandise were increased by the adoption of their own brands in addition to manufacturers' brands which were asked for by their clientele. Another executive, however, stated that total inventory had been reduced in some product categories by building a demand for the company's own brand among its customers. Customer demand for its brands permitted the dropping of some manufacturers' brands which then were not frequently called for. Aside from turnover costs, several executives mentioned the fact that their brands involved the costs of testing merchandise for quality.[9] This cost, however, was small. Moreover, some companies had found it necessary to tie up capital in labels for canned and bottled products, but again this was a minor expense item.

---

[9] Methods employed for testing by the reporting concerns are discussed in Chapter XXII, p. 631.

Promotion of Distributors' Brands

The character of the promotional and selling effort devoted to the selling of their private brands is indicated by the summary of replies to a check list, which is as follows:

Check the promotional and selling efforts employed by you to increase the sale of your own label merchandise—

TYPE OF EFFORT	NUMBER OF MENTIONS BY				TOTAL REPLIES
	20 Corporate Food Chains	13 Corporate Drug Chains	11 Voluntary Food Chains, Wholesaler Members	7 Voluntary Food Chains, Headquarters	
Newspaper listing..............	18	11	11	6	46
Handbills....................	17	6	10	6	39
Window streamers............	13	5	10	6	34
Window display..............	19	10	11	7	47
Prominent shelf space.........	12	7	10	2	31
Counter display..............	18	11	11	5	45
Price comparison displays......	6	2	3	2	13
Recommendations by clerks....	18	11	9	....	38
PM's to clerks...............	3	9	2	....	14
Other methods...............	7	1	1	....	9

It will be noted that newspaper listing, handbills, window display, prominent shelf space, counter display, and recommendation by clerks were most commonly mentioned by the 51 firms that replied. Price comparison displays, PM's to clerks, and miscellaneous methods were less commonly named.

The distributors interviewed varied in the aggressiveness with which they advertised and promoted their own brands. This was shown by the replies to several questions, but was specifically brought out in the following question, the replies to which are indicated:

Please check your policy with regard to aggressiveness in advertising and promoting your own brands of merchandise—

NUMBER AND TYPE OF ORGANIZATION ANSWERING	NUMBER OF MENTIONS		
	Generally give preference to own brands over other brands in our advertising and store promotion	Generally give about same emphasis to our own as to other brands	Generally give less emphasis to our own than to other brands
20 Corporate food chains...........	11	8	1
13 Corporate drug chains...........	1	8	4
11 Voluntary food chains, wholesaler member......................	9	2	....
7 Voluntary food chains, headquarters......................	1	6	....
5 Dry goods or department store chains........................	5	....	....
5 Limited price variety chains......	1	1	1
4 Department stores..............	4	....	....
Total replies.................	32	25	6

As shown in this table, 32, or approximately half of the 63 organizations replying to this question, stated that they gave preference to their own brands in their advertising and store promotion, a policy which would lead to higher promotional and advertising costs on these brands than on manufacturers' brands. Twenty-five concerns, or 40%, stated that they followed a policy of giving the same emphasis to other brands as to their own. Six concerns, or 10% of those replying, followed the policy of giving less emphasis to their own brands than to other brands in their advertising and promotion.

Comments of Cooperators Regarding Selling Costs

As might be expected, the comments made and the illustrations given by those who provided information were more illuminating regarding their selling costs than were the generalized answers tabulated above.

Whenever policies of aggressive advertising and promotion of their own brands were in force, the replies of the distributors invariably reflected the viewpoint that their selling costs for such brands were greater than for competing advertised brands. For example, a voluntary food chain executive said, "Some items, such as cake flour, need extra publicity. That is the greatest single additional expense in selling one of our brands as compared with a manufacturer's. But this does not apply to all items; hence the question of difference in costs varies with different items."

An executive of a corporate drug chain said that his company's selling methods for its own brands were such that costs were appreciably higher than for manufacturers' advertised brands. The company spent money to train its selling force to promote its own brands. Moreover, advantageous display was given to them and clerks were given PM's for their sale. A house organ also was devoted largely to sale of the store's brands.

In contrast, organizations which did not have a policy of aggressive advertising of private brands did not consider the selling costs of their own brands appreciably higher than those for manufacturers' advertised brands. Such was the situation with several non-advertising variety chains previously mentioned. Their brands were sold through display just as were competing manufacturers' brands.

Among the few distributors interviewed who sold their own brands of high-price mechanical products, such as refrigerators, radios, and washing machines, considerable expenditures were made for advertising. These few companies stated, however, that their advertising outlay was not so great as that of manufacturers.

That a policy of private branding need not involve large advertising outlay was indicated by the fact that one large and successful dry goods chain, which in 1939 sold 90% of all its merchandise under its own brands, had an advertising expense well below the common figure for department stores. However, many of the product lines handled by this company did not compete with manufacturers' heavily advertised brands.

Effect of Retailers' Contact with Consumers

The view was expressed by executives of a considerable number of organizations that their selling costs were only slightly higher for their own brands than for manufacturers' advertised brands because they made no appreciable out-of-pocket expenditures for selling private brand items after they once had established a customer following for them. In interview after interview, executives stated that first or early costs of selling a particular private brand item were high, but later such costs were little above those of manufacturers' brands. For example, an executive of a chain department store with large sales of its own brand of men's overalls stated that salesmen had to exert sales effort to make first sales, but the ready acceptance of the product thereafter had made selling relatively easy. Following the introductory period, the product had become a leading sales item with only normal selling effort devoted to it.

Another point stressed by those interviewed was the strategic position they held in securing consumer acceptance of their brands without large promotional outlay. The daily contact with customers and the reliance of customers upon them as a result of continued satisfactory dealings made it possible through advantageous display and salesmen's suggestions to obtain customer trial of their brands, particularly when good values were stressed. Repeat sales then depended largely on customers' satisfaction with the merchandise. As pointed out by several of those interviewed, the opportunity for the retail salesman to offer the distributors' brands when the customer did not name a brand, or to recommend them when the called-for brands were not carried, or to suggest them as additional items of purchase, gave the retailers a great opportunity to promote their own brands without appreciable increase in expense over their costs of selling manufacturers' brands. While an allocation of salesmen's time devoted to the selling of private brands as contrasted with that given manufacturers' advertised brands would undoubtedly show a larger selling cost for private brands, it should be recognized that the managements generally believed that salesforce expense as a whole was not appreciably increased as the result of the selling effort employed. Accordingly they looked with favor upon efforts by the salesforce to shift demand to their brands, from which they hoped to obtain greater profits than from manufacturers' brands.

That retailers are in a strategic position to recommend purchase of their own brands and thus gradually to build up demand for them is indicated by the replies to a question regarding the extent to which salesmen were authorized to recommend purchase of the stores' own brands. The replies to this question are recorded in Table 115. Among 53 organizations from whom replies were received, relatively few, about 25%, said that they followed the policy of recommending their own brands when customers specifically asked for a manufacturer's brand carried in the store. On the other hand, the great majority of stores directed their salespeople to recommend their own brand when a specific brand asked for was not carried in the store. Likewise they were directed to offer or recommend the store's brands when the customer did not specify a brand. Furthermore they were encouraged to name the distributors' brands when suggesting further items the customer might wish to buy.[10]

While sales practices such as those mentioned probably entail a somewhat higher personal selling cost than is involved when no substitution policy is employed, the difference in selling costs is probably of no great practical significance, as substitution is practiced by most of the reporting firms. The offering of the distributor's brand to the buyer when no brand has been called for entails no increased selling

---

[10] The extent to which dealers press substitutions and the extent to which they may influence the purchases of customers is shown in the results of a survey conducted by the Scripps-Howard Newspapers in 16 cities in 1938. The following is a summary of findings regarding dealer influence on the substitution of brands as shown from the interviews among some 53,000 housewives:

	GROCERS	DRUGGISTS
Percentage of consumers reporting offering of substitutions by retailers..........	30.9%	40.1%
Percentage of above housewives who said they accepted substitutions offered	62.7	44.1

Scripps-Howard Newspapers, *Market Records, 1938*, pp. 42 and 46.

TABLE 115

REPLIES TO QUESTIONS AMONG CERTAIN LARGE-SCALE RETAILERS REGARDING THE
EXTENT TO WHICH SALESMEN WERE AUTHORIZED TO RECOMMEND PURCHASE
OF DISTRIBUTORS' BRANDS, 1939

QUESTIONS	NUMBER OF MENTIONS BY:					
	20 CORPORATE FOOD CHAINS	13 CORPORATE DRUG CHAINS	10 VOLUNTARY FOOD CHAINS WHOLESALER MEMBER*	6 VOLUNTARY FOOD CHAINS HEADQUARTER OFFICE*	4 VARIETY CHAINS	TOTAL REPLIES
1. Are salespeople directed to recommend own brands when customer has asked for another brand carried in store?						
Yes.............	4	2	4†	0	0	10
No.............	15	9	6‡	6‡	4	40
2. Are they directed to offer or recommend your brands when customer asks for specific brand not carried?						
Yes.............	18	10	10†	6†	2	46
No.............	1	2	0	0	2	5
3. Are salespeople directed to offer or recommend your brands when customer has not specified a brand?						
Yes.............	19	11	10†	5	2	47
No.............	0	2	0	0	2	4
4. Are they encouraged to name your brands of merchandise when suggesting further items the customer might wish to buy?						
Yes.............	17	11	9†	3	1	41
No.............	2	2	1‡	0	3	8

* In this instance the headquarters were asked what the practices of retail members were.
† Reply of "often" listed as "yes."
‡ Reply of "seldom" or "never" listed as "no."

charge. Moreover, salesmen's suggestions of additional items for purchase is a common selling practice and the cost of suggesting private brands is no greater than that of suggesting known brands, although the response to the suggestion may not be so great. Finally, the opportunity of the salesperson over a period of time to recommend merchandise to the customer without reduction of his sales productiveness is present in most retail stores.

Summary of Evidence Regarding Costs from Survey

Although the evidence from the survey discussed above lacks the authority that would attend a large scale and detailed study of costs of selling under competing methods of marketing, still the evidence is believed to be significant. Distributors generally incur greater costs in selling their own brands of merchandise than in selling brands promoted by manufacturers. On products for which manufacturers' brands hold strong leadership, particularly on products relatively new to the market (so-called specialties), the distributor's selling costs evidently are appreciably higher for his own brands than for manufacturers' brands. The selling costs for private brands of such products are particularly high when the distributor is attempting to establish such brands. On many items where manufacturers' brand leadership is not strong, however, the distributor apparently can introduce his own brand without incurring selling costs appreciably larger than those for manufacturers' brands. Once a distributor has established a customer following for a private branded item which is acceptable to his clientele, however, his selling costs on this item often apparently are not materially larger than for manufacturers' brands.

This conclusion is significant because, whenever a private brand policy is followed, the manufacturer is almost fully relieved of advertising and promotional outlay.[11] Consequently, it is believed that in many instances the total promotional costs and the total marketing costs of distributors and manufacturers combined have been less under the system of distributors' brands than they have been under a system of promotion under manufacturers' brands. Whether this has been true in specific cases could be determined only by detailed data which are not available, except for the few instances given in the first part of this chapter. These confirm the tentative conclusion. In a later chapter data relating to prices and pricing practice for certain articles give a strong implication that the total costs of selling under distributors' brands often have been less than those of selling under manufacturers' brands.

In many instances the retail distributors interviewed volunteered the statement that the sales they secured for certain items under their own brands were favorably affected by the advertising of manufacturers in that this advertising built and maintained a primary demand for the type of product. For example, an executive of one chain expressed a conclusion, which is believed correct, that the substantial

---

[11] The above statement does not hold, of course, when the private brander is the manufacturer of a product. As manufacturer and distributor combined, he carries on the promotional function.

sales of the chain's brand of corn flakes, priced at a lower figure than manufacturers' brands, were obtained in part because the Kellogg and the Postum companies widely advertised corn flakes to the public. Likewise, a large department store, which followed the policy of simulating under its own brands several highly advertised drug and cosmetic specialties, enjoyed a large volume of sales for these because it offered them as economical substitutes for merchandise for which demand was stimulated by manufacturers' advertising. Numerous other instances might be cited. The statements bring out the important fact already mentioned at the first of the chapter that private branders seldom develop and promote the demand for new products, but enter fields for which demand has been established.

The full significance of the fact that private branders have low advertising costs because manufacturers' advertising stimulates primary demand will be discussed in Chapter XXIV.[12] It suffices to point out here that private branders generally are imitators who ride on the coattails of manufacturers who build a demand for a product. This fact suggests that some part of manufacturers' advertising should be looked upon as a growth cost, i.e., a cost which contributes to the growth of an industry.

THE WASTES OF ADVERTISING

Attention is turned now from the question of the relative costs under different methods of distribution to another aspect of the size of advertising costs, namely, the wastes of advertising, which increase the burden of costs entering into price. These wastes are of two types: (1) those arising from the inefficient use of advertising and (2) those attributable to competition in advertising.

The numerous ineffective and wasteful practices which lead to high advertising costs and low profits for individual businesses, whatever marketing formulae they follow, were outlined in considerable detail in Chapter V and need not be restated. As there pointed out, these ineffective and wasteful uses have come primarily from the immaturity of management techniques and from the varying capacities of business executives in using advertising. They are similar to the wastes and

---

[12] Page 710 ff.

inefficiencies found in all fields of business administration. They have occurred in spite of efforts of businessmen to reduce them. Like inefficiency in other lines of endeavor, they represent from an economic standpoint a waste of effort and resources which is highly undesirable but nevertheless bound to occur in an imperfect world. Just as economies from improved techniques and controls in manufacturing are to be desired, so greater efficiency in marketing technique and control are much needed. Fortunately, the urge to reduce such inefficiencies has been present in our free economy and much progress has been made in recent years to improve advertising practice.

The waste arising from ineffective and imperfect use of advertising is to be clearly differentiated, however, from what is more frequently termed "advertising waste" by certain critics, namely, the competitive costs of persuasion, the costs of extensive advertising and other promotional procedure undertaken by competing sellers to induce consumers to buy their products at prices which cover such costs. They are the costs incurred by sellers in a free economy to consummate sale of new and of differentiated merchandise. Illustrations of competition in advertising and selling were found in the case of cigarettes, dentifrices, sheets, and numerous other products. Moreover, it was noted that whenever manufacturers' brands have been heavily advertised, retailers have had to exert considerable selling effort to establish a demand for their own brands. That advertising and selling costs have been high for some products is evident from the cost figures given in preceding pages. These costs have not only been high, but there is always the threat that increasing competition in advertising might make them higher. It is important, therefore, from a social standpoint, to determine whether there are forces operating to reduce these costs and how strong these forces may be. What is to prevent the danger that more and more economic effort will be directed toward advertising?

The Checks on High Costs Arising from Competition in Advertising

In the chapter on the place of advertising in economic theory it was pointed out that any checks to prevent increase or to bring reduction in the costs of advertising and aggressive selling must come from a competition in price. Such checks exist when opportunity is given to consumers to make free choice between products which bear a heavy.

advertising cost and products which are offered at a relatively low price because they involve low advertising and aggressive selling costs. The availability of such choices to consumers depends upon a free competition between firms using different marketing procedures and upon competitors with low costs reflecting them in their prices. Thereby consumers may weigh price differences against product differences and product reputation. A study of the checks against large advertising costs arising from competition in advertising is dealt with not in this chapter on cost but in later chapters on price and pricing practice.

Before this discussion of possible social wastes from competition in advertising is dropped, it is well to point out that such competitive wastes apply to many types of costs incurred by producers. There has been a tendency on the part of some writers to single out advertising and selling costs as being different from other costs because they are used instead of price to gain sales volume. Such a distinction is not sound. Advertising is not the only functional cost which a business management may keep at a high level in order to attract patronage. Just as sellers may sometimes increase advertising cost in order to influence patronage, so they may increase costs of materials, labor, and overhead in order to gain differentiation in product quality to attract patronage. Likewise they may offer efficient delivery service, easy credit, attractive stores, and other costly devices to gain a profitable volume of business. In all instances their prices must reflect these costs of operation.[13]

The layman can understand the character of the checks which must operate to keep down advertising costs from his observation of similar checks which have operated against other non-price forms of competition. Examples of these forms are competition in delivery, credit, repair, liberality in warranty, and liberality in acceptance of returned merchandise.

Determination of the amount consumers will pay for such services has rested to a large extent with the consumers. The amount which they have been willing to pay for such services in turn has determined in considerable degree the costs incurred for the services by sellers. In

---

[13] The costs of non-price competition have received considerable attention in recent years. Numerous students of marketing have commented upon the large expenditures devoted to service and selling functions. For example, the study of distribution costs of the Twentieth Century Fund devoted a chapter to the reasons for the high costs of marketing, and pointed out the costs incurred in elaborate services to consumers and those arising from competitive personal selling and advertising. P. W. Stewart and J. F. Dewhurst, *Does Distribution Cost Too Much?* (New York, The Twentieth Century Fund, 1939).

the quest for profit, sellers who have not resorted to competition in these services, have set prices accordingly. Buyers have had opportunity to exercise an option. A clear illustration of such option, which has been observed by most laymen, is found in the case of retail distribution.

Each retail firm has had to determine the services to offer to its clientele and the prices to charge. Since it could not ignore prices of competing stores offering services similar to its own, it has been under pressure to manage its functional services so efficiently that it could realize a profit at a level of prices forced upon it by competition. But a service store has had to consider not only competitors offering similar services, but competitors offering more limited services and lower prices. It has had to decide to what extent services given would offset the tug of lower prices offered by nonservice competitors.

In recent years most cities have had different types of stores offering different services, different degrees of elaboration in store decoration and fixtures, differences in merchandise selection, and differences in reputation. These competing institutions with varying costs have come to exist side by side because consumers have elected to give patronage on numerous bases and not solely on price. Undoubtedly the carelessness, the indifference, and the ignorance of consumers in their buying, let alone the sheer difficulty of buying wisely, have permitted many inefficient, high-cost retail institutions to exist. Stores at various service levels probably have not gained patronage in strict accordance with the values given in merchandise and service. Yet there has been a tendency toward continuation, at each service level, of those firms which have given the most in product and service values at that level. Competition between stores at the same level has been chiefly in efficiency in service. In turn, the competition from nonservice stores has been a further urge to efficiency in providing these services and a check against relying on them too heavily as a means of getting patronage.

The tendency toward price competition with elimination of high service costs in retailing is found in the evolution of retail grocery institutions. In the course of time competition brought the chain stores, with lower costs than held for the independent-wholesaler method of distribution as it existed some years ago. Independents and wholesalers have been forced to revise their methods to meet this chain competition. In turn, the chains have been subjected in recent years to the low-cost, price-featuring competition of the super-markets and have in some instances adopted their methods. Imperfect as retail competition has been, it has tended to bring to consumers the option of buying from service stores or stores incurring a minimum of service costs. These low-cost retailers, in turn, have provided a check against unrestrained competition in services by service retailers. High-cost retailing has not been eliminated, but consumer option of using it or turning to low-cost retailers has provided a check against undue rise of costs.

Existing checks against excessive advertising must operate through free competition similar in many respects to that which checks retail. service costs. The checks depend upon competition in marketing procedures and become effective through choices given to consumers to weigh price differences against product differences and product reputation. The extent to which such options have been made available to consumers and the extent to which consumers have used them are questions of fact which will be inquired into in the chapter on price and pricing practice. But before that subject is taken up, evidence regarding the effect of advertising upon production costs will be discussed in the next chapter.

CHAPTER XIX

THE EFFECT OF ADVERTISING ON PRODUCTION COSTS

THE theoretical effects of advertising upon the costs of producing goods were discussed at length in Chapter VI. As was there indicated, the costs of stimulating an increased volume of business through advertising and aggressive selling may be compensated for in whole or in part by lower unit costs of production which may occur with an increased scale of operations. This condition is referred to by economists as one of decreasing costs. On the other hand, if costs are constant, i.e., if lower costs do not occur with increased size, the unit costs of manufacturing a product are not affected by increased volume.[1] While the behavior of costs in the logic of theory is clearcut, factual data regarding them is meager. The present chapter presents such evidence as was obtainable regarding possible effects of advertising upon production costs.

How Production Costs May Be Affected by Increased Size of Operations

In a study of production costs, a basic distinction must be drawn between the concept of lower costs which come from increasing utilization of an existing plant up to plant capacity, in which case lower costs are attained as fixed overhead is spread over an increasing number of units, and the concept of lower costs which comes from attainment of an optimum size of plant, i.e., a plant which gives greatest efficiency and hence lowest costs. It is this latter concept to which attention is directed first. The question of use of advertising by a management to gain full utilization of its plants is discussed in the latter part of the chapter.

Theoretically, in all industries there is an optimum size of plant, although practically not much is known regarding the matter. It has been learned that in many industries lower costs may be attained up to a particular size, then decreasing costs no longer hold. Were decreasing costs to continue with increasing size of operations, then

---

[1] In view of the fact that conditions of increasing costs are not commonly met in manufacturing industries, discussion of this situation is omitted.

logically, one concern might be expected eventually to have all the business. But this does not happen. In fact, evidence indicates that after a certain point no further economies follow, or increasing size may even lead to increasing costs for a time. So long as the principle of decreasing costs is operating, the efficiencies from increased size may come from a number of directions. Larger size may permit better organization within a plant. Specialized operations which allow economical planning and low labor costs may be instituted. Special-purpose machinery, which may greatly reduce unit costs, may be established, and an efficient flow of production operations may be set up. For example, in the automobile industry special-purpose presses to stamp out fenders and bodies have brought low costs, yet such special-purpose machines were not feasible until a large-scale of operations was attained. Attending such specialized production of parts, low-cost devices for conveying materials to workers were installed, and efficient assembly lines established. Again, increased size may permit economies in buying materials, not only because specialists in purchasing may be employed, but also because large-scale buying from certain sources may enable those sources in turn to get economies in their production and distribution.

Optimum size of plant in any industry is not fixed, but is subject to change. For example, it may change materially from time to time with technological development, as has occurred in the case of cigars, where the perfection of a cigar-making machine changed the optimum size of factories from small to large. Or optimum size of plant operations may be reduced by demand changes, as in the case of shoes, for which fashion made standardization and large-scale, mass production methods beyond a certain point unprofitable. The quick shifts of fashion made short production runs rather than long production runs desirable.

Questions to Be Considered in Factual Study

In making a factual study of specific business enterprises to determine the effects of advertising upon their production costs, two questions have been kept in mind: To what extent has advertising contributed a volume of sales resulting in an increased size of plant? To what extent have production costs been affected by size of operations? In view of the fact that the preceding chapters have dealt at length with the first issue regarding the effect of advertising upon demand, discussion of this point has received only a brief consideration in this chapter. The method followed is that of pointing out merely whether a management has or has not used advertising as an element in a program to attain increased sales giving larger scale of operations and whether advertising apparently has had appreciable effect in attaining this end. Analysis is centered largely on the issue of whether increased size attained with advertising help has given lower production costs.

It would not suffice, however, merely to determine whether specific business enterprises have attained low production costs with the aid of advertising. It is desirable from a social standpoint to inquire further to see whether equally low production costs have been attained by competing enterprises which have made smaller use of advertising and aggressive selling. In the end it would be desirable to know how large are the combined marketing and production costs of companies competing under different methods of marketing, for consumers are interested in low total costs which may be reflected in low prices. Unfortunately, the data obtainable do not permit such precise and satisfactory cost comparisons, but the question of such combined costs is raised in the pages ahead in numerous instances, and conclusions are drawn as far as evidence permits.

Sources of Evidence Regarding Production Costs

Evidence regarding the effect of advertising and aggressive selling on production costs was sought from several sources. One source was historical treatises relating to the Industrial Revolution. A second source was governmental documents and other books giving cost data relating to the specific industries which are dealt with in the chapters on demand. A third source was primary evidence gained in field trips, in case data, and through correspondence with business concerns regarding their costs.

None of these sources gave evidence permitting a clear and certain measurement of the effect of advertising on costs of production. In the case of historical treatises, the relation of advertising and aggressive selling to the lowered production costs which have been attained by industry must be inferred. Advertising and production cost data relating to specific industries, whether drawn from primary or secondary sources, are not fully satisfactory because business firms do not keep their records in a form which fits the needs of such economic analysis. The cost data obtainable are usually incomplete and usually cover only a short time span. In addition, the number of variables which bear upon the size of costs are too many to permit a sure determination of causal relations between increased size of operations and the size of production costs.

Even though the shortcomings of the data were realized in advance of the investigation,[2] a determined effort was made to secure information and to trace the effects of advertising upon production costs. Although the effort has given answers that in considerable part are indeterminate, the evidence is presented because it serves to indicate a significant conclusion, namely, that lack of information does not justify many of the positive statements which are sometimes made regarding the effect of advertising upon production costs. It is necessary to fall back on the logic of theory to draw conclusions regarding the effect of advertising upon production costs. But some of the conclusions indicated by theoretical analysis cannot be fully verified by the evidence available.

Evidence from Historical Treatises

Before the costs of specific enterprises are studied it is desirable to get an historical perspective. The part played by advertising and other forms of aggressive selling historically in making possible the establishment of the factories with large-scale output and low costs has been dealt with and need not be repeated at length.[3] Many of the early factories found it necessary to seek demand beyond the environs of their plants. To gain needed sales they dispatched salesmen over wide territories. Only in this way could they get volume adequate to keep their factories running. Later they made increasing use of advertising. The increase of industrialization brought lower costs of production.

The studies of specific industries contributed several illustrations of how advertising has played an important part in helping managements to attain a volume of sales necessary for employment of low-cost methods of production in their factories. One of these instances was found in the history of cigarettes.[4] Until the early 1880's cigarettes were made by hand and consumption was small. By 1883, however, Duke had perfected the Bonsack cigarette-making machine, which had been

---

[2] The Harvard Graduate School of Business Administration has had a long experience in gathering expense data from business concerns through its Bureau of Business Research. This experience indicated that figures to be obtained from manufacturing concerns relating to production costs would be nonuniform and difficult to obtain.

[3] Chapter II, pp. 21 to 51. Also see Chapter XXIV, p. 682 ff.

[4] Chapter VIII, p. 221.

placed on the market seven years before. One machine was able to make 100,000 cigarettes a day, the output of 40 to 50 hand workers. It reduced the cost of manufacture from 80 cents to 30 cents a thousand. Duke had two machines in his factory and needed to stimulate sales in order to absorb the output. "The Bonsack machines turned out cigarettes more rapidly than they could be sold; the first year there was a large overproduction, and warehouses were piled with excess stock."[5] His factory had to be closed. To attain sales he cut the price from 10 cents to 5 cents a package of 10 cigarettes, a cut made possible in part by his reduced costs and in part by a reduction in the internal revenue tax on cigarettes from $1.75 to 50 cents a thousand. At the same time he launched a heavy selling and advertising program. Under the impetus of the price cut and selling program, Duke sold 30,000,000 cigarettes in the next nine months and shortly enlarged his factories.

Relation of Advertising to Low Production Costs of Cigarettes in Recent Years

The Duke incident illustrates specifically how advertising proved to be a helpful tool to a business management in building a volume of sales which permitted low-cost manufacturing operations. But it sheds no light upon the question of whether continued advertising since that early date has been essential to cigarette manufacturers to attain a volume sufficient to give low manufacturing costs. Nor does it tell whether adequate volume at low production costs might have been attained by a cigarette manufacturer since that time without advertising expenditure. No complete answers to these questions are possible. The very fact that competition in the cigarette industry has taken place so largely on an advertising basis has meant that few companies have ever tried to operate without advertising expenditure. Yet some facts regarding these questions are available in the history of the 10-cent cigarette. Here for the first time cigarette manufacturers gained appreciable volume of sales without large use of advertising. It will be recalled that these cheaper cigarettes were introduced with little or no advertising, but in view of the effect of advertising in influencing consumer valuations of cigarettes, they found it necessary to do some advertising. Yet their advertising expenditures have probably been only about one-fifth as much per unit as those devoted to the leading brands. Accordingly, it may be asked whether the relatively

5 J. W. Jenkins, *op. cit.*, pp. 69 and 71–72.

large unit advertising expenditures made for the leading brands are offset by decreased production costs, or whether the manufacturers of 10-cent cigarettes have attained low production costs with their smaller promotional expenditures.

Just how large a volume of production is necessary to give minimum manufacturing costs for cigarettes is not known, because evidence regarding the optimum size of cigarette manufacturing plants was not obtained in this research study. Discussions with a few executives indicated that relatively small, well-managed units in the industry probably have obtained manufacturing costs comparing favorably with those of larger producers. Supporting data for this opinion were not available, however. It may be noted that the processing costs of the relatively small manufacturers of 10-cent cigarettes were not a barrier to keep them from entering the market in the early 1930's. Estimates of costs and profits on 10-cent and 15-cent cigarettes prior to January, 1933, as presented in a memorandum by manufacturers of 10-cent cigarettes to a subcommittee of the Committee on Ways and Means of the House of Representatives of the 73d Congress, by three separate, "careful students of the industry, after investigation," were reported as shown in Table 116.

Since these estimates emanated from a biased source, they cannot be looked upon as indubitable evidence of the effect of size of plant

TABLE 116

ESTIMATES OF COSTS AND PROFITS OF TEN- AND FIFTEEN-CENT CIGARETTES, 1934
Estimate No. 1 (Cost per Package Basis)

	"10-CENTERS"*		"15-CENTERS"†	
	Per Package	Percentage of Net Selling Price	Per Package	Percentage of Net Selling Price
United States internal-revenue tax......	$0.0600	71.599	$0.0600	49.669
Tobacco‡............................	.0094	11.217	.0196	16.225
Manufacturing costs§.................	.0098	11.695	.0160	13.245
Advertising..........................	.0000	.000	.0086	7.119
Profit...............................	.0046	5.489	.0166	13.742
Total..........................	$0.0838	100.000	$0.1208	100.000

* Wholesale, $4.75, less 10 percent and 2 percent, $4.19 net; $0.0838 per package, net.
† Wholesale, $6.85, less 10 percent and 2 percent, $6.04 net; $0.1208 per package, net.
‡ 1,000 cigarettes contain from 36 to 40 ounces of tobacco. Prices of domestic tobacco vary from a few cents a pound up to 30 or 40 cents. Turkish tobacco costs about as much, plus transoceanic shipping charges and a customs duty of 35 cents per pound. Obviously, there cannot be much Turkish in the "10-centers." Turkish in the "15-centers" runs from 15 to 25 percent. About 30 percent of tobacco's weight is lost in stemming and redrying.
§ This item includes plant and labor costs, administration, other materials, income and property taxes, insurance, bonus, sales, and shipping expenses.

Estimate No. 2 (Cost per Package Basis)

	Leading Brands, Cents	Percentage to Manufacturers' Net Sales Price	10-Cent Brands, Cents	Percentage to Manufacturers Net Sales Price
Retail price.	15.00	....	10.00	....
Retailer's profit.	2.98	....	1.62	....
Manufacturers' gross return.	12.04	100.000	8.38	100.000
Less revenue tax.	6.00	49.834	6.00	71.600
Total.	6.04	....	2.38	....
Manufacturing cost.	.98	8.140	.98	11.694
Total.	5.06	....	1.40	....
Advertising expense.	1.20	9.967	.04	.477
Total.	3.86	....	1.36	....
Less cost of tobacco.	1.37	11.379	.87	10.382
Total.	2.49	....	.49	....
Executive bonus.	.19	1.578	None	None
Total.	2.30	....	.49	....
Federal income tax.	.30	2.491	.06	.716
Net profit.	2.00	16.611	.43	5.131

From the above it can be seen that the wholesale price differential of 3.66 cents per package in favor of 10-cent brands is made up by—

	Cents
Lower tobacco costs.	0.50
Elimination of advertising.	1.16
Reduction of profit.	1.57
Elimination of bonuses.	.19
Lower Federal income tax.	.24
Total.	3.66

Estimate No. 3 (Cost per 1,000 Basis)

	10-center	Percentage to Retail Sales Price	15-center	Percentage to Retail Sales Price
Government tax stamps.	$3.0000	60.000	$3.000	40.000
Tobacco (at 25 cents per pound on the factory floor for 10-center, 39 cents for 15-center).	.5700	11.400	.900	12.000
Dealers.	.8105	16.210	1.464	19.520
Factory costs (labor and materials).	.1850	3.700	.210	2.800
Delivery.	.0500	1.000	.050	.667
Selling and advertising.	.0900	1.800	.550	7.333
Depreciation and administration.	.0630	1.260	.100	1.333
Total.	4.7685	....	6.274	....
Profit.	.2315	4.630	1.226	16.347
Retail price.	$5.0000	100.000	$7.500	100.000

Source: Hearings before a Subcommittee of the Committee on Ways and Means, House of Representatives, Seventy-third Congress, Second Session, *Tobacco Taxes* (Washington, U. S. Government Printing Office, 1934), pp. 201–202.

upon cigarette manufacturing costs. Moreover, two of the estimates do not separate manufacturing costs from material or selling costs. But Estimate No. 2, in which manufacturing (processing) costs are segregated from material and selling costs, gives the same processing costs for the 10-cent brands as for leading brands. Although the evidence is subject to doubt, it substantiates opinions expressed by certain cigarette manufacturers. Accordingly, it seems safe to conclude that so far as processing costs alone are concerned, companies relatively small in the industry as it now exists have been able to attain the economies of large-scale manufacturing.

This tentative conclusion leads to a further one, namely, that the large unit expenditure for advertising by leading cigarette companies has not been wholly offset by decreased processing costs, which have attended their increasing size. In fact, the relatively small manufacturers of 10-cent cigarettes have evidently been large enough to get such efficiencies in manufacture as come from size and, consequently, with their small promotional outlay, have had lower combined processing and promotional costs than the leading brands have had. Thus, the large advertising expenditures of leading brands cannot be justified on the grounds of bringing low production costs. On the other hand, the fact that lower manufacturing costs do not come after a certain point, has prevented large companies from becoming larger because of decreasing manufacturing costs; relatively small companies have been able to compete with them on a manufacturing cost basis, and by their use of ‘price competition have gained an increasing share of the cigarette market.

The Relation of Advertising to Production Costs of Cigars

A further example of the relationship of advertising to the attainment of volume essential for low-cost production was noted in the cigar industry. In this case, the tendency to concentration because of decreasing costs is still present. In contrast to the cigarette industry, which had favored large-scale operations after the perfection of the cigarette-making machine in 1883, cigars continued to be made by hand, and their manufacture was little subject to the advantages of large-scale operations until the cigar-making machine was perfected in 1917. It was estimated in 1931 that one operator on a combined cigar-making and cellophane-wrapping machine could wrap, band, and pack three times the number of cigars banded by a hand operator.[6] The machine has offered savings estimated to be as much as $5.50 to $6.00 a thousand cigars, even after royalty and overhead were allowed.

The extent to which a few large, machine-equipped, low-cost factories have tended to replace the thousands of small, hand-making factories since 1917 was noted in Chapter IX. Whereas in 1912 there were over 20,000 manufacturers of cigars in the United States, by 1938 the number had been reduced to some 4,400, and among these, 28 companies accounted for over 60% of total output. As decreasing costs have become possible with large-scale operations, leading companies, such as Bayuk and the General Cigar Company, have concentrated their selling efforts on a limited number of brands and have accorded them substantial advertising support in order to gain uniformities of demand among consumers that would permit large-scale machine-equipped factories. Although substantiating evidence is not available, it is believed that the large-scale advertising programs of these leading companies, which have helped them to build sales volume, have been made possible in part by the low costs of machine-equipped factories. Thus it may be said that although advertising has played a part in building for these companies a demand which has permitted low-cost production, in turn low-cost production has given the companies gross margins which have permitted more extensive advertising than could be undertaken by their smaller competitors.

Here again the question may be raised as to how far increased size of operations need go in order to enable a cigar manufacturer to attain low manufacturing costs. Has the increased size of operations of the leading companies been attended by a continuing decrease in manufacturing costs, or have the companies long since attained the optimum size as far as production is concerned? Again, definitive answers to these questions cannot be given, but the evidence indicates that the sales volume of certain leading cigar companies probably has gone far beyond the quantity needed to permit lowest costs of manufacture.

The size of cigar factory required for lowest production costs is not known to the author. In 1931, however, it was stated in the *Monthly Labor Review* that "With four experienced operators working an average full-time week of 48 hours, one machine will produce

---

[6] "Technological Changes in the Cigar Industry and Their Effects on Labor," *Monthly Labor Review*, p. 15.

approximately 20,000 cigars per week, or, with an average of 50 full weeks per year, approximately 1,000,000 cigars per year."[7] Another government study, made by the National Recovery Administration in 1936, stated "More efficiency can be provided when machines are installed in batteries; the skilled labor necessary to run 10 machines costs but little more than the skilled labor cost to run one machine."[8] From these meager data one cannot be sure what size is necessary for lowest cost, but it would appear that a factory with a capacity of 10,000,000 cigars or more a year was essential for lowest costs at that time. Many companies had not reached this point; the largest companies had gone far beyond it. It is well to point out, however, that one cannot draw final conclusions regarding the optimum size of a concern from the size for an efficient factory, because there may be a different optimum from the standpoint of manufacturing costs and of marketing costs. Hence, a cigar company with several low-cost factories in different places in the country might gain economies in marketing not realized by a company with only volume enough to support one low-cost factory. Be that as it may, whether or not 10,000,000 cigars a year is the right figure for the most efficient factory is not highly important. The important consideration is that there is some such figure which marks the point at which increasing size is no longer encouraged by processing economies. The fact that there is such an optimum size from a manufacturing standpoint may be significant in helping to shape the character of future competition in the industry, in view of the fact that certain companies may find it feasible to gain this volume without as large costs of advertising and aggressive selling as those expended by other cigar manufacturers. Such a phenomenon occurred finally in the case of cigarettes. Whether this will happen in the cigar industry, only time can tell.

Relation of Advertising to Production Costs for Shoes

In contrast to the cigar industry, the optimum size of shoe factory in the United States has tended to stabilize at a relatively low level in the period following World War I, since fashion has become an increasingly important element in demand.[9] Long manufacturing runs

---

[7] *Ibid.*, p. 13.

[8] U. S. National Recovery Administration, *The Tobacco Study* (Washington, U. S. Government Printing Office, March, 1936), p. 178.

[9] Information and data upon which the generalizations regarding shoe production were based were the following:

of standardized shoes have not provided a profitable manufacturing policy. Large companies, such as International Shoe Company, are reported to have found it desirable to abandon efforts of product standardization and to divide plants in order to obtain efficient operation for the nonstaple product characteristic in most lines. In 1937, a factory capacity of 2,500 pairs a day was reported as being large for style lines. Furthermore, since much of the principal machinery for shoe manufacturing has been obtainable upon lease, with royalty depending upon the volume produced, overhead has not been so important a cost factor to a producer as would have been the case were machines purchased. Accordingly, small-scale operators have been able to attain manufacturing costs permitting competition with large-scale producers.

In contrast to cigarette and cigar manufacturers, who generally have found it necessary initially to advertise to an appreciable extent in order to attain sales volume permitting an optimum size of manufacturing plant, the shoe manufacturer from early days has not had to resort to advertising in substantial amounts to attain sufficient volume for low-cost manufacture. Manufacturers of shoes have several marketing alternatives which may be profitably followed. Some advertise; others find they can dispose of the output of their factories on an unbranded basis, under private brands, or even under their own trade-marks with little advertising directed to consumers. In these cases, aggressive personal selling and a limited amount of advertising to the trade are employed, but advertising is held at a low point. Yet these producers are able to attain the economies of large-scale production. Accordingly, in the case of shoes it is well to note the limitations to the generalization that mass selling methods must accompany mass production. In this case "mass selling" cannot be taken to mean strong reliance on advertising. As will become increasingly clear, sales volume large enough to give low manufacturing costs need not necessarily involve the extensive use of advertising, although advertising often is essential to build volume to support low manufacturing costs for types of products which are new to the market.

E. M. Hoover, *Location Theory and the Shoe and Leather Industries* (Cambridge, Harvard University Press, 1937).

U. S. National Recovery Administration, Division of Review, *Report of Survey Committee on the Operation of the Code for the Boot and Shoe Manufacturing Industry* (Washington, July 16, 1935).

Standard Statistics Company, Inc., *Standard Trade and Securities*, "Leather and Shoes, Basic Survey," Dec. 2, 1936. Case material, files of Harvard Business School.

Relation of Advertising to Production Costs for Sugar

In the sugar industry, manufacturing economies have attended large-scale production, but attainment of volume adequate for low cost operation has not necessarily required much use of advertising by a refiner. In 1937, 23 refineries supplied the cane sugar requirements of the United States. Once a refinery is established, the large, fixed investment places a premium on full utilization of plant. Overhead is a large factor in costs. Yet advertising has not been an essential to attainment of sales volume required for low manufacturing costs. Discussions with executives in the industry indicated that the relatively small, so-called "pocket-size" refineries have had low manufacturing costs. These small refiners, like the larger refiners, have needed full utilization of plant to get low manufacturing costs. This sales volume has generally been obtainable within a short radius of the refineries. As a rule, the small refiners have promoted sales not by advertising but by personal selling, by good delivery service, or by other forms of non-price competition, since refiners quickly have met competitors' prices. The refiners employing advertising generally have been the larger companies, which have offered full lines of sugar and have sought markets over wide areas in order to get the volume needed to keep their large plants operating.

Hence the conclusion regarding sugar is similar to that expressed concerning shoes. Advertising may be a helpful tool to certain managements to attain a volume necessary for low manufacturing costs. On the other hand, it is not used by other managements in order to attain an efficient scale of manufacture.

Relation of Advertising to Production Costs for Refrigerators

In contrast to the shoe and sugar industries, refrigerators represent a product for which advertising during the period studied clearly has played an important part for all manufacturers in bringing a scale of operations permitting low costs of production. During this period advertising played an essential part in building primary demand for the product as well as selective demand for specific manufacturers. Demand for refrigerators had to be established before the economies of large-scale production could be attained by any company. As demand grew, swiftly advancing technology contributed to a rapid decrease in costs. The industry was one in which specialized production methods favored large operations. Undoubtedly special-purpose machinery became an increasing contributor to low costs as demands of individual companies grew. That manufacturing costs were materially decreased as volume increased is indicated by the very large decrease in average retail prices per unit which occurred between 1920 and 1935, even after allowance is made for changing levels in the general price structure during this period. (Table 92, p. 397, and Table 124, p. 571.)

While advertising thus far has been used by all sellers to build a sales volume permitting low cost operation, it is apparent that certain companies, such as Sears, Roebuck and Company and its factory supplier, have attained this size with smaller advertising costs than have certain other companies.[10] Although it is not known for sure, it is doubtful whether the companies spending more heavily for aggressive selling have had offsetting economies in production coming from their larger scale of operations.

Summary from Industry Studies

From the preceding instances, which are illustrative of a large number of cases studied in less detail, it is apparent that individual manufacturers who have used advertising to help gain sales volume have thereby been able frequently to secure economies in manufacture which have offset in varying degree their advertising expenditures. In certain instances in which advertising played an important part in building primary demand, the economies gained through increased size of factory as industry demand grew were greater than the promotional expenditures made. Among the few cases used for illustration this condition probably held in the early days of the cigarette business. It appears clearly to have been present in the case of refrigerators. Once primary demand was well established, however, it was possible in both these industries for other producers to seek a volume of sales permitting low cost manufacture through use of the price appeal. Their low prices were made possible in part by their adoption of marketing approaches which incurred low advertising and promotional costs. These manufacturers were able to profit from the public acceptance of products which others had stimulated.

All industries, however, have not had to rely upon extensive stimulation of advertising to build a primary demand sufficient to support

---

10 The fact that private branders generally do not share the burden of building primary demand has already been mentioned and will be developed further.

low-cost manufacturing operations. The sugar industry and the shoe industry, for example, grew to large size without much influence upon primary demand from advertising. In keeping with this development, sugar and shoe concerns since early times have not necessarily had to advertise to an appreciable extent in order to secure adequate volume to allow low cost operations, and it cannot be claimed for advertising in these industries that advertising costs of individual companies have ever been offset by economies from increased size of operations. In the case of the cigar industry, consumer demand had been fully established and was on the decline before technological advance in the form of the cigar machine increased the optimum size of cigar plant. Subsequently, selective advertising here was used to help build volume for individual concerns permitting low cost operations. In turn, large machine-equipped factories, once established, gave margins which permitted the companies to advertise more heavily than could their higher cost competitors.

It is evident from all these instances that once an adequate consumer demand for a type of product has been established in the country, advertising by all units in the industry upon a scale used by leading advertisers is not necessary to an individual concern in order to attain a size permitting low manufacturing costs. In the demand chapters, it was shown that the large advertising expenditures of certain companies sometimes serve in the early stages of the marketing of a product to build a demand permitting large-scale, low-cost production by numerous concerns in the industry. This building of public acceptance for a product in turn has the evident effect in some instances of making the demand curve for the product elastic. Enough people come to want the product so that a price appeal is likely to attract many buyers. Consequently, when once elasticity has been established, it becomes possible for certain concerns to secure a substantial volume of sales by making a bid for business on a price basis without incurring much advertising and promotional expenditure. At this juncture, the advertising carried on by certain manufacturing companies helps to maintain demand for the industry, and from this advertising the nonadvertisers benefit. As previously stated, these nonadvertisers ride on the coat-tails of those who by their advertising stimulate demand. In short, the large advertising expenditures of certain companies probably help to build and to keep production costs for a whole industry low, but to what extent this is true cannot be measured. In turn, it may be said that the nonadvertisers serve to check competition in advertising by the advertising concerns.

To what degree advertising may be essential to attainment of optimum manufacturing size after primary demand has been established depends upon the character of competition which develops within the industry. In the sugar industry and in the shoe industry, from early days companies employing advertising have competed against others not using it and both have secured volume permitting low manufacturing costs. Even in the cigarette industry, where competition over a long period has been carried on largely through advertising, certain companies in the last decade have been able through use of price as the chief means of attracting sales to secure a size of operations giving low production costs. In the dynamic, expanding refrigerator industry, which has been subject to decreasing costs and in which advertising has played a very important part in building both primary and selective demand, the same phenomenon of certain sellers using relatively small amounts of advertising appeared also. As demand became established, these sellers found it feasible, through use of price appeal, made possible in part by low cost marketing methods, to attain a volume permitting low manufacturing costs.

From an economic standpoint it is significant in all these cases that the principle of decreasing manufacturing costs does not continue beyond a certain point, for if it did, low manufacturing costs would tend to bring monopoly. Instead, a certain size of plant permits low manufacturing costs, and companies may compete by different marketing methods and with different appeals to attain volume permitting this size of plant. Some companies may elect to use low price, made possible by low distribution costs, to attain this size; other companies may choose to compete in product differentiation, in services, in advertising, and in other non-price forms of competition.

EFFECTS OF ADVERTISING ON PRODUCTION COSTS AS INDICATED BY A COST STUDY AMONG MANUFACTURERS

In addition to the evidence drawn from historical treatises and from documents consulted in the industry studies, a project was included in this study for the purpose of collecting from manufacturers figures of sales and operating costs over a period of years. It was hoped that these data might throw light upon the effects of advertising upon the costs of producing and marketing merchandise. Certain significant data regarding marketing costs obtained from this study have already been presented. Unfortunately, however, the determined efforts thus made to get evidence which might permit definitive conclusions regarding advertising's effects upon production costs were not successful.[11] The chief difficulties were two: (1) Many manufacturers found it difficult to cooperate because their books were not kept in a form to permit furnishing the figures requested, or they did not cooperate because they were loath to disclose such intimate information. Consequently, the sample did not permit comparison of costs between manufacturers in the same industry operating under different conditions of manufacture and marketing. (2) The character of the data obtainable was such that clear-cut conclusions regarding the effects of advertising upon production costs were impossible. Nevertheless a description of the project and a presentation of the evidence is warranted, not only because the evidence is of some value, but because the experience indicates the lack of extensive and satisfactory factual data to substantiate theoretical reasoning regarding the effect of advertising upon production costs.

Description of Cost Study

Briefly, a large number of manufacturers were asked to provide for individual products or brands of merchandise the following detailed data covering a considerable number of years: net sales in dollars and units; production costs broken down into direct material, direct labor, and manufacturing overhead; marketing expenses broken down according to salesforce expense, advertising and sales promotion expenses, and other marketing expenses. The form employed is reproduced as Appendix VI.

In solicitation of cooperation for the cost study, personal visits were made to 25 companies, and questionnaires were mailed to 737 companies. Thirty-seven companies sent in figures, the number of years

---

[11] As stated on page 492, it was recognized that it would be very difficult to secure data from manufacturers which would permit definitive conclusions concerning the effects of advertising on production costs. The experience of the School in collecting such data gave first-hand knowledge of the difficulties to be met in the data obtainable. It was felt, however, that the study would be incomplete without effort to get such information. Accordingly, one of the major projects was that described in the paragraphs above. The experience indicates that an attempt to secure such cost data, even on a larger scale, would probably be unproductive, because of the limitations of the information obtainable and the difficulty of tracing a causal relationship when so many variables are present.

covered by each ranging from 3 to 12. About half the cooperating companies were unable to supply all the detailed data requested. Eight of the cooperators were solicited through personal interview, while 29 were among those solicited by mail. The figures provided by cooperators covered a wide variety of products, ranging from mint candy to heavy machinery, as indicated in Table 106, page 444. Both consumers' goods and producers' goods were included. Large, medium, and small advertisers reported. Among them were companies relying heavily upon advertising and companies placing small reliance upon it.

Uncertainty in the Data

Conclusions regarding causes of changes in size of operations and of changes in unit product costs could not be determined from the operating figures with certainty because so many variables were involved, and knowledge regarding them was incomplete. Resources did not permit the sending of investigators to all cooperators to get detailed and lengthy histories regarding sales operations, plant operations, product developments, and fluctuating material and labor costs. Even had full histories been obtainable, it is doubtful whether positive conclusions could have been reached regarding the effects of advertising upon unit costs of production. The difficulty of appraising the effects of so large a number of variables as were concomitant with changing sales volume and changing production costs probably would have nullified efforts to determine definitively the effects of advertising efforts on unit costs. Some evidence of sales methods which would help in interpretation of operating figures was obtained from questions on the schedule form. In addition, personal interviews with eight of the concerns gave some additional information regarding their operations. But even here the information obtainable was incomplete and the effects of advertising on size of operations and the effect of operations on unit manufacturing costs could not be traced with certainty. The difficulties met in analyzing the data will be pointed out in connection with individual cases.

Among the 37 companies which supplied figures, only seven showed a growth in volume of sales great enough to involve material increase in size of their manufacturing operations. Since this analysis seeks to determine effect of increasing size on production costs, consideration in this chapter is limited to these seven companies. All used advertising. The exact contribution of advertising to growth of sales volume was not determinable from the data but the analysis proceeded on the assumption that advertising played an integral part in the attainment of their sales volume. To support this assumption was the fact that the managements had employed advertising because they considered it an essential and desirable element in the conduct of their enterprises. In the case of all seven companies there was clear reason to assign to advertising an important part in the attainment of their sales volume, because it was either the sole or a predominant selling method. Even so, it must be recognized that it would be an error to ascribe attainment of or changes in the sales volume to advertising alone. For example, one company which was a leader in its field made heavy use of advertising, but during part of the period covered by data it adopted a policy of greatly reducing its price and consequently its profit margins in order to maintain its leadership in the field. Price reduction was a large factor in bringing the increased volume which followed.

It must be recognized further that this study comprehended for each manufacturer an analysis of data for only a given program of marketing. It did not throw light on whether a size of operations giving low production costs might have been attained had other marketing methods been employed.

Evidence Regarding Specific Companies

Company No. 10, Table 106, produced an electrical appliance for which advertising was a major element in the marketing program. Of total marketing costs of 12.5% of sales, advertising and promotion accounted for 7.8%. For the first year of the 11-year period covered by the data, sales amounted to about 20,000 units. Toward the end of the period the number of units sold had increased 10-fold. During the period the unit costs had decreased in approximately the scale indicated below:

Year	Direct Material	Direct Labor	Manufac-turing Overhead	Total Production Costs
1926	$99.00	$20.20	$24.60	$143.80
1936	54.60	12.90	19.15	85.55

(Actual figures have been multiplied by a constant to protect against disclosure of identity.)

This illustrates clearly the difficulties met in any attempt to analyze the effect of size of operations upon costs of a company operating in a dynamic market. When so many variables operate, the effect of individual items cannot be definitely measured. Certainly much more detailed and elaborate analysis was needed than was possible with the information available in this study. The full explanation of the 40% decrease in product costs over this 10-year period is not ascertainable from the figures given above. In the first place, the appliance was subject to constant change and improvement in design. The average unit at the end of the period was believed to be better than at the beginning of the period, and consequently the reduction in cost was really more than 40%. In the next place, the sharp decrease in material costs was attributable in part to the falling price structure for raw materials, and in part to lowered costs of fabricated parts arising from improved technology. Whether these technological developments would have come without increase in size of operations is not known for certain, but it is assumed that many of them were encouraged by increased size of operations. Moreover, whether material costs were less as a result of large purchases called for by the scale of operations of the company was not determinable. In the next place, decreased labor costs per unit were attributable not only to lower wage rates which came as depression set in but also to reduced labor per unit coming from improved machines and manufacturing methods, which may or may not have been available with a smaller scale of operations. To what extent increased size of plant made possible an improved division of labor or more efficient production methods is not known. Finally, decrease in the overhead cost raised unanswered questions. The lower overhead may have come in part from the reduction in the prices of the variable costs included in overhead; it may have been affected in part by the ratio between fixed overhead and number of units produced for the last year as compared with this ratio for the first year. In short, it was impossible to tell whether the reduction in overhead was influenced by increase in the size of plant.

In the end, only a rough judgment could be made. In this instance a very material decrease in production costs over an 11-year period appears to have been far greater than would have occurred had not the increasing volume permitted and encouraged operating efficiencies. The company was operating in a field where opportunities to use specialized processes with increasing volume were great. Accordingly, in this instance it appears sound to conclude that reductions in manufacturing cost were far greater than would have occurred without the increase in size gained with the help of advertising.

Company No. 7, which also produced an electrical appliance, but of another type, had material reduction in unit costs over a nine-year period. For this product demand was stimulated largely by the use of advertising during the period covered by the data. Advertising expenditures accounted for more than half of marketing costs and were twice as large as personal selling costs. During the first year, less than 10,000 units were sold, but toward the end of the period covered by the data the number of units sold averaged about 200,000 a year. The relation between the elements of production cost for the first and last years of the period was as follows:

YEAR	DIRECT MATERIALS	DIRECT LABOR	MANUFAC-TURING OVERHEAD	TOTAL PRODUCTION COSTS
1927	$84.80	$27.76	$41.62	$154.18
1935	38.55	11.11	15.68	65.35

(Actual figures have been multiplied by a constant to protect against disclosure of identity.)

The usual difficulties were met in determining to what extent the increased volume, attained largely through advertising, had contributed to the marked reduction in unit costs. Again it was necessary to resort to a rough judgment; and as in the previous case, it was concluded that the very marked reduction in costs over the period was greater than would have occurred had the operations of the company continued on the scale which existed at the beginning of the period.

Company No. 8 used much advertising to build demand for an entirely new type of drug sundry. The author concurs with the management of the company in its conclusion that advertising was an important factor in building not only selective but primary consumer demand for this product. During a considerable part of the 12-year period covered by the data the item was clearly in the pioneering stage when public acceptance was being built for it. In this period sales approximately doubled in dollar value, but because of numerous price reductions this doubling of dollar sales represents a six-fold increase in the number of units manufactured.

Product costs at the end of the period were only approximately 40% of what they were at the beginning of the period, but unfortunately the composition of these costs was not obtainable. Accordingly, the extent to which the reduction in costs might have been the result of lower material and labor prices, of technological improvements in manufacturing methods, of changes in design of product, and of lower

costs resulting from lower overhead per unit is not known. In view
of the character of manufacture employed for the product, it was concluded that reduced production costs were probably attributable in
great degree to the lowered price structure for material and labor.
Some economies had probably come from technological development,
but on the whole it appeared that size of operations in itself did not
offer great opportunity for reduction of product costs. Apart from
the figures, knowledge regarding the industry led to the opinion that
the large volume of demand built by this company presumably did not
enable it to manufacture at appreciably lower costs than were obtained
by smaller competitors.

Company No. 24 produced a cosmetic product for which, during the
period covered, a reduction in price and increased advertising brought
a marked uptrend in the number of units sold. Four years after the
new prices and advertising policies were embarked upon, sales in units
had increased almost 400%, an increase presumably requiring manufacturing additions. The changes in production costs during this period
were as follows:

YEAR	DIRECT MATERIAL	DIRECT LABOR	MANUFAC-TURING OVERHEAD	TOTAL PRODUCTION COSTS
1935	$0.177	$0.029	$0.035	$0.241
1939	0.14	0.035	0.022	0.197

Again, it is not clear to what extent the lower costs of the later year
were attributable to the increased size of operations. The major part
of the reduction came in material costs and apparently was not a result
of increased capacity attributable to advertising. This probably was
not a situation in which increased size of plant gave much opportunity
for cost reduction.

Cosmetic manufacturer No. 29, who relied primarily upon advertising as a method of gaining sales, was able in the 10-year period
covered by the data to double the number of units sold. During this
period production costs per unit varied thus:

YEAR	DIRECT MATERIAL	DIRECT LABOR	MANUFAC-TURING OVERHEAD	TOTAL PRODUCTION COSTS
1926	$0.62	$0.05	$0.06	$0.73
1935	0.42	0.03	0.05	0.50

Total production costs decreased materially as volume increased, but it is not known how much the fall was the result of increased efficiency gained through increased size of operations. Again it was concluded that in view of the character of the manufacturing processes involved, increased size of plant did not contribute largely to reduced manufacturing costs.

Proprietary remedy manufacturer No. 28 increased unit sales almost 450% in a seven-year period largely through advertising efforts. During this period, production costs per unit (case) varied as follows:

Year	Direct Material	Direct Labor	Manufac- turing Overhead	Total Production Costs
First year.......	$1.05	$0.20	$0.25	$1.50
Seventh year....	0.96	0.10	0.13	1.19

In this instance the increase in sales occurred during a period when prices of labor and materials were relatively stable. The data indicate that the management apparently was able to effect some economies as a result of the increased size.

Company No. 12 manufactured a household appliance whose demand in general was expanding. Over the eight-year period covered by the data, sales of this company increased almost three-fold. In obtaining this increase, a substantial program of advertising was employed. For the years 1930 and 1937, unit production costs were as follows:

Year	Direct Material	Direct Labor	Manufac- turing Overhead	Total Production Costs
1930	$2.46	$0.49	$1.09	$4.04
1937	.99	.34	.51	1.83

In this instance, there was a marked decrease in costs over the period. Unit costs in 1937 were only 45% of those in 1930; however, the product was not constant. And, even if constancy is assumed, to what extent the decrease was due to increased plant size is not determinable, because of the fluctuations of the many variables entering into costs. But since the manufacturing operations were of a type which might be expected to bring decreasing costs, it was concluded that the increased capacity gained with the aid of advertising contributed to the lower unit costs.

Summary of Findings from the Cost Study

The analysis of specific operating figures of the above seven companies did not prove highly fruitful in giving positive conclusions regarding the extent to which advertising enabled them to attain lower unit costs. Only rough judgments could be drawn. In three instances the increased plant capacity obtained with advertising aid was not apparently in itself the cause of the lower production costs. In four instances the lower costs attained might well have been attributable in appreciable part to the larger manufacturing operations made possible in part through advertising and aggressive selling methods.

Probably the chief significance of this cost study rests in the fact that it serves to show the limitations of manufacturing cost and sales data as a basis for measuring the effects of advertising upon production costs.

THE RELATION OF ADVERTISING TO OVERHEAD COSTS

Now that the effect of advertising upon production costs through its effect upon the size of plant operations has been considered, attention is turned to the question of the effect of advertising upon the overhead costs of manufacturers. Under this heading, three different analyses are made. First, the issue as to whether advertising serves to give stability of operations to individual concerns is explored, for in so far as a business can get stable operations at a high level it can have low overhead costs. Secondly, the issue as to whether advertising is helpful to business concerns in overcoming seasonal demand and thereby in attaining a utilization of plant giving low overhead costs is discussed. Third, the question of the importance of overhead as an element in manufacturers' costs, as indicated by data from the cost study among manufacturers, is presented.

Advertising as a Stabilizer of Demand for Individual Concerns

In value theory, the question of the stability of the individual firm or of its costs is not a matter of moment in price determination. It is assumed that individual firms appear and disappear. Those whose costs permit them to meet the normal price find a demand and persist; the less efficient ones perish. Moreover, full employment in the economy is assumed.

In the real world, however, stability of demand to the individual firm is a matter of first importance; it affects costs and profits, and may even determine the life of an organization. Accordingly, the businessman will look with favor upon any means which promise stability of demand for his products, particularly if the demand is at prices which more than cover costs. Previous analyses have shown that businessmen generally cherish the constancy of demand that attends a strong brand preference for their products among ultimate users.

There are conflicting claims among writers as to whether advertising enables a concern to attain stability of operations. Since advertising has been one of the chief tools used by businessmen to build brand preferences and to establish goodwill, which brings repeat purchases, advertising accordingly has been praised by them as an important vehicle to make possible stability of operation. They claim further that this stability has permitted them to give steadiness of employment and to attain low operating costs through constant utilization of plant. While this claim for advertising has been presented by businessmen, some writers conversely have criticized advertising as being a cause of instability to the operations of individual firms. Demand, they say, has tended to shift among brands in accordance with the skill or good fortune with which advertising efforts have been directed by competitors.

Relative Stability of Advertising and Nonadvertising Manufacturers

Here, as is so often the case, apparently opposing claims both contain an element of truth. In particular industries where brands are important in guiding demand, an organization which has established a consumers' preference for its brands generally is in a more stable position than is one in the same industry which has not done so. Manufacturers generally prefer to be in the position where an insistent consumer demand requires tradesmen to stock and sell their products at whatever retail prices are required by the manufacturer's selling price rather than to be subject to the price bidding of retailers for unbranded or private-brand merchandise. The manufacturer of unbranded merchandise or of private brands may find himself in an uncertain position owing to the fact that his sales are made to a relatively small number of large buyers, the loss of any one of whom would materially affect his operations. He is not subject to the conditions of pure competition as assumed in economic theory. In his market there are not a large number of buyers and of sellers, each indifferent as to whether patronage is with particular individuals. The number of customers available to a manufacturer for private brands or unbranded merchandise may be relatively few, and individual contracts may be large. The business of a particular buyer can be very important. The buyer accordingly may be in a position to bring heavy pressure to drive price down. The commanding position of the large buyers, for example, led a limited number of manufacturers[12] to support legislation such as the Robinson-Patman Act, designed to reduce the power of these large-scale buyers.

Again, case evidence indicates that in many trades the unknown, unadvertised manufacturer's brand often has had a relatively hard time in securing and holding sales volume, as contrasted with the advertised item. Often the nonadvertising firm has not enjoyed a stability as great as that of the advertising firm with well-established brand. For example, it was noted that in the shoe business individual firms frequently employed consumer advertising in the belief that it offered stability. This goal also was back of such sugar advertising as was carried on. In the sugar industry, overhead costs are particularly high, and constant utilization of plant is greatly to be desired. In other industries studied, certain managements used advertising because they felt it offered greater security of sales volume. In short, the relative security of advertising firms enjoying well-established brand preferences, as compared with nonadvertisers not enjoying such brand preferences, has provided the basis for the praise bestowed upon advertising as a stabilizer of business for the individual firm.

Lack of Assurance of Stability from Advertising Usage

Examination of industries in which competition has been carried on largely through advertising indicates, however, that advertising does not necessarily assure stability of demand to the individual firm. This fact was brought out clearly in the case of cigarettes and dentifrices, and the same condition holds true for a large number of commodities for which advertising is an important sales tool, such as soap, cosmetics, and food specialties. It was concluded in the study of denti-

---

[12] The groups most interested in bringing about passage of the Robinson-Patman Act were certain associations of wholesalers and retailers, notably in the drug field. Only a relatively small number of manufacturers, largely in the drug field, actively supported the bill.

frices and cigarettes that advertising has been practically essential to any firm aspiring to have a considerable volume of demand in those fields. Hence, advertising has been deemed a requisite for stability by most firms operating in those fields under the system of competition that has evolved, although some small organizations have carried on without advertising. It must be recognized, however, that the advertising has not given assurance of constant sales to those concerns using it. Competition has been carried out very largely through advertising. Prices have tended to be relatively steady at levels which have provided margins adequate to cover advertising costs. Under such conditions the relative standing in their industries of individual companies has turned in considerable degree upon the good fortune or the skill with which they have been able to devise their advertising programs.

In addition to the evidence of the shifting of demand among cigarette and dentifrice manufacturers attributable to advertising, which was presented in the chapters on demand, the author had opportunity to note the relative brand standings of manufacturers of certain grocery specialties over a period of years, as given in the reports of the A. C. Nielsen Company. Study of these reports led to the same conclusion, namely, that where competition has been carried on to a large degree through advertising, shifts in demand have been attributable in part [13] to the varying effectiveness of the advertising and promotional programs of competing companies. In short, under conditions of strong competition in advertising, advertising in itself has not assured stability of demand to these concerns. To attain stability here a seller has to be not merely an advertiser but a relatively skillful advertiser and a good merchandiser at all times. The tool employed by a concern to gain stability may, in turn, be used by others to upset that stability.

To sum up, it may be stated that advertising has been used by many businesses to help gain the relative stability of demand which may come when a firm builds strong brand preference. As compared with concerns not having such goodwill and whose customers are few, these advertisers often have a relatively high stability of operations. On the other hand, in an industry in which competition is carried on largely in advertising, stability in demand of the advertiser depends not merely upon his being an advertiser, but upon his being an effective advertiser.

---

[13] As pointed out in previous chapters, the forces affecting relative sales volume of competing concerns are many. Here only advertising is under consideration.

Advertising as a Means of Overcoming Seasonal Fluctuations

Discussion is turned now to the second issue relating to the problem of advertising's effect on overhead costs, namely, the issue as to whether advertising helps business to overcome seasonal demand and thereby affects overhead costs through bringing more complete utilization of plants and organizations.

Seasonal fluctuation in demand, which usually affects industries, is clearly an undesirable thing not only for the individual company but also for society. To the individual company, seasonal demand for its merchandise means partially used factories, unemployed workers during off seasons, and inefficient use of permanent personnel. Consequently, costs are higher than those resulting from better plant utilization, and probably there is an adverse effect on profits. From the standpoint of the total economy, incomplete use of productive resources of individual businesses and industries, as outlined above, results in smaller total output to be consumed than could be produced with full utilization.

Advertising has proved a useful tool in some instances to help correct seasonal demand and to overcome seasonal production. It has been employed to promote new uses of products in off seasons, to stimulate sale of products adapted to off-season uses, and to announce and help carry through various management programs designed to overcome seasonal demand. Such programs, employing advertising, have included among others the promotion of complementary products whose demand might smooth out the sales curve, the stimulation of sales organizations and dealers to increased selling effort, the changing of seasons for introduction of new models, and the reduction of prices in off seasons to stimulate demand.

Conditions Governing Seasonal Consumption

The seasonal demand for many products is determined to considerable degree by temperature and weather conditions that govern consumer habits of product use. Overcoats are worn in the winter; skis are in demand only when there is snow; cold drinks are increasingly desired in hot weather; bathing suits are worn in the swimming season.

The seasonal consumption of some products may be determined to a marked degree by consumer habits and attitudes for which there may not be such well-established physical and physiological reasons. For example, the timing of new models of such products as automobiles, radios, refrigerators, and so on is a trade custom which may be changed with a consequent effect upon the sales and production curve, since introduction of new models is a stimulant to sales. Again, some foods have, without apparent reason, become associated with certain seasons. For example, turkey has long been the traditional dish for Thanksgiving and Christmas, and consumption has been limited primarily to the short holiday season,[14] although turkey should taste as good at other times. Walnuts have been a fall and holiday item, though suited for year-round use. Whether or not desirable from the standpoint of child psychology, 80% of toy sales have been concentrated in the two months of November and December.[15] Other products with many potential uses have been used primarily for one purpose during a particular season. For instance, lemons formerly were used mostly for cold drinks, in spite of their many possible year-round uses for cooking, salads, and as a cosmetic.

Conditions Governing Reduction of Seasonal Demand

In view of the undesirability of seasonal sales and consequent seasonal production, sellers have tried various means to equalize their production and sales. Successful plans have been the ones devised to fit the particular needs of specific products and companies. Whether advertising has been a helpful tool to a business management has turned generally on the question of whether consumer behavior could be altered at not too great a cost.

For companies with products whose seasonal demand has arisen from basic physical determinants or such deep-seated tradition that consumers' habits could not be readily altered, the most successful method to assure an even sales volume has been to add complementary products having a seasonal sales curve inverse to that of established product lines rather than to attempt to correct the seasonal of either product. Examples of this method are numerous. Manufacturers of radios, such as Crosley and Grigsby-Grunow, took on the manufacture and sale of refrigerators to complement production of their receiving sets. The Philco Radio and Television Company in

---

[14] F. G. Chambers, "Expanding the Turkey Season," *Harvard Business Review*, Autumn, 1939, p. 107.

[15] "Beating the Seasonal Slump," *Printers' Ink Monthly*, April, 1935, p. 76.

1939 undertook the distribution of air conditioners for the home. The A. C. Gilbert Company, manufacturer of toys, in 1914 started to manufacture and market electric fans and other electrical appliances as an offset to the seasonal demand for toys. In such instances the basic correction of seasonal has rested in the new products chosen, and advertising and aggressive selling have merely been the usual tools of management to secure demand for the new lines.

Cases in which advertising may be given greater credit for overcoming the undesirable seasonal demand are those in which it has been employed to stimulate off-season consumption for a product or for some adaptation designed to make the product suitable for off-season use. Whether advertising can profitably be used in this way depends upon whether consumers respond readily to suggested new uses or to the appeals presented. Examples of both successful and unsuccessful attempts to change the sales curve are to be found. Among cases in which there seems to have been a certain degree of success are the following, although the data on which to judge advertising's full contribution are lacking in most instances.

The California Fruit Growers Exchange was experiencing insufficient demand for its lemons in the winter season because they were used primarily for a hot-weather drink. In order to even out demand, this association has carried on over the years a consistent program to build up other uses to equal the summer demand. Recipes for cooking, such as lemon pie and salad dressing, and suggestions for use as a garnish with sea foods and with tea have been advertised in the off season. Use of lemons for cosmetic purposes, as a hair rinse and as a skin beautifier, also has been stressed, as well as hot lemonade as a remedy for colds. Furthermore, the 1938 Annual Report of the association (p. 24) stated, "Over a period of several years, successively more inclusive tests have been made of the sales effectiveness of a new lemon use: i.e., with soda in water daily for its tonic and laxative value. This use was chosen as it required one lemon per user per day the year around." Nearly half of 1939 lemon advertising was devoted to this appeal.[16]

Variation in recipes featured in different seasons has been used by other food manufacturers to build new habits of use and to help overcome seasonal demand. This practice has been followed, for example, by the California Fruit Growers Exchange not only for

---

[16] Annual reports of the California Fruit Growers Exchange.

lemons but also for oranges; it has been done by the salmon packers, by the California Walnut Growers Association, and by the Cranberry Canners, Inc.[17]

Certain cosmetics, such as Hind's Honey and Almond Cream[18] and Frostilla, which at one time had highly seasonal demand because they were used primarily for chapped hands, were able to overcome seasonal demand to some extent when they were featured as preventives and cures for sunburn.

In 1932 and 1933, Canada Dry Ginger Ale, Inc., found that it was able to create a considerable demand for its ginger ale during winter months whereas previously ginger ale had suffered from an extreme seasonal decline during those months.[19] Its new factories in the United States were, accordingly, more effectively used than had been anticipated.

A somewhat different situation is involved in those instances in which manufacturers have introduced models or designs adapted to off-season use. For example, in 1933 the seasonal sale of radios was corrected to some extent by the introduction of automobile radios, whose seasonal demand tended to be inverse to that of home radios.[20] To accomplish the same result, the R.C.A. Victor Company introduced a portable radio phonograph to meet summer needs.[21] With similar objective, the Kenwood Blanket Company in the spring and summer of 1932 carried on an advertising program to stimulate sales for a new light-weight blanket designed for warm weather needs.[22]

When the strategy for overcoming seasonal slump has involved reduced prices during off seasons or a change in date of introduction of new models, advertising has been an important vehicle for carrying through the policy. For example, in 1935, when the automobile industry agreed to change the date of introduction of new models from January to early fall, the new model publicity ordinarily released in January was moved ahead to the fall months. Again, the

---

[17] N. H. Borden, *Problems in Advertising* (3d ed., New York, McGraw-Hill Book Co., 1937), cases of Associated Salmon Packers and California Walnut Growers Association, pp. 3 and 535.

[18] Case files of Harvard Business School.

[19] N. H. Borden, *Problems in Advertising* (3d ed.), case of Canada Dry Ginger Ale, Inc., p. 358.

[20] A. P. Hirose, "Radio Beats Seasonal Slumps with Auto Sets," *Printers' Ink*, January 4, 1934, p. 33.

[21] "Beating the Seasonal Slump," *Printers' Ink Monthly*, April, 1935, p. 78.

[22] Ralph Crothers, "New Products for Summer Sales," *Printers' Ink*, June 23, 1932, p. 10.

Grigsby-Grunow Company sought, not very successfully, to reduce seasonal demand for its radio receiving sets in 1929 not only by introducing its new models in the summer instead of in the fall, but also by offering a temporary price reduction to help stimulate summer demand. In accordance with this plan, extensive advertising was scheduled for the summer months and the temporary price reduction was publicized.

Limitations upon Overcoming Seasonal

Numerous other strategies involving the use of advertising to overcome seasonal have been employed, which need not be recounted. As indicated above, the efforts have not met with uniform success, and the contribution of advertising to overcoming seasonal should not be overestimated. Managements seek to secure profitable sales results from their advertising. Accordingly, when featured new uses have not been readily adopted or programs such as that tried by Grigsby-Grunow have not met with favorable sales results, the advertising efforts have usually been dropped. For example, the Grigsby-Grunow Company's plan to shift sales of radio sets to the summer was not successful. Subsequently, to overcome seasonal production, the company undertook the production and sale of refrigerators. Again, the Pines Winterfront Company, which sold winterfronts for automobiles through the trade in the days before new cars were equipped with such devices, attempted in 1926 to lengthen the season of sales and use for its product, but did not meet with success in its efforts.[23] Fixed traditions and habits are often difficult to change, and consequently manufacturers find it better to conform to established buying and use habits for a product rather than to attempt to change them. On the other hand, in cases such as those mentioned above, where consumers' habits have been alterable without great effort or where changed products or new products have been accepted and have thus afforded means for leveling demand and production schedules, advertising has been a helpful economic tool in overcoming seasonal demand.

---

[23] N. H. Borden, *Problems in Advertising* (2d ed.), case of Pines Winterfront Company, p. 468.

The Relative Importance of Overhead Costs as an Element of Manufacturers' Total Costs

In the pages just preceding, evidence relating to advertising's effect upon stability of manufacturing operations and hence upon the degree of utilization of plants has been given.[24] Just how important are these overhead costs as an element in the total costs of manufacturers?

There has been a tendency at times to overemphasize the part of overhead as an element of product costs and, consequently, to overemphasize the importance of advertising in reducing overhead charges. Loose statements have been made to the effect that advertising has had a marked effect in keeping down production costs by enabling managements fully to utilize their plants. As already noted, advertising does not in itself assure stable sales volume for a concern. In addition, for many products manufacturing overhead costs represent so small a part of total product price that such fluctuations as occur in utilization of plant capacity do not materially affect total product costs. Accordingly, in such instances, these fluctuations may not have much effect upon price, in so far as a manufacturer is guided by manufacturing costs in his pricing. It must be kept in mind that the items which manufacturers classify as overhead for their accounting records are not uniform between manufacturers nor are they uniform in the same concern from time to time. Costs which at one time may be included in overhead accounts may later be charged directly to products and not indirectly through allocation of overhead. Consequently, accounting records of overhead costs must be studied with this lack of uniformity in mind. Ordinarily all concerns classify as overhead certain fixed costs which continue irrespective of the extent of operations, such as the charge for interest on plant and the salaries of permanent supervising organization. In addition, however, there are many expenditures classified as overhead that change as the volume of business varies, such as nonpermanent supervisory personnel, maintenance, indirect labor and supplies, and so on. Because these variable costs can be reduced when demand falls away, a management is able to reduce its overhead to a considerable degree in times of low demand. When the variable parts of overhead in a plant are relatively a large part of the whole and the fixed charges are not large, the

---

[24] The question of lack of full utilization of plant because of cyclical fluctuation and advertising's relation thereto are discussed in Chapter XXV.

overhead charges in years of reduced production may not be appreciably higher than in years of large production.

The cost data secured from manufacturers provided an opportunity to observe the effects of fluctuations in sales upon their unit manufacturing overhead costs. For many of these products the fixed elements of overhead costs were such that even large reduction in the volume of sales did not bring material increase in unit overhead costs. In a few cases where the fixed elements were relatively large, reduced volume had an appreciable effect upon unit costs, of course. There was, however, no positive correlation between the degree to which this group of manufacturers made use of advertising and aggressive selling and the pressure under which they operated to maintain volume of sales because of size of fixed overhead costs. In fact, the percentage of net sales devoted to advertising and marketing tended to be largest for products which had relatively small manufacturing overhead costs.

Eighteen companies gave information in enough detail to permit

TABLE 117

COMPARISON OF PRODUCTION COSTS AND ADVERTISING AND MARKETING COSTS OF CERTAIN MANUFACTURERS AS A PERCENTAGE OF NET SALES RANKED BY ASCENDING SIZE OF MANUFACTURING OVERHEAD EXPENSE, 1937

| Co. No. | Product | PRODUCTION COSTS | | | | MARKETING COSTS | | | |
		(1) Direct Materials	(2) Direct Labor	(3) Manufacturing Overhead	(4) Total Production Costs	(5) Advertising and Sales Promotion	(6) Sales force	(7) Other	(8) Total Marketing Costs
31	Proprietary Remedy....	9.6%	3.1%	*	12.7%	55.4%	0.0%	0.0%	55.4%
30	Toilet Article..........	21.62	0.2	0.9	22.6	43.5	0.0	6.7	50.2
26	Grocery Specialty......	28.5	0.3	1.4	30.4	23.9	7.3	7.6	38.9
20	Confection.............	18.8	5.8	2.0	26.6	16.5	9.9	1.9	28.3
28	Proprietary Remedy....	12.4	1.4	2.7	16.6	33.6	6.9	3.9	44.4
29	Cosmetic..............	30.0	2.5	3.6	36.1	27.4	13.7	4.9	46.0
18	Grocery Specialty......	51.9		6.5	58.4	6.9	19.1		26.0
24	Cosmetic..............	35.2	7.1	7.1	49.4	28.5	7.6	....	36.1
27	Clothing Item.........	36.0	11.7	7.8	55.4	13.5	12.8	15.7	41.9
25	Fountain Pens.........	30.6	8.3	11.5	50.4	15.9	10.0	11.1	37.0
16	Jewelry Product........	36.7	8.8	11.6	57.1	8.0	6.8	9.0	23.8
13	Tires.................	55.3	8.0	12.6	75.8	2.9	7.0	10.2	20.1
0	Electrical Appliance....	38.4	9.1	13.7	61.2	7.8	4.7		12.5
19	Hosiery...............	33.2	34.4	15.2	82.8	2.2	6.1	3.9	12.1
7	Electrical Appliance....	37.8	10.9	15.4	64.1	6.9	3.4	0.5	10.8
1	Watches...............	38.1	18.9	17.3	74.2	5.1	2.6		7.7
19	Rubber Footwear.......	35.0	19.3	17.8	72.0	3.7	7.8	16.7	28.3
5	Hosiery...............	25.2	45.5	17.9	88.6	1.6	4.0	4.6	10.2
12	Household Appliance...	42.4	14.6	21.8	78.9	10.2	4.2	4.8	19.2

* No costs allocated to manufacturing overhead.

a breakdown of production costs between direct materials, direct labor, and manufacturing overhead. As shown in Table 117, for half of these the manufacturing overhead in 1937 was less than 10% of net sales. Even the company with the heaviest overhead in this year allocated only 21.8% of net sales income to manufacturing overhead.

As these organizations kept their records of overhead costs, a substantial part of them showed only a slightly larger overhead burden per unit in lean years than they did in years of heavy production. The examples given in Table 118 illustrate the variation in unit costs in years of differing sales volume when apparently the same plant capacity was available for the two years. In the case of toilet article manufacturer No. 30 a loss of physical sales volume of 27% produced a 47% increase in overhead charge. The absolute amount,

TABLE 118

VARIATION IN MANUFACTURING OVERHEAD COSTS PER UNIT FOR VARIOUS PRODUCTS
IN YEARS OF LARGE AND SMALL OUTPUT

Company Number	Product	Approximate Retail Price of Product		Index of Physical Production	Manufacturing Overhead Costs per Average Unit
30	Toilet Article.........	$0.10 to $0.40	Year of large volume.	100	$0.0023
			Year of small volume	73	0.0034
24	Cosmetic.............	0.10 to 1.00	Year of large volume	100	0.041
			Year of small volume	74	0.044
29	Cosmetic.............	0.10 to 1.00	Year of large volume	100	0.064
			Year of small volume	80	0.063
27	Clothing Item........	2.00 to 10.00	Year of large volume	100	0.13
			Year of small volume	36	0.21
10	Electrical Appliance...	125.00 up	Year of large volume	100	14.75
			Year of small volume	66	16.03
7	Electrical Appliance...	125.00 up	Year of large volume	100	13.07
			Year of small volume	41	12.05
12	Household Appliance..	2.00 to 25.00	Year of large volume	100	0.51
			Year of small volume	75	0.61
9	Hosiery...	0.60 to 1.50	Year of large volume	100	0.054
			Year of small volume	68	0.053
5	Hosiery.............	0.60 to 1.50	Year of large volume	100	0.14
			Year of small volume	54	0.12
19	Rubber Footwear.....	1.00 to 5.00	Year of large volume	100	0.21
			Year of small volume	62	0.24

however, was small in terms of selling price. Overhead went from 3 cents to 4 cents per average unit, which had a selling price of about 25 cents. A 26% decrease in physical volume for cosmetic manufacturer No. 24 increased his overhead charge by only 7%. Again the absolute amount was small, only three mills per average unit, which had a selling price of approximately 30 cents. A 20% decrease in physical volume for cosmetic manufacturer No. 29, produced practically no difference in his overhead charge. A 64% decrease in physical volume for clothing manufacturer No. 27 increased the overhead charge per average unit from 13 cents to 21 cents, or 8 cents, but this increase is small as related to the selling price, which was over $2.50.

In the case of electrical appliance manufacturer No. 10 the year 1938 brought a 34% decrease in physical volume from the 1937 level; the consequent increase in overhead charge per unit was $1.28, or 9%. Selling price was in the neighborhood of $100. Appliance manufacturer No. 7, however, with a 59% decrease in sales in 1938 showed an overhead charge of $1.02 less than that for 1937, or a decrease of 8% in overhead. This indicates either that the manufacturer's classification of expense items in overhead was changed at this time, or that the company instituted unusual economies in the variable costs entering into overhead, or that both of those things occurred.

In the remaining items of the table, products for which manufacturing overhead made up an appreciable part of total costs, the overhead was not appreciably larger in years of reduced production than in years of large volume. In short, from these examples it is seen that appreciable changes in physical output did not produce for many products substantial increases in manufacturing overhead charges per unit.

Study of Table 118 shows that among these companies there was lack of positive correlation between size of manufacturing overhead (column 3) and the percentage of sales devoted either to advertising (column 5) or to total marketing (column 8). In fact, the correlation is negative. Products with low overhead, such as proprietary remedies, cosmetics, confections, and so on, had heavy advertising and total marketing costs, while the companies with heavy overhead had low advertising costs and low marketing costs. That there was a negative correlation is probably a matter of chance in this small sample, but that there was lack of positive correlation is not surprising. This study has indicated that the chief determinant governing use of advertising by a manufacturer is the opportunity profitably to stimulate demand for his merchandise, and not the composition of his production costs. This fact was illustrated clearly in the case of sugar. Heavy pressure to get full utilization of plant because of large fixed costs has not led manufacturers generally to use advertising to attain the desired volume, although it has probably been a factor in the case of those who have advertised.

Summary Regarding Advertising's Effects on Overhead Costs

Advertising has been of value to individual manufacturers in attaining relative stability of operations. Stability of industrial operations is greatly to be desired from the standpoint both of society and of the individual company. However, the importance of this stability as a factor in determining total product costs should not be overemphasized. The evidence upon costs indicates that for many products substantial changes in output of manufacturing plants did not result in appreciable increases in manufacturing overhead charges per unit, although in certain instances where fixed costs were large the effects were substantial. Moreover, the evidence shows that the pressure of large fixed costs has not been for most concerns an important factor in determining the degree of their use of advertising.

PART IV

The Relation of Advertising to Prices and Pricing Practice

CHAPTER XX

THE RELATION OF ADVERTISING TO PRICES
AND PRICING PRACTICE

IN THIS and the following chapter effort is made to trace the
effects of advertising upon the prices of specific merchandise.
Prices measure the balance, or equilibrium, of demand and supply factors. While certain evidence regarding demand and costs has
been presented, the conclusions and measurements thus far given are
not adequate to support conclusions regarding the effects of advertising upon price. Further evidence is needed, for prices are determined not merely by the demand schedules of consumers and the
costs of producers and distributors. They are affected also by the
character of the competition between sellers, that is, whether competition tends to turn largely on price or on non-price forms, whether
sellers are few or many, and whether certain sellers exercise appreciable influence over market prices.

The Issues Involved in the Price Study

In these price chapters the problem is largely one of tracing the
character of competition and of observing the behavior of prices
resulting from that competition. Conversely, from a study of the
price history of products it is often possible to surmise the character
of the competition which has existed in an industry and roughly to
measure the combinations of production and marketing costs resulting
from different operating methods employed by competing sellers.

The reasoning of value theory regarding effects of advertising upon
price was given in detail in Chapter VI and need not be repeated here.
It will help, however, to recall the specific issues indicated by theory,
which have guided the factual investigation for this and the following chapter. The more important of these issues are as follows:

(1) Is the control over price obtained through differentiation practically important in the whole economic picture, or is it relatively unimportant?

(2) To what extent is competition carried out through advertising
and other non-price forms in specific product fields?

527

(3) To what extent do competing sellers employ alternative selling methods with varying costs?

(4) Is there effective competition from sellers with lower operating costs which serves to check the use of advertising and
other forms of aggressive selling?

    (a) Are consumers given the option of buying unadvertised or
little-advertised products at prices reflecting their low
selling costs?

    (b) To what extent do consumers exercise the option of low
price extended to them?

(5) To what extent in specific industries does domination of leading concerns depend upon advertising?

(6) To what extent is entry into these industries made difficult
because of the advertising of the leading concerns?

    (a) What is the evidence regarding entry of new concerns?

(7) To what extent have leading concerns whose dominance has
been built through advertising been able to influence prices as
a result of their advertising?

    (a) Does this control over prices involve relatively large price
differences, or are the differences small?

    (b) Are prices of leading concerns in the industry evidently
set with reference to the prices of competitors?

(8) To what extent have smaller firms set prices with reference to
those of leading concerns?

(9) For products which have been widely advertised, what is the
price history over a period of time?

    (a) To what extent have any economies from large-scale pro-
duction and from technological development been passed
on in lower prices?

    (b) To what extent have they been retained, or spent for ag-
gressive selling?

    (c) To what extent have manufacturers of advertised products
reduced their prices and their gross margins as their relatively new, differentiated products (specialties) have
tended to lose their individuality and to become closely
similar to competing merchandise?

The data bearing on prices, product qualities, and profits are not
so complete as might be desired; nevertheless they are adequate to
support certain conclusions.

Lack of Definite Standards by Which to Judge Price Differences

Because the variations in price between competing goods in the market relate to differentiated merchandise, difficult problems are met in determining just how much price variation between these competing goods may be deemed justifiable socially. Likewise it is difficult to determine the points at which advertising costs for differentiated merchandise or the net profits taken by sellers, both of which enter into price, shall be considered too large. No standards by which to decide these questions are available beyond the judgments of individual critics. The purpose of this study primarily is to state the facts it finds. In the presentation of the facts, however, two basic considerations have been kept in mind as guides to social judgments regarding prices. First, the consumer should have a freedom of choice among a wide range of merchandise. For reasons which will be developed more fully in later chapters, it is believed that consumer satisfactions are greatest when such choices are available. However, the offering of differentiated merchandise by sellers may lead to extensive aggressive selling and advertising on their part to secure consumer preference; this may result in added costs. From a consumer's standpoint, costs should be kept low. The second guide to judgment, therefore, is that there should be adequate checks in the economic system to prevent these advertising and aggressive selling costs from becoming unduly large. Not all advertisers and sellers should compete through advertising and non-price forms. It is desirable socially if, among their choices, consumers have adequate opportunity to buy merchandise on a price basis, without costs of product differentiation, services, and other non-price competitive forms entering in appreciable amount. Not only does the opportunity to buy some merchandise on a price basis widen consumer choice, but it tends to check those whose competition is in non-price forms.[1] Accordingly, in various situations studied, effort has been made particularly to determine to what extent competition in price has been present alongside the competition among other sellers using non-price forms. In this part of the study dealing with price, as well as in subsequent chapters, these two guides to social judgment are followed. It is recognized that they are arbitrarily selected; they necessarily must be because they are dictated by ideology.

---

[1] It is recognized that the problem of consumers' ignorance exists. Advertising may have undue influence on some consumers. The possible check upon advertising influence from consumer education is discussed in Chapters XXII and XXIII.

In this study of price behavior the method of presentation will be to work according to product fields.[2] Not only the data obtained in the various research projects undertaken in this study, but data obtained from numerous published sources are used. Evidence regarding the specific products studied in the demand section which may afford significant comparisons or contrast will be adduced first.

THE RELATION OF ADVERTISING TO THE PRICE OF WALNUTS

Since its advent in 1912, the California Walnut Growers Association has been the dominant supplier in the market, controlling in recent years approximately 85% of the walnut crop, and the management of the association has been the chief determiner of prices at which walnuts were offered.[3] It has been the policy of the association's management each crop-year to name opening prices which they expected would move all the available supply of merchantable, unshelled walnuts into consumption within the crop-year. Other walnut packers have tended to follow the leadership of the association, but have set prices for comparable grades of nuts from 1 cent to 2 cents a pound under those of the association.

In his study of the pricing by the association management, Mr. H. C. Hensley arrived at the following conclusion:

> In summary it is seen that prior to the 1932–33 season the management of the association was very successful in setting prices which would avoid carry-overs with their depressing effect on the prices of the following crop year. Moreover, an examination of the movement of the crops into market indicates that the association generally named prices which were probably close to the maximum that might be maintained in view of the competition with other nuts.[4]

Clearly it has been the aim of the association to get the highest price possible for its members. To accomplish this aim it has used advertising to stimulate primary demand. In years of large crops it has advertised more heavily than in years of short crops.

The association has not been able, of course, to control the supply

---

[2] The products investigated were selected so as to give a range that would show the varying influence of advertising upon price. They included a number of products for which advertising has been soundly criticized as contributing to high prices.

[3] See H. C. Hensley and N. H. Borden, *Marketing Policies of the California Walnut Growers Association* (Bulletin No. 10, Farm Credit Administration, Washington, D. C., March, 1937).

[4] *Ibid.*, p. 99.

coming upon the market in any year, for this supply has been determined by growing conditions.[5] In this respect walnuts are in contrast to some manufactured products studied. The walnut prices set by management have been adjusted in accordance with size of the crop to be disposed of. On the other hand, in the case of some of the manufactured products studied, the supplies produced and placed on the market, particularly over short periods, have been adjusted largely in accordance with the volume which would be accepted by the market at the prices set by the managements.

Entry of new growers has been easy, also, so that in the long run, price, and not the management of the association, has been the determinant of supply. Accordingly, even though the association has administered prices, it has not held the full power of a monopolist, because it has not been able to control supply. In fact, in so far as its effective marketing has brought high prices, increased planting of new orchards, which high prices have encouraged, has operated to keep price down. Thus has it been the poor fortune of good agricultural marketing managements to have their own marketing efficiency create difficulty for themselves and their organizations through stimulation of supply.

In the walnut growers' experience, the sales volume stimulated by advertising has held forth no promise of production economies which would offset advertising costs. Even were such economies attainable, it is probable that, under the price control exercised by the association, they would have been retained for the benefit of the growers.

Since advertising has been undertaken by the California Walnut Growers Association for the clear purpose of getting better prices for its products than it would have obtained without advertising, what have been the results? What have been the limitations against undue expenditure?

Although the association received from 1 cent to 2 cents more a pound for its walnuts than did other packers, this differential could not be attributed solely to the effect of advertising. It had come in part from the careful grading of the association. It was the final conclusion of the government's study that the advertising had probably brought returns to the growers that were somewhat greater than the expenditure made; the amount was not so large as to make advertising's contribution easily determinable.

---

[5] A partial control over the season supply as a means of preventing low price was obtained beginning with the 1932–33 crop year, when part of the crop was taken from the domestic market through the plan of marketing agreements established under the Federal Agricultural Adjustment Administration.

If this conclusion is sound, the maximum effect upon price would have been not much, if any, more than ¾ cent a pound upon a product whose retail selling price averaged about 25 cents a pound over the years. For the period studied, the advertising expenditure per unit was somewhat greater in later years than in early years. From 1918 to 1926 advertising expenditures averaged less than ½ cent a pound, representing approximately 2% of the association's sales value; after 1926 the average was about ¾ cent a pound, or 4% of the association's sales value. The expenditure has tended to rest at this point, representing the "feel" of management that larger expenditure probably would be unprofitable. In only one year, 1932–1933, when the management was faced with the task of trying to move a very large crop in a period of extreme depression, did advertising expenditures exceed appreciably the average figure of ¾ cent a pound. In that year the expenditure represented 1.48 cents a pound, an amount which probably was not passed on to consumers, for the association's average selling price fell to an all-time low. The expenditure probably was derived in considerable part from reduced returns to growers.

This case shows clearly the limitations placed upon a management in its advertising expenditure when it is practically free from direct competition. The limitations came from indirect competition of other nuts and other food products, against which the pull of the advertising appeals was not particularly strong. Accordingly it was not worth while for the management to try to affect prices by an advertising expenditure appreciably beyond that which it made. To have done so would have been to reduce the return to growers rather than to have added to their returns. In short, advertising may have enabled the California Walnut Growers Association to get a somewhat larger price for its output than it otherwise would have obtained, but the amount has been small, probably not 3% of retail value. Moreover, since there has been no direct control of supply, prices over the years have tended downward to a level giving small returns to most growers.

THE RELATION OF ADVERTISING TO THE PRICE OF ORANGES

In many respects the story regarding the effects of advertising on the prices of oranges is similar to that recounted for walnuts; in others it is different.

While the California Fruit Growers Exchange has played an important part in the marketing of oranges, it has not administered the prices of oranges. The pricing of oranges has depended upon free competition between buyers and sellers in the important distributive markets. In order to get desirable prices for its members, the Exchange has sought carefully to control the quality of its branded products, to direct shipments so as to avoid market gluts of its produce at distributive centers, and to carry on aggressive promotion to create consumer demand for oranges and preference for its brands.

The Exchange, however, has not been in a position fully to control supply in the city markets. It has controlled the marketing of about three-quarters of the California and Arizona crops, but over the years Florida and other orange-growing states have accounted for an increasing percentage of the oranges marketed. For the six-year period, 1927–1932, California and Arizona accounted for 69% of car-lot shipments of oranges, and other orange-producing states for 31%; for the six-year period 1933–1938, California and Arizona accounted for 60% of car-lot shipments, and other states for 40%.[6] Accordingly, in certain years the exchange has marketed somewhat over 50% of the oranges sold; in other years, as in 1938–1939, it controlled only a little over 30%.

The continued growth of supply from new orchards, with a consequent reduction of prices, was recited in Chapter XIII. The increase in Florida production has been particularly large. As with walnuts, there has been no effective monopolistic control of supply.

In addition to competition on a price basis, there has also been some competition in advertising. In large part this latter type has come from substitute products, such as pineapple juice, tomato juice, and other fruits, such as prunes and apples, which have been advertised to consumers. In addition, since 1935 there has been a substantial amount of directly competitive advertising expenditure between California and Florida.

The extent to which the advertising and promotion of orange growers have enabled them to get a better price than they would have obtained without advertising cannot be stated with precision. Yet it is believed that growers have received in their prices more than they

---

[6] Based on report of car-lot shipments as given in U. S. Department of Agriculture, *Agricultural Statistics, 1939* (Washington, U. S. Government Printing Office, 1939), p. 189.

have expended upon advertising, and the consumers accordingly have paid more than merely advertising costs. Even in years of largest appropriations for the advertising of oranges, the expenditure was at the rate of 7 cents a box, or about ¾ cent a dozen. Had this small amount a dozen been passed on to consumers in lower prices, demand probably would not have been stimulated to such an extent as occurred from the use of this money for advertising. In other words, without advertising the large volume of oranges consumed would have been taken only at considerably lower prices, or possibly this large quantity would not have been absorbed by the market.

While advertising has probably given the growers better prices than they would have received without advertising, yet with no control over supply, the price of oranges has tended steadily downwards, with the index of orange prices in recent years generally below that of the Bureau of Labor Statistics all-commodity index. The sales returns have yielded only small profits to growers, particularly in recent years.

The advertising of the California Fruit Growers Exchange has had an effect not only on the price of oranges generally, but on the prices of its own brands. Its primary advertising probably has helped all growing regions to obtain a higher price than would have prevailed without such advertising. In addition, its brands have brought higher prices than have those of Florida oranges. It will be recalled that California navels sold over the 15-year period 1924–1938 for an average of 5.5 cents a pound in the New York auction market; Floridas for 4.1 cents a pound. This difference clearly cannot be attributed solely to reputation established by advertising, for the products have been different. California fruit has been more carefully graded and its market entry has been better regulated. But probably part of the difference is attributable to the reputation established through advertising. Whatever the basis has been, however, the differential was established through free play in the market.

As the supply of oranges has grown and the difficulty of selling them has increased, advertising expenditures per unit have increased, even as price has decreased. Florida has added a substantial advertising program to that of California, and the latter's advertising has become directly competitive. In spite of these increased costs for advertising, there is great pressure upon a marketing organization such as the California Fruit Growers Exchange to keep its marketing costs down so that the net returns to growers will be as high as or higher than those received outside the cooperative. Accordingly it is to be expected that increases in advertising expenditure find a natural competitive check from nonadvertised oranges sold through channels other than the cooperatives.[7] So far as consumers are concerned, while they will pay some differential for a brand whose quality is maintained, the opportunities for individualization by producers through such quality control are limited.

In addition to the check of price competition from nonadvertising orange packers, oranges have faced competition from other fruits and juices. While some of these, such as pineapple juice and tomato juice, have used aggressive advertising, even within these product fields not all sellers have employed aggressive selling, with the result that their advertising and promotional expenditures have been kept at relatively low levels. Low prices of some of these substitutes provide a check against orange price's becoming unduly loaded with selling and promotion charges.

To what extent competitive advertising of oranges will increase, only time will tell. The opportunities for free competition between advertisers and nonadvertisers, and the competition from substitute products lead one to doubt whether promotional expenditures will be permitted to increase appreciably. Thus far the cost of advertising to the consumer has been a small part of his outlay for the product.

THE RELATION OF ADVERTISING TO THE PRICE OF CIGARETTES

In March, 1915, Mr. Joseph E. Davies, United States Commissioner of Corporations, issued a report on the tobacco industry dealing with prices, costs, and profits of numerous manufacturing companies. The study was undertaken to determine how far the 1911 decree of

[7] Evidence of a check upon advertising expenditures through cooperative ventures is found in the following trade paper report:

"The Florida citrus growers have never been especially noted for their unity. Most of them are banded together in separate little groups which frequently scrap with one another. But for some years the whole industry has backed the Florida Citrus Commission in a yearly advertising campaign now grown to $1,000,000 annual proportions. Last fortnight the campaign struck a snag.

"One of the Commission's biggest backers, a separate trade group, called the Florida Citrus Producers Trade Association, caused the difficulty. It announced to the Commission that its members were 'not satisfied with results of the Commission's advertising program.' What bothered the dissenters was that, despite the whopping campaign, Florida growers were shipping less fruit this year than last and getting lower prices for it." Source: "Citrus Conflict," *Tide*, February 1, 1941, p. 28.

dissolution of the Tobacco Combination had succeeded in establishing effective competition between the seven parts of the Combination which were set up as distinct companies. The findings of this report provide an excellent background for study of the character of competition in the cigarette industry since 1911 and the place of advertising in that competition. The following extracts from the summary of the study are pertinent.

PRINCIPAL FACTS REGARDING THE COMBINATION

The Combination originated in 1890 with the formation of the American Tobacco Co., which, through the expansion of its business and the affiliation of numerous other concerns, acquired a dominating position in the tobacco industry. This Combination was dissolved by judicial decree in 1911.

The salient points brought out in this part of the report relative to the business of the Combination, so far as it was engaged in the manufacture and sale of tobacco in the United States, are as follows:

(1) That the Combination from 1902 to 1910 had a monopolistic position in each of the chief branches of the tobacco business, except in cigars, the minimum proportion of the annual output in the several branches ranging from two-thirds, to over five-sixths of the total output of the country, while in cigars the maximum proportion in any year was only one-sixth of the total.

. . . . .

(2) That for the Combination high rates of profit have followed monopolistic control, the greater the degree of control the greater the rate.

. . . . .

In the cigarette branch the Combination had practically a complete control from the organization of the American Tobacco Co. in 1890. In this branch the rates of profit were also high, particularly during the earlier years of the Combination's existence. The gradual decrease in the profits in the cigarette branch, without any marked decline in its proportion of the total output, was due in part to the fact that it was necessary in order to hold its position to shift during the latter part of the period to newer brands which, on account of the expense of exploitation, afforded a lower rate of return.

. . . . .

(3) That for most types of manufactured tobacco the Combination's rates of profit were ordinarily more than double those of its competitors, though for a few types it had no advantage.

. . . . .

In scrap tobacco, Turkish cigarettes, and cigars, on the other hand, the rates of profit of the Combination were generally less than those of the principal independent companies.

(4) That selling costs were materially reduced as the volume of the Combination's business increased.

. . . . .

In the cigarette branch the selling cost was practically uniform throughout the 18-year period covered. There was no marked increased in volume of sales in this branch until 1908.

. . . . .

(5) That generally there were material decreases in advertising expenditures of the Combination after a controlling proportion of the total production had been secured.

. . . . .

In the cigarette branch, while the Combination from its organization maintained a controlling position, its advertising expenditures varied considerably. This, however, is explained by the fact that when Turkish cigarettes became popular, their production was controlled by independent manufacturers, and the Combination made heavy advertising expenditures in order to increase its proportion of control in this type.

. . . . .

(7) That during 1901 and 1902 the internal-revenue tax was reduced 6 cents per pound on manufactured tobacco, 42 cents per thousand on cigarettes, and 46 cents per thousand on little cigars, but the Combination made practically no change in the prices to the jobber, while the prices to the consumer also remained unchanged, so that the Combination profited by substantially the whole extent of the tax reduction, though it was presumably intended for the benefit of the consumer.

. . . . .

(9) That there were practically no changes in prices to the consumer for the Combination's principal brands of manufactured tobacco, cigarettes, and little cigars from 1901 to July, 1910.

. . . . .

(10) That, while there were practically no changes in prices to the consumer from 1901 to July, 1910, for the Combination's principal brands, there were substantial increases in prices to jobbers, thus reducing the margins between these prices.

. . . . .

(11) That the most profitable years of the Combination's existence were from 1903 to 1908—the period of low tax, moderate leaf costs, decreased advertising expenditures, and highly monopolistic control.

. . . . .

PRINCIPAL FACTS REGARDING THE SUCCESSOR COMPANIES

By the term "successor companies" is meant the seven companies that succeeded, under the decree of dissolution, to the domestic tobacco manufacturing business formerly conducted by the Combination.

· · · · ·

The salient points brought out by this part of the report relative to the business of the successor companies, covering the two-year period following the dissolution of the Combination (1912 and 1913), are as follows:

(13) That the several successor companies established in accordance with the plan of dissolution were much larger producers of tobacco products than any of the other companies.

· · · · ·

(16) That, although there were no important changes in prices, the results for certain branches, particularly smoking and cigarettes, tend to show competition for business in 1912 and 1913 and an effort on the part of the several successor companies to fill in gaps in types of their business in which they were weak, though for certain other branches, particularly snuff, such competition has not been apparent.

· · · · ·

In the cigarette branch the R. J. Reynolds Tobacco Co. at the time of the dissolution did not manufacture cigarettes, but began the manufacture of them in 1913. The P. Lorillard Co. at the time of the dissolution manufactured no blended cigarettes, but since then has engaged in the manufacture of this type of product.

· · · · ·

(18) That the cost of leaf tobacco used by the successor companies in 1912 and 1913 in the plug, fine-cut, and cigarette branches was less, while in the smoking, snuff, and little-cigar branches it was more, than the cost of that used by the Combination in 1909 and 1910.

· · · · ·

(19) That the factory costs, other than leaf, of the successor companies in 1912 and 1913 and of the Combination in 1909 and 1910 were not materially different.

· · · · ·

(21) That increases in selling cost after the dissolution were general, resulting from the duplication of selling organization and increased overhead expense, due to the division of the business.

· · · · ·

(22) That there was a marked increase in the advertising expenditure of the successor companies as compared with that of the Combination.

· · · · ·

(23) That the aggregate amount of profit of the successor companies in 1913 was slightly less than that of the Combination in 1910 in spite of a larger volume of sales.

. . . . .

In domestic and blended cigarettes, the profit of the Combination in 1910 amounted to $3,977,571, or 76 cents per thousand, and to only $3,209,918, or 27 cents per thousand, for the successor companies in 1913.

. . . . .

(24) That the ratios of profit to net receipts less tax for the successor companies in 1913 were, in general, comparatively low in those branches or types in which competition for business was most pronounced, e.g., plug-cut smoking and domestic and blended cigarettes, and very high in those in which competition was slight, e.g., snuff.

. . . . .

(27) That there have been no material changes in prices to the jobbers since the dissolution of the Combination.

(28) That for all principal brands of the successor companies there have been practically no changes in prices to the consumer since the dissolution of the Combination.

. . . . .

(29) That the high profits taken in conjunction with the practically unchanged wholesale and retail prices of tobacco indicate that there has been but little competition in price, but this is explained in large part by the customary retail prices and other peculiar price-making conditions of the tobacco trade, including statutory provisions, which make it impracticable in most cases to increase the quantity sold at the customary price.

. . . . .

PRINCIPAL FACTS REGARDING OTHER COMPANIES

(31) That for companies other than the Combination and successor companies there were marked decreases in the proportions of their collective output in the plug, smoking, snuff, cigarette, and little-cigar branches, from 1905 to 1913.

. . . . .

(32) That compared with both the Combination and successor companies the manufacturing costs of the other companies covered by the investigation were extremely high in practically all branches.

. . . . .

(33) That compared with either the Combination or the successor companies the selling costs per unit of product of other companies investigated were extremely high in all branches. . . . In cigarettes, also, the selling cost of

other companies was markedly greater than that of the Combination and successor companies. This is particularly true after 1907. A part of the great increase in selling cost by companies other than the Combination and successor companies was undoubtedly due to the fact that the Combination was constantly becoming a more important factor and that only by increasing selling and advertising expenses was it possible for the independent companies to compete with the Combination.

·   ·   ·   ·   ·

(34) That the larger margins above manufacturing and selling costs of the Combination and successor companies enabled them in most branches to spend from three to five times as much per unit of product for advertising or competitive purposes as the other companies investigated and at the same time to obtain practically the same or even greater rates of profit.

·   ·   ·   ·   ·

(35) That compared with the Combination and successor companies the other companies investigated made an exceedingly poor showing of profits and that there was a marked decrease in profits of these companies in navy plug and Turkish cigarettes since the dissolution of the Combination.[8]

The general conclusions reached by the commissioner from his study were contained in the last two paragraphs of his Letter of Submittal to the President:

In conclusion it may be stated that the study of prices, costs, and profits in the tobacco industry, without taking into consideration other factors in the competitive situation, indicates that the decree of dissolution has resulted in the successor companies' competing with each other for business in most branches of the industry, but has not affected wholesale or retail prices. The successor companies have also competed with the smaller tobacco concerns and, collectively, have won business from them in some branches and lost to them in others. As a consequence of competition the rate of profit of the successor companies has been reduced, although their rate of profit is still high. In general, this competition had seriously reduced the profits of the other companies.

This reduction in profits has not been caused by increased cost of manufacture, but by increased expenses of distribution, and principally by the increase in expenditures for advertising. As the sale of tobacco products depends largely on the advertisement of brands, competition in the tobacco business necessarily increases advertising expenditure. In other words, for tobacco products, and it may be true also for other brand articles, the social cost of the system of competition is largely found in extraordinary advertising expense, and this would seem to be inevitable for brand articles so long as they have a proprietary character.[9]

---

[8] U. S. Bureau of Corporations, *Report of the Commissioner of Corporations on the Tobacco Industry* (Washington, U. S. Government Printing Office, 1915), Part III, pp. 1–28.

[9] Ibid., p. xxxii.

In the above study, issued over a quarter of a century ago, is found one of the most detailed and completely documented pictures ever published of the behavior of prices, costs, and profits under conditions of imperfect competition. The study is particularly pertinent because the situation for two years subsequent to the dissolution is compared with that which existed under the relatively extreme monopoly conditions of the Combination.

The commissioner concluded that, during the two-year period following the decree, competition took place, but not in prices. The struggle for business was centered in selling and advertising efforts. Marketing costs rose above those of the Combination; profits were lowered.

Competition Since 1911

Since the dissolution of the Combination in 1911, numerous governmental investigations and individual studies of the tobacco business have furnished the outline of the history of competition and of prices in the cigarette business. That there has been a struggle for business seems evident from these studies. During the years immediately following 1911, the successor companies were constantly introducing new brands of various products in an attempt not only to increase their proportion of the products allotted them under the decree, but also to branch into lines in which they were weak. The various companies had their ups and downs. It will be recalled from Chapter VIII that the R. J. Reynolds Tobacco Company, which was allotted no cigarette business by the decree, brought out its domestic blend, Camel, in 1913, and with it in a comparatively short time attained leadership. On the other hand, Lorillard, which was allotted 19% of the Combination's cigarette business, or 16% of the total cigarette business of the United States, lost out in the succeeding years because its Turkish blends lost favor. During the 1920's and 1930's it was relegated to a relatively minor position in the cigarette field, although it tried to regain its place after 1926 with Old Gold. The American Tobacco Company, which emerged from the disintegration with over 40% of the cigarette business of the country, accounted for only 35% in 1913, while by 1921 the company's proportion had fallen to about 20%.[10] Then followed its subsequent drive to leadership. The competition in

---

[10] Reavis Cox, *Competition in the American Tobacco Industry* (New York, Columbia University Press, 1933).

advertising and merchandising among the leaders was outlined in Chapter VIII.

In short, among the leading companies in the cigarette business there has been keen competition, but not on a price basis. Instead, the leading companies have sought for consumer favor through their blending of tobacco and through advertising and aggressive selling efforts.

Price History of Cigarettes

No intimate record is available of the moves by the several tobacco companies in pricing cigarettes and the reasoning of the executives about the prices named. A complete record of price changes for Lucky Strike cigarettes, including discounts, has been provided by the American Tobacco Company, however, and is shown in Table 119.

The price history of this brand closely resembles that of other lead-

TABLE 119
PRICES OF LUCKY STRIKE CIGARETTES, 1917–1940

Date	Price per 1,000	Revenue Tax per 1,000	Net per 1,000 after Discount and Revenue Tax	Federal Excise Tax per Package of 20 Cigarettes	Wholesale Price per Package after Discount and Federal Excise Tax	Lucky Strike Price Index 1926 = 100	B.L.S. Combined Index of Wholesale Prices 1926 = 100
October 19, 1917.....	$5.00	$1.25	$3.405	$.025	$.0681	127	118
March 9, 1918.......	5.8333	2.05	3.3808	.041	.0676	126	131
July 27, 1918........	6.00	2.05	3.536	.041	.0707	131	131
October 1, 1918......	7.50	2.05	4.723	.041	.0945	176	131
November 11, 1918..	6.00	2.05	3.368	.041	.0673	125	131
February 25, 1919....	7.50	3.00	3.615	.06	.0723	134	154
November 4, 1919...	7.80	3.00	3.8796	.06	.0776	144	154
November 27, 1919...	8.20	3.00	4.2324	.06	.0846	157	154
December 18, 1919...	8.00	3.00	4.056	.06	.0811	151	154
December 5, 1921....	7.75	3.00	3.8355	.06	.0767	143	98
January 19, 1922.....	7.50	3.00	3.615	.06	.0723	134	97
March 7, 1922.......	6.80	3.00	2.9976	.06	.06	112	97
August 24, 1922.....	6.20	3.00	3.076	.06	.0615	114	97
October 31, 1922.....	5.80	3.00	2.684	.06	.0537	100	97
August 8, 1923......	6.45	3.00	2.6889	.06	.0538	100	101
April 21, 1928.......	6.00	3.00	2.292	.06	.0458	85	97
October 5, 1929......	6.40	3.00	2.6448	.06	.0529	98	95
June 24, 1931........	6.85	3.00	3.0417	.06	.0608	113	73
January 1, 1933......	6.00	3.00	2.292	.06	.0458	85	66
February 11, 1933....	5.50	3.00	1.851	.06	.037	69	66
January 9, 1934......	6.10	3.00	2.3802	.06	.0476	88	75
January 20, 1937.....	6.25	3.00	2.5125	.06	.0503	93	86
July 1, 1940.........	6.53	3.25	2.5095	.065	.0502	93	....

Sources:
The American Tobacco Company and Its Service to the Public (Published by the American Tobacco Company, July, 1940), p. 26.
B. L. S. Index: *Statistical Abstract of the United States, 1939*, p. 316.

ing brands, because the price moves of any of the leaders have been quickly met by competitors. For example, the Federal Trade Commission[11] found that between 1926 and 1934 the leading four brands changed prices either on the same day, or at the most within four days of one another. Of seven price changes made during that period, the R. J. Reynolds Company was the first to announce price change on four occasions, and the American Tobacco Company on two occasions.

In its study, the Federal Trade Commission made careful inquiry into the nature and extent of cooperative activity or collusion among those in the industry. It stated that:

> The companies concerned have consistently denied that they ever exchange information regarding price or contemplated price changes or arrive at any understanding concerning them. The circumstances stated suggest that there are advance understandings but there is no evidence to support a conclusion contrary to the representations by the manufacturers. Their statements, which are supported by documentary evidence, show that it is entirely possible for the price changes to be accomplished almost simultaneously without any previous understandings.
> From the statements and evidence submitted by the manufacturers it appears that as soon as the trade is advised of a price change by one of them, news of it is immediately conveyed to other manufacturers by jobbers, field representatives, and others who are anxious to know what the other manufacturers will do. As soon as practicable, which means a matter of minutes or hours, the other companies, acting separately, call their boards of directors or responsible officials together to determine their action.[12]

As pointed out by the Federal Trade Commission, in an industry so completely dominated by a few companies the development of common prices and common marketing practices was to be expected. The large cigarette manufacturers have been of substantially equal strength. An attempt of one to secure a price advantage over the others would be met immediately by them. Continued efforts to establish an advantage would lead to price wars. As the Commissioner's report further stated:

> The result is that manufacturers of the "big four" cigarettes follow the price changes of any one of them upward or downward, regardless of their economic justification.[13]

An interpretation of price moves of cigarette companies for the period 1912–1931 has been given by Professor Reavis Cox in his study

---

[11] Federal Trade Commission, *Agricultural Income Inquiry*, Part I, Principal Farm Products (Washington, U. S. Government Printing Office, 1938), p. 447.
[12] *Ibid.*, p. 449.
[13] *Ibid.*, p. 445.

of *Competition in the American Tobacco Industry*,[14] from which the following paragraphs are quoted:

Cigarettes of the kind selling since 1922 at a "standard" retail price of fifteen cents for twenty were selling before 1914 at five cents for ten, or ten cents for twenty. During 1912–1914, the list price for such cigarettes ranged from about $3.90 to about $4.00 for 1,000 cigarettes, the unit customarily used in quoting wholesale cigarette prices; and fifteen-cent cigarettes, such as "Fatima" and its competitors, were around $6.00 per 1,000.* With the outbreak of the war in Europe, Turkish cigarettes began to advance almost immediately.† Other products climbed slowly during 1915 and 1916, the advance becoming quite general in the latter half of 1916.‡ With the beginning of 1917, substantial advances began; but the companies did all they could to soften the blow to the consumer by reducing package sizes and eliminating special discounts and prices rather than directly advancing their lists by large amounts.§ What the manufacturers particularly dreaded was to break from the custom of quoting retail prices in multiples of five cents. Lorillard tried the water early in 1917 with a wholesale price list necessitating odd-cent prices to consumers, but lost its courage and restored its earlier prices.‖ The new revenue act of 1917 forced a decision. Reynolds met the situation frankly by raising "Camel" cigarettes to $5.25 per 1,000, an increase of 70 cents at one move, and suggesting to retailers that they sell the brand at thirteen cents.¶ American Tobacco tried to meet the situation by putting out packages with 16 cigarettes each instead of 20 to sell at the old prices, but after a short struggle realized the futility of trying to keep ahead of war inflation by this method and reverted to the old sizes at higher prices.** The first step taken, prices continued to climb. The end of the war resulted in a few spasmodic price movements, meaningless reductions and advances alternating; but the renewal of inflation and the increase of taxes in 1919 forced a renewal of the advance. Prices reached their peak late in that year when "Camel," "Chesterfield," "Sweet Caporal," "Lucky Strike," and similar brands touched $8.00 per 1,000, with a suggested retail price of twenty cents.††

For two years prices held steady; then competition asserted itself. "Lucky Strike" dropped 25 cents to $7.75 per 1,000.‡‡ "Camel" replied with a cut to $7.50, and the other brands followed. George J. Whelan, of the United Cigar Stores, said this reduction cost the Reynolds Company $2,400,000 in rebates on

---

[14] Reavis Cox, *op. cit.*, pp. 204–207.
  * *United States Tobacco Journal*, Jan. 1, 1912, p. 12; Sept. 28, 1912, p. 9; Dec. 14, 1912, p. 7; Jan. 11, 1913, p. 27; July 25, 1914, p. 9.
  † *Ibid.*, Aug. 22, 1914, p. 20.
  ‡ *Ibid.*, July 22, 1916, pp. 5, 12; Sept. 9, 1916, p. 25; Oct. 21, 1916, p. 31.
  § *Ibid.*, April 7, 1917, p. 30; April 14, 1917, p. 31; June 23, 1917, p. 32.
  ‖ *Ibid.*, June 23, 1917, p. 18; June 30, 1917, p. 8.
  ¶ *Ibid.*, Nov. 10, 1917, p. 30; Nov. 24, 1917, p. 24.
  ** *Ibid.*, Oct. 27, 1917, pp. 24, 30; Feb. 9, 1918, p. 3; April 6, 1918, p. 6.
  †† *Ibid.*, Nov. 23, 1918, p. 20; Nov. 30, 1918, p. 3; Nov. 29, 1919, p. 20; Dec. 6, 1919, p. 5.
  ‡‡ *Ibid.*, Dec. 10, 1921, p. 8.

stocks held by the distributors and that it reduced the profit margin on cigarettes from $1.10 per 1,000 to 60 cents for "Camel" and from $1.20 per 1,000 to 70 cents for "Lucky Strike." He attributed the cut to Reynolds' determination to get "Camel" back into the fifteen-cent class. The American Tobacco Co. had made a similar attempt not by cutting the price of "Lucky Strike" but by introducing a new brand, "One-Eleven." "Reynolds, having no fifteen-cent cigarette brand, has opened a tobacco war, the end of which may be rather disastrous if it is not fixed up very quickly, which Whelan hopes it will be."§§ The hopes were not fulfilled, for in March Reynolds again cut, this time to $6.80, and in November to $6.40, forcing the other manufacturers to follow suit and dealers to sell at fifteen cents a pack or less.|| || Three things were accomplished by these reductions: (1) Allowance being made for increases in taxes, prices were now back within hailing distance of pre-war days. (2) Thanks to the pressure of public demand for cheaper cigarettes, retail prices had been lowered more than list prices, thus reducing the distributors' margin. (In the decade which followed, chains and cut-rate stores were to reduce that margin still further.) (3) Sales were stimulated, so that output in 1922 climbed to a total above that for 1919, the previous high year.

Prices were somewhat unsteady for a few months after this outbreak, but settled after a time at $6.40 for "Camel" and "Chesterfield" and $6.45 for "Lucky Strike." Since then there have been only three general changes in cigarette list prices. The first came after almost six years when, in April, 1928, the Reynolds Company again took the initiative and reduced "Camel" to $6.00. The others followed, "Chesterfield" and "Lucky Strike" dropping to the same price, while "Old Gold," which was now in the market, dropped to $6.10. This reduction was considered in some quarters an effort to check the growth of "Old Gold," in others a move to discourage any attempt by the British-American Co. to make its invasion of the American market an aggressive one, in still others an attempt to checkmate the newly projected Union Tobacco Co.; but the more plausible reasons were those advanced by the trade journals, which said that the reduction came as the result of Reynolds' determination to recover volume which its competitors had taken from it and, specifically, to force another unidentified manufacturer to stop giving specially low prices to large buyers.¶¶ Just before the stock market collapse in 1929, the Reynolds Company, continuing its role as leader, reversed itself and announced an increase to $6.40, which was followed by the other three companies.*** This advance has never been explained. Even more mystifying was the most recent price change, when the "big four" on June 24, 1931 again raised prices, this time to $6.85.††† Coming in the midst of a severe business depression, with prices of all other commodities, including leaf tobacco, tumbling, this advance aroused severe criticism even in Wall Street.‡‡‡

§§ Pound and Moore, *They Told Barron*, p. 224.
|||| *United States Tobacco Journal*, March 18, 1922, p. 12; Nov. 4, 1922, p. 3.
¶¶ *Ibid.*, April 28, 1928, p. 7; *Printers' Ink*, May 3, 1928, p. 182.
*** *United States Tobacco Journal*, Oct. 12, 1929, pp. 7, 38.
††† *New York Times*, June 25, 1931.
‡‡‡ Barney, *The Tobacco Industry*, 1931, pp. 22–24.

Until 1920 pricing moves of cigarette companies were guided to a large degree by the desire of selling companies to adhere to customary retail prices in multiples of 5 cents. Since that date, this custom evidently was a factor in the pricing of Philip Morris cigarettes and of one or two other leading brands. Undoubtedly it also entered into the pricing considerations of the producers of 10-cent cigarettes. Their products were introduced at first in states in which taxes did not prevent a 10-cent price. The increases in federal and state taxes and the variation in taxes between states, however, have made adherence to customary prices difficult for any producer. Pricing to permit customary prices has not been practiced by the Big Four since 1920. Accordingly, the managements did not have to fear upsetting traditional retail prices when they advanced wholesale prices as they did in June, 1931.

Whatever may have been the reasons for the price advances made at that date, the danger to the leading companies of establishing so wide a margin between manufacturing costs and selling price quickly became evident. Competitors relying upon low price and no advertising as bases for securing demand gained a foothold which they have held since. The rise of the 10-cent cigarettes as real factors in competition has been outlined in Chapter VIII. In June, 1931, when the Big Four advanced prices, 10-cent brands accounted for 0.28% of the market; 17 months later they had nearly 23% of the market (Table 34, page 235). The leading brands suffered marked decreases in sales. A retail price differential between leading brands and 10-cent brands of 4 cents to 5 cents was sufficient to overcome quality differences and reputation advantages of the former. The smaller companies gained sales at the expense of the leaders.

In order to check the inroads of these lower-price cigarettes, the leading companies sharply reduced prices in January and February, 1933. Sales of 10-cent cigarettes were checked, but with leading brands priced after 1934 so as to permit a retail price advantage of 2 cents to 4 cents a package for the new brands, sales of the latter grew until they accounted for 17% of the market in 1939.

Of the effectiveness of advertising in influencing consumers' cigarette valuations there can be no doubt. That there are definite limits to this effectiveness, however, is demonstrated in the history of the 10-cent brands. As stated by the Federal Trade Commission in its 1937 report:

The establishment of 10-cent brands of cigarettes in this country on a volume basis undoubtedly places serious competitive checks upon the leading brands, and imposes definite restrictions upon the freedom with which the dominant manufacturers may manipulate the price of their products. It is probable that in future changes the 'Big Four' manufacturers will be compelled to take into consideration the price and competitive position of the 10-cent brands.[15]

Inflexibility of Prices

That the prices of cigarettes have been relatively inflexible and have not moved with the prices of commodities in general is indicated by the number of price moves reflected in Table 119. In the 23-year period, 1917–1940, cigarette prices of leading manufacturers were changed only 23 times, of which 14 changes occurred in the unstable war and post-war years of 1917–1922. In other words, in the 18-year period, 1922–1940, there were only 9 price changes. This inflexibility is pointed out in view of its bearing upon the discussion relating to cyclical fluctuation in a later chapter. It is evidence, also, of the fact that competition in this field has not been centered upon price.

Profits

Figures showing the profits of the tobacco companies upon their cigarette sales are not available. That the prices at which the leading brands have sold have permitted a substantial profit in spite of large promotional expenditures seems evident. The estimates of the three experts testifying for the manufacturers of 10-cent cigarettes in their hearing before a congressional committee (Chapter XIX, page 494) indicated a profit per package to the manufacturers of from 1.67 cents to 2.4 cents, when the relatively high list price of $6.85 a thousand cigarettes was in effect. Apart from these uncertain estimates, it is known that the companies have been profitable and that, reputedly, a substantial part of their profits has come from their cigarettes.[16]

Extent of Concentration of Demand among Suppliers

That the dominant position established by the Big Four with the help of advertising has made difficult the entry of smaller companies into the cigarette field is indicated by the history of the industry.

---

[15] Federal Trade Commission, *op. cit.*, p. 463.

[16] This statement is based on evidence from a number of sources, primarily from the financial reports of tobacco companies. Also see report of the Federal Trade Commission, *op. cit.*, p. 832 ff. The *Fortune* report on The American Tobacco Company, referred to in Chapter VIII, stated that cigarette sales accounted for 65% of The American Tobacco Company's profits.

Nevertheless, the fact that smaller companies with acceptable blends and able management can compete successfully with the dominant companies has been shown not only by 10-cent brands, which have used price appeal plus advertising to get their hold, but by the cases of Philip Morris and other brands, which in recent years have adopted the prices of the leaders and relied chiefly on product quality and advertising to gain an increasing share of the market.

Up to 1931, the selling and pricing policies followed by the Big Four enabled them not only to hold but also to increase the market dominance which they inherited from the Combination. In 1910 the Combination had produced, roundly, 84% of all cigarettes, smaller companies 16%. In 1913, two years after the dissolution, the three successor companies allotted the cigarette business, through their use of aggressive selling, had gained 90.5% of the total; R. J. Reynolds Tobacco Company, a successor company not allotted cigarette brands and just entering the field with Camel, had 0.2%, while the smaller companies' share had fallen to 9.3%. By 1931, although marked shifts in their own relative positions had occurred from time to time, the Big Four, with their advertising, had acquired almost 97% of the total market; the smaller companies held only 3%. By 1939, however, the share of the Big Four had fallen to 70%, that of the others had risen to 30%.

The dominance of these large companies prior to 1932 and the lack of entry and growth of small competitors before that date rested primarily on two factors: First, the cigarette industry has been one requiring large financial backing. Large inventories of tobacco have been necessary, because three years of curing have been customary. Moreover, expensive storage and manufacturing facilities have been required. Secondly, the securing of demand in competition with the leading brands has been difficult. Until the entry of the 10-cent brands, substantial advertising had been considered necessary to gain sales enough to secure good distribution among retailers.

Until the past decade, small companies trying to enter the market have had high selling costs. In his report of conditions in 1912 and 1913 the U. S. Commissioner pointed out that the selling costs of the independents per unit of product were extremely high. "Only by increasing selling and advertising expenses was it possible for the independent companies to compete with the Combination." Likewise, it was indicated in Chapter VIII (Chart II, p. 244) that on the average the advertised brands, other than the three leaders, showed during the '30's a considerably larger advertising space expenditure for each billion of cigarettes sold than the leading three brands incurred. Since 1930, however, certain lesser brands which have relied on advertising have not had advertising costs above those of the leading brands. Particularly successful in entering the market without unduly large advertising costs per unit was the Philip Morris brand. Marketed by a minor company, this brand fared far better than the Old Gold brand, which was put out by Lorillard, one of the Big Four.[17]

Summary

In summary, the advertising of the leading cigarette manufacturing companies has given them a domination permitting considerable freedom in pricing policies. Each has met the price changes of others, but competition has taken place largely on advertising rather than on price. They have adopted substantially the same price schedules. Prices have been relatively inflexible. Smaller companies employing advertising have followed the price leads of the large companies. Entry of small competitors has been difficult because of strong brand domination, but lesser brands have made headway during the last decade. More significant has been the entry of the 10-cent brands, which have used little advertising and have relied on low prices to stimulate demand. They have come to represent a check against the freedom in pricing previously enjoyed by the leading advertised brands. Accordingly they serve as a check against undue profits or undue competitive advertising expenditures for the leading brands. Competition on a price basis became effective when prices of advertised brands permitted an attractive price differential to consumers to offset the quality differences and the reputation of the leading brands. Because advertising has substantial effect in guiding consumer valuations, a differential of several cents has apparently been necessary for the 10-cent brands to attract patronage from the advertised brands. This differential has represented in part the effect of advertising and in part the differences in quality between the two groups.

---

[17] For details of advertising costs, see Chapter VIII.

THE RELATION OF ADVERTISING TO THE PRICE OF CIGARS

The evidence regarding competition in the cigar industry is fragmentary. It indicates, however, that there has been substantial competition between producers on a price basis, with limited competition in advertising and other forms of aggressive selling.

Extent of Concentration of Supply

The number of companies engaged in cigar production has favored competition on a price basis. Cigars are in striking contrast to cigarettes in that competition has not been restricted to a few companies but has been carried on among thousands of companies; yet the tendency toward concentration of production in large units has made considerable headway since the advent of the cigar-making machine, 28 companies having accounted for 61.3% of total production in 1938. But the small number of large-scale manufacturers with national recognition, such as General Cigar Company, Inc., Bayuk Cigars, Inc., Consolidated Cigar Company, G.H.P. Cigar Company, and Congress Cigar Company, have always been in competition with smaller manufacturers distributing their brands regionally or locally. It will be recalled that in 1938, for example, 235 brands of cigars were being sold in Milwaukee. In that year there were still over 4,000 cigar factories in the United States. Large manufacturers have not dominated as they have in the cigarette field. The combined sales of the two leading producers, General Cigar Company and Bayuk Cigars, Inc., in recent years have been less than one-fourth of the total volume.

Competition in Quality at Traditional Prices

Published price data relating to cigars are likely to give a mistaken impression that competition on a price basis has not been present in this field. Manufacturers have priced their brands of cigars to meet customary retail prices. Consequently, price data for cigars appear to reflect a relatively inflexible price structure. For example, the report for the T.N.E.C., *Price Behavior and Business Policy,* lists cigars by the investigators' measures of price flexibility as one of the least flexible of products.[18] Yet the equivalent of keen competition in price has occurred, because consumers have had the option of buying cigars in a wide range of price lines, spaced at close intervals: 2 for 5 cents, 3

---

[18] Temporary National Economic Committee, *op. cit.,* p. 207.

for 10 cents, 5 cents each, 2 for 15 cents, 3 for 25 cents, 10 cents each, and so on. During the past 20 years peak demand has steadily shifted to lower price classes, until in 1935, 88% of all cigars retailed for 5 cents or less, whereas in 1920 only 24% of the demand was in this class. (Table 38, p. 251.) Manufacturers have had to seek consumer preference by offering in any price class a cigar of such quality and size that it would compare favorably not only with cigars in that class but with those in nearby classes. Given the option of buying inexpensive cigars, consumers have turned more and more to them.

There is no clear statistical evidence available to indicate to what extent the quality of leaf used in cigars of specific price classes, particularly the low price classes, has improved. Discussion with tobacconists and correspondence with executives of cigar manufacturing companies, however, has led to the conclusion that there has been a general improvement in the quality of the low-price cigars during the past two decades. The fact that cigar smokers have been willing in such large numbers to accept low-price cigars tends to confirm this conclusion.

Competition has largely been in quality differences within price classes.[19] Although there are no objective measures of cigar quality, in the course of time consumers discern the differences in quality of leaf used. It is more difficult to maintain uniformity of quality in cigars than in cigarettes, for which long aging of tobaccos and blending from large inventories is the custom. Success of cigar brands to a large extent has been determined by the ability of manufacturers to maintain blends pleasing to consumers. Different consumers have different tastes, and variation is found in the preference of different localities. Yet failure to give a quality equal to that of competing cigars of similar type brings unfavorable consumer reaction in the course of time. Wide acceptance of this view among cigar manufacturing executives has led to competition in quality at. the established prices. Quality improvement at a price is one form of price reduction.

That there has been improvement in quality of some brands in low price classes was brought out by the investigation of the Federal Trade Commission in 1937,[20] as indicated in the following paragraphs:

. . . since 1929 . . . many brands of cigars, among them some of the most popular which formerly retailed at 10 cents each or other prices above 5 cents were

---

[19] The conclusions presented in this paragraph, which must be looked upon as tentative, are based on evidence gained from cigar manufacturers and tobacconists, from case studies, and from correspondence.

[20] Federal Trade Commission, *op. cit.*, pp. 454–455.

reduced to the 5-cent class. An instance of this is the White Owl (General Cigar Co.) which in 1930 was listed at $53.50 per thousand less 12 percent and 2 percent, representing an ordinary retail price of three for 20 cents. In February, 1931, the price was reduced to $48 per thousand less 10 percent and 2 percent, representing a 6-cent retail price which is extremely unusual. On June 15, 1931, the price was further reduced to $40 per thousand less 5 percent and 2 percent, bringing it into the 5-cent class. On October 20, 1933, the discounts were increased to 8 percent and 2 percent and on January 2, 1934, to 10 percent and 2 percent. Another such instance is the Bayuk Phillies brand which in 1932 was listed at $75 per thousand less 12 percent and 2 percent and retailed at 10 cents each. On January 2, 1933, the list price was reduced to $40 per thousand less 12 percent and 2 percent, bringing it into the 5-cent class. On October 2, 1933, the discount was changed to 10 percent and 2 percent where it now remains.

The instances cited are typical of many similar reductions which have occurred since 1930. When a brand which has enjoyed popularity in the 10-cent retail class is reduced to the 5-cent class, undoubtedly its 10-cent reputation gives it prestige as a 5-cent cigar and places it in a definitely advantageous position. Certain manufacturers have frankly admitted that their formulae were altered when the prices were reduced and others have stoutly maintained that the quality of their cigars was unchanged. There is no accurate method for determining the comparative quality of cigars before and after price changes and no standard by which relative qualities of competitive cigars can be satisfactorily measured. These are matters which must be left to consumer determination.

Savings from Technological Development

That at least some of the saving from the reduction in labor costs brought by machine manufacture since 1917 has been passed on to consumers in the form of better quality has been suggested above. Cost evidence, too meager to be fully satisfying, indicates that the increase in consumption of machine-made cigars over handmade cigars may have been brought about in part because of the better quality of materials used in the machine-made cigars of a particular price class. This conclusion is indicated in the following statement from a U. S. National Recovery Administration study:

A survey of the costs of production of five-cent cigars was made in 1933 by the Census of Manufactures at the request of the National Recovery Administration. Eleven manufacturers of machine-made, combination hand and machine-made, and hand-made cigars were covered. These eleven manufacturers produced about 24.4 percent of all cigars made in 1933. . . .

Inspection of . . . [the evidence] discloses the startling fact that although tobacco costing $14.80 per 1,000 cigars was used for the machine-made product and tobacco costing only $11.52 per 1,000 cigars was used for the hand-made product, the total cost per 1,000 of the machine-made product was $25.68 as compared to $26.66 for the hand-made product. This advantage in both price and quality in favor of the machine-made product would seem to provide sufficient incentive for future mechanization.[21]

It should be mentioned in connection with the above statement that part of the higher material costs for machine-made cigars was attributable to a greater waste of leaf in machine manufacture than in hand manufacture; but evidence regarding leaf quality showed higher cost materials used in the machine-made product. It would appear, therefore, that the economies of technological development have been passed along to some degree at least to consumers in the form of better products in the traditional price classes, although part of the saving evidently has been used by large companies for advertising. Low price, handmade cigars probably have lost out in the competitive battle, in part because they have not been so satisfying to consumers, in part because machine-made cigars have had better advertising support. This view was found to be commonly held by tobacconists and cigar manufacturing executives interviewed during the study.

Competition in Advertising

The evidence of Chapter IX shows that advertising has had an effect upon consumer valuations and that competition has taken place in part in advertising. Yet competition in quality of product at traditional prices has been keen enough to prevent margins permitting large expenditures per unit for competition in advertising. Moreover, efforts by certain leading companies to gain dominance by competing in advertising on a large scale have not been successful. One example of this kind of unsuccessful attempt occurred at the beginning of the century, when the Tobacco Combination tried to strengthen its position in the cigar field.

The advertising expenditures in 1902 amounted to 37.5 per cent of the net price less tax, and in 1903 to 49.9 per cent, or almost exactly one-half. In these two years, as already noted, especially heavy losses were incurred on account of the unusually large advertising expenditures. In 1906 the advertising cost had fallen to 7.2 per cent, and in 1910 to 4.8 per cent, or less than one-tenth the proportion in 1903.

The profit in relation to the net price less tax fluctuated greatly. During the first four years of the period the domestic-cigar business showed a loss ranging from 0.6 per cent to 22.5 per cent of the net price less tax. The Combination, apparently discouraged in its attempt to acquire any large proportion of the

---

[21] U. S. National Recovery Administration, *op. cit.*, p. 170.

cigar industry, greatly reduced its advertising expenditures after 1905, with the result that the profit in 1906 and 1907 was 10 per cent. After 1908, due to a greater increase in costs than in prices, the ratio of profit was considerably less.

The rates of profit on domestic cigars were exceptionally low compared with those on other products.[22]

Another example of this kind occurred in the determined drive of The American Tobacco Company in 1930 and 1931 to establish Cremo as a dominant 5-cent cigar.[23] Advertising expenditures on this brand for a year or more were reportedly at the rate of $2,000,000 a year. Against this drive competing companies answered with both increased advertising and reduced prices. In February, 1931, General Cigar Company reduced prices of its well-known White Owl from 3 for 20 cents retail to 6 cents each; then on June 15, 1931, to 5 cents. Increased advertising support was also given the brand. The advertising drive on Cremo was dropped.

Some evidence of the effect of advertising upon the demand for brands and upon the prices obtainable from the trade is contained in the lower trade discounts given to the more extensively advertised brands of cigars. The Federal Trade Commission reported for 1937[24] that manufacturers' list prices of cigars showed a striking uniformity on the brands that were directly competitive. For example, the leading 5-cent cigar brands, such as White Owl, Bayuk Phillies, Muriel Senator, Harvester, La Azora, and Recollection, were all listed by the manufacturers at $40 per 1,000. White Owl and Bayuk Phillies, the brands having largest advertising expenditures, carried a discount of 10% and 2%; the other brands, discounts of 12% and 2%. Other cigars with smaller advertising support carried wider discounts to the trade. Since consumers paid the regular 5-cent price on all these brands, retailers received a smaller gross margin on the leading advertised brands than on the lesser brands. The Commission reported that the list prices of cigars designed to sell at 5 cents ranged from about $37.50 to $41 per 1,000.

While there has been some competition in advertising in the cigar business, it has been accompanied by a competition among producers to give consumers desired quality in traditional price classes. Quality in low-price cigars has improved and demand has shifted to these

---

[22] U. S. Bureau of Corporations, *op. cit.*, pp. 199–200.
[23] See Chapter IX, p. 261.
[24] *Op. cit.*, p. 453.

classes. The economies of technological development have been passed on in part to consumers in the form of improved quality. Although a part of these economies has gone into advertising, price competition among the large number of producers has been present in such degree as to prevent large unit expenditures for advertising competition.

THE RELATION OF ADVERTISING TO THE PRICE OF DENTIFRICES

The evidence contained in Chapters XI and XVIII clearly indicates that advertising costs have made up a substantial part of the price paid by consumers for dentifrices. Competition in this field has been very keen, but it has been largely competition in advertising. Consumers have been given the option of buying numerous forms of dentifrice at lower prices than those asked for the leading advertised brands, but so strong has been the influence of advertising that consumers have been willing to pay substantially higher prices for the advertised brands than for the unadvertised. Consequently, manufacturers have turned for the most part to competition in advertising rather than to competition in price. The different brands have varied in formula and also in quality. It is not known just how much these differences in quality have affected manufacturers' costs.

Entry Into the Dentifrice Business and Concentration of Supply

The number of manufacturers of toothpaste is not determinable from census statistics because dentifrice manufacturers are classed with manufacturers of perfume, cosmetics, and toilet preparations, of whom there have been some 500-odd in recent years.

The manufacture of a dentifrice does not require a large outlay of capital for plant; hence entry into this field should be relatively easy so far as needed capital is concerned. Some evidence of the ease of entry is shown by the fact that in Milwaukee in 1938 there were 83 brands of toothpaste on the market and 76 brands of tooth powder (Tables 66 and 67, page 311).

In spite of the small capital required for a dentifrice manufacturing plant, the major share of demand for dentifrices has been concentrated in a relatively small number of brands, the advertised brands. Ten advertised brands have apparently accounted for 90% of toothpaste demand, no brand getting over 20% of the market. The same condition has held true for tooth powder except that one brand, Dr. Lyon's, has had a substantial part of the tooth powder demand, probably from one-third to one-half. A few brands have dominated the new liquid dentifrice market.

Competition has been keen not only between these advertised brands in each product form but between the forms. It has been competition in advertising with a wide margin between price and manufacturing cost and with much of this margin devoted to advertising. For advertised brands, manufacturing costs have often represented less than 20% of retail selling price.

Entry to the field has involved large risks in advertising outlay for those companies which have desired to compete for a substantial volume of demand under their own brand. Manufacturers willing to sell to private branders or to sell their own brands to large-scale distributors on an exclusive agency arrangement, however, have not had to undertake such selling expense.

Prices

The prices of competing advertised brands have not been the same. Moreover, the consumer has been given the opportunity of buying unadvertised or little advertised brands at different prices, often, though

TABLE 120

RETAIL PRICES IN BOSTON STORES FOR CERTAIN BRANDS OF TOOTHPASTE, FEBRUARY, 1941

BRAND	SIZE OF TUBE	RETAIL PRICE PER TUBE	PRICE PER OUNCE
Bost	2.4 oz.	$0.32	$0.133
Briten (United Drug)	4.5	.39	0.087
Colgate	3.0	.33	0.11
Iodent	3.0	.33	0.11
Ipana	2.6	.39	0.15
Kolynos	2.0	.39	0.185
Klenzo (United Drug)	3.5	.39	0.111
Listerine	4.1	.33	0.08
Mi. (United Drug)	5.25	.50	0.095
Pebeco	3.25	.39	0.12
Pepsodent	3.25	.39	0.12
Phillips	3.6	.36	0.10
Rexall Milk of Mag. (United Drug)	3.75	.33	0.088
Squibb	3.0	.33	0.11
St. 37	1.75	.23	0.131
Worcester	3.0	.31	0.103
Craig-Martin (Woolworth)	5.5	.20	0.036
Sears (Sears, Roebuck and Co.)	2.5	.24	0.096
Approved Milk of Mag. (Sears, Roebuck and Co.)	4.0	.27	0.057

not always, less than the prices of advertised brands. Table 120 shows the prices at which certain brands of toothpaste were sold in selected Boston stores in February, 1941. The prices varied from $0.036 an ounce for Craig-Martin, an unadvertised brand sold in Woolworth's, to $0.185 an ounce for Kolynos, a well-advertised brand. An ounce of some of these toothpastes goes farther than an ounce of others. This fact has a bearing on prices. Of the well-advertised brands, Listerine sold for $0.08 an ounce, which was less than certain manufacturers' brands given little advertising, such as St. 37, Klenzo, and Briten. Of the relative qualities and effectiveness of the various brands this study has no evidence, nor are figures for manufacturing costs available. The least expensive brand, Craig-Martin, was permitted, however, to use the Seal of Approval of the American Dental Association, an indication that its low price did not mean lack of merit. Practicing dentists have given evidence that no dentifrices have substantial therapeutic value; their chief merit rests in their cleansing quality.

Further evidence that competition on a price basis has been available to many consumers who have wished to avail themselves of low-price dentifrices is shown in price evidence obtained from the survey of private brand practices of chain drug stores, variety chains, and department stores.

A large city department store offered under its own brand various types of toothpaste which it said were similar in formulae to certain advertised brands and contained identical quantities. In January, 1939, it sold its milk of magnesia type of toothpaste for $0.16 a tube, taking a low markup of 12½%. On a leading advertised milk of magnesia toothpaste selling under fair trade contract for $0.33 a tube it received a higher markup. For another paste, which was manufactured to compete with a leading brand then selling at $0.39 a tube, the store charged $0.19 a tube. At this price it received a markup of 37% as against approximately 20% on the advertised brand.

Among the 13 corporate drug chains supplying information in the survey, 9 sold toothpaste under their own brands. Seven provided data regarding their selling prices and markup on the two leading manufacturers' brands which they sold and on their own private brands. Their own tubes of toothpaste were as large as or larger than those of the two leading advertised brands. The following tabulation summarizes the prices charged per tube for the advertised and private brands and the gross margins taken on them:

	AVERAGE PRICE, MEDIAN*	APPROXIMATE INTERQUARTILE PRICE RANGE†	AVERAGE GROSS MARGIN, MEDIAN*	APPROXIMATE INTERQUARTILE GROSS MARGIN†
Distributors' brands..........	$0.29	$0.21 to 0.29	63.0%	50%—69%
Leading advertised brand......	0.39‡	0.39*	27.5	26 —29
Second advertised brand.......	0.33‡	0.33*	28.0	27 —31

* The median item in a statistical array is the middle item.
† The interquartile items in an array are those between the upper and lower fourth of the array.
‡ Price maintained.

The above figures show that the private brands of these drug chains were priced on the average from 4 to 10 cents a tube under the leading manufacturers' brands as a means of attracting patronage. Still the average percentage of gross margin obtained by the chains at the lower prices on their own brands was over twice as large as that taken on the advertised brands at their maintained prices. The various brands of paste were differentiated, and the comparable qualities are not known. The chains all stated that they believed their brands as good in quality as advertised brands.

With the price differentials indicated in the above instances, there was varying response among the clientele of the stores. The large city department store mentioned devoted substantial newspaper advertising and store display to its own brands and stated that it had had a rapid gain in sales of its own brands. Early in 1939, its own brand of milk of magnesia toothpaste was outselling the leading advertised manufacturers' brand at the rate of about 6 to 1. The other type was outselling the similar manufacturers' brand at the rate of 3 to 1. The corporate drug chains had no such outstanding experience in gaining patronage. Of the seven giving information, five reported an upward trend and two a downward trend of sales of their own brands. Sales of their own brands in five out of seven instances were less than those of the leading manufacturers' brand.

Further evidence that low price in itself has not been particularly effective in leading consumers to adopt a brand is had in the case of Listerine toothpaste. This brand has been on the market over 20 years at a price below that of other advertised brands, as reflected in Table 120. It has had a large amount of national advertising since 1925[25] and the economy appeal has been stressed. Yet this brand has not had a demand that approaches that attained by the three leading brands of Ipana, Colgate, and Pepsodent. The *Milwaukee Journal's* survey[26] of

[25] Figures for advertising expenditures are given in Table 63, Chapter XI, p. 306.
[26] *The Milwaukee Journal*, "Consumer Analysis of the Greater Milwaukee Market," 1941, p. 98.

consumer use in 1941 showed Listerine holding fourth place among toothpastes in the Milwaukee market with 5.0% of consumers using it as compared with 23.9% using Pepsodent, 22.9% using Colgate, and 17.0% using Ipana. The Scripps-Howard survey[27] in 16 cities showed Listerine in 1938 used by 6.1% of toothpaste users as contrasted with 19.3% for Ipana, 19.2% for Colgate, and 18.4% for Pepsodent. Thus it is seen that even when low price has been extensively advertised, consumers have not responded in large measure.

Inflexibility of Prices of Dentifrices

Detailed price data over a period of years for a large number of brands were not available, but conversation with retailers and wholesalers indicated that few changes in the wholesale prices of leading brands were made over long periods of time. Price data obtained for one of the leading brands showed that between 1930 and 1937 prices were reduced only about 5%. In some instances recognition of changing price levels has been given in changes in the net contents of containers, but such changes have not been substantial.

For many years dentifrices were one of the items frequently used as a price leader by retailers. Consequently, leading brands often were obtainable at far below the suggested resale prices. The margins of retailers under the stress of retail price competition sometimes became very narrow. After price maintenance legislation was enacted, practically all the manufacturers offered price maintenance contracts. The price structures of some manufacturers were adjusted at that time in order to afford retailers an acceptable margin at the minimum contract price, which generally became the retail price in chains and many independent stores.

At times the equivalent of price reductions has been given in special deals or combination offers directed either at the trade or at consumers. Such deals, however, have been temporary promotional drives for business; they do not materially alter the conclusion that prices have been inflexible.

Advertising has played an appreciable part in building up the use of dentifrices. With such demand established, growing competition on a price basis has been present in recent years. Such competition has not been highly effective thus far, however, in driving down the price of leading brands or in securing for the low-price brands an

---

[27] Scripps-Howard Newspapers, *Market Records*, 1938, Vol. I, p. 206.

appreciable part of the dentifrice market. Competition in advertising has prevailed and advertising costs still continue to represent a considerable part of the price paid by consumers for dentifrices.

THE RELATION OF ADVERTISING TO THE PRICE OF SUGAR

Quite clearly, the small amount of advertising employed for sugar has had little or no effect upon its price. Primary demand grew without the use of advertising. Whatever influence advertising has had in building brand preference for this almost standardized product, it has not made it possible for any seller to secure a price differential for his brand. There has been no private branding of sugar because distributors have not been able to buy more cheaply under their own labels than under manufacturers' labels or to secure a better retail price.

Only two large refiners have been consistent advertisers, and their expenditures have represented only a fraction of one per cent of their sales. Most of the 23 cane refiners have not advertised at all. The two large refiners have hoped to recover their advertising expenditure by securing not a higher price for their brands but manufacturing economies that might attend such stability of operations as came from the brand preference established.

THE RELATION OF ADVERTISING TO THE PRICE OF SHEETING

In Chapter XII the character of competition in the sheeting industry and the effects of advertising upon the price structure of sheeting were outlined in such detail that it is necessary here only to give a summary statement regarding the situation.

Conditions in the sheeting industry have been such as to bring about competition on price and a limitation on competition in advertising. The number of suppliers in this industry has been large; i.e., 100 or more sheeting producers have been in the market in recent years, and these various sellers have followed different patterns of marketing. Some manufacturers have sought consumer preference on a basis of product differentiation supported by advertising. Others have sold under their own brands without advertising. Alongside these there has been much private brand selling. Although mills have sought to differentiate their products, the product has tended to be standardized within grades.

The price history has been as follows: The advertised brands under each construction have been sold by the mills at approximately the same prices. These advertised brands have apparently commanded prices at from 5% to 15% above those of mills which have not advertised, and have commanded prices from 10% to 15% or more above those for sheets of similar texture packaged under distributors' brands. These differences in prices at the mill have not been uniformly reflected in retail prices. The private brands of certain chains, such as J. C. Penney Company, Sears, Roebuck and Company, and Montgomery Ward & Co., Incorporated, have sold at substantial differentials under the manufacturers' brands in the retail market. For example, in 1938 the retail prices for sheets of a 68 x 72 construction of one of these chains were from 20 cents to 30 cents under prices generally charged for leading mill brands of similar size. Apparently the promotional expenditures by some of these chains have been no greater, and in some instances less, than those spent by retailers upon sheeting generally. Their total expenses have been such as to permit them to sell their private brand merchandise on a price appeal. Likewise, certain department stores stressing price in their appeal for patronage have set prices below those of the leading mill brands. On the other hand, some department stores have sold their private brand merchandise at approximately the same prices as they have asked for the leading advertised brands. In so doing, they have received wide margins on their private brand merchandise because they have bought it at lower prices than those paid for advertised mill brands, for as has been mentioned previously, manufacturers ask less for private brand merchandise in view of the fact that they pass the promotional function on to the distributor.

Whether the differences in price between the advertised and the private brand merchandise have been so large that demand has shifted away from the advertised brands is not known definitely, although some informants in the sheeting industry and in the dry goods trade stated that the private brands of such chains as J. C. Penney Company, Sears, Roebuck and Company, and Montgomery Ward & Co., Incorporated, had experienced rapid growth in recent years.

In short, the tendency of competition to shift to price is clear. There has been sharp competition among marketing methods, some methods making greater use of advertising than others. Competition on a price basis has clearly been effective enough to prevent margins above manufacturing costs which would permit appreciable competition in advertising. Manufacturers' advertising has been limited to a range from approximately 1% to 3% of sales. Manufacturers said they could not profitably spend more. Intensive competition in advertising, which was started during the '20's and was dropped, has not been resumed.

THE RELATION OF ADVERTISING TO THE PRICE OF SHOES

To determine the effects of advertising upon the price of shoes is very difficult. The lack of standardization in the product makes interpretation of differences in prices between brands uncertain. Fashion as an element in guiding consumers' valuations has been present and often has completely overshadowed differences in quality of materials or of selling efforts as a determiner of values. Although fashion and differentiation in quality have prevented anything approaching the close buying on price that occurs on standardized merchandise, nevertheless conditions have favored active competition upon a price basis for much of the merchandise sold. Correspondingly, this competition upon price has operated against intense competition in advertising and aggressive selling.

Conditions Tending toward Competition in Price

The large number of suppliers and the ease of entry of new suppliers have favored the development of price competition alongside competition in non-price forms. In recent years there have been over 1,000 manufacturers of shoes, none of whom had a dominant position. Since optimum size of manufacturing plant has been relatively small, large producers have not had appreciable manufacturing advantages. New producers have entered the market rather easily because the practice of leasing machinery has kept low the capital requirements for factories. Moreover, the opportunity of new producers to sell to the trade, even though they have not had well-established brands, has relieved them from incurring large initial expenditures for promotion.

In the marketing of shoes there has been free competition among different types of marketing methods with varying costs. In the matter of branding, manufacturers' advertised brands, manufacturers' unadvertised brands, distributors' brands, and unbranded merchandise have all been sold in substantial quantities. In the matter of distribution channels, some shoes have been sold through wholesalers, but the great majority have been sold direct to retailers. Competing in the market have been independent shoe retailers and chains. Some of the latter have involved an integration of manufacturing and retailing functions; others have done no manufacturing. Like manufacturers, the retailers, who have conducted much of the advertising and promotion, have had varying promotional costs. These differing policies and methods of branding, distribution, and promotion have given varying total costs, which have been reflected in prices.

The availability of shoes in a large variety of price lines has given consumers the option of buying at desired prices and has had an effect on the pricing policies of sellers. Adults' shoes have been obtainable at numerous prices from $2 to $25 a pair. Shoes in any price class have had to be sold in competition not only with others within their price class, but also with those in other price groups.

A study of the price history of branded shoes is complicated by the fact that many concerns have at times, particularly up to the depression of 1930, followed the practice of holding to established retail prices and of adjusting quality with changing costs of materials and labor. Some concerns even went so far as strongly to associate their brand names with particular prices. For example, a number centered on the price of $5, others $3, and so on. While this policy operated without undue difficulty during periods of relatively stable prices, it was not satisfactory in periods of rapidly changing prices. In times of rapidly falling prices it was possible, of course, to put better materials into their shoes, but it was not strategic to hold to established prices when the prices of competing shoes were falling. The demand of consumers in such times changed to lower price lines, and a manufacturer who held to his old price lost volume. In times of rapidly rising prices, these concerns had difficulty in keeping the quality of materials in their shoes at a high enough level to maintain brand reputation. While under a fixed price plan quality could be varied within narrow ranges, any appreciable change was a threat to future patronage. As a result of these difficulties, the custom of advertising brands at fixed prices has been abandoned by most concerns since 1929 and the prices of branded shoes are changed with changing material and labor costs. For example, in the case of the Thursby Shoe Company[28] the management has followed the definite policy of maintaining quality of its shoes and has revised retail prices whenever manufacturing costs have changed by as much as 10%.

[28] Chapter XIV, p. 386 ff.

Conditions Tending toward Non-Price Competition

While the conditions outlined above have tended to bring competition in price, the presence of fashion as a determiner of consumers' valuations and the lack of standardization in materials signify the presence of very imperfect competition. One should not expect shoe prices to guide demand to suppliers according to the rational pattern given in the theory of pure competition. Consumers' buying necessarily has been inexpert and irrational. Consumers have not been good judges of quality of material or workmanship, and style valuation is outside the realm of reason. Yet in the long run, according to evidence given by executives in case histories, demand for a brand has turned in large degree upon the ability of the seller to offer at favorable prices the combination of material, fit, workmanship, and style which they sum up under the term "shoe quality."

Advertising has been employed, of course, as a tool to influence consumers, but its effects on prices have varied in different situations. That it has aided some companies to build reputations which have been reflected in the prices charged was indicated earlier. In none of the cases, however, was the reputation built by advertising apparently strong enough to build a large demand at an appreciable price premium. Nor did the use of advertising necessarily mean that a brand was priced in the market above non-advertised shoes of similar quality.

The varying effect of advertising upon price was reflected in the three cases which were given at some length in Chapter XIV. In the case of the Thursby Shoe Company, the adoption of advertising after a large volume of sales had been built without advertising apparently did not affect the prices of Thursby shoes. The company gained a relatively important place in the industry without use of advertising as a result of its policy of giving good value in the low price field. It sought to offer its shoes at low prices and still to make a profit by effecting economies in both production and distribution. When the management later employed advertising it did not consider that the reputation established thereby should be made the basis for higher prices. It employed advertising in any locality only so long as it gained sales volume thereby at the low advertising cost of 5 cents a pair, which it could spend without threat of raising its marketing costs.

In contrast, in the case of the Burwind Company,[29] advertising was

---

[29] *Ibid.*, p. 391 ff.

used to build reputation which undoubtedly was reflected in the prices which the company got for its shoes. A relatively large unit expenditure for a shoe manufacturer, about 40 cents a pair, was made to establish demand for the company's orthopedic shoes after the company had been unable to secure a substantial volume of sales without advertising. Sale of such shoes apparently has depended upon the reputation established for brand as designating sound, corrective shoes. Buyers have preferred even to pay more for shoes of known reputation than for those of unknown virtue. At a price of $10 to $13 a pair there has been a wider spread between manufacturing price and retail price for these shoes than has held in the case of many medium- or low-price shoes, such as those sold by the Thursby Shoe Company. Accordingly, advertising has played an important part in the determination of the price charged for these shoes. Yet after 1929 the company experienced a very marked decrease in sales. Under the stress of depression, sales of high-price shoes as a whole suffered materially, for demand shifted to lower price lines. The Burwind Company, which had been slow to make price adjustments, did not begin to regain lost sales volume until it had made a drastic price cut in 1932. Such a case shows that in this industry even a company which has a relatively well differentiated shoe must keep its prices in line with competitive prices if it is to avoid loss of sales.

In the case of the Holburn Company, advertising was used to make effective a material reduction in price. A price of $10 for shoes which the new management later sold for $6 was probably higher than it should have been relative to competitive prices. Failure to obtain large volume was probably attributable in part to high price. A $6 price without sacrifice in material quality, however, was predicated upon economies in production coming from large volume, upon relatively economical selling costs, and upon a reasonable unit profit. While the management shrewdly judged the effect of price upon quantities that it might sell, it made advertising also an integral part of the program. The phenomenal sales success indicated that the new price was attractive, but advertising also played an important part in bringing volume to permit low production and marketing costs. The new experience was in contrast to the previous failure of advertising to bring volume at the higher price.

Evidence Regarding Price Spreads

Only limited evidence of the spreads between manufacturers' costs and retail selling prices for shoes is available. Table 121 shows the price spreads for leather shoes obtained from "certain representative manufacturers"[30] in 1936, which were presented in the Twentieth Cen-

TABLE 121

COSTS AND PRICE SPREADS OF LEATHER SHOES, 1936

ARTICLE	MANU-FACTURER'S PRODUCTION COST	MANU-FACTURER'S SELLING PRICE TO JOBBER	JOBBER'S SELLING PRICE TO RETAILER	RETAILER'S SELLING PRICE	SPREAD BETWEEN PRODUCTION COST AND RETAIL PRICE		
					Amount	Per Cent of Cost	Per Cent of Retail Price
Men's							
Work shoe........	$1.23	$1.28	$1.50	$1.98	$ .75	61.0	37.9
"Every day" shoe.	1.33	1.38	1.60	2.19	.86	64.7	39.3
Side leather-calf tip shoe............	1.73	1.80	2.10	3.00	1.27	73.4	42.3
Calf-skin shoe.....	2.08	2.16	2.60	4.00	1.92	92.3	48.0
Women's							
Low-price.........	1.12	1.19	1.27	1.98	.86	76.7	43.4
Medium-price.....	1.35	1.57	1.62	2.45	1.10	81.5	45.0
Moderate-price....	2.35	*	2.92	5.00	2.65	112.8	53.0

* This manufacturer's products are distributed direct to retailer at $2.92 a pair.

Source: P. W. Stewart and J. F. Dewhurst, *Does Distribution Cost Too Much?* (New York, The Twentieth Century Fund, 1939), p. 46.

tury Fund's study of distribution costs. It was pointed out in that study that these spreads were small in comparison with those for other articles of wearing apparel. While the evidence is very limited, these figures probably are indicative of a relatively low price spread in the shoe industry generally. Exceptions will be found for orthopedic shoes and for certain highly styled specialty lines. As has been indicated in other fields studied, the presence of such a low spread is a good indicator that competition in an industry has turned largely on a price basis. It indicates further that competition in aggressive selling has not been highly effective in influencing the prices consumers would pay. In short, this evidence supports the conclusions obtained from the other evidence presented regarding shoes. The fact that total advertising expenditures, manufacturers' as well as trade, have been in the neighborhood of 3% of retail value, indicates that competition in advertising has been limited in shoes as compared with many products studied. Competition in price has existed alongside competition in non-price forms. Consumers have had a wide range of choice.

---

[30] Whether these manufacturers could be termed "representative" is uncertain, in view of the fact that the table indicates that distribution was through jobbers.

CHAPTER XXI

THE RELATION OF ADVERTISING TO PRICES AND
PRICING PRACTICE—Continued

THE RELATION OF ADVERTISING TO THE
PRICES OF MECHANICAL REFRIGERATORS

MECHANICAL refrigerators, more than any of the products studied, have had large economies in costs attending growth in size of operations. These economies flowed from technological development as the machines and manufacturing processes were perfected and large-scale operations developed. They also reflected decreases in the costs of selling. As refrigerators became known and wanted by consumers, expensive personal solicitation of prospects in their homes, with its attendant costly supervision, was much less widely employed than previously. To determine to what extent these economies have been passed on to consumers in lower prices is one of the main objectives of this analysis of competition in the industry and of the prices coming from this competition.

Number of Suppliers and Concentration of Demand

Attention is directed first to the number of suppliers, the degree of concentration of demand among them, and the entry of new concerns.

In the early days of the industry there were hundreds of companies in the field, each apparently hopeful of perfecting a machine which would permit it to profit in the expected expansion of the industry. Hull states that there were "several hundred concerns producing or developing household refrigerating equipment" during the 1920's.[1] As in the developmental stages of many industries, many of these companies never were appreciable factors in the market. Gradually after 1923 a leadership of brands began to develop as certain companies entered the competitive race: Kelvinator, Frigidaire, Servel, Copeland, General Electric, Electrolux, Westinghouse, and Norge.

A heavy mortality occurred after 1933. *The Electric Refrigerator*

---

[1] H. B. Hull, *Household Refrigeration* (Chicago, Nickerson & Collins Company), Foreword.

News in May, 1933, stated that 250 companies producing in 1932 had been reduced to 75. Of those disappearing, 24 had merged with other manufacturers, 110 were reported as having gone out of business, and 41 were assumed to have liquidated, since they could not be reached by mail. Among the companies continuing there was keen competition.

The number of brands of electric refrigerators which had been sold in preceding years in a single city market and the degree of concentration on brands is recorded in surveys made by the *Milwaukee Journal* and the Scripps-Howard Newspapers. In the Milwaukee survey, shown in Table 103, page 419, 62 brands were found in 1938, of which 6 accounted for approximately 75% of total sales. The Scripps-Howard survey in 16 cities (shown in Table 102, p. 418) indicated 70% of ownership concentrated among the six leading brands. In addition, 8.2% of the families surveyed owned Servel Electrolux gas refrigerators.

According to the 1937 surveys of the above papers and discussion with executives in the trade, the leading brands were as follows: Frigidaire clearly was the top; General Electric held second place; Nash Kelvinator Corporation, with its Leonard subsidiary, was third; Norge was fourth; and Servel Electrolux, Westinghouse, and Coldspot followed closely.

Further evidence regarding the number of manufacturers and the degree of concentration of business among them is given in the price study of the T.N.E.C., which secured its data from the U. S. Bureau of the Census. As shown in Table 122, there were in 1937,

TABLE 122

TOTAL PRODUCTION OF DOMESTIC ELECTRIC REFRIGERATORS AND PRODUCTION OF FIRST FOUR COMPANIES, SHOWING PERCENTAGE OF CONCENTRATION, 1937

	Production of First Four Companies	Percent of Total	Total Production	Number of Companies
Capacity under 6 cubic feet:				
Number	754,130	69	1,093,026	21
Value	$58,464,364	69	$84,458,077	
Capacity 6 to under 10 cubic feet:				
Number	728,660	74	991,022	25
Value	$73,739,375	77	$95,985,895	
Capacity 10 cubic feet and over (including those not reported by size):				
Number	*	*	*	14
Value	$2,406,123	77	$3,130,046	

* Data not available.

Source: Temporary National Economic Committee, *Price Behavior and Business Policy, op. cit.*, p. 163.

25 companies manufacturing domestic electric refrigerators, with over 70% of the business distributed among the first four companies.

Since 1937 new brands, such as Philco and Gibson, have entered the market with aggressive selling methods. In addition, while private branding by department stores had not become common by 1940, there was evidence that an increasing number of department stores were selling under their own brands, as shown by advertisements observed in 1940 and 1941 in metropolitan newspapers of the East and Middle West.

In short, in the refrigerator industry, as in many manufacturing industries, there has developed a relatively high degree of concentration among producers. Many producers have disappeared. While new concerns occasionally have entered the field, there have not been many. In addition to the complexity of manufacture and large investment involved, the difficulty of securing distribution and sales for an unknown brand and the difficulty of making a new brand known have operated against easy entry into the market.

Competition in Aggressive Selling and Advertising

That there has been strong competition among these suppliers in aggressive personal selling and in advertising was developed at length in Chapter XV. This competition in large degree was to secure a primary demand, to lead consumers to buy refrigerators instead of making other use of their money, particularly in the early years, when home solicitation of prospects was common. The growth of demand, upon which lower costs of production were predicated, was attributable in considerable degree to this aggressive selling. At all times, of course, there was also competition between the brands through appeals based upon superiority of mechanism, value, and differentiating features. The manufacturers generally spent between 5% and 10% of their sales value for advertising; private brands, such as those of Sears, Roebuck and Company and Montgomery Ward & Co., Incorporated, were also aggressive advertisers, but their expenditure per unit was apparently lower than under the customary wholesaler-retailer type of distribution.

Competition in Product Differentiation

Accompanying the competition in advertising and selling was a vigorous competition in quality, which is discussed at length in

Chapter XXII. Here was a relatively new product, not yet perfected. Increased sales depended in appreciable degree upon its perfection, particularly in the reduction of the cost of its operation. Producers sought consumer preference by constant striving for points of differentiation that consumers might look upon as improvements.

In any analysis, price data must be interpreted in the light of rapidly changing quality. As shown in Table 133, page 617, a six-foot model of the General Electric refrigerator in 1940 was priced at only $132.75, approximately 43% of the $310 charged for the same size model of 1927. But the six-foot refrigerator of 1940 was not the refrigerator of 1927; food storage was greater, kilowatt-hour consumption was less, noisiness was reduced, ice cubes froze more quickly, and the life of the refrigerator was about three times as long. Since manufacturers have had to match competitors' quality, it is assumed that these figures are indicative of a general advance of all refrigerators after 1927, and 1927 refrigerators were far superior to those of 1920.

Data showing the increase in expected life for all electric refrigerators are found in a table of estimated durability of electric refrigerators, given by Mr. Saul Nelson in his price study for the T.N.E.C. and shown here in Table 123. According to this estimate the average life expectancy grew from 6 years in 1920 to 15 years after 1937. This evidence like that above shows a large improvement in quality, which must be considered in interpreting price data.

Price History—Extent of Price Competition

To what extent there was competition in price among the various sellers must be judged largely from the price record. The average

TABLE 123
ESTIMATED DURABILITY OF ELECTRIC REFRIGERATORS

Year of Manufacture	Life Expectancy, Years*	Year of Manufacture	Life Expectancy, Years*
1920	6	1930	13
1921	7	1931	13
1922	8	1932	13
1923	9	1933	13
1924	10	1934	14
1925	11	1935	14
1926	11	1936	14
1927	12	1937	15
1928	12	1938	15
1929	12		

* The figure for each year is an average of data compiled from a sample study which was made by a large manufacturer of refrigerators.

Source: Temporary National Economic Committee, *op. cit.,* p. 149.

retail price per unit and an indication of its relation to prices generally is shown in Table 124.

The evidence indicates that during the period 1920 and 1933 competition in price was in effect to considerable degree. Prices fell rapidly and continuously from $600 to $170, while the machines improved. The $170 average refrigerator of 1933 was far better than the $600 product of 1920. Sellers turned to price reductions as well as to aggressive selling and product improvement to get sales volume. The profit of the producers is not known, but it appears that much of the saving in production during this period was passed on in lower prices. Moreover, while aggressive selling continued, the amount expended per unit fell as prices were reduced.

Prices since 1933

From 1933 on, the average price remained practically constant. Competition between the leading brands during these years was carried on largely on two grounds: (a) product improvement and (b) aggressive selling and advertising.

In recent years the price structures of the leading brands of electric refrigerators, other than distributors' brands, have been similar.

TABLE 124

UNIT PRICES OF MECHANICAL REFRIGERATORS, 1920–1940

YEAR	AVERAGE RETAIL PRICE PER UNIT		B.L.S. COMBINED INDEX OF WHOLESALE PRICES 1926 = 100
	Dollars	Index, 1926 = 100	
Up to 1920...	$600	154	154.4
1921	550	141	97.6
1922	525	135	96.7
1923	475	122	100.6
1924	450	115	98.1
1925	425	109	103.5
1926	390	100	100.0
1927	350	90	95.4
1928	334	86	96.7
1929	292	75	95.3
1930	275	71	86.4
1931	258	66	73.0
1932	195	50	64.8
1933	170	44	65.9
1934	172	44	74.9
1935	162	42	80.0
1936	164	42	80.8
1937	171	44	86.3
1938	172	44	78.6
1939	168	43	77.1
1940	152	39	....

Sources: Table 92, p. 397, and *Statistical Abstract of the United States, 1940*, p. 323.

TABLE 125

List Prices of Electric Refrigerators, Principal Companies, 1938*

Size, Cubic Feet	Frigidaire	General Electric	Westinghouse	Kelvinator	Crosley	Leonard	Norge	Stewart Warner	Universal Cooler	Coldspot
3.0 to 3.9:										
Size	3.1	....	3.2	3.16	3.16	3.14	3.12	....	....	4.2
Model	D3	....	HDS-32	K3-38	KB5-31	L3-38	R32-8	....	....	3804
Price	$119.50	....	$119.50	$118.95	$117.50	$118.95	$117.50	....	....	$114.50
4.0 to 4.9:										
Size	4.1	4	4.2	4.15	4.3	4.1	4.14	4.5	....	....
Model	N4-38	B-4	HDS-42	K4-38	KB5-43	L4-38	R41-8	458	....	....
Price	$144.50	$144.50	$144.50	$142.95	$142.50	$142.95	$142.50	$144.75	....	....
5.0 to 5.9:										
Size	5.1	5	5.2	5.16	5.07	5.12	5.15	5.64	5.25	....
Model	Sp. 5-38	JB-5	HS-52	KS5-38	KB5-50	LS5-38	S52-8	550	AD-538	....
Price	$164.50	$164.95	$169.50	$162.95	$162.50	$162.95	$162.50	$164.75	$164.95	....
6.0 to 6.9:										
Size	6.1	6.1	6.2	6.13	6.0	6.09	6.15	6.3	6.51	6.3
Model	Sp. 6-38	JB-6	HS-62	KS6-38	KB5-60	LS6-38	S62-8	770	AD-658	3816
Price	$184.75	$184.75	$189.50	$182.95	$182.50	$182.95	$182.50	$179.75	$184.95	$169.50
7.0 to 7.9:										
Size	7.2	7.1	7.2	7.19	7.1	7.3	7.14	....	7.45	....
Model	Sp. 7-38	JB-7	HS-72	KS7-38	KB5-71	LS7-38	S71-B	....	AD-758	....
Price	$204.75	$204.75	$209.50	$202.95	$202.00	$202.95	$202.50	....	$204.95	....
8.0 to 8.9:										
Size	8.25	8.1	....	....	....	....	8.11	....	....	8.6
Model	M8-38	B-8	....	....	....	....	R81-8	....	....	3838
Price	$264.50	$264.50	....	....	....	....	$259.50	....	....	$179.50

* Prices are lowest price comparable model in each size group.

Source: Temporary National Economic Committee, *op. cit.*, p. 162, which cites *Air Conditioning and Refrigeration News*, Business News Publishing Co., March 9, 1938, as the original source.

This similarity is indicated in Table 125 which shows list prices for 1938 of comparable models of the leading brands, although comparability here does not mean that they are identical or necessarily equivalent. Of the leading brands, all comparable models were priced within a few dollars of one another. Coldspot, the Sears, Roebuck and Company brand, however, was priced below the others; for example, the 6-cubic foot size was priced at $169.50, as against $179.75 to $189.50 for other models.

In the refrigerator industry, as in many other industries, producers and sellers have faced an important merchandising problem in trying to balance lower price against product improvement. Refrigerator manufacturers have been criticized by those outside the industry for apparently centering competition to too great a degree upon product improvements and for apparently having shown a disinclination to produce low-price models without the various niceties with which they were trying to attract consumer favor. The stability of refrigerator price structures between 1932 and 1940 and the stress on improvements have been cited as evidence.

Be this a fair criticism or not, in 1940 the experiment of seeking demand for a low-price, "stripped" model was launched by one of the leading manufacturers. In 1940 Kelvinator, concentrating production on 6-foot and 8-foot models, took the lead in offering a price list substantially under that of 1939 and featured as a leader a 6.25 cubic foot stripped model at $119.95. It was presented as a "low-priced model for families of limited budget, giving size, perfect refrigeration, and convenience."

Other companies, which had already announced prices similar to their 1939 prices, immediately had to revise their schedules to meet Kelvinator prices, and most of them also brought out stripped models at prices as low as $114.75. Sears, Roebuck and Company offered a stripped model at $89.95. The delivered prices of leading brands in Boston in 1940 are shown in Table 126.

That the lower prices of 1940 were a stimulant to sales was indicated by the all-time high in number of boxes sold, 2,600,000. The average price dropped from $169 to $152. A number of dealers interviewed in the Boston area stated that while they emphasized higher-price models in their selling efforts with consumers, a substantial percentage of sales were of the stripped models. For some dealers stripped models represented as high as 40% of the total number of

TABLE 126

RETAIL PUBLISHED LIST PRICES OF ELECTRICAL REFRIGERATORS, 1940
(DELIVERED, BOSTON, MASSACHUSETTS)

NORGE			FRIGIDAIRE		
Model	Cubic Feet	Price	Model	Cubic Feet	Price
VR3S	3.25	$119.95	SV3	3.00	$119.50
VR3	3.33	119.95	SV4	4.00	119.50
VR4	4.22	144.95	Master 5	5.10	149.50
DR5	5.62	197.50	Cold Wall Master 5	5.00	169.50
SR5	5.62	219.95	DeLuxe	5.00	174.50
UR6	......	159.95	SVS6	6.00	114.75
MR6	6.75	189.95	Super Value 6	6.00	129.50
DR6	6.65	219.95	Master 6	6.00	159.50
SR6	6.65	244.95	DeLuxe 6	6.00	189.50
DR8	8.75	249.95	Cold Wall Master	6.00	184.50
SR8	8.75	279.95	Cold Wall	6.00	214.50
			Cold Wall (porcelain)	6.00	239.50
WESTINGHOUSE			Super Value	8.00	169.50
			Master 8	8.00	199.50
Model	Cubic Feet	Price	Cold Wall	8.00	254.50
			Cold Wall (porcelain)	8.00	279.50
U3	2.90	$119.75			
H5	5.25	169.75	GENERAL ELECTRIC		
H6	6.25	179.75			
A5	5.25	189.75	Model	Cubic Feet	Price
A6	6.25	204.75			
A8	8.25	254.00	JB4	4.00	$129.75
A135	13.50	419.50	JB5	5.00	169.75
A200	20.10	489.50	JB6	6.00	179.75
E6	6.25	234.50	B3	3.00	119.75
E8	8.25	279.50	B5	5.00	197.75
E135	13.50	469.50	B6	6.00	214.75
E200	20.10	549.50	B8	8.25	259.75
S3	3.25	119.75	PB5	5.00	219.50
S4	4.25	129.75	PB6	6.10	239.50
LS6	6.20	114.75	PB8	8.24	279.50
S6	6.20	139.75	PB12	12.00	453.00
S8	8.25	179.75	PB16	16.00	557.00
D6	6.25	224.75	LB6B	6.00	114.75
D8	8.25	264.75	LB3	3.00	119.75
			LB6	6.00	139.75
KELVINATOR			LB8	8.00	179.75
Model	Cubic Feet	Price	COLDSPOT		
			Model	Cubic Feet	Price
SS6	6.25	$119.95			
S6	6.25	139.95	4046	6.50	$ 89.95
HS6	6.00	169.95	4066	6.50	112.95
R6	6.25	179.95	4096	6.30	129.50
HD6	6.10	209.95	4016	6.20	149.50
S8	8.20	189.95	4018	8.30	169.50
R8	8.20	209.95			
HD8	8.00	239.95			

Source: Dealers' literature.

boxes sold. These sales were said to have been made largely to consumers in low income brackets who previously had not considered purchase of electric refrigerators.

By 1940 in most city markets an appreciable business in recondi-
tioned refrigerators had developed. As in the case of the automobile
industry this second-hand business gave promise of tapping a market
among low-income bracket groups not reached by the lower prices
initiated for new boxes in 1940. In 1941 the price schedules again
were reported to represent reductions. Stripped models started at
approximately the same level as in 1940, $114.75 for 6-foot models.
In the better models there were numerous reductions, and sales efforts
according to trade paper reports were directed to these. In turn, the
offering of improvements again was evident in the new models of
the various producers.[2]

Summary

To sum up: in the history of the mechanical refrigerator industry
there is clear evidence of competition in price accompanying strong
competition in advertising, selling, and quality improvement. Competition in price has been strong enough to give to consumers much of the
production economy effected, and it appears to have brought a reduction
in the advertising and promotional expenditure per unit by the manufacturers. In addition to the direct price competition between leading
manufacturers there has been effective competition between the usual
wholesaler-retailer type of distribution used by leading brands and
the integrated distribution of the large chains and mail order houses
with their private brands. The latter method has undoubtedly involved
lower selling and distribution costs in some instances and these private
branders have priced their boxes appreciably below manufacturers'
brands to attract business. Such competition has served as a check
against growth of the selling costs incurred in the usual distributive
set-up. Growth of such competition may be expected to force reduction
of selling costs in the course of time.

RELATION OF ADVERTISING TO THE PRICES AND PRICING
STRUCTURE OF CERTAIN DRUG, COSMETIC,
AND GROCERY SPECIALTIES

In order to widen the range of evidence regarding the effect of
advertising upon prices of merchandise, information on the prices and
pricing practice for a number of drug, cosmetic, and grocery specialties

---

[2] "Review and Forecast," *Electrical Merchandising*, January, 1940, p. 16.

was sought. These are heavily advertised products and it has been charged that in these areas the most extreme effects of advertising in increasing price are likely to be found. In the investigation of these products evidence was taken from printed reports of certain other investigators and a large amount of additional new evidence was secured in the survey among large-scale retailers, which has already been described.[3]

The Relation of Advertising to the Price of Drug Specialties—Aspirin

The margins between manufacturing costs and selling prices which have persisted for many brands of proprietary drug products have been so wide as to bring severe criticism. These wide margins have been particularly noticeable in the case of items which have had to conform to the U. S. Pharmacopoeia or the National Formulary. Certain brands in some instances have been able to claim refinements not possessed by similar articles which nevertheless do meet government standards; yet the price differentials enjoyed by the branded articles have often been wide indeed. One of the most frequently cited articles of this type is aspirin. In June, 1938, Bayer's aspirin, the leading advertised brand, for which a high degree of solubility was claimed, had a wholesale price of 75 cents an ounce. At the same time, aspirin under its generic term of acetylsalicylic acid was available at wholesale at 13 cents an ounce, or about 17% as much.[4]

In recent years, consumers have been given the option of buying aspirin at a price much lower than that charged for Bayer's. In the survey among corporate drug chains in the early months of 1938, 7 out of 13 chains reporting sold aspirin under their own brands, as did several of the department stores and department store chains interviewed. Among the seven drug chains the prices asked for different brands of aspirin are shown in the following summary:

BRAND	CONTAINER SIZE	MEDIAN PRICE, CENTS	PRICE RANGE, CENTS	MEDIAN GROSS MARGIN OBTAINED	RANGE OF GROSS MARGINS OBTAINED
Distributors'.......	100's	37	29–39	59.0%	50–70%
Bayer's...........	100's	59	59*	27.5	26–28
Squibb's..........	100's	39	39*	36.0	33–36

* Maintained price.

[3] See Chapter XVIII, p. 473 ff.

[4] Temporary National Economic Committee, *op. cit.*, p. 81, which cites the Blue Price List Section of the *American Druggist*, July, 1938, as the source of price data.

The prices of the distributors' brands of aspirin were from 49% to 66% as much as the Bayer brand, even though the distributors took appreciably larger markups on their brands than they did upon the Bayer brand. In turn, distributors' brands sold at amounts ranging from 75% to 100% of the price asked for Squibb's aspirin, which had the benefit of the family brand of a leading pharmaceutical house, although it did not have the benefit of much specific advertising such as had been accorded Bayer's. The Squibb Company priced its aspirin about 33% below the Bayer brand.

One of the large department stores included in the survey was selling its own brand of aspirin at 18 cents for 100 tablets, as against the Bayer maintained price of 59 cents and Squibb's maintained price of 39 cents. At the retail selling price of 18 cents the store obtained a mark-up of 39% of selling price and sold large amounts of the item. It should be added, however, that this store evidently bought this item on an advantageous contract that was not available to other private branders. The aspirin was used as a special price leader to help build a reputation of low price to be had under the store's brands.

The extent to which the low prices on distributors' brands have led consumers to switch their patronage from the high-price brands is not known, but apparently this competition had begun to have its effect by 1938. Among the 7 drug chains handling their own brands of aspirin, sales in 1938 were distributed as follows between their own brands and manufacturers' brands:

Company Number	Percentage of Business on Own Brand	Percentage of Business on Manufacturers' Brands
1	41	59
2	39	61
3	28	72
4	27	73
5	20	80
6	5	95
7	5	95

Companies 1 to 4, inclusive, those with largest sales under their own brands, i.e., from 27% to 41% of the total sales of aspirin, stated that the trend of such sales had been upward during the preceding years. Company No. 5 stated that the sales of aspirin under its own brand had been approximately stationary, while companies 6 to 7 indicated that sales under their own brands had been downward. In these two instances the managements had ceased to push their own brands vigorously after the advent of price maintenance on manufacturers' brands.

While the above data provide some evidence that low price has had an effect in attracting demand for this widely used drug, it is evident that a large part of total demand has gone to manufacturers' brands at wide margins. It should be noted that consumers generally have had a choice open to them, but only a minority have exercised the low price option available. The majority have thus evidently preferred to pay relatively high prices for certain differentiating qualities and for the reputation for integrity of manufacture which they attach to the well-known brands. The question may be raised, however, as to whether a substantial number of these buyers have been acquainted with the fact that all brands of aspirin have had to conform to the U. S. Pharmacopoeia and that this conformity has insured the consumer protection as to quality and efficacy of the drug. It is in areas such as this that consumer education might possibly in time have appreciable effect in making consumers more responsive to price and thus check the continuation of the wide margins indicated.[5]

The Relation of Advertising to Prices of Proprietary Remedies with Secret Formulae

Proprietary remedies, whose formulae had usually been secret until the 1938 Food and Drug Act made it mandatory to list contents upon labels, have provided extreme cases of freedom from direct price competition. Their competition has come wholly from substitutes, each with its own secret formula. Competition on those proprietaries promoted to consumers rather than to doctors has been largely through advertising which has stressed primary appeals. Without advertising there would be little demand for such proprietaries. Accordingly, companies selling them have followed the only operating method which has given promise of profitable operation. Pricing in such cases

---

[5] Able students of consumption have expressed to the author their serious doubt that consumers will respond readily to education that tries to make them save money on relief for their ailments. Those interested in the consumer movement and private branders have frequently called attention of consumers to the wide differential in prices of various brands of aspirin which meet official standards; yet demand has continued to go predominantly to the Bayer brand. Since the mind has an important relation to ailments and since the desire for physical well-being is so great, consumers apparently are willing to pay a considerable differential for the remedy which gives them even slight promise of greater efficacy. As one student of consumption stated to the author: "After all, a person who imagines he has a headache does not mind paying 1.18 cents for two tablets which he imagines may relieve it; he may be quite indifferent to assertions that for .36 cents or .47 cents he may obtain two physically equivalent tablets that have less control over his imagination."

has presented the problem of balancing the pull of advertising against the value of the dollar to consumers. The manufacturer's price for such articles has often represented a small part of the retail selling price.

To illustrate, a family squabble gave the world the financial history of the Lydia E. Pinkham Medicine Company for the period from 1908 to 1935, inclusive. The report of a master, appointed by Massachusetts courts to take evidence in a suit between two factions of this company, revealed "All costs apart from advertising have mounted and now amount to about 30% of the gross sales."[6] For many years previous to the suit, the nominal retail list price for Lydia E. Pinkham Compound was $1.25 a bottle, and the price to wholesalers $10 a dozen, or approximately 80 cents a bottle. Total costs, aside from advertising, accordingly, were approximately 24 cents a bottle. Advertising costs, as disclosed by data submitted in the suit, over the years averaged approximately 40 cents a bottle, indicating a profit to the company of 16 cents a bottle. Here is a clear example of limited monopoly. There has been competition only from substitutes sold by similar methods.

Cost figures submitted by certain manufacturers of proprietary remedies which have been given in Table 106, page 444, illustrate similar wide margins between selling prices and manufacturing costs with large advertising costs. Manufacturing costs of company No. 28 in 1937 were only 16.6% of its selling price, advertising and sales promotion costs were 33.6% and total marketing costs 44.4%. Manufacturing costs of company No. 31 were only 12.8% of selling price, and advertising costs, which made up total marketing costs, were 55.4% of sales. Further examples of wide spreads of proprietary remedies are given in Table 127.

The Relation of Advertising to the Prices of Cosmetics

Like proprietary remedies, many cosmetics with their secret formulae have been completely individualized products. For example, the opportunities for variation in hand lotions are legion. Cosmetics frequently have sold with wide spreads between manufacturing costs and retail price, spreads which have been devoted very largely to advertising and aggressive selling. Table 127 shows the estimated

---

[6] N. H. Borden, *Problems in Advertising* (3d ed., New York, McGraw-Hill Book Company, Inc., 1937), case of Lydia E. Pinkham Medicine Company, p. 103.

TABLE 127

COMPARISON OF RETAIL PRICES OF DRUGS, COSMETICS, AND FOODS, WITH THE COSTS OF THEIR INGREDIENTS

Product Name	Advertised Use	Quantity	Cost of Ingredients		Retail Price Under Brand Name
			Wholesale	Retail	
Proprietary medicines:					
Carpentier's Compound	Cure for TB and ulcers of stomach	Per jar	$0.50		$7.00
Currier's Tablets	Ulcers of stomach, hyperacidity, general gastric distress	100 tablets		$1.85	5.00
Renesol	Phenobarbital and baking-soda tablets	65 capsules		.98	4.50
Electrovita	Stomach	1 gallon		.02	2.00
Mouthwashes: Listerine			Few cents		About $1.00
Dental remedy: Ora-Noid	Dental remedy	Per can	$0.10		$2.00
Reducing agent:					
Germania Herb Tea		Per package	$0.15		1.50
Lesser	Bathing salts	Per package	Few cents		1.00
Min-amin	Vitamin food	5 ounces	Few cents		1.00
Pomay Rx	Salve	8 ounces	About $0.40		10.00
Stardom's Holly-Diet	Reducing food	Package	2 cents to 3 cents		$1 to $2
Cure for baldness:					
Downing's Cure		4 bottles of different substances	$0.65		$5.00
Cosmetics:					
Cory's Dusting Powder		4.708 ounces		.157	.75
Cory's Face Powder		1.818 ounces		.120	.75
Elizabeth Arden Face Powder		5.345 ounces		.338	3.00
Elizabeth Arden Dusting Powder Venetian		11.244 ounces		.466	3.00
Harriett Hubbard Ayer Face Powder		2.262 ounces		.066	.60
Harriett Hubbard Ayer Ayeristocrat Bath Powder		10.170 ounces		.220	1.65
Daggett and Ramsdell Dusting Powder		4.883 ounces		.160	.85
Daggett and Ramsdell Face Powder		2.934 ounces		.094	.85
Max Factor Face Powder		4.584 ounces		.118	.75
Helena Rubenstein Face Powder		2.644 ounces		.100	1.00
Bourjois Sales Corp. Poudre Java		3.332 ounces		.098	.50
Evening in Paris Bath Dusting Powder		5.020 ounces		.164	1.10
Evening in Paris Face Powder with Perfume				.174	1.10
Richard Hudnut Face Powder Marvelous		2.479 ounces		.065	.55
Luzier's Face Powder		1.872 ounces		.077	1.00

TABLE 127 (Continued)

Product Name	Advertised Use	Quantity	Cost of Ingredients		Retail Price Under Brand Name
			Wholesale	Retail	
Cosmetics—Continued					
Luzier's Cleansing Cream		5.700 ounces		$0.197	$2.50
Luzier's Lu Mar Massage Cream		1.802 ounces		.140	3.00
Luzier's Lutone Skin Cream		2.109 ounces		.061	1.00
Coty Rouge Refill		0.148 ounce		.037	.38
Max Factor Dry Rouge		0.300 ounce		.082	.38
Luzier Rouge		0.317 ounce		.143	1.00
Harriett Hubbard Ayer Cream Rouge		0.315 ounce		.038	.55
Elizabeth Arden Venetian Lip Paste		0.357 ounce		.024	1.00
Springtime in Paris Lipstick		0.140 ounce		.737	1.25
Bourjois Sales Corp. Lipstick		0.070 ounce		.031	.55
Coty's Special Astringent		4.000 ounces		.071	1.00
Harriett Hubbard Ayer Special Astringent		11.993 ounces		.088	1.75
Primrose House Skin Freshener		4.000 ounces		.061	.85
Luzier Skin Refreshener		1.910 ounces		.087	2.50
Elizabeth Arden Venetian Dermatex Depilatory		2.323 ounces		.190	2.00
Evening in Paris Perfume		0.550 ounce		.268	2.75
Springtime in Paris Double Vanity		0.058 ounce		.252	1.75
Barbara Gould Cuticle Remover		0.566 ounce		.053	.55
Barbara Gould Hand Lotion		3.999 ounces		.082	.45
Food:					
Ovaltine		14 ounces		.100	.75
Instant Alberty's Food		16 ounces		.200	1.35
Chemm		16 ounces		.140	.59

Source: Temporary National Economic Committee, *Price Behavior and Business Policy*, *op. cit.*, pp. 82–83.

retail cost of physical ingredients and the retail price of certain brands of cosmetics and proprietaries, as estimated by the American Medical Association and by the Bureau of Health of the State of Maine. The table is a summary compiled for the study on *Price Behavior and Business Policy* of the T.N.E.C. It is not a statement of manufacturers' total costs. Manufacturers of cosmetics generally find that attractive and relatively costly containers greatly influence consumers' choices. Yet these container costs, which are an important cost element, are apparently not allowed for in the table. Consequently, such a table gives an exaggerated impression of the spread between manufacturers' costs and retail prices for many of these items. Nevertheless, even after material allowance is made for this exaggeration, a comparison of retail value of ingredients and of retail price is indicative in these instances of a wide spread between final price and manufacturing costs. Here again, sellers have been immune from direct competition upon price. Competition has been largely in advertising and aggressive selling, because these have been the effective methods for obtaining sales.

Evidence as to the relatively wide margins between selling price of manufacturers and their manufacturing costs and the extent to which this margin is devoted to advertising is contained in the cost data submitted by cosmetic manufacturers, which were included in Table 106, page 444. The manufacturing costs of cosmetic manufacturer No. 24 were 49.4% of sales; advertising and promotional costs were 28.5% of sales; while total marketing costs were 36.1% of sales. The manufacturing costs of manufacturer No. 29 were 36.1% of sales; advertising and promotional costs were 27.4% of sales; and total marketing costs were 46% of sales. The manufacturing costs of manufacturer No. 32 were 37.7% of sales; advertising costs were 37.1% of sales; while total marketing costs were 56.3% of sales. All these companies were among those with widest spreads between manufacturing costs and selling prices.

In the selection of cosmetics, consumers have undoubtedly been influenced more by strong emotional ideas associated with various brands than by reason based on scientific knowledge of the constituents and performance of products. Competing products have had secret formulae, and each brand has developed its own reputation. For many cosmetics it is difficult for the consumer through usage to determine with certainty the relative efficacy of different brands. Consequently, reputation built through advertising and through other aggressive selling methods has had much influence upon valuations. Consumers have been prone to avoid unknown or little known brands, even though the latter have been priced much lower than the known brands. To illustrate, a department store[7] which sold high-grade cosmetics under its own brand at prices materially below well-known brands in the market secured unsatisfactory sales volume at such prices. When, however, it set its prices just slightly below those of certain leading brands and made quality comparisons with such brands, it obtained a substantial volume of sales. Consumers looked upon a wide price differential as indicative of inferior quality. Subsequently a higher price and an association of ideas of quality with the product brought consumers' confidence.

In the field of cosmetics, entry into manufacture has been easy, and consumers have had opportunity to direct their purchases among many brands, some of which have sold at low prices. The ease of entry from a manufacturing standpoint is indicated by the fact that neighborhood druggists can compound hand lotions, and often do so to sell to their local clientele. The ease of entry into this field is indicated by *The Milwaukee Journal's* survey of the use of liquid hand lotions in its market area in 1936.[8] Effort was made in this survey to limit consideration to brands of manufacturers, wholesalers, and chains. Excluding brands of local pharmacists, 175 brands of hand lotion were being used among the families interviewed as of January 15, 1936. Only 9 of the brands, however, were used by at least 1% of the families; 166 brands were distributed among only 8.7% of the families. Consumer brand preference in that market was as follows:

BRAND	PER CENT OF ALL FAMILIES BUYING THIS TYPE OF PRODUCT WHO USE EACH BRAND—1936
Campana	50.8
Hinds	15.7
Jergen's	11.3
Mary King	6.3
Chamberlain's	2.5
Woodbury	1.9
Hess	1.6
Frostilla	1.3
Dame Nature	1.0
Miscellaneous*	8.7

* Including all brands used by less than 1 per cent of the total consumers of liquid hand lotion. (1936—166 brands).

Source: *The Milwaukee Journal, op. cit.,* 1936, p. 85.

[7] Based on confidential case material.
[8] "Consumer Analysis of the Greater Milwaukee Market," 1936,   p. 85.

Evidence was gathered in our survey among large-scale distributors regarding the prices charged for the distributors' own brands of hand lotion and for the fastest selling manufacturers' brands. The number of brands carried per store varied between 8 and 18. The prices charged for the two leading manufacturers' brands and for distributors' own brands, together with the margins obtained, are given in the following table:

BRAND	SIZE OF CONTAINER OUNCES	RETAIL PRICE	PRICE PER OUNCE	APPROX. GROSS MARGIN OBTAINED BY DISTRIBUTORS
Jergen's	6.5	$0.39*	$.065	22%
Hinds	4.5	.39*	.087	20
Brand of Drug Chain No. 1..	6.0	.29	.048	54
Brand of Drug Chain No. 2..	8.0	.29	.036	60
Brand of Drug Chain No. 3..	8.0	.37	.046	50
Brand of Drug Chain No. 4..	6.0	.39	.065	60
Brand of Drug Chain No. 5..	4.0	.33	.082	67
Brand of Drug Chain No. 6..	6.0	.33	.055	51

* Maintained price.

The formulae for these various lotions were different and consequently there was wide room for variation in appeal to consumers' likes and dislikes among them. The distributors' brands generally, though not in all cases, were priced below the manufacturers' brands. They ranged from $.036 an ounce to $.082 an ounce, whereas Jergen's Lotion sold for $.065 and Hinds Honey and Almond Cream for $.087 an ounce. Yet at the lower prices received for their brands, the chains took very liberal markups, that is, from 50% to 60% or more as against 20% to 22% on the advertised brands.

The extent to which these chains secured sales of their own lotions varied, the range being from 1% to 26% of total sales of lotion. Two chains reported that they had an upward trend of sales; two reported that sales were relatively constant; and two others stated that their sales trend was down.

The evidence obtained in this study as well as that taken from other investigations indicates clearly that in the case of cosmetics as well as of proprietary drugs competition in advertising has been the rule rather than competition on price. Consumers have had wide choice, including the opportunity of buying on price appeal. They have not availed themselves of such opportunities, however, and have preferred to buy well-known brands at higher prices. Consequently, most producers have followed the policy of pricing these products with wide margins between production costs and consumer price, and have devoted substantial parts of these margins to advertising. Private branders have not priced their products closely as a rule because low price has evidently not been highly effective in attracting patronage.

The Relation of Advertising to the Prices of Certain Grocery Specialties

Attention is turned from drug and cosmetic items to the findings regarding the prices of certain grocery specialties, of which the first is all-purpose flour. The prices current in the early months of 1939 of the distributors' brands of all-purpose flour were obtained from 16 corporate chains, and the corresponding current prices of two leading manufacturers' brands, Gold Medal and Pillsbury. The following table is a summary of the prices charged and the margins obtained, as reported by these chains:

	CONTAINER SIZE, POUNDS	MEDIAN PRICES, CENTS	RANGE OF PRICES, CENTS	MEDIAN GROSS MARGINS OBTAINED	RANGE OF GROSS MARGINS OBTAINED
Distributor's brand.	24½	59	53–75	20%	13–35%
Gold Medal........	24½	90	83–103	14	9–21
Pillsbury	24½	85	83–103	14	9–21

Prices of distributors' brands ranged from 53 cents to 75 cents, as against a range of 83 cents to $1.03 for the advertised brands. The low price of 53 cents represented a short-time price leader quotation. The median charge for distributors' brands was 59 cents, as against 90 cents for Gold Medal and 85 cents for Pillsbury. In spite of the fact that the distributors' brands were sold at appreciably lower prices, the distributors took a larger markup on the average on their own brands than they did on the manufacturers' brands, 20% on the former, as against 14% on the latter. No effort was made in the study to judge the qualities of the various brands of flour. Among the 16 private branders, 9 stated that their flour was of equal quality to the manufacturers' brand; 1 claimed a somewhat higher quality; 4 stated that their product was of lower quality; but these claims were not checked.

Indicative of the pull of price and store promotional methods, these chains reported that a large percentage of flour sales was of their own brands. Fifteen out of the 16 chains said that the trend of sales of their own brands as a part of total flour sales had been upward during the preceding 10 years. One stated that the percentage had been relatively constant. The percentage of total sales secured for their own brands for 1938 varied from 32% to 85%.

That a very large percentage of flour demand among consumers generally goes to the advertised brands was shown by the Scripps-Howard "Nation-Wide Inventory," 1938.[9] Among the 50,379 homes having all-purpose flour, Gold Medal was found in 37.7%; Pillsbury's Best in 14%; while the remaining 48.3% was distributed among a large number of brands. *The Milwaukee Journal*[10] for that year reported Gold Medal among 41.2% of all flour users; Pillsbury's among 33.5%; while the remaining 25.3% of families accounted for some 51 brands.

In summary, it appears that in the flour industry there is no lack of active price competition; yet reputation and possible quality differences permit a substantial price differential to persist.

Relation of Advertising to the Prices of Canned Milk

Price data on canned milk were obtained in the survey because in the canned milk industry all producers must meet government standards; consequently, the product approaches standardization. While there is some variation above government standards, few products bought by the consumer so closely approach being identical. Among the corporate chains interviewed, 13 had their own brands of canned milk.[11] Twelve claimed that their brands were equal in quality to the advertised, manufacturers' brands; one claimed somewhat higher quality. The prices at which the distributors' brands and the two leading manufacturers' brands were currently being sold by these chains in the early months of 1939, and the margins which they took, were as follows:

	CONTAINER SIZE, OUNCES	MEDIAN PRICES, CENTS	RANGE OF PRICES, CENTS	MEDIAN GROSS MARGINS OBTAINED	RANGE OF GROSS MARGINS OBTAINED
Distributors' brands.	14½	6.25	5.5–6.3	12.0%	4–21%
Carnation	14½	7.0	6.0–7.67	15.0	6–22
Pet	14½	7.0	6.25–7.00	15.0	6–16

The median price on the distributors' brands was 6.25 cents, or 4 cans for 25 cents. The range in their prices was from 5.5 cents to 6.3

---

[9] *Market Records*, 1938, *op. cit.*, p. 54.
[10] *Op. cit.*, 1938, p. 36.
[11] Some of the organizations interviewed manufactured their own canned milk.

cents. A somewhat higher price was asked for the advertised manufacturers' brands, the median price for both being 7 cents. The range for Carnation was 6 cents to 7.67 cents, somewhat higher than for Pet, which was 6.25 to 7 cents.

The distributors' margins on canned milk were in contrast to the margins obtained for many of the products studied. The margins secured on the somewhat lower prices of their own brands were not on the average as high as those secured on the manufacturers' brands, the median gross margin for distributors' brands being 12%, for manufacturers' brands 15%.

It will be noted that the behavior of prices for canned milk conforms to the pattern previously mentioned for products which have small opportunity for differentiation. The reputation established by the manufacturers has permitted them to get a slightly higher price than the less-advertised distributors' brands; yet the differential in this case is relatively narrow.

At their lower prices the chains were apparently attracting a considerable volume of business from the manufacturers' brands. The percentage of total canned milk sales on their own brands was reported to vary all the way from 21% to 91%. Most of the chains, however, reported over 50% of their canned milk being sold under their own brands.

The Scripps-Howard survey in 16 cities showed Carnation milk used by 21.6% of the families using such a product and Pet by 17.2%, while the remaining 61% was distributed among various manufacturers' and distributors' brands. *The Milwaukee Journal's survey* for 1939 showed Carnation to be used by 32.3% of the families consuming canned milk; Whitehouse (A. & P. brand), 18.1%; Gehl (regional brand), 24.1%; Pet, 11.4%; while some 15% of the families distributed their patronage among some 36 brands.

Relation of Advertising to the Prices of Breakfast Food

Generally speaking, distributors have not put out highly specialized breakfast foods under their own brands; yet a fair number have their own brands of corn flakes. Six corporate chains, for example, out of 19 interviewed, had their own brands of corn flakes in 1939, of which four put out an 8-ounce package comparable to the 8-ounce package of the leading brands. Three of these chains priced their 8-ounce packages of corn flakes at 5 cents; one, at 6½ cents. Kellogg's corn flakes, the predominant manufacturer's brand, was sold by three of them at that time at 7 cents a package, while one chain was selling it at 6 cents. Typically, the margin taken on the manufacturers' brands and on their own brands was about 15%.

At the price differential of 1 to 2 cents a package, the organizations stated that their own brands made up from one-fourth to one-half of their total corn flake sales. Among the consuming group as a whole, however, as indicated by the surveys of the Scripps-Howard papers and *The Milwaukee Journal,* Kellogg's corn flakes and Post Toasties together probably held 80% of the total corn flakes market.

In the course of the study an interview with a manufacturer of breakfast foods brought out the significant statement that the differentials between manufacturers' brands and distributors' brands, which were found to be small in this survey, had been wider some years previously. He pointed out that the margin of difference had tended to narrow because the manufacturers of breakfast foods had come to recognize that they could obtain for their brands only a small margin over private brands. In other words, private brand competition, he said, had forced down the price of the manufacturers' brands.

Additional cost data on the prices and margins of other grocery and drug items [12] were secured in the survey among large-scale distributors, but they need not be recounted because those already given serve to illustrate the wide range of competitive conditions found in the distribution of various consumer goods. These data do not show differences in price between manufacturers' advertised brands and manufacturers' unadvertised brands. Information was sought regarding manufacturers' unadvertised brands, but the data obtainable were too scattered to permit tabulation. The comparison between distributors' brands and leading manufacturers' brands, however, provides the information most significant for illustrating the offering of low price by one group of sellers to secure patronage in competition with manufacturers who place large reliance on advertising.

No single pattern of pricing practice was found to be used by distributors for their private brands. Not always did they put prices below those of manufacturers' brands. Moreover, the pricing practices for different types of merchandise of a particular organization varied. Wide differences were found in the gross margins taken upon their own brands for different classes of merchandise. For example, the

---

[12] In all, data were obtained for 12 drug items and 10 grocery items.

median gross margin taken upon private brand coffee among the chains was 28%; upon canned milk, 17%. Each product category must be studied separately to determine the competitive pattern and the pricing practice followed.

EVIDENCE REGARDING PRICING POLICIES OF LARGE-SCALE DISTRIBUTORS

In addition to specific price and margin data, such as have been presented, general statements as to the policy followed by distributors in pricing their brands, as their prices relate not only to those of manufacturers' brands but also to those of other distributors' brands, were obtained from the organizations interviewed in the survey. Such generalized statements are, of course, not highly satisfactory evidence, but they serve to show the general attitudes of the managements toward competitive prices.

Policy of Pricing Private Brands Relative to Manufacturers' Advertised Brands

As shown in Table 128, 48 out of the 61 organizations stated that their policy was to set the prices on their own brands below those of equivalent manufacturers' advertised brands; 12 stated that they set them at the same level as manufacturers' brands. Thus in most in-

TABLE 128

REPLIES OF LARGE-SCALE DISTRIBUTORS REGARDING PRACTICES GENERALLY FOLLOWED IN PRICING EQUIVALENT MERCHANDISE SOLD UNDER THEIR OWN BRANDS, AS RELATED TO PRICES OF LEADING MANUFACTURERS' BRANDS, 1939

NUMBER AND TYPE OF ORGANIZATIONS REPORTING	POLICY GENERALLY WAS TO PRICE MERCHANDISE UNDER OWN LABELS:		
	Above Prevailing Prices of Leading Manufacturers' Brands	At Same Level as Prices of Leading Manufacturers' Brands	Below Prevailing Prices of Leading Manufacturers' Brands
20 corporate food chains..............		4	16
13 corporate drug chains..............		2	11
11 voluntary food chains, wholesaler members*......................		4	6
7 voluntary food chains, headquarters...		2	5
5 limited price variety chains*........			5
5 dry goods or department store chains†			5
Total replies....................	0	12	48

* One organization stated that it priced its own brands in most instances on a cost plus desired markup basis.
† Two organizations stated that they priced their own brands in most instances on a cost plus markup basis. The resulting price was usually below manufacturers'.

TABLE 129

REPLIES OF LARGE-SCALE DISTRIBUTORS REGARDING RELATIONSHIP IN GENERAL BETWEEN
GROSS MARGIN RECEIVED ON ARTICLES SOLD UNDER OWN BRANDS COMPARABLE
WITH THOSE SOLD UNDER MANUFACTURERS' BRANDS, 1939

NUMBER AND TYPE OF ORGANIZATION REPORTING	GENERALLY SPEAKING, GROSS MARGINS ON OWN BRANDS AS RELATED TO GROSS MARGINS ON COMPARABLE MANUFACTURERS' BRANDS WERE:		
	Higher	About the Same	Lower
20 corporate food chains..............	19	1	....
13 corporate drug chains..............	12	1	....
11 voluntary food chains, wholesaler members..........................	10	1	....
7 voluntary food chains, headquarters...	7	....	....
5 limited price variety chains..........	4	1	....
5 dry goods and department store chains	5	....	....
Total replies.....................	57	4	0

stances the chains offered a price inducement to get sales, relying
in addition upon point-of-purchase promotion, customer friendship,
limited advertising, and satisfaction from use, to develop patronage.

While offering lower prices, they normally took much more liberal
markups on their own brands than they did on comparable manufacturers' brands. Fifty-seven out of 61 organizations stated that generally
they received a higher markup on their own brands (Table 129).
Large markup was acknowledged as one of the great inducements to
selling under their own brands.

The evidence gathered indicates that in pricing their own brands,
the chains and other large-scale distributors have been influenced
primarily by two considerations: the prices of the leading manufacturers' brands and the desire for a satisfactory margin. They have
had in mind price savings which, added to the point-of-purchase promotion and selling employed, would gradually overcome the preferences enjoyed by manufacturers' brands. Often they have deemed it
wise, particularly in the early stages of marketing private brand items,
when they have been developing a following for these items, not to
place their prices too far below those of the well-known brands, because
they had found that to do so might lead consumers to question the
quality of their items. In some instances, however, in the initial stages
private branders have priced their brands on certain items at wide
differentials below the advertised manufacturers' brands. The following instances were cited: When advertised brands of cake flour were
generally retailing for 25 cents a package, one chain brought out a
private brand for 17 cents and another chain launched its brand at

13 cents. When a leading dessert was retailing for 10 cents a package, a large chain brought out a competing item for 5 cents. From the data it is evident that the initial pricing of private brands in relation to the prices of advertised manufacturers' brands varies widely and follows no single pattern. It is clear, however, that when private branders have set their prices at a differential which will give needed volume, they ordinarily have received relatively large gross margins. They have desired to take better margins on their private brands than on manufacturers' brands, in part, because they have recognized a somewhat higher cost for selling their own brands; in part, because they have felt that such margins have been necessary to show a satisfactory profit on their total operations. They have felt that on well-known manufacturers' brands they have had to stand the brunt of fierce price competition among retailers, with resultant margins often becoming too narrow to satisfy them. A number of those interviewed pointed out that when the retailer feels forced, because of customers' demand, to sell certain types of merchandise at margins which do not cover his full cost of operations plus a profit, he must seek to increase his margin on other types of merchandise in order to show an overall profit or even to continue in business; hence his desire for good margins. Generally distributors have cut the margins on their own brands as low as those received on manufacturers' brands only when forced to do so to get sales.

While the evidence of the survey showed a tendency for distributors frequently to price with reference to manufacturers' prices, such was not always the case. On numerous items they reported taking a normal gross margin, even though the prices of manufacturers' brands might have permitted them to take more. Some organizations followed this practice more than others. In February, 1941, two years after the survey was made, an executive of a large chain stated that his organization had in recent years tended to change its pricing methods on its own brands. Instead of pricing them with reference to manufacturers' brands, it more frequently followed the practice of applying a desired markup on cost of merchandise. As a result, for numerous items the spread between manufacturers' brands and their own brands had widened. He expressed the opinion that this practice was being adopted by other chains. Time did not permit further inquiry to see whether this practice was becoming general among chains.

Pricing Policy as Related to Competing Distributors' Brands

In spite of the fact that distributors generally set the prices on their own brands with reference to competing manufacturers' brands, there was evidence of a substantial price competition between distributors' brands. This competition has generally come in the stage after distributors' brands have become well known in the market and have become acceptable to a considerable group of consumers. Then low price has been an effective means of attracting volume. Case material indicated that numerous large-scale retailers have used their own brands in recent years as leaders to attract trade. The fact that some chains, mail-order houses, and department stores have made an appeal for patronage on the basis of not being undersold has led them to give close attention to competitors' prices of private brands as well as manufacturers' brands. Upon manufacturers' brands, competitive prices clearly have had to be met if these stores were to maintain their reputations. When these stores have competed with private brands, such exact comparisons of price have been avoidable because the merchandise of the two suppliers has not been identical. Nevertheless, these organizations have recognized the danger of permitting prices of their own brands to be much higher than those of other retailers. In the survey it was found that all the distributors recognized the need of keeping their private brand prices in line with those of competitors unless superiority of merchandise, or store service, or location permitted them to set higher prices. Evidence of this is found in the fact that 50 out of 61 organizations covered in the survey stated that they sought to price their brands at the same levels as those adopted for competing retailers' brands of comparable quality (Table 130). One corporate chain sought to price its brands under competitors' brands; four placed their prices above those of competitors.

Although the statistical evidence showing the extent of price competition among distributors' brands is not conclusive, observation as well as the evidence given leads to the belief that direct competition among distributors' brands, particularly among chains, has tended in time to turn upon price rather than upon extensive use of advertising and promotion, although there has been some of the latter. That they have not turned to advertising competition in large volume is indicated by the fact that there has been little evidence of growth in advertising costs of such organizations, but inspection of adver-

TABLE 130

REPLIES OF LARGE-SCALE DISTRIBUTORS REGARDING PRACTICES GENERALLY FOLLOWED
IN PRICING MERCHANDISE SOLD UNDER THEIR OWN BRANDS AS RELATED TO COM-
PARABLE MERCHANDISE SOLD UNDER COMPETING RETAILERS' BRANDS

NUMBER AND TYPE OF ORGANIZATIONS REPORTING	POLICY GENERALLY WAS TO PRICE MERCHANDISE UNDER OWN LABEL:		
	Above Prices of Comparable Competing Retailers' Brands	At Same Level as Prices of Comparable Competing Retailers' Brands	Below Prices of Comparable Competing Retailers' Brands
20 corporate food chains..............	2	18	....
13 corporate drug chains..............	2	9	1
11 voluntary food chains, wholesaler members*......................	....	10	....
7 voluntary food chains, headquarters†..	....	6	....
5 limited price variety chains*.........	....	4	....
5 dry goods or department store chains‡	....	3	....
Total replies....................	4	50	1

* One organization stated that it priced its own brands in most instances on a cost plus markup basis.
† One organization stated that it did not pay much attention to prices of competing distributors' brands.
‡ Two organizations stated that they priced their own brands in most instances on a cost plus markup basis.

tisements indicates that some chains give a relatively larger amount of space to their own brands and less to manufacturers' brands than was true some years ago.

In so far as competition on price has tended to drive down prices on distributors' brands, manufacturers' brands in turn have been affected. When a private brand item reaches a stage at which it is well known in its market and is acceptable to many consumers, it will be taken in large volume if it is offered at an attractive price. When this stage is reached, manufacturers must take care to see that they do not permit the differential between their brands and such distributors' brands to become too wide, because the evidence not only of this survey but of case material has indicated that whenever too much of a price differential has been sought by an advertiser for his product, sales have tended to shift to lower-price merchandise.

Considerations Determining Entrance of Distributors' Brands

Distributors with private brands do not attempt to establish their brands on all products they sell. This fact is illustrated by the responses of grocery concerns which were asked in the survey to indicate whether they sold certain selected items under their own brands. The answers from 20 corporate food chains, 9 wholesaler members of voluntary food chains, and 7 headquarters officers of voluntary food chains are

TABLE 131

NUMBER OF ORGANIZATIONS SELLING CERTAIN SPECIFIED ARTICLES UNDER THEIR OWN
BRANDS AMONG TWENTY CORPORATE FOOD CHAINS AND SIXTEEN VOLUNTARY
FOOD CHAINS SUPPLYING DATA, 1939

ARTICLE	NUMBER OF ORGANIZATIONS HANDLING SPECIFIED ARTICLES UNDER OWN BRANDS			
	Among 20 Corporate Food Chains	Among 9 Voluntary Food Chains Who esaler Members	Among 7 Voluntary Food Chains Headquarters	Total
Coffee..........................	20	9	7	36
Canned vegetables...................	18	9	7	34
Salad dressing.....................	18	9	6	33
Bread........................	17	1	5	23
All-purpose flour..................	17	8	6	31
Canned fruit......................	16	9	7	32
Canned milk.....................	14	7	7	28
Prepared pancake flour..............	14	9	6	29
Canned salmon....................	11	8	7	26
Spices..........................	9	6	6	21
Fruit gelatin.....................	9	7	7	23
Farina.........................	6	2	4	12
Baking powder....................	5	2	5	12
Corn flakes......................	5	7	6	13
White soap flakes..................	3	2	5	10
Granulated soap flakes..............	3	5	6	14
Canned soup.....................	2	7	5	14
Perfumed soap....................	2	6	6	14
Kitchen cleanser...................	1	3	6	10
Floating soap.....................	0	1	5	6
Baking soda......................	0	2	4	6

shown in Table 131. Coffee, canned vegetables, salad dressing, flour,
canned fruit, and canned milk were mentioned by over 30 of the
36 organizations replying. On the other hand, products such as baking
soda, soaps of all kinds, kitchen cleansers, and canned soups were
among items mentioned by less than half the organizations.

The considerations determining whether retailers will seek to sell
specific products under their own brands are many and vary not only
for different products, but also among concerns. A few of the conditions which are especially pertinent in this study are brought out by the
evidence of the survey and by case material.

In the survey the concerns were asked to state why they did not
handle certain specific items and the reasons they gave indicate conditions which govern their entry into the private branding of various
items. For example, only two out of the 20 corporate food chains
supplying data stated that they carried a tomato soup to compete with
the Campbell brand. The reasons specified for not carrying the product under their own brand were the following: Ten stated that the

advertised brands were too strongly entrenched to permit the development of satisfactory volume; one organization stated that it had not been able to find a suitable supply for such a product; three stated that they were satisfied with the margin obtained on advertised brands; three stated that the margin to be obtained on their own brand was not sufficient to make it worth while; and another three stated that the expense of promoting their own brands to secure the needed demand would be too heavy. Another consideration which was mentioned was the difficulty of getting sufficient volume of sales in early stages to support good purchasing contracts or to permit obtaining desired turnover on stocks specified in purchasing contracts.

Similarly, among the 20 corporate chains, only two had their own brand of white soap flakes to compete with Lux and Ivory flakes. Among the 18 which did not carry such private brand flakes, 13 stated that the advertised brands were too strongly entrenched to permit them to develop satisfactory volume; two stated that no suitable source of supply was available; two stated that the margins obtainable on their own brand would not be sufficient to make it worth while; and three averred that the expenses of promoting their own brands to secure suitable volume would be too great. Similar reasons were given by the chains for not having their own brands of farina and corn flakes.

In short, in all the above instances, two conditions apparently were the chief preventives of entry into these merchandise fields: (1) the high cost of getting consumers to accept distributors' brands in substantial volume in competition with highly advertised manufacturers' brands; and (2) inability of distributors to buy such merchandise at prices which would permit them to offer an attractive price differential to consumers and at the same time to secure an attractive profit margin.

In contrast, these conditions did not hold for the items in Table 131 which were branded by the great majority of stores interviewed, such as coffee, canned vegetables, canned fruits, canned milk, salad dressing, and all-purpose flour. On these items it has been relatively easy for distributors to establish their brands. They are items in large demand. Moreover, favorable initial response to selling effort has not been too difficult to attain, for although there have been strong manufacturers' brands in certain of these fields, yet the storekeepers have found it possible to induce many consumers to shift brand allegiance. Again, they are products for which there have been numerous suitable sources of supply desirous of securing private brand contracts. In short, distributors have established their private brands first where conditions have made it easy to get a quick and profitable volume.

More detailed accounts of the reasoning of retailers regarding the branding of particular items were obtained from case reports. The views of two managements toward the branding of soaps and of another toward canned soup serve to illustrate the conditions and attitudes governing decisions.

The president of one large chain explained why his organization had never attempted to establish its own brand of soap. He stated that although soap had been a large volume grocery item, sales had been spread over many different types of specialized soaps. Leading soap companies had done much in improving their brands. He added that the competition among soap manufacturers had kept the wholesale price low, while competition among retailers had driven down retail prices until margins were at the vanishing point. Because of these margins his company would have liked to establish its own brand on numerous types of soap. But, according to the executive, it had been unable to buy good soaps at prices low enough to permit it appreciably to undersell the established brands and still have a desired gross margin. He thought a price differential of several cents a bar or package would be needed to win consumers away from the manufacturers' brands, and even with this differential considerable promotional outlay would be necessary.

In the latter months of 1938, executives of another large chain gave specific data regarding a possible entry into the selling of powdered soap under its own brand. This account is somewhat at variance with the preceding case in regard to the matter of opportunity to buy at a favorable price. It had under consideration the making of a contract with a soap manufacturer for a private brand of powdered soap to compete with Lever Brothers' Rinso and Procter & Gamble's Oxydol. At that time a case of 2 dozen 24-ounce packages of Oxydol cost the chain $4.46, while a similar size case of Rinso, in 23½-ounce packages, cost $4.48. The chain had opportunity to purchase a powdered soap at the favorable price of $2.67 a case of 2 dozen, 24-ounce packages. At that time, the chain was selling both Oxydol and Rinso at 19 cents a package, and securing a gross margin of approximately 2%. In spite of the fact that it could put out its own brand of soap powder at a price which would permit it to undersell the well-known brands by as much as 5 cents a package and still get a gross margin of 20%, the management hesitated to do so. There was some doubt as to whether the source would continue to offer the product on the same terms. Moreover, the chain was not sure whether consumers would like its brand of soap as well as the manufacturers' brands, even though the product had been given a good laboratory report. Because of these uncertainties the contract was not made, but early in 1941 the chain reported that it had found a dependable source and was about to put out its own brand of powdered soap. The executive interviewed stated that several acceptable sources for private brand soaps were then available.

Other case evidence gave similar reasons for the decision of a certain chain not to undertake sale of its own brand of canned soup. Executives did not think that they could attain a suitable volume with the desired net profit because manufacturers' brands sold at prices which the chain could not undersell. The secure position of manufacturers' brands was said to depend in part upon their advertising, in part upon the fact that consumers liked the quality, in part upon the low prices at which these products sold at retail. The chain found it difficult to buy private brand merchandise of suitable quality which it could offer at a saving which would attract consumers.

These more detailed reports indicate that when the prices of manufacturers' brands have been placed low enough to make it difficult for distributors or nonadvertising manufacturers to offer equally acceptable merchandise at attractive savings, private brand entrance has not been frequent. In the course of the study, certain manufacturers stated that the potential threat of private brand competition has led them to keep their prices low, with the result that such brands have not entered their fields.

That a manufacturer's pricing policy may play a dominant part in helping him to hold a leading position in a product field is illustrated in the case of Jell-O. In an address before the American Marketing Association in May, 1938,[13] Mr. Clarence Francis, President of General Foods Corporation, gave some facts regarding the pricing history of Jell-O and its unit advertising costs. He stated that when General Foods took over the Jell-O Company in 1925, Jell-O was selling to the consumer for an average of 12 cents a package. In 1938, the prevailing retail price was around 5½ cents to 6 cents a package. The total advertising cost at that date was under ½ cent a pound.

---

[13] Clarence Francis, "A Challenge to Marketing Men," *The Journal of Marketing,* July, 1938, p. 31.

Further evidence regarding the retail pricing of Jell-O and private brands of fruit gelatin was available in the survey among corporate and voluntary food chains. It was found that these organizations, in order to get desired gross margins on their private brands of fruit-flavored gelatins, had to sell them at prices which were only one-half cent a package below the retail price of Jell-O. Other manufacturers of fruit-flavored gelatins, such as Royal, sold at prices approximately the same as those for Jell-O. At a differential of one-half cent certain chains obtained substantial sales of their own brands of gelatin, but demand predominantly went to the manufacturers' brands. This leadership of manufacturers' brands is indicated by the consumer preference report of the Scripps-Howard survey in 1938,[14] which showed that among homes having gelatin desserts on hand at the time, 57.6% had Jell-O; 23.5%, Royal; 6.5%, Knox; 4.6%, Sparkle (A. & P. brand); while other brands accounted for 7.8%. In this instance large sales volume permitted substantial advertising of Jell-O at a low unit cost. In turn, the manufacturer's price did not include a large profit margin.

All the evidence given above regarding items offered under private brands indicates that in some fields the consumer does not have so great an option to buy distributors' brands on a price basis in competition with manufacturers' brands as he does in other fields. This limited option occurs particularly when manufacturers' specialty products have dominant brand leadership and the retail prices are so low that it is hard for the private brander to offer an effective price appeal under his brand. The fact that the retail prices of manufacturers are this low in such instances means that availability of the option would not be of large significance to consumers for they already get the products without unusually wide spread between manufacturer's cost and retail price.

Although the entry of private brands into some of these specialty product fields, such as the soap and canned soup fields, has been relatively slow, interviews with distributors showed a strong desire on their part to establish their brands on the items, because generally their gross margins and net profits, as a result of the price competition among retailers, have not been satisfactory to them. Consequently, in spite of the difficulties of entry, there has been a gradual extension of private branding into one after another of these fields. Thus consumer options in specialty fields have tended to increase.

---

[14] *Market Records*, 1938, p. 164.

In connection with this discussion of the options available to consumers in their purchasing, it should be pointed out that the choices available to consumers vary according to locality. In metropolitan districts where numerous retail organizations compete, one with the other, the options of the consumer are greater than in small towns and rural districts which cannot support such a large number of suppliers. Moreover, evidence regarding prices, obtained from extensive confidential surveys of prices in retail stores carried on by a private research organization, shows that price competition in metropolitan areas on both manufacturers' and private brands tends to be more intense than in small towns and rural areas, where suppliers are fewer. The prices which independent retailers pay and the prices which consumers pay are usually less in cities than in small towns and rural areas.

Varying Price Differentials between Distributors' Brands and Manufacturers'

Distributors' brands have made their greatest gains in sales during periods of depression, when differentials between manufacturers' and distributors' brands have tended to widen and such savings have had increased appeal to consumers because consumers have become penny conscious at such times. Generally speaking, the prices of manufacturers' heavily advertised brands have not been sensitive. They have tended to be "sticky," particularly in periods of falling price, although there are numerous exceptions.[15] This characteristic is illustrated in the grocery field. Price indexes of foods in several categories were made available to our investigators by a large grocery distributor who built these indexes from his own purchase figures. These data, only selected items of which are given in Table 132, show that the index of advertised grocery items declined less frequently and less widely than did the index of all food prices. Its fluctuations were far less wide and less frequent than those of an index of so-called "grocery trading items," whose prices are so closely governed by the fluctuations of basic commodities that neither distributors nor manufacturers have appreciable influence over prices. Examples of such items are butter and flour. On the basis of October, 1929, as 100, the index of adver-

---

[15] The fact that individual manufacturers with strongly advertised brands may follow a policy of adjusting prices in accordance with changing business conditions was shown in the case of one large company which sold numerous advertised grocery specialties. The average of this company's prices during the 1930 depression showed greater reduction than did the average prices for all foods.

TABLE 132

INDICES OF PRICES OF ALL FOODS, GROCERY TRADING ITEMS, AND GROCERY ADVERTISED
BRANDS OF A CORPORATE FOOD CHAIN—FOR SELECTED DATES FROM OCTOBER,
1929, THROUGH DECEMBER, 1938. OCTOBER, 1929=100

	PRICE INDEX NUMBERS (OCTOBER, 1929 = 100) FOR		
	All Foods	Grocery Trading Items	Grocery Advertised Brands
October, 1929..........................	100	100	100
December, 1930........................	84	75	95
December, 1931........................	75	64	90
December, 1932........................	66	58	85
February, 1933........................	62	52	75
December, 1933........................	70	68	80
December, 1934........................	76	77	85
December, 1935........................	84	78	87
December, 1936........................	83	81	87
March, 1937...........................	82	85	88
March, 1937...........................	80	74	88
March, 1938...........................	75	64	86

tised grocery items reached a low of 75 in February, 1939. The price
index of grocery trading items as of that date had fallen to 52; whereas
the index for all food, including advertised items, grocery trading
items, perishables, and meat, was about 62. Again, in the recession
of 1937–1938, the index number of grocery trading items fell from
approximately 82 in March, 1937, to a low of 65 for August, 1938.
The index number for advertised brands kept rising, however, until
September, 1937, when it was 89, and fell to a low of 86 in August,
1938.

Just as the prices of the advertised brands as a whole were shown
by the data to be sticky in periods of depression, so they tended to be
sticky in periods of rising prices; that is, the index for advertised
brands did not rise so rapidly relatively as did the index for grocery
trading items or the index for all foods. Consequently the spread between the index of the advertised brands, on the one hand, and the
index of grocery trading items and that for all foods, on the other
hand, widened in periods of depression and became narrower in times
of rising prices, as is indicated in Table 132. For example, at the
depth of the depression in February, 1933, there was a spread of
23 points between the index number of grocery trading items and that
of grocery advertised brands. In the months of relatively good business of late 1936 and early 1937, there was a spread of only 3 to 6
points between these two indices.

The executive of one large chain stated that the private brand sales
of his organization had made great strides during the 1929–1933

depression and again in the recession of 1937–1938. He claimed that at such times the chain had revised the prices of its merchandise downward more rapidly than had manufacturers as a whole. With the return of consumer buying power, he stated, and the narrowing of the spread between the chain's private brand prices and those of advertised brands, part of the advances reverted to the manufacturers' brands, but the chain's brands held an appreciable percentage of their gains. Executives of other chains gave similar evidence regarding appreciable gains on their own brands during depression, but did not claim retention of so large a part of their gains as did the executive mentioned above.

A specific example of a situation in which price differentials widened was provided by one chain, although this instance did not deal with a heavily advertised product. The chain increased its sale of green peas as a result of decreasing its prices more than those of a leading manufacturer's advertised brand during the depression of 1937–1938. The cost, pricing, and sales experience were as follows:

LEADING MANUFACTURER'S BRAND—303 CAN—17 OUNCES

Year	Cost per Case	Retail Price per Can	Approximate Sales, in Cases
1937................	$3.02*	18 cents	3,000*
1938................	2.92*	17 cents	2,600*

DISTRIBUTOR'S BRAND—No. 2 CAN—20 OUNCES

| 1937................ | $1.10† | 15 cents | 21,000† |
| 1938................ | 0.80† | 2/25 cents | 22,000† |

* Case of 24 cans.
† Case of 12 cans.

In this instance the manufacturer's advertised brand was reduced about 3%, while the chain got its private brand peas at a reduction of 26%. The retail price of the manufacturer's brand was reduced 5.5%; the private brand, 16.7%. Sales of its brand increased 5% while sales of the manufacturer's brand decreased 13%. These ratios should be looked upon as merely those found in one case rather than as typical, for it is doubtful whether there is a typical case. The situation, however, illustrates the fact that private branders have gained when their prices have been lowered during depressions more than those of manufacturers' brands.

While this evidence regarding the relative sensitivity of prices of private brands and manufacturers' brands is too meager to support definitive conclusions regarding the pricing practice of the two groups in periods of falling prices, still it is sufficient to suggest that manufacturers of many advertised brands might well consider whether they have permitted their prices to get out of line with private brand prices in periods of depression. They should give careful consideration to the effect of price upon the demand for their products and inquire whether they have taken a mistaken view that their advertising has created an inelastic demand for their brands.

Summary of Price Evidence

From the evidence which has been gathered in this study regarding prices and pricing practice, what helpful generalizations may be drawn?

These studies have shown that competition among manufactured products has been far from that idealized under the theory of pure competition.[16] Each of the industries has presented a different pattern. The extent to which competition has turned upon price has varied from industry to industry. The extent to which individual brands have been freed from meeting competing prices also has varied. In those industries in which product differentiation has been feasible and for which buying motives other than price have been effective among consumers, brands have become important guides in buying, and competition has turned toward advertising and aggressive selling rather than toward price.

Yet, even in those industries in which competition has been directed in large degree to non-price forms, a tendency toward price competition has been strong. Competition upon price invariably has appeared and this has in turn tended to limit competition on non-price forms. Even in the cigarette industry, in which consumer values have been particularly susceptible to advertising influence, and in which dominant companies have been prone to battle in advertising rather than on price, the 10-cent cigarettes in 18 months gained 25% of total consumer demand, when a retail price differential of 4 cents to 5 cents was permitted them. And since that time they have remained in the market, providing consumers with the option of balancing price consideration against superior product quality and reputation

---

[16] Attention of the layman again is called to the fact that under the theory of pure competition, competition is assumed to be based on price. The theory of imperfect competition recognizes that competition does not take place on price alone.

built by vigorous advertising. Thereby a check against increasing margins between manufacturing costs and final selling price has been provided. In the grocery field, advertised specialties such as gelatin and breakfast foods in time have had imitators whose price competition has driven down the prices and gross margins of the originators and thereby has brought a limitation on the competition in non-price forms and on the profits of the originating manufacturers. In the case of dentifrices, consumers have been given the option of balancing price against product difference and reputation; yet in this instance so strong have been the appeals applicable to dentifrices that consumers in large numbers have not availed themselves of low price. Demand has gone to the relatively high-price, advertised brands. Advertising has continued to be a chief element in the price of dentifrices. In striking contrast is sugar, for which advertising apparently has had little or no effect on the price charged.

For none of the products studied has competition between sellers been solely upon price. Product differentiation and appeals other than price have been employed; but in every instance there has been a distinct limit to the pull of differentiation and non-price selling appeals as against the price appeal to which some competing sellers have turned. In every case some sellers have seen opportunity to try for profits by turning to price as a means of gaining sales. Consumers have been given a choice of low price versus brand reputation. When sellers of differentiated products have attempted to secure a price difference for their brands which consumers have deemed too high, demand has flowed toward the lower-price products. This result was seen in the case of cigarettes, cigars, sheeting, and shoes. It apparently has occurred upon private brands of grocery products in periods of depression. Although price competition for these products has not acted in the quick, precise method indicated by the logic of the theory of pure competition with its assumption of identical merchandise, nevertheless price competition has been present and has provided a check against a high degree of freedom in pricing.

These instances show that each well-known brand has what may be termed a reputation value. Its reputation permits it to obtain from consumers a price somewhat above that obtained by merchandise which has comparable objective characteristics but which has not had the advantage of being made well known. Numerous examples which support this generalization have been cited.[17] In most instances, of course, reputation has been backed up by and built around product differentiation of some kind. Hence it is usually impossible to disentangle reputation value built by advertising and the value which is solely dependent upon objective product differences which the consumer learns from product use. The evidence indicates, however, that for most products the brander can permit to the less-known brand a certain price advantage without losing his competitive position. When he puts too high a value on reputation and differentiation, then demand flows away.

As the analysis has shown, the opportunity to build reputation value varies for different products. For sugar it cannot be expressed in terms of price at all. At the other extreme, however, are dentifrices; with wide differences in prices between the well-known and the unadvertised brands of dentifrices, demand still has continued to flow to the products with reputation established through advertising.

The areas in which price competition probably has been least effective, in which competition in advertising and aggressive selling has been most intense, and in which margins between manufacturing costs and selling price have been widest, are the drug, toilet goods, and cosmetics fields. Consumer buying here has been more emotional and less informed than in most product fields. Not only have advertising appeals to the motives of health, beauty, and romance been powerful, but consumers generally have lacked a basis for appraising product quality. The results from usage have not been subject to close check. Consumers' satisfaction with such products often has depended in large degree upon ideas implanted by advertising. They have not been able to appraise rival formulae. They have known that some drugs may be dangerous; hence they have been willing to pay heavily for brand familiarity. Moreover, the price differentials in many instances have probably not appeared important to consumers in view of the relatively small usage and consequent infrequent purchase of the items.

In a society in which product differentiation and influence in selling is permitted, it appears that reputation value is inevitable as a part

---

[17] The value of reputation in terms of price and quantities is clearly illustrated by the experiment conducted in 1932 by the Cannon Mills to test the sales effectiveness of its brand. In seven cities towels bearing the Cannon label were placed on sale side by side with identical towels which were unbranded. Although the branded towels were priced 10% above the unbranded towels, they outsold the latter in the ratio of 3.6 to 1. F. A. Williams, "Advertised Brands Prove to Be Best Profit Makers," *Printers' Ink*, September 29, 1932, p. 3.

of consumers' valuations, and it is not to be expected that competition will take place through price alone. The evidence indicates that when product differentiation is important in the mind of the consumer, and motives other than price are weighty in guiding consumer purchase, competition tends to turn from price to advertising and other non-price forms. Moreover, the more competition employs non-price forms, the greater is the spread between manufacturing cost and the price which consumers pay.

The evidence clearly leads to the conclusion that in the economic structure there are strong forces to counterbalance any tendency for competition to turn solely to non-price forms. In most fields, in the course of time organizations and sellers appear who elect to offer consumers opportunity to buy merchandise on a price basis. Thus the consumer may choose between differentiation and reputation, on the one hand, and price on the other. For example, the data regarding prices and pricing practices of corporate and voluntary chains and other large-scale distributors indicate that a large and important group of sellers have elected to compete with manufacturers by using price as one appeal for business. On many items they have set their prices below those of leading manufacturers' brands in amounts which they think will attract consumers. In so setting their prices they have been able to take wide gross margins, because their method of buying cuts down the functions which the manufacturer must perform. In some instances they have found that prices too much below the leading brands have not been productive of sales, because consumers apparently have regarded low price as indicative of poor quality. There is evident, however, a tendency for these private branders to compete with one another on a price basis. Since many of them have attained generally low operating costs through integration and through elimination of services, they have been able to make effective price appeals. It is concluded that these organizations in competition with one another and with manufacturers have in recent years afforded an important check against excessive competition in advertising.

By and large, however, the private branders cannot be credited with bringing product innovation and progress in merchandise. With relatively few exceptions they have been imitators and have benefited from the building of demand for various types of differentiated merchandise by manufacturers. They have not incurred the growth cost which some manufacturers have, but they enter with a price appeal when demand has been built. In so doing they provide a check against manufacturers retaining permanently the benefits of successful pioneering in merchandise.

Among industries studied which have had expansion of demand and for which important production economies have been realized as a result of increased size of operations and technological developments, competition in price has been keen enough to cause these economies to be passed along in large degree to consumers in the form of lower prices and better product quality. This fact was clearly illustrated in the instances of the electric refrigerator and of cigars. These two industries are believed to be merely illustrative of what has occurred in a large number of industries which have expanded with the help of advertising and aggressive selling and which have experienced decreasing costs. The prices of many products have fallen as their demands have grown under the stimulus of aggressive selling. This has been true not only of whole industries but it has been true of the operations of individual companies studied.

The manufacturers' prices of many advertised products have been relatively insensitive. This insensitivity was found particularly in the case of cigarettes and dentifrices, but it was present also in varying degree in other products. This lack of flexibility indicates that many manufacturers who have established consumer brand preferences for their products tend to assume that advertising has made the demand for their brands inelastic and that they can hold their prices relatively stable in times of general price decline without loss of volume. The evidence indicates, however, that many of them may be mistaken in this assumption, for private branders, who have been more flexible in their pricing, have usually gained business on their brands in periods of depression.

PART V

The Effect of Advertising on the Range of Products, on Quality, and on Consumer Choice

Chapter XXII

THE EFFECT OF ADVERTISING ON THE RANGE AND QUALITY OF PRODUCTS

ISSUES relating to the possible effects of advertising upon the range and quality of products available to consumers and to the worth of advertising as a guide to consumer purchasing are the subjects of inquiry in this and the following chapter (Part V of the volume). The range of products upon the market has widened amazingly since the advent of industrialization. Additions to this range have come from two sources: (1) new inventions that mark a major departure from existing products and (2) minor differentiations and developments of products already upon the market. This increase in the range of merchandise has had an important bearing on the satisfactions available to consumers. It has brought advantages, but it also has been a source of difficulties. In particular some students have questioned whether widening of choice through product differentiation has brought a positive contribution in satisfactions to consumers. In the chapter on value theory, the issue relating to differentiation raised for investigation is whether the practice of product differentiation contributes in any way to economic progress and thereby increases the satisfactions of consumers. Or whether, conversely, the differentiations employed by sellers in their attempts to get away from direct price competition are inconsequential and therefore undesirable from the standpoint of consumer satisfactions to be derived from them. Does this differentiation lead to undesirable complexity in consumer buying which might be avoided? And does it increase costs because of the resulting large number of brands (with but minor differences among them) which distributors must carry?

The increased range of merchandise available clearly has made buying more complex than formerly, and advertising has been criticized as a poor aid to consumers in guiding their choices among the intricate array of merchandise available to them. Since consumers' satisfactions are determined by their choices, advertising should be examined critically to determine how well it serves consumers. The investigation of this problem calls for answers to issues regarding the extent to which advertising, as conducted, has served as a desirable guide to consumers, whether it has led to correct valuations or to incorrect valuations, and the basis for determining what are correct and what are incorrect valuations. Also involved are the questions of whether advertising and aggressive selling are necessary functions in a modern, free economy, and to what extent there are effective substitutes for advertising to provide information and education.

The issues relating to the effect of advertising upon the range and quality of merchandise will be dealt with in this chapter and advertising's worth as a consumer guide will be treated in the next chapter. In this chapter the inquiry is directed first to the question of what part, if any, advertising has played in increasing the range of products through important new inventions, and then to the part of product differentiation in adding to product range.

Advertising's Influence on New Inventions

The striking character of the contribution to the range of products from new inventions is demonstrated in a list of consumer products that were not available 100 years ago. Only a few of the more important need be mentioned: sewing machines; electric lighting; the whole gamut of electrical appliances, washing machines, mechanical refrigerators, ranges, toasters, oil burners, and automatic stokers; cameras; automobiles; phonographs; telephones; safety razors; vitamin tablets, one of a whole array of medical products; and so on. The above list includes the more spectacular inventions, but it can be extended to include hundreds of articles, formerly unknown but now in everyday use among consumers, as a result of the efforts of enterprisers to profit from invention, articles such as fruit gelatin, blown soaps, zippers, batteries, rayon, nylon, plastics, frozen foods, prepared flours, decaffeinated coffees, prepared breakfast foods, and so on.

New inventions involving radically new product ideas have been more numerous in our society since advertising and selling have assumed an important place in business procedure than formerly, but the offering of new inventions cannot be ascribed to these forces except as they are important elements in an economic system that has fostered invention. The inception of ideas and the development of experimental plans and designs for major product innovations depend upon natural inventive genius and, in recent years, upon the extensive and well-organized programs of product research supported by industrial organizations. Undoubtedly many inventors have not been driven by profit as their chief motive for finding a solution to some product idea, but others have been. Moreover, the growing practice of industrial concerns during the past 50 years to conduct product research has been dictated primarily by the desire for profit. Underlying inventive work has been basic scientific research. Adaptation of technical discoveries to consumers' products has been stimulated by the existence of an economy which has offered large opportunity for profit by introduction of products. In turn, pure research has flourished in our vigorous society that has had the means to support universities and scientific laboratories.

Aggressive selling and advertising have played only an indirect but nevertheless important part in stimulating new invention through giving promise of a larger and more speedy profit than would occur without such methods. This has been true particularly in the case of research initiated by industrial concerns. These concerns have relied upon aggressive selling and advertising as means of speeding adoption of new inventions not only to enable them to recover research expense but also to afford a basis for new investment from which to profit. In many instances industrial concerns have not been responsible for the development of a new product idea, but they have adopted inventors' ideas and have carried out the necessary function of perfecting the products for the market. Frequently the expenditure made for research to perfect a new type of product has been large and concerns have been induced to carry on because they have hoped for an expanding market which would repay their experimental risks. In such cases the presence of aggressive selling may not have had material influence in the development of the original invention, but it has often influenced the important research necessary to make the idea marketable. As noted in the study of the mechanical refrigerator, which is believed to have followed a pattern similar to that of many major product innovations, perfection of a commercially satisfactory mechanical refrigerator for home use required years of experimentation. The idea of mechanical refrigeration had long been known and employed in industrial plants. Domestic refrigerating units were offered as early as 1915, but these were crude as judged by later standards. Many individuals and organizations were engaged in experiments to perfect acceptable machines. Most of them were led to do so because they saw possible profit in the idea. But even after fairly acceptable refrigerating units were available, sales were secured only as a result of highly aggressive personal selling and advertising.

Advertising and selling were not directly responsible for the idea or for its perfection. The undertaking of experimental programs by various concerns to perfect the idea of the refrigerator was spurred on by the hope of a profit, a profit, however, which the business managements from experience realized would come only as a result of aggressive cultivation of the market and from educating consumers to realize the satisfactions they might get from a new product. Thus aggressive selling played a part in this product introduction in that it was an important part of the profit system which made product experimentation worth while.

If aggressive selling did not have an immediate influence on the launching of the mechanical refrigerator, it did lead to much more rapid consumer adoption of refrigerators than would have come without its use. This rapid adoption depended not only upon manufacturers' building public acceptance for the new idea and influencing consumers to buy, but also upon their perfecting the product and selling it at a low price. Only with product perfection and low prices could widespread purchase and usage be consummated. Perfection of the product was stimulated by competition in quality, which will be discussed shortly. Lower prices depended upon the development of large scale demand and an accompanying technological development which has come with large scale demand. In the case of the mechanical refrigerator, the gaining of public acceptance, the perfection of the product, the reduction of prices to relatively low levels, and the growth of usage among a substantial part of the public were accomplished in the short period of 15 years from the time the first crude domestic refrigerating unit was placed upon the market.

This rapid public acceptance, perfection of product, and lowering of prices has occurred in the case of one after another of the new major inventions offered in the past 75 years, and in all of them advertising and other forms of aggressive selling played a part in the speeding up process. Such is the story of the automobile, the phonograph, the movies, the radio, electrical appliances, oil burners, stokers, and so on. In short, advertising and aggressive selling have played only an indirect part in stimulating such new inventions, but they have played a direct part in speeding up their wide adoption and use by consumers. In the course of the study it became evident from case material that many manufacturers have carried on extensive research to find and perfect new products largely because the opportunity for aggressive stimulation of the market for any newly found product has provided a basis for hope of quickly recovering their developmental outlay and of getting a profit. Without this hope of profit from market stimulation, their urge to carry on the search for new products would have been small. The indirect influence of aggressive selling upon the conduct of product research has been particularly important in the case of new types of products whose demand has depended very largely on advertising effort. For example, an executive of a large company in the grocery field stated that his concern would have spent little effort or money in the development of numerous new specialties which it had worked out in its laboratories and placed on the market if it had had to rely on the insignificant sales which would have come without advertising and other aggressive selling effort. All in all, with the growth of industrialism, aggressive selling has been an important, even though an indirect influence upon the development of significant new inventions.

Advertising's Part in Developing Range of Merchandise through Product Differentiation

The influence of advertising and aggressive selling in widening the range of merchandise through the stimulation of product differentiation among brands has been much more direct than their influence in widening the range through new inventions of major character; i.e., inventions incorporating radically new merchandise ideas. The desire on the part of producers to offer specific brands of products which would be preferred by consumers has led them to constant experimentation with possible combinations of desirable product qualities. Technology has been called upon to help develop new virtues in a product that might gain consumer favor. This procedure has been a force constantly tending away from standardization of merchandise among producers. The study of demand for various products has shown competing brands to differ in greater or less degree from each other, even when the differences are very small, as in the case of sugar or sheeting. In instances when brands have stood for no specific individualizing points, they often have had meaning in assuring the consumer of maintenance of quality.

A large mass of case material as well as numerous conversations with businessmen provide evidence of the constant quest by manufacturers and their advertising counsel for ideas for product improvement which might be used in advertising and selling. Both manufacturers and advertising agents seek, of course, to make the most of existing individualizing characteristics of their products. They are constantly spurred on, however, to find new differentiating innovations. In order to determine what changes might bring consumer favor, manufacturers have made numerous surveys among consumers and distributors. This viewpoint towards product differentiation is widespread and prevalent and is influenced to a marked degree by the desire for ideas to use in advertising and selling. Accordingly, modern advertising practice is believed to have had an appreciable effect in intensifying the drive for product differentiation in recent decades.

Product Differentiation as Related to Product Improvement

While this constant striving for product differentiation has tended to increase the range of consumers' products, students of consumption have often expressed doubt regarding many of the variations which have been offered consumers. Often the differences developed by sellers and stressed in advertising have appeared of doubtful significance to these students. Accordingly advertising has been charged with helping to bring "meaningless" or "inconsequential" product differences.

An appraisal of this issue calls for a clear understanding of the way in which product improvement is brought about in a free economy and the basis for determining what are "worth-while" innovations.

On the whole, students of consumption have been inclined to be less critical of persuasive selling and advertising as applied to major new inventions than as applied to products long upon the market and subjected to differentiation. For example, they have approved of the introduction of the automobile, but have been critical of later differentiating innovations, particularly what may be termed gadgets: radiator grilles, double horns, and so on. They have reasoned that it is desirable for consumers to enjoy the possible satisfactions to be had from new inventions. They have recognized that a persuasive educational program probably has been necessary to establish such products, particularly if the economies of large-scale production were to be made available without the long delay that would probably attend non-aggressive selling. To them many major inventions have represented worth-while products, but many of the small differentiations have been meaningless and not worth while.

One faces a dilemma, however, if he seeks to limit aggressive selling to worth-while new products. The very term *worth-while* indicates someone's judgment of the products, while a free society presumes self-determination by the individual consumer of what is worth while to him. Every new product differentiation made by producers in a free economy must be viewed in economic theory as being a new product, an improvement which may or may not give consumer satisfactions. Whether or not it is worth while rests upon consumer decisions. Such a view accords with that taken by the businessman when he experiments with product differentiation. He has found that consumer demand is the crucible for determining what is worth while in product innovations. This statement holds for small points of differentiation as well as for large.

Striking product innovations are relatively few in any year. Most radically new inventions at first have been crude articles produced commercially only long after the basic idea had been conceived. This fact is brought out clearly by Dr. S. C. Gilfillan in a chapter entitled "The Prediction of Inventions," in a study published by the U. S. National Resources Committee:

Taking 19 inventions voted most useful, introduced in 1888–1913, the average intervals were: Between when the invention was first merely thought of, and the first working model or patent, 176 years; thence to the first practical use, 24 years; to commercial success, 14 years; to important use, 12 years, or say 50 years from the first serious work on the invention. Again, in the study of the most important inventions of the last generations before 1930, in Recent Social Trends [written by President Hoover's Committee], a median lapse was found of 33 years between the 'conception date' . . . and the date of commercial success.[1]

Commercial models have improved under the stress of competition for product differentiation. Acceptable changes have soon been copied by competitors. Those not wanted have been dropped. Thus has consumer selection among new developments served to bring product

---

[1] *Technological Trends and National Policy* (Washington, U. S. Government Printing Office, 1937), p. 19.

There is also an excellent summary of the growth of technology in the testimony of Dr. Theodore J. Kreps before the Temporary National Economic Committee, *Verbatim Record of the Proceedings of the Temporary National Economic Committee*, Vol. 13, April 8, 1940–May 13, 1940 (Bureau of National Affairs, Inc., 1940), pp. 2 to 23.

forms better designed to give consumer satisfaction than were the forms that went before.

The tendency of competitors to adopt or copy innovations that have proved desirable and acceptable has represented a force leading towards uniformity of products with the general standard or norm of product quality and performance in succeeding years on higher levels. Thus, there are two divergent forces in operation: one, the quest for differentiation, which tends to non-uniformity of merchandise; the other, the imitation or copying of successful product innovations, which tends to product uniformity. The working of these two forces is evident in the instances that are discussed below:

Examples of the gradual improvement of quality resulting from the drive for new individualizing characteristics may be found in many product fields. While new, complex products which have been subject to advancing technology supply the more striking examples, yet even mature products are found to be subject to improvement. For instance, the efficient, convenient mechanical refrigerator of 1940 did not spring into full being as a result of an inventor's idea. Ammonia refrigeration was discovered in 1860. Commercial refrigeration had been on the market for many years before 1915, when the first refrigerating units for household use were offered. Hull, in his volume on *Household Refrigeration,* stated in 1933:

> The household refrigerating machine has been under development for the past 40 years. This work includes problems in mechanical, electrical, and chemical engineering. It has proven very difficult to construct a machine which will start and stop at required intervals, which will be self-regulating and self-oiling under all conditions, and which will be fool-proof and of such simplicity that an unskilled person can operate it without danger of interrupting the required refrigeration.[2]

The machines of early years were crude and inefficient judged by today's standards, and were manufactured to be attached to the relatively inefficient ice refrigerators then in use. From the start competing commercial units were marketed not on the basis of a price appeal for identical units, but upon the satisfactions to be had from product improvements. Manufacturers have striven constantly to produce more satisfactory machines. Some of the improvements which have been the subject of advertisement and selling appeal from year to year are

---

[2] H. B. Hull, *op. cit.*

low operating cost, adequate ice cube capacity, convenient food storage space, drawers to eliminate food dehydration, beautiful design, lighting of the box interior, easy ice cube removal, and quiet mechanism. Popular innovations brought out by one seller have had to be matched by others. Competition in succeeding years has been on a progressively higher quality level.

The extent of product improvement in this field is illustrated in the price and performance history of the General Electric refrigerator, shown in Table 133. In connection with interpretation of this table it should be remembered that the launching of the General Electric

TABLE 133

GENERAL ELECTRIC REFRIGERATORS, PRICE AND PERFORMANCE HISTORY, 1927–1940

YEAR	AVERAGE ZONE NO. 1 DELIVERED PRICE		CAPACITY* 1927 = 100%	AVERAGE* KW.-HR./MONTH 1927 = 100%	NOISE EFFECT ON EAR* 1927 = 100%	ICE FREEZING RATE* 1927 = 100 %
	All Models	6′ Model				
1927.......	$370	$310.00	100	100	100	100
1928.......	340	310.00	100	100	83	100
1929.......	300	285.00	100	100	83	100
1930.......	283	280.00	115	100	83	151
1931.......	266	275.00	119	84	68	167
1932.......	235	253.00	119	84	68	270
1933.......	199	235.00	141	74	36	270
1934.......	190	220.00†	141	74	36	270
1935.......	173	199.00	156	44	25	309
1936.......	172	199.00	156	44	22	309
1937.......	175	173.00	156	40	22	314
1938.......	179	178.00	156	40	22	314
1939.......	178	142.50	156	40	22	314
1940.......	162	132.75	156	40	22	314

* For 6 cubic foot models.
† No 6 cubic foot models in 1934. Price is an estimate of what the price would have been had one been made.
NOTE: The potential life of the 1940 machine is estimated to be about three times that of the 1927 unit.

refrigerator in 1927 came several years after the first electric refrigerator had been placed on the market; accordingly the improvement indicated in these statistics does not cover the full history of electric refrigeration. Yet the table tells an amazing story. Food storage capacity of the so-called six-foot model in 1940 was 56% greater than that of the corresponding 1927 model. The average monthly kilowatt-hour consumption was only 40% as great. The noise effect on the ear was only 22% as great. It froze ice cubes in one-third the time. Its potential life was estimated to be about three times as great. All these improvements were offered, not at increased, but at decreased price. A six-foot model in 1940 with all the improvements noted and others not listed cost only 43% as much as a six-foot model in 1927.

Improvement of the Automobile through Differentiation

Another example of continuous product improvement through competition in differentiation is found in the case of the automobile. The first automobile in this country was built by Duryea in 1892. Almost threadbare are the recitals comparing the pioneering automobiles of Duryea's day with their descendants of today. Duryea's Road Wagon covered 52.5 miles in a *Chicago Times-Herald* race, with an average speed of 7½ miles an hour, times for necessary stops being deducted. By 1903 as many as 11,000 cars were made in one year, with one- or two-cylinder motors placed under the front seat. Hazardous cranking was required; few models had windshields; steering wheels had just replaced tiller bars; shock absorbers had just been introduced; chain drives were employed; tires were of uncertain durability and hard to change; the few accessories available were expensive extras.

The transition from the undependable, inefficient automobile of Duryea to the smooth riding, powerful, and dependable car of 1940 was the result of the constant striving for product differentiation, of one refinement after another developed by laborious and expensive research of manufacturers seeking thereby to gain consumer preference. Always being sought were features which would command consumer preference. In the background was the desire of management for effective points to stress in advertising and personal selling. Over the years the list of improvements is long; only a few will be named here: the electric self-starter, electric ignition and lighting, improved carburetion, the demountable rim, the cord tire, the balloon tire, demountable wheels, four-wheel brakes, shatter-proof glass, controlled ventilation, all-steel bodies, improved springs and shock absorbers, enduring lacquer finishes, silent gears and synchronized shifting, sealed bearings and air-intake cleaners to keep from bearing surfaces the grit and water which shortened car life and increased wear and repairs, improved motors designed to provide smooth power and to reduce vibration. In economic terms such improvements have meant increased satisfaction in consumption.[3]

---

[3] Criticisms that consumers have had to buy more power and gadgets than they desire and have not had the option of getting the combination of product qualities desired at low prices is discussed in later pages (see page 652 ff).

TABLE 134

PASSENGER CAR SEQUENCES BASED ON GROSS SPECIFICATIONS

Make and Series	Year	Weight, Pounds	Wheelbase, Inches	Brake Horsepower	Delivered Price	Percentage of 1920's Price
Chrysler						
Plymouth Roadking	1939	2,824	114	82	$ 685	21.6
Chalmers 35.......	1920	3,100	117	45	3,170	
General Motors						
Chevrolet Master...	1939	2,820	112	85	648	26.6
Oldsmobile 37 B....	1920	2,739	112	44	2,435	
Graham-Paige						
Graham Standard...	1939	3,250	120	90	940	28.8
Paige 6-42........	1920	3,150	119	43	3,260	
Hudson						
Hudson 112........	1939	2,634	112	86	775	25.7
Essex A...........	1920	2,955	109	55	3,010	
Hupp						
Hupmobile Std. 6...	1939	3,280	112	101	995	29.3
Chandler N.S......	1920	3,400	123	45	3,400	
Nash-Kelvinator						
Nash-Lafayette....	1939	3,200	117	99	810	24.7
Nash 685..........	1920	3,455	121	35	3,285	
Packard						
Packard 6.........	1939	3,390	122	100	964	17.2
Packard Single 6...	1920	3,170	116	75	5,620	
Studebaker						
Studebaker Comm. 6	1939	3,160	116	90	955	34.4
Studebaker Light 6.	1920	2,900	112	45	2,780	
Willys-Overland						
Willys 4...........	1939	2,300	100	48	555	33.1
Overland 4-90......	1920	2,152	100	35	1,675	
*Average**.......	1939	2,934	114	85	795	27.6
	1935	2,933	114	83	806	28.0
	1930	2,930	113	64	1,118	38.9
	1925	2,875	113	50	1,387	48.2
	1920	2,981	114	43	2,877	100.0

* The averages are unweighted, and omit Packard because no comparable models were made in 1930 and 1935.

Source: A. T. Court, *Men, Methods and Machines in Automobile Manufacturing* (New York, Automobile Manufacturers Association, 1939), p. 6.

NOTE: No comparison is practicable on the Ford cars. All prices refer to cheapest 4-passenger closed car in series. Figures for 1939 are stated as of the month of May. Delivered prices estimated by adding 13½% to f.o.b. list. This has not always been exactly applicable to all makes, but the error involved is negligible for the purposes of this presentation.

As with the mechanical refrigerator, the improvements of one manufacturer have had to be matched by competitors. Competition has taken place on a higher level of quality from year to year. Technology applied to production methods and increased volume has made possible improved cars at lower prices. The story is told in part in a comparison of the gross specifications and prices of certain leading makes for the years 1920–1939, as shown in Table 134.

As shown in the table, the lowest-price cars in 1939 had greater power and size and better mechanical and riding qualities than the cars of 1920 which, on the average, cost consumers nearly twice as much in terms of dollars of constant value.[4] In addition, they had comfort features unknown to any motor car of the 1920's.[5]

Further striking evidence of the improvement in the automobile is contained in the testimony[6] of H. S. Vance, Chairman of the Studebaker Corporation, before the T.N.E.C., in which he gave data regarding the total operating costs of a popular-size automobile, including depreciation costs, for selected years between 1902 and 1938. While part of the decrease in operating cost is attributable to lowered prices of gasoline and oil, a larger part is attributable to the lowered price and increased efficiency and durability of the automobile and its replaceable parts, such as the tires, batteries, and spark plugs. The figures given for selected years are as follows:

Year	Total Operating Costs per Mile Including Depreciation	Miles of Automobiling for $300 a Year
1902	18.0 cents	1,667
1912	11.4	2,631
1920	7.4	4,054
1925	5.3	5,660
1930	4.2	7,143
1935	3.3	9,090
1938	3.1	9,667

[4] The table shows that in 1920 the cars compared cost four times those of 1939, but price comparisons based on this table are distorted by the fact that 1920 was a year of high prices. The B.L.S. Wholesale Price Index for all commodities (1926=100) shows the index number for 1920 to be 154.4 while that for 1939 is 77.1.

[5] An interesting description of the application of advancing technology to motor car production and the results attained thereby will be found in a study by A. T. Court, *Men, Methods and Machines in Automobile Manufacturing* (New York, Automobile Manufacturers Association, 1939); also see Paul McCrea, "American Free Enterprise Built the Motor Car," *Nation's Business*, November, 1939. The need of taking account of improved product quality in commodity price indexes, as illustrated by the automobile, will be found in the study of A. T. Court, *Hedonic Price Indexes with Automotive Examples*, paper presented at a joint meeting of the American Statistical Association and the Econometric Society in Detroit, Michigan, December 27, 1938 (General Motors Corporation, 1939).

[6] *Verbatim Record of the Proceedings of the Temporary National Economic Committee*, Vol. 9, October 26, 1939, to December 8, 1939, p. 506.

In industry after industry are found stories of slow but sure progress in product improvement from crude beginnings as a result of the constant striving of manufacturers to differentiate their products to gain consumer favor. For example, the first process for making rayon was introduced in 1884, but not until 1924, after the passage of 40 years, had the product reached a stage which afforded even moderate consumer satisfaction; since 1924 rapid improvement has brought rayon fabrics greatly superior to those of 1924.

The first patent on a typewriter was issued by the British Patent Office on January 7, 1714, but it was not until 1867 that an experimental machine was made that could write accurately and rapidly; not until 1873 that the first commercial typewriter was produced; not until 1878 that the first shift-key model was made; not until 1883 that the first type bar typewriter was introduced in which the type was visible to the operator without the necessity of his raising the carriage; and not until about 1923 that a noiseless machine was produced.[7]

The illustrations given above relate to so-called dynamic products, which have been particularly subject to improvement through competition in differentiation derived from technological developments; but even products apparently fully developed have over long periods had further significant improvements as a result of efforts to differentiate. Criticisms have been leveled at the practice of manufacturers' seeking differentiating characteristics which they may stress in advertising and selling, particularly in cases of products which have tended to be standardized. But study of such instances often shows that too short a time viewpoint may lead one to overlook significant improvements that come in the course of time from efforts to differentiate standardized products.

Improvement in Gasoline through Differentiation

Gasoline is a product whose development one must observe over some time-span in order to recognize the improvement that comes from efforts to differentiate. The advertising of gasoline has been criticized as questionable because at any one time advertised gasolines differ from one another only slightly; yet over a period of years competition in differentiation has brought important improvements in gasoline. In some quarters the claims of brand differences have appeared incon-

---

[7] *The Story of the Typewriter, 1873–1923*, published in 1923 in commemoration of the fiftieth anniversary of the invention of the writing machine, by the Herkimer County Historical Society.

sequential. Experts in petroleum production maintain, however, that the differences among competing gasolines upon the market are not meaningless or inconsequential.[8] Rather they often represent differences in opinion of petroleum engineers as to desirable combinations of conflicting product qualities. But even though the differences may be deemed small at any one time, they assume a long-range significance because the story of gasoline has been one of steady improvement under the drive of producers to find improvements which they could broadcast as a means of gaining sales preference. Moreover, improvement in commercial gasoline takes on added meaning because it has permitted adoption of high compression motors, which have offered increased operating efficiency.

The indirect effect of advertising on the improvement in gasoline quality was brought out in the testimony of several petroleum executives at the T.N.E.C. hearings[9] regarding the petroleum industry. The following testimony of Mr. Sidney A. Swensrud, vice president of the Standard Oil Company of Ohio, relates to the point made above:

More important than this consideration is the significance of competitive advertising in stimulating companies to improve products. It is claimed that there are only minor differences among the many advertised gasolines today. Since all gasolines must be manufactured to drive the same group of automobiles, the differences among them cannot be too great. Obviously, there may be many definitions of what constitutes a minor difference. What may be important to the technical expert may be unnoticed by the layman. Actually there are current differences among gasolines which affect the operation of automobiles. Two examples from many in the records of a single company in the East are cited.

For instance, in South Carolina in the summer of 1936 there was a variation in vapor pressure for samples of advertised brands of gasoline from 5.9 to 9.7 pounds. Vapor pressure, which can be controlled in some of the most up-to-date refining processes, is the factor which principally affects mileage per gallon because of its relation to the relative richness of mixture. In South Carolina summer weather, the lower vapor pressure gasoline will give substantially more mileage, which means an important saving to the consumer. Also, in a test made in Newark in 1936, samples of branded advertised gasoline revealed a difference of four octane numbers between the best and poorest "regular" gasolines. It should be kept in mind that the foregoing comparisons refer only to well-known brands. If the comparison had included local brands or unbranded gasolines, the differences would have been greater.

---

[8] The question as to whether advertising gives adequate information regarding product differences is discussed in the next chapter.

[9] *Verbatim Record of the Proceedings of the Temporary National Economic Committee*, Vol. 6, September 25, 1939–October 7, 1939, p. 661.

Further evidence of differences in gasolines is provided in the report of the octane committee of the Western Petroleum Refiners Association. The accompanying table lists the "lows" and "highs" of the specifications reported by the various companies:

COMPILATION OF THE ANALYSES OF SAMPLES OF MOTOR FUEL SHIPPED FROM MID-
CONTINENT REFINERIES FOR SUMMER USE, SHOWING THE RANGE AMONG
SAMPLES OF THE SAME GRADES AS WELL AS COMPARISON OF THE
ANALYSES OF THE DIFFERENT GRADES

	ETHYL	REG "O"	67 OCTANE	THIRD GRADE
I.B.P.	85–100	85–105	89–106	85–110
10% point	120–150	120–152	120–140	125–160
20% point	135–179	140–181	150–170	140–200
50% point	195–254	220–258	220–275	180–270
90% point	295–390	329–384	347–385	334–387
End point	365–410	360–414	390–415	375–430
Octane L3	76–81	70–74–1	67–69	45.67.3
Gum (copper dish)	0–25	0–25	2.4–25	0.25
Vapor pressure	7.5–11	7.8–10	8–10.1	6.6–10.1

Source: *National Petroleum News,* July 5, 1939, p. 11.

The compilation shows, for instance, that among 29 companies reporting on "Ethyl Premium" the octane value ranged from 81 down to 76, and on house brands from 74.1 down to 70. Other variations are also significant.

Whatever disagreement there may be about the importance of current differences among gasolines, there can be no disagreement as to the importance of the improvements effected over the years. Present-day gasoline is an altogether different product from that sold under the same name 15 years ago. There has been a constant improvement in gasoline, not so much as a result of remarkable new discoveries as by a succession of small changes. These small changes have been made in accordance with improvements in automobiles, for technical developments in the petroleum industry necessarily go hand in hand with technical developments in the automobile industry. The opportunity to capitalize, through advertising, on the preferences of some customers resulting from this steady flow of improvements has been a potent force in bringing about the improvements. That is to say, concentration on the small differences among gasolines at any one time neglects the highly dynamic character of the industry and does less than justice to the importance of competition in bringing about improvements in quality.

The improvements in gasoline quality over a period of years, to which Mr. Swensrud referred in his testimony, were presented in the specific terms of volatility and octane rating in the testimony of Mr. Robert E. Wilson, president of the Pan American Petroleum & Transport Company. The figures regarding these characteristics are shown in Table 135. In the course of 15 years the octane number of commercial gasoline improved from 50 to approximately 70.

TABLE 135

CHANGES IN THE VOLATILITY AND ANTI-KNOCK QUALITY OF GASOLINE PRODUCED IN
THE UNITED STATES OVER A PERIOD OF YEARS

Year	VOLATILITY AS FAHRENHEIT TEMPERATURE AT WHICH THE INDICATED PERCENTAGES DISTILLED			ANTI-KNOCK QUALITY OCTANE NUMBER
	10%	50%	90%	
1938	138	243	352	69.9
1937	139	244	353	69.1
1936	140	244	353	68.7
1931	139	254	366	65.4
1930	144	258	369	64.9
1929	151	263	379	....
1928	151	263	379	....
1927	154	266	382	....
1926	159	265	381	....
1925	165	271	384	....
1924	166	269	386	....
1923	173	268	379	50*
1922	172	269	376	50*
1921	173	261	377	50*
1920	187	265	379	50*
1919	....	261	361	50*

* All figures except the estimated octane numbers are from Bureau of Mines publications. Figures
for the years 1920 to 1930, inclusive, and for 1936 and 1937 are unweighted averages for sets of samples obtained in winter and summer. The 1931 figures are for winter samples only.
    The 1936, 1937, and 1938 series of samples differentiated between samples, representing grades
designated as "Premium," "Regular," and "Third Grade." Weighted averages were computed on
the basis of the assumption that the total volume of gasoline represented was 7.5% Premium, 80%
Regular, and 12.5% Third Grade.
    Source: *Verbatim Record of the Proceedings of the Temporary National Economic
Committee*, Vol. 6, p. 615.

The exact significance of the development of such qualities as octane
rating and volatility is at any time open to argument among scientific
men, but progress has been made by the experimentation by competing
companies to find improved gasoline. The testimony of Mr. Wilson
explains how the difficult problem of combining conflicting product
virtues may lead to differences of opinion as to the soundness of claims
of brand superiority to be found at any one time. Quotation of a few
paragraphs indicates that differences in gasoline are not meaningless:

Technologists in the industry are frequently asked whether the frequent
claims of improvements in gasoline quality and the superiority of a given company's products can be substantiated by the facts.

Without attempting to assume responsibility for, or to justify all of the
industry's advertising, there are two points which can properly be emphasized
in this connection. In the first place, scarcely a year has passed since 1920 which
has not seen a measurable improvement in one or more of the important properties of gasoline. Accordingly, the oft-repeated claims for improved products,
while doubtless exaggerated in some cases, do have a basis in fact. In the second
place, the quality of gasoline is not a function of only two or three properties,
but really depends upon a combination of a wide variety of properties, some of

which are more or less contradictory in nature. It is therefore quite possible for each of a half dozen different gasolines to excel the others in one or two respects, particularly since properties which are quite important in one engine or in one climate, are of less importance in another engine or in another climate. For instance, even today there is not complete agreement among leading technologists as to the best volatility of gasoline in certain seasons, or as to the proper method of determining the anti-knock value of gasoline. To explain the basis for these general comments it seems desirable to discuss briefly the actual practical significance of some of the more important properties of gasoline.

Of all the numerous properties of gasoline, volatility and anti-knock rating are undoubtedly the two of greatest importance, but even in referring to these two as the important properties there is great danger of over simplification because both of them are very complex properties, and a gasoline which may be better in volatility or anti-knock for one engine may be distinctly worse in these respects in some other engine, or under some other operating conditions.[10]

To summarize, it is found in the case of gasoline that what may appear to be inconsequential differences between brands at any one time may have real meaning, even though at the time experts do not agree on the meaning. Moreover, when product differences are projected over a period of time they take on material significance. The sum of small differences produced by the research of competitive organizations has resulted in product progress which leads to increased satisfaction in consumption.

Improvement in Sheeting through Differentiation

A product longer upon the market than gasoline and one which has been less subject to improvement through advancing technology in the past 40 years is sheeting. As indicated in previous discussion of that product, the advertised brands of particular texture have tended at any one time to present small differences. But investigation indicates that as a result of the drive to find this or that point which might gain consumer approval, sheeting manufacturers have introduced innovations which continued usage proves to be improvements from the consumers' standpoint. Here, as with other products mentioned, copying of successful innovations has led to competition on a higher quality level than previously. For example, the 66 x 72 construction, which has become the standard for medium-price muslin sheets, was not marketed in quantity until Pequot carried on experiments and testing in the hope of finding a product that consumers would prefer to competing products. At a later date Wamsutta and others carried on

10 *Ibid.*, p. 604.

extensive experimentation to develop an improved fine-count percale sheet.[11] Again, at the turn of the century, Pequot and others, seeking consumer favor, offered manufactured sheets and pillow cases, and since then practically all demand has turned to this form of product.

Case material indicates numerous other attempts by sheeting manufacturers to find desired innovations, and these have been received with varying response. They include a tape selvage to give added strength to sheets, which has been generally adopted; a tab, now universally used, showing the size of the sheet and placed so as to be easily visible when the sheet is folded; a tapered weave, which has a higher thread count at the place where wear is hardest, introduced by the Pepperell Manufacturing Company as being more durable (not yet widely copied); colored sheets and colored hems, once popular, but like many fashion characteristics, later discarded; and better packaging.

Some improvement in sheet quality apparently has come also from the drive of manufacturers to develop manufacturing methods which would insure uniform quality under their brands. This improvement in quality has come also as a by-product of efforts to find lower-cost production methods and should, of course, not be confused with the drive for product differentiation, except in so far as the offering of uniform quality is a basis for gaining brand preference. Not only the sheeting manufacturers but also the manufacturers of textile machinery have sought to develop improved methods in making yarn, in weaving, and in bleaching. Improvements which have promised more nearly uniform quality or lower costs made by one manufacturer have generally had to be met by competing manufacturers selling under their own brands.[12] Among the operating mill heads and executives of textile machinery companies consulted, there was a universal opinion that the decided improvements in cotton textile machinery during the past 20 years have made it possible to produce a more nearly uniform and better product than formerly, and at lower cost.[13]

[11] Between 1920 and 1938 Wamsutta Mills, in its effort to keep ahead of its competitors in producing fine percale sheets, made six basic changes in its product. During this period a good deal of experimental work in yarn construction and in weaving was carried on.

[12] It is recognized that the advances in textile technology have not offered enough in the way of savings in cost or improvement in quality to necessitate quick modernization of mills, particularly after bankruptcy has given old mills low overhead costs. Yet mills selling under their own brands have had to meet the quality of competitors to hold their own.

[13] Among textile machinery developments of the past 15 years which have tended to improve quality, the following may be mentioned:
Opening and blending machines. These have made possible a truer cotton mix; more

Other Examples of Improvement through Differentiation

Numerous other products long upon the market present a pattern somewhat similar to that of sheeting. Product improvement as a result of differentiation is not so marked as with relatively new, dynamic products; yet from time to time innovations have taken hold and their general adoption indicates them to be improvements from the consumer's standpoint. In the discussion of sugar it was pointed out that sugar companies have developed certain specialties which have been desired, such as thermophilic sugar, powdered sugar, and brown sugar, to meet special consumer uses. So far as granulated sugar is concerned, the only marked differentiating element developed over a long period of time has been that of packaging. That this practice represents an improvement to some consumers is indicated by the fact that in the course of 30 years package sales have increased until almost one-half the volume of granulated sugar for household use is sold in packages. Table salt for many years was just salt. In 1912 the Morton Salt Company, seeking a means of individualizing its product in a highly competitive field where there was little choice among brands, learned as a result of experimentation that salt could be made relatively impervious to moisture by being dusted with ordinary baking soda. The dusting process was found to be simplified and more efficient if salt was produced in cubic crystals rather than in the usual irregular flakes. Therefore the company changed its manufacturing processes. Free-running salt for household use was a distinct improvement, and it soon became necessary for all salt manufacturers to develop such a product.[14] For many years vegetable shortening

bales can be mixed and blended more thoroughly than previously. This has assured a greater uniformity of yarn.

Pickers. Improved pickers have given better results with less labor and less space than previous pickers.

Drawing machines. Cotton formerly went through three processes of drawing. One machine has been invented which cares for all three processes with a better result than the previous machine.

Roving frames. One machine does what used to be done by three. Not only have costs been lowered but the new machine produces a better quality of yarn than formerly.

Spinning frames. Improved spinning frames developed in the last 20 years have afforded lower costs of manufacturing yarn.

Winding and spooling. A machine which was perfected for tying knots greatly reduced the cost of this operation.

Warping. A new warping machine was developed which wound 1,000 yards of thread a minute instead of the 40 or 50 of previous years.

Slashing. A new machine was developed which operated at 80 yards a minute as contrasted with the 30 yards of the unimproved machine.

Looms. Recent looms have greatly reduced the need of operating supervision and at the same time have tended to improve quality of cloth.

[14] N. H. Borden, *Problems in Advertising* (3d ed., New York, McGraw-Hill Book Company, Inc., 1937), case of the Morton Salt Company, p. 84 ff.

had not been materially improved. Then as a result of experimentation by Lever Brothers to find an improved product to launch under its brand, creaming of shortening was developed. Competitive brands had to be treated in this way to hold their own in consumers' eyes.

The Desirability for Freedom of Opportunity for Differentiation

Such instances could be multiplied, but enough examples have been cited to indicate clearly how the desire to profit from product differentiation has provided a strong force for product improvement in our free economy. Advertising and aggressive selling, elliptically speaking, may be deemed partial causes of the improvement, because the sellers' desire to have effective selling points has been a driving force for differentiation. For certain dynamic products the improvement over a period of years has been striking; for products long upon the market the improvement has been less marked, yet often significant.

Any change in the economic system which had the force of denying or decreasing opportunity to profit from product differentiation, such as mandatory quality specifications, unless these were merely minimum standards, would remove what probably has been the strongest force in the economy for improvements in products and for increasing the range of products.

In this connection it may be pointed out that in the Middle Ages the guilds under their monopoly grants set up controls and regulations that permitted little or no aggressive selling by the guild members and little opportunity on their part to offer differentiated merchandise to meet consumers' desires. It was a sterile, static economy. Product forms were few, and they did not change or increase materially. Little was done to meet consumer wants. In fact, this rigid, static product control was a large factor leading to the gradual downfall of the guilds after the fourteenth century. The merchants, who emerged as a separate group from the craftsmen, could not readily sell what the craftsmen made; but the guilds stubbornly held to their product restrictions. In order to have things made that markets wanted, merchants turned to workmen outside the guilds; and the domestic, or "putting out," system developed. This change, wherein sellers took the initiative in seeking out buyers and profited from offering them new and desirable merchandise, gradually ushered in a more dynamic, progressive society than that which had gone before. Not until then did the range of merchandise widen appreciably.

The Practice of Withholding Improvements

There is one further aspect of the practice of product differentiation which should be mentioned before attention is turned in other directions, namely, the fact that manufacturers do not always introduce new product developments as soon as they are ready to place upon the market. Accordingly these manufacturers have been criticized at times for failing to give consumers the benefits of technological developments as rapidly as they might.

The withholding of new improvements is generally dictated by profit considerations. Manufacturers desire to secure all the profits possible from existing improvements before introducing new developments. They hesitate to incur the costs and risks attendant upon introduction. In spite of such hesitation, the stress of competition in differentiation is generally a sufficient force to prevent the withholding of significant product improvements for long periods.

At this point the practice of withholding improvements is mentioned in order that the mistaken impression that differentiations always are introduced as rapidly as possible may be avoided. The question of withholding improvements will be discussed further in Chapter XXIV, when technological developments and growth costs are discussed.

The Effect of Advertising upon Product Quality

Advertising not only has had an influence upon improvement of product quality through competition in differentiation, outlined in the preceding pages, but it has exercised some influence upon product quality in another way, namely, in leading producers to maintain quality under brands. Since frequent reference has been made to the relation of advertising to brand quality, at this point the subject will merely be briefly recounted. The system of branding evolved as a workable scheme for giving protection in product quality to consumers, because the self-interest of sellers has led them to guard carefully the quality of merchandise sold under their brands. It must be recognized, however, that the brand is not necessarily a guarantee of uniformity of product quality. It is affixed by an interested party, and he is free to tamper with or change quality as he sees fit, or through inefficiency he may have inadequate quality control. Not infrequently are examples found where knowingly or through inadvertence manufacturers have failed to maintain quality standards under their brands. For example, one cigarette manufacturer cited the action of a previous management of substituting cheaper tobaccos, when tobacco prices rose, in an attempt to keep the company's cigarettes profitable without altering their price of 10 cents a package. In the shoe field, some manufacturers admitted altering quality in times of rising costs in order to continue existing price lines. Again, in the sheeting field, a sales executive cited a mill superintendent who, in order to give his department a good profit showing, altered the mix of cotton and took certain other cost reducing measures which reduced the quality of the company's product. He did these things without informing his superiors. A sugar manufacturer cited an instance where for three days his refinery manager had failed, through inadvertence, to bring the sugar up to the customary standard of whiteness. A hosiery manufacturer told of a period during which his inspection force, as a result of labor trouble, failed to maintain the standards of inspection desired by the management. Many such examples were found in cases and in field work.

One must recognize also that changes may be made in branded products in the belief that they are desirable improvements; but they may not prove acceptable to consumers. For numerous products, such as automobiles, radios, refrigerators, and washing machines, manufacturers have produced new models annually. The new models have not always proved as acceptable to consumers as those of previous years and the companies have lost their relative position in the industry.

In spite of all such difficulties and shortcomings, branding has usually proved to be a workable device to assure consumers that they obtain merchandise which, by use or by reputation, they have come to know and to rely upon. The long-range profit viewpoint previously discussed usually leads a seller to go to great lengths to protect the goodwill which he has built around his brand. Brand reputation ordinarily has been established at too high cost and its importance to the future of his business is too great for him to be negligent of or to tamper with quality maintenance.

The danger to sellers of permitting product quality to deteriorate is illustrated by all the cases cited above, for the managements encountered subsequent difficulties. The sheeting manufacturer received complaints and lost sales. The sugar manufacturer stated that certain distributors withdrew their patronage and the company still had been unable to regain it after the lapse of 10 years. Sales of the cigarette fell as a result of the slighting of quality, and the new management which took over the business had trouble in regaining the lost ground. In the automobile field, manufacturers cited instances where defects in new models had led to consumer ill will which was reflected in the sales of subsequent models. Shoe manufacturers generally dropped the policy of selling at fixed prices, partly because of bad trade reaction to lower quality in times of rising prices.

Relation of Advertising to Quality under Brands

The desire of a seller to maintain quality under his brand does not depend upon his being an advertiser. He maintains quality under his brand in order to enjoy the benefits of patronage of satisfied customers, whether he advertises extensively or not. Thus, the survey made by this study [15] of the selling of private brand merchandise by large-scale distributors disclosed that these concerns were maintaining some kind of control over the quality of products sold under their labels. The methods reported by the various types of organizations are shown in Table 136. Since these concerns employed different methods for different types of products, the totals of methods reported exceed the number of concerns interviewed. The most common practices reported were periodic submittal of samples of merchandise to laboratory test and dependence upon suppliers in whom they had confidence to maintain quality control. A large percentage reported that they physically inspected merchandise. Some organizations had established their own laboratories. For example, 10 out of 20 corporate food chains interviewed had their own testing laboratories, 5 out of 13 corporate drug chains, and 2 out of 11 voluntary food chains. Others submitting products to laboratory check used commercial laboratories. The adequacy of these control systems was not closely studied, but every management was alert to the need of maintaining quality.

Some manufacturers supplying private brands to distributors stated that they exercised less rigorous quality control over merchandise manufactured for distributors' brands than over that sold under their own brands. This was true, for example, of one sheet manufacturer and of a hosiery manufacturer. Others, however, stated that their control over private brand merchandise was as rigorous as that given to their

---

[15] See Appendix V.

TABLE 136

METHODS EMPLOYED BY CERTAIN LARGE SCALE DISTRIBUTORS TO MAINTAIN QUALITY
OF MERCHANDISE SOLD UNDER THEIR OWN BRANDS, BUT NOT
MANUFACTURED BY THEM, 1939

METHOD EMPLOYED FOR CHECKING QUALITY*	NUMBER OF REPLIES AS TO METHODS USED AMONG:						
	20 Corporate Food Chains	13 Corporate Drug Chains	11 Voluntary Chains Wholesaler Members	7 Voluntary Food Chains Headqtr.	5 Limited Price Variety	5 Dry Goods & Dept. Store Chains	Total
(a) Keep inspectors in suppliers' plants............	1	0	0	3	0	0	4
(b) Use systematic physical inspection of merchandise.	16	0	10	3	1	3	33
(c) Submit samples periodically to laboratory test...	14	8	6	4	4	3	39
(d) Rely upon grading by government inspectors (applies to meats and canned foods)	4	0	4	6	0	0	14
(e) Depend primarily upon suppliers to maintain quality of specification or of sample submitted........	14	10	5	0	5	5	39
(f) Rely on integrity of supplier without specification or sample..............	1	0	0	0	0	0	1

* Many organizations reported using different methods for different products. Hence the total reported methods are greater than the number of concerns reporting.

own brands, and in many instances identical merchandise was sold under the producer's brand and distributors' brands.

While maintenance of quality for a brand does not depend upon advertising, advertising usually intensifies the desire of a manufacturer to maintain quality in order to protect the goodwill which adheres to his brand. Manufacturers are wary of letting quality deteriorate when they have a large volume of business gained at considerable cost. It was found in field work that without exception manufacturers had established quality controls for their advertised branded products. The efficiency of their control systems was not studied, but the importance they attached to maintaining quality was evident.

The Range of Products Available

The advent of new inventions and the quest for product differentiation have brought an enormous number of products on the market from which consumers may choose. This fact is indicated in the following quotation:

At any one time, there are now available about a quarter of a million distinct goods, each vying for a share of the consumer's dollar. A committee of experts, working for the Consumer's Advisory Board, recently listed about 100,000 important commodities, of which at least 2,000 were of key significance. The 1929 catalogue of Sears, Roebuck and Co. described more than 46,000 items; while the drug department alone of Macy's in New York City offers its customers their choice of some 20,000 items. No attempt has been made to count the total number of things sold throughout the store. Nor has any such census been made for the nation as a whole.[16]

The number of distinct commodities on the market is large, but such a figure is small in comparison with the number of brands in the country, because each commodity has many suppliers who brand their goods. No one knows how many there are. The study of shoes indicated that there were in excess of 6,000 brands of shoes on the market. Estimates of unknown validity have been published regarding the number of brands of various other products, e.g., 300 brands of canned pineapple, 1,000 of canned salmon, 4,500 of canned corn, 2,500 of perfume, 1,200 of face powder, 500 of mustard, 10,000 of wheat flour, and so on.[17] In the neighborhood of 375,000 certificates of registration for trade-marks had been issued by the U. S. Commissioner of Patents through 1940, but such a figure fails to reflect the number of brands on the market, because many marks in use, particularly marks not in interstate commerce, are not registered.

While astronomical figures of number of brands may be compiled, a better idea of the array of brands from which consumers may choose is conveyed by the list of brands for specific products to be found in individual city markets, for many brands have only limited distribution. A list of brand choices available for selected consumer products in the Greater Milwaukee market is given in Table 137. This table shows for these products not only the number of brands in the market but also the number carried by individual stores and the distribution of demand among the various brands available, facts upon which comment will be made later. The choices available in a market such as Milwaukee

---

[16] C. S. Wyand, *The Economics of Consumption* (New York, The Macmillan Company, 1937), p. 117.

[17] Such estimates have appeared in a number of books on consumption, but it has been impossible to trace the estimates to original sources.

Products—Usage by Brands and Retailer Stocking of Brands

Commodity	% of Families Reporting Use of Product	No. of Brands Reported in Use	Percentage of Families Consuming Product Who Used Leading Brands			No. of Brands Used by Less than 1% of Consumers
			No. 1	No. 1-3 Inc.	No. 1-5 Inc.	
Packaged Coffee	84.0	148	25.0	52.0	65.0	129
Coffee Subst. & Decaffeinated	9.5	12	56.0	100.0	....	9
Packaged Cocoa	85.0	80	34.0	76.0	86.0	71
Corn Breakfast Foods	78.0	10	90.0	102.0	....	7
Bran Breakfast Foods	36.0	12	43.0	80.0	101.0	6
Wheat Breakfast Foods	51.0	29	24.0	72.0	96.0	19
Quick Oat Breakfast Foods	75.0	25	93.0	95.0	97.0	21
Rice Breakfast Foods	34.0	15	50.0	100.0	....	12
Canned Peaches	57.0	102	68.0	82.0	88.0	91
Canned Pineapple	76.0	99	62.0	84.0	90.0	90
Canned Soups	84.0	50	84.0	100.0	103.0	45
Canned Milk	67.0	39	32.0	75.0	93.0	30
Canned Pork and Beans	82.0	41	72.0	97.0	99.0	34
Bottled Catsup	86.0	76	45.0	88.0	91.0	70
Tomato Juice	27.0	80	37.0	59.0	70.0	61
Wheat Bread	88.0	27	28.0	57.0	76.0	14
Packaged Soda Crackers	94.0	38	69.0	89.0	93.0	30
Packaged Cookies	28.0	26	80.0	90.0	96.0	19
Packaged Macaroni	78.0	108	57.0	79.0	85.0	99
Baking Powder	99.0	44	65.0	84.0	95.0	37
Baking Chocolate	74.0	24	71.0	96.0	100.0	18
Prepared Cake Flour	55.0	20	66.0	100.0	101.0	16
Flour	94.0	66	41.0	78.0	88.0	57
Packaged Comp. Yeast	45.0	8	52.0	102.0‡	102.0‡	8
Quick Dessert Powders	66.0	81	46.0	74.0	88.0	68
Packaged Cheese	61.0	43	52.0	85.0	94.0	31
Salad Dressings—Boiled	45.0	32	69.0	92.0	96.0	25
—Mayonnaise	40.0	53	40.0	87.0	95.0	47
Sugar in Cartons	14.0	9	49.0	99.0	99.0	6
Gran. Sugar in Cloth Bags	88.0	61	25.0	60.0	80.0	48
Smoked Ham	63.0	28	49.0	87.0	100.0	23
Packaged Bacon	71.0	31	47.0	85.0	98.0	25
Toilet Soap	99.0	86	29.0	80.0	104.0	76
Packaged Soap Flakes	82.0	72	38.0	79.0	98.0	60
Granulated Soap or Soap Beads	56.0	36	69.0	146.0	173.0	30
Washing Powder	10.0	44	69.0	80.0	87.0	34
Scouring Cleansers	90.0	43	45.0	80.0	93.0	35
Brown Laundry Soap	65.0	36	65.0	90.0	99.0	31
White Laundry Soap	58.0	28	53.0	94.0	99.0	23

Commodity	% of Families Reporting Use of Product	No. of Brands Reported in Use	Percentage of Families Consuming Product Who Used Leading Brands			No. of Brands Used by Less than 1% of Consumers
			No. 1	No. 1-3 Inc.	No. 1-5 Inc.	
Aspirin	78.0	71	88.0	95.0	....	68
Cigarettes	72.0	29	30.0	78.0	95.0	19
Pipe Tobacco	45.0	87	14.0	37.0	51.0	71
Perfume	49.0	181	56.0	69.0	77.0	166
Mouth Wash	69.0	118	47.0	78.0	88.0	111
Tooth Paste	82.0	99	24.0	53.0	72.0	86
Tooth Powder	33.0	63	67.0	85.0	89.0	55
Safety Razor Blades	87.0	127	56.0	78.0	89.0	121
Shaving Cream	55.0	100	39.0	67.0	79.0	89
Brushless Shaving Cream	18.0	44	27.0	68.0	94.0	33

Source: Based on data from *The Milwaukee Journal*, "Consumer Analysis of the Greater Milwaukee Market—1935."

—Selected Products in the Greater Milwaukee Market—1935

Percentage of Retailers Carrying Number of Brands Indicated							Percentage of Coverage among Retailers by Brands with Standing							
							No. 1		No. 3		No. 5		No. 10	
0	1	2	3	4	5	Over 5	Indp. Grocers	Chain	Indp. Grocers	Chain	Indp. Grocers	Chain	Indp. Grocers	Chain
....	2.5	2.0	7.5	7.5	11.0	70.0	0.0	33.0*	60.0	100.0	27.0	100.0	0.0	33.0*
14.5	39.5	30.5	14.5	1.0	....	....	78.0	100.0	27.0	100.0	....	‡		
1.5	22.5	34.0	28.5	10.0	2.0	1.5	69.0	100.0	27.0	67.0	....	....		
0.5	18.0	48.5	31.5	1.5	....	....	96.0	100.0	45.0	33.0	....	....		
3.0	12.0	22.5	27.5	26.0	6.5	2.5	86.0	100.0	77.0	100.0	30.0	100.0		
2.0	2.0	8.0	11.5	14.0	18.0	45.0	83.0	100.0	77.0	100.0	51.0	100.0	0.0	33.0*
0.5	68.0	25.5	5.5	0.5	....	....	94.0	100.0	0.5	33.0	....	....		
4.5	15.5	40.0	33.0	6.0	1.0	....	74.0	100.0	59.0	100.0	....	....		
1.5	16.5	32.0	24.0	10.5	8.0	7.5	29.0	100.0	0.0	33.0†	7.0†	0.0	3.0†	0.0
1.0	16.0	21.5	27.0	18.5	8.0	8.0	33.0	67.0	30.0	33.0	0.0	33.0*	....	....
0.0	3.5	9.0	16.5	23.5	18.5	29.0	97.0	100.0	52.0	100.0	0.0	67.0*		
0.5	10.5	29.0	36.5	16.5	3.5	3.5	79.0	100.0	25.0	100.0	64.0	0.0		
0.0	11.0	28.5	36.5	20.0	2.5	1.5	90.0	100.0	8.0	66.0	0.5	0.0		
0.5	7.0	18.5	30.0	24.0	12.0	8.0	82.0	100.0	26.0	0.0	0.0	33.0		
16.5	46.5	21.5	7.5	4.0	1.5	2.5	20.0	100.0	9.0	67.0	18.0	0.0	4.0	33.0
0.0	1.5	1.5	14.5	34.0	32.5	16.0	90.0	33.0	0.0	0.0	65.0	0.0	0.0	33.0
0.5	41.0	33.0	16.0	6.0	3.0	0.5	89.0	0.0	29.0	0.0	1.0	33.0		
14.5	32.0	28.5	10.5	8.0	4.5	2.0	40.0	0.0	1.0	33.0	0.5	33.0		
0.5	36.5	40.5	17.5	3.5	1.5	0.0	76.0	100.0	14.0	33.0	3.0	0.0		
0.5	8.5	14.0	25.5	28.5	17.5	5.5	95.0	100.0	38.0	100.0	0.0	0.0		
1.0	35.5	44.5	16.0	3.0	....	....	92.0	100.0	24.0	100.0	3.0	0.0		
6.0	38.5	27.5	24.5	3.0	0.5	0.0	81.0	100.0	51.0	100.0	....	....		
0.0	20.0	32.5	20.5	16.5	6.0	4.5	45.0	100.0	40.0	0.0	0.0	33.0		
1.0	51.5	47.0	0.5	....	....	....	72.0	67.0	only 2 brands given					
....	4.5	5.0	9.5	10.5	13.0	57.5	86.0	100.0	66.0	100.0	46.0	67.0	13.0	33.0
3.5	5.5	9.0	17.0	17.5	20.0	27.5	84.0	100.0	23.0	0.0	63.0	100.0	20.0	67.0
0.5	30.5	38.0	22.5	8.0	0.5	....	91.0	100.0	57.0	67.0	0.0	33.0		
3.5	38.5	36.5	16.5	4.5	0.0	0.5	74.0	100.0	41.0	100.0	4.0	0.0		
18.0	64.5	16.0	1.5	....	....	....	56.0	33.0	17.0	0.0	....	....		
37.0	45.5	16.5	0.5	0.5	....	....	8.0	0.0	21.0	33.0	0.0	33.0	0.5	0.0
69.0	22.5	7.0	1.0	0.5	....	....	9.0	100.0	5.0	100.0	0.0	0.0		
58.0	38.5	3.0	0.5	0.0	....	....	11.0	100.0	9.0	33.0	2.0	0.0		
Under 5 brands			0.5	....	99.5		89.0	100.0	92.0	100.0	99.0	100.0	0.0	0.0
....	1.5	8.0	11.5	14.0	14.0	51.0	31.0	100.0	77.0	100.0	68.0	100.0	22.0	100.0
0.5	3.0	7.0	17.0	28.5	28.0	16.0	97.0	100.0	83.0	100.0	24.0	100.0	....	....
10.0	45.5	29.5	12.0	2.5	....	0.5	83.0	100.0	21.0	0.0	0.0	0.0	4.0	0.0
0.5	2.0	9.0	12.5	26.0	22.0	28.0	88.0	100.0	54.0	100.0	78.0	67.0	....	....
1.0	14.0	32.0	32.0	19.0	1.5	0.5	88.0	100.0	37.0	100.0	49.0	67.0	....	....
0.5	18.5	49.0	23.0	7.0	2.0	0.0	92.0	100.0	99.0	100.0	1.0	0.0	....	....

Percentage of Druggists Carrying Number of Brands Indicated							Percentage of Coverage among Druggists by Brands with Standing							
							No. 1		No. 3		No. 5		No. 10	
0	1	2	3	4	5	Over 5	Indp. Druggists	Chain	Indp. Druggists	Chain	Indp. Druggists	Chain	Indp. Druggists	Chain
....	2.0	23.0	48.0	15.0	9.0	3.0	99.0	Yes	0.0	Yes	....	....	....	....
....	....	....	....	....	....	100.0§	96.0	Yes	94.0	Yes	91.0	Yes	90.0	Yes
....	....	1.0	....	....	....	99.0	93.0	Yes	91.0	Yes	94.0	Yes	86.0	Yes
....	....	41.0	....	....	....	59.0	89.0	Yes	21.0	Yes	50.0	No	25.0	No
....	....	....	....	....	....	100.0	95.0	Yes	97.0	Yes	0.0	No	....	....
....	....	....	....	....	....	100.0	92.0	Yes	82.0	Yes	91.0	Yes	96.0	Yes
....	....	....	3.0	8.0	5.0	84.0	97.0	Yes	59.0	Yes	54.0	No	....	....
....	....	....	3.0	....	5.0	92.0	97.0	Yes	71.0	Yes	82.0	Yes	....	....
....	....	....	....	2.0	1.0	97.0	80.0	Yes	83.0	Yes	85.0	Yes	1.0	Yes
....	....	....	4.0	7.0	6.0	83.0	97.0	Yes	79.0	No	49.0	No	19.0	No

* Chain brands.
† Wholesaler or cooperative chain brand.
‡ Only two brands given.
§ Range—3 to 25 brands; Mode—15 to 20 brands.

are numerous for most products: 148 brands of packaged coffee, 10 brands of corn breakfast foods, 29 brands of cigarettes, 87 brands of pipe tobacco, 99 brands of tooth paste, 100 brands of shaving cream, and so on. The number of brands available in city markets is, of course, far larger than the number available in small towns and rural districts, where the number of retailers is smaller.

Advertising's Relationship to the Number of Brands

While advertising and aggressive selling strengthen the tendency toward nonstandardization of merchandise and have encouraged continuous attempts at new differentiation, strangely enough advertising has been a force which has often tended to decrease the number of brands upon the market. The number of brands in any merchandise category is attributable not to the practice of advertising, but to the number of suppliers who find it profitable to sell such merchandise under their brands. Instead of being a force to increase the number of brand choices, advertising is a force tending to concentrate demand upon certain brands. Those employing selective advertising hope to attract a large volume of demand for their brands.

Many forces, of which advertising is but one, enter into determination of the number of suppliers of particular products in any market. Important among these forces is the presence or absence of decreasing production costs with increasing scale of operations. Chiefly because of the economies of large-scale operation, the number of companies is small in the automobile, electric refrigerator, and sugar industries. Accordingly, brands are few. In contrast, the advantages from large scale operation have not been present in such degree in the manufacture of canned fruits, shoes, macaroni, or flour; and the number both of suppliers and of brands has been relatively large. Among other considerations which have a bearing on the number of suppliers are the capital outlay required (usually associated with the phenomenon of decreasing costs), the effect of freight charges, and the volume of demand in the market to support a number of suppliers. To the above, advertising may be added as another force which has often been employed to bring concentration of demand on a few suppliers. In bringing concentration of demand it has had some, though not strong, influence in keeping down the number of brands. That advertising has some influence on the number of brands has been shown in the analyses of competition in the cigarette and dentifrice fields. Likewise in the cigar industry, advertising, since 1917, has been added to the force of decreasing manufacturing costs to bring concentration of demand, to reduce the number of suppliers, and thus to reduce the number of brands. Whenever advertising has been effective in building strong brand discrimination, this discrimination for established brands has been one factor to discourage the entry of new brands into the market, and has required any new entrant to make considerable outlay for aggressive selling costs to secure substantial volume. A number of cases were found in which manufacturers decided against entry into certain product fields because of the strongly entrenched positions of leading advertised brands. Again, the survey among chains showed that private branders have delayed entry into product fields in which the strong domination of manufacturers' brands has made the establishment of private brands difficult and expensive.[18]

Varying combinations of the forces governing the number of suppliers in the market account for the varying number of brands in different fields, such as are shown in Table 137. While advertising has had some effect on the entry of brands into the market, it has apparently not been a strong force in itself in keeping down the number of brands. In a number of fields in which advertising has played an important role in marketing and in which manufacturers' brands have been dominant, the total number of brands has continued to be large because forces other than advertising have favored easy entry of suppliers. For example, in 1935 there were 99 brands of tooth paste used in the Greater Milwaukee market. In this field it has been feasible for a large number of suppliers to enter manufacture, and to sell small volume with some profit, because little capital outlay has been required and no great production economies have attended large-scale manufacture. Yet advertising has been a force to discourage an even larger number of brands, as shown by the fact that 72% of the demand for tooth paste was concentrated in five extensively advertised brands. Likewise with shaving cream, the lack of economies in large-scale production and the small amount of capital required for manufacture led 100 concerns to put out shaving cream under their brands in the Milwaukee market, but nearly 80% of the demand was concentrated in five advertised brands. In contrast, in the case of cigarettes, the large outlay required for starting to manufacture was one force tending to hold the number of brands of cigarettes to 29, but on top of this

---

[18] See Chapter XXI, p. 593 ff.

was the restraining influence of the large advertising outlay needed to establish new brands, until the manufacturers of 10-cent brands entered the market without such outlay.

Thus when considering the problem of consumers' difficulties in getting the "best" value among a large number of brands in the market, one should realize that advertising in itself has been a force tending to bring uniformities of demand. It has led consumers to center concentration upon a smaller array of brands than probably would have been present were advertising not a strong factor in influencing selective demand.

While advertising has been a force tending to keep down the number of brands in some fields, at the same time its effect has been to keep alive in the minds of consumers the possible benefits of the differences offered in various brands. Consequently for many convenience products retailers have found it advisable to carry a substantial number of the available brands in order to meet the preferences of their clientele. Thus Table 137 shows that in Milwaukee 70% of the retailers carried over five brands of packaged coffee; 99.5% carried more than five brands of toilet soap; every retailer found it necessary to carry over five brands of cigarettes, and the modal number carried was 15 to 20 brands in spite of the fact that the total number of brands in the market was small in comparison with those for many other product groups. And so on with other products, such as tooth paste, tooth powder, safety razor blades, and shaving cream, for which differentiation and brand preferences were strong, the number of brands carried by retailers was large.

In contrast, for products for which brand discrimination was low and consequently advertising was not an important marketing tool, the number of brands carried by individual retailers tended to be small in relation to the total number of brands in the market. Retailers did not need to carry many brands, because consumers did not have strong enough brand preferences to make the offering of a wide variety of brand choice on the part of the retailer necessary. Although there were 102 brands of canned peaches in the market, the great majority of retailers found it necessary to handle only three brands or less; and so it was with canned pineapple, wheat bread, flour, mayonnaise, and many other products.

The number of brands carried by retailers appears to be a function of variety of choice demanded by consumers. When differentiation among competing brands has appeared of importance to consumers, the retailer has found it necessary to carry a considerable number of brands to satisfy demand. Where brand has offered differentiation of little consequence, the retailer has not been pressed to carry a large number of brands.

It is concluded from the above discussion that advertising in itself has been a force tending to reduce the number of brands upon the market, but it may have increased the number carried by individual retailers in some categories because it has helped to make product differentiation of consequence to consumers in guiding their demand.

Summary

The evidence of this chapter shows that advertising, as an important element in an aggressive, free enterprise, has been an indirect influence in bringing the remarkable range of products now available to consumers. It has thus contributed to an enhancement of consumer satisfactions. It has helped in the growth of product range through its part in speeding up the adoption of major inventions. It has had an even greater influence on range of merchandise through its encouragement of product differentiation. Because of their desire to find products which might prove desirable to consumers and which accordingly they might aggressively promote to consumers, sellers have been led to constant experimentation in combining product qualities.

In thus stimulating differentiation advertising has had an influence in bringing progress in merchandise development. Improved products have come on the market which better fill consumer desires and needs than the old products. This product improvement has been rapid and striking in the case of relatively new products such as automobiles, refrigerators, and other mechanical products. But even for merchandise long on the market the improvement has been substantial over a period of time. The constant striving for product improvement has brought significant improvements in products such as gasoline and sheeting, which at any time appear to critics to be relatively standardized. A time span must be observed if one is to discern the full effect of the drive for differentiation upon product improvement.

In addition to its effect in stimulating improvement, advertising has also influenced maintenance of product quality under brands, because sellers have been anxious to retain the goodwill which brand advertising has helped to build.

In the next chapter the advantages and disadvantages arising from the tremendous increase in the range of products will be discussed.

CHAPTER XXIII

ADVERTISING AS A GUIDE TO CONSUMPTION

WHILE advertising indirectly has played a part in increasing the range of merchandise available to consumers, such an increase has not been an unmixed blessing. The growth in number of products on the market has brought problems in consumption which have received increasing attention in recent years. The bright side of the picture is presented first.

Advantages of a Wide Range of Merchandise

The sum of consumer satisfactions has been increased by the widening range of products. New wants have been filled; old wants have been better met. Increased income has made it possible for a large number of consumers to enjoy many of the new things offered. Only a few of the increased satisfactions that have come from new inventions need be mentioned. The electric motor has brought alleviation from drudgery when applied to one household appliance after another, the washing machine, the vacuum cleaner, the oil burner, the coal stoker; the automobile has given greater mobility to the population; the telephone has made ease of communication possible. The movies, the radio, and the phonograph have contributed inexpensive entertainment. Improved home heating devices have given personal comfort. Numerous prepared foods have added to the variety of the diet and have helped to make the housewife's lot an easier one than formerly. New methods of sanitation and products contributing to better diets, better personal hygiene, and better medical service have made for a healthier populace.

The widened range of products both from new inventions and from differentiation has presented to consumers a freedom of choice permitting them to seek those things giving them the greatest satisfaction. Free choice among a wide range of products may give greater enjoyment than expenditure on a narrow range. Consumers have been able not only to apportion their expenditures among many new types of products, but as a result of the constant drive of sellers to gain sales by differentiation of their products, they have been able to seek out product characteristics which best meet their individual desires. The oft-expressed fears that mass production methods and intensive advertising, which tend toward uniformity of choice, would choke the chance for individuality to express itself in consumption are belied, in part at least, by the statistics of range of choices open to consumers. Consumers generally have the chance to satisfy their particular likes and dislikes because the number of suppliers of any type of product is generally fairly large and these suppliers seek to find those variations which some group of consumers wants. Some exceptions to this statement were noted in previous chapters.

While manufacturers and merchants may be criticized for failing to make their merchandise just what individual consumers like, this failure is not the result of their lack of desire to give what is wanted, but rather the result of the difficulties of knowing what the tastes of consumers are, of manufacturing products in advance of sale to meet all the whims of individual consumers, and of offering desired qualities at prices which will induce effective demand.[1] In an industrial society, where manufacturing commonly is done largely in advance of sale, expression of individuality such as is attainable when craftsmen manufacture in accordance with individual desire cannot be had. Yet within the limits imposed by the industrial machine, with its separation of producer and consumer and its requirement of uniformity in each manufactured lot of merchandise, there is ever present the tendency of individual producers to seek bases of differentiation which will appeal to some segment of the market. From the large number of producers in the economy comes a wide variety for individual choice. In the case of clothing and other fashion merchandise, where individual characteristics are especially desired by consumers, the industrial machine has adjusted itself to offering a wide variety of merchandise. Small runs of differently styled merchandise are characteristic in all the cutting-up trades and in shoe manufacture. At the other extreme, in the case of products for which wide choice has not been desired, the merchandise of different producers has tended to be standardized, as in the cases of salt, sugar, and sheeting.

---

[1] For a more complete discussion of the problems of producing merchandise to meet consumer desires, see H. R. Tosdal, "The Study of Consumer Demand in Relation to Capitalistic Society," *Business and Modern Society* (Cambridge, Harvard University Press, 1938), p. 313.

Difficulties Attending a Wide Range of Merchandise

While a wide variety of choice of merchandise gives consumers opportunity to increase satisfactions, nevertheless this variety gives rise to problems. In the first place, critics raise an ideological issue of the inherent desirability of a wide range of merchandise. In the second place, a wide variety of choice may cause difficulties for consumers in the selection of products.

Although many economic writers have taken the views that consumption is the sole end and purpose of production and that the aim of the economy should be to develop a high material welfare as expressed in the consumption of goods and services, other writers have questioned whether human happiness is necessarily furthered by ownership of a large variety of things. They raise the issue of whether people have sought happiness in a multiplicity of gadgets and have forgotten the art of simple living. This question can be posed; but the answer cannot be furnished by a factual investigation. The answer rests rather in ideological belief as dictated by sentiments. In the American society, where consumers and producers have had freedom of action, the guiding viewpoint thus far has been to increase the goods and services which satisfy consumer wants. But the need for leisure in which to enjoy them has not been overlooked. Moreover, material comforts in themselves need not cause loss of high-mindedness. While the level of material welfare attained in this country is high when measured in the light of history, yet it is low when measured in terms of consumption attained by the average consumer in the United States, far below that which most people hold desirable. As was explained in the first chapter, this study does not seek to find an answer to the ideological issue as to whether the desire for material things is undesirable for the individual and for society. One of the basic postulates laid down was that an individual's happiness and welfare depend in appreciable measure upon the degree to which his wants are satisfied; another was that the stimulation of wants is not considered counter to his welfare and happiness. In keeping with these postulates a correlative premise was adopted, namely, that a widening range of products is to be desired, particularly if high productivity will permit extensive use of products by consumers.

Once the viewpoint of the desirability of wide range of choice was accepted, the pertinent question raised for investigation was whether consumers have been able to buy these products at low prices. The investigation sought to determine to what extent various products have borne high costs for differentiation and advertising, and particularly whether consumers have been given the option of buying at relatively low prices merchandise which has not borne large costs for differentiation and promotion. The amount of advertising costs for various types of merchandise was shown in the cost chapter. The extent to which the option of buying on a price basis was found available in various product fields was discussed in the price chapters. It is necessary only to recall that the degree to which such an option has been present has varied with different product classes, but in the course of time consumers have usually had the option of buying on a price basis. In short, the study has indicated that a wide range of products, which is deemed desirable for consumer satisfaction, has been available in the product fields studied, and among the options the consumer has usually had opportunity to buy merchandise on a price basis.

The Difficulty of Selecting Wise Patterns of Consumption

A second group of issues arising from the increased range of merchandise relates to the difficulties met by the consumer in making wise choices when faced by a multiplicity of goods and services. One difficulty is to make a wise choice among the many types of products offered, that is, to select those things which give a desirable pattern of consumption. The problems here are largely ideological. What is a desirable pattern of consumption? What are correct valuations to place on one type of product as related to another? Some writers hold that experts should somehow guide the consumption patterns of consumers. A number have expressed the view that those who are actuated by profit should not be permitted to influence or manipulate consumption.

Again, such ideological questions are beyond the scope of investigation in this economic study. The postulates laid down assume a society in which consumers are free to determine their patterns of consumption and sellers are free to use influence in dealing with customers, so long as ethical dictates are observed, just as influence is used in other human affairs.

The Difficulty of Selecting among Numerous Brands

Beyond the difficulties of wise choice among types of commodities are the difficulties of selecting the best values in any one product field among the many brands with their numerous points of differentiation. Determination of "best" values among the large number of brands found in many classes of commodities is an Herculean task. But critics say that businessmen make the task more difficult for the following reasons: (1) they play up what the critics term "meaningless" or "inconsequential" product differences; (2) they fail to give adequate information about their merchandise to guide consumers; and (3) they attempt to lead untutored consumers to pay more for these differentiated products than is warranted. The critics argue that aggressive selling leads consumers to make "incorrect" valuations.

The Criticism of Meaningless Differentiation

In a free system many things that have been offered as product improvements have been merely sellers' judgments as to what certain consumers might want. Often their judgments or hopes as to what are worth-while differentiations are at variance with the views of individual consumers. Consequently consumers have been offered and advertising has played up differentiations that have appeared to be of questionable significance to many students of consumption.

Anyone who makes a study of the nonidentical merchandise on the market and the points of product differences that are stressed in advertising is very likely to agree that the number of individualizations which appear foolish or meaningless to him is large. Likewise he may conclude that the emphasis placed upon the differentiating points may lead to consumer confusion and questionable evaluation. A free system is not one that promises a product array selected according to some well-reasoned plan. It proceeds on a trial and error basis. What is offered at any one time is in accord not with the ideas or dictates of some one expert's ideas of desirable merchandise, but rather with the various ideas of an uncontrolled producing group, which is striving at all times to meet the many varied tastes it finds among a large population of nonuniform consumers. The only direction available to the producing group has come from consumer response to its offerings, together with such analysis and investigation as it has made in advance of manufacture to learn what product forms consumers desire.

It is unnecessary to cite a long list of examples to establish the fact that the merchandise world is full of what some people may deem minor differentiations. New inventions and major product improvements come at infrequent intervals. In the meantime sellers exercise ingenuity to find minor differentiations that will get consumer favor. Illustrations are legion: there is floating soap and soap that sinks, soap of all perfumes and colors. One can eat shredded, puffed, rolled, or crinkled cereals for breakfast. Radios come equipped with numerous gadgets; no longer does one have to "stoop, squint or squat" when tuning to a station; he presses a button instead of turning a dial. In refrigerators numerous minor points are played up: interior lighting, easy methods of cube removal, streamlined boxes, special food containers. In the case of cigarettes, toasting has been advertised heavily by one manufacturer; special tips by others; improved packaging by some; denicotinization by still others. Automobile tires have been offered in many and numerous varieties of treads whose virtues are proclaimed. For many lines of merchandise, when nothing else new has been available, improved packages have been devised. After one company had packaged salt, another offered a package with a pouring spout. Catsup put in a bottle with a wide spout has had the wide opening played up as a virtue. It is unnecessary to extend the list. The complaint of students of consumption is not merely that what they deem minor differences are built into products, but that advertising writers frequently seize upon these small differences and magnify them beyond their due, thus inducing in untutored consumers questionable valuations. Before the evidence regarding the character of advertising is presented, attention is directed to certain difficulties involved in distinguishing between what are significant and what are meaningless product differentiations and in setting valuations upon them. What standards exist by which to classify a differentiation as minor or as meaningless?

Difficulties in Evaluating Products for Consumers of Varying Tastes

The difficulties of evaluating product differentiations arise chiefly from two sets of facts: (1) consumers have widely varying tastes and incomes, which, in a free society, lead them to place varying evaluations on different product characteristics; (2) merchandise is often a complex combination of product qualities which are in conflict with one another, with the result that even experts cannot agree as to what combinations are best or what differentiations are significant. These two points are discussed in the order listed.

The problem of what determines correct valuation in a free society is difficult to understand and appreciate, because valuations represent the judgments of widely varying, untutored, and emotionally guided people of different incomes working under the stress of persuasion. The result is that many consumers, particularly those of small means, spend their money in ways which other people consider foolish and pay too much for this, that, or the other differentiated product, according to the judgment of observers or the "experts." But one person's judgment, even if he is an expert, need not necessarily be in accord with the views of other individuals. A valuation of merchandise by one person is not suitable for all groups of consumers, nor can a product differentiation that is deemed meaningless by one individual or organization necessarily be said to be meaningless to all consumers. To hold otherwise is to assume that all consumers are alike and that their evaluations of products will be the same. Quite clearly, such is not the case. Consumer desires and tastes are widely varied. The manner in which the diverse characteristics of consumers affect their preferences for merchandise is discussed in a published monograph on *Merchandise Testing as a Guide to Consumer Buying,* which was issued as a by-product of this study of the economics of advertising.

Theoretically it no doubt is possible to appraise merchandise without reference to the interests of any particular group. Such appraisals, however, would be no more than meaningless abstractions and could have little practical value as guides to product selection.* . . .

---

* W. A. Shewhart, "Some Aspects of Quality Control," *Mechanical Engineering,* December, 1934, p. 726. In this paper Mr. Shewhart recognizes three types of quality, any one of which it may be the object of a test to measure.
   "Quality of Type 1 is that which characterizes a thing itself independent of all other things and of human volition and interest.
   "Non-critical common sense attributes to every thing or object about us certain quality characteristics independent of human interest . . .
   "In so far as these common-sense quality characteristics may be observed either in the form of the pointer readings of the physicist and chemist such, for example, as those interpreted as mass, density, resistance, capacity, and velocity, or in the form of direct sensations, such as color, they become experimentally verifiable and have objective meaning.
   "Quality of Type 2 is that which characterizes a thing A in its relation to another thing B as a part of a whole and independent of human volition and interest.
   "This is the sense in which one speaks of a piece part in its relation to the whole of which it is a part or in the sense that parts of a telephone circuit, for example, contribute to the transmission characteristics of the circuit. Other typical examples are . . . the quality of a conduit to resist corrosion; the quality of a chemical compound as a plant fertilizer; and the quality of a drug as a medicine . . .
   "Quality of Type 3 is that which makes a thing wantable by some one or more persons.
   "Thus far we have considered the meaning of the quality of a thing as independent of human interest or volition. Fundamentally, however, the ultimate goal of the producer under conditions which we are here considering is to produce a product the quality of

In most discussions of consumer buying problems, consumers are conveniently lumped under the phrase "the consumer." It must be recognized, however, that the word consumer indicates no homogeneous group. In a sense, the word is meaningless.† All consumers are people, and to that extent alike. But consumers easily can be found among whom the similarity extends no further.

Consumers' Wants Influenced by Purchasing Power

Purchasing power of course constitutes one clear basis for classifying consumers. An evaluating program suitable for helping the Morgans and the Vanderbilts, for example, very likely would prove totally inadequate if applied to the problems of the humble Polinskys who have $1,500 for a family of seven. In economic terminology the marginal value of a dollar is different for people in different income groups. This difference in the marginal values of dollars dictates the necessity for evaluating merchandise with a specific income group in mind.‡

. . . . .

Other Factors Influencing Consumers' Wants

Purchasing power, while the most important, is only one of many significant consumer differences which must be taken into account by programs of objective merchandise evaluation. Cutting across any lines that might be drawn on the basis of purchasing power are other significant lines of difference: age, nationality, religion, occupation, geographic location, intelligence, skill, education, and cultural background. Certain magazines appraised highly by the educated are of little interest to the uneducated. Certain phonograph records that are prized by the musically cultured have no attraction for the devotee of popular music. Some people place high value on the appearance of food; others are concerned primarily with its taste;§ and others are interested only in the satisfaction of

---

which will be adequate, satisfactory, and dependable to the consuming group. This makes it necessary to consider the wantableness of a thing as the ultimate goal at which the producer is aiming in the control of quality of a product."

† Robert S. Lynd points out the meaninglessness of such abstract terms as "society," "labor," and "public good," and speaks of "Obfuscation due to preoccupation with abstracted entities," while at the same time he makes liberal use of the phrase "the consumer." Robert S. Lynd, "The Consumer Becomes a Problem," *The Annals of the American Academy of Political and Social Science*, May, 1934, p. 3.

‡ An official of the American Standards Association has stated that, for purposes of standardization work on consumers' goods, the association regards the population as being divided into three income groups, with, roughly speaking, 30% of the population falling in the lowest group at the present time, 60% in the middle group, and 10% in the upper group. It is toward helping the middle group, according to this official, that the association believes its efforts should be directed primarily, so far as consumers' goods are concerned. This official explains: "Style plays a prominent part in many of the purchases of the upper 10% and standards should not be concerned with style. Standards would naturally be of value to consumers in the upper and lower groups but would probably be of more direct value to those consumers in the middle group."

§ Mrs. Bert W. Hendrickson says, for example, in *National Consumer News*, January, 1938, p. 7: "Consumers with whom I have talked also wish manufacturers would put emphasis on flavor rather than looks. Gentlemen may like their women beautiful but dumb, but women want their food not merely beautiful, but also tasty, and if they must choose, they prefer flavor." This of course does not settle the question of *what* flavor.

their hunger. A cautious person would wish to sacrifice speed for safety. Many women, and not only the wealthy, gladly sacrifice durability in their clothes for the sake of more sophisticated styling or for the prestige given by the label of a particular store. One person likes a tooth paste with a peppermint flavor, while another prefers a different flavor. Often what theoretically might be considered of slight importance, such as tooth paste flavor, in reality is of real importance to the user if his own satisfaction is permitted to be the criterion. To some persons the noisiness of an electric icebox motor may offset such solid virtues as low initial cost and low operating expense. Even such a seemingly little thing as the ease with which the ice cubes can be extracted may be more important to certain users than the cubic contents of the box.

A difference in the conditions under which a product is used, furthermore, may be sufficient to determine its measure of satisfactoriness. And most products are used under very varied conditions. The same soap, for example, will be used in waters of different degrees of softness, in hot water, and cold water, for white clothes, and for colored. Tooth paste will be used by smokers and by non-smokers. Blankets will be used in heated and unheated houses. Paints will be used in wet areas and in dry. In any group of women discussing hosiery there will be one whose stockings always wear out in the toes; one who has no trouble with the toes but finds the heels a terrible problem; one who specializes in runs; one who cannot get stockings long enough; one who cannot get them short enough; one who, if she gets them large enough for her feet, finds them too large for her legs; and even perhaps one who is quite content.

The varying skills and aptitudes of people also help to determine the satisfactoriness of merchandise to them. One woman finds a certain can opener marvelous; her neighbor finds it impossible to operate it at all. An intricate camera will take beautiful pictures for the expert, but may be useless to the unskilled operator. Anyone who has had experience riding with a number of motorists will realize the vast opportunity there is for different styles of car operation. The brakes can be jammed on or they can be made to take hold gradually; the clutch can be slipped at will; gasoline can be fed to the motor at almost any rate; the car can be made to leap into action like a kangaroo or to start forward as smoothly as a ball on a gentle slope; tires can be skidded and made to scrape the curb; bumps can be taken at high speed or at low; the car may be oiled properly or neglected.[2]

Difficulties of Evaluation Arising from Combinations of Conflicting Product Qualities

While the varying use habits, varying purchasing power, varying environment, varying skills, and varying tastes of consumers, as described above, provide the basis for varying evaluations of differentiated products, the problem of evaluation of product differences is

---

[2] M. T. Gragg in collaboration with N. H. Borden, *Merchandise Testing as a Guide to Consumer Buying* (Harvard Business School, Business Research Studies, No. 22, October, 1938), p. 3 ff.

accentuated by the complexity of merchandise itself and the difficulties involved in determining just what combinations of product characteristics may produce differentiations of significance to consumers. Experts frequently cannot agree as to what are and what are not significant product differentiations. It will be recalled that in the case of gasoline [3] there was disagreement among petroleum engineers as to the significances of the differences among gasolines upon the market. Gasoline, like every other product, is, from the consumer's standpoint, a complex of product virtues which are in part conflicting.

The monograph [4] quoted above is drawn on again:

One of the most important characteristics of merchandise from the point of view of its evaluation arises from the fact that certain product virtues are antagonistic if not directly contradictory; if a product is "best" in one respect, it commonly follows that the product cannot be best in some other respects. The breaking strengths of textiles increase up to a point as the number of threads per inch is increased, but air permeability, on the other hand, is lowered. Those soaps and cleansers that loosen dirt most quickly and easily cannot be the gentlest in their action. The most effective insect poison may not be the safest to use under conditions in which children and pets must be considered. No one blanket can combine the virtues of maximum warmth, maximum strength, and minimum weight. Those bath towels which absorb water most rapidly are not the ·ones which can absorb the greatest quantity of water, nor are they the strongest. No one paint can possess the special virtues of a flat finish and an enamel finish. The sheerest silk stockings cannot give the longest wear. Doors that open to the right cannot open to the left.

In the case of automobiles, a high-speed motor gives certain advantages to the user, but only at the expense of certain other advantages offered by a different type of motor. The following is quoted from a publication of the Department of Commerce.*

Means of measuring vehicle performance have been under development for some time. It is found that the desirable qualities cannot all be secured at the same time. *Every design necessarily is a compromise in which some qualities must be sacrificed to secure others.* Thus, while each different model may excel in some particular respect, taking all factors into account, the merits of the different designs are remarkably near the same in any given price class. *There is no best design for all purposes.* If one were interested only in one or two qualities, such as looks or easy riding, regardless of the others, he might perhaps select one model which excelled the others in these respects. (Italics not in original.)

---

[3] See Chapter XXII, page 621 ff.
[4] M. T. Gragg, *op. cit.,* p. 6 ff.
* *Services of the National Bureau of Standards to the Consumer* (U. S. Department of Commerce, National Bureau of Standards), p. 9.

A writer in the magazine *Purchasing,* to cite an example from the industrial field, gives an interesting description of the irreconcilable virtues which would be encountered in the ideal leather belt for power transmission purposes.†

> In considering what really constitutes quality in a leather belt for power transmission purposes it will be well to start out with a brief statement of what may be looked upon as the conception of the ideal. This would be a belt of high enough strength to meet all requirements safely; of no thickness—in order to have no bending stresses; of no weight in order to have no centrifugal stresses; completely homogeneous—in order to have no weak spots at the joints or between the plies; almost a positive grip on the pulleys, or in other words, a maximum coefficient of friction; perfect elasticity, i.e., it must have no permanent elongation under continual stress when the belt is traveling around the pulleys. Such a belt could be installed on a drive at very low tension, and since it would never stretch permanently, it would continue to maintain its initially installed tension indefinitely. And since it would have a pulley-gripping ability approaching, but never quite reaching, the grip of a chain, the drive in all practical ways would be positive and yet would have all the desirable features of the flexible system of power transmission.

The need for compromise is inescapable in the case of most, if not all products. We cannot have everything. As Somerset Maugham remarks: ". . . the gods never make any of their gifts without adding to it a drawback."

Price in Conflict with Other Product Virtues

In a discussion of conflicts in product qualities, the factor of price cannot be overlooked. Since the goods would not exist if someone did not expect them to be purchased, and since they can be of no use to consumers unless they are purchased, their prices are as much a part of them as are their other properties. This involves further compromise, for it is unlikely that the best can often be the cheapest.

The following statement concerning paper towels is quoted from a circular of the National Bureau of Standards:‡

> . . . In evaluating paper towels, therefore, the main consideration, in addition to absorptiveness and softness, is the strength. *It is difficult to secure such a combination of desirable properties in the same sheet of paper.*

> The natural softness and absorptiveness of wood fiber are considerably lessened by the usual treatment given to develop its maximum strength for paper making. Generally, at one extreme, are associated in paper towels rapid absorption, softness, and weakness, and at the other extreme, slow absorption, hardness, and high strength. Those of the first class must be used as a blotter, or they may tear, while those of the second class require

---

† Francis A. Westbrook, Consulting Engineer, "What Constitutes Quality in Leather Belting," *Purchasing,* February, 1938, p. 12.

‡ Bourdon W. Scribner and Russell W. Carr, *Standards for Paper Towels,* (U. S. Department of Commerce, Circular of the National Bureau of Standards C407, March, 1935), p. 2.

considerable rubbing to complete the drying operation . . . *It is true that some towels have the two desirable properties of high absorptiveness and strength combined, but they are usually relatively high priced.* (Italics not in original.)

In view of the many differences which exist among consumers and the practical impossibility of bringing into combination conflicting product virtues, it is clear that no single product form can be best for everyone. This statement, that no single product form can be best for everyone, is true even as of a given time, without regard for the possibility that, no matter how excellent a product form is, it may suffer a rapid loss in suitability through production changes or changes in users' needs or desires. Were it not for the matter of price, it would be possible, in theory at least, to combine in one form all the virtues that can be possessed by a product of that type except the mutually irreconcilable ones. However, inasmuch as cost and price seldom can be ignored, the producer in planning his product finds it possible to choose only a limited number of virtues from among those available. And, since low price is not the least of these virtues, he must decide whether the addition of some possible merit will more than offset an increase in price.

Illustrations from Manufacturers' Experiences of the Difficulties of Evaluating Differentiations

Manufacturers have great difficulty in knowing whether a new product or a new differentiation will meet the desires of a substantial number of consumers, even though correct judgment is highly important to them. They cannot offer merely what they think consumers should like, but, rather, what consumers will like and buy. It is evident, of course, that in launching any new product differentiation under his brand, a manufacturer ordinarily is drawing upon his best judgment as to what a substantial group of consumers will like. His profit depends upon such acceptance, and failure of consumers to accept his new product form may entail considerable loss. Often the products offered are commercial failures even though considerable advertising and persuasion may be employed to influence consumer acceptance. New differentiations that have failed to "click" have been legion, even though their inventors or sponsors usually have been enthusiastic about them and have looked upon their offerings as improvements over other available products. In previous chapters several such unsuccessful products were mentioned: the rubber sponge window cleaner, the nonslip webbing to be used as a curtain in trousers, the easily-erasable paper, the dentifrice which required a brushing and massaging of the gums, deemed desirable by dental experts consulted. All these products had characteristics which producers hoped would commend them to consumers. But consumers did not accept them as improvements, even though their virtues were publicized.

Often products which are considered worth while by outside authorities are turned down by the majority of consumers. One of the large sugar refining companies, for example, introduced in 1936 a product made from raw sugar, purified by a patented process which permitted the retention of most of the original mineral properties. In spite of the health value of this product and its exclusive character, sales volume was unsatisfactory. Extensive advertising was not employed because the volume attainable did not justify it. In addition, market tests of the product were not promising. Many people apparently hestitated to pay the slight price premium asked by the company, and others did not like the product because it was brown in color and consequently did not look so pure as refined sugar. In short, to most people the product did not represent an improvement over ordinary sugar, or the price was too high.

An interesting example of the lack of certainty which can be attached to the judgment of individuals regarding what combination of product qualities consumers will accept in large enough quantity to afford commercial success is found in the experience of automobile manufacturers in their attempts to market inexpensive, small automobiles stripped of all gadgets and designed primarily to give cheap transportation. At various times automobile manufacturers[5] have been criticized for not making available a low-price automobile without numerous minor differentiating appurtenances. That automobile manufacturers have attempted to market such low-price cars without success was brought out during the T.N.E.C. hearings when Mr. H. F. Vance, Chairman of the Board of the Studebaker Corporation, and Mr. Paul G. Hoffman, president of that company, discussed with Mr. Leon Henderson of the Committee the probable acceptability of such a car to consumers. The discussion served to bring out the fact that consumers, when given such a choice, have not responded in large enough numbers to make the production of such a car profitable. They have preferred rather to buy at comparable prices used cars equipped with various gadgets and fine appointments. The following evidence[6]

[5] Similar criticisms have been leveled against manufacturers of other products, such as refrigerators.

[6] *Verbatim Record of the Proceedings of the Temporary National Economic Committee* (Washington, D. C.), Vol. 9, p. 507.

summarizes the industry's experience in the judgment of these two executives of high standing in the automobile field.

Mr. Hoffman: I think there is one point there that in a free economy the customer has a choice and the customer has demonstrated that he much prefers a used car with what you call the gadgets and comforts to a new car that might be sold at a comparable price.

Mr. Henderson: But I don't know that that is complete freedom of choice because nobody in your group or the big three has ever undertaken to get down to that other level.

Mr. Hoffman: I think history would raise a question about that statement of yours because there have been numerous exceptions when the public has been offered a stripped car and the public has not purchased it. You get right down to the fact that if you offer a customer a stripped car (and such cars have been offered) the customer won't buy it. He will buy a used car that in his opinion represents better transportation value.

Mr. Vance: On the point of whether manufacturers have attempted to offer so-called low-priced cars, from 1907 to 1939 there were a total of 110 different makes of cars offered to the public at prices ranging from $100 to $600 and the great majority of them were between $351 and $450.

Mr. Henderson: This isn't a comment to end all comments, but I would say that the general public would certainly welcome a lower-priced new car that was something more than a stripped car. Whether they can get it or not in the economics of the industry with the high values of the used car and the number of them, that is another question, but certainly the public hasn't completely dissipated its idea that it might get a brand-new car at something like Ford was thinking about at a dollar a day when he put out the first Lizzie. I know that from the raft of correspondence that I got when I was making a study of this industry, and the number of people who feel that they ought to get a new car at less than the average price is for the standard makes is tremendous.

Mr. Vance: Of course the public would always like to get what they want for less money. That goes without saying. You speak of Ford. Three years or so ago Ford brought out another model car, what they called a 60 model, and the first year that it came out it differed very little from the 85, the standard model which had been in production several years, except with respect to engine size, appointment, and a few things of that sort.

He made a difference of $50 in the price of the two cars. The Sixty, the lowest-priced car, never did get over, according to the best information we have been able to get. It never accounted for more than 20% of his production. He still sold, out of five cars, four [sic] of the higher-priced models than he did of the lower priced models, with this difference of $50 between them.

Now I think that that is an illustration of the point we are trying to make, and that is that people, even in the low-priced field, do, when they buy an automobile, want a certain level of standard of accommodation, if we may call it that, including in the word "accommodation" all the various things that make up for convenience and comfort and so on.

Mr. Henderson: And the psychological advantage of having a new car.

Mr. Vance: That's right, and it is the psychology of it that has resulted in Ford sales still being predominantly of the higher-priced model.

Mr. Fischer: Would you regard the Crosley product as a stripped car product?

Mr. Vance: It is more than a stripped car. It is a sub-standard car in size. Have you ever seen a Crosley?

Mr. Fischer: Yes, I have. That is why I asked the question. It appears to me to be somewhat depleted of much equipment.

Mr. Vance: It is a car that not only has been stripped of equipment, but it has been reduced in size as well, because neither the reduction in size or taking of equipment off would have produced the low price which was the objective of the manufacturer.

. . . . .

We cannot overemphasize the importance of visible advancing value in the new car in discussing the relationship of price to volume. For example, during the past several years, the buyers of low-priced automobiles which were offered in both deluxe and standard models have bought considerably more of the former than of the latter, electing to pay from $50 to $60 for the added features of the deluxe models; features contributing to convenience, to appearance and to improved service.

The public demand for more car is self-evident.

Further Examination of Bases for Varying Consumer Valuations of Product Differentiations

The above examples and many others which might be cited show the futility of trying to judge consumer buying by standards which any particular critic might set up as representing correct valuations. As has been indicated, the valuations placed on goods by consumers are not determined by a definite, scientific weighting of objective characteristics which can be readily measured and translated into dollar values, but rather by consumers' subjective valuations, i.e., by their ideas regarding the satisfactions which they may derive from goods. These subjective valuations placed upon products cannot be reduced to any single standard, because different men, who are free to act as they please, have different likes and different dislikes, and because they are guided by different sets of motives or desires and have different levels of income.

Some basis for believing that the product valuations of particular consumers are questionable or incorrect at times may be found in their lack of knowledge regarding the objective qualities and performance of products. In so far as consumers are ignorant of product qualities and performance and cannot thus know how well products will fulfill certain desires, they may arrive at valuations different from those which they would hold if their knowledge were complete. For example, a man may fail to set as high a valuation on a certain make of automobile as he would if he knew precisely its qualities and its performance. Again, the fact that some consumers are ignorant regarding the significance of conformity of drug products with the U. S. Pharmacopoeia or the National Formulary, may lead them to undervalue little-known brands of drugs which conform to these official standards. They do not realize that the safety and efficacy which they desire are assured by the official mark.

At times, valuations of certain consumers may be considered open to question because consumers attribute to products the ability to satisfy desired objectives which scientific experiment would show the products could not deliver. In other words, these consumers have subjective knowledge or views which would not be supported by objective facts.[7] Thus a man may attribute to a certain automobile mistaken ideas regarding its cost of operation or its acceleration or other performance characteristics, and thus may arrive at what may be deemed an incorrect valuation. Or some consumers may purchase a nostrum to cure a specific disease, whereas medical knowledge indicates that this nostrum will not cure the disease. It should be pointed out, in connection with this latter example, that consumers' reliance on mistaken ideas does not prevent them from getting satisfaction from their purchases, provided they continue in their belief even after using the products. Thus some consumers continue to get satisfaction from use of nostrums because their continued belief in the efficacy of these products permits them to derive satisfaction from use of such products, even though they may not be benefited physically.

---

[7] A significant classification of the behavior of men has been made by Pareto, who distinguishes between *logical* actions and *non-logical* actions. As Pareto points out, men's actions are not ordinarily illogical. They follow behavior which they hope will attain desired ends. They are guided by subjective ideas, some of which may not conform to the best objective knowledge available. Thus, Greek sailors plied their oars to drive their ships over the waters, but at the same time they offered sacrifices to Poseidon to make sure of a rapid and safe voyage. Objective knowledge indicates that plying the oars would attain the end. The view that sacrifice to Poseidon would attain the same end is doubtful, however, in the light of advanced knowledge. Pareto applied the term *logical actions,* to "actions that logically conjoin means to ends, not only from the standpoint of the subject performing them, but from the standpoint of other persons who have a more extensive knowledge"; in other words, to actions that are logical both subjectively and objectively. Other actions he termed *non-logical.* (Vilfredo Pareto, *The Mind and Society,* edited by Arthur Livingston; New York, Harcourt, Brace and Company, 1935, p. 75). This significant classification of the actions of people applies to and is helpful in a study of the buying action of consumers.

While ignorance or mistaken ideas about product qualities and performance may lead at times to what may be deemed questionable valuations, there is no sound reason for calling certain valuations correct and others incorrect when the basis for the differing valuations is found in differences attached subjectively by different consumers to various product qualities and product performances of which they have adequate knowledge. The desires of one person are not necessarily those of another. The flavor which one person likes in a food is not so highly esteemed by another. One wants fashion in a dress; another may buy for durability or warmth. One man wants economical transportation in an automobile; another wants something which will impress his neighbors. Accordingly, even if consumers could be furnished with full and complete objective information and could be disabused of mistaken beliefs regarding performance, yet the valuations placed upon competing products by different people would not be the same. Nor, from an economic standpoint, is there reason to hold one valuation as correct and another incorrect. In a free society one man's preferences in merchandise economically are not to be deemed superior to those of another. Each man seeks those things which give him happiness.

An examination of various instances of buying behavior which have been cited by critics as being directed by questionable valuations will serve to indicate to what extent either lack of knowledge, or mistaken ideas, or variation in subjective valuations are operative. The explanations of buying behavior in the cases below are surmised from individual experience and from observation of consumer behavior.

Why do many consumers spend 20 cents to 40 cents for a tube of tooth paste, when a mixture of baking soda and common salt will, according to some dentists, do as satisfactory a job of tooth cleansing? Lack of information may account in part for such behavior by some consumers. They probably do not know that many dentists have given the inexpensive salt and soda solution a good rating as a tooth cleanser. Again, mistaken ideas undoubtedly lead some consumers to continue to buy the relatively expensive tooth paste. They attribute to certain brands a therapeutic power which many competent dentists deny. Or some consumers attribute to particular brands a relative cleansing power that they do not possess. But ignorance or mistaken ideas do not account for all buying of tooth pastes. Many consumers continue to buy well-known brands, not because of ignorance or mistaken ideas, but because they are willing to part with the money involved, which may seem relatively small to them, in order to have the convenience of a handy tube of paste. They just don't want to be bothered with mixing a salt and soda solution. Or they may greatly prefer the taste of the commercial dentifrice. Or they may simply associate clean teeth and all that clean teeth imply with commercial dentifrice and get satisfaction from using it. In short, the buying behavior of consumers for dentifrice may be explained in part by consumer ignorance and mistaken ideas, but much of the buying is determined by the character of consumers' desires.

Why do women wear fragile, sheer silk hosiery, when heavy silk, cotton, or wool stockings give more protection against the weather and last longer? It is clear in this instance that consumer ignorance regarding warmth and durability are not the explanation of buying behavior, nor do mistaken ideas of consumers explain it. In their purchase of hosiery, women are moved more by desire to conform to fashion than by desire to keep their legs warm or to have hose that give many months of wear.

Why should people buy fine percale sheets, when more durable muslin sheets can be had at a much lower price? Some may be ignorant regarding the relative wearing qualities of grades and brands, or they may have mistaken ideas. But in large degree the high-price sheet is selected because its buyers are willing to part with their money to own fine things. They get satisfaction from expensive possessions, either because they feel it is good to live with things of fine quality, or because such possessions may impress their friends and neighbors. Objective measurements of durability have little effect in guiding these consumers' choices when desires such as those noted have so much influence over their selections.

Why should a young swain buy fancy chocolates at $1.50 a pound, when other chocolates, fully as tasty and also attractively packaged, may be had for 60 cents a pound? Here again, consumer ignorance of product quality is not the explanation of the buying behavior, nor do mistaken ideas account for it. The young man's chief desire is to impress his lady friend. She is likely to be impressed by the expensive, well-known brand, into which refinements in manufacture and in packaging have gone, and for which promotion has helped to build a reputation. She is flattered by being brought a box of candy which represents sacrifice. The young man spends his money to attain his desired end, although his own senses have told him that cheaper chocolates taste good.

Why do consumers buy toasted wheat flakes at a fancy price, when cracked wheat can be bought for a small fraction of that price? While some consumers may not be aware of the relatively high price they are paying per calorie in buying dry cereals, undoubtedly many continue to buy such products in spite of the fact that they know well the cost involved. They like dry cereals and are willing to pay the price necessary to get them.

And so on and on, instances might be cited which show that consumers' buying choices do not conform to any individual critic's judgment of what is sensible and reasonable behavior, largely because the desires and motives of many consumers are different from those of the critic. Consumers are not guided solely by what may be termed rational motives; i.e., they do not think solely in terms of such practical things as durability, efficiency, dependability, and economy; instead, they are moved frequently by desires that have a less practical tinge. Hence they are not likely to reduce their selection of products to a reasoned appraisal of objective qualities. At the moment, if one is to judge certain products and services offered consumers, it is impossible to prove on an objective basis that short hair for women, permanent waves, open-toe shoes, and crimson fingernails are improvements, yet many women unquestionably regard them as such.

Among the differentiating techniques employed by sellers, the packaging of food products has frequently been cited as an undesirable development involving costs that must be borne by consumers, who, it is argued, might better direct their expenditure in more essential ways. In spite of 30 years of attacks on food packaging as an undesirable development, because costly, yet, packaged foods have largely displaced food sold in bulk. This development has occurred because consumers have preferred packaged food, whether it is more expensive or not. The condemnation of packaging has rested upon the critics' rationalization of the way in which the consumer should value packaging. They have concluded that consumers have failed to arrive at correct valuations regarding packaged as against bulk foods.

The Nature of Consumer Satisfactions

The failure of consumer buying in such instances as those cited above to be guided solely by practical, objective product considerations, points to the need of careful study of the nature of consumer satis-factions. The examples given indicate that consumers' desires and wants are complex and varied. They do not fit into a simple pattern of practical considerations which can be expressed in objective product measurements with fixed dollar value. Much consumer buying be-havior is in contrast to that of industrial buyers. A business concern makes its purchases for business reasons. An industrial purchase is likely to be carefully weighed to determine how well competing products may contribute to an operating profit. Hence, industrial buy-ing is usually guided by rational motives. In contrast, consumer buying is likely to be influenced by desires to satisfy many personal whims and wishes which often have strong emotional character. Many con-sumers pay high prices for fashionable clothing, big automobiles, and countless articles which they think will help them to appear well in the eyes of others. They know they pay high prices to get styles and trade-marks that satisfy this desire. This desire for social distinction, or emulation, or vulgar ostentation, whatever it may be called, is a powerful motive and leads to valuations that some critics may term questionable, if the standards adopted for valuation are based on certain objective characteristics of products which contribute to fulfillment of certain practical wants or desires. The desire to emulate is but one of a long list of emotional motives that guide the buying actions of consumers.

The criticism is sometimes raised that sellers play upon such motives and build up subjective values to the point where consumers lose sight of objective product qualities and practical considerations. That sellers act thus is true, for in selling they appeal to those motives which are likely to induce preference for their product and to lead to buying action. The art of persuasion has always called for appeal to the strongest motives. Yet it must be recognized that the only sound basis for valuation on the part of the consumer rests in subjective considerations. His satisfactions are subjective. Objective qualities of a product have value meaning for him only so far as particular qualities make the product desirable to him subjectively. Hence, if the bases for subjective satisfactions are established as the results of persuasion, which is ethically directed,[8] it must be assumed in a free society that the consumer is getting what he desires for his money, particularly if he continues to purchase the article.

[8] A discussion of the ethics of selling is given in Chapter XXVII.

In short, since a large share of consumer buying is not directed by rational motives, rationalizations regarding the worth of product differentiations may be misleading, if a free society is assumed. Significant differentiations to the consumer are those things which give him satisfaction, and he expresses his judgment of them by buying or refusing to buy. Hence in a free economy whether or not differentiations are meaningless or inconsequential must be determined in the end by consumers' behavior. Every individual may have his ideas as to what is desirable consumption for himself, for others, and for society; and he may try to have his views prevail, on the ground that the other person's valuations and choices may not be good for society. Moreover, he may help the consumer to maximize his satisfactions by aiding him to widen his fund of information regarding products and patterns of living. But in the end he must expect the individual to make his own choices; one of the postulates of a free society is that the individual determines for himself what contributes to his welfare and happiness. In arriving at his decisions, it is further assumed, he may be subject not only to the many forces that make up his environment, but also to numerous forms of influence. This influence may come not only from sellers of merchandise but also from educational institutions and movements of various kinds, many of which may be initiated by consumers themselves.

It must be recognized, of course, that sellers may offer fraudulent merchandise and in their use of influence may depart from the ethical standards which are recognized in the community. Moreover, merchandise may be offered which the social group has banned as undesirable. The important issues relating to social and ethical control of selling operations are recognized, but their discussion is reserved for a later chapter.

The Need for Information by Consumers

That it is desirable for consumers in an advanced economy to have extensive information and knowledge regarding the wide array of products available to them may be stated as axiomatic. If consumers are to get a maximum of satisfactions from their expenditures, they should have opportunity to appraise the probable satisfactions that will attend their choices. They should have knowledge of what is on the market, for the greater such knowledge is, the more enlightened can be their choice of goods. Moreover, since goods are not identical, they should know the qualities of competing goods. The quantity of such information that may be used is large indeed, for the data regarding objective qualities of numerous products are many. In addition to knowledge regarding objective qualities of products consumers should have knowledge regarding the satisfactions that might come from use of various kinds of products and regarding the care of products to assure greatest satisfaction. Furthermore, in the quest for greatest satisfaction consumers should have knowledge regarding the satisfactions that come from various patterns of living. Such knowledge is dependent upon education, and it is assumed that in a free society the individual will be free to choose that pattern which he will follow.

The question is now raised as to whether advertising has done a satisfactory job of supplying this information which consumers should have. Further inquiry is made as to whether additional means of providing desired information are needed.

The Persuasive Character of Advertising

A study of advertisements and advertising material, particularly brand advertising, shows that usually they are designed not to give complete and detailed information about products, but rather to build certain mental associations and beliefs which may lead to ultimate buying action. The ideas presented in brand advertising are usually informative in some degree regarding the product advertised, for they usually tell something about product design and qualities, about performance, and about primary wants or desires of the consumer which may be satisfied by the product. But the information given usually is not detailed or complete. Moreover, it cannot be considered as unbiased, for advertisements are presented by an interested party. In short, advertisements must be viewed as persuasive documents designed to influence consumers' valuations.

The Use of Emotional Appeals

A large proportion of consumer advertisements should be classified as emotional rather than rational. Their appeal is largely to basic consumer desires or drives to action, which do not involve close reasoning regarding objective product characteristics. The associations or beliefs implanted often can be put to no objective tests or experimental checks. The consumers' acceptance of the idea of a product's efficiency in fulfilling the wants or desires presented may largely determine the satisfaction actually obtained from use. To illustrate, a host of products, such as automobiles, floor coverings, silverware, sheets, damask linen, have been pictured in fine surroundings, used by people worthy of emulation. Thus ideas of emulation, social prestige, or of pride in ownership, which in themselves might provide part of the satisfaction arising from the use or ownership of such products, are built around these products by the advertising. Advertisers proceed on the theory that a desire for distinction or social prestige which comes from ownership of a product may be more potent in inducing and in guiding purchase than the knowledge of objective characteristics relating to durability or economy.

Thus advertising is used to build into products ideas or beliefs that may be very effective in motivating purchase, that is, it builds mental associations about brands. Such associations might not develop around brands at all without advertising, or at least not develop in such a degree. The list of examples that might be cited is long. The belief in attainment of romance through use of cosmetics, the belief in glowing health or manly dominance that might come from drinking milk or eating cereals or swallowing vitamins, the belief that gifts of sterling silverware or of certain brands of chocolates or of a diamond ring may mark one as a discriminating giver—all these are examples of ideas that have been associated with products through advertising, ideas against which there are generally no logical objective tests that can be applied.

The extent to which advertisers have relied upon appeals to emotional motives has been shown in various advertising studies. For example, in 1924 in a study of buying motives, Copeland [9] analyzed 936 advertisements of consumers' products carried in general magazines and farm magazines then current. In his classification of buying motives he distinguished between emotional buying motives, that "have their origin in human instincts and emotions and represent impulsive or unreasoning promptings to action," and rational buying motives, aroused by stimulating the faculty of reasoning in consumers' minds. There may be question as to how clear a line of demarcation should be drawn between emotional and rational motivation. The distinction between what is logic and what is sentiment is often hard to make.

[9] M. T. Copeland, *Principles of Merchandising* (Chicago, A. W. Shaw Company, 1924), pp. 162 and 185.

Emotional appeals are often rationalized. It is possible, nevertheless, to classify advertisements, as Copeland has done, according to whether they make appeal to desires which are recognized as having an emotional basis or whether the reasons presented for buying a product relate to such buying motives as "efficiency in operation or use," its "dependability in use," its "durability," its "economy in use," or its "economy in purchase." Even with such categories established it is often difficult to classify an advertisement as being clearly emotional or rational, as defined by Copeland. Some advertisements are mere announcements of merchandise for sale and may be said to make no appeals or to contain no elements of influence. Others have both rational and emotional elements. Generally, however, the main appeal or the atmosphere of an advertisement permits fairly clear classification.

Copeland's distribution of the 936 advertisements is shown in Table 138. Counting only the advertisements classifiable as emotional or rational carried in both general and farm magazines, 61% of the appeals were to emotional buying motives, 39% to rational. Among general magazines, 72% of the appeals were classified as emotional; whereas among farm papers the order was reversed and 77% of the appeals were of a rational character. He found that rational motives were most commonly employed to stimulate purchase of "utilitarian" articles.

A study by the author of 897 consumer advertisements current in 1939 and early 1940 in general magazines and women's magazines showed a division between emotional and rational appeals much like that of Copeland for the earlier year. Approximately 75% were classed as emotional, 25% as rational.

The Employment of Persuasive Techniques

Not only have advertisers relied largely on emotional motives, but they have been careful students of the art of persuasion and have employed numerous techniques for influencing people to buy. This is a logical development, for businessmen desire to make their advertising resultful. They look upon advertising as being designed to influence. To make influence effective is not in itself unethical.[10] In order to attain a positive tone in their advertisements, they have generally presented the virtues of the products advertised without telling of shortcomings for particular uses; neither have they mentioned superior

---

[10] A discussion of the ethics of advertising is contained in Chapter XXVII.

TABLE 138

CLASSIFICATION OF CHIEF APPEALS FOUND IN 936 MAGAZINE ADVERTISEMENTS, 1924

EMOTIONAL BUYING MOTIVES	GENERAL MAGAZINES WOMEN'S MAGAZINES NATIONAL WEEKLIES	FARM PAPERS	TOTAL
Distinctiveness	27	1	28
Emulation	37	1	38
Economical Emulation	6	10	16
Pride of Personal Appearance	71	3	74
Pride in Appearance of Property	31	4	35
Social Achievement	9	0	9
Proficiency	10	1	11
Expression of Artistic Taste	17	0	17
Happy Selection of Gifts	16	4	20
Ambition	5	1	6
Romantic Instinct	8	0	8
Maintaining and Preserving Health	30	3	33
Cleanliness	19	2	21
Proper Care of Children	18	1	19
Satisfaction of the Appetite	22	2	24
Pleasing the Sense of Taste	31	1	32
Securing Personal Comfort	48	5	53
Alleviation of Laborious Tasks	13	7	20
Security from Danger	9	3	12
Pleasure of Recreation	9	0	9
Entertainment	17	4	21
Obtaining Opportunity for Greater Leisure	5	0	5
Securing Home Comfort	23	1	24
Total Emotional Buying Motives	481	54	535
RATIONAL BUYING MOTIVES			
Handiness	29	8	37
Efficiency in Operation or Use	10	12	22
Dependability in Use	21	16	37
Dependability in Quality	36	21	57
Reliability of Auxiliary Service	1	2	3
Durability	37	6	43
Enhancement of Earnings	2	13	15
Enhancing Productivity of Property	0	13	13
Economy in Use	19	22	41
Economy in Purchase	32	42	74
Total Rational Buying Motives	187	155	342
No Motives Used	50	9	59
Grand Total	718	218	936

Source: M. T. Copeland, *Principles of Merchandising* (Chicago, A. W. Shaw Company, 1924), pp. 178 and 185.

virtues of competing products for particular uses. Advertisements have carried the voice of authority, sometimes that of the man of science, again that of a person in a high place who must surely know what is right; or it may have been the humble neighbor who has commended the product. This method has been used because people are influenced by what others say without being highly critical of the adequacy of the authority cited. Often advertisements have relied merely on the force of a general assertion without citing authority. In other instances advertisers have relied on the force of the command to use a product. Again, since nothing succeeds like success, the idea that "everybody is using it" has been widely employed. As a rule, not cold reason based on a tabulation of facts, but warm emotion has been employed.[11]

The Lack of Detailed Product Information

Generally speaking, advertisements to consumers, whether based on emotional or rational appeals, have not included detailed and specific data of an objective character concerning either product qualities or product performance. Advertisements appealing primarily to the emotions, of course, rely for effectiveness not on factual data but upon sentiment and suggestion. Even when the appeals used might be classed as rational, the information given has often been presented in general terms rather than in precise, technical terms. Also, when advertisements have carried specific data they have not afforded a complete presentation of all that is pertinent for a fully rational choice. Detailed tabulations to establish the truth of this statement are not necessary. Several such tabulations have been made,[12] but brief observation by anyone of the indirect-action advertising carried in magazines, newspapers, car cards, outdoor posters is sufficient to establish the point.

Circumstances Accounting for Lack of Full
Information through Advertising

A number of circumstances account for the fact that advertising has not furnished and does not now furnish consumers the full, unbiased data which many consumers apparently feel it should give.

---

[11] Numerous treatises on advertising contain discussions of the techniques employed to influence consumers. A few sources are the following:

C. C. Hopkins, *My Life in Advertising* (New York, Harper & Brothers, 1927).

H. C. Link, *The New Psychology of Selling and Advertising* (New York, The Macmillan Company, 1932).

John Caples, *Tested Advertising Methods* (New York, Harper & Brothers, 1932).

K. M. Goode, *How to Write Advertising* (New York, Longmans, Green & Company, 1936).

[12] For example, see: M. G. Reid, *Consumers and the Market* (New York, F. S. Crofts & Company, 1938), ch. XIX.

R. S. Vaile, *Economics of Advertising* (New York, The Ronald Press Company, 1927), ch. III.

C. S. Wyand, *Economics of Consumption* (New York, The Macmillan Company, 1937, ch. 10.

The primary reason for the lack of detailed product information is that manufacturers use advertising to influence consumers; therefore they employ those advertising techniques which experience or current advertising practice leads them to consider effective in inducing buying action; and the supplying of detailed information often is not one of the effective means. From the manufacturer's standpoint promotional expenditure must be judged in terms of desired response. Effective use of an advertising appropriation requires that he follow the tenets of a behavioristic psychology. The careful advertiser tries to determine the effectiveness of his advertising in attracting consumer attention, interest, and buying action; hence the widespread effort of recent years to develop research techniques for testing and checking advertising response. If advertisers have largely employed emotional appeals and have veered away from extensive use of objective data, they have done so because they have deemed such practice to be most conducive to desired consumer response. Since the aim is to influence, advertising approaches have been determined by the fact that people's actions are guided not so much by objective logic and fact as by sentiment. Case data show that many advertisers have found purely factual advertising to be far less resultful than advertising using emotional appeals. For them to employ only factual advertising would entail an undue cost and hence a wasteful expenditure.

Other important considerations determining the small quantity of information given are the limitations imposed by advertising space and the relatively short period of attention that can be expected from readers and listeners. The objective information permitted by these limitations is far from what might be considered essential to a fully rational choice. The message that can be presented in a radio or periodical advertisement contains only a few hundred words; in a car card, poster, or point-of-purchase advertisement the limitations are even greater. Since the time that can be expected from readers or listeners is likewise limited, ideas must be conveyed quickly and impressed upon the reader's mind through repetition. It has become a common practice to build advertising campaigns around central themes or "core ideas" in order to make certain that the motivating ideas which may lead to brand preference are deeply impressed upon consumers; and with most humans the ideas likely to be effective in leading to subsequent buying action are appeals to the sentiments.

While space advertising and radio commercials have necessarily been limited in informational content, consumers generally have been given a substantially larger quantity of information regarding product qualities, care of products, and proper product usage, through labels and product literature accompanying merchandise or available at point of purchase. There is lack of uniformity in the satisfactoriness of this material, however. While some of it contains a substantial volume of helpful information, in other instances it has not been fully satisfactory to many consumers, as is attested by the considerable agitation for informational labeling in recent years.

Character of Advertisements of Industrial Goods

Typically, industrial goods advertisements differ from consumers' goods advertisements. Whereas consumers' goods advertisements predominantly make their appeal to emotional buying motives, industrial product advertisements almost invariably appeal to rational buying motives. This reliance on rational motives in industrial advertising is understandable because an industrial buyer makes his purchases ordinarily to help arrive at a profit. Accordingly the seller finds it advantageous to show how his product will help the buyer in this quest. Thus the ways in which a machine or material will reduce costs or will enhance the productivity of a plan, or will make the product of the buyer more salable, are driven home. To a very marked degree, industrial advertisements employ a performance type of copy designed to show the reader the business objectives which the product will solve for him.

Another contrast between the advertising of consumers' goods and of industrial products by manufacturers rests in the greater use by industrial goods advertisers of patronage motives. Often in the sale of industrial goods one of the most effective appeals which can be presented by a firm to secure the business of an industrial buyer is the statement of the reasons for patronizing the seller's firm rather than competing firms; such reasons as his ability to give engineering and designing service needed to solve installation and operation problems, his ability to give punctual delivery, his ability exactly to fill specifications, and so on.

Because industrial goods advertisers make an appeal to rational buying motives, industrial advertising has a higher informational content regarding products and product performance than does consumers' goods advertising. Just as with consumers' goods advertising, however, the space advertising of industrial goods does not present a complete and unbiased presentation of data essential for a rational choice. The advertisement of each manufacturer is designed to influence. It is an *ex parte* document. The advertiser seeks to use those techniques which will attract interest and which will convince and persuade. Moreover, just as with consumers' products, only a relatively brief product presentation can be made in the space available. Hence there is the same tendency dramatically to convey through a series of advertisements a few dynamic ideas to impress upon the readers the superiority of the advertiser's product. The aim is to establish the idea of product desirability or product leadership, so that when the buyer is approached by salesmen or when he is in the market, he will give favorable attention to the advertised product among those that are available to him.

An important part of industrial goods advertising consists of catalogues and product literature, which are often complete in their specific information regarding product construction, use, and care. Many industrial goods catalogues are looked upon by users as the most valuable technical texts available regarding the care and use of machines or other products of the type dealt with.

The relatively high proportion of informational content of industrial advertising is believed ascribable primarily to the fact that industrial goods buyers are equipped to use and, accordingly, want and demand such information from sellers. The supplying of such desired information is part of the influencing process in the sale of industrial goods. This fact suggests that sellers of consumers' goods would supply similar information if they felt that consumers would be influenced thereby. The lack of informational content in consumer goods advertising is attributable in considerable degree to the fact that consumers frequently do not carefully weigh objective facts in terms of price. The lack may be due in considerable part also to the fact that manufacturers have not been adequately aware that substantial numbers of consumers apparently want and would be influenced by more complete product information, particularly at the point of sale.

Lack of Informational Sources Other than Advertising

In spite of the informational weaknesses in advertising which have been outlined, it must be realized that advertising has been the only organized and substantial source of information available to consumers, and in spite of any inadequacies has been essential to the functioning of the economy. In an economy in which buyers and sellers are separated, the function of information, which is essential for exchange, has to be performed. Advertising has been one of the important methods to provide information, and as the American economy has evolved, no effective and economical substitute for it has been developed. In an advanced economy the only way in which consumers can learn of the wide range of merchandise available is for them either to seek out information directly themselves from the sellers, or to have sellers seek them out to inform them of the satisfactions to be had from the products offered at the prices asked, or for the two to share the task. Without agreement between buyer and seller, exchange cannot take place. The task of furnishing information has generally been assumed by sellers, for individual consumers have not been able to spend the time or money needed to assemble and appraise the information required for making selection among the many items of merchandise which they use.

In the case of large-scale buyers,[13] such as industrial organizations, it is not unusual to have purchasing departments seek out and compile their own information regarding the merchandise and reliability of various suppliers. But even most purchasing departments of industrial companies rely upon sellers to seek them out to provide much of the information needed to guide their buying decisions.

Industrial firms buying merchandise in large quantity can undertake a considerable part of the task of seeking out sources, of investigating merchandise, of testing it, and of making decisions regarding it, but consumers are in no position to follow such a procedure. The number of articles which they buy is so large and their purchases of each so small in value that it would not be feasible for them to seek out numerous sources of supply to learn the virtues of their offerings; neither could they afford the cost. In short, in the American economy, the initiative in exchange and in providing the information essential to exchange has rested with sellers. And advertising has been one of the chief methods used in conveying information to consumers. As the economy has developed no other means adequate for supplying the information essential to exchange has been established. Coopera-

---

[13] For a more complete discussion regarding the differences in product evaluation by governmental and industrial buyers, as contrasted with individual consumer buyers, see M. T. Gragg, *op. cit.*, ch. VII.

tive buying by consumers permits the individual consumer in some degree to pass on to a management which represents him the task of seeking out product information and of making choices for him. A cooperative may be large enough to search for sources and to buy economically. But in this country consumer cooperatives have not progressed far. Moreover, informational product services supported by consumers, such as Consumers' Research and Consumers' Union, have been subscribed to by only a fraction of one per cent of the populace. Moreover, while the information given by such services may be helpful to subscribers, it does not displace the need for much of the informational function performed through advertising, for such services cannot report on all products. In addition, many subscribers find that they cannot place full reliance for product choices on these organizations because they cannot always agree with the product recommendations made. The recommendations of such organizations can be based only on objective considerations and the subjective views of the particular people who make the judgments. The likes and dislikes of these people often do not correspond with those of subscribers.

Forces Counterbalancing *Ex Parte* Selling

In spite of the fact that the advertisements of individual manufacturers have been short on information and have been biased, the consumer has had numerous aids to help him guide his choices among individual sellers employing persuasion. For one thing the competing advertising and selling messages of numerous suppliers in a market have enabled him to compare the claims of one seller against those of others. Often he has had advice from retail merchants, although such advice frequently has been influenced to some extent by self-interest. Again, he has had helpful ideas from formal and informal education, from articles in newspapers, magazines, and books. Moreover, he has been able to secure the suggestions of other users, and he has been able to test his satisfaction through personal use, which method, for a large number of items of repeat purchase, probably forms the soundest basis for judging the satisfactions to be obtained from expenditures. Finally, he has had knowledge that he is in a market place in which sellers are actuated by self-interest and that he must use his own wits to protect his interests. When wise, he has placed considerable reliance on the doctrine of *caveat emptor*. The evidence regarding consumer buying indicates, however, that many consumers have apparently not relied as much as they should upon this doctrine.[14]

Consumer Requests for Further Information

Although these various means of supplementing the information contained in advertising have proved helpful, there have been numerous evidences of consumers' desire for further information. For example, in recent years certain consumer organizations and individuals have advocated that producers and retailers provide more definite information regarding the objective characteristics of their products in advertisements and particularly on selling tags and labels. The request for such information arises largely from the inadequacies of product information contained in advertising. It shows the desire of some consumers, at least, for detailed information to help them make more rational and intelligent choices than are possible without such information. The difficulties met in providing informational labels are many, and generally are not fully comprehended by the layman. There is the troublesome question of what information to place on the label, in view of the fact that product characteristics are many and often conflicting, and the interests and desires of consumers vary. Again, there is difficulty in determining how to express the data. Merchandise tests are likely to be highly technical and to have only limited significance. How properly to translate technical information so that it will mean the same thing to all consumers and not be misleading is often far from easy. In other instances it is hard to get the members of an industry to agree upon standard nomenclature and standard tests which might become known. In many instances manufacturers have difficulty in inducing distributors to use the labels which they are willing to furnish.[15] One of the most discouraging aspects of informative labeling from the standpoint of certain manufacturers is the apparent lack of attention given labels and package messages by a large proportion of buyers. One executive cited the instance of receiving a letter from a woman asking that the ingredients of a food product be made known. He replied that for several years

14 Better Business Bureaus have carried on substantial campaigns among consumers in an effort to make them wary buyers. These Bureaus have popularized the slogan, "Investigate before You Invest" and have applied it to the buying both of securities and of merchandise.

15 The difficulties of informational labeling and of other methods of guiding consumers are contained in the monograph previously mentioned, as a by-product of this economic study. M. T. Gragg, *op. cit.*

the ingredients had been stated in large letters on the front panel of every package of the product, in accordance with law.

One should not condemn the movement for informational labeling, however, merely because of the difficulties. It may take a long time to solve them; yet such labels carry enough promise to warrant experimental use by manufacturers and private branders. That compliance with the request for these labels may in itself be a basis for securing the favor of consumers who desire additional information is indicated by case reports from several manufacturers and retailers who have adopted the method. Unfortunately some manufacturers have given the impression of being opposed to providing detailed data regarding product qualities. Often their failure to give more detailed data has been based on honest doubts regarding the efficacy of such a method as applied to their products. Consumers, however, have gained the impression that these manufacturers wish to withhold specific information, and this impression is harmful from the standpoint of consumer-producer relations.

The Need of Consumer Education beyond Advertising

The incompleteness of information in manufacturers' advertising has accounted not only for the interest of some consumers in informational labeling, but also for other moves by consumer groups to increase the fund of information regarding varying patterns of consumption and regarding the wise selection and proper use of products. Among the methods adopted by them are consumer education in schools and colleges and the formation of organizations to advise consumers regarding product choices.

From the standpoint of maximizing consumer satisfactions, such movements and activities are to be deemed natural and desirable developments. A free society assumes the necessity of self-interest to guide the actions not only of producers but also of consumers. This assumption requires that consumers know what their interests are. As the range of products has increased, consumers have lacked the complete information needed to be certain of choosing the most satisfying of the options open to them. Moreover, sellers have been in a relatively dominant position in the matter of using influence in the exchange process. Each seller has been able to know his merchandise well, whereas the untutored buyer has had to learn the merits of thousands of items. Any moves made to strengthen the position of the buyer are deemed desirable, whether these be designed to make him wary in his buying, to help him get information which might supplement that gained in selling presentation, to train him how to use products in order to gain the greatest satisfactions from them, or to let him see clearly the probable satisfactions coming from alternative patterns of consumption. In spite of the many shortcomings of these consumer efforts they have come into existence to meet a need, namely, to help consumers improve their choices among merchandise offered.

It is believed that sellers should recognize both the right and the desirability of individual consumers and consumer groups to be aggressive in furthering methods to educate other consumers and to provide additional desired product information. In keeping with the postulates of a free economy, this study of advertising has advocated freedom of choice and freedom in the use of influence. But the use of influence permeates a democratic society. If sellers use influence in their advertising and personal selling, then they must recognize that consumers on their part should be equally free to use influence.

The reasoning that consumer choice is the determinant of value in a free society, which has been voiced several times in this volume, is ideologically correct; but it must be recognized that consumer valuations of some products may be materially affected if consumers, through education of one kind or another, are led to secure and use more product information. More complete knowledge may lead consumers to make product choices different from those which they make without such knowledge. Their willingness to pay price differentials for specific brands may well be affected. In short, information obtained outside of advertising may offset the effect of advertising appeals. An instance of the possible effect on consumer values from more widespread knowledge and use of facts is suggested by the data in the price chapter. For example, the wide variations in prices paid by consumers for drug products such as aspirin, which are manufactured to comply either with the U. S. Pharmacopoeia or the National Formulary, would probably not persist if consumers generally were fully aware of the significance of the statement of compliance with the standards of these institutions. Just as the valuations of these drug products might be affected by consumer education, so many other products might be valued differently if the attitudes of numerous consumers were affected by such education.

The Difficulties of Guiding Consumer Choice

The problem of aiding consumers in their choices of merchandise is formidable. To devise means to provide consumers with data relating to objective product qualities and product performance, which they can and will use, is very difficult. Many of the proposals advanced to aid consumers accept the merchandise test as the appropriate and adequate tool by which to assemble evidence regarding merchandise values. The variations in consumers' likes and incomes, the complexity of merchandise qualities, the shortcomings of testing methods, and the difficulties of interpreting and broadcasting results render the merchandise test of only limited value as a consumers' guide.

It is beyond the compass of this volume to explore in detail all the proposals that have been made to help the consumer spend his income more wisely, in the sense of obtaining a maximum of satisfactions therefrom. Some of these have been given attention in the monograph on *Merchandise Testing as a Guide to Consumer Buying,* to which reference has been made. The following quotation summarizes some of the conclusions reached in that report:

The purpose of this final chapter has been to suggest fruitful objectives for programs designed to aid consumers. Objectives in conflict with the fundamental principles of our social and economic order have not been considered. And objectives incapable of realization within that order have been rejected.

The numerous considerations which limit the usefulness of merchandise evaluations have been set forth in earlier chapters: the variegated nature of consumers, with their wide differences in purchasing power, interests, tastes, and skills; the peculiar nature of merchandise, with its multiple, ever shifting, and often conflicting characteristics; and the special problems inherent in the process of evaluation—determination of meaningful product groupings, selection of appropriate criteria for judging worth, designing of test methods that will measure the criteria in terms that have meaning from the point of view of actual service, determination of how many and which units to examine, and translation of the test results into a language or a form that will be correctly interpreted by consumers. It has been concluded that the guidance which can be given consumers in making their choices of merchandise is of a decidedly incomplete character. Blanket ratings or appraisals can be used to separate very good from very poor merchandise, but ordinarily they cannot be depended upon to indicate finer distinctions in probable product satisfactoriness to consumers. Factual information concerning products, although it may be enlightening, as to specific product characteristics, seldom can be complete without also being confusing.

Nevertheless, within the limitations imposed by the nature of the situation, there are various important things that can be done for consumers: to improve merchandise; to aid consumers in making their choices; and to encourage the proper utilization of goods purchased. These things, which it is believed constitute proper objectives for programs of consumer aid, are summarized in the following paragraphs. It is entirely possible that there are worth while objectives not included in this list; in any event, whatever objectives are set up must, if they are to be capable of realization, recognize the limitations outlined in this study.

Objective 1. Development in certain areas of identifying classifications of goods; and promotion of their common and honest use by manufacturers, distributors, and consumers.

Certain types of goods, notably those for which producers' standards have been developed, lend themselves to classifications which can be useful in guiding the choices of consumers. These class groupings may be identified by standard terms indicating compliance with standard specifications, by grade notations, or otherwise. The value of the class groupings to consumers will depend primarily not upon any objective evaluation implied by the grade or other standards observed. The principal value will arise, rather, from the indication given that the goods are of a definite type, and the extent of the help received by consumers will depend upon their ability to familiarize themselves with the meaning of the identifying notations or descriptions. To be useful, such identifying classifications obviously would have to be honestly, as well as widely, employed.

Objective 2. Development of classifications aimed at simplification.

It is evident that the fewer the classes into which goods reasonably can be grouped, the simpler will be the purchaser's task of selection. And there are instances in which the number of classes of consumers' goods can be reduced to advantage, not by moving the lines marking class divisions farther apart, but by arbitrarily limiting the number of varieties to be classified. Just as there are in industry instances in which the economies and convenience resulting from standardization offset whatever is lost in the way of product suitability, so also there are similar instances in the case of consumers' goods. There is no inherent reason, for example, why the quart and the pint are the best measures for milk or why milk should be sold to consumers in those units only. The advantage of having the number of possible measuring units reduced, however, outweighs the disadvantage of not always being able to get milk in the exact quantity that may be needed for the day.

There are a good many instances of this kind: number of class sizes of beds, sheets, and blankets; number of shapes and sizes of containers; fill of containers; size groupings of various types of clothing; and so on. The reduction in the number of product classes which follows from this process of limiting varieties, usually referred to as simplification, reduces confusion in buying. Any sacrifice that may be entailed in cases of this kind in respect to product suitability is more than compensated for by greater simplicity and perhaps greater economy in buying. Considerable progress in simplification already has come about through cooperative action by trade and government groups. It is not always easy in cases of this kind to arrive at sound decisions as to variety limitations; usually decisions, as with decisions concerning other industrial standards, are reached only after a long period of investigation and mutual discussion by interested parties. Unless the standards adopted are in accord with sound manufacturing practices, convenience in selection may be won at the expense of economy.

Objective 3. Development of a dictionary of understandable terms and definitions covering significant product qualities; and promotion of their common and honest use by manufacturers, distributors, and consumers in describing merchandise.

Achievement of this objective would do much to remove confusion from buying and to reduce both intentional and unintentional misrepresentation. There are, of course, many important product qualities incapable of being reduced to definitions that can have meaning to consumers; even the simplest terms no doubt will be misunderstood by some. Nevertheless, the use of standard nomenclature to whatever extent is feasible introduces a certain discipline and order into the sales picture that is beneficial both to buyers and to sellers. Not only does use of standard terms in product descriptions serve to simplify product selection, but it also provides a clearly defined basis for checking the honesty of the claims made.

Objective 4. Prevention of the manufacture and sale of harmful and fraudulent merchandise.*

It is clear that consumers should have this very important protection. They should be able to make their selections of merchandise with the assurance that, regardless of whether they are obtaining the best goods for their expenditures, they are safe from injury and outright fraud. It is in this area that mandatory standards are essential. Whatever the limitations may be upon testing procedures designed to compare sound merchandise, such procedures can be accepted as providing a fundamental and for the most part adequate basis for the detection of injurious and misrepresented goods. It already has been pointed out that the development of standard definitions to be used in product descriptions provides a helpful basis for the detection of misrepresentation and fraud.

Objective 5. Formulation and dissemination for consumer use of fundamental factual data as to the characteristics of the various types of goods, their uses, and their care.

This is an educational task. Its adequate realization should lead to a more intelligent approach to the problems of merchandise selection on the part of consumers. Not only would they be helped to allocate their incomes wisely among the different types of available merchandise and to obtain the maximum satisfaction from the goods they purchase, but they also would be provided with a sound defense against false and exaggerated sales claims.

---

* It should be pointed out that for many years there have been extensive and reasonably effective controls against the manufacture and sale of harmful and fraudulent merchandise as the result of a succession of federal and state laws. As new dangers to consumers have appeared, there have been moves to meet these dangers through legislation. For a discussion of such legal protection, see M. G. Reid, *op. cit.,* ch. XXI-XXV inclusive.

Objective 6. Support of basic product research aimed at product improvement rather than at product evaluation.

No matter how clearly the merits of merchandise were indicated for consumers, satisfaction would not follow use unless the merchandise itself was satisfactory. Choice obviously is limited by what is available. In our economy, as we have seen, the responsibility for merchandise experimentation rests largely upon private enterprise, although valuable assistance is received from government, academic institutions, and other agencies that engage in merchandise and related research. It is here that the merchandise test finds its most important use.

The need for laboratory experimentation to be supplemented by use of products under actual service conditions must not be overlooked. In other words, if consumers are to have the advantages of improvements in products, it is necessary for them to cooperate in the experimental work by using the goods offered. The cheerful cooperation extended by consumers in the development of the modern motorcar from its humble beginnings is one of the most interesting examples of this kind. While experimentation is bound to result in some failures, the wastes involved should be held within reasonable limits.

Objective 7. Furtherance of all movements that tend toward improvement of business management and growth of pride in integrity in business dealings.

This final objective has not been mentioned explicitly heretofore although its importance has been implicit throughout the entire discussion. The ultimate dependence of buyers upon the integrity of those who supply them with merchandise is a conclusion that cannot be escaped no matter how unsatisfactory it may seem to some to be.

As used here, integrity refers not alone to honesty and wellmeaningness, although certainly it does include those qualities. In addition it entails an intelligent alertness to and a skillful handling of responsibilities. A retailer who unwittingly permits injurious goods to be sold in his store is lacking in integrity if, by exercising reasonable care, he could have discovered their nature and prevented their purchase. The producer who through lack of attention to the details of management, or lack of reasonable competence, manufactures a product that is less sound than it might otherwise have been is lacking in integrity. So likewise is the producer or distributor who, whether by reason of greed or of inefficiency, overprices his goods. In the long run manifestations of lack of integrity in the management of business have a tendency to redound to the disadvantage of the business concerned. It is this fact that commonly is looked to for the protection of the public. There is no reason, however, why standards of integrity in business, that is, of honest, sound, and constructive management, cannot be improved by training and through the evolution of professional consciousness and pride on the part of business executives. Perhaps the most important achievement of the consumer movement will be found to arise from its effect in keeping producers and distributors alive to a sense of their responsibilities.

The producer, if that term may be applied to the more or less constant group of individuals responsible for the production of a given item, knows a great deal and determines a great deal about his product that cannot be reduced to words or made the basis for testing. In the case of many types of goods, for one thing, the points at which the goods might fail are so numerous that practical considerations alone make it impossible for the buyer to consider them all. A truck or automobile provides an excellent example of this. Suppose it is decided to cut an extra notch in a structural part in order to avoid some more costly method of making a necessary connection. The added notch may have the effect of weakening the part in such manner that, under some unusual but possible type of strain, it will give way. What buyer will foresee or allow for this? Who will count and measure the notches? Or, if this is done, who can judge the significance of this detail? What are the chances that a performance test will provide the identical type of strain that the part cannot withstand? Yet the vehicle will be less sound than it otherwise would have been, and the producer, and only the producer, will be in a position to know this. Almost any producer has numerous opportunities for cutting corners in ways impossible of outright detection no matter what policy is pursued as to specifications and tests. He may save on inspections; he may pass a few items here and there that might better be rejected. True, in the long run his product is likely to acquire an unsavory reputation, though users may be at a loss to know why they do not care for it.

Employee relations represent another aspect of producer responsibility. Relations may be good and the employees may take pride in their workmanship, or relations may be strained and the employees may merely live up to the letter of the demands made upon them. The effects of the presence or absence of pride in workmanship upon the goods produced often are incapable of definite measurement; nevertheless the effects may be real.

The distributor likewise is in an advantageous position, through his contacts with the trade and his familiarity with merchandise, for judging product soundness. Although he cannot say which of two sound articles is the better, he should be able to sift out the worthless, the unsound, and the possibly harmful. He, like the producer, has many opportunities for cutting corners in ways impossible of detection or of prevention.

These and many similar considerations enter into the question of the vendor's integrity, and it is partly for these reasons that industrial buyers set store by the seller's reputation and their previous experience in using his products.

In the last analysis it is upon the integrity of producers and distributors that buyers must rely. No quantity of laws and no amount of supervision can suffice for the production of sound goods, or for the selection of sound goods by distributors, if the producers have no interest in making their goods sound and if the distributors have no interest in offering sound merchandise. No amount of specifications, testing, and grading can definitely assure the soundness of merchandise unless there is a presumption of integrity behind it.[16]

---

[16] M. T. Gragg, *op. cit.*, pp. 81–84.
See also:
M. G. Reid, *op. cit.*
C. S. Wyand, *op. cit.*
S. H. Slichter, *Modern Economic Society* (New York, Henry Holt & Company, 1931).

PART VI

The Effect of Advertising on Investment and Volume of Income

CHAPTER XXIV

THE EFFECT OF ADVERTISING ON NATIONAL
INCOME—INVESTMENT

THIS chapter deals with the important issue of what effect, if any, advertising has had upon the total demand and supply of goods and services, that is, upon the size of the national dividend, which determines the standard of living or the sum total of satisfactions enjoyed by consumers. The economy has expanded and grown enormously, as shown by figures of national income. As it has expanded, consumer satisfactions have been increased. An adequate explanation of such growth in the economy is needed. Accordingly, an effort is made in this chapter to analyze available evidence to see whether in it may be found an explanation of the growth of the economy and to inquire specifically whether advertising and selling may have played a part in this growth. Their contribution to growth must have come in one or both of two ways, (1) through influence on investment, or (2) through influence upon technological development, for increase in national income has come from these two sources, from the development of management technique, and from discovery of natural resources. Consequently, the investigation seeks to determine the relationship, if any, between advertising and investment and between advertising and technological development.

The evidence gathered will be examined also to determine the correctness of the assumption employed by certain economists in their value analyses, that advertising and selling costs are normal costs which enter into the balance or equilibrium of demand and supply. Although they treat advertising and selling as normal costs, nevertheless they object to them because they conclude that advertising and aggressive selling, aside from the minimum amount necessary to provide information in an economy where producers and consumers are not in contact with one another, have represented in large part a wasteful competitive cost. There is reason to question whether the treatment of these selling costs as normal costs is sound. As pointed out in the chapter on value theory, such a treatment of advertising and selling costs from a theoretical standpoint is based upon a static concept and fails to explain how the economy gets from one level of production and consumption to another. In the evidence relating to possible explanations of the growth of the economy an answer is sought to the question of whether some part of advertising costs should be looked upon as growth costs.

It is impossible to trace statistically advertising's effect upon national income, which roughly measures the total consumption of the country. So many are the factors which determine the amount of income produced in any period that any attempt to isolate the effect of advertising or of aggressive selling is hopeless. This study can only set up hypotheses regarding its effects on the basis of known facts.

The Growth of National Income

In order that the reader may have clearly in mind what has happened to national income, the facts regarding its behavior are shown in Table 139. Attention is directed to two outstanding facts regarding national income in the past 100 years: first, the amazing increase in the size of income, both total and per capita; secondly, the marked fluctuations from boom to depression years. The table gives estimates of the national income for the period 1850–1938 in terms both of actual dollars and of 1926 dollars. In 1850 per capita income was only $95. It must be recognized, of course, that this figure probably represents a marked increase over the per capita income of 100 or even 50 years preceding, although income data to support such a statement are meager. Income rose to a high of $668 in 1929, the average for the 1920's being slightly above $600. Subsequent to 1929, however, it fell as low as $320 in 1932, while the average for the period 1930–1938 was only $442.

In order to remove the effects of the changing value of the dollar and thus more closely to determine what consumption may have been in terms of actual commodities, these amounts have been converted to a constant dollar by use of the index of wholesale prices of the Bureau of Labor Statistics, 1926=100. In such terms the increase over the period and the cyclical fluctuations are not so great as when expressed in actual dollars; yet the data present wide contrasts. In 1850, the average per capita income in terms of 1926 prices was $152; by 1870 it had risen to $201; by 1900 to $420; in 1929 to $702; in 1932 it fell to a low of $493. The marked growth in per capita income and the cyclical fluctuations involve two separate questions for investigation in this study: (1) What part, if any, have advertising and aggressive selling played in helping this country to attain a high level

TABLE 139

UNITED STATES NATIONAL INCOME, SELECTED YEARS, 1850–1938

YEAR	(a) TOTAL (BILLIONS)	(b) PER CAPITA	(c) BLS ALL COMMODITY WHOLESALE PRICE INDEX 1926 = 100	EXPRESSED IN CONSTANT PRICES 1926 = 100	
				(d) a ÷ c = d Total	(e) b ÷ c = e Per Capita
1850	$ 2.2	$ 95	62.3	3.5	152
1860	3.6	115	60.9	5.9	189
1870	6.7	174	86.7	7.7	201
1880	7.4	147	65.1	11.4	226
1890	12.1	192	56.2	21.5	341
1900	18.0	236	56.1	32.0	420
1909	29.2	322	67.6	43.2	476
1910	30.7	333	70.4	43.6	473
1911	30.6	327	64.9	47.2	504
1912	33.2	349	69.1	48.0	504
1913	35.0	363	69.8	50.2	520
1914	34.1	348	68.1	50.0	511
1915	37.1	373	69.5	53.4	536
1916	45.8	455	85.5	53.5	532
1917	53.3	522	117.5	45.4	444
1918	58.9	569	131.3	44.8	433
1919	67.4	641	138.6	48.6	463
1920	68.1	639	154.4	44.1	413
1921	50.7	468	97.6	52.0	479
1922	58.7	535	96.7	60.7	553
1923	68.0	610	100.6	67.6	606
1924	67.9	600	98.1	69.1	612
1925	72.8	633	103.5	70.4	612
1926	75.0	643	100.0	75.0	643
1927	73.8	624	95.4	77.4	655
1928	77.6	648	96.7	80.3	670
1929	81.1	668	95.3	85.3	702
1930	68.3	555	86.4	79.1	643
1931	53.8	434	73.0	73.7	594
1932	40.0	320	64.8	61.7	493
1933	42.3	336	65.9	64.1	509
1934	50.1	395	74.9	66.8	527
1935	55.2	433	80.0	69.1	541
1936	63.5	494	80.8	78.6	612
1937	69.8	540	86.3	80.9	626
1938	61.5	472	78.6	78.2	601

Sources:

Columns a and b: *Verbatim Record of the Proceedings of the Temporary National Economic Committee* (Washington, D. C., January 11, 1939), Vol. 1, Reference Data Section III, p. 41.

The table contains the following statement of sources:

U. S. Department of Commerce, for 1929–38; Kuznets in *National Income and Capital Formation*, 1919–1935, the National Bureau of Economic Research, on 1919–1928; and W. I. King, in *Wealth and Income of the People of the United States*, for 1850–1918; spliced into a single reasonably comparable series by the Department of Commerce. Reduced to a per capita basis by use of population estimates for the Continental United States prepared by the Census Bureau.

Column c: *Statistical Abstract of the United States, 1940.*

of income in recent decades as compared with previous years? (2) In the recent period, what is the relation of advertising and aggressive selling, if any, to the wide variations in the level of income; in other words, what is their relation to cyclical fluctuations and unemployment? The first question is the issue of this chapter, while the second will be dealt with in the following chapter.

Lack of Studies Fully Explaining Rising Standard of Living

The process by which a high standard of living has come about in the society of western countries has not been fully explored; nor is it feasible in this study to do much more than draw on theories already advanced by certain economic historians and to note to what extent the facts developed in this study fit these theories.

Economic historians, as a rule, have given relatively little attention to the demand factor in their studies of the Industrial Revolution. Their thoughts have turned more toward supply factors, such as the effects of power on productive capacity, the effects of technology upon manufacturing processes, the growth of transportation, the spread of industrial specialization with an increasing division of labor, the development of management skills needed in large-scale industry, and so on. The significance of these and other factors needs only be mentioned, because they have been treated comprehensively in other places.

Certain Factors Involved in Increased Productivity

It is quite clear that the high standard of living of the United States could not have been attained unless this country had built a large-scale productive machine and had evolved methods of distributing its output to consumers. Material resources, coal, oil, metals, and water power, have been harnessed. Factories with intricate machines have come to dominate the economy. Efficient systems of transportation and communication, essential to the other developments, have come into being. In his economic endeavors man has sought new techniques, striving ever to invent new products and to apply the laws of science to productive processes in order to gain larger output at lower costs than before. Improved technology has been necessary to give an abundance never known before.

To the student of history it is also evident that the high material welfare enjoyed in this country could not have been realized had not the industrial system developed management skills which made possible efficient direction of large aggregates of men and machines. Essential also has been the growth of corresponding management skills needed to direct the large-scale marketing activities that have evolved for distributing the output of large-scale factories to consumers. The creation of management techniques has been similar in its effects to technological inventions in the matter of contributing to increased productivity.

Conditions Calling Increased Productivity into Being

But why did such a development of productive resources come about? What were the conditions that fostered its growth, and what were the mechanisms that brought a change from the static society of the Middle Ages, with its low living standards? Do advertising and aggressive selling deserve any of the credit for this economic expansion?

The possibility that advertising and selling efforts might have played a part in increasing the productiveness of the economic machine through stimulating consumers to greater effort has been recognized by some economists;[1] it has also been a common theme of popular defenders of advertising and aggressive selling. Their reasoning is that advertising and aggressive selling have led people to want things; and to get desired products they have been induced to work harder than they would have otherwise, with consequent increase in goods produced.

Such a view undoubtedly contains some truth, but it is clearly an inadequate explanation in itself of the growth in production and consumption. One serious limitation is readily evident in the fact that many individuals have had to depend upon others for opportunity to work and have not been able at will to step up their earnings through harder work. Moreover, the study of demand led to the conclusion that environment and social conditions have been stronger forces than advertising and selling in increasing people's wants for products. Accordingly it is necessary to inquire further regarding the environmental and social conditions which may have accounted for expansion of demand. In addition, the supply side must be studied

---

[1] See D. Braithwaite and S. P. Dobbs, *op. cit.*, p. 88; F. W. Taylor, *op. cit.*, p. 44; Elizabeth W. Gilboy, "Demand in the Industrial Revolution," an essay in *Facts and Factors in Economic History* (articles by former students of Edwin F. Gay; Cambridge, Harvard University Press, 1932), pp. 620 ff.; Hazel Kyrk, *A Theory of Consumption* (Boston, Houghton Mifflin Company, 1923), p. 65.

to determine what conditions there may account for investment in factories and for the adoption of ever-improving technology. Advancing technology gave the factories increased productive power upon which the rising standard of living has depended. In short, inquiry must be made, on the one hand, regarding the forces which account for expansion of demand, and, on the other hand, regarding the mechanisms of investment and technological development. Advertising and aggressive selling must be fitted into their proper places as part of the explanation.

Social Changes Underlying Growth of Demand and Production

In order better to understand the conditions which account for the growth and changes in demand which have accompanied increased productivity, it is desirable to have the perspective given by history. For those who have known only a society of large productive capacity, enjoying a wide range of products and a high standard of living among a considerable share of the population, it is well to consider the changes that have occurred since times when oat bread was the common staff of life for the great majority of people and such items as tea, sugar, and wheat bread were luxuries available only to the few. Corresponding to the amazing growth in productive capacity since medieval times there had to be a corresponding increase in demand which would and could absorb the output of a productive machine brought into being because entrepreneurs hoped for a profit from investment in their enterprises. There had to be both a willingness and an ability of people to consume the output of the increasingly productive economic machine.

In an illuminating essay, Mrs. Elizabeth W. Gilboy [2] has advanced theories regarding changes in demand which have been essential to development of large-scale industry. She has pointed out that the factory form of organization had been known in ancient Rome, in medieval Florence, and other places previous to the Industrial Revolution, but prior to the eighteenth century it had not become typical. She presents the thesis that the factory system could not have become the typical mode of production until demand had become extended and had become sufficiently flexible among all groups in a population to consume the products of large-scale industry. In other words, social

[2] *Op. cit.*

conditions favorable to wide consumption of products had to come as a prelude to growth of the industrial machine.

Higher standards of living have not been a mere concomitant of growth in population. Population increase would not itself call into existence increases and improvements in production. As a matter of fact, the pressure of population upon means of subsistence, with a reduction of the standard of living to a bare minimum of existence, was a thesis popularized by Malthus and Ricardo. In addition, the examples of China, India, and other so-called backward countries illustrate the point. In these countries increase in population has failed to call forth an improvement in production corresponding to that known in the United States and other western countries. Rigid class systems have hampered development of demand among the great bulk of these Asiatic populations, a demand essential to the growth of a factory system.

Mrs. Gilboy names four necessary concomitants of growth of large-scale production, concomitants which have been noted in the study of demand in this volume. They are as follows: (1) mobility of individuals within and among the various classes of the population; (2) an introduction of new wants; (3) a shift in demand schedules of the entire population, that is, an increase in demand; and (4) changes in the shape of demand schedules, or, in the nature of demand at various layers of consumption within the general population.

Importance of a Mobile Society to the Growth of Demand and Production

A mobile society has been fundamental to the industrial change that has taken place. A society with standards of consumption set by traditional class lines does not provide a fertile soil for industrial change. During the medieval period custom and tradition fixed the consumption standards of each class, and there was little hope of rising above one's class. The luxuries of commerce were limited primarily to the consumption of a wealthy, leisure class. It was a static society, and until the barriers against mobility of the individual from his social group were broken down, conditions were unfavorable for the extension of demand upon which, in turn, industrial development depended.

In the Middle Ages, consumption of the lower classes was very limited. Commerce was in such luxuries as tea, sugar, and silk.

It was not until the seventeenth and eighteenth centuries that the ordinary individual would or could begin to include such goods in his own consumption. It did not occur to the average villein or serf to desire spices or jewels or silken robes. He expected to live and die in his own stratum, content with a simple diet and coarse and unornamented clothing. Envy of the upper classes, closely followed by an attempt to imitate them, what Defoe called "aping one's betters," is a comparatively modern phenomenon. The removal of political, legal, and economic restrictions upon the lower classes, the breakdown of feudal and manorial customs, were essential to its development.[3]

Importance of New Wants to Growth of Demand and Production

The process of the spreading of new wants among consuming groups, which is listed above as the second concomitant to growth of large-scale production, has been emphasized in the study of demand of this volume. It has been noted that, in a mobile society such as that of the United States, wants first adopted by the rich and well-to-do later have spread to other income classes. Products which at one time have been luxuries later have come to be regarded as necessities by large segments of the population. Individualistic competition has flourished. The individual has been free not only to aspire to consume products previously used only by higher income classes but also by his own efforts to improve his economic status. That emulation has been a potent force in inducing consumption has been indicated in the study of the demand for various products—electric lights, automobiles, refrigerators, tobacco, and so on. Consumers, in order to obtain desired items, have drawn on savings; or if they have had no surplus they perhaps have skimped on necessities; or, as has been previously suggested, some may have worked harder to obtain wanted products. In the recent period they have resorted more and more to instalment buying, mortgaging future earnings to get desired products. Historically, whatever have been the means whereby members in lower income levels came to purchase desired articles, the basis for large-scale production was established merely by their ability and willingness to buy. If consumption of new articles or of luxury articles had continued to be limited by custom to a small top stratum, as in the Middle Ages, the factory could not have become the typical productive unit.

The factors of shifts in the demand curves and of changes in the

---

[3] *Ibid.*, p. 626.

shape of demand schedules, which were listed by Mrs. Gilboy as concomitants to the growth of large-scale production, need not be elaborated on here because their relation to large-scale production has been brought out in previous chapters. Expansion in the demand of a product may permit large-scale production to develop, as was illustrated in the case of refrigerators and cigarettes. A change in the shape of schedules may occur when a product comes to be desired by large numbers of people. Then lower prices offered by a producer may permit an increased scale of production on his part. Historically, such changes in the shape of demand schedules and the shifts of demand schedules occurred at the close of the Middle Ages as rigid class distinctions broke down and society became mobile.

Social Changes in England Accompanying Growth of Demand and Production

Several centuries passed before the change from a stable, static society to a mobile society was brought about in England. When once individuals could aspire to pass to higher social and economic levels, an economic system was called forth which as compared with that which had gone before was fluid and elastic. "The fluid and elastic system was not entirely created by the Industrial Revolution. It existed prior to the development of the Industrial Revolution—or such a great economic change could not have happened when and where it did—and was then enhanced in turn by the industrial development."[4]

The changing characteristics in England which marked the transition leading up to the Industrial Revolution can be traced. During the eighteenth century England changed from a country predominantly rural, in which industry was carried on in homes under the putting-out system, to a country in which factories were fast supplanting the home as a producing unit. The data, though hard to evaluate, indicate that real wages probably rose during the century. Luxury items—sugar, tea, wheat bread, cotton cloth, and silk cloth—were more frequently consumed by the common classes. Pamphlets of the time remarked upon and often expostulated against the spread of luxuries among the laboring classes. There were signs of the social instability and of the freedom in individual consumption necessary for growth of large-scale demand and production which were evolving.

[4] *Ibid.*, p. 627.

The Entry of Aggressive Selling as a Factor in Demand Growth

Concurrent with the social changes discussed above, significant developments were taking place in marketing methods, and aggressive selling entered as a factor in influencing demand. The development of a mobile society encouraged the growth of a more aggressive group of entrepreneurs. By this time the restrictions of the guilds upon product form and quality had become progressively weaker. The merchant class had broken away to a considerable degree from the prejudices and restrictions against aggressive selling which had existed under the guilds.[5] During the eighteenth century there were further developments of aggressive selling methods, a departure from the system of making buyers seek out sellers and the substitution therefor of the system of sellers seeking out buyers. In short, manufacturers adopted methods of stimulating a demand which changing social and economic conditions made feasible. Salesmen who rode on horseback or by stage to buyers in distant towns were common by the middle of the eighteenth century.[6] This system increased as power machinery developed and factories grew. There evolved the commercial traveler.[7] Catalogues and other types of advertisement later were adopted. Advertising influence grew and became a factor in conditioning consumers to demand both the new and the old products offered.

---

[5] See page 28 ff.

[6] J. Aikin, *A Description of the Country from Thirty to Forty Miles Around Manchester* (1795), pp. 183–184.

[7] For statements regarding marketing aspects of the Industrial Revolution, see the list of references given on page 16, Chapter II. A specific treatment is given by G. B. Hotchkiss, *Milestones of Marketing*, ch. IX. A good account of the manufacturers' sales methods used in England after the Industrial Revolution was well launched may be found in *The Merchants' Magazine and Commercial Review*, Freeman Hunt, editor, July, 1839, p. 29.

"Not an uninteresting feature of the internal traffic of Great Britain, is the system commonly styled commercial travelling. This institution, though now in its wane, is still exercised to a very considerable extent throughout the United Kingdom. Almost every commercial house there, of any note, employs one or more agents, whose business it is to travel about the country and procure custom for their principals. The commercial traveller, (as the agent is denominated) is generally a young and very shrewd individual, possessing great suavity of manner, and a remarkable ability to suit himself readily to all the varied moods of his very various customers. Furnished by his principals with choice samples of their goods, he steps into his chaise or the stage, and with a light heart commences his circuit. It is not considered unusual if nearly a year elapses before he returns to his employers. At each town upon his route, he tarries at the principal inn, where he is sure to find a hearty welcome. After thus ensconcing himself in comfortable quarters, he arranges his samples, and, if it be forenoon, puts them under his arm and issues forth to visit the shopkeepers in the place. Wherever he goes, he is met with cordiality. Like all travellers, he is full of anecdote, and has at his command the rarest news of the time. None are more glad to see him than the shopkeepers' wives and daughters. To these he imparts the most recent scandal and the latest fashions, and affords them subjects for gossip until his

Social Conditions in America Favoring Growth in Demand and Productivity

From its start America had a mobile society free from the strong lines of class distinction which held back change in Europe. Moreover, it was relatively free from Europe's prejudices against changes in methods of production and against aggressive selling methods, vestiges of the guild system. Accordingly, it proved fertile soil for a changing and growing demand and the development of a correspondingly dynamic factory system, after industry was once established here in the nineteenth century. Members of the American society always have been free to rise from the lowest to the highest class. Consequently, they have provided a promising market for a constant succession of new products offered by the aggressive entrepreneur group which developed.

While the promising markets offered by the mobile society of this county served to encourage the formation of an aggressive entrepreneur group, in turn the entrepreneurs' activities in introducing new products and in aggressively selling them have unquestionably had an important influence in further conditioning the consumer group to a high degree of willingness to consume the widening range of products offered. Many of the products introduced and accepted in themselves became an important part of environment leading to new wants. In Chapter VII the far-reaching effect of the automobile in changing the consumption patterns of the populace was noted. Other new inventions have had similar effects. The economy has tended to become increasingly dynamic; and the American people, through habituation to change, have been prone to accept the new. In addition, advertising and aggressive selling efforts have been a force contributing to this willingness to accept the new.

The Role of Advertising and Selling in Inducing a Willingness to Consume

From a long range point of view aggressive selling and advertising probably have played a considerable but undeterminable part in the

next visit to the town. To the tradesmen he lauds his samples with all the eloquence and ingenuity of which he is capable, and seldom leaves them without making considerable bargains in behalf of his principals. He then collects monies due on former purchases, and, if in convenient shape, forwards the funds, together with his customers' orders for goods, by mail, to his employers.

"Nearly the whole of the country trade is managed by the commercial travellers. Each has his list of customers, who recognize his house only in him. Of them his principals are comparatively ignorant. To the discretion of the agent, it is left to determine who shall have credit, and to what amount that credit shall extend."

formation of mental attitudes necessary for a high level of consumption among the population of this country. The study of demand in this volume has indicated that what people want is determined largely by their social backgrounds and habits. New products have been accepted but the demands for them have grown relatively slowly. Once the new products have been accepted by a few consumers, however, consumption has usually expanded through much of the social group. Imitation and emulation have apparently been powerful forces in leading to widespread consumption. In time, use of new products has tended to become habitual, continuing until new developments have thrown them into disuse. While the attitudes which favor consumption of various products are determined by the entire milieu, aggressive selling and advertising have been important forces leading to the adoption and then general acceptance of new products. They have played a particularly important part in bringing first sales, upon which emulative consumption depends.

The scale on which advertising and aggressive selling have been conducted in the United States supports the theory that they have probably been forces of considerable consequence in influencing people's views and attitudes. Advertising expenditures in the last 20 years have been at a rate of some $2,000,000,000 a year, and personal selling expenditures have been greater. Much of the advertising and selling have been carried on by men trained in the techniques of influencing people's attitudes and beliefs. Consequently they probably have been contributors to the propensity to consume, a propensity which is absent among people who have not had similar social backgrounds and have not been subjected to such conditioning, with the result that they have not developed similar consumption habits. Traders among primitive people have always found it essential to carry to them not advanced merchandise but simple things which fit in with their existing wants. German traders in backward regions of the world are said to have complained of the *verdammte Bedürfnislosigkeit* (damned wantlessness) of the natives for the products they had to offer.[8] That lack of buying has not been due solely to lack of purchasing power is shown by the fact that companies carrying on construction projects in the tropics and in backward communities often have had difficulty in inducing workmen to stay on the job. This has been

---

[8] F. C. Mills, *Economic Tendencies in the United States* (New York, National Bureau of Economic Research, 1932), p. 285.

true, for example, in California with Indians employed in public utility construction work. A few days of work a week has been sufficient to supply them with funds necessary to satisfy their few, simple wants.

References to the variation in the propensity of different societies and individuals to consume and in the efforts which they put forth to fill the wants which have been fashioned by their environment and their individual makeup are to be found in many writings on economics. For example, Taussig in his *Inventors and Money-Makers* states:

> It is by no means obvious that all men desire to obtain additional wealth. On the contrary, there are whole races among whom satiety is reached at what may seem to the artificialized modern man a very early stage; races whose members cease to labor when a few simple wants have been gratified, and care for no additional wealth even if it can be got with but the slightest sacrifice. And among the advanced races themselves there is a very large proportion of persons, not only among the manual laborers, but among the property-accumulating members of the prosperous classes, whose wants are simple and limited, to whom leisure and relaxation appeal quite as much as additional wealth.[9]

Again, Marshall in his *Principles of Economics,* presents a similar conclusion:

> No universal rule can be laid down; but experience seems to shows that the more ignorant and phlegmatic of races and of individuals, especially if they live in a southern clime, will stay at their work a shorter time, and will exert themselves less while at it, if the rate of pay rises so as to give them their accustomed enjoyments in return for less work than before. But those whose mental horizon is wider, and who have more firmness and elasticity of character, will work the harder and the longer the higher the rate of pay which is open to them; unless indeed they prefer to divert their activities to higher aims than work for material gain.[10]

Such statements concerning the lack of wants of backward and primitive people indicate that the extensive wants and desires for most people in this and other advanced countries are the result of generations of conditioning for a high standard of consumption. This high standard has come in part because one product after another, over a long period, has been added to the category of things which

---

[9] F. W. Taussig, *Inventors and Money-Makers* (New York, The Macmillan Company, 1915), p. 77.
[10] Alfred Marshall, *Principles of Economics* (8th ed., New York, The Macmillan Company, 1920), p. 528.

may satisfy wants. People in large degree want what those about them have. Thus new products, which have been accepted slowly at first by people with money and willingness to experiment, later have been desired by many people. The luxuries of one generation have become the necessities of succeeding generations. Consumers have become habituated to a high standard of living, and aggressive selling has been an element not only in hastening this development but even in bringing it about.

The Role of the Entrepreneur in Adding to Investment and in Increasing the Standard of Living

The changes in social conditions and the employment of aggressive selling outlined above provide a logical explanation of growth and willingness of a population to consume, but a further explanation is needed regarding the mechanism by which it has been possible for consumers to fulfill this desire to consume. Willingness to consume must be accompanied by the availability of products and services which may be purchased, and by consumer income with which to purchase. Both the existence of products and the income of consumers depend upon risk-taking by entrepreneurs, businessmen who see an opportunity for profit and are willing to risk capital and effort to make that profit. They risk the savings of themselves and others when they see an opportunity to make and sell goods which they think consumers will want. Their risk activities bring the investment in factories and production facilities of various kinds, which not only produce goods for consumption but which employ the labor and pay the wages and the return upon capital upon which consumer income depends. In short, the activities of entrepreneurs create the markets for their own products. These activities provide the income with which consumers can secure the satisfactions from the goods which they produce. Without the risk activities of businessmen in launching and conducting enterprise, a free economy cannot expand. The effects of these risk-taking activities will be apparent in instances which are discussed in the pages ahead.

As economists from Adam Smith on have pointed out, businessmen in carrying on their activities have not been conscious of the social implications of their work; but their search for profit opportunities, their willingness to take risks and the attendant increase in factory capacity and productivity have had high social significance. In the activities of entrepreneurs and the volume of investment which they make possible lies a vital part of the explanation of the rising standard of living which has brought men from the meager levels of the Middle Ages to the relatively liberal standards of today. These activities account in large degree for the rise in real per capita income in the United States from $152 in 1850 to over $600 in recent decades. An account of the growth in consumer satisfactions arising from increased productivity must give an important place to the activities of the business enterpriser.

The Interest of Entrepreneurs in Promoting New Products

Increased capacity of the economic machine has come in large measure from the activities of businessmen in developing and promoting new and differentiated products. The new product has been a great lure to investment. Businessmen are constantly seeking new inventions which will be in demand and improvements upon already established products which will win consumer preference. To gain this end they spend considerable sums in product research and then risk further sums in personal selling, advertising and other costs to place these on the market. Previous chapters have enlarged upon these points and numerous examples have been cited of the quest for new and differentiated products to sell. As there brought out, advertising and aggressive selling have not been the causes of the launching of new enterprises, but they often have been important elements whereby the new enterprises might hope to gain a profitable demand. In addition they frequently have been helpful in speeding up a demand which has called for increasing investment. By such means have factories been built, men employed, and the products and incomes for increasing consumer satisfactions established.

A few of the examples cited heretofore are briefly reviewed to indicate how new products have been launched, demand established, and investments increased. The first American automobile was produced in 1892. The luxury product of the 1890's became the necessity of the 1930's. In this latter decade there were roughly three passenger cars registered for every four families. Such a demand was ushered in and grew under the stimulus of aggressive selling. While the expenditures of consumers for automobiles were shown by the studies of the National Resources Committee[11] in 1939 to vary

---

[11] *Consumer Expenditures in the United States* (Washington, U. S. Government Printing Office, 1939), p. 23.

largely with income, yet automobiles were used even in the lowest income groups. In families with incomes under $500, automobile expenses averaged only $15 annually per family, while for those with incomes of $20,000 they represented $1,759 per family. The proportion of car owners in the large income group, of course, was much higher than that in the low income levels. Nevertheless, these data show that in the American society even those with low incomes can aspire to own and use an article used by high income classes. The mobile society, even with widely different incomes, has provided a market through all social strata for this high-price item.

Amazing in its impact has been the investment called for by this new consumers' product and the resulting effects upon national income. Whereas there had been no investment in automobile factories previous to 1892, in 1937 the net tangible assets of motor vehicle manufacturing plants located in the United States, not counting parts, accessories, body, or tire manufacturers, were almost $1,370,000,000. The number of wage earners in motor vehicles and parts factories was 517,000, with wages of $806,000,000; while the number employed directly and indirectly in highway transportation was in excess of 6,000,000 people, approximately one-seventh of all the workers in the country.[12]

While the automobile stands as the most revolutionary of new products in its economic consequences, yet on a smaller scale the effects of other new products upon investment and upon consumer income have been similar. In the case of domestic refrigerators it was shown that only 1.1% of wired homes had electric refrigeration in January, 1925. Fifteen years later, 56% of wired homes had electric refrigeration. Here again is illustrated the fact that with the aid of aggressive selling and lowered prices resulting from large-scale demand, a new product in a relatively short time may be consumed in a mobile society by even low-income families. Although the data of investment and employment are not available, it is evident from the sales data that in the course of a few years large increases in investment were made and that considerable productive capacity was added to the economy.

It is unnecessary to recount the facts for other new products, motion pictures, phonographs, rayon, radio, and so on. The story is similar.

---

[12] Automobile Manufacturers Association, *Automobile Facts and Figures* (1938 edition).

For many of these products aggressive selling and advertising have been important parts of the free system under which entrepreneurs have launched the products, and these selling forces played a part in speeding up demand which brought increased investment and productive capacity. The advertising brought an acceptance which paved the way for wide usage when low prices were possible as the result of large-scale production and technological development.

Increased Investment in Long-Established Industries

It is recognized, of course, that not all increase in investment in factories and machines and other productive equipment has been for new products and services, for a considerable part of the increase in investment has been devoted to building productive capacity for what might be termed mature products and services. Previous chapters have noted the increased per capita production of oranges, sugar, tobacco products, lettuce, and other items which from a short-range point of view certainly could not be called new, although in historical perspective they should not be called old. The growth of such industries is as significant from a social standpoint as the entry of new products. If the variety of goods offered over a long period of time were held constant, consumer well-being might be increased by producing more of the same goods per capita. That there is wide room for increased consumption of most products is indicated by the differences in quantities consumed by different income groups, goods which all might agree upon as desirable things of life, foods needed in a well-rounded diet, the right kind of recreation, proper medical and health care, good housing, and so on.[13] To a large degree what is called a desirable standard of living hinges on an increasing consumption of these items.

The increased investment in these mature industries has in some instances been attended by the use of advertising; in other instances it has not. In those cases in which advertising has been used, entrepreneurs have generally displayed an attitude towards making investment such as is held by those venturing into new product fields. They have tried to foresee profit from some new product differentiation in these old fields which they might offer and promote. Thus, in

---

[13] These facts were brought out clearly in the study of the National Resources Committee, *op. cit.* They were also developed by Maurice Leven, H. G. Moulton, and Clark Warburton, in *America's Capacity to Consume* (Washington, The Brookings Institution, 1934).

recent years cigarette manufacturers have offered new tobacco blends, new hygroscopic agents, or lower prices as the basis for getting demand. In other instances, the enterpriser working in an old field has not relied on new differentiation but has seen a chance to tie in with favorable product trends which might be exploited, as in the case of the California Fruit Growers Exchange. In those product fields, such as lettuce and sugar, where advertising has not been used to appreciable extent the entrepreneurs have found that their profit opportunity has not been dependent on use of advertising, but they have relied to some extent on other forms of aggressive selling. In short, aggressive selling and advertising have been employed as helpful tools to establish and increase a demand calling for investment in production facilities in many established industries.

The Use of Advertising to Protect Investment in Declining Industries

Adverse trends of demand arising from the advent of new products or from social causes, which were discussed in previous chapters, have often tended to render investment in established industries unproductive. In such instances, it was shown that advertising has been used in attempts to protect the old industry from the inroads of the new. In the smoking tobacco, cigar, and shoe industries, for example, advertising has been used by numerous sellers, and it was concluded that the effect of their advertising probably has been to slow down adverse trends.

In the refrigerator industry, manufacturers of ice refrigerators have cooperated with the ice industry in combatting the inroads of mechanical refrigerators.[14] Likewise the gas industry has fought the inroads from newly developed electrical equipment.[15] In those instances where industries have fought a rear-guard action against new types of competition, however, hope of success has generally depended upon the older businesses changing their products to compete favorably with the new products. Thus, under the stimulus of competition from mechanical refrigeration, ice refrigeration was greatly improved and has in recent years been advertised extensively. Likewise, gas stoves, in order to hold their own against the inroads of electric ranges, were redesigned

---

[14] "Ice on the Offensive," *Printers' Ink*, November 21, 1935, p. 29.
So They Never Come Back? Pamphlet of National Broadcasting Company, 1938.
[15] N. H. Borden, *Cooperative Advertising, op. cit.*, case of New England Gas Association, p. 190 ff.

and sold aggressively. Coal sellers, in their battle against sellers of domestic oil burners, have promoted improved coal stokers. The use of advertising in protecting these old industries may thus be two-fold, it may serve not only as a means of preventing dislocation from the impact of too rapid loss of sales by these industries, but also to stimulate demand for new improvements that not only may keep the industry alive, but even give it a new life cycle calling for investment.

Investments in Plants to Produce Industrial Goods

Increase in the capacity of enterprise from investment is not, of course, accomplished solely by the investment in plants producing consumers' goods and services as described above. Much of the increase in investment in industry, which has accounted for employment and income to consumers, has been made in enterprises which have come into existence to produce the major plant and accessory equipment, the primary materials, the fabricated materials and parts, and the supplies needed in the operation of all kinds of business firms.[16] The development and size of these industries catering to business needs has, of course, depended ultimately upon the growth of the consumer goods industries. But even though its growth has depended upon the growth in demand for consumer goods, it has been able to contribute to the growth of consumption in consumer goods through its contribution to the improvement of manufacturing processes.

The Increase in the Standard of Living
Arising from Technological Developments

While the activities of entrepreneurs in making investment in new and old enterprises in order to promote profit-promising products have increased in large measure the per capita productiveness of the economic machine, their activity in developing and adopting technological improvements has also greatly added to the capacity of industry. Not only have new factories and machines been brought into being, but their productiveness has been subject to continuous improvement. Technological improvements have come in considerable degree

---

[16] No effort is made to describe in detail the full structure of the American economy, nor to show the relative importance of the various types of efforts and their interrelationships. The reader is referred to such sources as: National Resources Committee, *The Structure of the American Economy* (Washington, U. S. Government Printing Office, 1939).

S. S. Kuznets, *Commodity Flow in Capital Formation* (New York, National Bureau of Economic Research, 1938), Vol. I.

as the result of the activities of producers of industrial goods. The spur to such producers to bring out improved machines has come from the chance to profit from meeting the desires of industrial goods buyers.

The Attitudes of Industrial Goods Producers towards Technological Advance

The manufacturers of industrial equipment have in their fields followed the same pattern of behavior as have the manufacturers of consumers' goods and in so doing have furthered technological advancement. They have been led to the launching of enterprises when they have seen an opportunity to profit. They have been interested in finding new products of interest to industrial goods buyers. In order to improve their profit outlook they have sought to differentiate and improve their products in such ways as to make them more wantable by business concerns. The result has been a continuous succession of improvements in industrial products. Through such activities the industrial goods producers have played an important part in furthering technological advance and thereby have helped to increase the output of consumers' goods and services, to improve their quality, and to make their costs lower.

Manufacturers of installation and accessory equipment have played a particularly important role in bringing the technological advances in machines and production methods which have so greatly reduced merchandise costs and increased productive capacity. Power machinery, the turbine, electric motors, boilers, and internal combustion engines have been subject to continuous improvement since first introduced.[17] Machines used in the manufacture of practically all types of products have become more efficient and more economical to operate with the passing of time, as was illustrated in the study of sheeting.

The reason for the drive of installation and accessory equipment manufacturers to produce more efficient machines is evident. Among the strongest motives for purchase of a particular machine or process is the promise it may hold either for reduced operating cost or for improvement in the manufactured product into which it enters. Accordingly, in their search for product differentiation, manufacturers

---

[17] An account of increases in boiler, turbine, and engine efficiency will be found in the study of L. P. Alford, "Technical Changes in Manufacturing Industries," an essay in *Recent Economic Changes, op. cit.*, Vol. I, p. 129 ff.

of industrial machines have sought improvements on which they might utilize such appeals. A study of industrial goods advertisements has shown that the appeals of reduced costs from use of a machine, material, or process, or of increased salability of a product made by the improved manufacturing processes have been among the appeals most frequently used.[18] In many instances the industrial goods manufacturer seeks opportunity in his advertising and selling to work closely with manufacturers who are his customers in the solution of production problems. An example of this was given in the case of the Corning Glass Works in the promotion of Pyrex Glass.

Manufacturers of fabricated parts and materials likewise have sought profit by offering new and improved materials and parts to their customers. Here again technology has given striking improvements which often have had quick effect in improving consumer products or in lowering their costs. Examples of advances in fabricated materials are many and various—plastics, cellophane, pliofilm, rayon, nylon, cellular latex, stainless steel, and Monel metal—to name but a few which have been perfected in recent years by industrial firms. Many fabricated parts manufacturers have played an important role in bringing improvements to consumers' finished products into which their materials enter. For example, in the automobile industry independent product research and product improvement by parts manufacturers, such as Bendix, the tire manufacturers, the axle manufacturers, the body manufacturers, and electric headlight manufacturers, have contributed to the improvement as well as to the lower costs of automobiles. As previously related, increase of automobile engine efficiency was dependent upon the improvement of gasoline by the oil companies.

Aggressive Selling of Improved Industrial Products

Manufacturers of industrial products, like manufacturers of consumer products, in order to benefit from their product differentiation and in order to secure large enough demand to make possible large-scale operation, have resorted to aggressive selling methods, even though their markets generally have been much more clearly defined and much less widely scattered than have been consumers' goods markets. Personal selling has played a more important part than has

[18] See M. T. Copeland, *Principles of Merchandising* (Chicago, A. W. Shaw Company, 1924), ch. VII.

advertising in industrial selling programs, but advertising has generally been an essential element. Industrial product manufacturers have not found it feasible to sit back and wait for buyers to come to them. Particularly when they have offered differentiated products or processes, their potential customers have had to be informed, educated, and urged to buy. Even more than the consumer market, however, the industrial goods market has been responsive to new products so long as they have carried the promise of profit opportunities.

In brief, in the industrial goods market aggressive selling as a vehicle for profit realization indirectly has been a stimulant to technological development and, thus, to increased productivity and lower costs, which such development makes possible. In addition, the activities of entrepreneurs to develop and promote new and improved industrial goods products have led to a huge investment in industrial goods industries, which have become an important part of the complex modern economy.

Resistance to Technological Advance

While the free economy has brought forth a quest for product differentiation which has been conducive to technological advance in the fields of both industrial goods and consumers' goods, it has also provided resistances to advancing technology, which should be mentioned. That consumers have provided much resistance in their slowness to accept new products has been indicated in the study of demand. They have distrusted the unknown. Such was true with the steam train, the automobile, the airplane, household gas, and the zipper, to name but a few instances. The high costs and low efficiency of first commercial models have often contributed to slow adoption, as illustrated in the case of electric refrigerators and the automobile. Moreover, manufacturers enjoying a profitable and satisfactory market for one type of product not infrequently have hesitated to adopt radical innovations with the uncertainties entailed, innovations whose commercial success has not been certain. For example, motion picture producers hesitated to adopt sound films.[19] In other instances industries threatened by a new product innovation of a competitor have attempted to create antagonism to its success through ridicule or other methods. Reference is made again to the motion picture industry; its history abounds with tales of personal struggles of promoters who started

---

[19] Case of Warner Brothers Pictures, Inc., files of Harvard Business School.

on a small scale with meager financial resources and whose efforts were met by derision and by opposition from the legitimate stage. The early railroads suffered from resistance of owners of stage coaches, turnpike companies, and tavern keepers.[20] Later the railroads themselves opposed the growth of trucking.

Manufacturers have often held back from adopting improved machines or improved power equipment, not because of inertia or ignorance, but because of the cost of the obsolescence of the equipment displaced. Not until it is clear that improved machines will produce savings that make scrapping of old machines appear worth while to individual managements do they install new equipment. This is brought out in evidence adduced by President Hoover's conference on unemployment:

> A questionnaire sent to 800 of the larger and more representative manufacturing concerns of the United States sought to disclose the policy pursued when purchasing new equipment. The question bearing upon this point read: "Has your company a policy against the purchase of new equipment unless the production savings will return the initial investment within a definite period. If so, what is this period?"
>
> Nearly 200 replies were received to this questionnaire, disclosing that 3.6 percent of the companies required that new equipment should return its cost through savings in a period of two years or less, and that 64.1 percent required that it should pay for itself in three years or less. . . .
>
> The existence of a policy of this kind indicates the nature of the technical efforts being put forth not only to improve the capacity of manufacturing machinery, but also to increase its economy. Without doubt this is a most important element in the cost-reduction program of 1919 to date.[21]

Another type of resistance has been that encountered from labor. From the beginning of the Industrial Revolution, labor has resisted technological advances when rapid introduction of labor-saving machines has threatened dislocations entailing unemployment.[20]

The Greater Strength of Forces for Improvement

The evidences of resistance to technological innovation are many in the history of product development, but forces to bring adoption have been stronger. Apart from the resistance of consumers and of labor, examples of resistance of businessmen, such as recounted above,

---

[20] B. J. Stern, "Resistances to the Adoptions of Technological Innovations," in *Technological Trends and National Policy*, National Resources Committee (Washington, U. S. Government Printing Office, 1937), p. 39.

[21] L. P. Alford, *op. cit.*, p. 139.

have been not at all uncommon. Yet in the economy the force of competition in product differentiation among businessmen has been potent enough to overcome such resistance. In most areas competition has been free enough so that some producers have seen an opportunity to profit from promotion of innovations, and sooner or later, if these have proved worth while, competitors have been forced either to adopt them or to counter with something to match them. Many of the large, dominant industrial firms have supported research laboratories seeking new products and cost-reducing processes. But even when large companies have failed to produce promising new products or processes, or to launch them when perfected, capital has generally been available to new companies sooner or later to launch the profit-promising products or cost-reducing innovations developed outside of large industrial laboratories.

A few examples will be cited to illustrate some of the different types of situations found.

In the textile field, northern mills were slow to adopt the improved machines that were gradually developed. Receiverships and resulting low capital costs to succeeding operators tended to delay such adoption; yet their adoption by new, southern mills has brought competition which has gradually forced an increased use of improved technology.

In the motion picture industry the large, dominant companies were slow to adopt sound films even after the Western Electric Company had perfected processes sufficiently to insure successful operation. Their profits in silent pictures had been satisfactory, and they hesitated to threaten certain profit by the adoption of a radical and uncertain innovation which would upset existing operating methods. Yet Warner Brothers, then a relatively small company, was willing to gamble, and the success of sound films in a very short period forced their general adoption.[22]

Another example of a new product sponsored by a small company[23] to compete with established machines sold by two dominant and well-entrenched companies is a new process launched in 1940 for recording dictation and other verbal statements. This device makes use of radio principles and electric recording as contrasted with mechanical recording, which has heretofore been used in dictating machines

---

[22] Case of Warner Brothers Pictures, Inc., files of Harvard Business School.
[23] See "SoundScriber, A New Recorder by That Name Hits the Market," *Tide*, July 1, 1941, p. 30.

ever since Edison invented the phonograph. Should this new development prove commercially successful, it will represent technological advance sponsored by an outsider with an idea. Its chance to succeed in the end will depend on the opportunity for this new company to carry to potential buyers the story of what it considers an improvement by means of aggressive personal selling and advertising. Without such aggressive selling effort its chance of succeeding will be small indeed.

In short, the urge of entrepreneurs to profit from product improvement has brought in the United States an amazing application of scientific knowledge for improvement of products and processes, even though the free system may have many frictions. Whether another form of society with other incentives might remove some of the resistances met in the capitalistic system and might bring a more rapid application of scientific knowledge to production is a hypothetical supposition. It is not known how successful another form of society or economic organization would be in calling forth technological advance. Rarely today is the complaint of insufficient technology met. The present economy has provided a material welfare which has made possible generous support of institutions furthering pure research; in turn, industry has made wide use of such scientific knowledge to add to material welfare. Several investigations of recent years have shown the extent to which modern industry has established research laboratories to develop improvements. One of the most extensive of these was made by President Hoover's Committee on Recent Economic Changes.[24] The data given in the chapter on "Technological Changes in Manufacturing Industries" provide strong evidence of the constant drive under the free system towards greater productivity, the continuous increase in the output per worker. Similar evidence was presented to the T.N.E.C.[25] Thus it is seen that although the free economy has had resistances and frictions which operate against the adoption of technological advance and against investment in new enterprises involving improved products, yet the profit urge of enterprisers has been a force more than strong enough to overcome such resistances.

---

[24] National Bureau of Economic Research, *Recent Economic Changes*, ch. II.
[25] Testimony of Dr. Theodore J. Kreps before the Temporary National Economic Committee, *Proceedings of the Temporary National Economic Committee*, Vol. 13, April 8, 1940–May 13, 1940.

Economic and Social Problems Attending Technological Advance

While the growing, changing demand has called into being investment giving an ever-increasing productive economic machine from which has come a rising standard of living, it has also entailed difficult economic and social problems to which brief attention is called here, for it is well recognized that while the dynamic economy which advertising and selling helps to produce is in the main desirable, it has its shortcomings and drawbacks.

Neither investment in plants producing new products nor investment in labor or capital-saving machines has brought clear gain to the consuming group. Generally change has brought dislocations of one kind or another which have entailed loss. The study of demand has provided numerous examples. The automobile brought displacement of the horse and buggy industry, wagon makers, harness makers, livery keepers, and blacksmiths. The many and devious effects of the automobile upon consumers' living habits, and hence upon consumption habits in general, have adversely affected numerous industries. Mechanical refrigeration has made strides in part at the expense of the ice refrigerator business. Cigarette consumption has come largely at the expense of cigars and other types of tobacco. In the food field particularly have new developments brought loss to other food producers.

The losses from obsolescence, though they may sometimes seem large, are not to be overemphasized. Demand generally does not switch all at once, nor are products in use among either consumers or industrial users thrown at once on the scrap heap as innovations appear. Automobiles are resold several times before going into disuse; second-hand markets in mechanical refrigerators and radios have developed; old clothes are passed on to the less fortunate. Demand for old types of products generally continues for some time; consequently the plants producing them are not complete losses. Furthermore, the plants may be converted to new uses; some wagon and bicycle manufacturers became automobile manufacturers. Ice refrigerator manufacturers turned to the manufacture of mechanical refrigerators. Battery manufacturers became producers of radio receiving sets.

In so far as cost-reducing innovations are concerned, they must be able to pay their own way before old machines will be discarded, as was indicated in the evidence of practices governing adoption of new machines, quoted from the Hoover survey.[26]

Business management has undertaken the burden of being alert to change, of trying to foresee change and to make such shifts as will permit continuation of operation. Management has become more complex and difficult. Companies in many industries in stable, mature fields have not faced unduly hard problems in keeping up with technological change. Such has been true, for example, of the sheeting, sugar, and tobacco products industries. In contrast, however, some industrial firms have found it necessary to look for stability in change. Only through attention to product research have they been able to achieve success. New products have been needed, not simply for expansion but to replace products whose demand had fallen away. Such, for example, was true of the pharmaceutical firm previously mentioned, which dropped 15 to 20 items a year from its line, with the result that in 1940 only a small proportion of its 450 items had been manufactured and marketed for as long as 15 years. Few businesses today can succeed without careful attention to the changes that affect them. Alertness to change has become a prime requisite of good management.

In spite of losses and dislocations that have been incurred in the process of change and growth, the balance, so far as consumer incomes and rising standard of living are concerned, has clearly rested in favor of change. While there is uncertainty as to whether productive capacity may have decreased during the 1930 decade, the secular trend since the advent of the Industrial Revolution has been constantly upward.[27] As previously indicated, only as the productive machine increases may there be hope for a high degree of material welfare.

The Effect of Stability on Investment

Advertising serves in another way as an indirect stimulant to investment, namely, through such promise as it gives to an entrepreneur of building a stability of demand for his enterprise. The prospect of stability in an industry and in an enterprise increases the outlook for profit and thus leads to a willingness to invest. Although investors

---

[26] Page 703.
[27] Statistical measurements of production increase will be found in such volumes as: F. C. Mills, *op. cit.*, ch. I.
E. G. Nourse and associates, *op. cit.*
National Resources Committee, *The Structure of the American Economy.*

may be attracted to a new industry which gives promise of expansion, investment is made slowly until the promise of stability from growing primary demand has been established as a result of the aggressive selling efforts of the first pioneers. Moreover, as was indicated in Chapter XIX, many business managements look with favor on advertising because they believe that a business with well-established brand preference among consumers promises greater stability and greater profits than it would yield without such preference. The establishment of such stability is a positive influence to investment.

In still another way advertising has had an influence on investment. In contributing to the size of individual companies it has had an indirect influence in permitting the establishment of product research, which has become customary with large aggressive industrial concerns. Such product research departments have been an important force in bringing increased investment needed to produce the new or improved products.

Advertising and Aggressive Selling Costs as Growth Costs

In the preceding pages the thesis has been presented that advertising and aggressive selling have played roles of considerable consequence in increasing the production of goods and services. In the long run these selling forces have been one means by which people have developed the willingness to consume which has been essential to the growth of the industrial system. In turn, many entrepreneurs have relied upon these selling tools to make investment in their enterprises profitable. Particularly in the case of new inventions and important product differentiations, advertising and selling often have been used to develop a demand essential to increased investment, upon which increases in productivity, consumer income, and a rising standard of living depend. The force of aggressive selling has played an important part in bringing about the advance of the economy from one level to another.

This hypothesis leads to a rejection of the view that aggressive selling and advertising have had no effect in creating a net additional demand. Further, it supports the view that advertising and selling costs have not been merely normal costs of a wasteful type, but that in some immeasurable degree, those costs, particularly when devoted to new products and to new differentiations, should be looked upon as growth costs, costs incurred by entrepreneurs in raising the level of economic activity. From the standpoint of individual enterprise, they represent costs to establish a business and, like research expenditures incurred in developing a new product, they contribute to the growth of an industry. They are outlays made not to maintain an equilibrium between the forces of supply and demand for a product but to facilitate investment necessary to establish an industry and to reach a new equilibrium between the forces of supply and demand at a higher level.

The Character of Growth Costs

Companies which have incurred innovation or growth costs of various types include these costs in their prices and seek by various means to recover their outlays. The costs of product research are generally treated as overhead costs which must be recovered over a period of time in the prices of the products sold, particularly the new items produced for the market. A considerable part of the high price of newly-launched articles is frequently attributable to the loading for research. But all research costs cannot be loaded onto a product at once, for to attempt too quick recovery of such costs would result in prices which would make entry difficult. The research costs are often allocated over the sales of several years. Moreover, the organized research of an industrial concern entails risk. Part of its research effort usually is unproductive; either no product improvements suitable for the market are forthcoming, or the products developed are market failures. Yet the business venture hopes to recover all its research costs and, if feasible, loads its successful products with the research costs of its failures. The costs of these research failures are part of the price of progress and are to be included with the costs of research successes, as growth costs.

On top of product research costs must come aggressive selling costs incurred for gaining demand for new products. Here again, the aggressive selling costs for launching new products are often so large as related to sales that they prevent a net profit during the early years of operation. Examples of the practice of incurring large costs in product developing and early marketing, and of seeking to recoup these over a period of time, have been numerous in the case material studied. A good illustration is found in cases of pharmaceutical concerns which, in view of the fast pace at which medical knowledge is progressing, find it necessary to spend large sums in research to perfect new items. But these concerns have innovation expenditures other than those incurred in perfecting the new merchandise. They find it essential to promote their new medicines aggressively through salesmen and through advertising to physicians. A considerable part of this selling expense, particularly in the early stages of marketing, is analogous to the expenditure made for research. The expenditure in early periods is large as related to volume sold, and new products often are unprofitable for considerable periods until demand is built. Yet such outlays are a necessary part of the business process if the concerns are to profit from the new items which they have perfected and launched on the market. The prices of pharmaceuticals generally contain wide gross margins which the manufacturers justify in part by their innovation costs, including both the product research costs and the aggressive selling costs incurred. Frequently these costs have to be borne by relatively small volumes of merchandise.

Going concerns usually incur marketing losses on new products which prove to be market failures. In some instances they may hope to recover these losses, in part at least, through the prices which they receive for successful products. Thus, the marketing costs of new product failures, like the costs of unsuccessful product research, may be looked upon as a part of the costs of progress.

This illustration of growth costs is similar in principle to what is found in industry after industry. Numerous examples of the costs of product research undertaken to find desirable new products on the market have been cited in preceding chapters. In turn, demand for these product innovations has been built through aggressive selling and advertising. Automobiles, mechanical refrigerators, the new type of blown soap represented by Rinso, creamed vegetable shortening, new types of grocery specialties, such as puffed cereals and shredded wheat are examples which have been described.

The Entry of Imitators

Not all companies undertake such growth costs, and consequently those which do not are frequently in a position to set prices without inclusion of such costs. Every successful product has its imitators. In many instances these imitators incur relatively small product research costs. They benefit from the research efforts of the pioneers. Likewise they do not take on any of the costs of building consumer acceptance for the type of product which they sell. Generally they come into the market with a price appeal made possible in part by the fact that they have incurred little or no innovation costs. In short, the growth costs incurred in establishing an industry are not a part of the normal costs at which an equilibrium is established in the industry.

Such imitators, entering the market after the original concerns through aggressive selling and advertising have built a wide consumer acceptance for the product, depend upon the elasticity of demand built thereby to get needed sales volume. The entry of imitators and the elasticity of demand which they exploit are made possible by the aggressive efforts of the innovators. As was pointed out in Chapter XVI, advertising which has brought wide acceptance for a product frequently has had the effect not only of shifting the demand curve to the right, but also of changing its shape. By making a product wantable it may make a lowering of price by certain sellers highly effective in bringing a large number of purchasers into the market, particularly consumers in low income brackets to whom low price is an effective appeal. Thus the aggressive selling and advertising of companies which have entered the market early may pave the way for imitators who find their profit opportunities in making a bid for sales volume on a price basis.

Numerous examples of the practice of imitation were found in case material, and illustrations may be drawn from material that has been previously discussed. For example, private branders, with few exceptions, have been imitators. It has been pointed out that private branders generally have placed their brands on products for which demand has been well-established and for which entry has been relatively easy. Gradually they have worked into specialty product fields after demand in such fields has been established, even though manufacturers may have clearly established brand leadership there. On several occasions in comments to field investigators, they gave recognition of the fact that the advertising and promotional efforts of manufacturers help them to establish and maintain a demand for the types of products which they sell under their private brands. Thus a chain grocer recognized that sales of his brand of corn flakes were made possible because of demand created by the aggressive selling of corn flakes by certain manufacturers. Again, the seller of a private brand of electrical refrigerator recognized that he benefited from a demand established by the aggressive efforts of companies which had cultivated the market before he entered it.

A particularly clear example of the avoidance of growth costs is found in the case of so-called style piracy in the fields of fashion merchandise. Some concerns in those fields spend considerable sums in designing their merchandise in the hope of profiting through having some of their styles successful. Their profit depends generally on their receiving wide gross margins which reimburse them for their designing costs. On the other hand, certain concerns operate with little or no design expense and rely largely on copying styles which they know to be popular. They offer these imitations on a price basis to stores which appeal to clientele wanting fashion merchandise at a low price.

The Effort to Recover Growth Costs

In cases such as that just cited and in most instances in which manufacturers have incurred innovation costs of one kind or another, they seek to protect themselves in some way to make sure that they recover not only their own growth costs but profit from their enterprise. Without great success, producers of fashion goods have sought protection through design patents and through trying to prevent imitators from seeing their designs until the goods have been placed on the retail market. In other fields manufacturers have sought to get protection through patents on the design of their products or on the processes by which they are made. In many instances the innovators have relied upon advertising and aggressive selling to build a reputation for their brands which might give consumer preference that would afford some protection against imitators. Advertising often exhorts consumers to avoid imitations and to ask for the original. Early and aggressive development of a market often provides protection against later entrants. For example, the dominant position gained by Bayer in the aspirin field has undoubtedly been a great aid to that company and has been one of the factors accounting for its ability to make large sales at prices substantially above those of later comers.

These various examples of efforts to protect outlay in growth costs makes clear the significance of the statement by Professor Richard S. Meriam, previously quoted in Chapter VI: "If the nature of growth costs is clearly understood, the paradoxical proposition that a certain amount of monopoly is a necessary condition of economic progress is seen to be no nonsense." In other words, if the prospect of recovering growth or innovation costs is present, enterprises are more likely to take the risk of incurring such costs than when such prospect is absent. The prospect for the recovery of such costs is enhanced if the innovator has in view the protection afforded by presence, in some degree, of monopoly elements, such as patents or a firmly established brand preference. In short, the chance to have such protection in some degree is a stimulant to the investment upon which increased national income depends.

As was pointed out in a previous chapter, the imitator who rides in on the coat-tails of the innovator performs a real social service. He serves as a means of helping to hold down competition in advertising and other price forms by which some innovators hope to keep on benefiting from such improvements as they have given to the market. At the same time, the innovator also should be given credit for the social service which he performs; he develops new product forms which give improvement and he builds for these products a public acceptance and demand which calls into being the investment made by himself and which paves the way for the investment of the imitators.

CHAPTER XXV

THE RELATION OF ADVERTISING TO CYCLICAL FLUCTUATIONS

THIS chapter deals with the investigation of the relation of advertising to the cyclical fluctuations in business activity which have characterized the economy for centuries. Whatever part advertising and aggressive selling may have played in helping to bring into existence a highly productive economic machine under the system of free enterprise, unfortunately this machine has not operated at maximum capacity even in the best of times; and worse still, output periodically has fallen far below productive capacity. Consequently there have been the undesirable fluctuations in production of merchandise and services shown in the figures of national income in Table 139. In 1929, average per capita income was $702, as expressed in 1926 prices; in 1932 this dropped to $493. Men who have wanted to work have not been able to obtain employment. Machines and factories which could produce commodities needed by consumers have operated far below capacity. In agriculture, land has been left uncultivated and commodities for which there has been no effective demand have been destroyed. The magnitude of loss is indicated in the following quotation:

Had we made full utilization of our productive resources in the years from 1922 to 1929 the income of the American people would have been increased to the extent of approximately 113 billion dollars, or an average of 14 billion dollars a year. In the four years 1930 to 1933 the loss of potential income aggregated something like 135 billion dollars (1929 prices) or approximately 34 billion dollars a year. In addition, the expansion of productive capacity, upon which depend higher standards of living in the future, was held in abeyance.

The magnitude and significance of the lost, or unrealized, income of the first four years of the depression may best be made clear by certain comparisons. The amount (135 billion dollars) represents a value in terms of goods and services equal to nearly 30 per cent of the entire accumulated wealth of the nation. It is four times the value of the nation's farms; nearly six times the value of the nation's factories; 14 times the value of all mercantile establishments; and more than 25 times the value of the 26,500,000 automobiles registered in 1929.[1]

[1] H. G. Moulton, *Income and Economic Progress* (Washington, The Brookings Institution, 1935), pp. 27–28.

It is generally agreed among economists and social students that the greatest shortcoming of the free economy and the most severe threat to continuance of its way of life rests in the severe cyclical fluctuations which periodically have disrupted economic life and brought widespread discontent.

The Relative Importance of Advertising as a Causal Factor in Cyclical Fluctuations

It is beyond the scope of this study to outline the possible theories for the failure of the economy to operate at full capacity or to appraise the possible remedial measures.[2] Each of the many writers on cycles usually stresses one or more sets of causal factors. Among others the following have been emphasized by various writers as causes of cycles: wars, discoveries, inventions, and other "accidents"; changes in population; oversaving; underconsumption; the elastic commercial banking system; the lack of correspondence in saving and investment; periodic overinvestment by the capitalistic system; the variations in activity induced by the profit motive; maladjustments occurring in the exchange of goods; the psychological factor of overconfidence and lack of confidence; and deficiency in demand as it affects investment. It appears safe to conclude that the cycle can be ascribed to no single cause. "A broadly eclectic theory giving latitude to the operation of several causes in varying proportions at different times offers a considerably more realistic interpretation of the facts; there is at least a strong presumption that the economic universe is a pluralistic one.[3] It suffices here to point out that in none of the theories of causes have advertising and selling been named. Accordingly, instead of seeking to

---

[2] Many volumes may be consulted for discussions regarding possible explanations of business cycles and remedies therefor. A classification of cycle theories with comments thereon will be found in the following sources:

Business and Modern Society, "Business Cycle Theories: Some Comments for the Layman," by M. P. McNair; "The Adjustment to Instability," by S. H. Slichter (Cambridge, Harvard University Press, 1938).

S. H. Slichter, *Towards Stability* (New York, Henry Holt and Company, 1934).

J. P. Wernette, *The Control of Business Cycles* (New York, Farrar & Rinehart, 1940).

A. H. Hansen, *Business-Cycle Theory: Its Development and Present Status* (Boston, Ginn and Company, 1927).

W. C. Mitchell, *Business Cycles: The Problem and Its Setting* (New York, National Bureau of Economic Research, Inc., 1927).

Gottfried Haberler, *Prosperity and Depression: A Theoretical Analysis of Cyclical Movements* (Geneva, League of Nations, 1937).

W. M. Persons, "Theories of Business Fluctuations," *Quarterly Journal of Economics*, November, 1926, pp. 94–128.

[3] An article by M. P. McNair, "Business Cycle Theories: Some Comments for the Layman," in *Business and Modern Society*, p. 231.

relate advertising to various intricate theories of fluctuation, the purpose of this chapter is to try to determine the part which advertising has played towards either accentuating or alleviating fluctuations.

Although it is not generally classed as a cause of cycles, advertising may have some direct effect upon the size of cyclical fluctuations in two ways. First, as a form of business activity employing men and material, advertising may either accentuate or alleviate cyclical swings, according to the extent to which it is used in good times and in bad times. Second, as a force to influence the demand for products, it may either reduce or increase fluctuations in sales and thus in business activity, according to whether the volume used is in inverse or direct relationship to cyclical swings. Accordingly, attention is directed first to the relationship between advertising and business activity.

The Relationship of Advertising to Various Indices of Business Activity

There is no index of advertising activity which includes all types of advertising expenditure in its composition with which to compare the swings of business activity. The index most widely used and one having a wide base is that constructed by Dr. L. D. H. Weld, generally known as the *Printers' Ink* Index of General Advertising Activity. It is based upon the linage figures for a substantial part of the advertising carried in farm papers, magazines, and newspapers; upon time costs of the leading radio chains; and upon the expenditures for approximately 50% of the outdoor advertising of the country. It does not include linage for industrial publications or for direct advertising, which account for a substantial part of total advertising expenditure of producers of consumers' goods and industrial goods. All in all, however, it is a good indicator of fluctuations in advertising activity as a whole, because expenditures for advertising consumers' products greatly outweigh expenditures for industrial goods advertising, and the index contains a substantial part of total advertising activity for consumers' goods.

In the course of the investigation, this index of general advertising activity was compared with the following indices which reflect business activity: the Federal Reserve Index of Industrial Production; the Index of Production and Trade of the Federal Reserve Bank of New York; the Index of Production of Consumer Goods of the Federal Reserve Bank of New York; the Federal Reserve Board Index of

Department Store Sales; the U. S. Trade Barometer, published in Dun's Review; and the Standard Statistics Index of Bank Debits.[4] Since the comparisons among the various indices point to the same general conclusions with regard to the relation of advertising activity either to the fluctuations in production of consumers' and industrial goods or to the flow of trade, only two of the comparisons made are discussed here.

Chart V (p. 718) shows the relationship between the Index of General Advertising Activity, and the Index of Production and Trade of the Federal Reserve Bank of New York, which is a good indicator of the changes in business activity generally. The Index of Production and Trade reflects not only the production of industrial and consumers' goods, but also the activities involved in the distribution of these products, such as car loadings and various retail sales series. In addition, it includes miscellaneous services, such as communication, railway travel, postal receipts, and magazine and newspaper advertising, the latter two weighted but lightly in the whole.

Advertising activity and industrial activity, as measured by these indices, in general have fluctuated together. Changes in the upward or downward trend of industrial conditions usually have preceded changes in advertising activity by several months, although this relationship has not held true invariably.

All the indices of industrial production studied showed this tendency for production changes to precede advertising changes. Such a relationship is in accord with budgeting practice of business firms, as

---

[4] From time to time Dr. L. D. H. Weld has compared his Index of General Advertising Activity with various indices reflecting business activity of one sort or another. Among the articles showing such relationships are the following:

"Newspaper Advertising Volume as Influenced by Sales of Department Stores," *Printers' Ink*, July 26, 1940, p. 19 (Index of Newspaper Advertising vs. Federal Reserve Board Index of Department Store Sales, 1921–1940).

"Advertising Upturn Indicated by Banking Operations: A P. I. Index Study," *Printers' Ink*, September 27, 1940, p. 23 (General Index vs. Standard Statistics Index of Bank Debits, 1922–1940; General Index vs. bank deposits, 1922–1939; General Index vs. volume of commercial loans, 1922–1940).

"Advertising for First Quarter Disappoints, but Pick-up for Year Seems Likely," *Printers' Ink*, April 27, 1939, p. 21 (General Index vs. U. S. Trade Barometer, 1928–1939; General Index vs. Federal Reserve Board Index of Industrial Production, 1922–1939; General Index vs. production of consumer goods, 1928–1938).

"Electric Power Production and Advertising," *Printers' Ink Monthly*, February, 1937 (General Index vs. electric power production, 1922–1936).

"Chains and Advertising," *Printers' Ink*, July 22, 1937, p. 76 (General Index vs. variety store sales, 1929–1936).

"Advertising and Retail Trade," *Printers' Ink*, August 12, 1937, p. 49 (General Index vs. retail trade, 1929–1936; Newspaper Index vs. retail trade, 1929–1936; Magazine Index vs. retail trade, 1929–1936, Radio Index vs. retail trade, 1929–1936, General Index vs. department store sales, 1922–1937).

CHART V

Relationship between Advertising and Business Activity Generally, 1919–40

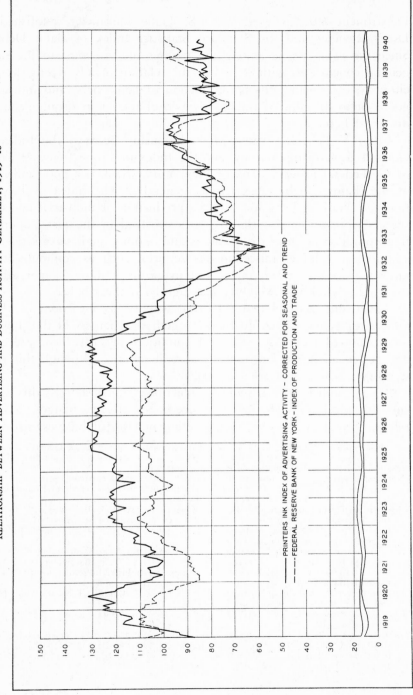

PRINTERS INK INDEX OF ADVERTISING ACTIVITY – CORRECTED FOR SEASONAL AND TREND
FEDERAL RESERVE BANK OF NEW YORK – INDEX OF PRODUCTION AND TRADE

will be discussed shortly. It is counter, however, to an impression which was found among some businessmen that advertising change preceded general business change.[5]

The Index of General Advertising Activity correlates even more closely with indices reflecting the flow of consumers' goods trade than with indices of industrial production. This correlation is to be expected, since the index of advertising relates almost solely to consumer advertising and advertising is adjusted to sales. Chart VI, which furnishes the basis for the above comparison, shows the relationship between the Index of General Advertising Activity and the Federal Reserve Bank Index of Department Store Sales. Department store sales in themselves are too small a segment of retail sales to be a fully satisfactory reflector of the flow of retail goods and services; yet they indicate the general trend of retail sales. It will be noted that there is a very close relationship between the advertising index and that of department store sales. The same close relationship was found to exist between the index of advertising and the U. S. Trade Barometer, published in *Dun's Review,* an index constructed to reflect the flow of trade through commercial channels, which is composed of the following four factors: bank debits, department store sales, new car sales, and life insurance sales. It will be noted that changes in advertising expenditures do not tend to lag behind changes in retail sales, as they do changes in industrial production. The changes in advertising activity as shown in this graph sometimes precede and sometimes follow changes in retail sales, but all in all the two move remarkably closely together. Such a relationship was true likewise of the change in advertising activity and the flow of trade as reflected in the U. S. Trade Barometer.

Advertising Budgeting Practice as Related to Cyclical Fluctuation

The fluctuation of advertising expenditure in the manner indicated above is to be expected in view of the advertising budgeting practices of business organizations. Advertising tends to be closely related to sales outlook. Sales outlook for any product or service is influenced largely by business conditions. Advertising expenditures, like other

---

[5] The conclusion that advertising change tends to precede change in general business activity was reached by W. L. Crum in his study, *Advertising Fluctuations, Seasonal and Cyclical* (Chicago, A. W. Shaw Company, 1927), in which he related advertising linage of magazines and newspapers to bank debits.

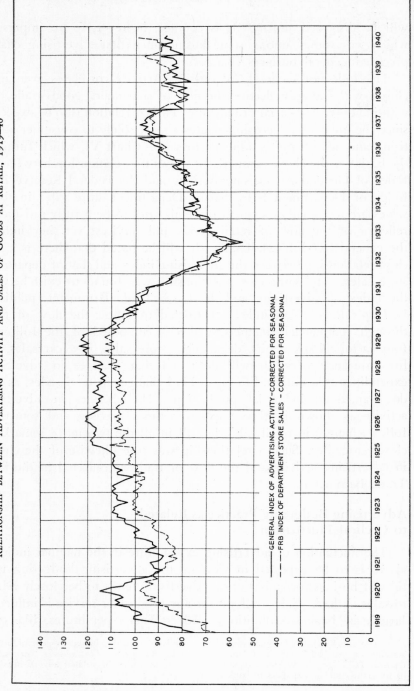

CHART VI

RELATIONSHIP BETWEEN ADVERTISING ACTIVITY AND SALES OF GOODS AT RETAIL, 1919–40

——— GENERAL INDEX OF ADVERTISING ACTIVITY – CORRECTED FOR SEASONAL

- - - - FRB INDEX OF DEPARTMENT STORE SALES – CORRECTED FOR SEASONAL

expenditures, are ordinarily adjusted from time to time in accordance with current sales behavior and the probable trend. The extent to which sales, and accordingly advertising, are affected by cyclical swings, varies with types of products. For example, foods do not suffer such wide fluctuations as consumer durable goods, while large installation equipment in the industrial product group may suffer from extreme fluctuations.

The extent to which business firms are guided by current sales in their advertising expenditures is shown by various studies of the bases for budgeting appropriations. For example, the following is a summary of the bases upon which 1935 advertising budgets of 215 national advertisers of consumers' goods were determined as reported by the Association of National Advertisers: [6]

CATEGORY NUMBER	BASIS OF 1935 ADVERTISING BUDGET	NUMBER OF COMPANIES	PER CENT OF TOTAL
1	A percentage of 1934 actual sales............	19	9
2	A percentage of 1935 estimated sales..........	65	30
3	A percentage of 1934 sales and 1935 estimated sales	28	13
4	A percentage of sales (year not given)........	5	2
5	Estimated amount needed for adequate campaign	48	22
6	Estimated amount for adequate campaign and percentage of 1934 sales..................	2	1
7	Estimated amount for adequate campaign and percentage of 1935 estimated sales..........	20	9
8	Estimated amount for adequate campaign and percentage of 1934 and 1935 estimated sales..	9	4
9	A certain amount per unit of sale............	4	2
10	Other methods	15	7

Of the 215 companies, 54% (categories 1 to 4 inclusive) stated that their appropriations were a predetermined percentage of sales, either of the past year or the year of the budget. Another 16% (categories 6 to 9 inclusive) were guided in part by a percentage of sales or a fixed amount per unit sale. Even in the cases in which budgets were based in whole or in part on a so-called task basis, i.e., the amount needed for an adequate campaign, it is evident that advertising appropriations would necessarily be adjusted in accordance with sales receipts.

The budgets of these companies were made up for relatively short periods and were adjusted in accordance with changing outlook. With

[6] Association of National Advertisers, Inc., *A Survey of 299 National Advertising Budgets, 1934–1935*, p. 84. A further report on advertising appropriation methods will be found in "How 150 Figure the Advertising Budget," *Printers' Ink*, April 15, 1937, p. 6.

few exceptions the advertising budgets were made up a year in advance. Replies from approximately half of the companies indicated, however, that periodic revision of the budget in accordance with changing conditions was the rule. Of those answering, the A.N.A. report states that the largest number bring up the matter of revision every three months and others semiannually, monthly, and at other intervals, i.e., weekly or irregularly.

A survey by the National Industrial Advertisers' Association gives similar evidence of budgeting practice for industrial advertisers in 1939. Replies from 383 industrial advertisers showed 28% using a fixed percentage of sales with the remainder apparently adopting a varying percentage based on judgment of conditions, as shown in the following summary:[7]

BASIS FOR DETERMINATION OF ADVERTISING BUDGET	NUMBER OF COMPANIES	PER-CENTAGE
As a fixed percentage of		
(a) Expected net sales volume for year ahead............	76	20
(b) Expected net sales volume of previous year..........	31	8
As a varying percentage, depending on conditions of		
(c) Expected net sales volume for year ahead............	54	14
(d) Net sales volume of previous year...................	24	6
On a lump sum basis set by..............................		
(e) Management alone	66	17
(f) Advertising department in conference with management.	132	35
	383	100%

Approximately 80% of the companies made up their budgets annually, while 5% made them quarterly, 5% semiannually, and 5% monthly. Over 50% of the companies reported that they made adjustments every 6 months; nearly 30% made theirs quarterly; while 20% made theirs monthly.

The Budgeting Practice of Retailers

Retail advertisers likewise have fallen into the habit of guiding advertising appropriations by percentages of sales evolved out of past experience. For example, department stores have customary percentages of expenditure for different departments. The reports of the Controllers' Congress of the National Retail Dry Goods Association show that the average percentages spent upon particular departments from year to year, while not fixed, move in a narrow range.

---

[7] National Industrial Advertisers Association, Inc., *A National Survey of Industrial Advertising Budgets for 1939*, p. 13.

The Variation of Advertising Expenditures for Specific Products

The actual amounts of traceable advertising expended for specific products, whose demand was studied in Part II of this volume, and for a few other products, show the degree to which advertising has been controlled by cyclical swings. They reflect as well the varying effects of these swings upon expenditure for different types of products. Table 140 summarizes the expenditure behavior for these products for the period 1929–1939. In this table, traceable advertising expenditures for 1929 equal 100.

TABLE 140

INDICES OF VOLUME OF TRACEABLE ADVERTISING EXPENDITURES BY MANUFACTURERS
FOR VARIOUS TYPES OF CONSUMERS' PRODUCTS, 1929–1939
(1929=100)

YEAR	CIGA-RETTES	CIGARS	SHEETS	SHOES	DENTI-FRICES	SUGAR	RE-FRIGER-ATORS	RADIOS	PAS-SENGER CARS*	TRUCKS*	ORANGES	WAL-NUTS†
1929....	100	100	100	100	100	100	100	100	100	100	100	100
1930....	125	100	60	62	100	102	100	66	86	97	60	99
1931....	182	91	43	80	92	95	123	26	72	76	130	77
1932....	136	55	34	40	77	56	82	14	42	34	68	175
1933....	132	37	36	30	78	48	52	13	31	35	58	80
1934....	152	39	50	44	79	51	67	18	40	57	84	77
1935....	140	36	56	49	79	25	77	22	51	72	145	......
1936....	156	44	64	50	87	26	74	25	62	91	62	......
1937....	147	44	94	69	116	29	89	33	59	88	111	......
1938....	130	41	83	53	90	31	45	14	47	69	143	......
1939....	115	46	82	54	103	19	56	8	67	87	80	......

* Magazine advertising only.
† Crop year 1929–1930=100.

Sources: Based on tables of traceable expenditures shown in Chapter VII (not including radio). The radio figures were compiled in the same manner as those of the other tables. Automobiles and Trucks are based on magazine expenditures only, as shown in Curtis Publishing Company, Advertising Department, *Leading Advertisers* (Philadelphia).

In the case of cigarettes an expanding demand maintained sales at so high a level during the depression that advertising expenditures for every year were above those of 1929, a behavior in marked contrast to that for every other product. In fact, advertising for cigarettes was built to an all-time high in 1931, almost two years after the advent of the depression. The expenditures were 182% of those of 1929. Although there was a material decrease from this high in later years, the totals still were well above those of 1929.

Cigar advertising shows a more marked effect from depression. Expenditures held up in 1930, but thereafter the decline was rapid, with 1933 expenditures only 37% of those of 1939. In the case of sheets and shoes, semidurable products, the declines were rapid and extreme. Depression expenditures were about one-third those of the boom year. In contrast to shoes and sheets, dentifrice advertising showed no such extreme contraction, because prices in dentifrices did not fall, nor did sales fall to such an extent. Advertising, the main prop of dentifrice marketing, was maintained at a fairly constant percentage of sales. The low point in 1932 was 77% of 1929 expenditures.

Sugar advertising fell markedly after 1930, nor was there a corresponding recovery in 1937 and 1939 as in the other fields. This failure to recover was probably accounted for by the fact that the use of advertising for sugar represented a marginal expenditure. Managements did not find it hard to dispense with this particular expense.

Refrigerators provide an example of a durable, consumers' product which ordinarily is extremely affected by business recession. Consumers will more readily undertake a major expenditure for such a product in times when income is certain than in periods of uncertainty. Moreover, as previously noted, the reduced incomes of depression years require so large a percentage of the family budget for nondurable necessities and rent that the demand for durable goods generally falls away. Consequently the expanding sales of refrigerators during the period 1929–1937 was unusual, although the demand came only with material price reductions. The effect of depression upon advertising expenditure is, nevertheless, evident. Expenditures in 1933 were only approximately one-half of those of 1929 and 1930. Yet the fact that refrigerators enjoyed an expanding demand resulted in a far smaller decrease in advertising expenditure for this durable product than for other such products which were not in the expanding demand stage.

A clear contrast is found in the behavior of the advertising of radios, which by 1929 had been bought by a substantial percentage of American homes. The fluctuations in advertising expenditures for radio were far greater during the period 1929–1939 than they were for refrigerators. Expenditures for radio in 1932 and 1933 were only a sixth of what they were in 1929. They fell to even lower levels in 1938. Refrigerator advertising held up relatively well; yet for 1938 it shows the extent to which managements will contract their advertising expenditures when demand fails to develop. The business recession of 1938 gave the expanding refrigerator business its first sharp setback. Corresponding to this loss in sales volume, 1938 advertising expenditures were cut to one-half those of 1937.

A further contrast with refrigerator advertising is shown in the advertising of passenger cars and trucks. The advertising index for these products is based solely on magazine advertising and hence is not so satisfactory as the broader base for the other products. Accordingly, the index may be subject to greater error, but it serves to reflect the wide variation in the advertising both of a durable, consumers' product, in the case of passenger cars, and also of an industrial goods accessory, in the case of trucks. For both products, magazine advertising at the depth of the depression was only one-third as great as that of the peak year, 1929. Both, likewise, showed a marked setback during the sharp recession of 1938.

While the indices of traceable advertising expenditures for oranges and walnuts reflect in part the effect of cyclical swings, they reflect even more the effect of wide variation in size of crop from year to year.

The Adjustment of Retailers' Advertising to Cyclical Fluctuation

The manner in which retailers adjusted their advertising expenditures to business conditions subsequent to 1929 is shown in Table 141, which gives the median figures of newspaper space costs and total publicity costs for department stores of various sizes. Department stores did not keep their newspaper space expenditures or their total

TABLE 141

DEPARTMENT STORE NEWSPAPER SPACE AND TOTAL PUBLICITY COSTS AS PERCENTAGE OF SALES, 1930–1939

YEAR	\$500,000 TO \$1,000,000		\$1,000,000 TO \$2,000,000		\$2,000,000 TO \$5,000,000		\$5,000,000 TO \$10,000,000		OVER \$10,000,000	
	Newspaper Space Cost, %	Total Publicity Cost, %	Newspaper Space Cost, %	Total Publicity Cost, %	Newspaper Space Cost, %	Total Publicity Cost, %	Newspaper Space Cost, %	Total Publicity Cost, %	Newspaper Space Cost, %	Total Publicity Cost, %
1930	2.7	4.1	2.7	4.8	2.9	4.6	3.3	4.8	3.3	4.6
1931	3.1	5.1	3.1	5.0	3.5	5.3	3.7	5.6	4.0	5.3
1932	3.1	5.0	3.3	5.3	3.7	5.9	3.7	5.6	4.2	6.1
1933	3.1	4.9	3.1	4.6	3.7	5.7	3.4	5.7	4.5	6.2
1934	2.5	4.3	3.1	4.7	4.4	5.6	4.0	6.0	4.2	6.2
1935	2.6	4.3	3.2	4.7	3.6	5.4	3.8	5.8	3.8	5.7
1936	2.8	4.6	3.0	5.0	3.4	5.0	3.8	5.6	3.8	5.7
1937	2.6	4.5	3.0	5.1	3.4	5.2	3.5	5.5	4.0	5.8
1938	2.7	4.7	3.2	5.4	3.6	5.3	3.8	5.8	4.3	5.9
1939	2.7	4.7	2.9	5.3	3.3	5.1	3.3	5.5	3.7	5.3

Source: Annual reports of the Controllers' Congress of the National Retail Dry Goods Association, 1930–1939.

space expenditures at a fixed percentage of sales. During the years of deepest depression, 1931, 1932, and 1933, these costs were somewhat higher on a percentage basis than during the years of relatively good business, such as 1930 and 1937. Yet the decrease in actual sales volume was so extreme[8] that the slightly larger percentages of expenditure gave a much reduced expenditure in dollars.

Theory That Advertising Is a Mitigator of Fluctuation

During the 1920's and since then, the theory has been advanced that advertising could be used by business organizations as a mitigator of cyclical fluctuation. This possibility has been discussed not only by economists but also by business executives;[9] references to it have been frequent in the trade press. The effect of depression is to alter the demand curve by moving it to the left. The objective of advertising and aggressive selling is to shift the curve to the right. Theoretically, then, aggressive selling might be used to offset the effect of depression.

One case was obtained in which a business management in 1927 stated that it had been committed since 1914 to a policy of regulating its selling and advertising activities inversely to swings in business conditions.[10] In harmony with this practice the management said that it had adopted a policy of avoiding expansion of its plants to meet the sales volume that might be attained in boom times through sales pressure. Instead it held capacity at a level for which sales could readily be secured in normal times and through intensive sales effort in depression times. The management even went so far as to explore the possibility of setting up a liquid reserve during periods of boom to serve as an advertising and promotional fund in periods of depression, but it had not carried out such action. However, in the extreme

---

[8] The Federal Reserve Bank Index of Department Store Sales showed a drop in sales from 111 in 1929 to 67 in 1933 (1923–1925=100), *Federal Reserve Bulletin,* September, 1941, p. 917.

[9] R. S. Vaile discussed the possibilities of the use of advertising to reduce cyclical swings in his *Economics of Advertising* (New York, The Ronald Press Company, 1927). Among numerous articles directed to businessmen, which have dealt with the subject, the following are more or less typical:
"Advertising Continuity," *Printers' Ink,* April 28, 1938, p. 11.
A. T. Falk, *Advertising as a Stabilizing Force in Business* (Bulletin of Advertising Federation of America, 1931 Series No. 5).
F. E. Fehlman, "Does Advertising Pay During a Depression?", *Advertising & Selling,* May 24, 1934, p. 18.
Forging Ahead During Depression (press release of U. S. Departmnet of Commerce), November 27, 1931.

[10] N. H. Borden, *Problems in Advertising* (3d ed., New York, McGraw-Hill Book Company, Inc., 1937), case of Ettrick Company (A) and (B), pp. 377 and 384.

depression following 1929, the company had to drop its avowed policy of applying selling pressure inversely to business conditions. Like other organizations, the management found it necessary to adjust its advertising and selling appropriations to the greatly reduced sales volume of those periods, and this adjustment resulted in considerable retrenchment in selling activities.

In 1927 Professor Roland S. Vaile made a study of the sales behavior of over 200 companies,[11] which followed apparently different advertising practices during the period 1920–1924; some increased advertising during the period, others were nonadvertisers, while others decreased their advertising. The actual sales of the nonadvertising firms were 20% lower in 1921 than in 1920. In contrast this slump was only 12% for firms which increased their advertising, but 26% for those which reduced advertising. In this study Vaile based his estimates of volume of advertising on magazine expenditures alone, a somewhat inadequate base in view of the fact that the use of advertising media by individual firms often varies markedly from year to year, particularly in periods of depression. Moreover, he was unable to follow results through to profit; nor did he have evidence regarding changing merchandising and pricing policies that may have accompanied these differing advertising practices. Hence he recognized that his results as a guide to executive policy could not be considered other than tentative and connotative.

Lack of Business Adherence to the Theory of Mitigation

Whatever theory may be expounded with regard to the desirability of business management's adjusting advertising and aggressive selling efforts in such a way as to reduce cyclical swing, such a theory has meant little in practice, for as pointed out in the statistics of expenditure, the behavior of business managements as a whole has been the opposite. Businessmen whose industries are subjected to cyclical fluctuation generally have felt it necessary to adjust their operating policies thereto. The more their products have been affected by fluctuations in sales, the more they have found it advisable, in order to protect profits or to avoid losses, to adjust selling expense to those sales. As indicated above, companies selling durable products, whose purchases are postponable in character, have felt it advantageous to reduce their

---

[11] R. S. Vaile, *op. cit.*, p. 121.

expenditures even more than companies selling products whose use does not permit much postponement of purchase. Even more have industrial advertisers found it desirable to adjust their advertising expenditures with the swings of sales volume. For example, case material indicates that companies selling heavy installation goods have generally concluded that it is unwise from an operating standpoint to undertake heavier than normal advertising and personal selling expenditures during periods of extreme depression, when a so-called "vacuum" market exists for their products. In their opinion, such efforts would be unproductive in sales and wasted.

Conditions Permitting Expansion of Advertising and Promotion During Depression by Business Concerns

While the above evidence indicates that advertising expenditures have been used in such a way as to accentuate cyclical fluctuations, the potentiality of advertising as a tool to help reduce fluctuations is illustrated in the cases of individual companies which not infrequently go counter to the general practice of their industries by maintaining or even expanding their advertising activity at a time when other firms are contracting. Study of such cases indicates that the increased advertising schedules in periods of recession cannot rest on a mere theory of putting on selling pressure when it is needed. Business concerns cannot afford such expenditures unless they are producing profitable sales volume. As a general rule, mere increase of advertising expenditure in depression does not by itself produce profitable sales results. A possible exception is found in cases when individual business firms maintain or increase their volume of advertising while competitors cease to maintain their efforts. Generally, however, increased advertising efforts by a concern during depression, in order to be effective and profitable, must be accompanied by merchandising efforts which bring about the offering of particularly desirable products at attractive prices. This statement is supported by numerous cases which show that companies successfully maintaining or increasing advertising expenditures in depressions have been astute enough or fortunate enough to produce new wantable varieties of merchandise at prices which induce demand.

The manner in which vigorous advertising and selling were used to increase the number of refrigerators sold during the 1930's has been noted. In order to accomplish this result, sellers reduced prices of refrigerators at the same time that they introduced improvements.

An example of an individual firm going counter to the advertising expenditure practice of an industry is the Philco Radio and Television Company in the period following the collapse of 1929. The extreme degree to which the advertising of radios generally was reduced during this period is shown in Table 142, a drop from $16,000,000 in 1929

TABLE 142

Estimated Value of Advertising for Radio Receiving Sets, Placed by Manufacturers in Newspapers, General Magazines, Farm Journals, and Chain Radio, 1929–1939

Year	Newspapers*	General Magazines	Farm Journals	Radio	Total	Index of Advertising 1929 = 100
1929	$12,128,220	$2,832,815†	$127,451§ᵃ	$1,576,596§ᵇ	$16,665,082	100
1930	6,109,885	3,636,386‡	96,577§ᵃ	1,197,195§ᵇ	11,040,043	66
1931	2,495,249	1,760,454‡	24,262§	....	4,279,965	26
1932	686,097	1,487,923‡	7,188§	96,806§ᵃ	2,278,014	14
1933	621,997	979,949‡	6,480§	586,373§ᵃ	2,194,799	13
1934	1,147,564	1,220,726‡	61,258‖	640,733‖	3,070,281	18
1935	1,168,924	1,448,418‡	157,937‖	910,881‖	3,686,160	22
1936	1,184,622	1,917,554‖	96,019§ᶜ	908,366§ᵈ	4,106,561	25
1937	1,606,518	1,634,433‖	178,268‖	2,096,580‖	5,515,799	33
1938	559,650	644,083‖	121,661‖	1,065,515‖	2,390,909	14
1939	424,528	620,347‖	111,909‖	118,065‖	1,275,849	8

ᵃ Extended from 11 months.
ᵇ Extended from 10 months.
ᶜ Extended from 9 months.
ᵈ Extended from 8 months.

Sources:
* 1929–1939 linage taken from Media Records, Inc., *Newspapers and Newspaper Advertisers*; 1938–1939 dollar figures from American Newspaper Publishers' Association, *Expenditures of National Advertisers*. Conversion ratio calculated from data for 1938 and 1939 — 25.7 cents per line applied to other years.
† Crowell Publishing Company, *National Markets and National Advertising*.
‡ Curtis Publishing Company, *Leading Advertisers*.
§ National Advertising Records, Inc., *National Advertising Records*.
‖ Publishers' Information Bureau, Inc., *National Advertising Records*.

to approximately $2,000,000 in 1933. In contrast, Philco expanded its advertising efforts after 1929 and maintained them at a high level during the depression. This policy is reflected in the figures of advertising which are available from published records, as shown in Table 143.

The Philco management was in a position to spend such increased amounts profitably because the low-price table models which it launched in 1930 enjoyed a large demand, not merely because they were low in cost in comparison with all models that had gone before, but also

TABLE 143

ADVERTISING EXPENDITURES OF PHILCO RADIO AND TELEVISION COMPANY IN MAGAZINES, FARM PAPERS, NEWSPAPERS, AND CHAIN RADIO, 1929–1936

YEAR	MAGAZINE	FARM PAPERS	RADIO	TOTAL MAGAZINE, FARM PAPER AND RADIO	NEWSPAPER LINAGE
1929	$263,530	....	$173,478*	$ 437,028	2,205,055
1930	527,690	....	233,241	760,931	2,028,833
1931	650,050	....	192,496	842,546	1,314,655
1932	933,570	....	104,384	1,037,954	742,465
1933	660,880	....	463,695	1,124,575	1,085,916
1934	617,596	$26,143	446,421	1,090,160	1,955,499
1935	673,484	47,205	556,989	1,277,678	2,428,728
1936	751,984	28,820	745,020	1,525,824	2,071,238

* Extended from figures for eight months.

Sources:

Farm papers, magazines, radio:
1929–1933, National Advertising Records, Inc., *National Advertising Records.*
1934–1936, Publishers' Information Bureau, *National Advertising Records.*
Newspapers:
Media Records, Inc., *Newspapers and Newspaper Advertisers.*

because they gave good broadcast reception and were convenient.[12] In 1931 the company continued to push the sales of its table models, but it also gave particular attention to the designing of higher-price radios in an effort to induce purchase by those who were still in the market for such models. Again in 1931 the company started intensive promotion on automobile radios, a new development. Aggressive selling was combined with skillful merchandising throughout this period to attain successful sales results. Thus is illustrated the generalization that increased advertising and selling effort in depression must be accompanied by astute merchandising and pricing to produce profitable sales volume.

Such cases as that of Philco represent the exception rather than the rule, although many individual examples can be found wherein managements have profitably maintained advertising and selling efforts during depression. These organizations generally have been able to improve their relative positions in their industries. Such situations are to be contrasted with that for refrigerators, in which a whole industry moved ahead in depression years.

To what extent there is hope that business managements generally will adjust their selling and advertising operations as an aid in reducing cyclical swings is unknown. It must be realized that the basic mal-

---

[12] S. M. Ramsdell, "How Philco Doubled Sales during the Depression," *Printers' Ink,* October 22, 1931, p. 17.

adjustments to which individual business managements must adapt themselves strongly influence any decisions regarding advertising and selling efforts. Moreover, it is probably to be expected that the waves of optimism and pessimism that influence business decisions generally will continue to influence their selling operations. Again, the opportunities to offer merchandise innovations and to apply technological improvements so as to reduce costs in times of depression vary widely with different products. Just as better use of credit and pricing practices which may bring quicker adjustments in depression is to be hoped for, so it is to be desired that an increasing number of individual managements may learn to adjust their selling operations in conjunction with their merchandising and other operations so as to reduce cyclical fluctuations. This goal would require the avoidance of excessive promotional effort and the corresponding expansion of productive capacity in boom periods. In turn, adjustment in periods of depression would probably be speeded by far-sighted merchandising planning which would involve the launching of new designs with prices adjusted so as to induce purchase at times when price change might stimulate demand. In addition, the situation would probably be helped if a larger proportion of advertisers developed more logical and scientific methods of budgeting and appropriating advertising funds to meet the needs of marketing plans than those now used. The method, now so often employed, of appropriating a more or less fixed percentage of the current or past year's sales tends to accentuate cyclical fluctuations. Means for determining more precisely the tasks and objectives of advertising than is now generally possible, and the practice of appropriating funds to accomplish these objectives are to be desired.

New Product Development as an Alleviator of Depression

It does not appear likely that entirely new inventions of known worth can be timed for introduction during depression periods as a means of aiding recovery. Instead, recovery appears to rest more upon bringing about adequate and quick price revisions of new merchandise designs for products which have already been widely accepted. Apart from the fact that significant new inventions cannot be timed as desired, the launching of radically new products during a depression does not appear promising in bringing business recovery, because new products, particularly when they are major purchases, are not likely to enjoy a large volume demand until they have gone through the years of improvement and the hard introductory selling that must precede broad market acceptance. Depression markets for new products generally cannot be stimulated by low prices until the demand has been made elastic by some cultivation. Moreover, only after such a long introductory period have technological development and decreasing costs progressed far enough to make possible price levels which permit a broad market. Once new products have reached the stage where they have proved their desirability, and emulative consumption has entered, however, they provide a helpful basis for economic recovery. It was noted in the study of demand in this volume that refrigerators and automobiles did not gain a large sales volume at the period of introduction, but only after years of selling effort and gradual price reduction. The automobile proved, however, to be a highly valuable product in helping to bring about economic recovery after the depressions of 1907, 1914, and 1920, during a period when it was greatly desired throughout the population, and demand was still expanding. Likewise, mechanical refrigerators, whose demand had just begun to mount to large proportions in 1929, were a highly effective product in providing business activity during the extreme depression of the 1930's. They provided a basis for employment not merely in the refrigerator industry but in the industrial goods factories which supplied the needs of refrigerator manufacturers.

Indirect Effects of Advertising through Price Rigidities

Advertising may have a possible indirect effect upon cyclical maladjustments in that the prices of advertised products tend to be relatively inflexible or rigid. Among the maladjustments of cyclical fluctuations those of price relationships loom large. Theoretically, if price competition in merchandise were free and labor and capital were mobile, adjustments in price relationships would automatically take place. New equilibria between demand and supply of various products would be established so as to utilize productive resources. But labor and capital are far from being mobile, and the prices of many products are relatively inflexible.

Some economists have laid much emphasis upon the rigidity of prices of manufactured goods as a cause of cyclical fluctuation, or at least they have taken the view that the price rigidity of these products as contrasted with agricultural products has accentuated cyclical maladjustments and has tended to prolong cyclical depression. Advertising in such a case is not charged with being the cause of price rigidities, but merely with being a significant element in the imperfect competition which produces such rigidities.

That the prices of many advertised products have tended to be relatively inflexible was brought out in the price chapter. Such was the case, for example, with cigarettes, smoking tobacco, and dentifrices. It was indicated, also, that private branders in the food field often were quicker in readjusting prices to changing price levels than were manufacturers. It was also shown that while advertised items were relatively inflexible, other items, termed "grocery trading items," such as butter and flour, have had relatively flexible prices. This is true because their prices are so closely governed by the fluctuation of basic commodities that neither manufacturers nor distributors have appreciable influence over prices. It is unnecessary to produce additional evidence, for extensive studies[13] of the relative price flexibility of many classes of products have been made, and these indicate that numerous product categories in which advertising plays an important part have been relatively inflexible.

On the other hand, many factors other than advertising are involved in the determination of the degree of price flexibility of a product, and often these are far more important than advertising in determining the degree of inflexibility. For example, grocery trading items such as flour and butter receive some advertising, yet they are very flexible. On the other hand, certain items which have relatively inflexible prices,[14] such as men's and women's underwear, coal, iron and steel products, paint and paint materials, chemicals, glassware, window shades and furniture, receive relatively little advertising.

Moreover, the recent government studies on price flexibility tend to disprove the thesis that price rigidities can be looked upon as a chief causal factor in fluctuations of production of various products. The following excerpt taken from the conclusions of the chapter on "Price Flexibility" of the T.N.E.C. study of *Price Behavior and Business Policy* is pertinent:

It has been shown that, within very broad limits, there was a tendency for production to fall less where prices fell more during the 1929–33 recession. Conversely, where prices were maintained production fell much more sharply.

---

[13] See T.N.E.C., Monograph No. 1, *Price Behavior and Business Policy* (Washington, U. S. Government Printing Office, 1940).

[14] For a rating of the flexibility of prices, see *Ibid.*, p. 172 ff.

It has been emphasized that there were very many exceptions to this generalization. It has been pointed out moreover that the existence of this limited correlation does not of itself imply any causal relationship.

For any individual commodity, price is but one, and not necessarily the most important, of the factors which affect its production. Thus the relatively sharp decline in the consumption of most durable goods between 1929 and 1933 was probably aggravated by the stability of their prices, but it seems likely that the postponable nature of their demand in combination with lower family incomes was of at least equal or of greater importance. With the spread of unemployment and a marked curtailment of purchasing power, the sale of goods whose purchase is relatively more postponable will usually decline regardless of price; the sale of articles designed to satisfy wants which cannot be long deferred is likely to be fairly well maintained, again regardless of price.

Moreover assuming any specific set of market conditions, or any given level of purchasing power, the effect of a change in the price of any commodity upon the purchases of that commodity may be slight. This is tantamount to saying that demand for many products, particularly during periods of depressed business activity, varies little regardless of price. Among the most notable examples of such "inelastic demand" are products such as steel castings, which find no independent market but whose demand is part of a joint demand for some more complex finished goods of whose total cost they constitute but a small part. In cases of this sort, isolated changes in price may have no discernible effect upon consumption whatever. Nor can isolated price changes during periods of curtailed purchasing power expect to influence materially the sales of such products as absolute necessities of life or capital equipment for industries operating at fractions of their capacity.

·   ·   ·   ·   ·

There is little doubt that the behavior of prices intimately affects the rate of business activity. Nevertheless it seems equally evident that no simple, single approach to prices as such will solve the problem of increasing and maintaining industrial activity. The problem is far too complex.[15]

In view of the evidence of these studies and of the uncertain weight to be given to advertising as an element in inducing inflexibility, it is concluded that the importance of advertising as a causal factor in cyclical fluctuations is not large.

Summary

The analysis indicates that advertising has not, in itself, been a causative factor of appreciable moment in cyclical fluctuations. However, as used, it has tended to accentuate fluctuations because expenditures for advertising have varied directly with business activity. As

---

[15] *Ibid.*, p. 51.

an employer of men and materials, advertising has been subject to the same fluctuations as business generally. As a stimulant to demand for products and services, it has been most extensively used in boom times and most lightly used in depressions. Thus employed, it has tended to accentuate the swings of demand. Indirectly it may have had some influence on fluctuations in so far as its use has accompanied inflexible prices, but the effect here is not deemed significant.

Unfortunately, cyclical fluctuations appear to be inevitable in a free, profit-directed economy, but there is hope of overcoming the degree of unemployment from which the country suffered during the 1930 decade, and advertising may play a part. This hope rests in the expansion of the economy through investment in new enterprise. The theories of the Keynes school of thought with regard to unemployment and its relation to investment were briefly outlined in Chapter VI with comment on the relation of advertising to these views. That advertising may have a desirable effect in developing a propensity of people to consume, which in turn may help overcome unemployment, was there indicated. But it is not enough merely to induce people to consume in order to cut down their saving and thus reduce the deficiency in demand, a factor which looms large in the Keynes theory. The surest remedy would come from a revival of the spirit of enterprise and of risk-taking, which would bring the industrial activity that overcomes unemployment.

Much current economic thinking and writing tends to minimize the importance of risk-taking by businessmen. Investment is treated as a mechanical process which simply comes about through someone's building factories to make goods which people need. Such a view fails to appraise the attitude of the risk-taker and the spirit of enterprise. The risk-taker must see an opportunity for profit. He must be enthusiastic regarding his opportunities and willing aggressively to promote his products. Unless there is confidence in the profit outlook, investment does not readily take place, as is attested by the low rate of investment or even the possible decline in investment in this country in the 1930 decade.

One of the critical economic and social issues today turns upon the question as to why there has not been more risk-taking by businessmen in recent years. This lack of willingness to venture accounts for the failure of the economy to rally from depression during this period. It is beyond the scope of this study to investigate this problem. The reasons are probably many. But among them the public attitude toward risk-taking, which has come as a result of economic discussion during the period, is of some consequence. In particular, the viewpoint that this nation has become a mature society and that further expansion and investment are likely to proceed much more slowly has received wide publicity and much acceptance. Such a viewpoint does not instill the confidence in which enterprises flourish and investments are made. In view of the possibilities for finding new wantable products which the present expanding technology holds forth, there is little basis for believing that expansion is a thing of the past. Moreover, there is large reason to desire expansion, for few members of the community have incomes to satisfy their many wants and desires. The attainment of these satisfactions would be furthered by a resumption of risk-taking, such as occurs when there is an atmosphere of confidence in the future. A bullish attitude on the future rather than a view that America has reached the end of the trail is clearly essential to encourage investment and to bring the rising standard of living which is to be desired. It behooves businessmen who favor retention of the free system to rise above the difficulties and to keep alive the spirit of enterprise and risk.

PART VII

Ethical Aspects of Advertising

CHAPTER XXVI

CONSUMERS' APPRAISALS OF ADVERTISING

I N THIS and the following chapter a study is made of the ethical and moral views of consumers, of businessmen, and of the community generally which govern advertising and selling activity. As was pointed out in the first chapter, the functioning of a free capitalistic economy is fashioned in large degree by constantly changing ethical and moral views and rules. Although people speak of a free society, there is no such thing. Freedom is but a relative term. Businessmen, like all members of society, have had to conduct their activities with reference to those about them and to act in accord with dictates laid down by the social group to protect the individual who cannot adequately protect his own interests.

The tasks laid out in the investigation for these chapters were two: (1) To find out what the views of consumers towards advertising might be, thereby to learn whether businessmen have transgressed moral sentiments of consumers. (2) To trace the changing ethical attitudes of society which have determined codes of business conduct and legalistic control of advertising. The views of consumers are presented and discussed in this chapter; the historical treatment of codes in the following chapter.

The Significance of Consumer Attitudes toward Advertising

The attitudes of consumers towards advertising may provide a clue as to whether advertising has or has not contributed to their satisfactions and whether it has violated moral sentiments. The word *clue* is used advisedly, because it is realized that consumers' attitudes at any moment may not give a true measurement of the actual contribution of advertising to their satisfactions or of its conformity to ethical practice.

Consumers' attitudes are the result of numerous forces. More often than not they are compounded of emotional experience rather than of cold reason applied to fact. They are determined in part by consumers' experiences in the market place. What have been their experiences with advertised and nonadvertised merchandise? What have been their satisfactions from the two? How frequently have they been misled by advertising? Attitudes are determined also by advertising itself as a form of literature and art which is showered upon them. Has it pleased them or has it irritated them? What is the feeling aroused by the ever-present advertisement, the billboard, the radio commercial, the mail piece, the magazine, and the newspaper?

Again, attitudes are influenced largely by what people have been taught or led to believe. In recent years there has been much propagandizing about advertising. It has been subjected to a barrage of criticism in books and magazine articles, some of which have had wide circulation. Often they have been vitriolic in their denunciation. In turn, the organized advertising interests have countered with praise of advertising. Newspapers, magazines, and radio stations have given generous space and time to such messages.

A serious difficulty in studying and appraising attitudes arises from the uphill task of actually finding out what consumer attitudes are, of measuring their intensity, and of judging their significance as guides to consumer action. Such difficulties will be apparent as studies which have been undertaken are discussed.

Since attitudes are formed as they are, and are so hard to determine, much weight probably should not be attached to them when the economic and social effects of advertising are being appraised. Nevertheless, if the sources of attitudes are kept in mind, and if the shortcomings of attitude studies are clearly realized, the reports of attitudes coming from these studies may have some value for students of advertising. At least they may serve to show to businessmen possible causes of friction in advertising and marketing practice which may need attention.

Numerous Studies of Consumer Attitudes

In the last half-dozen years, with increasing public attention being placed upon problems of consumption, many studies have been aimed at uncovering various aspects of consumers' attitudes toward advertising and advertised goods. A few of these studies have attempted to contact many consumers, returns being obtained from 1,000 to 10,000 persons. The majority of the studies, however, have made use of small samples, locally distributed. Sales and advertising trade papers, advertising associations, and professors of marketing and advertising have been the chief instigators of such surveys.

Inasmuch as the individual studies differ in specific objectives, in questions asked, and in methods of sampling, interviewing, and reporting, it is, of course, impossible to pool results. Later in this chapter, however, some comparisons are shown between results obtained in the study which was undertaken as a part of this economic investigation and results obtained by others working in this general area.

No attempt will be made here either to describe the surveys referred to or to appraise their merits and shortcomings. It must be recognized, however, that the very nature of the problem—that of finding out people's attitudes by the simple process of asking them questions—places decided limitations on the realism which the results may be assumed to possess. The form of the question asked to a considerable degree determines the answers received. In these circumstances literal acceptance of exact percentages of any of the studies presented in this chapter is to be guarded against. It is by studying the general trend of the answers and the distribution of answers to one question with reference to the distribution of answers for related questions that one may hope to develop an over-all sensing of public sentiment.

The Special Survey of Attitudes Undertaken

In making the field survey of consumer attitudes, which was directed by the author, the Harvard Business School was fortunate in having the assistance of Alpha Delta Sigma, National Advertising Fraternity, with chapters in numerous colleges located in all sections of the country. Indeed, without the assistance of the members of this fraternity, who conducted all the interviews, this survey could not have been undertaken. It is fitting to say that whatever the shortcomings of the survey may be, every evidence points to confidence in the intelligence and conscientiousness with which the interviews were conducted and reported.

The survey was divided in two parts. For one part, questionnaire Form A was used, and for the other part, questionnaire Form X was used, both of which will be found in Appendix VII, page 947 ff. Form A was aimed at uncovering consumers' attitudes toward general questions concerning advertising, such as whether advertising helps people to buy wisely, whether advertising of various types is liked or disliked, what degree of governmental control over advertising should be adopted, and so on. Form X was designed to determine attitudes toward specific advertisements. This double approach was used in the belief that one set of questions in which consumers were faced with the general and another in which they dealt with the specific would give a surer basis for determining attitudes than would a single approach.

To test the correctness of this theory, as well as to test the adequacy and clearness of the statements suggested for inclusion in the two types of forms, several hundred interviews were obtained in the vicinity of Boston before the questionnaires were put in final form and distributed for use nationally.

Partly because it might have proved confusing to consumers to be faced with two forms, and partly because they very well might have resented being asked to devote so much time to the project, different consumers were approached with the two types of forms. The instructions to interviewers are shown in Appendix VII, pages 951 and 963.

THE SURVEY OF CONSUMERS' OPINIONS REGARDING SPECIFIC ADVERTISEMENTS

Questionnaire Form X dealt with consumers' opinions about specific advertisements. Such a test was deemed to promise significant information because many of the advertisements were of types which have been adversely commented upon both by critics and by defenders of advertising practice.

The shortcomings and weaknesses of such a test were realized. It forced consumers to become conscious critics of advertisements, and accordingly one cannot be certain that the views thus expressed would have developed under normal conditions of advertisement reading. Nevertheless, a consciously critical attitude was expected to give some clues regarding what consumers deem undesirable practice and to show what kinds of advertisements might be sources of consumer ill will toward advertising as an institution. Moreover, such a test complemented the general attitude technique used in Form A and the various testing methods found in numerous other surveys, which generally had not employed specific advertisements.

The test was not designed to develop any quantitative measurement of consumers' attitudes toward advertising practice as a whole. The 20 advertisements presented were not a true cross section of advertising practice. They were consciously chosen to get examples of what many critics have characterized as undesirable practice. The advertisements as a group were expected to show a higher frequency and a more intense degree of criticism than would be found for advertisements generally. The reader, therefore, should keep in mind in connection with the detailed analyses of replies which are presented that the test is in large part a critical consumer reaction to what many deem the more questionable aspects of advertising practice, although the practices illustrated have not been infrequent.

Methods Employed in Survey

In all, 20 magazine advertisements were used in the survey. These were grouped into four sets of five advertisements each. Each consumer interviewed was shown one set of the advertisements. In most instances, the consumers gave their reactions to all five of the advertisements shown; sometimes, however, they were unable or unwilling to give the time necessary for examining the full set. For the purpose of the survey, the advertisements were reproduced in black and white on stiff paper. Interviewers recorded the responses.

Altogether, 14,798 individual sets of responses to specific advertisements were obtained from 3,032 consumers. The smallest number of responses received for any one of the 20 advertisements was 617, and the largest number was 933; that is, each advertisement was examined and reported on by 617 to 933 persons.

The questions which the consumers were asked to answer and the categories of answers recorded were as follows:

Questions	*Answers*
1. Do you find anything objectionable in this advertisement?	1. Yes
If so, what?	No
If answer is "Yes," check one or more of the reasons listed.	Uncertain
	Comment:
(Note: The responses were not prompted or suggested. The list opposite was found in the testing of the method to cover the answers given and was thus set up to expedite the interview.)	In bad taste
	Indecent or suggestive
	Negative—uses fear motive
	Repulsive ideas
	Unattractive advertisement
	Exaggerated
	Not true
	Misleading
	Silly
	Testimonial is objectionable
	Object to product
	Other (state)

2. (To be asked only when answer to question 1 is "Yes.") Would you have the things that you object to prohibited by law?	2. Yes No Uncertain
3. Have you ever used the product?	3. Yes No Uncertain
4. Do you think the product (probably) is as good as the advertisement says?	4. Yes No Uncertain Comment
5. Do you think the product (probably) is a good product?	5. Yes No Uncertain Comment
6. How do you think the product (probably) compares in quality with competing products selling at about the same price?	6. Best on market Better than most About the same Inferior Uncertain Other (state) Comment

Distribution of the 14,798 individual answers to the 20 advertisements by sex, income, occupation, and education of the persons answering is shown in Table 144. As already explained, the same person ordinarily, although not always, gave answers for five different advertisements. The distribution of persons interviewed was heavily overbalanced in the upper income brackets and among people with college and high school education.[1] It was not judged worth while, in presentation of composite returns, to make a correction for these factors because such correction did not alter distribution enough to affect conclusions. Answers to the questionnaire are shown separately for the four income groups so that anyone interested in working out adjusted figures may do so.

Advertisements Used for the Survey

In the selection of advertisements to be used with Form X in this consumer survey, it was desired to cover a representative group of products and various types of advertising. Some products of low unit

---

[1] There is strong reason to suspect the distribution of answers as to education is in error. Tests have shown that peoples' replies to questions regarding the extent of their education are not accurate and dependable.

TABLE 144

DISTRIBUTION OF COMBINED ANSWERS TO TWENTY ADVERTISEMENTS ACCORDING TO SEX,
INCOME, EDUCATION, AND OCCUPATION OF PERSONS ANSWERING

	NUMBER	PERCENTAGE
Sex		
Male	6,864	46.5
Female	7,858	53.0
No answer	76	0.5
	14,798	100.0
Family Income		
A—$5,000 and over...................	1,580	10.7
B—$2,000–$4,999	6,357	43.0
C—$1,000–$1,999	5,303	35.8
D—Less than $1,000...................	1,200	8.1
No answer	358	2.4
	14,798	100.0
Education		
College	6,561	44.4
High School	6,097	41.1
Grade School	1,711	11.6
Less	183	1.2
No answer	246	1.7
	14,798	100.0
Occupation		
Housewife	5,296	35.8
Domestic worker	505	3.4
Professional	1,690	11.4
Business executive or owner.............	1,368	9.2
Clerical, sales, stenographic.............	2,210	14.9
Skilled labor	964	6.5
Unskilled labor	354	2.4
Unemployed	363	2.5
Student	1,697	11.5
Other	351	2.4
	14,798	100.0

value and frequent use, heavily advertised and widely popular, were
included; some of high unit value and more limited use and popularity; some products of questionable worth and some of indisput-
able soundness; some advertisements of a cheerful nature and some
of the fear-inspiring type; some advertisements with illustrations; some
without; some advertisements with testimonials; some full of exaggerations; some with copy irrelevant to the product's merit; some with
straightforward descriptive copy. Because of the limited number of
advertisements which could be tested, it was not feasible to include
all types of advertisements that have been criticized. And, clearly, the
advertisements did not represent a true cross sample of advertising.

In the selection of these advertisements, one further factor also was considered: namely, the attitude of a professional advertising committee toward the advertisements. The views of this group were made available to the author by one of the advertising associations. This group had previously examined for the association a large number of advertisments and had reported as to whether they violated in any way the Copy Code jointly adopted by the American Association of Advertising Agencies and the Association of National Advertisers. Also, for the purpose of this examination, they had added two points to the seven points of the code. For the consumer survey, some of the advertisements rated by this committee were selected which according to the committee offended the various requirements of this code, and some advertisements were selected which were judged by the advertising committee to be inoffensive. The use of these advertisements in the survey allowed a comparison between the attitude of certain individuals in the advertising profession itself and the attitude of a group of consumers. It should be recognized, however, that the opinion of the small committee of advertising men cannot be taken as necessarily representative of the views of all advertising men.

The nine points on the basis of which the examining committee checked the advertisements were as follows:

1. False statements or misleading exaggerations.
2. Indirect misrepresentation of a product or service, through distortion of details or of their true perspective, either editorially or pictorially.
3. Statements or suggestions offensive to public decency.
4. Statements which tend to undermine an industry by attributing to its products, generally, faults and weaknesses true only of a few.
5. Price claims that are misleading.
6. Pseudoscientific advertising, including claims insufficiently supported by accepted authority, or that distort the true meaning or practicable application of a statement made by professional or scientific authority.
7. Testimonials which do not reflect the real choice of a competent witness.
8. Trade puffery which is so extravagant or ridiculous as to harm advertising.

9. Advertising of products which are in themselves dishonest or unworthy.

Description of Advertisements Used in Survey

Because specific products and advertisements are stigmatized as undesirable, the advertisements are not reproduced here. They will be described briefly as follows without specific details. It must be realized that it has been necessary to describe the advertisements as the author has seen them, and in such general terms as to avoid disclosure. Hence, there is editorial opinion as to the products and the advertisements which could not be avoided. The effort was made to be objective and to give such evidence of advertising practices as will enable the reader to typify each of the advertisements from his own observation.

Advertisement 1.—A toothbrush advertisement based on alleged scientific facts supported by photographs and the statement that "dentists by the thousands say . . . ." Competitors' products are referred to unfavorably. The advertisement seeks to arouse fear as to the oral effects of using other brands of toothbrushes. The product itself has been widely advertised for years, is among the best of its type on the market, and sells at the price of leading brands.

Criticized by the advertisers' committee on the ground of code point 1: "false claims or misleading exaggerations."

Advertisement 2.—This advertisement introduces an improvement in a well-known brand of kitchen utensils. These utensils are of unquestioned merit. Although the unit prices of these utensils are not large, they are high compared with the prices of other products which can be used for the same purposes. The advertisement contains a series of pictures of the product in use. The headline, which contains the keynote or theme of the advertisement, by implication is a disparagement of competing types of utensils. This theme, which is played up in the text, would probably be regarded by some critics as an exaggeration. The advertisement is largely devoted to a description of the positive merits of the product; only by implication are competitive products suggested to be undesirable or inferior.

The advertisers' committee made no unfavorable criticism.

Advertisement 3.—This advertises a well-known dental product. An illustration showing a close-up of the head and shoulders of a beautiful and happy-looking woman lying in bed while her husband bends over her is the prominent feature of the advertisement.

The tone of the illustration, the headline, and the first paragraph of the text is positive and cheerful, playing up happy marital relations, to which the product might contribute. Later paragraphs point out dangers from failure to use the product but nevertheless maintain the positive and hopeful tone of the first part of the advertisement.

Advertisers' committee made no unfavorable criticism.

Advertisement 4.—This advertises a washing machine. It contains a large picture of the washer and small inserts illustrating different fabrics for which the machine can be used successfully. One of these small illustrations is of a girl in her underwear putting on a silk stocking. The text discusses the exclusive features of the machine as they contribute to excellent laundry results.

In general the advertisement is of a conservative type; it is conservative in appearance, and while the claims made in the text may be deemed exaggerated, they are expressed in a simple, straightforward manner.

No unfavorable criticism by advertisers' committee.

Advertisement 5.—A textile product which is said to be mothproofed. The advertisement contains an illustration in which a magnified moth is prominently displayed. The text deals chiefly with the superiority of this product to competing products, particularly "cheap" articles of the kind.

No unfavorable criticism by advertisers' committee.

Advertisement 6.—This advertises a well-known brand of cigarettes. It contains pictures of and testimonials from socially prominent persons. One illustration shows women in low-cut evening gowns. Some of the statements regarding the physiological effects of cigarettes probably would be deemed questionable by physiologists.

The advertisers' committee criticized it on five grounds: code point 1, misleading exaggerations; point 2, indirect misrepresentation; point 5, price claims that are misleading; point 6, pseudoscientific claims; and point 7, testimonial not reflecting real choice of competent witness.

Advertisement 7.—This is an advertisement of a typewriter. It is gloomy, and one would have to be charitable indeed not to consider its theme far-fetched. This theme is an elaboration of the dire things that will happen to children who do not have typewriters. The advertisement displays a coupon prominently and urges installment purchase. The product itself is well known and entirely reputable.

Criticized by the advertisers' committee on the grounds of code point 1: misleading exaggerations, and code point 6: pseudoscientific claims.

Advertisement 8.—This advertises a well-known and widely used food product. It contains a large and attractive illustration of the product ready to be served. The emphasis of the headlines and text is upon the importance of the flavor and of getting the "genuine" product. In the original this advertisement was in vivid color, and black and white reproduction used in the survey was less satisfactory in this case than it was in the case of most of the other advertisements.

The advertisers' committee criticized this advertisement on the grounds of code point 2: indirect misrepresentation of a product or service, through distortion of details, or of their true perspective, either editorially or pictorially.

Advertisement 9.—This also advertises a well-known and widely used food product. It is cheerful and positive in tone, emphasizing the advantages of buying the product ready-made rather than making it in the home. As with advertisement 8, attractiveness was greatly diminished by loss of color in the reproduction.

No objections from the advertisers' committee.

Advertisement 10.—This is an advertisement of a cosmetic, appealing to the desire for a fine skin and beauty. It plays upon fear of results from improper skin care but emphasizes the happy solution. It has a large illustration of pseudoscientific character, and it contains testimonials from socially prominent women.

This advertisement is criticized by the advertisers' committee on the grounds, point 6, that it is pseudoscientific.

Advertisement 11.—This advertises a well-known food product. It contains, among others, illustrations of two women: one, with a displeased expression, is sampling a competing product, while the other, looking very happy, is sampling the advertised product. Relying largely on illustration, it has little text.

Criticized by the advertisers' committee, not on any of the code points, but for being unfair to other advertising.

Advertisement 12.—This also advertises a widely used food product.

Several famous children are featured as users. The general theme of the advertisement is that the product has specific vitamin and health value.

Criticized by the advertisers' committee for being pseudoscientific, point 6.

Advertisement 13.—This is a whiskey advertisement. It is pictorially attractive and the text says simply that the makers have had long experience and make a high-class product.

This advertisement was chosen as a means of obtaining some indication of the influence which people's attitudes toward products have upon their attitudes toward advertisements of those products.

No criticism by advertisers' committee.

Advertisement 14.—A preparation for the hair is advertised here. The advertisement relies almost entirely upon fear, both in illustration and text, to induce buying action. The text presents the product as a cure for dandruff and an aid to prevention of baldness.

This advertisement was the only one used which was not rated by the committee.

Advertisement 15.—This advertises a well-known toilet soap. The tone of the advertisement is cheerful. The main illustration shows a beautiful, nude girl. To support its claims as an aid to good complexion, unnamed scientists are quoted. Many of the claims undoubtedly would be deemed exaggerations by many critics.

The advertisers' committee made no unfavorable criticism.

Advertisement 16.—Medium-price shoes for women are the subject of this advertisement. It undertakes to arouse interest by means of a puzzling headline and illustration. The text emphasizes the effect of comfortable shoes on the beauty of the wearer and also the attractiveness of the shoes.

The advertisers' committee criticized the advertisement on the grounds of point 1, false statements or misleading exaggerations, and also on the grounds, point 6, that it is pseudoscientific.

Advertisement 17.—A cigarette advertisement of a humorous type, pointing out the merits of the product. Emphasis upon one point carries the implication that other cigarettes are faulty in this respect.

The advertisers' committee criticized it for point 4: statements which tend to undermine an industry by attributing to its products, generally, faults and weaknesses true only of a few.

Advertisement 18.—This advertises a product for increasing one's weight. The headline is of cartoon type, the words coming from the mouth of a professional-looking man, probably a doctor. A well-developed young woman in a bathing suit is also featured. Emphasis in the copy is placed on fear of being unattractive because thin, but the general tone is cheerful, inasmuch as the cure for this situation is at hand. Scientists and vitamins are referred to. There is a money-back guarantee and a special free offer.

The advertisers' committee criticized the advertisement, point 9, for the advertising of products which in themselves are dishonest or unworthy.

Advertisement 19.—This is a proprietary remedy advertisement of clearly questionable type. An all-text advertisement, it promises immediate relief of many physical disorders or money back.

The advertisers' committee criticized it, point 9, as advertising products which are in themselves dishonest or unworthy.

Advertisement 20.—This advertises a well-known toilet soap. It is of the cartoon type, with the unpopular, unhappy girl finally finding romance and happiness.

The advertisers' committee offered no unfavorable criticism.

Comparison of Attitudes of Professional Advertising Committee and Consumers

Table 145 shows a comparison between the criticisms made of the 20 advertisements by the group of professional advertisers and the objections cited by the consumers interviewed. In interpreting this exhibit and various others in this section, one must remember that each consumer could enter as many objections as he wished to each advertisement. Moreover, it must be kept in mind that those interviewed had no specified standards to guide them regarding the characteristics to which they might object, such as untruth, exaggeration, indecency and so on.

It will be seen that little correlation appeared between the attitudes of the two groups. For example, the advertisers' committee found nothing objectionable in advertisement 3, that of the dental product, showing a boudoir scene, whereas 35% of consumers had some objection to make, 13% finding it indecent, 6% finding it not true, 7% finding it misleading, and 12% finding it exaggerated. A similar

TABLE 145

Criticisms Made of Twenty Advertisements by Professional Advertising Committee
and
Certain Criticisms Made of Same Advertisements by Consumers Interviewed

Advertisement Code Number	Product Advertised	Advertising Committee's Attitude	Percentage of Persons Interviewed Who Had One or More Objections	Percentage of Persons Interviewed and Grounds of Objection*					
				Not True	Misleading	Exaggerated	Indecent	Objection to Product	Testimonial
1	Toothbrush	False statements or misleading exaggerations (Copy Code 1)	31	3	3	7	0	0	1
2	Kitchen Utensil	No objection	14	1	1	2	0	0	0
3	Dental Product	No objection	35	6	7	12	13	2	1
4	Washing Machine	No objection	13	2	2	4	1	0	0
5	Textile Product	No objection	18	2	2	3	0	0	0
6	Cigarette	False statements or misleading exaggerations (1); indirect misrepresentation (2); misleading price claims (5); pseudoscientific (6); testimonials (7)	42	9	7	13	1	3	18
7	Typewriter	False statements or misleading exaggerations (1); pseudoscientific (6)	50	12	14	23	0	1	1
8	Food Product	Indirect misrepresentation of a product (2)	18	1	1	6	0	0	0
9	Food Product	No objection	10	1	1	2	1	0	0
10	Cosmetic	Pseudoscientific (6)	37	5	8	14	0	1	1
11	Food Product	Unfair to other advertising (11)	31	1	4	13	0	1	3
12	Food Product	Pseudoscientific (6)	24	2	3	7	1		9
13	Whiskey	No objection	18	1	2	2	1	9	0
14	Hair Preparation	(not rated)	51	10	10	19		2	1
15	Toilet Soap	No objection	41	8	9	14	17	0	2
16	Women's Shoes	False statements or misleading exaggeration (1); pseudoscientific (6)	25	2	3	11	0	0	0
17	Cigarette	Statements which tend to undermine an industry (4)	18	2		4	0	3	0
18	Proprietary Remedy	Dishonest or unworthy product (9)	60	15	17	27	9	6	3
19	Proprietary Remedy	Dishonest or unworthy product (9)	70	24	21	28	2	12	2
20	Toilet Soap	No objection	61	13	8	6	27	4	4

* Not all the grounds of objection are included in this table. See questionnaire form Appendix VII for complete list.

situation is found for advertisements 15 and 20, the soap advertisements with extreme appeals to beauty and romance. In these cases, although the committee made no unfavorable criticism, 41% and 61%, respectively, of consumers found something to object to, many of them on serious grounds. For example, 17% of consumers found advertisement 15 indecent, and 27% had the same objection to advertisement 20.

Again, in one or two cases in which the committee made complaints against the advertisements, relatively few consumers objected. Advertisement 17, the cigarette advertisement, in which the committee found unfair competitive statement, is an example of this.

The closest association between objection by the committee and by consumers occurs with advertisements 18 and 19, dealing with proprietary remedies which the committee held to be unworthy. Here, although only 6% of consumers in the case of advertisement 18 and 12% in the case of advertisement 19 objected specifically to the products advertised, 60% and 70%, respectively, did have some objection to the advertisements.

Great significance cannot be given to the exact nature of the differences appearing in Table 145. The data are offered merely as an indication that consumers and persons actually engaged in advertising work do not always see eye to eye. This fact suggests that some advertising men may not be fully alert to the ways in which some advertisements violate consumers' sentiments.

Other research workers also have commented on this lack of agreement between the two groups. For example, Mr. Byron Moore, in reporting in *Market Research,* November, 1934, on a survey among 1,113 consumers in which they were asked to state their particular dislikes among advertisements, remarked:

Perhaps as interesting as any point is that the dislikes of the advertising men and women are at variance with those of other respondents. For example, Lifebuoy advertising is very much disliked except by advertising men. On the other hand, Camel advertising is strenuously objected to by advertising men and women, but this advertising does not seem to ruffle the Pittsburgh women or the subscribers to the women's magazine.

In this same connection it will be noted later that in the case of the Harvard Questionnaire, Form A, dealing with consumers' general attitudes toward advertising, the business groups were more favorably inclined toward advertising than were the other groups.

TABLE 146

SUMMARY OF CONSUMERS' ANSWERS TO FIVE QUESTIONS OF QUESTIONNAIRE FORM X, SHOWING PERCENTAGE OF ANSWERS IN AGREEMENT AND PERCENTAGE IN DISAGREEMENT (IN ORDER OF PERCENTAGES OF OBJECTIONS FOUND)

ADVERTISE-MENT CODE NUMBER	PRODUCT ADVERTISED	ANYTHING OBJECTIONABLE IN THE ADVERTISEMENT?		IF THERE IS SOMETHING OBJECTIONABLE, WOULD YOU HAVE IT PROHIBITED BY LAW?		HAVE YOU EVER USED THE PRODUCT?		PRODUCT AS GOOD AS ADVERTISEMENT SAYS?		PRODUCT A GOOD ONE?	
		Yes	No	Yes	No	Yes	No	Yes	No	Yes	No
9	Food Product.	10%	89%	8%	69%	94%	3%	82%	12%	96%	2%
4	Washing Machine....	13	86	16	72	9	88	43	14	69	2
2	Kitchen Utensil.....	14	85	5	82	63	35	78	7	91	1
5	Textile Product	18	79	8	71	22	73	49	16	67	5
8	Food Product.	18	81	8	82	94	4	68	23	95	2
13	Whiskey......	18	81	61	27	37	56	48	20	63	11
17	Cigarettes.....	18	81	19	65	49	49	40	30	60	14
12	Food Product.	24	76	22	63	90	7	69	19	93	3
16	Women's Shoes	25	73	8	72	12	82	37	25	62	6
11	Food Product.	31	68	9	76	74	18	35	29	88	4
1	Toothbrush...	31	68	22	55	64	28	57	22	85	5
3	Dental Product	35	65	28	57	86	13	46	44	75	17
10	Cosmetic.....	37	61	19	66	46	53	35	41	70	10
15	Toilet Soap...	41	58	38	46	75	22	44	42	84	5
6	Cigarettes.....	42	57	30	54	59	39	33	46	74	11
7	Typewriter....	50	48	15	70	58	39	57	25	90	3
14	Hair Preparation.	51	47	19	63	15	82	17	50	34	24
18	Proprietary Remedy....	60	39	35	52	12	86	11	61	30	34
20	Toilet Soap...	61	36	21	54	80	18	34	53	70	21
19	Proprietary Remedy.....	70	27	47	37	6	91	8	63	13	49

Table 146 summarizes the consumers' answers to the first five questions of Form X. Reference to these figures will be made in connection with more detailed tables which follow.

Nature and Frequency of Consumers' Objections

Table 147 shows the frequency with which various types of objections were made to each of the 20 advertisements and the distribution of total number of objections among the advertisements. When the number of objections of the various types were combined for all the advertisements, it was found that the most often named objection was "exaggerated," which accounted for 20% of total number of complaints reported. The second most common objection was "unattractive," with 17% of the total complaints. This response is not deemed of great significance in throwing light on consumers' objections to advertising that may be meaningful to advertisers. It indicates that

TABLE 147

PERCENTAGE DISTRIBUTION OF OBJECTIONS MADE TO SPECIFIC ADVERTISEMENTS

Adver-tise-ment Code Number	Bad Taste	Inde-cent	Nega-tive Fear Motive	Re-pul-sive Ideas	Unat-trac-tive	Ex-ag-ger-ated	Not True	Mis-lead-ing	Silly	Testi-monial	Un-worthy Prod-uct	Other	Total	Number of Objections as Percentage of Total for All Advertisements
1....	6	1	9	14	26	18	8	8	2	2	0	6	100	3
2....	3	0	1	4	54	14	5	7	1	1	0	10	100	2
3....	12	19	3	4	7	18	10	10	11	1	3	2	100	5
4....	2	4	1	1	31	23	12	15	2	2	1	6	100	1
5....	5	0	6	8	39	14	8	9	3	0	0	8	100	3
6....	6	1	2	2	8	18	12	10	4	25	5	7	100	6
7....	3	0	17	2	10	26	14	16	6	1	1	4	100	7
8....	4	0	1	0	36	29	6	6	8	1	1	8	100	2
9....	0	0	0	0	47	15	7	8	7	0	4	12	100	1
10....	5	1	5	8	18	23	9	12	3	11	2	3	100	5
11....	7	0	3	4	27	28	3	8	5	6	2	7	100	4
12....	3	1	1	2	16	21	7	10	2	26	0	11	100	2
13....	26	2	1	8	1	6	4	7	1	2	38	4	100	2
14....	11	1	13	10	19	17	10	9	6	1	2	1	100	12
15....	11	25	1	1	5	21	12	13	5	4	0	2	100	7
16....	4	0	3	2	22	34	6	10	14	2	1	2	100	2
17....	6	2	1	2	16	17	7	10	16	0	13	10	100	3
18....	13	7	1	5	12	21	12	13	8	2	5	1	100	11
19....	10	1	4	9	20	16	14	12	3	1	7	3	100	13
20....	15	8	3	8	10	22	7	5	14	3	3	2	100	9
Aver-age.	9	5	5	6	17	20	10	11	6	4	4	3	100	100%

NOTE: Figures are based on number of objections, not number of people objecting. Many people objected on several grounds.

those interviewed were in a critical frame of mind and were looking for possible objections to the advertisements. Accordingly, they presented opinions on the attractiveness of the advertisements, whereas the interest of this study relates to opinions having moral, social, or economic implications, which may affect consumer goodwill toward advertising, such as was found in the objection to exaggeration. Third and fourth places for number of complaints were held by "misleading," with 11%, and "not true," with 10%. Thus, in all, the three related complaints, exaggerated, misleading, and untruthful, account for 41% of the total number of mentions of complaints.

In this connection it is interesting to note that in a survey made for *Sales Management* by the Ross Federal Corporation and reported in the September 1, 1938, issue of that magazine, 51.4% of the persons interviewed when asked, "What is your chief criticism of advertisements?" distributed their replies among "exaggeration, over-exaggeration, and lack of truth."

The least criticized advertisements, as shown in the last column of Table 147, were number 4 (washing machine) and number 9 (food product), each of which received but 1% of total number of objections. The three most criticized advertisements were number 19 (proprietary remedy), with 13% of the total, number 14 (hair preparation), with 12%, and number 18 (proprietary remedy), with 11%. An even division of objections would, of course, have given each advertisement 5% of the total, a figure with which the above extremes may be compared.

Inasmuch as selected advertisements were used, it cannot be assumed that the data in Table 147 indicate what consumers object to most commonly in connection with advertising as a whole. The advertisements used in the survey probably were more open to objections on various of the grounds named than is typical of advertisements in general. However, when the nature of the objections made by consumers is compared with their belief as to whether or not the objectionable things should be prohibited by law, evidence is obtained as to the sort of failings regarded by consumers as serious.

Objectionable Characteristics Deemed Serious by Consumers

Since each consumer could specify as many objectionable characteristics of the advertisements as he wished, it is, unfortunately, impossible to be sure which he had in mind when his answer to Question 2 was "Yes, I would have the objectionable things prohibited by law." As a matter of fact, when saying that he would have objectionable things prohibited, he was probably moved to say so by a combination of things considered undesirable. Consequently, in determination of what faults of advertisements were deemed serious by those interviewed, two approaches were taken: (1) To make an array of the advertisements in accordance with the intensity of objection, as indicated by the extent to which interviewees would have the objectionable features prohibited by law, along with an accompanying array of the objections made, that is, the percentage of people examining the advertisement who objected on various specified grounds. (2) To examine the advertisements deemed most blameworthy in the light of the objections made to them.

Table 148 shows the percentage of persons answering the questionnaire who objected to the various advertisements on 11 specified grounds, as compared with the percentage who said that they would like to have the objectionable things in the advertisements prohibited by law.

TABLE 148

PERCENTAGE DISTRIBUTION OF CONSUMERS' OBJECTIONS TO TWENTY ADVERTISEMENTS, BY NATURE OF OBJECTION, COMPARED WITH PERCENTAGES OF TOTAL PERSONS ANSWERING FORM X WHO REPORTED THEY WANTED SOMETHING IN THE ADVERTISEMENTS PROHIBITED BY LAW

Advertisement Code Number	Product Advertised	Percentage of Total Persons Answering Who Would Like to Have Something About the Advertisement Prohibited by Law	Percentage of Total Persons Answering for Each Advertisement* Who Objected on the Following Grounds:										
			Not True	Misleading	Exaggerated	Indecent or Suggestive	Bad Taste	Repulsive Ideas	Silly	Fear Motive	Objection to Product	Testimonial	Unattractive
9	Food Product	1	1	1	2	0	0	0	1	0	0	0	6
2	Kitchen Utensil	1	1	1	2	0	0	1	0	0	0	0	9
4	Washing Machine	2	2	2	4	1	0	0	0	0	0	0	5
5	Textile Product	2	2	2	3	0	1	2	2	2	0	0	10
8	Food Product	2	1	1	6	0	1	0	2	2	0	0	8
16	Women's Shoes	2	2	3	11	0	1	1	5	1	1	3	7
11	Food Product	3	1	4	13	0	3	2	2	1	1	0	12
17	Cigarettes	4	2	3	4	0	2	1	4	0	3	9	4
12	Food Product	5	2	3	7	0	1	1	2	0	1	7	5
10	Cosmetic	7	5	8	14	1	3	5	2	3	3	1	11
1	Toothbrush	7	3	3	7	0	3	6	1	4	1	1	11
7	Typewriter	8	12	14	23	0	3	2	5	15	0	1	9
3	Dental Product	10	6	7	12	13	8	3	7	2	1	1	4
14	Hair Preparation	10	10	10	19	1	12	10	6	14	2	1	21
13	Whiskey	11	1	2	2	1	6	2	0	0	9	0	0
6	Cigarettes	13	9	7	13	1	5	4	4	2	3	18	6
20	Toilet Soap	13	13	8	6	27	9	18	17	10	4	4	11
15	Toilet Soap	16	8	9	14	17	8	1	4	0	0	2	1
18	Proprietary Remedy	22	15	17	27	9	16	6	10	1	6	3	15
19	Proprietary Remedy	33	24	21	28	2	17	15	5	7	12	2	34

* The number of persons judging individual advertisements varied from 617 to 933. The percentages for each class of objection is the ratio between the count of objections for that class and the number of people examining the advertisement.

As mentioned previously, the frequent objections as to the unattractiveness of the advertisements (last column) can be dismissed, because the layman's offhand appraisal of the artistic merits of the advertisements is not pertinent. It does not bear strongly upon the problem of consumer goodwill toward advertising.

The array of Table 148 indicates that the related objections of "not true," "misleading," and "exaggerated" are most frequently cited for all the advertisements, but their weighting becomes particularly heavy for advertisements in the lower half of the list, those for which over 5% of the consumers would have the objectionable features prohibited by law. Moreover, for this list of objectionable advertisements, additional undesirable characteristics came in with relatively large percentages of objectors. These latter were only infrequently mentioned for the advertisements in the first half of the list, or those least criticized. Certain of these objections may be brought together as violations of good taste, namely, "indecent or suggestive," "bad taste," "repulsive ideas," and "silly." To the above two related groups were added as particularly objectionable in certain instances the use of fear, the advertising of unworthy products and the use of questionable testimonials. Thus is built the array of factors most responsible for consumer ill-will: namely, misleading or untrue statements, bad taste, use of fear, use of questionable testimonials, and the advertising of unworthy products.

Types of Advertisements Most Frequently Found Objectionable

Examination of advertisements found most objectionable shows them, with three exceptions, to be advertisements of proprietary remedies, cosmetics, and toilet goods. Advertisements in these fields probably more than in any other have been the butt of severe criticism on the part of commentators. These advertisements and the objections made, as shown in Table 148, will be examined starting at the bottom with the most blameworthy advertisement and working upward, in view of the fact that the advertisements are arranged in descending order of the votes as to their delinquency.

Advertisement 19 dealt with a proprietary remedy cited by the advertising committee as an unworthy product. Although 91% of those interviewed had never used the product, 12% immediately classified the advertisement as presenting an unworthy product. It was scored by them because of its extreme claims, stated or implied, of relief from numerous ills. It was frequently criticized also on the ground of bad taste.

Advertisement 18 also dealt with a proprietary remedy, cited by the advertising committee as unworthy. Again an appreciable number of consumers condemned the advertisement as presenting a product of questionable merit, as using misleading or exaggerated statements, and as being in bad taste.

Advertisement 15, a soap advertisement, although not objected to by the advertising committee, was deemed to be exaggerated and misleading in its pseudoscientific claims as an aid to beauty. Moreover, the use of a nude female figure probably led to a relatively high vote that it showed bad taste.

Advertisement 20, another soap advertisement, employing a cartoon to tell a story of romance and happiness gained through use of the product, was deemed by many to be untrue, misleading, exaggerated, or in bad taste.

Testimonial advertisement 6, of cigarettes, was objected to by consumers most heavily on the ground that the manner in which it used testimonials of prominent people represented undesirable practice. Likewise, a considerable number regarded the claims as to beneficial physiological effects of cigarettes as untrue, misleading, or exaggerated.

Advertisement 13, for whiskey, undoubtedly suffered because of the sentiments of some people against alcoholic beverages. The objection to the advertisement itself was low on most scores other than the objection to the product. The willingness to prohibit advertising by law was undoubtedly directed against a product which some people feel should not be advertised or even marketed.

Advertisement 14, for a hair preparation, was considered untrue, misleading, and exaggerated as a cure for dandruff and a preventive of baldness. It was voted against in like measure as being in bad taste.

Advertisement 3, for a dental preparation, promising that the product would contribute to happy marital relations, was scored about equally as being untrue, misleading, exaggerated, and in bad taste.

Advertisement 7, of a typewriter, was particularly criticized as being untrue, misleading, or exaggerated. In fact, the claims were so exaggerated as to be untrue in the direction of the ridiculous rather than in the direction of the deceptive. Thus while 23% said it was exaggerated and 12% and 14%, respectively, looked upon it as untrue and misleading, only 8% would have prohibited the undesir-able practices by law. In this instance there was a heavy vote against it also on the ground that it dealt with a fear motive.

Advertisement 1, of a toothbrush, was looked upon by a consider-able number as being untrue, exaggerated, and in bad taste.

Advertisement 10, for a cosmetic, which employed testimonials and scientific claims for the product as an aid to beauty, was voted against because it was deemed untrue, misleading, exaggerated, and in bad taste, and because its testimonials did not reflect real choices of competent witnesses.

This examination of the advertisements rated as objectionable enough to warrant their practices being prohibited indicates that although advertising methods such as those employed may produce profitable business, yet they are definitely classified as undesirable by an appreciable number, even though a small minority, of consumers. Such violation of the sentiments of consumers has provided the basis for the material criticism of advertising that has manifested itself in recent years.

Evidence that Consumers Expect Puffery

Examination of the data suggests that consumers have a consider-able tolerance for exaggeration and puffery in advertising. Apparently they do not expect advertisements to be absolutely honest documents, just as an absolute honesty is not expected in connection with most human activities. They undoubtedly expect advertisements to be biased and to present merchandise in an attractive light. It is only when there is undue violation of claims that an appreciable number of persons express their belief that the undesirable practices should be prohibited by law. These generalizations are supported by an analysis of Table 149.

In this table the advertisements are listed according to the number who would prohibit the undesirable practices by law, shown in column (1). In columns (2), (3), and (4), are shown the percentages of persons who objected to the respective advertisements on grounds that they were not true, misleading, or exaggerated. Column 5 gives the totals of these objections, but inasmuch as each person appraising an advertisement could, if he wished, name all three of these grounds for objection, it is likely that the totals in column 5 contain duplications.

TABLE 149

PERCENTAGE OF PERSONS COMPLAINING OF THE TWENTY ADVERTISEMENTS ON THE GROUNDS THAT THEY ARE NOT TRUE, MISLEADING, AND EXAGGERATED, COMPARED WITH THE NUMBER REPORTING THAT THEY DO NOT BELIEVE THE ADVERTISED PRODUCT TO BE AS GOOD AS THE ADVERTISEMENT SAYS

ADVER-TISEMENT CODE NUMBER	PRODUCT ADVERTISED	(1) PERCENTAGE OF TOTAL PERSONS ANSWERING WHO WOULD LIKE TO HAVE SOMETHING ABOUT THE ADVERTISEMENT PROHIBITED BY LAW	PERCENTAGE OF PERSONS OBJECTING ON FOLLOWING GROUNDS:				(6) PERCENTAGE OF PERSONS BELIEVING PRODUCT NOT SO GOOD AS ADVERTISEMENT SAYS
			(2) Not True	(3) Mis-leading	(4) Exag-gerated	(5) Total*	
9	Food Product........	1	1	1	2	4	12
2	Kitchen Utensil......	1	1	1	2	4	7
4	Washing Machine...	2	2	2	4	8	14
5	Textile Product......	2	2	2	3	7	16
8	Food Product........	2	1	1	6	8	23
16	Women's Shoes......	2	2	3	11	16	25
11	Food Product........	3	1	4	13	18	29
17	Cigarettes..........	4	2	3	4	9	30
12	Food Product.......	5	2	3	7	12	19
10	Cosmetic...........	7	5	8	14	27	41
1	Toothbrush........	7	3	3	7	13	22
7	Typewriter.........	8	12	14	23	49	25
3	Dental Product.....	10	6	7	12	25	44
14	Hair Preparation.....	10	10	10	19	39	51
13	Whiskey............	11	1	2	2	5	20
6	Cigarettes..........	13	9	7	13	29	46
20	Toilet Soap.........	13	13	8	6	27	53
15	Toilet Soap.........	16	8	9	14	31	42
18	Proprietary Remedy..	22	15	17	27	59	61
19	Proprietary Remedy..	33	24	21	28	73	63

* Inasmuch as each person could, if he wished, say that an ad was not true, was mis-leading, and also was exaggerated, the percentages in this column cannot be compared without proper interpretation with those in the last column. The percentages in the "Total" column, in other words, are relatively large; if the duplications were taken out, the percentages in the Total column would be even smaller than they are, in most cases, in relation to the percentages in the last column.

Comparison of column 1 with columns 2 to 5, inclusive, shows that the complaints, particularly on the score of exaggeration, are far more numerous than the number of those who would prohibit such undesirable practices by law. Thus it would appear that overstatement and questionable claims must be extreme before consumers favor resorting to legal prohibition. Only towards the end of the column, when the number of citations of "not true" and "misleading" becomes high, do the percentages of those who would resort to legal prohibition rise above the 10% mark.

Again, that consumers take advertising with a grain of salt is indicated by a comparison of column 6 with column 5. Column 6 gives the percentages of those replying to question 4, which read, "Do you think the product is as good as the advertisement says?"

Several facts stand out in a comparison of columns 5 and 6. In the first place, as would be expected, there is a positive association between the number who objected to the advertisement on the ground of over-statement and the number who expressed the view that the products did not live up to the claims in the advertisements. Overstatement naturally produced doubt or unbelief in claims. It is even more significant that in most instances the percentages of those expressing the view that the products did not live up to the advertising claims (column 6) were appreciably larger than the percentages of those objecting on grounds that claims were misleading or exaggerated (column 5). In every instance the percentage of doubters (column 6) is much larger than the percentage looking upon the advertising claims as untrue or misleading (columns 2 and 3). Thus the data appear to support the view that consumers expect puffery; and since they would resort to legal control only for more extreme untruth, have a tolerance to biased and exaggerated statements in advertising.[2] Even in the extreme cases of advertisements 18 and 19, drug products, which were regarded as of questionable worth, only 20% said they would resort to legal prohibition.

Further evidence that consumers have come to expect advertising to be biased is indicated from the data of Table 150, which compares affirmative answers to questions 4 and 5 of questionnaire Form X. It shows the number of consumers who, although they believed the advertising claims to be exaggerated, nevertheless had confidence in the products advertised. The differences between the percentages of persons who thought the product a good product and the percentages who thought it to be as good as the advertisement said ranged, for the 20 advertisements, from 5% for the patent medicine to 41% for cigarette advertisement number 6. Similar evidence was found in answer to Questionnaire A. According to data which will be presented, consumers in that survey showed greater faith in the advertised merchandise than in the advertising.

Objections Made by Occupational Groups

Table 151 shows distribution of complaints by the various occupational groups. For this table, answers to all 20 advertisements were

---

[2] Various statutes designed to prevent untrue and misleading statements are discussed in the next chapter. Among these the Wheeler-Lea Act prohibits statements that are "misleading in any material respect."

TABLE 150

CONSUMERS' BELIEFS AS TO GOODNESS OF ADVERTISED PRODUCT COMPARED WITH THEIR BELIEFS AS TO ACCURACY OF ADVERTISING CLAIMS

CODE NUMBER	PRODUCT ADVERTISED	PERCENTAGE OF PERSONS BELIEVING:		
		Product a Good One	As Good as Advertisement Says	Difference
9	Food Product...............	96	82	14
8	Food Product...............	95	68	27
12	Food Product...............	93	69	24
2	Kitchen Utensil.............	91	78	13
7	Typewriter.................	90	57	33
11	Food Product...............	88	55	33
1	Toothbrush.................	85	57	28
15	Toilet Soap.................	84	44	40
3	Dental Product.............	75	46	29
6	Cigarettes..................	74	33	41
20	Toilet Soap.................	70	34	36
10	Cosmetic...................	70	35	35
4	Washing Machine...........	69	43	26
5	Textile Product.............	67	49	18
13	Whiskey....................	63	48	15
16	Women's Shoes.............	62	37	25
17	Cigarettes..................	60	40	20
14	Hair Preparation...........	34	17	17
18	Proprietary Remedy.........	30	11	19
19	Proprietary Remedy.........	13	8	5

TABLE 151

DISTRIBUTION BY OCCUPATIONAL GROUPS OF CONSUMERS' SPECIFIED OBJECTIONS TO TWENTY ADVERTISEMENTS*

NUMBER OF APPRAISALS 20 ADS COMBINED	OCCUPATION	BAD TASTE	INDECENT	NEGATIVE FEAR MOTIVE	REPULSIVE IDEAS	UNATTRACTIVE	EXAGGERATED	NOT TRUE	MISLEADING	SILLY	TESTIMONIAL	UNWORTHY PRODUCT	OTHER	TOTAL
1,697	Student......	7%	3%	6%	5%	15%	17%	9%	9%	6%	4%	2%	2%	85%
1,690	Professional.	7	3	4	3	12	16	8	9	5	5	3	4	79
2,210	Clerical....	6	2	3	4	12	13	7	8	3	3	2	3	66
1,368	Business....	4	3	3	3	11	14	7	7	2	3	3	3	63
354	Unskilled Labor.....	5	3	3	3	9	10	6	4	2	2	2	3	52
363	Unemployed	5	4	2	3	8	10	6	7	2	1	2	0	50
964	Skilled Labor.....	5	2	2	2	8	10	3	5	3	2	2	2	46
505	Domestics..	4	3	2	2	7	9	5	6	2	1	3	1	45
5,296	Housewife..	3	2	1	2	4	9	2	2	2	1	2	1	31

* Number of answers in column one represent total number of appraisals made of all 20 advertisements combined; in most cases each person interviewed studied 5 advertisements so that number of appraisals is about five times as great as number of *different* persons interviewed. The percentages in the body of the table indicate the number of appraisals in which the various objections appeared. The percentages in the Total column indicate the ratio of total complaints, including all those made by each person answering, and combined answers as shown in the first column.

combined. For example, 20 advertisements received a total of 5,296 appraisals by housewives, each housewife ordinarily accounting for five of these appraisals. In 3% of the appraisals by housewives, the complaint of "bad taste" was entered; in 2%, the complaint of "indecent" was entered; and so on. Percentages in the final column of the table indicate the relation between total number of complaints and total number of appraisals. For example, the number of complaints registered by housewives was 31% of the total number of appraisals made by them.

This table indicates in a very general way some of the differences in the attitudes of the respective occupational groups. As will be indicated in a later discussion of returns to Form A, students and professional people appear to be the most critical. In the Form A survey, these two groups showed themselves most unfavorably inclined toward advertising in general, just as in this test of specific advertisements, Form X, they show themselves most critical of specific advertisements.

The probable greater articulateness of professional people and students than the other groups interviewed may account in part for the relatively high complaint ratios of those groups, as shown in Table 151; they may have been better able than certain of the other groups to formulate and state a variety of objections. However, when the number of separate objections is disregarded, and the comparison is made merely on the basis of number of appraisals in which at least one complaint was registered as related to total number of appraisals, the professional and student group still appear to be the most critical. For example, 38% of the appraisals made by professional people and 44% of the appraisals made by students contained at least one objection, whereas the corresponding percentage for housewives was 29; for domestic workers, 24; and for businessmen, 34.

When considering specific advertisements, the business and clerical groups, while raising fewer objections than the professional and student groups, show themselves considerably more critical than they did in the case of the general attitude test for which Form A was used. The relatively large technical advertising knowledge of these groups and their professional interest in advertisements probably account for this situation.

Perhaps the most significant feature of the data in Table 151 is the relatively tolerant attitude of housewives when faced with specific advertisements. In only 2% of their appraisals did they raise the objection of "not true," whereas the corresponding figure was 8% for the professional group, 7% for the business group, and 9% for students. In the case of the objection "misleading," the situation is similar. Housewives there were more critical on the grounds of "exaggeration" than they were on the grounds of "not true" and "misleading," but even here only 9% of their appraisals contained this complaint, whereas in 16% of the professional group's appraisals, 14% of the business group's appraisals, and 17% of the student appraisals, the criticism "exaggerated" was cited.

These evidences of relatively favorable attitude toward advertising on the part of housewives serve to support the findings of the Form A survey. Of all the occupational groups whose opinions were sought in that study, the housewives, after the business groups, tended to be most favorably inclined toward advertising.

Objections Made by Income, Educational, and Sex Groups

As among income groups, the survey showed persons in the A income groups, with incomes of $5,000 or over, to be more critical of the 20 specific advertisements shown them than were the other groups. When the total number of specific objections made is compared with total number of appraisals made of the 20 advertisements, the following percentages appear: A income group, 77%; B group, 46%; C group, 51%; and D group, 50%. When the number of appraisals in which at least one objection is raised is expressed as a percentage of total number of appraisals for the 20 advertisements, the figures for the four income groups are as follows: A, 45%; B, 35%; C, 28%; and D, 27%. Thus, persons in the A group not only specified more objectionable characteristics per appraisal than the lower income groups specified, but in a larger number of their appraisals they found something objectionable in the advertisements.

For the education groups,[3] persons claiming college educations showed themselves more critical than persons with less formal education. In 40% of total appraisals made by persons claiming college education, at least one objection was cited. For the three lower educational groups, the corresponding percentages ranged from 25% to 29%.

The men interviewed were more critical than were the women. In 36% of the men's appraisals, as against a figure of 30% for the

---

[3] Evidence from questionnaire studies indicates that there may be considerable error in replies by consumers to questions of the amount of education which they have had. In their answers, they tend to "save face" and claim more than the facts warrant.

women, some objection was raised. This result, of course, follows naturally from the relatively tolerant attitude of the large number of housewives interviewed.

The Relationship of Belief in Product Merit to Belief in Advertising Claims

The final question in Form X was "How do you think the product (probably) compares in quality with competing products selling at about the same price?" The answers to this question were related to the answers to other questions to determine whether liking for a product might have an effect upon belief in its advertising claims, and conversely whether acceptance of advertising claims was the cause of belief in product superiority.

While the data suggested that consumers' judgments of specific advertisements are probably colored in many instances by their liking for products advertised, it was impossible to say with certainty what was cause and what was effect. There is, however, close association between the data showing esteem for the products and the data of advertisement criticism, that is, when products were known and well thought of, the criticism tended to be less.

Another analysis was made to determine to what extent users and nonusers of products differed in their criticisms of the advertisements. Except in two instances the proportion of users citing objections to the advertisement was not greatly different from the proportion among nonusers. It appears, therefore, that for the most part consumers' attitudes toward the advertisements were determined less by their opinions of products acquired by use than it was by their opinions acquired through reading advertising or through word-of-mouth knowledge. One of the exceptions related to advertisement 13, that of whiskey. Inasmuch as the chief objections made to this advertisement were that it concerned an objectionable type of product, it is natural that volume of complaints should be greater for nonusers than for users. The other exception related to patent medicine, No. 19. Here again apparently many nonusers objected on principle to the advertising of such a product, whereas among users such a feeling did not exist.

Summary of Survey with Specific Advertisements

It must be emphasized that the returns to the Form X study should be regarded as indicative rather than as conclusive. Percentages can justifiably be taken only as rough measures. Moreover, it must be kept in mind that the test was a consciously critical estimate by consumers of advertisements which in large part embodied what critics have deemed questionable practice. The test was not a measurement of attitudes towards advertising practice in general.

The study does, on the other hand, provide a general picture that is not without significance. Consumers are sensitive to many failings in magazine advertisements such as were exhibited in these tests, which while not a true sample of advertising, were representative of a considerable body of advertising. For most of these failings they have rather a wide tolerance, not carrying their criticisms to the point of wanting legal prohibitions placed on the advertisers. Except in the two cases, in which the advertised products themselves were in question, not more than 16% of the persons interviewed wanted any legal action to banish objectionable characteristics. For many of the products only a very small percentage had serious objection. It seems fairly certain, however, that the consumers had little tolerance for what they regarded as untrue, although it also appears that they were inclined to be lenient in their interpretation of what was true and what was false. Moreover, even though the majority would not resort to legal prohibition even for the worst advertisements, the large percentages who criticized on the score of exaggerated or untrue claims, of bad taste, of use of fear motives, or of use of questionable testimonials, furnish evidence that these criticisms have provided fertile ground for the growth of the ill-will against advertising which has manifested itself.

THE SURVEY OF GENERAL ATTITUDES TOWARDS ADVERTISING

Form A represents a type of attitude questionnaire which has been used occasionally in recent years. The attitudes to be measured are those widely voiced by proponents and opponents of advertising. They were divided about equally between opinions favorable to advertising and those unfavorable. The consumers were given the opportunity to indicate varying intensity of feeling in that they could agree strongly, agree, disagree, disagree strongly, or express uncertainty toward the opinion expressed. Those interviewed themselves read the statements and marked their views.

As is generally true of opinion tests, the form of the statements had much influence upon the responses given, and in interpreting the data the reader should make allowance for this fact. In many instances the replies given should not be accepted as reflecting well-considered and clearly-defined attitudes of many of those questioned, but rather snap judgments to ideas which had not been given much previous thought. Moreover, the form of the statements undoubtedly aroused sentiments of one type or another which affected replies. While the percentages of various responses are recorded, the reader is again cautioned that they should not be accepted as careful measures of well-defined opinions, but rather as rough clues by which to arrive at an ultimate estimate of consumer attitudes. When one studies carefully the responses in the light of the specific questions and compares them, he may get a sense of consumers' views toward advertising.

Methods Employed in the Survey

In the formative stage of the test, experiments were made to develop a form which could be scored statistically along the lines developed by Professor L. L. Thurstone,[4] Dr. Rensis Lickert,[5] and other experimenters of attitude testing in the educational field. Such scoring methods involve use of elaborately devised rating scales of opinion or the weighting of the intensity of view when the statements and replies are drawn, as in Form A. It was finally deemed advisable merely to give a simple numerical ranking of replies to each question without attempt to get an overall score.

In all, 4,575 sets of answers were obtained, by personal interview, to Form A. Distribution of this sample is shown in Table 152 by occupation, education, age, sex, family income, city size, and state of residence.

The distribution of the sample clearly is overbalanced in certain respects when compared with distribution of the country's population as a whole. The chief lack of balance results from undue emphasis on the upper occupational, educational, income, and city-size groups. It was not judged worth while to undertake to correct the results of the study for each of the distribution factors because an attempt to adjust for all factors would have involved complex, questionable, and

---

[4] See L. L. Thurstone, "Theory of Attitude Measurement," *Psychological Review*, Vol. 36, p. 222.

[5] See Rensis Lickert, "Technique of Attitude Measurement," *Psychological Archives*, 1932.

incomprehensible computations. However, weights were applied to the returns to adjust for differences between income distribution of the

TABLE 152

CLASSIFICATION OF 4,575 PERSONS ANSWERING QUESTIONNAIRE A

OCCUPATION			ESTIMATED FAMILY INCOME		
Occupation	Number	Percentage		Number	Percentage
Housewife............	1,452	31.7	$5,000 and over......	506	11.0
Domestic worker......	129	2.8	$2,000 to $4,999......	1,788	39.0
Professional..........	602	13.2	$1,000 to $1,999......	1,688	37.0
Business executive or			Less than $1,000......	444	10.0
owner.............	484	10.6	Unclassified.........	149	3.0
Clerical, stenographic,					
or sales.............	803	17.6		4,575	100.0
Skilled labor.........	297	6.5			
Unskilled labor........	141	3.1			
Unemployed..........	133	2.9			
Retired..............	101	2.2			
Farmer..............	16	0.4			
Student..............	392	8.6			
Other...............	6	0.1			
No answer...........	19	0.3			
Total.............	4,575	100.0			

EDUCATION			SEX		
	Number	Percentage		Number	Percentage
College..............	2,019	44.0	Male...............	2,250	49.3
High School..........	1,951	42.7	Female.............	2,287	49.9
Grade School.........	474	10.4	Not indicated.......	38	0.8
Less................	40	0.9			
No answer...........	91	2.0	Total............	4,575	100.0
Total.............	4,575	100.0			

AGE			CITY SIZE		
	Number	Percentage		Number	Percentage
16 to 20.............	296	6.5	Farm................	81	1.8
20 to 29.............	1,506	32.9	Town under 10,000...	905	19.7
30 to 44.............	1,324	28.9	10,000 to 25,000......	623	13.6
45 to 59.............	1,142	25.0	25,000 to 100,000.....	596	13.1
60 and over..........	268	5.8	Over 100,000.........	2,294	50.1
No answer...........	39	0.9	No answer...........	76	1.7
Total.............	4,575	100.0	Total.............	4,575	100.0

STATE REPRESENTATION

Western	Number	Percentage	Middle	Number	Percentage	Eastern	Number	Percentage
California......	1,233	27.0	Illinois........	27	0.6	Massachusetts..	37	0.8
Oregon........	101	2.2	Indiana........	364	7.9	New Jersey....	149	3.3
Washington....	350	7.6	Kentucky.......	132	2.9	New York.....	987	21.6
			Missouri.......	245	5.4	Pennsylvania...	810	17.7
			Ohio..........	74	1.6	No answer.....	66	1.4
						Total........	4,575	100.0

persons interviewed and distribution of the total population by income groups, because it was believed that this represented probably the most important single characteristic. It may be added, however, that the application of this correction did not alter the conclusions based on unweighted figures, for the percentages of reply were accepted as only rough measures involving considerable error.

The persons making the questionnaire interviews were asked to classify the persons interviewed into four family income groups on the basis of several observable factors. (See Appendix VII for directions given interviewers.) It is of course impossible to be sure that, in all instances, the families interviewed have been placed in the proper income group. However, examination of data obtained as to home ownership, home value or rental, automobile ownership, and education indicated that the classifications were substantially accurate. The nature of the variations shown in attitudes between the four income groups, furthermore, serves to strengthen this opinion.

The sample obtained compares with actual reported income distribution for the United States as follows:

Family Income Group	Division of Persons Interviewed		Actual Distribution* Families and Single Individuals
	Number	Percentage	
A—$5,000 and over..................	506	11.5	2.4
B—$2,000 to $4,999.................	1,788	40.4	15.8
C—$1,000 to $1,999.................	1,688	38.1	35.3
D—Less than $1,000................	444	10.0	46.5

* Source: National Resources Committee, *Consumer Incomes in the United States, Their Distribution in 1935–1936* (Washington, 1938), Table 2, p. 6.

It was on the basis of these figures showing distribution of sample interviews for income groupings and actual distribution of population as a whole that weights were applied to produce the composite figures such as given in certain tables that follow.[6]

The Distribution of Replies as a Whole

The combined replies to the various attitude statements, corrected for income distribution, are shown in Table 153. To make the data more readily understood it appeared desirable to combine the "strongly agree" and "agree" answers in one category and the "strongly dis-

---

[6] Returns for each of the four income groups are shown separately later in this chapter, Table 154, so that attitudes of persons in the different economic classes can be compared.

agree" and "disagree" answers in a second category. The ratios appearing in the final column of the table indicate the relation between the number of answers which can be construed as favorable to advertising and the number which appear to reflect an unfavorable attitude. In the computations of ratios, the "uncertain" or "indifferent" answers were disregarded. In the case of statement 1, for example, there were 2.1 times [7] as many answers (after adjustment had been made for distribution by income groups) that were favorable to advertising as there were unfavorable answers. So far as this first statement is concerned, answers in disagreement were taken as favorable to advertising and answers in agreement as unfavorable.

TABLE 153

FORM A: CONSUMERS' RESPONSES, ALL GROUPS COMBINED, SHOWING PERCENTAGE DISTRIBUTION OF ANSWERS AND RATIO OF ANSWERS FAVORABLE TO ADVERTISING AS COMPARED WITH UNFAVORABLE ANSWERS; FIGURES SHOWN HAVE BEEN ADJUSTED TO ALLOW FOR DIFFERENCES BETWEEN INCOME DISTRIBUTION OF SAMPLE AND ACTUAL INCOME DISTRIBUTION OF THE POPULATION

	AGREE*	UN-CERTAIN*	DIS-AGREE*	RATIO OF RESPONSES† FAVORABLE TO ADVERTISING TO THOSE UNFAVORABLE
1. The consumer usually gets better value for his money in unadvertised brands of products than in advertised brands................	27	16	58	2.1
2. Present-day advertising is desirable because it encourages people to want things........	73	10	18	4.1
3. Manufacturers could sell their products for less if they did not spend so much on advertising...................................	50	14	37	0.7
4. The advertising that is done by *retail stores* generally helps consumers to buy wisely....	68	15	17	4.0
5. The advertising that is done by *manufacturers* generally helps consumers to buy wisely....	57	19	23	2.5
6. The only real justification for advertising is to give product information; advertising should not seek to induce or persuade people to buy products........................	62	8	30	0.5
7. It is all right for manufacturers to use advertisements that need to be taken with a grain of salt..................................	16	10	74	0.2
8. Widely advertised products usually prove disappointing to the people who buy them....	21	18	61	2.8
9. Manufacturers' advertisements should be replaced by impartial statements published by the government or some other organization established to examine and test products....	49	17	34	0.7
10. The products of advertisers usually live up to the promises of quality and performance made in their advertisements.....................	47	18	35	1.3

* As a result of rounding off the decimals of these various categories, the adjusted figures give a sum of the three items which in some instances is slightly more or less than 100%.

† The ratio in this column is obtained by a division of the answers to any question which can be construed as favorable to advertising by the number which appear to reflect an unfavorable attitude. In these computations "uncertain" or indifferent answers were disregarded.

(Continued on next page.)

[7] Those disagreeing with the statement, 58%, divided by those agreeing, 27%, equals 2.1.

TABLE 153—*Continued*

	Approval* or Liking	Un-concern* or In-differ-ence	Irrita-tion* or Disap-proval	Ratio of Responses† Favorable to Advertising to Those Unfavorable
11. *In general* my attitude toward *billboard* advertising is one of............................	30	34	36	0.8
12. *In general* my attitude toward *magazine* advertising is one of............................	70	24	6	11.7
13. *In general* my attitude toward the advertising in *radio* programs is one of...............	38	25	37	1.0
14. *In general* my attitude toward *newspaper* advertising is one of........................	70	26	*4	17.5
15. *In general* my attitude toward *mail* advertisements is one of...........................	20	34	46	0.4
16. The government should exercise the following degree of control over advertising:				
(a) Rigid control: Establish a special board to censor *all* advertisements before publication to prevent objectionable advertising.............................			34	1.9
(b) Strict control: Establish a special board to censor all advertisements after publication to stop further use of material judged objectionable.................				
(c) Moderate control: Leave to the regular law-enforcement officers the task of investigating and stopping objectionable advertising which they observe or which is called to their attention............. 58				
(d) Minimum control: Permit interference with advertising only in cases of clear-cut dishonesty or fraud................... 66				
(e) No governmental control: Leave control of advertising entirely in the hands of the advertisers..................... 8				

* As a result of rounding off the decimals of these various categories, the adjusted figures give a sum of the three items which in some instances is slightly more or less than 100%.
† The ratio in this column is obtained by a division of the answers to any question which can be construed as favorable to advertising by the number which appear to reflect an unfavorable attitude. In these computations "uncertain" or indifferent answers were disregarded.

Attitudes toward Truth and Informative Character of Advertising

Examination of Table 153 indicates a belief among consumers that advertising should be strictly true and purely informative. Statements 6, 7, and 9, all of which bear on this point, were answered by a majority of consumers in this way: 62% agreed that the only justification for advertising is to give product information, while only 30% disagreed; 74%, as against 16%, were of the opinion that advertisers should not rely on the public to supply the traditional grain of salt; and, more serious yet from the point of view of advertisers, 49% agreed, while 34% disagreed, with the statement that manufacturers' advertising should be replaced by impartial statements issued by the government or some other independent agency. It is recognized that statement 7 has a strong appeal to moral sentiments. People generally will agree that honesty in statement should prevail. Moreover, statement 8 probably arouses a sentiment in many people against persuasion or inducement. Yet the responses to this test as a whole indicate the existence of a conscious sentiment among a substantial number of people against a not uncommon type of advertising—that which employs puffery, superlatives, vague assertions, and cajoling or aggressive persuasiveness, although the test of specific advertisements under Form X showed a considerable tolerance for such practices.

Attitude toward Price of Advertised Goods and toward Media

In the matter of price, a majority of people with definite opinions expressed the belief that manufacturers could sell their products for less if they did not spend so much on advertising; 50% agreed with this statement and 37% disagreed.

In the line-up of opinion, furthermore, the vote on billboard (statement 11), radio (statement 13), and mail advertising (statement 15) was adverse; that is, more people expressed irritation or disapproval than expressed approval or liking for these forms of advertising.

Attitude toward Advertised Merchandise

On all the remaining statements, large majorities of consumers gave answers favorable to advertisers, although there were substantial minorities who were adverse. It will be noticed that two of these statements, 1 and 8, have to do with merchandise itself rather than with the form or merits of advertising. On statement 1, to the effect that consumers usually get better value in unadvertised brands of products than they do in advertised brands, 27% of the consumers agreed and 58% disagreed, a ratio of 2.1 to 1 in favor of advertised goods. Again, on statement 8, that widely advertised goods usually prove disappointing to the people who buy them, only 22% agreed and 61% disagreed, giving a favorable ratio of 2.8 to 1. It seems fair to conclude that responses to these two questions reflect a rather high opinion of advertised merchandise by a large majority of consumers although advertisers cannot take comfort in the numbers who were critical.

A friendly feeling toward advertised goods is further emphasized by the responses to statement 10. The replies to this question in conjunction with those to statements 1 and 8, give some evidence that consumers have a better opinion of advertised products than they have of the advertising itself. Statement 10 reads: "The products of advertisers usually live up to the promises of quality and performance made in their advertisements." Of total answers, 47% were in agreement and 35% in disagreement, a ratio of 1.3 to 1. That the margin of favorable feeling was considerably smaller on this statement than on those which dealt simply with advertised merchandise, with no reference to advertising claims, probably is an indication that there is greater liking for the products than there is belief in the advertisements. In other words, a great many people, although they do not believe that advertised merchandise lives up to advertising claims, nevertheless are not disappointed in the products; they evidently do not expect them to be so good as the advertisements claim because they expect advertisements to be biased.

In short, consumers in their answers to this questionnaire, taken altogether, paid a tribute to advertised merchandise; nevertheless, there was evidence that many people looked favorably upon the values of unadvertised merchandise and that advertising overstated the worth of the products. It must be noted here that well-known distributors' brands may have been grouped by consumers with the "advertised brands," although the instructions given to interviewers to guide them in their interviews stated: " 'Widely advertised brands' are the brands of manufacturers who advertise nationally. 'Unadvertised brands' include producers' and distributors' brands, which are advertised little or not at all in national media. Chain store brands, mentioned in retail newspaper advertising, are regarded here as among the 'unadvertised' brands."

Attitudes toward Advertising Practice

What now may be said to be the consumer's attitude toward advertising itself, as reflected in answers to the questionnaire? As already noted, there is apparently a conscious belief that advertising should be strictly true and purely informative. Also, there are many people who, although not disappointed in advertised products, nevertheless, according to their answers, do not believe that they live up to advertising claims of quality and performance. The ratio on this question, nevertheless, still is favorable to advertising; i.e., 1.3 persons to 1 stated that advertised products *do* live up to advertising claims. The distribution of answers to this statement is not such as to give advertising a clear record.

Answers to questions 4 and 5 show that the respondents looked upon both retail store advertising and manufacturers' advertising as helpful to the consumer. On question 4 the vote is 4.0 to 1 in support of the belief that retail advertising generally helps consumers to buy wisely; and on question 5 the ratio is 2.5 to 1 that manufacturers' advertising is helpful. The somewhat lower ratio for manufacturers' advertising and the relatively great degree of uncertainty expressed on this question are to be noted.

The remaining statement in the first group of 10 is number 2: "present-day advertising is desirable because it encourages people to want things." Responses to this were 4.1 in agreement to 1 opposed. Uncertainties were relatively low, amounting to 10% of the total answers. Here the good old American faith in the value of materialistic ambition finds expression.

That the response to question 2 does not constitute a wholesale approval of advertising, however, is apparent when the consumer responses to the questions relating to information and exaggeration are considered. The answers to statement 2 appear to contradict the answers to statement 6. It may be that consumers approve the underlying effect of advertising in building up demand for various types of merchandise, but, at the same time, feel that this effect can and will be produced by true and strictly informational advertisements and that highly competitive, boastful advertisements aimed not at increasing primary demand but rather at securing favor for a particular brand, are undesirable. More likely, the discrepancy in the answers to the two questions may merely represent consumer rationalizations and hence indicate a weakness in the test; i.e., the answers to statement 6, as well as the confirmatory answers to statements 7 and 9, may be merely reflections of consumers' sentiments toward honesty and influence rather than of any well-defined attitude regarding advertising.

On the whole, however, it seems reasonable to say that consumers' answers to the first 10 statements of Form A reflect a friendly attitude by a large percentage of consumers, both to advertised products and to advertising; at the same time, however, they show that a large group of consumers would appreciate stricter adherence to truth and a more informational presentation of facts than now typify advertising.

Attitudes toward Media

Consumers' attitudes to specific advertising media, as reflected by answers to questionnaire statements 11 through 15, show billboard, radio, and direct advertising to be more frequently the source of irritation than magazine and newspaper advertising. Comments revealed that the outdoor medium violated their sentiments toward aesthetics. Radio advertisements were said by many to be irritating. The objection to mail advertising was that it was a nuisance to receive much second class mail.

For newspaper advertising the ratio of approvals to disapprovals is 17.5 to 1, and for magazine advertising the ratio is 11.7 to 1. For magazine advertising only 6% of total answers, and for newspaper advertising, only 4%, expressed irritation or disapproval. Both media unquestionably showed themselves acceptable to consumers, although in both cases approximately a quarter of the answers professed unconcern or indifference.

When the answers to questions 12 and 14 are compared with the answers to questions 5 and 4, respectively, some pertinent facts come to light. The percentage of persons liking newspaper advertising is very nearly the same as the percentage of those finding retail store advertising helpful. The percentage of those expressing irritation or disapproval of newspaper advertising, however, is much lower than the percentage of those who do not find retail store advertising helpful. A similar discrepancy appears when the disapprovals of magazine advertising are compared with the disagreements with statement 5. In the case of magazine advertising, however, the percentage of persons liking or approving it is appreciably larger than the percentage who think such advertising helps consumers buy wisely. While it is dangerous to reason too closely regarding these expressions of opinion, the above comparisons suggest a general conclusion: advertising may be liked by some consumers and approved of on grounds other than its effectiveness as an aid to wise buying. The high measure of liking and approval which consumers answering this questionnaire expressed for magazine and newspaper advertising, when looked at in the light of the answers given to the other questions, seems to indicate that advertising can, and in these media does, perhaps, serve ends which are approved of by consumers but which are not directly related to the function of providing a rational buying guide. What these ends are may be guessed at. The advertisements are of human and often of aesthetic interest. They are full of color, of life, and of novel ideas, often even ridiculous ideas. They suggest possibilities; they stimulate thought. They are, in short, interesting.

Another conclusion also is suggested when the smallness of the volume of disapproval expressed toward magazine and newspaper advertising is considered in the light of the strictness which consumers showed on some of the other questions. The conclusion indicated is that the significance of the evidence must be appraised in the light of the questions asked. When consumers begin to think about actual advertisements and to get away from a consideration of general statements which arouse sentiments as to honesty or against persuasion, a change in reaction takes place. For example, many consumers are led by their sentiments to respond affirmatively to the statement that the only justification for advertising is to give product information. On the other hand, when faced with the question of whether they dislike magazine advertising, which most certainly has not limited itself to giving rational product information, their answers do not conform with those to the first statement. The feelings toward magazine advertising actually obtained from experience led them to say they liked it.

Specific consideration of media, however, did little to soften consumers' judgments in the case of billboard, radio, and direct-mail advertising. Thirty per cent of consumers were favorably disposed toward billboard advertising, while 36% expressed irritation or disapproval; 38% liked radio advertising, and 37% were irritated by it; only 20% expressed a liking for mail advertisements, and 46% regarded them with irritation or disapproval. Unconcern or indifference, it will be noted, ranged from 25% to 35% for the five media.

In fairness to radio as a medium, it should be observed that the statement as worded in the questionnaire refers to the "advertising in radio programs" and not to the programs as a whole. Many people voluntarily spoke of their fondness for, and their appreciation of, the entertainment provided by radio advertisers. Many also, however, spoke with a violent dislike of the advertising inserts.

Attitudes toward Governmental Control of Advertising

In order to make an interpretation of the answers to statement 16, that dealing with the degree of control to be exercised by the government, it has been judged wise to combine the answers for (a) and (b) and also to combine those for (c) and (d). A certain measure of confusion was evident in consumers' answers to this statement, a confusion arising from the statements which follow the various degrees of control set forth. These statements were intended merely as suggestions as to the type of supervision each degree of control might call for. In some instances, however, consumers placed the emphasis, in making their answers, upon the suggested nature of the supervision rather than upon the degree of control it was intended to represent. With the answers combined as indicated, this difficulty is largely obviated. There are, then, 34% of the consumers in favor of rigid or strict control, 58% in favor of moderate or minimum control, and 8% in favor of no government control. The "no control" answers are grouped with those favoring moderate or minimum control, and this combination gives a figure of 66% classed as having a favorable attitude towards freedom in advertising. The ratio favorable to advertising is 1.9 to 1. Here, as in the earlier questions, the distribution of answers shows that a majority of consumers have no antipathy to advertising or to advertisers strong enough to cut down the freedom of advertising, but none the less a large minority by their statements adhere to the view that strict governmental control is advisable in order to secure the elimination of objectionable advertising. If these questionnaire returns can be accepted as evidencing public sentiment in at least a general way, it seems clear that a substantial portion of the public would be willing to give a favorable reception to proposals which have been made to bring severe regulation of advertising. The fact that 49% of consumers interviewed expressed themselves as favoring the rather revolutionary notion that manufacturers' advertising should be replaced by impartial statements published by the government or some other organization established to examine and test products should not be accepted at its face value as a measurement of considered opinion. There is little doubt that the answers of a large majority of those interviewed represented snap judgments on an idea to which they had given little or no thought beforehand. But even after the evidence is discounted because of uncertainty as to the exact significance of responses to the statements used, the large number giving voice to a willingness for legalistic control provides some indication that advertising practice has to an appreciable degree transgressed the ethical standards which many consumers believe should be followed.

Effect of Income upon Attitudes

The comments so far made as to consumers' attitudes were based on the combined answers of all persons interviewed, corrected as has been explained to allow for the difference between the income grouping of those persons and the reported income distribution of the total population. In order to allow a comparison of the attitudes of persons in different income classes, there are shown in Table 154, for the four income groups used, the percentages of persons agreeing and disagreeing with the statements used in questionnaire Form A.

While there appeared to be no drastic difference in attitude among the several income groups, nevertheless differences greater than might be attributable to mere chance in size of samples did show up. These followed what appears to be a logical pattern. For example, on statement 1, to the effect that the consumer usually gets better value for his money in unadvertised than in advertised brands, 31% of the lowest income group, as compared with 23% of each of the other three groups, were in agreement.

Again, on statement 10, that the products of advertisers usually live up to the promises of quality and performance made in their advertisements, a definite division of opinion is shown between the D group, with incomes of less than $1,000, and the other groups: 50%–52% of the three upper groups agreed with this statement whereas only 41% of the lowest income group agreed.

Similarly, statement 8, that widely advertised products usually prove disappointing, was agreed to more generally among the low income than among the upper income groups. Again, the poor were more firmly of the opinion than were the well-to-do that manufacturers could sell their products for less if they did not spend so much on advertising. The lower the income group, furthermore, the stronger appeared to be the belief, statement 9, that manufacturers' advertisements might well be replaced by impartial statements.

In the case of the statements so far mentioned, the attitude of the lower income groups has been less favorable to advertising than the attitude of those in the upper groups. In the matter of attitude toward media, however, disapproval of billboard and radio advertising decreased as income fell.

These variations in attitude among income groups, and others which can be observed in Table 154, seem to follow a logical pattern, but in view of the size of the samples and the uncertainty of consumer

TABLE 154

PERCENTAGE DISTRIBUTION, BY FAMILY INCOME GROUPS, OF CONSUMERS' RESPONSES TO FORM A STATEMENTS*

STATEMENT	PERCENTAGE AGREEING — INCOME GROUPS				PERCENTAGE DISAGREEING — INCOME GROUPS			
	A	B	C	D	A	B	C	D
1. The consumer usually gets better value for his money in unadvertised brands of products than in advertised brands..........................	23	23	23	31	62	61	61	53
2. Present-day advertising is desirable because it encourages people to want things..............	72	72	72	73	20	19	19	16
3. Manufacturers could sell their products for less if they did not spend so much on advertising.......	43	47	50	51	45	41	38	33
4. The advertising that is done by *retail stores* generally helps consumers to buy wisely............	61	66	67	68	24	22	16	16
5. The advertising that is done by *manufacturers* generally helps consumers to buy wisely............	54	59	57	57	29	24	21	23
6. The only real justification for advertising is to give product information; advertising should not seek to induce or persuade people to buy products....	53	55	59	66	40	36	32	25
7. It is all right for manufacturers to use advertisements that need to be taken with a grain of salt..	11	11	11	17	82	81	78	71
8. Widely advertised products usually prove disappointing to the people who buy them..........	16	16	20	25	74	69	64	54
9. Manufacturers' advertisements should be replaced by impartial statements published by the government or some other organization established to examine and test products......................	43	45	47	52	45	40	36	30
10. The products of advertisers usually live up to the promises of quality and performance made in their advertisements...............................	51	52	50	41	31	32	34	40

STATEMENT	PERCENTAGE APPROVING — INCOME GROUPS				PERCENTAGE DISAPPROVING — INCOME GROUPS			
	A	B	C	D	A	B	C	D
11. *In general* my attitude toward billboard advertising is one of†.................................	26	27	30	32	41	41	34	33
12. *In general* my attitude toward *magazine* advertising is one of†....................................	77	76	70	67	4	4	5	7
13. *In general* my attitude toward the advertising in *radio* programs is one of†......................	29	34	37	41	44	39	36	36
14. *In general* my attitude toward *newspaper* advertising is one of†...................................	73	71	70	68	3	3	4	4
15. *In general* my attitude toward *mail* advertisements is one of†...................................	18	19	18	21	43	43	45	47

STATEMENT	PERCENTAGE FAVORING RIGID OR STRICT GOVERNMENTAL CONTROL				PERCENTAGE FAVORING MODERATE, MINIMUM, OR NO GOVERNMENTAL CONTROL			
	A	B	C	D	A	B	C	D
16. The government should exercise the following degree of control over advertising:..............	32	34	34	32	67	64	64	66

* The income groups were as follows:
A—Family income $5,000 and over
B—Family income $2,000 to $4,999
C—Family income $1,000 to $1,999
D—Family income less than $1,000

† The responses to these statements, which might be checked by the person answering, were as follows: approval or liking, unconcern or indifference, irritation or disapproval. For the form, see Appendix VII.

responses to these questions, the differences are too small to hold much significance. However, they point in the direction of the conclusion that the attitudes among those who compose the great mass market is possibly less friendly towards advertising than the attitudes of higher income groups.

Attitudes of Men and Women Compared

Distribution of answers by sex is shown in Table 155. The male sample was overbalanced with business executives and professional men. In all, 484 business executives and 602 professional persons were interviewed. While not all these were men, it is likely that most of them were.[8] Inasmuch as the total number of men interviewed was 2,250, it is possible that almost half were in these two categories. Hence the distribution of male responses may have been influenced by the unrepresentative character of the sample in occupational distribution.

The chief differences of opinion shown by men and women appeared in the case of statements 3, 4, 6, 8, 9, and 14. These differences are not great in most instances and in general they are in directions that might well be expected. For example, on the matter of price, women were more inclined than men to think that advertising increases prices; women found retail advertising more helpful than did men; on statements 6 and 9, regarding truth and information, the women showed themselves more strict; they were more inclined than were men to think that advertised products disappoint users; and they expressed considerably greater liking for newspaper advertising (as they did on related statement 4) than was shown by the men.

Attitudes of Occupational Groups

Probably the most significant and interesting differences which the study reveals in consumer attitudes are those among the various occupational groups. Table 156 (page 784) shows ratio of responses favorable to advertising and responses unfavorable for nine occupational groups. These ratios, as already explained, were obtained by dividing total number of answers favorable to advertising by total number unfavorable, disregarding "uncertain" and "indifferent" answers.

Inspection of this table provides basis for conclusions regarding the

---

[8] A cross-computation between sex and occupation was not made; hence the distribution of the occupations among men and women was not available.

TABLE 155

PERCENTAGE DISTRIBUTION, BY SEX, OF CONSUMERS' RESPONSES TO FORM A STATEMENTS

STATEMENT	PERCENTAGE AGREEING		PERCENTAGE DISAGREEING	
	MALE	FEMALE	MALE	FEMALE
1. The consumer usually gets better value for his money in unadvertised brands of products than in advertised brands................	23	24	62	60
2. Present-day advertising is desirable because it encourages people to want things........	70	73	20	17
3. Manufacturers could sell their products for less if they did not spend so much on advertising..	44	52	45	33
4. The advertising that is done by *retail stores* generally helps consumers to buy wisely....	63	69	23	17
5. The advertising that is done by *manufacturers* generally helps consumers to buy wisely....	56	58	26	21
6. The only real justification for advertising is to give product information; advertising should not seek to induce or persuade people to buy products.......................	51	63	41	27
7. It is all right for manufacturers to use advertisements that need to be taken with a grain of salt...........................	12	12	79	78
8. Widely advertised products usually prove disappointing to the people who buy them....	15	22	70	62
9. Manufacturers' advertisements should be replaced by impartial statements published by the government or some other organization established to examine and test products....	43	50	44	32
10. The products of advertisers usually live up to the promises of quality and performance made in their advertisements..............	50	49	32	32

	PERCENTAGE APPROVING		PERCENTAGE DISAPPROVING	
	MALE	FEMALE	MALE	FEMALE
11. *In general* my attitude toward *billboard* advertising is one of*........................	27	30	40	36
12. *In general* my attitude toward *magazine* advertising is one of*........................	73	73	4	5
13. *In general* my attitude toward the advertising in *radio* programs is one of*..............	35	35	37	40
14. *In general* my attitude toward *newspaper* advertising is one of*........................	66	74	4	3
15. *In general* my attitude toward *mail* advertising is one of*................................	21	17	42	46

	PERCENTAGE FAVORING RIGID OR STRICT GOVERNMENTAL CONTROL		PERCENTAGE FAVORING MODERATE, MEDIUM OR NO GOVERNMENTAL CONTROL	
	MALE	FEMALE	MALE	FEMALE
16. The government should exercise the following degree of control over advertising......	32	35	66	63

* The responses to these statements, which might be checked by the person answering, were as follows: approval or liking, unconcern or indifference, irritation or disapproval. For the form, see Appendix VII.

general feeling which persons in the various groups have toward advertising. Business executives and owners, closely seconded by persons in the clerical, stenographic, and sales category have a more favorable attitude toward advertising than is shown by the other groups. This fact is not surprising, but neither is it without significance. It might be expected that persons closely associated with business have interest in and friendliness to advertising inasmuch as they use it. On the other hand, the results strongly suggest that the businessman's personal attitude is not that of other people. Persons in the professional group, doctors, lawyers, engineers, architects, and so on, were consistently less favorably inclined toward advertising than were the businessmen. Students also showed a relatively strong disposition to be critical of advertising, although their answers to statements 1 and 8 showed a good opinion of advertised products. Students also were considerably above the average in approval of magazine advertising, but still showed far less enthusiasm for this advertising than businessmen did.

On the question of degree of control to be exercised over advertising by the government, number 16, businessmen showed clearly a relatively strong antagonism to strict outside regulation. More than three-quarters of them favored moderate, minimum, or no control, whereas the other groups were divided somewhat less than 2 to 1 in favor of comparatively light control. So far as liking or approval of newspaper and magazine advertising is concerned, furthermore, opinion of businessmen was distinctly out of line with the opinion of all other groups except the clerical, stenographic, and sales group. In fact, in the case of all the advertising mediums, business opinion was consistently more favorable than was opinion of other occupational groups.

Attitudes of Housewives

Because of the importance commonly attached to the attitude of housewives toward advertising, and also because the sample for this group, 1,452 persons, was more adequate than were the samples for some of the other occupational groups, Table 157 (page 786) is included to show in detail housewives' attitudes.

In general, housewives, next to the business groups, were most favorably inclined toward advertising. More than half of them, however, believed that advertising increases the prices of merchandise; more than two-thirds were of the opinion that advertising should be limited to giving product information; four-fifths thought that advertisements which need to be taken with a grain of salt should not be

TABLE 156

RATIOS OF RESPONSES FAVORABLE TO ADVERTISING TO RESPONSES UNFAVORABLE TO ADVERTISING FOR OCCUPATIONAL GROUPS ANSWERING FORM A

STATEMENT	HOUSE-WIVES	PRO-FESSIONAL	BUSINESS EXECUTIVES	CLERICAL, SALES, ETC.	STUDENTS	SKILLED LABOR	UN-SKILLED LABOR	DOMESTIC	UN-EMPLOYED	ALL
1. The consumer usually gets better value for his money in unadvertised brands of products than in advertised brands.	2.3	2.4	2.9	3.2	3.7	2.6	1.9	1.6	1.8	2.6
2. Present-day advertising is desirable because it encourages people to want things.	4.7	2.1	8.3	4.8	2.0	5.2	3.2	4.0	2.8	3.8
3. Manufacturers could sell their products for less if they did not spend so much on advertising.	0.6	0.7	1.2	1.2	1.0	0.9	0.7	0.7	0.7	0.8
4. The advertising that is done by *retail stores* generally helps consumers to buy wisely.	5.4	2.2	3.5	5.4	1.3	4.2	3.3	3.9	2.2	3.3
5. The advertising that is done by *manufacturers* generally helps consumers to buy wisely.	3.5	1.6	2.7	2.3	1.2	2.8	1.8	3.3	1.2	2.4
6. The only real justification for advertising is to give product information; advertising should not seek to induce or persuade people to buy products.	0.3	0.6	1.3	0.8	1.0	0.5	0.4	0.3	0.5	0.6
7. It is all right for manufacturers to use advertisements that need to be taken with a grain of salt.	0.2	0.1	0.1	0.1	0.2	0.2	0.2	0.3	0.2	0.2
8. Widely advertised products usually prove disappointing to the people who buy them.	2.6	4.3	6.2	5.9	4.6	2.7	3.3	1.5	2.8	3.6
9. Manufacturers' advertisements should be replaced by impartial statements published by the government or some other organization established to examine and test products.	0.6	0.9	1.6	1.0	0.8	0.7	0.4	0.6	0.4	0.8
10. The products of advertisers usually live up to the promises of quality and performance made in their advertisements.	1.9	1.1	2.4	1.8	0.8	1.8	1.0	1.0	1.0	1.6

Statement	House-wives	Pro-fessional	Business Executives	Clerical, Sales, etc.	Students	Skilled Labor	Un-skilled Labor	Domestic	Un-employed	All
11. *In general* my attitude toward *billboard* advertising is one of*	0.8	0.4	0.9	0.9	0.7	1.0	1.3	0.8	1.0	0.8
12. *In general* my attitude toward *magazine* advertising is one of*	13.4	11.9	34.2	27.8	20.0	14.6	13.1	10.9	10.3	15.7
13. *In general* my attitude toward the advertising in *radio* programs is one of*	1.0	0.5	1.3	1.1	0.6	1.3	1.8	1.2	0.7	0.9
14. *In general* my attitude toward *newspaper* advertising is one of*	23.3	12.6	39.3	34.8	16.9	17.5	19.2	9.6	10.3	19.8
15. *In general* my attitude toward *mail* advertisements is one of*	0.3	0.4	0.8	0.5	0.4	0.4	0.5	0.5	0.4	0.4
16. The government should exercise the following degree of control over advertising:										
a. Rigid control: Establish a special board to censor *all* advertisements *before* publication to prevent objectionable advertising....										
b. Strict control: Establish a special board to censor *all* advertisements *after* publication to stop further use of material judged objectionable....										
c. Moderate control: Leave to the regular law enforcement officers the task of investigating and stopping objectionable advertising which they observe or which is called to their attention....	7.9	1.7	3.2	1.9	1.9	1.9	1.8	1.3	1.9	1.9
d. Minimum control: Permit interference with advertising only in cases of clear-cut dishonesty or fraud....										
e. No governmental control: Leave control of advertising entirely in the hands of the advertisers....										

* The responses to these statements, which might be checked by the person answering, were as follows: approval or liking, unconcern or indifference, irritation or disapproval. For the form, see Appendix VII.

used; and almost half were in favor of manufacturers' advertisements being replaced by impartial statements published by the government or some other organization established to examine and test products. On the other hand, a large majority indicated confidence in advertised products as shown by their answers to statements 1 and 8. Relatively large percentages found retail, and to a lesser extent national, advertising an aid to wise buying and correspondingly approved or liked newspaper and magazine advertising.

TABLE 157

PERCENTAGE DISTRIBUTION OF HOUSEWIVES' RESPONSES TO FORM A STATEMENTS

Question	Percentage Agreeing	Percentage Disagreeing	Percentage Uncertain	Ratio of Responses Favorable to Advertising to Those Unfavorable
1. The consumer usually gets better value for his money in unadvertised brands of products than in advertised brands.	24	61	16	2.5
2. Present-day advertising is desirable because it encourages people to want things.	74	16	9	4.6
3. Manufacturers could sell their products for less if they did not spend so much on advertising.	53	31	15	0.58
4. The advertising that is done by *retail stores* generally helps consumers to buy wisely.	74	14	12	5.3
5. The advertising that is done by *manufacturers* generally helps consumers to buy wisely.	62	18	19	3.5
6. The only real justification for advertising is to give product information; advertising should not seek to induce or persuade people to buy products.	67	23	9	0.34
7. It is all right for manufacturers to use advertisements that need to be taken with a grain of salt.	12	78	9	0.15
8. Widely advertised products usually prove disappointing to the people who buy them.	23	60	16	2.6
9. Manufacturers' advertisements should be replaced by impartial statements published by the government or some other organization established to examine and test products.	48	31	19	0.64
10. The products of advertisers usually live up to the promises of quality and performance made in their advertisements.	53	27	19	1.9

	Percentage Approving	Percentage Disapproving	Percentage Indifferent	
11. *In general* my attitude toward *billboard* advertising is one of*.	29	37	34	0.78
12. *In general* my attitude toward *magazine* advertising is one of*.	73	5	21	14.6
13. *In general* my attitude toward the advertising in *radio* programs is one of*.	37	38	25	0.98
14. *In general* my attitude toward *newspaper* advertising is one of*.	75	3	21	25.0
15. *In general* my attitude toward *mail* advertisements is one of*.	16	47	35	0.34

TABLE 157—*Continued*

Question	Percentage Favoring Rigid or Strict Governmental Control	Percentage Favoring Moderate, Medium, or No Control	Ratio of Responses Favorable to Advertising to Those Unfavorable
16. The government should exercise the following degree of control over advertising:			
a. Rigid control: Establish a special board to censor *all* advertisements *before* publication to prevent objectionable advertising..........................	34		
b. Strict control: Establish a special board to censor *all* advertisements *after* publication to stop further use of material judged objectionable.................			
c. Moderate control: Leave to the regular law-enforcement officers the task of investigating and stopping objectionable advertising which they observe or which is called to their attention............		64	
d. Minimum control: Permit interference with advertising only in cases of clear-cut dishonesty or fraud...............			
e. No governmental control: Leave control of advertising entirely in the hands of the advertisers......................			1.9

* The responses to these statements, which might be checked by the person answering, were as follows: approval or liking, unconcern or indifference, irritation or disapproval. For the form, see Appendix VII.

Attitudes of Educational Groups

As shown in Table 158, with few minor exceptions the trend of opinion was the same for the educational groups as for the income groups; that is, opinion for high income, medium income, and low income groups tended to vary in the same direction as did opinion of those with high education, medium education, and low.[9] As was true of income variation, the differences generally are too small to be deemed significant.

Attitudes of Age Groups

From Table 159, page 792, which gives consumers' attitudes classified by age groups, it appears that age had some influence on certain attitudes, but for the most part the differences were not large enough to be deemed highly significant in view of the character of the questions and the small number in the groups under age 20 and over 60.

[9] Because the number with less than grade school education was so small, the returns were incorporated with the grade school group.

Attention is called also to the uncertainty of replies of those interviewed as to their education, which was discussed in the footnote on page 765.

Attitudes of Consumers by Size of Town

Influence of size of town upon consumers' attitudes is reflected in Table 160. The farm sample was so small as to involve a high degree of chance error. When recognition is given to this fact, the percentages of answers by size of town show a relatively high degree of uniformity.

TABLE 158

PERCENTAGE DISTRIBUTION, BY EDUCATIONAL LEVELS, OF CONSUMERS' RESPONSES TO FORM A STATEMENTS

STATEMENT	PERCENTAGE AGREEING			PERCENTAGE DISAGREEING		
	College	High School	Grade School or Less	College	High School	Grade School or Less
1. The consumer usually gets better value for his money in unadvertised brands of products than in advertised brands.	20	25	30	64	60	51
2. Present-day advertising is desirable because it encourages people to want things.	65	77	75	24	14	16
3. Manufacturers could sell their products for less if they did not spend so much on advertising.	45	47	57	43	39	29
4. The advertising that is done by *retail stores* generally helps consumers to buy wisely.	59	71	75	27	15	12
5. The advertising that is done by *manufacturers* generally helps consumers to buy wisely.	52	61	61	29	20	19
6. The only real justification for advertising is to give product information; advertising should not seek to induce or persuade people to buy products.	52	59	66	41	30	21
7. It is all right for manufacturers to use advertisements that need to be taken with a grain of salt.	10	13	16	88	76	71
8. Widely advertised products usually prove disappointing to the people who buy them.	15	20	26	71	64	56
9. Manufacturers' advertisements should be replaced by impartial statements published by the government or some other organization established to examine and test products.	43	45	52	41	36	28
10. The products of advertisers usually live up to the promises of quality and performance made in their advertisements.	46	44	51	36	29	27
	PERCENTAGE APPROVING			PERCENTAGE DISAPPROVING		
	College	High School	Grade School or Less	College	High School	Grade School or Less
11. *In general* my attitude toward *billboard* advertising is one of*.	23	32	33	42	35	31
12. *In general* my attitude toward *magazine* advertising is one of*.	74	75	64	6	5	7
13. *In general* my attitude toward the advertising in *radio* programs is one of*.	29	39	44	43	36	30
14. *In general* my attitude toward *newspaper* advertising is one of*.	66	74	75	4	3	
15. *In general* my attitude toward *mail* advertisements is one of*.	16	21	22	44	45	42

TABLE 158—*Continued*

STATEMENT	PERCENTAGE FAVORING RIGID OR STRICT GOVERNMENTAL CONTROL			PERCENTAGE FAVORING MODERATE, MEDIUM, OR NO CONTROL		
	College	High School	Grade School or Less	College	High School	Grade School or Less
16. The government should exercise the following degree of control over advertising:						
a. Rigid control: Establish a special board to censor *all* advertisements *before* publication to prevent objectionable advertising......						
b. Strict control: Establish a special board to censor *all* advertisements *after* publication to stop further use of material judged objectionable...........................	35	32	34			
c. Moderate control: Leave to the regular law-enforcement officers the task of investigating and stopping objectionable advertising which they observe or which is called to their attention...............						
d. Minimum control: Permit interference with advertising only in cases of clear-cut dishonesty or fraud.......................				64	66	63
e. No governmental control: Leave control of advertising entirely in the hands of the advertisers...........................						

* The responses to these statements, which might be checked by the person answering, were as follows: approval or liking, unconcern or indifference, irritation or disapproval. For the form, see Appendix VII.

Comparison of Form A Results with Results of Other Studies

The results of various consumer studies which have been made by other organizations can be compared on some points with those of the Harvard study. The question of the effect of advertising upon price, for example, repeatedly has been the subject of inquiry. Some of the results obtained are cited in the table on page 790, where percentage of answers favorable and unfavorable to advertising are given for various related questions.[10]

The questions used in these various surveys were not the same, nor were the methods of sampling and interviewing or the scope of the studies by any means identical. It is perhaps all the more interesting for these reasons to observe that general attitudes recorded agree as closely as they do. All but one show consumers to believe that advertising increases the prices of merchandise.

[10] Footnote references to the various studies will be found at the end of the chapter, pages 799–800.

STATEMENT OR QUESTION GIVEN	PERCENTAGE OF RESPONSES FAVORABLE TO ADVERTISING	PERCENTAGE OF RESPONSES UNFAVORABLE TO ADVERTISING	UNCERTAIN
Harvard Study: Manufacturers could sell their products for less if they did not spend so much on advertising..........................	37	50	13
University of Toledo:[1] Stores could sell for less money if they didn't advertise so much......	46	39	15
Advertising Age:[2] Do you believe that you are paying a premium for widely advertised goods, because of the large amount of money spent for advertising by the manufacturer of these goods?...........................	49	51	0
Sales Management:[3] One pays more for advertised articles than for those distributed without advertising..............................	22	53	25
Ladies' Home Journal:[4] Do you think products that are advertised widely cost more than products that are not advertised?..........	49	52	0
Psychological Corporation of America:[5] Do you believe that advertising makes the things you buy cost more or less in the long run?...	24	40 (17 neither)	19
Sales Management:[6] Do you believe that widely advertised mass production articles cost more because they are advertised?..............	64	36	0
Association of National Advertisers:[7] Do you think that advertising increases or decreases the cost of things you buy?..................	15	72	13
Sales Management:[8] Too much money is spent for advertising...........................	47	53	0

Only one study, one of those reported in *Sales Management,* showed a majority expressing belief that advertising did not increase prices. The relatively low percentage of unfavorable answers to the question, "Do you believe that widely advertised mass production articles cost you more because they are advertised?" may be explained by the fact that the two preceding questions on the questionnaire directed attention to the possible effect of mass production and broad markets upon price. The question itself repeated the phrase "mass production."

The Gallup survey for the Association of National Advertisers shows the highest percentage of persons believing that advertising increases prices. This survey was one of the most extensive made, 5,000 persons being interviewed. Dr. Gallup reported, "Interviews were distributed properly by states, small towns, cities, by ages, income groups, farms, etc." The interviewing work was done by the field organization used regularly by the Institute of Public Opinion. It is also the most recent of all the surveys cited. In view of these considerations it may be concluded that probably more than half of the adult population of the country are of the opinion that advertising increases prices.

Another attitude frequently measured has related to the relative qualities of advertised and unadvertised goods. Results of six different surveys are shown below:

STATEMENT OR QUESTION GIVEN	PERCENTAGE OF REPLIES		
	Favorable to Advertising	Unfavorable to Advertising	Uncertain
Harvard Study: The consumer usually gets better value for his money in unadvertised brands of products than in advertised brands........	57	27	16
Widely advertised products usually prove disappointing to the people who buy them......	61	22	17
Sales Management:[8] Highly advertised brands are more dependable.....................	54	46	0
Fortune:[9] When you buy canned goods, groceries, drugs, and toilet items, do you think the difference in price between nationally advertised brands and unadvertised brands represents a worth-while difference in quality?	47	33 (No difference in price—5%)	15
Sales Management:[3] A good name on a quality product justifies a somewhat higher price.....	58	19	23
Advertised articles are frequently worth additional money.........................	43	32	29
Association of National Advertisers:[7] Are you willing to pay more for nationally known products?............................	73	27	0
The American Consumer:[10] Do you believe, generally speaking, that you are getting full value in quality and quantity at reasonable prices when you buy today?.....................	37	46	17

In every survey except one the number of replies showing a favorable attitude toward quality of advertised products was appreciably greater than the number with an unfavorable attitude. Yet the proportion of unfavorable replies was not such as to give comfort to advertisers. Since the questions and statements used to determine consumer attitudes were dissimilar in character, close uniformity of results could

TABLE 159

PERCENTAGE DISTRIBUTION, BY AGE, OF CONSUMERS' RESPONSES TO FORM A STATEMENTS

STATEMENT	PERCENTAGE AGREEING					PERCENTAGE DISAGREEING				
	Under 20	20–29	30–44	45–59	60 & over	Under 20	20–29	30–44	45–59	60 & over
1. The consumer usually gets better value for his money in unadvertised brands of products than in advertised brands.	21	23	24	23	31	61	62	61	60	51
2. Present-day advertising is desirable because it encourages people to want things.	66	69	72	76	69	21	22	18	15	19
3. Manufacturers could sell their products for less if they did not spend so much on advertising.	49	45	51	47	55	41	44	37	38	31
4. The advertising that is done by *retail stores* generally helps consumers to buy wisely.	50	58	70	74	76	32	26	16	14	10
5. The advertising that is done by *manufacturers* generally helps consumers to buy wisely.	41	50	62	64	62	37	30	19	19	15
6. The only real justification for advertising is to give product information; advertising should not seek to induce or persuade people to buy products.	51	53	60	60	65	42	40	31	30	25
7. It is all right for manufacturers to use advertisements that need to be taken with a grain of salt.	18	11	13	10	15	67	78	78	82	74
8. Widely advertised products usually prove disappointing to the people who buy them.	17	16	17	21	31	62	69	68	64	52
9. Manufacturers' advertisements should be replaced by impartial statements published by the government or some other organization established to examine and test products.	55	48	44	42	49	31	37	38	40	35
10. The products of advertisers usually live up to the promises of quality and performance made in their advertisements.	31	44	54	56	53	50	38	28	26	26

Statement	Percentage Approving					Percentage Disapproving				
	Under 20	20–29	30–44	45–59	60 & over	Under 20	20–29	30–44	45–59	60 & over
11. *In general* my attitude toward *billboard* advertising is one of*	33	30	28	27	18	27	33	39	42	50
12. *In general* my attitude toward *magazine* advertising is one of*	69	73	75	74	63	5	4	5	5	9
13. *In general* my attitude toward the advertising in *radio* programs is one of*	31	33	37	36	34	42	40	38	37	37
14. *In general* my attitude toward *newspaper* advertising is one of*	61	66	73	75	69	5	3	4	3	5
15. *In general* my attitude toward *mail* advertisements is one of*	14	18	19	20	18	44	44	45	43	47

Statement	Percentage Favoring Rigid or Strict Governmental Control					Percentage Favoring Moderate, Minimum or no Control				
	Under 20	20–29	30–44	45–59	60 & over	Under 20	20–29	30–44	45–59	60 & over
16. The government should exercise the following degree of control over advertising:										
a. Rigid control: Establish a special board to censor *all* advertisements *before* publication to prevent objectionable advertising..........	33	35	34	31	32					
b. Strict control: Establish a special board to censor *all* advertisements *after* publication to stop further use of material judged objectionable..........										
c. Moderate control: Leave to the regular law enforcement officers the task of investigating and stopping objectionable advertising which they observe or which is called to their attention..........						66	63	64	67	65
d. Minimum control: Permit interference with advertising only in cases of clear-cut dishonesty or fraud..........										
e. No governmental control: Leave control of advertising entirely in the hands of the advertisers..........										

* The responses to these statements, which might be checked by the person answering, were as follows: approval or liking, unconcern or indifference, irritation or disapproval. For the form, see Appendix VII.

TABLE 160

PERCENTAGE DISTRIBUTION, BY SIZE OF TOWN, OF CONSUMERS' RESPONSES TO FORM A STATEMENTS

Statement	Percentage Agreeing					Percentage Disagreeing				
	Farm	Under 10,000	10,000-25,000	25,000-100,000	Over 100,000	Farm	Under 10,000	10,000-25,000	25,000-100,000	Over 100,000
1. The consumer usually gets better value for his money in unadvertised brands of products than in advertised brands	26	24	21	24	24	60	62	62	61	60
2. Present-day advertising is desirable because it encourages people to want things	65	70	69	71	74	22	20	18	19	18
3. Manufacturers could sell their products for less if they did not spend so much on advertising	59	50	48	46	48	25	38	39	40	40
4. The advertising that is done by *retail stores* generally helps consumers to buy wisely	49	68	70	64	64	30	14	16	21	22
5. The advertising that is done by *manufacturers* generally helps consumers to buy wisely	57	57	58	59	57	20	22	20	24	26
6. The only real justification for advertising is to give product information; advertising should not seek to induce or persuade people to buy products	64	58	58	54	57	22	33	32	35	35
7. It is all right for manufacturers to use advertisements that need to be taken with a grain of salt	15	11	11	12	12	75	76	79	76	80
8. Widely advertised products usually prove disappointing to the people who buy them	26	20	16	20	18	56	65	68	63	67
9. Manufacturers' advertisements should be replaced by impartial statements published by the government or some other organization established to examine and test products	62	43	43	52	46	27	38	37	33	39
10. The products of advertisers usually live up to the promises of quality and performance made in their advertisements	36	49	51	48	50	43	32	28	33	32

Statement	Percentage Approving					Percentage Disapproving				
	Farm	Under 10,000	10,000–25,000	25,000–100,000	Over 100,000	Farm	Under 10,000	10,000–25,000	25,000–100,000	Over 100,000
11. *In general* my attitude toward *billboard* advertising is one of*	27	34	26	27	31	43	43	35	41	35
12. *In general* my attitude toward *magazine* advertising is one of*	62	72	73	71	74	2	5	5	6	4
13. *In general* my attitude toward the advertising in *radio* programs is one of*	36	37	35	31	35	36	36	36	43	39
14. *In general* my attitude toward *newspaper* advertising is one of*	69	68	72	69	71	4	4	3	4	3
15. *In general* my attitude toward *mail* advertisements is one of*	28	19	18	17	19	36	44	42	49	44

16. The government should exercise the following degree of control over advertising:*	Percentage Favoring Rigid or Strict Governmental Control					Percentage Favoring Moderate, Minimum, or No Governmental Control				
	Farm	Under 10,000	10,000–25,000	25,000–100,000	Over 100,000	Farm	Under 10,000	10,000–25,000	25,000–100,000	Over 100,000
a. Rigid control: Establish a special board to censor *all* advertisemens *before* publication to prevent objectionable advertising	37	31	32	32	35					
b. Strict control: Establish a special board to censor *all* advertisements *after* publication to stop further use of material judged objectionable										
c. Moderate control: Leave to the regular law enforcement officers the task of investigating and stopping objectionable advertising which they observe or which is called to their attention						60	67	67	67	63
d. Minimum control: Permit interference with advertising only in cases of clear-cut dishonesty or fraud										
e. No governmental control: Leave control of advertising entirely in the hands of the advertisers										

* The responses to these statements, which might be checked by the person answering, were as follows: approval or liking, unconcern or indifference, irritation or disapproval. For the form, see Appendix VII.

not be expected. In Dr. Gallup's study for the Association of National Advertisers the simple question, "Are you willing to pay more for nationally known products?" brought the largest percentage of replies indicating favorable attitude. The final statement, used by *The American Consumer,* which showed a questionable attitude toward the values received in merchandise by consumers, is not directly comparable to the others, for it does not distinguish between advertised and unadvertised goods. Neither does it reflect a cross section of public opinion, since interviews were limited to the educational field and to leaders in consumer education. The distribution of answers to this question is included here because of the basic interest of the question and the replies of this particular group.

The following comparisons are made of results obtained in different studies as to consumers' attitudes toward the truthfulness of advertising claims.

| | PERCENTAGE OF RESPONSES | | |
STATEMENT OR QUESTION GIVEN	Favorable to Advertising	Unfavorable to Advertising	Uncertain
Harvard Study: The products of advertisers usually live up to the promises of quality and performance made in their advertisements.....	47	35	18
Advertising Age:[11] Did you buy any products in the past year which failed to live up to claims made for them by the manufacturers?........	88*	11†	1
Ladies' Home Journal:[4] During the last year have you bought any widely advertised products which did not turn out as advertised?.......	82	18	0
Sales Management:[12] Most advertising statements are based either on reasonable facts or exaggerated claims. Which do you find most often to be the case?........1934 survey....	51	49	0
1938 survey....	42	58	0
Ladies' Home Journal:[4] On the whole, do you believe advertising today is truthful?........	51	49	0
Sales Management:[8] Most advertising fools the public....................	46	54	0
University of Toledo:[1] Most retail advertising fools the public.........................	35	52	13

* Answered no or named local brands.
† Mentioned national brands.

Again the form of questions asked led to widely varying response. When specific questions were asked in the *Ladies' Home Journal* and

Advertising Age surveys as to whether consumers in their own experience found that products did not live up to advertising claims, 82% of consumers in one case and 88% in the other gave a favorable response as to the truthfulness of advertising claims. When general opinions or attitudes regarding the truthfulness of advertising were sought, then approximately half either stigmatized advertising claims as exaggerated, misleading, or untruthful, or were uncertain as to its honesty.

The question of governmental control of advertising also has been raised in several of the studies, as indicated in this summary:

STATEMENT OR QUESTION GIVEN	PERCENTAGE OF REPLIES		
	Favorable to Advertising	Unfavorable to Advertising	Uncertain
Harvard Study: The government should exercise the following degrees of control over advertising: rigid or strict control; moderate, minimum, or no control...................	66	34	0
Manufacturers' advertisements should be replaced by impartial statements published by the government or some other organization established to examine and test products......	34	49	17
Sales Management:[8] Advertising should be replaced by daily governmental bulletins......	59	41	0
The government should control the trustworthiness of advertising.................	26	74	0
Association of National Advertisers:[7] Do you think there is need for stricter laws to regulate what is said in advertisements?............	41	59	0
University of Toledo:[11] The government should impose stricter regulations on the retail advertiser and make advertising more truthful and accurate...........................	20	69	11
The American Consumer: [10] Do you think it would help consumers if there were more regulation of *business* or less?........................	32	43	25*

* Qualified answers.

The divergence which occurs in percentages of favorable and unfavorable answers on the matter of government control is understandable from the nature of the different statements used. The important conclusion which can be drawn from the data is that at least a third of the public expressed themselves in favor of rather strict governmental control of advertising.

One other comparison of the results of the various studies is made, that concerning the helpfulness of advertising to consumers.

| | PERCENTAGE OF REPLIES | | |
STATEMENT OR QUESTION GIVEN	Favorable to Advertising	Unfavorable to Advertising	Uncertain
Harvard Study: The advertising that is done by retail stores generally helps consumers to buy wisely..................................	68	17	15
The advertising that is done by manufacturers generally helps consumers to buy wisely.....	57	23	19
University of Toledo:[1] Most retail store advertising is a valuable help in educating the consumer....................................	71	18	11
Without advertising the consumer would be seriously handicapped in shopping..........	76	16	8
Sales Management:[6] Do you believe that if that product (a favorite to be named by the person interviewed) had never been advertised you would have discovered its value anyway?....	65	35	0
Advertising Age:[2] Do you believe that advertising renders the consumer a valuable or helpful service?..............................	89	11	0
Sales Management:[3] Advertising is valuable consumers' education.......................	79	21	0
Only through advertising can the public know what is on the market....................	77	23	0
Buying by advertisements helps you to save much money...........................	54	46	0
Ladies' Home Journal:[4] Should advertising matter be left out of newspapers and magazines, out of radio programs?..........Magazines.....	95	5	0
Newspapers....	96	4	0
Radio.........	80	20	0

Taken altogether, these answers seem to indicate that a substantial majority of consumers have an underlying acceptance of and a friendly feeling for advertising as it may aid them in knowing merchandise; yet a substantial minority express discontent with advertising practice.

Summary of Survey Findings

In spite of the shortcomings of many of these opinion surveys, including the Harvard Study, and in spite of doubt as to the exact meaning of the replies, the general tenor of the responses found in all the studies should give and undoubtedly has given advertisers food for thought. They show that although a substantial majority of consumers are not unfriendly to advertising, nevertheless a considerable group of people do not bear goodwill toward advertising. Or, if the general attitude of many consumers is not unfriendly, the unfavorable opinions, directed against exaggeration, poor taste, or lack of information, provide a fertile background for further destruction of confidence in advertising as an economic tool.

The analyses of the demand, cost, and pricing effects of advertising made in this volume have indicated a basis in business practice for the views which are accepted regarding the effects of advertising on price. The views regarding honesty, or truthfulness, are understandable in the light of some current, familiar advertising, even though it represents a small part of the whole.

The evidence of this chapter is believed to be of greatest significance to businessmen themselves. Instead of looking in the material for crumbs of satisfaction to be had from the fact that the majority of consumers are friendly to advertising, they should consider carefully the evidence of the minorities whose replies are critical. These facts indicate that advertising and business practice are violating the sentiments of a substantial number of consumers as to what is good taste, honesty, or desirable behavior. Businessmen must realize that ethical attitudes, which are subject to constant evolution, govern the conduct of business. Consequently they should be alert to changes in ethical viewpoints and adapt themselves to the moral and ethical sentiments of the community. Blindness to them can only result in legal compulsion.

FOOTNOTES TO TABULATED MATERIAL ON PP. 790, 791, 796 AND 797

[1] H. A. Frey, *What Your Customers Think about Your Retail Advertising Methods and Media* (University of Toledo, 1935). (Weights have been removed from Mr. Frey's figures to make them comparable to others in the tables.)

[2] "93 Per Cent See Advertising as Economic Force," *Advertising Age*, January 13, 1936, p. 25.

[3] "Growing Army of Young Skeptics Imperils Success of Sales Drives," *Sales Management* (Survey made by Market Research Corporation of America), January 15, 1936, p. 80.

[4] H. F. Pringle, "What Do the Women of America Think about Advertising?" *Ladies' Home Journal*, May, 1939, p. 22.

[5] Henry C. Link, *Consumer Research and Consumer Good-Will* (Boston Conference on Distribution, 1938), p. 60.

[6] "Should Advertising be Afraid of the 'Consumer Movement'?" (Survey made by the Ross Federal Research Corporation for *Sales Management*), *Sales Management*, September 1, 1939, p. 18.

[7] George Gallup, "The Consumer Movement—the Scope and Penetration Nationally Among the Consuming Public," *Proceedings, Thirtieth Annual Meeting, Association of National Advertisers*, October, 1939, p. 17.

8 "Attitude Test Shows Women and Old People Favor Advertising Most" (Survey made by Market Research Corporation of America for *Sales Management*), *Sales Management*, January 1, 1936, p. 26.

9 *Fortune*, "The Fortune Quarterly Survey: IX," July, 1937, p. 104.

10 "Results of Business-Consumer Survey Conducted by *The American Consumer*, 1938" (typed). (Interviews limited to educational field and consumer leaders.)

11 "383 Consumers Tell of Products Which 'Failed to Meet Expectations,'" *Advertising Age*, October 28, 1935, p. 18.

12 "What the Consumer Thinks of Advertising—1938 and 1934" (Survey made by Ross Federal Research Corporation for *Sales Management*), *Sales Management*, September 1, 1938, p. 18.

CHAPTER XXVII

THE RELATION OF ADVERTISING TO ETHICAL
AND MORAL RULES

THE evidence of the preceding chapter was hardly needed to show that the advertising practices of some sellers in recent years have violated the moral and ethical sentiments of a number of consumers. Although these consumers have apparently expected advertising to carry the biased viewpoint of the seller and to be characterized by puffery, nevertheless they have indicated that some sellers have employed advertising practices which they considered improper. Their responses both to general statements about advertising practice and to specific advertisements indicate that they do not look with favor upon the use of exaggeration, untruth, pseudoscientific appeals, and illustrations and copy which they deem in bad taste. Moreover, they dislike the offering and sale of products which they think are worthless or possibly harmful, particularly items in the drug and cosmetic fields. Although these practices are limited to a small percentage of advertisers, they have been employed frequently enough to color the attitudes of these consumers toward advertising as an institution, and toward selling practice in general. While the products deemed harmful or undesirable are evidently few and for the greater part are sold by small concerns, the advertising practices which were designated as undesirable have been employed by certain leading advertisers and consequently have been frequently before the public.

The significance of this evidence lies in the fact that the attitudes and views of the consumer group in considerable measure determine what products may be sold and the character of the selling influence that may be employed. If sellers offend the moral and ethical sentiments of consumers, they will in time be made to conform through legislation to consumer dictates of proper behavior. The student of economic history cannot but be impressed with the importance of ethical and moral views as determinants of economic and business practice. Hence, an analysis of the ethics of advertising and selling is pertinent to a study of the economics of advertising.

The Approach to the Ethical Problem

The fundamental ethical issues raised in this chapter regarding advertising and selling are the degree to which influence and persuasion on the part of sellers are to be permitted, and the manner in which they may be used. The use of influence in commercial relations is one of the attributes of a free society, just as persuasion and counter-persuasion are exercised freely in many walks of life in our free society—in the home, in the press, in the classroom, in the pulpit, in the courts, in the political forum, in legislative halls, and in government agencies for information. In each of these areas there are ethics governing the use of influence. In each, pragmatic considerations determine the formation of ethical rules or standards which apply; they are designed to meet the needs of people in specific social relationships at particular times. A study of ethics shows that ethical standards are in constant evolution and hence vary with the passage of time. Rules that meet the needs of one period are not suitable for those of another. Moreover, codes of ethics and ethical standards for different callings or occupations at any one time are not uniform. They are appropriate to the needs of particular circumstances. Thus, the ethical standards which govern the conduct of a judge are not those which apply to the lawyer, whether he be prosecutor or defense counsel. Ethical rules require that a judge be impartial, but a lawyer is expected to present one side of the case to the best of his ability. Again, because relationships between a doctor and his patient are different than those of a businessman and his customer, the ethical standards which have evolved to guide the physician in the solicitation of clients are different from those applied to the businessman in the sale of merchandise.

The purpose of this chapter is to inquire into the present status of the ethics of advertising, to determine what forces underlie present standards, to appraise the criticisms of present practice and to indicate the direction of present tendencies to which businessmen must adjust themselves. Most people agree as to the desirability of preventing clear misrepresentation and falsehood. The extent of misleading and false advertising is shown in evidence given in this chapter regarding certain legal and extra-legal bureaus dealing with questionable advertising practice. But the prohibition of certain types of advertising brought about by these bureaus is not enough to satisfy all critics. Some of the attitudes recorded in the preceding chapter show the tendency of some consumers to favor restriction of the use of influence even beyond the prevention of what may be termed the grosser forms of misrepresentation. The viewpoint is more clearly brought out in the statements of certain writers who have been severe critics of advertising and selling practice. In order to sharpen appreciation of the basic ethical problem relating to use of influence in advertising, the statements of certain of these critics are discussed. Then in order to provide perspective on the issue of the place of influence in the modern economy, effort is made to trace the changing ethical rules which have governed the use of influence and the reasons therefor, in so far as these changes are reflected in legalistic controls and in codes of business practice. The character of the codes followed by businessmen is noted and an effort is made to see what progress in the light of present ethical standards has been made in improving buying and selling practices. Some of the important forces which have governed the relations of buyers and sellers are outlined, and forces which may be operating currently to bring changes to which businessmen should be alert are indicated. Finally the issue of whether influence is to be deemed ethical in a free society and the economic implications of its prohibition are discussed.

Evidences of Questionable Use of Influence in Advertising, as Shown in Reports of Legal and Extra-legal Bureaus

Just how much of advertising is to be deemed unethical depends upon the viewpoint and the standards of the individual critic. But an indication of the quantity deemed undesirable by certain legal and extra-legal policing organizations is given in the reports of governmental enforcement agencies and from the Better Business Bureaus.

The annual reports of the Federal Trade Commission give the best available information of the extent and the character of false and misleading representations in advertising. This government agency scrutinizes a vast volume of advertising material and reports not only the number of advertisements tentatively marked as being possibly misleading but also the number of complaints which it has launched against advertisers and the number of stipulations entered into with advertisers to cease certain advertising practices. Many of the advertisements which the Commission's employees mark as possibly questionable do not prove upon investigation to warrant complaints by the Commission or to necessitate negotiations which might entail administrative action. Yet the figures regarding the number of advertisements which its employees survey and mark as deserving further study give a rough indication of the extent of advertising which certain individuals in the employ of the Commission deem questionable. The following excerpts from the annual report for the year ending June 30, 1940, are pertinent to the work of the Commission in its investigation of advertising:

Advertising matter as published in newspapers, magazines, catalogs, and almanacs and as broadcast over the radio is surveyed and scrutinized for false and misleading representations by the Commission through its radio and periodical examining staff on a continuing current basis. This work includes duties devolving upon the Commission with the enactment of the Wheeler-Lea amendment to the Federal Trade Commission Act.

The survey of magazine and newspaper advertising was inaugurated by the Commission in 1929, and the surveying of commercial advertising continuities broadcast by radio was started in 1934. As expanded in 1939, this survey includes mail-order catalogs and domestic newspapers published in foreign languages.

Apparent and probable misrepresentations detected through this survey are carefully investigated, and where it appears from the facts developed that the advertising is false or misleading and circumstances warrant, the advertisers are extended the privilege of disposing of the matters through an informal procedure, more fully explained at page 123, which permits their executing stipulations in which they agree to cease and desist from the use of the acts and practices involved. A large majority of the cases are adjusted in this manner. In those cases where this informal procedure is not applicable or does not result in the elimination of the misleading claims, and the facts so warrant, formal procedure is instituted.

. . . . .

Newspaper and magazine advertising. In examining advertisements in current publications, it has been found advisable to call for some newspapers and magazines on a continuous basis, due to the persistently questionable character of the advertisements published. However, as to publications generally, of which there are some 20,000, it is physically impossible to survey continuously all advertisements of a doubtful nature; also, it has been found unnecessary to examine all the issues of publications of recognized high ethical standard whose publishers carefully censor all copy before acceptance.

Generally, copies of current magazines and newspapers are procured on a staggered monthly basis, at an average rate of three times yearly for each publication, the frequency of the calls for each publication depending upon its circulation and the character of its advertisements.

Through such systematic calls for magazines and newspapers during the fiscal year ended June 30, 1940, the Commission procured 1,631 editions of representative newspapers of established general circulation and 1,339 editions of magazines and farm journals of interstate distribution representing a combined circulation of 122,995,074. Among these periodicals were included representative foreign-language publications having a combined circulation of 1,417,587 copies.

The Commission examined 300,741 advertisements appearing in the aforementioned newspapers and magazines and noted 24,104 as containing representations that appeared to be false or misleading. The 24,104 questioned advertisements provided current specimens for check with existing advertising cases as to their compliance with orders of the Commission and stipulations accepted from advertisers, and also formed the bases of prospective cases not previously set aside for investigation.

. . . . .

In the examination of 15,208 pages of the mail-order advertising, 441 pages have been marked by the preliminary reviewing staff as containing possibly false, misleading and deceptive material, and have been set aside for investigation. A wide variety of commodities (including food, drugs, devices, and cosmetics) is included in this questioned advertising.

Radio advertising. The Commission, in its systematic review of advertising copy broadcast over the radio, issues calls to individual radio stations, generally at the rate of four times yearly for each station. However, the frequency of calls to such individual broadcasters is varied from time to time, dependent principally upon transmittal power, the service radius or area of specific stations, and the advertising record of certain types of stations, as disclosed in analyses of previous advertising reviews.

. . . . .

During the fiscal year ended June 30, 1940, the Commission received 759,-595 copies of commercial radio broadcast continuities, amounting to 1,518,237 pages of typewritten script. These comprised 1,072,537 pages of individual station script and 445,700 pages of network script.

The staff read and marked 684,911 commercial radio broadcast continuities, amounting to 1,398,561 pages of typewritten script. These comprised 436,700 pages of network script and 961,861 pages of individual station script. An average of 4,570 pages of radio script were read each working day. From this material 22,556 commercial broadcasts were marked for further study as containing representations that might be false or misleading. The 22,556 questioned commercial continuities provided current specimens for check with existing advertising cases as to their compliance with orders of the Commission and stipulations accepted from advertisers, in addition to forming the bases for prospective cases which may not previously have been set aside for investigation.

. . . . .

Source of radio and periodical cases. Examination of current newspaper, magazine, radio, and direct mail-order house advertising, in the manner described, has provided the basis for 79 percent of the radio and periodical advertising cases handled by the Commission during the fiscal year ended June 30, 1940. Information received from other sources including information from other divisions of the Commission, and from other Government agencies, formed the basis of the remainder of this work.

Analysis of questioned advertising. An analysis of the questioned advertising which was assembled by cases and given legal review discloses that it pertained to the following classification of 3,014 commodities in the proportions indicated:

CLASSIFICATION OF PRODUCTS

Commodity	Per cent	
Food, drugs, devices and cosmetics:		
Food	11.2	
Drugs	33.4	
Cosmetics	12.8	
Devices [for use in diagnosis, prevention, or treatment of disease]	2.3	
		59.7
Other products:		
Specialty and novelty goods	11.2	
Automobile, radio, refrigerator, and other equipment lines...	4.9	
Home study courses	2.8	
Tobacco products	1.2	
Gasoline and lubricants	1.6	
Poultry and livestock supplies and equipment, including hatchery products, etc.	2.0	
Miscellaneous, including apparel, coal and oil fuels, house furnishings and kitchen supplies, specialty building materials, etc.	16.6	
		40.3
Total		100.0

In the item of drug preparations listed above, a substantial proportion of the related advertising contained positive misrepresentations or representations which encompassed possible injurious results to the public and for that reason were given preferred attention.

Number of cases handled. During the fiscal year the Commission sent questionnaires to advertisers in 739 cases and to advertising agencies in 109 cases, and negotiated 190 stipulations, which were accepted and approved by the Commission.

A total of 532 cases were disposed of by the various methods of procedure. Of this number, 188 cases were considered settled upon receipt of reports showing compliance with previously negotiated stipulations. The remaining 344 cases were closed without prejudice to the right of the Commission to reopen if warranted by the facts: 333 of them for such reasons as no evidence of violation, lack of jurisdiction, and insufficient public interest; 2 because the Post Office Department had issued fraud orders against the advertisers, and 9 because the Post Office Department had accepted from the parties concerned affidavits of discontinuance of business.

In addition, the Commission, in 36 cases, ordered issuance of complaint: in 17 instances where advertisers failed to stipulate; in 1 case in which the advertiser was not given an opportunity to stipulate because of gross deception, and in 18 involving violation of the terms of existing stipulations previously accepted and approved. In 41 cases field investigations were ordered, including 13 wherein it appeared that application for injunction or criminal proceedings might be warranted. Also, 3 cases were referred to other governmental agencies as concerning matters more appropriately coming within their jurisdiction.

Seven hundred forty-three radio and periodical cases were pending on July 1, 1939, and 979 were pending on June 30, 1940.[1]

Questionable Retail Advertising

There is no record which shows just how much retail and local financial advertising is misleading or false. Reports of the Better Business Bureaus, which carry out the organized efforts of local merchants to prevent fraud and misrepresentation in the 55 communities in which they operate, give a clue; but most of the efforts of such bureaus are devoted to preventive work. To illustrate, the Boston Better Business Bureau, in the report at its annual meeting[2] held in May, 1941, stated that it had received and acted on 377 consumers' complaints of misrepresentation or fraud. It submitted evidence to governmental authorities in 83 cases, and the evidence which it presented was used in prosecution or in other government action in 41 cases. On the other hand, the Bureau issued 10,927 reports to answer inquiries from consumers concerning the soundness of products or securities advertised or the activities of various concerns. In other words, in these cases the Bureau was presumably asked to give advice to consumers before they acted on sales presentations of one kind or another. What percentage of these inquiries involved questionable advertising practice was not stated. The Bureau also worked with retailers to secure their cooperation in censoring advertisements before publication; it also issued reports on 2,497 advertisements which it investigated after publication.

---

[1] U. S. Federal Trade Commission, *Annual Report of the Federal Trade Commission for the Fiscal Year Ended June 30, 1940* (Washington, U. S. Government Printing Office, 1940), pp. 119–123.

[2] Boston Better Business Bureau, Inc., *The Bulletin*, May 7, 1941.

A fairly definite idea of the extent to which inaccuracies are found by the Better Business Bureaus throughout the country among the advertisements which they read and scan while carrying out the activities described above is given in the following statement, based on evidence from the annual report of the National Association of Better Business Bureaus:

During the past year [1940–41] Better Business Bureaus have read and scanned more than 3,500,000 advertisements. Of this number, the Bureaus actually shopped advertisements suspected of being inaccurate or misleading, totaling more than 150,000. These investigations, however, revealed inaccuracies totaling less than 51,000. In the vast majority of cases, adjustments and revisions of advertising copy or radio continuity were satisfactorily procured. It is to be noted that of the suspicious advertisements actually shopped, approximately one-third were found to be inaccurate. The number of inaccurate or misleading advertisements disclosed by these investigations, when compared with the number of advertisements read and scanned, represents less than two per cent of the total. Furthermore, it should be made clear that an advertisement, classified by the Bureaus as inaccurate, is not necessarily misleading but may be so classified because it fails to meet the highest retail advertising standards, incorporated in the "Guide for Retail Advertising and Selling," a Bureau publication.[3]

The Proportion of Misleading and False Advertising

The evidence from the reports both of the Federal Trade Commission and of the Better Business Bureaus leads to the conclusion that a relatively small percentage of advertising material is of such a character as to be misleading or false under the definitions adopted by those organizations. For example, the figures of the Federal Trade Commission given above show that its first survey of magazine and newspaper advertising, made in an unrepresentatively large number of periodicals with low standards of censorship, showed somewhat less than 8% marked for further investigation. Somewhat over 3% of radio scripts were so marked, and less than 3% of mail-order pages. From study of this material, which involved the thousands of advertisements noted in the quotation from the report, the Commission sent questionnaires to 739 advertisers and to 109 advertising agencies whose names it obtained from this marked advertising and from other sources. Of the cases which were handled during the year, 612 were either disposed of or had been made the basis of further action which had not been concluded. Of the 612 cases, 344, or 56%, were closed

---

[3] Boston Better Business Bureau, Inc., *The Bulletin*, September 3, 1941.

for such reasons as "no evidence of violation, lack of jurisdiction, and insufficient public interest"; 188, or 31%, were closed upon reports showing compliance with previously negotiated stipulations to desist from misleading practices; while the remaining 80, or 13%, were of a character which led the Commission either to enter complaints, to make field investigations looking toward complaints, or to refer the cases to other governmental agencies. The number of cases involving stipulations and the number in which action was ordered represented a small fraction of the advertising surveyed. In the instance of the Boston Better Business Bureau report, the number of advertisements which warranted investigation and the number of complaints are indeed small in the light of the volume of advertising and the number of business transactions in that city. Moreover, less than 2% of advertisements read and scanned by the Bureaus throughout the country were found to be inaccurate or misleading when judged by their fairly rigid standards. In short, from these reports it is concluded that the number of instances of misleading or false advertising as defined by the organizations is small as compared with the vast quantity of advertising which is accepted as honest and accurate; yet it has been great enough to provide a basis for the opinion of some consumers that there is a substantial volume of questionable advertising.

The Viewpoint against Use of Advertising Influence as Expressed by Certain Writers

While the record above shows that a small percentage of advertising is of such a character as to be deemed misleading by governmental policing agencies and by the policing bureaus set up by businessmen, nevertheless many individuals may be found who class a much larger proportion of advertising as dishonest, or at least as representing questionable use of influence. The attitudes of certain consumers toward exaggeration and the biased character of many selling messages were shown in the last chapter; but in order to bring into sharper focus the viewpoints of the more severe critics of business honesty as found in advertising messages, two men whose conclusions, though perhaps extreme, are believed to be representative of a group, are quoted. Their views crystallize the issues regarding the place of influence in economic affairs and the manner in which influence may be exercised.

Professor Max Radin, in a scholarly and interesting series of essays,[4]

---

[4] Max Radin, *op. cit.*, p. 47 ff.

arrives at the conclusion that if advertisers were to be strictly honest and were to follow the dictates of good taste, as recognized among gentlemen, they would be led to the system of advertising ascribed to the English Quaker, George Cadbury, who advertised his cocoa "without pictures or devices and without commendatory adjectives or descriptions, simply by the words 'Cadbury's Cocoa.' " Radin contrasts with this simple announcement the coercive force generally employed by advertisers to guide the judgment of the buyer. He calls attention to examples of self-laudation (while self-praise is not immoral, it is not considered good taste among gentlemen), and to examples of deviation from the truth, varying from mild puffing to claims that are clearly untrue. Proceeding, he points out, "To tell nothing but the truth and to omit laudatory adjectives may be the beginning of advertising morality, but it is not the end. There are those less obvious forms of falsehood which in casuistry and in law are called the *suppresio veri* and the *suggestio falsi,* concealing the truth and hinting a lie, methods which certain types of advertising have carried to a pitch of skill and success that leaves us breathless." As an example of the latter method he cites a soap that its producers have made famous by advertising that it floats, when, according to advice offered by chemists, floating is not a virtue in soap; on the contrary, good soaps should not float. Parenthetically, it seems strange that in spite of all that the chemists told Professor Radin, millions of people over a period of seven decades have continued to buy this floating soap after using it, although they have had the option of buying soaps that do not float.[5] This fact suggests that a chemist's concept of what is "truth" in soap has not tallied with many consumers' ideas.

To Professor Radin the efforts of sellers to influence buyers through application of studied psychological techniques to attract consumers' attention and to arouse desire and conviction smacks of the training received by the "artful dodger." "When a benevolent old gentleman is invited by an affable stranger to look up at a new kind of airplane passing overhead, the affable stranger may be interested in a striking aerial phenomenon or he may be trying to pick the benevolent gentleman's pocket. It is an ambiguous device, this solicitude to gain a man's attention."

Professor Radin's definition of honesty and good taste apparently recognizes no basis for the seller in his advertising to employ suggestion

---

[5] Further comment upon this example is made on page 831.

or artful presentation in order to induce the consumer to want a product. "Morals, with law following or preceding, may some day bring us to the Cadbury system of advertising."

Another recent critique of advertising is that of the English professor, A. S. J. Baster, who, in *Advertising Reconsidered,* states his view that most advertising is deceptive.

. . . Now the major part of informative advertising is and always has been a campaign of exaggeration, half-truths, intended ambiguities, direct lies, and general deception. Amongst all the hundreds of thousands of persons engaged in the business it may be said about most of them on the informative side of it that their chief function is to deceive buyers as to the real merits and demerits of the commodity being sold.

. . . All advertisements which give true information are selective (i.e., selective of facts used). That they could not be otherwise because the whole truth is much and space expensive is not the real reason; their authors would not tell it if they could. Their natural aim is to select the most pleasant truths which place the product in the most favorable light, after the fashion of the publisher, who prints only the most favorable part of an approving *Times* review, without reproducing the faint praise with which the *Herald Tribune* damned his book; or the businessmen in Honolulu, who arrange that much shall be said in the newspapers about the coral sand, the whispering surf and the tropic breeze, but nothing about the distressing incidents of the last few years, culminating recently in the murder of a native.

. . . Advertisements of the *non*informative kind present a psychological museum of rare interest, but with some depressing exhibits. . . . All advertisements except signs showing only the name of the product, contain more or less matter that is completely irrelevant to the formation of a rational judgment by the consumer, and that is, in many cases, specially designed to hamper it. Appeals to reason are heavily frowned upon in expert advertising circles as very much out of date, and the modern tendency is to steer clear of the consumer's rational faculty altogether.

. . . One way (perhaps the most depressing exhibit of all) to get people to buy a product is simply to command them to do so. "Drink Coca-Cola" or "Eat More Fruit." If the command is put into a simple phrase, printed in large type across the page of a newspaper every day for a few weeks, flashed imperiously from an electric sign, or painted in staring colours on prominent billboards up and down the country, experience shows that in a profitably large number of cases, it will be obeyed. The desired end may be reached in a slightly more complex way by giving the same publicity to a slogan which, at its best, develops into a cleverly compressed informative advertisement, and, at its worst, is a pithy way of saying something about a product that is neither entirely irrelevant to the question of judging its worth, or so short as to be mere empty boasting, "They Satisfy," "Eventually—Why Not Now" . . .

. . . But the new tactics of the more progressive publicity agents substitute for the indiscriminate heavy bombardment described above a searching, raking fire of a much more terrifying sort. This takes the form of the appeal to instincts, generally of the less socially desirable kind, such as the acquisitive instinct, or the instinct of self-assertion and self-display. The appeal is couched in language calculated to arouse emotions which give rise to the instinctive activities desired by the advertiser, namely the purchase of his goods, the language being assisted where possible by suitable pictures.

.   .   .   .   .   .

. . . Great efforts are made by copy writers to invest the most commonplace processes and objects with an emotional content. Syrup is "bucketed in the far North Woods by snowshoed woodsmen, and hauled to camp on oxen-drawn bobsleds." One wonders whether it is any better syrup for being thus bucketed and thus hauled. The behavior of banana fritters in a certain brand of cooking fat, which "takes these puffy little balls right into its deep heart and seals them in amber crispiness," begins a very moving description of what everybody formerly mistook for a rather ordinary kitchen experiment; and the well-known panegyrics on "the soup that makes the meal happier," "the soup with the racy flavour, and the sparkling, sunny smile" are in a similar vein.

.   .   .   .   .   .

. . . The direct function of the words and pictures of the noninformative part of an advertisement, enshrouded as it is in the kind of irrelevant emotional verbiage described above, has become that of a veiled appeal to instinct, with studied avoidance of any rational judgment. In the animal world, where instinctive behavior has developed to a very high level because of urgent biological needs, this sort of advertising would precisely fit the conditions. The whole complicated technique devised to make human beings want more things and work harder to get them could certainly be applied with perfect suitability to a community of wasps. But in human affairs, the application of the rational test has led people to discard numerous routines of instinctive behavior because they are not only useless in modern conditions but often positively harmful. The great aim of high-pressure salesmanship is to prevent the use of any such test.[6]

A considerable number of critics lay particular stress upon one of the points mentioned above in the quotation from Baster, namely, the failure of advertising to give to consumers adequate informative data about the physical characteristics of the merchandise and its performance in use. Advertising is deemed not to conform to honesty in the strictest sense, both because it fails to give adequate objective data and substitutes emotional appeals which build subjective values deemed by them to be of questionable merit, and because the information given fails to tell the full truth. The consumer is led to want a product because favorable data are skillfully presented, while data

---

[6] A. S. J. Baster, *op. cit.*, p. 50 ff.

which might help the skillful buyer in this product appraisal are withheld. In short, the practices followed are held not to conform to a strict code of honesty in statement.

Viewpoints such as those held by Professors Radin and Baster, when carried to their logical conclusion lead to a doctrine which denies a proper place for influence or persuasion by sellers in economic affairs. The use of influence, even in moderate degree, is characterized as dishonest and in bad taste; and the critics evidently would like to see it greatly restricted. The economic implications of such views are profound, but before they are discussed it is proposed to inquire into the development of existing legal controls and the effects of changing business environment upon selling practice. As previously noted, the ethics of selling, like all ethics, are subject to constant evolution and are governed by pragmatic principles. The intent of this inquiry is to see what social and economic changes have occurred that account for present standards, to ask what the present standards of honesty of businessmen are, to note to what extent influence is permitted, and to try to determine what forces now operating may portend changes in the social viewpoint toward the use of influence to which businessmen should adjust themselves, changes to which businessmen may be forced to adjust themselves.

The Viewpoint of Businessmen toward Use of Influence in Selling

The barrage of criticism which holds business up to scorn as being dishonest not only hurts the feelings of most businessmen but confuses their thinking. Most businessmen believe that they are honest and upright in their selling operations. Against practices of misrepresentation and dishonesty they themselves have spoken out and have taken action through their trade associations and Better Business Bureaus.[7] But they fail fully to comprehend the charge of dishonesty directed against many practices which seem to them to be normal selling procedures. Their codes of commercial conduct do not term as dishonesty a seller's action in enthusiastically or even boastfully

---

[7] In an address before the Associated General Contractors of America, in Washington, in February, 1938, Edwin L. Davis, of the Federal Trade Commission, in describing the practices and experience of that Commission, stated: "The vast majority of members of industry are honest and ethical. Unfortunately, however, there is a small percentage in nearly every line of enterprise who persist in sharp practices. It has ever been thus. The desire to possess, a generally prevalent human instinct, has resulted in the employment of unfair and predatory practices throughout the life of mankind."

presenting his merchandise and in fashioning his presentation of appeals primarily with the aim of leading the consumer to want his product and to buy it. Their codes of selling conduct represent the evolution of over two centuries in a free, individualistic economy, and give recognition to the fact that the seller, in a dynamic economy, in order to dispose of his merchandise and to make a profit—seeks out buyers and makes known to them his claims as to the merits of his products and of the service he gives. Such a viewpoint is reflected in almost all codes of commercial practice, although different sellers have different codes.

Need of Study of Long-Time Forces to Understand Ethics of Selling

An understanding of modern codes of commercial practice requires that they be viewed in the light of history and the bearing of the numerous forces which determine such codes. Why and how rules governing buying and selling relations have developed is a matter for lengthy research by the legal and philosophical scholar. In this study lack of time and of resources compels the author merely to outline a tentative theory about such rules and their relationships. If the theory is in error at any point or incomplete, that fact is of no great consequence, because the main consideration in this study is that of the economic consequences of such rules as exist or may be set up.

To begin with, it must be recognized that the moral and ethical rules which have governed the relationships between buyers and sellers are found in two sources: first, common and statutory law give the formal rules which society as a political body has provided as its means of making certain that those actions are carried out which the group deems necessary to insure just relationships among individuals; second, the codes of ethics of individual businessmen or of groups of businessmen reflect their ideas of the proper rules to apply in their dealings with buyers. Both legal rules and private codes governing selling have been subject to change in association with changing social conditions, which are briefly traced in the pages ahead.

The Changing Character of the Law of Fraud

The basic legal control which has guided businessmen in their selling transactions is contained in the rules of law governing fraud, which have been evolved over several centuries in the common law and have been supplemented by statutory law.[8] *Corpus Juris* states the elements of actionable fraud to be as follows:

(1) A representation. (2) Its falsity. (3) Its materiality. (4) The speaker's knowledge of its falsity or ignorance of its truth. (5) His intent that it should be acted upon by the person and in the manner reasonably contemplated. (6) The hearer's ignorance of its falsity. (7) His reliance on its truth. (8) His right to rely thereon. (9) And his consequent and approximate injury.[9]

It will be noted from study of these elements that for fraud to exist there must be misrepresentation by the seller of some material fact with the intent of deceiving, but in sales transactions the buyer is not looked upon as one utterly unable to defend himself or look after his own interests. He knows that the seller is actuated by self-interest; accordingly he is expected to use due prudence or diligence. It must be shown that he was misled and that under the circumstances he had a right to rely on the statements made or withheld which led to his injury. The law has recognized that the seller ordinarily is expected to puff his wares. The law through the years has been subject to changing interpretation as to what is fraud and as to the relative position of buyer and seller. For example, under what conditions puffing is to be deemed misrepresentation is not and never has been clearly defined. What has been held to be fraudulent has changed with the passage of time. What juries under judicial guidance have considered as fraud has depended upon the facts and circumstances surrounding particular cases. Various legal students have made note of the fact that over a period of time the tendency has been to give greater protection to the buyer and less to the seller. For example, *Corpus Juris* comments thus:

The tendency of modern decisions is not to extend but to restrict the rule requiring diligence, and similar rules, such as *caveat emptor,* and the rule granting immunity for dealers' talk, and to condemn the falsehood of the fraud feasor rather than the credulity of his victim.[10]

Radin has pointed out that in the early Colonial days and for long after, the Common Law, "Having in contemplation two men equally

<hr>

[8] For a discussion of the various legal devices for consumers' protection, see Nathan Isaacs, "The Consumer at Law," *Annals of the American Academy of Political and Social Science*, May, 1934. In the comments above we have not included statements regarding breach of warranty, protection of title, and certain other remedies provided the consumer by the law, because our interest is to trace the relationship of the law to the honesty of statements made by sellers. This relationship is comprehended primarily through a study of the law of fraud and deceit.

[9] 26 *Corpus Juris* 1062.

[10] *Ibid.*, p. 1144.

able to take care of their interests, it grimly bade them fall to and let the better man win,"[11] whereas in more recent years, "Courts are becoming more definite in regard to fraud in contracts. 'Sellers' talk' is reduced to smaller and smaller proportions."[12]

The Effect of Changing Social Conditions on Ethical Rules

Professor Nathan Isaacs has commented more fully on the significance of social changes as they may bear upon the laws which are developed to govern selling transactions. He notes the important fact that the rules that have applied at different times are those which changing economic and social viewpoints have called into being.

The market conditions that the business world demands of the law have undergone a complete transformation since the days of Lord Coke. The picture of the buyer before the eyes of the law has ceased to be that of a very cautious, designing sort of person well able to take care of himself. On the contrary, every effort is made by means of the licensing of dealers and manufacturers, by means of the registration and inspection of products, by blue sky laws, by imposing penalties for misbranding, adulteration, and fraudulent advertising, by safeguarding competition and condemning unfair methods of doing business, to make the market safe for purchasers. Let us contrast the conditions in older systems of law that looked rather to the protection of the seller. In Roman law, for example, there developed the idea that a seller would repudiate an extremely bad bargain though there was no corresponding provision for a disillusioned buyer.[*] Such law was, of course, appropriate in a comparatively noncommercial society where the selling of goods outside of the ordinary course of business was a sign of distress on the part of the more or less unwilling and unfortunate owner. The buyer was looked upon as a wealthy person taking advantage of the distress of his neighbor, much as if he were lending him money for usury. This picture has changed completely. The buyer represents today the average member of society, while the seller is looked upon as the party better able to take care of himself. The development of the modern point of view in recent times is illustrated in the development of the law of implied warranties of quality[†] or of title[‡] and the disappearance of that extent of *caveat emptor*.

The particular details as to which the public puts a buyer under its protection are, of course, constantly changing. Today the danger is from misbranding, false advertising, inadequately described securities. Yesterday the emphasis was rather on the danger of lack of skill in professional men, mechanics, and others who have been subjected to licensing laws. Tomorrow the dangers may be

---

[11] Max Radin, *op. cit.*, p. 52.
[12] *Ibid.*, p. 55.
[*] Manuel Girard, *Elementaire de Droit Romain* (6th ed. 1918), p. 552.
[†] Williston, *Contracts* (1920) § 976.
[‡] *Ibid.*, § 983.

different and the emphasis may be shifted to prevent the abuse of high-powered salesmanship accompanied by intriguing installment devices.[13]

What are the forces that have brought changing legal and ethical rules governing sales transactions, such as are noted in the above quotation? It is impossible to list them all and to follow their many interactions, for they involve the whole social environment and their investigation is beyond the scope of this economic study. Among the more important of the forces clearly are religion, the environment surrounding business activity, the influence of legal codes already established, the activity of producer or consumer groups, education, and the ideologies which have developed not only from the above but from the peculiar characteristics of our land and of the people who have developed it.[14] Only a few of the more evident relationships are pointed out here.

The Effect of a Changing Business Environment on the Ethics of Selling

That a changing business environment has been important in the development of changing rules governing selling is certain. As men have emerged from a simple handicraft economy to the involved industrial economy of today, with its division of labor in the production of merchandise and the removal of the maker from intimate contact with the final buyer, new methods and new procedures have been devised which have called for new rules of selling conduct. One of the most significant changes attending this development has been the gradual evolution of sellers to a relatively more powerful position than formerly. Formerly, buying and selling transactions of consumers were relatively few and simple as contrasted with the present time. The number of buyers in the market has greatly increased, and the range of products which they buy and consume is far wider than ever before. The consumer's ability to judge these products and the satisfactions that might come from them is limited. Clearly the ultimate consumer is an inexpert judge of much of the merchandise he buys. He must rely largely on the seller's representations. Sellers today are far better organized for trade than are consumer buyers; their knowledge of

---

[13] Nathan Isaacs, "Business Postulates and the Law," *Harvard Law Review*, June, 1928, p. 1020.

[14] For an analysis of physical and racial factors which may in part explain American business behavior, see C. F. Taeusch, *Policy and Ethics in Business* (New York, McGraw-Hill Book Company, Inc., 1931), chs. 1 and 2.

the characteristics of the merchandise they sell is ordinarily much greater. While the consumer of 1941 is far from being the helpless individual sometimes pictured in current literature, nevertheless in his buying transactions he is no longer in a position to deal with the seller at arm's length, as comprehended in the Common Law of several centuries ago. Hence the law of fraud has given more and more protection to the buyer.

The Effect of Self-Interest of Sellers on
Their Codes of Practice

The very development and growth of commerce itself has meant that self-interest has led businessmen to appreciate the need of a different code of selling conduct from that held when buying transactions were relatively infrequent and simple. If business is to flow uninterruptedly, it is necessary that it be done in an atmosphere of trust and confidence, so that transactions can be facilitated. The tremendous volume of sales of the thousands of items that are offered consumers in the American economy could not be consummated if every sales transaction consisted in the haggling and jockeying that formerly characterized consumer buying and still does in some countries. Moreover, and this point is one to which emphasis has been given in preceding chapters, businessmen greatly prize continued patronage. One-time sales are not usually profitable; continued patronage carries the promise of profit because it gives stability of sales volume which is the goodwill that is so highly prized by successful businesses. Business has come to be conducted largely under a scheme of brands, whereby the consumer can recognize merchandise in repurchase. Or, if he does not buy by brand, he ordinarily deals with a retailer who expects to continue in business. The self-interest of sellers has led them to realize that success depends not upon a one-time sale, but upon having the buyer purchase again and again. Hence from the standpoint of self-interest, if for no other reason, most businessmen have found it desirable not to misrepresent products in such a way that their patronage would be endangered or lost through ill will thereby created.

Self-interest has also been an important element in leading many businessmen to attempt to secure among the business community widespread adherence to a high standard of commercial conduct, through formulation of codes and through various plans for self-regulation of trade. Such efforts have probably been brought about in part by the desire to have business transactions facilitated through creation of a general trust on the part of consumers, in part through fear of imposition of government regulations which might prove costly and cumbersome, in part as a result of criticism of business activity by reformers or by organized consumer groups, in part by the crusading spirit of leaders interested in seeing their own, private moral codes of commercial conduct more generally accepted. This widening appreciation of the desirability of a high standard of commercial conduct has led to numerous instances of group action by businessmen in laying down codes of ethics. This group activity has probably had an influence in continuously raising the general standards of fair dealing between buyer and seller. Examples of such codes are those of professional groups; those formulated by the Better Business Bureaus, both local and national; the Advertising Copy Code of the American Association of Advertising Agencies; and the codes formulated by numerous trade associations.

Proceeding beyond the mere drawing of formal codes to serve as guides, businessmen have promoted voluntary regulating agencies designed to police the activities of a business community or industry. Such activities are exemplified in the work of the local Better Business Bureaus, the National Better Business Bureau, the Audit Bureau of Circulations, and the Proprietary Association, all designed to raise standards of honesty in commercial transactions.[15]

Self-interest also accounts in large degree for the efforts undertaken by groups of businessmen themselves, in conjunction with consumer groups, to bring about legislation to curb business methods which tend to disturb the trust of buyers in sellers generally or in the advertising messages they have to offer. Businessmen, for example, were largely responsible for the enactment in many states of the *Printers' Ink Statute,* designed to prevent fraud and misrepresentation in advertising. Again, businessmen have always played an important part in the enactment of some of the most restrictive legislation, such

---

[15] For a more detailed discussion of such activities, see:
Chamber of Commerce of the United States, *The Service of Advertising* (Washington, D. C., 1937).
H. J. Kenner, *The Fight for Truth in Advertising* (New York, Round Table Press, Inc., 1936).
M. G. Reid, *op. cit.*
John Richardson, "Business Policing Itself through Better Business Bureaus," *Harvard Business Review,* October, 1930.
W. C. Waite and R. Cassady, Jr., *op. cit.*

as the Pure Food and Drug Act. Some business interests have done what they could to sabotage such bills, and others have been opposed to certain provisions because they have feared them or disagreed as to the extent and type of control which should be enacted; nevertheless, there has always been considerable activity on the part of businessmen in the food and drug industries to bring about the enactment of such legislation because they have deemed a low grade of moral practice by other men in their industry not only to violate their ideas of moral behavior but even to harm business itself.[16]

Other Forces Affecting Businessmen's Codes of Practice

While self-interest has been an important force influencing sellers to raise the standard of honesty in dealing with buyers, numerous other changing forces, difficult to trace and impossible to measure, have entered to mould the ideas of businessmen as to a proper course of commercial action. The moral codes laid down by religions; the rules inculcated by moral philosophies; the ideas showered from the press, from the pulpit, from the schoolroom rostrum—each has had its bearing. The importance of these influences is evident when one asks himself the question, "Where do men get their ideas of honorable conduct?" The ideas come from many sources and they affect the behavior of men in all walks of life.

The Enactment of Legal Rules Governing Selling Behavior.

Whenever the number of businessmen in the community who have followed questionable selling practices has grown large enough to be considered threatening, the social group has usually brought about enactment of laws to restrict the business group. As noted above, businessmen because of self-interest have played a part in securing such legislation, but in large degree legislators have passed laws restricting sellers as a result of the crystallization of public attitudes. These public attitudes generally have not been spontaneous, but have been generated by those in a position to propagandize and arouse public interest. Under leadership there have been waves of moral indignation among the consuming public whenever an appreciable number of sellers have followed practices deemed dangerous to the

---

[16] For a detailed discussion of activities leading up to the enactment of the Food, Drug, and Cosmetic Act of 1938, see D. F. Cavers, "The Food, Drug, and Cosmetic Act of 1938: Its Legislative History and Its Substantive Provisions," *Law and Contemporary Problems* (Duke University), Winter, 1939, p. 2.

public and against which the individual has not been able adequately to protect himself. These crusades have developed as a result of changes in the business environment which have made the buying group relatively unable to care for its own interests. They have occurred whenever the law and business practice lag too far behind the sentiment of the community. A militant campaign of the early part of the century led by the editors of important magazines and newspapers called attention to the too frequent instances of adulteration and misbranding of drugs. The resulting clamor brought enactment of the Pure Food and Drug Act of 1906. Again, the evidence indicates that the law and business practice were too far behind public sentiment for several years previous to 1935. Then the spirited drive by relatively small but effective groups interested in obtaining additional protection for consumers played an important part in the enactment of the Pure Food and Drug Act of 1938; the Wheeler-Lea Act,[17] which provided against dissemination of false advertisements concerning foods, drugs, medical devices, and cosmetics, the fields in which misstatement has been most frequent and most dangerous to the individual; and the Wool Labeling Act, which made provision for information desired by consumers.

Such campaigns have not merely resulted in laws; they have led businessmen to give serious thought as to whether their methods have needed changing. In part the fear of onerous governmental restrictions or control leads businessmen voluntarily to follow acceptable selling methods rather than to be subject to regulation by a government bureau. But beyond dislike of government control in the minds of many businessmen lies appreciation of the fact that the goodwill of consumers is essential to a business. A firm wishes, if possible, to avoid the stigma of any public condemnation of its selling methods or its brand name. Even more significant is the fact that a great number of businessmen have a high sense of honor which they apply as much to their business activities as to their activities in other walks of life. They sacrifice their own interests when those interests do not conform with their ideas of honorable conduct.

---

[17] Many recent volumes dealing with the consumer elaborate in more or less detail the various pieces of legislation designed to protect the consumer. For example, see W. C. Waite and R. Cassady, Jr., *op. cit.*, chs. VII and VIII. M. G. Reid, *op. cit.*, chs. XXI and XXV.

The Effect of Legal Enactment on Business Practice

Just as the law itself has been changed, in part as least, at the urge of business groups, to make it conform more closely to what some deem a higher moral standard, so the enactments of ethical rules into legal edict have reacted upon business to raise the standards of mercantile honesty generally followed.[18]

As the changing views of the courts toward fraud have had an effect in raising the standards of business honesty, the activities of quasi-judicial bodies, such as the Federal Trade Commission, have had a tendency to raise the standards followed by many business organizations. The Federal Trade Commission, until the passage of the Wheeler-Lea Act, had looked at advertising and other selling methods primarily from the standpoint of preventing unfair competitive practices. Its rulings dealt with the honesty of selling statements, because it deemed dishonest selling an unfair form of competition, in that it might harm the competitor who was honest. The Wheeler-Lea Act employed a somewhat different legal theory. It empowered the Commission in the case of advertisements of foods, drugs, medical devices, and cosmetics to regulate advertising statements with consumer welfare and public interest as its guide. Its rulings have come to form a sort of policeman's guide as to what cannot be said in advertising. In its 1940 report the Commission stated its belief that its work in the field of examining and preventing false and misleading advertising "contributes substantially to the improvement that has been evident in recent years in the character of all advertising."[19] In addition, the activities of the Commission in recent years in its Fair Trade Practices Conferences, in which industries or trades have been brought together to reach agreement upon practices relating to selling and buying, have helped to build up codes of behavior which in time promise to be accepted as normal guides of proper action, rather than as mere threats of policing by a governmental agency. Such a social mechanism tends in time to generate a higher average of moral conduct.

Protection of Buyers through Private Codes of Ethics

From the account given in the preceding pages it is evident that the protection of the buyer in selling transactions has not rested in

---

[18] See Max Radin, *op. cit.*, p. 15.
[19] U. S. Federal Trade Commission, *Annual Report 1940, op. cit.*, p. 119.

the law alone. Outside of any legal restraints, most businessmen, like most citizens generally, have learned to guide their behavior toward others more honestly and decently than the minimum standard required by the law. It is fair to state that the general morality applied to buying and selling activities is and generally has been for years, on a higher plane than that required by law. The great bulk of buying and selling transactions involving consumers is carried on with a high degree of trust and satisfaction. Most sellers conduct themselves without thought as to whether the eyes of the policeman are turned in their direction. This fact was indicated in the evidence given above regarding the work of the Federal Trade Commission and Better Business Bureaus. The relation of law to the conduct of business has been thus stated by Isaacs:

. . . We may venture two propositions: first, that the legal system of any given time or place contributes heavily to the fulfillment of our expectations; and second, that the legal system is by no means alone in this function. The first of these propositions is, of course, generally taken for granted. It is our purpose here not to prove it, but to find out just how the law comes to the aid of the business world. The second proposition, however, is very generally overlooked. Legal specialists talk occasionally as if the sole deterrent from crime in the world today were criminal law.* Little wonder, then, that the layman looks to the law to accomplish single-handed the greatest of wonders, and in turn criticizes the law for its failure to do that which he frequently assumes, in the first place, it can do. When everything goes wrong he says: "There ought to be a law against this or that." He expects a legislative *fiat* to make men moral, to make men sober, to make men efficient. We must therefore emphasize the limits of effective legal action.† When it actually was necessary to look behind every tree for a possible Indian, the best code in the world could not have done away with that necessity any more than we can today put an end to war by such a simple device as declaring it unlawful. Yet with the aid of law and a hundred other elements we have succeeded in reaching a measure of internal peace and we may hope to achieve a corresponding measure of world peace eventually. The point is that law does not and cannot work alone. The development of law is but a phase of the development of civilization.[20]

While the law undoubtedly has been a highly important element in the development of codes of ethics regulating selling practices in accord with changing social conditions, the codes voluntarily followed by the great majority of businessmen have been even more important. It must

---

* Cf. Wigmore's Introduction to Train, *The Prisoner at the Bar* (1907).

† Cf. Pound, *The Limits of Effective Legal Action* (1916) 22 Pa. Bar Ass'n Rep. 221, (1916) 3 A.B.A.J. 55; (1916) 27 Internat. J. of Ethics 150.

[20] Nathan Isaacs, "Business Postulates and the Law," *op. cit.*, pp. 1014–15.

be recognized, however, that there is no single code of commercial conduct followed by business. At no time have all businessmen in the community followed the same code or set of rules. Individual businessmen and firms have their own private moral codes of commercial conduct. Only when there is a widespread adherence to a certain code may it be termed a public, or moral, code.[21] There have been and probably always will be those who do not follow the code most generally accepted and followed at any time. The activities of these individuals in modern commercial communities account largely for the dangers from which the public has sought protection under the common law and under statutory law.

Varying Levels of Business Codes

The private codes of commercial honesty and good taste of businessmen may be classified at different levels. At one level some sellers may be found who in their sales statements attempt to live up to the practice of telling the "full truth" called for by some of the more precise critics of current business practices, such as were quoted earlier in the chapter. Such a code would evidently require the seller to avoid artful appeals and to disclose all the shortcomings as well as the merits of his product, and possibly might even go so far as to require disclosure as to whether or not the price asked made the product the best buy for the consumer. The author does not recall ever having met a businessman who so conducted his selling operations. He knows of certain retail advertisers who at times have frankly stated the shortcomings of merchandise offered or have even disparaged the goods advertised, but such practice has thus been employed because its novelty has made it an effective selling approach. Such advertisements have not represented a copy approach which would be generally practicable, for common adoption of the method would eliminate the novelty and, hence, the effectiveness.

Another high level code would restrict the seller from saying anything other than that he sold a certain type of merchandise, as suggested by Radin. It would avoid dishonesty because it would take no chances in stating anything that might not really be true. Such a code would recognize that the "truth" about merchandise is often not easily determinable, and that the seller cannot tell in strict honesty whether

---

[21] For an able analysis of moral codes as related to business executives, see C. I. Barnard, *The Functions of the Executive* (Cambridge, Harvard University Press, 1938), ch. XVII.

his product and price represent the most desirable buy for particular consumers. The advertising of some businessmen conforms to this simple announcement practice, but among most businessmen such advertising is deemed ineffective and wasteful because it fails to produce a profitable volume of sales.

Different from the moral codes dictated by a perfectionist's definition of honesty are those codes more generally practiced, which apply a utilitarian basis for judging the honesty of sales statements. Those who follow such codes deny that the self-interest of sellers makes impossible the application of a high level of honesty in selling transactions. They hold that the ethical basis and the profitable basis of selling are identical; that any sale, to be successful, must involve mutual benefit to buyer and seller. The seller must get a price which makes it attractive to him to continue in business; the buyer, satisfactions from use which compensate for the sacrifice he has made. Only as buying transactions result in satisfaction can the seller expect continued patronage and good reputation, which provide the basis for profitable operation of a continuing business. Accordingly, the codes require the seller to offer honest merchandise, to tell the truth about what he offers, and to reveal material facts, concealment of which might mislead. On the other hand, an attractive, enthusiastic, or even boastful sales or advertising presentation featuring the consumer's problems which the product might solve, or suggesting the desires, the hopes, or aspirations which the product might help him attain, is not considered dishonest so long as the product gives satisfaction. All statements the seller has to make about prices and relative values are true, but he does not expect specifically to say whether his article is a better or a worse buy for the consumer than competitive articles, first, because frequently he is not in a position honestly to make any such statement, and secondly, because he might thereby violate an ethic governing his relations with competitors. On the other hand, he is permitted to describe his merchandise glowingly and to indicate his conviction that the product is a desirable purchase for the consumer and one that will give him satisfaction.

The codes of ethics drawn up by associations and business organizations, to which reference has already been made, represent the ideal of business conduct at the present time. They probably do not describe the public moral code, i.e., the level of practice generally followed. While the conduct of many business organizations measures up to the precepts laid down, that of others does not. Unfortunately, as is true in other walks of life, there are too many who seek to keep barely within the level of the law or are intent on practicing misrepresentation and fraud in the hope of evading the law. Illustrative of codes of selling ethics to which business concerns might aspire is the 10-point Fair Trade Code formulated by the National Association of Better Business Bureaus, as follows:

(1) Serve the public with honest values.
(2) Tell the truth about what is offered.
(3) Tell the truth in a forthright manner so its significance may be understood by the trusting as well as the analytical.
(4) Tell customers what they want to know—what they have a right to know and ought to know about what is offered so that they may buy wisely and obtain the maximum satisfaction from their purchases.
(5) Be prepared and willing to make good as promised and without quibble on any guarantee offered.
(6) Be sure that the normal use of merchandise or services offered will not be hazardous to public health or life.
(7) Reveal material facts, the deceptive concealment of which might cause consumers to be misled.
(8) Advertise and sell merchandise or service on its merits and refrain from attacking your competitors or reflecting unfairly upon their products, services, or methods of doing business.
(9) If testimonials are used, use only those of competent witnesses who are sincere and honest in what they say about what you sell.
(10) Avoid all tricky devices and schemes such as deceitful trade-in allowances, fictitious list prices, false and exaggerated comparative prices, bait advertising, misleading free offers, fake sales and similar practices which prey upon human ignorance and gullibility.

Modern Commercial Codes Compared with Those of the Past

No evidence exists which reveals with clarity and certainty what the prevalent codes of commercial honesty at different times have been. Adequate descriptions and comments upon usual selling practices for periods other than recent years are few. Comments carried in Hunt's *Merchants' Magazine and Commercial Review* seem to indicate that in the 1840's and 1850's there was a considerable quantity of sharp practice among retailers in New York. Here, however, it is not certain whether the comments upon the sharp practice were directed against that which was common or against that which was unusual. At the present time in any large city so-called "borax" establishments exist, employing the same type of sharp practice complained about 100 years ago. Such shops are the exception, not the rule. They are the butt of the activities of Better Business Bureaus, and receive considerable comment in the literature of those organizations.[22] They represent not normal practice but an undesirable sore spot which other business interests are trying to stamp out.

In so far as advertisements provide a record of the selling representations of businessmen, the current standard appears to be above that of 100 years ago,[23] although much advertising of that time conformed to high standards. A study of old files of magazines and newspapers shows that advertising during the nineteenth century was devoted in large part to lotteries, transportation, books, auctions, and patent medicines. One of these items, lotteries, represents a type of consumer expenditure which has since been banned as immoral. Many of the books featured in advertisements were of a sensational and questionable character. The patent medicine advertising which made up a very substantial percentage of the advertising revenue of publications,[24] was a sore spot and undoubtedly accounted in considerable part for the stigma attached to advertising at the time. In the best publications appeared many advertisements of proprietary remedies and of charms to make the user well, strong, or beautiful, which would be found only in the lowest grade magazines of the present time. In contrast, however, many of the advertisements of manufactured products, books, and transportation services, published in both magazines and newspapers, were simple, direct, and dignified, and certainly characterized by no more puffing or overstatement than is found in current advertising,[25] perhaps less. Much of the advertising of retailers consisted of simple statements of importations or domestic purchases available.[26] Occasionally merchants featured competitive prices which would tax belief; but even at the present time, in spite of the exhortations of Better Business Bureaus and of merchant leaders, questionably phrased promises of unusually large price savings are found in the daily papers.

---

[22] The bulletins of Better Business Bureaus carry current reports of activities directed against transgressors of honest practice. Also see H. J. Kenner, *op. cit.*

[23] For examples of advertising of various periods, see Frank Presbrey, *op. cit.*

[24] Discussion of such advertising is found on page 289 ff., *ibid.* According to Presbrey, patent medicine advertising contributed more than half the advertising linage in many papers. After the Civil War, the volume of such advertising was even greater.

[25] For examples, see *ibid.*, pp. 229, 250, 285, 288, 367.

[26] For examples, see *ibid.*, pp. 209, 249, 251, 257, 273, 324 ff., 345.

A review of the more important forces which have played a part in shaping the moral codes now followed by businessmen gives a better perspective on the charges of dishonesty which are now leveled against the selling methods employed by business. The history of the law, as it reflects the moral codes followed by sellers at different times, the changing social forces which have served to generate moral values underlying codes of conduct, and the history of industry and the actions taken by businessmen themselves to regulate their commercial conduct, all lead to the conclusion that on the whole an appreciably higher standard of honesty in selling relationships holds now than held in former times. Judged on a long-time span it is amazing that men have learned to exchange commodities on so vast a scale as they do today with so little friction. On the other hand, if an abstract and precise definition of honesty, which states that nothing shall be said by the seller which is not literally true and that no material facts shall be withheld, is applied to present conduct, the public can be shocked at what it finds. Or, if a less rigorous definition than strictest truth is applied, one can be moved to moral indignation by a catalogue of the sinners who have failed to live up to what may be accepted as the current moral code of commercial conduct. It is not surprising that those who set out to look for evidence of what they might term dishonesty can build a long and imposing list of transgressors. How much of current selling shall be termed dishonest depends entirely on the definition of honesty which the critic would apply. This matter of definition explains why certain critics of advertising at the present time hold practically all, or at least a very large part, of current advertising to be a tissue of lies and deceit. They apply to advertising and personal selling an abstract definition of honesty, a definition which seldom applies to the actions of men in any walk of life.

The Inevitability of Influence

A pragmatic test does not support a viewpoint which denies a place for influence or persuasion by sellers in economic affairs. Whether one likes persuasion or not, it appears inevitable in a free society that sellers should try to influence buyers. An individual, capitalistic system relies on the self-interest of buyers and sellers to make the system work at all. The history of mankind reveals that when men wish to interests through influence. The development of aggressive selling further interests in which other men are involved, they further those in western economies indicates that free men, left to their own resources, resort to persuasion in exchange operations. When the economist speaks of self-interest as the director of economic endeavor in a dynamic economy he should, if he is a realist, expect the seller to be aggressive in the distribution of merchandise and should make room for the costs and for the effects of persuasion in his economic analysis. To deny the use of influence to seekers of profit is tantamount to denying such an economy, especially to denying the dynamic aspects of such an economy.

It is essential when one is appraising the honesty of advertising to try to arrive at a realistic understanding of the way in which people behave. Advertising is written and presented by men or firms impelled by self-interest to induce others to buy their products. Yet certain extreme critics of advertising, even while recognizing its biased source, appear to expect from advertisers an unbiased statement about the merchandise which is being featured, a statement measured by a standard of abstract truth.

Messages of any kind which are designed to persuade and to influence others generally do not measure up to the standards of abstract truth. When advertisements are judged as biased or persuasive messages, they accord with what men have come to expect in persuasive messages in all walks of life. The same charges of bias, and hence of dishonesty, may be applied to the statesman in his pronouncements designed to influence the viewpoints of other statesmen, to the politician seeking votes, to the lawyer in his plea to the jury, or even to the pulpit orator seeking to save the sinner.

Need of Pragmatic Test of Honesty

The above statements are not meant to condone departures from truth, but they indicate a need for a pragmatic test of honesty. In all human affairs the precepts of abstract moral law serve as guides to deter men from departing from the paths of honesty or uprightness. The threat of condemnation which may come if others detect dishonesty plays a part in keeping them upright. Nevertheless, men trying to influence others resort to biased statement. In the end, for most human endeavors a pragmatic basis in judging human actions is required. The intent of the doer and the end attained guide judgment as to the goodness of actions.

Although advertising is a biased statement, and although it departs

from the standards of an abstract truth, the buyer is not left unpro-
tected. His protection comes in part from the fact that he realizes
that advertisements are biased messages. Advertising is propaganda,
but it is a frank sort of propaganda, for every advertisement bears
the signature of its source. The reader knows who speaks; he knows
the special interests of that man or firm, and usually he knows his
reputation for integrity and for veracity.[27] In contrast there are certain
other types of publicity for which the source is not evident to the
reader.

The buyer has protection also in the statements of competing
sellers. No one seller presents all the views to which the buyer is
subjected. The statements of competing sellers tend to offset one
another. This counterbalance found in the statements of competing
sellers undoubtedly has an important effect upon the ethics governing
use of influence. The situation is somewhat as in the law, though not
exactly parallel. In the court the lawyer presents a biased argument
for his client. The plea of the plaintiff is balanced against the plea
of the defendant. In business each seller presents a biased statement.
But that fact is understood by the buyer. He gets some protection
from a comparison of sellers' claims.

He has the further protection mentioned previously, namely, that
the self-interest of the seller, his desire for continued patronage, ordinarily will insure that the presentation made will contain no essential
untruths or promises of satisfactions that will not be delivered. Yet
in a world where the best men are not perfect and the worst are very
bad, and where not all sellers are guided by long-range viewpoints of
profit, the buyer should always have a fair regard for the doctrine of
caveat emptor in directing his own affairs,[28] and the survey among
consumers indicates that fortunately such an attitude exists, though
probably not to such a degree as is desirable.

When judging the veracity of advertising statements, just as when
judging statements in other lines of human endeavor, one should
realize that the truth is often not easily determinable. Although information for consumers is deemed desirable, yet facts concerning the
physical characteristics and the performance in use of merchandise

---

[27] As was brought out in the preceding chapter, the surveys among consumers regarding their attitude toward honesty of advertisements show a large degree of discrimination as to the reputation for integrity or honesty of different manufacturers or distributors.

[28] "He who buys needs a thousand eyes; he who sells but one." *Poor Richard's
Almanac.*

are often difficult to obtain and impart to consumers. Furthermore, these facts have varied significance to different buyers. As a result, many of the statements of advertisements which have been and are being attacked as untrue are actually of debatable truth. An illustration is provided in the quotation from Radin, given above. Professor Radin cited as an example of *suppressio falsi* the advertising which featured that a certain soap floated, whereas competent chemists had advised him that floating was not a virtue, but a fault in soap. Yet that very characteristic of floating has commended the soap to many consumers; even though they may be buying air or a low specific gravity in such a soap, they prefer it. Apparently there is something to be said for a soap that is readily retrieved in the tub, for every leading soap manufacturer in the United States has found it advisable to offer consumers a floating soap.

When one looks upon advertising as a message designed to influence, he finds the underlying reason for attractive presentation and for use of appeals to the emotions and instincts. This latter type of appeal is the rule followed from time immemorial by astute men desiring to influence the action of others.

Nor is the charge of the impropriety of self-laudation or puffing in advertising and selling efforts to be taken very seriously. True, self-laudation is generally recognized as poor manners among gentlemen in their personal intercourse. This sentiment carries over to personal selling and advertising, for excessive boastfulness in an advertisement is likely to arouse a feeling of resentment and thus to defeat an advertiser's effort to get favorable attention and action from buyers. But that the taboo against self-laudation in social intercourse should apply with equal force to relations between the buyer and the seller does not necessarily hold. The merchandise offered by different sellers is generally not identical. Ordinarily the merits and utility to consumers of any vendor's merchandise can be known only from use, from the recommendation of other users, or from what the vendor tells. Consumers want to know about the merits of products offered and expect sellers to tell them. The testimony of sellers indicates that the reflection of sincere enthusiasm for their merchandise in selling statements, which might well be considered self-laudation in personal intercourse, is not resented generally by buyers and is inducive to conviction on the part of buyers.

Summary

In summary, the lack of adherence to abstract truth in selling statements is explained by the fact that any advertisement must be judged as a statement issued by a party at interest. The advertisement is designed to influence, and hence it is likely to follow the pattern employed in all persuasive statements, by making appeals to the emotions and instincts. Judged upon such a basis, advertising statements are deemed to compare favorably in honesty with persuasive statements in other lines of endeavor. That they do so is explained in large part by the self-interest of those engaged in business; they desire continued patronage, and experience has led them to realize that even an *ex parte* statement should not be couched in phrases that will lead consumers to expect satisfactions that they will not realize.

If one thinks in terms of action designed to attain a high standard of honesty in sellers' statements, it appears futile to look solely to the law. The law almost perforce must limit itself to efforts designed to prevent the grosser departures from probity. To attempt to make sellers speak without bias would present a hopeless problem in enforcement. Sale of dangerous or immoral products can be banned. A seller's recommendations for use of drugs or other products in harmful quantities fortunately can be ostracized by law. Fraud and gross misrepresentation can be legislated against with some success. But even the most ardent reformers cannot hope to prevent men from putting their best foot forward when trying to persuade other people.

Those who would banish persuasion in the exchange of products must find a solution in some form of an authoritarian, planned economy, such as socialism. To the socialist, aggressive selling, whether personal or advertising, is anathema, because it is actuated by the drive for profit; and the quest for profit is deemed by the socialist to bring the inequalities and the exploitation that make the individual, capitalistic system undesirable in his eyes. But even in a socialistic state, advertising would probably not be more honest than in a capitalistic state. At least, it would employ influence. As yet there is no adequate evidence of just what form advertising would take in a fully socialized, industrial state offering a wide variety of merchandise to consumers. From the evidence of practice in Russia, however, and from *a priori* reasoning, it is presumed that advertising would be employed by a central planning authority to influence consumption of certain products, either to effect full utilization of existing equipment or to arouse desire for new products deemed beneficial for the social group. Advertising employed to accomplish these ends might well be similar to much present advertising. If the advertising was to be effective, it would probably be emotional in character, just like the competitive advertising of our present system, because the mainsprings to action lie primarily in emotions. To use advertising which did not actually induce action would be just as wasteful as a poor copy approach is an ineffective or wasteful expenditure for a businessman. Thus, unless men change, it is logical to expect advertising under a different system to be persuasive and to reflect some of the same inaccuracies and emotional and instinctive appeals which are now condemned in the commercial advertising of the capitalistic system.[29]

Since an underlying postulate of this study is the maintenance of a system in which consumers have freedom of choice, it is assumed that consumers will find the way to the good life in the midst of the persuasive efforts of thousands of sellers, and that the protection of the consumer will rest in his own exercise of his native-given wits, in the growing protection given by law, in the group efforts of consumers to further their own interests, and in those forces that lead sellers of merchandise to adopt progressively higher moral codes.

All in all, the evidence regarding ethical attitudes gives little reason to believe that abstract definitions of honesty, which would deny to sellers the right to use influence, are likely to be adopted by the social group. Ethical and moral values change slowly, not rapidly. Moreover, the quick denial of the use of influence to sellers could occur only as the result of a revolutionary change in our economic order, which is not in prospect. While the use of selling influence undoubtedly will continue to be an aspect of our economy, nevertheless the long-time trends described in this chapter indicate that sellers, either voluntarily or through force, will have to give increasing recognition to the fact that consumers in the modern complex economy need and evidently will secure for themselves increasing protection and aid in their buying. If a substantial number of businessmen persist in using questionable selling methods, consumers will rely on

---

[29] A. S. J. Baster, *op. cit.*, p. 121, notes with some dismay that the British government in its "Buy British" Campaign resorted to what he deems questionable tactics in its advertising and promotional efforts to induce good Britons to Buy British. He concludes, "To use appeals to patriotism in this way to persuade people to buy what they do not want, with the notion that it will help the nation economically, bears a suspicious resemblance to the equally convincing, if less ingenious activity of persuading people to sell their sovereigns because it will save the Gold Standard," p. 123.

legislation such as the Wheeler-Lea Act for protection against false and misleading selling. Moreover, it is to be expected that slowly but persistently they will seek aids to intelligent buying for themselves. Some of their efforts will take the form of advice to consumer groups, and some the form of educational work. It is also to be expected that they will increase their pressure upon sellers to provide helpful information. In turn, it is believed that sellers should recognize this growing desire for information on the part of consumers and experiment with methods of fulfilling it. Such procedure does not involve abandonment of the use of influence, and it gives promise that in the course of time the satisfaction of consumers will be increased.

PART VIII

Summary

CHAPTER XXVIII

A SUMMARY

AFTER the long and detailed analyses of the many issues relating to the economic effects of advertising comes the task of final appraisal. There is need for selecting, out of all the many judgments given along the way, those that are most significant, and for arranging them in such a manner that a view of the undertaking may be presented in true perspective. To attain this end, the project and its findings are discussed under seven headings. Under the first, the character of the broad economic problem is outlined with statements as to its magnitude, the criticisms met, the point of view adopted, the criteria of appraisal employed, and the major economic issues considered. In the second section, the conclusions reached on the major questions are given at length, with indication of how definitive an answer to each question is warranted by the evidence. Third, the possible dangers involved in the use of advertising, as shown by the study, are pointed out. This section is followed in turn by a discussion of such counterbalancing forces as were found to exist in the economy which offset in whole or in part the dangers and shortcomings of advertising. The remaining discussion deals in turn with questions of ethical aspects, constructive criticisms, and the place of advertising in the capitalistic economy of the United States.

STATEMENT OF THE ECONOMIC PROBLEM

The Size of the Advertising Expenditure

The size and importance of the economic problem of advertising is shown by the fact that in the 1920 decade, advertising expenditures averaged in excess of $2,000,000,000 a year, during the 1930 decade somewhat less than this figure, or 3% of the national income. The sum is 7% of the total amount spent for the distribution of goods and services. The figure of $2,000,000,000 is a gross expenditure, however, and is offset in part by the contribution which advertising makes to the publication of newspapers and magazines, which are sold at low cost to consumers, and to radio broadcasting, which provides free consumer entertainment. It was estimated that the contribution of advertising to publishing and broadcasting, based on a survey of the year 1935, was roughly one-fifth of total advertising expenditure.

It is evident that the potentialities for waste are great when such large sums are involved. But the possible economic significance of advertising is not limited to the potential wastes arising from ineffective employment of the men and resources represented by the large annual expenditure. Advertising has important effects upon the functioning of the economic system, and about these effects there has been much controversy.

Principal Criticisms of Advertising

The more significant criticisms of advertising arising from this controversy may be grouped under three main heads: ideological, ethical, and economic. Persons who have criticized advertising on ideological grounds have basic objections of one kind or another to the functioning of our free, capitalistic system. Some object because they feel that an economic system which is directed and driven by free individuals impelled by a desire for profit is socially undesirable. They would substitute therefor some system whereby the production and distribution of goods are directed and controlled by government or socially controlled agencies. To such critics, advertising, which is one of the most evident of the tools used for gaining profit, is naturally objectionable. Other persons who object on ideological grounds condemn advertising along with many other activities of our economy because these activities encourage desire for material things. These critics speak out against advertising particularly because it is one of the most apparent of the forces leading to what they deem an undesirable materialism.

This study has made no effort to find the answers to these ideological criticisms, partly because there is no logical, scientific way of determining the answers, and partly because the task laid out for this study was an analysis of the facts regarding advertising within the framework of the existing free, capitalistic society. Such a society is one which relies on private initiative to supply desired goods and services; permits individuals to seek happiness in material welfare, if they so desire; and recognizes that in all social intercourse individuals may use influence to attain their ends, so long as they observe the ethical rules established by the social group.

The criticisms of advertising on ethical grounds arise primarily from three practices of advertisers: (1) the use of advertising to sell certain products which the critics hold to be undesirable and hence immoral and unethical; (2) the employment in some advertising of false and misleading statements which violate accepted ethical standards; (3) the employment of illustrations and statements which offend the critics' ideas of good taste. The criticisms of this sort are numerous because different individuals have different ideas as to what is ethical and in good taste. Some critics would practically rule out advertising because they look upon use of influence as dishonest and unethical, at least its use by the profit-seeker.

The adverse criticisms of advertising on economic grounds which have been made by various writers are numerous; the more significant are the following: (1) that much advertising represents wasteful expenditure because sellers compete in advertising, with the result that their efforts and resources go into reputation making, which, it is alleged, is of doubtful social value; (2) that through building a strong brand following, advertisers avoid price competition and consequently often secure high prices, and that the wide margins between price and production costs have been taken as profits by the sellers or have been used for wasteful advertising expenditure; (3) that advertising has contributed to the concentration of supply among a small number of producers and that this has tended to prevent a free play of price competition; (4) that advertising has encouraged meaningless product differentiation, thereby adding to the cost of goods and tending to make the consumers' buying problem unnecessarily complex and confusing; (5) that through its persuasive methods advertising has led consumers to make incorrect valuations of merchandise, and has induced them to divert their expenditures to advertisable products to the neglect of possibly more socially desirable products; (6) that advertising has contributed to the violence of cyclical fluctuations through its encouragement of price rigidity and its excessive use in boom times and under-use in depressions.

Definition of Significant Points of View

In the investigation undertaken to appraise these criticisms it has been essential to recognize the distinct points of view from which the issues may be considered. On the one hand, there is the point of view of the individual businessman, whose interest is in profit. Ordinarily he takes a long-range view of profit, and in so doing attempts to give the consumer those satisfactions which will bring constant patronage. Nevertheless he constantly has to make short-run decisions in terms of his long-run plans. The pressure of making a desirable profit showing over the short-run and of conserving his cash resources in times of stress may lead him to depart from long-run policies. Further, his is a restricted, selfish, individual point of view. In the conduct of his business he frequently is not fully aware of the social consequences of his business acts; yet those acts are fraught with social significance. His viewpoint towards advertising was treated in this study only because an appraisal of the economic effects of advertising requires a knowledge of how it is used by the businessman.

A second point of view is that of the consumer. His is a short-run point of view also, and his interest in advertising turns largely on whether it enables him to secure desirable merchandise at low prices. He desires a maximum of satisfactions from his limited resources. In the end, however, the welfare of consumers as measured by their satisfactions must be the gauge of the social results of economic processes.

The point of view of ethics concerns the question of what is fair, honorable, and decent in the use of influence in economic affairs. Ethical behavior is a constantly evolving phenomenon. It comes from the flux of social forces and is the result of the effort of the social group to protect its members from dangers of one kind or another. It has a bearing upon economics because it restricts and controls economic processes. Yet in a study of the economics of advertising it has been treated separately, and the study has been made under the assumption that relatively free use of influence is ethical and that the seller is expected to put his best foot forward in selling transactions.

The viewpoint of economics is the general social viewpoint. It seeks to determine how all members of the society are affected by economic processes and to indicate the practices which may detract from the material welfare of the social group. The economic point of view has governed this investigation, except for the chapters which describe and analyze the use of advertising by businessmen and those on ethics.

Criteria of Appraisal

The criteria of appraisal employed in the study are determined from the point of view of economics. The ultimate aim of economic processes is assumed to be the economic welfare of the social group. Hence the chief criterion by which advertising is appraised is whether it enhances consumers' satisfactions and hence their welfare.

Use of this criterion, however, requires that the nature of consumer satisfactions be clearly understood. Many critics of advertising condemn it because it appeals to the sentiments and emotions of consumers, builds up undesirable subjective values, and fails to give what they deem proper emphasis to objective product characteristics and the prices to pay therefor. The evidence of consumer buying, however, indicates that criticism from such a viewpoint fails adequately to appraise the nature of consumer satisfaction. It must be remembered that in a free economy the happiness and welfare of the individual are determined by himself. In the market place he can show what is satisfying to him only by his purchases, provided he has free choice. His buying actions, like most of his actions, are guided not solely by logic but to far greater extent by emotion, whether influence has been used in the selling process or not. If the criterion of consumers' satisfactions is to be employed and the assumption of personal freedom of choice is to hold, then it is futile to try to define consumer satisfaction in terms of any critic's rationalizations as to what correct consumers' satisfactions and valuations should be.

Since attainment of a maximization of consumers' satisfactions is the chief criterion for appraisal, the study has adopted a further criterion to apply, namely, that the consumer should have in the market place a wide freedom of choice among products, in order that his particular desires may be met. Among the choices should be that of getting desired product qualities and, for those who wish, products at low price. Those things which interfere with freedom of choice this study has deemed undesirable. Moreover, the view has been accepted that improvements in the quality of products contribute to the satisfactions of consumers, and that those things which have brought product improvement are to be deemed desirable economically.

When criteria by which to judge advertising were set up, it was believed that a search for checks and balances in the economic system should be made. If certain effects of advertising which might threaten a maximization of consumer satisfactions are offset by counterbalancing forces, then recognition should be given to the existence of such checks.

In the establishment of criteria it was deemed sound to accept a long-run point of view in judging the possible contribution of advertising to consumer satisfactions arising from increase in real national income. Consumers' material welfare and satisfactions have increased many fold in the past two centuries, because the per capita productivity of the economy, upon which consumption depends, has increased. Since the enhancement of material satisfactions has been so dependent upon a growing, dynamic economy, this study has adopted the criterion that forces which have encouraged enterprise and have contributed to opportunity of investment are desirable economically.

Major Economic Questions

The major economic questions to which investigation has been directed grow out of economic analysis which has as its criterion a maximization of consumer welfare. The outline of economic analyses which have indicated these questions was given in some detail, and at this point only the questions are listed:

(1) Does advertising tend to increase demand?
   (a) For a product as a whole.
   (b) For individual companies.
   (c) Total demand.
(2) Does advertising affect elasticity of demand?
   (a) Does it make demand for products on the whole more or less elastic?
   (b) Does it make individual companies' demand more or less elastic?
(3) Does advertising tend to increase or decrease distribution costs?
(4) Does advertising tend to reduce production costs?
(5) Does advertising tend to promote concentration of supply?
(6) Do all advertising costs enter into equilibrium costs or are some advertising costs growth costs?
(7) Does advertising tend to injure or destroy price competition, thus preventing a normal behavior of a free competitive system?
(8) Does advertising tend to increase price rigidity?
(9) Does advertising affect the fluctuations of the business cycle?
(10) Does advertising improve quality and range of products?
(11) Does advertising tend to increase or decrease the real national income?

QUESTIONS AND ANSWERS REGARDING ECONOMIC EFFECTS OF ADVERTISING

The first economic question dealt with in the study is whether advertising increases the demand for products in the following classifications: (1) types or classes of products (primary demand); (2) products of individual companies (selective demand); and (3) all products (total demand as measured by national income).

Does Advertising Increase Demand for Types of Products as a Whole?

Study of demand for a wide range of products leads to the conclusion that basic trends of demand for products are determined primarily by underlying social and environmental conditions, and that advertising by itself serves not so much to increase demand for a product as to speed up the expansion of a demand that would come from favoring conditions, or to retard adverse demand trends due to unfavorable conditions. The demands for some products, for example, lettuce, sugar, green vegetables, and professional services, have grown even though the products are little advertised, for underlying social and environmental conditions have been favorable to expansion of their demand. Other industries for which there have been underlying conditions favorable to demand expansion have had their demand more rapidly expanded through use of advertising than would have occurred without such advertising. Among the products studied, this quickening of expansion has occurred in the case of cigarettes, dentifrices, oranges, automatic refrigerators, and other mechanical products such as automobiles, radios, and electric washers. On the other hand, for certain products for which underlying conditions caused adverse demand trends, demand was found to continue to contract in spite of considerable expenditures for advertising and promotion. Such was the situation with cigars, smoking tobacco, furniture, wheat flour, and men's shoes. In these instances advertising was powerless to reverse underlying declining trends, although it probably served to retard the declines. In other instances, certain products have had relatively constant per capita consumption over a period of years, even though substantial advertising was devoted to them. In short, such contrasting demand situations as mentioned above led to the conclusion that consumers' wants for products are determined by the character of consumers and their existing environment. Advertising has not changed people's characteristics; it has changed environment only as it has contributed indirectly over a long period in helping to bring a mobile society and a dynamic economy. In speeding up demand for new products it has contributed to the dynamic character of the economy.

Does Advertising Increase Demand for Individual Concerns?

Advertising can and does increase the demand for the products of many individual companies, but the extent to which it does so varies widely and depends upon the circumstances under which an enterprise operates. An individual company can use advertising profitably to increase sales only when it serves to stimulate a volume of sales at prices which more than cover all costs including the advertising outlay. Advertising's effectiveness in profitably stimulating sales for a concern depends upon the presence of a combination of conditions, of which the following are important.

First, advertising is likely to be more effective if a company is operating with a favorable primary demand trend than if it is operating with an adverse trend. With the industry's sales expanding, each concern has opportunity to strive for part of an increasing whole. Thus in the tobacco industry some companies in recent decades have put much of their advertising and promotional effort on cigarettes, because the demand for cigarettes has been expanding and promotional effort given to them has been particularly promising of results in the form of increased volume of sales. On the other hand, their advertising of cigars, smoking tobacco, and chewing tobacco has not been carried on with such favorable trends; and although advertising has been profitably used, each producer has been seeking to get a share of a contracting total demand.

Secondly, advertising is particularly helpful to individual companies in stimulating demand when their products provide large chance for differentiation. Conversely, advertising is of smaller help when there is a marked tendency for the products of various producers to become closely similar. Product differentiation provides the opportunity for influencing consumers to prefer one brand to another brand. Advertising provides the means for pointing out to consumers the significance of differentiating qualities. Moreover, when differentiations of significance to consumers are found, the seller often can secure wider gross margins than when such differentiations are absent, for when significant differentiations are effectively advertised, consumer valuations are affected. Wide margins, in turn, provide funds with which to support advertising. Among the products studied, smoking tobacco, cosmetics, dentifrices, soaps, electric refrigerators, and automobiles are products which have provided opportunities for product differentiations, and these individualizing points have been advertised. Conversely, sugar, salt, canned fruits, and sheeting are illustrative of products which have tended to be closely similar, with consequent limitations upon the use of advertising to increase the demand of individual companies.

A third condition having a bearing upon the effectiveness of advertising in increasing selective demand is the relative importance to the consumer of hidden qualities of the products, as contrasted with external qualities which can be seen and appreciated. For example, consumers attach importance to the hidden qualities of mechanical products, such as automobiles, watches, and washing machines, for satisfactory operation of the machine depends upon these hidden qualities. Manufacturers of such products find advertising helpful in building mental associations regarding the dependability of their products. Likewise, consumers are apt to give great weight to the purity, potency, and other hidden qualities of such products as drugs and cosmetics. Conversely, one reason why advertising has not been valuable to producers of green vegetables is the fact that the buyer can inspect the articles and judge their worth at the time of purchase. The seller's trade-mark can stand for no hidden qualities of great significance to the buyer, particularly in view of the perishable nature of the product. Similarly, in the case of fashion merchandise the consumer can judge the elements of style, such as color and design, and tell whether the product suits his fancy. These external characteristics often are more important to the buyer than are hidden product qualities which may be associated with a seller's trade-mark. This fact accounts in considerable part for the relatively small use of advertising to influence the demand for the branded merchandise of producers of fashion goods.

A fourth condition having a highly important bearing upon the effectiveness of advertising in increasing the demand for products of individual concerns is the presence of powerful emotional buying motives to which the concerns can appeal in their advertising. Thus in the case of oranges effective appeals to maintenance of health have helped to build demand for the products of the California Fruit Growers Exchange. Similarly, manufacturers of cosmetics, drugs, and food specialties have found in their products bases for appeal to strong consumer buying motives. Cosmetics are bought because they promise personal beauty and romance; food and drugs are bought because they promise health. Often such emotional appeals have material effect on consumers' valuations of the advertised products, a fact clearly illustrated in drug and cosmetic products. In contrast to the above, sugar manufacturers, walnut growers, sheeting manufacturers, and numerous other sellers have found their products less adapted to the use of strong emotional appeals.

A fifth condition of prime importance to the use of advertising for increasing the demands of individual companies is whether the company's operations provide substantial sums with which to advertise and promote their products. The matter of an advertising fund for any period turns upon the number of units of the product which can be sold in the period and upon the margin available for advertising. The size of the margin depends very largely upon the effectiveness of advertising in influencing consumer valuations for a product. This influence of advertising is dependent upon the extent and significance of product differentiation present and upon the strength of appeals which may be employed to present differentiated qualities. The amount of margin available for aggressive selling work depends also upon conditions of competition within an industry. Cigarettes and dentifrices are illustrative of products which are purchased by large numbers of consumers at relatively frequent intervals and on which the margins available for advertising have been substantial proportions of selling prices. In consequence, many sellers in these fields have had large advertising appropriations. In contrast, although sugar has had large sales volume, its price has provided very narrow margins available for advertising. Again, the number of units of electric refrigerators sold is not large as compared with the above products, but the size of unit sale has been large enough to provide a relatively large margin per unit and, consequently, large total advertising appropriations to individual companies. In contrast, manufacturers of products of high price but of thin demand, such as expensive clocks and pipe organs for the home, have been small advertisers because they have not sold enough units to support substantial advertising programs.

The effectiveness of advertising in influencing selective demand depends upon the extent to which the five conditions outlined above are present. The combination of conditions which exist rather than any one condition determines the effectiveness of advertising in influencing selective demand. The possible combinations are almost innumerable, and each demand situation as it relates to advertising use must be studied separately. Of the conditions, those which are particularly important in rendering advertising an effective means for increasing the demands of individual companies are the chance for significant product differentiation, the opportunity to use strong emotional appeals, the existence of hidden qualities of importance to buyers, and the existence of circumstances favoring the accumulation of substantial sums to support advertising.

The study of demand shows that the opportunity for the use of advertising to increase demand varies markedly among different products. Although advertising for some products can be a very important means of increasing sales for the advertiser, yet, contrary to the view of many laymen, advertising does not always pay. Moreover, the use of advertising, like other business expenditures, involves risk for businessmen.

The study of demand shows further that even in product fields for which advertising may be used effectively by some concerns to increase their demand, other producers find opportunity to gain sales volume by other means. For example, by eliminating or greatly reducing the advertising and promotional functions, some manufacturers gain desired business by selling at a low price. Moreover, some sellers elect to use larger proportions of personal selling or other forms of promotion and less of advertising.

Does Advertising Increase Demand for All Products?

The question of whether advertising has had any effect in increasing the demand for all products has meaning only as advertising may have played a part in increasing the size of national income. Demand for all products can increase only as income from production increases. Over the past 100 years real national income has increased four-fold, and during this period aggressive selling and advertising were increasingly used. The part which advertising may have played in helping to bring the increase in national income will be summarized in connection with the review of advertising's effect on investment.

Does Advertising Affect Elasticity of Demand for Products?

Now that the effect of advertising in increasing the demand for products and for individual companies, i.e., its effect in shifting demand curves, has been summarized, its effect on elasticity, or the shape of demand curves, is reviewed. The evidence regarding the effect of advertising on elasticity of demand is not comprehensive and complete, and conclusions must be based largely on inference from comparisons and contrasts of the demand behavior of different products.

Does Advertising Increase the Elasticity of Primary Demand for Products?

First is the question, does advertising make the demand for classes of products as a whole more or less elastic? That is, has it made the demand for products, such as sugar, cigarettes, and dentifrices, more or less responsive to price changes?

It appears likely that for products whose demand is inherently inelastic, i.e., whose consumption by individuals is limited by the character of the products, advertising does not materially affect the elasticity of demand. For example, although salt has been advertised to consumers, it seems unlikely that advertising has materially shifted or changed the shape of the demand curve for salt. Its demand is and has been inelastic. Again, although advertising has helped in greatly expanding the demand for cigarettes, i.e., in shifting the demand curve, advertising does not appear to have greatly changed the shape of the curve. The sales of cigarettes fell somewhat in the 1930 depression, when leading companies generally held cigarette prices firm, an action which was equivalent to a normal price rise. But the decrease was relatively slight as compared with the decrease for many other products. This behavior of cigarette demand is in keeping with what would be expected from the fact that cigarette use is habitual with most buyers and their purchases are not appreciably affected by price change. In short, while advertising has helped induce some persons to acquire the use habit and thus has influenced total cigarette demand, advertising has not affected the shape of the demand curve, that is, the responsiveness of demand to price change.

In contrast to the above examples, for certain products advertising not only has had the effect of increasing their demand, i.e., of shifting the demand curves, but has apparently altered the shape of the curves. For example, many new products give evidence, in their early stages of marketing, of having small and relatively inelastic demand. Consumers are usually skeptical of a new product. They are not responsive to a price appeal at such times because of this skepticism and lack of an aroused desire for the product. Moreover, limited use of a product prevents the important selling forces of emulation and imitation from coming into play. As advertising and aggressive selling are employed, however, to build public acceptance for a new product and widening use brings the force of emulation into play, the shape of the product's demand curve evidently is altered. Large numbers of people come to desire the product. In short, in such cases the advertising and promotion have the effect of making demand more elastic. When public acceptance is once established, lowering of price generally serves to bring a large number of buyers into the market. Mechanical refrigerators are an example of a product whose elasticity of demand was increased by advertising and aggressive selling. Demand was built up slowly at first by aggressive selling. After the introductory period, as prices dropped, large numbers of buyers were brought into the market. Other new mechanical products which have been heavily promoted are also believed to have had their demand curves thereby rendered more elastic, products such as automobiles, radios, oil burners, and a long list of electrical appliances. Likewise, in other fields, it is believed that advertising has had the effect of increasing the elasticity of primary demand. For example, in the food field advertising and promotion have probably increased the elasticity of demand for such products as prepared breakfast foods, prepared desserts, and numerous other food innovations which have enjoyed substantial expansion of demand following their introduction to the market.

While conceivably there are products whose total demand becomes less responsive to price rise as the result of the building of strong consumers' preference for the products through advertising, no examples of this kind were found during this study, and they are believed to be few, if any. Dentifrices are a product which from *a priori* reasoning was expected to behave in this way. It was thought that the strong health and beauty appeals employed for dentifrices would have built such a strong desire for the product that an increase in price would not materially affect consumption. This reasoning was not borne out in the 1930 depression, however. When the price structure for dentifrices generally was held quite rigid in the depression, an action equivalent to a price rise in that period of declining prices, per capita sales for dentifrices fell some 25%. The contraction of dentifrice demand on this equivalent of a price rise suggests that demand for the product might be stimulated in turn by a general reduction of price. That this would actually happen is not supported by evidence. Strangely enough, price appeal has not been highly effective to individual companies in attracting selective demand.

Does Advertising Make Demand for an Individual Company's Product More or Less Elastic?

From the question of the effect of advertising upon the elasticity of demand for types of products as a whole (primary demand), the review is turned to the question of whether advertising makes the demand for products of individual concerns more or less elastic.

The evidence indicates that the advertising of brands tends to make their demands relatively inelastic for varying periods of time. The data which support this conclusion are found in the relatively rigid prices of many advertised articles. That brand advertising would have this effect is natural, for an objective of brand advertising is to build consumer preferences. Some consumers will stick by a brand even though its price relationships with competing brands are disturbed. Clearly the establishment of strong brand preference has led some manufacturers to act as though these preferences made the demand for their brands relatively inelastic. Rarely have they tested the inelasticity of their brands by raising and holding up their prices when competitors have failed to follow a similar procedure. Yet numerous examples were found in which manufacturers in periods of depression held their prices rigid while prices generally and the prices of some competitors were being lowered.

In all such instances price competition was found to come into play sooner or later, and either demand shifted to sellers with lower prices or a reduction of prices was forced. The quickness with which price competition comes into play varies in different product fields. In the fields of proprietary remedies, the highly individualized nature of branded products and the tendency of consumers to build strong attachments to brands have given these brands an inelastic demand over relatively long periods of time. Even in these instances, however, price competition eventually has developed. Proprietaries which have become popular have been copied by other manufacturers or by private branders, who have then used the same appeals as the imitated brands and also have featured the price appeal. Thus, for example, certain leading antiseptics have been imitated and forced to reduce price. In the aspirin field, the Bayer Company has held its prices relatively constant over long periods, but competing aspirins have gained ground.

The demands for individual brands of dentifrices, which are believed to follow a pattern of price behavior similar to that of many toilet goods and cosmetics, have been relatively inelastic. Prices have been held relatively rigid, and although consumers have been given opportunities to buy dentifrices at lower prices than those of leading advertised brands, demand has gone primarily to the advertised brands. Notwithstanding, price competition has entered this area and gives promise over a long period of gaining headway.

Similarly, the demand for cigarette brands has been relatively inelastic. Nevertheless, during the 1930 depression, 10-cent cigarettes became generally established when the price differences between leading advertised brands and 10-cent brands became substantial, and since that date 10-cent cigarettes have come to claim nearly one-fifth of the market.

In the food field, manufacturers of food specialties were found frequently to hold their prices relatively rigid with the onset of depression and thus to treat the demand for the products as inelastic, although there were numerous exceptions to this practice. The evidence indicates, however, that when this policy has been followed and private branders have adjusted their prices more rapidly than the manufacturers, demand has tended to flow to the private brands. In such instances manufacturers of advertised brands either have lost ground or have been forced to reestablish normal price relationships in order to hold sales volume. In these areas the effects of price competition were felt relatively quickly.

Does Advertising Tend to Increase Distribution Costs?

The review of evidence and conclusions is directed now to the question of whether advertising has tended to increase the costs of distributing merchandise.

The answer to this question is indeterminate from the evidence available. One cannot be certain to what extent the increased distribution costs which have attended the growth of industrialism are attributable to advertising. Yet the evidence, though conflicting in some aspects, is complete enough to dispel certain misconceptions sometimes met in the literature relating to advertising regarding the effects of advertising upon distribution costs.

The rising trend of distribution costs which was concomitant with the Industrial Revolution was inevitable. In the simple village economy which preceded the growth of the factory system, the few purchases of consumers were made without appreciable marketing costs. With the exception of the limited number of items then in general commerce, the exchange of merchandise was effected by direct contact between the buyer and the maker. After the factory system was established, the growth of large-scale, specialized units producing a tremendous variety of merchandise necessarily was accompanied by increasing costs of bringing about exchange. In addition to such essential marketing costs as those for transportation, warehousing, and credit, it was necessary also to incur the costs of bringing buyers and sellers together in the market. Sellers had to be informed of buyers' wants, and buyers had to be informed of merchandise available, if exchange was to take place. The costs of the selling process, i.e., providing the information and persuasion needed to effect exchange, became larger as the industrial organization became more complex.

But sellers have incurred selling and distribution costs greater than the minimum which may be deemed necessary to effect exchange. They have resorted to competition in advertising, personal selling, and other non-price forms of competition, all of which involve cost. The charge that advertising increases the costs of distribution is attributable in considerable part to the competition in advertising that occurs in some industries.

In a number of the product fields studied there was substantial competition in advertising and consequently these products had high advertising costs relative to certain other products. In fields in which such intensive competition in advertising has existed, the use of advertising, like the use of other forms of non-price competition, has increased the costs of distribution, or at least has held these costs at high levels. In many of these instances, however, consumers have shown a willingness to pay for the costs which attend the vigorously advertised products, for in large numbers they have not exercised the options open to them of buying lower-price, non-advertised merchandise. Instances of this kind were found in many fields, but especially clear were the instances in the dentifrice, cigarette, and grocery fields.

The sweeping generalization sometimes made that high advertising costs result in low personal selling costs and other marketing costs was not substantiated by the evidence of this study. Sometimes this statement is true, many times it is not. The managements of individual concerns frequently experiment to reduce their selling costs by using advertising instead of personal selling or other forms of promotion. Often in such instances advertising is an economical alternative, although in other instances it is not. Frequently advertising proves to be an economical and effective complement to personal selling. In other cases, sellers increase advertising costs per unit, not with the thought of reducing unit selling costs, but rather with the idea of increasing the volume of sales or of affecting consumer valuations in such a way that aggregate net profit may be increased. In short, sellers do not necessarily use advertising to attain the lowest possible costs of marketing, but to attain a desired marketing objective of selling certain volumes of merchandise at certain prices.

It is not possible to trace on a large statistical scale the full effects of advertising by manufacturers on the expenses and margins of distributors who handle advertised products. Whenever advertising builds a ready demand for a branded product, the costs of selling that product by the trade tend to be low. Thus, manufacturers' advertised brands of cigarettes, grocery products, and numerous other items have low costs of selling among distributors. Upon such items distributors ordinarily receive lower margins than they do on similar products bearing their own private brands or sold unbranded. But low selling costs apply to many staple commodities in ready demand which have relatively little advertising by producers, such as sugar, butter, potatoes, and so on. Moreover, distributors' private brands, once established, may enjoy low selling costs. Whether the reductions in trade margins of numerous advertised brands are more or less than sufficient to cover the manufacturers' costs of advertising is uncertain. The evidence is inadequate and conflicting.

Indication that high advertising costs do not necessarily entail low distribution costs was gained from a comparison of the costs of distributing merchandise under competing methods of marketing. It was found that those methods which involved highest advertising costs did not necessarily have lowest total costs of distribution. For example, in certain instances in which distributors sold under their own brands, the total selling and advertising costs and the total distribution costs incurred between factory and consumer were less than corresponding costs for competing marketing methods in which the manufacturers sold under their own brands. It should be pointed out, however, that in such cases the manufacturers primarily shouldered the burden of promoting and stimulating the demand for the products of their industries and that the private branders benefited from this promotion and advertising.

There was evidence in numerous cases that advertising has played a large part in contributing to the size of enterprises, but the data also showed that increased size does not necessarily mean lower distribution costs. In fact, there was evidence, though contradictory, that large concerns may have relatively high marketing costs. It should be recognized, however, that such a result is not undesirable, provided the increase in scale permits production costs that more than offset increased marketing costs.

While the evidence regarding advertising and distribution costs was adequate to warrant the conclusions outlined above, no answer was possible to the question of whether advertising has tended to increase distribution costs as a whole. The distribution cost picture is obscured by the fact that advertising and distribution cost data of business concerns relate to numerous combinations of products and of functional services and these combinations are subject to constant shifting. The overall effects of advertising on total distribution costs cannot be traced.

Does Advertising Tend to Reduce Production Costs?

The answer to the question of advertising's effects on production costs is indeterminate. While there is much affirmative evidence of striking economies in the costs of production which have attended the concurrent growth in size of industries and in use of advertising and aggressive selling, it is impossible from cost data to trace a clear causal relationship between decreased production costs and advertising. Only limited and tentative conclusions regarding advertising's effect on production costs are warranted by the evidence.

Over a long time span, aggressive selling and advertising have played a more or less important part in different industries in making possible the volume of demand necessary for the establishment of factories whose costs have been low as compared with the costs of handicraft methods of production. Advertising evidently has had an indirect effect in reducing production costs in numerous industries, not only through its contribution to growth in scale of operations but through its contribution to technological development, points which are summarized later.

In the study of specific industries, numerous instances were noted in which manufacturers employed advertising to help gain sales volume and in which the increase in size was attended by economies, which in varying degree offset advertising expenditures. In certain instances studied, advertising played a considerable part in building industry demand, and the economies gained through increased size of factories as industry demand grew were apparently greater than the promotional expenditures. Among products discussed at length, this condition evidently held in the early days of the cigarette industry and clearly in the case of mechanical refrigerators; less intensive study of numerous other industries indicates that the condition has frequently held true.

Not all industries, however, have had to rely upon the stimulus of advertising to build a demand sufficient to support low-cost manufacturing operations. The sugar, shoe, and sheeting industries, for example, grew to large size without much influence from advertising in stimulating primary demand, although aggressive selling in other forms was used.

Once industry demand has been established, it is possible for producers to seek a volume of sales large enough to permit low costs of manufacture without employment of a substantial amount of advertising. This generalization applies clearly to industries such as the sugar industry, which never has been a substantial user of advertising, but it applies as well to industries in which many producers are advertisers. Thus, not only do numerous sugar refineries attain low costs of production with little advertising, but the same is true of certain producers of cigarettes, mechanical refrigerators, dentifrices, and numerous other products, who are operating in industries which have relatively high average ratios of advertising costs. As pointed out elsewhere, in the latter instances the advertisers have assumed the burden of building demand for these products and the non-advertisers have benefited therefrom.

Sweeping claims of production economies resulting from and maintained by advertising are not in accord with the facts given above. In many industries concerns which are nonadvertisers or are relatively small users of advertising have low production costs. These concerns have been able to attain a profitable volume of sales through special contracts with large customers, through an appeal to consumers on the basis of price, or through some form of promotion and selling other than advertising.

Production economies, furthermore, do not always attend large-scale operations. In some industries relatively small plants may enjoy low production costs. This condition may be the result of the character of manufacturing processes, or it may be attributable to a type of demand which necessitates small runs of a product, as in the cutting-up trades and in the shoe industry. In these instances fashion has made the use of standardization of production runs and mass production methods beyond a certain point unprofitable. Accordingly in these industries relatively small firms often operate with production costs as low as those of large concerns.

Apart from the question of advertising's effect on production costs through economies that might be gained in size, there is the question of the value of advertising as a means of attaining low overhead costs. The question posed is whether advertising serves to bring stability of demand and relatively constant use of plant, with subsequent lowering of overhead costs.

The contribution of advertising as a means of attaining low overhead costs in this way has frequently been overstated. To begin with, advertising in itself does not insure stability of operations to a concern. While it helps many businesses to gain the relative stability of demand which comes when a firm builds strong consumer brand preference, nevertheless in an industry in which competition is carried on largely through advertising, the relative standing of sales of individual companies turns not so much on whether the concerns advertise, as on how skillfully they advertise in comparison with competitors. Moreover, stability of sales depends upon good merchandising and numerous factors other than advertising. In the next place, the importance of stability as a factor in costs depends upon the amount of fixed costs under which a concern operates. The study indicates that businessmen do not have uniform and clear-cut ideas of their fixed and variable costs. Accordingly what some of them class as overhead costs are not always in accord with the economist's definition of fixed costs. When fixed costs are taken into consideration, the evidence shows that for many products substantial fluctuation in the output of manufacturing plants does not produce appreciable changes in overhead charges per unit, although in certain instances where fixed costs are large, variations in costs are appreciable with fluctuation of output.

While the evidence regarding production costs warranted the conclusions which have been stated in this section, the evidence relating to production costs is especially unsatisfactory. Advertising and production cost data concerning specific industries, whether drawn from primary or secondary sources, are not satisfactory because business firms do not keep their records in a form which fits the needs of such economic analysis. The cost data obtainable are usually nonuniform and incomplete and generally cover only a short time span. In addition, the variables which bear upon size of production costs are too many to permit a sure determination of causal relations between size of operations and size of production costs. Because of these difficulties it is doubtful whether adequate and satisfactory cost evidence will ever be available.

Do All Advertising Costs Enter into Equilibrium Costs?

In effect the question as to whether advertising costs enter into equilibrium costs is an inquiry as to whether all advertising costs are costs which are incurred in the maintenance of an equilibrium, or balance, between the forces of supply and demand. Or are some advertising costs to be looked upon as growth or innovation costs which have the effect not of maintaining an equilibrium, but of raising the level of demand and supply in an industry, i.e., in establishing a new equilibrium?

Analysis of evidence regarding the growth of industries leads to the conclusion that in some immeasurable degree advertising and selling costs, particularly those devoted to new products and product differentiations, should be looked upon as growth costs, costs incurred by entrepreneurs in raising the level of economic activity. From the standpoint of the individual enterprise, they represent costs to establish a business, and like research expenditures incurred in developing a new product, they contribute to the growth of an industry. Their outlay is made not to maintain an equilibrium but to facilitate investment necessary to establish an industry and reach a new equilibrium.

For many commodities, in order to build a large primary demand which will make profitable the investment in an enterprise, business concerns often spend large sums on advertising and aggressive selling.

Like the sums spent on product research, the advertising and selling outlays for developing a market often are not included in the current prices, but managements expect temporary losses and anticipate their recovery from profits on the increased sales volume of later years. Case evidence shows that it is common experience for new product ventures to show losses for several years after being launched, losses due in considerable part to the advertising and aggressive selling efforts incurred.

In most industries which have been built by the aggressive selling efforts of innovators, imitators enter the market to profit from the demand that has been built up. Often these new entrants make small outlay either for product research or for advertising and selling effort by which to maintain the demand of an industry at existing levels, or to raise it to new levels. Frequently they make their bid for business on a price appeal made possible by low costs. Their entry into the market and the elasticity of demand which they exploit are made possible by the aggressive selling efforts of innovators. In short, the imitators often ride on the coat-tails of the innovators.

The extent to which growth costs enter into equilibrium costs and prices depends upon the date of entrance of the imitators and on the marketing strategy which they use. If they enter at an early point and employ price competition, the growth cost of the innovator may not be fully recovered. In short, under these conditions growth costs may not fully enter into equilibrium costs and prices. In a far larger number of cases the innovators recover their growth costs and then continue advertising and aggressive selling costs at a high level. In numerous instances a condition of competition in advertising and other non-price forms exists. Under these conditions the advertising costs tend to enter equilibrium costs and be borne by consumers in prices.

Because of the tendency of business firms to maximize profits and to compete in advertising and non-price forms, the imitator who enters the market and makes his bid for business on a price basis performs a significant social service. By keeping his selling and marketing costs low and by offering consumers the option of low prices, he serves to help hold down competition in advertising and other non-price forms. In short, he serves to help bring low costs and low prices in established industries. On the other hand, the innovator should be given credit for the important social service he performs. He develops improved products and builds for them a public acceptance and demand which calls into being the investment made by himself. Likewise he paves the way for imitators.

The innovator must have the prospect of recovering growth costs if advancement in the economy is to occur, and such recovery makes necessary some degree of monopoly, such as is provided in patents, secret processes, brands and so on. If the prospect of recovering growth or innovation costs is present, enterprisers are more likely to take the risk of incurring such costs than if such prospect is absent. The prospect for recovering such costs is enhanced if the innovator has in view the protection afforded by some degree of monopoly elements such as patents, secret processes, or the establishment of strong brand preference from early and aggressive development of a market. In short, the chance to have such protection in some degree is a stimulant to investment, upon which economic progress depends.

Does Advertising Tend to Promote Concentration of Supply?

No clear-cut answer of general application can be given to the question of the degree to which advertising tends to promote concentration of supply. In certain industries advertising has been employed to bring concentration of demand upon a few suppliers. In bringing concentration of demand it has probably had some, though not strong, influence in keeping down the number of suppliers. Whenever advertising has been effective in building strong brand discrimination this buyer preference for established brands has been one factor to discourage the entry of new brands into the market, because it has required any new entrant to make considerable outlay for aggressive selling costs to secure substantial volume. A number of cases were found in which manufacturers or distributors decided against entry into certain product fields because of the entrenched positions of leading advertised brands. On the other hand, other forces appear to have a much more important bearing on concentration of supply than does advertising. In a number of fields in which advertising has played an important role in marketing and in which manufacturers' advertised brands have been dominant, the total number of brands in the market has been large because forces other than advertising have favored easy entry of suppliers. Thus there are many brands of dentifrices even though demand is concentrated among a dozen or so brands. Similarly, numerous brands and suppliers are to be found in cosmetic and grocery product fields in which there is a relatively high degree of concentration of demand. In such industries, not only a potentially but an actually large number of suppliers exist in spite of advertising's effectiveness in building brand leadership for a limited number of concerns.

In industries studied it was found that some entrants by using price competition have found it possible to establish themselves without the risk of advertising expenditure. Thus the 10-cent cigarette manufacturers entered the market with small advertising outlay, and similarly certain manufacturers of dentifrices and food products have obtained business from private branders without use of advertising. These are examples of a widespread phenomenon.

In some of the industries studied, in which there is concentration of supply, the leading companies are large advertisers, but forces other than advertising have an important bearing on the degree of concentration. Thus, in the cigarette field, the need of heavy capital outlay for tobacco inventories and for plant investment has tended to keep down entry probably as much as the risk of capital for the promotional outlay to establish new brands. Again, in the automobile, refrigerator and petroleum industries, although the leading companies are advertisers, advertising does not appear to be among the more important factors in bringing about the concentration in those industries. The reasons for concentration of industries are numerous and have not been investigated in this study, except for an appraisal of the part which advertising has played in the instances studied. In numerous industries in which a T.N.E.C. study[1] shows relatively high concentration, such as the meat, copper, iron and steel, rayon yarn, sugar, and electric bulbs, advertising has played practically no part in bringing concentration. In short, although advertising has been a factor in the development of concentration in certain industries, it does not loom large among the causes.

Does Advertising Tend to Injure or Destroy Price Competition, Thus Impeding Normal Behavior of the Competitive System?

The evidence indicates that in many industries advertising tends to impede quickly-acting price competition, but in no case does it prevent it ultimately. Each of the industries studied has presented a different pattern of competition. The extent to which competition has turned upon price has varied from industry to industry; the extent

---

[1] Temporary National Economic Committee, Monograph No. 27, *The Structure of Industry* (Washington, U. S. Government Printing Office, 1941).

to which individual brands have been free from meeting competing prices has also varied. In industries in which the opportunity for product differentiation has been great and for which buying motives other than price have been effective among consumers, brands have become important guides to buying; and competition has tended to turn toward advertising and aggressive selling rather than toward price. Thus in certain industries studied, notably the cigarette, smoking tobacco, cosmetics, and drug industries, most producers have elected to compete on product differentiation and non-price forms; and price competition in numerous instances has been postponed for a long time. The areas in which price competition has been least effective, in which advertising and aggressive selling have been most intense, and in which margins between manufacturing cost and selling cost have been widest are the drug, cosmetics, and toilet goods fields. Consumer buying here has been less influenced by price than in most product fields. The advertising appeals to motives of health, beauty, and romance have been powerful; and consumers generally have lacked a basis for appraising product quality or performance since results from usage have not been subject to close check. Demand has gone primarily to the advertised products, and the degree of price competition found in many other industries has not been present.

In contrast to the situation in the drug and cosmetics field, competition in advertising in many fields is limited, and competition in price acts more quickly. This effective price competition does not allow margins permitting extensive advertising. The evidence shows that each well-known brand in any product field has what may be termed a "reputation" value, which permits it to obtain from consumers a price somewhat above that obtained for merchandise which has comparable objective characteristics but which has not had the advantage of being made well-known. In most instances brand reputation has been backed up by and built around product differentiation of some kind. Thus the price difference between the brands is associated with differences in product qualities as well as differences in reputation built through advertising. For most products the well-known brander can permit to the less-known brand a certain price advantage without losing his competitive position, but when he puts too high a value on reputation and product differentiation, then demand flows away.

The freedom of pricing by sellers and the opportunity to carry out competition on non-price forms rather than on price were found to be limited in all product fields. Even in industries in which consumers have been particularly susceptible to advertising influence and in which leading companies have been prone to battle in advertising rather than in price, competition in price ultimately has entered. For example, in the 1930 depression the 10-cent cigarettes entered a market long dominated by advertising competition, and in 18 months gained 25% of total consumer demand, when sold at a retail price differential of 4 cents to 5 cents a package under the prices of leading brands. In the case of dentifrices, toilet goods, drugs, and numerous other products in which advertised brands are dominant, consumers have been given the options of buying little-advertised private brands and manufacturers' brands at low prices, although they have not availed themselves of the opportunities in large numbers. In all such instances they have had the chance to balance price against the product differences and reputation offered in the advertised brands.

The evidence leads clearly to the conclusion that in the economic structure there are strong forces to counterbalance any tendency for competition to turn solely to non-price forms and for sellers to be free from price competition. In most fields in the course of time sellers appear who elect to offer consumers opportunity to buy merchandise on a price basis. For instance, numerous data relating to private branding practices of distributors show them to be an important counterbalancing force against those who choose to compete in product differentiation, advertising, and other non-price forms. They provide consumers with the option of buying on a price basis or of choosing the differentiated product with special characteristics made known through advertising.

There was considerable evidence to indicate that price competition tends to reassert itself particularly in periods of depression. Many manufacturers of advertised products have tended to hold their prices relatively rigid at a time when the value of money to the consumer is increasing. Such times have been fruitful for those sellers who make their appeal on a price basis. Thus it was found that large-scale distributors who have been more flexible in pricing their brands than manufacturers have increased the sales of their private brands in competition with advertised brands. Again, the 10-cent cigarettes provide an example.

One of the charges made against advertising as it affects prices is that it tends to bring concentration of supply, and that concentration leads sellers to set prices with reference to the potential retaliatory action of competitors. Thus normal price competition is said to be hindered because prices are not determined free from the influence of individual sellers.[2] Do large advertisers who provide a considerable share of the total supply follow a live-and-let-live policy in their pricing, that is, do they set prices with reference to competitors' actions and establish their prices at points which maximize profits? Direct evidence from advertisers upon this point is not available, and conclusions have to be drawn by inference from price data. In certain fields where competition has been carried out among a small number of companies largely through advertising, and in which consumers in large numbers have not been attracted by the price appeal of non-advertisers, pricing data give the impression that leading companies in numerous instances have been guided in their pricing policies with reference to the activity of competitors. In such instances, since competition in advertising rather than competition in price has given promise of greatest profit, these concerns have elected to compete on that basis. In other instances, however, in which there has been high concentration of supply, there is no evidence that such a live-and-let-live pricing policy has been followed. The managements have apparently set their prices without particular reference to competitors' actions, but at the level they have felt necessary to gain desired business or to hold their positions in the market. Under conditions of relatively high degrees of concentration of supply, different pricing practices are encountered in different industries and among different concerns. Concentration is determined by numerous forces other than advertising, and advertising in itself apparently has little to do with the pricing practices followed. The evidence indicates that the assumption frequently made that sellers have a perfect knowledge of costs, of the character of the demand curves for their products, and of the behavior of other sellers, which permits them to set prices so as to maximize profits, is far from reality. Prices are often set with great ignorance on the part of sellers as to supply and demand conditions.

The study has led to the conclusion that for new industries some delay in adjustment to strict price competition may be socially desirable in order to provide profit opportunities that will attract investment. Managements are likely to make investment when their chances of

---

[2] It is recalled for the general reader that the theory of pure competition assumes that individual sellers and buyers have no appreciable influence on the determination of market price.

recovering their growth costs and of making a profit are bright. Accordingly some slowing down in price competition in early periods may in the long run help to bring an advance in the level of national income which more than offsets the prices which consumers pay as a result of the lack of active price competition. On the other hand, businessmen in their efforts to maximize profits often are inclined to try to put off entering into active price competition. For this reason the imitators who enter the market to exploit the elasticity of demand made possible by pioneers in the field perform an important social service.

Does Advertising Tend to Increase Price Rigidity?

Attention is given to this question because of the emphasis placed by certain economists on price rigidity as a possible cause of failure of the economic system, particularly as it may be a possible cause of cyclical fluctuation or, at least, a force to accentuate cyclical maladjustments and to prolong cyclical depressions.

The evidence shows that advertising has contributed to price rigidity. The prices of many advertised items have been relatively insensitive. In many fields manufacturers have been slow to reduce prices in times of depression and, likewise, slow to raise prices in periods of upswing. Among the industries studied, this insensitivity of prices was found, particularly in the tobacco, drug, toilet goods, and cosmetics industries, but it was also present in varying degree in others. From studies made by the T.N.E.C. and other agencies it has generally become accepted that advertised goods have fewer price changes than unadvertised goods, although there are many exceptions to this rule. This relative stability of prices is to be expected, for advertisers generally make their appeal to buying motives other than price.

The lack of sensitivity of prices of advertised products indicates that manufacturers who have established consumer preferences for their products generally assume that advertising has made the demand for their brands inelastic and that they can hold prices relatively stable in times of general price decline without loss of volume. An impression gained from the study is that advertisers as a rule, although there are numerous exceptions, have become unduly wed to the notion of price rigidity and that they are loath to explore the possible degree of elasticity of demand for their products. In many instances they do not venture to experiment to determine the effect of lower prices as a means of gaining sales volume. The evidence indicates that many concerns which have held to rigid prices apparently have been mistaken in their assumption of the inelasticity of their brand demands, for competing private branders who have been more flexible in their pricing have generally gained business from these concerns in periods of depression.

Does Advertising Aggravate the Fluctuations of the Business Cycle?

Advertising cannot be classed as an important causal factor in cyclical fluctuations, although the way in which businessmen have used advertising leads to the conclusion that it has tended to aggravate cyclical fluctuations. None of the students of cyclical fluctuation have named advertising as an important causal factor. Moreover, fluctuations occurred before advertising became an important factor in the economy.

Advertising as used has tended to accentuate cyclical fluctuations because expenditures for advertising have varied directly with business activity. As a considerable employer of men and materials, advertising has thus contributed to fluctuations in the use of economic resources. As a stimulant to demand for products and services advertising has been most extensively used in boom times and most lightly used in depressions. When thus employed it has tended to accentuate the swings of demand.

The potentiality of advertising as a tool to help reduce fluctuations is illustrated in the case of certain individual companies which have been farsighted or fortunate enough to develop merchandising and promotional plans which have permitted them profitably to go counter to the general practice of their industries. They have maintained or even expanded advertising activities at a time when other firms were contracting. They could do so because they were in a position to offer product improvements at prices which permitted them to gain large sales volume even though buying power was down. Such concerns, however, represent the exception rather than the rule. Again, in past depressions certain important industries whose demand was expanding at the time of the advent of depression employed advertising and aggressive selling during the depressions as one force among a number to help stimulate a demand that aided in bringing readjustment. For example, the automobile proved a highly valuable product in helping to bring about economic recovery after the depressions of 1907, 1914, and 1920. Likewise, mechanical refrigerators, whose demand had just begun to mount to large proportions in 1929, were extensively advertised throughout the depression and enjoyed an expanding demand during that period. The behavior of these industries is, however, an exception and is counter to the behavior of industries which did not have exceedingly favorable demand trends at those times.

One of the principal hypotheses according to which advertising might be deemed a possible indirect cause of cyclical fluctuation rests in its contribution to rigid prices. Although prices of advertised products have tended to be relatively inflexible, recent studies relating to price flexibility tend to disprove the thesis that price rigidities can be looked upon as a chief causal factor in cyclical fluctuations. Accordingly it was concluded that advertising as a causal factor through its effect upon price rigidities was not significant. The most that can be said is that advertising is an integral part of a business system subject to fluctuations. Many activities of businessmen have some bearing on cyclical fluctuation, and of these advertising is one; but there are numerous other parts of the economic system, such as the use of money and credit, which are much more important causes of fluctuations.

Does Advertising Tend to Improve the Quality and Range of Merchandise?

The answer to the question of whether advertising tends to improve the quality and range of merchandise is decidedly affirmative. Advertising and aggressive selling have made an important contribution to the satisfactions of consumers through their part in stimulating the development of a wide range of merchandise and of product improvement. The part of advertising and aggressive selling here has been indirect, but nevertheless real and important. These two forces have played an integral part in a free enterprise system that has given a growing, dynamic economy. Business managements have relied on these selling forces to speed up the adoption of important inventions and product improvements, not only to enable their enterprises to recover research expenses devoted to product development, but also to afford a basis for new investment from which to profit.

In the matter of new major inventions, advertising's part has been that of affording to enterprise a larger and more speedy profit than would occur without such selling methods. New inventions do not

come into the world in full perfection, but as relatively crude, inefficient products which are gradually perfected through painstaking,
laborious efforts. Business is spurred on to such development effort
by the hope of profit, but profit on new products and improvements
has generally been realized only as a result of aggressive cultivation
of the market and of educating and influencing consumers to a realization of the satisfactions the new products would give.

Advertising and aggressive selling have led to much more rapid
adoption of major inventions than would have come without their
use. Consumer adoption is slow; it depends not only on stimulation
by the producer but also on the perfection of the product and on low
selling prices. Advertising and aggressive selling have contributed
to fulfillment of all these requirements. In building consumer acceptance, they have led to a relatively quick establishment of large-
scale demand, upon which low prices have often depended. In turn,
they have been a stimulant to product improvement.

Advertising and aggressive selling have had their most direct and
important influence in widening the range of merchandise through
the part they play in stimulating product differentiation among brands.
The desire of producers to offer under their specific brands products
which will be preferred by consumers has led them to a constant experimentation with possible combinations of desirable product qualities.
Technology has been called upon to develop new and improved products which some group of consumers might prefer. The quest is for
the desirable product, but always management has in mind aggressively
promoting the improved product and is influenced by its desires for
ideas which it may use in its advertising and selling efforts. Thus,
advertising and selling are an integral part of the system, and out of
the system has come a tremendous range of merchandise.

As part of the process of stimulating product differentiation, advertising has contributed to progress in merchandise improvements. As a
result of the process of constantly offering new differentiations, enterprise has placed on the market improved products which better fill consumers' desires and needs than did previous products. This product
improvement has been rapid and striking in the case of relatively new
products, such as automobiles, radios, refrigerators, washing machines,
and other mechanical contrivances. Over a relatively short period of
years such products have been made far more efficient and dependable
than those which preceded them and have been offered at prices

which generally have been but a small fraction of the prices of earlier years. But even for merchandise long on the market, the improvement has been substantial over a period of time; this is true, for example, of products such as gasoline and sheeting, which at any one time appear to critics to be relatively standardized. One must employ a time span to discern the full effect of the drive for differentiation on product improvement. Always the improvements of one manufacturer which have proved desirable have had to be matched by competitors. Competition has taken place on a higher level of quality from year to year.

In addition to its effect in stimulating improvement, advertising has also had an effect on product quality through its influence on maintenance of quality of products sold under brands. While brands are not necessarily a guarantee of uniformity of product quality, the desire of businessmen to profit from continued patronage usually has led them to maintain quality. Although maintenance of brand quality is not entirely dependent upon advertising, nevertheless advertising has some influence because the advertised brand usually represents a goodwill asset which has been built at considerable expense and injury to which would represent a business loss.

In their practice of differentiation, businessmen have placed upon the market many product differentiations that have appeared trivial and foolish to many people, but out of the process has come a remarkable product advancement. What is significant in product differentiation can be determined in a free society only by the action of consumers in the market place. Differentiations criticized as meaningless often prove to be significant to some consumers. Only through trial and error in the market can progress be made in merchandise development.

Does Advertising Tend to Increase or Decrease the Real National Income?

Advertising and aggressive selling as integral parts of the free competitive system have been a significant force in increasing the investment in productive facilities and in advancing the technology of production, two developments which have largely accounted for the four-fold increase of real national income per capita during the past 100 years. The tremendous advance in material welfare which has come since the Middle Ages would have been impossible without the building of a large-scale productive machine employing improved technology and management skills. But such an improved productive machine was called into being only as the result of strong social forces. On the one hand, there were forces to increase the willingness and desire of people to consume at a high quantitative level, for this willingness is not inherent in a population. On the other hand, there were forces leading to investment in productive facilities and to improvement in technology.

The willingness and desire of peoples in western countries to support a high level of consumption is basically attributable to social changes that have given these countries a mobile society in which individuals have been free to rise from the lowest to the highest class and have been able to aspire to the consumption of all types of products in the market. With the development of social mobility, the introduction of new wants and an increase in consumption were possible. Such changes were essential to the growth of industrialism and a dynamic economy.

From a long-range point of view, aggressive selling and advertising probably have played a considerable but undeterminable part in the formation of mental attitudes necessary for a high level of consumption. The study of demand in this volume has indicated that what people want is determined largely by their social backgrounds and habits. New products have been accepted by people, but the demand for them has grown relatively slowly. Once new products have been accepted by a few consumers, however, consumption usually has expanded through much of the social group. By helping to expand the use of products, advertising and selling have permitted the strong buying motives of emulation and imitation to come into play relatively quickly. They have played a particularly important part in bringing first sales, upon which emulative consumption depends. The new wants and new products which they have helped to bring in turn have become a part of environment influencing the further expansion of wants and desires of consumers.

While changes in social conditions and the forces of selling provide an explanation of growth of wants and willingness of the population to consume, this willingness could not have been satisfied had not the productive machine been called into existence. The productive machine which makes the products available provides the consumer income with which to purchase products. The existence of both the products and the income of consumers depends upon risk-taking by businessmen who see an opportunity for profit through making and selling goods which they think consumers will want. Their risk-taking activities bring the investment in factory and production facilities, which not only produce goods for consumption but employ labor and pay the wages and the return on capital upon which consumer income depends. In short, the activities of entrepreneurs create the markets for their own products.

Advertising and aggressive selling have an influence upon investment because they are important, integral parts of the system which leads to investment. Advertising and aggressive selling in themselves have not been the causes of the launching of new enterprises, or of the expansion of old, but they have been important elements whereby the new or enlarged enterprises might hope to gain a profitable demand. They frequently have been helpful in speeding up a demand which has called for increasing investment. They have promised the stability of demand and of profit to an enterprise which is attractive to investment. By such means have factories been built, men employed, and the products and incomes for increasing consumer satisfactions been established.

While advertising and aggressive selling have probably had greatest influence upon investment in new industries, they have also played a part in helping to increase the demand of established industries, which has called for investment to expand productive facilities. Even in the case of declining industries, the selling force has been employed to try to hold demand and thus to protect the investment in those industries against the inroads of the new industries. In some instances selling has also served to stimulate demand for new improvements in the products of declining industries and thus has served to give to the industry a new life cycle calling for investment.

Advertising and aggressive selling have also had a close relationship to the improvement in technology, which is one of the important explanations of the increase in national income. Technological improvements have come in considerable degree as the result of the activities of the producers of industrial goods. The spur to such producers to bring out improved machines has come from the opportunity to profit from meeting the desires of industrial buyers for more economical and efficient machines and materials. In turn, in the industrial goods field advertising and aggressive selling have played a part in promising to the enterpriser a profitable demand and thus have attracted investment.

In the free economy there have been frictions and resistances to technological advance and to investment in new enterprises producing improved goods; but the profit urge of enterprisers has been a force more than strong enough to overcome such resistances.

It is generally recognized that while the dynamic society which advertising and selling helps to produce has brought a high standard of living and in the main is desirable, it has serious shortcomings and drawbacks. Neither investment in plants to produce new products nor investment in labor-saving or capital-saving machines has brought unmixed gain to the consumer group, for the new has caused obsolescence of the old. It is believed, however, that the losses from obsolescence, though they sometimes seem large, are not to be overemphasized. Demand for a declining industry generally does not disappear all at once; nor are products in use either among consumers or among industrial users made useless thereby. Consumers' goods are generally used through second- and third-hand markets until their usefulness has gone. New machines are not substituted for old until the new are certain to pay their way. Moreover, business has learned to adapt itself to rapid change when necessary. In spite of losses and dislocations that are incurred in the process of change and growth, the balance so far as consumer incomes and rising standards of living are concerned has clearly rested in favor of change.

POSSIBLE DANGERS

Now that the answers to the more important economic questions have been reviewed, possible dangers associated with the use of advertising which the study has indicated are summarized. Counterbalancing forces which tend to offset some of these dangers are not discussed at length here, but are noted at a later point.

Insufficient Freedom of Choice by Consumers

The first of these possible dangers is that in some product fields in which advertising has been particularly effective in building brand preferences it has probably been a factor in reducing the opportunity of wide choice by consumers among products, particularly in so far as the option of buying low-price merchandise is concerned. One of the criteria employed in this investigation into the economic effects of advertising has been that the consumer should have in the market place a wide freedom of choice and particularly that among choices there should be products of low price.

The evidence indicates that in most product fields consumers do have a wide freedom of choice, including opportunities to buy low-price merchandise in competition with higher-price merchandise which is differentiated in some way to command the higher price asked. In certain fields, however, advertising has been so powerful a force that many consumers have not had readily available choices of buying low-price merchandise. The brands generally available have been the extensively advertised brands. Most of the leading brands available in these fields bear considerable costs for advertising and for other non-price forms of competition. Price competition has been slow to gain a foothold. Among the products studied this situation has been true especially of certain drug, cosmetic, and certain grocery specialty items. Private branders and others seeking demand on a price basis have made little headway in establishing their brands. The consequence has been that consumers have had in those fields a limited choice because of the domination of advertised brands and the lack of an appreciable number of competing low-price brands which are well established and widely distributed.

It should be pointed out, however, that private branders or others who make an appeal for business on a price basis have failed to enter some of these fields because the prices of the advertised brands have been so low as to make the price appeal of the unadvertised brands ineffective. The saving which the private branders have been able to offer consumers has not been sufficient to overbalance in the minds of many consumers the differentiating qualities and repuation of the advertised brands. Some manufacturers have been well aware that prices containing an unduly wide margin for promotion and net profit invite the entry of competition. Hence they have followed the policy of lowering their margins to discourage the entry of competition. In these cases the threat of price competition has been effective in reducing margins. In those instances in which manufacturers have maintained their dominating positions as a result of a policy of price reduction, consumers have not suffered appreciably from the relative lack of nonadvertised brands in the market, for the prices of the advertised brands have contained relatively small advertising costs and net profit margins.

It was found also that opportunity for wide choice by consumers varies considerably by localities. In small-town and local communities the choice available is not so wide as it is in cities. The number of retail establishments is smaller and, consequently, the number of stores of private branders, who have widened the range of choice through the offering of low-price merchandise; moreover, private branders and other price competitors are not equally active in all sections of the country.

Undoubtedly in many instances consumers fail to realize the opportunities of choice open to them. Evidence indicates that in many of their purchases consumers are not well informed or careful. They are not aware of the qualities of products available to them or of the satisfactions that might attend their use. Again in certain product fields appeals which the advertisers use are so strong that they are particularly effective in attracting consumers who are not well informed regarding merchandise qualities. In short, the evidence indicates that there is need of consumer education regarding products beyond that attainable from the persuasive messages of advertisers. In a free economy consumers need to be equipped to look out for themselves and should be trained to be wary in their buying.

Insufficient Freedom of Entry into Industries

Closely related to the danger just noted above is another possible danger, namely, the insufficient freedom of entry of new concerns in certain fields in which competition is carried out largely through advertising. In these fields the entry of new producers or of new brands has been made difficult and expensive because of the dominant position of the extensively advertised brands. As has been pointed out previously, however, it is believed that the restriction attributable to advertising is not large. While entry of firms desirous of competing through advertising is made expensive and risky through the need for large advertising outlay, other firms willing to compete on a price basis usually have found opportunity to enter sooner or later without heavy risk in advertising. They have found this opportunity because large-scale distributors gradually have tended to seek out sources through which to get merchandise to establish themselves even in industries where advertised brands have been strongest. Moreover, in fields where there is an appreciable amount of sales, entry on a price basis is likely to occur if the prices of the dominating brands become high enough to afford opportunity for effective price appeal by those desiring to compete on price. It should be pointed out also that in many product fields in which there is concentration of demand and in which entry is difficult, the difficulty of entry is attributable not so much to advertising as to other causes.

The evidence indicates further that in most product fields where an entrant has a really superior product, that is, a differentiation worth promoting, he ordinarily can establish himself in the market. In such cases advertising is for him an essential tool with which to make his product known. He has little hope of gaining appreciable sales volume without its use.

Too Little Price Competition

In some product areas, among them those discussed under the two previous headings, there has been evidence that demand has been concentrated among a limited number of producers and that there has been too little competition in price on the part of many concerns and too much reliance on competition in advertising and other non-price forms. The entry of effective price competition in some of these fields has been too long delayed.

The presence of active price competition in any product field, after primary demand has once been well established, is highly desirable from a social standpoint. It serves as a means of holding down competition in non-price forms with its attendant costs. The virtues of non-price competition are appreciable and are worthy of repeating in this connection. From it comes progress in product development. It encourages a wide range of merchandise. In addition, when there is competition in services, such as delivery and credit, consumers may choose these services, even if they must pay for them. Their option is widened by such choice. But alongside this competition in differentiation and other non-price forms should be competition based largely on price to afford the economy a check against increasing cost of non-price competition. Effective price competition tends to reduce or to hold down the costs of distribution when once the advantages of growth in an industry have been largely attained. While active price competition was found in most fields studied, in a limited number it was not present in appreciable degree.

Danger of Waste in Distribution

The danger of too little price competition is, in effect, the danger frequently mentioned by critics, namely, waste in distribution attending the use of advertising. When competition is carried on to a large extent in advertising and other non-price forms, competitive waste may develop in that distribution costs become high or remain high. The point need not be developed further, for the conclusion is adequately reviewed above. In so far as advertising and selling costs incurred by a concern are more than offset by production economies which result from increased scale of operations, there can be no complaint that advertising and selling costs are high and lead to competitive waste. In certain product fields, however, where advertising and selling costs are high, there is no evidence that these high costs are offset by production economies of the concerns which incur them. The high costs persist because effective price competition has been prevented by the existence of other strong appeals which have affected consumers' valuations.

The Lack of Sufficient Consumer Information

The long persistence of relatively high advertising and distribution costs in some fields is attributable in appreciable degree to the emotional and the uninformed character of the buying of consumers. In large part they have not made use of such information as has been available to them in advertising and other sources regarding objective product characteristics. To a large extent they have not been guided in their buying by a careful rationalization of objective product characteristics in terms of price, and this study has pointed out that the character of consumer satisfaction does not lead to the belief that for much of their buying they may be expected to follow such a behavior. The evidence indicates, however, that there is a substantial minority of consumers desirous of more information to guide their buying.

In this connection there is the danger from the consumers' standpoint that advertising in itself does not provide the information which will permit consumers wishing to buy on a logical, informed basis to do so. Advertising is influence, and it provides information only as information is effective to induce buying action. Since detailed factual information has not in itself been an effective means of stimulating large demand for many products, advertisers generally have not provided such information.

That it is desirable for consumers in an advanced economy to have extensive information and knowledge regarding the wide range of products available to them is axiomatic. If consumers are to get a maximum of satisfaction from their expenditures, they should have opportunity to appraise the probable satisfactions that will attend their choices. They should know what is on the market, for the greater their knowledge, the more enlightened can be their choice of goods. Moreover, since goods are not identical, consumers should have knowledge regarding the qualities of competing goods and the use and care of these goods. Since there is the danger that advertisers will fail to provide a sufficient amount of information to satisfy the consumers desiring to buy on a logical and informed basis, there is need of counterbalancing forces to meet this difficulty.

COUNTERBALANCING FORCES

Since advertising incurs the possible dangers summarized above, what forces exist in the economic system which tend to counterbalance these dangers? Attention is directed first to forces tending to counterbalance the dangers arising from intensive competition in advertising.

Development of Concerns Electing to Compete on a Price Basis

· The evidence has indicated that the best protection against the dangers arising from intensive competition in advertising and other non-price forms of competition is the presence of concerns which elect to reduce advertising, selling, and other non-price competitive costs and to make their bid for patronage on the basis of price appeal. These concerns serve to give to consumers the option of low-price purchases; they reduce the danger of excessive competition in non-price forms and help to assure that the degree of non-price competition which persists is giving to consumers satisfactions for which they clearly are willing to pay.

Among the strongest forces in the economy serving as a corrective of this kind against excessive brand advertising are the large-scale distributors, who in recent decades have become increasingly active in establishing their own brands in various product fields and in offering them on a price basis. These include many, though not all, of the chains, mail-order houses, voluntary chains, and supermarkets, and a lesser proportion of department stores. Through an integration of marketing functions they often have been able when selling under their own brands to attain economies in overall marketing costs not attained when the manufacturer carries out the advertising and promotional functions. Many of the chains, though not the department stores generally, have greatly reduced their competition in offering services to consumers. In instances in which they have followed this policy, they have generally made their bid for business on a price basis. In addition, because of their size they have had strong bargaining power, which has often enabled them to buy merchandise at favorable prices, which, in turn, they have passed on, in part at least, to consumers.

They have established their own brands first in those fields in which they have been able to get volume of sales readily and without undue promotional costs. Many of them have been desirous, however, of extending their brands into fields strongly dominated by manufacturers' brands. Gradually they have done so, although the number of private brands in some product fields dominated by manufacturers' brands is still small. Once these brands have become established, the effectiveness of their price competition has tended to become greater. Thus they have become an increasingly strong force to limit competition in advertising and non-price forms in all the fields in which they have entered with their own brands.

The Counterbalancing Force of Consumer Education

The danger that advertising will fail to give adequate information to consumers desiring to buy on a logical and informed basis has been counterbalanced in part by the development of the so-called consumer movement, which includes a wide range of activities, among them consumer education in schools and colleges and the formation of organizations to advise consumers regarding product choices.

From the standpoint of maximizing consumer satisfactions, such movements and activities are deemed natural and desirable developments. As yet consumer education has made little headway, but it is gaining in strength.

ETHICAL ASPECTS

The summary turns now to a brief review of the evidence and conclusions upon ethical issues.

The evidence from reports both of the Federal Trade Commission and of Better Business Bureaus leads to the conclusion that a relatively small percentage of advertising material is of such a character as to be misleading or false under the standards applied by those organizations. Yet the volume of such advertising has been great enough to provide a basis for the feeling on the part of a substantial minority of consumers that there is a considerable volume of undesirable advertising. Part of this adverse attitude is attributable to a sentiment held by some persons that the use of influence by businessmen is unethical. This attitude has been frequently reflected in the writings of certain critics of advertising.

A postulate accepted for this study is that influence is an integral part of a free system and that it is no more denied to men in their economic transactions than it is to men in their educational, religious, political, and other social intercourse. The question involved is one of determining what is to be deemed ethical in the use of influence.

Ethics is a constantly evolving concept, and what is deemed ethical in selling transactions has changed materially over the centuries. When a long time span is employed the evidence indicates that an appreciably higher standard of honesty in selling relationships holds now than held in former times. Furthermore, there has been a growing attitude that the consumer shall be given more and more protection and that the seller shall be subject to increasing limitations on his use of influence. This change is attributable to the fact that since handicraft days, when exchange was limited and direct, sellers have gradually attained a relatively more powerful position than they held formerly. As the range of products bought by consumers has increased, consumers have become relatively weaker in the matter of using influence in the exchange process. The seller now knows his merchandise well, whereas the untutored buyer has to learn the merits of thousands of items. The consumer group, consequently, has received more and more protection.

This tendency to greater protection of buyers does not mean a denial of the use of influence to sellers. It means merely that they must adapt themselves to this tendency in ethical concepts. The evidence indicates that the social group will accept a pragmatic test of honesty. The group will judge the goodness of the actions of sellers by their intent and by the end they attain. If business is to avoid restrictive legislation, however, it must find a way of curbing the unethical activities of the relatively few sellers who transgress consumers' sentiments regarding what is ethical, moral, and in good taste.

CONSTRUCTIVE CRITICISM

Out of this study of the use of advertising by businessmen have come impressions regarding certain business practices and business attitudes which have been commented upon along the way and are reviewed here.

Price Strategy

One of these impressions relates to a tendency on the part of many advertisers to fail to give proper attention to the elasticity of demand either for the type of products which they sell or for their brands. Consequently, in the opinion of the author, they fail fully to realize the effect of price upon their sales volumes.

In the case of products which are relatively new on the market or which are important new differentiations, advertising often has the effect of greatly increasing the elasticity of demand. Hence, a tremendous increase in volume can be realized sometimes through price decreases. New buyers in lower income levels than have been reached theretofore can be brought into the market by low prices. While in many instances producers are fully cognizant of the effect of price and use it to bring expansion, in others they fail correctly to appraise the effect of price and do not take the risk of reducing price to test thereby the effect upon volume and profits. Again, they do not include in their lines of merchandise inexpensive models that might reach new buying strata. Often as a result of failure to bring prices down, the leading innovators have paved the way for relatively easy entry of the imitative concerns which come in and exploit the elasticity of demand which the innovators' activities have built. This study indicates the wisdom from the standpoint of the business concern of carefully considering the profits it could gain from greater attention to price strategy.

Attention has been called also at various points to the tendency of some advertisers to overestimate the extent to which advertising has made the demand for their brands inelastic, that is, the extent to which advertising has freed them from price competition. This fact accounts in part for the relatively high degree of rigidity in the prices of many intensively advertised items. While brand advertising does build consumer preferences which permit some freedom from price competition, every advertiser should realize that when he permits normal price relationships to become disestablished, he is likely to lose volume. Numerous cases were found of businesses which lost much ground in their industry standing by overestimating the inelasticity induced by the advertising of their brands.

Supplying Product Information

Another point to which many business concerns might well give careful consideration is the supplying of further product information to consumers. This study has recognized that advertising is essentially influence and that the provision of information in advertising is determined largely by its effectiveness in inducing consumer purchases. In recent years an increasing number of consumers have given evidence of wanting increased information. To the requests of this group, among whom are militant advocates of informative advertising, some concerns have turned a deaf ear or have voiced opposition, thereby harming the consumer relations of business. Other concerns have recognized that by adopting informative labeling they have had an opportunity to win the favor of the group requesting it. Since a broad survey of advertising usage indicates that when detailed information is provided it is because buyers desire the data, concerns in many fields should give careful thought to furnishing the sort of information which consumers may want and from which they may benefit. Thereby the busines firm itself may profit. Such a procedure need not detract from the interest, attractiveness or persuasiveness of an advertising campaign, which is essential to low advertising costs.

Business concerns should realize that the consumer educational movement, which is relatively new and weak, is a natural development resulting from the growing complexity of merchandise available. From an economic standpoint it is a desirable development because it promises to make consumers able to look after their own interests. Accordingly, as in the case of other broad social developments, businessmen would do well to study this movement sympathetically and to adapt themselves to it.

THE PLACE OF ADVERTISING IN A CAPITALISTIC ECONOMY— A FINAL STATEMENT

In the end, what role of social significance does advertising play in our capitalistic economy? On the whole, does it add to consumer welfare? The discussion has shown that its use is accompanied by certain dangers, particularly those attending the tendency of business-men to compete in advertising and thus to bring into prices a large amount of selling costs. On the other side of the ledger, what is adver-tising's offsetting contribution, if any?

Advertising's outstanding contribution to consumer welfare comes from its part in promoting a dynamic, expanding economy. Adver-tising's chief task from a social standpoint is that of encouraging the development of new products. It offers a means whereby the enter-priser may hope to build a profitable demand for his new and differ-entiated merchandise which will justify investment. From growing investment has come the increasing flow of income which has raised man's material welfare to a level unknown in previous centuries.

In a static economy there is little need of advertising. Only that minimum is necessary which will provide information regarding sources of merchandise required to facilitate exchange between buyers and sellers who are separated from each other. Clearly in a static econ-omy it would be advisable to keep informational costs at a minimum, just as it would be wise to keep all costs at a minimum.

In a dynamic economy, however, advertising plays a different role. It is an integral part of a business system in which entrepreneurs are striving constantly to find new products and new product differentia-tions which consumers will want. Without opportunity to profit relatively quickly from the new products which they develop, entre-preneurs would not be inclined either to search for them or to risk investment in putting them on the market. Advertising and aggressive selling provide tools which give prospect of profitable demand.

The critic must realize that progress in product improvement comes slowly; merchandise does not come on the market in full perfection. The constant seeking for product improvements, with which advertis-ing and aggressive selling are intimately related, has been essential to an ever-increasing variety of new merchandise.

For much of this new merchandise advertising and other forms of aggressive selling play the significant role of aiding the expansion of demand and the responsiveness of demand to price reductions upon which widespread enjoyment of the products among the populace depends. Widespread usage is made possible by low prices, which in turn require low costs. For many industries low costs of produc-tion depend upon large-scale operations which are not possible until there is a large volume of sales not only for the industries, but also for individual producers. Advertising may make increased sales possible not only through shifting demand schedules but also through increasing the elasticity of demand for products. Thereby it provides business concerns with the opportunity to increase dollar sales volume through price reductions and makes it worth their while to do so as production costs decrease. In past years in industry after industry the economies which have come from large-scale operations and technological development have been passed along in lower prices.

As an industry matures and new differentiations, upon which expansion rests, become less important, then it is particularly desirable that counterbalancing forces which tend to check and reduce competition in advertising, and which prevent innovators from profiting over long periods of time from their innovations, should have free opportunity to operate. Probably the most important of these counterbalancing forces is that provided in the competition of business firms which do not make substantial outlays in development work on which growth depends, either in product development or in promotion of new merchandise. The price competition of these concerns serves to hold down the costs of competition in advertising and other non-price forms. The price competition of such concerns is to be encouraged rather than discouraged by restrictive price legislation, such as has been embodied in recent years in price control acts of one type or another.

To the counterbalancing force of price competition may be added that of increased education of consumers permitting them to choose intelligently among the variety of goods offered them.

Since advertising has in large part been associated with the promotion of new and differentiated merchandise, a substantial part of advertising costs should be looked upon economically as growth costs. They are the costs incurred in raising the economy from one level to another. From the standpoint of social welfare these costs have been far more than offset by the rise in national income which they have made possible. Such costs should not be prevented or decried. In the future if man's material welfare is to be raised to higher levels in our free economy, the spark of enterprise must be kept glowing brightly; the chance to profit from the new should continue to exist. So long as individual enterprise flourishes and a dynamic economy continues, advertising and aggressive selling will play a significant social role.

NOTE ON SOURCES OF INFORMATION
AND METHODS OF STUDY

IN THE preparation of *The Economic Effects of Advertising,* many sources of information have been tapped and many special studies have been made. There is repeated mention of these studies in the text, but limitations of space have made it impossible at any point to describe in detail the method and content of each. In the collection of material, all approved scientific methods have been utilized. The literature in appropriate fields has been carefully examined, analyzed, and evaluated. Extensive correspondence has been carried on and important use has been made of mail questionnaires in securing information from business firms. Much more reliance has been placed upon personal investigations and more or less extensive interviews with business executives, consumers, and others who are concerned with advertising and its effects. Trained research personnel was engaged to do the principal interviewing work under the personal and continuing supervision of the author. For certain portions of the study, the case studies which have been made through the Harvard Business School since 1920 have proved most useful. These cases provided primarily for teaching purposes in the Harvard Business School bring out in detail the problems, policies, and results of advertising for many different business enterprises. Five hundred and seven of these cases had been collected specifically in the advertising field under Professor Borden's direction prior to the beginning of the study. Sixty more were collected in connection with the present investigation. Some of these studies have been published in the various editions of Borden's *Problems in Advertising;* others, particularly those relating to cooperative advertising, are published in Volume 11 of the *Harvard Business Reports;* but many more are in the confidential case files of the Harvard Business School. Among over 15,500 cases collected by the Harvard Business School, over 3,500 case studies relate to general marketing, sales management, retail distribution, and industrial marketing. These have all been available to the author and have been examined for what they might offer in connection with problems of the study. Case materials have been of special usefulness in showing the issues confronting businessmen and have indicated how businessmen think about their promotional problems.

Because of its broad scope, the study of *The Economic Effects of Advertising* comprised numerous smaller projects and special studies which may, for convenience, be grouped under four headings:

1. General studies
2. Consumer studies
3. Studies of distributors' advertising
4. Studies of producer and manufacturer advertising

1. Among the general studies was the preliminary, exhaustive study of the literature relating wholly or partly to advertising. Economic, advertising, and business literature which has appeared both here and abroad was examined and analyzed to furnish a clear basis for determining the scope and precise nature of criticisms of advertising. All available cost studies which might throw light upon the costs of advertising were scrutinized.

2. Special study was made of the volume of advertising in the United States. Going beyond the examination of printed sources of information, personal interviews were conducted with some 75 executives of various media organizations. A special questionnaire was directed to 300 newspapers and 200 magazines, and a large amount of special correspondence carried on in connection with the effort to get an accurate estimate of volume elicited many hundreds of replies.

3. In an effort to measure the advertising contribution to the revenue of newspapers, magazines, and radio broadcasting stations, both library research techniques, numerous field interviews and a questionnaire study directed to 100 newspapers and 50 magazines were utilized.

4. Two other general studies were not productive of useful information: (1) A survey designed to measure on an historical basis the growth in volume of advertising for new products. It developed that much of the advertising for new products was done by companies already selling established products and the records of media did not permit a breakdown between the amounts devoted to new and old products. (2) A study of census data by means of which it was hoped that the increase in the range of products offered consumers might be traced was not successful. In the general area covered by these two inquiries, much useful information was obtained from individual firms on a case study basis. But over-all figures for the market or for classes of products could not be obtained.

The key position of the consumer in any study of the economics of advertising was clearly recognized at the outset and several types of studies were deemed advisable:

1. Literature relating to the consumer, the consumer interest, and the consumer movement was carefully studied.

2. An intensive study of merchandise testing was conducted. In addition to the examination of literature, field interviews with retailers, manufacturers, testing organizations, and industrial and ultimate consumers were conducted, and a voluminous correspondence was carried on in order to arrive at conclusions on merchandise testing and its relation to the consumer and advertising. The results of this part of the investigation were separately published in "Merchandise Testing as a Guide to Consumer Buying." [1]

3. The consumer relationship to advertising was studied from a different angle through a consumer attitude survey made on the basis of personal interviews. Interviewers using two different questionnaire forms obtained answers from 3,032 persons on one questionnaire, and from 4,575 on the other. In carrying out these interviews the Harvard Business School was fortunate in having the assistance of Alpha Delta Sigma, National Advertising Fraternity.

4. A third study of buying appeals made to consumers in the 897 advertisements of businessmen was made following the method first used by Professor Copeland in the Harvard Business School in the 1920s.[2] The method consists essentially of an intensive study of a large number of advertisements with a view to grouping and classifying the appeals used by advertisers in selling to readers of the advertising. Presumably these reflect buying motives or more accurately advertisers' ideas as to,buying motives of purchasers.

5. A study in which attempt was made to classify advertising according to ethical criteria did not produce useful information. The principal difficulty was the inability to devise a practically useful classification of what was ethical and what was unethical.

Of the various classes of businessmen engaged in the purchase and sale of commodities, the retailer comes closest to the consumer. While from general sources and many personal contacts a mass of information was available, certain special studies of this relationship to the economics of advertising were considered necessary:

1. A review of literature and all appropriate case material in the Harvard Business School files dealing with advertising by distributors.

2. A field study involved extensive personal interviews with 52 large distributive organizations, corporate and voluntary chains, department store and mail order concerns, in order to secure data upon brand policies, prices, and pricing policies.

3. A mail questionnaire sent to 92 corporate and voluntary chains, likewise dealing with brand policies, prices and price policy, brought 25 replies.

Detailed information upon the advertising and marketing operations of manufacturers is so meager and difficult to secure that several special studies were attempted.

---

[1] M. T. Gragg, in collaboration with N. H. Borden: *Merchandise Testing as a Guide to Consumer Buying* (Harvard Business School, Division of Research, Business Research Studies, No. 22, November, 1938).

[2] M. T. Copeland, *Principles of Merchandising*; A. W. Shaw Company, Chicago, 1924.

1. These were preceded by the usual examination of literature and pertinent case material.

2. The first special study was one relating to marketing and production costs of manufacturers, involving interviews with 25 firms and the collection of a large amount of information from each.

3. A questionnaire was sent to 737 companies seeking similar information on marketing costs, production costs and volumes. This produced 29 replies, a disappointingly small proportion, but not surprising in view of the long, detailed and complex data requested.

For reasons outlined in the text, these efforts by field interviews and questionnaire to discover more facts about the relationship between advertising and manufacturing costs did not provide as much useful information as had been hoped.

4. An intensive analysis was made of cost data regarding advertising available in the offices of the Association of National Advertisers.

5. A similar analysis of cost data regarding marketing and advertising costs was made from information in the files of the Harvard Bureau of Business Research.

6. Of a different type but relating to marketing operations of manufacturers was the analysis of the records of four different manufacturing industries selling consumer goods for which a private research organization makes continuing confidential studies of product demand. These studies revealed the flow into consumption of competing manufacturers' products and the record of promotional efforts and the movement of prices. The author found this a valuable supplement to other library research and field investigations.

No brief statement as to the basis for conclusions contained in the text would be complete without taking into account the long period of experience and research in advertising and related fields represented by the author and members of the advisory committee. The philosophy of the Harvard Business School and basic teaching methods have compelled members of this group to maintain continuous research and active contact with business enterprise and with problems of the social impact of business upon the community for 20 years or more. That experience and contact was invaluable in appraising the material as it appeared and in reacting to it scientifically.

NOTES, REFERENCES, AND COMPUTATIONS CONCERNING THE VOLUME OF ADVERTISING IN THE UNITED STATES

A. NEWSPAPERS

THE *Biennial Census of Manufactures,* 1935, U. S. Bureau of the Census, page 575, gives newspaper advertising revenue as $500,022,708. The Bureau was unable to state whether this sum represented net advertising revenue of newspapers or a gross revenue before deduction of advertising agency commissions. To determine this point the author of this study sent a questionnaire to 300 leading newspapers selected at random over the entire United States. Returns from 175 papers showed that approximately two-thirds had reported a net figure and one-third a gross figure. In accordance with this result, the census figure was increased some $19,000,000, an amount representing two-thirds of the estimated agency commissions paid by newspapers. The figure for discount or commissions allowed agencies by newspapers was based on data from the U. S. Bureau of the Census, *Census of Business, 1935:* "Advertising Agencies." (See notes on Advertising Agency Commissions, Appendix I, p. 913).

Distribution of Newspaper Advertising between National and Local

The basis for distribution of newspaper revenue between local advertising, $361,000,000, and national advertising, $158,000,000, was determined by reference to the figures shown in Appendix Table 1 and Appendix Table 2, which indicate that somewhat over 30% of newspaper advertising in 1935 was national. This figure is above that shown in the distribution of linage as reported in the studies made by Media Records, Inc., Year 1935, in which general, automotive, and financial advertising accounted for 25% of the total linage of 369 newspapers in 95 leading cities (476,000,000 lines out of a total of 1,901,000,000 lines). The *Census of Business, 1935,* "Advertising Agencies," page 4, states that 37.7% of agency billings were for newspaper

APPENDIX TABLE 1

ESTIMATES OF NATIONAL, LOCAL, AND TOTAL NEWSPAPER ADVERTISING, 1915–1938

YEAR	NATIONAL ADVERTISING	PERCENTAGE OF TOTAL	LOCAL ADVERTISING (Including Classified)	PERCENTAGE OF TOTAL	TOTAL ADVERTISING
1915.	$ 55,000,000	20.0	$220,000,000	80.0	$275,000,000
1916.	75,000,000	20.0	300,000,000	80.0	375,000,000
1917.	80,000,000	20.0	320,000,000	80.0	400,000,000
1918.	90,000,000	20.0	360,000,000	80.0	450,000,000
1919.	150,000,000	30.0	350,000,000	70.0	500,000,000
1920.	200,000,000	30.8	450,000,000	69.2	650,000,000
1921.	180,000,000	27.7	470,000,000	72.3	650,000,000
1922.	200,000,000	28.6	500,000,000	71.4	700,000,000
1923.	205,000,000	28.9	505,000,000	71.1	710,000,000
1924.	200,000,000	28.6	500,000,000	71.4	700,000,000
1925.	220,000,000	29.5	525,000,000	70.5	745,000,000
1926.	235,000,000	30.4	540,000,000	69.6	775,000,000
1927.	225,000,000	29.0	550,000,000	71.0	775,000,000
1928.	235,000,000	29.0	575,000,000	71.0	810,000,000
1929.	260,000,000	30.2	600,000,000	69.8	860,000,000
1930.	230,000,000	31.5	500,000,000	68.5	730,000,000
1931.	205,000,000	31.3	450,000,000	68.7	655,000,000
1932.	160,000,000	30.8	360,000,000	69.2	520,000,000
1933.	145,000,000	30.8	325,000,000	69.2	470,000,000
1934.	163,000,000	31.2	357,825,000	68.8	520,825,000
1935.	167,000,000	30.4	382,515,000	69.6	549,515,000
1936.	188,000,000	30.9	421,500,000	69.1	608,500,000
1937.	191,000,000	30.3	439,000,000	69.7	630,000,000
1938.	148,000,000	27.2	396,000,000	72.8	544,000,000

Source: Bureau of Advertising, American Newspaper Publishers' Association, *Expenditures of National Advertisers in Newspapers*, 1915–1938.

APPENDIX TABLE 2

ESTIMATES OF NATIONAL, LOCAL, AND TOTAL NEWSPAPER ADVERTISING, 1933–1936

YEAR	GENERAL, AUTO AND FINANCIAL ADVERTISING	PERCENTAGE OF TOTAL	RETAIL AND CLASSIFIED ADVERTISING	PERCENTAGE OF TOTAL	TOTAL ADVERTISING
1933.	$145,000,000	33.0	$295,000,000	67.0	$440,000,000
1934.	163,000,000	33.2	327,000,000	66.8	490,000,000
1935.	167,000,000	31.8	358,000,000	68.2	525,000,000
1936.	190,000,000	32.8	390,000,000	67.2	580,000,000

Source: *Editor & Publisher*, February 27, 1937, Sec. II, p. XVIII. Estimates by Robert S. Mann.

advertising, among those agencies reporting receipts in detail. On the basis of the census estimate that total agency billings in 1935 were approximately $500,000,000, it is judged that about $188,000,000 worth of newspaper space was handled through agencies. This entire amount cannot be looked upon as national advertising, however, for commissions were probably granted on some local advertising.

B. PERIODICALS OTHER THAN NEWSPAPERS

The figure for total advertising income for periodicals other than newspapers is reported as $186,097,701 in the *Biennial Census of Manufactures,* 1935, p. 575. The above figure was increased by approximately $14,000,000 to represent agency commissions not included in the reports of magazine publishers to the Census Bureau. Questionnaires were directed to 200 leading magazine publishers in various classes, and returns from 95 of these showed that 60% reported to the census a net figure, not including advertising commissions, while 40% reported a gross figure. It was necessary, therefore, in order to determine advertisers' total expenditures in magazines, to increase the Census figure by 60% of the advertising agency discount or commissions paid by magazines, estimated to be approximately $23,000,000. (See notes on Advertising Agency Commissions, Appendix I, p. 913.)

General Magazines and National Farm Magazines

Figures for general magazines, $120,811,000, and for national farm magazines, $5,565,000, are those reported by *National Advertising Records,* Publishers' Information Bureau, Inc., "Magazine Totals, 1935." The figures used are for 1935.

Trade and Business Publications

The figure for trade and business paper advertising, $43,241,000, is an estimate derived from data supplied by the management of Associated Business Papers, Inc. The volume of advertising carried by publications with membership in this organization is shown in Appendix Table 3.

Executives of Associated Business Papers, Inc., stated that a sampling study which they had carried on several years previously indicated that the Associated Business Papers publications represented be-

APPENDIX TABLE 3
PAGES OF ADVERTISING CARRIED IN ASSOCIATED BUSINESS PAPERS PUBLICATIONS, 1935–1936

Year	Number of Publications	Pages Paying Commissions		Pages Not Paying Commissions		Total Pages	
		Number	Income	Number	Income	Number	Income
1935........	135	28,502	$5,167,406	60,165	$9,246,311	88,667	$14,413,717
1936........	149	54,746	9,337,197	63,771	9,668,239	118,517	19,005,436

tween 30% and 35% of total advertising in the business and trade paper field. On the assumption that the $14,413,717 shown in Appendix Table 3 represented one-third of the total for all business paper advertising, the final figure of $43,241,000 was derived ($14,-413,717 $\times$ 3 = $43,241,151).

The figure of $30,383,000 for Other Periodicals is the difference between the sum of the figures for general magazines, national farm magazines, and trade and business publications, as given in the table, and the total figure for periodicals other than newspapers. This amount covers expenditures for advertisers who spent too little to be covered in the reports of the Publishers' Information Bureau, for the general and farm periodicals not included in those reports, and expenditures for advertising in classifications not measured at all, such as religious, educational, medical, and legal. Publishers' Information Bureau, covered only 90 magazines in its measurements and the estimate for business and trade papers would include some 2,000 publications listed by *Standard Rate & Data Service* in recent years. That there are many publications included in this "other" classification is indicated by the fact that the *Biennial Census of Manufactures, 1935,* gave 4,018 as the number of periodicals other than newspapers.

Postage on Periodicals

A figure for postage might possibly be included in advertising expenditures for newspapers and periodicals. In the *Annual Report of the Postmaster General, Fiscal Year Ended June 30, 1936,* p. 42, it is stated, "The weight of the advertising portions of publications subject to the zone rates mailed during the year was 368,366,868 pounds, on which $8,643,580.68 was collected." In view of the fact that this sum was paid by the publishers rather than by the subscribers, and presumably was looked upon by publishers as a cost deductible from their advertising revenue, which is elsewhere included, postage was not included in Table 2, page 54, as an additional cost.

C. RADIO BROADCASTING

Radio Time

All estimates of time costs were taken from the *Census of Business, 1935,* "Radio Broadcasting." Estimates made by the National Association of Broadcasters, which were in excess of the Census of Business figures, were considered, but consultations with executives in the industry led to the conclusion that the federal census figures were more nearly accurate.

Talent for National and Regional Network Programs

Talent costs for these network programs were computed as 40% of radio time costs, on the basis of estimates obtained from the following sources:

Herman S. Hettinger, *A Decade of Radio Advertising* (Chicago, University of Chicago Press, 1933), page 111, estimated that talent costs were from one-third to one-fourth of time costs. This average applied apparently to both network and local programs. He stated that experts (15 station managers and several network officials) seemed to be in fair agreement on this.

The Bureau of Advertising of the American Newspaper Publishers' Association in a sales promotion bulletin, *Yardsticks on the Air, 1935,* on the basis of a study of 79 broadcast programs, says, "The average cost (per program) among the 79 programs considered in this study was $8,052, of which 35.6% represented cost of talent."

The Association of National Advertisers' study, *A Survey of 299 National Advertising Budgets, 1934–1935,* pages 134–135, states:

> The ratio of talent costs to time costs for the 28 companies reporting in 1935 was 48%. In order to determine how representative this was of network advertisers, averages were calculated for the figures reported by 19 of those companies which were definitely identified as network advertisers. The ratio of talent to time costs of these 19 advertisers was only one point lower, or 47%.

Clark-Hooper, Inc., in its *Coincidental Radio Advertising Report* (1935), gave the findings of a study of the radio advertising of 72 companies, all using network facilities. In this report, estimated average costs of talent were 51% of estimated average time costs. Time costs were gross costs in most, if not all, instances.

In January, 1938, the following statement was received from an executive of one of the large broadcasting systems:

> We are proceeding with the analysis of network accounts, and a preliminary estimate would place the current figure for talent cost somewhere between 40% and 50% of time costs. I recall that you were interested in the figure for 1935, but I feel certain that talent costs have risen rather sharply during the past couple of years. I would estimate that 35% to 40% would be a safer figure to use for the talent-time ratio as of 1935.

Letters received from two regional network executives estimated that the cost of talent for regional network broadcasts was from 35% to 45% of time costs.

Talent Costs for Local Programs and for National and Regional Spot Programs

Estimates of talent costs for national and regional spot advertising and for local advertising were complicated by the fact that some programs involved personal renditions, others employed transcriptions, others used phonograph records, and still others consisted merely of announcements. The ratio of program talent costs to time costs varied widely for these different types of rendition, being practically nil in the case of announcements, and frequently very high for live talent.

Live Talent Costs

For local and spot programs using live talent, it was estimated that the talent cost amounted to 45% of the time charges. This estimate was derived as follows: *A Survey of 299 National Advertising Budgets, 1934–1935*, p. 134 gave a talent cost of 48% for 28 companies. Nineteen of these companies recognized as network advertisers had a talent to time ratio cost of 47%. This statement would imply, although one cannot be certain, that the ratio of talent to time costs for non-network advertisers was slightly over 48%.

Personal interviews and correspondence with six broadcasting station managers produced estimates typically ranging from 35% to 45% of time charges devoted to talent, although one station manager estimated that live talent costs for his station might run as much as 75% of time costs. While the sample of stations interrogated was small, it seemed safe, in view of the corroboratory data of the Association of National Advertisers' study, to estimate that live talent costs for non-network broadcasting were conservatively 45% of time costs.

Transcription Costs

It was impossible to get a fully satisfactory estimate of transcription costs of radio advertisers for 1935. One estimate was secured from an executive of a large broadcasting chain which does a considerable business in making transcriptions. This estimate was backed by a research conducted within his company. He estimated that the cost of transcriptions to advertisers for the year 1937 lay somewhere between $3,000,000 and $4,500,000 and that for the year 1935 they were probably between $2,000,000 and $4,000,000.

An executive of another leading organization engaged in the manufacturing of transcriptions and records looked upon these estimates as being probably too high. When, however, differences in definitions of costs of the two men were considered, it seemed fair to assume that total transcription costs for sponsored broadcasts by advertisers for the year 1935 were as much as $3,000,000.

In order to obtain a ratio of transcription costs to time costs for transcription programs it was necessary to turn to federal census figures to determine time sales for transcription programs, both spot and local. According to the *Census of Business, 1935,* "Radio Broadcasting," page 54 and following, replies from 215 broadcasting stations reporting revenue by type of rendition, 38.6% of all stations reporting to the census, indicated a distribution of time sales as shown in Appendix Table 4.

APPENDIX TABLE 4

REVENUE RECEIVED FOR TIME, FOR NATIONAL AND REGIONAL SPOT BROADCASTS, BY TYPE OF RENDITION, 215 STATIONS, 1935

TOTAL REVENUE	TRANSCRIPTIONS	LIVE TALENT	ANNOUNCEMENTS
$4,971,000	$2,043,000	$1,466,000	$1,462,000
100%	41.1%*	29.5%	29.4%

* Includes records accounting for 1.3% of total revenue.

If the percentage for transcriptions, 41.1%, is extended to the national and regional spot business of all stations, total time costs for transcription programs for 1935 may be estimated to have been $5,672,000 (i.e., 41.1% of $13,805,200, the census figure for time costs of national and regional spot advertising of all stations.)

The *Census of Business, 1935,* "Radio Broadcasting," page 52 and following, states that 51.8% of the broadcasting stations gave a breakdown of time revenue by types of rendition for local programs, as shown in Appendix Table 5.

If we extend the ratio of 11% for transcription time to local advertising income for time for all stations in the United States, we may judge that approximately $2,868,000 of local advertising revenue was obtained from time sales for transcription broadcasts (11% of $26,074,-476, the total revenue from time sales for local advertising broadcasts).

APPENDIX TABLE 5

REVENUE RECEIVED FOR TIME FOR LOCAL ADVERTISING BROADCASTS BY TYPE OF
RENDITION—289 STATIONS, 1935

TOTAL REVENUE	MECHANICAL RENDITION		PERSONAL RENDITION	
	Transcriptions	Records	Programs	Announcements
$13,393,000	$1,467,000	$1,327,000	$4,930,000	$5,669,000
100%	11%	9.9%	36.8%	42.3%

The total time revenue of broadcasting stations for transcription
broadcasts, therefore, can thus be estimated:

Spot broadcasts $5,672,000
Local broadcasts 2,868,000

$8,540,000

With this figure, the ratio of transcription costs to time costs may be
determined thus:

$$\frac{\text{Estimated transcription costs } \$3,000,000}{\text{Estimated time costs } \$8,540,000} = 35\%, \text{ ratio of}$$

transcription costs to time costs.

Record Costs

According to Appendix Table 5, 9.9% of the revenue from time
sold for local advertising programs was for programs using phonograph records. These records for the most part probably were sold to
advertisers from the program service libraries of the stations, which in
turn had leased them from companies in the recording business.

An executive of a company engaged in making records which are
leased to stations for sustaining programs estimated that local stations
in 1935 probably paid between $800,000 and $1,000,000 for records
for sustaining programs. There was no basis for telling to what extent
these sustaining program records were resold to broadcasters, or for
what price. He guessed, however, that as much as 50% might have
been resold. It appears, then, that broadcasters spent as much as
$400,000 for the use of records in connection with their local broad-
casts—a pure guess.

The income of local stations from programs using records was approximately $2,600,000 (9.9% of $26,074,776, total local advertising
time sales for all stations). From this figure is derived a ratio for
record costs to time costs as follows: $\dfrac{\$400,000}{\$2,600,000} = 15\%.$

Weighted Ratio of Talent Costs to Time Costs for National and Regional Spot and for Local Advertising

In the above paragraphs the relation of time costs to program costs for live talent, transcriptions, and records has been estimated, and in the tables the percentages of revenue received by stations for programs using the various types of rendition have been shown. To arrive at a final single ratio of talent costs to time costs for national and regional spot advertising and for local broadcast advertising, it was necessary in the averaging process to weight the ratios of talent to time costs for each type of rendition in accordance with the percentage of revenue received by the broadcasting stations from programs using that type of rendition. The data employed in this computation and the final weighted averages are shown in Appendix Table 6.

APPENDIX TABLE 6

DETERMINATION OF AVERAGE RATIOS OF TALENT TO TIME COST FOR NATIONAL AND REGIONAL SPOT ADVERTISING AND FOR LOCAL ADVERTISING, 1935

Type of Rendition	National and Regional Spot Advertising			Local Advertising		
	(1) Ratio of Talent to Time Cost	(2) % of Total Spot Revenue	(3) Weighting (Col. 1 x Col. 2)	(4) Ratio of Talent to Time Cost	(5) % of Total Local Revenue	(6) Weighting (Col. 4 x Col. 5)
Live Talent.......	45%	29.5%	13.28%	45%	36.8%	16.56%
Transcriptions....	35	41.1	14.39	35	11.0	3.85
Records..........	....	....	....	15	9.9	1.49
Announcements...	0	29.4	0	0	42.3	0
Totals.........		100.0%	27.67%		100.0%	21.90%

The ratios of talent to time costs assumed are as follows:

National and regional spot advertising.......................28%
Local advertising 22%

Once the ratios of talent costs were estimated, it was possible to devise the dollar value of talent costs as shown in Appendix Table 7, by application of the ratios to time costs as shown in the census.

APPENDIX TABLE 7

EXPENDITURES FOR RADIO ADVERTISING, BROADCAST TIME AND TALENT, 1935

	(1) Expenditures for Time	(2) Ratio of Talent Cost to Time Cost	Estimated Talent Cost (Col. 1 x Col. 2) (Approx.)
National and Regional Network Advertising..	$39,737,867	40%	$16,000,000
National and Regional Spot Advertising.......	13,805,200	28	3,865,000
Local Advertising.........................	26,074,472	22	5,736,000
	$79,617,539	32%	$25,601,000

D. ADVERTISING EXPENDITURES FOR SIGNS AND ADVERTISING NOVELTIES

For signs and advertising novelties, the figure of $74,000,000 was derived from two sources.

(1) The federal *Biennial Census of Manufactures, 1935,* gives the value of products for 1,075 "establishments engaged primarily in manufacturing or assembling electrical and mechanical signs and advertising devices, and stamped, embossed, and painted signs of metal, wood, glass, and other materials; (and also establishments engaged in the) manufacture of advertising novelties, such as tools, utensils, and other small articles intended primarily for advertising purposes." The painting of outdoor signs and printing of advertising matter is not included in this category. The following items from the census tables have been selected as representing expenditures for advertising.

Signs and advertising novelties......................		$60,243,208
Neon-tube signs	$17,469,619	
Other electric signs and advertising devices.............	1,904,797	
Cards and posters.................................	1,403,281	
Window and lobby cutouts and displays...............	5,819,008	
Metal signs	7,455,970	
Process signs	5,056,264	
Outdoor signs not specified above....................	2,867,065	
Other signs	4,218,909	
Advertising novelties	12,256,334	
Signs and advertising novelties not reported in detail......	1,791,961	
Receipts for custom, contract, and repair work.............		1,943,109
Total signs and advertising novelties...............		$62,185,597

(2) The *Census of Business, 1935,* "Service Establishments," Vol. II, gives data showing the value of products of sign painting shops. These sign painting shops were engaged in office-door and window lettering, commercial poster work, and canvas lettering. The receipts from the establishments were stated to be primarily from sign painting work, although some revenue was derived from the sale of signs as well as from the maintenance of signs. In all there were 5,035 establishments with total receipts of $14,048,000. It is probable that some indeterminate amount of the total receipts of this industry were derived from noncommercial work, but it is thought that the greater part of the income was for signs that might be considered advertising. Arbitrarily, $12,000,000 was taken as the amount representing the receipts of sign painting shops to be added to the $62,185,597 for establishments engaged in the manufacturing of signs and advertising novelties, as indicated above.

E. OUTDOOR ADVERTISING

Space Costs, 24-Sheet Posters, 3-Sheet Posters, Electric Spectaculars, and Painted Displays

The *Census of Business, 1935,* "Service Establishments," Vol. I, page 1, gives the figure of $26,897,000 for billboard advertising service of 491 establishments, which are described as follows on page xii:

Billboard Advertising Service. Establishments included in this classification are engaged chiefly in the preparation and presentation of poster displays (principally outdoor) on their own or rented signboards. The revenue of these establishments is derived from rentals of space on display boards and from other sources, such as fees received for the preparation of display advertisements. The receipt figures reported include amounts passed on as commissions to advertising agencies and to the various organizations engaged in the sale of billboard space. Operative employees of these establishments are engaged in the repairing and maintenance of display boards and the posting of advertisements. Usually the selling function is undertaken by a separate organization, and for this reason few plants maintain an extensive sales force.

The census figure of $26,897,000 was considered incomplete in view of the small number of establishments reporting. The submittal of figures for this census was voluntary. The reports covered only 491 establishments, whereas the Traffic Audit Bureau reported that in 1936 it had 1,114 plant members in the United States and Canada,[1] of which over 1,000 were in the United States, and the Outdoor Advertising Association reported that it had 983 member companies in 1938.

The *Census of Business, 1935,* "Advertising Agencies," page 5, states that of the total billings of the agencies reporting, 5.7% was for car cards, outdoor advertising, and window display services, thus indicating approximately $28,500,000 of business for these media. From conversations with advertising agency executives it was concluded that this figure was mostly for the outdoor media. Car cards did not offer agency commissions until 1938. Window display service billings by agencies are relatively small. The $28,500,000, further, would be mostly for national advertising. Assuming that 20% to 25% of outdoor advertising was local business, a considerable part of which probably did not involve agency commissions, the total figure for outdoor advertising would be in excess of $35,000,000.

---

[1] Traffic Audit Bureau, Inc., *Standard Circulation Values of Outdoor Advertising, 1936* (New York, The Bureau, 1936), p. 9. Correspondence with the Bureau indicated that about 6% of its member plants were in Canada.

Executives of Outdoor Advertising, Inc., reported a total sales volume for 1935 of $28,000,000, as indicated in Appendix Table 8.

APPENDIX TABLE 8

VOLUME OF OUTDOOR ADVERTISING HANDLED BY OUTDOOR ADVERTISING, INC.,
1932–1937*

YEAR		DOLLAR VOLUME
1932	....	$20,000,000
1933	....	18,000,000
1934	....	21,000,000
1935	....	28,000,000
1936	....	33,500,000
1937	....	40,000,000

* All national advertising, no local.

This organization acts as selling agent for approximately 85% of the plant owners; these clients, in turn, control 90% to 95% of the panels of the industry and account for 90% to 95% of the total volume of national advertising for 24-sheet posters, painted displays, and electric spectaculars. These figures were confirmed by Mr. H. E. Fisk, General Manager of the Outdoor Advertising Association of America.

The distribution of outdoor advertising as 20% to 25% local and 75% to 80% national was determined from correspondence and conversations with executives of Outdoor Advertising, Inc., the Outdoor Advertising Association, and outdoor plant operating companies. It is based on the estimates of the men interviewed, supported in most instances by operating data. In large cities the percentage of local business is considerably larger than it is in towns and small cities.

The above figures would indicate an expenditure for 24-sheet posters, painted displays, and electric spectaculars of $37,500,000 to $40,000,000, thus:

National advertising, $30,000,000 (the $28,000,000 of Outdoor Advertising, Inc., taken as 90%—95% of total national).

Local advertising, $7,500,000 to $10,000,000 (Local advertising, taken as 20% to 25% of the total).

A letter from Mr. H. E. Fisk stated: "The normal capacity of standardized outdoor advertising plants, including electric spectaculars, painted displays, 24-sheet posters, and 3-sheets, is approximately $50,000,000 annually. . . . This capacity was consumed about 70% during 1935." This statement would indicate a total of $35,000,000 spent on outdoor advertising.

On the basis of all the available evidence it was decided that $34,000,000 would constitute a conservative figure for 24-sheet posters, painted displays, and spectaculars. Information supplied by Outdoor Advertising, Inc., indicated that 82% of this amount, or $28,000,000, was for 24-sheet posters and the remainder, $6,000,000, was for painted displays and spectaculars.

To the $34,000,000 for these outdoor media there was added $1,000,000 for 3-sheet posters. This estimate was based on correspondence with an executive of a company controlling a major share of this type of business.

Outdoor Advertising—Printing and Lithographing Costs

Traffic Audit Bureau, Inc., *Standard Circulation Values of Outdoor Advertising,* 1936, p. 9, states that the plants whose circulations records it had audited "contain 135,340 poster panels, or substantially more than 50% of the estimated total capacity of the poster advertising medium." In 1937, it reported in *Circulation Characteristics of Poster Advertising Plants,* p. 21, that "it may be estimated with a considerable degree of accuracy, that the industry now maintains approximately 257,000 panels." On the assumption that the panels were used to 70% of capacity, the conclusion is reached that the equivalent of 180,000 panels were in full use for the year: $257,000 \times .70 = 179,900$.

It was then assumed that posters were changed monthly and that the average production cost per poster was $1.50. H. E. Agnew and W. B. Dygert, *op. cit.,* page 331, state that "Posters cost from $1 to $2 in lots of 1,000, depending on the number of colors used and the cost of the original design."

A lithographing cost of approximately $3,000,000 for 24-sheet posters is thus derived: $144,000 \times 12 \times \$1.50 = \$3,240,000$. To this sum, something might be added for 3-sheet posters; in view of the roughness of the computation, however, it was judged advisable to let the figure remain at $3,000,000.

F. CAR CARDS

Space Costs

Expenditures for car card space have been variously estimated from $2,000,000 to $20,000,000.

Robert S. Mann, in *Editor & Publisher,* February 27, 1937, Section

II, p. xviii, gives expenditures for car cards as possibly $2,500,000 to $2,000,000; no reliable figures were available. These figures are clearly inadequate, for the New York area alone, according to information obtained from several sources believed reliable, produces something over $4,000,000 of car card business.

Frank Presbrey, *The History and Development of Advertising* (New York, Doubleday Doran & Company, Inc., 1929), page 591, gave a figure of $20,000,000 for car card advertising (1928), but offered no supporting evidence.

The Bureau of Advertising, American Newspaper Publishers' Association, in a bulletin, *1932 Sales Promotional Service,* No. 9, page 12, states, "Total street car advertising receipts are said by its representatives to amount to $14,000,000 a year, of which about half represents national advertising."

Executives of companies engaged in the car card business were interviewed. One in whom considerable confidence was placed estimated 1935 volume at $10,000,000, with a possible range from $9,000,000 to $12,000,000. Another man well versed in the industry gave as his opinion that the total varied in 1935 between $10,000,000 and $20,000,000 and expressed the belief that in previous years it may have been well above this figure.

After these conversations and after a consideration of possible revenue from the number of card positions available, an estimate of $12,000,000 was submitted to the late Mr. Barron Collier for his confirmation, in view of his dominating position in this industry. He stated in a letter:

While some years in the past this amount may have been exceeded and in some of the leaner, poorer years that the medium has endured the amount may have been less, I still feel that the results of your investigation warrant your assumption of this amount as a fair estimate of the value of money spent in street railway advertising media during the year 1935,—that it is nearly enough correct for me to agree with you.

Computations of probable card positions for sale, of average rental space charges, and of percentage of capacity utilized provide only an uncertain basis for estimating since most of the underlying estimates are shaky.

Agnew and Dygert, *op. cit.,* page 352, state: "The rental of space runs from 50 cents a card in smaller districts to $3 a month in New York City. The average is perhaps 60 to 75 cents a month per card.

. . . Most of the street cars will not accommodate over 50 or 60 cards; 35 is a high average for the smaller cities."

It should be pointed out that the number of cards carried in busses, approximately 25% of all transit vehicles in 1935, probably averages not over 20 cards. A weighting for the number of cards carried in the various classes of vehicles, shown in Appendix Table 9, gave an average of 40 cards per car for all cars.

C. A. Faust in the *Transit Journal,* January, 1936, indicated approximately 75,000 transit vehicles for 1935 (average of January 1, 1935, and January 1, 1936, as shown in Appendix Table 9).

APPENDIX TABLE 9

SUMMARY OF NUMBER OF ALL TYPES OF PASSENGER TRANSIT VEHICLES OWNED BY TRANSIT COMPANIES IN THE UNITED STATES FOR 1935–1936 (AS OF JANUARY 1)

	1935	1936
Surface rail cars	44,676	40,767
Rapid transit cars	10,437	10,314
Suburban electric cars	3,112	3,123
Total rail cars	58,225	54,204
Busses	17,411	19,100
Trolley busses	448	648
Total	76,084	73,952

Source: "Vehicle Purchases Set 23-Year Record," by C. A. Faust, *Transit Journal,* January, 1936, p. 19.

On the basis of the above figures an estimate of $23,400,000 was arrived at as the total capacity revenue for car card space in 1935: 75,000 (cars) $\times$ 40 (average car space) $\times$ 12 (months) $\times$ 65 cents (average space cost) = $23,400,000. This figure, compared with the estimated $12,000,000 expenditure for car card space, would indicate that something over 50% of capacity was sold in 1935. Computations made from average figures so uncertain as these, however, have no great virtue.

Car Card Printing and Lithographing Cost

The estimate of $1,500,000 for printing and lithographing costs for car cards is based in part on the same uncertain data just discussed.

National advertisers buy more expensive cards on the average than do local advertisers, according to information received from executives in the industry. Agnew & Dygert, in *Advertising Media,* page 352, state that card costs will depend upon the number prepared and the expense of the design. In lots of 10,000 they cost from $10 to $25 per thousand. This would indicate costs of 10 cents to 25 cents a card.

Conversations with printers and lithographers engaged in manufacturing car cards and with executives of street car card companies indicated that a conservative average cost for cards used by national advertisers would be 15 cents a card, and for local advertisers 7 cents a card, not including art costs.

Conversations with executives of car card companies indicated that business was divided approximately evenly between local and national advertising. Assuming an average cost of 65 cents a month for car card space (Agnew & Dygert), a total of approximately 18,500,000 card-space months were sold, i.e., $\dfrac{12,000,000}{.65}$ (estimated total space costs) (estimated monthly cost per space). An even division between national and local accounts would mean 9,250,000 for each of the two types.

Interviews with car card operators indicated further that while cards for local accounts were changed monthly, the cards for national accounts generally were allowed to run for two months.

On the basis of the preceding data and the following calculations, a rough estimate of $1,350,000 for card costs was reached:

Cards for local accounts:

9,250,000 × $.07   = approximately $650,000.

Cards for national accounts:

.5 × (9,250,000 × $.15) = approximately $700,000.

G. DIRECT ADVERTISING

Postage for Direct Mail Advertising

The estimated expenditure of $87,000,000 for postage was judged to be divided among first, third, and fourth-class mail, approximately as follows:

First class $16,700,000
Third class 62,900,000
Fourth class 7,600,000

The figure for first-class postage is based on the assumption that 5% of first-class mail revenue in 1935 was from advertising pieces. Total postal revenue from first-class mail, except air mail, in the year ending June 30, 1936, according to the Annual Report of the Postmaster General for that fiscal period, page 109, was $335,409,708. Five per cent of this amount equals $16,770,485.

Mr. Leonard J. Raymond, President of Dickie-Raymond, Inc., and a former president of the Direct Mail Advertising Association, has carried on extensive investigations to estimate volume of direct mail advertising. Writing in *Printers' Ink,* April 25, 1935, page 68, he said: "One hardly dares hazard a guess as to what part of this first-class $332,000,000 revenue [for 1933] carries direct-mail advertising. Postal experts tell me that 5% is a conservative figure."

And, again writing in *Printers' Ink,* January 27, 1938, page 20, Mr. Raymond said: "What percentage of first-class mail is now advertising mail? I have received estimates as high as 33⅓%; as low as 2%. Today a generous allowance appears to be 5%."

Mr. Homer J. Buckley, President of Buckley, Dement & Company, of Chicago, and a former president of the Direct Mail Advertising Association, in a letter dated October 25, 1937, estimated that for the year ending June 30, 1936, 33⅓% of first-class mail pieces were advertising matter.

Mr. Raymond's estimate of 5% was supported by his own sample counts of first-class mail as well as by estimates of postal authorities and of executives of several mailing organizations. Accordingly, his figure was accepted in place of the higher estimate, which probably reflects more the situation when first-class postage was two cents instead of the three cents that applied in 1935.

The figure for third-class postage is based on the assumption that practically all this class of mail is advertising material. Total postal revenue from this source was $62,974,797.86 in the year ending June 30, 1936. While a limited quantity of third-class mail is small packages, it was believed that this might be disregarded in the computations.

The figure for fourth-class postage, primarily catalogues and advertising booklets, is taken from an estimate made by Mr. Buckley, contained in the previously mentioned letter of October 25, 1937. Mr. Buckley estimated that 20% of fourth-class pieces for local, first, second, and third zone mailings was advertising. The total number of fourth-class pieces in 1935 (Postmaster General's report), was 617,790,781. Mr. Buckley, basing his estimate on his own experience and that of other mailing operators, estimated an average postage cost of 8 cents per piece for fourth-class mailings. His estimate of total fourth-class postage for advertising material in 1935 was $7,680,000.

Duplicating, Addressing, Mailing, and Mailing List Service

A round item of $9,000,000 was included for this service from data supplied in the *Census of Business, 1935,* "Service Establishments," which describes the classification as follows (Volume 1, page xiii):

Duplicating, Addressing, Mailing, and Mailing List Service. Establishments engaged principally in providing mimeographing, multigraphing, rotaprinting, multilithing, planographing, addressographing, and mailing services are included in this classification. Establishments engaged in the compilation and sale of mailing lists are also included. Printing plants frequently provide such services. (Printing plants are included in the Biennial Census of Manufactures whenever they report annual receipts in excess of $5,000. When the receipts are less than $5,000, they are included as service establishments under the classification "Printing and Publishing Shops.") Many of the establishments included conduct stenographic, typewriting, or mailing services as minor phases of their business. Establishments engaged solely in writing copy for direct mail advertising are not included in this classification but are covered in "Other Business Services."

The reported receipts were as follows (Vol. I, page 1):

Number of establishments	1,257
Receipts	$9,813,000

It was assumed that the major portion of the work of these establishments was devoted to advertising.

Production Costs for Direct Mail

The production costs for direct mail by classes was estimated as follows:

First-class mail	$ 20,000,000
Third-class mail	147,000,000
Fourth-class mail	80,000,000
	$247,000,000

Raymond's estimates of average costs of mail pieces including postage, determined from extensive investigation,[2] were as follows:

First-class mail	6 cents per piece
Third-class mail	4.5 cents per piece

Since the average postage for all first-class mail was 2.791 cents per piece, and for all third-class mail 1.347 cents (according to the Postmaster General's annual report), the following production cost figures for advertising pieces can be derived from Raymond's estimates of total costs including postage:[3]

---

[2] See *Printers' Ink*, January 27, 1938, p. 19.

[3] These estimates of production costs are higher than estimates provided by Mr. Buckley, which were: First-class, 2.5 cents; third-class, 2.0 cents.

First-class mail ....3.20 cents
Third-class mail ....3.15 cents

On the basis of 636,550,000 pieces of first-class mail (5% of the total handled by the Post Office Department) and of 4,674,000,000 pieces of third-class mail (virtually all of that class), the estimated production costs of approximately $20,000,000 for first-class mail and $147,231,000 for third-class mail were reached.

The estimate of $80,000,000 for production of fourth-class mail was provided by Mr. Buckley.

Production Costs for Direct Advertising Other Than Mail: Printing and Lithography Expenditures for Advertising

According to census reports, total commercial printing and lithographing amounted to approximately $735,000,000 in 1935, while the volume for the entire graphic arts industries was about $1,900,-000,000. It was concluded that the printing and lithography expenditures allocable to advertising totaled $409,000,000, made up as shown in Appendix Table 10:

APPENDIX TABLE 10
ESTIMATED PRINTING AND LITHOGRAPHY EXPENDITURES FOR ADVERTISING, 1935

Commercial Printing (Census of Manufactures).........................	$340,000,000
Printing and Publishing Shops (Census of Business).....................	15,000,000
Lithographing (Census of Manufactures).............................	54,000,000
	$409,000,000

The *Biennial Census of Manufactures, 1935,* page 573, gave total receipts for Commercial Printing as shown in Appendix Table 11. Figures for Printing and Publishing by Newspapers and Periodical Publishers are not included in this table.

APPENDIX TABLE 11
CENSUS OF MANUFACTURES REPORT ON COMMERCIAL PRINTING, 1935

Commercial printing total	$603,797,270
Newspapers and periodicals printed for publication by others..........	67,391,090
Books and pamphlets printed for publication by others..............	63,188,623
Ready prints	1,209,907
Music printed for others..	1,086,832
Maps and atlases made for others................................	1,334,963
Other commercial printing, total.................................	469,585,855
Labels:	
Printed	$ 32,128,903
Embossed	282,965
Direct Mail:	
Books and pamphlets..	12,103,988
Letters, circulars, etc.......................................	9,835,410
Other	485,131
Greeting cards	15,967,088
Tags and seals	9,295,751
Legal	6,366,787
Railroad tariff	3,624,559
General commercial printing	379,495,273

It was concluded that the following amounts from Appendix Table II were chargeable to advertising:

Maps and atlases made for others	$ 1,000,000
Labels	32,000,000
Direct mail	22,425,000
General commercial printing	285,000,000
	$340,425,000

The above conclusions as to what part of the printing bill should be charged to advertising activity are little more than arbitrary guesses, based on conversations with advertising men, commercial printers, and Census Bureau employees. Of the large item of General Commercial Printing, 75% was taken to be advertising. The total figure is probably conservative, because considerable printing done by publishers and not included in Appendix Table 11 was probably advertising material.

In Appendix Table 12 are shown the expenditures for lithographing reported in the *Biennial Census of Manufactures, 1935*, page 602.

APPENDIX TABLE 12

CENSUS OF MANUFACTURES REPORT ON RECEIPTS OF LITHOGRAPHERS, 1935

Lithographing		$99,647,083
Color (posters, calendars, etc.)	$40,126,699	
Commercial forms	25,438,889	
Labels	19,332,458	
Music	1,064,682	
Tags and seals	1,007,523	
Greeting cards	6,143,995	
Maps and atlases	1,041,758	
Metal lithographing	4,557,663	
Paper patterns	933,416	

Of the total receipts of lithographers, the following portions were judged to represent expenditures for advertising:

Color	$30,000,000
Labels	19,000,000
Maps and atlases	1,000,000
Metal lithographing	3,500,000
Tags and other items	500,000
	$54,000,000

As with printing, the allocations of lithographing receipts to advertising are no more than guesses determined from conversations with executives in the industry. Certain officers of the National Association of Lithographers expressed the opinion that the Census total for lithography was probably not a complete report, owing to the fact that in recent years lithography has been taken up by many letter press printers and that these were not apparently fully covered in the lithography census. These officials estimated total lithographing for 1935 to be between $125,000,000 and $150,000,000. Because of this uncertainty and because of the lack of a sound basis for determining the portion of lithographing allocable to advertising, the estimate of $54,000,000 must be accepted with a large grain of salt.

The *Census of Business, 1935,* "Service Establishments," Vol. I, gives the following description of printing and publishing shops and report of receipts, p. xxiii and p. 2.

Printing and Publishing Shops—This classification includes printing and publishing establishments not reporting in connection with the Biennial Census of Manufactures, because the value of product for the year was less than $5,000. Many of these establishments are engaged in the printing and publishing of rural newspapers. The receipts for this classification include revenue from the sale of advertising, from subscriptions, and from job printing. Establishments engaged essentially in retailing stationery, though rendering a printing service as well, are included in the Census of Retail Trade.

Number of establishments	12,640
Receipts	$31,891,000
Service sales $31,488,000	
Sales of merchandise................. 350,000	
Other 53,000	

Of the above receipts, $15,000,000 was assumed to be the portion allocable to advertising.

Of the $409,000,000 of printing and lithographing attributed to advertising on the basis of the estimates just described, $251,500,000 has been accounted for as follows:

Car cards —printing and lithographing costs..........$ 1,500,000	
Posters —printing and lithographing costs.......... 3,000,000	
Direct mail—printing and lithographing costs.......... 247,000,000	
	$251,500,000

There is a remainder, therefore, of $157,500,000, which is assigned to display materials, salesforce, dealer and consumer literature, labels, and other direct advertising expenditures.

An unpublished figure, obtained from the Bureau of the Census, of $2,587,000 receipts for 206 window display service establishments, which is included in the *Census of Business, 1935,* "Service

Establishments," as a part of Business Services, Other, was not listed separately here, in view of the fact that the omnibus item of $157,-500,000 was deemed adequate to cover direct advertising costs other than mail.

Direct Advertising Costs Computed from Advertising Budget Data

Studies of advertising budgets by various organizations provided a means, though a very uncertain one, for establishing ratios between direct advertising costs and total advertising costs, and thus for estimating the dollar volume of direct advertising. The percentages of expenditure for direct advertising which are reported in the budget studies for different product groups among manufacturers and for different groups of local advertisers unfortunately show a wide range, and the data needed for arriving at a weighted average for all advertisers are not available. Accordingly, the figures employed as averages, 30% for regional and national advertisers and 20% for local advertisers, must be taken as very uncertain.

A Survey of 1935 Industrial Advertising Budgets, published for the National Industrial Advertisers' Association, reports for 79 advertisers that 13.87% of the total advertising budget was for direct mail, 22.13% was for catalogues, and 5.15% was for house organs, a total of 41.15% for direct advertising.

In a study made by the Association of National Advertisers, *A Survey of 299 National Advertising Budgets, 1934–1935,* are tables showing for various manufacturing groups the expenditures for dealer helps, direct mail, house organs, and sales and service literature expressed as percentages of the total advertising budgets. The sums of these classifications for the various industry groups are given in Appendix Table 13.

Whether the limited number of companies cooperating in this study were representative of their respective product groups is questionable. Moreover, there is no way of weighting the percentages for the various product groups to derive a satisfactory average figure for all industry. Inspection would indicate that a common figure would be in the neighborhood of 30%; but this figure possibly may be high in view of the fact that drug and toilet article, food, and proprietary medicine advertisers, who are relatively small users of direct advertising, are heavily weighted in the whole picture of advertising expenditure.

PERCENTAGE OF TOTAL ADVERTISING BUDGET DEVOTED TO DIRECT ADVERTISING, 1935

INDUSTRY	NUMBER OF COMPANIES REPORTING	PERCENTAGE OF TOTAL ADVERTISING BUDGET SPENT FOR DIRECT ADVERTISING
Consumer Products		
Agricultural Equipment	6	31.79
Auto Accessories	8	31.06
Auto Trucks	2	24.47
Beer	4	29.12
Beverages (Soft and Carbonated)	4	31.68
Clothing and Accessories	8	22.23
Confections and Ice Cream	4	36.49
Drug Sundries	6	28.07
Drugs and Toilet Articles	16	15.13
Food and Grocery Products	37	16.29
Footwear	7	29.36
Hardware	4	30.33
Heating, Air Conditioning, etc.	9	35.41
House Furnishings	8	33.91
Household Electrical Equipment	7	35.31
Knit Goods, Hosiery, etc.	7	22.44
Office Equipment	6	58.85
Paints, Varnishes, etc.	7	36.78
Petroleum Products	8	16.28
Proprietary Medicines	7	3.68
Service Organizations	2	17.35
Silverware, Clocks, etc.	7	28.26
Sporting Goods, etc.	5	27.16
Textiles	5	14.51
Travel and Transportation	9	16.92
Industrial Products		
Auto Equipment	8	37.02
Building and Construction Materials	10	34.59
Chemicals	5	31.86
Electrical Equipment	3	21.33
Machinery and Supplies	15	31.42
Miscellaneous	5	47.79
Paper and Paper Products	7	38.31
Steel and Other Metals	14	18.30

Source: Based on table, pp. 82–83, Association of National Advertisers, *A Survey of 299 National Advertising Budgets, 1934–1935.*

Satisfactory figures for volume of direct advertising by retailers and other local advertisers are not available. Indications, however, are that the percentage of the retail advertising budget devoted to direct advertising, while smaller than that applicable to producers' advertising, is still appreciable.

According to the *Data Book* of the National Retail Dry Goods Association, Sales Promotion Division, June, 1936, page 1217, the average department store in 1935 spent 3% of its advertising budget for direct mail, 11% for display cost, and 4% for miscellaneous media, part of which is chargeable to direct advertising, a total of 15% to 20%.

According to a statement by Preston E. Reed, executive vice president of the Financial Advertisers' Association, in an article on "How to Build Budgets for a Bank," [4] a "mean average of scores of budgets" indicated that direct mail was allotted 17% of the budget, window and lobby display 7%, and financial publications 4.5%, a total of 28.5%. These items combined indicate a larger percentage for direct advertising than is used by department and dry goods stores. On the other hand, the advertising of the latter type of institution bulks much larger than does the advertising of financial institutions; hence in the estimates of an average for local advertisers, greater weight was given to the department store category than to financial advertisers, and an average figure of 20% was assumed.

Since the direct advertising carried on by national advertisers was assumed to be 30% of their total advertising expenditure, and that conducted by local advertisers was only 20% of their total expenditure, it was necessary to get separate figures of total advertising expenditures for manufacturers and retailers to which to apply these percentages.

An uncertain approximation was reached by working from the distribution of newspaper advertising between national and local, as estimated from data furnished by the American Newspaper Publishers' Association. Assuming that $361,000,000 of newspaper advertising was local (see notes on newspapers, Appendix I, page 887) and that this sum represented about 60% of the expenditures of local advertisers,[5] a total for local advertisers of $600,000,000 was reached. If the total advertising bill be taken as $1,700,000,000, there then remains for national and regional advertising a sum of $1,100,000,000.

From these totals were derived direct advertising costs, as follows:

National and regional advertisers, 30% of $1,100,000,000 = $330,000,000
Local advertisers, 20% of $600,000,000   = 120,000,000
                                                             _____
                                                            $450,000,000

---

[4] See table, p. 916, Appendix I.

[5] *The Data Book* of the National Retail Dry Goods Association, Sales Promotion Division, June, 1936, p. 1217, reported 64% of the advertising budget of department and dry goods stores was spent for newspaper linage. See p. 915, Appendix I. Financial advertisers apparently spent a smaller percentage on newspapers, 40% of the appropriation. See p. 916, Appendix I. Greater weight was given to the department-dry goods store group than to the financial advertisers in arriving at a newspaper percentage representative of local advertisers.

This figure of $450,000,000 is to be compared with the figure of $500,000,000 arrived at by a compilation of estimated postage and production costs for mail and arbitrary allocation of printing and lithographing data from the census. The $500,000,000 figure was chosen because it represented a material reduction from original estimates based on allocation of census figures and was thought to be nearer the true cost than the lower figure.

Estimates derived by either method are based on such inadequate data as to be clearly unsatisfying; yet they are presented as the result of analysis of available figures, and are probably as near to the truth as available information permits.

H. ADVERTISING THROUGH MOTION PICTURES

The *Biennial Census, 1937,* "Motion Pictures," gave as the production costs of advertising and news reel films for 1935 a value of $4,939,964. This figure is highly unsatisfactory not only because it combines news reels and advertising films, but also because it includes none of the distribution costs for films, which in some instances are appreciable. As a means for arriving at an estimate, executives of leading companies in the industry were asked to give their opinions as to the value of advertising films for the year 1935. A commonly named figure for production and distribution costs for all business films was $10,000,000. Of this amount approximately one-half was judged to be strictly advertising film.

I. ART WORK, PLATES, AND OTHER MECHANICAL COSTS

Census of Business, 1935, "Advertising Agencies," page 5, states that 6.4% of total agency billings for those agencies reporting their billings in detail were for art and mechanical charges.

Various other figures on production costs are available.

The *Data Book* of the National Retail Dry Goods Association, June, 1936, page 1217, states that "the average department store during 1935 spent 5% of its total 'publicity' budget for 'production.'"

A Survey of 1935 Industrial Advertising Budgets reports that 6.5% of the total advertising budgets of the 79 companies reporting was spent for "Art Work, Engraving for Trade Paper Space and Annual Condensed Catalogs," and that 0.64% was spent for "Production Expense."

A Survey of 299 National Advertising Budgets, 1934–1935, page 83, reports that "Space Production Costs" for consumer advertisers range from 2.42% of total advertising budget for proprietary medicines, to 11.56% for hardware. For industrial advertisers, page 95, corresponding figures for space production costs range from 2.92% for building and construction materials to 10.59% for steel and other metals. "Space Advertising Production Costs" are stated to include "cost of art work, engravings, mats, electros, etc., used in magazines, newspapers, car cards, outdoor, and other space advertising."

On the basis of these various indications, the figure of 6.4% for art and mechanical charges as given in the *Census of Business, 1935,* "Advertising Agencies," does not seem to be an unreasonable one to apply to all space advertising, whether billed through an agency or not. Estimated space charges, as indicated below, were $1,170,-000,000. Application to this total of the census percentage, 6.4%, indicates that total art and mechanical charges were about $75,000,000. Of this amount, it can be assumed that $32,000,000 was billed through agencies (6.4% of the census estimate of $500,000,000 total agency billings).

Newspapers	$ 519,000,000
Magazines	200,000,000
Outdoor	35,000,000
Car cards	12,000,000
Direct	404,000,000
	$1,170,000,000

Census figures on photoengraving are pertinent in this connection. *Biennial Census of Manufactures, 1935,* states: "The establishments in this industry are engaged primarily in making photoengraving plates for printing illustrations, art work, post cards, greeting cards, half-tone engravings, etc. These establishments do not, as a rule, print from the plates they make, but prepare them for use by others."

1. Photoengraving not done in printing industry, all products total value....$53,342,208
2. Photoengraving 50,625,651
3. Products not normally belonging to the industry...................... 2,716,557
4. Photoengraving, secondary activities in establishments in other industries.. 6,199,661
   Photoengraving, aggregate value (2 + 4).............................. 56,825,312
   Of this total, rotogravure was.. 8,798,190

J. AGENCY COMMISSIONS

No separate figure for advertising agency commissions is included in Table 2, page 54, because estimates for the various media are gross figures which include agency commissions. As stated in the text, the census figures for newspaper and magazine expenditures had to be modified because reporting of publishers to the Census Bureau was not on a uniform basis. To determine the correction needed, a sample survey was made among 300 newspaper and 200 magazine publishers to find the proportion which reported gross figures, including advertising agency discount or commission, and the percentage which reported net figures of revenue. Replies from 176 newspapers showed that 66% reported net figures and 34% reported gross figures. Replies from 98 magazines gave a division of 61% reporting net figures and 39% reporting gross figures.

The total amount of agency discount or commission paid by publishers in 1935 was determinable from data in the *1935 Census of Business,* "Advertising Agencies." The percentages of total agency billings applicable to newspapers and magazines were there reported as follows (page 5):

Newspapers	37.7%
Periodicals other than newspapers	30.4%

Application of these ratios to a figure of $500,000,000, estimated total agency billings, indicated, as shown below, the volumes of business handled in these media and the agency commissions allowed.

	VOLUME OF BUSINESS HANDLED	COMMISSIONS AT 15%
Newspapers	$188,500,000	$28,275,000
Periodicals other than newspapers	152,000,000	22,800,000

To the Census figure of newspaper advertising revenue, therefore, was added $19,000,000, i.e., approximately two-thirds of $28,255,000. To the census figure of advertising revenue for periodicals other than newspapers was added $14,000,000, i.e., approximately 60% of $22,800,000.

K. ADVERTISING DEPARTMENT ADMINISTRATION

The cost of administration for the advertising departments of business firms is estimated to represent roughly 10% of total expenditures for advertising. This estimate is based upon studies of various advertising budgets, pertinent figures from some of which follow:

A Survey of 299 National Advertising Budgets, 1934–1935, Association of National Advertisers, Inc., page 23:

Figures as follows for 117 consumer advertisers:

ADMINISTRATIVE EXPENSES OF THE ADVERTISING DEPARTMENT

	ARITHMETIC AVERAGE PERCENTAGE OF TOTAL BUDGET 1935
Salaries	6.62
Traveling expenses	.75
Rent	.29
Other	1.06
Total advertising department administrative expense	8.72

Figures as follows for 39 industrial advertisers, page 98:

ADMINISTRATIVE EXPENSES OF THE ADVERTISING DEPARTMENT

	ARITHMETIC AVERAGE PERCENTAGE OF TOTAL BUDGET 1935
Salaries	10.66
Traveling expenses	1.09
Rent	.63
Other	.71
Total advertising department administrative expense	13.09

A Survey of 1935 Industrial Advertising Budgets, National Industrial Advertisers' Association, Inc., November 1, 1935, 70 out of 750 questionnaires returned.

DIVISION OF ADVERTISING BUDGET IN PERCENTAGES

Trade paper space	29.78
Annual condensed catalogues	3.16
Art work for above	6.50
Advertising to general public	
Publications	1.97
Radio	.57
Other media	.09
Production expense	.64
Own catalogues, etc.	18.97
Direct mail	13.87
House organs	5.15
Conventions	2.89
Editorial publicity	.80
Motion pictures, etc.	1.00
Administrative expense	10.73
Miscellaneous	3.88

National Retail Dry Goods Association, Sales Promotion Division, *Data Book,* June, 1936, page 1217, states:

The following figures indicate how the publicity dollar was spent by the average department store during 1935:

Newspaper linage ....$ .64
Production .... .05
Miscellaneous media .... .04
Radio broadcasting .... .01
Direct mail .... .03
Advertising payroll .... .08
Total display .... .11
All other .... .04

$1.00

National Retail Dry Goods Association, Sales Promotion Division, *Retailers' Calendar and Promotional Guide for 1938*, by Thomas Robb, p. 5.

HOW THE AVERAGE STORE HAS BEEN DISTRIBUTING ITS PUBLICITY DOLLAR

Newspaper space...$ .62
Advertising payroll .... .08
Production costs.. .05
Display total .... .11
Direct mail .... .04
Radio broadcasting .... .02
Miscellaneous media .... .05
All other .... .03

$1.00

Harvard Business School, Bureau of Business Research, Bulletin No. 100, *Operating Results of Department and Specialty Stores in 1935*, by Carl N. Schmalz, Tables 16, 21, 22, 29, 30.

Department Stores—net sales $500,000 to $2,000,000
   Publicity—payroll .... 0.70% to 0.80% (of net sales)
   Publicity—total cost .... 4.30% to 4.80% (of net sales)
Department Stores—net sales $2,000,000 to $10,000,000
   Publicity—payroll .... 0.65% to 0.70% (of net sales)
   Publicity—total cost .... 5.10% to 5.60% (of net sales)
Department Stores—net sales $10,000,000 or more
   Publicity—payroll .... 0.60% to 0.65% (of net sales)
   Publicity—total .... 4.65% to 5.05% (of net sales)
Specialty Stores—net sales $1,000,000 to $2,000,000
   Publicity—payroll ....   0.80% (of net sales)
   Publicity—total cost ....   6.25% (of net sales)
Specialty Stores—net sales $2,000,000 or more
   Publicity—payroll .... 0.60% to 0.80% (of net sales)
   Publicity—total cost .... 5.20% to 6.35% (of net sales)

Financial Advertising Budgets:

The following was presented as "a mean average of scores of budgets" of financial advertisers, by Preston E. Reed, in an article "How to Build a Budget for a Bank," in the *Bulletin* of the Financial Advertisers' Association, September, 1930, page 319.

Newspapers	40.0%
Direct mail	17.0
Outdoor	14.0
Window and lobby displays	7.0
Financial publications	4.5
Advertising specialties	4.0
Car cards	2.0
Mass plan	2.0
Miscellaneous	9.5
	100.0%

Secondary source: L. D. Meredith, *Merchandising for Banks, Trust Companies, and Investment Houses* (Bankers Publishing Company, 1935).

ESTIMATES OF THE VOLUME OF TOTAL SALES
TRANSACTIONS IN BUSINESS, 1935

IN THIS appendix are given the bases for the estimates of volume of sales transactions of a selected group of businesses in which advertising was used in appreciable amounts in 1935 and of the total volume of sales transactions for all business for that year. These estimates were compared with advertising expenditures in Chapter III, p. 58 ff.

Estimate for Businesses Using Appreciable Advertising

The estimates for the selected group of businesses deemed users of advertising in appreciable amounts, the character of the data used, and the sources of the data are shown in Appendix Table 14. For some classifications the data are reported sales figures, representing complete coverage of the field; in others they are admittedly incomplete. In some instances, as with finance and insurance, it is difficult to determine what data may be said to represent sales. Comment on some of the problems met and shortcomings of the estimates follow:

In Group I the large sums shown for manufacturers' sales, wholesalers' sales, retailers' sales, and construction sales, accounting for almost 80% of the total of the table, are census data of practically complete coverage. The wholesalers' sales figure, item 2, does not include sales of manufacturers' sales branches, bulk stations, and agents and brokers, which are included in the totals of the federal wholesale census, because the sales of such branches were included in the figures of manufacturers' sales and involved no actual additional sales transactions. In the case of real estate, item 5, an estimate of the sales and rental value was reached by multiplying by 20 the census figure for fees received by real estate agencies, the assumption being that fees received approximated 5% of sales or rental value. The total value of real estate sales and rentals was, of course, greatly in excess of this figure, for many real estate transactions were not handled by agencies.[1]

---

[1] The Twentieth Century Fund, Inc., Committee on Old Age Security, estimated real estate sales of $6,000,000,000, and rents and royalties of $5,188,000,000 for 1934. See *The Townsend Crusade* (New York, The Twentieth Century Fund, Inc., 1936), p. 76.

APPENDIX TABLE 14

DETERMINABLE SALES OR COMMISSIONS FROM SALES OR RELATED FIGURES FOR TYPES OF
BUSINESS IN WHICH ADVERTISING WAS EMPLOYED IN APPRECIABLE AMOUNTS—1935

TYPE OF BUSINESS	CHARACTER OF DATA	DOLLAR VOLUME (000 omitted)
Group I—Sales of Tangible Products—Total		$96,087,000
1. Manufacturers	Sales	38,821,280
2. Wholesalers	Sales	20,124,702
3. Retailers	Sales	33,161,276
4. Construction Industry	Sales—Work Done	1,622,862
5. Real Estate Sales through Agencies	Fees Received × 20 ($117,844 × 20)	2,356,880
Group II. Sales of Various Services—Total		4,285,924
6. Service Establishments	Sales	2,029,302
7. Power Laundries and Cleaning	Sales	369,452
8. Hotels	Sales	720,145
9. Tourist Camps	Sales	24,300
10. Places of Amusement	Sales	699,051
11. Motion Picture Producers	Production Cost	188,470
12. Radio Broadcasting	Sales, Broadcasting Stations	86,493
13. Advertising Agencies	Commissions Received	70,840
14. Public Warehousing	Sales	97,871
Group III. Sales of Transportation—Total		5,711,340
15. Motor Bus Transportation	Sales	167,933
16. Motor Trucking for Hire	Sales	530,860
17. Railways, Freight	Freight Revenue	2,831,139
18. Railways, Passenger	Passenger Revenue	358,423
19. Street Railways (Electric, Motor Bus)	Operating Revenue	666,633
20. Civil Aeronautics	Estimated Passenger and Express Revenue	16,450
21. Pullman	Gross Operating Revenue	48,428
22. Express Companies	Total Operating Revenue	91,474
23. Water Transportation	Estimated Operating Revenue	1,000,000
Group IV. Financial Services—Total		11,256,292
24. Banks	Estimated Gross Earnings	1,600,000
25. Security Dealers	Sales of New Securities	3,782,143
26. Financial Institutions Other than Banks and Security Dealers	Payroll × 2	324,520
27. Insurance, Life	Premiums	3,692,128
28. Insurance, Fire and Marine	Premiums	871,414
29. Insurance, Casualty	Premiums	953,380
30. Insurance, Mutual, Accident, and Sick Benefit	Premiums	32,707
Group V. Communication, Light, Heat, and Power Services—Total		3,530,836
31. Electric Light and Power	Revenues from Sales of Current	1,975,304
32. Natural Gas*	Revenue from Consumers	374,546
33. Telephone	Operating Revenue	1,048,815
34. Telegraph and Radio Telegraph	Operating Revenue	131,171
Total		$120,871,392

* Manufactured gas included in the Census of Manufactures Item 1.

APPENDIX TABLE 14—Continued

Sources:

1. Manufacturers' Sales: *Census of Business, 1935,* "Distribution of Manufacturers' Sales." From the census figure of $43,801,214,000 is deducted $4,350,415,000, representing transfers among plants in own organization and $629,139,000 representing sales to own retail stores.

2. Wholesalers' Sales: *Census of Business, 1935,* "Wholesale Distribution," gave a total figure for all wholesale distribution of $42,802,913,000. Included in this figure were the sales by manufacturers' sales branches, manufacturers' sales offices, bulk tank stations, and agents and brokers. These were omitted, in view of the fact that they represented no actual sales transaction other than had already been accounted for in the figure for manufacturers' sales.

3. Retailers' Sales: *Census of Business, 1935,* "Retail Distribution," Volume I.

4. Construction Industry: *Census of Business, 1935,* "Construction Industry."

5. Real Estate Sales through Agencies: *Census of Business, 1935,* "Real Estate Agencies."

6. Service Establishments: *Census of Business, 1935,* "Service Establishments," Volume I.

7. Power Laundries and Cleaning: *Biennial Census, 1935,* "Power Laundries."

8. Hotels: *Census of Business, 1935,* "Hotels."

9. Tourist Camps: *Census of Business, 1935,* "Tourist Camps."

10. Places of Amusement: *Census of Business, 1935,* "Places of Amusement."

11. Motion Picture Producers: *Biennial Census, 1935,* "Motion Pictures."

12. Radio Broadcasting: *Census of Business, 1935,* "Radio Broadcasting."

13. Advertising Agencies: *Census of Business, 1935,* "Advertising Agencies."

14. Public Warehousing: *Census of Business, 1935,* "Public Warehousing."

15. Motor Bus Transportation: *Census of Business, 1935,* "Motor Bus Transportation."

16. Motor Trucking for Hire: *Census of Business, 1935,* "Motor Trucking for Hire."

17. Railways, Freight: *Statistical Abstract of the United States, 1938,* p. 387.

18. Railways, Passenger: *Statistical Abstract of the United States, 1938,* p. 389.

19. Street Railways: *Statistical Abstract of the United States, 1937,* pp. 394 and 400. (Figures for 1932).

20. Civil Aeronautics: *Statistical Abstract of the United States, 1938,* p. 409.

21. Pullman: *Statistical Abstract of the United States, 1937,* p. 393.

22. Express Companies: *Statistical Abstract of the United States, 1937,* p. 393.

23. Water Transportation: This figure is based on an estimate made for 1934 of $940,000,000 for water and air transportation, by the Twentieth Century Fund in its study, *The Townsend Crusade,* page 77. It is derived by estimating labor income as 40% of gross revenue.

24. Banks: U. S. Board of Governors of the Federal Reserve System, *Federal Reserve Bulletin,* vol. 22, p. 520 ff., gave a figure for total current operating income for 8,729 state banks, whose deposits were insured in 1935, of $690,764,000. The *Annual Report* of the Comptroller of Currency for the year ending October 31, 1936, reports, page 650, the total earnings for 5,392 active national banks for the year ending December 31, 1935, of $794,156,000.
The annual report of the comptroller stated that there were 15,803 active banks for the year ending June 30, 1936. The earnings report, therefore, covered over 91% of the active banks. On the basis of these figures, an estimate of $1,600,000,000 gross earnings for banks is derived.

25. Security Dealers: *Second Annual Report of Securities & Exchange Commission,* Fiscal Year Ended June 30, 1936, p. 109.

26. Financial Institutions Other than Banks and Security Dealers: *Census of Business, 1935,* "Financial Institutions Other Than Banks."

27. Insurance, Life: *Insurance Year Book, 1936.*

28. Insurance, Fire and Marine: *Insurance Year Book, 1936.*

29. Insurance, Casualty: *Insurance Year Book, 1936.*

30. Insurance, Mutual, Accident, and Sick Benefit: *Insurance Year Book, 1936.*

31. Electric Light and Power: *Statistical Abstract of the United States, 1938,* p. 359. (Figure for 1932.)

32. Natural Gas: *Statistical Abstract of the United States, 1938,* p. 736.

33. Telephone: *Statistical Abstract of the United States, 1938,* p. 351.

34. Telegraph and Radio Telegraph: *Statistical Abstract of the United States, 1938,* pp. 351-352.

In Group II, all data were from Census Bureau reports. In the case of motion pictures, item 11, production cost was used because the federal census does not supply the sales revenue for motion pictures. The figure for advertising agencies, item 13, is the census figure for commissions received and is somewhat less than the probable total, because all agencies were not covered by the census.

Category IV, banks and financial institutions of various kinds, which do a considerable volume of advertising, presented perplexing questions with regard to the proper figures to use. A figure exactly comparable to the sales figures of businesses in other categories is not to be had. In the case of commercial banks, item 24, the gross earnings were available for national banks and for state banks whose deposits are insured, which include some 14,121 banks out of a total of 15,803. From these figures an estimate of gross earnings was made. For the 7,224 brokers and security dealers, item 25, the figure used was that of new capital issues, other than government issues. This figure is clearly a compromise, for much of the activity of such dealers is devoted to sales of other than new issues. Moreover, many new issues receive little or no advertising other than that required in issuing a prospectus. Yet it was deemed unwise to inflate the sales figure of advertising business (Appendix Table 14) by including all over-the-counter sales, and clearly unwise to include sales on exchanges. In the case of financial institutions other than banks and security dealers, item 26, no good basis for estimating gross earnings was available. The closest approach was the payroll figure provided by the *1935 Census of Business.* This is far less than the gross earning figure of such institutions; it was multiplied by two on the basis of an uncertain judgment that payroll was approximately one-half operating revenue for such institutions. A proper base to use for insurance, items 27–30 inclusive, was particularly perplexing. An insurance contract is merely a contractual arrangement between the insurance company and the policyholder. It was decided that instead of the face amount of the policies a more desirable figure to use was premium income. While the total income figure of $11,256,292,000 for financial services of various kinds may be subject to question, any other estimate would probably be equally or more open to challenge.

Estimate of Total Sales Transactions of Business

To arrive at a figure of total sales transactions of business for 1935, some $70,000,000 must be added to the total of $120,900,000,000 given in Appendix Table 14. This amount represents sales of products and services in which advertising was not used in large enough amounts to justify inclusion in that table. They are listed in Appendix Table 15.

APPENDIX TABLE 15

VOLUME OF SALES TRANSACTIONS FOR SELECTED PRODUCTS AND SERVICES NOT EMPLOYING APPRECIABLE ADVERTISING, 1935

(a) Estimated Cash Income from Farm Marketings	$ 6,507,000,000
(b) Total Fisheries, United States and Alaska	80,121,000
(c) Total Mineral Products	3,650,000,000
(d) Nonprofit Organizations	404,312,000
(e) Sales of Various Products and Securities on Organized Exchanges (Estimated)	38,800,000,000
(f) Sales by Individuals, by Small Businesses, and Miscellaneous Sales Unreported in Any Census or Reporting Service	indeterminate
(g) Pipe Lines, Operating Revenue	197,368,000
(h) Sales of Professional Services	2,000,000,000*
(i) Over-the-counter Security Sales	20,000,000,000*
Approximate Total	$72,000,000,000

* Probably underestimated.

Sources:
(a) Estimated cash income from farm marketing: *Statistical Abstract of the United States, 1938*, p. 616.
(b) Total fisheries in the United States and Alaska: *Statistical Abstract of the United States, 1937*, p. 691.
(c) Total mineral products: *Statistical Abstract of the United States, 1937*, p. 695.
(d) Nonprofit organizations: *Census of Business, 1935*, "Nonprofit Organizations, Office Buildings, and Miscellaneous Businesses."
(e) Sales of various products and securities on organized exchanges: The Second Annual Report of the Securities & Exchange Commission, Fiscal Year Ended June 30, 1936, gave the volume of sales on registered exchanges for the fiscal year as $25,704,000,000.
   Sales on commodity exchanges were estimated at $15,168,480,000 by taking the figure of $3,950,544, tax on sales of produce for future delivery, as a base. This tax represented 3 cents on each $100 transaction.
(g) Pipe lines, operating revenue: *Statistical Abstract of the United States, 1937*, p. 732.
(h) and (i) Sale of professional services and over-the-counter security sales: These estimates are based on 1934 figures of Committee on Old Age Security of the Twentieth Century Fund, *The Townsend Crusade*, p. 76.

Considerations which were weighed in the placing of certain of these items in the above table instead of in Appendix Table 14 are given below:

Some of the products of farms, item (a), are advertised by the producers in appreciable amounts, particularly in the case of farm marketing cooperatives selling citrus fruits, walnuts, apples, and cranberries. Otherwise farm producers do little advertising. The advertised items are relatively small in the total of farm marketings.

Many of the products of agriculture, fisheries, and mines, items (a), (b), and (c), become advertised and sold aggressively as soon as they are fabricated or are put into the channels of trade. They are therefore included in Appendix Table 14 in various categories after they have reached the second or third stage of their march to consumption.

Some of the nonprofit organizations, item (d), and some of the miscellaneous businesses included in item (d) employ advertising to a certain degree, for example, civic organizations, welfare and relief organizations, and certain miscellaneous businesses included in the census figure. Since the larger part of the businesses included under item (d) did not employ an appreciable amount of advertising, however, and since inclusion or omission of the item did not make a relatively great difference in the total of advertising business, it was thought advisable to place it in Appendix Table 15 rather than in Appendix Table 14.

A sales figure of tremendous size, over $38,000,000,000, placed in the table of businesses using little advertising, is that of sales on the organized exchanges of various kinds. There is, of course, almost no advertising charge assessable against such sales. Likewise, over-the-counter sales of securities, which were in excess of $20,000,000,000, were omitted from Appendix Table 14 for reasons indicated in the discussion of financial data of that table.

There was no satisfactory basis for estimating item (f), sales of individuals and small businesses not included in censuses. Probably a fair share of such sales were consummated with the help of advertising. But since the amount was not only indeterminable but also relatively small in relation to the total for businesses using advertising in appreciable amount, the item was placed in Appendix Table 15.

NOTES ON CONTRIBUTION OF ADVERTISING TO PUBLISHING AND BROADCASTING

THIS appendix describes the bases on which the net contribution of advertising to newspaper and magazine publishing and to radio broadcasting were estimated. The summary of findings was given in Chapter III, p. 68 ff.

Advertising Revenue and Newspaper Publication

In an effort to get evidence of the extent to which advertising supports newspaper publishing, 100 newspapers selected at random were requested to furnish the following data: the revenue from advertising and from circulation in dollars or percentages of total revenue; the approximate advertising linage and approximate other linage; and a breakdown of expenses which permitted a computation of percentage of expenses directly or indirectly chargeable to advertising. In all, usable data were secured from 23 daily newspapers. An analysis of these data is contained in Appendix Table 16. The sample is small and it is uncertain how closely the median figures presented correspond to common figures for the newspaper publishing industry; yet they are presented as being at least indicative. The returns were from cities in 16 widely scattered states. The cities varied in size from one of approximately 35,000 population to New York City. The percentages of revenue from advertising and from circulation for the group were almost identical with those shown for all newspapers in the *Biennial Census of Manufactures, 1935.* On the other hand, the wide range of the data supplied indicates that considerable error may be involved in a sample so small.

The essential facts regarding these newspapers for the year studied are as follows:

(1) Approximately 65% of income was from advertising, and 35% from circulation. This distribution relates solely to advertising and circulation income and does not include the small percentage of revenue from other sources enjoyed by some of the publishers studied.

APPENDIX TABLE 16

ANALYSIS OF INCOME AND EXPENSE DATA, 23 DAILY NEWSPAPERS, 1938

	MEDIAN PERCENTAGE	RANGE OF PERCENTAGES	NUMBER OF PAPERS SUPPLYING DATA
1. Revenue from Advertising..................	64.9	55.3 to 86.8	23
2. Revenue from Circulation.................	35.1	13.2 to 44.7	23
3. Proportion of Advertising Linage to Total Linage.......................................	35.5	25.5 to 44.1	22
4. Proportion of Other (News, Editorials, Features) to Total Linage............................	64.5	56.0 to 74.5	22
5. Expense Directly Chargeable to Advertising (Total Expense=100%).....................	7.9	3.6 to 15.6	22
6. Editing and News Expense (Total Expense= 100%)...................................	17.5	12.4 to 29.1	22
7. All Other Expense (Total Expense=100%)....	75.0	60.0 to 78.1	22
8. Part of "All Other" Expenses Suggested by Managements as Allocable to Advertising Activities................................	35.0	22.3 to 47.5	13
9. Expense Attributable to Advertising, Direct and Allocable (Total Expense=100%)...........	34.5	22.0 to 46.0	13
10. Expense Attributable to Publishing, Exclusive of Advertising..............................	65.5	54.0 to 78.0	13
11. Percentage of Advertising Revenue Available for Publishing and for Profit after Direct and Allocable Advertising Expense Deduction:			
a. As Derived from All Papers after Allowing for a Net Profit of 6.6%.................	50.3	....	....
b. As Derived from Dollar Income and Expense Data of 7 Papers........................	54.3	40.8 to 66.4	7
Net Margin or Profit Indicated (Revenue from Advertising and Circulation=100%)......... 12.	6.6	0.0 to 14.2	7

(2) Approximately 35% of total linage was given to advertising, and 65% to news, editorials, and features.

(3) Approximately 8% of total expense was directly chargeable to advertising, i.e., advertising salesmen's salaries and commissions, traveling expenses, advertising engraving costs, and so on.

(4) Editing and news expense, against which no advertising expense can be allocated, represented approximately 17% of total expense.

(5) All other expenses, such as those of the composing room, the press room, stereotyping, paper, material and supplies, accounting, administration, circulation activities, overhead, and so on, which are chargeable in part against advertising and in part against the publishing apart from advertising, accounted for about 75% of total expense.

(6) Thirty-five per cent of this "other" expense item, or approximately 26% of total expense, was suggested by the advertising managements supplying the data as allocable to advertising. It will be

noted that the percentage employed is approximately the proportion of advertising linage to total linage carried in the newspapers.

(7) The expense attributable to advertising, including direct expense and allocable expense, was therefore approximately 35% of the total expense incurred.

(8) It follows from the preceding point that the expense attributable to publishing, exclusive of advertising, was approximately 65% of total expense.

(9) From seven papers which furnished dollar data as well as percentage figures, it was possible to derive a median figure of net margin or net profit of 6.6%. The small number of cases involved make this figure very uncertain as representative of either the entire group studied or of the newspaper publishing business as a whole for the year 1938. In view of the absence of any better data, however, it was utilized to reduce the expenditure figures from a percentage of total expense to a percentage of total revenue; i.e., total expense was taken to represent 93.4% of revenue. The expense attributable to advertising, therefore, was 32.2% of revenue.

(10) Approximately 50% of the advertising revenue may be considered to have been contributed for publishing and profit after the expense attributable to advertising activities had been deducted; i.e., 64.9% (total advertising revenue)—32.2% (advertising expense) = 32.7% (remainder), which is approximately an even division of advertising revenue between expenses attributable to advertising and revenue remaining for publishing activities other than advertising and for profit. The data of the seven publishers who submitted their dollar figures indicated only a slightly higher percentage (54.3%) of advertising revenue remaining for publishing other than advertising (Item 11b, Appendix Table 16).

In interpreting the expense data, one must realize that the suggested allocation of expenses to advertising as against allocation to other publishing activities is arbitrary and to a considerable degree uncertain. Accordingly, the figure of total advertising cost must not be taken as a careful measurement but, at the best, as only an approximation. It makes possible, however, a tentative conclusion that for the year 1938 advertising accounted for approximately 65% of the income of the papers studied, and was responsible for perhaps 35% of the cost of operating the business. After the expenses attributable to advertising had been allowed for, approximately one-half of the revenue was available to support the elaborate newspapers that were published, to be sold to readers at the low price of 2 or 3 cents for daily papers and 10 cents for Sunday papers.

Although advertising accounted, according to the survey, for 35% of newspaper publishing expenditure on the average, this does not mean that the elimination of advertising would reduce the expense of publishing the same paper by 35%. Many of the costs are joint costs, and elimination of advertising would not necessarily bring a reduction so great as is indicated by an arbitrary allocation of expense to advertising in accordance with the percentage of advertising linage carried in the paper. Moreover, the effect of elimination of advertising revenue would vary considerably with different papers. Nevertheless, for this group of papers it seems safe to assume that had the publishers attempted to maintain papers on the same scale of news reporting and of features that they followed in 1938, without the aid of advertising they would probably have had to extract from subscribers a sum at least equal to one-half the advertising revenue of their papers, and probably in excess of this amount. This sum means roughly that circulation revenue would have had to be doubled.

The net contribution of advertising to newspaper publishing for 1935 is taken to be one-half the known advertising revenues for that year. The *Biennial Census of Manufactures* reported a total income of newspapers for 1935 of $760,274,048, of which $500,022,708 came from advertisers, and $260,224,340, from subscriptions. The figure of $500,022,708 is not the net income from advertising, but the net was probably only slightly below this.[1] Consequently the net contribution of advertising to the publishing of newspapers for that year is estimated to have been $250,000,000.

Advertising Revenue and Magazine Publishing

A request for operating figures from a limited group of leading magazine publishers did not elicit enough specific operating figures or ratios to permit an analysis of the effect of advertising upon publishing magazines, such as has been presented for newspapers. From these magazine publishers, however, were obtained opinions to supplement data from published sources which give a rough picture of the contribution of advertising toward magazine publishing costs.

---

[1] As was pointed out in the section dealing with the compilation of advertising expenditures, approximately one-third of newspaper publishers included discounts or commissions allowed advertising agencies in their reports to the Census Bureau. Accordingly the net advertising revenue was probably some $9,000,000 less than the census figure.

A substantial number of magazines operate with little or no advertising revenue. The outstanding example is probably *Reader's Digest,* which was reported to have a circulation of 1,801,400 copies in October, 1936,[2] at a price of 25 cents a copy, or $3 a year. The unusual editorial policy of this magazine, that is, the offering of digests of selected articles from other magazines, undoubtedly makes it atypical among magazines of large circulation, so far as its operating costs are concerned.

More common in the magazine field than magazines without advertising revenue are magazines which forego revenue from circulation. We refer here to the so-called "controlled circulation" papers which are presented without charge to selected lists of desired readers.[3] While there are a few examples of such magazines directed to consumers, they are found with greatest frequency and have enjoyed greatest success in certain trade and business fields. In these areas advertisers are interested in coverage of an industry or particular parts of an industry. To secure and hold such coverage of paid subscribers is not only difficult but may involve circulation costs in excess of the revenue to be obtained. Accordingly the publishers rely upon the editorial interest of the medium to potential readers to bring a reading which will make the magazines desirable advertising media.

Among magazine publishers there are between these extremes of operating policy varying degrees of reliance upon revenue from subscriptions on the one hand and advertising on the other. Accordingly, common figures or averages would be less applicable for magazines then for daily newspapers, for which the operating methods are more nearly uniform. Among magazines, particularly leading consumer magazines, will be found those with expensive and elaborate editorial makeup, sold at a very low price, whose main source of income is advertising. For example, the Curtis Publishing Company sells *The Saturday Evening Post* at 5 cents a copy, or $2.00 a year; the *Ladies' Home Journal* at 10 cents a copy, or $1.00 a year; and the *Country Gentleman* at 5 cents a copy, or 25 cents a year. The annual reports of this company indicate that in recent years approximately 75% of its gross revenue has come from advertising and only 25% from circulation. It is readily seen that if an attempt were made to support

[2] See "The Reader's Digest," *Fortune,* November, 1936, p. 121.

[3] See: Oscar Dystel, *An Analysis and Appraisal of Controlled Circulation among Business Papers* (New York, Controlled Circulation Audit, Inc., 1938).

publications of this kind without advertising revenue, the cost to the consumer would have to be substantially increased, probably from two to three times, in order to yield an amount equivalent to the net contribution of advertising to the publication. In contrast, publications such as *The Nation* or *New Republic*, which carry relatively little advertising and which are priced at 15 cents a copy, would not be so greatly affected by the elimination of advertising.

In the case of publications with expensive editorial content and large circulation, there would, of course, be grave question whether the circulation to maintain this editorial content could be attained even at the substantially increased price that would be necessary were advertising eliminated. There are several reasons for this doubt. First, the evidence of consumer surveys indicates that the advertising pages represent an element of considerable value and interest to many readers. Their elimination, therefore, might be considered a deduction from the value of periodicals. In the next place, the increased prices, according to the workings of economic law, would lead to expectation of decreased demand. To secure large circulation would involve heavy promotional expenditure, if one may judge from the experience of publishers. As has been pointed out, in the trade and business paper field many publishers have resorted to the controlled circulation method in large part because the expense involved in getting desired circulation is so great. Likewise, in the consumer magazine field, one of the costs that should be assessed against advertising for some publications is the promotional and selling effort exerted to keep circulation at a certain level either to meet circulation guarantees for a particular advertising rate or to avoid giving the impression of retrogression in circulation. Often this last increment of circulation is obtained or maintained only at a cost in excess of receipts.

In spite of the uncertainty or vagueness provided in an average or over-all picture of advertising's contribution in the magazine field, a rough approximation of what this may be can be arrived at from government figures supplemented by cost estimates.

According to the *Biennial Census of Manufactures, 1935,* the distribution of revenue for periodicals other than newspapers in 1935 was as follows:[4]

---

[4] As explained in Appendix I, some magazine publishers included agency discounts in the figure reported to the Census Bureau. Accordingly their net income from advertising was about $9,000,000 less than shown above. But for the rough calculations made here, a refinement of the above is not required.

	Revenue	Percentage
Subscriptions and sales....................	$143,466,166	43.5
Advertising revenue	186,097,701	56.5
	$329,563,867	100.0

Approximately this same division of revenue between subscriptions and advertising held also in the 1937 census, although the proportion of advertising revenue was higher, 63%, in 1929, when the volume of advertising was high, and lower, 52%, in 1933, when the volume of advertising was low.

The ratios of advertising linage and reading linage of magazines vary widely in accordance with the importance of the magazine as an advertising medium. The proportions maintained in *The Saturday Evening Post* have been approximately 55% for advertising and 45% for reading. Among leading magazines generally, at least 25% of linage is advertising, and in many, from 40% to 50% is advertising linage. Agnew[5] reports that measurement of 70 issues distributed among 59 leading general, farm, class, and women's publications, showed 52.2% reading matter and 47.8% advertising.

The percentages of reading and of advertising matter for magazines and newspapers as a whole are obtained from the reports of the Postmaster General. For the fiscal year ending June 30, 1936, the weight of the advertising portions of publications subject to zone rates mailed during the year was 61% reading matter and 39% advertising matter.[6] From the study of newspapers and from confirmatory statements obtained from executives in the newspaper field, the distribution in newspapers for the year 1938 was believed to approximate 65% reading and 35% advertising matter. Accordingly it may be concluded from the Postmaster General's figures and from the estimate of the distribution of newspaper linage that the proportion of reading matter for magazines generally must be somewhat higher than is indicated in Agnew's study of leading magazines. For 1935 it seems reasonable to estimate that approximately 55% was reading matter and 45% was advertising.

---

[5] H. E. Agnew, *Advertising Media* (New York, D. Van Nostrand Company, Inc., 1932), pp. 136–137.

[6] This does not include mailings of newspapers and periodicals of religious, educational, scientific, philanthropic, agricultural, labor, and fraternal organizations, which paid a flat rate, and whose advertising portions are not subject to a zone rate. See *Report of Postmaster General, Fiscal Year Ended June 30, 1936.*

The conclusion is that in 1935 advertising contributed approximately 55%[7] of the revenue of magazines and probably made up about 45% of linage. Conversely, subscriptions contributed 45%, while reading matter, for which subscriptions were presumably paid, made up 55% of the linage.

How much expense should be allocated against advertising operations is not known, but opinions obtained from publishers and appraisal of the data presented above lead to the opinion that the percentage of advertising revenue available to support publication after allowance for advertising expense is less for magazines than for newspapers. Statements secured from publishers support the conclusion that among consumers' magazines the direct cost for securing advertising was from 5% to 30% of the advertising revenue. If an average figure of 15% is taken, this would represent a direct advertising expense of 9% of the total publishing revenue (i.e., if advertising revenue represents 55% of total revenue). According to certain publishers, an allocation to advertising of expense, other than editorial expense, would involve probably an additional 30% to 35%, bringing direct and allocable expense chargeable to advertising roughly to 40% of total publishing expense. How much profit magazines as a whole earned is not known, but it is assumed that there was profit and, hence, that the percentage of total income used for advertising costs was somewhat less than the figure of 40%, which is a percentage of expense. Since advertising revenue represented 55% of total income of magazines, and direct and indirect advertising expenses in this rough estimate were somewhat less than 40% of total income, it is concluded that from one-fourth to one-third of the advertising revenue of 1935 may have been considered as a net contribution to publication. In other words, of the total advertising revenue of $177,000,000,[8] probably as much as $50,000,000 may be considered to be advertising's net contribution to magazine publication. This estimate is, of course, based on scanty evidence and may be subject to large error. It is believed, however, to be an understatement rather than an overstatement of the net contribution.

---

[7] A somewhat lower percentage of advertising revenue than is shown in the Census distribution of revenue is employed on the assumption that the $186,097,701, advertising revenue, is gross income, at least for part of those reporting, from which agency commissions should be deducted.

[8] The Census of Manufactures' figure of periodical revenue of $186,000,000 is deemed to contain approximately $9,000,000 of advertising agency commissions or discounts. (See section on magazine advertising expenditures).

Advertising Income and Broadcasting

The advertising revenues of broadcast stations and networks of the United States serve not only to·pay for the broadcasts of sponsored programs, but also for the entire operation of the commercial stations and the networks, including the sustaining programs. In addition they provide the profit realized by the stations and networks.

It is estimated that of the total advertising expenditures for radio in 1935, $105,000,000, as shown in Table 2, page 54, some $77,-000,000, may be considered to be the amount expended in providing free radio entertainment to the public. This statement should not be taken to mean that a system of government broadcasting would cost listeners this amount, because fewer broadcasting stations probably would be employed, and the prices paid for talent probably would be less under government operation than under the commercial system. However, it can be said that the wide variety of programs made available to listeners over the large number of broadcasting stations cost consumers for entertainment around $77,000,000, and for advertising, $28,000,000, a total of $105,000,000. This estimate was derived as described in the following paragraphs.

Appendix Table 17 presents an operating statement for all networks and for 629 broadcasting stations operating on a commercial basis in 1937.

It will be noted in Appendix Table 17 that the ratio of advertising, selling, and publicity expense to income from time sales was 5.4%, leaving a ratio for all other expenditures to time sales of 83.8% (89.2% — 5.4% = 83.8%). These were the normal operating expenses that apparently would be incurred were there no advertising. On the assumption that these 1937 percentages were applicable, with no great error, to the year 1935, it was concluded that 83.8% of the net time revenues of approximately $69,000,000 [9] for stations and networks was expended in providing the broadcasting facilities and the sustaining programs given to listeners that year by stations and networks. This amount is roundly $58,100,000. [10]

A deduction from this amount must be made, however, for the time consumed in broadcasting commercial messages. Commercially sponsored programs accounted for only 35% of broadcast time. It is

---

[9] This figure represents the time revenue reported in the Census less 12.9% for commissions, the rate shown in Appendix Table 17.

[10] 83.8% of ($79,617,543 — $10,270,663 [estimated commission]).

APPENDIX TABLE 17

ANALYSIS OF NET REVENUE FROM BROADCAST SERVICES, ALL NETWORKS AND 629
BROADCAST STATIONS OPERATING ON A COMMERCIAL BASIS, 1937

REVENUES	AMOUNT	RATIO TO REVENUE FROM TIME SALES
Time Sales by Networks and Stations....................	$117,908,973	
Sale of Talent and Other Revenue.......................	13,296,893	
Total Gross Sales.......................................	$131,205,866	
Commissions to Agents and Brokers (12.9% of Gross Sales).	16,982,960	
Total Net Revenue of Networks and Stations..............	$114,222,906	
Estimated Total Net Revenue from Time Sales (Time Sales Less 12.9% Commission)............................	$102,698,402	
EXPENSES		
Salaries to Officers......................................	$ 4,817,466	4.7%
Salaries to Others, except Program, Advertising and Selling Staffs	15,616,243	15.1
Payments for Use of Communication Lines Used in Program Transmission	7,489,065	7.3
Payments for Rent of Complete Broadcast Stations and Equipment Leased from Others.............................	693,438	0.7
Program and Talent Expense, Including Sustaining Programs Purchased	32,500,677	31.6
Advertising, Selling, and Publicity Expense................	5,551,202	5.4
Repairs, Maintenance, and Supplies.......................	2,490,403	2.4
Light, Heat, Power, and Miscellaneous Rents..............	4,836,527	4.7
Depreciation of Assets Devoted to Broadcasting............	3,936,158	3.8
Amortization of Intangible Assets Devoted to Broadcasting....	485,593	0.5
Taxes Applicable to Broadcasting (Except Federal Income Taxes)	2,017,696	2.0
Unclassified Broadcast Expenses of Stations................	3,066,323	3.0
All Other General Expenses (Including Rents Paid for Use of Land)	8,155,520	7.9
Total Expenses	$91,656,311	89.2%
Net Profit from Broadcast Services (before Federal Income Taxes)	$22,566,595	

Source: *U. S. Federal Communications Commission, Fourth Annual Report*, Fiscal Year Ended June 30, 1938. Adapted from Table I, Appendix H, pp. 213–214.

estimated that not over 15% of the time of commercial broadcasts was devoted to advertising messages.[11] Consequently 5.25% of total broadcasting time was devoted to advertising messages, and a charge against advertising for this amount of time would bring the charge for entertainment time costs down to around $55,000,000.

On the assumption that a government-conducted radio would incur no brokerage cost for talent, the figure of $25,600,000 included in Table 2, p. 54, for talent employed in commercial programs should

[11] See H. S. Hettinger and W. J. Neff, *op. cit.*, pp. 195–197.

be reduced by the probable commissions paid (assumed that ratio of commissions to total talent cost = 12.9%) in order to arrive at a net talent cost for the commercial programs. The result is $22,300,-000. Hence the total costs for broadcasting entertainment in 1935 is estimated to have been as follows:

For operation of broadcasting facilities and for sustaining programs. . $55,000,000
For commercial talent.................................... 22,300,000

Approximate total $77,000,000*

The corresponding cost incurred for obtaining, handling and broadcasting the advertising, for brokerage on talent and for profit was $28,000,000.

Total Amount Considered Deductible for Advertising's Contribution to Periodicals and Broadcasting

From the preceding sections the conclusion is reached that the total amount that might possibly be considered deductible from the advertising bill for 1935 as representing the net contribution of advertising revenue to publishing and broadcasting entertainment is as follows:

Newspapers $250,000,000
Magazines 50,000,000
Radio 77,000,000

Approximate total $380,000,000*

Such a deduction would reduce the estimated advertising cost to consumers for 1935 to approximately $1,320,000,000.

---
* Total rounded off to indicate probable inaccuracies of estimates.

APPENDIX IV

EXPLANATION OF DERIVATION OF CONVERSION RATE
APPLIED TO NEWSPAPER LINAGE

IN THE various tables in the chapters on demand the volume of newspaper advertising in many cases has been determined by a so-called "cenversion rate," which has been applied to the linage figures as compiled by Media Records, Inc. Since the conversion rate employed in different tables is not uniform, this appendix note serves to explain the reason therefor. Briefly the method followed was this:

The regular reports, *Newspapers and Newspaper Advertisers,* issued by Media Records, Inc., from which the newspaper linage of advertisers was compiled, covered for the period 1929–1939 approximately 100 cities. Figures of dollar expenditures in newspapers were not available until 1939, when the Bureau of Advertising of the American Newspaper Publishers' Association issued its report, *Expenditures of National Advertisers in Newspapers in 1938.* These figures on dollar expenditures were based not only on the advertising placed in the 100 cities carried in the linage reports of Media Records, Inc., but on that for a great many additional cities. In all, daily and Sunday newspapers of 760 cities of 10,000 population or over in the United States were included in the A.N.P.A. report for 1938.

In order to obtain a conversion rate which might be applied to the linage for advertisers over the full period covered by Media Records, Inc., the following formula was used. The dollar value of newspaper advertising for the 760 cities as reported in *Expenditures of National Advertisers in Newspapers in 1938 and 1939* was divided by the total linage of advertisers for these two years, as reported by Media Records, Inc., in *Newspapers and Newspaper Advertisers.*

This procedure had definite shortcomings which were recognized; yet it was adopted because it was thought that its merits outweighed its shortcomings. The procedure assumes that over the period of years advertisers had approximately the same proportions of newspaper advertising in small cities and large cities as held for the years 1938 and 1939. In so far as this assumption is not far wrong, the conversion rate gives a better estimate of the newspaper advertising expenditures than would multiplication of the linage figures of Media Reports, Inc., for each year by a constant conversion rate of around 30 cents to 35 cents. The latter method would fail to provide for newspaper advertising in small cities. It was realized that advertisers' distribution of newspaper schedules between large cities and small towns is not constant from year to year. Accordingly there is room for appreciable error in the statement of newspaper expenditures of advertisers for years where the assumption is far wrong. In spite of this difficulty, however, the plan was adopted in the belief that the error would not be unduly large. In any case, the error resulting from this procedure would not be great enough in the estimates of total advertising expenditures for advertisers or industries to alter conclusions of analyses in which advertising expenditures are involved. It must be recognized that the figures of traceable advertising given for individual advertisers, other than for the years 1938 and 1939 for which the A.N.P.A. reports were available, are rough estimates only, derived from the best data that were available to the author.

Appendix V

FORMS USED IN SURVEY AMONG LARGE-SCALE DISTRIBUTORS

Please return to
Professor N. H. Borden   A939
Soldiers Field   *Strictly Confidential*
Boston, Massachusetts   Code No._____

HARVARD GRADUATE SCHOOL OF BUSINESS ADMINISTRATION

Confidential Questionnaire Regarding Distributors' Branding Policies

Note to Cooperating Firms: The information which you send will be held as strictly confidential. Care will be taken in use of the information to combine it with data supplied by others in such a way that identity will not be revealed. If you have no private brand merchandise, please answer questions 10 and 18i.

(1) Please check your policy with regard to increasing your private brands:

    a. Our policy is to increase the number of items under our our label.   _____

  b. Our policy is not to increase the number of items under
  our own label.   _____

  c. Our policy is to reduce the number of items under our
  own label.   _____

Comment:

(2) Please check your policy with regard to aggressiveness in
advertising and promoting your own brands of merchandise:

  a. Our policy is generally to give our own brands preference
  over others' brands in our advertising and store promotional effort.   _____

  b. Our policy generally is to give our own brands about the
  same emphasis in advertising and promotional efforts as
  others' brands.   _____

  c. Our policy generally is to give our own brands less emphasis in advertising and promotional efforts than we give
  others' brands.   _____

Comment:

. . . .

(This section is to be detached on receipt of questionnaire)

Code No._____

Firm Name_____ No. of Stores_____

Street_____ City and State_____
Individual to whom correspondence should be addressed

_____ Position_____

(3) Please check the questions below to indicate the extent to
which salesmen are authorized to recommend purchase of
your brands of merchandise:

  a. Are they directed to recommend your brands when
  customer has asked for another specific brand which is
  carried in the store?   Yes_____

                                                            No _____

  If "Yes," does this apply to all customers?   _____
                   only customers of long standing?   _____

  b. Are they directed to recommend your brands when customer has asked for another specific brand which is not
  carried in the store?   Yes_____

No _____

c. Are they directed to offer or recommend your brands when the customer has not specified a brand?

Yes_____

No _____

d. Are they encouraged to name your brands of merchandise when suggesting further items the customer might wish to buy?

Yes_____

No _____

Comment: _____

(4) Approximate number of items carried under your private label. _____
(By items we mean a specific type of merchandise of a particular grade or price line; different sizes of container or unit of a grade of merchandise *should not* be counted as separate items.)
If more convenient, simply send us a copy of your warehouse or store order form which would give us the desired information.

a. How does the number now carried compare with the number carried 10 years ago?

Considerably larger _____
Somewhat larger _____
About the same _____
Smaller _____

Comment: _____

(5) Approximately what percentage of your total dollar sales is of merchandise bearing your own labels? _____
a. How does this percentage compare with that of 10 years ago?

More _____
Same _____
Less _____

Comment: _____

(6) Please check for the following products whether they are sold under your label, and if so, the sources of supply of your private label merchandise, as indicated by column headings:

Product	Check if sold under your label	Check for each product the column which indicates current sources of supply of your brand of merchandise		
		Your own manufacture or pack	Manufacturer who also sells under well-known brand of his own	Manufacturer selling primarily dealer label merchandise
Canned vegetables				
Canned fruit				
All-purpose flour				
Prepared pancake flour				
Canned milk				
Canned salmon				
Coffee				
Spices				
Salad dressing				
Baking soda				
Fruit gelatin				
Baking powder				
Canned soup				
Floating soap				
White soap flakes				
Granulated soap				
Kitchen cleanser				
Farina				
Bread				
Corn flakes				
Perfumed soap				

(7) Check the promotional and selling efforts employed by you to increase the sale of your own label merchandise:

Newspaper listing _____   Counter display _____
Hand bills _____   Displays showing price com-
Window streamers _____   parisons with competing
Window display _____   brands _____
Prominent shelf space_____   Recommendation by clerks _____
                                         P. M.s to clerks _____
                                         Other: _____

Comment:

(8) In your own business, what has been the effect of price maintenance laws on your private labelling policy?

    a. Effect has been to increase our emphasis on our own brands. _____

    b. Effect has been to decrease our emphasis on our own brands. _____

    c. No appreciable effect. _____

Comment:

(9) In your own business, what has been the effect of the Robinson-Patman Act on your private labelling policy?

    a. Effect has been to increase our emphasis on our own brands. _____

    b. Effect has been to decrease our emphasis on our own brands. _____

    c. No appreciable effect. _____

Comment:

(10) Have you made any studies regarding costs of handling and
selling your own brands vs. handling and selling manufacturers' brands of merchandise?   Yes_____

    No _____

    a. If your answer just above is "yes," what did your findings
indicate?
Expenses for handling and selling private brand of merchandise, as compared with manufacturers' brands, are:

               Appreciably higher   _____

               Slightly higher   _____

               About the same   _____

               Slightly less   _____

               Appreciably less   _____

               Varies widely with
different merchandise _____
(If so, please comment)

Comment:

    b. If your answer to above question (number 10) is "no," do
you think that in general the costs of handling and selling
private brands of merchandise, as compared with manufacturers' brands, are:

Appreciably higher   _____

Slightly higher   _____

About the same   _____

Slightly less   _____

Appreciably less   _____

Varies widely with
     different merchandise _____
     (If so, please comment)

Comment:

c. Aside from the question of cost of handling and selling, how does rate of turnover of your own brands compare with that of national brands?

Appreciably higher   _____

Slightly higher   _____

About the same   _____

Slightly lower   _____

Appreciably lower   _____

Varies with
     different merchandise _____

Comment:

(11) Please check methods employed by you to maintain quality of merchandise sold under your own brands, when not manufactured by yourself or a subsidiary. Please give examples of products to which the methods checked are applied.

a. We keep our own inspectors in our suppliers' plants.   _____
(Examples of products for which used.)

b. We have a plan for systematic physical inspection of merchandise.   _____
(Examples of products for which used.)

c. We submit samples of merchandise periodically to laboratory tests.   _____
(Examples of products for which used.)

d. We rely upon grading by government inspectors.   _____
(Examples of products for which used.)

e. We depend primarily upon suppliers to maintain quality under specifications we have made or to meet a sample.   _____
(Examples of products for which used.)

f. We shop around and rely entirely on integrity of suppliers without giving specifications or furnishing a sample.   _____
(Examples of products for which used.)

Comment:

(12) Do you have your own laboratory to test merchandise?   Yes_____

No _____

(13) Please indicate under the questions below the practices followed in pricing merchandise sold under your own label:

    a. Is it your policy generally to price merchandise under your
own label:

      Above prevailing prices of leading manufacturers' brands
of equal quality   _____

      At same level as prevailing prices of leading manufacturers'
brands of equal quality   _____

      Below prevailing prices of leading manufacturers' brands
of equal quality   _____

Comment:

    b. Is it your policy generally to price merchandise under your
label:

      Above prices of comparable competing retailers' private
brands   _____

      At same level as prices of comparable competing retailers'
private brands   _____

      Below prices of comparable competing retailers' private
brands   _____

Comment:

(14) Generally speaking, the *gross margin* received on articles sold
under our own label

Is *higher* than received on manufacturers' brands   _____

Is *about the same* as received on manufacturers' brands   _____

Is *less* than received on manufacturers' brands   _____

Comment:

(15) Can you cite products bearing your label on which you get a
relatively large gross margin because competitive price levels
for those types of products are set by heavily advertised brands
and are set at a relatively high level above manufacturing
costs?

Examples:

Are instances of this sort relatively frequent?   ————————

infrequent?   ————————

(16) Can you cite products bearing your label on which you get a relatively low gross margin because the competitive price levels for those types of products are set by heavily advertised brands and are set at a relatively low margin above manufacturing costs?

Examples:

Are instances of this sort relatively frequent?   ————————

infrequent?   ————————

(17) Can you cite products bearing your label on which it is your practice to take only a normal gross margin (for the type of product) above cost of merchandise, although the prices of comparable manufacturers' brands would probably permit you to take more?

Examples:

Are instances of this sort relatively frequent?   ————————

infrequent?   ————————

NOTE:

In the questionnaire sent to *drug* distributors the following drug products were listed under question 6, page 938:

Aspirin	Chocolate Laxative Tablets
Alkalate Tablets	Milk of Magnesia
After-Shave Lotion	Mouth Wash
Brushless Shave Cream	Nose and Throat Drops
Cod Liver Oil	Razor Blades
Cold Cream	Rubbing Alcohol
Cough Syrup	Toilet Soap
Cream Deodorant	Toothbrush
Face Powder	Tooth Paste
Hand and Face Lotion	Tooth Powder

In all other respects the questionnaire was the same as that sent to grocery distributors.

umn?

Farina	All-Purpose Flour	Canned Peas (Choice grade)	Canned Milk	Salad Dressing	Bread	Coffee

as the example.

	TOMATO SOUP (Campbell grade)	WHITE SOAP FLAKES (Lux grade)	CORN FLAKES
a. Do you have private label on the product* (If *not*, jump to question I, next page)			
1. Brand name			
2. Size of fastest selling container			
3. Regular current selling price for above container			
4. Your gross margin on this item (%)			
5. Regular price at which member retailers sell this item			
b. Leading advertised brand—name			
1. Size of fastest selling container			
2. Regular current selling price			
3. Your gross margin on this item (%)			
4. Regular price at which member retailers sell this item			
c. Second place advertised brand—name			
1. Size of fastest selling container			
2. Regular current selling price			
3. Gross margin (%)			
4. Regular price at which member retailers sell this item			
d. Approximate number of brands carried of this type of product			
e. Any manufacturers' unadvertised brands carried			
1. Size of fastest selling container			
2. Regular current selling price			
3. Gross margin (%)			
4. Regular price at which member retailers sell this item			
f. Sales, 1938, or other recent year—all size containers (Ratios, if you prefer)			
Your brand			
Manufacturers' advertised brands			
Manufacturers' unadvertised brands			
Bulk			
g. Trend of sales of your brand as part of whole during last 10 years			
1. Up			
2. About same			
3. Downward			
h. Quality of private label product, named above, as compared with leading advertised brand			
1. Higher quality			
2. Equal quality			
3. Lower quality			
i. If any of the listed products are *not* carried under your label, please check the most important reasons for not having your own brand.			
1. Advertised brands too strongly entrenched to develop satisfactory volume			
2. Source of supply of suitable product not found			
3. Satisfactory margins can be obtained among advertised brands			
4. Margins to be obtained on own brand not sufficient to make it worth while			
5. Expenses of promoting own brand to secure needed demand are too heavy			
6. Other Comment			

* If you have your own brand name on more than one price line of any product, use your fastest selling brand

FORM USED IN SURVEY OF MARKETING AND PRODUCTION COSTS OF MANUFACTURERS

Strictly Confidential

Please Return to
Professor N. H. Borden
Soldiers Field,
Boston, Massachusetts

STUDY OF THE ECONOMICS OF ADVERTISING
GRADUATE SCHOOL OF BUSINESS ADMINISTRATION
HARVARD UNIVERSITY

Code No.............................

SCHEDULE FOR COST DATA ON AN ADVERTISED PRODUCT

NOTES

Three sets of data are requested covering a specific advertised brand or product: (1) net sales in dollars and units; (2) production costs; and (3) marketing costs.

Brand or Product upon Which to Report Data

Where several brands are manufactured and advertised, cost data should be given on the most important brand judged on the basis of contribution to sales volume.

Where Brand Selected Is Made in Several Grades or Sizes

Where the company decides to report data on a brand made in several grades or sizes, we should like to have such figures as can be furnished by the company in the form in which it segregates its costs. Below is outlined the desired segregation of data:

Where a single brand name is applied to several grades of product:
1. If only one grade is advertised, sales and cost data should be reported on the advertised grade; in addition, summarized costs should be reported for the brand (including all grades). For example, assume that a rubber company manufactured Brand A of tires in a first, second, and third grade. Suppose, also, that the company advertised only the first grade Brand A tire. Under these circumstances, sales and cost data should be reported on the first grade of Brand A; in addition, summary figures should be reported on all three grades of Brand A.
2. If all grades are advertised, sales and cost figures should be reported separately on each grade of the brand, if possible. For example, if the rubber company referred to above advertised separately Brand A Grade 1, Brand A Grade 2, Brand A Grade 3, then sales and cost data should be reported on each grade of Brand A.

When to report data by sizes:
1. Where a given brand is produced in only two or three sizes (e.g., toothpaste—25 cent size, 50 cent size) sales and cost data should be reported by sizes, if possible.
2. Where a given brand is manufactured in a large number of sizes (e.g., automobile tires, shoes) it is not necessary to break down the data by sizes.

Period to Be Covered

1. In general, data are desired for a period of time which will reflect the long-term changes in sales volume and costs during the period of advertising. Although the period of time to be covered will vary with different businesses, data are desired for a minimum of 10 years. If, in the opinion of the cooperator, a longer period should be covered in order to present a fair picture, then figures may be given for 15 years, 20 years, or whatever period is deemed necessary.
2. If data for a 10-year period are provided, figures should be presented for every year during that period. If, however, it is necessary to cover a 20-year period, data should be given for every other year. If the data cover an even longer term, it is sufficient to report at less frequent intervals in order to minimize the work involved.
3. When to report data covering years prior to advertising:
   a. Companies that have initiated advertising within the past 10 years should, if possible, report data for at least two or three years prior to the start of advertising.
   b. Companies that have been advertising for a period of longer than 10 years need not report data prior to the start of advertising. If, however, such data can be obtained without undue expenditure of time and effort, we should appreciate getting them.
4. Where it appears unwise to give data for recent years, it will be satisfactory to cover a period ending with any year desired.

Where Company Sells Both to Consumers and to Industrial Users

Where the company sells its product both to consumers (through wholesalers and retailers, through retailers, or direct to the consumer) and to industrial users, data should be reported separately upon that portion of the product sold to consumers and that sold to industrial users.

Directions for Cases Where Complete Costs by Products Are Not Kept

Even where complete costs by products are not kept it will be of value if the cooperator will report as many of the requested data as are available. Thus, Net Sales, in dollars and units, together with space advertising costs would provide data of distinct value. Again, where production costs and only a part of marketing costs are allocated to the product, these data would be decidedly helpful. In short, the cooperator is requested to fill in the schedule as far as his accounting and statistical records will permit, even though complete figures are not available.

(This section is to be detached on receipt of schedule.)

Code No.............

Brand or Product for
which Cost Data are given...

Firm Name...

Street...City and State.....................................

Individual to whom correspondence should be addressed:

....Position ....

(Please Print Name)

COST DATA ON A PRODUCT OR BRAND—(Please omit cents)

YEAR	NET SALES		PRODUCTION COSTS			
	Dollars	Units	Direct Materials	Direct Labor	Manufacturing Overhead	Total Production Costs

DEFINITIONS

Net Sales

1. *In Dollars.* Gross Sales less Returned Goods, Allowances to Customers, Cash Discounts taken by Customers, and Other Discounts to Customers.

2. *In Units.* What is desired here is a figure indicating the physical volume of net sales. The unit chosen can be whatever unit of sale is used in recording such information in company records.

Production Costs

1. *Direct Materials.* The term, Direct Materials, includes all those materials that are used directly in producing the product—to the extent that they can be definitely measured and charged to the product or brand. For example, the cost of the lumber used in making furniture is considered a direct material cost of the furniture.

2. *Direct Labor.* The wages of those employees working directly on the product or brand—to the extent that they can be definitely measured and charged to the particular unit.

3. *Manufacturing Overhead.* Manufacturing Overhead (or Manufacturing Burden) includes all manufacturing costs which are not capable of being directly charged to the product; in other words, it includes all costs of production except Direct Labor and Direct Materials. Among others, Manufacturing Overhead includes the following items: depreciation, taxes, insurance, interest, indirect materials, supplies, superintendence, supervision, inspection, indirect factory clerical, designing, drafting, heat, light, power, spoilage, inside trucking, etc.

4. *Total Production Costs.* Sum of Direct Materials, Direct Labor, and Manufacturing Overhead.

Marketing Expenses

1. *Salesforce Expense.* This group represents the expenses incurred in securing orders for the company's products. Salesforce Expense includes salaries, commissions, and bonuses; travelling expenses (including direct and indirect expense of salesmen's automobiles); other salesforce expenses (including salesmen's samples, sample cases, sales manuals, portfolios, price books, report blanks, etc.).

COST DATA ON A PRODUCT OR BRAND—(Please omit cents)

Salesforce Expense	MARKETING EXPENSES						
	Advertising and Sales Promotion Expenses				Other Marketing Expenses	Total Marketing Expenses
	Space Advertising	Field Promotion	Other Advertising and Sales Promotion	Total Advertising and Sales Promotion		

DEFINITIONS

2. *Advertising and Sales Promotion.* The Advertising and Sales Promotion group of expenses covers the direct charges for those activities which have as their purpose securing recognition and stimulating demand for a company's products.

a. *Space Advertising.* Includes cost of space purchased in general, farm, and class magazines, newspapers, radio, trade papers, professional periodicals, outdoor (poster and painted display), street cars, mechanical display and other space mediums. Also, it includes salaries and wages of the company's own copywriters and other space advertising expense.

b. *Field Promotion.* This group of expenses covers those sales-stimulative or promotional activities which in general are carried on in the field, frequently under the supervision of, or closely coordinated with, the salesforce activities. This item includes salaries and wages of company employees engaged in field promotional activities (missionary salesmen), travelling expense, cost of samples, cost of dealer helps and displays, cost of booklets and leaflets, cost of supplies and equipment, and other expenses incurred for field promotional activities.

c. *Other Advertising and Sales Promotion Expenses.* This item includes direct mail advertising, premium advertising, and miscellaneous sales promotion and advertising expenses incurred at the home office (except administration covered in 3c below).

3. *Other Marketing Expenses.* Included under this heading are:

a. Shipping, transportation, district warehousing, and delivery expenses.

b. Credit and collection expenses.

c. Marketing administration expenses including salaries and wages, travelling expenses, office expenses, and other marketing administration costs.

4. *Total Marketing Expenses.* Sum of Salesforce, Advertising and Sales Promotion, and Other Marketing Expenses.

Note: If your classifications of expense differ significantly from those presented above, use your own classifications in reporting data. Where this is done, please substitute your classifications on the Schedule and indicate in a footnote what these classifications cover.

Interpretive questions appear on the following page.

Answers to the following questions will assist greatly in analyzing the report.

1. **Products.**
   What types of merchandise do you sell? Please specify.

   ....

   ....

   ....

   ....

   ....

   With respect to the product on which cost data are given, approximately what percentage of total dollar sales volume does this product represent? ....%

2. **Channels of Distribution.**   *Please check*
   Is the product covered in this report sold to:
   a. wholesalers?   ....
   b. retail chain stores?   ....
   c. direct to independent retailers?   ....
   d. other?   ....

   With respect to the relative number of   *State*
   retailers through which the product is   *Yes or No*
   distributed:
   a. Are retail outlets granted exclusive
      agencies?   ....
   b. Is the product sold through selected
      retailers in each locality?   ....
   c. Is the product sold through all re-
      tailers who will stock it in a given
      locality?   ....

   Please state the number of outlets through   *Number*
   which the product was sold in 1938.   ....

3. **Extent of Sales Area.**   *State*
   Is the market for the product: *Yes or No*
   a. Local? (Less than 100 miles)   ....
   b. Sectional? (Up to 500 miles)   ....
   c. National?   ....
   Was there any change in extent of sales area
   during the period covered by cost data?   ....

If so, please specify the nature of the change.......................

....

....

....

4. Approximate ratios of advertising expendi-   *% of total*
   ture for the product, by media, in recent   *advertising*
   years: *expenditure*

   Newspapers   ....

   Magazines   ....

   Radio   ....

   Outdoor and car card   ....

   Mail to consumers   ....
   Trade and industrial papers and mail to
   trade

   Dealer helps   ....
   Other advertising expenditures
   (administration, production costs, etc.) ....

5. Do you use missionary salesmen to solicit   *State*
   orders from retailers for the account of   *Yes or No*
   wholesalers?

6. Do members of your regular salesforce en-   *State*
   gage *actively* in the following functions in   *Yes or No*
   addition to securing orders for your own
   account:
   a. Securing missionary orders from re-
      tailers for the account of wholesalers? ....
   b. General educational work with re-
      tailers?   ....
   c. Making demonstrations to consum-
      ers?   ....
   d. Supervising field promotion activities?...................

7. Average number of full-time salesmen in   *Number*
   1938:
   a. Regular salesforce   ....
   b. Missionary salesforce   ....

FORMS USED IN SURVEY OF CONSUMER ATTITUDES TOWARD ADVERTISING

FORM X

ALPHA DELTA SIGMA
NATIONAL ADVERTISING FRATERNITY

SURVEY OF CONSUMER ATTITUDES TOWARD ADVERTISING

•

EXPLANATION OF THE SURVEY

This consumer survey is being conducted by Alpha Delta Sigma, National Advertising Fraternity, as its contribution to a study which the Harvard Graduate School of Business Administration is making of the Economics of Advertising.

The object of the survey is to determine to what extent advertising is serving, or is failing to serve, consumers satisfactorily.

Consumers are asked to examine three to five advertisements and then answer a few simple questions concerning them.

Names of cooperators are not recorded, nor will the cooperators be approached further.

FORM X: PART I

QUESTIONS	ADVERTISEMENT	ADVERTISEMENT
	Code Number............................	Code Number............................
	Product Name............................	Product Name............................

1. Do you find anything objectionable in this advertisement? If so, what?

	ADVERTISEMENT	ADVERTISEMENT
1.	Yes . . . . ☐	1. Yes . . . . ☐
	No . . . . ☐	No . . . . ☐
	Uncertain . . . . . . ☐	Uncertain . . . . . . ☐
	Comment............................	Comment............................

If answer is "Yes," check one or more of the reasons listed:

	ADVERTISEMENT	ADVERTISEMENT
	In bad taste . . . . . ☐	In bad taste . . . . . ☐
	Indecent or suggestive . . ☐	Indecent or suggestive . . ☐
	Negative — uses fear motive ☐	Negative — uses fear motive ☐
	Repulsive ideas . . . . ☐	Repulsive ideas . . . . ☐
	Unattractive advertisement ☐	Unattractive advertisement ☐
	Exaggerated . . . . . ☐	Exaggerated . . . . . ☐
	Not true . . . . . . ☐	Not true . . . . . . ☐
	Misleading . . . . . ☐	Misleading . . . . . ☐
	Silly . . . . ☐	Silly . . . . ☐
	Testimonial is objectionable ☐	Testimonial is objectionable ☐
	Object to product . . . ☐	Object to product . . . ☐
	Other (state)............................	Other (state)............................

2. (To be asked only when answer to question 1 is "Yes") Would you have the things that you object to prohibited by law?

	ADVERTISEMENT	ADVERTISEMENT
2.	Yes . . . . ☐	2. Yes . . . . ☐
	No . . . . ☐	No . . . . ☐
	Uncertain . . . . . ☐	Uncertain . . . . . ☐

3. Have you ever used the product?

	ADVERTISEMENT	ADVERTISEMENT
3.	Yes . . . . ☐	3. Yes . . . . ☐
	No . . . . ☐	No . . . . ☐
	Uncertain . . . . . . ☐	Uncertain . . . . . . ☐

4. Do you think the product (probably) is as good as the advertisement says?

	ADVERTISEMENT	ADVERTISEMENT
4.	Yes . . . . ☐	4. Yes . . . . ☐
	No. . . . . . . ☐	No. . . . . . . ☐
	Uncertain . . . . . ☐	Uncertain . . . . . ☐
	Comment............................	Comment............................

5. Do you think the product (probably) is a good product?

	ADVERTISEMENT	ADVERTISEMENT
5.	Yes . . . . ☐	5. Yes . . . . ☐
	No . . . . ☐	No . . . . ☐
	Uncertain . . . . . . ☐	Uncertain . . . . . . ☐
	Comment............................	Comment............................

6. How do you think the product (probably) compares in quality with competing products selling at about the same price?

	ADVERTISEMENT	ADVERTISEMENT
6.	Best on market . . . ☐	6. Best on market . . . . ☐
	Better than most . . . ☐	Better than most . . . ☐
	About the same . . . . ☐	About the same . . . . ☐
	Inferior . . . . . . ☐	Inferior . . . . . . ☐
	Uncertain . . . . . . ☐	Uncertain . . . . . ☐
	Other (state)............................	Other (state)............................
	Comment............................	Comment............................